DI
TH

TEXT AND MATERIALS

AUSTRALIA
Law Book Co.
Sydney

CANADA and USA
Carswell
Toronto

HONG KONG
Sweet & Maxwell
Asia

NEW ZEALAND
Brookers
Auckland

SINGAPORE and MALAYSIA
Sweet & Maxwell Asia
Singapore and Kuala Lumpur

DISCRIMINATION LAW: THEORY AND CONTEXT

TEXT AND MATERIALS

First Edition

by

NICHOLAS BAMFORTH, B.C.L., M.A. (Oxon)
Fellow in Law, The Queen's College, Oxford

MALEIHA MALIK, L.L.B., B.C.L.
Reader in Law, King's College, University of London

COLM O'CINNEIDE, B.C.L., L.L.M., B.L. (King's Inns)
Senior Lecturer in Laws, University College London

With an Introduction by

SIR GEOFFREY BINDMAN,
B.C.L., M.A. *Solicitor, Visiting*
Professor of Law at University College London and
at London South Bank University,
Senior Consultant at Bindman & Partners

LONDON
SWEET & MAXWELL
2008

Published in 2008 by
Sweet & Maxwell Limited of
100 Avenue Road
London NW3 3PF
(http://www.sweetandmaxwell.co.uk)
Typeset by YHT Ltd, Uxbridge, Middlesex
Printed by
Ashford Colour Press, Gosport, Hants

First Edition..2008

A CIP catalogue record for this book
is available from The British Library

ISBN 978–0–421–55440–5

FOREWORD

This book seeks to provide a comprehensive account of discrimination law understood as an articulation of constitutional law concerns rather than—as the subject has traditionally been presented in the UK—just as a specialist branch of employment law. In the USA, Canada, South Africa and numerous other jurisdictions to which English common lawyers pay attention, protections against invidious forms of discrimination are treated primarily (although not exclusively) as matters of constitutional law. We argue that the UK's membership of the EU and the European Convention on Human Rights requires discrimination lawyers to pay proper attention at national level to the constitutional dimensions of the subject.

The organisation of the book reflects these concerns, and as a result may appear somewhat unusual to employment and discrimination lawyers. In Part A, we outline our conception of the subject, including the key questions which any system of discrimination law must answer. We then consider, partly by reference to these questions, how discrimination is regulated in domestic law. In doing so, we begin by considering EU law and the Convention (and the resulting "constitutional" dimensions), before seeking to explain their relationship with the more traditional statutory prohibitions on discrimination. Finally, we continue the constitutional and comparative themes by exploring the large debates in legal philosophy concerning principled justifications for the legal regulation of invidious forms of discrimination. In Part B, we present what are essentially overviews of some of the organising concepts in discrimination law: direct and indirect discrimination; positive action; and harassment and hostility. In doing so, we take care to move well beyond the "traditional" framework of employment law. The constitutional dimensions of the subject also come through in our discussion of clashes between different prohibited grounds of discrimination, and between non-discrimination and other legally protected human rights. In Part C, we explore the law's treatment of the six key prohibited grounds of discrimination within the UK: sex, sexual orientation, race, religion, disability and age. In doing so, we adopt a comparative and (where necessary) theoretical form of analysis, and seek to explore the interactions between EU law, the European Convention and "domestic" statutory measures. Finally, in Part D, we consider individual and collective remedies.

The government's *Discrimination Law Review* was published whilst we were working on the book, and it seems likely that an attempt will soon be made to clarify and rationalise discrimination law via the introduction of a single statute to regulate all the prohibited grounds. Such a development would undoubtedly be welcome, but one clear conclusion to emerge from this book must be that a single statute cannot, without more, reduce the complexities resulting from the influence on domestic law of two sometimes divergent bodies of "European" law (EU law and the Convention), each with its own constitutional "weight" at national level.

Some authors have referred to the body of law with which we are concerned as "anti-discrimination law"; others describe it as "non-discrimination law". We have opted for "discrimination law" since this seems to be the term which is now most commonly in use. When describing the various discrimination-related Directives emanating from the EU, we use—also for ease of reference—the day-to-day labels attached to the Directives by the EU institutions—for example, "Employment Equality Directive" and "Race Equality Directive"—rather than the more technical "Framework Directive" and "Racial Discrimination Directive". Again for the sake of simplicity, we generally refer to "EU law" rather than distinguishing between EC and EU law.

Whilst this is a joint project, the responsibility for this book is divided as follows. Part A sets out a framework for understanding discrimination law. This forms the structure within which we analyse central concepts (Part B), prohibited grounds (Part C), and remedies (Part D). We have formulated ten key questions as set out in Chapter 1, the "key Issues and Questions in Discrimination Law", which was written by Nicholas Bamforth. Chapter 2 on the "Sources and Scope of Discrimination Law" explores these questions through a discussion of the main legal provisions. Nicholas Bamforth and Maleiha Malik jointly undertook the research and preparation of a number of drafts of this chapter, and the final version was written by Nicholas Bamforth. Chapter 3, which was written by Maleiha Malik with valuable contributions by Nicholas Bamforth, is an analysis of the theoretical foundations of discrimination law. Nicholas Bamforth wrote Chapter 11, and he jointly wrote Chapter 5. Maleiha Malik wrote Chapters 4, 8, 9, 10, 12, 13 and 16, and she jointly wrote Chapters 6, 7 and 17, with valuable contributions from the other authors. Colm O'Cinneide wrote Chapters 14 and 15, and he jointly wrote Chapters 5, 6, 7 and 17. Maleiha Malik and Colm O'Cinneide owe a debt of gratitude to Nicholas Bamforth for his help and guidance on the substance of their chapters, and for editing large parts of the manuscript. All the authors are indebted to Geoffrey Bindman for initiating this project, and his participation and guidance during all its stages.

We would also like to thank Rebecca O'Rourke, Victoria Blanshard and Kevin Symons at Sweet and Maxwell for doing huge amounts to bring this project to fruition; and to Krysia Domaszewicz, Nia Murphy, Claire Sharp and Samantha Siddle for their production-related work. In addition, Nicholas Bamforth would like to thank his father, sister, brother-in-law and nephew, as well as Peter Leyland, David Richards and Dan Sarooshi; Maleiha Malik would like to thank her colleagues, friends and family, and to dedicate this work to her grandfather, M. Y. Peerzada; and Colm O'Cinneide would like to thank his parents. All three co-authors would like to thank Aileen McColgan and Robert Wintemute for their helpful and expert comments at important stages.

The book takes account of case law and other materials available up to August 31, 2007. However, we have attempted wherever possible to include references to subsequent developments.

Nicholas Bamforth
Maleiha Malik
Colm O'Cinneide
London, February 8, 2008

ACKNOWLEDGMENTS

Adams, Lorna, Fiona McAndres and Mark Winterbotham, *Pregnancy Discrimination at Work: A Survey of Women*, EOC Working Paper Series No.24, EOC: Manchester, Winter 2004/2005, pp.71–74.

Alexander, Larry, 'What Makes Wrongful Discrimination Wrong?' (1992–1993) U. Pa. L. R. 154, at 219. With the kind permission of Univeristy of Pennsylvania Law School (Copyright ©) and William S. Hein & Company, Inc.

Asad, Talal, *Reflections On Laïcité & The Public Sphere*, Keynote address at the "Beirut Conference on Public Spheres," October 22–24, 2004, *http://www.ssrc.org/publications/items/v5n3/index.html*.

Background paper for the expert meeting on the Gender-Related Aspects of Race Discrimination, November 21–24, 2000, Zagreb, Croatia, World Conference Against Racism, Selected Documents and Links (*http://www.wicej.addr.com/wcar_docs/index.html)* (accessed August 20, 2006), Durban, South Africa, August 31—September 7, 2001.

Baker, Aaron, 'Comparison Tainted by Justification: Against a "Compendious Question" in Art.14 Discrimination' [2006] P.L. 476, 476–7.

'Bakke's Case: Are Quotas Unfair?' and 'What Did The Bakke Case Really Decide?', *A Matter of Principle* (Oxford: Clarendon Press, 1986) pp.293–395.

Barnard, Catherine, *The Substantive Law of the EU: The Four Freedoms* (Oxford: Oxford University Press, 2004), pp.23–4.

Bamforth, Nicholas 'Sexual Orientation Discrimination after Grant v. Southwest Trains' (2000) 63 M.L.R. 694, 701, 703–6. With permission from Blackwell Publishing.

Bell, Mark, *Anti-Discrimination Law and the European Union* (Oxford: Oxford University Press, 2002), pp.5, 6–7, 27–8, 29, 147–8 (excerpts).

Benhabib, Seyla, *The Claims of Culture: Equality and Diversity in the Global Era*, (Princeton University Press, 2002).

Best Value. Best Equality, (1998) Equal Opportunities Review, Published by IRS, London, May 1, 1998.

Bouteldja, Naima, 'The Reality Of L'affaire Du Foulard', *The Guardian*, February 25, 2005.

Brown, Jonathan, How Two Racists Faced Each Other In Court, Then Shunned Prejudice To Become Friends, *The Independent*, London: September 9, 2006.

Cane, Peter, *Responsibility in Law and Morality* (Hart Publications: Oxford, 2002), pp.2–5; 40; 44.

Collins, Hugh, 'Discrimination, Equality and Social Inclusion' (2003) 66 Modern Law Review 16, at pp.41–43.

Coussey, Mary, 'The Effectiveness of Strategic Enforcement of the Race Relations Act 1976', in B. Hepple and E. Szyszcak (eds.) *Discrimination: The Limits of Law* (Mansell: London, 1992). By kind permission of Continuum International Publishing.

Crenshaw, Kimberle, 'Demarginalising the Intersection of Race and Sex: A Black Feminist Critique of Antidiscrimination Doctrine, Feminist Theory and Antiracist Politics (1989) UO, Chi. Legal F. 139.

Cretney, Stephen, *Same-Sex Relationships: From 'Odious Crime' to 'Gay Marriage'* (Oxford: Oxford University Press, 2006) pp.1–2.

Dhami, Dr Ravinder Singh, Professor Judith Squires and Professor Tariq Modood—'Developing Positive Action Policies: Learning from the Experiences of Europe and North America', Research Report No. 406, Department for Works and Pensions.

'Discrimination: Burden of proof finally reversed in direct discrimination claims' 820 (2005) IRS Employment Review Publisher IRS, on March 25, 2005.

Dworkin, Ronald, *The New York Review of Books*, Vol.50, No.8, May 15, 2003, The Court and the University (excerpts).

Easton, Susan, *Pornography As Incitement to Sexual Hatred* (1995) Institute of Feminist Legal Studies pp.89–104.

EOC case summaries on race and sex cases—multiple discrimination *http://www.eoc.org.uk/Default.aspx?page=15655* (accessed May 2006).

Ellis, Evelyn, 'The Definition of Direct Discrimination in European Sex Equality Law'(1994) 19 E.L.R., 561, 564–6.

Equality: A New Framework. Report of the Independent Review of the Enforcement of UK Anti-Discrimination Legislation (Oxford: Hart, 2000), para.1.5.

'Equality Commissions Publish Annual Reports', (2006) 156 Equal Opportunities Review.

'Facts and figures about the situation of women in Europe', Published by European Women's Lobby *http:www.womenslobby.org* (accessed July 2007)

Fathers and the Modern Family, EOC Research, EOC: Manchester, 2007 (available at *www.eoc.org.uk*—accessed August 22, 2007).

Fiss, Owen, ' Groups and the Equal Protection Clause', (1976) 5 Philosophy and Public Affairs, pp.107–177.

Fredman, Sandra, 'The Age of Equality', in S. Fredman and S. Spencer, *Age as an Equality Issue* (Oxford: Hart, 2003), 21–69, 46–50.

Fredman, Sandra, 'Equality: A New Generation' (2001) 30 I.L.J. 145, pp.163–5.

Fredman, Sandra, *Discrimination Law* (Oxford: Oxford University Press, 2002), pp.67–8.

Fredman, Sandra , *Women and the Law* (Oxford: Clarendon Press, 1999) pp.226–227.

Freeman, Alan David, 'Legitimising Racial Discrimination Through Anti-discrimination law: A Critical Review of Supreme Court Doctrine' (1978) 62 Minnesota Law Review 1049.

Gardner, John, 'Discrimination as Injustice' (1996) 16 O.J.L.S. 367.

Gardner, John, On the Ground of Her Sex(uality) (Spring 1998) 18 O.J.L.S. 167–187 (excerpts).

Gooding, Caroline and Anna Lawson (eds.), *Disability Rights in Europe* (Oxford: Hart, 2004), 199–218, 211–214.

Grimshaw, Damian and Jill Ruberry, *Undervaluing Women's Work*, EOC Working Paper Series No.53, Equal Opportunities Commission: Manchester, Spring 2007, pp.v-x.

Hannett, Sarah, 'Equality at the Intersections' (2003) 23 O.J.L.S 65–86, at 78.

Hill Jr., Thomas E., *Autonomy and Self-Respect* (Cambridge: Cambridge University Press, 1991), pp.31–37.

Holmes, Elisa, 'Anti-Discrimination Rights Without Equality' (2005) 68(2) M.L.R. 175–194, at p.186.

Identity Cards Bill: CRE Briefing, House of Commons: Committee Stage, January 20, 2005, para.12.

ILO Equal Remuneration Convention, 1951 (No.100)—articles 2.1 and 3.3. Copyright © International Labour Organization 1951.

Issacharoff, Samuel, and Erica W. Worth, 'Is Age Discrimination Really Age Discrimination? The ADEA's Unnatural Solution' 72 N.Y.U.L. Rev. 780, 780–783.

Iyer, Nitya, 'Categorical Denials: Equality Rights and the Shaping of Social Identity', (1993–1994) 19 Queen's L. J. 179, at 193 (excerpts).

Joseph, Sarah, Jenny Schultz and Melissa Castan, *The International Covenant on Civil and Political Rights: Cases, Materials, and Commentary* (Oxford: Oxford University Press, 2nd edn., 2004), pp.13–4.

Lester, Anthony, and Geoffrey Bindman, *Race and Law* (London: Longman, 1972), p.100.

Lewis, Melina, *Asylum: Understanding Public Attitudes*, (Institute for Public Policy Research: London 2005), p.39.

Loury, Glenn C., *The Anatomy of Racial Inequality* (Cambridge, Mass: Harvard University Press, 2002) pp.151–152.

McConnell, Michael W., 'Free Exercise Revisionism and the Smith Decision', (1990) 57 U. Chicago L. Rev. 1108, at p.1152.

McCrudden, Christopher, 'Rethinking Positive Action' (1986) 15 I.L.J. 219.

McCrudden, Christopher, 'Institutional Discrimination' (1982) 2 O.J.L.S. 303 (excerpts).

McCrudden, Christopher, 'Changing Notions of Discrimination' in S. Guest and A. Milne (eds.), *Equality and Discrimination: Essays in Freedom and Justice*, Archives for Philosophy of Law and Social Philosophy, (Stuttgart: Franz Steiner Verlag Wiesbaden GMBH, 1985). With permission from

Franz Steiner Verlag GmbH, Birkenwaldstr. 44, D-70191 Stuttgart, Germany.

MacKinnon, Catherine A., 'Difference and Dominance' in *Feminism Unmodified* (Cambridge, Mass.: Harvard University Press, 1987), at pp.37–38.

MacKinnon, Catherine A., *Sexual Harassment of Working Women: A Case of Sex Discrimination* (New Haven: Yale University Press, 1979). With permission from Yale University Press.

Mason, Andrew, 'Political Community, Liberal Nationalism and the Ethics of Assimilation', (1999) 109(2) Ethics 261–286.

Meenan, H., 'The Future of Ageing and the Role of Age Discrimination in the Global Debate' [2005] The Journal of International Aging, Law & Policy 1–41, 6–11.

Modood, Tariq, *Multicultural Politics* (USA: University of Minnesota Press, 2005), pp.38–39, 42–45.

O'Cinneide, Colm, 'The Commission For Equality And Human Rights: A New Institution For New And Uncertain Times' 36(2) Industrial Law Journal 141–162, 147–149.

O'Donovan, Katherine, *Sexual Divisions in Law* (London: Weidenfeld and Nicolson, 1985) at pp.16–18.

O'Donovan, Katherine, and Erika Szyszczak, *Equality and Sex Discrimination Law* (Oxford: Blackwell Ltd, 1988). With kind permission of Blackwell Publishing.

Parfitt, D., ' Equality and Priority' in A. Mason (ed.) *Ideals of Equality* (Oxford: Blackwell, 1998). With kind permission of Blackwell Publishing.

Peach, Professor Ceri, Centre for the Environment, Oxford University, Letter to *The Guardian*, September 28, 2005.

Postema, Gerald J., *Bentham and the Common Law Tradition* (Oxford: Clarendon Press, 1986).

Raz, J., *Ethics in the Public Domain*, (Oxford: Clarendon Press, 1994) at p.26.

Raz, J., *The Morality of Freedom* (Oxford: Clarendon Press, 1987) at p.228.

Sargeant, Malcolm, 'The Employment Equality (Age) Regulations 2006: A Legitimisation of Age Discrimination in Employment' (2006) 35 I.L.J. 209–227.

Schwarzenbach, Sybil A., 'On Civic Friendship' (October 1996) 107 (1) Ethics 97–128, at p.102.

Simmonds, Nigel E., *The Decline of Juridical Reason: Doctrine and theory in the legal order* (Manchester: Manchester University Press, 1984), p.8.

Solomos, John, *From Equal Opportunity to Anti-Racism: Racial Inequality and the Limits of Reform*, Policy Paper in Ethnic Relations No.17, Centre for Research in Ethnic Relations, Warwick: University of Warwick, 1989.

Statement Of The Equal Opportunities Commission: 'New EOC Research shows bigger challenges in the workplace for ethnic minority women' April 7, 2006 *http://www.eoc.org.uk/Default.aspx?page=18589* (accessed May 20, 2006).

Sooben, Phillip N., 'The Origin of the Race Relations Act', Research Paper in

Ethnic Relations, No.12 (Centre for Research in Ehnic Relations: Warwick, 1990).

Swift, Jonathan, 'Justifying Age Discrimination' (2006) 35 Industrial Law Journal Vol.232.

Taylor, Charles, *Multiculturalism and "The Politics of Recognition"*, (Princeton University Press), pp.37–44.

The U.N. International Covenant on Civil and Political Rights (ICCPR) 1966, Art.26.

van Dijk, P., and G.J.H. van Hoof, *Theory and Practice of the European Convention on Human Rights* (Antwerp: Insertia, 4th edn, 2006), pp.718–720.

Waddington, L., *Implementing and Interpreting the Reasonable Accommodation Provision of the Framework Employment Directive: Learning from Experience and Achieving Best Practice* (Brussels: E.U. Network of Experts on Disability Discrimination, 2004) 31–34.

Waldron, Jeremy, 'Indirect Discrimination' in *Equality and Discrimination: Essays in Freedom and Justice*, Archives for Philosophy of Law and Social Philosophy (Stuttgart: Franz Steiner Verlag Wiesbaden GMBH, 1985). With permission from Franz Steiner Verlag GmbH Birkenwaldstr. 44, D-70191 Stuttgart, Germany.

Waldron, Jeremy, *Law and Disagreement* (Oxford: Oxford University Press, 1999), p.264.

Weber, Mark C., 'Disability and the Law of Welfare: A Post-integrationist Examination' (2000) University of Illinois Law Review 889.

Westen, Peter, 'The Empty Idea of Equality' (1982) 95 Harv. L. R. 537.

Winant, Howard, 'Theoretical Status of the Concept of Race, In Les Black and John Solomos (eds.), *Theories of Race and Racism: A Reader* (London: Routledge, 2000).

Wintemute, Robert, 'From "Sex Rights" to "Love Rights": Partnership Rights as Human Rights', Ch.6 in Nicholas Bamforth (ed.), *Sex Rights: the Oxford Amnesty Lectures 2002* (Oxford: Oxford University Press, 2005), pp.187–191.

Wintemute, Robert, 'Sexual Orientation and Gender Identity', Ch.10 of Colin Harvey (ed.), *Human Rights in the Community: Rights as Agents of Change* (Oxford: Hart, 2005).

Wintemute, Robert, *Sexual Orientation and Human Rights: The United States Constitution, the European Convention, and the Canadian Charter* (Oxford: Clarendon Press, 1995).

Young, Iris Marion, *Justice and the Politics of Difference* (NJ: Princeton University Press, 1990), Chapter 2.

Abdulaziz, Cabales and Balkandali v United Kingdom (1985) 7 EHRR 471.

Broeks v The Netherlands (172/84), April 9, 1987.

Clark v TGD Ltd t/a Novacold [1999] ICR 951.

De Freitas v Permanent Secretary of the Ministry of Agriculture, Fisheries, Land and Housing [1999] 1 A.C. 69.

Dudgeon v United Kingdom (1982) 4 EHRR 149.

Employment Division v Smith, 494 U.S. 872 (1990), US Supreme Court, April 17, 1990.

Goodwin v Post Office [1999] I.C.R. 302, 308.

Granovsky v Minister for Employment and Immigration [2000] 1 S.C.R. 703, S.C.C. 28.

Griggs v Duke Power Co (1971) 401 US 424, 430–1.

King v Great Britain-China Centre Court of Appeal, CA (Civ Div) [1992] I.C.R. 516.

Multani v Commission Scolarie Marguerite-Bourgeoys [2006] SCC 6 (excerpts).

Orok v Shepherds Bush Housing Association Ltd, 17 May 2006; Case No.3306338/05, Reported in (2007) 165 Equal Opportunities Review, published by IRS on June 1, 2007.

Peake v Automotive Products Ltd [1977] I.C.R. 968 (alternative citations [1978] QB 233; [1978] I W.L.R. 853; [1978] I All. E. R. 106).

R. (On the Application of Shabina Begum) v Headteacher and Governors of Denbigh High School (Shabina Begum). R. v Secretary of State for Education and Employment Ex p. Williamson, House of Lords, February 24, 2005, [2005] H.R.L.R. 14.

Smith v Gardner Merchant Ltd [1999] I.C.R. 134, Court of Appeal, CA (Civ Div).

Sandra Lovelace v Canada, Communication No. R. 6/24, U. N. Doc. Supp. No. 40 (A/36/40) at 166 (1981).

Strathclyde Regional Council v Porcelli [1986] I.C.R. 564,

Timishev v Russia 55762/00; 55974/00, [2005] ECHR 858 (December 18, 2005).

University of California Regents v Bakke 438 U.S. 265 (1978).

TABLE OF CONTENTS

TABLE OF CASES

TABLE OF STATUTES

TABLE OF STATUTORY INSTRUMENTS

TABLE OF CODES OF PRACTICE

INTRODUCTION

The publication of this book now could not be more timely. The creation of a single administrative agency, the Equality and Human Rights Commission, is about to be followed by a Single Equality Act, which will codify in one statute the discrete laws which at the time of writing prohibit discrimination on different grounds. We are also at a critical stage in the development of our conception of the underlying purposes and place of anti-discrimination law in the legal system and in both domestic and global society. An important question, examined in this book, is whether anti-discrimination law reflects or embodies a constitutional principle.

I have been fortunate to have had a series of favourable vantage points from which to observe the piecemeal growth of anti-discrimination law in Britain and to compare it with what has been happening elsewhere. The earliest legislation was of course the Race Relations Act 1965. In its original form the Bill from which the Act sprang applied the ordinary criminal law to acts of unlawful discrimination which were to be made criminal offences. A group of members of the Society of Labour Lawyers, some of whom were familiar with the legal system in the United States, found this approach surprising. It reflected a strategy for confronting racial discrimination which dated back to the period after the Civil War and the ending of slavery in the 1860s. It had been abandoned in the US because it had been found ineffective.

After the second world war, to the successful outcome of which black people in the United States had made a major contribution, it came to be acknowledged that old patterns of de facto segregation and discrimination needed to be contested vigorously. Starting in the industrial states of the east coast, a series of statutory commissions were created with wide powers. Their task was to investigate complaints of racial discrimination and seek to resolve them, not by the imposition of penalties, but by recommending constructive measures within corporations and institutions to promote equal treatment, coupled with payment of compensation where merited.

The UK government in 1965 changed course and the Bill was amended to adopt this US framework. The 1965 Act created the Race Relations Board which was meant to be modelled on the US commissions. These now included the Equal Employment Opportunities Commission, a federal body established by the Civil Rights Act 1964.

Political compromises produced what was sadly but a pale shadow of the US model—unlike them it had no power to conduct public hearings or to bring proceedings—but the germ of a viable legal framework for anti-discrimination law was there. Roy Jenkins, who had become Home Secretary after the Act came into force but before any steps had been taken to implement it, appointed his friend Mark Bonham-Carter to be chairman of the new Board. The other members were Learie Constantine (Lord Constantine) the famous West Indian cricketer, and Alderman Langton, Lord Mayor of Manchester. John Lyttle, a former official of the Labour party, was made chief executive and there was a small staff of about seven people. I was appointed the Board's legal adviser on a part-time basis, a position I held for the whole of the Board's ten year existence.

Bonham-Carter made it a condition of accepting the appointment that he be allowed to report on the effectiveness of the new law. Two independent committees were appointed: one—administered by the organisation Political and Economic Planning—was to investigate the extent of discrimination in employment, housing, and other spheres not covered in the 1965 Act; and the other to examine the state of anti-discrimination law in the US and other countries. I was one of the three members of the latter committee. The chairman was the late Professor Harry Street. The third member was Geoffrey Howe Q.C., the future Foreign Secretary and now Lord Howe of Aberavon. We were able to travel to see the US laws in operation, as well as those in Canada, which was virtually the only other country in the world with anti-discrimination law in a developed form.

The aims of anti-discrimination law in the 1960s were moulded by the social and political needs of the time. Though, in America, gender and other grounds were embraced by the legislation, in Britain race was the only focus. Immigration from the Caribbean and Indian sub-continent had been encouraged by the demands of the post-war economy for labour. Citizens of the Commonwealth saw Britain as their motherland and there were virtually no immigration restrictions before 1968. The findings of the PEP study that there was widespread discrimination in housing, employment and the provision of goods facilities and services to the public and the recommendations of the Street Report that the law should be extended to these areas enabled the Labour government of James Callaghan to balance its acceptance of the case for extending the law to restrict immigration with greater protection for those immigrants who had been allowed to settle in Britain. Hence the cynical coupling of the Race Relations Act 1968 with the illiberal Commonwealth Immigrants Act in the same year.

The conception of discrimination underlying the statutes of 1965 and 1968 was influenced by the overt hostility to black people by many white employers, landlords, and others wielding economic power. Acts of discrimination by them were often conscious and visible. The focus of the law was thus on disparate treatment—on overt individual instances of direct discrimination. Only such discrimination was targeted by the 1968 Act. Later, the prevalence of hidden forms and patterns of discrimination began to be understood by those responsible for government policy. In the United States it was not until the Supreme Court decision in *Griggs v Duke Power Company* (1971) 401 U.S. 424 that it became clear that treatment which was equal in form but discriminatory in effect could be unlawful. Whereas the US legislation allowed the definition to be extended by judicial interpretation to embrace indirect discrimination, that possibility did not appear to exist under the 1968 Act.

Furthermore, the Race Relations Board had very limited investigatory powers and rarely made use of them. Although—an advance on the 1965 Act framework—the 1968 Act gave the Board power in the last resort to take county court proceedings against those alleged to have unlawfully discriminated, opportunities to pursue substantial cases were very few, especially in employment. The problem was that the legislation had built into the enforcement process an obligation to seek conciliation. Only if conciliation failed could proceedings be brought and there was little opportunity to control the conciliation process which was entrusted to a series of voluntary committees. In employment cases the delays and weak compromises were particularly acute because the appointment of committees was delegated to employers' organisations and trade unions, neither of which were committed to the legislation. They rarely reached a compromise or recognised a failure to achieve a result, without which the Board could take the matter no further. As the Board's legal adviser and solicitor, I was responsible for preparing all the cases brought by the Board during its lifetime between 1966 and 1976. It was a frustrating experience. There was a total absence of employment cases. Those few cases which were pursued seemed trivial—at least in the context of widespread and serious discrimination of which we were increasingly aware. Many seemed to be concerned with refusal of service in public houses and bars, for which the accepted tariff of compensation was £5.

What has been called the second generation of discrimination law came into existence with the Sex Discrimination Act 1975, which was followed by the Race Relations Act 1976 adopting a similar structure and powers. Roy Jenkins was again Home Secretary. He visited the United States and was clearly much influenced by developments there. The Government had published a White paper based on that experience. The Equal Opportunities Commission was given much stronger investigatory powers than the Board and the EOC's powers were replicated in the Commission for Racial Equality which replaced the Board under the 1976 Act.

Now of course the prohibition of indirect discrimination had been enacted and the commissions had the wide investigatory powers which the Street Committee had recommended in 1967 and which were intended to enable the commissions to uncover and act against patterns and practices of discrimination. These were manifestly causing widespread injustice to ethnic minorities and to women but were beyond the range of the prohibition of direct discrimination and indeed of the individual complaint. The compulsory conciliation process was dropped and individuals could now bring cases themselves in employment tribunals and county courts. The legislation of the mid-1970s is that currently in force at the time of publication of this book. Its operation is analysed in great detail in the ensuing chapters.

In addition to that legislation and the Disability Discrimination Act which followed it in 1995, a third generation of anti-discrimination laws began in mainland Britain to emerge at the beginning of the 21st century, though it was prefigured in Northern Ireland legislation against religious discrimination from 1989. The Race Relations (Amendment) Act of 2000 enacts a challenge to inequality which was recognised only in token form in the 1976 Race Relations Act (though not in the Sex Discrimination Act). Section 71 of the 1976 Act required local authorities "to make appropriate arrangements with a view to securing that their various functions are carried out with due regard to the need (a) to eliminate unlawful racial discrimination; and (b) to promote equality of opportunity, and good relations, between persons of different racial groups." This convoluted requirement had no sanctions attached to it and was expressed in such vague language as to make it impossible to police. But the concept of a positive duty to promote equality is hugely important and has been expanded and developed in the 2000 Act, and now, by the Equality Act 2006, extended to gender as well as race.

A further vital dimension in the development of anti-discrimination law has been the growing influence of European law, which has impelled the UK government to extend anti-discrimination law to a range of other areas: age, sexual orientation, religion. This plethora of laws is examined in great detail in the following chapters.

The accretion of new prohibited areas of discrimination and the introduction of refinements to the scope of the legislation and the enforcement procedures by amendments and regulations have created a nightmare of legal complexity. In 1995, the Disability Discrimination Act added a new anti-discrimination commission to the CRE and EOC. Adding further grounds of prohibited discrimination forced the government to face the impracticality of a continuing proliferation of separate bodies and separate laws all seeking the elimination of a single source of injustice. The Equality Act 2006 has now abolished the separate commissions and has established the Equality and Human Rights Commission to replace all of them, take responsibility for all anti-discrimination issues, and in addition to fulfil belatedly the role of a human rights commission, nearly ten years after the Human Rights Act 1998, which it is designed to promote. What remains to be done is to rationalise and co-ordinate the multiplicity of legislation. A Single Equality Act is now promised to accomplish this task.

Although in 1965 the original notion of criminalising racial discrimination was abandoned, the Act of 1965 contained a new criminal offence of incitement to racial hatred. This has been perpetuated in the subsequent legislation,with various changes, and in 1986 was transferred to the Public Order Act, where it properly belongs. The law has been controversial and variably enforced under successive governments. The decision to prosecute requires the consent of the Attorney-General. Some have been unwilling to give their consent. In 2005, new legislation controversially extended the scope of the criminal law to include incitement to religious hatred. Certainly, the absence of such a law gave rise to anomalies because the borderline between the ethnic and religious characterisation of some groups was problematical. It was the political context of increasing anti-Muslim racism which mainly motivated the government to promote it. The issue of emerging anti-Muslim racism is addressed in chapter 12 on race discrimination, and hate speech is discussed in chapter 8.

The overriding justification for this book is the transformation of anti-discrimination law from a particularised and, for many, marginal topic into a central plank of a newly developing constitutional dispensation in which human rights are the bedrock of our democratic system. This book is a thorough and profound exploration and exposition of the current complexities of discrimination law and its place in the constitutional framework. It is made especially important by recent legislative changes and those which are about to come. It will be an immensely valuable key to the understanding of a vital area of law and social policy.

Sir Geoffrey Bindman, November 25, 2007

PART A

THE NATURE OF DISCRIMINATION LAW

1

KEY ISSUES AND QUESTIONS IN DISCRIMINATION LAW

I. Introduction

At the start of the twenty-first century, the existence of legal protections against invidious forms of discrimination is treated as a central feature of the constitutional architecture of liberal democracies.[1] The US Bill of Rights, the Canadian Charter of Rights and Freedoms, and the post-apartheid South African Constitution are among the more obvious examples of constitutional codes which contain protections against discrimination. In western Europe, the European Convention on Human Rights now contains a stand-alone protection against discrimination in the form of Art.14 (although, since the United Kingdom has not acceded to Protocol 12, Art.14 may only be invoked in conjunction with another Convention right before domestic courts[2]), whilst the European Union now has a comprehensive Treaty-based commitment to combating discrimination on various grounds as well as its own Charter of rights.[3] The grounds of discrimination which are explicitly prohibited, the range of actions which fall within the ambit of relevant non-discrimination provisions, and the areas of life which are affected by those provisions, inevitably vary to some extent according to the jurisdiction and the constitu-

1 The first part of this chapter draws on Nicholas Bamforth, "Conceptions of Anti-Discrimination Law" (2004) 24 O.J.L.S. 693.

2 For criticism of the UK's position concerning Protocol 12, see Urfan Khaliq, "Protocol 12 to the European Convention on Human Rights: a step forward or a step too far?" [2001] P.L. 457; Sandra Fredman, "Why the UK Government should Sign and Ratify Protocol 12" (2002) 105 Equal Opportunities Review 21; Robert Wintemute, "Filling the Article 14 'Gap': Government Ratification and Judicial Control of Protocol No.12 ECHR: Part 2" [2004] E.H.R.L.R. 484.

3 For analysis, see Mark Bell, *Anti-Discrimination Law and the European Union* (Oxford: Oxford University Press, 2002) and "Article 13 EC: The European Commission's Anti-Discrimination Proposals" (2000) 29 I.L.J. 79; Sandra Fredman, "Equality: A New Generation?" (2001) 30 I.L.J. 145; Elspeth Guild, "The EC Directive on Race Discrimination: Surprises, Possibilities and limitations" (2000) 29 I.L.J. 416; Lord Lester, "New European equality measures" [2000] P.L. 562; Lisa Waddington, "Article 13 EC: Setting Priorities in the Proposal for a Horizontal Employment Directive" (2001) 29 I.L.J. 176. For discussion specifically of the Charter, see Sandra Fredman, Christopher McCrudden & Mark Freedland, "A EU Charter of fundamental rights" [2000] P.L. 178; Bob Hepple, "The EU Charter of Fundamental Rights" (2001) 30 I.L.J. 225; Sionaidh Douglas-Scott, "The Charter of Fundamental Rights as a Constitutional Document" [2004] E.H.R.L.R. 37.

tional or treaty provision in issue. Furthermore, different legal systems invoke divergent justifications—whether at a policy level or in terms of basic constitutional principle—when deciding which activities count as examples of the type of impermissible discrimination that the law should prohibit. In addition, some societies grant wide powers to courts when it comes to recognising new grounds of prohibited discrimination or when reinterpreting or refashioning existing rules, whilst others prefer to leave such issues to the legislature where this is practicable.

Despite the existence of these (and other) important differences, it is nonetheless clear that there is quite a lot more to unite than to divide contemporary systems of protections against discrimination, whether in terms of their perceived social role or in terms of their apparently settled place in the constitutional structure.[4] This unity of purpose and place is underlined by the increased judicial citation of comparative authority in cases involving discrimination issues,[5] something which would be impracticable in the absence of the common point of reference which the existence of legal protections against discrimination in so many jurisdictions provides. This is not to say, of course, that the scope of those protections—even down to the issue of whether particular questions count as "discrimination" questions at all—is uncontroversial: in all of the jurisdictions concerned, there has been legislative and/or juridical debate about the ambit of protections against discrimination, particularly where those protections touch on areas which involve cultural sensitivity. What seems uncontroversial, however, is the claim that at the start of the twenty-first century, constitutional democracies are expected and, in practice, try to articulate a public commitment to challenging invidious forms of discrimination as part of their basic concern to safeguard human rights (whether they are successful in doing so is a different question). Furthermore, that commitment is, as a matter of almost universal practice, expressed in legal provisions of a constitutional nature or importance in the society concerned. This premise forms the starting point for the exploration of discrimination law to be conducted in this book.

This chapter provides an overview of some of the key issues which must be considered if we accept the premise that a realistic understanding of discrimination law must provide a proper account of its constitutional dimensions. In Section II, we consider the constitutional dimensions of discrimination law in greater detail, and contrast our preferred constitutional

[4] A unity which may be reinforced by the overlapping historical origins of some of the anti-discrimination concepts in play in the USA and the UK: see further chapter 2.

[5] See, for example, *Lawrence v Texas* (2003) 123 S. Ct. 1406 (overruling *Bowers v Hardwick* (1986) 106 S. Ct. 2841); *National Coalition for Gay and Lesbian Equality v Minister of Home Affairs (No.2)* (2000) 2 S.A. 1; *R. (Carson) v Secretary of State for Work and Pensions* [2005] UKHL 37. For commentary, see Lord Steyn, "Human Rights: The Legacy of Mrs Roosevelt" [2002] P.L. 473, 481; William Eskridge, "*Lawrence v Texas* and the imperative of comparative constitutionalism" (2004) International J. of Constitutional Law (I-CON) 555. For critical analysis, see Christopher McCrudden, "A Common Law of Human Rights? Transnational Judicial Conversations on Constitutional Rights" (2000) 20 O.J.L.S. 499.

conception of the subject with a more traditional approach in the United Kingdom, whereby protections against discrimination are treated as the creature of a narrower legal discipline: namely employment law. In Section III, we consider the central conceptual questions which must be tackled by any system of discrimination law, and which provide a backdrop to our consideration of domestic discrimination law in this book. The constitutional dimensions of discrimination law become still clearer when many of these questions are considered.

II. Employment-focused and Constitutional Conceptions of Discrimination Law

At least when dealing with the subject at a general level rather than in relation to specific heads of discrimination, scholars of discrimination law in the United Kingdom have often approached their material from the direction of employment law instead of treating it primarily as the embodiment of a constitutional commitment which happens in practice to have a particular impact on the regulation of the employment relationship.[6] Viewed historically, this focus is understandable. For in the United Kingdom, discrimination has traditionally been tackled through statutes which prohibit specific types of discrimination in a specified range of social contexts, principally the employment relationship (although also including, for example, the provision of goods and services). The Sex Discrimination Act 1975, Race Relations Act 1976 and Disability Discrimination Act 1995 follow this model—subject to certain variations as between the different measures—as, generally-speaking, has EU law when dealing with prohibited grounds of discrimination.[7] It therefore comes as little surprise that anti-discrimination protections should have attracted detailed attention principally from employment lawyers: a response which, one might imagine, has probably also been driven by the fact

[6] The words "happens in practice" should not be taken as meaning that the impact is random: as several authors have explained, the social power of employers may well explain why the law regards it as right to place them under a duty not to discriminate, by contrast with other private actors (see, e.g., John Gardner has argued in "Liberals and Unlawful Discrimination" (1989) 9 O.J.L.S. 1, 11 and "On the Ground of Her Sex(uality)" (1998) 18 O.J.L.S. 167, 167; Andrew Koppelman, *Antidiscrimination Law and Social Equality* (New Haven: Yale University Press, 1996), p.14; on the more general social significance of the employment relationship, see Hugh Collins, *Employment Law* (Oxford: Oxford University Press, 2003), pp.3–5).

[7] Although note the slight variations in coverage of the Racial Equality Directive (Directive 2000/43) and Employment Equality Directive (Directive 2000/78): see further Mark Bell, *Anti-Discrimination Law and the European Union*, n.3 above, Ch.5; see also Ch.2 of this book. Nationality discrimination has always been prohibited in a broader range of contexts in E.C. law (see, e.g., Paul Craig & Grainne de Burca, *EU Law: Text, Cases and Materials* (Oxford: Oxford University Press, (4th edn, 2008), Chs 18 and 19 (goods), 21 (workers), 22 (establishment); Catherine Barnard, *EC Employment Law* (Oxford: Oxford University Press, 3rd edn., 2006), Ch.4 (persons)).

that discrimination law might be said to be motivated by similar concerns for social justice as those which are often associated with employment law.[8] Text books have tended to reflect this, with detailed treatment of protections against discrimination being found mainly in works concerning employment law.[9] As Sandra Fredman has argued, "anti-discrimination law in Britain has emerged from labour law, and pre-dates human rights law by a long way".[10]

The parameters of discrimination law, conceived of from an employment-centred perspective, are powerfully illustrated by the first edition of Aileen McColgan's work on the subject.[11] In her text-length treatment, McColgan's main focus was on the areas regulated by domestic anti-discrimination statutes, reinforced where appropriate by EU law and the European Convention. By and large, McColgan treated the concept of discrimination as being, for practical purposes, pretty much synonymous with the subject-matter of the specific statutes she analysed. In consequence, the overwhelming focus of her analysis was on discrimination on specified statutory grounds in the contexts of employment and access to goods, facilities and services. Even when the focus switched to the common law's regulation of discrimination, or the presence of discrimination-related issues in other contexts such as immigration, this appeared to be by way of contrast to the coverage provided by the anti-discrimination statutes.[12] Discrimination law thus appeared, for McColgan, to be concerned almost entirely with the workplace.[13] Although McColgan was keen to acknowledge the contribution made by EU law and the European Convention on Human Rights, and indeed to cite materials from non-European jurisdictions where this was relevant, it was not important to her project to stress the broader constitutional dimensions of protections against discrimination. McColgan's first edition provided, in other words, a

[8] For a general survey of the history of employment law, see Hugh Collins, "Labour Law as a Vocation" (1989) 105 L.Q.R. 468, 468–471.

[9] See, classically, Paul Davies & Mark Freedland, *Labour Law: Text and Materials* (London: Weidenfeld & Nicolson, 2nd edn., 1984), pp.41–80, 369–421,521–6; Lord Wedderburn, *The Worker and the Law* (London: Sweet & Maxwell, 3rd edn., 1986), Ch.6. More recently, see Simon Deakin & Gillian S. Morris, *Labour Law* (Oxford: 4th edn, Hart Publishing, 2006), Ch.6 (but see also pp.51–52 and 99–105), Hugh Collins, K.D. Ewing & Aileen McColgan, *Labour Law: Text and Materials* (Oxford: Hart, 2nd edn., 2005), Chs 3 & 4 (Ch.6, entitled "Human Rights and Labour Law", also deals entirely with "workplace issues" (p.609)); A.W. Bradley & K.D. Ewing, *Constitutional and Administrative Law* (Harlow: Pearson/Longman, 14th edn., 2007) deals with discrimination issues rather sporadically and in diverse areas such as EU law, the Convention and the composition of the judiciary—see, e.g. pp. 132–133, 388, 422–432, 465–466.

[10] *The Future of Equality in Britain*, Equal Opportunities Commission Working Paper No.5 (Manchester: EOC, 2002), p.35.

[11] In her book *Discrimination Law: Text, Cases and Materials* (Oxford: Hart, 2nd edn., 2005).

[12] See the discussion at n.11 above, pp.4–20. Clear summaries of the scope of McColgan's work can be found at pp.33 & 35.

[13] As Hugh Collins observes, the "primary focus" of employment law "always concerns the contractual relation of employment, which is the legal expression of the economic and social relationship through which work is performed" (*Employment Law*, n.6 above, p.5). In fairness to McColgan, it must be noted that her book was written before the Human Rights Act 1998 came into force, and contains an acknowledgement that the Act might have a relatively wide influence (whatever the substantive effects of that influence): n.11 above, pp.2, 23–7, Ch.11.

classic example of a comprehensive, stand-alone exposition of the subject from an employment-focused perspective. While the second edition of her work, published in 2005, is concerned to integrate EU and Convention material as far as this is possible, the organisation of the discussion still closely parallels the prohibited statutory grounds of discrimination and does not attempt to consider, for example, the general character of the Art.14 prohibition on discrimination contained in the European Convention, nor its potential reach outside of the established grounds or contexts in which discrimination is prohibited.[14]

There are two reasons for claiming that an employment-focused conception of discrimination law[15] by no means accounts—at least, without considerable stretching—for the range of situations in which particular forms of treatment tend nowadays to be categorised (whether morally or legally) as invidious forms of discrimination. A good example is provided by the (now-repealed) s.28 of the Local Government Act 1988 in the United Kingdom, which prohibited local authorities from "intentionally promot[ing] homosexuality" or promoting "the teaching in any maintained school of the acceptability of homosexuality as a pretended family relationship". Whilst the repeal of this provision was driven by the argument that it constituted an unjust form of legislative discrimination on the basis of sexual orientation, the provision had no direct connection with employment: it was a public law provision which imposed a specific statutory duty on local authorities in relation to public education and service-provision, and was enforceable via the public law application for judicial review procedure. In reality, highly significant anti-discrimination issues arise, sometimes within the ambit of the Human Rights Act 1998 and sometimes not, in the context of the criminal law,[16] police practice,[17] judicial review (particularly in the context of immigration law),[18] family law and property law[19]—a point which is amply reflected in the range

[14] *Discrimination Law: Text, Cases, and Materials* (Oxford: Hart, 2nd edn., 2005), especially Chs 2 to 4. McColgan notes at p.2 that:

> "the implementation in the UK of the Human Rights Act 1998 has had the effect that Article 14 of the European Convention on Human Rights, together with a number of other provisions of the Convention which are particularly relevant to discrimination, have been given a form of effect in domestic law. The contours of these provisions are considered at various points throughout the book and there is a brief explanation . . . of how the HRA operates. *But the discussion of the HRA is only by way of context and background for the most part in a book whose focus is on the detailed statutory regulation of discrimination*" (emphasis added).

[15] The most authoritative definition of a conception in the legal context is probably that provided by John Rawls in *A Theory of Justice* (Oxford: Oxford University Press, revised edn., 1999), p.5.

[16] See, for example, the interest in regulating "hate crimes": Maleiha Malik, "'Racist Crime': Racially Aggravated Offences in the Crime & Disorder Act 1998 Part II" (1999) 62 M.L.R. 409.

[17] See, for example, the *Report of an Inquiry by Sir William MacPherson of Cluny* (the Stephen Lawrence Inquiry), Cm.4262–I, 1999.

[18] In the immigration context, see *R. v Entry Clearance Officer, Bombay, Ex p. Amin* [1983] 2 A.C. 818. In the non-immigration context, see *R. v Secretary of State for Employment, Ex p. Equal Opportunities Commission* [1995] 1 A.C. 1; *R. v Ministry of Defence, Ex p. Smith* [1996] Q.B. 517 (successfully appealed to the European Court of Human Rights as *Smith v United Kingdom* (2000) 29 E.H.R.R. 493).

[19] See *Ghaidan v Godin-Mendoza* [2004] UKHL 30.

of subject-matters which are litigated by specialist discrimination law practitioners. There are in fact common principles and goals which motivate the legal regulation of discrimination in a wide range of areas, including but not limited to employment law.[20] By adopting an overly employment-focused conception of discrimination law, we risk losing sight of this broader perspective, leading to a fragmented and piecemeal treatment of the issues.[21]

The second, related reason is comparative and explicitly constitutional: namely that the protections against discrimination which are to be found in the US Constitution, the Canadian Charter, and the European Convention on Human Rights clearly have as their principal focus (albeit to differing degrees, even within the same instrument) the actions of state bodies or the operation of laws. Many key cases which articulate non-discrimination norms have involved a state body as defendant and have turned on a point or points of constitutional interpretation.[22] Courts have also sometimes suggested that a broader range of factors may be involved in cases involving the state than are involved in cases—including employment disputes—between private parties.[23] One might, in consequence, argue that there is much to be lost at the level of simple understanding if we fail to acknowledge the constitutional dimensions of discrimination law, particularly when there appears to have been cross-fertilisation between the United States, western European and other jurisdictions in developing the prohibited heads of discrimination.[24] This claim cannot be rebutted merely by citing cases in which constitutional protections against discrimination have been found—at least where the correct account of their scope has been used—to touch on private law relationships. For, while such protections have often been extended by interpretation or by analogy to private actors, this has characteristically been via consideration either of the nature of the constitutional right involved or of the role of the state (and, by

[20] For a practitioner's survey of the very wide range of contexts in which discrimination issues might currently be felt to arise, see Anthony Lester, "Equality and United Kingdom Law: Past, Present and Future" [2001] P.L. 77.

[21] In this sense, the argument assumes that an appropriate conception is one which "fits" the law: see further Ronald Dworkin, *Law's Empire* (London: Fontana, 1986), pp. 228–232, 245–6, 255.

[22] For a classic illustration in the context of US law, see Paul Brest, "In Defense of the Antidiscrimination Principle" (1976) 90 Harvard L. Rev. 1. While Brest's definition of the "antidiscrimination principle" may be somewhat narrow (its scope can be seen by comparing pp.1, 5 & 52), he clearly articulates the notion that an essentially similar core basis exists for challenging discrimination in the contexts of the constitutional review of legislation, judicial review of executive action, and judicial scrutiny of employment decisions by the lower courts. In the context of the European Convention, see Andrew Clapham, *Human Rights in the Private Sphere* (Oxford: Clarendon Press, 1993).

[23] In the context of sexual orientation discrimination, compare the Supreme Court of Canada's decisions in *Egan v Canada* [1995] 2 S.C.R. 513 (constraints on the *public* purse as a reason for not recognising that state social security provisions should apply to same-sex as well as opposite-sex couples) with *M. v H.* (1999) 171 D.L.R. (4th) 577 (statutory framework for the division of *private* assets on the breakdown of a relationship could not justifiably be confined to opposite-sex couples).

[24] See the materials cited in nn. 4 and 5 above.

analogy, private actors) under the instrument concerned and in relation to the relevant right[25]: in other words, via judicial decision-making concerning essentially "constitutional" questions. For example, to the extent that particular Convention rights (including Art.14) have had a "horizontal" effect at common law under the Human Rights Act 1998, this has been due to judicial analysis of the nature of the right(s) in question and of the rules of interpretation embodied within or promoted by the Act itself: again, typically "constitutional" questions.[26] At a broader level, it is also useful to recall that many of the key non-discrimination provisions in the contemporary legal world—at least, if we adopt a comparative perspective—are to be found in international treaties, which have a more or less "constitutional" effect in the decisions of domestic courts, depending upon the treaty and the national legal system in issue.[27]

In consequence, the sheer range of circumstances in which non-discrimination norms tend nowadays to be invoked would seem, at minimum, to favour the inclusion of a constitutional dimension within our conception of discrimination law. This, of course, raises the question of how large that dimension should be and, in turn, of how constitutional our conception of discrimination law should be. How, for example, should we deal with employment–related prescriptions against discrimination, if they are no longer to be given an exclusive centre-stage role? Should they be ignored, or treated as something quite distinctive from explicitly constitutional protections against discrimination, or should we seek to present an integrated analysis of the whole range of situations in which the law seeks to counter invidious

[25] See, for example, *Retail, Wholesale and Department Store Union v Dolphin Delivery* [1986] 2 S.C.R. 573; *Mrs W. v United Kingdom* (1983) 32 D.&R. 10; *Mrs W. v Ireland* (1983) 32 D.&R. 211.

[26] This point is neatly captured by considering the intensive academic and judicial debate concerning the reach of European Convention rights (including the Art.14 right to non-discrimination in the enjoyment of Convention rights) in domestic United Kingdom law under the Human Rights Act 1998: see further *Douglas and Zeta-Jones v Hello! Ltd* [2001] Q.B. 697; *A v B Plc* [2002] 3 W.L.R. 542; *Campbell v Mirror Group Newspapers Ltd* [2004] UKHL 22; Nicholas Bamforth, "The Application of the Human Rights Act 1998 to Public Authorities and Private Bodies" (1999) 58 C.L.J. 159, "The True 'Horizontal Effect' of the Human Rights Act 1998" (2001) 117 L.Q.R. 34 and "A Constitutional Basis for Anti-Discrimination Protection?" (2003) 119 L.Q.R. 215; Sir Richard Buxton, "The Human Rights Act and Private Law" (2000) 116 L.Q.R. 48; Murray Hunt, "The 'Horizontal' Effect of the Human Rights Act" [1998] P.L. 423; Ian Leigh, "Horizontal Rights, the Human Rights Act and Privacy" (1999) 48 I.C.L.Q. 57; Lord Lester & David Pannick, "The Impact of the Human Rights Act on Private Law: the Knight's Move" (2000) 116 L.Q.R. 380; Gavin Phillipson, "The Human Rights Act, 'Horizontal Effect' and the Common Law" (1999) 62 M.L.R. 824; Sir William Wade, "Human Rights and the Judiciary" [1998] E.H.R.L.R. 520 and "Horizons of Horizontality" (2000) 116 L.Q.R. 217. The assertions contained in the text should not be taken to suggest that the Human Rights Act (or any other statute) can or should be *formally* identified as a "constitutional" statute with distinctive properties, as Laws L.J. controversially suggested in *Thoburn v Sunderland City Council* [2002] EWHC 195 Admin, para.[62].

[27] In relation to the reception of the European Convention into national legal systems, see Conor Gearty (ed.), *European Civil Liberties and the European Convention on Human Rights: A Comparative Study* (Dordrecht: Martinus Nijhoff, 1997). For discussion of discrimination on the basis of religion in terms of US constitutional law and public international law, see Michael Perry, *Religion in Politics: Constitutional and Moral Perspectives* (New York: OUP, 1997), Ch.1.

forms of discrimination, whether using constitutional measures, employment-related rules, or any other type of provision? Perhaps predictably, some of the most powerful accounts in the United States adopt an exclusively (or almost exclusively) constitutional focus by analyzing the role of the federal courts in prohibiting discrimination under the auspices of the US Constitution and Bill of Rights. For judicial interpretation of the Fourteenth Amendment to the US Constitution has provided some of the key US case law concerning protections against discrimination,[28] and the federal courts' approach to the interpretation of this provision is frequently treated as a key indicator of their approach to constitutional interpretation more broadly.[29] In consequence, those who seek to explain why and how far it is right to use the Fourteenth Amendment to challenge invidious forms of discrimination must clearly employ theories whose central concern is with constitutional interpretation and constitutional law. Such theories have implications for the employment relationship—to the extent that the US Constitution and Bill of Rights impacts upon it—but that relationship is very far from centre-stage.

This is particularly evident in David Richards's analysis. Richards is concerned to present an "interpretive proposal for how, in light of the history and political theory of the Reconstruction Amendments"—including the Fourteenth Amendment—such Amendments "should be interpreted in contemporary circumstances".[30] Richards suggests that, viewed historically and as a matter of constitutional law, the "Reconstruction Amendments are best understood ... as a set of ramifying principles all interpretive of the central judgment of political morality at the heart of the abolitionist movement [relating to slavery], namely, the fundamental moral wrongness of slavery because it abridges fundamental human rights".[31] Reasoning by analogy,[32] Richards argues that the "normative conception of *moral slavery* is ... the best interpretation of the prohibition of slavery in the Thirteenth Amendment".[33] This conception "condemns a structural injustice marked by two interlinked

28 Most famously in *Brown v Board of Education* (1954) 347 U.S. 483.

29 For prominently examples, see John Hart Ely, *Democracy and Distrust: A Theory of Judicial Review* (Cambridge: Harvard University Press, 1980), especially Ch.6; Ronald Dworkin, *Law's Empire*, n.23 above, Ch.10, especially pp. 379–397. It also seems clear that David A.J. Richards's interpretation of the role of the US Constitution in discrimination cases falling within its ambit is merely a part of his broader theory relating to the correct constitutional interpretation of the Reconstruction Amendments (that is, the Thirteenth to Fifteenth Amendments): see *Conscience and the Constitution: History, Theory, and Law of the Reconstruction Amendments* (Princeton: Princeton University Press, 1993), especially p.17. Note also, however, the argument that the Civil Rights Act 1964 has itself impacted upon interpretation of the Fourteenth Amendment: William Eskridge and John Ferejohn, "Super-Statutes" (2000–1) 50 Duke L.J. 1215, pp.1237–1242, 1246 ff.

30 Richards, *Women, Gays, and the Constitution: the Grounds for Feminism and Gay Rights in Culture and Law* (Chicago: University of Chicago Press, 1998), p.3; Richards's preferred interpretative approach is sketched out at pp.18–19, 27–32. Richards analyses the general significance of the Reconstruction Amendments in *Conscience*, n.29 above, esp. Chs 4 & 8.

31 Richards, *Women, Gays*, n.30 above, p.132; see also p.262.

32 See, e.g., Richards, *Women, Gays*, n.30 above, pp.137–140, 142–3.

33 Richards, *Women, Gays*, n.30 above, p.3.

features: first, its abridgment of the basic human rights of a group of persons, and second, the rationalization of such abridgement on inadequate grounds reflecting a history of unjust treatment (involving the dehumanization of the group)",[34] and can be used by analogy to justify (using a "historically informed normative analysis"[35]) the prohibition under the Fourteenth Amendment of provisions which discriminate on the bases of sex and sexual orientation.[36] Such provisions should be seen as suspect under the Fourteenth Amendment, Richards argues, because "they use a basis for laws condemned by the constitutional prohibition of moral slavery. They enforce the culturally constructed basis for the unconstitutional moral slavery of a group ... and are condemned, for this reason, as a fundamentally illegitimate basis for law".[37] At a practical level, Richards applies this argument to justify the constitutional prohibition of sex discrimination[38] and to argue for the striking down, under the Fourteenth Amendment, of laws which either discriminate in general terms against lesbians and gay men or which specifically exclude them from marriage rights and military service.[39] Moral slavery, for Richards, "powerfully illuminates the common grounds of constitutional principle that condemn extreme religious intolerance, racism, sexism, and homophobia".[40]

Richards's arguments are purely constitutional, relating as they do to the interpretation of the Thirteenth to Fifteenth Amendments (the "Reconstruction Amendments"). Yet their central concern—within the context of the US Constitution and Bill of Rights—is with the protection against invidious forms of discrimination of historically disfavoured groups. Another US writer, Andrew Koppelman, provides an account which, while being similarly constitutionally-focused, is slightly broader in scope. Koppelman aims to provide a justification for what he characterises as the "antidiscrimination project": that is, a project which "seeks to reconstruct social reality to eliminate or marginalize the shared meanings, practices, and institutions that unjustifiably single out certain groups of citizens for stigma and disadvantage".[41] As Koppelman repeatedly acknowledges, this project—if executed to its max-

34 David A.J. Richards, *Identity and the Case for Gay Rights: Race, Gender, Religion as Analogies* (Chicago: University of Chicago Press, 1999), p.3; for earlier formulations, see Richards's *Women, Gays*, n.30 above, pp.3 and 155 (also pp.106, 114–124, 458).

35 Richards, *Women, Gays*, n.30 above, p.4.

36 See, on a cumulative basis, Richards, *Women, Gays*, n.30 above, pp.137–140, 142–3, 174, 176–8, 182, 199–200, 203, 261, 464–5. At *Women, Gays*, p.263, Richards suggests that "To interpret the Reconstruction Amendments in this way makes powerful normative sense of their volcanic significance in American constitutional history and interpretation" (see also *Identity and the Case for Gay Rights*, n.34 above, pp.53, 108, 156, 171–2). For an evaluation of recent Fourteenth Amendment case law from the standpoint of the moral slavery theory, see *Women, Gays*, pp.283–6. For analysis of case law concerning lesbian and gay rights claims, see *Women, Gays*, pp.346–373, 402–5, 407–8; for earlier analysis covering race, gender and sexuality, see *Conscience*, n.29 above, Chs 5–7.

37 Richards, *Women, Gays*, n.30 above, p.5.

38 Richards, *Women, Gays*, n.30 above, Chs 2 & 3, especially pp.92 and 100.

39 Richards, *Women, Gays*, n.30 above, p.3, Chs 7 & 8.

40 *Identity and the Case for Gay Rights*, n.34 above, p.3.

41 n.6 above, p.8; see also p.116.

imum justifiable extent—would not be confined to requiring the federal US government, or even the state governments, to act in opposition to invidious forms of discrimination: instead "[t]he social reality this project seeks to reconstruct operates on several levels: the beliefs and values shared by members of society; the practices that are constructed by (and, in turn, construct) those beliefs; and the distribution of wealth and power that emerges out of those practices".[42] For Koppelman, a counter-discrimination commitment should, in other words, affect *private bodies* (or some of them) as much as it would the state.[43] However, despite his commitment to social reconstruction as something which potentially involves private employers as well as the state, it is clear that Koppelman's arguments are of a fundamentally constitutional nature. For although Koppelman deploys three theories—which he describes as the process theory, the social stigma theory and the group disadvantage theory—when determining which groups should be able to claim the protection of non-discrimination norms, these theories derive from and are tied throughout the argument to an interpretation of the Equal Protection Clause of the Fourteenth Amendment.[44] In consequence, while Koppelman's three theories can be used to differing extents to justify regulation of the private employment relationship, the intellectual basis of any justification is tied very firmly to principles which originate and mainly operate in the constitutional sphere. It is only by demonstrating the existence of appropriate constitutional arguments for coercing private actors, as well as appropriate analogies between the private employment relationship and the constitutional sphere, that Koppelman can explain why the three theories are capable of justifying—to the extent that they do—a project of social reconstruction involving private actors.[45] What Koppelman categorises as the "antidiscrimination project" is, in short, essentially a project of constitutional law.

Richards and Koppelman offer fascinating constitutional analyses of the Fourteenth Amendment, and it should be stressed that it was never the intention of either author to provide an account of discrimination law as a discrete discipline.[46] Nonetheless, our discussion of their analyses should hopefully show (particularly if we compare them with McColgan's account) that an *exclusively* constitutional conception of discrimination law—that is, one which left the private employment relationship wholly out of the discussion, or viewed it entirely as an appendage of a particular constitutional provi-

[42] n.6 above, p. 92.

[43] For examples, see n.6 above, pp.140, 242, 244, 248.

[44] See especially n.6 above, pp.115–6.

[45] See n.6 above, Chs 1 to 4.

[46] Some recent studies of distinctive aspects of discrimination law (or of areas in which the law arguably fails to offer protection against invidious forms of discrimination, or itself discriminates) published in the United Kingdom have either diluted the previously-dominant employment-related focus or have explicitly treated the availability of protections against discrimination as a matter of comparative constitutional law: see, e.g., Mark Bell, n.3 above; Robert Wintemute, *Sexual Orientation and Human Rights: The United States Constitution, the European Convention, and the Canadian Charter* (Oxford: Clarendon Press, 1995).

sion—would fall just as short of providing a complete account as does a purely employment-focused conception. To construct an account which encompasses all the contexts in which protections against discrimination now operate—particularly when dealing with the position in the United Kingdom—we must therefore find a place for discrimination law's treatment of the employment relationship (and of other analogous relationships), albeit *within* a broader constitutional framework. An adequate constitutional conception of discrimination law must, in other words, be capable of locating and explaining the employment-related aspects of the subject. In this respect, Sandra Fredman's concise account of the subject is promising.[47] Fredman deals in detail with the employment law aspects, but considers in equal detail the potential of constitutional instruments for combating discriminatory social practices in many different social contexts. For example, she examines the treatment of protections against discrimination at different constitutional levels (purely UK, European, international); as a matter of comparative constitutional law (by comparing, in different contexts, the types of legal protection available in western Europe, Canada, the United States and South Africa, and their extents); *and* by reference to some of the theoretical justifications which have been advanced in order to explain the normative legitimacy of such protections.[48] As we will see in the next section, she also considers one of the important constitutional question focused on by Richards and Koppelman: namely, how far it is right for courts to develop the boundaries of protections against discrimination via judicial interpretation. Although Fredman does not explicitly state her support for a constitutional conception, her understanding of discrimination law clearly fits within this bracket: her account seeks to give proper weight to the constitutional dimensions of the subject without unjustifiably down-playing the importance of its employment-related aspects.

It is possible, at an analytical level, to go still further than Fredman in integrating the employment aspects of the subject within a constitutional framework. We can see how this might be done by considering the United Kingdom's incorporation of EU law via the European Communities Act 1972, and its bringing into domestic law of much of the European Convention on Human Rights via the Human Rights Act 1998.[49] These developments have created new rules of statutory interpretation: statutes must be read so far as this is possible in the light of directly effective provisions of EU law, including

[47] *Discrimination Law* (Oxford: Oxford University Press, 2002). The employment-focused and constitutional conceptions are not the only possible ways of viewing discrimination law: see Mark Bell, n.3 above, Ch.6 & pp.198–202, for further possibilities.

[48] Chapter 1 deals with theoretical justifications for anti-discrimination protections, and Ch.2 with the historical and social background. Chapters 3 to 6 then examine different types of legal and extra-legal measures in a variety of jurisdictions.

[49] For analysis of competing accounts of the authority of EU law and Convention norms within domestic UK law, see Nicholas Bamforth, "Courts in a Multi-Layered Constitution", Ch.11 in Nicholas Bamforth & Peter Leyland (eds.), *Public Law in a Multi-Layered Constitution* (Oxford: Hart, 2003). Sandra Fredman analyses some of the resulting overlaps and differences between specific statutory heads of prohibited discrimination and the Human Rights Act 1998 in *The Future of Equality in Britain*, n.10 above, pp.35–9.

protections against discrimination,[50] and of Convention rights including the Art.14 prohibition on discrimination (enjoyed, in the UK, in relation to other rights).[51] Where a statute cannot be read in this way, it must—where direct effect is in operation—be "disapplied" in a case involving EU law.[52] In a case involving Convention rights, a declaration of incompatibility may be issued concerning the statute, although it continues to have effect and must be applied by the court.[53] It would seem that courts also regard themselves as bound to interpret the common law in the light of Convention rights.[54] In consequence, statutes must in principle be read subject to the EU law and European Convention prohibitions on discrimination: a requirement which is of *general* application, covering statutes dealing with employment discrimination just as much as statutes dealing with other subject-matters.[55] This requirement can be characterised as being of a constitutional nature for two reasons. Firstly, it deals with a classic question of constitutional law: namely how courts should interpret statutes. This question is "constitutional" in the sense that it deals with the powers and spheres of action of vital state institutions: for in determining which rules of statutory interpretation to apply, we are concerned with the proper approach of the courts when dealing with and applying the products of the legislative process.[56] Secondly, the requirement derives its authority (at least for domestic courts) from statutes—the European Communities Act 1972 and the Human Rights Act 1998—which, however their particular provisions are understood, are generally (and rightly) seen as central features of the United Kingdom's current constitutional architecture: both statutes seek to lay down ground rules for the division of power between different "layers" (national, EU and Convention-related) within the contemporary constitutional structure,[57] and at a purely national level both have important implications for the powers of the executive, the courts and the legislatures (the Westminster and devolved legislatures in the case of EU law; the devolved legislatures, in the case of the Convention).[58]

[50] *Marleasing v La Comercial* [1990] E.C.R. I-4135; in the domestic context, see *Webb v EMO Air Cargo (UK) (No.2)* [1995] 1 W.L.R. 1454.

[51] *Ghaidan v Godin-Mendoza* [2004] UKHL 30; *R. (Carson) v Secretary of State for Work and Pensions* [2005] UKHL 37.

[52] *R. v Secretary of State for Transport, Ex p. Factortame (No.2)* [1991] 1 A.C. 603; see *R. v Secretary of State for Employment, Ex p. Equal Opportunities Commission*, n.18 above, for "disapplication" of a statutory provision in the sex discrimination context.

[53] Human Rights Act 1998, ss.4 & 10, Sch.2.

[54] See the materials considered at n.26 above.

[55] In the case of the *Marleasing* interpretative obligation, n.50 above, the domestic statute must simply cover the same subject-matter as the relevant EU provision; in the case of the Human Rights Act 1998, a Convention right must be in issue in the litigation in which the court is asked to interpret the statute or common law provision.

[56] See further Jeremy Waldron, *Law and Disagreement* (Oxford: Oxford University Press, 1999), Chs 1–6.

[57] See further Nicholas Bamforth & Peter Leyland, Ch.1 (especially pp.1–10) in Nicholas Bamforth & Peter Leyland (eds.), *Public Law in a Multi-Layered Constitution*, n.49 above.

[58] As was made clear at n.26 above, this is not to suggest that the Human Rights Act 1998 can or should be *formally* identified as a special "constitutional" statute.

The requirements of the rules dealing with interpretation, "disapplication" and declarations of incompatibility will be considered in further detail in Chapter 2. It is the *existence* of these rules which is relevant for present purposes. For, if it is right to characterise these rules as imposing requirements of a constitutional nature, then each time a court deals with a case involving discrimination within the employment relationship, it must—in so far as either EU law or the European Convention is relevant to that case—deal with the subject-matter in the light of those constitutional requirements.[59] The requirements provide a filter through which the subject-matter of the case must pass in order for the court to pronounce judgment, and circumscribe the possible judgments which are open to the court. In consequence, a heavily constitutional "gloss" could be said to apply to judicial decision-making in employment discrimination cases, even though such cases may formally count as private law disputes between an employer and employee. Such an argument could be made with even greater force in relation to the USA or Canada, where the non-discrimination aspects of the relevant constitutional instruments (the Fourteenth Amendment to the US Constitution and s.15 of the Canadian Charter) form a central aspect of constitutional law, and where compatibility with those aspects is a test of the constitutional validity of ordinary statutes.

In and of itself, however, the existence of such a "gloss" is not enough to justify the contention that the employment discrimination case law can and should be integrated into a constitutional conception of discrimination law, viewed as a whole. For if a constitutional "gloss" applies in employment discrimination cases, it must surely also apply in *every* area of domestic law—contract, tort, property, etc.—to which the rules dealing with interpretation, "disapplication" and declarations of incompatibility apply. Whilst it seems uncontroversial to suggest that these latter subjects now have a constitutional dimension,[60] it would be an exaggeration to claim that they have been integrated in an analytical sense with constitutional law considerations, or that they must be understood in the light of a constitutional conception. A further factor is therefore needed in order to explain why this stronger claim can be made about discrimination law. Such a factor can be provided if we apply

[59] This point seems to be implicit in a comparison drawn extra-judicially by Lord Steyn between common law human rights (including the right to non-discrimination) and human rights (including the right to non-discrimination) under the Human Rights Act 1998: "What is the significance of classifying a right as constitutional? It is meaningful. It is an indication that added value is attached to the protection of the right. It strengthens the normative force of such rights. It virtually rules out arguments that such rights can be impliedly repealed by subsequent legislation. Generally only an express repeal will suffice. The constitutionality of a right is also important in regard to remedies. The duty of the court is to vindicate the breach of a constitutional right, depending on its nature, by an appropriate remedy" ("Democracy Through Law" [2002] E.H.R.L.R. 723, 731). We do not necessarily endorse the characterisation of constitutional rights in this quotation.

[60] For a good illustration, see the substantive chapters of Richard Clayton & Hugh Tomlinson in relation to the Human Rights Act 1998: *The Law of Human Rights Volume 1* (Oxford: Oxford University Press, 2000).

Hugh Collins's scheme of legal categorisations, initially devised in order to explain the nature of employment (or, as he calls it, labour) law. Having set out two rival conceptions of employment law, Collins suggests that:

Hugh Collins, "Labour Law as a Vocation" (1989) 105 L.Q.R. 468

p.473: "This investigation of the coherence of these two conceptions of Labour Law rests upon certain assumptions. My standard of coherence comprises three elements: an investigation of the social problem, or family of problems, to be addressed; a gathering together of the legal materials relevant to that problem; and finally, a normative vision of how those problems might best be resolved through the instrument of law. Notice that there is no suggestion that coherence requires the identification and reasoned elaboration of a few elementary principles of law into an entire regulatory scheme. Although some fields of law such as contract and crime are marked by the quest for coherence according to a small set of principles, Labour Law like other contextual fields such as Family Law, has never aspired to such conceptual unity. What I suggest brings coherence to Labour Law as a distinct field of legal studies is a sense of vocation. This vocation springs from a conviction that urgent social problems need to be addressed, and blossoms into a vision of justice in this sphere of social life in which law plays its appropriate role. The sense of vocation marks out a field of inquiry, establishes criteria of relevance of legal materials, and finally constructs a critical vantage-point from which to assess the substance and techniques of current law."

Given the contextual nature of discrimination law, its historical link to employment law, and its concern with issues of historical and contemporary social justice, it is easy to view the employment-related and constitutional conceptions of the subject in terms of Collins's "vocational" categorisation. For example, the "urgent social problems" which have characteristically formed the focus of employment law, broadly conceived—namely the allocation, operation and regulation of power within the employment relationship—might be said to carry over into the employment law conception of discrimination law, as does the "sphere of social life"—namely, the workplace—with which employment law is concerned.[61] For supporters of the employment law conception of discrimination law, the subject is merely a specialist branch of the broader discipline: it is concerned with the social problem of power being allocated or exercised within the workplace (by employers, employees or trade unions) in a way which involves impermissible discrimination, or—arguably—being exercised by the government or legislature (for example, by the passing of regulatory rules) in a discriminatory fashion which affects the workplace. For supporters of the constitutional conception of discrimination law, by contrast, the workplace is but one example of a far wider range of social situations in which it is relevant to talk of impermissible discrimination,

[61] And, on one view, the regulation of the employment market more broadly: see Hugh Collins, n.8 above.

the sources of such discrimination lying in the actions of individuals, employers, trade unions, the police, the courts, the government, the legislature, and so on. The discriminatory allocation or exercise of power within the employment relationship is, from this perspective, but one example—albeit an important one—of the social evil(s) which discrimination law is intended to counter.

What this analysis reveals is a point of basic common sense: namely, that for supporters of a constitutional conception of discrimination law, the sense that there is a particular social injustice which the law should seek to fight is prevalent in every area of the subject. We might say that government has a special obligation not to discriminate, or a special duty to take steps to counter discrimination,[62] but it is clear that the basic social evil which is involved in acts of invidious discrimination (as to which, see Chapter 3) is similar in whatever context such acts occur.[63] This being so, it makes very good sense to view all of these areas as an integrated whole when considering the law's response. It is this factor—deriving from the "sense of vocation" in play in all non- discrimination cases—that explains, when coupled with the existence of a constitutional "gloss" in ordinary employment discrimination cases, why an integrated constitutional conception of the subject is ultimately to be preferred. Such a conception will be applied throughout this book.

It has been argued in this section that a constitutional conception of discrimination law—albeit one which gives suitable weight to the employment relationship—is to be preferred to what has been categorised as the employment-focused conception. It is easy to see why, historically-speaking, an employment-focused conception should until recently have played a leading role in UK scholarship, but it does not fit the contemporary circumstances. By approaching discrimination law from a constitutional standpoint, we can understand the law's response to invidious forms of discrimination more fully. In the next section, we begin to examine the law's role in identifying particular forms of discrimination as invidious, and the organisation of systems of discrimination law more generally.

III. Key Questions in Discrimination Law

Understood in its most general sense, "to discriminate" means to make a selection between options, whatever they are, or to draw some type of distinction.[64] This being so, the term does not always refer to decisions or selec-

[62] Or, with Andrew Koppelman, that the "antidiscrimination project" encompasses private employers as well as government: text to nn.41 to 45, above.

[63] This is not to say that additional constitutional evils are not involved in cases involving government.

[64] This paragraph is taken from Nicholas Bamforth, "Prohibited Grounds of Discrimination under EU Law and the European Convention on Human Rights: Problems of Contrast and Overlap" (2007) *Cambridge Year Book of European Legal Studies*, Ch.1.

tions that are regarded as wrongful: a point which has both analytical and normative dimensions. The analytical dimension is captured in Lord Walker's observation in *R. (Carson) v Secretary of State for Work and Pensions* that impermissible discrimination "must always be on some ground. Completely blind, motiveless malevolence may be anti-social and abhorrent but it cannot amount to discrimination, because it is indeed indiscriminate".[65] Normatively, many or most of the distinctions or selections made in everyday life are perfectly acceptable: as John Gardner suggests, if "you keep befriending vain people, or falling in love with bullies, the explanation may be that you are insufficiently discriminating."[66] In consequence, the concern of discrimination law is not to prohibit *all* selections or distinctions as a matter of principle. Instead, it is to counter those selections or distinctions that are regarded as *invidious*: for example, those made on the basis of race, sex, sexual orientation, age, disability, or religion. Furthermore, such distinctions or selections may not be impermissible in every context in which they occur. Sometimes, competing rights or values (depending upon the jurisdiction)—for example, expression or privacy—or policy goals (for example, military efficiency or business necessity) are deemed to assume a higher priority. Differentiating between permissible and impermissible distinctions or selections is a core task of any system of discrimination law.

In Chapter 3, we consider the theoretical justifications which are offered for the prohibition or regulation of impermissible forms of discrimination, and/or for the promotion of various types of non-discrimination measure or strategy. Such justifications can help, particularly when coupled with empirical data concerning patterns of disadvantage, in characterising the nature of the social problem which discrimination is felt to represent, and in consequence in explaining which distinctions or selections *should*, in normative terms, be identified as examples of invidious discrimination properly falling within the law's reach.[67] Relevant justifications can therefore be used to inform and to criticise the results of boundary-setting exercises conducted by legislatures and courts. The present section is concerned to evaluate exercises of this type, given that they lie at the heart of all systems of discrimination law, and often serve to highlight the constitutional properties or dimensions of the subject (despite the differences between the protections against discrimination in force in different jurisdictions). In practice, at least nine questions can be associated with attempts to differentiate between permissible and impermissible distinctions or selections. In any system of discrimination law, a tenth question—dealing with extra-legal methods of addressing discrimination—must also be

65 [2005] UKHL 37, para.[50].

66 "On the Ground of Her Sex(uality)" (1998) 18 O.J.L.S. 167 at 167. For specific discussion in the context of Art.14 of the European Convention, see P. van Dijk & F. van Hoof, *Theory and Practice of the European Convention on Human Rights* (Antwerp: Insertia, 4th edn., 2006), pp.1034–9.

67 See Nicholas Bamforth, "Setting the Limits of Anti-Discrimination Law: Some Legal and Social Concepts", Ch.5 in Janet Dine and Bob Watt (eds.), *Discrimination Law: Concepts, Limitations, and Justifications* (Harlow: Longman, 1996), pp.56–8.

considered. We begin merely by listing these questions, given that most of them are dealt with in detail in subsequent chapters and all of them are referred to when we introduce the central elements of domestic discrimination law in Chapter 2. We next move on to consider the first question—namely, the respective roles taken by courts and legislatures in deeming particular grounds or instances of discrimination to be impermissible—at greater length given that it is of *particular* significance to the constitutional character of discrimination law. We then explore an issue closely associated with the fourth and fifth questions highlighted here—namely, whether it is possible to identify a "generational" approach to protections against discrimination—given that it is of significance when considering the general character of the protections against discrimination in force in any given legal system. Finally, we consider the eighth question—concerning the differences between "discrimination" as understood in common-sense or colloquial terms and legal terms—an issue which is of practical importance given that many cases which might be thought on a common sense basis to involve discrimination issues are in fact litigated under headings which have no necessary connection with discrimination law. A full understanding of discrimination law demands that we consider these cases as well as those which are categorised in legal terms as involving discrimination issues.

A. *The Ten Questions Outlined*

It should be stressed that the following division of questions is approximate, and that other divisions are possible. Furthermore, aspects of the various questions overlap. Nonetheless, it is useful to present the questions as a list so as to offer some keys to understanding the main aspects of discrimination law systems: aspects which we shall consider in later chapters. The questions are as follows:

(1) Who is protected?

Which grounds of discrimination—sex, race, and so forth—are prohibited, and which institution—the legislature or the judiciary—is empowered (or primarily empowered) to determine that a given ground is impermissible? To the extent that the judiciary is involved in this exercise, a closely related issue is what test or standard it is to deploy in scrutinising discriminatory behaviour. For example, is the same test to be employed, or employed in the same way, regardless of the ground of discrimination in issue, or does the test employed and/or intensity of judicial scrutiny vary depending upon the ground concerned? We consider this question in the next section, and (in detail) in Chapter 2.

(2) When are they protected?

In which contexts is discrimination on an impermissible ground to be prohibited or otherwise regulated? Is the primary focus of protections against discrimination to be discrimination in employment and in the provision of goods, facilities and services, or is the prohibition of discrimination also a concern when testing the legality of public authorities' actions, in the interpretation of legislation, or even (where permitted) in judicial review of legislation? We consider this question in Chapter 2 and in the chapters dealing with the different prohibited grounds of discrimination (chapters 10 to 15).

(3) Who has to protect them?

Who are the permissible claimants and defendants? Are protections against discrimination enforceable only by individual litigants who claim to be victims of impermissible discrimination, or can public enforcement agencies play a part? And are such protections enforceable mainly or only against employers and service-providers, or are public authorities placed under a distinct or even a special duty not to discriminate on impermissible grounds? We consider this question in Chapters 2, 16 and 17.

(4) How wide are the protections?

To what extent is the law concerned to prohibit indirect (or "disparate impact") discrimination, whereby the application of an apparently neutral practice or criterion produces an outcome which is unfavourable to members of the disadvantaged group, as well as direct (or "disparate treatment") discrimination, which involves the drawing of overt (usually intentional) distinctions between members of an advantaged and a disadvantaged group?[68] To what extent are affirmative action and analogous "positive" measures to be permitted, and discriminatory forms of harassment prohibited? These issues form part of a broader debate about the extent to which the law should be focusing on and penalising individual instances of identifiable discrimination, and how far it should be concerned with promoting general, positive duties to establish a non-discriminatory environment. We consider this debate below, and question (4) in chapters 2, 4 and 5, and in the chapters dealing with the different prohibited grounds of discrimination (chapters 10 to 15).

(5) Can discrimination sometimes be justified for policy reasons?

When (if at all) are measures which appear to involve impermissible discrimination on a *prima facie* basis nonetheless capable of justification for policy reasons? Which test is used to determine whether a measure may be justified? This latter point tends to involve standards such as proportionality or, in the United States, "heightened" or "strict" scrutiny. We consider this question in

[68] The exact operation of the test for each type of discrimination of course varies slightly as between jurisdictions.

Chapters 2, 4 and 5, and in the chapters dealing with the different prohibited grounds of discrimination (chapters 10 to 15).

(6) What happens when protection from discrimination clashes with other rights or values?

How are clashes between different prohibited grounds of discrimination (and, in consequence, the right to non-discrimination in relation to each of these grounds), or a prohibited ground of discrimination (and, in consequence, the right to non-discrimination in relation to that ground) and a competing human right to be dealt with? An example of the first of these situations might be the question whether it is lawful for a religious institution to refuse for doctrinal reasons which constitute a part of its right to religious freedom to employ a gay man or lesbian, and an example of both the first and second might be the question whether it is lawful for such an institution publicly to espouse, for doctrinal reasons, homophobic or sexist policies, or the extent to which racist "hate speech" should be permitted as an aspect of freedom of expression.[69] Analogies can be drawn between these issues and the policy-related justifications considered under question (5), given that the boundaries of protections against discrimination are in issue in both cases and proportionality or proportionality-style tests tend to be used in each. Nonetheless, the cases are separable in so far as question (6) deals with clashes between competing rights rather than, as under question (5), protections against discrimination and a competing policy interest. We consider this question further in Chapters 8 and 9 and in the chapters dealing with the different prohibited grounds of discrimination (chapters 10 to 15).

(7) Are there other exceptions to protection from discrimination?

Are there exceptions from the duty not to discriminate which can lift cases out of the scope of protections against discrimination altogether? This question is distinct from the previous two in that, although situations falling within its scope may still involve the issue of competing rights or policies, we are concerned here with the wholesale exclusion of protections against discrimination (for example, for reasons of national security or immigration control) rather than case-by-case justification. We consider this question further in the chapters dealing with the different prohibited grounds of discrimination (chapters 10 to 15).

(8) How far can other human rights be used to combat discrimination?

How far can challenges to the adverse treatment of members of particular social groups be brought under constitutional or other legal headings which are not explicitly focused on the prohibition of discrimination? For example, cases which might be thought to raise discrimination issues in terms of their

69 See, for analysis of expression and non-discrimination as competing rights, David A.J. Richards, *Free Speech and the Politics of Identity* (Oxford: Oxford University Press, 1999).

facts are sometimes litigated using constitutional rights such as privacy (sometimes associated with due process of law) and dignity. We consider this question further below and in Chapters 2, 10, 11 and 13.

(9) What legal remedies are available, and who may seek them?

If impermissible discrimination is found to have taken place, what legal remedies are available to claimants? Do the available remedies differ according to the identity of the defendant? What are remedies intended to signify or achieve? How closely connected must a remedy be to a definable wrong committed by the defendant? In some circumstances, public enforcement agencies may seek to bring discrimination-related proceedings (even though they have not themselves been harmed by the discriminatory actions which form the subject-matter of the proceedings), so that the question whether a legal remedy is available is not always synonymous with the question of who is protected by the law in relation to invidious discrimination. We explore this question further in Chapters 2, 16 and 17.

(10) How far should we look outside the law for solutions?

On the assumption that law can solve only a part of the social problem posed by invidious discrimination, what is the role of extra-legal strategies such as supply-side measures, contract compliance and social policy? We consider this question in Chapter 17.

To some extent, each of these questions serves to highlight the constitutional properties or dimensions of the subject. The first three questions are particularly significant in this regard in that possible answers are likely—in any system with a written constitution, or even just (as in the United Kingdom) certain legal provisions that appear to be of particular constitutional significance—to turn on judicial interpretation or application of such provisions. Statutory protections against discrimination in areas such as employment must, in the jurisdictions concerned, always be interpreted in the light of relevant constitutional provisions (or, in the United Kingdom, provisions of particular constitutional significance), and legislation may in the USA and Canada be set aside for incompatibility with those provisions. For this reason, many of the key "constitutional" cases involving non-discrimination issues tend to be concerned with one or more of these three questions. The fourth to seventh questions can also have constitutional dimensions, although they are sometimes slightly less visible than in relation to the first three questions. For, depending upon the law of the jurisdiction in issue, direct and indirect discrimination arguments might be made in explicitly "constitutional" cases involving judicial review of executive action or legislation, and in private law cases focusing typically on discrimination in the workplace: that is, cases with a less obvious (but still present) constitutional "flavour". The sixth and eighth key questions, while emphasising the constitutional dimensions of the subject, sit at the intersection between discrimination law and the broader discipline of human rights law, and tend to arise in any jurisdiction with a set of clearly articulated positive rights.[70]

B. *The Roles of Courts and Legislatures in Challenging Discrimination*

Under both the employment-related and constitutional conceptions of discrimination law—but in particular under the constitutional conception, given its explicit focus on the role of courts in interpreting non-discrimination provisions—it is important to consider the extent to which it is appropriate for courts, as opposed to legislatures or executive agencies, to play a significant role in combating invidious forms of discrimination. In practice, this issue usually arises when we consider how far courts may recognise that protections against discrimination should extend to groups which are not explicitly recognised as falling within their scope, and how far such decisions should be left to the legislature. This issue needs to be considered at two levels, the first of which is normative and general, the second related specifically to discrimination law.

Starting at a normative, general level, the role of courts in combating invidious forms of discrimination merely constitutes one facet of a far broader debate—of potential relevance in every area of the legal system, and a central topic of discussion in legal philosophy—concerning the proper role of courts and (or, as opposed to) legislatures. It is useful to consider this debate since arguments which arise at the general, normative level often inform more specific arguments within discrimination law. The nature of the debate within legal philosophy has been neatly captured by Jeremy Waldron:

Jeremy Waldron, *Law and Disagreement* (Oxford: Oxford University Press, 1999)

p.264: "Judgement foreshadows disagreement, and in politics the question is always how disagreements among the citizens are to be resolved [. . .] this includes disagreements about rights and justice and thus disagreements about the things covered by the abstract moral principles to which the people have committed themselves in their constitution. Different forms of government amount to different answers to the question: whose judgement is to prevail when citizens disagree in their judgements?"

Slightly earlier in his account, Waldron develops this point at greater length:

[70] Discrimination law forms one component part of human rights law.

pp.243–4: "... since people disagree about what rights we have or ought to have, the specification of our legal rights has to be accomplished through some political process.

Rights, in other words, are no exception to the general need for authority in politics. Since people hold different views about rights and since we have to settle upon and enforce a common view about this, we must ask: 'Who is to have the power to make social decisions, or by what processes are social decisions to be made, on the practical issues that competing theories of rights purport to address?' As political philosophers, our task is to inquire into the principles and criteria by which this question of authority is to be answered. ... When someone asks, 'Who shall decide what rights we have?', one answer (*my* answer) is: 'The people whose rights are in question have the right to participate on equal terms in that decision.' But it is not the only possible answer. Instead of empowering the people on the grounds that it is after all their rights that are at stake, we might instead entrust final authority to a judicial or scholarly elite, on the ground that they are more likely to get the matter right."

Very clearly, questions relating to the grounds on which and the circumstances in which particular forms of discrimination should be legally prohibited fall within the group of issues—those relating to justice and to rights—that Waldron is discussing here. This helps explain why the extent to which the legislature rather than the courts should take the leading role in acting to combat discrimination, or the circumstances in which either institution should do so, is such a central question within discrimination law (a point also implicit in our earlier discussion of the arguments advanced by Richards and Koppelman). Answers will vary, as Waldron indicates: as should be evident from his somewhat loaded reference to a "judicial elite", Waldron himself favours a leading role for the legislature and a subsidiary role for the courts.[71] However, other legal theorists—typified, in the present context, by Ronald Dworkin—favour a stronger role for the judiciary, not least in checking the activities of the legislature.[72] Our preferred answer will in fact depend upon our background theory of justice (that is, a theory concerning the proper distribution of entitlements as between people or peoples), and more particularly our background theory of political morality (that is, a theory concerning the proper roles of constitutional institutions such as the courts, the executive and the legislature).[73] We consider the various theories of justice from which philosophical justifications for the existence of anti-discrimination protections can be derived in Chapter 3. It is these justifications which can explain why invidious forms of discrimination should in principle be legally prohibited, and in consequence why certain forms (that is, certain grounds of discrimination) deserve to be seen as invidious. In order to explain how *courts*

[71] Jeremy Waldron, *Law and Disagreement*, n.56 above, especially Chs 1,4, 5, 10, 11–13; *The Dignity of Legislation* (Cambridge: Cambridge University Press, 1999), especially Ch.1; "The Core of the Case Against Judicial Review" (2006) 115 Yale L.J. 1346.

[72] See, e.g., Dworkin's *Law's Empire*, n.21 above, *Life's Dominion: an argument about abortion and euthanasia* (New York: Knopf, 1993). David Richards and Andrew Koppelman (considered above) would also seem to fall within this group.

[73] The two sets of theories frequently being, in practice, interconnected. For an analogous exploration in the US context, see David A.J. Richards, *Toleration and the Constitution* (New York: Oxford University Press, 1986), Ch.1.

and legislatures should develop and enforce protections against discrimination, however, we must connect whichever justification is being invoked to a theory of political morality.

In domestic law, the strongest illustration of the practical importance of disagreements about the appropriate roles of different institutions can be seen in public law scholarship. In consequence, it is worthwhile considering this area briefly to see what lessons it can offer. Within public law scholarship,[74] three basic models of the appropriate roles of the courts and the legislature and/or the executive have been developed. These models have been labelled red light (or conservative normativist), green light (or functionalist), and amber light (or liberal normativist).[75] Summarising these models, Adam Tomkins has suggested that red light theorists or conservative normativists believe that "law is autonomous to and superior over politics", that the state must be kept in check by the law, that "the preferred way of doing this is through rule-based adjudication in courts", and that "the goal of this project should be to enhance individual liberty ... an idea of liberty which is best realised by having small government."[76] The red light model rests on support for the notion of a balanced constitution, with the executive being controlled politically by Parliament and legally by the courts. By contrast, in Harlow and Rawlings's words, green light theorists or functionalists are "inclined to pin their hopes on the political process".[77] They believe, according to Tomkins, that "law is nothing more than a sophisticated (or elitist) discourse of politics", that activist government is to be welcomed and that the law should serve to encourage good administrative practices, that "the best institutions to achieve these aims will not necessarily be courts" and that "the goal of this project should be to enhance individual and collective liberty where liberty is conceived of as something which is, if not constituted by the state, then ... at least facilitated by it, and ... certainly not necessarily threatened by it."[78] Such theorists therefore rely on political and administrative institutions rather than the courts as agents of social change (thereby coming close to the position advocated by Waldron).[79] Finally, amber light theorists or liberal normativists believe that "law is both discrete from and superior to politics" (in line with

[74] The term "public law" is taken here to include both constitutional and administrative law: see P.P. Craig, *Public Law and Democracy in the United Kingdom and the United States of America* (Oxford: Clarendon Press, 2000), Ch.1.

[75] See further Carol Harlow & Richard Rawlings, *Law and Administration* (London: Butterworths, 2nd edn., 1997), esp. Chs 1–4; Martin Loughlin, *Public Law and Political Theory* (Oxford: Clarendon Press, 1992).

[76] Adam Tomkins, "In Defence of the Political Constitution" (2002) 22 O.J.L.S. 157, 158; see also Martin Loughlin, *Public Law and Political Theory*, n.75 above, pp.60–61 (note that Loughlin is only talking only about *conservative* normativism at this point).

[77] Harlow & Rawlings, n.75 above, p.67. As Loughlin demonstrates (n.75 above, pp.190–206), caution is however necessary at this point: for different functionalist writers have subtly divergent views concerning the role of courts and the law.

[78] Tomkins, n.76 above, pp.158–9; see also Martin Loughlin, n.75 above, pp.60–1.

[79] Harlow & Rawlings, n.75 above, pp.76, 79. See also Martin Loughlin, *Sword and Scales: An Examination of the Relationship Between Law and Politics* (Oxford: Hart, 2000), pp.208–213, Ch.15.

red light theorists), that "the state can successfully be limited by law, although that law ought properly to allow for the administration to enjoy a degree—albeit a controlled degree—of discretionary authority", that "the best way of controlling the state is through the judicial articulation and enforcement of broad principles of legality", and—perhaps most distinctively—that "the goal of this project is to safeguard a particular vision of human rights".[80] Amber light theorists or liberal normativists thus stress that rights may sometimes trump policy considerations. They focus on judicial remedies, like their red light counterparts, but prioritise the constitutional role of the judiciary to a far greater extent.

This three-fold distinction is not perfect,[81] but it is helpful for present purposes since each model rests on a distinctive theory (or set of theories) of justice and of political morality. Red light theorists are characterised as being concerned as a matter of justice to prioritise the private rights of individuals and to protect them from incursions by the state, a concern which justifies as a matter of political morality extensive judicial intervention in defence of relevant private rights. Green light theorists, by contrast, are associated with the view that widespread government intervention in pursuit of social and economic goals is desirable as a matter of justice, and that courts are essentially conservative bodies which should be kept within defined limits in order to prevent them from resisting the policy-based decisions of elected authorities (an argument of political morality). Finally, amber light theorists are seen as prioritising an essentially liberal conception of individual rights as a matter of justice, and to favour—within certain limits—the notion that support for such rights should be given priority by any institution which is empowered to do so. While many of the arguments which feature in the debate between the three models concern the respective roles of the legislature and the courts in checking executive power, it seems clear that a more basic question—namely the degree of trust or leeway which should presumptively be given to actions or decisions of the executive and/or the legislature in a constitutional democracy—is also involved. This question is, of course, relevant not just in relation to judicial review of executive action, but also in relation to the role of the courts in *any* area in which the executive or the legislature seeks to act. That this should be so is hardly unexpected: after all, it is a basic concern of liberal theories of justice and political morality that legislative acts require a clear normative justification *whatever* their subject-matter, given their inherently coercive nature.[82] The public law debate cannot be transplanted unmodified into a discussion of discrimination law, at least if we assume that

80 Tomkins, n.76 above, p.159.

81 See Nicholas Bamforth, "Courts in a Multi-Layered Constitution", Ch.11 in Nicholas Bamforth & Peter Leyland (eds.), n.49 above, pp.301–9.

82 As an example, see the treatment of common law, statutory and constitutional interpretation in Ronald Dworkin's *Law's Empire*, n.21 above, Chs 8–10.

discrimination law should regulate private actors as well as the state.[83] However, analogous approaches to those which are in play in the public law debate can certainly be applied when considering the roles of the various institutions in discrimination law. For example, theorists who adopt a functionalist position in the public law debate would presumably be keen for Parliament to take the lead in developing protections against discrimination through specific statutes, while normativists of either type would presumptively be keen for the courts to play a broader role (although conservative normativists might entertain suspicions about an excessively human rights-focused approach).

The importance of thinking in normative terms about the roles which should be played by different institutions is also evident in the US literature about in discrimination law. For example, having presented his three accounts of US protections against discrimination, Andrew Koppelman uses them to suggest that:

> "The question whether any group should be protected by antidiscrimination law turns on the following inquiry: does the prevailing understanding of that group unjustifiably stigmatize or socially construct its members in a way that reduces the group's political power, material wealth, and autonomy?"[84]

If this question (which is predominantly a question of justice) is answered affirmatively, then Koppelman suggests that courts are entitled—as a matter of political morality—to interpret the Fourteenth Amendment Equal Protection Clause so as to bring members of the group concerned within its protection.[85] Rival theories of justice and/or political morality will justify different amounts of judicial (or legislative) activity. John Hart Ely, for example, argued in favour of a "participation-oriented, representation-reinforcing approach to judicial review" under the Fourteenth Amendment and parallel constitutional provisions.[86] According to this view, judicial intervention "can appropriately concern itself only with questions of participation, and not with the substantive merits of the political choice under attack".[87] Judicial invalidation of legislation or of executive decision-making—among other reasons, because it constitutes invidious discrimination—is thus merited only where the existing *processes* of political representation seem inadequately fitted to the representation of minority groups, even where the members of those groups possess a vote.[88] Judicial intervention is justified in order to protect minorities from a denial of

83 Given that the positions in the public law debate are concerned with institutions of the state (although some positions in the debate have implications for or overlaps with the position of private parties).

84 n.6 above, p.116.

85 n.6 above, pp.14–5; practical examples of such reasoning are to be found in Chs 3 (women) and 4 (lesbians and gay men).

86 Ely, n.29 above, p.87.

87 Ely, n.29 above, p.181.

88 Ely, n.29 above, p.86.

equality of concern and respect (essentially an argument of justice), Ely's focus on the processes of political participation being explained by a concern to prevent judicial review from undermining the legitimate claims of majority rule (rather more an argument of political morality).[89] The key point to note here is that the theory of political morality implicit in Ely's justification of constitutional review—being process-based and excluding considerations of substance—is only capable of justifying a narrower reach for anti-discrimination protections than is Koppelman's theory.[90]

Given their practical as well as theoretical dimensions, these arguments show how close the connection is between the first (normative) and second (day-to-day, and specifically discrimination law-focused) levels at which the appropriate role of courts needs to be discussed. At the second, day-to-day level, it is necessary to specify how, in any given system of discrimination law, certain grounds of discrimination are to be singled out for prohibition. This, in turn, raises the question whether the courts or the legislature are to take the lead in doing this, and what legal test a court should employ where it takes the lead (as indicated above, answers will be informed by our general normative theories and are open to criticism in the light of them). These practical questions have been explored in the work of Robert Wintemute and Sandra Fredman.

Robert Wintemute "Filling the Article 14 'Gap': Government Ratification and Judicial Control of Protocol No.12 ECHR" [2004] E.H.R.L.R. 484

p.491: "All courts interpreting general equality or non-discrimination clauses, in national constitutions and international human rights treaties, face the same dilemma. Because the business of governments and legislatures is to make distinctions or provide different treatment, the vast majority of distinctions or differences in treatment *must* be justifiable. Otherwise, governments and legislatures would be paralysed. In upholding the vast majority of differences in treatment, courts must decide whether to acknowledge in advance that the strictness of their review will vary depending on the *ground* on which the difference in treatment is based, or the nature of the *opportunity* denied."

[89] Ely, n.29 above, pp.86–7, 100–1.

[90] For Koppelman's general critique of Ely, see n.6 above, Ch.1, esp. pp. 49 & 55. For Koppelman's own view of the possible role of the regulation of private companies, see n.6 above, pp.43–6. For Ely's view of the practical ambit of anti-discrimination protections which his theory might justify in relation to women, lesbians and gay men, see n.29 above, Ch.6, especially pp.163–7. David Richards, *Women, Gays* (see pp.204, 465–6), n.30 above, also supports the view that protections against discrimination can affect private organisations, and at pp.453–7 argues against Cass Sunstein's assertion (in "Homosexuality and the Constitution" (1993) 70 Indiana L.J. 1) that courts should tread warily when dealing with lesbian and gay rights issues. In *Identity and the Case for Gay Rights*, n.34 above, pp.10–1 (see, more generally, *Conscience*, n.29 above, pp.9–12 and *Toleration and the Constitution*, n.73 above), Richards criticises Ely's theory (*inter alia*) for affording too weak a range of constitutional protections against discrimination.

Sandra Fredman, *Discrimination Law* (Oxford: Oxford University Press, 2002)

pp.67–8: "What sort of distinctions should be outlawed by the law as illegitimate and unacceptable? We could search for a unifying principle which explains existing grounds of discrimination and generates the answer to new questions. Or we could argue that the decision is simply a political one, reflecting the balance of opinion in society at a particular time. Shadowing this set of issues is the debate about which institution should make the decision: the courts or the legislature. It could be argued that since one of the main reasons for providing protection for particular groups is their political powerlessness, it is counterproductive to rely on the majority to enact anti-discrimination laws through the political process. On this view, the decision as to which groups should be protected is one for the judiciary. However, this assumes that there is a set of principles which guide the judges in making decisions as to whether a particular group should be protected. If there is no such set of logical principles, then a political decision or value judgement is being delegated to unelected judges. A different solution could be to create a list of protected groups at international level, enshrined in a treaty such as the International Covenant for the Protection of Civil and Political Rights. This transcends the particular balance of power in any participating State. But it runs the risk of doing no more than establishing a lowest common denominator.

It is also important to view the democratic dimension as embracing more than just legislature and courts. In fact much modern equality theory stresses that the participation of affected groups in decision-making is a central value. This is equally true for the courts, which need to be adapted to be inclusive in this way. Equally complex is the question of how a group is defined. Is it enough for a set of individuals to believe themselves to constitute a group, or is it necessary to formulate objective criteria? And how does the law deal with those who belong to more than one specified group, such as black women?

There are three types of response to these questions. The first is to frame a broad open-textured equality guarantee, stating simply that all persons are equal before the law, without specifying any particular grounds. This approach takes the decision out of the political process, and instead leaves it to judges to decide when a classification is prohibited . . . A second approach, at the other end of the spectrum, is to formulate legislation containing an exhaustive list of grounds. This contrasts with the first approach in that the choice of ground is made wholly within the political process with no discretion left to the judges. Grounds can be added or removed only legislatively and not judicially . . . In between these two extremes is the third approach, which specifies a list of grounds of discrimination, but indicates that the list is not exhaustive . . . This approach gives judges some discretion to extend the list according to a set of judicially generated principles; but judicial discretion is bounded by the existence of enumerated grounds."

The general analyses offered by both authors can be applied to any of the discrimination law systems mentioned in this chapter. Wintemute and Fredman make particular reference to the general non-discrimination provisions in force in the United States, Canada, the Convention and the European Union. These provisions are worded as follows:

Fourteenth Amendment to the United States Constitution

"(1). [N]or shall any State ... deny to any person within its jurisdiction the equal protection of the laws."

Canadian Charter of Rights and Freedoms, section 15(1)

"Every individual is equal before and under the law and has the right to the equal protection and equal benefit of the law without discrimination and, in particular, without discrimination based on race, national or ethnic origin, color, religion, sex, age or mental or physical disability."

European Convention on Human Rights, Article 14

"The enjoyment of the rights and freedoms set forth in this Convention shall be secured without discrimination on any ground such as sex, race, colour, language, religion, political or other opinion, national or social origin, association with a national minority, property, birth or other status."

Article 13(1) EC

"Without prejudice to the other provisions of this Treaty and within the limits of the powers conferred by it upon the Community, the Council, acting unanimously on a proposal from the Commission and after consulting the European Parliament, may take appropriate action to combat discrimination based on sex, racial or ethnic origin, religion or belief, disability, age or sexual orientation."

Fredman suggests that the principle of the equal protection of the laws embodied in the Fourteenth Amendment to the US Constitution typifies what she described as the "first approach", and that the second—which she also dubs the "fixed category" approach—is to be found in the UK and under EU law. Fredman associates her "third approach" with Art.14 of the Convention and with s.15(1) of the Canadian Charter, although the passage of the Human Rights Act 1998 also creates a role for it within the UK[91]—suggesting that, at least unless the constitutional law of a jurisdiction precludes it, it may be

[91] Acknowledged by Fredman in *Discrimination Law*, p.76.

possible for a legal system to combine aspects of either the first and second or second and third approaches (the first and third being directly contradictory). As Fredman goes on to argue, however, each approach has its problems. The "fixed category" approach, "because it is based on the assumption of clearly delineated boundaries, has the effect of excluding groups only marginally outside of those boundaries. This creates great pressure on the judiciary to redraw the margins, resulting in even more complex and anomalous distinctions."[92] This comment demonstrates that even in a legal system in which prohibited grounds of discrimination are set out exclusively in legislation, judges retain some measure of interpretive freedom, allowing them to expand (or contract) the scope of the relevant provisions. Fredman also argues that the assumption that clear boundaries can be drawn encourages the false characterisation of groups on the basis of apparently fixed attributes, and may generate problems in cases of cumulative or intersectional discrimination (where individuals experience discrimination on more than one ground) since such discrimination "is not fully described by simply adding two kinds of discrimination together"[93] as the idea of fixed categories might imply. All three approaches, according to Fredman, raise the issue of accessibility, in the sense of the degree to which courts (or legislatures) are appropriately open to concerned groups.[94] Meanwhile, the first and third approaches raise the contentious issue of what criteria courts should employ when determining which groups fall within the scope of relevant constitutional protections against discrimination.[95]

Fredman's differentiation is helpful at a general level since it highlights the fact that, *unless* one subscribes to the view that Parliament should take the lead in developing protections against discrimination, with judges taking a clearly secondary role (for example, with only very limited ability to engage in statutory interpretation),[96] it becomes an actively important matter to consider whether (and how far) courts should be free to develop the scope of protections against discrimination. With this in mind, it is clear that the first and third approaches raise questions concerning the intensity with which courts should scrutinise particular distinctions in order to determine whether they

[92] *Discrimination Law*, p.68; see, more broadly, pp.68–74.

[93] *Discrimination Law*, p.75; see also Bob Hepple, Mary Coussey and Tufyal Choudhury, *Equality: A New Framework, Report of the Independent Review of the Enforcement of UK Anti-Discrimination Legislation* (Oxford: Hart, 2000), paras 2.61–2.62.

[94] *Discrimination Law*, p.67.

[95] For an illustration, see Kenji Yoshino's argument that the US Fourteenth Amendment Equal Protection Clause "heightened scrutiny" jurisprudence entails courts in comparing would-be protected groups with currently protected groups—an exercise in promoting assimilation rather than diversity—in order to see whether they deserve protection: "Assimilationist Bias in Equal Protection: The Visibility Presumption and the Case of 'Don't Ask, Don't Tell'" (1998) 108 Yale L.J. 485, especially 487.

[96] As, for example, in relation to how widely an established head of discrimination should be recognised as extending (see, in relation to sex discrimination, *P. v S. and Cornwall CC* [1996] ECR-I 2143, a judicially recognised expansion in the concept of direct sex discrimination which was nonetheless given a basis in legislation at national level: Sex Discrimination Act 1975, s.2A).

should be categorised as prohibited (should all distinctions receive the same intensity of scrutiny, or should it vary?), and also concerning the appropriate boundaries of judicial scrutiny (should the courts be more deferential to elected authorities in cases where sensitive policy choices are involved? How far does the law's treatment of discrimination in itself involve sensitive policy questions that are better left to elected authorities?).[97] Robert Wintemute outlines how courts in the relevant jurisdictions have dealt with these questions in relation to an open-ended non-discrimination guarantee (Fredman's "first approach") or a list of grounds of prohibited discrimination to which they may add (Fredman's "third approach"):[98]

Robert Wintemute "Filling the Article 14 'Gap': Government Ratification and Judicial Control of Protocol No.12 ECHR" [2004] E.H.R.L.R. 484

pp.491–3: "Three possible approaches are exemplified by the case law of the US Supreme Court, the Supreme Court of Canada, and the ECJ [European Court of Justice]. Under Amendments XIV and V to the US Constitution, the US Supreme Court has traditionally adopted a 'levels of scrutiny' approach, which announces in advance that the use of certain 'suspect' or 'quasi-suspect' grounds of distinction, and the denial of certain opportunities that represent 'fundamental rights', will receive 'heightened scrutiny'. Distinctions based on all other grounds, or affecting all other opportunities, will receive highly deferential 'rational basis review'. The Supreme Court of Canada decided in 1989 not to bother with residual 'rational basis review', and instead limited the scope of s.15(1) of the Canadian Charter of Rights and Freedoms to the nine grounds of discrimination 'enumerated' in s.15(1) (race, national or ethnic origin, colour, religion, sex, age, mental or physical disability) and grounds that are 'analogous' to these grounds. In contrast, in applying its general principle of equality or non-discrimination, the ECJ does not yet appear to announce in advance that certain grounds are excluded altogether or will receive only deferential review, and instead examines on a case-by-case basis whether each challenged difference in treatment has an objective and reasonable justification.

The approach of the ECJ resembles the original definition of 'discrimination' adopted by the ECtHR [European Court of Human Rights] in the *Belgian Linguistic Case* in 1968 [(1968) 1 E.H.R.R. 252 at [1.B.10]]:

> '[T]he principle of equality of treatment is violated [there is "discrimination"] if the distinction has no objective and reasonable justification ... assessed in relation to the aim and effects of the measure ... A difference of treatment ... must not only pursue a legitimate aim: Art.14 is likewise violated when it is clearly established that there is no reasonable relationship of proportionality between the means employed and the aim sought to be realised.'

[97] *Discrimination Law*, pp.76–82.

[98] The one more direct correlation is that intensity of scrutiny or level of deference tests are unlikely to be relevant (or as relevant) in a jurisdiction which relies upon Fredman's second, "fixed category" approach.

However, since at least 1985, the ECtHR has (like the Supreme Courts of the United States and Canada) indicated several times that differences in treatment based on certain 'sensitive grounds' are harder to justify than differences in treatment based on other 'non-sensitive' or 'ordinary grounds', whether or not the 'sensitive ground' is mentioned in Art.14. To date, these 'sensitive grounds' appear to be sex, birth out of wedlock, religion, race (or ethnic or national origin), nationality, and sexual orientation. For all of these grounds (which are similar to those treated as sensitive by the Supreme Courts of the United States and Canada), the ECtHR requires (explicitly or implicitly) that the respondent government present 'very weighty reasons' or 'particularly serious reasons' to justify use of the ground as the basis for a difference in treatment. The Court has not yet had the opportunity to make similar statements with regard to disability or age."

It is worth noting just how far different the constitutional law of the four jurisdictions mentioned here is. The United States and Canada are both federal legal systems in which legislation and executive action may be judicially reviewed for compatibility with federal non-discrimination guarantees (the equal protection provisions of the Fourteenth Amendment and s.15(1) of the Charter, respectively). Courts may thus set aside incompatible measures and actions by public authorities, as well as legislation enacted so as to prohibit discrimination in private employment and the provision of goods and services, using the tests mentioned by Robert Wintemute. The European Union aspires towards being a federal system, in which—due to the unique principles of EU law supremacy and direct effect—the European Court of Justice may cause national courts to set aside national level measures for incompatibility with Art.13 EC (national courts may also do so without referring the case to the Court of Justice). More conventionally, the Court may also judicially review decisions taken and measures adopted by EC institutions for compatibility with Treaty provisions. However, the Court does not itself set aside national measures, and there exists (at least at a theoretical level) an ongoing dialogue concerning national versus EU-level sovereignty.[99] The Convention, by contrast, is a standard international treaty. Signatory states are required (by Art.13) to grant a minimum level of protection to Convention rights—including the Art.14 right to non-discrimination—and may be held to account by the Court of Human Rights if they do not. Nonetheless, the extent to which Convention rights may be enforced by national courts—whether against public authorities or in litigation between private parties—is a matter for signatory states. By contrast with the European Union, legislation cannot be passed or executive action taken at Convention level. In terms of discrimination law, it is extremely significant that despite the differences highlighted here between the four jurisdictions, similar questions arise (as we have seen) when we consider the respective roles of courts and legislatures.

We have seen in this section that in jurisdictions in which selected grounds

[99] Note also that courts in different member states have adopted variable positions as to whether national or EU law has the ultimate say in disputes concerning the compatibility of EC measures with fundamental national level constitutional guarantees (Paul Craig & Grainne de Burca, *EU Law: Text, Cases and Materials* (Oxford: OUP, 4th edn., 2008), Ch.10).

of discrimination are prohibited, it may be the courts or the legislature which take the lead in the selection process, and that some systems contain a fixed list of prohibited grounds whereas in others the list may be added to. Where courts are charged with deciding whether new prohibited grounds of discrimination should be recognised, tests of variable intensity and involving variable levels of deference to the elected authorities are seemingly employed. At a more theoretical level, considerations of political morality—that is, considerations concerning the proper roles of different institutions—are crucial when determining which institution should take the lead. This point might be felt to further illustrate the power of the constitutional conception of discrimination law, by contrast with the employment-focused alternative. Questions of political morality relate directly to a society's constitutional arrangements and are clearly important *whichever* conception of discrimination law is adopted. This being so, it seems sensible to suggest that the preferable conception of discrimination law is that which is better equipped to handle such questions in an informed fashion. Given its constitutional *focus*, it is clearly the constitutional conception which is the better equipped.

C. *A "Generational" Approach to Protections against Discrimination? Direct Discrimination, Indirect Discrimination, and Beyond*

While the prohibition of direct and indirect discrimination forms the centrepiece of contemporary systems of discrimination law (whether relevant prohibitions focus on discrimination in employment or have a wider, explicitly constitutional reach), jurisdictions vary in the extent to which they prioritise the two categories of prohibited discrimination rather than adopting additional strategies for preventing or penalising invidious discrimination. It has sometimes been regarded as appropriate, for example, to move beyond direct and indirect discrimination and impose positive duties on designated bodies, such as public authorities, requiring them to act to prevent discrimination, to support affirmative action measures, and so on. Some theorists have used these differences as a basis for categorising systems of discrimination law according to the types of non-discrimination protection which they contain and/or prioritise, such categorisations helping in turn to provide an indication of how we are to understand the reach and ambition of the discrimination law system in issue. Such categorisation exercises can operate both historically, using the development of a given system of discrimination law to show how that system is evolving on a "generational" basis, and analytically, using the reach of the protections contained within the system to draw conclusions about its conceptual nature.

The "generational" approach has been employed by the *Report of the Independent Review of the Enforcement of U.K. Anti-Discrimination Legislation* (the "Hepple Report"), taking the development of protections against discrimination in the United Kingdom as its point of reference. The Hepple Report categorised the initial, limited use of the criminal law to penalise overly hostile discriminatory behaviour as a "first generation" anti-discrimination measure, and the development of limited private law remedies for instances of overt discrimination as "second generation". The Sex Discrimination Act 1975 and Race Relations Act 1976, involving broader public and private law enforcement together with the prohibition of indirect as well as direct discrimination, constituted "third generation" measures.[100] The Hepple Report confined this analysis to domestic law, but it nonetheless provides a useful basis for analysing discrimination law more broadly. For "first generation" measures might be said to categorise impermissible discrimination as a serious public wrong (thus justifying the use of the criminal law) but as something with which the law is concerned only comparatively rarely and in highly visible situations (hence the exclusion of private law liability for discrimination in the workplace). "Third generation" measures, by contrast, treat impermissible discrimination as a pervasive private as well as public wrong, in relation both to the contexts in which it is deemed to occur—private employment and service-provision as well as within areas for which public bodies are responsible—and to those who are subject to an enforceable duty not to discriminate: namely, private employers and service-providers as well as public bodies. Under this approach, discrimination law is concerned to remedy deeper-seated forms of discrimination alongside overt acts of hostility: hence the prohibition of indirect discrimination.[101] Nonetheless, as the Hepple Report notes, the "essential feature" of such measures "remains a negative prohibition on discrimination, rather than a positive duty to promote equality".[102]

The Hepple Report went on to argue, again by reference to UK domestic law, that "fourth generation" measures have now begun to emerge—an argument taken still further by Sandra Fredman, who draws on examples from Canada and the EU as well as from domestic law. In doing so, she highlights the implications of "fourth generation" measures for how we think about discrimination law, as well as some of their limits.

100 Bob Hepple, Mary Coussey and Tufyal Choudhury, *Equality: A New Framework; Report of the Independent Review of the Enforcement of U.K. Anti-Discrimination Legislation* (Oxford: Hart, 2000), paras 1.2 to 1.7.

101 See Christopher McCrudden, "Institutional Discrimination" (1982) 2 O.J.L.S. 303; see further Ch.5.

102 Hepple Report, n.100 above, para.1.2.

Sandra Fredman "Equality: A New Generation" (2001) 30 I.L.J. 145

pp.163–5: "The recognition of the limits of both direct discrimination and indirect discrimination has led law-makers to strike out in a new direction, namely the imposition of positive duties to promote equality, rather than just the negative requirement to refrain from discriminating. Such 'fourth generation' duties move beyond the fault-based model of existing discrimination law, where legal liability only rests on those individuals who can be shown to have actively discriminated, whether directly or indirectly; and the remedy is to compensate the individual victim. At the root of the positive duty, by contrast, is a recognition that ... [e]quality can only be meaningfully advanced if practices and structures are altered proactively by those in a position to bring about real change, regardless of fault or original responsibility. Positive duties are therefore proactive rather than reactive, aiming to introduce equality measures rather than to respond to complaints by individual victims.

This has important implications for both the content of the duty and the identification of the duty[-]bearer. In order to trigger the duty, there is no need to prove individual prejudice, or to link disparate impact to an unjustifiable practice or condition. Instead, it is sufficient to show a pattern of under-representation or other evidence of structural discrimination. Correspondingly, the duty-bearer is identified as the body in the best position to perform this duty. Even though not responsible for creating the problem in the first place, such duty[-]bearers become responsible for participating in its eradication. A key aspect of positive duties, therefore, is that they harness the energies of employers and public bodies. Nor is the duty limited to providing compensation for an individual victim. Instead, positive action is required to achieve change, whether by encouragement, accommodation, or structural change...

The proactive nature of positive duties thus changes the structure of equality law, but positive duties are only meaningful if they are targeted towards particular aims. It is therefore still important to focus on what we are trying to achieve by means of positive action. Is the aim to achieve the removal of prejudice and harassment; or to redistribute resources; or to accommodate diversity? And which principle of equality is being utilised: [...] equality of results, equality of opportunity or some other substantive value? Many positive duties appear to be furthering a redistributive aim; in that they are formulated in terms of improving the representation of minorities or women in a given sector. As such, [their] limitations should not be ignored, particularly in that there may be no impetus to change underlying discriminatory structures. Thus the representation of minorities might be improved because more of [their] members have felt compelled to assimilate to dominant cultures; more women might be in higher positions because they have chosen not to have children, or delegated their child-care responsibilities to other women who remain low paid and are given little social status. Positive duties to be truly effective must do more than just change the colour or gender make-up of existing structures, but also reshape them."

As Fredman makes clear, "fourth generation" measures raise an important question of justification: namely, which variety of equality argument can be used to explain and justify them, or whether some other argument—such as autonomy/dignity—is needed.[103] This question is particularly acute given that such measures dispense with the need to relate the award of a remedy, or indeed the making of any legal order, back to a specific act by an identifiable

[103] See further Ch.3.

wrong-doer: a radical re-casting of the assumptions on which many attempts to justify discrimination law are constructed. The de-coupling of remedy from specific wrong-doer also raises important practical questions. Can "fourth generation" measures now single out any organisation or individual as a potential "duty-bearer"? If not, where are the limits to be set? Might "fourth generation" measures entail an abandonment of the requirement, characteristic of direct and indirect discrimination, that the claimant find a similarly-placed "comparator" from the mirror-image group (or possessing the mirror-image characteristic) to their own, who has been better treated?[104]

At a broader level still, we might ask whether the appearance of "fourth generation" measures ought to entail the replacement of the existing "third generation" concepts of direct and indirect discrimination, as seen in the USA, Canada, the European Union and the United Kingdom, or whether the different types of measure can comfortably sit alongside one another. This is an especially pertinent issue given that none of the jurisdictions mentioned has instituted a *general* move towards "fourth generation" measures: in fact, such measures are rather few and far between, begging the question whether they in fact constitute a general way forward for discrimination law or examples of a more sporadic phenomenon.

Mark Bell's analysis of the discrimination law regimes in force in the national laws of European Union member states raises similar questions to the "generational" approach, but unlike the "generational" approach does not adopt an historical perspective when considering the range of protections in force in the legal systems in issue. Bell draws a distinction between what he characterises as "discrimination laws" and "equality laws".

Mark Bell *Anti-Discrimination Law and the European Union* (Oxford: Oxford University Press, 2002)

pp.147–8: "In examining the Member States' existing legal provisions, it may be said that there are, broadly speaking, three levels of legal protection. These will be termed 'equality laws', 'anti-discrimination laws', and an 'absence of any specific legal provision'. Whilst the latter is more or less self-explanatory, the first two categories need additional clarification.

In the majority of Member States, one finds the existence of *anti-discrimination* laws. These may be summarised as largely a set of negative obligations, focusing on actions that employers must refrain from, as opposed to the imposition of positive duties on employers to act in favour of equal opportunities. Thus, there is a focus on providing a legal remedy for individuals in the face of manifest discrimination, but much less attention to the need to identify and challenge the discriminatory structures in the labour market which may perpetuate disadvantage for vulnerable groups. The legislation is founded on

[104–105] For a critique of this requirement, see Aileen McColgan, "Cracking the Comparator Problem: Discrimination, 'Equal' Treatment and the Role of Comparisons" [2006] E.H.R.L.R. 650.

the notion of individual litigants enforcing non-discrimination through recourse to the legal protection provided by the law. Therefore, the major legal questions which arise concern issues such as the definition of discrimination, access to justice, the nature of the judicial process, the burden of proof, protection from victimisation and remedies.

In practice, individuals face a wide range of barriers to litigation, such as costs (financial and emotional), information and awareness, and legal procedures . . . this model possesses serious deficiencies in terms of the effective enforcement of equal treatment. In contrast, states with *equality* laws have recognised the limits of an anti-discrimination strategy dependent on individual litigants and have responded principally in two directions. First, institutional provision has been made to support individual litigants, with a view to rendering more effective and accessible the right to non-discrimination. Second, measures have been adopted which break the link with the individual plaintiff, thereby focusing on collective mechanisms to combat discrimination. This frequently manifests itself in the adoption of certain forms of positive action. Such measures include making public procurement contracts conditional on firms meeting equality requirements (contract compliance), monitoring the workforce for its gender/ethnic/religious profile, and targeting advertisements at groups currently underrepresented in the workforce."

It may be unduly simplistic, linguistically or analytically, to draw a firm distinction between "discrimination" and "equality" laws, given that many popular justifications for discrimination laws rest, as we shall see in Chapter 3, on notions of equality. Nonetheless, Bell's categorisation scheme, like the "generational" approach, might be felt to provide a useful basis for charactising the nature of the protections against discrimination in force in a given legal system, and in turn the goals of that system. Despite the (perhaps inevitable) questions raised in this section, this method of categorisation will be useful in Chapter 2 when analysing anti-discrimination protections in England and Wales.

D. *Discrimination in Language and Law*

Theorists often argue that the definitions of impermissible discrimination in play in a particular legal system are too wide or too narrow, and therefore open to criticism. Any such criticism, being of a normative character, must in logic presuppose a vision, held by the critic, of the range of conduct which discrimination law *should* prohibit or regulate. The critic's view of what constitutes impermissible discrimination will, in other words, differ from the law's current view, and the critic will seek to argue that the normative strength of their preferred vision is such that the law's boundaries should be adjusted. For this reason, it is important to remember that the law's definition of "discrimination" may in fact be contestable. One of the co-authors has argued that this may give rise to confusion, although this can be alleviated by being clear about what our normative vision of discrimination law (our philosophical justification for its existence) consists of:

Nicholas Bamforth, "Setting the Limits of Anti-discrimination law: Some Legal and Social Concepts" in J. Dine and B. Watt (eds.), *Discrimination Law: Concepts, Limitations and Justifications* (Harlow: Longman, 1996)

pp. 57–9:[106] "[C]ourts and tribunals are often willing to re-interpret the legal concepts of discrimination [...] The boundaries of the legal concepts are, therefore, somewhat fluid. However, this analysis tells us only that the range of conduct deemed [non-discriminatory] by anti-discrimination law various over time. We need also to consider a deeper question, which is whether the conduct justified or penalised as a result of the boundary alteration exercises can properly be described as 'discrimination' [...]

This question goes beyond the legal concepts of direct and indirect discrimination, and can only be answered satisfactorily by employing a notion of discrimination which is independent of the law [...] Unfortunately, lawyers often lose sight of this point, understanding 'discrimination' solely in terms of the legal concepts. A clear example of this tendency is Lord Fraser's assertion, in *Amin* v. *Entry Clearance Officer, Bombay*, that the first section of the 1975 [Sex Discrimination] Act *defined* discrimination, which was then made unlawful by the subsequent sections of the Act.[107] In fact, discrimination against women and ethnic minorities had been recognised as a social problem long before the Act. All the Act did was to establish specific legal devices which were to be deployed in tackling some aspects of this problem.

There are other ways in which the adoption of a wholly law-centred view of the word 'discrimination' can blur the debate over anti-discrimination law. First, it can obscure the fact that the law exists to serve social goals—i.e. to counter behaviour which is seen as sexually or racially discriminatory. Blurring can occur because the law's effectiveness in this task can only meaningfully be measured by comparison with extra-legal notions of 'discrimination'. A wholly law-centred view may, secondly, cause us to forget that the law's social goals can also be served by extra-legal devices such as contract compliance. Again, blurring can occur since a decision whether to use law or extra-legal methods often turns on tactical considerations, and can only be made coherently if an extra-legal notion of 'discrimination' is kept in mind.

To decide whether judicial boundary alteration exercises result in the justification or penalizing of conduct which can properly be described as 'discrimination' . . . we must find a [philosophical] justification . . . for the law's anti-discrimination provisions which will characterise the *nature* of the social problem which discrimination is felt to represent. Such a philosophical justification will reveal the common link between practices penalised under the legal notions of direct and indirect discrimination which merits treating them in this way."

This approach might be felt to reflects observations made by Nigel Simmonds and Gerald Postema about the nature of legal analysis more broadly. Although Simmonds begins by discussing legal rights, the idea that certain types of discrimination are invidious would seem to be an obvious candidate for inclusion in his list of concepts which "link legal ideas to a wider context".

[106] See also John Gardner, "On the Ground of Her Sex(uality)", n.6 above, 167–9.
[107] [1983] 2 All E.R. 864 at 871.

Nigel E. Simmonds, *The Decline of Juridical Reason: Doctrine and theory in the legal order* (Manchester: Manchester University Press, 1984)

p.8: "The law cannot settle any philosophical dispute about the nature of legal rights simply by enacting a stipulative definition: for the concept of a 'right' has important uses outside the law, in our moral life, and it seems to be that feature of the concept that gives it its theoretical interest. It is true that the concepts of 'motor vehicle' or 'building' may have uses both within and without the law. But those concepts which have been of interest to legal theorists appear to link legal ideas to a wider context in a more fundamental way. We might think of the concepts of right, duty, power, person and responsibility (or some not dissimilar list) as constituting a framework that makes legal discourse possible. Far from being *defined by* the law, such concepts provide the location of law and legal ideas within the moral and social life of which they are a part. The essential task of legal theory is best seen as the tracing out of such connections, to link legal discourse to wider forms of moral life. In this way, legal theory would provide 'foundations' for legal knowledge, not in the sense of supposed epistemological certainty, but rather in the sense of a locus, a place within which legal ideas are perfectly intelligible and at home."

Simmonds goes on to suggest that:

p.9: "Fully to understand legal discourse one should aim at a cultural knowledge that is both rich and deep. In particular . . . because discursive concepts cannot be prised off from the social formations which give them sense so also they cannot be understood apart from the historical experience that has shaped them."[108]

An analogous point is made by Gerald Postema, as part of his analysis of Jeremy Bentham's critique of the common law:

Gerald J. Postema, *Bentham and the Common Law Tradition* (Oxford: Clarendon Press, 1986)

p.334: "Jurisprudential theory . . . even when it appears to be engaged in conceptual analysis, is focused on the task of giving an account of legal institutions, and the practice and 'sensibility' that breathe life into them. This accounting can never limit itself to simple description. It is essentially a matter of *characterization* or interpretation. For these practices are not mere and mindless habits, or behavioural routines with no intrinsic significance to those who execute them. They are intelligible social practices with a certain, perhaps very complex, *meaning* or *point*. In fact, the law is not merely a device for regulating behaviour; it is a complex structure of discourse within which behaviour is *construed* (and on this construal action is taken and evaluations of it are formed). The context of law gives behaviour meaning; sense is made of it. And this constructive, interpretative power is rooted in the collective resources of the practice."

108 For further analysis, see Nigel E. Simmonds, *The Decline of Juridical Reason: Doctrine and theory in the legal order* (Manchester: Manchester University Press, 1984), pp.11–13.

Both Simmonds and Postema therefore challenge the view that the analysis and exposition of rules of law can proceed in a fashion which is oblivious to background social factors, whether these are social concepts of particular types (such as a right or a discriminatory act) or the social context (for example, patterns of disadvantage suffered by particular disempowered social groups). This is particularly true of discrimination law, given its strong social focus.

By appreciating that actions which might be perceived in common sense terms or described colloquially as "discriminatory" are not always synonymous with the law's definition of discrimination, we can also make sense of the phenomenon—highlighted in the eighth question articulated earlier in this section—whereby cases which might be thought in common sense terms to be "about" discrimination are frequently litigated under headings which are not expressly concerned with discrimination. Two obvious examples spring to mind. Firstly, in the United States, the Supreme Court held in *Lawrence v Texas* that legislation which prohibited consenting, private sexual activity between adult men breached the right to private life protected by the Due Process Clause of the Fourteenth Amendment to the US Constitution.[109] Although, viewed in common sense terms, the Supreme Court could clearly be said to have declared a key example of direct discrimination on the basis of sexual orientation ('gay people may not engage in sexual activity with one another; straight people may do so') to be unconstitutional, the case was not litigated or decided under the Equal Protection Clause, which is explicitly concerned with non-discrimination. Secondly, the European Court of Human Rights decided in *Smith and Grady v United Kingdom* that the automatic discharge of lesbian and gay service personnel from military employment, after intrusive inquiries by the military police, violated the right to respect for private life guaranteed by Art.8 of the European Convention.[110] The Court declined to give judgment in terms of Art.14, the Convention right to non-discrimination, even though—viewed in common sense terms—the fact situation represented another example of direct sexual orientation discrimination. It is clear from both cases that it would be impossible to gain a proper understanding of the contemporary legal protections against sexual orientation discrimination without looking beyond the provisions of the US Constitution and European Convention which deal expressly with the right to non-discrimination: in fact, "discrimination" issues, understood on a common sense basis or colloquially, frequently arise outside of those provisions and must be included within any study of discrimination law.

[109] (2003) 123 S. Ct. 2472.

[110] (1999) 29 E.H.R.R. 493; see also *Lustig-Preen and Beckett v United Kingdom* (1999) 29 E.H.R.R. 548.

IV. Conclusion

In this chapter, we have considered the constitutional and employment-focused conceptions of discrimination law. We have argued that the traditionally dominant employment-focused conception (traditionally dominant in England and Wales, that is) fails in a critical sense to provide an integrated account of the nature of protections against discrimination. By contrast, provided that proper account is taken of the statutory rules and case law which concern the employment relationship, a constitutional conception of discrimination law provides a more complete and satisfactory account: a conclusion which is perhaps unsurprising given the close association which is now drawn in many jurisdictions (including England and Wales) between constitutional law and human rights and the fact that freedom from discrimination is recognised as a key human right in many jurisdictions, including all of those considered in this chapter.[111] We have also introduced, and in some cases explored in detail, the key conceptual questions and issues which face systems of discrimination law, and as part of this have compared the roles of courts and legislatures in protecting against invidious forms of discrimination in different jurisdictions. These questions and issues will be relevant to our evaluation, starting in Chapter 2, of domestic discrimination law in England and Wales.

[111] On the role of freedom from discrimination as a human right in UK law, see Richard Clayton & Hugh Tomlinson, *The Law of Human Rights Volume 1*, n.60 above, Ch.17; Stephen Grosz, Jack Beatson & Peter Duffy, *Human Rights: The 1998 Act and the European Convention* (London: Sweet & Maxwell, 2000), paras C14–01 to C14–25. For discussion of human rights and domestic constitutional law more generally, see, e.g., Lord Hope, "Human Rights—Where Are we Now?" [2000] E.H.R.L.R. 439; Lord Steyn, "The New Legal Landscape" [2000] E.H.R.L.R. 549, "Democracy Through Law", n.59 above.

2

SOURCES AND SCOPE OF DOMESTIC DISCRIMINATION LAW

I. Introduction

As David Feldman notes, the "structure of the law relating to discrimination in England and Wales is now immensely complex, consisting of a large number of inter-woven strands."[1] The rules prohibiting the various grounds and instances of unlawful discrimination have a variety of sources and rationales, helping to give rise to a collection of overlaps and divergences. Since domestic constitutional law might nowadays be described as "multi-layered", given the United Kingdom's membership of the European Union and the bringing of the European Convention on Human Rights ("the Convention") into domestic law via the Human Rights Act 1998, prohibited grounds and instances can have their origins in one or more of three sources: national statutory provisions, EU law, and/or Convention case law. Other international treaties sometimes also have an influence. The rules emanating from these different sources are not always consistent with one another, and national courts are required to give variable weights to rules emanating from different sources. Furthermore, no attempt has yet been made to gather into one comprehensive statute even the prohibited grounds of discrimination that were originally dealt with primarily or exclusively under national law: instead, an ever expanding body of primary and secondary legislation, of differing ambits and dealing with different but often overlapping subject-matters, has been allowed to develop.[2]

This chapter seeks to introduce and provide an overview (rather than a full account) of domestic discrimination law, before we explore the key concepts found within it—and the key contexts in which it applies—in later chapters. After providing an analysis of some of the key issues in Section II, in which it will become apparent that discrimination law is being viewed increasingly in

1 *Civil Liberties and Human Rights in England and Wales* (Oxford: Oxford University Press, 2nd edn., 2002), p.146.

2 *Equality: A New Framework. Report of the Independent Review of the Enforcement of UK Anti-Discrimination Legislation* (Oxford: Hart, 2000), paras 2.1 to 2.4, Appendices 2 and 3. For an outline (albeit now somewhat outdated) of relevant complexities, see paras 2.60 to 2.84.

human rights (or constitutional law)-focused rather than employment-focused terms, we consider the different influences on and sources of domestic discrimination law: international non-discrimination provisions to which the United Kingdom is a signatory but which have not been brought into national law (in other words, provisions other than those found in the Convention and EU law) (Section III); the Convention (Section IV); EU law (Section V); and non-discrimination provisions which have their origins (or originally did so) "purely" in national law (Section VII). In Section VIII, we discuss the extent to which the current complexities might be resolved by consolidating discrimination law into a single statute encompassing all aspects of prohibited discrimination. We consider the Convention before looking at EU law (despite the fact that domestic courts were given the power to apply EU norms before they had the power to apply Convention rights directly, and despite the stronger legal weight at national level of directly effective EU norms) because EU law and the judgments of the European Court of Justice are sometimes influenced by the Convention. The overlaps and divergences between the two—at "European" as well as national level (see Section VI)—can thus be better understood if the Convention is considered first. This ordering is not perfect, for two connected reasons. The first is the mere fact that the Convention and EU law overlap in certain areas. The second is that it is somewhat artificial to talk of "purely" national protections against discrimination, given the expansive jurisdictions of the Convention and EU law and the fact that both are brought into national law via statutes passed by the Westminster Parliament (the Human Rights Act 1998 and European Communities Act 1972 respectively). In fact, it is highly unlikely that there is now any discrimination-related statutory provision passed by the Westminster Parliament which is not in some way affected by EU law and/or the Convention. We discuss relevant "national" measures separately here purely for ease of explanation, given that such measures are often discussed without extensive consideration of EU law or the Convention in the case law and academic literature. Nonetheless, we stress throughout the chapter the need constantly to bear in mind the influence of EU law and the Convention on the interpretation and—in the case of EU law—application by national courts of "national" measures concerning discrimination, as well as the overlaps between the Convention and EU law. In order to emphasise the integral role of Convention and EU law provisions at national level, we consider the operation of each in domestic law immediately after outlining their general nature, rather than in a separate "domestic" section.

We try to offset the complexity of domestic discrimination law by conducting our analysis, wherever possible, by reference to the list of key questions outlined in Chapter 1.[3] In summary, the questions are as follows. Firstly, who is protected against discrimination (which grounds of discrimination are deemed to be invidious)? Secondly, when are they protected? Thirdly, who

[3] Ch.1, Section III.

has to protect them? Fourthly, how wide are the protections (which includes consideration of whether indirect as well as direct discrimination is prohibited)? Fifthly, when can otherwise discriminatory acts or measures be justified for policy reasons? Sixthly, what happens when protections against invidious discrimination clash with other protected rights? Seventhly, are there other exceptions to protections against discrimination? Eighthly, how far can human rights which are not specifically associated with discrimination (for example, the right to respect for private life) be used in cases which, in common sense or colloquial terms, seem to involve discrimination? And ninthly, what legal remedies are available? The tenth question, concerning the extent to which we should look outside the law for solutions, is not relevant when conducting an outline of the legal protections. Obviously, not every question will be as relevant in each part of the analysis.

II. Central Historical, Conceptual and Legal Issues

In Chapter 1, we explored the "generational" analysis of discrimination law—that is, the notion that discrimination law systems can be categorised according to whether they involve mainly criminal law ("first generation") penalties for prohibited discrimination, limited private law ("second generation") enforcement,[4] broader public and private law enforcement including the prohibition of indirect discrimination ("third generation" mechanisms), or the imposition of positive duties to redress structural inequalities without a clear nexus always needing to be shown between the duty-bearer and the claimant ("fourth generation" measures)—as well as the idea that systems of discrimination law can be identified according to the extent to which they allow courts to recognise new grounds of prohibited discrimination rather than confining this task to the legislature. In this section, we analyse domestic discrimination law in the light of these points, in order to provide a background to the detailed discussion of domestic legal provisions in later sections. We also introduce, between discussion of the "generational" analysis and the roles of the legislature and the courts, an argument which is crucial to the analysis in the rest of this chapter and book: namely, that the United Kingdom now has what might be termed a "multi-layered" constitutional structure, something which is of overriding importance to the operation of discrimination law.

Beginning with the "generational" analysis, discrimination law in England and Wales was initially imported from the United States,[5] and the earliest anti-

[4] See, for a "second generation" example, the Race Relations Act 1968. For a discussion of the legal regulation of race discrimination in the 1960s, see Anthony Lester and Geoffrey Bindman, *Race and Law* (Longman: London, 1972), Pt 1.

[5] See, e.g., Christopher McCrudden, "Institutional Discrimination" (1982) 2 O.J.L.S. 303, especially pp.305, 317, 335, 345–6, 358.

discrimination legislation contained only criminal offences and accompanying "first generation" penalties. This was rapidly found to be disadvantageous:

Anthony Lester and Geoffrey Bindman,
***Race and Law* (London: Longman, 1972)**

p.100: "Th[e] preference for administrative rather than criminal enforcement was partly based on [the] conclusion that criminal proceedings would be much less likely to be brought. [It] also referred to several other disadvantages of the criminal process.

For example, in view of the obvious difficulties of obtaining evidence of racial discrimination, it would often be impossible to satisfy the criminal burden of proof beyond reasonable doubt, whereas it would be practicable to satisfy the civil standard of proof on the balance of probabilities. Criminal proceedings would be brought by the police or a public prosecuting authority, neither of which would be especially skilled in problems of race relations. Cases would be tried summarily by magistrates or on indictment by a jury; the former would often lack the necessary time or expertise, especially when dealing with the complexities of employment and housing; the latter might sympathise more with the accused, than with the victim of his crime. On the other hand, an administrative agency would have specialist skills; proceedings in civil courts would conveniently explore the complex issues involved in allegations of unlawful discrimination; and the courts could be assisted in their adjudication by lay experts in the fields of employment, housing and commerce, and race relations. Criminal proceedings would generate wide publicity in a punitive context, which might cast the discriminator in the role of a martyr rather than a law breaker. And perhaps most importantly of all, the punishment of the wrongdoer, by fine or imprisonment, would not provide any remedy for the wrong suffered by his victim."

Anti-discrimination remedies thus expanded into private law via the Equal Pay Act 1970 (concerning equal pay for equal work by men and women), the Sex Discrimination Act 1975 ("SDA") and the Race Relations Act 1976 ("RRA")—the latter two pieces of legislation also having public law implications due to the statutory duties which they placed upon public authorities and the public law enforcement mechanisms for which they provided.[6] These developments are captured in the following passages, the first of which is taken from the "Hepple Report" (named after its first named author):

***Equality: A New Framework. Report of the Independent Review of the Enforcement of UK Anti-Discrimination Legislation* (Oxford: Hart, 2000)**

para.1.5: "The inspiration for British and Northern Irish legislation in the 1960s and 1970s was found in the USA and Canada. The Street Report of 1967 made a study of the workings of anti-discrimination in North America, and contained detailed proposals for a

[6] The enforcement mechanisms having since been consolidated in Pt 1 of the Equality Act 2006.

'second generation' Race Relations Act to replace the limited first Act of 1965. This Report had some influence on the shape of the Race Relations Act 1968, but it was not until the 'third generation' legislation—the SDA and RRA—that its most important advice was heeded, particularly by strengthening the commissions and the enforcement provisions. The White Papers which preceded the 1975 and 1976 Acts ... marked a major turning point. The resulting legislation provided a right for individuals to bring proceedings for compensation for unlawful sex and race discrimination in industrial (later employment) tribunals, or for damages in designated county and sheriff courts in non-employment cases, while at the same time entrusting strategic enforcement in the public interest to the E[qual] O[pportunities] C[ommission] and C[omission for] R[acial] E[quality]. The Acts also imported the novel American concept of adverse impact or indirect discrimination."

Phillip N. Sooben "The Origin of the Race Relations Act" Research Paper in Ethnic Relations, No.12 (Centre for Research in Ethnic Relations: Warwick, 1990)

"Serious political recognition in Britain of the example of American anti-discrimination law can perhaps be dated from 1967 and the report of the Street Committee ... their report exercised some influence over the terms of the 1968 Race Relations Act. The Committee had sought to examine the value of legislation in other countries, especially in the United States but also in Canada, in more detail than had previously been carried out in Britain, and they had recommended a broadening of the scope of British law and a strengthening of the enforcement machinery. However, the situation in America had clearly progressed somewhat by the mid-1970s and a fresh appraisal was required. Although there existed some significant differences between the British and American cases, there were certainly a number of areas and recent developments from which much could be learnt, and both the Home Secretary and the Select Committee on Race Relations and Immigration drew on these sources in their consideration of possible reforms in Britain."

The SDA and RRA borrowed their main structure and concepts from US civil rights legislation. The impetus for the civil rights movement in the USA was the *de facto* segregation of African Americans who were excluded from access to key public and private services and employment opportunities.[7] The legal response to the movement's political demands was the Civil Rights Act 1964, which removed segregation and introduced the principle of non-discrimination in the provision of public and private services (Title II) and in employment (Title VII). The grounds on which discrimination in these areas was rendered unlawful included race, religion, national origin and sex. The Civil Rights Act 1964 thus provided the "civil law" paradigm for the SDA and RRA. What identified the SDA and RRA as "third generation" measures was their inclusion of the concept of indirect discrimination (stipulating, broadly speaking, that provisions that are formally neutral but which have a disproportionate impact on minorities or women are not permitted unless they

[7] See, e.g., David A.J. Richards, *Disarming Manhood: Roots of Ethical Resistance* (Ohio: Swallow Press, 2005).

can be justified),[8] their strengthening of the ability of individuals to litigate (an individual who could establish a cause of action in direct or indirect discrimination had a right to damages and/or some forms of injunctive relief), and their reliance on public enforcement bodies such as the Commission for Racial Equality and Equal Opportunities Commission alongside private litigants and private law remedies. The Commissions were created to support individual litigants, to use investigatory and advice-giving powers to promote the aims of discrimination law, and to litigate in a public capacity (in addition, the Disability Rights Commission was created under the Disability Rights Commission Act 1999, supplementing the Discrimination Act 1995, a "third generation" measure dealing with disability discrimination; the three Commissions were later amalgamated under the Equality Act 2006 into one single body called the Commission for Equality and Human Rights[9]). As the Hepple Report also makes clear, the 1975 and 1976 legislation did *not* import the American concept of affirmative action, which was employed only in the context of religious discrimination under legislation applicable in Northern Ireland.[10] The "essential feature" of the 1975 and 1976 Acts was instead "a negative prohibition on discrimination, rather than a positive duty to promote equality".[11]

As the Hepple Report notes, the "third generation" legislation developed in part "under the strong influence of EU law", particularly that relating to unlawful sex discrimination.[12] However, domestic impetuses have also encouraged the development of discrimination law. The Fair Employment Act 1989, applicable to religious discrimination in Northern Ireland, "shifted the emphasis from the elimination of unlawful discrimination on grounds of religion or political opinion"—the "third generation" approach adopted in its predecessor from 1976—to "the reduction of structural inequality in the labour market, whether caused by discrimination or not."[13] This approach has been taken further in subsequent legislation applicable in Northern Ireland, was echoed in the Stephen Lawrence Inquiry's emphasis on institutional racism in the police, and in later legislation imposing positive duties on public authorities not to discriminate.[14] The Hepple Report thus suggests that:

"Pressures are now growing ... for the UK as a whole to move towards a fourth generation of legislation prescribing positive duties on public authorities, employment and pay equity plans, and contract compliance regimes.

[8] Recognised in US law in the Supreme Court decision in *Griggs v Duke Power Co* (1971) 401 U.S. 424. Section 1(1)(b) of the SDA 75 and RRA 76 employ what is essentially the *Griggs* definition of indirect discrimination in statutory form.

[9] See Equality Act 2006, Pt 1.

[10] para.1.6.

[11] para.1.2.

[12] para.1.7.

[13] para.1.3.

[14] para.1.4. The legislation concerned is the Race Relations (Amendment) Act 2000 and the Equality Act 2006.

Several models now exist ... such as employment and pay equity legislation in Canada, affirmative action for women in Australia, and ... employment equity legislation in South Africa."[15]

The "fourth generation" model emphasises "promoting equality in addition to eliminating discrimination", and aims for a "positive, inclusive approach which encourages the assumption of responsibility by organizations and individuals to achieve change."[16] In considering the non-discrimination measures outlined in later sections, it will be useful to ask how closely they fit into the "generational" analysis.

The Hepple Report's reference to EU law brings us to the most decisive influence on the shape of contemporary discrimination law, and arguably one of the key reasons for its complexity: namely, the fact that the domestic constitution can now be described as "multi-layered".

Nicholas Bamforth and Peter Leyland, "Public Law in a Multi-Layered Constitution", Ch.1 in Nicholas Bamforth & Peter Leyland (eds.), *Public Law in a Multi-Layered Constitution* (Oxford: Hart, 2003)

pp.1–3: "The restructuring of the constitutional architecture of the United Kingdom in the past thirty or so years—in particular, since 1997—has been fundamental ... In practical terms, power (both legislative and political) has been spread away from the Westminster Parliament, both 'upwards' to the European Union and 'downwards' to the devolved assemblies. There has also been what might be seen as a rebalancing of the roles of the courts and Parliament in holding the executive to account, given the development by the courts—particularly since 1977—of a comprehensive regime of judicial review, a regime which has arguably been strengthened by the passage of the Human Rights Act 1998. The domain of government has also been altered by the processes of privatisation and contracting out...

The various changes ... have been prompted by a diverse collection of rationales, justifications and ideologies ... Nonetheless, the *overall consequence* has been to bring about a profound constitutional change, in that the United Kingdom could now be said to possess what might be described as a *multi-layered* constitution ... there has been a two-way redistribution of power from Westminster level to the European Union and the devolved levels of government, and the European Convention on Human Rights now plays a direct role in national law. Elected public bodies and courts must—to varying degrees—take account of and reflect such changes [. . .] the permissible scope of executive action—whether at UK or at devolved level—is [now] regulated by general United Kingdom-level laws, by the requirements of EC law and the European Convention (via the European Communities Act 1972 and Human Rights Act 1998 respectively) *and*, to varying extents, by the rules delimiting the powers of the devolved institutions."

[15] para.1.6.
[16] para.2.14.

The requirement that courts give effect to relevant provisions of EU law and the Convention is particularly important in the discrimination field. For both EU law and the Convention contain protections against invidious forms of discrimination. EU law has long been concerned to combat discrimination on the grounds of sex and nationality, and has more recently begun to tackle discrimination on the bases of race, sexual orientation, age, religion or belief and disability. Article 14 of the Convention is also concerned with these grounds—some explicitly, some through judicial interpretation—as well as others such as birth status, and discrimination-related claims are sometimes brought using other Convention rights.

There are two dimensions to the complexity arising from the UK's membership of the European Union and the Convention. Firstly, in certain areas of discrimination law, both bodies of law appear to have jurisdiction. However, at a level of detail the two bodies also differ in many ways: for example, in the contexts in which they apply, in their treatment of justifications for prima facie acts of discrimination, and in the extent to which direct and indirect discrimination are prohibited. Secondly, and at the heart of the "multi-layered" issue, is the role played in the national legal systems of EU member states by directly effective provisions of EU law and Convention rights (all EU member states also being signatories to the Convention). The most significant divergence between the two, both in relation to protections against discrimination and more generally, concerns what might be described as the legal weight of directly effective EU legal norms and rights protected under the Convention. Directly effective EU provisions take priority over conflicting rules of national law, which must in appropriate circumstances be disapplied by national courts.[17] Furthermore, national courts must interpret national legislation, as far as this is possible, in the light of those norms,[18] and damages may be granted against national authorities where national legislation or executive action contravenes them.[19] By contrast, the Convention, while granting the citizens of signatory states the right to an effective remedy where Convention rights are violated (Art.13) has such force at national level as the constitutional systems of the signatory states allow. As the Court of Human Rights made clear in *Smith and Grady v United Kingdom*, the "effect" of Art.13 is to:

"require the provision of a domestic remedy allowing the competent national authority both to deal with the substance of the relevant Convention complaint and to grant appropriate relief. However, Art.13 does not go so far as to require incorporation of the Convention or a particular form of remedy,

[17] Case 6/64, *Costa v ENEL* [1965] E.C.R. 505 at 593–4 (supremacy); Case 26/62, *Van Gend en Loos* [1963] E.C.R. 1 (direct effect); Case C-213/89, *R. v Secretary of State for Transport, Ex p. Factortame* [1990] E.C.R. 1–2433 (disapplication of national norms).

[18] Case 14/83, *Von Colson and Kamann v Land Nordrhein-Westfalen* [1984] E.C.R. 1891; Case C-106/90, *Marleasing SA v La Comercial Internacional de Alimentacion SA* [1990] E.C.R. I-4135.

[19] Case C-46/93, *Brasserie du Pecheur SA v Germany* [1996] E.C.R. I-1029.

Contracting States being afforded a margin of appreciation in conforming with their obligations under this provision."[20]

A litigant who feels that they have not obtained a satisfactory remedy at national level may take a case to the European Court of Human Rights, but the effect at national (as opposed to international) level of any remedy granted depends upon how, if at all, Convention norms and Convention jurisprudence are treated within the national legal system.[21] As such, it is possible to categorise directly effective EU law norms, including directly effective anti-discrimination protections, as having potentially stronger legal weight than Convention rights in the domestic law of EU member states.[22]

Since England and Wales is a dualist jurisdiction in which the legislature deliberately sought to place limits on the extent to which courts may apply Convention rights, the phenomenon of differing legal weight is particularly visible in national discrimination law. For, while the Human Rights Act 1998 echoes EU law by requiring that domestic legislation be interpreted, so far as its wording allows, in the light of Convention rights,[23] legislation may not be set aside for incompatibility: instead, the court may issue a declaration of incompatibility, leaving it to Parliament to decide whether and how to alter the legislation concerned.[24] The permissible scope of executive action is now regulated by "purely" national law, by the requirements of EU law *and* by those of the Convention, with the courts having assumed a powerful role in holding the executive to account via judicial review, under which proportionality review is applied when EU law or Convention rights are in issue (including in cases involving discrimination issues).[25] The fact that national courts do not have the same power to apply Convention rights as they do with directly effective provisions of EU law, coupled with the differences of detail between the Convention and EU law, means that different protections against discrimination vary quite visibly in their scope and legal weight. The importance of this issue will be demonstrated throughout this chapter.

Another divergence between EU law and Art.14 of the Convention relates to the role of courts and legislatures in determining which grounds of discrimination to prohibit, a question which is closely tied to the standard of review to be used when evaluating different types of allegedly unlawful discrimination. The practical consequence of the influx of Art.14 into domestic

20 (1999) 29 E.H.R.R. 493, para.[135].

21 For illuminating comparative analysis, see the essays in Conor Gearty (ed.), *European Civil Liberties and the European Convention on Human Rights: A Comparative Study* (The Hague: Martinus Nijhoff, 1997).

22 See Evelyn Ellis, *EU Anti-Discrimination Law* (Oxford: Oxford University Press, 2005), p.37.

23 Human Rights Act 1998, s.3.

24 Human Rights Act 1998, s.4.

25 These features might be described as examples of the emergence of a "multi-layered" constitution: see further Nicholas Bamforth and Peter Leyland, "Public Law in a Multi-Layered Constitution", Ch.1 in Nicholas Bamforth and Peter Leyland (eds), *Public Law in a Multi-Layered Constitution* (Oxford: Hart, 2003).

law is that the discrimination law system in force now involves a mixture of what was described in Chapter 1 as a "fixed category" approach to the prohibited grounds of discrimination and a "non-exhaustive list" approach. In other words, in cases based upon EU law—either through the direct effect of Art.141EC or relevant Directives, or relying on national measures designed to bring such provisions into domestic law—or on national measures passed without reference to EU law, courts lack the freedom to recognise new prohibited grounds of discrimination, being confined to ruling on the ambit of those grounds declared unlawful in the relevant legislation (although, as *P. v S. and Cornwall County Council* revealed in the European Court of Justice, this still allows for judicial recognition of gender identity discrimination as a form of unlawful sex discrimination[26]). In Art.14-related cases brought under the Human Rights Act 1998, by contrast, national courts are entitled to determine whether a hitherto unrecognised ground of discrimination is in fact precluded under that Article, and indeed whether conduct which might appear in colloquial terms to be "discriminatory" in fact violates another substantive Convention right relied upon without reference to Art.14. This apparent disparity raises the question whether domestic law is coherent (or coherent enough), and whether courts should be given the freedom to recognise new prohibited grounds of discrimination in non-Convention cases. Furthermore, the list of prohibited grounds of discrimination is still not as lengthy as the Hepple Report advocated,[27] and significant inconsistencies remain—as we shall see in subsequent sections—between the different prohibited grounds.

It is unsurprising, given this background, that the Hepple Report made clear in 2000 (echoing the "multi-layered" dimensions of contemporary discrimination law) that:

Equality: A New Framework. Report of the Independent Review of the Enforcement of UK Anti-Discrimination Legislation (Oxford: Hart, 2000)[28]

para.1.17: "There are [. . .] numerous challenges to the present framework—dissatisfaction with the fragmentation and inconsistencies between four separate anti-discrimination regimes in the U.K. ... demands for the legislation to be made more comprehensible and user-friendly; international, European and domestic pressures to extend the grounds of unlawful discrimination; the commitment of government to impose positive duties on public authorities; the relative success of fair employment legislation in

[26] Case C-13/94, [1996] E.C.R. I-2143; see further Ch.11.

[27] See Hepple Report, paras 2.70 to 2.75 (traveller communities and possible genetic discrimination): although note that same-sex couples are now treated more generously, under the Civil Partnership Act 2004, than the Hepple Report recommended at paras 2.83 to 2.84.

[28] Bob Hepple, Mary Coussey and Tufyal Choudhury, *Equality: A New Framework* (Oxford: Hart, 2000).

Northern Ireland in reducing structural inequality; the continuing need to keep in line with EU law; the pressure from devolved legislatures and executives in the UK; and the building of a new legal and political culture of equality based on the ECHR and international human rights treaties."

para. 2.24 "The inconsistent and unsatisfactory nature of the existing legislation is a result of its history. Successive anti-discrimination statutes have each concentrated upon a particular target. Notwithstanding the similarities between the S[ex] D[iscrimination] A[ct], R[ace] R[elations] A[ct] and D[isability] D[iscrimination] A[ct], and the attempts of the courts to interpret them as a harmonious code, the legislation now present[s] a mass of inconsistent detail, with major gaps in coverage"

The government's Discrimination Law Review recommended in its June 2007 Consultation Paper that consideration be given to consolidating discrimination law into a single non-discrimination statute.[29] The creation of a "Single Equality Act", the Review suggested, would provide "the opportunity to create a coherent legislative framework for fairness".[30] Nonetheless, the Review was keen to stress that the anticipated legislation "should build on our current anti-discrimination legislative model"[31] and that there were "no real gains to be made from departing from the British model" of fixed and generally legislatively-established grounds of prohibited discrimination towards a general equality or non-discrimination provision of the type seen in US law.[32] We consider the merits of and problems associated with introducing a single statute in Section VIII. For the moment, it is important to note an apparent tension in the Report's approach. For, having commended the "current" model, it went on to note that:

"Alongside discrimination legislation, the Human Rights Act gives people a clear legal statement of their basic rights and fundamental freedoms in our democratic society. Rather than just ensuring equal treatment ... it puts in place standards of behaviour based on dignity and respect. Legislation must be interpreted in the light of these rights ... The application of human rights in an equality context has been demonstrated in a number of cases dealing with disability, sexual orientation, gender reassignment and religion or belief and in some cases has led to new discrimination law being brought forward."[33]

Despite its rejection of a general equality or non-discrimination provision, in other words, the Report implicitly accepts the existence of an inter-relationship between discrimination law, human rights, and constitutional law, given the emphasis placed on the role of the Human Rights Act 1998. This inter-relationship, which derives in very large part from the "multi-layered" nature of

[29] *A Framework for Fairness: Proposals for a Single Equality Bill for Great Britain* (London: Department for Communities and Local Government, 2007).
[30] *ibid.*, Pt 2, para.8.
[31] *ibid.*, Pt 2, para.8.
[32] *ibid.*, Pt 2, para.10.
[33] *ibid.*, Pt 2, para.11.

contemporary constitutional law, is clearly a central aspect of discrimination law in the United Kingdom.

We have tried in this section to set out some of the overarching issues in contemporary discrimination law. Having begun by considering the application of "generational" analysis, we moved on to explore the decisive influence of the contemporary "multi-layered" constitutional structure: something which, we argued, has in turn affected the extent to which discrimination law can now be understood in constitutional and human rights terms. These points will become further evident in our analysis of the Convention and EU law in later sections—prior to which, we consider the role of other international discrimination-related provisions.

III. International Law

Although the discrimination-related provisions in international treaties ratified by the United Kingdom but not brought into national law (in other words, treaties other than the European Convention and EC Treaties) are taken into account only infrequently by national courts, the fact that national law is *sometimes* evaluated by reference to them means that they must briefly be considered. Generally, treaty provisions have effect at international level by and against states. Their effect in national law depends upon the character of the national legal system concerned. Since England and Wales is a dualist jurisdiction, in which international provisions must be brought into national law by Parliament in order to be directly enforceable, national courts tend to take account of unincorporated provisions only when interpreting ambiguous areas of national law (although, as we shall see, the House of Lords arguably adopted a bolder approach in *R. v Immigration Officer at Prague Airport, Ex p. European Roma Rights Centre*, a case concerning racial discrimination[34]).

Relevant international provisions can be of three varieties: free-standing prohibitions on discrimination found in general human rights treaties; prohibitions on discrimination in the enjoyment of other rights protected in general human rights treaties; and treaties prohibiting discrimination or specific forms of discrimination. The UN International Covenant on Civil and Political Rights ("I.C.C.P.R."), to which the United Kingdom is a party, contains examples of the first two types of provision. Within the first category is Art.26[35]:

[34] [2004] UKHL 55.

[35] Note also Arts 1 and 2 of the Universal Declaration of Human Rights, which influenced the drafting of the I.C.C.P.R.: Sarah Joseph, Jenny Schultz and Melissa Castan, *The International Covenant on Civil and Political Rights: Cases, Materials, and Commentary* (Oxford: Oxford University Press, 2nd edn., 2004), paras 1.09 to 1.11.

The UN International Covenant on Civil and Political Rights (ICCPR) 1966, Article 26:

"All persons are equal before the law and are entitled without any discrimination to the equal protection of the law. In this respect, the law shall prohibit any discrimination and guarantee to all persons equal and effective protection against discrimination on any ground such as race, colour, sex, language, religion, political or other opinion, national or social origin, property, birth or other status."

Articles 2(1) and 3, by contrast, are examples of the second type of provision: Art.2(1) obliges signatory states to respect and to ensure to individuals within their territory and jurisdiction the rights recognised within the Covenant, without distinction on the same grounds as those recognised (or, presumably, other statuses allowed for) in Art.20, while Art.3 requires signatory statues to ensure the equal enjoyment of such rights by men and women.[36] A further example falling within the first category is Art.1 of International Labour Organisation ("I.L.O.") Convention 111, established in 1958 and relevant in the employment law context, which requires states to ensure equality and eliminate practices that differentiate on "the basis of race, sex, religion, national extraction or social origin". A further example falling within the second category is Art.2(2) of the UN International Covenant on Economic, Social and Cultural Rights ("I.C.E.S.C.R."), to which the U.K. is also a signatory. Article 2(2) obliges signatory states to ensure that the "rights enunciated in the present Convention will be exercised without discrimination of any kind". Provisions falling within the third category, relating specifically to discrimination or to certain forms of discrimination, include the 1966 International Convention on the Elimination of All Forms of Racial Discrimination and the 1979 Convention on the Elimination of All Forms of Discrimination Against Women.

All these provisions possess the standard legal properties associated with international treaty obligations. As Richard Clayton and Hugh Tomlinson suggest, they "guarantee the rights contained in them: this means that the UK Government is obliged, as a matter of international law, to secure in domestic law the protected rights and freedoms and to provide effective remedies before national authorities for breaches of the of the treaty provisions".[37] This has been captured specifically in relation to the I.C.C.P.R. by Sarah Joseph, Jenny Schultz and Melissa Castan:

[36] See also Arts 23, 24 and 25.
[37] *The Law of Human Rights*, Vol.1 (Oxford: Oxford University Press, 2000), para. 2.01.

Sarah Joseph, Jenny Schultz and Melissa Castan, *The International Covenant on Civil and Political Rights: Cases, Materials, and Commentary* (Oxford: Oxford University Press, 2nd edn., 2004)

pp.13–14: "[1.25] Though the ICCPR imposes duties upon States in the international plane of law, it is envisaged that the implementation of the rights therein is primarily a domestic matter. Indeed, article 2, the general obligation provision, requires States Parties to protect the ICCPR rights at the municipal level. International enforcement measures, such as the supervisory mechanisms of the H[uman] R[ights] C[ommittee], are designed to be a secondary source of ICCPR rights protection . . .

[1.26] Thus, States Parties have an international duty to translate the ICCPR guarantees into domestic rights for individuals. The actual domestic protection afforded to ICCPR rights depends on the legal and political system of the relevant State Party."

The Human Rights Committee is the international panel charged with explaining the meaning of the I.C.C.P.R.'s provisions, considering reports submitted to it by the signatory states concerning their compliance with the provisions, hearing inter-state complaints (provided both states agree that the Committee is competent to do so), and—in the case of states which have signed the First Optional Protocol—receiving complaints from individuals and recommending appropriate remedies.[38] However, the Committee is confined to making recommendations: its determinations are not legally binding.[39] In any event, since the United Kingdom is not yet a party to the First Optional Protocol, UK citizens cannot complain to the Committee.

Other treaties and their anti-discrimination provisions are administered in analogous ways. There is no individual complaints procedure concerning the I.C.E.S.C.R.[40] Meanwhile, Art.9 of the International Convention on the Elimination of All Forms of Racial Discrimination obliges signatory states to submit reports on the legislative, judicial and administrative measures it has adopted and which give effect to the Convention's obligations not to discriminate. These reports are submitted to the Committee on the Elimination of Racial Discrimination. Article 11 provides for an inter-state complaints procedure, but the United Kingdom has not accepted a right to individual petition.[41] Under Art.18 of the Convention on the Elimination of All Forms of Discrimination Against Women, signatory states must submit reports to the Committee on the Elimination of All Forms of Discrimination Against Women,

[38] Sarah Joseph, Jenny Schultz and Melissa Castan, *The International Covenant on Civil and Political Rights: Cases, Materials, and Commentary*, n.35 above, paras 1.31 to 1.61; see I.C.C.P.R., Arts 28 to 45.

[39] *ibid.*, para. 2.02.

[40] See, generally, Matthew Craven, *The International Covenant on Economic, Social and Cultural Rights: A Perspective on Its Development* (Oxford: Clarendon Press, 1998).

[41] See, generally, Richard Clayton & Hugh Tomlinson, *The Law of Human Rights*, *ibid.*, Vol.1, para.2.55.

which provides guidelines on the interpretation of the Convention.[42] Furthermore, as Clayton and Tomlinson have noted, the I.L.O. is a "specialist agency of the United Nations" concerned with employment law:

"[t]he United Kingdom must submit periodic reports on the measures it has adopted to give effect to ILO Conventions which are examined by a Committee of Experts. If an association of employers or workers wishes to complain that a state has failed to observe a Convention, the Governing Body of the ILO may communicate the compliant to the state and arrange a hearing before a special committee which then reports back to the Governing Body".[43]

Although the United Kingdom has ratified Convention 111, its general ratification record in relation to I.L.O. Conventions remains sporadic.

Perhaps the most visible body of discrimination-related reasoning relates to the I.C.C.P.R. The Human Rights Committee has interpreted Art.26 of the I.C.C.P.R. as prohibiting direct as well as indirect discrimination[44] and extending to discrimination in the enjoyment of social and economic rights as well as of civil and political rights.[45] The "other statuses" falling within its ambit have been held to include nationality, marital status, place of residence, school status, employment status, and sexual orientation,[46] reasonable and objective (i.e., proportionate) distinctions have been found to be capable of justification,[47] and some forms of affirmative action have been deemed permissible.[48] Some of these points are captured in the Committee's somewhat controversial opinion in *Broeks v The Netherlands*, concerning discriminatory provisions of national social security legislation.[49] As well as considering the general operation of Article 26, the Committee emphasised that its application could not be blocked by a potential overlap with other international protections against discrimination, and that within the I.C.C.P.R., Art.26 was broader than Art.2 (given its free-standing nature).

[42] See, generally, Richard Clayton & Hugh Tomlinson, *ibid.*, para.2.56.

[43] *The Law of Human Rights*, Vol.1, *ibid.*, para.2.58.

[44] Sarah Joseph, Jenny Schultz and Melissa Castan, *The International Covenant on Civil and Political Rights: Cases, Materials, and Commentary*, n.35 above, paras 23.31 to 23.40.

[45] *ibid.*, paras 23.09 to 23.19.

[46] *ibid.*, paras 23.20 to 23.30.

[47] *ibid.*, paras 23.41 to 23.67B.

[48] *ibid.*, paras 23.68 to 23.86.

[49] For criticism, see M. Schmidt, "The Complementarity of the Covenant and the European Convention on Human Rights—Recent Developments", in David Harris and Sarah Joseph (eds.), *The International Covenant on Civil and Political Rights and United Kingdom Law* (Oxford: Clarendon Press, 1995).

Case 172/84, *Broeks v The Netherlands*, April 9, 1987

[12.1]: "... The Committee is of the view that the International Covenant on Civil and Political Rights would still apply even if a particular subject-matter is referred to or covered in other international instruments, for example, the International Covenant on the Elimination of All Forms of Racial Discrimination, the Convention on the Elimination of All Forms of Discrimination Against Women, or, as in the present case, the International Covenant on Economic, Social and Cultural Rights. Notwithstanding the interrelated drafting history of the two Covenants, it remains necessary for the Committee to apply fully the terms of the International Covenant on Civil and Political Rights. The Committee observes in this connection that the provisions of article 2 of the International Covenant on Economic, Social and Cultural Rights do not detract from the full application of article 26 of the International Covenant on Civil and Political Rights.

[12.3]: For the purpose of determining the scope of article 26, the Committee has taken into account the 'ordinary meaning' of each element of the article in its context and in the light of its object and purpose (art. 31 of the Vienna Convention on the Law of Treaties). The Committee begins by noting that article 26 does not merely duplicate the guarantees already provided for in article 2. It derives from the principle of equal protection of the law without discrimination, as contained in article 7 of the Universal Declaration of Human Rights, which prohibits discrimination in law or in practice in any field regulated and protected by public authorities. Article 26 is thus concerned with the obligations imposed on States in regard to their legislation and the application thereof.

[12.4]: Although article 26 requires that legislation should prohibit discrimination, it does not of itself contain any obligation with respect to the matters that may be provided for by legislation. Thus it does not, for example, require any State to enact legislation to provide for social security. However, when such legislation is adopted in the exercise of a State's sovereign power, then such legislation must comply with article 26 of the Covenant...

[13]: The right to equality before the law and to equal protection of the law without any discrimination does not make all differences of treatment discriminatory. A differentiation based on reasonable and objective criteria does not amount to prohibited discrimination within the meaning of article 26."

As should be clear from this analysis, the mechanisms for enforcing protections against discrimination at international level are not especially strong. The same might generally be said about the impact of these provisions at national level. None of the provisions mentioned here has been brought into national law by legislation. As such, the general rule is that national courts may make reference to them only in order to resolve ambiguities in domestic legislation, something which has occurred only sporadically, but perhaps most frequently in relation to the I.C.C.P.R.[50] *R. v Immigration Officer at Prague Airport, Ex p. European Roma Rights Centre* may, however, be indicative of a bolder approach

[50] For illustrations of the general rule (albeit not in relation to the provisions under discussion), see *Salomon v Commissioners of Customs and Excise* [1967] 2 QB 116, 143–4 (Diplock L.J.), *R. v Secretary of State for the Home Department, Ex p. Brind* [1991] 1 AC 696. For discussion of circumstances in which provisions mentioned here have been invoked, and of competing views concerning when they should be invoked, see Richard Clayton and Hugh Tomlinson, *The Law of Human Rights*, Vol.1, *ibid.*, paras 2.44 to 2.46, 2.61 to 2.68.

by the House of Lords in the discrimination context.[51] Here, the majority supported Baroness Hale's invocation of Arts 2 and 26 of the I.C.C.P.R., together with Art.2 of the International Convention on the Elimination of all Forms of Racial Discrimination, as a basis (when coupled with arguments focused on the Race Relations Act 1976, as amended) for finding that the respondent had unlawfully directly discriminated contrary to the Race Relations Act in operating a scheme whereby Roma individuals who were seeking to travel to the UK from Prague airport were treated with more suspicion and subjected to more intensive and intrusive questioning than non-Roma travellers.[52] Baroness Hale appeared to treat arguments based on the international law provisions as conceptually distinct from those based on the drafting of the 1976 Act, and granted a declaration despite the absence of any obvious ambiguity in the latter.[53] Nonetheless, we should perhaps be wary of reading too much into the case. As Ralph Wilde has noted, the House of Lords merely "seemed to assume", without addressing important counter-arguments concerning the extraterritorial application of the I.C.C.P.R., that the Covenant could apply to the respondent's actions in operating the scheme at Prague airport.[54] It seems similarly to have been assumed, without thought having been given to the general rule about international legal provisions, that Arts 2 and 26 could be directly employed to support a finding of unlawful discrimination. The rather spartan reasoning in *Roma Rights* might thus be vulnerable when the role of the Covenant in supporting a finding of unlawful discrimination (whether involving extraterritorial application or not) is revisited in later cases.[55]

It is important for both practical and conceptual reasons not to overlook relevant international provisions. As a practical matter, we have seen that they may be relevant in terms of the UK's international legal obligations, and may be sometimes be referred to by national courts. Furthermore, the existence of these provisions—as a mechanism to be used when considering the drafting and interpretation of national legislation—serves to highlight in conceptual terms the constitutional dimensions of discrimination law (for, as noted in chapter 1, the interpretation of legislation is an essentially constitutional issue), as well as its broader-than-national character.

[51] [2004] UKHL 55.

[52] [2004] UKHL 55, paras [98]–[103] (Baroness Hale), supported by Lord Bingham at paras [10] and [31], Lord Steyn at paras [38] and [47] and Lord Hope at para.[48].

[53] [2004] UKHL 55, paras [98], [104].

[54] "The Extraterritorial Application of the Human Rights Act" (2005) 58 C.L.P. 47, 65.

[55] It is worth noting in this regard that *Roma Rights* has been distinguished by the House of Lords on the extra-territorial application point: *Al-Skeini v Secretary of State for Defence* [2007] UKHL 26, paras [21] (Lord Bingham) and [136] (Lord Brown).

IV. The European Convention on Human Rights[56]

In this section, we examine the working of Art.14 and other provisions of the Convention in so far as they deal with discrimination issues. Our initial focus is on Art.14 and other Convention rights which touch upon discrimination at European Court of Human Rights level. We consider the ambit of Art.14, in the sense of the subject-matters to which and situations in which it applies (encompassing the second and fourth key questions about discrimination law: "when are litigants protected?" and "how wide are the protections?"); followed by the tests used by the Strasbourg Court in determining whether a particular ground of discrimination is prohibited under Art.14 (the first, fifth and sixth key questions: "who is protected?", "can discrimination sometimes be justified for policy reasons?" and "what happens when protection from discrimination clashes with other rights or values?"). The eighth key question ("how far can other human rights be used to combat discrimination?") is particularly relevant when dealing with the ambit of Art.14 given that this Article can only be pleaded in UK cases *in conjunction with* another substantive Convention right, and many discrimination-related arguments have been made in cases brought under other Convention Articles not explicitly concerned with discrimination but wide enough to cover situations that, in colloquial or "common sense" (i.e., extra-legal) language, might be thought to involve discrimination. We mention the reception of Convention rights into domestic law where relevant in this part of the analysis. The focus switches directly to domestic law in the remainder of the section, in which we explore some of the main issues which have arisen in discrimination cases under the Human Rights Act 1998—including the operation of proportionality, judicial deference and the selection of a "comparator" for the discrimination claimant.

Our second and ninth key questions ("who has to protect claimants from discrimination?" and "what legal remedies are available, and who may seek them?") have different answers depending upon whether a case is before the European Court of Human Rights or a domestic court. The only permissible defendants at Strasbourg level are signatory states (even if states are sometimes held responsible, due to a failure to act, for rights violations committed by third parties),[57] and the only permissible claimants are "victims" (an individual, an association of individuals, or the spouse or parent of a deceased individual, whose Convention rights have allegedly been breached)[58] and signatory states. "Victims" may seek "just satisfaction" (including the award

[56] This section develops the analysis found in Nicholas Bamforth, "Prohibited Grounds of Discrimination under EU Law and the European Convention on Human Rights: Problems of Contrast and Overlap" (2007) *Cambridge Year Book of European legal Studies*, Ch.1.

[57] See, e.g. Andrew Clapham, *Human Rights in the Private Sphere; Osman v United Kingdom* (1999) 29 E.H.R.R. 245.

[58] Richard Clayton and Hugh Tomlinson, *The Law of Human Rights*, Vol.1 (Oxford: Oxford University Press, 2000), paras 22.14 to 22.49; *Norris v Ireland* (1988) 13 E.H.R.R. 186; *CCSU v United Kingdom*; for discussion, see Joanna Miles.

of damages), and signatory states are expected, by virtue of Art.13, to grant an effective remedy for the protection of Convention rights at national level.[59] However, Art.13 falls far short of the EU law principle of direct effect, in that national courts are not required to set aside national legislation where there is incompatibility.

At national level, by contrast, the Human Rights Act allows for proceedings to be brought by two routes, the permissible parties varying depending upon each. The first route is laid down in s.3(1), which states that "So far as it is possible to do so, primary legislation and subordinate legislation must be read and given effect in a way which is compatible with the Convention rights". As s.3(2)(a) makes clear, this duty "applies to primary legislation and subordinate legislation whenever enacted"—that is, to legislation passed both before and after the Human Rights Act came into force. It also arises *whoever* the parties to the case happen to be—in other words, whether either or both parties are private or public in nature—and regardless of the subject-matter of the case.[60] The main substantive constraint imposed on the operation of s.3(1) is that the statutory provisions in issue in the case must reveal an incompatibility with Convention rights using ordinary principles of interpretation—which are assumed to give courts less interpretative latitude—before s.3 may be used in an attempt to produce a compatible interpretation.[61] Subject to this constraint, s.3(1) may in principle be used to interpret any legislation—including the SDA, RRA and other provisions designed to combat specific examples of discrimination—in the light of Convention rights, including the Art.14 right to non-discrimination. As the words "so far as it is possible" imply, s.3 does not impose an absolute duty to interpret legislation compatibly with Convention rights. Where statutory provisions remain incompatible with Convention rights even when they are interpreted using s.3(1), they must be applied as they stand. Where a court is satisfied that a provision of primary legislation is incompatible with Convention rights, s.4(2) prescribes that "it may make a declaration of that incompatibility". However, such a declaration "does not affect the validity, continuing operation or enforcement of the provision in respect of which it is given" (s.4(6)(a)) and "is not binding on the parties to the proceedings in which it is made" (s.4(6)(b)).[62] There has, in consequence, been considerable debate in the cases and academic literature concerning the limits

[59] Richard Clayton and Hugh Tomlinson, *ibid.*, on Art.13, see *Smith and Grady v United Kingdom* (1999) 29 E.H.R.R. 493.

[60] *Ghaidan v Godin-Mendoza* [2004] UKHL 10, para. [106] (Lord Rodger).

[61] The formulations used in different cases and judgments vary: *R. v A.* [2001] UKHL 25, paras [10]–[15] (Lord Slynn), [29]–[43] (Lord Steyn), [68], [121], [136]–[137] (Lord Clyde), [155], [161]–[163] (Lord Hutton); *Poplar Housing and Regeneration Community Association Ltd v Donoghue* [2001] EWCA Civ 595, para.[75] (Lord Woolf C.J.); *Ghaidan v Godin-Mendoza* [2004] UKHL 30, paras [5]–[35] (Lord Nicholls).

[62] For the Parliamentary procedures for removing incompatibilities by "remedial order", see s.10 and Sch.2.

of the s.3(1) interpretative obligation.[63] The House of Lords attempted to rationalise the case law in *Ghaidan v Godin-Mendoza*, key aspects of their approach being captured in Lord Nicholls' judgment[64]:

Ghaidan v Godin-Mendoza [2004] UKHL 30

[32]: "... the mere fact the language under consideration is inconsistent with a Convention-compliant meaning does not of itself make a Convention-compliant interpretation under section 3 impossible. Section 3 enables language to be interpreted restrictively or expansively. But section 3 goes further than this. It is also apt to require a court to read in words which change the meaning of the enacted legislation, so as to make it Convention-compliant. In other words, the intention of Parliament in enacting section 3 was that, to an extent bounded only by what is 'possible', a court can modify the meaning, and hence the effect, of primary and secondary legislation.

[33]: Parliament, however, cannot have intended that in the discharge of this extended interpretative function the courts should adopt a meaning inconsistent with a fundamental feature of legislation. That would be to cross the constitutional boundary section 3 seeks to demarcate and preserve. Parliament has retained the right to enact legislation in terms which are not Convention-compliant. The meaning imported by application of section 3 must be compatible with the underlying thrust of the legislation being construed. Words implied must ... 'go with the grain of the legislation'. Nor can Parliament have intended that section 3 should require courts to make decisions for which they are not equipped. There may be several ways of making a provision Convention-compliant, and the choice may involve issues calling for legislative deliberation."

The second route under the Human Rights Act is laid down by s.6(1), which stipulates that it is "unlawful for a public authority to act in a way which is incompatible with a Convention right".[65] Section 7 allows the "victim" of an alleged violation of Convention rights—the same test as used by the Strasbourg Court—plus the Commission for Equality and Human Rights, as a statutory enforcement agency[66]—to bring proceedings against a public authority (according to ss.6(3) and 6(5), bodies "certain of whose functions are

[63] Key cases include *R. v A.* [2001] UKHL 25, paras [44] (Lord Steyn), [108] (Lord Hope), [162] (Lord Hutton), *Re S* [2002] UKHL 10, paras [39]–[40] (Lord Nicholls), *R. (Anderson) v Secretary of State for the Home Department* [2002] UKHL 46 and *Bellinger v Bellinger* [2003] UKHL 21. For general discussion, see Conor Gearty, "Reconciling Parliamentary Democracy and Human Rights" (2002) 118 L.Q.R. 248; Gavin Phillipson, "(Mis)-Reading Section 3 of the Human Rights Act" (2003) 119 L.Q.R. 183; Conor Gearty, "Revisiting section 3(1) of the Human Rights Act" (2003) 119 L.Q.R. 551 and *Principles of Human Rights Adjudication* (Oxford: Oxford University Press, 2004), pp.52–3, 141–5; Danny Nicol, "Statutory interpretation and human rights after *Anderson*" [2004] P.L. 274; Aileen Kavanagh, "Statutory interpretation and human rights after *Anderson*: a more contextual approach" [2004] P.L. 537 and 'Unlocking the Human Rights Act: The "Radical Approach to Section 3(1) Revisited" [2005] E.H.R.L.R. 259.

[64] See also paras [28]–[31] (Lord Nicholls), [38]–[39], [44]–[50] (Lord Steyn), [107], [110], [121]–[124] (Lord Rodger).

[65] An "act" is defined in s.6(5), and includes a failure to act.

[66] Equality Act 2006, s.30(3).

of a public nature" are included within the definition of a "public authority" in so far as their acts are not of a private nature).[67] Section 8(1) then stipulates that a court may grant "such relief or remedy, or make such order, within its powers as it considers just and appropriate": a power which, while subject to certain qualifications,[68] has been found to give the courts jurisdiction to allow for judicial review of[69] as well as damages actions against public authorities.[70] The range of permissible claimants and defendants is thus narrower than under s.3(1), but the range of remedies is arguably broader. As under ss.3 and 4, provision is made for incompatible legislation, in that s.6(2) specifies that a public authority will not have acted unlawfully contrary to s.6(1) if "as a result of one or more provisions of primary legislation" it could not have acted differently, or where it was acting "so as to give effect to or enforce" provisions of or made under primary legislation "which cannot be read or given effect in a way which is compatible with the Convention rights". In such a situation, the court will need to consider whether to make a s.4 declaration.[71] The courts also appear to have accepted that the inclusion of courts and tribunals within the list of public authorities in s.6(3)(a) entitles or obliges them to interpret and develop existing common law causes of action between private parties by reference to Convention rights, albeit without creating new causes of action.[72]

It should be emphasised that, by contrast with the role of courts in cases involving directly effective provisions of EU law, national courts have no power to "disapply" legislation which breaches Convention rights, including Art.14. In consequence, directly effective EU law rights have what might be described as greater legal weight than Convention rights at national level—for

[67] For discussion of the victim test in domestic law, see Joanna Miles, "Standing under the Human Rights Act 1998: theories of Rights Enforcement and the Nature of Public Law Adjudication" (2000) 59 C.L.J. 133 and "Standing in a Multi-layered Constitution", Ch.15 in Nicholas Bamforth & Peter Leyland (eds), *Public Law in a Multi-layered Constitution* (Oxford: Hart, 2003). For analysis of the nature of a "public authority" and functions of a "public nature", see *Parochial Church Council of the Parish of Aston Cantlow and Wilmcote v Wallbank* [2003] UKHL 37; *Poplar Housing and Regeneration Community Association Ltd v Donoghue* [2001] EWCA Civ 595; *YL v Birmingham City Council* [2007] UKHL 27.

[68] ss. 8(2) to 8(4), 9.

[69] See, most obviously, *R. v Secretary of State for the Home Department, Ex p. Daly* [2001] UKHL 26.

[70] See *Anufrijeva v Southwark London BC* [2003] EWCA Civ 1406; *R. v Secretary of State for the Home Department, Ex p. Greenfield* [2005] UKHL 14; L.Com. Report No. 226, *Damages Under the Human Rights Act*.

[71] See, e.g. *A v Secretary of State for the Home Department* [2004] UKHL 56.

[72] The most obvious judicial decisions to this effect (relying on Art.8) are *Douglas and Zeta-Jones v Hello! Ltd* [2001] Q.B. 697 (CA) and *Campbell v MGN Ltd* [2004] UKHL 22 (HL). For the background debate, see, e.g., Murray Hunt, "The 'Horizontal' Effect of the Human Rights Act" [1998] P.L. 423; Sir William Wade, "Human Rights and the Judiciary" [1998] E.H.R.L.R. 520 and "Horizons of Horizontality" (2000) 116 L.Q.R. 217; Sir Richard Buxton, "The Human Rights Act and Private Law" (2000) 116 L.Q.R. 48; Nicholas Bamforth, "The True 'Horizontal Effect' of the Human Rights Act 1998" (2001) 117 L.Q.R. 34.

they may be used to "disapply" incompatible legislation rather than, as with a s.4 declaration, leaving it to Parliament to remedy any anomaly.[73]

A. *The ambit of Article 14*

European Convention on Human Rights, Article 14

"The enjoyment of the rights and freedoms set forth in this Convention shall be secured without discrimination on any ground such as sex, race, colour, language, religion, political or other opinion, national or social origin, association with a national minority, property, birth, or other status."

As it is worded, Article 14 prohibits discrimination only in the enjoyment of other Convention rights—in practice, those contained in Arts 2 to 12 of the Convention or Arts 1 to 3 of the First Protocol—and one of these rights to be in play in order for a claimant to rely upon Art.14. According to the Strasbourg Court in *Rasmussen v Denmark*:

"Article 14 complements the other substantive provisions of the Convention and the Protocols. It has no independent existence since it has effect solely in relation to the 'enjoyment of rights and freedoms' safeguarded by those provisions."[74]

Robert Wintemute explains position this by reference to the circumstances and time of the Article's drafting:

Robert Wintemute "'Within the Ambit': How Big *Is* the 'Gap' in Article 14 European Convention on Human Rights? Part 1" [2004] E.H.R.L.R. 366

367: "Article 14 was a bold experiment in 1950 [when it was opened for signature]. It contained a prohibition of discrimination in '[t]he enjoyment of the rights and freedoms set forth in the Convention', resembling Art.2 of the unenforceable 1948 Universal Declaration of Human Rights (UDHR) (entitlement 'without distinction' to 'all the rights and freedoms set forth in this Declaration'), but combining such a prohibition with the

[73] As Paul Craig suggests, there is "therefore an incentive for those minded to challenge primary legislation to do so through EU rights where that is possible": *EU Administrative Law*, (Oxford: Oxford University Press, 2006), p.532.

[74] (1984) 7 E.H.R.R. 371, para.29; see further *National Union of Belgian Police v Belgium* (1975) 1 E.H.R.R. 578, para.45; *Schmidt and Dahlstrom v Sweden* (1976) 1 E.H.R.R. 632, para.39; *Petrovic v Austria* R.J.D. [1998]-II 579.

unprecedented enforcement mechanism of the European Court and Commission of Human Rights. Having agreed to be bound by judgments of the first international human rights court, Member States of the Council of Europe were understandably nervous about incorporating a general, independent, or 'free-standing' prohibition of discrimination, such as Art.7 UDHR ('[a]ll are . . . entitled without any discrimination to equal protection of the law') [. . .] the enforceability of Art.14 and the year of its birth explain its relative narrowness . . ."

Article 1 of Protocol 12 to the Convention, opened for signature in 2000 and in force since 2005 in those signatory states which have acceded to it, seeks to convert Art.14 into a free-standing protection against discrimination. Instead of tying Art.14 to any other right set forth in the Convention, Protocol 12 ties it to any right set forth by law:

(Optional) Protocol No.12 to the European Convention on Human Rights

Article 1. "The enjoyment of any right set forth by law shall be secured without discrimination on any ground such as sex, race, color, language, religion, political or other opinion, national or social origin, association with a national minority, property, birth, or other status."

Article 2. "No one shall be discriminated against by a public authority on any ground such as those mentioned in paragraph 1."

The United Kingdom has so far refused to sign Protocol 12, and so national courts may for the moment apply only the unamended Art.14.[75] Three issues arise in relation to the width of Art.14 as it currently stands: firstly, how a claimant is to show that a discriminatory act is closely enough connected with the enjoyment of another substantive Convention right that Art.14 may be pleaded in conjunction with that right; secondly, which areas of activity fall within the scope of Art.14 in its current form; and thirdly, to what extent Art.13 precludes indirect as well as direct discrimination.

In relation to the first issue, the derivative nature of Art.14 was explained in general terms by the Strasbourg Court in the *Belgian Linguistic (No.2)* case:

[75] For critical analysis of the UK's refusal, see Urfan Khaliq, "Protocol 12 to the European Convention on Human Rights: a step forward or a step too far?" [2001] P.L. 457; Sandra Fredman, "Why the UK Government should Sign and Ratify Protocol 12" (2002) 105 Equal Opportunities Review 21; Robert Wintemute, "Filling the Article 14 'Gap': Government Ratification and Judicial Control of Protocol No.12 ECHR: Part 2" [2004] E.H.R.L.R. 484.

Belgian Linguistic (No.2) (1968) 1 E.H.R.R. 252

para.9: "While it is true that this guarantee [of non-discrimination] has no independent existence in the sense that under the terms of Article 14 it relates solely to 'rights and freedoms set forth in the Convention', a measure which in itself is in conformity with the requirements of the Article enshrining the right or freedom in question may however infringe this Article when read in conjunction with Article 14 for the reason that it is of a discriminatory nature.

Thus, persons subject to the jurisdiction of a Contracting State cannot draw from Article 2 of the [First] Protocol (P1–2) [the right to education] the right to obtain from the public authorities the creation of a particular kind of educational establishment; nevertheless, a State which had set up such an establishment could not, in laying down entrance requirements, take discriminatory measures within the meaning of Article 14.

To recall a further example . . . Article 6 of the Convention [the right to a fair hearing] does not compel States to institute a system of appeal courts. A State which does set up such courts consequently goes beyond its obligations under Article 6. However it would violate that Article, read in conjunction with Article 14, were it to debar certain persons from these remedies without a legitimate reason while making them available to others in respect of the same type of actions.

In such cases there would be a violation of a guaranteed right or freedom as it is proclaimed by the relevant Article read in conjunction with Article 14. It is as though the latter formed an integral part of each of the Articles laying down rights and freedoms. No distinctions should be made in this respect according to the nature of these rights and freedoms and of their correlative obligations, and for instance as to whether the respect due to the right concerned implies positive action or mere abstention. This is, moreover, clearly shown by the very general nature of the terms employed in Article 14: 'the enjoyment of the rights and freedoms set forth in this Convention shall be secured'."

This position has been reiterated in domestic law at House of Lords level:

Ghaidan v Godin-Mendoza [2004] UKHL 30

LORD NICHOLLS

[10]: "Unlike [A]rticle 1 of the 12th Protocol, [A]rticle 14 of the Convention does not confer a free-standing right of non-discrimination. It does not confer a right of non-discrimination in respect of all laws. Article 14 is more limited in its scope. It precludes discrimination in the 'enjoyment of the rights and freedoms set forth in this Convention'. The court at Strasbourg has said this means that, for [A]rticle 14 to be applicable, the facts at issue must 'fall within the ambit' of one or more of the Convention rights."

Nonetheless, there is some controversy as to what exactly is meant by the notion that an Art.14 claim must fall "within the ambit" of another Convention right in order to be heard by a court.[76] The Strasbourg Court has taken a broad view in many cases. In *Rasmussen v Denmark*, for example, it stated that:

[76] For discussion of the present position, see Richard Clayton and Hugh Tomlinson, *The Law of Human Rights*, Vol.1 (Oxford: Oxford University Press, 2000), paras 17.86 to 17.88. For criticism and alternatives, see Aaron Baker, "The Enjoyment of Rights and Freedoms: A New Conception of the 'Ambit' under Article 14 ECHR" (2006) 69 M.L.R. 714.

"Although the application of Article 14 does not necessarily presuppose a breach [of] the other substantive provisions of the Convention, [and] to this extent it has an autonomous meaning, [there could be] no room for its application unless the facts at issue fall within the ambit of one or more of the latter."[77]

In *Petrovic v Austria*, it suggested that Art.14 could be relied upon whenever the measure complained of was "linked" to the exercise of another substantive Convention right,[78] or when the subject-matter of the disadvantageous treatment "constitutes one of the modalities" of the exercise of the right concerned.[79] At national level, Buxton L.J. relied on *Petrovic* to take a "wide view" at Court of Appeal stage in *Ghaidan v Godin-Mendoza*, citing with approval the suggestion that:

"even the most tenuous link with another provision in the Convention will suffice for [A]rticle 14 to enter into play".[80]

Keene L.J. suggested that it was necessary to show only that the facts fell within the ambit of one or more of the substantive Convention rights: an Art.14 claim did not require a substantive Convention right actually to have been breached. By contrast, it was been suggested in some later cases that this was to adopt an overly wide interpretation of prevailing Strasbourg case law.[81] At House of Lords level, neither Lord Nicholls in *Ghaidan*[82] nor Lord Hoffmann in *R. v Secretary of State for Work and Pensions, Ex p. Carson*[83] considered it necessary to give a final decision on the correct reading of Art.14.

One consequence of the present scope of Art.14 is that while its reach is *potentially* broader than that of EU law—after all, other Convention rights are

77 (1984) 7 E.H.R.R. 371, para [29]. See also *Van der Mussele v Belgium* (1983) 6 E.H.R.R. 163, para.[43]; *Abdulaziz, Cabales and Balkandali v United Kingdom* (1985) 7 E.H.R.R. 471, para.[71].

78 (2001) 33 E.H.R.R. 307, para.[28].

79 *ibid.*, para.[22].

80 At [2003] Ch 380, 387, para [9]; see also Keene L.J. The quotation comes from Grosz, Beatson and Duffy, *Human Rights: the 1998 Act and the European Convention* (London: Sweet & Maxwell, 2000), s. C14–10.

81 *R. (Erskine) v London Borough of Lambeth* [2003] EWHC (Admin) 2479, paras [21]–[22] (Mitting J.), *R. (Douglas) v North Tyneside Metropolitan BC* [2004] 1 All E.R. 709, 722, paras [53]–[54] (Scott Baker L.J.).

82 Lord Nicholls highlighted the differing views at para.[11], but stated at para.[12] that it was unnecessary to give a final view since it was common ground that para.2 of Sch.1 to the Rent Act 1977, which stipulated succession rights to statutory tenancies as between members of couples who lived together, fell within the ambit of the Art.8 right to respect for private and family life; see also Baroness Hale at para.[135]: "On any view", the "threshold is crossed here".

83 [2005] UKHL 37, para.[51].

relevant in an enormous range of circumstances—it has been argued that employment, or at least access to employment, is excluded from its scope given that it does not fall within the scope of other, substantive Convention rights.[84] However, this argument may be too broad: the Strasbourg Court has accepted that Art.8 precludes dismissal from military employment (albeit after intrusive investigation of individuals' private lives),[85] and Robert Wintemute has argued that the Strasbourg case law should be interpreted not as requiring the denial of an opportunity falling within the ambit of a substantive right in order for a case to fall within Art.14 (thus excluding employment), but merely as requiring that the ground on which the decision to deny the opportunity was based does so (thus including discrimination in employment, at least in relation to certain "sensitive" or "ordinary" grounds).[86] It should also be noted that while the exclusion of private employment is reinforced by the fact that the only permissible defendants before the Strasbourg Court are national authorities, courts are not confined by this restriction at national level.[87]

However this issue is resolved, to the extent that employment, private employment, or aspects of it are excluded from the ambit of Art.14, a gap emerges between the prohibition of discrimination under Art.14 and under EU law provisions, given that the latter have employment as their primary focus. If Art.14 is considered alone, there might thus appear to be a gap between employment-related discrimination—which falls within the scope of directly effective EU law when an EU-prohibited ground of discrimination is in issue—and discrimination in contexts falling within the scope of substantive Convention rights, in relation to which Art.14 is invoked. In reality, however, the gap may not always be so wide (regardless of one's view of the merits of signing and ratifying Protocol 12). As Judge Luzius Wildhaber has pointed out, cases which might be regarded, in colloquial terms, as raising issues of discrimination and in which the claimant has been successful can be divided into four groups: first, the "relatively few cases" in which the Strasbourg Court finds a breach of the substantive Convention Article when read in conjunction with Art.14, but not of the substantive Article read alone;[88] secondly, the "relatively frequent cases" in which the Court finds a violation of

84 See Judge Luzius Wildhaber, "Protection against Discrimination under the European Convention on Human Rights—A Second-Class Guarantee?" (2002) 2 Baltic Yearbook of International Law 71, 73 (access to employment); Stephen Livingstone, "Article 14 and the prevention of discrimination in the European Convention on Human Rights" [1997] E.H.R.L.R. 25, 26 (provision of employment).

85 *Smith and Grady v United Kingdom* (1999) 29 E.U.R.R. 493; *Lustig-Preen and Beckett v United Kingdom* (1999) 29 E.H.R.R. 548.

86 "'Within the Ambit': How Big *Is* the 'Gap' in Article 14 European Convention on Human Rights?" [2004] E.H.R.L.R. 366, 369–378; Wintemute relies for authority on *Thlimmenos v Greece* (2000) 31 E.H.R.R. 15, paras [41]–[42].

87 For an obvious Art.8 case at national level involving only private parties, see *Ghaidan v Godin-Mendoza* [2004] UKHL 30, [2004] 2 A.C. 557. Compare, in relation to the Court of Justice's position, Case C-144/04, *Mangold v Helm* [2005] E.C.R. I-9981, especially paras [75]–[78].

88 Luzius Wildhaber, *ibid.*, 78. See, as examples, *Abdulaziz, Cabales and Balkandali v United Kingdom* (1985) 7 E.H.R.R. 471; *Pine Valley Developments v Ireland* (1991) 14 E.H.R.R. 319; and *Schuler-Zgraggen v Switzerland* (1993) 16 E.H.R.R. 405.

the substantive Article but does not go on to consider Art.14 independently;[89] thirdly, the "exceptional cases" in which the Court finds a violation both of the substantive Article and of Article 14;[90] and fourthly, the "relatively frequent cases" in which the Court finds that Art.14 has been breached without considering independently whether the relevant substantive Article has been breached.[91] The boundaries between these categories do not seem to be clearly (or even consistently) drawn, but the existence of the large second category means that a number of cases which might be described colloquially as involving discrimination issues are resolved by the Court using provisions of the Convention other than Art.14. The way in which this might be seen as closing the gap between employment and non-employment cases is illustrated by *Smith v United Kingdom* (in which the Strasbourg Court found against the United Kingdom) in which a key question was the compatibility with Art.8 of the claimants' dismissal from public sector military employment because of their sexual orientation[92]: the type of claim which might be brought, before other courts, under the headings of sex discrimination or (where it is prohibited) sexual orientation discrimination.[93] A similar pattern is evident at national level, given that in *Ghaidan*, the House of Lords effectively prohibited unfair treatment on the basis of sexual orientation in the housing context—and, indeed, in most scenarios involving statutory interpretation—using Article 8 of the Convention, without going on to consider Art.14.[94]

[89] Luzius Wildhaber, *ibid.*, 78. Prominent examples include: *Airey v Ireland* (1979) 2 E.H.R.R. 305; *Dudgeon v United Kingdom* (1981) 4 E.H.R.R. 149, paras [67]–[70]; *X and Y v Netherlands* (1985) 8 E.H.R.R. 235; *Johnston v Ireland* (1986) 9 E.H.R.R. 203; *Smith and Grady v United Kingdom* (1999) 29 E.H.R.R. 493, paras [115]–[116]; *Lustig-Prean and Beckett v United Kingdom* (1999) 29 E.H.R.R. 548, paras [108]–[109]; and *ADT v United Kingdom*, application No.35765/97, E.C.H.R. 2000-IX, para.[41].

[90] Luzius Wildhaber, *ibid.*, 79; see also pp.76–7. For examples, see *Marckx v Belgium* (1979) 2 E.H.R.R. 330; *Canea Catholic Church v Greece* (1997) 27 E.H.R.R. 521; *Chassagnou v France* April 29, 1999.

[91] Luzius Wildhaber, *ibid.* 79; see also p.77. See, as examples, *Inze v Austria* (1987) 10 E.H.R.R. 394; *Hoffmann v Austria* (1993) 17 E.H.R.R. 293; *Gaygusuz v Austria* (1996) 23 E.H.R.R. 365.

[92] (1999) 29 E.H.R.R. 493.

[93] For attempts to challenge unfavourable treatment on the basis of sexual orientation before the European Court of Justice as an example of sex discrimination, see Case C-249/96, *Grant v South West Trains Ltd* [1998] E.C.R. I-621 and Cases C-122P and 125/99P, *D. v Council* [2001] E.C.R. I-4319; see Section V below for the present position.

[94] *Ghaidan v Godin-Mendoza, ibid.* The words "most contexts" make allowance for the declaration of incompatibility procedure established under s.4 of the Human Rights Act 1998, and also for the House of Lords' interpretation of Art.8 in *Secretary of State for Work and Pensions v M.* [2006] UKHL 11; [2006] 2 A.C. 91 (for criticism of which, see Robert Wintemute, "Same-Sex Couples in *Secretary of State for Work and Pensions v M.*: Identical to *Karner* and *Godin-Mendoza*, Yet No Discrimination?" [2006] E.H.R.L.R. 722; Nicholas Bamforth "'The benefits of marriage in all but name'? Same-sex couples and the Civil Partnership Act 2004" (2007) 19 C.F.L.Q. 133).

B. *Discrimination Claims and other Convention Rights*

As the preceding analysis has suggested, claims which might appear from their facts to involve "discrimination" issues (in that members of a minority group have been singled out for unfavourable treatment) are sometimes litigated under Convention rights other than Art.14, and the Court of Human Rights is somewhat variable in its willingness to decide cases on the basis of Art.14, Art.14 coupled with the other right involved, or solely using the other right. Claims which have been dealt with using Convention rights other than Art.14 include *Dudgeon v United Kingdom*,[95] in which the criminalisation of consensual homosexual acts in Northern Ireland was found to violate the right to respect for private life guaranteed by Art.8, while the claimant's Art.14 argument was not considered by the Court for the reason that it raised the Art.8 issue from a different angle. The Court noted that:

"Where a substantive Article of the Convention has been invoked both on its own and together with Article 14 and a separate breach has been found of the substantive Article, it is not generally necessary for the Court also to examine the case under Article 14, though the position is otherwise if a clear inequality of treatment in the enjoyment of the right in question is a fundamental aspect of the case".[96]

A similar stance was adopted in *Smith and Grady v United Kingdom*, in which the litigants successfully argued that their dismissal from military employment due to their sexual orientation violated their Art.8 right to respect for private life, and their Art.13 right to an effective remedy.[97] As we shall see below, the Court has nonetheless considered other cases concerning sexual orientation discrimination under Art.14. The Court's position on the use or otherwise of Art.14 must thus be described as somewhat unpredictable.

C. *Which Groups and Which Test?*

Article 14 of the Convention prohibits discrimination on specified grounds, but also on the basis of "other statuses", and the Court of Human Rights is charged with determining which "statuses" fall implicitly within Art.14. While the Court of Human Rights uses proportionality as its standard of review when a prohibited ground of discrimination (express or implied) is in issue, it has come to distinguish between "ordinary" and "sensitive" grounds,

[95] (1981) 4 E.H.R.R. 149.
[96] *ibid.*, para.[67].
[97] (2000) 29 E.H.R.R. 493.

requiring the production of particularly serious reasons in order to justify discrimination falling within the latter category. Nonetheless, given the frequent opacity of the Court's reasoning concerning proportionality and the so-called "margin of appreciation", the case law involves less clear-cut differences between the treatment of the different grounds than the Court's *dicta* may suggest.

Grounds of discrimination expressly prohibited in the text of Art.14 include race,[98] sex,[99] religion,[100] and nationality.[101] As the words "such as" and "other status" in Article 14 imply, other grounds can be—and have been—interpreted by the Court of Human Rights as being prohibited by implication. The general test was laid down in *Kjeldsen, Madsen and Pedesen v Denmark*, where the Court stressed that to fall within Art.14 by implication, a ground of discrimination must relate to a "status", defined as a "personal characteristic ... by which persons or groups of persons are distinguishable from each other."[102] Prohibited grounds recognised by the Court using this test include: sexual orientation,[103] marital status,[104] illegitimacy,[105] trade union membership,[106] military status,[107] conscientious objection;[108] professional status;[109] and imprisonment.[110] Although it has sometimes been suggested that the Court has moved beyond the *Kjeldsen* "personal characteristics" test, it continues to be followed in many cases and has twice been accepted as authoritative at House of Lords level in domestic law.[111] It was thus recognised in *Carson* that the "other status" heading could include discrimination based on place of residence.[112]

98 See *East African Asians v UK* (1973) 3 E.H.R.R. 76.
99 See *Abdulaziz, Cabales and Balkandali v UK* (1985) 7 E.H.R.R. 471.
100 See *Hoffmann v Austria* (1993) 17 E.H.R.R. 293.
101 See *Gaygusuz v Austria* (1996) 23 E.H.R.R. 365.
102 (1976) 1 E.H.R.R. 711, para.[56].
103 See *Salgueiro da Silva Mouta v Portugal* (2001) 31 E.H.R.R. 47.
104 See *Rasmussen v Denmark* (1984) 7 E.H.R.R. 371.
105 See *Marckx v Belgium* (1979) 2 E.H.R.R. 330; *Inze v Austria* (1987) 10 E.H.R.R. 394.
106 See *National Union of Belgian Police v Belgium* (1975) 1 E.H.R.R. 578.
107 See *Engel v Netherlands (No.1)* (1976) 1 E.H.R.R. 647.
108 See *X v Netherlands* (1965) 8 Y.B. 266.
109 See *Van der Mussele v Belgium* (1983) 6 E.H.R.R. 163.
110 See *RM v United Kingdom* (1994) 77-A DR 98.
111 At House of Lords level, see *R(LS) v Chief Constable of the South Yorkshire Police* [2004] UKHL 39, para.[48] (Lord Steyn) and *R (Carson) v Secretary of State for Work and Pensions* [2005] UKHL 37, paras [13] (Lord Hoffmann), [53]–[54] (Lord Walker); relevant recent Strasbourg cases include *Budak v Turkey,* App No.57345/00, 7th September 2004 and *Beale v United Kingdom,* App No.6743/03, October 12, 2004.
112 *Carson, ibid.*, para.[13] (Lord Hoffmann).

R. v Secretary of State for Work and Pensions, Ex p. Carson [2005] UKHL 37

LORD HOFFMANN

[13]: "... I am willing to assume that the reason for the alleged discrimination, Ms Carson's foreign residence, was a Convention ground. In *Kjeldsen, Busk Madsen and Pedersen v Denmark* ... the court said that article 14 applied only if the discrimination was on the basis of a 'personal characteristic'. That is the construction which has recently been adopted by the House of Lords: *R (S) v Chief Constable of the South Yorkshire Police* .... On the other hand, in *Wandsworth London Borough Council v Michalak* [2003] 1 WLR 617, 628, para 34 Brooke LJ said that Strasbourg seemed to have moved on since *Kjeldsen's* case and had applied article 14 in cases in which it was hard to say that the ground of discrimination was in any meaningful sense a personal characteristic. As the House of Lords has recently adopted the *Kjeldsen* test, I need not discuss the later Strasbourg jurisprudence. I am content to assume that being ordinarily resident in South Africa is a personal characteristic.

LORD WALKER

[52]: It will be apparent that the grounds of discrimination prohibited by article 14 extend a good way beyond sex and race. Its enumeration of grounds does not in terms include residence ... or age [...] The residual group, 'or other status' ... is far from precise [...] it is clear from the jurisprudence of the Strasbourg Court that the possible grounds of discrimination under article 14 are not wholly unlimited; nor are all possible grounds of equal efficacy in establishing unlawful discrimination...

[53]: In *Kjeldsen, Busk Madsen and Pedersen v Denmark* ... an early Strasbourg decision ... the court ... interpreted 'status' in article 14 as 'a personal characteristic ... by which persons or groups of persons are distinguishable from each other' [...] [and on the facts, an objection by a group of parents to their children receiving sex education at school was not accepted as equivalent to a religious belief protected under Article 14].

[54]: It was suggested in argument that the *Kjeldsen* test of looking for a personal characteristic is no longer part of the Strasbourg jurisprudence. But it has recently been followed by the Fourth Section of the European Court of Human Rights in two admissibility decisions, *Budak v Turkey* ... and *Beale v United Kingdom* .... In *Budak* the only relevant difference was in the criminal procedure adopted for two different types of offence. In *Beale* it was the different investigatory procedures appropriate for the police (on the one hand) and trading standards officers (on the other hand). In neither case was there any personal characteristic of the claimant which could be a ground for discrimination contrary to article 14. Moreover this House has recently applied *Kjeldsen* in *R (S) v Chief Constable of the South Yorkshire Police* ...."

While the general tests concerning proportionality and justification under Art.14 were first authoritatively set out by the Court of Human Rights in the *Belgian Linguistic Case*,[113] they have been usefully summarised by the court in *Abdulaziz*:

[113] (1968) 1 E.H.R.R. 252. For practical examples, see *East African Asians v UK* (1973) 3 E.H.R.R. 76; *Marckx v Belgium* (1979) 2 E.H.R.R. 330; *Fredin v Sweden* (1991) 13 E.H.R.R. 784; *Hoffmann v Austria* (1993) 17 E.H.R.R. 293; *Stubbings v United Kingdom* (1996) 23 E.H.R.R. 213; *Gaygusuz v Austria* (1996) 23 E.H.R.R. 365.

Abdulaziz, Cabales and Balkandali v United Kingdom (1985) 7 E.H.R.R. 471

[72]: "For the purposes of Article 14 (art. 14), a difference of treatment is discriminatory if it 'has no objective and reasonable justification', that is, if it does not pursue a 'legitimate aim' or if there is not a 'reasonable relationship of proportionality between the means employed and the aim sought to be realised'...

The Contracting States enjoy a certain margin of appreciation in assessing whether and to what extent differences in otherwise similar situations justify a different treatment in law [...] but it is for the Court to give the final ruling in this respect.

[78]: [...] Although the Contracting States enjoy a certain 'margin of appreciation' in assessing whether and to what extent differences in otherwise similar situations justify a different treatment, the scope of this margin will vary according to the circumstances, the subject-matter and its background..."

In *Belgian Linguistics*, the Court was more detailed in its explanation. It began by emphasising that only *some* distinctions are prohibited by Art.14, and that the "criteria which enable a determination to be made as to whether or not a given difference in treatment, concerning [...] the exercise of one of the [substantive] rights and freedoms" contravenes Art.14 are whether the relevant distinction has no objective and reasonable justification.[114] The existence of the justification must be assessed in relation to the aims and effects of the measure in issue; the difference of treatment must pursue a legitimate aim and there must be a reasonable relationship between the means employed and the aim sought to be realised. In conducting this exercise, the Court "cannot disregard those legal and factual features which characterise the life of the society in the State" concerned, and in "so doing it cannot assume the role of the competent national authorities, for it would thereby lose sight of the subsidiary nature of the international machinery of collective enforcement established by the Convention."[115] This last element is nowadays associated with the idea of the "margin of appreciation", authoritatively set out by the Court of Human Rights, in the context of Art.10, in *Handyside v United Kingdom*: namely that, "[b]y reason of their direct and continuous contact with the vital forces of their countries, State authorities are in principle in a better position than the international judge" at Strasbourg level "to give an opinion on the exact content of" the requirements of Convention rights "as well as on the 'necessity' of a 'restriction' or 'penalty' intended to meet them".[116]

As *Belgian Linguistics* demonstrates, the combination of the reasonable relationship test and the margin of appreciation sometimes makes it quite easy for a signatory state to establish a rational aim. In *Abdulaziz*, for example, UK Immigration Rules resulted in would-be immigrant husbands being refused

114 (1968) 1 E.H.R.R. 252, para.[I.B.10].

115 *ibid.*; see also para II.A.7. See, more generally, Jeremy McBride, "Proportionality and the European Convention on Human Rights", in Evelyn Ellis (ed.), *The Principle of Proportionality in the Laws of Europe* (Oxford: Hart, 1999).

116 *Handyside v United Kingdom* (1976) 1 E.H.R.R. 737, para.[48].

permission to join their wives who were already in the UK, whereas would-be immigrant wives were entitled to come in to join their husbands. This was found to discriminate on the basis of sex, but to serve the legitimate aim of protecting the domestic labor market.[117] Furthermore, the "margin of appreciation" has often assisted signatory states in the absence of a "European consensus". In *Petrovic v Austria*, for example, it was found that a decision to pay women but not men a parental leave allowance fell within the national government's margin of appreciation since there was no common standard among the signatory states as to whether such an allowance should be paid to men.[118] Nonetheless, the intensity of review adopted by the Court clearly varies. This has been expressed in relation to Convention rights in general by van Dijk and van Hoof:

Pieter van Dijk and Fried van Hoof (eds), *Theory and Practice of the European Convention on Human Rights* (Antwerp: Intersentia, 4th edn, 2006)

p.1045: "... the scope or the intensity of the review of the Court [of Human Rights] may and probably will vary according to the grounds of the distinction made. **Infra** it will be concluded from the case law of the Court that some distinctions have to be treated with a more strict scrutiny than others. Crucial seems to be whether a common ground can be said to exist. Another factor, however, that could play a role is the area in which a specific distinction has been made. When it concerns purely economic regulations the Court probably will be more reluctant to interfere than when it has to cope with a distinction that touches upon essential elements of freedom rights [that is, those which oblige public authorities to refrain from restrictive interference with individuals]."

Robert Wintemute has gone further, suggesting that *within* Art.14, the Strasbourg Court's approach to the intensity of review now varies depending upon the type of discrimination in issue, so that:

"To date, [the] [...] 'sensitive grounds' appear to be sex, birth out of wedlock, religion, race (or ethnic or national origin), nationality, and sexual orientation. For all of these grounds ... the [Strasbourg Court] requires (explicitly or implicitly) that the respondent government present 'very weighty reasons' or 'particularly serious reasons' to justify use of the ground as the basis for a difference in treatment. The Court has not yet had the opportunity to make similar statements with regard to disability or age."[119]

117 *ibid.*

118 RJD [1998]-II 579; see also *Rasmussen v Denmark* (1984) 7 E.H.R.R. 371.

119 Robert Wintemute, "Filling the Article 14 'Gap'", *ibid.*, pp.492–3; see also *R. v Secretary of State for Work and Pensions, Ex p. Carson*, para.[58] (Lord Walker). For earlier analysis, see Stephen Livingstone, "Article 14 and the Prevention of Discrimination in the European Convention on Human Rights" [1997] E.H.R.L.R. 25, 32–3. For an apparently differing view of Art.14, see Sandra Fredman, "Why the UK government should sign and rectify Protocol 12" (2002) 105 Equal Opportunities Review 21, 24 (heading 2).

However, Wintemute's statement must be read with some care. Discrimination relating to sex, illegitimacy, nationality and sexual orientation is recognised in the Art.14 case law as requiring "weighty" or "particularly serious" reasons.[120] However, this requirement has only been mentioned in relation to nationality in cases which involve arguable discrimination, colloquially speaking, but which have been decided on the basis of *other* Convention rights. The idea of "particularly serious" reasons has thus been used in the context of establishing a justification for actions which, prima facie, contravene Art.6[121] or Art.10,[122] rather than Art.14. In relation to sexual orientation, the notion that "particularly serious" reasons were needed arose first in Art.8 case law dealing with the adverse treatment of lesbians and gay men,[123] before also being recognised as applying to Art.14.[124] Furthermore, because of the Court's somewhat opaque explanation of the cases, it is not entirely clear how far the rhetoric of "particularly serious reasons" in fact translates into a more intense standard of review in practice.[125] In Art.14 cases in which the "margin of appreciation" has not played a strong role but "particularly serious reasons" have been required, the Court's evaluation tends to involve the same brevity as is seen in cases in which such reasons are not required: as such, it is often hard to tell what difference the requirement to have such reasons makes.[126]

The lack of clarity is seemingly greater in cases in which the Court has paid particular attention to the "margin of appreciation". As *Inze v Austria* illustrates, the operation of the "margin" in Art.14 cases varies according to the circumstances, the subject-matter and its background.[127] Its variability is particularly evident from the Art.8 and Art.14 case law dealing with adverse treatment on the basis of a person's sexual orientation. Art.8 has been found to preclude the criminal prohibition of consensual, private sexual activity between adults of the same sex,[128] or investigations into a person's private life

[120] On sex, see: *Abdulaziz, Cabales and Balkandali v United Kingdom* (1985) 7 E.H.R.R. 471, para.[78]; *Schmidt v Germany* (1994) 18 E.H.R.R. 513, para.[24]; *Van Raalte v Netherlands* (1997) 24 E.H.R.R. 503, paras [39], [42]–[44]. On illegitimacy, see: *Inze v Austria* (1987) 10 E.H.R.R. 394, para.[41]. On nationality, see: *Gaygusuz v Austria* (1997) 23 E.H.R.R. 364, para.[42]. On sexual orientation, see: *Karner v Austria* (2003) 38 E.H.R.R. 24, para [41] (by contrast with *Salgueiro da Silva Mouta v Portugal* (2001) 31 E.H.R.R. 1055, para.[36]).

[121] *Sander v United Kingdom* (2000) 31 E.H.R.R. 44, para.[23].

[122] *Jersild v Denmark* (1994) 19 E.H.R.R. 1, para.[30].

[123] See *Dudgeon v United Kingdom* (1982) 4 E.H.R.R. 149, paras [51]–[53]; *Smith and Grady v United Kingdom* (1999) 29 E.H.R.R. 493, paras [89], [90], [94], [105]–[110]; *Lustig-Prean and Beckett v United Kingdom* (1999) 29 E.H.R.R. 548, paras [80]–[83], [87]; *L and V v Austria* (2003) 36 E.H.R.R. 55, para.[45]. See also *Van Kuck v Germany* (2003) 37 E.H.R.R. 51, para.[72] (gender identity).

[124] See *Karner v Austria*, id. Note also that *Hoffmann v Austria* (1993) 17 E.H.R.R. 293, paras [33] and [36] do not appear, despite Wintemute's argument to the contrary, to assert the need for "particularly serious" reasons in relation to discrimination on the basis of religion.

[125] See also, for criticism of other related aspects of the Art.14 case law, Aaron Baker, "Comparison Tainted by Justification: Against A 'Compendious Question' In Article 14 Discrimination" [2006] P.L. 476, 488–493.

[126] See, e.g., *Inze v Austria* (1987) 10 E.H.R.R. 394, paras [41]–[44]; *Gaygusuz v Austria* (1997) 23 E.H.R.R. 364, paras [42]–[52]; *Van Raalte v Netherlands* (1997) 24 E.H.R.R. 503, paras [39]–[45].

[127] para.[41].

[128] See, e.g., *Dudgeon v United Kingdom* (1982) 4 E.H.R.R. 149; *Norris v Ireland* (1991) 13 E.H.R.R. 186.

followed by their automatic discharge from military service because of their lesbian or gay orientation.[129] In relation to justification, the Court has stressed that while Convention states enjoy a margin of appreciation when determining the necessity of a restriction for a reason set out in Art.8(2), since particularly serious reasons are needed (given that relevant restrictions concern a most intimate part of a person's private life[130]), the margin is narrow in this context.[131] When sexual orientation was first recognised as a prohibited ground under Art.14, the "ordinary" standard of review was employed, with the defendant state being required to demonstrate an objective and reasonable justification (in other words, that there was a legitimate aim or reasonable relationship of proportionality between the means employed and the aim being pursued).[132] The Court began to invoke the need for "particularly serious" or "very weighty" reasons in *Karner v Austria*, (dealing with discrimination on the bases of sex and sexual orientation),[133] where it also stressed that states had only a narrow margin of appreciation under Art.14 in relation to such types of discrimination.[134]

However, the Court also considered it "quite natural" in *Frette v France* (where the claimant's argument that "particularly serious" reasons were required was noted but not taken further[135]) that "the national authorities ... should enjoy a wide margin of appreciation when they are asked to make rulings" about the suitability of a single gay man—by contrast with a single heterosexual—to adopt a child.[136] In *this* context, it seemed that delicate issues were involved, there was little common ground among the signatory states, and the law appeared to be in a transitional stage when it came to adoption.[137] Decisions in which the "margin of appreciation" has been important to the Court are plainly context-sensitive, and it has been argued that differences in treatment are likely to be upheld where they fall within the "margin of appreciation", even if the Court officially requires "very weighty reasons" by way of justification.[138] The Court of Human Rights' treatment of prohibited grounds of discrimination thus appears, given the operation of the justification

[129] *Smith and Grady v United Kingdom* (1999) 29 E.H.R.R. 493; *Lustig-Prean and Beckett v United Kingdom* (1999) 29 E.H.R.R. 548.

[130] Fully spelt out in *Dudgeon v United Kingdom*: "not only the nature of the aim of the restriction but also the nature of the activities involved will affect the scope of the margin of appreciation. The present case concerns a most intimate aspect of private life. Accordingly, there must exist particularly serious reasons before interferences on the part of the public authorities can be legitimate for the purposes of paragraph 2 of Article 8" (para.[52]).

[131] *ADT v United Kingdom*, id., para.[38]; see also *Dudgeon v United Kingdom, ibid.*, para [52] and *Smith and Grady v United Kingdom, ibid.*, para.[89], in which the existence of a narrow "margin" is tied to the need for "particularly serious reasons".

[132] *Da Silva Mouta v Portugal* (2001) 31 E.H.R.R. 1055, paras [29]–[36].

[133] (2003) 38 E.H.R.R. 24, para.[37].

[134] *ibid.*, para.[41].

[135] (2002) 38 E.H.R.R. 21, para.[35].

[136] (2002) 38 E.H.R.R. 21, para.[41]. On the facts, this clearly involved a difference of treatment based upon sexual orientation: see paras [32]–[33].

[137] *ibid.*, paras [41]–[42].

[138] See the discussion in Robert Wintemute, "Filling the Article 14 'Gap'", *ibid.*, 495.

and proportionality standards, alongside the "margin of appreciation", to be considerably more context-dependent *within* each ground of discrimination than is apparent at first sight from Wintemute's division into "sensitive" and "ordinary" grounds. It is also worth noting that while the Court of Human Rights has been required to evolve its own standards for what may count as adequate reasons for differential treatment in the Art.14 case law, the permitted justifications for violating substantive "qualified" Convention rights (either on their own or when coupled with Art.14), including Art.8, are explicitly spelt out in the text of those rights[139] and are thus less open to generalistic interpretation than is the case with the judicially-recognised grounds which are invoked in EU law.

D. *Direct and Indirect Discrimination*

For much of its history, Art.14 had been thought to preclude only direct discrimination. As a result, the Strasbourg Court's case law concerning justification (tied to the issue of proportionality) has—by contrast with that of the Court of Justice—traditionally concerned the justification of acts of prima facie direct discrimination.[140] Direct discrimination has (at least since the *Belgian Linguistic* case) been capable of justification under Art.14, providing a strong contrast with EU law and causing Evelyn Ellis to suggest that Art.14 offers "a much weaker model for discrimination law than that adopted" by the Court of Justice.[141] However, as a result of *Thlimmenos v Greece*, Art.14 now appears also to prohibit, at least in some circumstances, indirect discrimination.[142] In *Thlimmenos*, the Court of Human Rights made clear that it had previously:

"considered that the right under Article 14 not to be discriminated against in the enjoyment of the rights guaranteed under the Convention is violated when States treat differently persons in analogous situations without providing an objective and reasonable justification ... However ... this is not the only facet of the prohibition of discrimination in Article 14. The right ... is also violated

[139] See, e.g., Art.8(2), Art.9(2), Art.10(2) and Art.11(2). For discussion of "qualified" rights, see See, e.g., Richard Clayton & Hugh Tomlinson, *The Law of Human Rights* Vol.1, *ibid.*, paras 6.86–6.92, 6.123–6.147A; Jeremy McBride, "Proportionality and the European Convention on Human Rights", in Evelyn Ellis (ed.), *The Principle of Proportionality in the Laws of Europe* (Oxford: Hart, 1999), especially p.24.

[140] See Karon Monaghan, "Limitations and Opportunities: A Review of the Likely Domestic Impact of Article 14 ECHR" [2001] E.H.R.L.R. 167, 174, invoking the *Belgian Linguistic Case (No. 2)* (1968) 1 E.H.R.R. 252.

[141] *EU Anti-Discrimination Law*, (Oxford: Oxford University Press, 2005), p.112 n.123.

[142] (2000) 31 E.H.R.R. 15.

when States without an objective and reasonable justification fail to treat differently persons whose situations are significantly different".[143]

On the facts, it was therefore impermissible for the state to apply a blanket rule which precluded all persons with serious criminal convictions from qualifying as a chartered accountant. The Court accepted that "as a matter of principle, States have a legitimate interest to exclude *some* offenders from the profession of chartered accountant".[144] However, a conviction (as here) for refusing on religious grounds to wear a military uniform could not, unlike other types of serious criminal offence, in itself "imply any dishonesty or moral turpitude likely to undermine the offender's ability to exercise this profession".[145] The Court accepted that the national authorities "had no option under the law but to refuse to appoint the applicant a chartered accountant", but nonetheless found that this did not absolve them of responsibility.[146] The thrust of the Court's reasoning seems to be that the application of a facially neutral blanket rule—"no person with a serious criminal conviction may qualify as an accountant"—may, if disproportionate, fall foul of Art.14 (considered as the primary Convention right in play in a case) if it impacts for no defensible reason on persons of *particular* religious beliefs.[147] Issues of proportionality and justification may now therefore be deployed under Art.14 in relation to indirect as well as direct discrimination.[148]

E. *Proportionality and Deference under the Human Rights Act 1998*

The importance of Art.14 in domestic law was stressed by both Lord Nicholls and Baroness Hale in *Ghaidan v Godin-Mendoza*:

143 *ibid.*, para [44]. For earlier argument to the effect that indirect discrimination falls within the ambit of Art.14, see Stephen Livingstone, "Article 14 and the Prevention of Discrimination in the European Convention on Human Rights" [1997] E.H.R.L.R. 25, 31.

144 para.[47], emphasis added.

145 para.[47].

146 para.[48].

147 For further discussion of the extension involved, see Judge Luzius Wildhaber, "Protection against Discrimination under the European Convention on Human Rights: A Second-Class Guarantee?" (2002) 2 Baltic Yearbook of International Law 71, 81; Robert Wintemute, "'Within the Ambit': How Big *Is* the 'Gap' in Article 14 ECHR?" [2004] E.H.R.L.R. 366, 377–8; "Filling the Article 14 'Gap'" [2004] E.H.L.R.R. 484, 496–9; Aaron Baker, "The Enjoyment of Rights and Freedoms: A New Conception of the 'Ambit' under Art.14 ECHR" (2006) 69 M.L.R. 714, 723–5.

148 For practical examples, see *Hoogendijk v Netherlands* (2005) 40 E.H.R.R. SE22; *D.H. v Czech Republic*, (2007) 43 E.H.R.R. 922, discussed in Chapter 5.

Ghaidan v Godin-Mendoza [2004] UKHL 30

LORD NICHOLLS

[9]: "It goes without saying that article 14 is an important article of the Convention. Discrimination is an insidious practice. Discriminatory law undermines the rule of law because it is the antithesis of fairness. It brings the law into disrepute. It breeds resentment. It fosters an inequality of outlook which is demeaning alike to those unfairly benefited and those unfairly prejudiced. Of course all law, civil and criminal, has to draw distinctions. One type of conduct, or one factual situation, attracts one legal consequence, another type of conduct or situation attracts a different legal consequence. To be acceptable these distinctions should have a rational and fair basis. Like cases should be treated alike, unlike cases should not be treated alike...

BARONESS HALE

[131]: When this country legislated to ban both race and sex discrimination, there were some who thought such matters trivial, but of course they were not trivial to the people concerned. Still less trivial are the rights and freedoms set out in the European Convention. The state's duty under article 14, to secure that those rights and freedoms are enjoyed without discrimination based on such suspect grounds, is fundamental to the scheme of the Convention as a whole. It would be a poor human rights instrument indeed if it obliged the state to respect the homes or private lives of one group of people but not the homes or private lives of another.

[132]: Such a guarantee of equal treatment is also essential to democracy. Democracy is founded on the principle that each individual has equal value. Treating some as automatically having less value than others not only causes pain and distress to that person but also violates his or her dignity as a human being ... it is a purpose of all human rights instruments to secure the protection of the essential rights of members of minority groups, even when they are unpopular with the majority. Democracy values everyone equally even if the majority does not."

This commitment to the importance of Art.14 was also articulated in the Court of Appeal in *Ghaidan*. Buxton L.J. stated that:

"issues of discrimination ... have high constitutional importance, and are issues that the courts should not shrink from. In such cases deference has only a minor role to play."[149]

Keene L.J. echoed the point about constitutional importance, albeit in relation more to the operation of proportionality than the ambit of deference.[150]

It is clear from *Ghaidan* and more particularly *Carson* that questions of proportionality and deference will be central to cases which either involve Art.14 pleaded in conjunction with another Article, or which arise solely under other Articles but involve decisions or actions which might be characterised as treating members of a particular group unfavourably. Proportionality and deference are both relevant whether a case arises in relation to s.3 or s.6 of the Human Rights Act, although their roles differ slightly under each heading. In

149 [2002] EWCA Civ 1533, para.[19].
150 para.[44].

s.3 cases, courts test the Convention-compatibility of potential interpretations of statutory provisions by seeing whether those interpretations involve a disproportionate restriction of a Convention right; in s.6 cases, proportionality is used when assessing the legality of public authorities' actions. Given the varying nature of the inquiries involved under each heading, questions of deference are more likely to relate in s.3 cases to the role of the legislature and in s.6 cases to that of the executive.[151]

After the Human Rights Act came into force, the House of Lords recognised the applicability of proportionality in *R. v Secretary of State for the Home Department, Ex p. Daly*.[152] Lord Steyn accepted that a "three point test", articulated in the Privy Council's judgment in the *De Freitas* case, should be adopted as the key formulation of the proportionality test in domestic law.[153]

De Freitas v Permanent Secretary of the Ministry of Agriculture, Fisheries, Land and Housing [1999] 1 A.C. 69

PRIVY COUNCIL (LORD CLYDE)

p.80: "Their Lordships were referred to three cases in which that phrase ['reasonably justifiable in a democratic society'] has been considered. In *Government of the Republic of South Africa* v. *The Sunday Times Newspaper* [1995] 1 L.R.C. 168 Joffe J. adopted from Canadian jurisprudence four criteria to be satisfied for a law to satisfy the provision in the Canadian Charter of Rights and Freedoms that it be 'demonstrably justified in a free and democratic society'. These were a sufficiently important objective for the restriction, a rational connection with the objective, the use of the least drastic means, and no disproportionately severe effect on those to whom the restriction applies. In two cases from Zimbabwe, *Nyambirai* v. *National Social Security Authority* [1996] 1 L.R.C. 64 and *Retrofit (Pvt.) Ltd.* v. *Posts and Telecommunications Corporation* [1996] 4 L.R.C. 489, a corresponding analysis was formulated by Gubbay C.J., drawing both on South African and on Canadian jurisprudence, and amalgamating the third and fourth of the criteria. In the former of the two cases [1996] 1 L.R.C. 64, 75, he saw the quality of reasonableness in the expression 'reasonably justifiable in a democratic society' as depending upon the question whether the provision which is under challenge 'arbitrarily or excessively invades the enjoyment of the guaranteed right according to the standards of a society that has a

[151] For examples in relation to s.3, see *R. v A.* [2001] UKHL 25, paras [35]–[38] (proportionality and deference) (Lord Steyn), [58], [99] (deference), [104] (proportionality) (Lord Hope); in the context of s.6, see *R. v BBC, Ex p. Prolife Alliance* [2003] UKHL 23. For discussion of the particular issues raised for proportionality analysis by legislation, see Philip Sales and Ben Hooper, "Proportionality and the Form of Law" (2003) 119 L.Q.R. 426.

[152] In reaching this decision, the House of Lords placed considerable weight on *Smith and Grady v United Kingdom, ibid.*, demonstrating that although Art.13 has not been brought directly into domestic law under the Human Rights Act, Art.13 case law (including *Smith*) can be and is taken into account, a possibility allowed for by the wording of s.2 of the 1998 Act. For general analysis of proportionality under the Human Rights Act, see Nicholas Blake Q.C., "Importing Proportionality: Clarification or Confusion?" [2002] E.H.R.L.R. 24; Ian Leigh, "Taking Rights Proportionately: Judicial Review, the Human Rights Act and Strasbourg" [2002] P.L. 265.

[153] para.[27]. Lord Steyn's reasoning was supported by Lord Bingham, Lord Cooke and Lord Hutton.

proper respect for the rights and freedoms of the individual'. In determining whether a limitation is arbitrary or excessive he said that the court would ask itself:

> 'whether: (i) the legislative objective is sufficiently important to justify limiting a fundamental right; (ii) the measures designed to meet the legislative objective are rationally connected to it; and (iii) the means used to impair the right or freedom are no more than is necessary to accomplish the objective.'

Their Lordships accept and adopt this threefold analysis of the relevant criteria."

Lord Steyn stressed in *Daly* that this test corresponded with the decision of the Strasbourg Court in *Smith v United Kingdom*.[154] He thus noted that proportionality "may require attention to be directed to the relative weight accorded to interests and considerations", and that the intensity of judicial scrutiny was "guaranteed by the twin requirements that the limitation of the [claimant's] right was necessary in a democratic society, in the sense of meeting a pressing social need, and the question whether the interference was really proportionate to the legitimate aim being pursued."[155] In *Huang v Secretary of State for the Home Department*, the House of Lords accepted that a fourth question—whether the measure in question included the striking of a fair balance between the rights of the individual and the interests of the community—must be employed in addition to those required in *De Freitas*.[156]

Since the Convention "margin of appreciation" is premised on the fact that the Strasbourg Court is an international court, it cannot—as Lord Hope accepted in *R. v DPP, Ex p. Kebilene*—filter directly into the work of national courts.[157] Nonetheless, a domestic deference principle is applied in Human Rights Act cases. In *Kebilene*, Lord Hope described this as the "discretionary area of judgment"—where the executive or the legislature had to make difficult policy choices between the rights of the individual and the needs of society:

> "[i]n some circumstances it will be appropriate for the courts to recognise that there is an area of judgment within which the judiciary will defer, on democratic grounds, to the considered opinion of the elected body or person whose act or decision is said to be incompatible with the Convention".[158–159]

Lord Hope offered only loose indications concerning the criteria to be used when calculating the appropriate degree of deference. It would, he suggested, be:

154 (1999) 29 E.H.R.R. 493. Lord Steyn expressly equated the two approaches (and that used by the European Court of Justice) in *R. v A.* [2001] UKHL 25, para.[38].

155 para.[27].

156 [2007] UKHL 11, para [19]. Note also the discussion in paras [11] and [13].

157 [2002] 2 A.C. 326, 380–1 (Lord Hope); for general analysis, see *International Transport Roth v Secretary of State for the Home Department* [2002] EWCA Civ 158, paras [81], [83]–[85], [87] (Laws L.J.).

158–159 [2000] 2 A.C. 326, 380–1 (Lord Hope).

"easier for such an area of judgment to be recognised where the Convention itself requires a balance to be struck" [i.e., where a "qualified" right was in issue] "much less so where the right is stated in terms which are unqualified. It will be easier for it to be recognised where the issues involve questions of social or economic policy, much less so where the rights are of high constitutional importance or are of a kind where the courts are especially well placed to assess the need for protection."

It is fair to say that the conceptual basis and practical operation of this principle remain somewhat obscure, however.[160]

We saw in Section C, above, that the proportionality test varies in intensity when applied by the Strasbourg Court, and the same is true at national level. Where discrimination is in issue (whether considered under Art.14 or another Convention heading), the House of Lords has stressed in *Ghaidan v Godin-Mendoza* and *Carson* that some grounds of discrimination demand a more intense application of proportionality than do others.[161] In *Ghaidan,* argued under s.3 of the Human Rights Act and concerning the tenancy-succession rights of same-sex partners, both Lord Nicholls and Baroness Hale stressed that intense review was necessary in cases involving differences based upon sexual orientation.

Ghaidan v Godin-Mendoza [2004] UKHL 30

LORD NICHOLLS

[9] "...The circumstances which justify two cases being regarded as unlike, and therefore requiring or susceptible of different treatment, are infinite. In many circumstances opinions can differ on whether a suggested ground of distinction justifies a difference in legal treatment. But there are certain grounds of factual difference which by common accord are not acceptable, without more, as a basis for different legal treatment. Differences of race or sex or religion are obvious examples. Sexual orientation is another ... Unless some good reason can be shown, differences such as these do not justify differences in treatment. Unless good reason exists, differences in legal treatment based on grounds such as these are properly stigmatized as discriminatory.[162]

BARONESS HALE

[136] ...sexual orientation is one of the grounds covered by article 14 on which, like race and sex, a difference in treatment is particularly suspect ... the grounds put forward to justify it require careful scrutiny."

160 See Lord Steyn, "Deference: A Tangled Story" [2005] P.L. 346; Murray Hunt, "Sovereignty's Blight: Why Contemporary Public Law Needs the Concept of 'Due Deference'", Ch.13 of Nicholas Bamforth and Peter Leyland (eds.), *Public Law in a Multi-Layered Constitution* (Oxford: Hart, 2003). Note also the House of Lords expression of disquiet on the language of deference in *Huang v Secretary of State for the Home Department* at para [16].

161 *ibid*.

162 Lord Nicholls cited in relation to sexual orientation *Frette v France* (2003) 2 F.L.R. 9.

Lord Nicholls noted that while protection of the traditional family unit could be "an important and legitimate aim" and a "cogent reason justifying differential treatment", this was only in "certain contexts" and in deciding whether its use was appropriate it was important to identify the *element* of the traditional family that the legislation in issue sought to protect.[163] This reasoning suggests that use of the "traditional family" justification must be tightly controlled. Similarly, Baroness Hale argued that what was "really meant by the 'protection' of the traditional family"—when used as a justification—"is the encouragement of people to form traditional families and the discouragement of people from forming others", and that it did not protect the traditional family to grant it a benefit denied to those who could not or would not become such a family.[164] There may be legitimate reasons to encourage people to marry and to discourage them from living together without marrying, but these did not justify legislation which encouraged heterosexual unmarried relationships but discouraged same-sex ones,[165] the aim of "discouraging homosexual relationships" being inconsistent with respect for private life under Art.8.[166]

The reasoning in *Ghaidan* was seemingly taken further by the House of Lords in *R. v Secretary of State for Work and Pensions, Ex p. Carson*, in which both Lord Hoffmann and Lord Walker stressed at length that some of the grounds of discrimination precluded by Art.14 were more sensitive than others and placed a stronger burden of justification on the respondent.[167]

R. v Secretary of State for Work and Pensions, Ex p. Carson; R. v Secretary of State for Work and Pensions, Ex p Reynolds [2005] UKHL 37

LORD HOFFMANN

[10] "Article 14 ... does not prohibit all discrimination but only in certain respects and on certain grounds ...

The principle that everyone is entitled to equal treatment by the state, that like cases should be treated alike and different cases should be treated differently, will be found, in one form or another, in most human rights instruments and written constitutions. They vary

163 para.[16]; see also Baroness Hale at para.[138].
164 para.[143].
165 para.[143].
166 para.[143], citing *Dudgeon v United Kingdom* (1982) 4 E.H.R.R. 149.
167 [2005] UKHL 37, paras [15]–[17] (Lord Hoffmann), [55], [57]–[58], [89] (Lord Walker). Lords Nicholls, Rodger and Carswell (paras [1], [42] and [92]) agreed with both judgments. Lord Hoffmann suggested that discrimination on a sensitive ground could not be justified merely by appeal to a "utilitarian" value such as the general public interest (para.[16]), while Lord Walker—echoing the Strasbourg Court—asserted that "very weighty reasons" would be needed. Lord Walker describes the sensitive grounds, by analogy with US 14th Amendment jurisprudence, as "suspect categories" (para.[58]), although his assertion (at para.[55]) that sexual orientation constitutes such a category in US law is, with respect, an over-simplification.

only in the generality with which the principle is expressed. Perhaps the broadest is contained in the 14th Amendment to the constitution of the United States: 'No state shall . . . deny to any person within its jurisdiction the equal protection of the laws.' The scope of article 14 is narrower in two ways. First, it has a restricted list of the *matters in respect of which* discrimination is forbidden. They are 'the enjoyment of the rights and freedoms set forth in [the] Convention'. Secondly, it has a restricted list of the *grounds upon which* discrimination is forbidden. They are 'any ground such as [the enumerated grounds] or other status'

[15] . . . Article 14 expresses the Enlightenment value that every human being is entitled to equal respect and to be treated as an end and not a means. Characteristics such as race, caste, noble birth, membership of a political party and (here a change in values since the Enlightenment) gender, are seldom, if ever, acceptable grounds for differences in treatment. In some constitutions, the prohibition on discrimination is confined to grounds of this kind and I rather suspect that article 14 was also intended to be so limited. But the Strasbourg court has given it a wide interpretation, approaching that of the 14th Amendment, and it is therefore necessary, as in the United States, to distinguish between those grounds of discrimination which prima facie appear to offend our notions of the respect due to the individual and those which merely require some rational justification: *Massachusetts Board of Retirement v Murgia* (1976) 438 US 285.

[16] There are two important consequences of making this distinction. First, discrimination in the first category cannot be justified merely on utilitarian grounds, eg that it is rational to prefer to employ men rather than women because more women than men give up employment to look after childen. That offends the notion that everyone is entitled to be treated as an individual and not a statistical unit. On the other hand, differences in treatment in the second category (eg on grounds of ability, education, wealth, occupation) usually depend upon considerations of the general public interest. Secondly, while the courts, as guardians of the right of the individual to equal respect, will carefully examine the reasons offered for any discrimination in the first category, decisions about the general public interest which underpin differences in treatment in the second category are very much a matter for the democratically elected branches of government.

[17] There may be borderline cases in which it is not easy to allocate the ground of discrimination to one category or the other and, as I have observed, there are shifts in the values of society on these matters. *Ghaidan v Godin-Mendoza* . . . recognised that discrimination on grounds of sexual orientation was now firmly in the first category. Discrimination on grounds of old age may be a contemporary example of a borderline case. But there is usually no difficulty about deciding whether one is dealing with a case in which the right to respect for the individuality of a human being is at stake or merely a question of general social policy.

LORD WALKER

[55] The proposition that not all possible grounds of discrimination are equally potent is not very clearly spelled out in the jurisprudence of the Strasbourg Court. It appears much more clearly in the jurisprudence of the United States Supreme Court, which in applying the equal protection clause of the 14th Amendment has developed a doctrine of 'suspect' grounds of discrimination which the court will subject to particularly severe scrutiny. They are personal characteristics (including sex, race and sexual orientation) which an individual cannot change (apart from the wholly exceptional case of transsexual gender reassignment) and which, if used as a ground for discrimination, are recognised as particularly demeaning for the victim.[168]

[57] . . . these distinctions are not so clearly signalled in the jurisprudence of the European Court of Human Rights. But [counsel for the respondent] [. . .] submitted, in my

[168] At para. [56], Lord Walker cited as examples *San Antonio School District v Rodriguez* (1973) 411 U.S. 1, 29 and *Massachusetts Board of Retirement v Murgia* (1976) 427 U.S. 307, 314.

opinion correctly, that the equivalent doctrine is to be found there. Where there is an allegation that article 14 has been infringed by discrimination on one of the most sensitive grounds, severe scrutiny is called for. As my noble and learned friend, Lord Nicholls of Birkenhead put it in *Ghaidan v Godin-Mendoza* ... para 19:

> '... where the alleged violation comprises differential treatment based on grounds such as race or sex or sexual orientation the court will scrutinise with intensity any reasons said to constitute justification. The reasons must be cogent if such differential treatment is to be justified.'

[58] In its judgments the European Court of Human Rights often refers to 'very weighty reasons' being required to justify discrimination on these particularly sensitive grounds. This appears, for instance (in relation to cases of discrimination on the ground of sex) in *Abdulaziz, Cabales and Balkandali v United Kingdom* (1985) 7 E.H.R.R. 471, 501, para 78; *Schmidt v Germany* (1994) 18 E.H.R.R. 513, 527, para 24; *Van Raalte v Netherlands* (1997) 24 E.H.R.R. 503, 518–519, para 39. When Harris, O'Boyle and Warbrick's valuable work, *Law of the European Convention on Human Rights*, was published in 1995, the authors recognised that the Strasbourg Court had its own suspect categories, identifying them as discrimination on the grounds of race, gender or illegitimacy. Since then religion, nationality and sexual orientation have, it seems, been added: see *Jacobs and White, European Law of Human Rights*, 3rd ed (2002), pp 355–6, citing *Hoffmann v Austria* (1994) 17 E.H.R.R. 293, 316, para 36; *Gaygusuz v Austria* (1997) 23 E.H.R.R. 364, 381, para 42 and *Salgueiro da Silva Mouta v Portugal* (2001) 31 E.H.R.R. 1055, 1071, para 36. Where an individual lives is in principle a matter of choice. So although it can be regarded as a personal characteristic it is not immutable. Nor is there anything intrinsically demeaning about an individual's place of residence. Social or business practices which amount to what is sometimes called a 'postcode lottery' might, if devoid of any rational basis, constitute discrimination. But that is not this case."

Lord Walker seemed to push the distinction between "sensitive" and "ordinary" grounds of discrimination further than Lord Hoffmann, suggesting that it was "clear" from the Strasbourg jurisprudence that "the possible grounds of discrimination under [A]rticle 14", under the "other status" heading, "are not wholly unlimited; nor are all possible grounds of equal efficacy in establishing unlawful discrimination."[169] Lord Walker accepted that discrimination on the grounds of place of residence and age did not count as particularly sensitive grounds,[170] a conclusion which differs from Lord Hoffmann's in relation to age. In relation to age, Lord Walker suggested that while age was a personal characteristic, it inevitably affected every human being. It may be "disheartening" for a person to be told that they had to retire at a given age, but "lines have to be drawn somewhere" in relation to "normal retirement ages"[171] and there was nothing "intrinsically demeaning" about this (so long as relevant line-drawing exercises did not involve different treatment on the basis of, for example, sex).[172]

Unfortunately, Lord Walker's approach is problematical in two ways. Firstly, it misstates the US case law, which does not currently treat sex, race

[169] *Carson*, para. [52].
[170] *Carson*, para. [59].
[171] *Carson*, para. [60]; see also paras [58]–[59].
[172] *Carson*, para. [60].

and sexual orientation as being subject to equal intensity of scrutiny: sexual orientation is not a suspect classification, although there are strong arguments that it should be recognised as being so.[173] Unfortunately, the direct analogy drawn by Lord Walker (with whose judgment Lords Nicholls, Rodger and Carswell agreed) with the Strasbourg case law rests on his categorization of US law. Secondly, the presence of the "margin of appreciation" in the Strasbourg case law—affecting the intensity of proportionality review on a case-by-case basis—suggests that there is not the clean progression of intensity of review that Lord Walker's comments imply. It should also be noted that since *Carson* involved a claim of direct discrimination, the use of proportionality reasoning in order to demonstrate that the difference in issue served a legitimate aim and was proportionate to that aim neatly demonstrates the central place of justification arguments in Art.14-based direct discrimination cases—in direct contrast with the official position in direct discrimination claims based upon EU law.

Domestic courts have not yet had the chance particularly to develop their reasoning concerning deference in discrimination cases under the Human Rights Act, although it is quite possible that the uncertainties which generally beset deference at Strasbourg and national levels will also operate in this area.[174] Particular uncertainty might relate to the role of the "discretionary area" in cases where a "sensitive" ground of prohibited discrimination is in issue. In *Ghaidan*, for example, Lord Nicholls suggested that while a court would be less ready to reach a different conclusion from Parliament about the meaning of legislation in an area like housing policy, in which Parliament had to strike a balance between the interests of landlords and tenants, if—*within such an area*—an alleged breach of Article 14 involved a "sensitive" ground of discrimination, the Court might adopt a more intense approach.

Ghaidan v Godin-Mendoza [2004] UKHL 30

LORD NICHOLLS

[13] "In the present case paragraph 2 of Schedule 1 to the Rent Act 1977 draws a dividing line between married couples and cohabiting heterosexual couples on the one hand and other members of the original tenant's family on the other hand. What is the rationale for this distinction? The rationale seems to be that, for the purposes of security of

[173] For general discussion of equal protection, see Kenji Yosino, "Assimilationist Bias in Equal Protection: The Visibility Presumption and the Case of 'Don't Ask, Don't Tell'" (1998–9) 108 Yale L.J. 485. For the US Supreme Court's use of distinctive "animus" reasoning in relation to sexual orientation, see *Romer v Evans* (1996) 547 U.S. 620. For argument that sexual orientation *should* be recognised as a suspect class, see Nicholas Bamforth and David A.J. Richards, *Patriarchal Religion, Sexuality and Gender: A Critique of New Natural Law* (New York: Cambridge University Press, 2008), Ch.6.

[174] For normative arguments, see Sandra Fredman, "From Deference to Democracy: the Role of Equality under the Human Rights Act 1998" (2006) 122 L.Q.R. 53.

tenure, the survivor of such couples should be regarded as having a special claim to be treated in much the same way as the original tenant. The two of them made their home together in the house in question, and their security of tenure in the house should not depend upon which of them dies first . . .

[19] . . . arguments based on the extent of the discretionary area of judgment accorded to the legislature lead nowhere in this case. . . . Parliament is charged with the primary responsibility for deciding the best way of dealing with social problems. The court's role is one of review. The court will reach a different conclusion from the legislature only when it is apparent that the legislature has attached insufficient importance to a person's Convention rights. The readiness of the court to depart from the view of the legislature depends upon the subject matter of the legislation and of the complaint. National housing policy is a field where the court will be less ready to intervene. Parliament has to hold a fair balance between the competing interests of tenants and landlords, taking into account broad issues of social and economic policy. But, even in such a field, where the alleged violation comprises differential treatment based on grounds such as race or sex or sexual orientation the court will scrutinise with intensity any reasons said to constitute justification. The reasons must be cogent if such differential treatment is to be justified."

Perhaps the flip-side to these observations can be found in Lord Walker's assertion in *Carson* that, even within Art.14 cases, any "issue of macro-economic policy [. . .] is eminently within the province of the legislature and the executive . . .".[175]

It is thus clear that, when assessing whether a breach of a "qualified" Convention right, including that contained in Art.14, can be justified, the Strasbourg Court deploys a proportionality test of variable intensity, coupled with the "margin of appreciation" principle. This is paralleled by the domestic courts' use of proportionality, and by their adoption of a national level deference principle known as the "discretionary area of judgment". As *Ghaidan* and *Carson* demonstrate, proportionality plays a key part in Human Rights Act discrimination cases, and it seems likely that the "discretionary area" will also have an important role. This being so, it will be important for national courts to be clearer in their understanding of the intensity of proportionality (especially given the difficulties in Lord Walker's judgment in *Carson*) and to think be careful in relating it to the "discretionary area", especially in cases where "sensitive" grounds of discrimination are in issue alongside sensitive policy arguments.

F. *Differently and Similarly Situated: the Comparator Problem*

Since prohibited discrimination involves a difference of treatment based on an impermissible ground, discrimination law tends to require the claimant to show that they have been treated *differently from* someone who did not possess the characteristic which is alleged to form the basis for discrimination but is in other ways analogous. How does one determine who is analogous, however?

175 *Carson*, para. [80]; see also Lord Hoffmann at paras [25] and [26].

How similar does this require the comparator to be? Is it possible for a court to conduct the comparison exercise without engaging either in explicit value judgments (in order to determine who is similar) or, at the other end of the spectrum, in mechanical and artificially rigid analysis? And does the requirement that a comparator be found mean that discrimination law is entrenching a "normalising" standard established by reference to the characteristics of members of the "majority" group in society? Such questions have long affected discrimination law, not least given now the US Civil Rights Act 1964, the Sex Discrimination Act 1975, Race Relations Act 1976 and other statutory protection against discrimination in the UK, together with most EU measures, use a comparative approach in establishing whether unlawful discrimination has taken place. As Aaron Baker has noted:

"Legal protection against discrimination exhibits an enduring dependence on the technique of comparing a claimant, or a group to which the claimant belongs, to some other group. Discrimination laws in the United Kingdom and the European Union, for example, define discrimination by reference to 'less favourable treatment'—explicitly requiring a comparison—or to comparisons of the relative impact on different groups of apparently equal treatment."[176]

Historically, domestic courts have adopted a relatively rigid approach to the comparator requirement, as was demonstrated by the extremely slow recognition—only finally achieved after the European Court of Justice's decision in *Webb v EMO Air Cargo (UK) Ltd*—that it was not always necessary obsessively to search for a male "comparator" for a pregnant female when bringing a claim based on the Equal Treatment Directive.[177]

After an initial, apparently rather rigid approach was adopted by the Court of Appeal, the House of Lords seems to have opted in *Ghaidan* and *Carson* for a more flexible approach to the comparator issue in Art.14 cases. The original approach was encapsulated in a series of questions, which became known as the "*Michalak* criteria" after the case in which they were first enunciated.[178] As will be obvious, it is questions (ii) and (iii) which are directly relevant to the comparator issue, while question (iv) moves on to deal with proportionality.

[176] "Comparison Tainted by Justification: Against a 'Compendious Question' in Art.14 Discrimination" [2006] P.L. 476, 476. See also Aileen McColgan, "Cracking the Comparator Problem: Discrimination, 'Equal' Treatment and the Role of Comparisons" [2006] E.H.R.L.R. 650, 650–3.

[177] Case C-32/93, [1994] E.C.R. I-3567. For more detailed analysis of the comparator problem, see the Hepple Report (*Equality: A New Framework. Report of the Independent Review of the Enforcement of UK Anti-Discrimination Legislation* (Oxford: Hart, 2000), paras 2.24 to 2.25, 2.51.

[178] The questions were first set out in, and taken in *Michalak* from, Stephen Grosz, Jack Beatson and Peter Duffy, *Human Rights: The 1998 Act and the European Convention* (London: Sweet & Macwell, 2000) para.C14–08.

***Wandsworth London BC v Michalak* [2003] 1 W.L.R. 617**

BROOKE L.J.

[20] "It appears to me that it will usually be convenient for a court, when invited to consider an article 14 issue, to approach its task in a structured way. . . . If a court follows this model it should ask itself the four questions I set out below. If the answer to any of the four questions is 'No', then the claim is likely to fail, and it is in general unnecessary to proceed to the next question. These questions are as follows. (i) Do the facts fall within the ambit of one or more of the substantive Convention provisions (for the relevant Convention rights, see section 1(1) of the Human Rights Act 1998)? (ii) If so, was there different treatment as respects that right between the complainant on the one hand and other persons put forward for comparison ('the chosen comparators') on the other? (iii) Were the chosen comparators in an analogous situation to the complainant's situation? (iv) If so, did the difference in treatment have an objective and reasonable justification: in other words, did it pursue a legitimate aim and did the differential treatment bear a reasonable relationship of proportionality to the aim sought to be achieved? The third test addresses the question whether the chosen comparators were in a sufficiently analogous situation to the complainant's situation for the different treatment to be relevant to the question whether the complainant's enjoyment of his Convention right has been free from article 14 discrimination."

Criticism of the questions was initially voiced in the House of Lords by Baroness Hale in *Ghaidan*:

***Ghaidan v Godin-Mendoza* [2004] UKHL 30**

BARONESS HALE

[134] ". . . In my view, the *Michalak* questions are a useful tool of analysis but there is a considerable overlap between them: in particular between whether the situations to be compared were truly analogous, whether the difference in treatment was based on a proscribed ground and whether it had an objective justification. If the situations were not truly analogous it may be easier to conclude that the difference was based on something other than a proscribed ground. The reasons why their situations are analogous but their treatment different will be relevant to whether the treatment is objectively justified. A rigidly formulaic approach is to be avoided."

The criticisms were developed in detail in *Carson*, where the House of Lords concluded that the questions should be abandoned. It is worth setting out the judgments at length, given that they associate the *Michalak* questions not only with problems of undue complexity, overlap and rigidity, but also with a misunderstanding of the Convention approach.

R. v Secretary of State for Work and Pensions, Ex p. Carson; R. v Secretary of State for Work and Pensions, Ex p. Reynolds [2005] UKHL 37

LORD NICHOLLS

[3] "I prefer [instead of using the *Michalak* criteria] to keep formulation of the relevant issues in these cases as simple and non-technical as possible. Article 14 does not apply unless the alleged discrimination is in connection with a Convention right and on a ground stated in article 14. If this prerequisite is satisfied, the essential question for the court is whether the alleged discrimination, that is, the difference in treatment of which complaint is made, can withstand scrutiny. Sometime the answer to this question will be plain. There may be such an obvious, relevant difference between the claimant and those with whom he seeks to compare himself that their situations cannot be regarded as analogous. Sometimes, where the position is not so clear, a different approach is called for. Then the court's scrutiny may best be directed at considering whether the differentiation has a legitimate aim and whether the means chosen to achieve the aim is appropriate and not disproportionate in its adverse impact.

LORD HOFFMANN

[14] ... Discrimination means a failure to treat like cases alike. There is obviously no discrimination when the cases are relevantly different ... There is discrimination only if the cases are not sufficiently different to justify the difference in treatment. The Strasbourg court sometimes expresses this by saying that the two cases must be in an "analogous situation": see *Van der Mussele v Belgium* (1983) 6 E.H.R.R. 163, 179–180, para 46.

[15] Whether cases are sufficiently different is partly a matter of values and partly a question of rationality....

[29] [The *Michalak* questions] are no doubt an accurate taxonomy of the various issues decided by the Strasbourg court. But I am not sure that they are always helpful as a framework for reasoning. Question (i) reflects the fact that article 14 is confined to discrimination as to a list of particular matters and, as Stanley Burnton J said in this case [at first instance] ... it would be logical to add the question of whether the discrimination was on one of the specified grounds. Unless the claim satisfies these requirements, article 14 is not engaged at all. Question (ii) identifies the nature of the claimant's case. It identifies the real or hypothetical person in comparison with whom he complains he is being treated differently.

[30] The real difficulty about the questions is the apparent overlap between questions (iii) and (iv). If an "analogous situation" in question (iii) means that the two cases are not relevantly different (no two cases will ever be exactly the same) then a relevant difference may be the justification for the difference in treatment. In what kind of case does one go on to question (iv) and ask separately about justification? Laws LJ [in the Court of Appeal] suggested that it might clarify matters to substitute for question (iii) a "compendious question":

> "Are the circumstances of X and Y so similar as to call (in the mind of a rational and fair-minded person) for a positive justification for the less favourable treatment of Y in comparison with X".

[31] But in my opinion there are two difficulties about this formulation. First, it appears to reduce question (iii) to asking whether there is, so to speak, a prima facie case of discrimination (do the facts "call for" a justification) and to treat question (iv) as dealing with whether the call has been answered. But this division of the reasoning into two stages is artificial. People don't think that way. There is a single question: is there enough of a relevant difference between X and Y to justify different treatment? Secondly, the invocation of the "rational and fair-minded person" (who is, of course, the judge) suggests that the decision as to whether the differences are sufficient to justify a difference in treatment will always be a matter for the judge. In many cases, however, the decision will be a matter for Parliament or the discretion of the official entrusted with statutory powers.

[32] It might be more logical to confine question (iv) to justification for different treatment of cases which were *not* relevantly different, eg to achieve some legitimate teleological or administrative purpose, such as correcting the effect of past discrimination or the administrative convenience of having clear distinctions. That would explain why in such cases the courts insist that the discrimination must be necessary and proportionate for the object to be achieved. But neither the Strasbourg court nor the English courts have approached the matter in this way . . . and it is certainly not expressed in the formulation of the questions.

[33] For these reasons I have found it better not to use the *Michalak* framework. . . .

LORD RODGER

[43] . . . a court faced with a case of alleged discrimination should not go mechanically through a series of questions. Rather, it should look at the facts of the case as a whole and identify the particular issue or issues which will have to be resolved in order to decide whether there has been discrimination contrary to article 14.

[44] Often, the critical question will be whether the person complaining of discrimination is really in an analogous situation to that of the person who is treated more favourably.

LORD WALKER

[63] One of the most powerful criticisms of a rigid, step by step approach based on comparators is [. . .] [that it is] [. . .] liable to obscure the real issue in the case, which was *why* the complainant had been treated as she had been treated. Until that question was answered, it was impossible to focus properly on the question of comparators. [. . .]

[64] My Lords, I think the time has come to say that in cases on article 14, the *Michalak* catechism, even in a corrected form, is not always the best approach. When the United Kingdom first enacted legislation against discrimination on grounds of sex or race, over 20 years before the Human Rights Act 1998, it was natural that Parliament felt bound to provide detailed definitions of discrimination suitable for statutes of a penal character. The definitions in the Sex Discrimination Act 1975 and the Race Relations Act 1976 are far removed from the broad sweep of language appropriate to a human rights instrument. Inevitably they gave rise to much learning on the subject of "comparators."

[65] The Strasbourg jurisprudence, by contrast, has made little direct use of comparators. The approach of the European Court of Human Rights has been described as follows by Professor David Feldman, *Civil Liberties and Human Rights in England and Wales*, 2nd ed (2002), p 144:

> "The way the court approaches it is not to look for identity of position between different cases, but to ask whether the applicant and the people who are treated differently are in 'analogous' situations. This will to some extent depend on whether there is an objective and reasonable justification for the difference in treatment, which overlaps with the questions about the acceptability of the ground and the justifiability of the difference in treatment. That is why, as van Dijk and van Hoof observe, and 'in most instances of the Strasbourg case law . . . the comparability test is glossed over, and the emphasis is (almost) completely on the justification test'. However, there are occasions on which the court has rejected applications under article 14 purely on the ground that the applicant has provided no evidence that the people who were treated differently had been in

analogous situations, or because the comparators are not genuinely in analogous positions."[179]

[68] In these cases (and numerous other cases in which there is even less discussion of the meaning of "analogous situations") the European Court of Human Rights was, without any elaborate analysis or discussion of comparators, reaching an overall conclusion as to whether in the enjoyment of Convention rights there had been unfair and unjustifiable discrimination on the grounds of some personal characteristic. This assessment calls for a process of judicial evaluation which must be sensitive to the factual context. Some analogies are close, others are more distant. As Brooke LJ recognised [in *Michalak*, at para [22]] [. . .] the evaluation process may not be assisted by setting out standard questions "as a series of hurdles, to be surmounted in turn."

[70] [I] would not, however, wish to suggest that there are not some circumstances in which justification must be considered as a separate issue. The clearest case [. . .] is that of "positive discrimination," in which a category of disadvantaged persons is accorded specially favourable treatment (and others are correspondingly worse treated) precisely because of some personal characteristic (such as race or gender) of the preferred group. That personal characteristic obviously cannot be taken into account as a relevant difference negativing "analogous circumstances"; positive discrimination must be justified, if at all, for reasons which focus on (and as it were make a virtue of) what would otherwise be a proscribed ground . . .

LORD CARSWELL

[97] Many discrimination cases resolve themselves into a dispute, which can often seem more than a little arid, about comparisons and identifying comparators, where a broader approach might more readily yield a serviceable answer which corresponds with one's instincts for justice. ... Much of the problem stems from focusing too closely on finding comparisons, an approach which may tend to place too much emphasis on finding answers to the four [*Michalak*] questions. ... These questions can supply an admirable analysis for some cases, but can form a Procustean bed if others are forced into their framework. Question (i) will be a constant in every consideration of article 14, but is not in issue in the present appeal. Question (ii) requires to be answered in some form, for the essence of discrimination is in the different treatment of persons who ought to be treated in the same or a similar fashion . . ."

Although *Carson* might look like a welcome rejection of undue rigidity, the judgments give rise to three important questions. The first is whether the House of Lords has left the lower courts with any real criteria for determining whether a claimant has been unfavourably treated. While it may well be undesirable to force claims into an unduly rigid framework, do the judgments open the way for lower courts to engage in *ad hoc* decision-making, shaped by their view of what justice, however defined, might require in an individual case? Secondly, *Carson* appears to represent a relaxation rather than an abandonment of the comparator requirement, given that Lord Hoffmann and Lord Walker placed considerable emphasis on the Strasbourg approach to comparisons, which they would appear to be content for domestic courts to

179 As Lord Walker noted at paras [66] to [67], examples included *Van der Mussele v Belgium* (1983) 6 E.H.R.R. 163, especially para. [46] (treatment of the Belgian bar by contrast with other professions) and *Johnston v Ireland* (1986) 9 E.H.R.R. 203, especially para. [60] (treatment of divorcees permanently resident in Ireland, and their children, by contrast with that of couples divorced abroad but resident in Ireland).

use. How far, nonetheless, does this relaxation represent a departure from the traditional understanding of discrimination law (at domestic level) as something which entails comparisons? Thirdly, how far is it acceptable for different approaches to comparators to be used in Art.14 cases, by contrast with non-Convention (including EU) cases before national courts? Lord Walker emphasized the difference in language in Art.14 (its "broad sweep") by contrast with the statutory prohibitions on discrimination, but is this difference sufficient to justify the distinct approach used in Art.14? It is also interesting to speculate, under this heading, about whether Lord Carswell might have been hinting—when advocating a "broader and simpler approach ... *certainly in cases* in which resort is had to the Convention"[180]—that he would support, given his condemnation "arid" disputes about "identifying comparators", a more flexible approach to comparators *outside* as well as within Art.14.

Carson has been the subject of powerful academic criticism. Aaron Baker has questioned whether, by abandoning the separation in the *Michalak* criteria between proportionality (question (iv)) and comparisons (questions (ii) and (iii)), the House of Lords might in fact have underscored a departure—despite the claims of Lord Hoffmann and Lord Walker to the contrary—from the Convention approach to Art.14. He suggests that:

Aaron Baker "Comparison Tainted by Justification: Against a 'Compendious Question' in Art.14 Discrimination" [2006] P.L. 476 at 476–7

"[I]t should rarely be possible to dispose of cases under Art.14 of the European Convention on Human Rights [...] by comparing the claimant to a person without a specific protected status, because the ECHR dies not forbid discrimination on a handful of protected grounds, but requires that any ground be 'justified': the European Court of Human Rights ... requires a review of the legitimacy of a challenged distinction in a justification inquiry that incorporates a proportionality balancing. A court might, therefore, properly use comparisons to reveal that the ground of discrimination is one not covered by Art.14, or that proffered comparators are not sufficiently analogous to identify on what ground, exactly, discrimination occurred. What is worrying, however, is the number of domestic cases in which a court—having accepted the alleged ground as one covered by Art.14—uses a comparison to prove the absence of discrimination, and disclaims any need to perform a justification inquiry involving proportionality. UK courts appear to be performing a minijustification as an integral part of their comparison, but one that is usually unacknowledged and always less rigorous than the formal justification analysis they reject as unnecessary."

[180] *Carson*, para.[97] (emphasis added). Note also Lord Carswell's observations in *R.(LS) v Chief Constable of the South Yorkshire Police*, paras [80]–[83], about the differences between direct and indirect discrimination cases in relation to comparators.

While it is easy, Baker suggests, for judges to dispose of discrimination cases under the traditional domestic statutes just be relying on comparison exercises, this is because of the rather exact drafting of the statutes themselves. Nonetheless, comparison exercises always entail at least implicit policy judgments.[181] By disposing of Art.14 cases—as is possible under the *Carson* approach—solely by reference to comparisons, domestic courts fail to give adequate weight to the justification exercise associated with proportionality and demanded by Art.14.

Aileen McColgan echoes aspects of Baker's criticisms, although her conclusion is rather different. She suggests, paralleling Baker, that Lord Hoffmann's "single question" (was there "enough of a difference between X and Y to justify different treatment?") "so emphasises the comparative exercise" as to leave, as Lord Hoffmann accepted, "little room for consideration of the question of justification as an independent head, except perhaps where positive discrimination was at issue. Everything boiled down to the question whether the ground on which the challenged distinction was based was 'relevant' to the legislative distinction".[182] Nonetheless, McColgan accepts that justification exercises do sometimes underlie comparison exercises in the Court of Human Rights' Art.14 case law,[183] and is keen—rather than treating comparison exercises as conclusive of the question whether unlawful discrimination has occurred—for the issues of comparison and "difference" to play a claimant-friendly role at the justification (i.e., proportionality) stage of the inquiry as an aspect of deep-level scrutiny into the legitimacy of the legislative purpose behind the distinction concerned.[184] As we will see in later chapters, the issue of comparators raises recurring questions in all areas of discrimination law at Convention, EU and domestic levels.

G. *Conclusion*

We have seen in this section that considerable uncertainties beset the Convention discrimination case law, both at Strasbourg level and before domestic courts. These relate to the closeness of the connection which needs to be established between Art.14 and whatever Convention right a litigant is relying on in conjunction with it (given the United Kingdom's refusal to accede to Protocol 12), which cases fall within the remit of Art.14, how readily the courts may bring new grounds of prohibited discrimination within the remit of

181 "Comparison Tainted by Justification", p.476. For analysis of this phenomenon in EU case law, see Aileen McColgan, "Cracking the Comparator Problem", *ibid.*, pp.658–9.

182 "Cracking the Comparator Problem", p.670; this refers to para.[31] of Lord Hoffmann's judgment.

183 "Cracking the Comparator Problem", pp.659–62.

184 As we argue in Ch.4, there are conceptual limits to the possibility of moving away from comparisons altogether.

Art.14 under the "other statuses" heading, the apparently variable intensity of proportionality review, judicial deference, and the treatment of comparators. Furthermore, the range of litigants and potential remedies differ as between national and Court of Human Rights level. As the next two sections will show, there are also considerable differences between the approaches used under the Convention and EU law, and EU law has greater legal weight than EU law at national level due to the principles of direct effect and the supremacy of EU law.

Despite the fact that Art.14 (and, in so far as they relate to discrimination, other Convention Articles) is less strongly protected in national law than EU discrimination norms, the passage of the Human Rights Act 1998 nonetheless heralds a significant shift in the nature of domestic discrimination law. Since s.3 obliges courts to interpret *any* legislation in accordance with Convention rights, Art.14 will have an influence far beyond the fields of employment and the provision of goods, facilities and services, which form the primary focus of previous national and (most) EU non-discrimination legislation. It may be fair to argue that s.3 heralds an important change of emphasis in in the United Kingdom: having once been the province of specific statutory protections in employment and analogous areas, the prohibition of invidious forms of discrimination now forms part of a general principle of statutory interpretation affecting every area in which the Human Rights Act applies.

V. The European Union

EU discrimination measures have been of enormous importance in the past thirty years, both as a reflection of the policy goals of the EC/EU and as a source of discrimination law at domestic level. The sheer number of directly effective EU discrimination measures, coupled with an expansive European Court of Justice case law, has given EU law a central role in shaping the development of discrimination law in England and Wales. In the first part of this section, we set out the main Treaty provisions and consider the policy goals of EU law, these goals being relevant to our evaluation of EU anti-discrimination measures. In the second part, we explore the content of those measures, together with the proportionality analysis used by the European Court of Justice: matters which are of real importance to national courts given their obligation, when interpreting and applying national law, to give effect to directly effective EU measures and Court of Justice decisions. In the third part we outline some relevant EU-related decisions in national law. As we noted in Chapter 1, EU law provides an example of what Sandra Fredman has characterised as the "fixed category" approach to discrimination law.[185] In consequence, we do not need—by contrast with our treatment of Art.14—to

[185] Chapter 1, Section IIIB.

engage in detailed analysis of how the prohibited grounds of discrimination are chosen (the first of our 10 questions outlined in Chapter 1). It is also clear that both direct and indirect discrimination are prohibited under EU law (answering our fourth question), and the ambit of the principle of direct effect helps to highlight the permissible defendants (our third question). However, our second, fifth, sixth and seventh questions (in which contexts is discrimination prohibited? Can discrimination be justified for policy reasons? How are clashes between different prohibited grounds treated? Are there other exclusions from protections against discrimination?) are all directly relevant when considering EU law, and proportionality analysis—used when answering the fifth question—plays an important part in the ECJ's case law. Nevertheless, given the role of direct effect in EU law, the reception of "EU" norms into domestic law does not give rise to such a wide range of questions as those which relate to the Convention and the Human Rights Act 1998.

A. *Treaty Provisions and Policy Goals*

The following sections of the EC Treaty (as revised) are relevant to discrimination law. These are:

Article 12(1) EC

Within the scope of application of this Treaty, and without prejudice to any special provisions contained therein, any discrimination on grounds of nationality shall be prohibited.

Article 13(1) EC

Without prejudice to the other provisions of this Treaty and within the limits of the powers conferred by it upon the Community, the Council, acting unanimously on a proposal from the Commission and after consulting the European Parliament, may take appropriate action to combat discrimination based on sex, racial or ethnic origin, religion or belief, disability, age or sexual orientation.

Article 141(1) EC

Each Member State shall ensure that the principle of equal pay for male and female workers for equal work or work of equal value is applied.

Despite EU law's use of a 'fixed category' approach to the grounds of prohibited discrimination, it was not until the amendment of the EC Treaty in 1997 (with the Treaty of Amsterdam) that a particularly lengthy list of grounds was in fact prohibited. Prior to 1997, the only heads of discrimination expressly prohibited in the Treaty were nationality (Art.12EC) and failure to adhere to the principle of equal pay for male and female workers (Art.141(1)EC). The Treaty of Amsterdam amendments expanded the scope of Art.141EC so as to confirm the existence of legislative competence to enact measures to ensure equal opportunities and equal treatment for men and women (Art.141(3)EC)[186]—a competence previously assumed by the EC institutions when legislating—and to permit affirmative action measures by Member States (Art.141(4)EC). Article 13EC was also created, establishing competence to legislate in relation to discrimination based on sex, racial or ethnic origin, religion or belief, disability, age and sexual orientation.[187] Extensive use has been made of secondary legislation, both prior to and since the Treaty amendments. Secondary legislation has been enacted to give effect to the principle of equal pay[188] and, under Art.308EC, to equal treatment for men and women in employment.[189] Both of these Directives (and others) have now been consolidated into the "recast" Equal Treatment Directive, which deals with all aspects of sex discrimination in employment, including direct discrimination, indirect discrimination and harassment.[190] However, certain aspects of sex discrimination—relating to state social security, access to and the supply of goods and services, pregnancy and parental leave, and the

186 See also Art.137(1)(i). More generally, Art.2 EC proclaims that the Community must promote equality between men and women as one of its tasks, while Art.3(2)EC states that it must aim to promote equality and eliminate inequalities between men and women in all of its specified activities.

187 See, generally, Evelyn Ellis, *EU Anti-Discrimination Law* (Oxford: Oxford University Press, 2005), pp.12–20.

188 Council Directive No.75/117, on the approximation of the laws of the Member States relating to the application of the principle of equal pay for men and women; for analysis, see Evelyn Ellis, *EU Anti-Discrimination Law*, *ibid.*, pp.187–207.

189 Council Directive No.76/207 (as amended), on the implementation of the principle of equal treatment for men and women as regards access to employment, vocational training and promotion, and working conditions.

190 Council Directive No.2006/54, on the implementation of the principle of equal opportunities and equal treatment of men and women in matters of employment and occupation (recast). This entered into force in July 2006, and national implementing measures (if any are needed, which is perhaps arguable given that the Directive is a consolidating measure) have not yet been passed in the UK.

self-employed—continue to be dealt with in other Directives.[191] Although Art.13EC is thought to lack direct effect, the Race Equality Directive[192] and the Employment Equality"[193] have implemented the expanded list of prohibited grounds of discrimination.[194] This expansion, as we will see, is thought to reflect the shifting rationales underpinning non-discrimination measures at EU level.

Apart from the expanded range of expressly prohibited grounds of discrimination,[195] the Court of Justice has sometimes made reference to the notion of equality as a general principle of EU law underpinning the specific non-discrimination provisions,[196] and famously used this notion in *P v S and Cornwall CC* to suggest that the sex discrimination provisions of the original Equal Treatment Directive were to be read as prohibiting discrimination on the basis of gender reassignment: in other words, discrimination associated more with gender identity than with a person's apparent physical sex.[197] What therefore seems to exist, at EU level, is a "fixed category" approach under which the range of prohibited grounds of discrimination has been expanded by Treaty amendment, but within the framework of which the Court of Justice felt empowered—in *P v S*—to offer a broad, if not expansive, approach to the

[191] See Council Directives No.79/7, on the progressive implementation of the principle of equal treatment for men and women in matters of social security; No.86/613 on the application of the principle of equal treatment of men and women engaged in an activity, including agriculture, in a self-employed capacity, and on the protection of self-employed women during pregnancy and motherhood; No.92/85, on the introduction of measures to encourage improvements in the safety and health at work of pregnant workers and workers who have recently given birth or are breastfeeding; No.96/34, implementing the framework agreement on parental leave; No.2004/113, implementing the principle of equal treatment between men and women in the access to and supply of goods and services. See further Chapter 10 and Noreen Burrows and Muriel Robison, "An Assessment of the Recast of Community Equality Laws" (2006) 13 E.L.J. 186.

[192] Council Directive No.2000/43, implementing the principle of equal treatment of persons irrespective of racial or ethnic origin.

[193] Council Directive No.2000/78, establishing a general framework for equal treatment in employment and occupation.

[194] The exact boundaries of Art.13EC are also a matter for debate: see further Mark Bell, *Anti-Discrimination Law and the European Union, ibid.*, pp.128–143.

[195] Note also the provisions contained in C.III of the Charter of Fundamental Rights: for discussion of the possible legal effects of which, see Paul Craig, *EU Administrative Law* (Oxford: Oxford University Press, 2006), pp.494–523, 537–9; Anthony Arnull, Alan Dashwood, Michael Dougan, Malcolm Ross, Eleanor Spaventa and Derrick Wyatt, *Wyatt and Dashwood's European Union Law* (London: Sweet & Maxwell, 5th edn., 2006), pp.299–303.

[196] In the context of agriculture, see Cases 117/76 and 16/77, *Ruckdeschel v Hauptzollamt Hamburg-St Annen* [1977] ECR 1753, para.[7] and Case 8/78, *Milac GmbH v Hauptzollamt Freiburg* [1978] ECR 1721, para.[18].

[197] Case C-13/94, *P v S and Cornwall County Council* [1996] ECR I-2143, paras [18]-[21]; more expansive than the judgment was the Opinion of Tesauro A-G. For analysis of the principle as set out in *P v S*, compare Catherine Barnard, "*P v. S*: Kite Flying of a New Constitutional Approach?", Ch.IV of Alan Dashwood and Siofra O'Leary (eds.), *The Principle of Equal Treatment in EC Law* (London: Sweet & Maxwell, 1997) with Grainne de Burca, "The Role of Equality in European Community Law", Ch.II of Dashwood and O'Leary (eds.), *ibid.* See also Evelyn Ellis, *EU Anti-Discrimination Law, ibid.*, pp.335–344.

range of cases which might be brought within one of those categories by interpretation.[198] One might not wish to make too much out of *P v S* given that the Court's boldness of spirit was not repeated in later cases in which it ruled (prior to the passage of the Employment Equality Directive) that discrimination relating to sexual orientation—arguably another example of gender identity-based discrimination—could not be litigated as an example of sex discrimination.[199] Nonetheless, *P. v S.* clearly identifies the potential for expansive judicial interpretation of the boundaries of the various "fixed categories" which now exist. The Court was similarly ambitious, albeit in a subtly different way, in *Mangold v Helm*, a case concerning the age discrimination provisions of the Employment Equality Directive. Here, the Court characterised the provisions as an application of the general background principle of non-discrimination on the basis of age, to which effect had to be given: in other words, judicial interpretation could be guided by the principle rather than merely the provisions.[200]

As noted, the expansion in the list of prohibited grounds of discrimination at EU level has been tied to a shift in the general purposes of EU law.[201] Catherine Barnard captures this changing agenda in the following passage:

Catherine Barnard *The Substantive Law of the EU: The Four Freedoms* (Oxford: Oxford University Press, 2004)[202]

pp.23–24: "The driving force behind the European Union is, and always has been, the consolidation of a post-war system of inter-state co-operation and integration that would make pan-European armed conflict inconceivable. This has been promoted through a vigorous emphasis on free trade, with all the economic benefits that entails, albeit not to the exclusion of all other interests . . . And as the EU's self-perception changed from a European *Economic* Community to a European Union, so its tasks and objectives have been broadened to take into account a broader range of policies which may complement, but may also obstruct, free trade. For example, Article 2 EC has been amended to add new tasks for the Community including a high level of employment and social protection, equality between men and women, environmental protection, and economic and social cohesion. The solidarity between citizens of the EU envisaged by these measures and the

198 For analysis of the Court of Justice's expansiveness in relation to sex discrimination, see Evelyn Ellis, *EU Anti-Discrimination Law, ibid.*, pp.24–8.

199 See Case C-249/96, *Grant v South-West Trains Ltd* [1998] ECR I-621; Cases C-122 and 125/99, *D and Sweden v Council* [2001] ECR I-4319.

200 Case C-144/04, *Mangold v Helm* [2005] ECR I-9981, paras [74]-[77]. Note, however, the somewhat more cautious Opinions of the Advocates General in Case C-277/04P, *Lindorfer v Council*, November 30, 2006, and Case C-411/05, *Palacios de la Villa v Cortefiel Servicios*, February 15, 2007.

201 See, generally, Evelyn Ellis, *EU Anti-Discrimination Law* (Oxford: Oxford University Press, 2005), pp.7–12; Catherine Barnard, *EC Employment Law* (Oxford: Oxford University Press, 3rd edn, 2006), Chs 1 & 3.

202 For analysis of non-discrimination norms in relation to nationality, goods and workers, see pp.18–19, 51, 91, 140, 234.

State/federal intervention they necessitate are a far cry from an ordo-liberal/neo-liberal agenda.

This change in orientation can be seen in the simple Statement by the Court in *Deutsche Post* [Joined Cases C-270/97 and C-271/97, *Deutsche Post* v. *Sievers* [2000] ECR-I 929, para.57], a case decided in 2000 on Article 141 on equal pay. The Court said that "the economic aim pursued by Article [141] of the Treaty, namely the elimination of distortions of competition between undertakings established in different Member States, is secondary to the social aim pursued by the same provision, which constitutes the expression of a fundamental human right". This is significant for it marks an important shift in emphasis—from a pure market-based, neo-liberal vision premised on deregulation, efficiency, and the assumption of formal equality between individuals—to one which recognises the need to accommodate a wider range of interests. Since the 1970s the Court has tried to balance market rights with traditional civil, political, and social rights. This approach has been legitimised by the adoption of the Charter of Fundamental Rights which now forms part of the draft [EU] Constitution. This rights-based approach has begun to shape the contours of the Court's case law, particularly in the field of citizens' rights. At a time when global movements are mobilizing forces against free trade which they see as both wasteful to sustainable resources and producing inequality . . . the EU would find itself significantly out of step with its citizens if it did not recognize the broader social and environmental issues at stake."

While not incompatible with Barnard's analysis, Mark Bell's characterisation of the development of EU competence (particularly in the areas of racial and sexual orientation discrimination) more in terms of a *dialogue* between two evolving policy—dubbed the "market integration" and "social citizenship" models—is perhaps more gradated. Bell explains the two models in the following terms;

Mark Bell *Anti-Discrimination Law and the European Union* (Oxford: Oxford University Press, 2002)

[pp. 6–7:] "Two theoretical models of European social policy may be identified. First, there is the *market integration model* which prescribes a limited social policy for the European Union. This is predicated on the assumption that the primary goal of the Union is to achieve economic integration. Therefore, the EU only intervenes in the social sphere when this is required to support and sustain the smooth functioning of the common market. Essentially this is a model for a social policy dependent on the economics of European integration. Alternatively, there is a model of social policy as an independent policy objective for the EU, foreseeing a social policy as vibrant and autonomous as the Union's activities in the economic sphere. This is centred around a role for the Union as a guarantor of fundamental social rights and may be described as the *social citizenship model*. It is within these policy frameworks that EU anti-discrimination law has developed."

Bell characterizes the market integration model as working from the assumption that especially marked differences in social costs among member states—such as those caused by nationality or sex discrimination—distort the common market, placing member states at a competitive disadvantage.[203] On this view, "EU intervention in employment regulation" is seen as "justified only where this is necessary to prevent unfair competition that could disrupt the smooth functioning of the internal market."[204] This model thus prescribes a role for social policy as supplementary to economic integration.[205] The social citizenship model, by contrast, sees "an expanded role for the Union in guaranteeing a range of fundamental social rights and hence building a sense of European citizenship among the benficiaries of those rights"[206] and "prescribes for the EU a role as a guarantor of fundamental human and social rights."[207] More generally, the:

"underlying aim of the social citizenship model is the generation of greater legitimacy for the Union and the cultivation of deeper support for European integration amongst the peoples of the Member States. In this respect, the sense of citizenship nurtured through the role for the Union as a protector of fundamental rights addresses the profoundly political objective of winning the 'consent' and 'trust' of citizens of the E.U. for the integration process."[208]

Bell goes on to discuss the development of EU law in terms of a dialogue between the two models, which have in any event evolved over time:

[pp. 27–8:] "[I]t is [currently] difficult to describe [European social policy] as neatly falling into either of the two models proposed. The market integration model is clearly evident as the original vision of the appropriate role for social policy. However, this model has mutated during certain periods, in the direction of a much broader social policy than that envisaged by the drafters of the Treaties; a social policy around establishing common minimum labour law standards. At the same time, it is important to recognise that this process has not been unidirectional. It is quite evident that the Delors vision of social policy which underpinned the 1989 Social Charter has since given way to a much more cautious assessment of the contribution the Union can make in this field.

[p.29:] [Furthermore], the market integration model now accepts the need for some basic labour law standards to combat destructive competition within the internal market. To the extent that these basic standards can be approximated to agreement on a limited core of fundamental social rights, then the two models have a meeting place where progress may be possible. Importantly, anti-discrimination law finds a location in both, whether as a tool against the gaining of unfair competitive advantages through cheap labour, or as a breach of the fundamental right to non-discrimination. As a result, this renders it an area fertile for an expanded EU role.

The theoretical models offer general explanations for the pattern of EU social policy. However, either model is limited when it comes to making sense of specifics in labour law.

[p.5:] Whilst progress has been made in building a set of basic labour law rights, social policy still remains linked to a market integration rationale. Nonetheless, the rise of new

203 *Anti-Discrimination Law and the European Union* (Oxford: Oxford University Press, 2002), p.8.
204 *ibid.*, p.2.
205 *ibid.*, p.9. See pp.9–12 for discussion of different versions of this model and market-integration based social policy.
206 *ibid.*, p.2.
207 *ibid.*, p.12.
208 *ibid.*, p.13; see also pp.191–2.

forms of EU regulation ... produced a shift away from the focus on market integration in favour of facilitating market participation. The emphasis on removing barriers to participation in the labour market has created a new space for anti-discrimination law, albeit in a different context form a fundamental rights rationale"

Bell is therefore keen to stress that the passage of Art.13, and the Directives designed to give effect to its general guarantees, cannot be seen as the final stage in a move towards the social policy model. The market integration model "has undergone some mutation", but "remains very much present".[209] While the Art.13 Directives are not central to the market integration project—for their central focus is on discrimination within the labour market, most instances of which "will have no connection to cross-border trade or the migration of workers"—and "can easily be placed within the wider aims of the social citizenship model", they do not necessarily represent a "new golden era of citizenship-based social policy; a body of social law founded on the guarantee of fundamental human rights".[210] Bell suggests that the Directives could help to build awareness of the diversity of the European populace, thereby strengthening the links between the EU and individual citizens, but that their capacity to do so should not be exaggerated—particularly given the uncertainties surrounding the concept of EU citizenship.[211] Furthermore, there may be a distinction between the two Directives. The Employment Equality Directive is concerned with employment and thus the "familiar market citizen".[212] By contrast, the Race Equality Directive extends beyond employment and into areas such as health care, education and housing. This suggests it may have the potential to embrace a vision of social citizenship. Bell notes that caution may nonetheless be necessary: for the boundaries of Art.13EC—and hence of EC legislative competence in this area—remain uncertain, so that a narrow reading of competence and of the boundaries of the Directive could confine it to the cross-border, private sector delivery of services such as health and education.[213] Thus, while there may have been, especially with Art.13, a move away from the market integration model towards the protection of fundamental rights, the social citizenship model may still remain more an aspiration than a reality.[214]

An overriding uncertainty at present is whether social citizenship and the further evolution of EU non-discrimination measures might be given impetus

209 *ibid.*, p.192.
210 *ibid.*, p.193.
211 *ibid.*, pp.192–5.
212 *ibid.*, p.195.
213 *ibid.*, p.195.
214 *ibid.*, pp.2–3, 15–6, 18.

by the EU Charter on Fundamental Rights.[215] The Charter was approved by the Member States in 2000. Although it was not legally binding,[216] the ECJ and other EC institutions sometimes referred to it when reaching decisions.[217] Article 1(8) of the Treaty of Lisbon (signed on December 3, 2007) grants the "rights, freedoms and principles" set out in the Charter and has "the same legal value" as the Treaty on European Union and the EC Treaty.[218] However, it also notes that the provisions of the Charter do not extend to the competences of the EU. Furthermore, the UK and Poland have negotiated a Protocol to the Treaty of Lisbon to the effect that the Charter does not extend the ability of the ECJ or domestic courts "to find that the laws, regulations or administrative provisions, practices or actions of Poland or of the United Kingdom are inconsistent with the fundamental rights, freedoms and principles" affirmed in the Charter.[219] The wording of the Protocol presents some questions. The assertion that the Treaty of Lisbon does not "extend" the competences of the ECJ and domestic courts suggests that any existing competence of those courts to make reference to the Charter is acceptable, while the reference to "inconsistent" domestic laws suggests that it will be acceptable for courts to reinterpret legislation so as to render it compatible with Charter rights, freedoms and principles, so long as the legislation in issue is not incompatible with them.

Turning to the text of the Charter, Chapter III—headed "Equality"—protects equality before the law (Art.20), declares that the European Union shall respect cultural, linguistic and religious diversity (Art.22), guarantees equality between men and women in all areas, including employment and pay, and allows Member States to adopt affirmative action measures (Art.23), seeks to protect the rights of children (Art.24) and of the elderly (Art.25), and seeks to promote the integration of persons with disabilities (Art.26). The broad scope of C.III, and in particular the fact that it does *not* appear (at face value) to be confined to the employment sphere, is most evident in Art.21, which goes some way beyond Article 13EC:

215 See generally, Mark Bell, *ibid.*, pp.23–7;"Equality and the European Union Constitution" (2004) 33 I.L.J. 242; Cathryn Costello, "Gender Equalities and the Charter of Fundamental Rights of the European Union", in Tamara Hervey and Jeff Kenner (eds), *Economic and Social Rights under the EU Charter of Fundamental Rights* (Oxford: Hart's Publishing, 2003).

216 See, e.g., Case C-540/03, *European Parliament v Council* [2006] ECR I-5769, para. [38]; Case C-131/03 P, *Reynolds Tobacco Holdings v Commission* [2006] ECR I-7795.

217 See *European Parliament v Council; Reynolds Tobacco Holdings v Commission;* Helen Toner, "Impact Assessment and Fundamental Rights Protection in EU law" (2006) E.L. Rev. 316.

218 Treaty of Lisbon, overriding the Treaty on European Union and the Treaty establishing the European Community, December 3, 2007, CIG 14/07.

219 Protocol on the Application of the Charter of Fundamental Rights of the European Union to Poland and to the United Kingdom, December 3, 2007, CIG 14/07.

Charter of Fundamental Rights of the European Union, Article 21 [2000] O.J. C364/01

(1) Any discrimination based on any ground such as sex, race, colour, ethnic or social origin, genetic features, language, religion or belief, political or any other opinion, membership of a national minority, property, birth, disability, age or sexual orientation shall be prohibited.

(2) Within the scope of application of the Treaty establishing the European Community and of the Treaty on European Union, and without prejudice to the special provisions of those Treaties, any discrimination on grounds of nationality shall be prohibited.

At present, the long-term significance of the Charter is a matter for debate. Bell suggests that the "diversity and breadth" of the Charter's commitments suggest "a genuine departure from the economic orientation of European integration".[220] However, the Charter's potential force is diminished by Art.51(2), which asserts that its provisions neither create any new power or task for the EC or EU nor modify the powers and tasks conferred by the existing Treaties.[221] Viewed from this perspective, the Charter looks more like a "logical progression from the existing fundamental rights case law of the Court".[222]

In consequence, Bell is of the view that while the Charter may encourage the EU to move further towards the social citizenship model, it does not in and of itself effect a fundamental shift in that direction.[223] Nonetheless, the drafting of Art.21, and C.III more broadly, is significant in so far as the absence of references to the workplace (save in Art.23, where employment is treated as an example rather than the defining limit of the Charter's application) suggests a shift towards a constitutional/human rights-driven conception of discrimination law, moving beyond (but incorporating) the market/employment conception which appears originally to have underpinned EU non-discrimination measures. This is, of course, a rather similar shift to that seen at national level.

Finally, it should be noted that a European Union Agency for Fundamental Rights has been established under Council Regulation 168/2007. This has the task of providing "the relevant institutions, bodies, offices and agencies of the Community and its Member States when implementing Community law with assistance and expertise relating to fundamental rights".[224] More specifically,

220 Mark Bell, *Anti-Discrimination Law and the European Union*, *ibid.*, p.23.

221 Art.51(1) also stipulates that the provisions of the Charter are addressed to the institutions and bodies of the EU, but to Member States only when implementing EU law. For further analysis of uncertainties associated with the Charter, see Piet Eeckhout, "The EU Charter of Fundamental Rights and the Federal Question" (2002) 39 C.M.L. Rev. 945.

222 Mark Bell, *ibid.*, p.24.

223 *ibid.*, p.25.

224 Council Regulation (EC) No.168/207 of February 15, 2007 establishing a European Union Agency for Fundamental Rights (O.J. L53/1, 22 February 2007), Art.2.

the Agency is charged with collecting, recording, analysing and disseminating information at national and EU level, engaging in analytical work, publishing an annual report on fundamental rights issues, and publishing thematic reports concerning its analysis and research. The Agency is required to refer specifically to the "fundamental rights" as defined in Art.6(2) of the TEU (including European Convention Rights), and the ninth recital in the preamble to Regulation 168/2007 also refers to the Charter of Fundamental Rights. As such, discrimination falls within the Agency's remit. This being so, it is interesting to note that while the Agency is formally defined as a research and information-providing body rather than as an enforcement body, it has nonetheless indicated that it is prepared to refer complaints concerning discrimination to national level enforcement agencies.[225]

B. *The Legislation*

Directives, given their greater level of specificity than Treaty Articles, are designed to provide a reasonably clear guidance to Member States who are expected to turn them into national legislation within a specified time limit.[226] It thus comes as no surprise that there are many similarities between the Directives dealing with different grounds of discrimination. They all preclude direct and indirect discrimination, as well as harassment. Direct discrimination is defined as the less favourable treatment of one person, on the relevant ground, by comparison with the current, past or possible future treatment of another person in a comparable situation.[227] The possibility of justification is not mentioned, although there has been speculation that the ECJ has implicitly recognised it in some circumstances.[228] Apparently indirectly discriminatory provisions, criteria or practices may, however, be redeemed if they are objectively justified by a legitimate aim, the means of achieving that aim being appropriate and necessary.[229] As the ECJ has recognised, the latter part of this formulation clearly allows for proportionality analysis. It has thus persistently found that examples of prima facie indirect discrimination are capable of justification by demonstrating that the allegedly discriminatory measure was necessary and proportionate to an approved policy goal. For the moment, however, proportionality is used only in relation to indirect discrimination (even if the Directives contain various specific exceptions from direct and indirect discrimination liability): for the ECJ has not yet clearly recognised that

225 See the Agency's website at *http://www.europa.eu/eumc/index.php*.

226 Mark Bell, *Anti-Discrimination Law and the European Union, ibid.*, p.147. In the absence of implementation, a Directive becomes directly effective.

227 Recast Equal Treatment Directive, Art.2(1)(a); Racial Discrimination Directive, Art.2(2)(a); Framework Directive, Art.2(2)(a).

228 See Ch.4.

229 Recast Equal Treatment Directive, Art.2(1)(b); Racial Discrimination Directive, Art.2(2)(b); Framework Directive, Art.2(2)(b)(i).

such analysis can be applied in cases of direct discrimination.[230] This, of course, represents a strong contrast to the position adopted by the ECHR in relation to Art.14.

Nonetheless, the Directives do not apply in identical ranges of circumstances.[231] The recast Equal Treatment, Race Equality and Employment Equality Directives all regulate conditions of access to employment or occupation for both public and private bodies. The Directives cover selection criteria, recruitment conditions and promotion, access to vocational guidance and training, employment and working conditions (including dismissals and pay), and membership of or involvement in workers', employers' or professional associations.[232] The Race Equality Directive also prohibits discrimination in relation to social protection (including social security and health care), social advantages, education, and access to and the supply of goods and services available to the public (including housing).[233] However, the recast Equal Treatment Directive makes no reference to these areas and the Employment Equality Directive specifically excludes from its scope payments made by state social security or social protection schemes.[234] What this shows, of course, is that even in a discrimination law regime based on "fixed categories" (see Chapter 1), relevant categories need not be treated exactly alike.[235]

We now outline some of the main Directives, arranged according to the ground(s) of prohibited discrimination which they cover.

(i) *Sex discrimination*

Council Directive No.2006/54, on the implementation of the principle of equal opportunities and equal treatment of men and women in matters of employment and occupation (recast), Article 1:

"The purpose of this Directive is to ensure the implementation of the principle of equal opportunities and equal treatment of men and women in matters of employment and occupation.

To that end, it contains provisions to implement the principle of equal treatment in relation to:

(a) access to employment, including promotion, and to vocational training;

(b) working conditions, including pay;

230 See further Evelyn Ellis, *EU Anti-Discrimination Law, ibid.*, pp.111–113.
231 For general analysis, see Evelyn Ellis, *EU Anti-Discrimination Law, ibid.*, Ch.5.
232 Recast Equal Treatment Directive, Art.14; Racial Discrimination Directive, Art.3(1)(a) to (d); Framework Directive, Art.3(1).
233 Racial Discrimination Directive, Art.3 (1)(e) to (h).
234 Framework Directive, Art.3 (3).
235 Note also the variations designed to cater for different grounds of discrimination: Framework Directive, Art.5 (reasonable accommodation for disabled persons) and 6 (age); for discussion, see Evelyn Ellis, *EU Anti-Discrimination Law, ibid.*, pp.283–289, 292–296.

(c) occupational social security schemes."

As mentioned above, the "recast" Equal Treatment Directive (the ETD) consolidates Directive 76/207 and the previous Equal Pay Directive in the light of the case law of the European Court of Justice since their original passage.

Article 2(1)(a) defines direct discrimination as occurring "where one person is treated less favourably on grounds of sex than another is, has been or would be treated in a comparable situation", while Art.2(1)(b) defines indirect discrimination as occurring where "an apparently neutral provision, criterion or practice would put persons of one sex at a particular disadvantage compared with persons of the other sex, unless that provision, criterion or practice is objectively justified by a legitimate aim, and the means of achieving that aim are appropriate and necessary". Discrimination includes (Art.2(b)) an instruction to discriminate against a person on the ground of sex, and (Art.2(c)) less favourable treatment of a woman related to pregnancy or maternity leave.

Article 4 of the recast ETD prohibits direct and indirect discrimination "with regard to all aspects and conditions of remuneration" where "the same work or [...] work to which equal value is attributed" is involved. Article 5 prohibits direct or indirect discrimination in relation to occupational social security schemes, including in relation to contributions and the calculation of benefits (see also Arts 6 to 8 for the full range of schemes and workers covered). Article 14(1) prohibits direct and indirect discrimination in the public or private sectors, including public bodies, in relation to conditions for access to employment, to self-employment or to occupation, access to all types and to all levels of vocational guidance and training, employment and working conditions, including dismissals, and membership of, and involvement in, employers' or workers' organizations. Article 15 regulates maternity leave. The scope of the prohibition of sex discrimination in Art.141 EC was also provided for in the Goods and Services Directive (GSD) of 2004.[236] GSD Art.3 states that the principle of equal treatment between men and women applies to provisions of goods and services which are available to the public, as regards both the public and private sectors, and which are offered outside the area of private life and family life.

Harassment and sexual harassment are specifically included as forms of discrimination within the recast ETD. Harassment is defined in the recast ETD Art.2(1)(c) as occurring where:

"unwanted conduct related to the sex of a person occurs with the purpose or effect of violating the dignity of a person, and of creating an intimidating, hostile, degrading, humiliating or offensive environment".

Sexual harassment is defined in Art.2(1)(d) as occurring where:

[236] Council Directive 2004/113/EC of December 13, 2004.

"any form of unwanted verbal, non-verbal or physical conduct of a *sexual* nature occurs, with the purpose or effect of violating the dignity of a person, in particular when creating an intimidating, hostile, degrading, humiliating or offensive environment".

Recast ETD Art.2(2) categorises harassment and sexual harassment as forms of prohibited discrimination.

There are exceptions to the equal treatment principle and the application of Art.141 EC and the recast ETD. Recast ETD Art.8 exempts varies types of contract from its scope, while Art.14(2) stipulates that:

"Member States may provide, as regards access to employment including the training leading thereto, that a difference of treatment which is based on a characteristic related to sex shall not constitute discrimination where, by reason of the nature of the particular occupational activities concerned or of the context in which they are carried out, such a characteristic constitutes a genuine and determining occupational requirement, provided that its objective is legitimate and the requirement is proportionate."

Article 141 EC and the recast ETD specifically include provisions that permit positive action, which is a departure from the strict principle of equal treatment and which would otherwise fall within the definition of direct or indirect discrimination. Article 141(4) EC stipulates that:

"With a view to ensuring full equality in practice between men and women in working life, the principle of equal treatment shall not prevent any Member State from maintaining or adopting measures providing for specific advantages in order to make it easier for the underrepresented sex to pursue a vocational activity or to prevent or compensate for disadvantages in professional careers".

Recast ETD Art.3 allows member states to "maintain or adopt measures within the meaning of Article 141(4) of the Treaty with a view to ensuring full equality in practice between men and women in working life."

There are a number of other relevant directives in the field of EC sex discrimination law. These include the Pregnancy Directive[237] which introduces special regime for the protection pregnant workers. The Parental Leave Directive[238] establishes a framework agreement as part of EC social policy to enable the reconciliation of work and family life and for the promotion of equal opportunities between men and women. The Parental Leave Directive includes, inter alia, a right to parental leave for at least three months which is subject to justifiable exceptions by employers and time off work for urgent

[237] Council Directive 1992/85/EC.
[238] Council Directive 1996/34/EC.

family reasons. The Part Time-Work Directive[239] is also established as part of EC social policy and enacts a Framework Agreement to remove discrimination against part-time workers who are disproportionately women. Finally, equal treatment between men and women in the area of social security is ensured by the Social Security Directive.[240] This prohibits direct and indirect sex discrimination in social security and its scope extends to areas such as statutory sick pay and invalidity schemes, accidents at work, unemployment benefit and accidents at work.

(ii) *Race discrimination*

Council Directive 2000/43/EC of June 29, 2000 prohibiting discrimination in employment on the grounds of race and ethnic origin (O.J. [2000] L 180/22), Article 2(1):

"For the purposes of this Directive, the principle of equal treatment shall mean that there shall be no direct or indirect discrimination based on racial or ethnic origin."

The Race Equality Directive (RED) gives voice to the principle of equal treatment between persons irrespective of racial or ethnic origin. It extends to a wide range of areas (RED Art.3): employment and vocational training; social protection; social security; healthcare; social advantages; education; goods and services; and housing.

Article 2 defines defines discrimination as including direct and indirect discrimination and harassment based on racial or ethnic origin. *Direct discrimination* (RED Art.2(1)) is defined as: "taken to occur where one person is treated less favourably than another is, has been or would be treated in a comparable situation on grounds of racial or ethnic origin." *Indirect discrimination* is (RED Art.(2)(2)): "taken to occur where an apparently neutral provision, criterion or practice would put persons of a racial or ethnic origin at a particular disadvantage compared with other persons, unless that provision, criterion or practice is objectively justified by a legitimate aim and the means of achieving that aim are appropriate and necessary." *Harassment* is (RED Art 2(3)): "deemed to be discrimination within the meaning of paragraph 1, when an unwanted conduct related to racial or ethnic origin takes place with the purpose or effect of violating the dignity of a person and of creating an intimidating, hostile, degrading, humiliating or offensive environment. In this context, the concept of harassment may be defined in accordance with the national laws and practice of the Member State."

There are two types of exception to the principle of non-discrimination in

[239] Council Directive 1997/81/EC.
[240] Council Directive 1979/7/EC.

the RED: genuine and determining occupational requirements; and positive action. Article 4 states that:

"Member States may provide that a difference of treatment which is based on a characteristic related to racial or ethnic origin shall not constitute discrimination where, by reason of the nature of the particular occupational activities concerned or of the context in which they are carried out, such a characteristic constitutes a genuine and determining occupational requirement, provided that the objective is legitimate and the requirement is proportionate."

RED Art.5 deals with positive action:

"with a view to ensuring full equality in practice, the principle of equal treatment shall not prevent any Member State from maintaining or adopting specific measures to prevent or compensate for disadvantages linked to racial or ethnic origin."

(iii) *Sexual orientation; religion; disability and age*

Council Directive No.2000/78/EC of November 27, 2000, establishing a general framework for equal treatment in employment and occupation and applies to age, religion or belief, disability and sexual orientation (O.J. [2000] L 303/16), Article 2(1):

For the purposes of this Directive, the principle of equal treatment shall mean that there shall be no direct or indirect discrimination whatsoever on any of the grounds referred to in Article 1 [religion or belief, disability, age, sexual orientation].

EC sex and race discrimination law give extensive protection in areas such as employment and goods and services, and in the case of race discrimination in the area of social security and the like. EC discrimination law has a more limited scope in relation to other prohibited grounds, by contrast. The Employment Equality Directive (EED)[241] ensures that non-discrimination on the grounds of sexual orientation, religion, disability and age is only prohibited in the sphere of employment and training. EED Art.2 makes clear that in relation to these grounds (set out in EED Art.1) the principle of equal treatment shall mean that there is "no direct or indirect discrimination whatsoever". This applies to the following areas (EED Art.3): access to employment; vocational training; employment and working conditions including dismissal and pay; and membership of a worker's or professional

[241] Council Directive 2000/78/EC of November 27, 2000.

organisation. Discrimination includes direct and indirect discrimination and harassment (EED Art.2). *Direct discrimination* "shall be taken to occur where one person is treated less favourably than another is, has been or would be treated in a comparable situation" in relation to any of the grounds referred to in Art.1 (i.e religion or belief, disability, age, sexual orientation). *Indirect discrimination* is defined as:

(a) where an apparently neutral provision, criterion or practice would put persons having a particular religion or belief, or particular disability, a particular age, or a particular sexual orientation at a particular disadvantage compared with other persons; unless

(b) that provision, criterion or practice is objectively justified by a legitimate aim and the mans of achieving that aim are appropriate and necessary.

There is a particular provision in relation to indirect disability discrimination which states that:

"as regards persons with a particular disability, the employer or any person or organisation to whom this Directive applies, is obliged, under national legislation, to take appropriate measures in line with the principles contained in Article 5 [broad justification of direct discrimination under limited circumstances] in order to eliminate disadvantages entailed by such provision, criterion or practice." (EED Art.2(b)(iii)).

Harassment is also included within the definition of discrimination under the EED. Harassment is:

"deemed to be a form of discrimination within the meaning of paragraph 1, when unwanted conduct related to any of the grounds referred to in Article 1 takes place with the purpose or effect of violating the dignity of a person and of creating an intimidating, hostile, degrading, humiliating or offensive environment. In this context, the concept of harassment may be defined in accordance with the national laws and practice of the Member States."

General exceptions in the EED are similar to those in other Directives. EED Art.4 provides that difference of treatment is justified where there is a "genuine and determining occupational requirement, provided that the objective is legitimate and the requirement proportionate." However, there are also a number of distinct exceptions contained within the EED. The provision in EED Art.2(b)(iii) that protects exceptions to the principle of discrimination in order to accommodate those with disabilities has already been mentioned. In addition, EED Art.2(5) provides a broad justification for provisions which would otherwise amount to prohibited forms of direct discrimination. It states that: "This Directive shall be without prejudice to measures laid down by national law which, in a democratic society, are necessary for public security, for the maintenance of public order and the prevention of criminal offences, for the protection of health and for the protection of rights and freedoms of others." This provision mirrors the justificatory provisions contained in Arts 8(2) to 11(2) of the ECHR. Another exception is EED Art.3(3) that ensures that the EED does not apply to "payments of any kind made by state schemes or similar, including state social security or social protection." This is a significant difference in light of the fact that legislation such as the recast ETD and the Social Security Directive specifically prohibit sex discrimination in the context of state payments of this type, and the fact that the RDD extends to social protection, social security, and health-care.

The EED also contains exceptions that are more specific and linked to the distinct grounds that it regulates. For example, there is a specific exception in relation to religion or belief. EED Art.4(2) ensures that churches and other organisations with a "religious ethos" are permitted to undertake different treatment based on religion or belief. There are two aspects to this. Firstly, in relation to discrimination in employment EED Art.4(2) provides for a situation where the religion or belief is a relevant requirement for the particular individual and states:

"Member States may permit a difference of treatment 'in the case of occupational activities within churches and other public or private organisations the ethos of which is based on religion or belief' [where] by reason of the nature of these activities or of the context in which they are carried out, a person's religion or belief constitutes a genuine, legitimate and justified occupational requirement, having regard to the organisation's ethos."

The provision makes clear however that "This difference of treatment [...] should not justify discrimination on another ground" e.g sex, racial or ethnic origin, disability, age, or sexual orientation. Secondly, Art.4(2) provides for a group exception and states that "Provided that its provisions are otherwise complied with, this Directive shall thus not prejudice the right of churches and other public or private organisations, the ethos of which is based on religion or belief [...] to require individuals working for them to act in good faith and with loyalty to the organisation's ethos."

Other examples of exceptions are as follows. First, there is an exception in relation to reasonable accommodation for disabled persons. EED Art.5 allows employers to "take reasonable measures where needed in a particular case, to enable a person with a disability to have access to, participate in, or advance in employment, or to undergo training, unless such measures would impose a disproportionate burden on the employer." Second, for age there is a broad general justification for direct discrimination contained in EED Art.6 which allows differences in treatment based on age provided that they are "objectively and reasonably justified by a legitimate aim, including legitimate employment policy, labour market and vocational training objectives, and if the means for achieving that aim are appropriate and necessary." EED Art.6(1)(b)/(c) gives specific examples of permissible justifications, such as minimum requirements of age, professional experience and seniority in service; and the fixing of a maximum age for recruitment which is based on the training requirements of the post in question or the need for a reasonable period of employment before retirement. Third, Employment Equality Directive has an exception for positive action. EED Art.7 permits such measures: "With a view to ensuring full equality in practice, the principle of equal treatment shall not prevent any Member State from maintaining or adopting specific measures to prevent or compensate for disadvantages linked to any of the grounds [i.e religion or belief, disability, age or sexual orientation] referred to in Art.1."

C. *The Proportionality Test*

As a general matter—that is, thinking more broadly than EU non-discrimination measures—proportionality review as applied by the ECJ requires that a measure be suitable or appropriate, as well as necessary, to achieve the desired end, as well as (at least in some cases) proportionate to that end in the sense of not imposing a burden on the claimant which is disproportionate to the benefits secured (termed "proportionality *stricto sensu*" by Paul Craig), the ends which count as "desirable" being identified by the Court.[242] Furthermore, the intensity of proportionality review varies. Grainne de Burca thus argues that factors which appear to influence the intensity with which the ECJ will "examine a measure for proportionality" include "not just the subject matter of the dispute and the nature of the interests concerned in the case, but also matters relating to the limits of the judicial role and the judicial process".[243] In further detail, it is:

"apparent that in reaching decisions, the Court of Justice is influenced not only by what it considers to be the nature and importance of the interest or right claimed by the applicant, and the nature and importance of the objective alleged to be served by the measure, but by the relative expertise, position, and

[242] Paul Craig, *EU Administrative Law* (Oxford: Oxford University Press, 2006), pp.655–8, 670–2; note, however, that this is also a label which Craig deploys in relation to proportionality review in domestic law: see his *Administrative Law* (London: Sweet & Maxwell, 5th edn., 2003), pp.622–3. See also, on the distinction between "two-pronged" and "three-pronged" proportionality, Walter van Gerven, "The Effect of Proportionality on the Actions of Member States of the European Community: National Viewpoints from Continental Europe", in Evelyn Ellis (ed.), *The Principle of Proportionality in the Laws of Europe ibid.*, at pp.37–42; cf. Takis Tridimas, "Proportionality in Community Law: Searching for the Appropriate Standard of Scrutiny", in Evelyn Ellis (ed.), at pp.68–9.

[243] "The Principle of Proportionality and its Application in EC Law" (1993) 13 YBEL 105, 105–6.

overall competence of the Court as against the decision-making authority in assessing those factors."[244]

De Burca suggests, in relation to the variable intensity of review, that proportionality "covers a spectrum ranging from a very deferential approach, to quite a rigorous and searching examination of the justification for a measure which has been challenged".[245] Craig has thus argued that this seems to depend in part upon whether the ECJ (or Court of First Instance) is reviewing a Community or national measure, and in part upon the context[246]: for example, discretionary policy choices relating to Community regulatory initiatives such as the common agricultural policy tend to involve low intensity review, coupled with a sympathetic approach to objective justification and the differential treatment of previous compartmentalised markets,[247] while cases where the Courts perceive that a fundamental right recognised by the Community legal order is infringed by a policy choice might sometimes involve a stricter form of review.[248] Close scrutiny tends, in turn, to be deployed in cases involving penalties and financial burdens.[249] Intense proportionality scrutiny is also used where national measures which arguably violate one of the freedoms of movement of workers, services, establishment and capital are in issue.[250]

As de Burca has noted, the ECJ's perception of the divisions of competence within the Community's legal architecture can also influence the intensity with which it is willing to review national measures.[251] These divergences, in terms of intensity, are sometimes reflected in practice at the third (categorised by Craig as "*stricto sensu*") stage of the proportionality inquiry. In *United Kingdom v Council* (the "Working Time Directive case"), for example, the Court noted that "the Council must be allowed a wide discretion in an area which involves the legislature in making social policy choices and requires it to carry out complex assessments. Judicial review of the exercise of that discretion must therefore be limited to examining whether it has been vitiated by manifest error or misuse of powers, or whether the institution concerned has manifestly exceeded the limits of its discretion."[252] In other contexts, as de Burca has noted, the Court has used "many apparently different tests for proportionality—such as normal control, minimal control, strict scrutiny, the costs/benefits analysis, the 'not manifestly appropriate' test, or the 'no less restrictive

244 "The Principle of Proportionality and its Application in EC Law", *ibid.*, 111.
245 "The Principle of Proportionality and its Application in EC Law", *ibid.*, 111.
246 See also Francis G. Jacobs, "Recent Developments in the Principle of Proportionality in European Community Law", in Evelyn Ellis (ed.), *The Principle of Proportionality in the Laws of Europe op. cit.*
247 *EU Administrative Law*, *ibid.*, pp.658–672; see also Grainne de Burca, *ibid.*, at pp.115–126.
248 *EU Administrative Law*, *ibid.*, pp.672–681.
249 *EU Administrative Law*, *ibid.*, pp.681–5.
250 *EU Administrative Law*, *ibid.*, pp.687–94; see also Grainne de Burca, *ibid.*, at pp.126–145.
251 de Burca, *ibid.*, p.127.
252 Case C-331/88, *R. v Minister for Agriculture, Fisheries and Food and Secretary of State for Health, Ex p. Fedesa* [1990] ECR I-4012, paras [15]–[17].

means' test", depending upon "the nature and context of the various interests at stake",[253] and has even spoken—most unusually—of Member States enjoying a "margin of appreciation" (albeit relating to specific circumstances such as choice of the measures capable of achieving the aims of their policy, rather than in the more general sense employed by the ECHR) when converting Community measures regulating agriculture into national law or in relation to social and employment policy.[254]

Even within the ECJ's treatment of the prohibited grounds of discrimination, variations in the application of proportionality can also be seen.[255] Thus, Paul Craig has argued that while the ECJ tends to adopt a "strident" approach towards nationality discrimination in the context of the freedom of movement of workers, services, establishment and capital and also Art.12EC,[256] entailing high intensity judicial review in these contexts,[257] the case law dealing with discrimination in the context of Community regulatory initiatives involves low intensity review.[258] In the context of sex discrimination, the Court has seemingly varied somewhat in the intensity of review applied.[259] High intensity review is generally used in the area of equal pay, where the Court has repeatedly asserted that in determining whether an apparently indirectly discriminatory employment practice or national measure was capable of objective justification, the practice or measure must be shown to correspond to a real need, to be appropriate with a view to achieving the objectives pursued and to be necessary to that end:[260] a test described by Evelyn Ellis as setting "a formidable hurdle for a respondent seeking to justify indirectly discriminatory conduct … if reasonable alternative means are available to the respondent to attain the objective, the behaviour will breach the non-discrimination principle."[261] Proportionality is also used, albeit using a subtly different formulation,

253 "The Principle of Proportionality and its Application in EC Law", *ibid.*, p.113. For a useful, more recent survey, see Takis Tridimas, "Proportionality in Community Law: Searching for the Appropriate Standard of Scrutiny" in Evelyn Ellis (ed.) *The Principle of Proportionality in the Laws of Europe, ibid.*

254 Case 5/88, *Wachauf v Germany* [1989] ECR 2609, discussed in Grainne de Burca, *ibid.*, pp.123–6; see pp.147–8 for a more general analysis of circumstances in which the Court is prepared to be deferential. In relation to social and employment policy, see Case C-317/93, *Nolte v Landesversicherungsanstalt* [1995] ECR I-4625, para. [33] and Case C-167/97, *R. v Secretary of State for Employment, Ex p. Seymour-Smith* [1999] ECR I-623, paras [73]–[75].

255 See, generally, Evelyn Ellis, "The Concept of Proportionality in European Community Sex Discrimination Law", in Evelyn Ellis (ed.), *The Principle of Proportionality in the Laws of Europe* (*ibid.*).

256 *EU Administrative Law, ibid.*, pp.547, 548, 549.

257 *EU Administrative Law, ibid.*, pp.604–5; see also Catherine Barnard *The Substantive Law of the EU: The Four Freedoms* (Oxford: Oxford University Press, 2004), pp.78–82, 112–7.

258 *EU Administrative Law, ibid.*, pp.585, 604–5.

259 *EU Administrative Law, ibid.*, pp.605, 695–701.

260 See, e.g., Case 170/84, *Bilka-Kaufhaus v Weber von Hartz* [1986] ECR 1607, para. [36]; Case 171/88, *Rinner-Kuhn v FWW Spezial-Gebaudereinigung GmbH* [1989] ECR 2743; Case 184/89, *Nimz v Freie und Hansestadt Hamburg* [1991] ECR 297; Case C-167/97, *R. v Secretary of State for Employment, Ex p. Seymour-Smith* [1999] ECR I-623, para. [77]; Case C-381/99, *Brunnhofer v Bank der Osterreichischen Postsparkasse AG* [2001] ECR I-4961, paras [67]–[68]; Case C-256/01, *Allonby v Accrington and Rossendale College* [2004] ECR I-873.

261 *EU Anti-Discrimination Law, ibid.*, pp.109–110.

where the ECJ is measuring whether a Member State has legitimately asserted an exception to the principle of equal treatment: such aims are required to be "appropriate and necessary for achieving the aim in view" and to reconcile the principle of equal treatment, as far as possible, with the decisive justification for the existence of the exception,[262] with the scope of the relevant exception being interpreted strictly.[263] Nonetheless, as Evelyn Ellis has observed, there remain a number of EU staff and social security cases in which the ECJ has applied surprisingly low intensity review when considering the compatibility of allegedly indirectly discriminatory national measures.[264] Thus, in *Kirsammer-Hack v Sidal*, the Court noted that even if indirect discrimination had been established on a prima facie basis (it had not been, on the facts), it could have been justified—it seems without more—by the need to alleviate the constraints burdening small businesses, a very wide proposition which does not seem to have involved any need to demonstrate a tight correlation between the measure concerned and the aim.[265]

D. *Enforcement in Domestic Law*

EU law requires that there are effective sanctions for breach of any of the provisions of the discrimination law Directives. Generally, these consist of "disapplication" of national legislation which is incompatible with directly effective EU provisions, reinterpretation of national legislation so far as this is possible to ensure conformity with directly effective Directives, and damages for acts (including national legislation or failures to legislate) which breach EC law.

At domestic level, the House of Lords accepted in *R. v Secretary of State for Transport, Ex p. Factortame (No.2)* that legislation could be "disapplied" for incompatibility with directly effective provisions of EU law (in this case, concerning free movement of services).[266] As was acknowledged in *R. v Secretary of State for Employment, Ex p. Equal Opportunities Commission*, "disapplication" (or a declaration highlighting the incompatibility of domestic legislation) might be available in the case of directly effective Treaty Articles both "vertically"—that is, against "emanations of the state"—and "horizontally", against private bodies.[267] By contrast, Directives—including, in this

[262] Case 222/84, *Johnston v Chief Constable of the EUC* [1986] ECR 1651, para. [38].
[263] *ibid.*, para. [36].
[264] "The Concept of Proportionality in European Community Sex Discrimination Law", *ibid.*, pp.175–181.
[265] Case C-189/91, [1993] ECR I-6185.
[266] *R. v Secretary of State for Transport, Ex p. Factortame (No.2)* [1991] 1 A.C. 603 (in response to the ECJ's decision in Case C-213/89, *R. v Secretary of State for Transport, Ex p. Factortame* [1990] ECR 1-2433; compare the House of Lords' earlier treatment of the case in *R. v Secretary of State for Transport, Ex p. Factortame* [1990] 2 A.C. 85).
[267] [1995] 1 A.C. 1, 25–7 (Lord Keith).

context, the recast Equal Treatment Directive, the Race Equality Directive and the Employment Equality Directive—are only "vertically" directly effective.[268] Legislation must be interpreted, so far as possible and in either "horizontal" or "vertical" situations, in the light of Art.141 or any of the Directives.[269] Litigants may seek judicial review of executive action for incompatibility with directly effective provisions, and sue public authorities for damages for loss resulting from a failure to bring national law into line with such provisions or for executive action which contravenes them.[270]

At domestic level, courts have deployed proportionality analysis, with varying intensity, in assessing whether prima facie acts of discrimination can be justified where EU measures (or national measures designed to give effect to them) are in issue. For the present, the best examples, under the EU heading, of proportionality scrutiny are found within the context of *sex* discrimination claims. A good example of proportionality review at House of Lords level can be found in the *Equal Opportunities Commission* case. The claimants argued that provisions of the Employment Protection (Consolidation) Act 1978 which stipulated that employees had to have worked continuously for a specified number of years, the number concerned being tied to the number of hours per week worked (which were also required to be above a fixed minimum) in order to qualify for compensation for unfair dismissal and redundancy pay, discriminated against women because considerably more women than men worked part-time. Lord Keith made clear that in determining whether the impugned statutory provisions violated Art.141 EC (the right to equal pay) the court had to ask whether they were objectively justified, the onus of establishing justification lying on the respondent. Lord Keith concluded that while the aim of brining about an increase in the availability of part-time work (the policy justification advanced for the legislation) was a beneficial social policy aim and could not be said not to be necessary, the central question was whether the provisions "have been shown, by reference to objective factors, to be suitable and requisite for achieving that aim".[271] Proportionality analysis required, in other words, a suitably tight fit between the legislative provisions and the legitimate policy goal—something which the respondent could not establish on the facts given in particular the nationwide application of the measures to all part-time workers.

It should also be noted that the RED and ETD make provision for enforcement by administrative agencies as a supplement to individual remedies in discrimination law. Article 13 of the RED requires that:

268 See Mummery J.'s general analysis of the applicability of Directives in the context of discrimination in *MacMillan v Edinburgh Voluntary Organisations Council* [1995] I.R.L.R. 536.

269 See Case 14/83, *von Kolson and Kamann v Land Nordrhein-Westfalen* [1984] ECR 1891; Case C-106/89, *Marleasing SA v La Comercial Internacional de Alimentacion SA* [1990] ECR I-4135.

270 On damages actions see Case C-46/93 and C-48/93, *Brasserie du Pecheur SA v Germany* [1996] ECR I-1029.

271 [1995] 1 A.C. 1, 29.

"Member States shall designate a body or bodies for the promotion of all persons without discrimination on the grounds of racial or ethnic origin. These bodies may form part of the agencies charged at national level with the defence of human rights or the safeguard of individual's rights".

The functions of such a body include: providing individual assistance to victims of discrimination in pursuing their complaints about discrimination; conducting independent surveys concerning discrimination; and publishing reports and making recommendations on any issue relating to such discrimination. A similarly worded provision applies with respect to sex discrimination via Art.20(a) of the recast ETD, which requires the creation of a similar body with the same functions to pursue equal treatment between men and women. As we shall see below, a single enforcement agency—the Commission for Equality and Human Rights—now has responsibility for policing all prohibited grounds of discrimination in domestic law.

E. *Conclusion*

The EU law approach to protection against discrimination therefore suggests that, even where courts are not given the freedom to add to the list of prohibited grounds of discrimination (the "fixed categories" approach), the scope of application of the measures concerning the protected categories may vary somewhat, and some room may be left for judicial interpretation of the range of litigants or groups who can claim the protection of those categories, as *P v S* suggests. For the moment, given the relatively recent passage of the Framework Directive and Racial Discrimination Directive, the key examples of discrimination-related proportionality review are to be found in the nationality and sex discrimination cases. Here, we have seen that high intensity review is generally (but not universally) used. One might therefore imagine, given the similar drafting of all the relevant Directives in this regard, that the ECJ will use similar intensities of review with the wider range of grounds of discrimination which are prohibited in the post-Treaty of Amsterdam period. What this would suggest, in turn, is that while the evolution of EU law's approach to discrimination has turned crucially on the addition of new "fixed categories" in the Treaty and the legislative response to this, the character of this approach has also depended upon the Court of Justice's explanation and application of proportionality review. Even under a "fixed category" approach to discrimination law, in other words, courts can play a crucial role.

VI. Overlaps and Differences between EU Law and the Convention

As has been noted in previous sections, the key difference between Convention rights and directly effective norms of EU law relates to their differing legal weight. In domestic law, no ability to "disapply" exists in relation to Art.14 of the Convention (or other Convention rights), by contrast with EU law. Legislation must be interpreted, as far as this is possible, in the light of Convention rights and may be the subject of a declaration of incompatibility if compatible interpretation is impossible, leaving it to Parliament to determine whether to rectify the incompatibility. In *Ghaidan v Godin-Mendoza*, the remedial question facing the House of Lords was thus whether to make a declaration of incompatibility under s.4 of the Human Rights Act or to reinterpret under section 3, the most that could have been issued under s.4 being a declaration.[272] In addition, executive action which is incompatible with Convention rights and not sanctioned by legislation may be set aside in proceedings (usually for judicial review) brought under s.6. Convention rights may also influence the development of common law causes of action in cases involving private parties. By contrast, directly effective EU law rights have greater legal weight. Similarities exist in so far as national courts must interpret legislation in the light of directly effective rules of EU law. However, as was shown in the discrimination context in the *Equal Opportunities Commission* case, legislation must be set aside for incompatibility with directly effective rules of EC law. As Paul Craig suggests, there is "therefore an incentive for those minded to challenge primary legislation to do so through EU rights where that is possible".[273] We have also identified other differences in previous sections. For example, since Convention rights may be pleaded only in relation to subject-matters which fall within their ambit, Art.8 might be invoked in relation to military employment or housing but it is far from clear whether Art.14 may be relied upon in the context of private employment. By contrast, employment forms the major focus of most EU discrimination provisions. Furthermore, national courts may read new grounds of prohibited discrimination into Art.14 but not into directly effective EU discrimination norms, and the "discretionary area" approach to deference is applied in cases involving Convention rights but not (or not openly) in those involving EU law.

Despite these various differences, it is nonetheless clear that a certain range of cases may involve an overlap between the two jurisdictions: a phenomenon which is visible in the case law of the European Courts of Justice and Human Rights as well as at national level. At "European" level, as we have seen, both

272 For general analysis, see *Ghaidan v Godin-Mendoza* [2004] UKHL 30, [2004] 2 A.C. 557. Compare also: Danny Nicol, "Statutory interpretation and human rights after *Anderson*" [2004] P.L. 274; Aileen Kavanagh, "Statutory interpretation and human rights after *Anderson*: a more contextual approach" [2004] P.L. 537 and "Unlocking the Human Rights Act: The "Radical Approach to Section 3(1) Revisited" [2005] E.H.R.L.R. 259.

273 *EU Administrative Law*, *ibid.*, p.532.

EU law and the Convention contain protections against discrimination which, despite their differing ambits, sometimes apply to the same sets of facts. More generally, as Sionaidh Douglas-Scott has noted, "the Court of Justice began [in the 1970s] to develop its own human rights jurisdiction ... A variety of situations can now arise in which the ECJ, or the Court of First Instance, may have to assess a measure for its compatibility with human rights and there are human rights cases aplenty" in those courts.[274] In addition, "claims have also been brought to the European Court [of Human Rights] in Strasbourg, challenging the compatibility of certain EC and EU measures with the European Convention. ... So there exists an overlap of jurisdiction between the two courts, with, on some occasions, cases arising from the same State conduct being heard in both courts".[275] The *Bosphorous* cases provide a prominent example of a challenge to a state's implementation of an EU measure involving litigation before both Courts,[276] while in the discrimination context it was only the Court of Justice's decision in *Grant* v. *South-west Trains* which prevented exactly the same issue (dismissal from military employment due to a person's sexual orientation) from being litigated in parallel before the two Courts.[277] Less dramatically, but more frequently, each Court has cited the other's human rights case law—although commentators have sometimes questioned (including in the discrimination context) whether particular citations have been made with sufficient sensitivity to the details of the other Court's case law.[278]

At a national level, cases involving an overlap provide a strong illustration of the complications which can potentially arise due to the existence of bases of claim of differing weights and ambits. In English law, a vivid example can be found in *Chief Constable of the West Yorkshire Police v A (No.2)*, albeit in a claim under Art.8 involving what might colloquially be described as discrimination rather than a claim turning on Art.14. The claimant, a male-to-female transsexual, had applied to become a police constable. Since her application preceded the passage of the Gender Recognition Act 2004, she was still legally classified as a man. The Chief Constable rejected her application on the ground that the claimant could not lawfully perform the full searching duties required

274 Sionaidh Douglas-Scott, "A Tale of Two Courts: Luxembourg, Strasbourg and the Growing European Human Rights *Aquis*" (2006) 43 C.M.L. Rev. 629, 629.

275 Sionaidh Douglas-Scott, *ibid.*, 629–30.

276 Case C-84/95, *Bosphorous Hava Yollari Turzim Ve Ticaret Anonim Sirketi v Ireland* [1996] ECR I-3953 (Court of Justice); *Bosphorous Hava Yollari Ve Ticaret Anonim Sirketi v Ireland* (2006) 42 E.H.R.R. 1 (Court of Human Rights). For detailed analysis of cases involving "overlaps", see Helen Toner, *Partnership Rights, Free Movement and EU Law* (Oxford: Hart, 2004), Ch.4; Paul Craig and Grainne de Burca, *EU Law: Text, Cases, and Materials* (Oxford: Oxford University Press, 4th edn., 2008), pp. 420–6.

277 Case C-249/96, *Grant* v. *South-west Trains* [1998] ECR I-. The military employment issue had previously been referred to the Court of Justice in *Perkins*, but the reference was withdrawn in the light of *Grant*. At the same time, however, two cases involving military employment were successfully litigated before the Court of Human Rights: *Smith v United Kingdom, Lustig-Preen v United Kingdom*; for commentary, see Nicholas Bamforth, "Sexual Orientation Discrimination after *Grant* v. *South-west Trains*" (2000) 63 M.L.R. 694 .

278 See, e.g., Sionaidh Douglas-Scott, *ibid.*, 640–4; Nicholas Bamforth, *ibid.*

of a police constable, it being a genuine occupational qualification under s.7 of the 1975 Act for a constable to be of the same sex as those being searched. Sections 54(9) and 55(7) of the Police and Criminal Evidence Act 1984 stipulated that suspects could be searched or subjected to intimate searches only by constables of the same sex, precluding the claimant from searching female suspects since she was still legally a man. Furthermore, since the applicable Code of Practice, prescribed under s.66 of the Act, stipulated that every reasonable effort had to be made to minimise the embarrassment caused to a person being searched, the claimant could not search men either: in Baroness Hale's words, "because to all intents and purposes she is a woman, a man might reasonably object to her carrying out a search upon him."[279] Given the requirement that national courts interpret legislation as far as it is possible to do so in the light of directly effective EU law and Convention rights, two connected questions arose in determining whether the denial of employment constituted unlawful discrimination contrary to the Sex Discrimination Act 1975: first, whether it was necessary to interpret the 1975 Act in the light of Art.8 of the Convention *as well as* the Equal Treatment Directive; and secondly, whether such interpretation should be conducted in the light of the Art.8 case law as it stood in 1998, when the Chief Constable had rejected the claimant's application, or as it stood at the time of the case. The second, timing-related issue was important due to a radical alteration in the position adopted in the Convention case law.

On the EU side, the ECJ's decision in *P. v S.*—from before *A (No.2)* arose in the domestic courts—had made clear that the Equal Treatment Directive prohibits, as a form of sex discrimination, unfavourable treatment in employment due to gender reassignment.[280] As a result, the 1975 Act had been amended by the Sex Discrimination (Gender Reassignment) Regulations 1999 so as clearly to prohibit discrimination against transsexuals. However, it was common ground in *A (No.2)* that since the case had arisen before the passage of the Regulations, it fell to be decided under the unamended 1975 Act (albeit interpreted in the light of *P. v S.*).[281] On the Convention side, the Court of Human Rights had determined in *Goodwin v United Kingdom*, in a very clear departure from its earlier case law,[282] that refusal to alter the sex of a post-operative transsexual as registered on their birth certificate (thereby preventing them from marrying a person of the opposite sex to their reassigned sex) violated the Art.8 right to respect for private life and the Art.12 right to marry.[283] As a result of *Goodwin*, the House of Lords had accepted in *Bellinger v*

[279] [2004] UKHL 21, para. [33]. See also the Court of Appeal decision at [2002] EWCA Civ 1584 and *R. (Amicus) v Secretary of State for Trade and Industry* [2004] EWHC Admin 869; [2007] I.C.R. 1176.

[280] Case C-13/94, [1996] ECR I-2143; see also Case C-117/01, *K.B. v National Health Services Pensions Agency* [2004] ECR I-541 (equal pay).

[281] See *A (No.2)* per Lord Rodger at para.[17].

[282] Namely *Rees v United Kingdom* (1986) 9 E.H.R.R. 56; *Cossey v United Kingdom* (1990) 13 E.H.R.R. 622; and *Sheffield and Horsham v United Kingdom* (1998) 27 E.H.R.R. 163.

[283] (2002) 35 E.H.R.R. 447.

Bellinger that s.11(c) of the Matrimonial Causes Act 1973 was incompatible with Arts 8 and 12 in so far as it prevented post-operative transsexuals from marrying—resulting in turn in the passage of the Gender Recognition Act 2004.[284] However, *Goodwin* had only been decided in 2002; at the time that *A (No.2)* arose, the proposition that Arts 8 and 12 did not require that transsexuals be allowed to alter the sex on their birth certificate was still good law at Strasbourg level. A finding that the 1998 interpretation of the Convention was to be applied might thus have appeared to create a conflict for domestic courts, while a finding that the post-*Goodwin* interpretation should be used might have been felt to strengthen the claimant's case.

The Court of Appeal ruled in *A (No.2)* that the 1975 Act had to be read in the light of the Equal Treatment Directive as it operated in 1998, which had *in turn* to be read in the light of the Court of Human Rights' interpretation of relevant Convention rights in *Goodwin*.[285] In consequence, the Chief Constable could not claim that he could legitimately treat the claimant unfavourably under the 1975 Act: the refusal of the 1975 Act, as it stood when the claim arose, to recognise the claimant's gender reassignment was a breach of her rights under Arts 8 and 12 of the Convention. In reaching this conclusion, the Court of Appeal crucially accepted that since decisions concerning the interpretation of EU measures normally operate retrospectively, the Equal Treatment Directive should be interpreted in the light of *Goodwin* despite the fact that the Strasbourg Court's change of position in *Goodwin* rested on its perception that the ambit of the "margin of appreciation" open to Convention signatory states when dealing with the legal rights of transsexuals had altered, meaning that the decision could be deemed only to operate "prospectively".[286] Buxton L.J. also pointed out that since Art.8 is a "qualified" Convention right, the national court might have to evaluate the Chief Constable's decision using the Art.8 proportionality test. This notion is of real significance, given that it suggests that a Convention test might be employed when interpreting the application of an EU Directive in *national* law.

Although the House of Lords affirmed the Court of Appeal's decision that the refusal to employ the claimant was impermissible under the 1975 Act, Lord Bingham and Baroness Hale—who delivered the key judgments—largely avoided the question of overlap between the Convention and EU law and instead interpreted the 1975 Act in the light of the Directive alone.[287] For Lord Bingham, *Bellinger v Bellinger* could be distinguished because it concerned marriage and "lacked any [European] Community dimension", including any reference to the decision in *P v S*.[288] Similarly, Baroness Hale categorized

[284] [2003] UKHL 21, [2003] 2 A.C. 467.
[285] [2002] EWCA Civ 1584; [2003] I.C.R. 161; note also Baroness Hale's summary in the House of Lords: *ibid.*, para. [46].
[286] See *A (No.2)* per Baroness Hale's summary at para.[47].
[287] Lord Rodger arrived at the same conclusion but using slightly different reasoning and without mentioning the Convention; Lord Steyn and Lord Carswell agreed with Lord Bingham and Baroness Hale.
[288] *ibid.*, para.[12].

Bellinger as being concerned (unlike the case at hand) with marriage rights, and observed that *P v S* had not in fact been cited to the House of Lords in that case.[289] Both stressed that more broadly, the Human Rights Act did not generally have retrospective effect, and the decision in *Goodwin* could be distinguished as being of an essentially prospective character given that it relied for its force on the notion that there had been a shift in the margin of appreciation.[290] Baroness Hale was clear that "the *Goodwin* decision did not require that the Equal Treatment Directive be interpreted as if *Goodwin* had been the law from the moment the Directive came into effect."[291] Instead, the case had to turn on the claimant's rights under the Equal Treatment Directive as it stood in 1998, albeit interpreted in the light of *P v S*, rather than upon the impact of *Goodwin*.[292] Lord Bingham and Baroness Hale were both clear that when interpreted in this light, the Directive gave effect to the rights of transsexual persons to be recognised in their reassigned gender and to be free from discrimination. When read in the light of this obligation, the same-sex requirement imposed for searching by the 1975 and 1984 Acts had to be taken to refer to the acquired gender of a post-operative transsexual, so that the Chief Constable was in breach of the 1975 Act when he refused to employ the claimant.[293]

Although the overlap question was avoided by the House of Lords in *A (No. 2)*, two points stand out as being of particular interest. The first is that both Lord Bingham and Baroness Hale took care to stress the common values shared by EC law and the Convention. Lord Bingham suggested that the "importance of the Convention in this appeal derives not from the decision in *Goodwin* but from the part which the Convention has played in shaping the current European understanding of what fundamental human rights require and mean."[294] Meanwhile, Baroness Hale stressed that the "human rights values which led to" the *Goodwin* decision "also underpin the EC legislation", that is, the Equal Treatment Directive.[295] While Lord Bingham's observation appears to be less specifically-focused than Baroness Hale's, by stressing the unity of values within the Convention and EU law (whether generally or specifically) both judges may well have been trying to indicate that, regardless of their origins (or consequent legal weight) legal protections against invidious forms of discrimination need to be understood as serving a common goal. The second point is that, while the House of Lords avoided the overlap problem in *A (No.2)* itself, this was only because of the interpretation placed on the *Goodwin* case. If the Strasbourg Court in *Goodwin* had not invoked the margin of appreciation so prominently, it is hard to claim with confidence—especially

289 *ibid.*, para.[41].
290 *ibid.*, Lord Bingham, para.[13] (note also his observaion that the House had adopted the same characterisation of *Goodwin* in *Bellinger*, at para. [24]); Baroness Hale, paras [41] and [53].
291 *ibid.*, para.[53].
292 *ibid.*, para.[50]; see also para.[63].
293 paras [10]–[11], [13] (Lord Bingham), [55]–[59], [63] (Baroness Hale).
294 para.[13].
295 para.[54].

given the emphasis placed on the common values of the Convention and EU law in the non-discrimination field—that the House of Lords would not have allowed the Directive to be interpreted in the light of the Convention. In an area such as racial discrimination, in which the EU is a relatively new actor on the scene by contrast with the Strasbourg Court, such an outcome might indeed be likely (and is certainly not precluded by *A (No. 2)*). Nonetheless, *A (No.2)* still serves to highlight the divergences between the Strasbourg and EU approaches to protections against discrimination, in so far as the weight of the Strasbourg approach at national level is weakened by the margin of appreciation—a phenomenon which is not present in the House of Lords' treatment of the Equal Treatment Directive.[296] *A (No. 2)* thus provides a vital illustration of the phenomenon of differing legal weight in the context of an individual case at national level.

VII. Domestic Statutory Protections against Discrimination

Nowadays there are a very large number of pieces of primary or secondary legislation—some inspired by domestic policy imperatives but generally designed to ensure compliance with EU law—dealing with the prohibited grounds of discrimination. The sheer number of measures is enough on its own to make contemporary domestic law appear extremely complicated, but further complexity stems from the fact that such measures operate against the backdrop of, and must be read in the light of, the various EU non-discrimination guarantees that have direct effect in domestic law, *as well as* of the Human Rights Act's protection of Art.14 and other Convention rights which are relevant in the discrimination context. Any attempt to harmonise or otherwise reform domestic law will therefore need to take account of the differing legal weight (discussed in previous sections) of Convention rights and rules of EU law: something which, as we will see in Section VIII, may undermine the recommendation of the government's Discrimination Law Review (DLR) (discussed in Section II) that a single statute be introduced to harmonise all the strands of domestic discrimination law.

In this section, we provide an introduction to relevant domestic primary and secondary legislation, which will be discussed further in later chapters. We discuss the different prohibited grounds of discrimination in thematic order, as in Pt C of the book, given the analogies or potential overlaps in coverage between some of them (for example, sex and sexual orientation, and race and religion). However, as the SDA and RRA historically preceded the prohibitions more recently created in the areas of sexual orientation, religion, dis-

[296] Note, however, that the ECJ sometimes takes account of what it deems to be a commonly held position among Member States: see *Grant v South-west Trains, ibid., D. and Sweden v Council, ibid.*, and *KB v Secretary of State for Health, ibid.*, discussed at length in Ch.11.

ability and age, it is no surprise that the earlier legislation tends to form a reference point for later primary or secondary legislation dealing with other prohibited grounds of discrimination. As such, the SDA and RRA might be described as the legislation which most clearly illustrates the form, content and procedures of domestic discrimination law. For this reason, this section focusses on these pieces of legislation in rather greater detail than on later primary or secondary legislation governing disability, sexual orientation, religious and age discrimination (all of which will be dealt with in Pt C).

Two general points are worth stressing at the outset. The first is that the "generational" development of discrimination law (discussed in Chapter 1 and in Section II of the present chapter), is illustrated in detail by the primary and secondary legislation discussed in the present section. The Equal Pay Act 1970 (EqPA), Sex Discrimination Act 1975 (SDA) and Race Relations Act 1976 (RRA) constitute "third generation" responses to sex and race discrimination, and, as such, focus on discrimination in employment, as well as offering some coverage in areas such as education, housing and the provision of goods and services.[297] Much of the more recent primary and secondary legislation has been designed to ensure compliance with EU discrimination law and thus covers additional grounds such as disability, religion, sexual orientation and age. However, the material scope of discrimination law has also shifted beyond the focus on employment to include areas such as the provision of public services. If the recommendations of the Discrimination Law Review are implemented, we will see a further "reform" stage that seeks to eliminate differences between the law's regulation of the different prohibited grounds of discrimination through a strategy of "harmonisation" via the passage of a single non-discrimination statute covering all prohibited grounds, replacing the large and sometimes incoherent collection of primary and secondary measures which currently exist.

The second general point is that, as in previous sections, relevant provisions are considered by reference to the key questions of discrimination law outlined in Chapter 1. In the context of domestic primary and secondary legislation, the first to fourth questions ('who is to be protected?'; 'when are they protected?'; 'against what are they protected?'; and 'how wide are the protections?') are of particular significance. Outside of the present section, they are also discussed in detail in Pts B and C of the book. The sixth question, dealing with conflicts between non-discrimination and other rights, is also important given that the proliferation of prohibited grounds of discrimination in domestic law increases the possibility of conflicts between grounds of discrimination as well as between non-discrimination and other rights which are protected, for example, under the European Convention on Human Rights. Outside of the present section, issues falling under this heading are dealt with

[297] For definitions of the terms "employment", "education", "housing" and "goods and services" see the discussion in Aileen McColgan, *Discrimination Law: Text, Cases and Materials*, (Oxford: Hart, 2nd edn, 2005), Ch.4.

in Chapter 9, concerning multiple discrimination and intersections between prohibited grounds, and in Chs 11 and 13 in relation to conflicts between non-discrimination on the grounds of sexual orientation and religion. Domestic legislation deals in detail with the sixth and seventh key questions (concerning situations in which otherwise discriminatory acts may be justified, and exceptions which can "lift out" protection from discrimination in some areas), for example under headings such as genuine occupational requirements and exceptions based on national security and immigration. Outside of the present section, such issues are dealt with in Pt C of the book. The ninth key question, concerning the availability of remedies for prohibited discrimination, is answered by domestic legislation in a variety of ways, varying in part according to the ground of discrimination in issue. "Individual" remedies are enforceable against private parties (such as employers) and also sometimes public bodies (e.g. local authorities), the forum for enforcement varying between specialist employment tribunals and the County Court. At a "collective" level, separate commissions—the Commission for Racial Equality, Equal Opportunities Commission, and Disability Rights Commission—were charged, prior to the Equality Act 2006, with the enforcement of protections against race, sex and disability discrimination respectively. The Equality Act 2006 has dissolved the individual commissions and transferred their key functions to a new single equality body called the Commission for Equality and Human Rights. Outside of the present section, the ninth key question (and the tenth, dealing with the use of non-legal solutions to discrimination) is dealt with in Pt D of the book. Since domestic legislation must be read in the light of directly effective EU requirements and (where relevant) Art.14 and other Convention rights, the ECJ's and ECHR's treatments of the key questions are of great practical significance to the treatment of non-discrimination provisions at a domestic level (and will be included wherever relevant in later chapters). However, since EU and European Convention non-discrimination provisions have been considered in detail earlier in the present chapter (in particular, in relation to the sixth and seventh key questions), they need not be discussed again in detail here.

A. *Sex Discrimination*[298]

The two main pieces of primary legislation dealing with sex discrimination are the EqPA and the SDA. The EqPA prohibits pay discrimination between men and women and ensures compliance with Art.141 of the EC. The SDA, which prohibits discrimination on the ground of sex in a range of areas, was introduced as part of a domestic political initiative designed to promote equality for women and ethnic minorities—a concept that was captured in the

[298] See further Ch.10.

pre-legislative White Papers *Equality for Women* and *Racial Discrimination*.[299] Subsequent developments in EU sex discrimination law have meant that the SDA has been subject to ongoing amendment, including piecemeal changes to the definition of discrimination and the burden of proof (see the earlier discussion of EU developments in Section IV). In consequence, the definitions of prohibited discrimination under the SDA now vary according to the sphere in which an alleged act of discrimination has occurred. In this sub-section, we therefore discuss the definitions of prohibited "sex" discrimination, the coverage of the relevant legal prohibitions, positive action and the duty to promote gender equality, and the exceptions to relevant prohibitions.

Significantly, the provisions of the SDA are symmetrical:[300] in other words, s.2(1) of the SDA states that the provisions of the Act "relating to sex discrimination against women, are to be read as applying equally to the treatment of men, and for that purpose shall have effect with such modifications as are requisite". This ensures that the answer to the first key question of discrimination law, namely "who is protected?", is that both women and men are protected. The fact that men are protected against sex discrimination under the SDA is not controversial. There are, however, certain distinct issues that relate to the characteristic "sex" that have caused problems. To take one example, the question of how to treat discrimination on the ground of pregnancy caused great difficulty, mainly because it was impossible to find an appropriate male comparator to a pregnant woman. We first encountered the issue of comparators in section III in the context of Art.14 of the Convention. The requirement to undertake a 'comparison' under the SDA is set out in s.5(3), which states that there must be a comparator in cases of direct and indirect discrimination (s.1) and discrimination on the ground of gender reassignment (s.2). The "relevant circumstances" in the case of the claimant are required to be "the same, or not materially different from" those which prevail in "the other"—i.e. in the case of the comparator. When determining whether unfavourable treatment of a pregnant female employee constituted sex discrimination, domestic courts struggled and, after initially suggesting that dismissing a woman because she was pregnant did not amount to direct discrimination, tried to use a hypothetical sick man as a comparator—a solution which was unworkable and arguably demeaning to women.[301]

The ECJ has intervened to resolve this difficulty by decreeing that a comparator is, in general, unnecessary in pregnancy cases (so that discrimination

299 Cmnd.5724 (London: H.M.S.O., 1974) and Cmnd.6234 (London: H.M.S.O., 1975) respectively.

300 For a critique of the symmetrical nature of sex discrimination law, see Nicola Lacey, 'From Individual to Group? A Feminist Analysis of the Limits of Anti-Discrimination Legislation?' in Nicola Lacey, *Unspeakable Subjects: Feminist Essays in Legal and Social Theory* (Oxford: Hart, 1998), p.19.

301 See, for example, *Turley v Allders Department Stores Ltd* [1980] I.C.R. 66 (but compare *Hurley v Mustoe* [1981] I.C.R. 490, dealing with a female employee with young children); *Hayes v Malleable Working Men's Club* [1985] I.C.R. 703.

on the ground of pregnancy is per se sex discrimination),[302] and s.3(A) of the SDA now makes special provision for pregnancy and maternity leave by stipulating that a person discriminates against a woman if, during the protected period of pregnancy or maternity leave, and on the ground of the woman's pregnancy, "the person treats her less favourably than he would treat her had she not become pregnant". Discrimination against a woman on the ground of her exercise (past, present or future) of the statutory right to maternity leave is also prohibited. Moreover, s.2(2) of the SDA states that in relation to the comparator requirement "no account shall be taken of special treatment afforded to women in connection with pregnancy or childbirth."

A second problematical example concerned the question whether discrimination on the ground of sex included discrimination due to a person's sexual orientation or gender reassignment. The ECJ found in *P v S and Cornwall County Council* that the term "sex" included gender reassignment in a claim based on Art.141EC,[303] but in *Grant v. South-west Trains Ltd.* that discrimination on the basis of sexual orientation did not constitute unlawful sex discrimination[304] (a position later confirmed in domestic law in relation to harassment and dismissal from employment.[305]) As a result of *P v S*, the SDA was amended, via the Gender Reassignment Regulations 1999, to prohibit discrimination on the ground of gender reassignment (see further below). Issues relating to those who choose to adopt different dress codes (for example, men who choose to wear female clothing or vice versa) are not covered by the provisions on gender reassignment. Sexual orientation discrimination is now precluded in its own right under domestic secondary legislation (see below) but—as we will see in Chapter 11—conceptual problems are posed by the question why discrimination on the ground of gender reassignment constitutes a form of prohibited sex discrimination while discrimination on the ground of sexual orientation does not.

The headings under which discrimination is prohibited are relevant when considering the fourth key question of discrimination law, namely the width of protections against discrimination. The definition of direct discrimination is set out in ss.1(1) and 1(2) of the SDA, and applies in all areas in which discrimination is prohibited including employment and training, housing, and the provision of education, goods, facilities and services. Direct discrimination occurs where "on the ground of her sex he [the alleged discriminator] treats her [the claimant] less favourably than he treats or would treat a man" (SDA, s.1(1)(a) and 1(2)(a)). In *James v Eastleigh Borough Council*, the House of Lords held (in an analysis which has also been applied to racial discrimination) that direct discrimination does not require that there be an intention to dis-

302 Case C-32/93, *Webb v EMO Air Cargo (UK) Ltd* [1994] E.C.R. I-3567, followed by the House of Lords in *Webb v EMO Air Cargo (UK) Ltd (No.2)* [1995] I.C.R. 1021.

303 Case C-13/94, [1996] ECR I-2143.

304 Case C-249/96 [1998] E. C. R. I-621.

305 *MacDonald v Advocate General for Scotland; Pearce v Governing Body of Mayfield School*[2003] UKHL 34.

criminate: all that is required is a causal link so that it is possible to say that "but for" the act of the discriminator the victim would not have suffered less favourable treatment.[306]

The definition of indirect sex discrimination, by contrast, varies depending on the context. Section 1(1) of the SDA therefore defines indirect discrimination in all areas except employment and training (e.g. education and the provision of goods, facilities and services); whereas s.1(2) of the SDA applies only to employment and training. Indirect sex discrimination under s.1(1)(b) occurs where "he [the alleged discriminator] applies to her [the claimant] a requirement or condition which he applies or would apply to a man but (i) which is such that the proportion of women who can comply with it is considerably smaller than the proportion of men who can comply with it, and (ii) which he cannot show to be justifiable irrespective of the sex of the person to whom it is applied, and (iii) which is to her detriment because she cannot comply with it".

Indirect sex discrimination in employment and training, by contrast, is defined under s.1(2) of the SDA in a different way so as to ensure compliance with EU law: it therefore occurs where a person applies to a woman "a provision, criterion or practice which he applies or would apply equally to a man, but (i) which puts or would put women at a particular disadvantage when compared with men, and (ii) which puts her at that disadvantage, and (iii) which he cannot show to be a proportionate means of achieving a legitimate aim". It is to be hoped, for the avoidance of confusion, that courts will interpret the two definitions in similar fashion (see further Ch.4). Domestic courts are gradually developing a more robust approach to the 'justifiability' defence in indirect sex discrimination cases.[307]

The SDA also prohibits sexual harassment and victimisation. Previous case law on sexual harassment under the SDA caused problems because of the need to find a comparator before treatment could be deemed to be "discriminatory" on the ground of sex.[308] This problem has now been overcome by the introduction of new definitions of discrimination in the ETD and EED, which explicitly state that harassment is a form of discrimination. First, s.4A of the SDA introduces the definition of harassment in the ETD into domestic law. It prohibits both harassment where "on the ground of her [the complainant's] sex" a discriminator "engages in unwanted conduct" or in "any form of unwanted verbal, non-verbal or physical conduct of a sexual nature" which in either case has the purpose or effect of "(i) violating her dignity, or (ii) of

306 [1990] 2 A.C. 751. See also *Nagarajan v London Regional Transport* [2000] 1 A.C. 501 (HL); *Khan v Chief Constable of West Yorkshire Police* [2001] I W.L.R. 1947 (HL); and *Shamoon v Chief Constable of Royal Ulster Constabulary* [2003] I.C.R. 337. The extent to which *James* remains unqualified by these subsequent cases see Ch.4; see also Lizzie Barmes, 'Promoting Diversity and the Definition of Direct Discrimination' (2003) 32 I.L.J. 200; Bob Watt, 'Goodbye 'but for', hello 'but why?' (1998) 27 I.L.J. 121.

307 *London Underground v Edwards* [1985] I. C. R. 574 (E.A.T.).

308 See, e.g. *Stewart v Cleveland Guest (Engineering) Ltd* [1996] I. C. R. 535 and *British Telecoms Plc v Williams* [1997] I.R.L.R. 668.

creating an intimidating, hostile, degrading, humiliating or offensive environment for her''. Whether there has been harassment is determined ''having regard to all the circumstances, including in particular the perception of the woman, it should reasonably be considered as having that effect'' (s.4A(2)). Less favourable treatment that is based on the rejection of, or submission to, sexual harassment as defined in s.4A of the SDA is also prohibited. The provisions relating to sexual harassment also apply to men (s.4A(5)), and harassment because of gender reassignment is prohibited (s.4A(3)).

Victimisation is defined in s.4(1) of the SDA as less favourable treatment of an individual by reason of the fact that the person victimised has: ''(a) brought proceedings against the discriminator or any other person'' under the EqPA, SDA or ss.62 to 65 of the Pensions Act 1995, or has ''(b) given evidence or information in connection with proceedings brought by any person against the discriminator or any other person'' under such legislation, or has ''(c) otherwise done anything under or by reference to'' such legislation ''in relation to the discriminator or any other person'', or has ''(d) alleged that the discriminator or any other person has committed an act which (whether or not the allegation so states) would amount to a contravention'' of such legislation. Victimisation can also be established when the discriminator knows that the person victimised intends to do any of those things, or suspects that the person victimised has done, or intends to do, any of them.[309] The victimisation provisions do not apply ''to treatment of a person by reason of any allegation made by him if the allegation was false and not made in good faith'' (s.4(2) of the SDA).

The second key question of discrimination law ('when are claimants protected?') is crucial in determining the range of subject-areas in which domestic sex discrimination law applies. The SDA prohibits sex discrimination in employment (Pt II) and in the provision of goods and services (Pt III). Section 6(1) of the SDA specifies that discrimination is unlawful in the arrangements an employer makes for the purpose of determining who should be offered employment, the terms on which employment is offered, and in the refusal or deliberate omission to offer employment. Section 6(2) of the SDA extends protection against sex discrimination to access to opportunities for promotion, transfer or training, to any other benefits, facilities or services, to refusals or deliberate omissions to afford access to them, and to dismissals or any other detriment. These protections apply to a woman whom the employer employs and to a woman who has applied for employment (s.2(A)).

Most of the requirements of the EU Goods and Services Directive (GSD) were already provided for in the SDA, but the Sex Discrimination Act 1975 (Amendment) Regulations 2007 have been brought into force to make provision for remaining disparities. Specific examples of goods and services are set out in Pt III of the SDA. Section 29(2) of the SDA includes access to and use of any place which members of the public or a section of the public are permitted

[309] See further Ch.4 and, for example, *Nagarajan v London Regional Transport* [2000] 1 A.C. 501 (HL).

to enter; accommodation in a hotel, boarding house or other similar establishment; facilities by way of banking or insurance or grants, loans, credit and finance; facilities for education; facilities for entertainment, recreation or refreshment; facilities for transport or travel; and the services of any profession or trade, or any local or other public authority. The types of conduct covered include refusing or deliberately omitting to provide a woman with goods, facilities and services, and refusing or deliberately omitting to provide a woman with goods, facilities or services of the like quality, in the like manner and on the like terms as are normal in his case in relation to male members of the public (s.29(1)).

These provisions will obviously cover explicit cases of discrimination such as a refusal to sell goods or to provide services to a woman or man. There is little case law, but prominent examples include the refusal of a wine bar to serve women unless they were seated,[310] a shop's refusal to extend credit facilities to a woman unless she used her husband as a guarantor,[311] the refusal by a magazine to accept an advertisement for a cook from a man,[312] and—in *James v Eastleigh*—differential charging for access to a swimming pool.[313] Exceptions include the area of insurance, where it is permissible for those who are involved in the assessment of risk to engage in differential treatment in reliance on actuarial or other statistical information from a source on which it was reasonable to rely, where such reliance was reasonable having regard to the data and other relevant factors (s.45 of the SDA).

The SDA also prohibits discrimination in the provision of housing. Section 30 provides that it is unlawful for a person to discriminate on the ground of sex in the provision of premises over which he has power or which he manages. This covers commercial and domestic lettings and includes the terms on which the premises are offered; refusal of applications; eviction; and access to benefits or facilities. It also covers short-term leases and the hire of rooms in houses. The hire of a hotel room which does not create a property right will be covered by the prohibitions on goods and services. There are limited exceptions to these provisions, as set out in ss.31(2) and 32 of the SDA. These include privacy-related situations where the discriminator or a near relative resides or intends to reside on the premises; or where the premises are "small premises", i.e. for residential accommodation this is in relation to no more than two households or where there are not normally more than six persons (in addition to the relevant occupier and his household) resident on the premises.

Positive action measures are generally not permitted under the SDA, but there are limited exceptions (this issue is therefore arguably relevant, depending upon one's view of positive action measures (see further Chapter 6), to the fifth key question of discrimination law, namely whether discrimination can sometimes be justified for policy reasons). First, s.47(1) of the

310 *Gill v El Vino Co Ltd* [1983] Q.B. 425.
311 *Quinn v Williams Furniture Ltd* [1981] I.C.R. 328.
312 *Bain v Bowles* [1991] I.R.L.R. 356.
313 *James v Eastleigh Borough Council* [1990] 2 A.C. 751.

SDA echoes EU sex discrimination law by permitting positive action in employment and vocational training where: (a) "it reasonably appears to" the person acting "that at any time within the 12 months immediately preceding the doing of the act there were no persons of the sex in question doing that work in Great Britain, or the number of persons of that sex doing the work in Great Britain was comparatively small"; or (b) "where it reasonably appears to that person that those persons are in special need of training by reason of the period for which they have been discharging domestic or family responsibilities to the exclusion of regular full time employment". Secondly, a significant form of positive action to promote the greater participation of women in politics is permitted.[314]

Section 42A of the SDA (inserted under the Sex Discrimination (Election Candidates Act) 2002) allows for positive action by political parties in selecting candidates where the measures are made by a registered political party and "are adopted for the purpose of reducing inequality in the numbers of men and women elected, as candidates of the party, to be members of the body concerned". This ensures that women-only short lists for election candidates are not covered by the general principles of domestic sex discrimination law.

In relation to positive duties, Pt 4 of the Equality Act 2006 (especially s.84) amends the SDA and the EqPA (as already amended by the Employment Equality (Sex Discrimination) Regulations 2005) by placing a statutory duty upon public authorities when carrying out their public duties to have due regard of the need to: (a) eliminate unlawful discrimination and harassment; and (b) promote equality of opportunity between men and women. These requirements are known as the "general duty". The general duty places a proactive responsibility upon all public bodies to ensure that their services, practices and policies are developed with the different needs of women and men in mind. It is designed along the same lines as the duty to promote racial equality which was first introduced into domestic law by the Race Relations Amendment Act 2000 (discussed below).

There are both general and specific exceptions to the coverage of the SDA. In the context of employment, there is a general exception for "genuine occupational qualifications" (GOQs) set out in s.7 of the SDA although it should be noted that this definition is narrower than the genuine occupational requirements contained in EU sex discrimination law (see section V above). Section 7(2) of the SDA makes it clear that being a man is a GOQ for a job only in limited circumstances, including: (a) where the essential nature of the job calls for a man for reasons of physiology, or in a dramatic performance, and where the essential nature of the job would be materially different if carried out by a woman; (b) where the job needs to be held by a man to preserve decency because of physical contact to which women may reasonably object or where

[314] For policy arguments, see Sarah Childs, Joni Lovenduski and Rosie Campbell, 'Women at the Top 2005: Changing Numbers, Changing Politics?' (Hansard Society: London, 2005). See also Rushnara Ali and Colm O'Cinneide, *Our House? Race and Representation in British Politics* (London: Institute for Public Policy Research, 2002).

men may object to contact with women because they are in a state of undress or using sanitary conditions; (c) where the job is likely to involve working or living in a private home; (d) where the nature of the establishment requires special care, supervision or attention in an all male environment (e.g. a prison or a hospital); and, (e) where the holder of the job provides individuals with personal services promoting their welfare or education, or similar personal services, and these services can most effectively be provided by a man.

The SDA also contains specific exceptions covering employment in the armed forces and religious institutions. Section 85 makes it clear that although the Act applies to "service in the armed forces, as they apply to employment by a private person", nothing in the Act "shall render unlawful an act done for the purpose of ensuring the combat effectiveness of the armed forces". By contrast with the Act's treatment of GOQs and the armed forces, which might be felt to fall within the seventh key question in discrimination law (concerning policy-based exceptions to the duty not to discriminate), the final specific exception—applicable to organised religions—brings into play the sixth key question, which concerns clashes between different grounds of non-discrimination or between non-discrimination and other rights. Section 19 specifies that the Act's prohibition of sex discrimination does not apply to employment for the purposes of an organised religion where the employment is limited to persons of one sex or to persons who have not undergone or are not undergoing gender reassignment so as either to comply with the doctrines of that religion or to avoid offending the religious sensibilities of a significant number of its followers.

B. *Sexual Orientation and Gender Identity Discrimination*[315]

As noted above, the term "sex" has been interpreted by EU and domestic courts as including gender reassignment but not sexual orientation, and the SDA has been amended to bring discrimination on the basis of gender identity within its ambit. Direct and indirect discrimination and victimisation due to a person's sexual orientation have since been prohibited in the areas of employment and training under the Employment Equality (Sexual Orientation) Regulations 2003 (SO Regs 2003) and in the areas of goods, facilities and services under the Equality Act (Sexual Orientation) Regulations 2007 (SO Regs 2007). Harassment is also prohibited in relation to employment and training under the SO Regs 2003. While the SO Regs 2003 were implemented in response to the EED, the SO Regs 2007 were introduced under s.81 of the Equality Act 2006.

There are detailed as well as wide-ranging exceptions to liability under both measures, suggesting that—by contrast with race discrimination and, to a

[315] See further Ch.11.

lesser extent, sex discrimination—the question whether an act of *prima facie* discrimination falls within an exception may come to assume greater practical significance when determining liability than the question whether an act falls within the remit of direct or indirect discrimination. Sexual orientation and gender identity also provide stronger illustrations than other grounds of prohibited discrimination of the existence of "discrimination issues" outside of the fields of employment and the provision of goods, facilities and services.

Two important pieces of recent legislation—the Gender Reassignment Act 2004 and Civil Partnership Act 2004—have been devoted to alleviating disadvantage faced by post-operative transsexuals and same-sex couples in family law (and, in the case of same-sex partners, any area of law relating to civil marriage). Furthermore, differences in the criminal law's regulation of the sexual activity of gay and heterosexual men have gradually been removed as part of an attempt to eradicate discrimination in the law itself.

Dealing briefly with gender identity, the Sex Discrimination (Gender Reassignment) Regulations 1999, passed in response to *P v S. and Cornwall CC*,[316] inserted a new s.2A into the Sex Discrimination Act 1975 so as to specify that discrimination due to the fact that a person "intends to undergo, is undergoing or has undergone gender reassignment" (s. 2A(1)), constitutes unlawful sex discrimination in the range of circumstances covered by the 1975 Act (employment, vocational training and the provision of goods, facilities and services, etc.).[317] Section 2A(3) makes clear that a person is also treated less favourably than others if, in making arrangements for that person's absence from work to undergo gender reassignment, they are treated less favourably than they would be if their absence was due to sickness or injury, or treated less favourably than they would be if their absence was due to some other cause and it is reasonable, having regard to the circumstances, for them to be treated no less favourably.

Section 82 goes on to define gender reassignment as "a process which is undertaken under medical supervision for the purpose of reassigning a person's sex by changing physiological or other characteristics of sex, and includes any part of the process."

Turning to sexual orientation and starting with the first key question of discrimination law—"who is protected?"—there is considerable potential for uncertainty about the definition of sexual orientation. Section 35 of the Equality Act 2006 defines sexual orientation as "an individual's sexual orientation towards—(a) persons of the same sex as him or her, (b) persons of the opposite sex, or (c) both". Apart from its apparent circularity, the definition poses some questions. To be deemed to possess a lesbian or sexual

[316] Case C-13/94, [1996] ECR I-2143.

[317] See *Chessington World of Adventures Ltd v Reed* [1998] I.C.R. 97, in which the Employment Appeal Tribunal suggested that the unamended Sex Discrimination Act could be interpreted to preclude gender identity discrimination. See also *Chief Constable of West Yorkshire Police v A (No.2), op. cit.*, for analysis of how national law is to be interpreted in the light of changing EU and Convention interpretations.

orientation, for example, is it sufficient for a person to be attracted to persons of the same sex as themselves, or do they need to have acted on that inclination and engaged in sexual relations with someone of the same sex? And at a deeper level, is it necessary for a man who has been unfavourably treated for having a sexual relationship with another man to self-identify as gay in order to claim the protection of discrimination law (something which might be problematical for a "closeted" gay man who does not self-identify as gay but is adversely treated by others when they become aware of his sexual relationship)?[318] Difficult issues of this type have yet to be addressed in the case law.

Turning to the second key question, there are some minor drafting differences in the definitions of direct and indirect discrimination in the 2003 and 2007 SO Regs (on which it seems unlikely that much will turn) as well as some potentially more important differences. Regulation 3.1 of the SO Regs 2003 defines direct discrimination as occurring where, on the ground of sexual orientation, the discriminator (dubbed "A") treats the claimant (dubbed "B") "on grounds of sexual orientation ... less favourably than he treats or would treat other persons". As with sex discrimination, the protection from discrimination is symmetrical and a comparator is required.

Regulation 2.2 thus makes clear that "A comparison of B's case with that of another person ... must be such that the relevant circumstances in the one case are the same, or not materially different, in the other." In a minor drafting difference, reg.3.1(1) of the SO Regs 2007 includes the comparator requirement in the definition of direct discrimination, specifying that: "a person ("A") discriminates against another ("B") if, on grounds of the sexual orientation of B or any other person except A, A treats B less favourably than he treats or would treat others (in cases where there is no material difference in the relevant circumstances)." A more significant difference between the two would appear to be reg.3(2) of the SO Regs 2007, which makes clear that direct discrimination liability can arise in cases of less favourable treatment due to a "sexual orientation which [a person] is thought to have" as well as one which they actually have—a provision which is not found in the SO Regs 2003.

Drafting differences can also be found in the definitions of indirect discrimination. Under the SO Regs 2003, indirect discrimination is defined as occurring where the discriminator applies to the claimant (dubbed "B") "a provision, criterion or practice which he applies or would apply equally to persons not of the same sexual orientation as B", which "puts or would put persons of the same sexual orientation as B at a particular disadvantage when

318 At a deeper level, the law also ignores the highly problematical debate about whether we can properly understand a sexual orientation as something which involves a fixed meaning or "essence", independent of social circumstances (an "essentialist" approach), or whether we understand ideas of sexual orientation as being a product of social circumstances (a "constructionist" approach), so that the very idea of sexual orientations (as opposed to socially permissible and socially impermissible sexual conduct) is a relatively recent one, historically-speaking. See further Nicholas Bamforth, *Sexuality, Morals and Justice* (London: Cassell, 1997), Ch.3.

compared with other persons'', ''puts B at that disadvantage'', and which the discriminator ''cannot show to be a proportionate means of achieving a legitimate aim'' (reg.2.1(b)). The comparator requirement found in reg.2(2) applies. Regulation 3(3) of the SO Regs 2007 stipulates, by contrast, that ''a person (''A'') discriminates against another (''B'') if A applies to B a provision, criterion or practice—(a) which he applies or would apply equally to persons not of B's sexual orientation; (b) which puts persons of B's sexual orientation at a disadvantage compared to some or all others (where there is no material difference in the relevant circumstances); (c) which puts B at a disadvantage compared to some or all persons who are not of his sexual orientation (where there is no material difference in the relevant circumstances); and, (d) which A cannot reasonably justify by reference to matters other than B's sexual orientation.''

There appear to be three differences here. First, the SO Regs 2007 require the claimant to have been put at a disadvantage rather than a *particular* disadvantage. Second, the comparator is included within the definition of indirect discrimination in the SO Regs 2007, by contrast with the SO Regs 2003. Third, reg.3(3)(b) and (c) of the SO Regs 2007 involve a rather sharper formulation of comparative disadvantage (''some or all others'' in part (b), followed by ''some or all persons ... not of his sexual orientation'' in Pt (c)) than is found in reg.2(1)(b) of the SO Regs 2003, according to which ''persons not of the same sexual orientation'' forms part of the description of the impugned provision, criterion or practice rather than sitting openly at the centre of the comparison exercise. It is unclear whether material differences will be found to result from these differences of drafting.

Both sets of Regulations prohibit victimisation, although the SO Regs 2007 do so on a slightly wider basis than the SO Regs 2003. Regulation 4(1) of the SO Regs 2003 prohibits victimisation of a person who has brought proceedings against the discriminator (dubbed ''A'') or any other person, or given evidence or information in connection with proceedings brought against A or any other person (in each case under the Regulations); or otherwise done anything under or by reference to the Regulations in relation to A or any other person; or alleged that A or any other person has committed an act which would breach the Regulations (reg.4(1) of the SO Regs 2003). The SO Regs 2007, by contrast, apply not only to cases where the claimant has brought proceedings, given information, etc., but also to cases where A knows or suspects that they have done so, where they intend to do so, or where A knows or suspects that they intend to do so (reg.3(5) of the SO Regs 2007). Protection against victimisation does not apply to a person who has made an allegation or given evidence or information where the allegation, evidence or information is false and not made or given in good faith (reg.4(2) of the SO Regs 2003; reg.3(6) of the SO Regs 2007); the SO Regs 2007 extend this exception to cases where claimant intends to make a false allegation or to give false evidence or information.

The SO Regs 2003 prohibit harassment, defined as ''unwanted conduct which has the purpose or effect of—(a) violating B's dignity; or (b) creating an intimidating, hostile, degrading, humiliating or offensive environment for B" (reg.5(1)). Regulation 5(2) specifies that conduct shall only be regarded as having this effect "if, having regard to all the circumstances, including in particular the perception of B, it should reasonably be considered as having that effect." The SO Regs 2007, by contrast, do not prohibit harassment on the basis of sexual orientation in the contexts of goods, facilities and services.

Turning to the second key question, concerning when protections against discrimination apply, reg.6 of the SO Regs 2003 makes clear that the obligation not to discriminate applies to arrangements made for determining who should be offered employment, the terms on which employment is offered and refusals or deliberate failures to offer employment, the terms of existing employees, promotion opportunities, dismissals and other detriments. Regulation 8 extends equivalent protections to contract workers. Provision is also made, for example, for appointment but not election to non-political office (reg.10), the police (reg.11), barristers (reg.12), trade organisations (reg.15), providers of vocational training (reg.17), government-provided statutory facilities for employment and training (reg.19) and institutions of further and higher education (reg.20). Generally, the Regulations apply to acts done by or for a Minister of the Crown or government department and to service in the armed forces (reg.36). Regulation 22 makes an employer liable for the actions of employees done in the course of their employment, and principals for the actions of agents acting with their express or implied authority. Under reg.23, it is unlawful to knowingly aid another person to do an act which is unlawful under the Regulations.

Regulation 4(1) of the SO Regs 2007 makes it unlawful to refuse to provide a person with goods, facilities or services, either at all or which are the same as or similar to, or of a similar quality to, those normally made available to the public or to a section of the public to which the claimant belongs; or to refuse to provide them in a manner which is the same as or similar to that in which the goods, facilities or services are normally provided to the public or to the section to which the claimant belongs. As reg.4(2) makes clear, these obligations apply in particular to access to public places; hotel accommodation; banking or insurance facilities for grants, loans, credit or finance; entertainment, recreation or refreshment facilities; transport or travel facilities; and the services of a profession or trade. Regulation 5 makes it unlawful to discriminate in the disposal of premises, while later Regulations apply to discriminatory practices (reg.9), discriminatory advertisements (reg.10), instructing or causing discrimination (reg.11), the police (reg.32) and the Crown (reg.33). Regulation 30 extends liability to employers and principals as well as employees and agents. Regulation 29 makes it unlawful to knowingly help another person to do an act which is unlawful under the Regulations, but employs a slightly different form of words from those used in reg.23 of the SO Regs 1993.

Turning to the fifth key question, reg.8(1) of the SO Regs 2007 imposes a general duty on public authorities not to discriminate on the basis of sexual orientation, and an analogous duty is imposed on educational establishments (including local educational authorities) under reg.7. The SO Regs 2003 do not impose a general duty on public authorities, although they do—unlike the SO Regs 2007—allow for positive action (a meaningful concept in the area of employment, but would be harder to understand when dealing with the provision of goods, facilities and services). Regulation 26 of the SO Regs 2003 thus makes clear that the obligation not to discriminate in employment on the basis of sexual orientation does not render unlawful any act done in or in connection with: (i) affording to persons of a particular sexual orientation access to facilities for training which would help fit them for particular work; or (ii) encouraging persons of a particular sexual orientation to take advantage of opportunities for doing particular work, provided that, in both cases, it reasonably appears that the act prevents or compensates for disadvantages linked to sexual orientation which are suffered by persons of that sexual orientation doing that work or likely to take up that work.

Despite the ambit of the SO Regs 2003 and the SO Regs 2007, and of the prohibition on discrimination due to gender reassignment under the SDA, the wide exemptions from liability for relevant acts of discrimination raise questions about the extent to which the general prohibitions on discrimination are meaningful. In relation to sexual orientation discrimination, there are specific and complete sets of exemptions from the requirements of both sets of Regulations, as well as provisions dealing with genuine occupational qualifications. Dealing first with specific exemptions, the SO Regs 2003 make clear that nothing done to safeguard national security is rendered unlawful so long as it is justifiable for that purpose (reg.24), a point replicated in reg.25 of the SO Regs 2007. The SO Regs 2007 also provide specific exemptions concerning: educational or welfare-related services provided for the special needs of sexual minorities (reg.13) and facilities for persons of particular sexual orientations (regs 17 and 18); provision of certain services in the home (reg. 6); and annuities, life insurance policies and the like, where the treatment is by reference to actuarial or other data from a source on which it is reasonable to rely, and is reasonable having regard to that data and any other relevant factors (reg.27); and blood donation services where a refusal to accept blood is based on a risk assessment which is reasonable with regard to recognised scientific data (reg.28).

In relation to genuine occupational qualifications, reg.7(2) of the SO Regs 2003 makes it clear that the non-discrimination obligation does not apply where, having regard to the nature of the employment or the context in which it is carried out, "being of a particular sexual orientation is a genuine and determining occupational requirement", "it is proportionate to apply that requirement in the particular case"; and either "the person to whom that requirement is applied does not meet it" or "the employer is not satisfied, and in all the circumstances it is reasonable for him not to be satisfied, that that person meets it". Regulation 7(2) also makes clear that genuine occupational qualifications may apply "whether or not the employment is for purposes of an organised religion", while reg.7(3) makes additional *special* provision (echoing the law relating to sex discrimination) for genuine occupational qualifications in the context of organised religion. It states that where employment is for the purposes of an organised religion and the employer applies a requirement related to sexual orientation so as to comply with the doctrines of the religion, or so as to avoid—because of the nature of the employment and the context in which it is carried out—conflicting with the strongly-held religious convictions of a significant number of the religion's followers, relevant protections against discrimination do not apply if the person to whom the requirement is applied does not meet it, or the employer is not satisfied (and in all the circumstances it is reasonable for them not to be satisfied) that the person meets it.

It is not meaningful to talk of genuine occupational qualifications in the context of goods, facilities and services, and, as such, the SO Regs 2007 make no provision for them. However, reg.14 of the SO Regs 2007 is similar in spirit to reg.7(3) of the SO Regs 2003 by granting special, wide exemptions to religious groups. Organisations whose purpose is to practice, advance or teach a particular religion or belief may thus restrict membership of or participation in the group, or the provision of goods, facilities and services by it, or the use of or disposal of premises which it owns or controls (reg.14). Ministers of religion may, in the course of activities carried on in the performance of their functions in connection with a religious organisation, restrict participation in the activities of the organisation or the provision by it of goods, facilities or services. In all cases, a restriction is permissible only if it is necessary to comply with the doctrines of the organisation or so as to avoid conflicting with the strongly held religious convictions of a significant number of the religion's followers. Regulation 15 grants exemptions to fostering organisations of a religious character.

The SDA makes provision for genuine occupational qualifications in its regulation of gender identity discrimination. Section 7A thus makes clear that discrimination is not unlawful if being male or female is a genuine occupational qualification for the job *and* the employer can show that the complained-of treatment is reasonable in view of s.7(2) and other relevant circumstances.[319] Furthermore, s.7B sets out additional specific privacy-related exceptions relating to gender reassignment where:

(a) the holder of the job is liable to be called upon to perform intimate physical searches pursuant to statutory powers;

(b) the job involves doing work or living in a private home and the degree of physical or social contact with a person living there, or the likely knowledge of intimate details of that person's life, mean that objection

[319] Note also the Gender Recognition Act 2004 Sch.6 para.2 which amends s.7A to make provision for the legal consequences of gender reassignment (see also paras 4 and 5).

might reasonably be taken to allowing a person who is undergoing or has undergone gender reassignment to do the job;

(c) it is impracticable for the holder of the job to live elsewhere than in premises provided by the employer, and the only available premises are such that reasonable objection could be taken, for the purpose of preserving decency and privacy, to the holder of the job sharing accommodation and facilities with either sex whilst undergoing gender reassignment, provided that it is not reasonable to expect the employer either to equip the premises with suitable accommodation or to make alternative arrangements; or

(d) the holder of the job provides vulnerable individuals with personal services promoting their welfare (or similar personal services) and in the reasonable view of the employer those services cannot be effectively provided by a person who is undergoing gender reassignment. There is also a special exemption for religion, paralleling that applicable in cases of sexual orientation discrimination.

The obligation not to discriminate due to a person's gender identity does not apply where the employment, or an authorisation or qualification, is for purposes of an organised religion and employment is limited to those who not undergoing and have not undergone gender reassignment to comply with the doctrines of the religion or avoid offending the religious susceptibilities of a significant number of its followers (s.19 of the SDA).

As presented so far, the provisions governing gender identity and sexual orientation can be viewed in the light of the same key questions that are relevant when considering sex discrimination. This is so despite the fact that the drafting of some provisions differs from those applicable in the case of sex discrimination. These differences are sometimes the result of policy concerns (i.e. pay is not an issue *per se* in instances of sexual orientation discrimination although making allowance for organisations concerned with the welfare of sexuality minority groups is. However, sometimes the differences occur for no real reason (such as the minor variations in drafting for those provisions concerning indirect discrimination). Furthermore, protections against hostile expression directed at lesbians and gay men are currently weaker than those applicable in cases of racist expression,[320] and while public authorities are obliged not to discriminate on the ground of sexual orientation, there is no positive equality-related duty of the type which applies. However, some of the provisions concerning gender identity and sexual orientation reach beyond the areas with which sex discrimination law is concerned, reflecting the fact that until very recently the law *itself* actively discriminated against sexual minority groups (as we will see in Ch.11, not only in its denial of partnership rights, but at a more basic level in the provisions of the criminal law regulating per-

[320] It is currently unclear whether the position will change: see Ch.11, section VI.

missible sexual activity). These provisions have also highlighted the fact that discrimination law is not confined to the areas of employment, goods, facilities and services.

The Gender Reassignment Act 2004 is thus intended to bring domestic law into conformity with the requirements of the European Convention by allowing post-operative transsexuals to be registered on their birth certificates with their reassigned gender rather than their birth gender, enabling them to marry a person of the opposite sex to their reassigned one.[321] Furthermore, the Civil Partnership Act 2004 allows same-sex couples to register their partnerships, granting almost all the same legal rights as are available in relation to marriage but without describing them as "married".[322]

C. *Race Discrimination*[323]

Race discrimination is regulated in domestic law by the Race Relations Act 1976 (RRA), as amended by the Race Relations (Amendment) Act 2000 (RRAmnd 2000), which extends the scope of prohibited race discrimination when conducted by key public bodies and introduces a positive duty to promote racial equality. One crucial difference from domestic sex discrimination law is that some instances of unlawful discrimination which fall within the RRA are categorised as falling outside the revised standards brought into domestic legislation so as to ensure conformity with EU law's Race Equality Directive (RED). All discrimination which is prohibited under the SDA falls, by contrast, within the scope of Art.141 of the EC and the ETD. As such, different legal requirements appear to apply in each set of cases and will be discussed at appropriate points. A further important difference between sex discrimination and race discrimination concerns the provisions relating to racist speech, which is criminalised in the public sphere through legislation on public order and incitement to racial hatred.[324]

By analogy with other prohibited grounds of discrimination, the first key question of discrimination law ("who is protected?") is brought into play when we attempt to define what "race" means for the purposes of race discrimination. The RRA prohibits both direct discrimination perpetrated on the basis of a person's "racial grounds" (namely their "colour, race, nationality or ethnic or national origins") and indirect discrimination which relates to a person's membership of a "racial group" (meaning "a group of persons

321 For relevant cases, see *Goodwin v United Kingdom* (2002) 35 E.H.R.R. 447; *Bellinger v Bellinger* [2003] UKHL 21.

322 Note also provisions dealing with civil partnership in the employment discrimination context: Civil Partnership Act 2004 s.251; SO Regs 2003 reg.25 (as amended); SO Regs 2007 regs.3(3) and 3(4).

323 See further Ch.12.

324 See for example Public Order Act 1986, Pt III.

defined by reference to colour, race, nationality or ethnic or national origins, and references to a person's racial group refer to any racial group into which he falls" (s. 3 of the RRA)).

Like the SDA, the RRA is symmetrical and gives protection to both the majority and the minority. Comparison is therefore essential to establish race discrimination. Section 3(4) of the RRA stipulates that "A comparison of the case of a person of a particular racial group with that of a person not of that group under section 1(1) must be such that the relevant circumstances in the one case are the same, or not materially different, in the other."[325]

In *Mandla v Dowell Lee*,[326] the House of Lords held that characteristics such as language, history and culture could be used as a guide to whether a group could be characterised as a racial group within s.3 of the RRA. However, there is confusion about how exactly this analysis applies—in particular this confusion concerns whether the *Mandla* criteria form an absolute inflexible minimum and whether the test is a subjective or objective one.

A series of post-*Mandla* decisions have produced divergent results concerning the range of groups falling within the protection of the RRA. Ethnic religious minorities (such as Sikhs and Jews)[327] have been found to constitute racial groups, but non-ethnic religious minorities (such as Muslims[328] and Rastafarians)[329] have not. This has led to accusations of inconsistency.

The EED (see Section IV above) and Employment Equality (Religion and Belief) Regulations 2003 render this distinction less relevant insofar as they protect non-ethnic religious minorities against religious discrimination in the context of employment and training—a protection extended by the Equality Act 2006 to goods, facilities and services. However, racial minorities and ethnic religious minorities enjoy greater protection than non-ethnic religious minorities in areas such as the provision of public goods (the RRA and RED), positive action and the positive duty to promote equality (under the RRAmnd Act 2000), and in various mainstreaming and extra-legal measures that give priority to tackling racial discrimination.

A further criticism of domestic courts' interpretation of the term "race" is that it uses an essentialist methodology that assumes that race is a fixed biological or scientific category. This line of argument suggests that the term "race" should be treated as a socially constructed concept rather than as a

325 For a discussion of how to choose the appropriate comparator see the discussion in Dhatt v MacDonald's Hamburgers [1991] ICR 238 (CA).

326 [1983] 2 A.C. 548.

327 *Seide v Gillette Industries Ltd* [1980] I.R.L.R. 427.

328 *J. H. Walker Ltd v Hussain* [1996] I.C.R. 291.

329 *Crown Suppliers v Dawkins* [1993] I.C.R. 517.

fixed category with a clearly discernible essence.[330] From this standpoint, it is more important to ask why we are interested in the category "race"; what function it performs in our social or legal analysis; and what harm it represents, captures and addresses.[331]

Section 3 of the RRA defines race in marked contrast to the blunt wording of the Racial Equality Directive (RED). The RED refers merely to "race" and "ethnic origin", with no reference to "national origins".[332] Where a case falls within the RED, the Directive's definition of discrimination will apply if the rules of direct effect so dictate. However, it is not clear how far the difference in definition is likely to be significant in practice, especially given that the RED applies in many contexts already covered by the RRA.

Turning to the fourth key question of discrimination law, concerning the width of available protections against discrimination, direct and indirect race discrimination, as well as harassment and victimisation, are prohibited in domestic law. However, the treatment of prohibited acts will depend upon whether a case falls within the revised tests introduced to ensure conformity with the RED, or with the original tests in so far as they still apply. Direct race discrimination is defined in s.1(1)(a) of the RRA as occurring where a person treats the claimant "less favourably than he treats or would treat other persons" on racial grounds. This is consistent with the definition of direct discrimination in the RED.

The definitions of direct discrimination in the SDA and RRA have so far been interpreted by the courts in a similar way. The "but for" test for direct discrimination therefore applies in direct race discrimination cases to the same extent that it does in cases of direct sex discrimination.[333] By contrast, indirect race discrimination is defined in s.1 of the RRA in two different ways. The first,

330 Bob Carter, *Realism and Racism: Concepts of Race in Sociological Research* (London: Routledge, 2000); Glenn C. Loury, *The Anatomy of Racial Inequality* (Cambridge, Mass: Harvard University Press, 2002); Rogers Brubaker, "Ethnicity without groups", in Stephen May, Tariq Madood *et al.* (eds), *Ethnicity, Nationalism and Minority Rights* (Cambridge: Cambridge University Press, 2004) at p.54; Kwame Anthony Appiah, 'Race, Culture, Identity', in Kwame Anthony Appiah and Amy Gutmann, *Color Conscious: The Political Morality of Race* (New Jersey, USA: Princeton University Press, 1996) at p.89. See also Seyla Benhabib's argument against conflating the politics of recognition with the politics of identity in Seyla Benhabib, *The Claims of Culture: Equality and Diversity in the Global Era*, (Princeton New Jersey, USA: Princeton University Press, 2002); note also Frederik Barth (ed.), *Ethnic Groups and Boundaries: The Social Organisation of Cultural Difference* (Waveland, 1998). For Muslims see, for example, Tariq Modood, *Multicultural Politics: Racism, Ethnicity and Muslims in Britain* (Edinburgh: Edinburgh University Press, 2005), esp. Chs 1–2.

331 Ron Mallon, 'Race: Normative, Not Metaphysical or Semantic' (2006) 116 Ethics 525 at 550-551.

332 One area of controversy may therefore relate to refugees, who are likely to be racialised on the basis of a lack of nationality rather than traditional concepts of race such as colour or ethnicity. For discussion of race discrimination and refugees, see for example Bernard Ryan, 'Employer Enforcement of Immigration; Law after Section Eight of the Asylum and Immigration Act 1996' (1997) 26 I.L.J. 136; Miranda Lewis, *Asylum: Understanding Public Attitudes* (IPPR: London, 2005) at p.40.

333 Set out in the context of sex discrimination in *James v Eastleigh Borough Council* [1990] 2 A.C. 751. See also the following House of Lords decisions: *Nagarajan v London Regional Transport* [2000] 1 A.C. 501; *Khan v Chief Constable of West Yorkshire Police* [2001] I W.L.R. 1947; *Shamoon v Chief Constable of Royal Ulster Constabulary* [2003] I.C.R. 337.

"new" definition, inserted in order to comply with the RED, is found in s.1(1A) of the RRA and applies in cases concerning race or ethnic or national origins. Section 1(1A) of the RRA stipulates that:

"A person ... discriminates against another if ... he applies to that other a provision, criterion or practice which he applies or would apply equally to persons not of the same race or ethnic or national origins as that other, but—(a) which puts or would put persons of the same race or ethnic or national origins as that other at a particular disadvantage when compared with other persons, (b) which puts that other at that disadvantage, and (c) which he cannot show to be a proportionate means of achieving a legitimate aim."

Section 1(1B) makes clear that this definition applies in cases involving employment (Pt II of the RRA), certain aspects of education (ss.17 to 18D), the provision of goods, facilities and services and the disposal or management of premises (ss.20 to 24), duties of public authorities relating to forms of social security, health care, social protection and social advantage which do not count as goods, facilities and services within s.20 (s.19B), pupillage and tenancy arrangements for barristers (ss.26A and 26B), various government appointments (ss.76 and 76ZA), and unlawful acts falling within the scope of Part IV of the Act.

The second, "old" definition is found in s.1(1)(b) of the RRA and applies in all other cases. Under s.1(1)(b), a person indirectly discriminates if:

"he applies to that other a requirement or condition which he applies or would apply equally to persons not of the same racial group as that other but—(i) which is such that the proportion of persons of the same racial group as that other who can comply with it is considerably smaller than the proportion of persons not of that racial group who can comply with it; and (ii) which he cannot show to be justifiable irrespective of the colour, race, nationality or ethnic or national origins of the person to whom it is applied; and (iii) which is to the detriment of that other because he cannot comply with it."

It is not entirely clear from the terms "racial group", "colour" and "nationality" how wide a range of claimants might fall within the "old" definition but not the "new", or how different the two tests are likely to be in practice. Regardless of how the two tests are defined at a general level, it is clear from s.1(1C) of the RRA that they are intended in practice to be mutually exclusive—we are told that where, by virtue of the "new" definition a person discriminates against another, the "old" definition will not apply.

Like the SDA, the RRA makes provision for prohibited harassment and victimisation. However, unlike the SDA and as is the case with indirect race discrimination the treatment of a harassment claim differs depending upon whether its subject-matter falls within s.1(1B). Where the case concerns a subject-matter or area listed in s.1(1B), s.3A(1) of the RRA applies. This section stipulates that a

"person subjects another to harassment . . . where, on grounds of race or ethnic or national origins, he engages in unwanted conduct which has the purpose or effect of—(a) violating that other person's dignity, or (b) creating an intimidating, hostile, degrading, humiliating or offensive environment for him".

Section 3A(2) specifies that conduct shall only be treated as having such an effect if

"having regard to all the circumstances, including in particular the perception of that other person, it should reasonably be considered as having that effect."

In practice, the application of s.3A of the RRA is therefore limited in *two* ways: it applies *only* to harassment on grounds of race or ethnic or national origins, not to harassment due to the victim's colour or nationality (reflecting its purpose, which was to secure compliance with the RED); *and* the harassment must occur in a situation to which s.1(1B) applies.

It seems possible to deal with cases falling outside these limits in two possible ways. First, certain provisions in Pt II of the Act prohibit harassment in specific contexts without reference to ss.1(1B) or 3A, suggesting that such instances of harassment might be litigated without reference to the earlier provisions. Section 4(2)(A) of the RRA thus applies specifically to racial harassment in employment, stipulating that it is "unlawful for an employer, in relation to employment by him at an establishment in Great Britain, to subject to harassment a person whom he employs or who has applied to him for employment"; s.20(3) prohibits racial harassment in the provision of goods, facilities and services; and ss.21(2A) and 24(1)(b) prohibit racial harassment in the disposal or management of premises and in decisions concerning assignment and sub-letting.

Secondly, given that ss.1(1B), 3A, 4(2)(A) and 20(3) of the RRA were placed within the Act by the Race Relations Act 1976 (Amendment) Regulations 2003, it seems likely that previous case law concerning situations in which harassment amounts to unlawful discrimination continues to apply where harassment is not caught by the provisions inserted in 2003.[334]

In addition, s.2(1) of the RRA prohibits victimisation of an employee, defined as less favourable treatment of an individual "by reason that the person victimised" has "brought proceedings against the discriminator or any other person" under the RRA, "given evidence or information in connection with proceedings brought by any person against the discriminator or any other person" under the RRA, "otherwise done anything under or by refer-

[334] See further Ch.8. Relevant cases include *Strathclyde Regional Council v Porcelli* [1986] I.C.R. 564 and *Pearce v Governing Body of Mayfield School* [2003] UKHL 34.

ence" the RRA "in relation to the discriminator or any other person", or "alleged that the discriminator or any other person has committed an act which .. would amount to a contravention" of the RRA. Protection under s.2(1), which employs the same definition of victimisation as under the SDA s.5 and the SO Regs 2007, extends to situations where the discriminator knows that the person victimised intends to do any of the things listed in s.2(1), or suspects that they have done or intends to do any of them. Protection does not extend to situations where an allegation is false and was not made in good faith (s.2(2) of the RRA).

The use of the words on 'racial grounds' have also been interpreted as prohibiting racial discrimination which arises from instructions (to third parties) to discriminate on the grounds of race.[335]

The RRAmnd Act 2000 amended Pt III of the RRA so as to ensure that public authorities are prohibited from engaging in race discrimination. Section 19(B)(1) thus states that it is "unlawful for a public authority in carrying out any functions of the authority to do any act which constitutes discrimination". Section 19(B)(1A) also makes provision for harassment by a public authority, which is defined in s.19(B)(2)(a) as including "any person certain of whose functions are functions of a public nature". However, s.19(B)(4) stipulates that in relation to a particular act, "a person is not a public authority" by virtue *only* of s.19(B)(2)(a) "if the nature of the act is private."

Section s.19(B)(3) of the RRA wholly excludes from the ambit of s.19(B)(1) the Houses of Parliament, a person exercising functions in connection with proceedings in Parliament, the Security Service, the Secret Intelligence Service, the Government Communications Headquarters, and any unit or part of a unit of the naval, military or air forces which is required to assist the Government Communications Headquarters. Section 19(C) provides for further exceptions for judicial acts, as well as for legislative activity such as the making, confirmation or approval of Orders in Council or instruments made by ministers under the authority of primary legislation. Sections 19(D) and (E) make provision for exceptions and monitoring in the exercise of immigration functions. Finally, s.19(F) creates an exception for decisions not to prosecute.

Moving on to consider the second key question of discrimination law, "when are claimants protected?", it is clear that with some exceptions, the coverage of the RRA is analogous to that of the SDA in key areas. Within employment and training (covered in Pt II of the RRA), s.4 prescribes that it is unlawful to discriminate in the arrangements an employer makes for the purpose of determining who should be offered employment, the terms on which employment is offered, and in the refusal or deliberate omission to offer employment. Similar protection applies to opportunities for promotion, transfer or training, to any other benefits, facilities or services, to refusals or

335 Showboat Entertainment Ltd v Owen [1984] I.C.R. 65.

deliberate omissions to afford access to them, and to dismissals or any other detriments. The RRA extends to education (ss.17 to 19ZA), public authorities (ss.19B to 19F), the provision of goods, facilities and services (s.20, defined in similar terms to those applicable under the SDA), housing (ss.21 to 24) and barristers and advocates (ss.26A and 26B).

Case law concerning race discrimination in the provision of goods, facilities and services has related, for example, to the grant of marriage licences[336] and to the provision of services by estate agents.[337] Although there is not a large number of such cases, evidence presented to the Commission of the European Communities concerning sex discrimination in the goods and services context suggests that a lack of cases is not in itself a reliable indicator of an absence of discrimination in practice.[338] There are two interesting differences from the provisions applicable in cases of sex discrimination. First, as we saw in the previous sub-section, harassment *as well as* direct and indirect discrimination is prohibited in relation to housing. Secondly, in relation to the provision of goods, facilities and services, the exceptions which allow limited sex discrimination in the use of actuarial evidence in the provision of insurance are not permitted in the case of race discrimination. It is not therefore permissible to use statistical evidence of risk between different racial groups to differentiate between them in the provision of insurance.

It has been held that an instruction by an employer to an employee to discriminate on the ground of race can fall within the definition of prohibited race discrimination.[339] Furthermore, the general statutory duty imposed on public authorities not to discriminate (under s.19(B)(1) of the RRA—see above) encompasses the provision of goods, facilities and services by public authorities, and thus overrides the decision in *R v Entry Clearance Officer, Bombay Ex p. Amin* that goods and services provided by public institutions under Crown prerogative powers fell outside the material scope of the RRA.[340]

As we saw in the context of sex discrimination, the fifth key question of discrimination law—the justification of discrimination for policy reasons—is in issue when considering positive action and the promotion of racial equality. Although positive action is generally not permitted, ss.36 to 38 of the RRA provide limited exceptions covering the provision of training to ethnic minorities. These are applicable on a similar basis to the provisions governing positive action under the SDA (discussed above). A series of measures

[336] *Tejani v The Superintendent Registrar for the District of Peterborough* [1986] I.R.L.R. 502.
[337] *R v Commission for Racial Equality, ex parte Cottrell and Rothon* [1980] 1 W.L.R. 1580.
[338] 'Proposal for a Council Directive implementing the principle of equal treatment between women and men in the access to and supply of goods and services' (presented by the EU Commission, Brussels, November 5, 2003, COMM 2003/657, final).
[339] *Showboat Entertainment Centre Ltd v Owen* [1984] 1 All E.R. 836.
[340] *Regina v Entry Clearance Officer, Bombay, ex p. Amin* [1983] 2 A.C. 818.

providing for the "mainstreaming" of racial equality in public services also exist, applicable for example to the civil service and police.[341]

More broadly, the RRAmnd 2000—introduced following concerns voiced in the Macpherson Inquiry Report[342] about institutional racism in public services generally, and the police in particular—places public authorities under a general statutory duty to promote racial equality, as part of an attempt to encourage change on a proactive basis. This duty, commonly referred to as the race equality duty, is set out in s.71(1) of the RRA, which imposes a general statutory duty on public authorities (the list of which is set out in Sch.1A to the and includes ministers of the Crown and government departments, the armed forces, the N.H.S., local authorities, education bodies, housing authorities and the police, but excludes—by analogy with s.19B—the security service, the secret intelligence service, and the Government Communications Headquarters) to the effect that a public authority shall,

"in carrying out its functions, have due regard to the need—

(a) to eliminate unlawful racial discrimination; and

(b) to promote equality of opportunity and good relations between persons of different racial groups".

Section 71(2) of the RRA empowers the Secretary of State to impose by order, "on such persons falling within Schedule 1A as he considers appropriate, such duties as he considers appropriate for the purpose of ensuring the better performance by those persons of their duties" under s.71(1). The Race Relations Act 1976 (Statutory Duties) Order 2001 thus required the publication of race equality schemes by specified public sector employers.[343]

There are both general and specific exceptions to the duty not to discriminate contrary to the RRA (thus answering the seventh key question of discrimination law, "are there other exceptions to protections from discrimination?"). By contrast with sex discrimination and sexual orientation discrimination, the RRA contains fewer exceptions which are designed to protect competing rights or prohibited grounds of discrimination (implicating the sixth key question of discrimination law). As in other areas of domestic race discrimination law, the application of the general exceptions—which

341 The Civil Service has thus launched "Pathways", a two year leadership development programme which will provide senior ethnic minority staff with the tools and direction to compete for Senior Civil Service posts. The programme provides opportunities for staff to demonstrate their potential and ability, as well as understanding more about the expectations attached to such posts. Participants work closely with senior civil servants who provide the direction, and in turn explore issues surrounding ethnicity. See: http://www.cmps.gov.uk/pathways/index.asp.

342 Cmnd 4262–I (1999), *The Stephen Lawrence Inquiry: Report of an Inquiry by Sir William MacPherson*. For a discussion of the term 'institutional discrimination' see also Christopher McCrudden, 'Institutional Discrimination' (1982) 2 O.J.L.S. 303.

343 S.I. 2001/3458.

concern only discrimination relating to employment—varies depending upon whether a case involves discrimination on grounds of race or ethnic or national origins (in which case compliance with the RED is necessary) or other types of race discrimination.

Section 4A of the RRA introduces the EU law concept of a "genuine and determining occupational requirement" (GOR). According to s.4A(2), a GOR will apply where,

"having regard to the nature of the employment or the context in which it is carried out—

(a) being of a particular race or of particular ethnic or national origins is a genuine and determining occupational requirement;

(b) it is proportionate to apply that requirement in the particular case; and

(c) either—

  (i) the person to whom that requirement is applied does not meet it, or
  (ii) the employer is not satisfied, and in all the circumstances it is reasonable for him not to be satisfied, that that person meets it".

Since s.4A of the RRA is designed to ensure compliance with the RED, it applies only in cases involving discrimination on the grounds of race or ethnic or national origins. A slightly different general exception, known as a "genuine occupational qualification" (GOQ) may apply, by contrast, in cases falling outside s.4A (in other words, to characteristics such as "colour" and "nationality").

RRA, s.5(2) stipulates that

"being of a particular racial group [in relation to those characteristics] is a genuine occupational qualification for a job only where—(a) the job involves participation in a dramatic performance or other entertainment in a capacity for which a person of that racial group is required for reasons of authenticity; or (b) the job involves participation as an artist's or photographic model in the production of a work of art, visual image or sequence of visual images for which a person of that racial group is required for reasons of authenticity; or (c) the job involves working in a place where food and drink is (for payment or not) provided to and consumed by members of the public or a section of the public in a particular setting for which, in that job, a person of that racial group is required for reasons of authenticity; or (d) the holder of the job provides persons of that racial group with personal services promoting their welfare, and those services can most effectively be provided by a person of that racial group".

GOQs are a long-standing feature of domestic sex and race discrimination law.

The key difference between GORs and GOQs would appear to be that GOQs are drafted in narrower terms and set out with far greater specificity the conditions under which there will be a valid exception.[344] A specific exception governing public authorities is found in s.19(D)(1) of the RRA, which states that it is not unlawful for the public authority to "discriminate against another person on grounds of nationality or ethnic or national origins in carrying out immigration and nationality functions".

D. *Religious Discrimination*[345]

The Employment Equality (Religion and Belief) Regulations 2003 (RB Regs)[346] give effect to the provisions of the EED by prohibiting religious discrimination in employment and training (reg.6). In addition, the Equality Act 2006 prohibits religious discrimination in the provision of private goods and services, education, housing and health (Equality Act 2006, ss.44–52). Particular examples of situations in which discrimination is prohibited are listed in s.46(2) and include:

(a) access to and use of a place which the public are permitted to enter;

(b) accommodation in a hotel or boarding house;

(c) banking or insurance facilities;

(d) facilities for entertainment, recreation or refreshment,

(e) facilities for transport or travel; and

(f) the services of a profession or trade.

In terms of the question "who is protected?" by these provisions, the RB Regs define "religion or belief" as meaning "any religion, religious belief, or similar philosophical belief" (reg.2; see also s.44 of the Equality Act). This open-ended definition leaves the matter of whether a particular religion or belief falls within the scope of the Regulations to courts and tribunals. The Department for Trade and Industry's guidance on the RB Regs explicitly follows the approach adopted under Art.9 ECHR by leaving open the precise definition of religion and belief, although it includes an open list of those religions which are recognised in Britain: namely, Christianity, Islam, Hinduism, Judaism, Buddhism, Sikhism, Rastafarianism, Baha'ism, Zorastrianism and Jainism.[347] Given the close connection and occasional overlap between

344 For discussion of "genuine occupational qualifications", see *Lambeth v Commission for Racial Equality* [1990] I.C.R. 768.

345 See further Ch.13.

346 SI 2003/1660.

347 ACAS, "Religion and Belief and the Workplace" (ACAS: London, November 2005), available at www.acas.org.uk (accessed August 20, 2006).

discrimination on the grounds of race and religion (see above), it seems likely that ethnic religious minorities such as Sikhs and Jews would be able to claim the protection of both race and religious discrimination provisions.

Turning to the second key question of discrimination law, direct and indirect discrimination, victimisation and harassment are prohibited. The definitions are similar to those found used in relation to other prohibited grounds in response to the EED. Regulation 3(1)(a) thus defines direct discrimination as less favourable treatment of the claimant (dubbed "B") on grounds of religion or belief, and indirect discrimination as the application to B of a provision, criterion or practice which [the defendant] applies or would apply equally to persons not of the same religion or belief as B, but—(i) which puts or would put persons of the same religion or belief as B at a particular disadvantage when compared with other persons, (ii) which puts B at that disadvantage, and (iii) which [the defendant] cannot show to be a proportionate means of achieving a legitimate aim."

The standard comparator requirement is included, reg.3(3) specifying that "A comparison of B's case with that of another person ... must be such that the relevant circumstances in the one case are the same, or not materially different, in the other."

By analogy with the drafting differences found between the SO Regs 2003 and SO Regs 2007, s.45 of the Equality Act applies slightly (but insufficiently seriously to be likely to make a practical difference) revised definitions of direct and indirect discrimination in the situations which it regulates, and makes provision for a claimant's apparent religion or belief (s.45(2)). ACAS guidelines provide advice to employers about the types of practice they should consider accommodating as part of their policy to eliminate direct and indirect discrimination. For example, ACAS lists the major religious holidays and requirements for prayers.[348] Regulation 4 prohibits victimisation, employing similar terminology when doing so to that found in the SO Regulations 2007. Regulation 5 prohibits harassment, defined as occurring where, on grounds of religion or belief, the defendant:

"engages in unwanted conduct which has the purpose or effect of—(a) violating B's dignity; or (b) creating an intimidating, hostile, degrading, humiliating or offensive environment for B", provided that, "having regard to all the circumstances, including in particular the perception of B, it should reasonably be considered as having that effect."

Limited positive action is also allowed for under reg.25, which permits acts done

[348] ACAS, 'Religion or Belief and the Workplace', November 2005, available at www.acas.org.uk (accessed on August 20, 2006).

"in or in connection with—(a) affording persons of a particular religion or belief access to facilities for training which would help fit them for particular work; or (b) encouraging persons of a particular religion or belief to take advantage of opportunities for doing particular work, where it reasonably appears to the person doing the act that it prevents or compensates for disadvantages linked to religion or belief suffered by persons of that religion or belief doing that work or likely to take up that work."

Further provisions governing trade organizations are found in reg.25(2).

Regulation 7 of the RB Regs allows for genuine occupational requirements to apply in two main situations. The first is where:

"having regard to the nature of the employment or the context in which it is carried out—

(a) being of a particular religion or belief is a genuine and determining occupational requirement;

(b) it is proportionate to apply that requirement in the particular case; and

(c) either—

(i) the person to whom that requirement is applied does not meet it, or
(ii) the employer is not satisfied, and in all the circumstances it is reasonable for him not to be satisfied, that that person meets it."

((reg.7(2), a provision which applies whether or not the employer has a particular religion or belief).

Secondly, reg.7(3) applies where an employer "has an ethos based on religion or belief", although it is drafted in more general terms than the religion-focused exemptions found in the areas of sex, sexual orientation and gender identity discrimination, which focus on the doctrines of the religion in issue. By contrast, reg.7(3) stipulates that where,

"having regard to that ethos and to the nature of the employment or the context in which it is carried out—

(a) being of a particular religion or belief is a genuine occupational requirement for the job;

(b) it is proportionate to apply that requirement in the particular case; and

(c) either—

(i) the person to whom that requirement is applied does not meet it, or
(ii) the employer is not satisfied, and in all the circumstances it is reasonable for him not to be satisfied, that that person meets it."

By analogy with sexual orientation discrimination, it would not be logical for the Equality Act to provide for genuine occupational requirements in relation to goods, facilities and services. However, the Act does contain exceptions to protect faith-based organisations from having to accept as members those of other faiths or beliefs. Section 57 thus specifies that an organisation:

"the purpose of which is—

(a) to practice a religion or belief,

(b) to advance a religion or belief,

(c) to teach the practice or principles of a religion or belief,

(d) to enable persons of a religion or belief to receive any benefit, or to engage in any activity, within the framework of that religion or belief, or

(e) to improve relations, or maintain good relations, between persons of different religions or beliefs" (s.57(1)),

and the sole or main purpose of which is not commercial, to restrict its membership, participation in its activities, the provision by it, on its behalf or under its auspices of goods, facilities or services, or to restrict the use or disposal of premises which it owns or controls (s.(57(3)).

Under s.57(4), a minister of religion may restrict participation in activities carried on in the performance of his or her functions in connection with or in respect of a religious organisation, or restrict the provision of goods, facilities or services in such a context. Under either sub-section, it is necessary to show that the restriction is imposed by reason or on the grounds of the purpose of the organisation, or to avoid causing offence on grounds of the religion or belief to which the organisation relates to persons of that religion or belief. Sections 58, 59 and 60 contain further exemptions covering religious charities, faith schools and conditions of membership.

There are also more specific exemptions for national security (reg.24; Equality Act, s.63) and in relation to Sikhs. Regulation 26 "deems" the requirement for Sikhs to wear a helmet on a construction site to be unjustifiable indirect religious discrimination. This perhaps further illustrates the extent to which domestic legislation attempts to address the sixth and seventh key questions of discrimination law, concerning situations in which otherwise discriminatory acts may be justified. In the case of reg.26, a legislative exception is introduced for one particular social group to accommodate their specific religious needs. Various privacy-related exceptions apply in the housing context under s.48 of the Equality Act, while s.46 excludes from the scope of the Act's non-discrimination requirements public authorities and situations which are covered by the RB Regs.

The RB Regs do not cover religious discrimination in Northern Ireland, where discrimination on the grounds of "religion and belief" has been prohibited since the Employment Acts 1976 and 1989 (a product of political concern over sectarian violence in Northern Ireland). The impact of the EED, in so far as it concerned religious discrimination, thus depended on its interaction with the existing Fair Employment and Treatment (Northern Ireland) Order 1998 (FETO), which constituted an attempt to consolidate policies of non-discrimination and affirmative action in Northern Ireland and was part of an attempt to achieve greater political, social and economic equality between Protestants and Catholics.[349] Significantly, the FETO provisions prohibit discrimination not only on the grounds of religion and belief, but also on the ground of "political opinion", thereby recognising the close connection between religion and sectarian politics in the Northern Irish context.

E. *Disability Discrimination*[350]

The Disability Discrimination Act 1995 (the DDA 95) prohibited disability discrimination at national level before the EED was introduced at EU level. Victimisation and harassment are prohibited in similar terms as those found under the SDA and RRA for victimisation and the SO and RB Regs for harassment.

The DDA differs from other discrimination legislation in that in general only persons defined as "disabled" under the Act can bring a claim for disability discrimination: the legislation is not, in other words, symmetrical in its application. However, there is a distinction between what the DDA and subsequent legislation has defined as constituting disability and what social practice tends to treat as being a disability. Not all "social" forms of disability are covered by legal regulation. This means that a key issue in this area concerns how the legal definition of disability discrimination is framed. Section 1 of the DDA defines disability as "a physical or mental impairment which has a substantial and long-term adverse effect on his ability to carry out normal day-to-day activities" and a "disabled person" means someone who "has a disability." This introduces a 'medical' paradigm which treats disability as a characteristic that is an individual impairment of the individual.

This wide definition of disability is elaborated in further detail in Sch.1 to the DDA 95 which is of great importance in understanding the precise nature of the protection against disability discrimination. Sch. 1 makes clear what is meant by the requirement in s.1 of the DDA that a disabled person means someone who "has" a disability, i.e. has a disability in the present and that this should have "substantial and long-term adverse effects". Schedule 1 s.2 of the DDA states that the effect of an impairment is long-term effect if: "(a) it has

[349] SI 1993/3162 (N.I. 21).
[350] See further Ch.14.

lasted at least 12 months; (b) the period for which it lasts is likely to be at least 12 months; or (c) it is likely to last for the rest of the life of the person affected." Moreover, in relation to these criteria of substantial long term effect Sch.1 s.2(2) of the DDA states that "Where an impairment ceases to have a substantial adverse effect on a person's ability to carry out normal day-to-day activities, it is to be treated as continuing to have that effect if that effect is likely to recur."

The requirement in the definition of disability in s.1 that the adverse effect should be "on his ability to carry out normal day-to-day activities" is further elucidated in Sch.1 s.4(1) of the DDA. This section states that an impairment is to be taken to affect the ability of the person concerned to carry out normal day-to-day activities only if it affects, *inter alia*, one of the following: mobility; manual dexterity; physical co-ordination; continence; ability to lift and carry etc.; speech, hearing or eyesight; memory or ability to concentrate; or perception of risk or danger.

The relationship between a disability and medical treatment is dealt with in Sch.1 s.6 of the DDA 95:

"An impairment which would be likely to have a substantial adverse effect on the ability of the person concerned to carry out normal day-to-day activities, but for the fact that measures are being taken to treat or correct it, is to be treated as having that effect."

Schedule 1 s.6A introduces a provision that ensures that persons with cancer, HIV infection or multiple sclerosis are "deemed" to have a disability for the purposes of the Act. In relation to progressive conditions, Sch.1 s.8 states that where (a) a person has a progressive condition; and (b) as a result of that condition, he has an impairment which has (or had) an effect on his ability to carry out normal day-to-day activities, but (c) that effect is not (or was not) a substantial adverse effect, then he "shall be taken to have an impairment which has such a substantial adverse effect if the condition is likely to result in his having such an impairment".

In order to be clear about the types of impairments that are *not* to be treated as disabilities under the DDA 95, the Disability Discrimination (Meaning of Disability) Regulations 1996[351] make it clear that addictions (to alcohol, nicotine or other substances) are not to be treated as an impairment, but that this does not apply to "addiction which was originally the result of administration of medically prescribed drugs or other medical treatment". Other conditions which are *not* to be treated as impairments under the DDA 95 include, *inter alia*: a tendency to set things on fire, to steal and towards physical or sexual abuse; exhibitionism and voyeurism; or the specific condition of seasonal allergic rhiniti. Moreover, tattoos and body piercing are not to be treated as a disability, nor is severe disfigurement. The Disability Discrimination

[351] SI 1996/1455.

(Amendment) Act 2005 has classified certain conditions, in particular HIV-positive status, which would not otherwise come within the original DDA definition of disability, as constituting a disability for the purposes of the legislation.

Disability discrimination is prohibited in a number of areas: employment and training; access to goods, facilities and services; the management, buying or renting of land or property; education and the performance of public functions. Section 19(3) of the DDA 95 lists the examples of goods and services in the same way as those for sex discrimination under the SDA, for example sale of material goods, hotels, banking, entertainment, transport and travel, or services of a profession or trade. In addition, s.19(3) also includes: access to and use of means of communication; access to and use of information services; and facilities provided by employment agencies. Special provisions govern the provision of transport services.

The definitions of discrimination in the DDA 95 vary from those found in the SDA and RRA. The first set of definitions of disability discrimination prohibit similar types of conduct as are prohibited under the definition of direct discrimination used across the other grounds, but includes a "justifiability" aspect. This definition has undergone serious modification in recent years. Originally, s.5 of the DDA stated that a person discriminates against another if:

"(a) for a reason which relates to the disabled person's disability, he treats him less favourably than he treats or would treat others to whom that reason does not or would not apply; and (b) he cannot show that the treatment in question is justified."[352]

Changes introduced under the Disability Discrimination Act (Amendment) Regulations 2003[353] to ensure compliance with the EED mean that direct discrimination on the ground of a person's disability is prohibited and can no longer be justified. Therefore, the original s.5 of the DDA 95 has been replaced by a new s.3A which provides that "less favourable treatment" of a disabled person for a reason related to their disability will constitute discrimination if it cannot be justified, so long as it does not amount to direct discrimination on the basis of a person's disability (which is incapable of justification). This distinction between direct discrimination on the ground of a person's disability and less favourable treatment on grounds related to an individual's disability is not altogether clear. However, it appears that a distinction is being drawn between discrimination directly based upon a person's disability itself (such as refusing to employ someone because they are blind), which cannot now be justified, and discrimination based upon the *consequences or impact* of a

[352] See *Clark v TDG Ltd Novacold* [1999] I.C.R. 951 where the Employment Appeals Tribunal held that the appropriate comparator to establish whether there had been discrimination was a non-disabled employee.

[353] SI 2003/1673.

disability upon a person's abilities (such as refusing to employ someone who is blind on the basis that they will not be able to access essential work-related information), which can be justified: see Ch.14 for more analysis of this distinction.

The second definition of disability discrimination, found in the new s.3A(2), is analogous to indirect discrimination (which is not prohibited *per se* in the context of disability) but introduces the concept of a 'duty to make reasonable adjustments' in relation to disability. Section 3(A)(2) thus stipulates that "a person ... discriminates against a disabled person if he fails to comply with a duty to make reasonable adjustments imposed on him in relation to the disabled person". Differing reasonable accommodation duties are imposed upon employers and providers of goods and services: a failure to make reasonable accommodation can be justified in the context of the provision of goods and servcies, but not now in the context of employment and occupation following the coming into force of the Disability Discrimination Act (Amendment) Regulations 2003. There is also statutory guidance on the factors, *inter alia*, that will be taken into account in determining whether "reasonable adjustment" has been made. These include: the extent to which making the adjustments would prevent the effect in relation to which the duty is imposed; the extent to which it is practicable to make the adjustments; the financial and other costs which would be incurred in making the adjustments; the extent to which making the adjustments would disrupt other activities; the availability of financial or other assistance in making the adjustments; and the nature and size of the undertaking. Concrete examples are also given and include, *inter alia*: altering the time of work; assigning a different place of work and training; acquiring and modifying equipment; modifying procedures for testing and assessment; and providing a reader or interpreter.

There is a positive duty to promote equality of opportunity for disabled persons imposed upon public authorities. This requires the removal of barriers to participation by disabled people, promoting equality of opportunity and embracing diversity (Pt 5A of the DDA). Preferential treatment of persons with disabilities and other affirmative action measures are uniquely not prohibited in domestic law and are subject to little if any legal constraints.

F. *Age Discrimination*[354]

The Employment Equality (Age) Regulations 2006 (Age Regs)[355] apply to age discrimination in employment and vocational training and implement the requirements of the EED. Their impact is confined to the field of employment and occupation: at present, age discrimination legislation does not extend to

[354] See further Ch.15.
[355] SI 2006/1031.

the provision of any form of goods or services. Age raises some distinct questions for discrimination law, and it is not immediately clear whether it is analogous to other prohibited grounds of discrimination.[356]

The Age Regs prohibit direct and unjustified indirect age discrimination on the ground of age. Direct discrimination is defined as less favourable treatment than is afforded or would be afforded to another person (reg.3(1)(a)), while indirect discrimination is defined (in reg.3(1)(b)) as the application of a provision, criterion or practice which is applied or would be applied equally to persons not of the same age group as the claimant (dubbed "B"), but

"(i) which puts or would put persons of the same age group as B at a particular disadvantage when compared with other persons, and (ii) which puts B at that disadvantage, and A cannot show the treatment or, as the case may be, provision, criterion or practice to be a proportionate means of achieving a legitimate aim."

Regulation 3(2) includes a standard comparator requirement, making clear that a comparison of B's case with that of another person "must be such that the relevant circumstances in the one case are the same, or not materially different, in the other." Victimisation is prohibited under reg.4, and harassment under reg.6. The Age Regs, which are a detailed body of complex rules, apply within employment and occupation (Age Regs, Pt 2). They are symmetrical in so far as they apply to people of any age, young or old. Certain forms of age discrimination, including mandatory retirement at 65, are deemed to be automatically justified (reg.30): however, the existence of these "block exceptions" in domestic law may themselves have to be shown to be objectively justified under EU law. Regulation 29(1) (note also reg.29(2) dealing with trade associations) allows for limited positive action, in the form of acts done in or in connection with:

"(a) affording persons of a particular age or age group access to facilities for training which would help fit them for particular work; or (b) encouraging persons of a particular age or age group to take advantage of opportunities for doing particular work; where it reasonably appears to the person doing the act that it prevents or compensates for disadvantages linked to age suffered by persons of that age or age group doing that work or likely to take up that work."

The Age Regs remove the upper age limit for unfair dismissal and redundancy rights, giving older workers the same rights to claim unfair dismissal or receive a redundancy payment as younger workers, unless there is a genuine retirement. They allow pay and non-pay benefits to continue which depend on

[356] C. O'Cinneide, 'Comparative European Perspectives on Age Discrimination' in Fredman and Spencer (eds), *Age as an Equality Issue* (Oxford: Hart, 2003), Ch.9, esp. at pp.214–5.

length of service requirements or which recognise and reward loyalty and experience and motivate staff (reg.32). They also remove the following restrictions: the age limits for statutory sick pay, statutory maternity pay, statutory adoption pay and statutory paternity pay, so that the legislation for all four statutory payments applies in exactly the same way to all. They remove the lower and upper age limits in the statutory redundancy scheme, but leave the current age-banded system in place (reg.33). They also provide statutory exemptions for many age-based rules in occupational pension schemes (Sch.2) and for certain types of retirement ages, which permit employers to retain a mandatory retirement age of 65. As compensation for the retention of mandatory retirement ages, employers will be subject to a duty to consider requests from employees to stay on beyond the fixed retirement age, who is obliged to give reasonable consideration to requests to work on, similar to their obligations in respect of part-time workers (regs 47 and 48, Schs 6 and 7). The retention of mandatory retirement has already proved to be a controversial issue in the EU context and is currently the subject of cases before the European Court of Justice from several different European countries.

G. *Remedies and Procedural Issues*

The ninth key question of discrimination law concerns the range of available legal remedies. Since the answer to this question is similar in relation to each of the prohibited grounds, it is dealt with here rather than separately in relation to each ground (and will be dealt with in greater detail in Chs 18 and 19). Remedies divide between those open to individual claimants (''individual remedies'') and those which may be sought by the Commission for Equality and Human Rights as the public body charged with enforcing non-discrimination legislation (''collective remedies''). The most common individual remedies are of a private law character, but some public law remedies are also available—generally in relation to the performance of statutory duties imposed by discrimination legislation. The operation of the burden of proof is crucial in claims for private law individual remedies, not least since the burden of proof is on the claimant but the complexity of many cases means that there is seldom direct evidence of discrimination and often a need to 'infer' its existence from the facts. The burden of proof is an area in which EU law has had a particular impact. Collective remedies are largely of a public law character.

In relation to unlawful discrimination in employment, individual claimants may bring private law proceedings before employment tribunals for damages and other related remedies.[357] In such cases, the tribunal may in general award

[357] See, for example, RRA, s.64; SO Regs 2003, reg.28; DDA, s.8; Age Regs, reg.36.

a successful claimant such of the following remedies "as it considers just and equitable":[358]

(a) an order declaring the rights of the complainant and the respondent in relation to the act to which the complainant relates;

(b) an order requiring the respondent to pay to the complainant compensation; and

(c) a recommendation that the respondent take within a specified period action appearing to the tribunal to be practicable for the purpose of obviating or reducing the adverse effect on the complainant of any act of discrimination to which the complaint relates.[359]

The time limit for bringing an action is three months from the date when the act complained of was done[360] although a tribunal can hear a complaint outside this period if, in all the circumstances of the case, "it considers it is just and equitable to do so".[361]

In relation to unlawful discrimination in relation to aspects of education, planning, the duties of public authorities, and goods, facilities and services, individual claimants may bring civil proceedings before the county court "in like manner as any other claim in tort" (s.57(1) of the RRA), "in the same way as any other claim in tort" (s.25(1) of the DDA) or "by way of proceedings in tort" (reg.20(1) of the SO Regs 2007), which may award all such remedies, including damages, as would be available in the High Court.[362] The Equality Act 2006 gives jurisdiction to the country court for religious discrimination in the provision of public and private goods and services (ss.65–72 of the Equality Act). However, outside of the disability context, damages are only available under this heading for intentional acts of indirect discrimination.[363] The time limit for bringing an action is six months from the date when the act complained of was done,[364] although there are circumstances in which a court can hear a complaint outside of this period.[365]

The Sex Discrimination (Indirect Discrimination and Burden of Proof) Regulations 2001 amended s.63 of the SDA so as to ensure conformity with the EU Burden of Proof Directive in individual claims: similar amendments will also have to be made to implement the burden of proof provisions in the

[358] See, for example, RRA, s.56; SO Regs 2003, reg.30; DDA, s. 8(2); Age Regs, reg.38.
[359] Note the slightly more detailed wording in RRA, s.56.
[360] See, for example, RRA, s.68(1); SO Regs 2003, reg.34(1); DDA, Sch.3(3); Age Regs, reg.42(1).
[361] See, for example, SDA, s.76; RRA, s.68(6); SO Regs 2003, reg.34(3); DDA, Sch.3(3)(2); Age Regs, reg.42(3).
[362] See, for example, RRA, s.57(2); SO Regs 2007, reg.22(1); DDA, s.25(5).
[363] See, for example, RRA, s.57(3); SO Regs 2007, reg.22(1)(c).
[364] See, for example, RRA, s.68(2); SO Regs 2007, reg.23; DDA, Sch.3(6)(1).
[365] Under the SDA, s.76 or RRA, s.68(6) this is if, in all the circumstances of the case, the court "considers it is just and equitable to do so"; under the SO Regs 2007 reg.23 and DDA Sch.3(6)(3), this is with the permission of the court.

Gender Directive 2004/113/EC.[366] As a result, where, in a claim before an employment tribunal or in a County Court, a claimant proves facts from which the tribunal or court could conclude in the absence of an adequate explanation that the respondent had committed prohibited sex discrimination, then the court or tribunal will have to uphold the claim unless the respondent proves that they did not commit or should not be treated as having committed the relevant act.[367] Similarly worded provisions are found in the SO Regs 2003 (reg.29) and SO Regs 2007 (regs 20(5) and 34(2)), which respectively deal with employment and with goods, facilities and services and other subject-matters falling within the SO Regs 2007, and in regs 37 and 40 of the Age Regs, which only apply to employment and occupation. In the race discrimination context, the operation of the burden of proof depends upon whether the subject-matter of a case falls within an area where standards of liability have been altered to ensure compliance with the RED. In cases of discrimination based on race, ethnic origins or national origins falling within Pt II of the RRA (concerned with employment), or provisions dealing with aspects of education, goods, facilities and services, and other related areas, or provisions concerned with harassment,[368] RRA ss.54A and 57ZA (inserted via the Race Relations Act 1976 (Amendment) Regulations 2003) apply the RED standard by specifying that where, in a claim before an employment tribunal or in a County Court, a claimant proves facts from which the tribunal or court could conclude in the absence of an adequate explanation that the respondent has committed an act of prohibited race discrimination or harassment, then the complaint is to be upheld unless the respondent proves that they did not commit the act in question.[369] In cases concerning the residual categories of colour and nationality, a different burden of proof applies. If the complainant establishes facts from which an employment tribunal or county court could conclude that they have suffered race discrimination, the tribunal or court will ask the alleged discriminator for an explanation. If the explanation is unsatisfactory, the tribunal or court may find that discrimination has occurred. As with other areas of race discrimination law, it is not clear how far the distinction between the two burden of proof standards is likely to prove significant in practice. A similar situation applies in the context of disability discrimination.

Individuals with standing may brings proceedings in judicial review against public bodies for their failure to carry out public law duties imposed on them by discrimination legislation (for example, the specific statutory duties imposed under RRA ss.19 and 71).[370] Proceedings brought by the Commission for Equality and Human Rights are of a public law character in so far as they

[366] SI 2001/2660.

[367] For the previous position, see *King v The Great Britain-China Centre* [1992] I.C.R. 516.

[368] See RRA, ss.54A(a) and 57ZA(a) for the exact list of situations.

[369] This also applies to cases where, under RRA, ss.32 and 33, the respondent is to be treated as having committed the act concerned.

[370] See, in relation to RRA, s.71, *Wheeler v Leicester CC* [1985] A.C. 1054; see, in the area of sexual orientation, also Employment Equality (Sexual Orientation) Regulations 2003, reg.27; Equality Act (Sexual Orientation) Regulations 2007, regs 19 and 22(1).

involve judicial review of the decisions or actions of public bodies. The Commission is also responsible for formulating codes of practice, conducting inquiries into the legality of behaviour given the specific legal duties not to discriminate, and helping individuals to bring proceedings.[371] Its responsibilities—to be considered in detail in Part D of the book—thus engage the tenth key question of discrimination law (concerning extra-legal measures) as well as the ninth.

H. *Conclusions*

In this section, we have outlined the coverage of domestic statutory discrimination law in relation to each of the prohibited grounds of discrimination. By framing the analysis in terms of the key questions of discrimination law outlined in Ch.1, it has become clear that while contemporary domestic provisions treat the SDA and RRA as key models for discrimination law, nonetheless the nature of the protections offered varies according to the ground in issue. Thus, the definitions of discrimination are different in the contexts of disability and age, additional exceptions are found in the contexts of sex and particularly sexual orientation, provisions designed to counter hate speech exist in relation to some grounds but not others, non-discrimination protections move into the public law sphere to differing extents, and in the area of sexual orientation what might be viewed as protections against discrimination on the basis of partnership status now play a key role in family law.

A second key difference between the grounds concerns the extent to which domestic law has been amended or developed to ensure compliance with EU law. As is particularly visible in the context of race discrimination, tests and standards vary depending upon whether there is an obligation to comply with standards imposed by EU law.

It should, finally, be reiterated that to describe the protections discussed here as "domestic" is to some extent artificial, and that it is inaccurate to regard domestic primary and secondary legislation (in terms of its coverage or as drafted more generally) as representing a conclusive statement of the UK's commitment to non-discrimination. For, wherever directly effective provisions of EU law or Art.14 of the Convention are in issue, any legislation—whether officially concerned with prohibited discrimination or not—must be interpreted in the light of relevant non-discrimination provisions of each system; and, where reinterpretation is impossible, disapplied or subjected to a declaration of incompatibility (depending on whether EU law or the Convention is in issue).

[371] Equality Act 2006, Pt I and Schs 1 and 2. See in particular Equality Act (Sexual Orientation) Regulations 2007, reg.19.

VIII. A Single Non-Discrimination Statute? Reform of Discrimination Law

We have seen in previous sections just how complicated domestic discrimination law now is. The various grounds of prohibited discrimination are dealt with under different pieces of primary and secondary legislation. Direct discrimination is open to justification in cases based on Art.14, but remains (subject to possible counter-examples) a strict liability wrong in cases involving EC law. While indirect discrimination is generally prohibited, this has only recently been the case in Art.14 cases, about which there is little case law. Courts have historically insisted on the need for a comparator, but the House of Lords has indicated that it is prepared to take a more relaxed approach towards this requirement in Art.14 cases. The range of subject-matters falling within different headings also varies: while EU law relates largely to the employment context, the application of Art.14 (and other Convention rights) is potentially far broader. The Equality Act 2006 sought to simplify the public enforcement of protections against discrimination by replacing the previously separate commissions dealing with race, sex and disability discrimination with a single Commission for Equality and Human Rights charged with the *general* promotion of equality and diversity (that is, regardless of the ground of discrimination in issue), for example by formulating codes of practice, conducting inquiries into the legality of conduct by reference to the specific legal duties not to discriminate, assisting individuals in bringing proceedings, and bringing proceedings itself.[372] At a more substantive level, however, the 2006 Act did nothing to consolidate the law dealing with all prohibited grounds of discrimination, which continue to exist in numerous differently-drafted and separate pieces of primary and secondary legislation.[373]

Given these complexities, it has been suggested that it would be beneficial to consolidate the existing substantive duties not to discriminate, and perhaps also the enforcement mechanisms, into one comprehensive non-discrimination statute.[374] For example, the Independent Review of the Enforcement of UK Anti-Discrimination Legislation (the "Hepple Report") has proposed the enactment of a "single Equality Act" designed to "eliminate unlawful discrimination and to promote equality regardless of sex, race, colour, ethnic or national origin, religion or belief, disability, age, sexual orientation, or other

372 Equality Act 2006, Pt I and Schs 1 and 2.

373 Parts 2 to 4 instead deal with discrimination on the ground of religion or belief; enable the creation of regulations to make detailed provision for discrimination on the ground of sexual orientation; and regulate public authorities' duties not to discriminate on the bases of sex, disability or race—a rather pragmatically-driven set of concerns.

374 See the Discrimination Law Review, *A Framework for Fairness: Proposals for a Single Equality Bill for Great Britain: A Consultation Paper* (Department for Communities and Local Government, June 2007), pp.11–12, 27–8.

status''.[375] The government-commissioned Equalities Review has asserted that the ''current legal framework is . . . inconsistent and complex. So an excellent starting point for creating a better framework for achieving equality is a simpler law: namely, a single Equality Act'' which ''focuses on a simpler, more coherent framework'', bringing all prohibited grounds of discrimination into one statute.[376] Furthermore, the Discrimination Law Review, working within the remit of the Department for Communities and Local Government and established to make detailed proposals concerning the future of non-discrimination legislation, is considering ''the opportunities for creating a simpler, fairer and more streamlined legislative framework in a Single Equality Act.''[377] In its 2007 Consultation Paper, this Review has stressed that a single Act would provide ''the opportunity to create a coherent legislative framework for fairness.''[378] Apart from promoting more effective enforcement by reducing or removing existing complexities and inconsistencies, it has been suggested that a single statute would emphasise the common policy concerns underpinning the law's attempts to counter discrimination on all of the prohibited grounds, thus acting against the prospect of balkanisation, and make it easier to deal with cases where claimants have been discriminated against on multiple grounds (for example, because they are black and because they are female). The Hepple Report has thus stressed that a single statute would ''recognise the indivisibility of the concept of equality. Sharing common ground would encourage links among groups facing discrimination, while at the same time focussing the attention of employers and service providers on the need for an inclusive approach.''[379] With a sensitively drafted statute, cases of ''multiple discrimination'' would become easier to deal with since it would no longer be necessary to determine whether to bring proceedings under (for example) separate sex or race discrimination legislation depending upon which basis for the act of discrimination was thought to be the more significant.

It has, however, been suggested that grouping all prohibited grounds of discrimination together in a single statute might cause some to become less visible or less well-prioritised, in terms of public enforcement, than others. The Hepple Report responded to this suggestion by asserting that ''this reservation confuses a 'general' concept with a unified one. The same concept of equality

[375] Bob Hepple, Mary Coussey and Tufyal Choudhury, *Equality: A New Framework: Report of the Independent Review of the Enforcement of UK Anti-Discrimination Legislation* (Oxford: Hart, 2000), p.xiv; see also p.25, Recommendation 1; p.xvii (Recommendations 1 and 2); p.xviii (Recommendation 14). The inclusion of ''other status'' indicates this to be an example of Sandra Fredman's ''third approach'', typified by Canadian law; note also Recommendation 8 (p.xviii) and paras 2.41 to 2.42 concerning the anticipated purposes of the legislation.

[376] *Fairness and Freedom: The Final Report of the Equalities Review* (2007), p.115; see also Bob Hepple, Mary Coussey and Tufyal Choudhury, *Equality: A New Framework, ibid.*, paras 2.3 to 2.7. For details of the Equalities Review, see its website: *http://www.theequalitiesreview.org.uk.*

[377] *http://www.womenandequalityunit.gov.uk/dlr/index.htm.*

[378] *A Framework for Fairness: Proposals for a Single Equality Bill for Great Britain: A Consultation Paper*, p.62.

[379] Bob Hepple, Mary Coussey and Tufyal Choudhury, *Equality: A New Framework, ibid.*, para.2.9.

can be applied to each ground of discrimination without undermining specific action against particular grounds of discrimination".[380] It might be ventured, of course, that in the absence of empirical evidence this response is no less speculative than the reservation. A clearer shortcoming of a single non-discrimination statute would be that, as should be clear from our analysis in preceding sections, the differing legal weight of directly effective EU law and Convention rights in domestic law would mean that instances of discrimination which are prohibited under the Convention would not, by definition, have the overarching legal force that EC law provides when dealing with directly effective provisions governing prohibited discrimination. Some grounds of prohibited discrimination, or some instances of some grounds, have stronger weight than others where their foundation lies in EU law. In consequence, it does not appear possible for domestic discrimination law to be consolidated completely (that is, in terms of remedies as well as the prohibited grounds of discrimination) by a single statute: the only ways in which something approaching a full consolidation could be achieved would either be for the Convention and EU law grounds to be harmonised at Convention/EU law level, most probably as a result of the EC joining the Convention as a direct party,[381] or for domestic courts to be given the same powers to set aside inconsistent legislation when dealing with EU law and Convention rights, going beyond the Human Rights Act's declaration of incompatibility procedure. Even then, though, the consolidation would still not be complete, given the somewhat different subject-matters of the two bodies of law, not least when it comes to employment.[382] Furthermore, as Paul Craig has pointed out, difficult technical choices would need to be made if the EC was to accede to the Convention: "Decisions would have to be made as to whether . . . to build in a preliminary reference relationship" between the Courts of Justice and Human Rights."[383] At national level, therefore, the passage of a single non-discrimination statute will not be sufficient to overcome the phenomenon of differing legal weight, which constitutes a key aspect of the complexity of domestic discrimination law.

IX. Conclusion

We have seen in this chapter that domestic discrimination law is exceptionally complex. This is mainly due to the "multi-layered" nature of the domestic

380 Bob Hepple, Mary Coussey and Tufyal Choudhury, *Equality: A New Framework*, *ibid.*, para.2.10.

381 As to which see Protocol Relating to Article 6(2) of the Treaty on European Union on the Accession of the Union to the European Convention on the Protection of Human Rights and Fundamental Freedoms, Treaty of Lisbon, 3rd December 2007.

382 It is not entirely clear whether this difficulty would be eliminated if Protocol 12 to the Convention was brought into force as well as the EU joining the Convention.

383 *EU Administrative Law* (Oxford: Oxford University Press, 2006), p.531.

constitution: a phenomenon which results in the existence of intermeshing networks of protections against discrimination of differing ambits and legal weights. At a more conceptual level, we can develop the argument of Chapter 1 by observing that domestic law has moved from the fixed category, legislatively-specified grounds of discrimination model through to a combination of models, something which is tied to the developing "generational" approach. Despite the complexities at the level of detail, therefore, it is possible to make sense of the development of domestic law in terms of the conceptual models outlined in the previous chapter, as well as versions of the ten key questions of discrimination law. Subsequent chapters will explore specific aspects of domestic discrimination law with these conclusions and the key questions in mind, the next chapter examines the theoretical justifications for having discrimination law. It undertakes an analysis of concepts such as "equality" which are often presented as deeper justifications for the legal regulation of discrimination.

3

THEORETICAL JUSTIFICATIONS FOR DISCRIMINATION LAW

I. Introduction

This chapter is concerned with the theoretical principles which justify the legal regulation of discrimination. Equality is the main principle that has been used, and continues to be used, to justify discrimination law. In this chapter we focus on equality and relate it to the discussion of discrimination law: we consider the different ways in which the concept of equality can be defined; and we also set out a number of critiques of equality. We also consider other justifications for the legal regulation of discrimination that rely on promoting goals such as autonomy, procedural justice and social inclusion.

There are a number of ways in which theoretical analysis and philosophical arguments can be related to discrimination law. At one level, any liberal political and legal system needs to be able to "justify" legal intervention which could have a potential impact on the liberty of the individual. At this most basic level, a precept such as Mill's requires that the only justification for an interference with the liberty of another is to prevent "harm to others".[1] There is also a second level of analysis, focusing specifically on the constitutional structure of the society concerned. Depending on the constitution in issue, arguments at this level can relate both to the powers of important institutions (e.g. legislatures and courts) and to the scope of the rights or values in the relevant society (e.g. to what extent are practices commonly perceived as discriminatory prohibited under legal rules or rights relating to discrimination, to what extent are those rights or rules couched in the language of equality, and to what extent do arguments about rights to autonomy, dignity or privacy play a role?). Although discrimination law has a short history, there is a substantial body of theoretical literature on the topic.[2] Some of the theoretical writing relates specifically to direct, indirect and positive discrimination and it is dealt with in Part B of the book.

[1] J. S. Mill, *On Liberty and other writings*, (Cambridge: Cambridge University Press, 1989), Chapter 4.

[2] C. McCrudden, *Anti-discrimination law*, (Aldershot: Dartmouth, 1991)

II Justifying Discrimination Law

Paul Brest has set out the contours of a more theoretical approach in the context of race discrimination. He argues that the "anti-discrimination principle" is a principle of justice that prevents and rectifies racial injustice. However, he insists that the anti-discrimination principle is not the only or predominant principle of justice; it can, in some instances, give way to other demands of justice. Moreover, in Brest's analysis, the "anti-discrimination principle" includes not only negative but also positive goals: so that, it is concerned with the exclusion caused by the malign use of racial criteria from decision making procedure; but it is also concerned with unjust results.[3]

Brest's analysis is an exercise in justifying the emerging body of US anti-discrimination law. It is worth noting that the term "justification" has a precise "legal" meaning in discrimination law. Indirect discrimination can be "justified" where a requirement or condition which the employer has applied may disproportionately disadvantage a member of a protected group but which can be explained by a legitimate reason such as business necessity.[4] In this chapter, justification is used in its non-legal sense to mean "the action of justifying or showing something to be just, right or proper;".[5] The goal of this enquiry is to identify the *ideas and principles* which justify the legal regulation of discrimination.[6]

There is a preliminary question which must be addressed before launching into this substantive enquiry: how are the theoretical justifications of discrimination law related to the legal rules, practices and policies which constitute discrimination law doctrine?

The legal definition of concepts in discrimination law needs to be preceded by theoretical and extra-legal analysis. In order to clarify the relationship between these two levels of enquiry we need a better understanding of the impact of theoretical concepts on legal doctrine, and vice versa. Neither the search for stipulative legal definitions nor the assertion of prior concepts is a sufficient explanation of this complex relationship. Nigel Simmonds has

[3] Paul Brest, (1976) The Supreme Court 1975 Term. Forward: "In Defense of the Anti-discrimination Principle", 90 Harvard Law Review 1–55. See also Larry Alexander, "What Makes Wrongful Discrimination Wrong" (1992–1993) 141 Univ. Pa. L. R. 219; Richard A. Wasserstrom, "Racism, Sexism and Preferential Treatment: An Approach to the Topics" (1977) UCLA L. Rev. 581; Alan Wertheimer, "Jobs, Qualifications and Preferences" (1983) 94 Ethics, 99.

[4] See N. Bamforth, "Setting the Limits of Anti-discrimination law: Some Legal and Social Concepts" in J. Dine and B. Watts (eds.), *Discrimination Law: Concepts, Limitations and Justifications* (London: Longmans, 1996)

[5] See N. Bamforth, "Setting the Limits of Anti-discrimination law: Some Legal and Social Concepts" in J. Dine and B. Watts (eds.), *Discrimination Law: Concepts, Limitations and Justifications* (London: Longmans, 1996) at 51.

[6] For the term "anti-discrimination principle" see Paul Brest, The Supreme Court 1975 Term. "Forward: In Defense of the Anti-discrimination Principle", 90 Harvard Law Review 1–55 (1976).

explored that relationship in the following passage (part of which was discussed in Chapter 1) in ways that are also relevant to understanding the relationship between the anti-discrimination principle and discrimination law:

Nigel E. Simmonds, *The Decline of Juridical Reason: Doctrine and theory in the legal order* (Manchester: Manchester University Press, 1984)

p.8: "The law cannot settle any philosophical dispute about the nature of legal rights simply by enacting a stipulative definition: for the concept of a 'right' has important uses outside the law, in our moral life, and it seems to be that feature of the concept that gives it its theoretical interest. It is true that the concepts of 'motor vehicle' or 'building' may have uses both within and without the law. But those concepts which have been of interest to legal theorists appear to link legal ideas to a wider context in a more fundamental way. [...]"

p.9: "The conditions of intelligibility are to be found within concrete forms of life. Fully to understand legal discourse one should aim at a cultural knowledge that is both rich and deep. In particular, it will be argued that because discursive concepts cannot be prised off from the social formations which give them sense so also they cannot be understood apart from the historical experience that has shaped them."

"Theory, doctrine and history

[...]

pp.11–13: "The wide separation between theory and reality rests above all on a failure to appreciate the extent to which 'a man's social relations with his fellows are permeated with his ideas about reality'. For changes in theory and belief are not simply sources of truth or error about reality: by transforming the significance of human practices, they may work a transformation in the nature of social reality itself. [. .]

Legal and political theories are not descriptions of brute facts. Nor are they merely postulated ideals or aspirations. Theories reflect and are reflected in our social relationships. And the historical development of our social life is itself a part of the intellectual evolution of our ideas. The attempt to implement a certain conception of freedom, for example, inevitably increases our understanding of what is involved in that conception, exposing it perhaps as one-sided or otherwise inadequate. In this way our ideas of freedom may be enriched, or at least complicated. And if understanding a moral or political concept is a matter of understanding the 'form of life' to which it belongs, an articulation of this or that conception may well require attention to its history. Moral and political values thus cannot and should not be discussed in isolation from the institutions and social histories that shaped them. What is required is a sensitive historical reconstruction, 'a retrospective reconstruction which is itself a form of conceptual analysis'."

This view of the relationship between theory and practice challenges the assumption that theoretical analysis should proceed as a separate level of enquiry which seeks to accurately describe the pre-existing body of legal rules and practices constituting legal doctrine. In order that concepts and terms in anti-discrimination law have clear meaning, there is a need to formulate "'pure' or 'ideal' types of the relevant kind which exhibit the internal coherence and unity at the level of meaning."[7] Yet, at the same time, theoretical enquiry extends beyond the accurate description of doctrine. It requires attention to a number of additional features: the connection of the legal concept to related phenomenon outside the law; the historical context within which the concepts developed; and the way in which they operate in present social and cultural contexts. Rather than developing theoretical justifications of anti-discrimination as an abstract principle, we need to trace through the context in which the concept of anti-discrimination has taken shape. These passages indicate that there are not two levels of enquiry: one theoretical and the other doctrinal. Rather, the development of concepts at a theoretical level can have an impact on doctrine, so that identifying concepts at a theoretical level will have an impact on legal issues at a more practical level. Moreover, the historical and present social context within which the concept of anti-discrimination has taken on shape in our culture are relevant to a theoretical discussion of the discrimination law. As Postema makes clear in the following passage, facts about law and complex social practices are not "brute facts" which lend themselves to accurate description. What is required is a "characterisation" or "interpretation" of these concepts.

Gerald J. Postema, *Bentham and the Common Law Tradition* (Oxford: Clarendon, 1986)

p.334: "Jurisprudential theory, then, even when it appears to be engaged in conceptual analysis, is focused on the task of giving an account of legal institutions, and the practice and 'sensibility' that breathe life into them. [. . .]

This must be refined: it may be true that law is merely an instrument for regulating social behaviour, but this is not a brute or 'objective' fact about the law (even less a brute fact about law in any society or any culture). If the claim is true, it is true by virtue of a social fact, a fact about the point or function of law as viewed by self-identified participants.

We must note here two important features of interpretations or characterisations. As Charles Taylor has pointed out, simple descriptions can be accurate or inaccurate, and their inaccuracy can be shown by pointing to new or overlooked facts or evidence, but when characterisations fail they distort the reality they seek to interpret. And after a point, no mere showing, or marshalling of more evidence, will settle a dispute regarding the truth of the characterization. That question will turn on the strength and plausibility of the sense, point or meaning attributed to those facts. Thus, because they do not merely ascribe properties to objects, but instruct us about how to think about them, characterisations do not leave the phenomenon unchanged. In consequence, characterisations are always open to challenge."

[7] M. Weber: "The Nature of Social Action" in W. G. Runciman (ed.), E. Matthews (Tr.) *Weber, Selections in Translation*, Cambridge: Cambridge University Press, 1978) at p.23.

A process of interpretation will require the theorist to attend to the point and significance which is attributed to these practices.[8] This in turn means that an atomistic treatment of the action of agents needs to give way in favour of an analysis which places the action of agents in a wider context: taking into account factors which lends significance to their actions and makes them explicable, such as their personal history or their membership of a wider communal group.

Postema also confirms that theoretical enquiry does not leave the "phenomenon" which is studied unchanged. This has important consequences in the context of discrimination law. First, the meaning which legislators and judges give to key concepts, and the consequent boundaries which they draw around terms such as "discrimination" and "equality", will depend in part on theoretical and extra-legal notions of these concepts. Clarity about the meaning of these concepts will be necessary for any critical understanding of their use in legal doctrine. However, as Simmonds argues, this does not mean that this should be a purely theoretical or analytical process that generates "essentialist" concepts. Rather, what is required is a method that relates theory to the historical, social and contemporary context within which discrimination law operates.

Second, if theoretical and legal concepts are not only descriptive but also contribute to the construction of behaviour and social practices, then discrimination law will have a profound effect upon its subject matter. Agents and institutions which perpetuate discrimination will look to the law to reflect back to them their existing behaviour. Legal regulation will also make available a pool of ideas and concepts which influences the self-perception of agents (individuals and institutions). Where legal regulation transforms behaviour in a positive sense, and promotes the aims of discrimination law, it may be justified and serve an important function. However, an error at the level of theory can also distort the reality which is its subject matter. When this occurs, discrimination law has the potential to cause harm: by reflecting back to agents a distorted view of their identity and their social practices; or by failing to capture some important feature of their self-definition. In these cases the ideas about individuals that are reflected in discriminaiton law may be rejected as false or alienating.[9]

These malign consequences take on greater significance as the definition of discrimination, and the scope of discrimination law, proliferates and extends its reach into daily activities and social practices. The consequences of such errors often go beyond the impact on individual perpetrators and victims of discrimination. They can also extend to members of minority and majority

[8] For a discussion of the way in which theroising about human practices is "interpretative" see Charles Taylor: "Interpretation and the Sciences of Man", *Philosophical Papers Vol.II* (Cambridge: Cambridge University Press 1985).

[9] For a detailed discussion of this approach see Maleiha Malik, "Faith and the State of Jurisprudence" in Peter Oliver et al (eds.), *Faith in Law: Essays in Legal Theory* (Oxford: Hart Publishing, 2000)

communities, as well as the relevant institutions and social practices. The use of legal regulation in pursuit of cultural transformation, and an ever increasing normative policy agenda for discrimination law, is therefore not a risk free project.

The fact that an error at the level of theory can cause significant harm raises the stakes in any discussion of theory and doctrine in discrimination law. Relying on familiar intuition and judgements to set the limits of discrimination law, and resolve these inherent risks, poses its own problems.[10] There is a danger that these intuitions may reflect the exact biases and prejudice that it is the aim of the discrimination law to eliminate. As Andrew Koppelman notes:

"To complicate matters further, unlike Burke, we cannot rely on our untutored prejudices and the ordinary decent person's opinions to see us through to the right balance, because these are among the things that the anti-discrimination project calls into question. Our biases are likely even to impair our ability to tell when racism [or other forms of prejudice *author's addition*] has affected, or is reinforced by, our actions. The disposition of character that the project seeks to foster is an unstable mix of courage and self-doubt: a willingness to say fearlessly what one believes, while remaining acutely aware that one's convictions are always in danger of being tainted by unconscious racism. The project requires us to make fine-grained practical judgements at the same time that we cultivate suspicion of our own powers of judgement."[11]

Discrimination law has expanded on a number of levels. The legal forms that it may take range from international human rights documents through to constitutional, European Union and statutory law. The scope of discrimination law has also broadened from employment and the provision of goods and services, through to private activities and criminal conduct. It is not uncommon to find overlapping legal obligations which derive from all these various sources. This vast expansion in the sources of anti-discrimination makes it even more important to develop a method that can respond to fine differences of historical, social and political context. This breadth in discrimination law has important consequences for the method of analysing the anti-discrimination principle.

First, it means that the search for a single unifying principle which explains discrimination law in all these contexts may be less helpful than an approach which sets out a range of possible justifications whose relevance depends on the context and form of legal regulation. Second, an expanded role for discrimination law precludes its treatment as a discreet or self-contained project which analyses concepts as they operate in their legal context. The concept of discrimination exists within legal doctrine but it is also an essential part of

10 See L. Lustgarten, "Racial Inequality and the Limits of Law" (1986) 49 Modern Law Review 1 68–85.

11 See Andrew Koppelman, *Anti-discrimination and Social Equality*, (New Haven, USA: Yale University Press, 1996), Introduction.

contemporary political philosophy and ordinary usage. Analysis must locate it within this wider frame of reference. Discrimination law is increasingly taking on a more ambitious project of cultural transformation which seeks to use legal and non-legal methods to eliminate the meanings, practices and institutions which unjustifiably discriminate, stigmatise or disadvantage members of groups in important areas of social life.[12] In this context, the need to clarify the theoretical foundations of discrimination law takes on a greater urgency. Yet, at the same time, these judgements are difficult because discrimination law often seeks to challenge exactly those practices which are deeply ingrained in our own attitudes and institutions.

Despite the increasing variety in the use of the term "discrimination", a recurring theme, in legal and non-legal contexts, is that the legal regulation of discrimination is justified because it promotes equality. The concept of equality is therefore an obvious starting point in any discussion of the anti-discrimination principle and it forms the main part of the analysis in this chapter.

III. Equality and Discrimination Law

Equality is used in a wide range of legal and non-legal discussions. In the context of "political equality" or "equality before the law" it is used as part of a commitment to liberal democracy and the rule of law. Analysis is further complicated by the fact that contemporary political theory has seen the proliferation of egalitarian theories of justice, as well as the rhetorical use of equality. This section is concerned with equality as a goal of discrimination law and policy. It is often assumed that equality is self-evidently a normative concept. Can the concept of equality provide a sufficient or adequate basis for the discrimination? The discussion of "equality" reveals that this pre-analytical confidence is not always well placed. It is far from clear that equality can provide us with evaluative criteria which are self-standing and cannot be re-stated by reference to other normative principles (such as autonomy or justice). The suspicion is that it is these principles, autonomy or justice, which provide the justification, whilst appeals to equality in these circumstances serve a rhetorical function which can also mask the foundations of discrimination law.

Equality has been used to justify the legal regulation of discrimination in the past, especially in domestic discrimination law where the White Papers that preceded the SDA and RRA cite sex and racial equality as a key goal of the legislation. It is also treated as an important constitutional right in many jurisdictions (e.g. Canadian Charter, section 15(1)). As we see in the next dis-

12 See Andrew Koppelman, *Anti-discrimination and Social Equality*, (New Haven, USA: Yale University Press, 1996), Introduction.

cussion, however, the concept of equality can have a number of different meanings. In some contexts, equality is used to connote "equality of opportunity" by contrast to "equality of results". Critics have argued that equality is an "empty concept" that is used as a marker for some other more substantial value. They also argue that equality is also sometimes used as "short hand" or as a "rhetorical value" for stating that all human beings deserve to be treated well. In some cases, these criticisms of the concept of equality have led commentators to argue that discrimination law can be justified using non-egalitarian goals such as autonomy or social justice. We consider these alternative ways of justifying discrimination law later in the chapter.

Even if we accept that there are valid criticisms of equality, it is still important to understand the relationship between equality and discrimination law. One way of relating the equality to the complex nature of discrimination law is to move beyond the idea that there is one "all or nothing" concept of equality towards an analysis, such as that of Derek Parfit[13] which is extracted and discussed later in the chapter, that recognises that "equality" has a range of meanings. On this analysis, although equality understood as the treatment of "like with like" may explain some outward features of discrimination law (e.g. direct discrimination) it cannot explain others (e.g. positive action). Equality understood as "the priority principle", on the other hand, would be more useful to explain the increasing focus of discrimination law on addressing the overall disadvantaged position of some social groups.

Analysis is further complicated because equality is a relational value whose underlying subject matter—the criteria for comparison between individuals or the goods which are the subject of distribution—can vary. Whether or not inequality is seen to be relevant, and to justify legal regulation, will depend on the weight given to these underlying factors. As Raz states in relation to egalitarian principles in moral and political theory:

"...we only have reasons to care about inequalities in the distribution of *goods* and *ills*, that is of what is of value or disvalue for independent reasons. There is no reason to care about inequalities in the distribution of grains of sand, unless there is some other reason to wish to have or to avoid sand."[14]

An analysis of equality is also important because it exposes the multifarious meanings of the term. Discrimination law covers a wide range of activities and goods. Once we move beyond comparison of similar behaviour or distribution of a simple good, and move towards more complex comparisons and the distribution of controversial goods, it becomes clear that definitions of equality involve a "complex relation of persons mediated by the goods we make, share, and divide among ourselves; it is not an identity of possessions."[15] This raises

[13] D. Parfit, 'Equality and Priority' in A. Mason, (ed.), *Ideals of Equality* (Oxford: Blackwell, 1998).
[14] Joseph Raz, *The Morality of Freedom* (Clarendon Press: Oxford: Clarendon Press, 1986) at 235.
[15] Michael Walzer, *Spheres of Justice* (Oxford: Blackwell, 1983) at 18.

a question about the scope of discrimination law: what type of behaviour or social goods are subject to regulation; should all individuals be subject to the principle in the same way; can exceptions be justified? Here, it could be argued that these complex variations make it impossible to isolate a single unifying definition of equality which will explain discrimination law. The concept of equality which is relevant may depend on context: the form of the legal regulation, e.g. constitutional, criminal or civil law; the type of behaviour which is prohibited, e.g. employer discretion, a criminal act or public speech; or the type of good which is being distributed, e.g. employment, housing or education. Moreover, the individuals who are subjects of comparison may be differentially placed from these goods (e.g. employment) because of factors such as poverty or class, which will in turn effect any analysis of equality. It is often assumed that "strict" or "simple" equality interpreted as identical treatment or the treatment of "like with like" provides the best explanation for discrimination law. However, as the next discussion shows, this assumption is not free of controversy.

Starting an analysis with a discussion of the concept of equality poses a danger. It could entrench existing assumptions that "equality" is a sufficient or predominant justification for discrimination law. As chapter 1 argued, there are a number of powerful critiques of the concept of equality. Critics argue that equality is an "empty" and incoherent concept: it is at best an insufficient explanation for discrimination law; and at worst it is an incoherent concept which is a barrier to understanding and implementing the central goals of discrimination law. These critics suggest alternative principles, e.g. autonomy or social exclusion, as a more coherent theoretical foundation for discrimination law. These criticisms are set out below. Nevertheless, there are a number of reasons why it remains important to have a detailed understanding of "equality", as well as its uses and applications in anti-discrimination law. The enduring use "equality" in discussions of constitutional and statutory discrimination law doctrine confirms that it remains a key concept that needs to be analysed. For those who challenge and question equality, it is important to understand why it is so stubbornly entrenched within discrimination law. For the critics, there is also the further question of "Why and how is the concept of equality being misused within discrimination law?". It is also important for proponents of "equality" to understand the different meanings of the term and its complex role within discrimination law. For these supporters, the question is: "How should we define the concept of equality to ensure that it is used appropriately and effectively within discrimination law?" For both critics and advocates, a detailed understanding of the concept of equality is essential for an analysis of discrimination law.

Early discussions of discrimination law in the White Papers which preceded the Sex Discrimination Act 1975 ("SDA") and Race Relations Act 1976 ("RRA") refer to the goal of equality as a reason for anti-discrimination legislation. In the US, the Fourteenth Amendment provides that "No State shall [...] deny to any person within its jurisdiction the equal protection of the laws" and uses the benchmark of "equality" to provide a constitutional guarantee against discrimination on grounds such as race, sex and disability. More recent developments have entrenched "equality" as a constitutional guarantee in a number of jurisdictions such as Canada and South Africa. At the EU level, Article 13 of the Treaty of Amsterdam provides the foundations for developing a general non-discrimination clause which has been translated into the Race and Employment Equality Directives.

A. *The Concept of Equality*

1. Equality of Opportunity and Equality of Results

Disagreement about the exact basis for equality underlie some of the most heated and controversial debates in discrimination law. The previous section has discussed the relationship between different definitions of equality, and the consequences of this difference for discrimination law. A recurring discursive devise in this context is the dichotomy between "equality of opportunity" (equality) and "equality of results" (difference). This debate reflects some of the points considered in the previous section and the failure of a formal definition of equality as the treatment of "like with like" as an organising principle for discrimination law. It is useful to explicitly place a discussion of the discrimination principle in this context because "equality of opportunity" was stated as being the main goal of UK discrimination law[16]

Katherine O'Donovan and Erika Szyszczak, *Equality and Sex Discrimination Law*, (Oxford: Blackwell Ltd, 1988)

pp.3–4: "The notion of equality which appears to have motivated the United Kingdom legislation on sex discrimination and equal pay is equal opportunity. The White Paper which preceded the legislation declared the government's resolution 'to introduce effective measures to discourage discriminatory conduct and to promote genuine equality of opportunity for both sexes.' In liberal discourse the notion of equal opportunity which was widely used in Parliament is employed to deal with perceived inequalities. Bernard Williams makes a distinction between inequality of need and inequality of merit. Need can be satisfied by simple distribution, whereas 'merit has a competitive sense [...] [I]t is appropriate to speak in the case of merit, not only of a distribution of the good, but of a distribution of the opportunity of achieving the good'. Competition on merit is what equal opportunity is about. To overcome the question of the relationship between need and merit liberal writers advocate minimal state provision for need, after which all compete on

16–19 The White Paper which preceded the SDA 76, Equality for Women, Cmnd.5724 (London: HMSO,1974), para.17 sets out the aim of the legislation as "to introduce effective measures to discourage discriminatory conduct and to promote genuine equality of opportunity for both sexes".

merit. Thus intervention because of need or inequality is a justification for state action, regulation or legislation. Thereafter the role of the state is to hold the ring for free competition."

As O'Donovan and Szyszczak suggest, the idea of "merit" was a core aspect of the idea of equality of opportunity. A number of writers have argued that "merit" is a core feature of discrimination law.[20] Merit is, however, a wide terms. As Christopher McCrudden has argued it requires more detailed analysis before it can be applied in arguments about discrimination and especially in contexts where "merit" is cited as an argument against the introduction of positive (affirmative) action.[21]

Equality of opportunity need not necessarily exclude all positive action. Sandra Fredman points out that there are two possible versions of the concept: procedural or substantive equality of opportunity. Fredman writes:

"On the procedural view, equality of opportunity requires the removal of obstacles to the advancement of women or minorities, but does not guarantee that this will lead to greater substantive fairness in the result. For example, the abolition of word-of-mouth recruitment or non-job-related selection criteria removes procedural obstacles and so opens up more opportunities. But this does not guarantee that more women or minorities will in fact be in a position to take advantage of those opportunities. Those who lack the requisite qualifications as a result of past discrimination will still be unable to meet job-related criteria; women with child-care responsibilities will still find it easier to take on paid work. [...] A substantive sense of equality of opportunity, by contrast, requires measures to be taken to ensure that persons from all sections of society have a genuinely equal chance of satisfying the criteria for access to a particular social good. This requires positive measures such as education and training, and family friendly measures. It may go even further, and challenge the criteria for access themselves, since existing criteria of merit may themselves reflect and reinforce existing patterns of disadvantage."[22]

This more substantive idea of equality of opportunity is reflected in the White Paper which preceded the Race Relations Act, discussed in the chapter on race, which has significant references to the need to supplement law reform with a focus on disadvantage and supply side measures.

Fredman goes on to distinguish equality of opportunity from equality of results which she writes is "primarily concerned with achieving fairer distribution of benefits; while formal equality is based on a notion of procedural fairness stemming from consistent treatment."[23] The idea may, as Fredman

[20] See D. Nolan's discussion of the "right to meritorious treatment" as a justification for anti-discrimination legislation, "A Right to Meritorious Treatment" in C. Gearty and A. Tomkins (ed.), *Understanding Human Rights* (London: Cassell, 1996)

[21] Christopher McCrudden, "Merit Principles", (1998) 18 O.J.L.S. 4 at 543–579.

[22] Sandra Fredman, *Discrimination Law* (Oxford, Clarendon Press, 2002) at p.15.

[23] Sandra Fredman, *Discrimination Law* (Oxford, Clarendon Press, 2002) at p.15, at p.11.

notes, often be too focused on one representative individual thereby ignoring the fact that other members of the group have different needs or cannot meet the same criteria. Moreover, a focus on the "exclusionary" criteria that are an obstacle to an equality of results may ignore the fact that certain individuals are excluded because they cannot meet that criteria, e.g. through a lack of qualification. Some of the strongest versions of "equality of results" may require the maintenance of a pattern without any proof of a discriminatory act or factor: "the mere fact of under representation is discriminatory; and action should be aimed at achieving equality of outcome."[24] These strong versions would justify preferential treatment, quotas and provisions such as female only short lists that are aimed at ensuring greater women's participation in politics. In this sense, equality of results may be a useful way to justify positive action measures that are aimed at overcoming the structural disadvantage of women and minorities. However, as Fredman notes, the focus on "results" which is encouraged by this idea of equality may be misleading. It may encourage monitoring results with a view to gaining parity rather than targeting the causes of structural disadvantage. Moreover, the focus on "equality" of results may lead to assimilative models, that ignore relevant difference, and that are themselves a potential cause of structural advantage. In these cases, it may be more useful to express the goal using the language of "priority" (discussed below as the "priority principle") and "structural disadvantage" rather than equality of results.

2. Simple Equality: "alike should be treated alike"

The force of the assumption that "alike should be treated alike" whilst things which are "unalike should be treated unalike" explains much of the normative appeal of the principle of equality.[25] This principle can be understood in two ways. First, as the *principle of formal equality* which requires persons to be treated equally unless there is some reason for treating them differently. Second, as the *principle of universal humanity*.

3. Formal Equality

At first sight this seems an obvious and attractive way of giving content to equality. However, the principle fails to provide any criteria for determining the respect in which the two persons are equal or the underlying basis for comparison. Scepticism about giving normative content to "equality" in this way are discussed in the following passages:

24 Sandra Fredman, *Discrimination Law* (Oxford, Clarendon Press, 2002) at p.13.
25 For the relationship between equality and justice see Aristotle, *Ethica Nicomachea* Vol.3.1131a–1131b (W.Ross trans. 1925)

J. R. Lucas, "Against Equality" (October 1965) XL Philosophy

pp.296–307: "This Equality, which is a by-product of rationality, is nothing other than the principle of Universalisability. I shall call it the principle of Formal Equality. It requires that if two people are being treated, or are to be treated, differently, there should be some relevant difference between them. Otherwise, in the absence of some differentiating feature, what is sauce for the goose is sauce for the gander, and it would be wrong to treat the two unequally, that is, not the same.

It is clear that the principle of Formal Equality by itself establishes very little. Indeed, if we accept the infinite variety of human personality, that no two people, not even identical twins, are qualitatively identical, then there will always be differences between any two people, which might be held to justify a difference of treatment. Many of these differences we may wish to rule out as not being relevant, but since the principle of Formal Equality does not provide, of itself, any criteria of relevance, it does not, by itself, establish much. It gives a line of argument, but not any definite conclusion."

Peter Westen, "The Empty Idea of Equality" (1982) 95 Harv. L. R. 537

"As the reader may have noticed, a more natural view of "like treatment" is suggested by the way "people who are alike" was interpreted. Just as no category of "like" people exist in nature, neither do categories of "like" treatment exist; treatment can be alike only in reference to some moral rule. Thus, to say that people who are alike in a certain respect "should be treated alike" means that they should be treated in accord with the moral rule by which they are determined to be alike. Hence, "likes should be treated alike" means that people for whom a certain treatment is prescribed by a standard should all be given the treatment prescribed by the standard. Or, more simply, people who by a rule should be treated alike should by the rule be treated alike.

So there it is: equality is entirely "[c]ircular." It tells us to treat like people alike; but when we ask who "like people" are, we are told they are "people who should be treated alike." Equality is an empty vessel with no substantive moral content of its own. Without moral standards, equality remains meaningless, a formula that can have nothing to say about how we should act. With such standards, equality becomes superfluous, a formula which can do nothing but repeat what we already know. As Bernard Williams observed, "when the statement of equality ceases to claim more than is warranted, it rather rapidly reaches the point where it claims less than is interesting."

The idea that equality is the treatment of "like with like" fits into the conception of equality associated with the rule of law and individual justice which requires that an adjudicator should not arbitrarily differentiate between like cases or take into account arbitrary factors in reaching a decision.[26] This idea of equality, therefore, may be especially attractive in areas where equality or the anti-discrimination principle are being used to allocate core political or legal

[26] See Peter Ingram, "Procedural Equality" in S. Guest and A. Milne (eds.), *Equality and Discrimination: Essays in Freedom and Justice,* Archiv Fur Rechts Und Sozialphilosophie, (Stuttgart: Franz Steiner Verlag, Wiesbaden, GMBH, 1985)

rights. However, this definition of equality does not provide the distinguishing criteria which identify the respects in which the two persons are alike. Therefore, this version of the principle of equality does not provide a sufficient guide to why two persons are categorised as being alike and qualify for equal treatment. Once it is accepted that there will be differences between persons which justify differential treatment, and that the principle of formal equality does not of itself provide a guide or limits to the application of these differences, the principle becomes limited in its use.

4. Equality as a Principle of Universal Humanity

The principle of universal humanity is another way of interpreting the requirement that "like should be treated with like". This principle is based on the idea that all persons are alike in one important respects: they are rational, sentient beings sharing a common humanity. It follows from this idea that all persons deserve a certain type of treatment by virtue of their humanity and membership of the human race. This definition of equality, which generates an all encompassing and universal principle, may be especially appropriate where the subject matter is fundamental human rights, or for analysis of discrimination provisions in human rights and constitutional documents (e.g. the International Covenant on Civil and Political Rights or the Canadian Charter). It may be possible, however, to state the principle of universal humanity without drawing on a concept of equality: is the principle of universal humanity necessarily linked with the concept of equality? Critics such as J. R. Lucas or Joseph Raz argue that the core value which underlies the principle of universal humanity is not equality but some other normative value, e.g. respect or recognition for a person as a human being.

J. R. Lucas, "Against Equality" (1965) Philosophy

pp.296–307: "And therefore it is proper to view the argument as one which starts from the universal common humanity of men—that all men are men—and ends with an injunction on how men are to be treated—that all men are to be treated alike, *in certain respects*. Although thus set out, the argument would not find favour with tough minded philosophers, it is a sound argument as far as it goes. Only it has little to do with Equality. It is, rather, an argument of Universal Humanity, that we should treat human beings, because they are human beings, humanely. To say that all men, because they are men, are equally men, or that to treat any two persons as ends in themselves is to treat them as equally ends in themselves is to import a spurious note of egalitarianism into a perfectly sound and serious argument. We may call it, if we like, the argument from Equality of Respect, but in this phrase it is the word 'Respect'—respect for each man's humanity, respect for him as a human being—which is doing the logical work, while the word 'Equality' adds nothing to the argument and is altogether otiose."

J. Raz, *The Morality of Freedom* (Oxford: Clarendon Press, 1987)

p.228: "Arguments and claims invoking equality but not relying on strictly egalitarian principles are rhetorical. This is not meant in a derogatory sense. It is simply that they are not claims designed to promote equality but rather to promote the cause of those who qualify under independently valid principles. They invoke equality sometimes to facilitate exposition (as in type (3) principles) and often to gain from the good name of equality in our culture. It was mentioned above that principles of equal respect or concern, etc., often amount to little more than an assertion that all human beings are moral subjects, to an assertion of humanism. Such principles can be asserted with equal ease without invoking equality. They are not designed to increase equality but to encourage recognition that the well being of all human beings counts. If their resort to fashionable egalitarian formulations makes them more attractive, so much the better. The price we pay is in intellectual confusion since their egalitarian formulation is less perspicacious, i.e. less revealing of their true grounds, than some non-egalitarian formulations of the same principles: 'Being human is in itself sufficient ground for respect' is a more perspicacious rendering of 'All humans are entitled to equal respect.'"[. . .]

As Raz points out, there are risks involved in using "equality" as a marker for harm in these cases. It can obscure the fact that it is the underlying wrong (a failure to grant respect or recognition) which is the actual harm. However, the use of equality as a foundation for claims that "being human is a ground for respect" can be useful as a rhetorical device, as Raz makes clear in the following discussion:

"Rhetorical invocation of equality is appropriate to a variety of contexts. A parent who gives medicine to the healthy child and not to the sick one, or who deceives one of his children and not the others, is treating them unequally. A person who keeps his promise to one person and breaks his promise to another is, likewise, treating them unequally. But in all these cases the wrong is the same as where a parent has only one child whom he deceives, or to whom he denies the medicine when he is sick, or when a person always breaks his promises to all. Accusing a person of unequal treatment in these and many other contexts is permissible if he behaves wrongly or badly towards some while behaving properly towards others. To accuse him of unequal treatment, however, is not to identify the nature of the wrong of creating or perpetuating inequalities. As my examples show the same wrong can exist in situations involving no inequality.

In these and in many other contexts in which equality is invoked it functions contextually rather than normatively. It indicates features of the situation in which the wrong is perpetrated which have nothing to do with the reasons for it being a wrong, nothing to do with the kind of wrong it is. This is not to say that such invocations of equality do not have useful argumentative functions. They are sometimes used *ad hominem*. "You seem to acknowledge the force of the reason in one case so why do you deny it in the other? They also sometimes indicate that something can be done to improve things. Here I have in mind not so much charges of unequal treatment as of inequality in the way things are. Poverty may be no worse in a society where it afflicts only some than in a society where all are poor. It is bad or regrettable in both to the same degree and for the same reasons. The charge of inequality which can be levelled against only one of these societies is used here rhetorically. The wrong is poverty and its attendant suffering and degradation, not the inequality. But the inequality is an indication that there may be resources which can be used to remedy the situation. It is relevant to an argument about what can be done, as well as to arguments about not doing enough to reduce the poverty.

I hope that these comments—and they are not meant to be exhaustive about the rhetorical use of equality—vindicate my claim that I am using 'rhetorical' literally and not pejoratively. The point is that in all those cases the offence is other than inequality and the action to be taken is not designed to achieve equality but some other good."

Used in this way, equality claims force a comparison which brings attention to the underlying wrong. Rhetorical equality will, therefore, be especially useful where social groups who have been traditionally excluded and disenfranchised are claiming access to rights or goods which have been monopolised by a dominant group. The claim for equality is, in this context, often used as a substitute for claims for inclusion. Although rhetorical equality is often used to highlight wrongful behaviour, they are also relevant to the distribution of goods. In this context comparison can conveniently point to the availability of resources which can be applied to remedy a grievance. This point is made most explicitly in the article by Hugh Collins which is extracted below which argues that equality claims, and anti-discrimination law, is increasingly using the paradigm of "social exclusion."[27]

B. *"A New Start"—Three Concepts of Equality*

The preceding sections discussed the way in which simple equality (formal equality and equality as universal humanity) can play a useful rhetorical role in promoting the goals of discrimination law. These formulations of equality are, therefore, especially appropriate in the context of human rights or constitutional texts. Does equality have any wider contribution to make to the anti-discrimination project? The increasing variety in the sources, form and content of discrimination law which will have important consequences for the way in which we define discrimination, as well as the scope of the legislation. One consequence will be that it may be unrealistic to expect any single concept of equality to provide a comprehensive justification for discrimination law in its multifarious forms. It may be more useful to identify a range of different definitions of equality that allow more refined analysis within discrimination law. Derek Parfitt provides three distinct formulation of equality that allow these distinctions. He defines these three versions of equality as:

(1) *Strict (Telic) Equality* is the claim that "it is in itself bad if some people are worse off than others."[28]

[27] Hugh Collins: "Discrimination, Equality and Social Inclusion" (2003) 66 M.L.R. 16. This is considered further below.

[28] D. Parfit, "Equality and Priority" in A. Mason (ed.) *Ideals of Equality*, (Oxford: Blackwell, 1998) at p.3.

(2) *Instrumental (Deontic) Equality* requires that "though we should sometimes aim for equality, that is *not* because we would thereby make the outcome better. On this view, it is not in itself bad if some people are worse off than others. When we ought to aim for equality, that is always for some other moral reason."[29]

(3) *The Priority Principle* requires that "Benefiting people matters more the worse off these people are."[30].

In the following discussion we will explore these three different claims of equality. This is not just an exercise in formal taxonomy. The failure to recognise the distinctions between these forms of equality is a major cause of confusion in discrimination law and policy. On a practical level, differences in our understanding of equality can influence a range of practical issues concerning scope, motive, causation and justifications in discrimination law.

1. Strict (telic) v Instrumental (deontic) Equality

D. Parfit, "Equality and Priority" in A. Mason (ed.) *Ideals of Equality*, (Oxford: Blackwell, 1998)

p.7: "We can now redescribe our two kinds of Egalitarianism. On the Telic view, the inequality is bad; on the Deontic view, it is unjust.

It may be objected that, when inequality is unjust, it is, for that reason, bad. But this does not undermine this way of drawing our distinction. On the Deontic View, injustice is a special kind of badness, one that necessarily involves wrong-doing. What is unjust, and therefore bad, is not strictly the state of affairs, but the way in which it was produced."

These differences manifest themselves in the context of anti-discrimination in a number of important ways. Strict and Instrumental Equality can provide justifications for different legal definitions of discrimination as well as concepts such as scope and causation in discrimination law. With strict equality, it is the end result which is important; how that end result is achieved will be less important than the fact that there is an equal outcome. For example, adherence to strict equality as a goal may require sacrificing other values and goods: this is most clear in the cases where courts of legislatures have responded to claims of discrimination by permitting the removal of a valuable resource or "levelling down". Strict equality will also be indifferent as to how the equality came about. Issues of motive and wrongdoing will not be as important in the context of strict equality as other equality formulations. By contrast, because instrumental equality is concerned with the underlying justice which is an end goal (i.e. the goal for which equality is being used as a

29 ibid at p.6.
30 ibid at p.12.

convenient marker), it will be more concerned that end results are achieved through means that are themselves just. Issues such as the motivation and state of mind of the discriminator will take on greater importance for instrumental equality. Moreover, the use of unjust means to reach equality (such as affirmative action which sacrifices the individual rights to non-discrimination in order to favour another) will be more difficult to justify.

Instrumental Equality may generate a more limited principle than strict equality in other respects. In particular, where there is a natural inequality in the distribution of a good, that cannot be distributed without unjustly sacrificing the rights of an individual, then instrumental (deonitc) equality may require no action. The fact that there is a substantial inequality in the distribution of resources, or substantive social-economic inequality between groups, will not necessarily be problematic on this analysis unless there are independent reasons of justice that require a distributive solution. Parfitt summarises this in the following passage:

"There is one case which most clearly separates these two views: those in which some inequality cannot be avoided. For Deontic Egalitarians, if nothing can be done, there can be no injustice. In Rawls' word, if some situation "is unalterable . . . the question of justice does not arise." Consider, for example, the inequality in our natural endowments. Some of us are born more talented or healthier than others, or are more fortunate in other ways. If we are Deontic Egalitarians, we shall not believe that such inequality is in itself bad. We might agree that, if we *could* distribute talents, it would be unjust or unfair to distribute them unequally. But, except, when there are bad effects, we shall see nothing to regret in the inequalities produced by the random shuffling of our genes. Many Telic Egalitarians take a different view. They believe that, even when such inequality is unavoidable, it is in itself bad. [. . .]"

2. Causation

In the context of causation, Parfit notes that instrumental equality will generate a more narrow principle than strict equality. (page 7)

p.7: "Consider next the question of causation. The Telic View naturally applies to all cases. On this view, we always have a reason to prevent or reduce inequality, if we can. If we are Deontic Egalitarians, we might think the same; but that is less likely. Since our view is not about the goodness of outcomes, it may cover only inequalities that result from acts, or only those that are intentionally produced. And it may tell us to be concerned only with the inequalities that we ourselves produce. On such a view, when we are responsible for some distribution, we ought to distribute equally. But, when no one is responsible, inequality is not unjust. In such cases, there is nothing morally amiss. We have no reason to remove such inequality by redistribution. Here again, since this view has narrower scope, this can make a great practical difference."

This view of causation has important consequences for the scope of the discrimination law. If instrumental equality is likely to be more concerned with issues of individual responsibility for acts or conditions that create inequality, then it is more likely to generate a narrower range of circumstances in which legal regulation to achieve equality is justified. There will need to be certain conditions in place before legal regulation can be justified: e.g. a causal link between the act of the discriminator and the wrong done to the victim of inequality; a greater focus on individual actors and wrong rather than the structural context that produces inequality; and greater interest in the state of mind (intention or motivation) of the discriminator. If the concern is with strict equality then these issues of individual responsibility, the state of mind of the discriminator and a causal link between the discriminatory act and the harm suffered will take on less importance. Moreover, instrumental equality is likely to justify non-discrimination in a narrower set of circumstances than strict equality. If there is a need for individual responsibility and causation, then it will be easier to justify legal regulation in cases where there is a clear relationship between the parties, e.g. a private contractual relationship. It will be more difficult to justify legal regulation, or why an individual should bear the burden of ensuring equality, where the relationship between the parties is more diffuse, because in these cases an individual or institution is being asked to take on responsibility (or costs) for achieving the goal of equality despite the fact that he has not created the inequality. This distinction will be especially relevant in discussions of positive action policies, e.g. remedies that require employers who have not engaged in discrimination to introduce programmes to train or employ women or minorities.

3. The Levelling Down Objection

Joseph Raz notes that one problem with equality is that it is prone to achieving its goal by "levelling down" and removing a benefit from all people. He states: "Egalitarian principles would be indifferent between achieving equality through taking away from those who have and giving to those who have not. The implausibility of such a view points to the existence of additional fundamental principles which at least establish a preference for the non-wasteful option. Most would agree that they will do more. They will override the egalitarian principles in at least some circumstances in order to avoid waste when equality cannot be achieved in any other way."[31] Parfitt also discusses this issue.

D. Parfit, "Equality and Priority" in A. Mason (ed.) *Ideals of Equality*, (Oxford: Blackwell, 1998)

pp.9–10: "A second objection is more serious. If inequality is bad, its disappearance must be in one way a change for the better, however this change occurs. Suppose that, in some

[31] J. Raz, *The Morality of Freedom* (Oxford: Clarendon Press, 1987) at pp.234–235:

natural disaster, those who are better off lose all their extra resources, and become as badly off as everyone else. Since this change would remove the inequality, it must be in one way welcome, on the Telic View. Though this disaster would be worse for some people, and better for no one, it must be, in one way, a change for the better. Similarly, it would be in one way an improvement if we destroyed the eyes of the sighted, not to benefit the blind, but only to make the sighted blind. These implications can be more plausibly regarded as monstrous, or absurd. The appeal to such examples we can call *the Levelling Down Objection*.

It is worth repeating that, to criticize Egalitarians by appealing to this objection, it is not enough to claim that it would be wrong to produce equality by levelling down. Since they are pluralists, who do not care only about equality, Egalitarians could accept that claim. Our objection must be that, if we achieve equality by levelling down, there is *nothing* good about what we have done. Similarly, if some natural disaster makes everyone equally badly off, that is not in any way good news. These claims do contradict the Telic Egalitarian View.

I shall return to the Levelling Down Objection. The point to notice now is that, on a Deontic view, we avoid this objection. If we are Deontic Egalitarians, we do not believe that inequality is bad, so we are not forced to admit that, on our view, it would be in one way better if inequality were removed by levelling down. We may believe that we have a reason to remove inequality only *when*, and only *because*, our way of doing so benefits the people who are worse off. Or we may believe that, when some people are worse off than others, through no fault or choice of theirs, they have a special claim to be raised up to the level of the others, but they have no claim that others be brought down to their level."

Although, as we mentioned earlier, instrumental equality is attractive because it avoids the levelling down objection, it cannot justify intervention in some situations such as the Divided World example where it is sometimes argued that there should be redistribution because of "inequality".

"Given these differences between the Telic and Deontic Views, it is important to decide which view, if either, we should accept. If we are impressed by the Levelling Down Objection, we may be tempted by the Deontic View. But, if we give up the Telic View, we may find it harder to justify some of our beliefs. If inequality is not in itself bad, we may find it harder to defend our view that we should often redistribute resources. And some of our beliefs might have to go. Reconsider the Divided World, in which the two possible states are these:

(1) Half at 100. Half at 200

(2) Everyone at 145.

In outcome (1) there is inequality. But, since the two groups are unaware of each other's existence, this inequality was not deliberately produced, or maintained. Since this inequality does not involve wrong-doing, there is no injustice. If we believe that (1) is worse, and because of the inequality, we must accept the Telic form of the Egalitarian View. We must claim that the inequality in (1) is in itself bad."

However, for Parfit, it does not follow that intervention in situation (1) has to draw on equality as a justification. The wrong in this case is not inequality, but rather the absolute lower standard of the group who have 100 (Group 100). The use of "equality" as a benchmark in these contexts can be explained in a number of ways. The comparison with the group which has 200 (Group 200) serves as a devise which either identifies the minimum threshold standard or confirms the availability of resources for redistribution. In addition, the use of equality in this context may perform a strategic or rhetorical function. The aim of redistribution in this context is not to maintain a pattern of equality. Rather, it is to give priority to Group 100 who have fallen below the relevant standard. This critical distinction—between claims of Strict Equality and the Priority Principle—are discussed in the following section.

4. The Priority Principle

D. Parfit, "Equality and Priority" in A. Mason (ed.) *Ideals of Equality*, (Oxford: Blackwell, 1998)

pp.11–13: "We might, however, give a different explanation. Rather than believing in inequality, we might be especially concerned about those people who are worse off. That could be our reason for preferring (2).

Let us now consider this view. [. . .]

The Priority View: Benefiting people matters more the worse off these people are. For Utilitarians, the moral importance of each benefit depends only on how great this benefit would be. For Prioritarians, it also depends on how well off the person is to whom this benefit comes. We should not give equal weight to equal benefits, whoever receives them. Benefits to the worse off should be given more weight. This priority is not, however, absolute. On this view, benefits to the worse off could be morally outweighed by sufficiently great benefits to the better off. If we ask what would be sufficient, there may not always be a precise answer. But there would be many cases in which the answer would be clear.

On the Priority View, I have said, it is more important to benefit those who are worse off. But this claim does not, by itself, amount to a different view, since it would be made by all Egalitarians. If we believe that we should aim for equality, we shall think it more important to benefit those who are worse off, since such benefits reduce inequality. If *this* is why we give such benefits priority, we do not hold the Priority View. On this view, as I define it here, we do not believe in equality. We do not think it is in itself bad, or unjust, that some people are worse off than others. That is what makes this a distinctive view.

The Priority View can be easily misunderstood. On this view, if I am worse off than you, benefits to me matter more. Is this *because* I am worse off than you? In one sense, yes. But this has nothing to do with my relation to you.

It may help to use this analogy. People at higher altitudes find it harder to breathe. Is this because they are higher up? In one sense, yes. But they would find it just as hard to breathe even if there were no other people who were lower down. In the same way, on the Priority View, benefits to the worse off matter more, but that is only because these people are at a lower *absolute* level. It is irrelevant that these people are worse off *than others*. Benefits to them would matter just as much even if there *were* no others who were better off.

The chief difference is, then, this. Egalitarians are concerned with relativities: with how each person's level compares with the level of other people. On the Priority View, we are concerned only with people's absolute levels. This is a fundamental structural difference. Because of this difference, there are several ways in which these views have different implications.

One example concerns scope. Telic Egalitarians may, I have said, give their view a wide scope. They may believe that inequality is bad even when it holds between people who have no connections with each other. This may seem dubious. Why would it matter if, in some far off land, and quite unknown to me, there are other people who are better off than me?

On the Priority View, there is no ground for such doubts. This view naturally has universal scope. If it is more important to benefit one of two people, because this person is worse off, it is irrelevant whether these people are in the same community, or are aware of each other's existence. The greater urgency of benefiting this person does not depend on her relation to the other person, but only on her lower absolute level.

These views differ in other ways, which I have no space to discuss here. But I have described the kind of case in which these views most deeply disagree. These are the cases which raise the Levelling Down Objection. Egalitarians face this objection because they believe that inequality is in itself bad. If we accept the Priority View, we avoid this objection. On this view, except when it is bad for people, inequality does not matter."

As Parfit's arguments suggest, instrumental equality is likely to generate a narrower principle than strict equality which seeks to maintain an egalitarian pattern as its central aim. One consequence of this narrower view (without any further conceptual supplement) is that it will lead us to sacrifice our impetus towards intervention in cases such as the divided world example where we feel that intervention is justified because of the unequal distribution of an important good to justify intervention. However, Parfit's argument reveals that this impetus towards intervention in the "divided world" example is in fact an aspect of priority rather than equality. Parfit's analysis also confirms that many of the concerns which are advanced under the label of "equality" are in fact arguments for the redistribution of resources to those who are disadvantaged. The persistence of the appeal to "equality" in these cases can be understood as the use of the concept in its "rhetorical" sense: as a convenient way of drawing attention to the need to give priority to a group, or as a convenient way of using relativities and comparison to establish the "absolute" level of need of those who deserve priority. The introduction of "priority" as a way of explaining some of our concern with "equality" has important consequences for discrimination law. For example, it may explain the increasing importance of positive action (and especially forms of positive action that require preferential treatment) and the greater focus on social policy as a way of alleviating disadvantage.

5. Three Concepts of Equality and Discrimination Law

Instrumental equality could be thought to explain many of the concepts and provisions in discrimination law. It is based on the view that inequality is sometimes bad because it is unjust. The injustice can arise in a number of ways. It may be a wrongful act or malign decision-making process.[32] Alternatively, it can be the failure to respect certain principles of justice. The focus

[32] For a discussion of the "stigma" theory of anti-discrimination see Koppelman, Andrew Koppelman, *Anti-discrimination and Social Equality*, (New Haven, USA: Yale University Press, 1996), Introduction and Ch.1.

of analysis in these cases is not the unequal outcome but rather the breach of the requirements of justice which are highlighted by the use of equality as an indicator (it is used as an instrumental value). This version of equality is concerned with the individual responsibility of the agent: e.g. voluntary acts; the motivation of the discriminator; the causal relationship between the action of the discriminator and the impact on the victim. Moreover, this instrumental equality is breached where there is a failure to comply with principles of justice which are the ultimate goal, such as avoiding malign preferences in decision-making or the failure to respect the principle of autonomy or avoiding oppression.

To the extent that it focuses on the state of mind and the action of the discriminator rather than results, the concept of direct discrimination can be placed within this category. A more pejorative label for this form of discrimination is the "perpetrator perspective" which was summarised by Alan Freeman as the:

"stance of society as a whole, or of a disinterested third-party gaze looking down on the problem of discrimination, and it simply does not care about results. Discrimination becomes the action of individuals, the atomistic behaviour of persons and institutions who have been abstracted out of actual society as part of a quest for villains."[33]

In part, the UK definition of direct discrimination which originated in the Race Relations Act 1968, and which is included within the SDA and RRA, can be placed within this category. Examples of direct discrimination in the UK include s.1(1) of the SDA which states that "A person discriminates against a woman if: (a) on the grounds of her sex he treats her less favourably than he treats or would treat a man [...]". The analogous provision in the RRA is s.1(1) which states: "A person discriminates against another ... if: (a) on racial grounds he treats that other less favourably than he treats or would treat other persons [...]". Although subsequent case law has confirmed that intention to discriminate is not necessary to establish direct discrimination under the SDA and RRA[34] the emphasis remains on the action of individuals. The crucial question is one of causation: has the victim been treated less favourably because of sex or race. This point is confirmed in the following comment of Lord Goff in *James v Eastleigh*:

"I incline to the opinion that, if it were necessary to identify the requisite intention of the defendant, that intention is simply an intention to perform the relevant act of less favourable treatment [...] It is not saved from constituting unlawful discrimination by the fact that the defendant acted from a benign

[33] A. D. Freeman, "Anti-discrimination Law: a critical review", in D. Kairys (ed.), *The Politics of Law* (New York: Pantheon, 1982) at 99.

[34] See for example *James v Eastleigh Borough Council* [1990] I.R.L.R. 208 (House of Lords)

motive. As I see it, cases of direct discrimination [...] can be considered by asking the simple question: would the complainant have received the same treatment from the defendant but for his or her sex?"[35]

A concern with results and the maintenance of a "pattern" of equality which we identified as a feature of strict equality has also influenced discrimination law. The reasons for a move away from equality (which are the main focus of instrumental equality) become less important on this analysis. Legal regulation can be justified whenever there is a deviation from an egalitarian pattern. This triggers the legislation whose goals include the maintenance of an egalitarian pattern rather than prevention of wrongful conduct. For strict egalitarians, any inequality is bad irrespective of how the inequality came about. Nor is the underlying good in respect of which the comparison is being made necessarily relevant to the analysis, unless it is specified as a limiting feature. A move towards a strict version of equality would considerably expand the range of legal regulation beyond the intentional direct acts of an individual to all indirect and unintentional acts which cause inequality. The focus of attention moves from processes to the results of acts and decision-making. In this respect, the distinction between instrumental and strict equality mirrors the distinction between equality of outcome and equality of results which is discussed below in para.(*).

It could be argued this version of equality provides a partial explanation of the concept of indirect discrimination which originated in US case law in *Griggs v Duke Power Co.*[36], and was adopted in the SDA and RRA. For example, s.1(1) of the RRA (the SDA has an analogous provision) states that a person indirectly discriminates against another if:

"he applies to that other a requirement or condition which he does apply or would apply to persons not of the same racial group as that other but:

(i) which is such that the proportion of persons of the same racial group who can comply with it is considerably smaller than the proportion of persons not of that racial group who can comply with it; and
(ii) which he cannot show to be justifiable irrespective of the colour, race, nationality or ethnic or national origin of the person to whom it is applied; and
(iii) which is to the detriment of that other because he cannot comply with it."

There are, however, some limits to the use of strict equality as an explanatory concept for indirect discrimination. It could be argued that the legal definition of indirect discrimination (as set out in the SDA and RRA) sits between instrumental and strict notions of equality, as Christopher McCrudden notes in the following passage:

35 *James v Eastleigh BC* [1990] I.R.L.R. at 294–295.
36 (1971) 401 U.S. 424.

Christopher McCrudden: "Changing Notions of Discrimination" in S. Guest and A. Milne (eds.), *Equality and Discrimination: Essays in Freedom and Justice, Archiv Fur Rechts Und Sozialphilosophie*, (Stuttgart: Franz Steiner Verlag Wiesbaden GMBH, 1985)

pp.84: "The principle on which the concept of indirect discrimination is based differs from the simple non-discrimination principle (which underlies the idea of direct discrimination) in being positive as well as negative in its requirements and in taking into account some of the prior existing disadvantages which black and women workers bring to the market place. The employer must, if he is not to be in breach of his duty, so operate his recruitment and promotion procedures, *etc* so as to positively offset the group related disadvantages which adversely affect a black or woman worker's chances of being hired or promoted. Also unlike the simple non-discrimination principle, it requires questions to be asked not only about the precise basis on which the good being distributed is deserved but also about the nature of the good being distributed.

The new concept of indirect discrimination is, however, like the simple non-discrimination principle in that neither assume that one particular pattern of distribution of goods should result from these procedures. Both look to how the distribution was arrived at rather than the outcome."

The passage suggests that although the focus on groups rather than individuals and inequality of results underlies indirect discrimination, the concept stops short of insisting on a strict pattern on equality. This ensures that indirect discrimination continues to operate as an individual rather than a group concept. The individual's right does not depend on others in the group, although the individual may be classified as part of a group, making a claim because of his membership of that group, and is claiming that the wrong is the disparate impact of conduct or a decision on that group. The fact that there is inequality of outcome is not the wrong. Rather, it is an indicator that there has been a decision or conduct which provides the individual with a right to complain of discrimination.[37]

As we will see later, some commentators seek to justify discrimination law using ideas of autonomy and social exclusion rather than equality. For those who support the notion that some version of equality justifies discrimination law, however, many of the disagreements concerning the appropriate goal of discrimination law, or its perceived inadequacies, can be traced back to confusions about what is meant by equality. Although legislation often gives effect to an instrumental equality through the use of motivation and causation, critics of the discrimination law sometimes use strict equality as their preferred evaluative criteria. If, on the other hand, the focus is on strict equality then the means by which this equality is achieved becomes less important than the ultimate result raising two particular problems. First, the prospect of the removal of an advantage or good is removed from the preferred group to achieve equality (*levelling down objection*). Second, the shift towards results

[37] See Owen Fiss, "Groups and the Equal Protection Clause", (1976) 5 Philosophy and Public Affairs 107, at 126–129.

rather than processes, and impact on groups rather than individuals, raises the spectre of "preferential treatment" or "affirmative action".

For advocates of equality some of these problems can be overcome once we move beyond the assumption that discrimination law has to reflect one sole rather than a mixed concept of equality. The mixed approach also asks further questions: which concept of equality is being deployed; is it the most appropriate version; what function do we want equality to perform; is equality promoting rather than obscuring the goals of discrimination law.

On this mixed approach, it would be possible to say that in some cases equality gives sense to the governing value in this case: e.g. the concept of alleviating disadvantage. This would also suggest that an appropriate response to a finding of equality is not the removal of a good because although this promotes strict equality it undermines other important values such as justice (reflected in instrumental equality) or alleviating disadvantage (reflected in the priority principle). To return to the levelling down problem, it should be possible to object to the levelling down objection by pointing to the fact that it undermines a central concern that is entailed by the use of equality within discrimination law: e.g. the priority principle which is concerned with the substantive alleviation of disadvantage. In this context priority mirrors the use of equality in its rhetorical sense: it is used to bring attention to the absolute and independent wrong which is suffered by an individual or group. Therefore one objection to the levelling down objection is that it gives effect to one aspect of equality (strict) whilst seriously undermining another (priority). Equality is often used as a way of drawing attention to the absolute disadvantage or needs of individuals or a group. This has important consequences in the context of the discrimination law and policy. Increasingly, it is being argued that certain criteria—such as membership of a disadvantaged group or the possession of a characteristic which is used as a basis for exclusion from a good—are in themselves, and without the need for comparison, a sufficient trigger for the discrimination law. The fact of comparison with others, in these circumstances, serves to draw attention to this wrong or to the availability of the means to remedy the situation. Comparison, in these contexts, does not give sense to strict equality: therefore, although levelling down is able to achieve equality between the comparators it is not a legitimate and appropriate response to a claim of inequality or discrimination. In areas such as pregnancy discrimination or harassment, for example, it is argued that there is a remedy in discrimination law without the need for a male comparator. Analogous arguments are made by those who argue that the absolute levels of disadvantage of certain racial groups justify affirmative action policies. The White Paper which preceded the RRA sets out the alleviation of "disadvantage" as one of the aims of the legislation. This concept of priority can also provide a justification for the use of supply side measures to overcome disadvantage (see EU Social Action Plan, Art.13 Treaty of Amsterdam).

Despite critiques, or calls for a more complex and nuanced approach, the concept of equality continues to be popular in justifying discrimination law.

One explanation for this may be that as well as being a concept that is used within statutory discrimination law, equality is also increasingly presented as a foundational constitutional value.

"Hugh Collins, Discrimination, Equality and Social Inclusion" (2003) 66 M.L.R. 16

pp.41: "My surmise is that equal treatment has been accorded such importance in anti-discrimination laws for two reasons. First, equal treatment is the normal rule required by the separate principle of respect for individual dignity or equal worth. We observed earlier that equal worth sometimes requires respect for difference, but we should not ignore how it also supports in most instances a requirement of equal treatment. This principle of equal respect is expressed by article 14 of the European Convention for the Protection of Human Rights and Fundamental Freedoms: 'The enjoyment of the rights and freedoms set forth in this Convention shall be secured without discrimination on any ground such as sex, race, colour, language, religion, political or other opinion, national or social origin, association with a national minority, property, birth or other status.' The independent value of respect for individual dignity thus strengthens the weight to be attached to the value of equal treatment.

A second reason why equal treatment has been given such a prominent role in the legislation is that the principle has provided a dominant constitutional principle within Western legal systems. A legal system, which has achieved autonomy from the political and economic systems, has its independent demands of fair process, of evidence and proof, of remedial devices, of legal justification, and, in general, of preservation of the integrity of its system."

As Collins makes clear, equality has become a key constitutional and human rights value. One consequence of this development is that equality is de-contextualised from the specific liberal foundations from which it emerges. This approach also tends to present equality as a universal normative value which is detached from the political, social and economic contexts in which it operates. A defence of egalitarian policies and discrimination law has usually been associated with liberal political theory. The next section sets out the different strands within liberalism and relates them to the discrimination law. The discussion makes clear that the relationship between liberalism and the evolving concepts of the non-discrimination are not as complimentary as it may appear. Discrimination law and policy has a tense relationship with liberalism. There has been increasing criticism that liberal discrimination law is too focused on concepts of individual rights and formal equality which cannot respond to the most significant causes of inequality and discrimination. This has led to the development of "critical" perspectives by feminists, critical race theorists and other radical critics: these critics argue that liberal discrimination law is not able to respond to the structural disadvantage that is a cause of inequality and discrimination. Liberal discrimination law has increasingly come under attack for a number of reasons: because of its focus on procedural and formal equality; its treatment of non-discrimination as an individual right; and because it deploys a sharp separation of the public and private sphere. These critics argue that liberal anti-discrimination law cannot address the fundamental and structural causes of inequality, social exclusion and oppression of minorities. The next section discusses liberalism and its critics in the context of discrimination law.

IV. Liberalism and Discrimination Law

Within the liberal justification of discrimination there are differences between those approaches that use a procedural form of liberalism and treat equality as a formal treatment of "like with like"; and those that base liberalism on deeper values such as autonomy, dignity or respect. Within the generic term "liberalism" there is significant difference between the neutrality based arguments of anti-perfectionists and the appeal to well being and the good which underlie the work of perfectionist liberal writers.[38]

Most liberal writers argue for and support discrimination law and policy, as an important means of securing justice for individuals in a liberal democracy. In the previous discussion we defined *Instrumental Egalitarians* as those for whom "though we should sometimes aim for equality, that is not because we would thereby make the outcome better. On this view, it is not in itself bad if some people are worse off than others: when we ought to aim for equality, that is always for some other moral reason."[39] In considering these other reasons it becomes necessary to examine the theories of justice which provide the underlying moral reasons for aiming for equality, and the justifications of discrimination law. Contemporary liberal theories of justice which often appeal to "egalitarianism" are an obvious starting point for analysis. Despite the common group of ideas of freedom, equality and individual rights which unite these theories, it is necessary to differentiate between the different kinds of liberal theories of justice which are relevant. The key distinction is between those theories of *procedural liberalism* associated with traditional liberal writers such as Rawls and Dworkin which are founded on the idea of the "priority of the right over the good". This is the claim (often stated as the claim of state neutrality) that individuals may rely on a range of conceptions of the good drawing on a variety of comprehensive doctrines in their private life. The state, however, must remain neutral between these conceptions. This contrasts with the claims of *perfectionist liberals* who argue that it is a function of the state to advance legitimate and important goal, e.g. autonomy, respect or recognition. This distinction is important for the discrimination law and policy. For

[38] For a perfectionist defence of constitutional judicial review see Joseph Raz, *Ethics in the Public Domain* (Oxford: Oxford University Press, 1994) at 55–58.

[39] See Derek Parfit, "Equality and Priority" in A. Mason (ed.) *Ideals of Equality*, (Oxford: Blackwell, 1998) at p.6.

procedural liberals, the discrimination law is a requirement of justice because of its contribution to the aim of ensuring neutrality as to concepts of the good. This can be secured in a number of ways. A policy of tolerance of minorities can be secured through respect for individual rights which leave individuals the freedom to pursue their preferred conception of the good in their private lives without interference by others or the state. In recent times, a specific right of non-discrimination has been recognised as part of this framework of individual rights. For perfectionist liberals, the discrimination principle is a requirement of justice because it advances a conception of the good, a valid goal, which the state should secure for its citizens, e.g. autonomy, respect or recognition. Raz, for example, states: "it is the goal of all political action to enable individuals to pursue valid conceptions of the good and to discourage evil or empty ones"[40]

These distinctions are relevant in the context of instrumental egalitarianism. For procedural liberals, the discrimination law and policy can be justified because of their contribution to the goal of state neutrality. For perfectionist liberals, on the other hand, they are justified because they allow the state to secure valuable goods such as autonomy for individuals.

A. *Procedural Liberalism*

In choosing an explanatory framework, Ronald Dworkin's discussion of liberalism is an obvious starting point because he makes the idea of treating citizens with "equal respect and concern" as central aspect of his version of liberalism.[41] In his summary of liberalism, Dworkin distinguishes between two kinds of moral commitments: on the one hand, there are concepts about what constitutes the good life; and on the other hand, there are ideas of what it is to treat others fairly, justly and in a way so as to respect their dignity as human agents (procedural principles).[42] Dworkin argues that it is a distinguishing characteristic of a liberal theory of justice that it takes no position as to the substantive views about the ends of a good life, but it remains strongly committed to safeguarding the principle of treating people with equal respect. Neutrality as to the substantive goals of individuals is essential for showing

[40] See Joseph Raz, *The Morality of Freedom*, (Oxford: Clarendon Press, 1986) at 133.

[41] Martin Loughlin, *Public Law and Political Theory*, (Oxford: Clarendon, 1992) concludes that "The main handle for promoting reforms based on this liberal normativist analysis has been the European Convention of Human Rights" (at 207) and "The jurisprudential foundations of this programme have been laid mainly by Ronald Dworkin who, during the last 20 years, has developed a normative theory of law based on liberal, rationalist premises." (at 207). For examples of liberal normativist support for a Bill of Rights see A Lester: "The Constitution: Decline and Renewal" in J. Jowell and D. Olive (eds.), *The Changing Constitution* 1st edn, (Oxford, 1985), Ch.12; A Lester et al., *A British Bill of Rights* (London, Institute of Public Policy Research, Consultation Paper No. 1, 1990). See also R. Dworkin, *A Bill of Rights for Britain* (London: Chatto and Windus, 1990).

[42] R. Dworkin, *A Matter of Principle* (Oxford: Oxford University Press, 1985), Ch.8.

each person equal respect and, thereby, respecting their dignity as agents. Given the diversity of goods that individuals can choose, a failure to remain neutral in relation to substantive principles would be tantamount to saying to those whose conception of the good is not preferred, that their views are not as worthy as those of other citizens. It would be a failure to accord them individual liberty and dignity.

Despite modification to his arguments since *A Theory of Justice*,[43] John Rawls also adopts this idea as a key feature of his liberalism in *Political Liberalism*.[44] In these contexts neutrality operates as a political principle. The requirement is not that all individuals should be neutral in relation to the good in their private lives. Rather, public decision-making should remain neutral between substantive principles, allowing an individual to choose and revise their own concept of the good[45]. Nor is it the case that the appeal to neutrality is an appeal to scepticism or relativism. According to Dworkin, neutrality is required "not because there is no right or wrong of the matter, but because that is what is right."[46] This support for neutrality takes claims about individuals as the initial starting point (as the input) for a theory of justice. For example, Dworkin analysis is based on the right of each individual to "equal respect and concern", whilst Rawls is committed to the idea that all citizens are "free, moral and equal". In addition, rights are the end product (the output) of this approach to politics. For Dworkin these are the fundamental principles of individual freedom which act as a "trump" over collective goals and policies.[47] In Rawlsian terms, a liberal theory of justice is characterised by a commitment to two principles of justice: first, there is individual freedom as embodied in a package of individual liberties which are distributed equally between citizens (ensuring an equal right to basic liberties such as integrity of the person and freedom of expression and association); second, there is the principle to equality of opportunity and a more equal distribution of the products of social co-operation.[48]

The substance and form of this version of liberalism (sometimes labelled procedural[49]) are immediately familiar. In terms of its contents, interests of the individual in liberty (i.e. freedom of speech, association, personal integrity and the values of the rule of law) are safeguarded. The form for protecting these interests is typically through the judicial review of the acts of the state. Despite variation in substance and form, this model provides the preferred structure

43 J. Rawls, *A Theory of Justice* (Oxford: Oxford University Press, 1972)

44 J Rawls, *Political Liberalism* (New York,: Columbia University Press, 1993) Lecture V.

45 See for example Rawls' discussion of "The Political Conception of the Person", *Political Liberalism* (New York,: Columbia University Press, 1993) at 29.

46 R. Dworkin, *A Matter of Principle* (Oxford: Oxford University Press, 1985) at 191 and 203.

47 See Ronald Dworkin's defence of this position in "Is there a Right to Pornography?", (1981) 1 O.J.L.S. 1

48 See John Rawls *Political Liberalism* (New York,: Columbia University Press, 1993) at Lecture VIII

49 This term is used and discussed in the context of the liberal—communitarian debate by Charles Taylor: "Cross Purposes: The Liberal—Communitarian Debate" in *Philosophical Arguments* (Cambs. Mass: Harvard University Press) at 186.

for a range of constitutional documents in western democracies, as well as international and regional human rights documents.

The traditional liberal approach requires that any involvement by citizens with voluntary, private or civil organisations must be uncoerced and consensual[50]. This draws upon the idea of a neutral public sphere as its essential structuring device and relegates issues of personal identity to the private sphere. It also relates to the anti-discrimination law and policy in a number of ways.[51]

First, the *toleration* of minorities is cited as one of the main advantages of individual civil rights and liberties. Citizens are free to express their particular identity in the private sphere, either individually or in association with others, without state interference. This approach to minority protection fits comfortably with the idea that it is no business of the state to prescribe what its citizens should believe, and that influencing citizen's beliefs is no part of the function of the state.

Second, recent strategy for the protection of minorities has supplemented toleration in the public sphere with an *individual right to non-discrimination*. Although most versions of this right permit a limited measure of discrimination in the private sphere, non-discrimination ensures that minorities have access to politics, the economy and key sectors such as public services and education. This clearly affects the way in which the majority will conduct not only their private but also some of their public affairs and it involves interference with private choices.

Recent liberal politics has increasingly adopted a third strategy of "recognition" in the public sphere as an important aspect of the well being of individuals. These are moves towards *multiculturalism, accommodation of difference, cultural pluralism* as a response to, and requirement for, minority protection.

The legal regulation of discrimination, and interference with individual choice, is justified from within the procedural liberal paradigm because discrimination is labelled a "malign criteria" and "illegitimate preferences". The argument is that a liberal political theory need not remain neutral about discriminatory preferences which are classified as malign preferences. Taking into account these malign preferences would be a failure to treat the victims of discrimination with equal respect and concern; and, therefore, procedural liberalism does not require a democratic decisiomaker to be neutral in this context.[52] This interference can be justified in two contexts: first, through

[50] Rawls discussion of the relationship between individual and groups is that individuals have political rights whereas groups are recognised as instrumental or associational. John Rawls *Political Liberalism* (New York,: Columbia University Press, 1993

[51] See Joseph Raz, "Multiculturalism" in J. Raz, *Ethics in the Public Domain* (Oxford: Clarendon Press, 1994).

[52] This provides an attractive model for justifying the anti-discrimination for a judicial process which is more comfortable with procedural rather than substantive principles of justice. This is a point made in the following extract by Owen Fiss in his analysis of the constitutional provision in the US constitution which guarantees equality. He argues that the attraction of grounding the anti-discrimination in a principle of neutrality appeals to a system of reasoning which is grounded in ideas of neutrality between persons. See Owen Fiss, "Groups and the Equal Protection Clause" (1976) 5 Philosophy and Public Affairs, pp.107–177.

restricting the illegitimate discriminatory choices of individuals; and second, through measures which distribute goods to minorities to compensate for their disadvantage which can be attributed to past or present discrimination.

Dworkin defends procedural liberalism (in the following passage he uses the term neutral utilitarian) in both contexts. He argues that a procedural (anti-perfectionist) liberal can justify the non-discrimination principle and need not remain neutral in the face of malign preferences for racism or other discriminatory choices. He states:

"Suppose the community contains a Nazi, for example, whose set of preferences includes the preference that Aryans have more and Jews less of their preferences fulfilled just because of who they are. A neutral utilitarian cannot say that there is no reason in political morality for rejecting or dishonoring that preference, for not dismissing it as just wrong, for not striving to fulfil it with all the dedication that officials devote to fulfilling any other set of preferences. For utilitarianism itself provides such a reason: its most fundamental tenet is that people's preferences should be weighed on an equal basis in the same scales, that the Nazi theory of justice is profoundly wrong, and that officials should oppose the Nazi theory and strive to defeat rather than to fulfil it. A neutral utilitarian is barred, for reasons of consistency, from taking the same politically neutral attitude toward the Nazi's political preference that he takes toward other sorts of preferences."[53]

He goes on to argue that malign preferences such as racism or other forms of discrimination are a failure to grant "equal respect and concern" to each individual which is a central requirement of liberal politics.

In addition to challenging prejudice as malign preferences, and an individual right to non-discrimination, procedural liberalism also justifies the distribution of resources to minorities. One argument in favour of discrimination law is that it re-distributes valuable resources to individuals and groups on the basis of need. Dworkin has argued that a liberal political theory needs to attend to the distribution of resources. Such a system must "place victims in a position as close as possible to that which they would occupy if prejudice did not exist" and it must "protect people who are the objects of systematic prejudice from suffering any serious or pervasive disadvantage from that prejudice."[54] These ideas underlying a liberal theory of justice generate a wider definition of discrimination law. They would justify not only an individual right to non-discrimination and protection from the most explicit forms of prejudice, but also policies (legal and non-legal) which redistribute resources to those who suffer social or economic disadvantage. Dworkin also concludes

53 See R. Dworkin, "Do We Have a Right to Pornography?", in *A Matter of Principle*, n.35 above at pp.361–62. See also Ely's response to this argument, Koppelman n.2 above at pp.21–22, that it is not because preferences are external (Dworkin's main concern) but rather because they are malign that they cannot be permitted.

54 R. Dworkin, "What is Equality? Part 3: The Place of Liberty," 73 (1987) Iowa L. Rev. 1 at 36–37

that redistribution of resources through affirmative action programmes is justified by the relationship between the present disadvantage of certain groups and a history of discrimination.[55] John Rawls' theory of justice includes principles of justice which require distribution of goods on the basis of equality. All inequalities are subject to the "difference principle" which requires that a move away from equality is only justified if it benefits the least well off. It is worth noting that there is a considerable overlap between these liberal principles of redistribution and the Priority Principle which Parfit argues is one idea underlying the commitment to egalitarianism. This aspect of the procedural liberalism response to minorities is important: it provides a justification for a legal definition of discrimination which goes beyond explicit acts of prejudice and also includes indirect discrimination and affirmative action programmes.

The distinctive feature of anti-perfectionist liberal theories, such as those of Rawls and Dworkin, is that although they argue for the neutrality of the state in relation to conceptions of the good in the public sphere, they simultaneously argue for state intervention in the free market to distribute resources as a requirement of justice. The contradiction between the claims to neutrality as a guarantee of individual rights and freedom, and policies of redistribution of resources has been discussed by critics of distributive justice.[56] Before moving on to discuss these liberal justifications for anti-discrimination law it is also worth mentioning that there are "libertarian" writers who argue from within the liberal paradigm but are opposed to anti-discrimination law. Those writers who are against regulation of free market relations and private contractual relationship have an objection to anti-discrimination law because it is a regulatory interference with freedom of contract. Richard Epstein, for example, makes a detailed "libertarian" argument against employment discrimination.[57]

B. *Perfectionist liberalism*

Support for a wider definition of discrimination is also provided by perfectionist liberal theories which rely on substantive principles of autonomy, dignity, respect or recognition. Perfectionist liberal theories also require attention to the distribution social and economic resources as a requirement of individual autonomy. However, they bypass the criticism that liberalism requires the state to remain neutral in relation to conceptions of the good. They explicitly affirm that rather than remaining neutral, a liberal state can justifiably intervene in the public sphere to create the optimal conditions for rea-

[55] R. Dworkin, "Bakke's Case: Are Quotas Unfair?" in *A Matter of Principle*, n.46 above.

[56] See R. Nozick, *Anarchy, State and Utopia*, (Oxford: Blackwells, (2001)), ch.7.

[57] Richard A. Epstein, *Forbidden Grounds: The Case Against Employment Discrimination Laws* (Cambridge: Harvard University Press, 1992).

lising a value such as autonomy.[58] Despite some similarities, e.g. the focus on individual choice and appropriate resources, there are significant differences between procedural and perfectionist liberal theories in the context of the discrimination law.

For perfectionist liberals, discrimination law is not justified because it contributes to state neutrality between citizen's concepts of the good. Rather, perfectionist liberal theories can defend anti-discrimination legislation because it can contribute to some positive valuable goal, which it is the function of the liberal state to secure. The goal can be autonomy and well being, dignity or respect and recognition. Procedural liberals justify the discrimination law because it contributes to a framework of rights which allows individuals to determine their own conception of the good; and perfectionist liberals justify discrimination law as an aspect of the good which it is the duty of the state to secure for its citizens.

Autonomy, dignity and well being are terms that require further analysis. Dignity, in particular, is increasingly cited as a core foundational principle of discrimination. As Sandra Fredman has noted, "the primacy of individual dignity and worth as a foundation for equality rights has been clearly articulated in a number of jurisdictions, both in constitutional or statutory documents and by courts". Fredman gives examples from the Canadian Supreme Court; the South African constitution; and the Germany Constitutional Court; the term "dignity" is also increasingly used as a justification for the statutory provisions which regulate discriminatory harassment.[59] Gay Moon and Robin Allen have also recently applied the concept of "dignity discourse" to discrimination law, particularly in areas such as harassment, in relation to comparators and justification and reasonable accommodation. Significantly, they also argue that "dignity" can be useful in the context of multiple discrimination and conflicts of rights, discussed further in Chapter 9. Some of the core issues about the substantive values of autonomy, well being and dignity are also discussed in the following passage by Thomas Hill.

[58] For a detailed discussion of the differences between anti-perfectionist and perfectionist liberalism see: Raz, *The Morality of Freedom*, n.17 and J. Raz, *Ethics in the Public Domain* (Oxford: Clarendon Press, 1994), Ch.5.

[59] Sandra Fredman, *Anti-discrimination Law*, (Oxford: Clarendon Press, 2002), page 18–19. See also Gay Moon and Robin Allen QC, *Dignity Discourse in Discrimination Law: A Better Route to Equality?* [2006] 6 E.H.R.L.R. 610–649.

Thomas E. Hill Jr., *Autonomy and Self-Respect* (Cambridge: Cambridge University Press, 1991)

pp.31–37: "*Autonomy as a psychological capacity*

[. . .] Autonomy on this view is not freedom from causal determinism, still less an ability to act independently of desire. It is a capacity and disposition to makes choices in a rational manner; and this means choosing in the absence of certain particular attitudes and inner obstacles, such as blind acceptance of tradition and authority, neurotic compulsions, and the like. [. . .]

Autonomy as a right

Sometimes the assertion that persons are autonomous is an attribution of a right rather than a psychological capacity. To say that persons have autonomy in this sense is not a descriptive statement that they are in fact free from certain influences (such as inner compulsions and slavery to convention) but instead a claim that they ought to be free from certain influences (inappropriate interference by others). [. . .] Though other rights have been associated with autonomy, the right I have in mind is a moral right against individuals (not the state) (a) to make one's own decisions about matters deeply affecting one's life, (b) without certain sorts of interference by others, (c) provided certain conditions obtain. The right presupposes a background of other moral rights and legal rights within a just system, which define an area of permissible conduct. [. . .]

Let us say that persons have autonomy, or live autonomously, in a final sense if the following is true: (1) They have the psychological capacities for rational decision making which are associated with autonomy; (2) they actually use these capacities when they face important choice situations; (3) they have the right of autonomy discussed previously, i.e., a right to make morally and legally permissible decisions about matters deeply affecting their own lives free from threats and manipulation by others; (4) other people actually respect this right as well as their other rights; (5) they are able and disposed to have distinctly human values; (6) others respect this capacity by not presuming that they value only good experiences for themselves and by not counting their comfort as more important than their declared values; and, finally, (7) they have ample opportunities to make use of these conditions in living a life over which they have a high degree of control."

Clearly the ability to make choices free of interference and coercion is a critical aspect of leading an autonomous life. Not only coercion or interference by others but also other factors such as the "harsh conditions" which result from social and economic deprivation can interfere with the meaningful realisation of autonomy. Hill's discussion of autonomy allows us to identify the relationship between autonomy and the discrimination law. There are a number of similarities between anti-perfectionist and perfectionist liberal theories. Like anti-perfectionist liberalism, a concern with autonomy as a principle of political morality generates a policy of toleration towards minorities. However, there are critical difference between the two. Whilst anti-perfectionist theories draw on scepticism in relation to the good: "The sceptical and semi-sceptical arguments are thought to buttress, among other things, the conclusion that, while we may guide our own lives by our beliefs about the nature of the good life, we should refrain from relying on these beliefs when we act politically."[60]

[60] See Raz, *Ethics in the Public Domain*, ibid at p.109.

Perfectionist liberalism, by contrast bases its commitment to tolerance on the goods of autonomy and pluralism. So Raz states, a commitment to autonomy "is valuable only if one steers a course for one's life through significant choices among diverse and valuable options" and "The emphasis here is on the range of options available to the agent. This points to a connection between autonomy and pluralism. A pluralistic society, we may say, not only recognizes the existence of a multiplicity of values but also makes their pursuit a real option available to its members. But it is not merely that autonomy and pluralism require the availability of a wide range of options. They are also at one in requiring that those be valuable options."[61] Tolerance in this context is justified as a requirement of the good of autonomy and pluralism rather than scepticism. Autonomy generates other arguments in favour of the anti-discrimination principle.

First, autonomy requires that individuals have "the psychological capacities for rational decision making which are associated with autonomy" and "they actually use these capacities when they face important choice situations." In the context of the discrimination law it will be obvious that explicitly discriminatory conduct will interfere with creating the conditions in which the victims can develop these capacities and exercise meaningful choice. Prejudice and direct discrimination can be understood as tantamount to a "stigma". In the US, stigma theory has been developed as the underlying basis for the Equal Protection Clause and the prohibition of racial discrimination. However, stigma theory has a potential application which goes beyond issues of race. Koppelman cites the following definition which links the harm of stigma with the failure to grant recognition, respect, belonging and equal citizenship on the victim[62].

In addition, Paul Brest whose defence of the "Anti-Discrimination Principle" includes procedural defects, also includes the malign results of discrimination and the "psychic" injuries associated with, for example, racial discrimination.[63] One of the psychic injuries that may be caused by discrimination is the failure to grant recognition, or misrecognition, of a core aspect of a person's personal identity which is increasingly becoming important as part of the contemporary "politics of recognition".

On this analysis, discrimination law is justified, in part, because it contributes to the eradication of social practices which stigmatise individuals on the basis of a characteristic (such as race or sex) which is "protected". In Chapter [*] we will consider the basis for attributing special protected status to certain characteristics, and discuss the range of legal protection in this area. Here, it is worth noting that unlike the anti-perfectionist liberal justification of the discrimination law, the present argument shifts the focus of analysis away

[61] ibid at pp.119–120.

[62] Andrew Koppelman, *Anti Discrimination Law and Social Equality* (New Haven, USA: Yale University Press, 1996), Ch.2.

[63] Paul Brest, *The Supreme Court 1975 Term. Forward: In Defense of the Anti-discrimination Principle*, (1976) 90 Harvard L.R. 1–55.

from the decisiomaking process of the discriminator and is more concerned with the impact on the victim. The harm identified is not that of "malign" decisionmaking but rather lack of respect and recognition, essential aspects of the well being for individuals. These differences are important because they explain the contemporary emphasis on "identity politics". Stigma and the failure to grant recognition also draw on various (and sometimes contradictory) uses of the term equality in contemporary discussions.

Joseph Raz, *Ethics in the Public Domain*, (Oxford: Clarendon Press, 1994)

pp.26: "It is futile to enumerate all the ways in which our actions affect other people's ability to have (well-deserved) self-respect. They range from conditions which are necessary for mental health, and the eradication of racism and other forms of bigotry. The latter constitutes the major part of the politics of identity. It concerns the fact that people born into societies which denigrate aspects of their being central to their own sense of who they are cannot but be affected by those attitudes. They may come to share them, sometimes even while they openly reject them as unfounded, and be tormented by self-hatred and self-doubt. Or they may reject them and pay the price of defying their society. The price is expressed in alienation from the society, and difficulty in engaging in pursuits which because of their social profile involve close integration in the society, and in many other ways. The current emphasis on the politics of identity in some countries may be a passing phase. But the pivotal importance of self-respect to the well-being of people is enduring and fundamental. The crucial importance of the fight against racism, homophobia, sexism, chauvinism, and the like, is a central element of the duties of well-being, even if its moral relevance may not be exhausted by its relevance to well-being."

C. *Autonomy, the Context of Choice and Multiculturalism*

Another aspect of perfectionist liberalism and the focus on autonomy is that it shifts the analysis beyond a focus on interference with individual choice. It gives greater weight to external factors that are outside the control of the individual but which nevertheless impact on his or her ability to be autonomous. Thomas Hill and Joseph Raz considers this issue in their discussion of autonomy.

Thomas E. Hill Jr., *Autonomy and Self-Respect* (Cambridge: Cambridge University Press, 1991)

pp.36: "This last point requires special explanation. One might at first think it sufficient for an ideal rational life to have the capacities, rights, and good treatment from others indicated in (1)–(6) (a list of factors important for autonomy—authors addition); but further reflection quickly shows otherwise. Even if (1)–(6) were true, people could still find themselves unable to make use of these favorable conditions for any of several reasons. For example, though rationally disposed to make the best of their situation and unhindered by threats and manipulation by others, they might be severely confined in the choices they could make by widespread poverty, disease, overpopulation, and absence of technology and culture. Even if it is no one's fault, when one has to labor in the fields all day to survive, one has little opportunity to live as a rational person controlling his life. The choice to labor may be perfectly rational, of course; but it may be almost the only rational choice one has a chance to make. Harsh conditions also restrict the range of morally permissible choices: one cannot do philosophy if one must mine coal to feed one's children. Opportunities to live an ideally rational life may be further restricted by pointless role-expectations and conformist attitudes, and the lack of what Mill called "experiments in living". And even though one may be able to select from many brands of soup and cosmetics, if communal values are lost in a capitalistic society then more significant options are effectively closed. Finally, and significantly for present purposes, opportunities for rational, self-controlled living are restricted when one does not know the realities of one's choice situation. I could be able and eager to seek information, to reflect critically, to be on guard against manipulation and neurotic patterns, and to decide rationally on the basis of my beliefs, but still I would not really be in rational control of my life if my beliefs about my situation were drastically mistaken. Opportunities to learn the relevant facts are also needed."

J. Raz, *The Morality of Freedom* (Oxford: Clarendon Press, 1987)

pp.373–375: "*The Adequacy of Options.* No one can control all aspects of his life. How much control is required for the life to be autonomous, and what counts as an adequate exercise of control (as opposed to being forced by circumstances, or deceived by one's own ignorance, or governed by one's weaknesses) is an enormously difficult problem.

[. . .]

The criteria of the adequacy of options available to a person must meet several distinct concerns. They should include options with long term pervasive consequences as well as short term options of little consequences as well as short term options of little consequence., and a fair spread between them. We should be able both to choose long term commitments or projects and to develop lasting relationships and be able to develop and pursue them by means which we choose from time to time. It if intolerable that we should have no influence over the choice of our occupation or of our friends. But it is equally unacceptable that we should not be able to decide on trivia such as when to wash or when to comb our hair. This aspect of the requirement of adequate choice is necessary to make sure that our control extends to all aspects of our lives. This is clearly required by the basic idea of being the author of one's life."

Both the Raz and Hill make clear that autonomy requires control, ability and the inner capacity to exercise choice; freedom from coercion. Autonomy also requires ample opportunities to make use of these conditions in living a life over which they have a high degree of control. This raises an issue about the context in which individual choice is exercised. Procedural liberalism is also concerned with issues of distributive justice. Perfectionist liberal theories provide a strong justification for state intervention in the public sphere by arguing for the creation of the right conditions in which individuals can exercise valuable options. Thus, concern with autonomy requires attention to the social and economic context within which choice is exercised: not only that there should be choice available for an individual, but that there should be an adequate range of choices. A concern with autonomy justifies special attention to the need for distributive justice. In the context of the discrimination law this is likely to generate legal definitions of discrimination which include indirect discrimination, positive action and extra legal measures for alleviating disadvantage. In addition, rather than operating in a vacuum, the meaningful exercise of autonomous choice will require a collective context. Therefore, a focus on autonomy may require support for cultural pluralism: a flourishing cultural context within which these choices take on meaning and significance for the individual, which are issues often discussed in the context of multiculturalism.[64]

V. Critiques of Liberal Discrimination Law

The idea of equality of opportunity is often equated with "procedural" or "formal" equality, which is contrasted with "substantive" equality. The contrast between the two definitions of equality is often used to highlight the limits of equality of opportunity with criticism in a number of contexts. In particular, this line of reasoning allows a critique of models of discrimination law that are based on formal procedural equality. This more "radical" critique of liberal discrimination law has a number of trajectories and overlapping features which we explore in the next section. However, despite this diversity, it is worth bearing in mind a number of common features of these critical perspectives: they criticise procedural and formal inequality for its inability to address the reality of the experience of discrimination by victims; they identify the symmetry and colour blind nature of formal procedural equality as problematic because it fails to accommodate legitimate differences between social groups; they identify discrimination in a context that is wider than "individual acts", they focus on the way in which discrimination impacts in distinct and asymmetrical ways on different social groups; and they define discrimination as a structural problem that causes not just the wrong of "individual injustice", but also contributes to wider oppression and social exclusion of some individuals and groups. Finally, critiques of liberal discrimination law focus on the public private division that is a central feature of traditional liberal theory. Critics argue that the claims to neutrality in the public sphere, and the defence of the private realm as a sphere which is beyond legal regulation and the "reach" of discrimination law, operate to entrench the real causes of dis-

[64] For a discussion of these issues in the context of liberalism see W. Kymlicka, *Liberalism, Community and Culture* (Oxford: Clarendon Press, 1989).

crimination. For example, feminists argue that the private realm of the home and personal relationships is exactly the area in which discriminatory attitudes and practices develop. Yet, discrimination law regulates spheres such as the workplace where the effects of these attitudes are manifested, rather than the personal sphere where fundamental causes of discrimination originate. We examine some of these issues in the discussions that follow.

A. *Accommodating Differences I: Groups, the Politics of Recognition and Multiculturalism*

A number of writers, such as Joseph Raz and Charles Taylor, have noted the relationship between individual well being and the communal context. Although there are important differences between them, these liberal writers emphasise that a concern with individual freedom and well being requires paying attention to social and communal practices. A number of consequences follow from recognising this connection. First, it means that an important source of well being and self-respect for individuals (earlier categorised by Hill as key components of autonomy) arise out of their identitification and attachment with social groups. Moreover, where these beliefs and social groups are denigrated this can, in turn, be a serious harm to individuals. Raz represents this concern as the "pivotal importance of self-respect to the well being of people" and notes that the harm includes "alienation from society."[65] This shift towards acknowledging the importance of respect and recognition means that the failure to grant recognition to an individual, or misrecognition by others, could be a type of harm.[66] This further raises an important point about the public recognition of private identities or the "politics of identity". It provides a way of challenging the state and public institutions that either fail to grant recognition to certain social groups, or represent their beliefs in a demeaning way. Charles Taylor argues that this concern with respect which, focuses on difference, generates contemporary forms of multiculturalism and "politics of recognition". He also argues that these new forms of politics emerge out of established ideas of universal individual dignity.

[65] Joseph Raz, "Duties of Well Being", in *Ethics in the Public Domain* (Oxford: Clarendon Press, 1994) at p.288.

[66] For further discussion of these issues see Maleiha Malik, "Faith and the State of Jurisprudence", in P. Oliver et al eds., *Faith and Law: Essays in Legal Theory*, (Oxford: Hart Publications, 2000)

Charles Taylor, Multiculturalism and "The Politics of Recognition" (Princeton, NJ: Princeton University Press, 1992)

pp.37–44: "I want to concentrate here on the public sphere, and try to work out what a politics of equal recognition has meant and could mean.

In fact, it has come to mean two rather different things, connected, respectively, with the two major changes I have been describing. With the move from honor to dignity has come a politics of universalism, emphasizing the equal dignity of all citizens, and the content of this politics has been the equalization of rights and entitlements. What is to be avoided at all costs is the existence of 'first class' and 'second class' citizens. Naturally, the actual detailed measures justified by this principle have varied greatly, and have often been controversial. For some, equalization has affected only civil rights and voting rights; for others, it has extended into the socioeconomic sphere. People who are systematically handicapped by poverty from making the most of their citizenship rights are deemed on this view to have been relegated to second-class status, necessitating remedial action through equalization. But through all the differences of interpretation, the principle of equal citizenship has come to be universally accepted. Every position, no matter how reactionary, is now defended under the colors of this principle. Its greatest, most recent victory was won by the civil rights movement of the 1960s in the United States. It is worth noting that even the adversaries of extending voting rights to blacks in the southern states found some pretext consistent with universalism, such as 'tests' to be administered to would-be voters at the time or registration.

By contrast, the second change, the development of the modern notion of identity, has given rise to the politics of difference. There is of course a universalist basis to this as well, making for the overlap and confusion between the two. *Everyone* should be recognised for his or her unique identity. But recognition here means something else. With the politics of equal dignity, what is established is meant to be universally the same, an identical basket of rights and immunities; with the politics of difference, what we are asked to recognize is the unique identity of this individual or group, their distinctness from everyone else. The idea is that it is precisely this distinctness that has been ignored, glossed over, assimilated to a dominant or majority identity. And this assimilation is the cardinal sin against the ideal of authenticity.

Now underlying the demand is a principle of universal equality. The politics of difference is full of denunciations of discrimination and refusals of second-class citizenship. This gives the principle of universal equality a point of entry within the politics of dignity. But once inside, as it were, its demands are hard to assimilate to that politics. For it asks that we give acknowledgement and status to something that is not universally shared. Or, otherwise put, we give due acknowledgement only to what is universally present—everyone has an identity through recognizing what is peculiar in each. The universal demand powers an acknowledgement of specificity.

The politics of difference grows organically out of the politics of universal dignity through one of those shifts with which we are long familiar, where a new understanding of the human social condition imparts a radically new meaning to an old principle. Just as a view of human beings as conditioned by their socioeconomic plight changed the understanding of second-class citizenship, so that this category came to include, for example, people in inherited poverty traps, so here the understanding of identity as formed in interchange, and as possibly so malformed, introduces a new form of second-class status into our purview. As in the present case, the socioeconomic redefinition justified social programs that were highly controversial. For those who had not gone along with this changed definition of equal status, the various redistributive programs and special opportunities offered to certain populations seemed a form of undue favoritism.

Similar conflicts arise today around the politics of difference. Where the politics of universal dignity fought for forms of nondiscrimination that were quite 'blind' to the ways in which citizens differ, the politics of difference often redefines nondiscrimination as requiring that we make these distinctions the basis of differential treatment. [. . .]

These two modes of politics, then, both based on the notion of equal respect, come into conflict. For one, the principal of equal respect requires that we treat people in a difference-blind fashion. The fundamental intuition that humans command this respect focuses on what is the same in all. For the other, we have to recognize and even foster particularity. The reproach that the first makes to the second is just that it violates the principle of nondiscrimination. The reproach that the second makes to the first is that it negates identity by forcing people into a homogenous mould that is untrue to them. This would be bad enough if the mould were itself neutral-nobody's mould in particular. But the complaint generally goes even further. The claim is that the supposedly neutral set of difference-blind principles of the politics of equal dignity is in fact a reflection of one hegemonic culture. As it turns out, then, only the minority or suppressed cultures are being forced to take alien form. Consequently, the supposedly fair and difference-blind society is not only inhuman (because suppressing identities) but also, in a subtle and unconscious way, itself highly discriminatory."

As this passage makes clear, the recent discussions of equality as the "recognition of difference" are a far cry from the classical definitions of equality as the "treatment of like with like". Moreover, as Taylor illustrates, both of these tendencies can be justified within the paradigm of contemporary concepts of equality and non-discrimination. The paradox is that both these often contradictory definitions of what is meant by equal treatment have a place within the modern commitment to non-discrimination. Many of the seemingly intractable conflicts within discrimination law and policy can be traced back to the co-existence between these two concepts: one pushing discrimination law towards universalism and strict equality of treatment; whilst the other pushes in the direction of the recognition of difference and specificity. These issues are especially relevant in the context of the modern demand for "multiculturalism" as the appropriate response to minority protection. This conflict also echoes the objection of feminist critiques which highlights the failure of liberal discrimination law to deal with important differences between men and women.

Debates about multiculturalism are discussed in more detail throughout the book, e.g. in the chapters on race, religion and multiple discrimination. Here it is worth noting that our societies are increasingly comprised of a diversity of races, cultures and religions. This "factual multiculturalism" is undisputed. What is more controversial is the normative claim that such diversity is a good thing and, more significantly, the demand that these groups must be accommodated within our public sphere. Increasingly, groups claim that the liberal democratic state should grant them autonomy in decision- making that affects their individual members; they claim distinct rights even where these are in many cases inimical to the interests of women. This is an important question for politics because the most urgent demands for social and political equality are no longer exclusively or predominantly the preserve of feminism. It is also an important question for law because the legal regulation of discrimination has now moved beyond the traditional categories of race and sex and now extends to religion and some of its cultural manifestations.

Multiculturalism is often presented as giving minorities in liberal democracies an unprecedented opportunity to live as equal citizens without suffering the worst excesses of forced assimilation. Multiculturalism is a wide term that requires some explanation.[67] At a normative level it includes the claim that is supported by the earlier discussion of Raz and Taylor: that different groups—defined along categories such as race, religion, gender and sexual orientation—can make legitimate claims for public accommodation of some of their practices. In this way, it challenges the classic liberal settlement of keeping the public sphere as a neutral space where citizens come together as equal citizens with recognised political rights. Of course, this classic liberal approach allowed minorities to flourish through guaranteeing individual civil and political rights, e.g. free speech; free association and free exercise of religion. This provided an over-arching framework allowing minorities to pursue their way of life in the private sphere.

It is worth reiterating that multiculturalism is not only a normative claim. It is also a social and political fact. Identity politics is an observable social phenomenon: there has been a significant change in the form and content of the political claims made by minority groups in recent times. Many no longer ask for the "same" rights as the majority. Some of the most vocal demands of minorities now take the form of calls for the accommodation of "difference" in the public sphere. This social change is especially problematic for liberal multiculturalism. Claims for accommodation vary greatly: the categories range from race, culture and religion through to gender and sexual orientation and disability.

In these circumstances, a definition of citizenship that uses a common race, culture or religion as its marker may necessarily and unjustly exclude large numbers of people. Any liberal democracy that has a large diversity of races, cultures and religions will find it difficult to simultaneously generate a meaningful "sense of belonging" to a political community and comply with the principle of equality. One alternative to these criteria is to develop a definition of citizenship that focuses on identification with public institutions. Developing citizenship along these lines of "institutional accommodation" requires attention to the needs of both the majority and the minority. If a "sense of belonging" to a political community and its national institutions is important for the minority then it is also important for members of the majority community.[68]

One way of developing a sense of belonging to key political and legal institutions is to ensure that the interests of women and minorities are represented in these forums. In some cases it is argued that it is also important

[67] See M. Malik, "Minorities and Human Rights", in *Sceptical Approaches to Human Rights*, T. Campbell, K. D. Ewing and A. Tomkins (eds.), Oxford: Oxford University Press, 2000.

[68] See M. Malik, "Minorities and Human Rights" in Campbell, Ewing, et al (eds), *Sceptical Approaches to Human Rights*, (Oxford, Oxford University Press, 2000).

for there to be representatives of these groups in these forums[69], which explains positive actions which permits the introduction of all women short lists which are exempt from the SDA.[70] The idea of institutional accommodation of minorities has, to some extent, been given a legal context by the increasing use of positive action, and the introduction of a general duty on public institutions to promote equality[71], e.g. the Race Relations Amendment Act 2000. There are a number of specific costs discussed in chapter 6 associated with institutional accommodation. In the short term it will rarely benefit the majority who are likely to resist this process. Put bluntly, this version of multiculturalism will often require the majority to give up their power and advantage as institutions are transformed from exclusively reflecting their vested interests and increasingly start to accommodate some of the most urgent needs of groups. There may be long terms benefits for the majority that compensate for these costs: a more principled treatment of minorities by the liberal state and a more stable political community. Minorities may also have to make painful adjustments through a limited assimilation to the shared values and practices (such as foundational constitutional and human rights norms) that are the agreed basis for a common public life. In practice, this will mean that they may need to compromise some of their most cherished values in order to become acceptable partners in any process of public accommodation. A process of multicultural accommodation may also create specific risks to vulnerable group members. This is especially true where there is accommodation of traditional racial, cultural or religious practices which often and predominantly harm women, gays and lesbians.[72] These are discussed in more detail in Chapter 9 on multiple discrimination and intersectionality.

The previous passage and the debates about the "politics of recognition" also raise two key issues which replicate the feminist critique of liberal anti-discrimination law in important respects. Minorities are no longer willing for their differences to be a matter of "tolerance" in private: they now demand political rights and accommodation in the public sphere. Feminists recognise this move immediately. Yet, at the same time, they also immediately recognise the way in which this challenge to the private-public dichotomy, especially by traditional cultures, is a threat to women. This is partly why the confrontation between feminism and multiculturalism is so painful. Like the insistence on the recognition of difference by the "politics of recognition", most accounts of feminism argues: (a) there are legitimate differences between men that should not be assimilated into a dominant majority norm; (b) public recognition and

[69] For an argument that there should be a focus on ideas rather than a focus on group representation, see Anne Phillips, *The Politics of Presence* (Oxford: Oxford University Press, 1998).

[70] For a discussion of policies to increase the representation of racial minorities in political processes and institutions see *Our House? Race and Representation in British Politics*, co-written with Rushanara Ali and C. O'Cinneide, (London: Institute for Public Policy Research, April 2002), pp.105

[71] [FOOTNOTE MISSING]

[72] Susan Moller Okin: *Feminism and Multiculturalism*, Ethics 108 (July 1998), 661–684.

accommodation of women's differences.[73] This is partly why the confrontation between feminism and multiculturalism is so painful. Feminism reflecting on multiculturalism often sees its own mirror image. Feminists are acutely aware that they have laid the foundations for a wider identity politics. However—as the "Is Multiculturalism Bad for Women" debate discussed in Chapter 9 on multiple discrimination confirms—despite this intimate connection at the level of theory the two movements are also often incompatible.

B. *Accommodating Difference II: Feminism and Discrimination Law*

A significant challenge has come from feminists who argue that this concept is insufficiently radical and ignores important differences between men and women which are relevant to discrimination law. Some of these concerns are summarised in the passage below:

Katherine O'Donovan and Erika Szyszczak, *Equality and Sex Discrimination Law*, (Oxford: Blackwell Ltd., 1988)

pp.7: "The question of whether equality is viewed as competition between women and men starting from the same point, or as a pluralistic recognition of different qualities and needs, is fundamental to theories of sex equality. The first approach, of an equal starting point, may fulfil the criteria defined for equality of opportunity. But it does rest on the twin assumptions that women do start from the same point as men; or that if not, they can do so. The starting point is, as it were, open to all. Differences between women and men are ignored. That women might find it difficult or impossible to get to the starting point is overlooked. This version of equality can be criticised as a procrustean bed into which the sleepers must be fitted through cutting or stretching. If the model for whom the competition (or bed) is designed is male then women may find it difficult to fit. They may be forced to accept a starting point and a competition which does not suit them. Their qualities and needs may be overlooked. Economic and social institutions, willing to admit women under a policy of equality, will not necessarily adapt to accommodate them. These institutions may regard their admission of women as more than sufficient to fulfil equality requirements.

If treatment as an equal implies respect for others, avoidance of stereotypes and viewing the world from another's point of view, then pluralism goes further than equal treatment. For it allows for differences in persons, their situations, their needs. It requires 'an effort at identification' in the way we treat others. In this guise equality does not mean giving or

[73] For an introduction and selected readings see W. Kymlicka, "Introduction", *Rights of Minority Cultures*, W. Kymlicka (ed.), Oxford: Oxford University Press, 1995. See also Jurgen Habermas on the relevance of cultural difference to liberal constitutional democracies, Jurgen Habermas, "Struggles for Recognition" in Amy Gutman (ed.), *Multiculturalism* (Princeton, N.J.: Princeton University Press, 1994).

receiving the same treatment, but rather giving or receiving equal concern. Each person is then taken account of in her particular environment.[. . .]

[. . . the passage then summarises the Westen argument that equality is an 'empty concept': author's note].

Although we may not go as far as Westen in the rejection of conceptions of equality as empty, his example does illustrate the centrality of the standard against which persons are to be measured. This is taken up also by Catherine MacKinnon. She suggests that existing inequalities should be taken into account in law-making and application. Her proposal is that in considering legal standards, a distinction should be made as to whether (a) a given standard is equally premised between women and men but unequally applied; (b) unequally premised but equally applied; or (c) equally premised and equally applied to an existing social inequality. Earlier, MacKinnon had argued that the focus in equal protection law should not be on whether the sexes are similarly or dissimilarly situated; nor on 'differences'; nor on whether differences are 'arbitrary' rather than 'rational'; but on inequality. The courts should consider whether legal treatment results in systematic disadvantage because of membership of a particular group. In the area of sex discrimination the 'only question for litigation is whether the policy or practice in question integrally contributes to the maintenance of an underclass or a deprived position because of gender status'.

[. . .]

It is pertinent to ask whether MacKinnon has disposed of 'the difference approach' in her focus on inequality. It seems rather that her proposal links inequality and difference. It allows in some pluralist ideas of equality by admitting that not everyone starts from the same position, or is similarly circumstanced. It gets away from equal treatment which limits itself to a comparison of treatment. Pluralism goes further than equal treatment because it allows the dissimilarities between the sexes to enter in. A focus on inequality puts differential treatment to the forefront. This is a deeper approach which enables the standpoint or perspective of those, unequal in social reality, to emerge. But instead of women's difference from men being a signal for unequal treatment to follow, as it has done in the past, it would be a sign for suspicion of the existing inequality, whether it existed in law, its application, or because of extraneous factors.

What MacKinnon's scheme for inquiry into inequalities highlights is that existing approaches of equal treatment or equal standard assume that women and men can be taken to be the same. This takes no account of inequalities and differences, whether they be of social, economic or biological origin. But it is an open question whether the differences approach is entirely avoided by a focus on inequality. Feminist analysis argues that differences should not be made the justification for unequal treatment. But differences, where they exist in biology or socioeconomic structures, cannot be ignored. The problem remains that, just as courts have justified differential treatment on grounds that women and men are not similarly circumstanced, so too may they justify inequality."

Two recurring themes within feminist theory are identified in these passages. First is the extent to which men and women are "equal" or "different"; second, is the critique of the private/public dichotomy which is a central organising concept in liberal political and legal theory.

1. Women and Men: Equality or Difference?

The first theme is the essential distinction between biological sex on the one hand, and the expectation and roles which are associated with the social and cultural construction of gender. The distinction between these two concepts has had a significant impact on sex discrimination law. Arguments concerning "biological" and natural differences between men and women, as well as social and economic difference, have led feminists to disagree about the foundations of the anti-discrimination law. Many feminists agree with those, such as Peter Westen, who criticise the concept of equality as the treatment of "like as like" as a formal and inadequate concept. These writers provide the basis for criticising equality of opportunity, with its emphasis on a "male comparator", as an inadequate response.

MacKinnon, for example, argues that analysis should focus on disadvantage rather than comparison on the basis of equality or difference between men and women.[74] Mackinnon has developed a feminist response to liberal equality of opportunity standard which uses the usual contrast between equality and difference as an essential organising idea. Some radical critics of liberalism, e.g. Iris Marion Young, argue that abstract liberal concepts of equality fail to recognise the real differences (social and economic) caused by patriarchy. These differences mean that men and women cannot compete for, and have access to goods, in a similar way. The application of the principle "like with like" in this context fails to alleviate women's disadvantage. Within feminist theory, there is an ongoing debate about whether the differences between men and women are "essential" or the product of "social construction". This debate has implications for the discrimination law because whether a definition of equality or discrimination applies in a practical contexts, such as pregnancy, child care or sexual harassment, depends on understanding the goal which women are seeking. Although feminists such as Mackinnon[75] have argued that there is a need to move away from equality towards the recognition of difference, some modern feminist writers have challenged their acceptance of the equality–difference dichotomy. For example, Drucilla Cornell's work uses of the idea of "double movement"—which builds on the technique of "double writing" introduced by Jacque Derrida—as a critique of more orthodox concepts in feminist writing.[76] Cornell challenges the value of

[74] Catharine Mackinnon, *Feminism Unmodified: Discourses on Life and Law.* Cambridge: Harvard University Press, 1987; *Toward a Feminist Theory of the State.* Cambridge: Harvard University Press, 1989.

[75] Catharine MacKinnon, "Difference and Dominance: On Sex Discrimination," in *The Moral Foundation of Civil Rights.* Ed. Robert K. Fullinwinder and Claudia Mills. Rowman and Littlefield, 1986.

[76] See Jacque Derrida: *Positions* (Chicago, USA: Chicago University Press, 1981). Derrida uses this technique in the following way. In Positions he argues for a general strategy of deconstruction. The first stage is the overturning where the existing binary opposition man/woman is overturned. Thus, the hierarchy is challenged by showing that the hierarchically superior could not exist without the inferior turn, i.e that it is marked by the trace of the other. Second, is a movement outside this phase which is still determined by the existing deconstructed system. We do this by through the emergence of a new concept that cannot be, and could never be, within the deconstructed system. This concept is new, resistant and challenging without ever emerging as a third term. Thus, in relation to this second phase he writes: "we must also mark the interval between inversion, which brings low what was high, and the irruptive emergence of a new 'concept', a concept that could no longer be, and never could be, included in the previous regime . . . resisting and disorganising it, without ever constituting a third term (p.42–43).

certain binaries: either women and men are equal or different; either essentialism (the claim that similarities or differences are determined by their essences) or constructivism (the claim that things have no knowable essence and are therefore historically or discursively constructed). Cornell argues that to use these binaries is to argue from within, rather than to challenge modern patriarchy's values.[77] The practical consequences of these issues are considered in Chapter 10 on sex discrimination which deals with issues of family, pregnancy and childcare.

There are also internal developments within feminism to recognise difference. Recent scholarship and political activism has focused on the way in which categories such as "gender", "sex" and "women" are too homogenous and often reflect the views of those who have greater social power within these groups. Those within these groups who are different, e.g. with respect to race or sexual orientation, call for a greater accommodation of these differences. This issue is considered in more detail in Chapter 9 on multiple discrimination.[78]

2. The Public and Private Distinction

Like other radical critiques, feminists challenge the liberal state's claim to neutrality and its failure to address the reality of oppression and domination. They argue that the chimera of neutrality, and the private-public distinction, prevents discrimination law from reaching into the precise spheres, e.g. the home and private relationships or the operation of free market, which cause discrimination and violence against women.

Katherine O'Donovan, *Sexual Divisions in Law*, (London: Weidenfeld and Nicolson, 1985)

pp.16–18: "The focus on the social construction of women's difference from men had an immediate consequence in terms of law. Feminists and liberals were agreed in questioning differential treatment of women and men in legislation. In particular, in the United States, a whole series of challenges to gender-based legislative classifications took place. [...] The aim was to eliminate women's differences as a source of subordination so far as possible by opening up the public sphere and assimilating women to men. But in their

[77] For examples of double movement feminism see the work of Drucilla Cornell and Judith Butler. See also an overview of the ideas in her essay Cornell: "What is Ethical Feminism?" in Benhabib, Butler, et al. (ed.): *Feminist Contentions: A Philosophical Exchange* (London: Routledge, 1995). See also the work of Judith Butler: *Bodies that Matter: On the Discursive Limits of "Sex"*, (London: Routledge, 1993).

[78] See the following literature for a discussion of these key issues: Susan Moller Okin: Feminism and Multiculturalism, Ethics 108 (July 1998), 661–684. S. Moller Okin, S. Moller Okin: "'Mistresses of Their Own Destiny': Group Rights, Gender, and Realistic Rights of Exit" Ethics 112 (January 2002).

alliance with liberal reformers feminists seemed to forget that element of the analysis of difference that identified the private sphere as the location of women's oppression.

With the focus on sexual division came the celebration of women's difference. The woman-centred analysis which developed from the mid-1970s studied women's culture, held up by some as a model for all persons. This meant an examination of mothering, of women's virtues, of female sexuality, of female experience as values for the culture as a whole, and a critique of masculinity. Celebrating women's difference as a source of strength rather than of oppression became an accepted mode of analysis. Important and perhaps even essential though this stage in the development of feminist theory was, it seemed to lose contact with the major early feminist dissection of the myths surrounding gender.

There is a curious similarity between the positions of feminist theorists of the 1960s and early 1970s who focused on eliminating women's differences and those from the mid-1970s onwards who celebrated difference. Both streams accepted the dichotomy between public and private. The first group favoured eliminating the differences between women and men, but not necessarily the division between private and public. The second group celebrated women's private existence.

Yet there is within feminist analysis a slogan 'the personal is political' which emphasises the falsity of the public/private dichotomy. Male hegemony has been identified as a continuum in relations between the sexes in all spheres. In the private arena, according to this analysis, relations of domination and subordination are masked by the ideology of love. In the public economic and cultural factors hide the reality. Gender relationships are power relationships.

This account of the feminist critique of the private thus far is a resume of radical feminist thought since the mid-1960s. There is also within feminist theory a marxian analysis which places class alongside gender in its account of women's oppression. [. . .]

Recently a series of questions about the state have been raised by the feminist lawyer Catharine MacKinnon. Pointing out that feminism has a theory of power but not theory of the state, she argues that the 'state's formal norms recapitulate the male point of view on the level of design'. Her view is that the liberal state's claim to objectivity rests on its allocation of public matters to itself to be treated objectively, and of private matters to civil society to be treated subjectively. 'But feminist consciousness has exploded the private . . . To see the personal as political means to see the private as public.' MacKinnon criticises both marxism and liberalism for transcending the private and for failing to confront male power and its expression in state and law."

As well as criticising the assimilationist effects of the equality of opportunity concept, the feminist challenge to the private/public dichotomy also provides an argument for extending the scope of discrimination law beyond public goods and employment to include spheres such as the home (domestic violence issues) and private speech (pornography) which are discussed in the chapter on sex discrimination, as well as the chapter on violence, harassment and hate speech.

The feminist critique is that the present structure of discrimination law replicates the arbitrary distinction between private and public spheres. By identifying certain spheres as falling within the ambit of anti-discrimination law (e.g. employment, delivery of private and public goods and services, and the provision of public services) the present arrangements leave the remaining spheres as areas in which discrimination is permissible. Discrimination law, feminists argue, fails to reach the private sphere where discriminatory attitudes are created and flourish. It is worth noting that there may good reasons for these limits. Liberal responses to this critique focus on the importance of maintaining a private sphere and the inherent limits of using law to deliver all the goals of discrimination law. John Gardner has noted, in the context of discrimination law, that there are certain inherent limits to the ability of all law (not just liberal discrimination law) to be able to achieve the full goals of equality and non-discrimination for women and minorities. Gardner's analysis challenges the argument, of feminists and others, that one way of facilitating this goal is to be more willing to cross the line between the public and the private sphere. Gardner argues that there are certain "direction sensitive" relationships which are not always amenable to wholesale legal regulation without a loss of value inherent in those relationships and cultures. Gardner concludes: "Law is a blunt tool, which destroys more readily than it creates. The social forms which are the source of the value in our lives are delicately shaped over time, whatever their defects. There is no quick way to get them into perfect shape, although the less direction-sensitive among them can be nudged by legal means in order to get some sort of gradual adjustment underway. It is easy to understand the frustrations of those critics who see the whole business as excessively protracted. But they waste their energy criticising the law for being the way the law necessarily is. They would be better employed arguing for improved government expenditure to increase the momentum for change. Even then, of course, they should not expect rapid transformation."[79]

C. *Critical Legal Studies and the "victim's perspective"*

The need to understand the social, economic and political structures within which structural disadvantage is created and sustained, and within which discrimination law operates, was also emphasised by the CLS movement. The CLS movement is important in the context of discrimination law for a number of reasons. By revealing the way in which formal rules can operate to reinforce existing hierarchies, a CLS approach suggests that the formal application of rules that prohibit discrimination is a limited response to the goals of discrimination law. CLS can, therefore, provide an explanation for seemingly contradictory rules and principles in the doctrine of discrimination law. As Unger argues, this is an outcome of judicial attempts to impose order on a system through rules without recognising the underlying ideological conflict that produces the contradictory rules.[80] Moreover, CLS has led to more spe-

[79] John Gardner, "Private Activities and Personal Autonomy: At the Margins of Anti-discrimination Law", Bob Hepple and Erika M. Szyszczak, in *Discrimination: The Limits of Law* (London: Mansell, 1995), at p.169.

[80] Roberto Mangabeira Unger, *The Critical Legal Studies Movement*, (Camb, Mass: Harvard University Press, 1983)

cialist analysis in areas that are at the heart of discrimination law: for example, critical race theory and critical gender studies. These specialist aspects of the CLS movement have (a) developed a sophisticated and detailed critique of liberal discrimination law; and also (b) developed an analysis of the way in which discrimination law can be used as a means of challenging and restructuring social hierarchies, rather than preserving liberal neutrality between equal citizens. The following section focuses on critical race theory which illustrates some of the central concerns of CLS.

Critical Race Theory was a particular form of the CLS movement. Writers such as Derrick Bell challenged the pace of change towards racial equality. They argued for a strategy that was different to liberal anti-discrimination law in a number of important respects. This strategy emphasised that race was a social rather than essential biological concepts; it argued that racist behaviour was not just part of the peripheral social life but was in many cases part of what is considered "normal" in social life; the decision whether and in what way to respond to racism was influenced by issues of power of social elites; and finally, race was understood as a complex phenomenon that intersected with other variables such as gender or class.[81]

One leading example of the Critical Race Theory movement is Kimberle Crenshaw, who argues that there was often little difference between conservative attitudes to race and the ambitions of liberal discrimination law and policy: both replicate the restrictive trends within discrimination law. Crenshaw argues that formal liberal reform has "repackaged racism" rather than replaced it. Moreover, although liberal discrimination law is able to regulate the symbolic aspects of racism, its neutral, colour blind approach and focus on individual rights leaves in place the material subordination and oppression of minorities such as African Americans.[82] Crenshaw has also used the methods of Critical Race Theory to argue that liberal "single axis" anti-discrimination law is unable to deal with issues of intersectionality that face those who are members of more than one protected group: e.g. black women.

Other features of Critical Race Theory emphasised the relevance and importance of racial minorities disrupting the predominant narratives and reframing the way in which they, their history and lives were presented. Richard Delgado, in particular, has emphasised the importance of challenging the "norm" that is established as the basis for comparison in discrimination law.[83] Delgado's work is also important because it is a precursor to the "politics of recognition" argument that has become popular in recent times. As discussed, feminist theory challenges (a) the distinction between the private

[81] Derrick A. Bell, Remembrance of Racism Past: The Civil Rights Decline. In Hill & J. E Jones (eds.) *Race in America: The Struggle for Equality* (Madison, USA: University of Wisconsin Press, 1993) at p.73–82

[82] Kimberele W. Crenshaw, Race Reform, Retrenchment: Transformation and Legitimation in Anti-Discrimination Law (1988) 101 Harvard L. R., 101. 1331–1387.

[83] Richard Delgado Legal Storytelling: Storytelling for Oppositionists and Others: A Plea for Narrative. In R. Delgado (Ed.) *Critical Race Theory: The Cutting Edge* (Philadelphia, US: Temple University Press, 1995)

and public sphere to argue that the "private is also political"; and (b) challenges the male norm to argue that female "difference" should be accommodated. Increasingly, racial, cultural and religious minorities are challenging the liberal solution of safeguarding the identity of minorities in the private sphere, whilst maintaining the public sphere as a neutral zone within which all citizens come together as "citizens".

We have already considered the feminist critique of liberal discrimination law which cites the abstraction of individuals from the reality of their social and economic circumstances, and the use of abstract concepts of equality, as an inappropriate response to the disadvantage of women. Feminists also argue that liberalism's focus on neutrality, and its use of the public-private distinction, fail to take up the perspective of women who are the primary victims of discrimination. These approaches are more concerned with the perspective of those who are victims of discrimination. The need for discrimination law to take up the victim's perspective is also developed by Alan Freeman in the context of racism in the following passage.

Alan David Freeman, "Legitimising Racial Discrimination Through Anti-discrimination law: A Critical Review of Supreme Court Doctrine", (1978) 62 Minnesota L. R. 1049

"1. The perpetrator perspective

The concept of "racial discrimination" may be approached from the perspective of either its victim or its perpetrator. From the victim's perspective, racial discrimination describes those conditions of actual social existence as a member of a perpetual underclass. This perspective includes both the objective conditions of life—lack of jobs, lack of money, lack of housing—and the consciousness associated with those objective conditions—lack of choice and lack of human individuality in being forever perceived as a member of a group rather than as an individual. The perpetrator perspective sees racial discrimination not as conditions, but as actions, or series of actions, inflicted on the victim by the perpetrator. The focus is more on what particular perpetrators have done or are doing to some victims than it is on the overall life situation of the victim class.

The victim, or "condition", conception of racial discrimination suggests that the problem will not be solved until the conditions associated with it have been eliminated. To remedy the condition of racial discrimination would demand affirmative efforts to change the condition. The remedial dimension of the perpetrator perspective, however, is negative. The task is merely to neutralize the inappropriate conduct of the perpetrator.

In its core concept of the "violation," discrimination law is hopelessly embedded in the perpetrator perspective. Its central tenet, the "anti-discrimination principle," is the prohibition of dependent decisions that disadvantage members of minority groups, and its principal task has been to select from the maze of human behaviours those particular practices that violate the principle, outlaw the identified practices, and neutralize their specific effects. Anti-discrimination law has thus been ultimately indifferent to the condition of the victim; its demands are satisfied if it can be said that the "violation" has been remedied.

The perpetrator perspective presupposes a world composed of atomistic individuals whose actions are outside of and apart from the social fabric and without historical continuity. From this perspective, the law views racial discrimination not as a social phenomenon, but merely as the misguided conduct of particular actors. It is a world where, but for the conduct of these misguided ones, the system of equality of opportunity would work to provide a distribution of the good things in life without racial disparities and where deprivations that did correlate with race would be "deserved" by those deprived on grounds of insufficient "merit." It is a world where such things as "vested rights," "objective selection systems," and "adventitious decisions" (all of which serve to prevent victims from experiencing any chance in conditions) are matters of fate, having nothing to do with the problem of racial discrimination.

Central to the perpetrator perspective are the twin notions of "fault" and "causation". Under the fault idea, the task of anti-discrimination law is to separate from the masses of society those blameworthy individuals who are violating the otherwise shared norm. The fault idea is reflected in the assertion that only 'intentional' discrimination violates the anti-discrimination principle. In its purest form, intentional discrimination is conduct accompanied by a purposeful desire to produce discriminatory results. One can thus evade responsibility for ostensibly discriminatory conduct by showing that the action was taken for a good reason, or for no reason at all.

The fault concept gives rise to a complacency about one's own moral status; it creates a class of 'innocents,' who need not feel any personal responsibility for the conditions associated with discrimination, and who therefore feel great resentment when called upon to bear any burdens in connection with remedying violations. This resentment accounts for much of the ferocity surrounding the debate about so-called 'reverse discrimination', for being called on to bear burdens ordinarily imposed only upon the guilty involves an apparently unjustified stigmatization of those led by the fault notion to believe in their own innocence.

Operating along with fault, the causation requirement serves to distinguish from the totality of conditions that a victim perceives to be associated with discrimination those that the law will address. These dual requirements place on the victim the nearly impossible burden of isolating the particular conditions of discrimination produced by and mechanically linked to the behaviour of an identified blameworthy perpetrator, regardless of whether other conditions of discrimination, caused by other perpetrators, would have to be remedied for the outcome of the case to make any difference at all. The causation principle makes it clear that some objective instances of discrimination are to be regarded as mere accidents, or 'causes,' cannot follow their successors in interest over time. The causation principle also operates to place beyond the law discriminatory conduct (action taken with a purpose to discriminate under the fault principle) that is not linked to any discernible 'discriminatory effect.'

The perpetrator perspective has been and still is the only formal conception of a violation in anti-discrimination law. Strict adherence to that form, however, would have made even illusory progress in the quest for racial justice impossible. The challenge for the law, therefore, was to develop, through the usual legal techniques of verbal manipulation, ways of breaking out of the formal constraints of the perpetrator perspective while maintaining ostensible adherence to the form itself. This was done by separating violation from remedy, and doing through remedy what was inappropriate in cases involving only identification of violations. But since one of the principal tenets of the perpetrator perspective is that remedy and violation must be coextensive, it was necessary to state that tenet and violate it at the same time, no mean task even for masters of verbal gamesmanship. For a while, the remedial doctrines seemingly undermined the hegemony of the perpetrator form, threatening to replace it with a victim perspective. In the end, however, form triumphed, and the perpetrator perspective, always dominant in identifying violations, was firmly reasserted in the context of remedies as well."

Freeman's critique focuses on a number of flaws in the traditional "perpetrator's perspective" in discrimination law. It criticises the individuation of discrimination law which uses concepts of fault, causation and remedy, thereby focusing on the individual conduct of the discriminator rather than the effect on the victim. Freeman's critique is especially relevant to domestic and EU discrimination law in so far as they rely on a private law paradigm to regulate discrimination. Freeman's argument is that the liberal response is inherently flawed because it draws a false distinction between discrimination as individual conduct and the prevalence of discriminatory attitudes in the wider society. It could be argued that Freeman's wide ranging criticism fails to pay sufficient attention to the different contexts in which discrimination law is applied. There may, as Freeman suggests, be a continuity between individual discrimination on the one hand, and discriminatory attitudes, practices and social and economic conditions which perpetuate discrimination. However, it does not follow that legal regulation is the appropriate response in all these various contexts. The use of legal regulation may be especially justified where the presence of individual fault or causation justifies a remedy against that individual perpetrator. Moreover, the nature of the legal regulation (e.g. the use of criminal, tort or administrative law) will depend on other features such as the gravity of the harm caused to the victim, as well as the state of mind of the perpetrator. For example, although tort law may be appropriate to deal with discrimination in the context of employment law, the discriminatory selection of victims for bodily harm or harassment may justify criminalisation. However, an comprehensive response to the underlying conditions of disadvantage which Freeman identifies may be outside the scope of legal regulation. A more appropriate response may also include extra legal action by the state in the form of support for education policies or supply side investment.

Freeman's critique is important for a number of reasons. First, it re-states the previous arguments about the weaknesses of a paradigm of liberal discrimination law that is based on individualism. This paradigm, it might be argued, uses symmetry and comparison to replicate and entrench the viewpoint of those in power rather than protecting those who are the victims of discrimination and inequality. Second, Freeman's critique is also important because it shifts the analysis towards a model of discrimination law that focuses on the impact of discrimination on disadvantaged groups, and the need to understand discrimination as a structural rather than individual wrong.

D. *The "Social Context" of Discrimination*

The move towards understanding discrimination as a response to current social problems, which is emphasised by the CLS movement and by Freeman also informs Larry Alexander's analysis of what makes discrimination a "wrong". Like Paul Brest, Alexander treats the "anti-discrimination principle" as one of many, rather than the only, goal that a state should pursue.

Larry Alexander, "What Makes Wrongful Discrimination Wrong?" (1992–1993) 154 U. Pa. L. R.

pp.219: "In short, in an otherwise just society, discriminatory preferences are intrinsically morally wrong if premised on error, moral or factual, about the dispreferred. Discriminatory preferences are extrinsically morally wrong if their social costs are large relative to the costs of eliminating or frustrating them. And if a discriminatory preference is morally wrong—and if there is no moral right that protects its exercise—then there is a legal case for legally prohibiting its exercise if the costs of legal prohibition and enforcement are low relative to the social gains to be achieved. Thus, I end with these whimpers and no bang. What makes discrimination wrong is usually quite complex as well as culturally and historically variable"

This shift in emphasis is discussed in the next two sections which re-frame the harm of discrimination: from an individual wrong caused by a procedural defect; to a collective social problem that is caused by deeper social, economic and political structural conditions. Davina Cooper, for example, develops an analysis of the relationship between law and the "politics of belonging" that is able to link issues of equality to a full range of issues relevant to culturally diverse and plural political communities. In *Governing Out of Order: Space, Law and the Politics of Belonging*,[84] these ideas are developed through an application of Foucouldian political analysis, discourse theory, socio-legal theory and cultural geography to explore the way in which citizens are excluded from meaningful participation in political processes through the arbitrary use of distinctions between categories such as the "public" and the "private". Cooper's advocacy of a different form of politics where institutions are willing to move between these boundaries, and to "govern out of order", provides one way of challenging the exclusion of some citizens from political participation. Cooper has applied these ideas to the question of equality and discrimination in *Challenging Diversity: Rethinking Equality and the Value of Difference*. In this book Cooper identifies a number of issues that are also relevant for discrimination law. For example, she asks "Gender, age, sexual orientation, race and disability have joined, and in some cases superseded, the left's traditional preoccupation with class. But what remains less clear are the criteria required for recognition of a social relation."[85]

[84] Davina Cooper, *Governing Out of Order: Space, Law and the Politics of Belonging* (London: Rivers Oram Press, 1998).

[85] Davina Cooper, *Challenging Diversity: Rethinking Equality and the Value of Difference* (Cambridge: Cambridge University Press, 2004), at p.3.

Cooper also poses the questions in terms of the relationship of the value of equality to issues of subordination and power by noting that: "What does equality mean in relation to dominant constituencies? If equality refers to something more complex than raising those with less, we might think about the application of equality to those subjectivities, preferences and conduct constituted through the terms of whiteness, hetereosexuality, masculinity and economic power. [...] How can equality be conceived in a way that recognises the relationship between being and doing, between social structures and individual agency, without losing the specificity of either?"[86]

Cooper's distinct contribution is to suggest a different method for the analysis of issues of inequality, subordination and discrimination that focuses on two strands of analysis: "The first concerns the ways in which assymetries circulate through social institutions as a result of the permeation of norms and values to which they are articulated. The second concerns the distinctive and constitutive relationship of principles of inequality to social dynamics, such as capitalism and the intimate/impersonal."[87]

These two poles of analysis, and this alternative method, opens up issues of inequality to a wider enquiry than is encouraged by liberal political analysis. On this analysis, liberal discrimination law replicates the public-private dichotomy thereby leaving issues of socio-economic exclusion and forms of inequality resulting from the "private sphere" outside its scope. Cooper's analysis also encourages the analysis of inequality and discrimination as structural problems related to "groups" rather than one off "wrongful" acts of individuals. In the context of domestic discrimination law and policy, the shift from individual fault to group structures has taken on an increasing importance because of the increasing focus on "social exclusion". As the next passage from Hugh Collins indicates, discrimination law is increasingly being placed as one of a number of responses to the problem of the exclusion of certain individuals and groups from mainstream political, social and economic processes and institutions.

Hugh Collins: "Discrimination, Equality and Social Inclusion" (2003) 66 Modern L. R. 16, at pp.42–43

Returning, finally, to the question posed at the outset—what are the aims of anti-discrimination laws?—my argument suggests that as well as upholding the ideal of respect for the dignity of individuals or equal worth, the legislation also must be understood as pursuing a distributive aim in order to account for deviations from the equal treatment

[86] Davina Cooper, *Challenging Diversity: Rethinking Equality and the Value of Difference* (Cambridge: Cambridge University Press) p.4.
[87] Davina Cooper, *Challenging Diversity: Rethinking Equality and the Value of Difference* (Cambridge: Cambridge University Press) p.10.

principle. I have argued, though certainly not conclusively, that this distributive aim or criterion of fairness may be discovered in the aim of social inclusion. Although the current law does not fit precisely with the principles suggested by the aim of social inclusion, the match is closer than might be initially supposed, and in several respects the aim of social inclusion explains features of the law that seem hard to account for by reference to other possible distributive aims such as equality of opportunity. In particular, the aim of social inclusion suggests a more determinate standard for the legitimacy of positive action than the tests of "proportionality" or "strict scrutiny". It suggests that deviations from equal treatment should be permitted where the discriminatory measure is necessary to achieve the result of social inclusion for members of a group that are presently largely excluded.

Moreover, an appreciation of the aim of social inclusion may provide an insight into the reasons why we may have reservations about some aspects of the current law. For instance, remember *James v Eastleigh Borough Council*, the case concerning free entry to a swimming pool. Although the majority of the House of Lords regarded the problem as a simple case of direct discrimination, because "but for" his sex Mr. James would have had a free swim, the minority were surely correct to doubt whether the aim of the law included preventing the local authority from increasing access to its facilities for those who might otherwise be excluded. We do not know whether the concession based upon state pensionable age served the goal of reducing the exclusion of a group that was otherwise disproportionately excluded from this public facility. That question was left answered, because the majority believed that ultimately the equal treatment principle provided an exclusionary rule that prevented any justification of direct discrimination. The aim of social inclusion explains why that question should have been relevant, and why a deviation from the equal treatment rule may have been justified in this instance. This exercise in examining the aims of the anti-discrimination laws in the light of the idea of social inclusion is not therefore merely an exercise in mapping, of interpretation, or of rationalisation, but it is also intended as a critical exploration of the assumptions and limitations of these laws.

Collins argument uses "social exclusion" as a category which allows a convergence between a number of fragmented aims in discrimination law: the concern with both direct discrimination with its focus on individual wrong and stigma which underlies the original concern with equal protection in jurisdictions such as the US; and the increasing concern with distributive justice and socio-economic inequalites which is clear in the emerging definitions of indirect discrimination and positive action. John Gardner has explained these twin goals from within liberal political theory as part of the commitment to autonomy: that seeks to remedy both the injury of stigma and at the same time is based on distributive justice.[88]

In order to develop an analysis of discrimination law as social exclusion there needs to be a more comprehensive and detailed enquiry into which groups are at risk of social exclusion; what conditions cause and exacerbate social exclusion; how the process of social exclusion operates. This analysis will allow a better understanding of discrimination as a structural problem as well as enabling a more refined understanding of the problem. It will also allow a better understanding on the remedial role of discrimination law and policy, i.e. how, and at what stage in the process of social exclusion, should

[88] See J. Gardner, "Liberals and Unlawful Discrimination", (1989) O.J.L.S. 9, 1; reprinted in Christopher McCrudden (ed), *Anti-Discrimination Law* (Aldershot: Dartmouth, 1991)

legal and policy interventions be introduced in order to eliminate or reduce the problem.

E. *Discrimination as Oppression*

Iris Marion Young's analysis which treats discrimination as a form of oppression against certain social groups provides one way of breaking down the category "social exclusion". Like other critics of liberal anti-discrimination principles and law, Young criticises the liberal paradigm as too individualistic to capture the importance of groups and their particular experience. Her main objection is that this vision of justice tends to "restrict the meaning of social justice to the morally proper distribution of benefits and burdens among members of society". As an alternative, Young proposes that a theory of justice should attend to factors other than individual rights and the distribution of resources: for example, the social structure and institutional context; issues of decisionmaking power and procedures; division of labor and culture. Her argument is that oppression, which she defines using five categories which she calls the "five faces of oppression" is a more appropriate method to capture this wider vision of social justice. Moreover, Young shifts the focus of analysis to the oppression of social groups rather than individuals. This critique of liberal discrimination law as too focused on individuals, and the shift of focus from individuals to groups, is a common theme in "critical" approaches to the subject. Traditional liberal theory, such as that of Dworkin or Rawls, has treated the individual as the focus for analysis, and treated the core of discrimination law as being an "individual right" to non discrimination or "equal respect and concern". A concern with groups is seen to be an instrumental aspect of this focus on the individual.[89] Paul Brest endorses some shift towards a group analysis in his writing, although he warns that "the fact is that most injuries of discrimination—even indirect and secondary ones—were inflicted on particular persons and only they are entitled to compensation. Where discrimination has undermined the unity or culture of a group, it may be appropriate to characterise the injury as one to the group; but the appropriate remedy then is one that reestablishes the group, an end that is not promoted by the fiction of treating individuals members as its agents."[90] However, Young's approach is not to treat individuals as agents of their groups but rather to challenge the focus on individual action in traditional liberal theory in favour of an approach that focuses on collective structural factors. This makes it easier to understand the experience of injustice and oppression of

[89] Rawls' discussion of the relationship between individual and groups is that individuals have political rights whereas groups are recognised as instrumental or associational. John Rawls *Political Liberalism* (New York: Columbia University Press, 1993).

[90] Paul Brest, *The Supreme Court 1975 Term. Forward: In Defense of the Anti-discrimination Principle*, 90 Harvard L.R. 1–55 (1976) at p.51–52.

"groups" as a distinct category rather than an amalgamation of individual actors.[91] The following discussion applies discussion of Young in the context of discrimination law.

Iris Marion Young, *Justice and the Politics of Difference* (NJ: Princeton University Press, 1990) Chapter 2

p.38–48: "I have proposed an enabling conception of justice. Justice should refer not only to distribution, but also to the insitutitonal conditions necessary for the development and exercise of individual capacities and collective communication and cooperation. Under this conception of justice, injustice refers primarily to two forms of disabling constraints, oppression and domination. While these constraints include distributive patterns, they also involve matters which cannot easily be assimilated to the logic of distribution: decisionmaking procedures, division of labor, and culture.

Many people in the United States would not choose the term 'oppression' to name injustice in our society. For contemporary emancipatory social movements, on the other hand—socialists, radical feminists, American Indian activists, Black activists, gay and lesbian actitivists—opression is a central category of political discourse. Entering the political discourse in which oppression is a central category involves adopting a general mode of analyzing and evaluating social structures and practices which is incommensurate with the language of liberal individualism that dominates political discourse in the United States.

A major political project for those of us who identify with at least one of these movements must thus be to persuade people that the discourse of oppression makes sense of much of our social experience. We are ill prepared for this task, however, because we have no clear account of the meaning of oppression. While we find the term used often in the diverse philosophical and theoretical literature spawned by radical social movements in the United States, we find little direct discussion of the meaning of the concept as used by these movements."

By shifting the focus of a theory of justice away from issues of individual freedom and distribution towards groups and structural inequality, Young identifies a range of issues which are not often included within discussions of the discrimination law. In particular, the shift in the analysis from the individual to the group suggests that oppression is a:

p.41: "structural concept rather than the result of a few people's choices or policies. Its causes are embedded in unquestioned norms, habits, and symbols, in the assumptions underlying institutional rules and the collective consequences of following those rules [...] In this extended structural sense oppression refers to the vast and deep injustices some groups suffer as a consequence of often unconscious assumptions and reactions of well-meaning people in ordinary interactions, media and cultural stereotypes, and structural features of bureaucratic hierarchies and market mechanisms—in short, the normal processes of everyday life. We cannot eliminate this structural oppression by getting rid of the

[91] See discussion of importance of groups in the context of British responses to minorities, Tariq Modood, *Multiculturalism*, (Cambridge: Policy Press, 2007)

rulers or making some new laws, because oppressions are systematically reproduced in major economic, political and cultural institutions."

Young goes on to derive five faces of oppression which reflect the oppression experienced by groups e.g. blacks, women, gays and lesbians. She identifies the "social group" as:

p.48: "a collective of persons differentiated from at least one other group by cultural forms, practices, or way of life. Members of a group have a specific affinity with one another because of their similar experience or way of life, which prompts them to associate with one another more than with those not identified with the group, or in a different way. Groups are an expression of social relations; a group exists only in relation to at least one other group. Group identification arises, that is, in the encounter and interaction between social collectivities that experience some differences in their way of life and forms of association, even if they regard themselves as belonging to the same society."

The shift of focus from individuals to groups represents an important alternative to liberal discrimination law. As we have seen a number of commentators have criticised the focus of liberal discrimination law on individual rights rather than groups and structural practices. This criticism has also identified the way in which Young goes on to identify five ways in which groups can be oppressed. In the following section these five categories are set out and related to the themes of discrimination law explored in this book.

Iris Marion Young, Justice and the Politics of Difference, NJ: Princeton University Press, 1990, Chapter 2, at pp.48–63.

"The Faces of Oppression

Exploitation

The central function of Marx's theory of exploitation is to explain how class structure can exist in the absence of legally and normatively sanctioned class distinctions.[...] Capitalist society, on the other hand, removes traditional juridically enforced class distinctions and promotes a belief in the legal freedom of persons.

The central insight expressed in the concept of exploitation, then is that this oppression occurs through a steady process of the transfer of the results of the labor of one social group to benefit another. The injustice of class division does not consist only in the distributive fact that some people have great wealth while most people have little [...] Exploitation enacts a structural relation between social groups. Social rules about what work is, who does what for whom, how work is compensated, and the social processes by which the results of work are appropriated operate to enact relations of power and inequality. These relations are produced and reproduced through a systematic process in which the energies of the have-nots are continuously expended to maintain and augment the power, status, and wealth of the haves. [...]

To summarize, women are exploited in the Marxist sense to the degree that they are wage workers. Some have argued that women's domestic labor also represents a form of capitalist class exploitation insofar as it is labor covered by the wages a family receives. As a group, however, women undergo specific forms of gender exploitation in which their energies and power are expended, often unnoticed and unacknowledged, usually to the benefit of men by releasing them for more important and creative work, enhancing their status and environment around them, or providing them with sexual and emotional services.

Race is a structure of oppression as basic as class or gender. Are there, then, racially specific forms of exploitation? There is no doubt that, racialized groups in the United States, especially Blacks and Latinos, are oppressed through capitalist superexploitation resulting from a segmented labor market that tends to reserve skilled, high-paying, unionized jobs for whites. [. . .]"

Young's definition of exploitation provides an explanation for discrimination law's focus on employment discrimination. Not only radical critics, but also liberals themselves recognise the importance of access to employment opportunities as a pre-requisite to the value of distributive justice that discrimination law should promote. For example, John Gardner justifies the priority given to employment discrimination within discrimination law by arguing that private employer's have the power to distribute an important public good in the form of the income and self-respect which follows from having a job.[92]

However, what is significant about Young's analysis is that it goes further than liberal responses by arguing that employment discrimination is a structural problem:

"these relations are produced and reproduced through a systematic process in which the energies of the have-nots are continuously expended to maintain and augment the power, status, and wealth of the haves." (see the extract above).

This has significant implications for the way in which the problem of employment discrimination is identified and also for what constitutes an appropriate remedial response. A traditional liberal response to employment discrimination will treat it as an individual failure by a one-off employer to meet the procedural requirements of formal equality (or equality of opportunity). Moreover, this definition will apply equally to all groups, irrespective of whether the group is particularly vulnerable to exploitation (e.g. women and racial minorities) or is a dominant majority. Once the problem is identified in these terms, the remedy for employment discrimination will be individual compensation (damages) for the harm caused by an individual employer who has committed a "wrong" against an individual employee. In Part B of the book we examine the way in which this model of employment discrimination as a procedural failure of the individual employer sits uneasily with concepts such as indirect discrimination and positive action. In Part D we note the way

[92] J. Gardner, "Liberals and Unlawful Discrimination", (1989) O.J.L.S., 1; reprinted in Christopher McCrudden (ed.), *Anti-Discrimination Law* (Aldershot: Dartmouth, 1991)

in which they are difficult to reconcile with an increasing focus on collective remedial action for discrimination. Young's analysis focuses more explicitly on the structural causes on employment discrimination which lead to the disproportionate exploitation of certain groups, and provides an analysis that shifts the focus from individuals to groups. Moreover, her identification of the way in which factors other than employment can exacerbate the problems of some social groups explains the increasing concern in discrimination law with spheres other than employment, e.g. the participation of social groups in political processes, and the provision of public services. Young identifies two ways in which social groups who are already exploited can become more oppressed as a result of the experience of other forms of discrimination in the political and social spheres.

"*Marginalization*

Marginalization is perhaps the most dangerous form of oppression. A whole category of people is expelled from useful participation in social life and thus potentially subjected to severe material deprivation and even extermination. The material deprivation marginalization often causes is certainly unjust, especially in a society where others have plenty. [...]

Powerlessness

This powerless status is perhaps best described negatively: the powerless lack the authority, status, and sense of self that professionals tend to have. The status of privilege professionals has three aspects, the lack of which produces oppression in nonprofessionals."

Young's identification of powerlessness as a process through which discrimination emerges and is exacerbated is important. The focus on traditional discussions of discrimination law tends to be on socio-economic goods: especially employment opportunities, pay, private and public goods and services. The focus on "powerlessness" makes explicit the precise ways in which an individual may be discriminated in accessing these goods. It is not just the access to certain goods, but also the way in which they are made available, that may contribute to oppression of groups. For example, in the context of employment discrimination, it is not just the fact that an individual has experienced unequal treatment in applying for a job, but also the fact that certain classes of jobs are classified as non-professional and of a lower status that may contribute to powerlessness. More generally, Young's analysis makes clear that the power of defining social meaning is relevant to understanding the experience of discrimination and oppression. For example, as the chapter on race and multiple discrimination makes clear, the unequal distribution of not just economic power in the form of job opportunities, but also social and political power more generally, mean that dominant groups may be able to define the very categories of discrimination law in ways that give them an advantage over less powerful groups. Moreover, this greater power of social definition also extends to establishing the norm in the public sphere in ways that exclude less powerful social groups. Young identifies this form of oppression as "cultural imperialism."

"*Cultural Imperialism*

Cultural imperialism involves the universalization of a dominant group's experience and culture, and its establishment as the norm. Some groups have exclusive or primary access to [. . .] the means of interpretation and communication in a society. As a consequence, the dominant cultural products of the society, that is, those most widely disseminated, express the experience, values, goals, and achievements of these groups. Often without noticing they do so, the dominant groups project their own experience as a representative of humanity as such. Cultural products also express the dominant group's perspective on and interpretation of events and elements in the society, including other groups in the society, insofar as they attain cultural status at all. [. . .]

Cultural imperialism involves the paradox of experiencing oneself as invisible at the same time that one is marked out as different. The invisibility comes about when dominant groups fail to recognize the perspective embodied in their cultural expressions as a perspective. These dominant cultural expressions often simply have little place for the experience of other groups, at most only mentioning or referring to them in stereotyped or marginalized ways. This, then, is the injustice of cultural imperialism: that the oppressed group's own experience and interpretation of social life finds little expression that touches the dominant culture, while that same culture imposes on the oppressed group its experience and interpretations of social life."

The previous section on "the politics of recognition" and cultural pluralism will have an obvious connection with this category. Therefore, the risk that racial, ethnic or religious minorities are unable to fully influence the public culture in which they live will be a distinct problem. This issue is dealt with in discussions of "cultural pluralism" or "multiculturalism" (see especially the chapters on race, religion and multiple discrimination). However, Young's argument has a wider application. Other protected groups, (e.g. defined along characteristics such as gender, disability and sexual orientation) may also find that their experiences are inadequately represented in the public sphere: either (a) because not adequately included; or (b) where they are included they are misrepresented and distorted. Women may want to argue that pornography and sexist advertising falls within this category. There may also be arguments against the use of legal regulation of speech and representations in this context and a preference for non-legal measures that enable vulnerable social group to enter into the public sphere to participate fully or remedy distortions and misrepresentations. In the most extreme cases, it could be argued that some forms of misrepresentations may verge on incitement to hatred (hate speech). In other cases there may actually be violence against individuals which is caused by their membership of a particular social group. This is discussed in Young's next, and final, category of the way in which oppression and social exclusion can target (and be experienced by) certain social groups.

"*Violence*

Finally, many groups suffer the oppression of systematic violence. Members of some groups live with the knowledge that they must fear random, unprovoked attacks on their persons or property, which have no motive but to damage, humiliate, or destroy the person. [...] What makes violence a face of oppression is less the particular acts themselves, though these are often utterly horrible, than the social context surrounding them, which makes them possible and even acceptable. What makes violence a phenomenon of social injustice, and not merely an individual moral wrong, is its systematic character, its existence as a social practice.

Violence is systematic because it is directed at members of a group simply because they are members of a group. Any woman for example, has a reason to fear rape. Regardless of what a Black man has done to escape the oppressions of marginality or powerlessness, he lives knowing he is subject to attack or harassment. The oppression of violence consists not only in direct victimization, but in the daily knowledge shared by all members of oppressed groups that they are liable to violation, solely on account of their group identity. Just living under such a threat of attack on oneself or family or friends deprives the oppressed of freedom and dignity, and needlessly expends their energy. [...]

Violence is a form of injustice that a distributive understanding of justice seems ill equipped to capture. This may be why contemporary discussions of justice rarely mention it. I have argued that group-directed violence is institutionalized and systemic."

Young's inclusion of violence as a form of oppression and as a relevant harm considerably expands the scope of discrimination law. For example, it is increasingly being argued that certain forms of violence raise an issue of discrimination because they specifically target women or minorities. This, in turn, justifies enhanced criminal penalties to reflect the additional harm caused by discrimination or animus that motivates the selection of the victim.[93] These "hate crimes" have become an increasingly popular legal response to the most extreme forms of violence against certain social groups, e.g. minorities, women, gays and lesbians. Certain well established forms of violence, such as rape or the trafficking of women, do not fall within the core of discrimination law. Yet, at the same time, they raise issues about prejudice, social powerlessness and oppression of social groups that are at the heart of discrimination law's concerns. Although these issues do not form a major part of the discussion in this text, Young's analysis is important because it makes clear that all of these forms of harms are often experienced by the same social group in an overlapping way that contributes to their experience of oppression and social exclusion. In this way it is a reminder of the relevance and continuity between the discrimination law as applied in areas such as employment discrimination and the increasing concern with the discriminatory impact of certain types of violence, e.g. hate crimes, rape and trafficking.

Young, like Freeman, argues that the focus of minority protection strategies should be on victims and results rather than perpetrators and intention, fault and causation. However, she concludes "it confuses issues to bring such a focus on results under the concept of discrimination. A much better strategy

[93] For a discussion of these issues in the UK context see M. Malik, "Racist Crime", at n.9 above.

for addressing the injustice suffered by disadvantage groups is to restrict the concept of discrimination to intentional and explicitly formulated policies of exclusion or preference, and to argue that discrimination is not the only or necessarily the primary wrong that women and people of color suffer. As groups, the primary wrong we suffer is oppression".[94]

Unlike many radical critiques of a liberal discrimination law, Young's theory of "discrimination as oppression" provides a detailed alternative. More specifically, by extending the range of harms caused by discrimination beyond a failure to "treat like with like" this justification of discrimination law is able to include harms such as violence and cultural alienation. This approach also connects two key debates in contemporary discussions of justice: redistribution and recognition. It is sometimes argued that the debate around the "politics of recognition" has marginalised the importance of "redistribution". There is increasing acceptance of the fact that that both "claims for recognition" and "claims for a more just distribution of goods and resources" are independent (albeit related) sources of injustice.[95] By including not only exploitation, marginalisation and powerless, but also cultural imperialism and violence in her theory, Young is able to provide an overarching framework that includes "recognition" and "redistribution" in its definition of oppression of certain groups. Young's alternative strategy significantly expands (a) the types of conduct that fall within the categories "inequality" or "discrimination"; and (b) the range of legal concepts that can be used to regulate these harms, e.g. civil and criminal law and also non-legal policies. These set of ideas are also able to connect the harms of exploitation and marginalisation (that are addressed through traditional regulation of employment discrimination) to the increasing concern with multiculturalism, hate crimes and hate speech. In the chapter on multiple discrimination and intersectionality we consider some of the critiques of this concern with "groups" and the way in which this can pose a distinct risk to the central goals of discrimination law. However, it is worth noting that by presenting an alternative to the individual as the predominant focus of discrimination law, Young's theory of group oppression can justify some of the key features of anti-discrimination law that are discussed in this book. For example, it explains the priority originally given to employment discrimination to overcome the marginalisation, economic exploitation and powerlessness of some social groups. It also explains the emerging focus on the processes through which the public sphere can exclude or distort some groups experiences as reflected in constitutional protection against discrimination. Finally, it explains the increasing concern with the violence that is experienced by women and minorities that justifies the increasing focus of discrimination law on hate crimes and hate speech.

94 See I. M. Young, *Justice and the Politics of Difference*, (Princeton: Princeton University Press, 1990) at p.196.

95 For a discussion of this conflict, see Nancy Fraser and Axel Honneth, *Redistribution or Recognition? A Political Philosophical Exchange* (London: Verso, 2003)

VI. Conclusion

This chapter has examined several possible theoretical justifications for discrimination law. It should be clear that the complexity of the debates we have examined, together with the complexity of discrimination law itself, makes it particularly difficult to provide one single justification. Nonetheless, because of the need to justify the use of law to regulate social life, theorists continue to see the task of justifying discrimination law as a necessary one. For this reason, theoretical analysis is often used to justify and explain at a more specific level many of the outward features of discrimination law, and to help answer what was characterised in chapters 1 and 2 as some of the key questions of discrimination law. Three examples will illustrate this, the first two of which are relevant to answering the fourth key question 'how wide are the protections?' First, there is a key debate about the extent to which particular ideas of equality and autonomy can be used to justify and explain the boundaries of, and distinctions between, direct and indirect discrimination.[96] Secondly, such ideas are also crucial when justifying and explaining the extent to which positive action is a legitimate concept in discrimination law. Turning to a third example, arguments about equality, autonomy or social exclusion can also be used to explain why particular groups enjoy protection from discrimination[97]—thereby helping to answer the first question, 'who is protected?'.

[96] Jeremy Waldron, 'Indirect Discrimination' in Stephen Guest and Alan Milne (eds.), *Equality and Discrimination: Essays in Freedom and Justice* (Stuttgart, Germany: Archiv Fur Rechts-Und Sozialphilosophie, 1985); John Gardner, 'Liberals and Unlawful Discrimination' (1989) 9 OJLS 1 and 'Discrimination as Injustice' (1996) 16 OJLS 353.

[97] John Gardner, 'On the Ground of Her Sex(uality)' (1998) 18 OJLS 167.

PART B

CENTRAL CONCEPTS IN DISCRIMINATION LAW

4

DIRECT DISCRIMINATION

I. Introduction

In this chapter we consider the concept of direct discrimination. How direct discrimination should be defined is related to the third of the ten key questions of discrimination law that we identified in chapter 1, given that it raises issues about 'how wide are the protections' of discrimination law. Direct discrimination is one of the main concepts that is used to regulate discrimination under all the prohibited grounds. In Chapter 2, we noted that the Sex Discrimination Act and the Race Relations Act borrowed their main structure and concepts from the US civil rights legislation, such concepts also being seen in EU discrimination law. The US civil rights movement was a response to slavery and segregation. Its main political and legal demand was the call for 'inclusion' of African Americans in mainstream US society on the same terms as the majority. In *Plessy v Ferguson* decided in 1896 after the American Civil War, the US Supreme Court had held the equal protection clause of the Fourteenth Amendment of the US Constitution to permit a law that required racial segregation.[1] A major focus of the legal struggle of the US civil rights movement in the 1950s and 1960s was to overturn this decision by declaring that government sponsored segregation was unconstitutional under the Fourteenth Amendment. This struggle resulted in a dramatic victory when the US Supreme Court held in *Brown v Board of Education* that racial segregation in schools violated was unconstitutional because it violated the equal protection clause.[2] Given this historical and political background, it is not surprising that the model of discrimination law that emerged out of the US context focused on symmetry and comparison. This model will be familiar to those who understand discrimination law as giving sense to a concept of equality as the treatment of 'like with like' (see further Chapter 3). One of the main issues that we consider in this chapter is the extent to which the focus on 'comparison' in

[1] *Plessy v Ferguson* 163 U. S. 538 (1986). The Fourteenth Amendment states, inter alia, " No State shall [. . .] deny to any person within its jurisdiction the equal protection of the laws."
[2] *Brown v Board of Education* 347 U.S. 483 (1954).

legal definitions of direct discrimination restricts the protection offered by discrimination law.

In many jurisdictions, notions of direct and indirect discrimination play a role in judicial interpretations of constitutional non-discrimination provisions. A good example is provided in the case law dealing with s.15(1) of the Canadian Charter of Rights.[3] Courts determine whether a ground of discrimination which is not expressly prohibited in s.15(1) in fact falls within its reach as an "analogous" ground, and s.15(1) has been found to preclude, in each case on the basis of one or more of the prohibited grounds, formal distinctions between the claimant and others, substantively differential treatment of the claimant and others due to a failure to take into account the claimant's already disadvantaged position, and provisions which are neutral in their language but which have adverse effects on a disadvantaged group—in other words, both directly and indirectly discriminatory provisions.[4] In the United Kingdom, by contrast, direct discrimination is a concept found mainly in domestic statutory protections against discrimination. However, it is also found—albeit with differences of formulation—within Art.14 of the European Convention on Human Rights and in EU law. In consequence, domestic legislation must where relevant be read in the light of those provisions (and may, in cases involving directly effective provisions of EU law, be 'disapplied' for incompatibility). How far notions of direct discrimination at these different 'levels'—the Convention, EU law and domestic legislation—are reconcilable is thus a key question for national courts. At a more theoretical level, a further question is how far Convention and EU law notions of direct discrimination operate in a "constitutional" fashion in domestic law. This question provides a direct illustration of the debate considered in Chapter 1 concerning the extent to which the Convention and EU law play a "constitutional" role in domestic law.

As such, it is important for us to focus on Art.14 and EU law towards the start of the chapter (we do so in sections II and III). We begin at a more theoretical level, however, by considering (building on Chapter 3) what may be thought to be wrong about direct discrimination.

II. Direct Discrimination and Equality

The main discussion in this chapter focuses on the legal definitions of direct discrimination. First, this section examines the relationship between equality and direct discrimination. In Chapter 3 we identified three different ways in

[3] For general analysis, see Richard Clayton & Hugh Tomlinson, *The Law of Human Rights: Volume 1* (Oxford: Oxford University Press, 2000), paras. 17.171 to 17.193.

[4] See, for example, *Eldridge v. Attorney-General of British Columbia* [1997] 3 S.C.R. 624; *Vriend v. Alberta* [1998] 1 S.C.R. 493; *Law v. Canada (Minister of Employment and Immigration)* [1999] 1 S.C.R. 497.

which the term equality is used. There may in fact be great value, as Holmes argues, in keeping law discrimination separate from equality.[5] Nevertheless, it is useful to investigate the role of equality because it is a recurring feature of the historical justification and contemporary defense of the concept of direct discrimination. In Chapter 3, strict equality was defined as the principle that requires using equality as the end goal: i.e. any inequality is intrinsically bad irrespective of how it comes about; and even when inequality is unavoidable it is deemed to be bad. Instrumental equality was defined as in terms of the pursuit of some deeper principle of justice: i.e. where inequality is used as a marker for pursuing some other goal or identifying some form of wrongdoing or harm. This means that when no-one is responsible then inequality may not be unjust; and the focus is on individual acts that result in the wrongdoing. Finally, the Priority Principle was defined in terms of the idea that benefiting people matters more the worse off they are and it appeal to equality is often rhetorical or a means of identifying the absolute standard for actions or distribution.

The concept of direct discrimination, as set out in legislation and developed in cases discussed in this chapter, can be related to strict equality, and is concerned with individual acts and decision-making. To this extent direct discrimination is concerned with controlling the decision-making and conduct of the discriminator rather than promoting a collective goal. The legislation operates by focusing on the acts and practices of private individuals and institutional actors. Where these acts/decisions and practices can be said to be on the grounds of a prohibited ground (sex, race, etc.), they translate into wrongful direct discrimination. The requirement for "but for" causation provides the essential link between the two parties in the action: the decision and conduct of the discriminator who has acted on a prohibited ground and the individual who is the victim of the discrimination. To this extent the action in direct discrimination mirrors a tort action with its focus on two individuals and wrongful conduct.

Another way of understanding the concept of direct discrimination is to notice that it is a version of instrumental equality. Within this analysis, equality is used as a marker for identifying a more fundamental injustice. Some commentators point out that within this analysis we are not really concerned with equality at all; instead, our main concern is with the underlying value that motivates the appeal to equality.[6] Analysis does need to address the central place of equality in discrimination. However, this indirect appeal to equality usefully allows us to identify: what is this more fundamental injustice that underlies direct discrimination? Some commentators treat direct discrimination as a failure in procedural justice which encourages a focus on challenging "stereotypes". This has, in the past, been a common way

[5] See Elisa Holmes, "Anti-Discrimination Rights Without Equality", (2005) 68 M.L.R. 2 at 175–194.

[6] See Elisa Homes, "Anti-Discrimination Rights without Equality", (2005) 68 M.L.R. 2 at 175–194.

of identifying the injustice (or harm) of direct discrimination. Others treat direct discrimination as a substantive harm to the autonomy or dignity of the individual, each of these arguments are examined in the section below. Here it is worth noting that treating direct discrimination as an example of instrumental equality, and distinguishing it from strict equality, has one distinct advantage. This approach avoids one of the most damning indictments of equality as a justification for discrimination law: the "leveling down objection".

As we saw in Chapter 3 the leveling down objection is a critique of strict versions of equality. This critique focuses on the fact that when equality is treated as an intrinsic end goal, there is no mechanism for specifying the way in which equality is achieved, and there is no substantive standard that can act as a redress to "levelling down" to achieve equality. Holmes has summarised the leveling down objection and its consequences in the following terms:

Elisa Holmes, "Anti-Discrimination Rights Without Equality" (2005) 68 M.L.R. 2 175–194

p.186: "We have already seen that equality must be of something. [. . .] In the case of that something being valuable because it is valuable to have, and so equalising it helps ensure that everyone has some. On this scenario, egalitarianism would be purely instrumental. Alternatively, the independently valuable thing might be something which it is important to an egalitarian to have equalised whether or not it is important for everyone to have: if anyone is to have it, it should be had in equal measure. In this way equality itself has some constitutive value: there is value in a particular other value being had in equal measure, not just in having the other value. Notice one important repercussion of this position: whatever level of that other value is had, it is valuable to have it equally, even if it is equalised by lowering the total level of that value, and by increasing no-one's share of that value. This is sometimes called the leveling down objection to equality. The same idea means that if a detriment has to occur to someone, there is value in imposing the detriment on everyone, even though the action is good for no-one."

Therefore, if the ultimate goal of discrimination law is equality then there is no reason why that end state cannot be achieved by taking resources from those who have them and giving them to those who do not. At its most extreme, a strict version of equality would permit achieving equality through the destruction of resources from those who have more of them to achieve a strict parity between the parties. There a number of examples where the levelling down objection has been used as a response to a claim of direct discrimination to reduce the protection and advantage for those discriminated against rather than raising the standard. One example is *Smith v Advel*[7] where the ECJ per-

[7] Case C-408/92, *Smith v Avdel* [1994] European Court Reports I-4435.

mitted compliance of a pension scheme with Art.119 (141) EC through raising rather than lowering the pension age for women: i.e. by equalising downwards. In *Smith*, the ECJ acknowledged that Art.119 (141) protection merely required that men and women should receive the same pay for the same work without imposing any specific level of pay, did not preclude measures which achieved equal treatment by reducing the advantages of the persons previously favoured. A notable example of "levelling down" to comply with a constitutional equality provision is the US Supreme Court decision in *Palmer v Thompson*, where it was held that that act of city in closing public swimming pools rather than attempting to operate them on a desegregated basis did not breach the 14th Amendment equal protection rights of African Americans[8]. It is worth noting that the decision of the city authorities in *Palmer* to close down certain of the pools was taken in the context of a general policy of desegregating its facilities. The closure of the pools in question was deemed to be necessary to preserve peace and order and that the integregated pools could not be economically operated. Nevertheless, the fact that levelling down was permitted in the context of a constitutional equality provision is a vivid illustration of the risk of "levelling down" as a solution to a discrimination claim.

The risk of levelling down can be overcome once we understand direct discrimination as instrumental rather than strict equality. On this construction, there is a reason to pursue equality where this ensures the overall justice (however defined) of the situation. In some circumstances the principle of justice may require that individuals are treated in the same way or have access to the same goods as another. However, it does not require that others are bought down to the same lower level in order to maintain equality between the parties.

Once direct discrimination is treated as instrumental equality it becomes important to specify the underlying principles of justice which "equality" is being used to track. There are two sets of arguments that are used to justify direct discrimination: first, direct discrimination a failure in procedure; and second, direct discrimination as a denial of a substantive value such as autonomy or dignity.

A. *Discrimination as a failure in procedure: Stereotyping, Prejudice and the Failure to Treat "Like with Like"*

Direct discrimination was in the past associated with stereotypes about protected groups such as women and racial minorities. Stereotypes are a generalised assumption about an individual (often because of their membership of a wider group) that fail to take into account the individual facts and cir-

[8] *Palmer v Thompson* (1971) 403 U.S. 217, 91 S.Ct. 1940.

cumstances that are relevant to an assessment of that individual. Discrimination law does not treat all stereotypes as invidious and worthy of legal prohibition. It is only those stereotypes and generalisations that are based on prohibited grounds that trigger the legal prohibitions in discrimination law. On one analysis of direct discrimination, this is a *procedural* failure.

Another way of expressing this concern with process, and challenging stereotypes, is by noticing that it appeals to a particular version of equality as the treatment of "like with like" and traditional definitions of "equality of opportunity". It is often seen as a "procedural" rather than "substantive" notion of equality. This requires investigating the way in which two entities—e.g. men and women—are similar and different. Different treatment in the face of similarities triggers allegations of discrimination but significantly it is also important to search for and establish the legitimate differences between the two entities (men and women) that should fall outside the label "discrimination". This reading of direct discrimination protects men and women, majorities and minorities, in a symmetrical way; moreover, a comparison that is central to establishing direct discrimination.[9]

In the following passage, Owen Fiss argues that this procedural version of equality is especially attractive as a judicial mechanism for regulating equality.

Owen Fiss, "Groups and the Equal Protection Clause", (1976) Philosophy and Public Affairs

pp.107–177: "First, the antidiscrimination principle embodies a conception of equality that roughly corresponds to the conception of equality governing the judicial process. When we speak of 'equal justice' we have in mind a norm prohibiting the adjudicator from taking into account certain irrelevant characteristics of the litigants—their race, wealth, and so on. This is the message conveyed by the icon of justice. The anti-discrimination principle also invokes the metaphor of blindness—as in 'color blindness'. The overarching obligation is to treat similar persons similarly, declaring certain individual characteristics-such as color-irrelevant.

It is natural for the Justices to seize upon the ideal of their craft in setting norms to govern others. Their craft sets the limits to their horizons, it influences their choice among the many meanings of equality. This limit on vision may have been reinforced by the fact that some of the early equal protection cases challenged exclusionary conduct occurring in the course of the judicial process. Moreover, the words 'protection of the laws' in the Clause may have led the Justices to think primarily of the administration of justice, and the concept of equality that governs judicial activity in general (equal justice). At some point in history the word 'equal' shifts its location so as to deemphasize the word 'protection'—it becomes understood that the clause guarantees 'the protection of equal laws,' rather than just the 'equal protection of the laws'; but the implications of the original version still linger.

[9] See SDA 75, s.5(3) and RRA 76, s.4.

Second, the antidiscrimination principle seems to further another supposed norm of the craft—value neutrality—that the judges not substitute their preferences for those of the people. The antidiscrimination principle seems to respond to an aspiration for a 'mechanical jurisprudence'—to use Roscoe Pound's phrase—by making the predicate of intervention appear technocratic. The anti-discrimination principle seems to ask no more of the judiciary than that it engage in what might at first seem to be the near mathematical task of determining whether there is, in Tussman and TenBroek's terms, 'overinclusiveness' or 'underinclusiveness,' or, in the terms of the contemporary commentators, whether there is the right 'fit' between means and ends. The terms used have an attractively quantitative ring. They make the task of judicial judgment appear to involve as little discretion as when a salesman advises a customer whether a pair of shoes fit. Moreover, under the anti-discrimination principle, whatever judgment there is would seem to be one about means, not ends, thereby insulating judges from the charge of substituting their judgments for that of the legislature. The court could invalidate state action without passing on the merit or importance of the end—a task, it might be argued, that is especially committed to the more representative branches of government."

Although Fiss developed his argument in the context of US 14th Amendment Equal Protection Clause, it has a wider relevance. Early cases under the SDA confirm the way in which direct discrimination can identify and seek to eliminate stereotypes. Three cases illustrate this point: *Hurley v Mustoe*[10], *Skyrail Oceanic Ltd v Coleman*[11] and *Horsey v Dyfed*.[12]

The stereotypical assumption at issue in *Hurley v Mustoe* is a good example of the point made earlier: of the way in which certain social roles are given weight and may seem to be natural or essential because they are entrenched. In *Hurley*, the complainant was challenging a policy of the employer not to employ women with young children. This policy was based on a general assumption that mothers have primary responsibility for the care of children and that they make unreliable employees. The EAT held that this policy, applied to women but not to men, did constitute direct discrimination under the SDA:

"Finally we should make it clear what we are not deciding. First, we are not deciding whether it is, or is not, desirable for women with young children to go out to work. Strong views are held on this point. But Parliament has legislated that it is up to each mother to decide whether or not she goes out to work and employers may not discriminate against them just because they are mothers. Secondly, we are not deciding whether or not women with children as a class are less reliable employees. Parliament has legislated that they are not to be treated as a class but as individuals. No employer is bound to employ unreliable employees, whether men or women. But he must investigate each case, and not simply apply what some would call a rule of convenience and others a prejudice to exclude a whole class of women or married persons because some members of that class are not suitable employees."[13]

10 [1981] I.C.R. 490 (EAT).
11 [1981] I.C.R. 864 (CA).
12 [1982] I.C.R. 755 (EAT).
13 [1981] I.C.R. 490 (EAT) at p.497.

The case illustrates the process approach to direct discrimination. The EAT refused to give a substantive view on the appropriate role of women. The issue of how to resolve issues of childcare between men and women was not the purpose of direct discrimination under this analysis. Rather, the focus was on treating women (and men) as individuals rather than as members of a particular class. Direct discrimination involves, according to this view, examining the facts of each case rather than applying a generalised assumption or general rule. This interpretation of direct discrimination was also confirmed in the *Skyrail Oceanic Ltd v Coleman* decision where the Court of Appeal held that an assumption that a man was the chief breadwinner in the family could be direct discrimination under the SDA. In *Horsey v Dyfed CC*, the applicant was a social worker who wanted to accept a training course so that she could be near her husband and therefore applied to the council for secondment to that course. The council refused her secondment because, since her husband had obtained full-time permanent employment, she would be unlikely to return to work for the council upon completion of her course. The EAT found that this generalised assumption was direct sex discrimination. They also found that direct discrimination can cover "sex plus" cases: ie where the employer claims that there are reasons other than sex that have motivated their decision. In their judgment the EAT stated:

"In our view it is now established by authority that those words do not only cover cases where the sole factor influencing the decision of the alleged discriminator is the sex, marital status or race of the complainant. The words 'on he ground of' also cover cases where the reason for the discrimination was a generalised assumption that people of a particular sex, marital status or race possess or lack certain characteristics, e.g. 'I like women but I will not employ them because they are unreliable.' 'I will not lend money to married women because they are not wage earners' or 'I will not employ coloured men because they are lazy.' Most discrimination flows from generalised assumptions of this kind and not from a simple prejudice dependent solely on the sex or colour of the complainant. The purpose of the legislation is to secure equal opportunity for individuals regardless of their sex, married status or race. This result would not be achieved if it were sufficient to escape liability to show that the reason for the discriminatory treatment was simply an assumption that women or coloured persons possessed or lacked particular characteristics and not that they were just women or coloured persons."[14]

Earlier case law such as *Peake* supported the view that the SDA did not seek to eliminate all differences between men and women and that differential treatment *per se* without more was not sex discrimination. Subsequent cases confirm that there is no requirement for the difference in treatment between men and women that is otherwise direct discrimination to also lead to a detriment. This issue was confirmed in *Gill and Coote v El Vino*[15], and in *Brennan v JH Dewhurst Ltd*. In *Brennan*, Browne-Wilkinson J. stated:

"To the extent that he is saying that in order to show discrimination within section 1, or,

[14] p.761.
[15] [1983] 1 All E.R. 398.

indeed, within section 6(1)(a), the applicant had to show a detriment to her, we are unable to accept that submission which is not justified by the words of the Act. As was pointed out in *Gill v. El Vino Co. Ltd.* [1983] Q.B. 425, the showing of a detriment is an essential feature of some causes of action under the Act but not of others. Where the establishment of a detriment is a necessary element in establishing a cause of action, the section so provides. It is not necessary in any other case."[16]

This line of cases confirms that general stereotypes are captured by the prohibition against direct discrimination. They also support the view that direct discrimination is aimed at ensuring a fair process: whether this is articulated as the equality principle of treating "like with like" and ensuring "equality of opportunity" or in terms of general procedural fairness of ensuring that malign reasons do not infect decisionmaking. The fact that there is no requirement to show detriment also supports this analysis of direct discrimination, in the sense that the mere presence of the malign reasons (and the fact of the defect in the process) itself constitutes the relevant harm. Without any need to prove that there has in fact been an unequal outcome.

The harm of direct discrimination arises, according to this analysis, from the way in which it breaches principles of fairness and procedural justice. At one level the concept of direct discrimination in the SDA 75 and similar legislation addresses exactly this defect. It focuses on individual conduct and requires the decisionmaker to discount stereotypes and prejudices that may prevent fair treatment. Generalised assumptions that there are sexual—or racial differences—can translate into important disadvantages for women and minorities. On this analysis stereotyping is a failure to take into account all the relevant information about an individual before making a relevant decision about them. In some cases this defect may collapse into prejudice: a preconceived opinion that is not based on reasons or actual experience. There is a danger that these prejudices can turn into dislike, hostility and unjust behaviour. Basing decisions on stereotypes and prejudice—and allowing malign principles to infect decisionmaking—is a particularly powerful argument where direct discrimination is justified by reference to "procedural liberalism."[17] Egalitarian liberal theories, such as those of Dworkin, that frame principles in terms of equality—as the fundamental right to equal respect and concern—will of course be especially relevant as justifications of direct discrimination.[18]

More recently, there has been a challenge to the assumption that the main harm of direct discrimination is stereotyping and a failure of "process". On this analysis, although direct discrimination can usefully challenge harmful stereotypes, it is dangerous to assume that direct discrimination is "solely"

[16] [1984] I.C.R. 52 at p.58.

[17] For a discussion of stereotyping and prejudice as a procedural failure see J. H. Ely, *Democracy and Distrust* (Cambridge: Harvard University Press, 1980) at pp.137–157.

[18] For a discussion of the idea of "equal respect and concern" and its application to the antidiscrimination principle see R. Dworkin, "Bakke's Case: Are Quotas Unfair", in *A Matter of Principle*, Cambridge, Mass: Harvard University Press, 1985). For a general discussion of equality see R. Dworkin,

about stereotyping. This alternative reading treats direct discrimination as a substantive harm to autonomy and dignity.

B. *Discrimination as Substantive Harm: autonomy and dignity*

There is, of course, a link between the harm of stereotyping and harms of autonomy and dignity. Socially constructed stereotypes perpetuate difference. They may force people into roles or choices that do not comply with the requirements to treat individuals as autonomous persons. One possible reading of the stereotypes in cases such as *Peake* and *Hurley v Mustoe* is that they reduce the range of choices that are available to individuals, e.g. the stereotype in *Hurley v Mustoe* that women are the primary carers of children may limit the pool of choices for action that are available to women to pursue valuable roles other than motherhood.

Another way of capturing the substantive harm of direct discrimination is by noting that decisions that are based on invalid grounds (especially immutable grounds such as race and sex) are not just a failure of process, they are also a substantive harm because they stigmatise the victim in a more fundamental way. Stigma theory, developed in the context of racial discrimination in the US, provides strong support for the analysis. It suggests that direct discrimination is a harm to a person's self respect, autonomy and dignity.[19]

Dignity has become an important source for justifying anti-discrimination norms.[20] That is not to say that "process" values cannot provide the foundations for constitutional discrimination law. In fact, in the US context, one of the ways in which the equal protection clause of the 14th Amendment has been justified is by reference to the importance of ensuring that constitutional decisionmaking and procedures are free from the taint of malign preferences.[21] Nevertheless, substantive values such as dignity increasingly provide the basis for contemporary constitutional and statutory discrimination law.

EU discrimination law also increasingly justifies key anti-discrimination provisions such as Art.141 EC and Art.13 EC by reference to fundamental rights. In the context of domestic discrimination law, the increasing use of Art.14 ECHR, which ensures non-discrimination in the exercise of key human rights provisions, as well as the potential that in limited circumstances racial discrimination could constitute inhuman and degrading treatment under Art.3 of the ECHR[22], suggest that dignity can be a useful substantive value that justifies direct discrimination.

[19] Andrew Koppelman, Anti-Discrimination and Social Equality, (New Haven, US: Yale University Press, 1996) at Ch.2.

[20] Gary Moon and Robin Allen Q.C., "Dignity Discourse in Discrimination Law: A Better Route to Equality?" (2006) 6 EHRLR 610.

[21] J. H. Ely, Democracy and Distrust (Cambridge, Mass: Harvard University Press, 1980)

[22] *East African Asians v United Kingdom* (1981) 3 EHRR 76.

Substantive values such as dignity, autonomy and respect have also become important because they provide a more credible justification for the use of the criminal law to deal with problems of prejudice and stereotyping that have typically been dealt with by the civil law (e.g. SDA, RRA).

The concept of direct discrimination is also increasingly important in contexts other than discrimination law, because it can usefully justify certain types of discriminatory conduct such as harassment or hate crimes that have never comfortably fit into the paradigm of direct discrimination as the failure to treat "like with like". For example, the substantive value of dignity is increasingly used to justify the legal regulation of harassment in constitutional cases where sexual harassment is treated as a failure to respect individual dignity.[23] Developments in domestic discrimination law's treatment of harassment confirm the preference for treating harassment as an example of direct discrimination which causes harm to individual dignity rather than as part of the requirement to treat "like with like".

C. *Direct Discrimination: Remedy for Discriminatory Effects or a Moral Wrong?*

John Gardner has argued that the paradigm case of direct discrimination is where the improper ground for discrimination figures in the operative premisses of the discriminator's thinking. For Gardner the justification for the prohibition on discrimination on certain grounds (i.e. sex, race, etc.) is that they violate autonomy based duties that we owe individuals. For Gardner, the paradigm of direct discrimination requires a focus on the discriminator's reasoning.

> "For these duties, as I explained when I introduced them, are precisely what makes it wrong to act on a proposal about women or black people or gay men etc, even when one is right to believe it. It follows that the wrongfulness of discrimination is fundamentally linked to the fact that an improper ground of discrimination figures in the operative premisses of the discriminator's thinking. That is the core or paradigm case of wrongful direct discrimination which emerges from our discussion of what makes a ground of discrimination an improper ground."[24]

Later in this chapter, we discuss *James v Eastleigh*[25] in which the House of Lords affirmed the "but for" test for direct discrimination, which shifts the analysis away from the motive and intention of the discriminator. Some commentators welcome a purely causal enquiry because this approach can overcome practical problems of proof of motive in discrimination cases. Commentators have argued that a "but for" test that concentrates on causation rather than the state

[23] S. Fredman, *Discrimination Law*, (Oxford: Clarendon Law Series, 2002) at pp.17–19 and p.120.
[24] *James v Easleigh* BC [1996] I.C.R. 554.
[25] John Gardner, "On the Grounds of Her Sex(uality)", (1998) 18 O.J.L.S. 167, at p.182.

of mind of the discriminator is a more appropriate test for direct discrimination.[26] Evelyn Ellis makes this point in setting out a model for direct discrimination which sees it as a remedial response to the problems of discrimination.

Evelyn Ellis "The Definition of Direct Discrimination in European Sex Equality Law" (1994) 19 European Law Review, 561, 564–6

"However, before enacting the sex, race, and religious and political anti-discrimination legislation of the mid-1970s, the United Kingdom legislature seems to have been particularly convinced by two specific explanations. The first, and less palatable, notion was that there was active prejudice in operation against theses disadvantaged sections of society. The second, and more subtle, was that discrimination had become 'institutionalised' in certain sectors, so that traditional and unquestioned practices were having the effect of unnecessarily and unfairly excluding equality of opportunity [. . .]

Three vital deductions follow from such an understanding of the origins of anti-discrimination laws. The first is that the anti-discrimination laws were created as devices for the relief of disadvantage; the law created was not intended to be in any sense criminal or punitive in nature. The logic understanding it is the compensation of the victims of the prior system and, by doing so, the deterrence of others in the future from repeating the injustices of the past. Thus, however, this may become disguised as a result of the technical legal definition and judicial interpretation, it is at the very heart of the notion of discrimination that it is the *effect* on its victims with which the law is truly concerned, not the precise nature of the conduct of perpetrators.

The second deduction is that the legislation has to recognise two different situations in which discrimination can occur; this has been reflected in the law's general acceptance of the twin concepts of direct and indirect discrimination, an acceptance made both by domestic systems and by the European Community system. Thirdly, however, it has to be concluded that these concepts are indeed twins, in other words that they are very closely related and have both sprung from identical roots. Their underlying rationale is the same and this means that they must both consist essentially of the same two elements: some sort of adverse impact on their victims and a prohibited classification underlying that impact. Adverse impact and causation, at least in a broad, non-technical sense, must as a matter of basic logic be the constituent elements which underpin all systems of sex-discrimination law. The question then becomes whether or not the definition of direct discrimination provided by a particular system of law, and thereupon applied by the relevant group of judges recognises this logic [. . .] What sometimes leads to confusion in cases of direct discrimination is the fact that the clearest instances of its occurrence is provided where the perpetrator makes plain an intention to disfavour the victim, in other words, the case of intentional discrimination. The temptation here is to extrapolate from the malign motive and to conclude that it is this element which renders the conduct offensive. This however is to fall into the trap of analysing discrimination as quasi-criminal in nature rather than treating the notion as essentially remedial in character. An intention to disfavour the victim simply helps to prove the case. It is *not* a necessary ingredient of the statutory tort."

[26] G. Mead, "The Role of Intention in Direct Discrimination,", (1990) 19 I.L.J., 250.

It is true that intention is not a requirement of the test for direct discrimination, as we see later in the discussion of the "but for" test. However, there are problems in any analysis that reduces direct discrimination to a purely "remedial" concept that only requires a focus on causation without any focus on the discriminator's reasoning, fault, or responsibility. Such an analysis risks collapsing important distinctions between concepts of direct discrimination on the one hand and indirect discrimination. Ellis states that direct and indirect discrimination spring from common roots and are twin concepts. Although it is true that direct and indirect discrimination are part of an overall framework of discrimination law, they are separate and distinct concepts that are defined in markedly different ways. Moreover, and crucially, direct discrimination cannot be justified whilst indirect discrimination can be justified in some circumstances. Gardner argues that core case of direct discrimination as dealing with cases where an improper ground for discrimination (sex or race) is motivationally relevant and figures in the operative ground of the discriminator's thinking. He points out that one advantage of this analysis is that it allows important distinctions between direct discrimination, indirect discrimination and positive duties/action programmes to be maintained. Gardner states at pp.182–183:

"Of course there can be moral reasons to extend the scope of wrongful discrimination beyond this core case. There are various moral arguments, for example, for attending to discriminationory side-effects of some decisions as well as the discriminatory grounds on which they were reached. These arguments supply the foundation of the secondary paradigm of indirect discrimination (or disparate impact discrimination) found in today's more sophisticated anti-discrimination statutes. For example: prohibitions on direct discrimination alone typically do rather little to expand the options of those who have been directly discriminated against in the past, when the world has been so comprehensively organized around their absence. Making progress with the problem may therefore require one not only to control perpetuation of the direct discrimination which was the original source of the problem, but also to add some positive duties to make the options from which those discriminated against were excluded genuinely acceptable and hospitable to them so that they aren't still excluded in effect even though not only on purpose. This is where the indirect discrimination paradigm comes in. But it does not replace the original paradigm of direct discrimination, on the moral significance of which, as my remarks have just illustrated, it depends for its own moral force. There may likewise be plenty of sound institutional reasons for expanding the law's definition of direct sex discrimination along James v Eastleigh lines, to include cases where sex figures only in the auxiliary premisses of the discriminator's thinking. Perhaps otherwise sex discrimination will be too hard to prove, or some complex cases will be likely to fall through a legislative loophole between direct and indirect discrimination., or lay tribunals will tend to get out of their conceptual depth. [*Gardner cites in a fn here: "This was an argument relied upon heavily by Lord Goff in his speech: ibid, at 618*] But these institutional considerations take us out to the moral margins of the phenomenon, within sight of the grey areas and borderline cases. They are not and cannot be the core or paradigm cases of direct discrimination, the ones which capture what is fundamentally wrong with it. In fact they obscure the point, which is that the wrongfulness of direct discrimination on a certain ground stems primarily from the ground figuring in the operative premisses of the discriminator's reasoning."[27]

As Gardner states, there may be good reasons to prefer the wider remedial model of direct discrimination. This may be especially relevant where, as Ellis states, direct discrimination operates as a statutory tort. There are, however, good reasons to preserve the paradigm case of direct discrimination as a moral wrong as Jeremy Waldron argues in the next passage.

Jeremy Waldron "Indirect Discrimination" in *Equality and Discrimination: Essays in Freedom and Justice, Archives for Philosophy of Law and Social Philosophy* (Stuttgart: Franz Steiner Verlag Wiesbaden GMBH, 1985)

"People at present respond differently to direct discrimination and what we are now to call 'indirect discrimination'; the point of extending the meaning of the emotive term 'discrimination' to encompass actions of both types is to persuade them to respond in the future to the two sorts of action in the same way. If only we can get them to describe actions of both sorts with the same word—the same emotive word—then w will have brought about a change in their attitudes so far as their practical and affective response to actions of the second kind is concerned.

I do not want to suggest that there is anything disreputable or objectionable about persuasive definitions of this sort. On the contrary, these processes go on all the time in discussions of morals and politics: they are part of the way in which our moral and political consciousness evolves. But we should be aware of the dangers that are involved when we attempt a persuasive definition. The danger is the possibility of a shift of emotive meaning in the reverse direction: instead of regarding indirect discrimination with the same abhorrence and condemnation as now regard direct discrimination, the attempt at a persuasive definition may have the effect that people come to regard the former with the same mild indifference as they presently regard the latter. 'Indirect discrimination' is as bad as direct discrimination' entails 'Direct discrimination is *no worse* than indirect discrimination'; there is, then a danger that an attempt to extend the meaning of 'discrimination' may have the effect of weakening or diluting the current level of feeling opposed to racial prejudice. Familiarity with the new and extended use of the concept may breed moral contempt for the moral attitudes that it was originally supposed to embody and discredit the wider campaign for racial and sexual equality.

The reality of this danger depends partly on how people respond in fact to the new definitions that the legislation is foisting on them; that is a matter for empirical research, though my hunch is that the main effect has been to weaken the moral force of the charge of discrimination. The gravity of the danger, however, depends also on our estimation of whether there *is* any real moral difference between direct and indirect discrimination. If there is not, then persuasive definition may seem an appropriate strategy, and all we need to ensure is that the moral indignation evoked by the two practices is pitched at the right (cardinal) level. But I am not convinced that direct and indirect discrimination are morally on a par. Intentional discrimination—that is, discrimination based on racist and sexist

[27] John Gardner, "On the Grounds of Sex(uality)", (1998) O.J.L.S. 167 at pp.182–183.

prejudice—seems a much nastier, more vicious phenomenon than indirect discrimination as that is currently understood. It seems to me that the law should reserve special sanctions and special procedures for dealing with it (probably to the extent of making it a criminal offence), marking out the special abhorrence that we ought to feel when someone deliberately chooses race or sex as a basis for inferior treatment. In other words, I think that the difference in attitude we noted earlier is morally justified, and therefore, to that extent, the attempt to assimilate attitudes towards these two morally different phenomenon is itself morally misguided."

Discussion of whether the distinction between direct and indirect discrimination lies in the significance of the discriminator's reasons for action in relation to the former, and the disproportionate impact of the discriminator's action in relation to the latter, has tended to focus on the role of direct and indirect discrimination under legislation such as the SDA or RRA. However, as we saw in Chapter 2, the law's regulation of invidious forms of discrimination can also encompass measures dealing with hate speech or sentence-enhancement for criminal offences motivated by discrimination. Given criminal law's focus on wrongdoing, the "moral wrong" analysis of direct discrimination (distinguishing it from indirect discrimination or positive action) may provide a mechanism for understanding the criminal law's treatment of hate speech and hate crimes.

III. The European Convention and Direct Discrimination

We considered the role played by Convention rights—particularly Art.14—in discrimination law at a general level in Chapter 2. In this section, we briefly summarise the main aspects of the Convention's treatment of direct discrimination. We do not, however, consider relevant points in great detail, given that a full discussion can be found in Chapter 2, section IV.

As we saw in Chapter 2, in order to show that there has been a violation of Art.14, a claimant must first establish that the subject-matter of the case falls within the ambit of another Convention right, given that Art.14 currently relates, in so far as UK cases are concerned and until the UK accedes to Protocol 12, to the enjoyment of other Convention rights (raising questions, for example, about whether discrimination in the context of employment falls within Art.14).[28] The claimant must also establish that they have been discriminated against on one of the grounds listed in Art.14 (namely sex, race, colour, language, religion, political or other opinion, national or social origin, association with a national minority, property and birth) or by reference to one of the judicially-recognised "other statuses" (including sexual orientation). Given that indirect discrimination was not acknowledged in the Convention case law until comparatively late (see chapters 2 and 5), the vast majority of

[28] See, e.g., *Belgian Linguistic (No.2)* (1968) 1 E.H.R.R. 252, para.[9].

Art.14 cases concern direct discrimination. Direct discrimination has been succinctly defined by the ECtHR as a "difference in treatment".[29] However, as the court made clear in *Belgian Linguistic (No.2)*, since "absurd results" would be produced if Art.14 prohibited "every difference in treatment in the exercise of the rights and freedoms recognised" in the Convention, the main focus of judicial scrutiny is on "the criteria which enable a determination to be made as to whether or not a given difference in treatment ... contravenes Article 14. On this question the Court, following the principles which may be extracted from the legal practice of a large number of democratic States, holds that the principle of equality of treatment is violated if the distinction has no objective and reasonable justification."[30] As we noted in chapter 2, a proportionality test is deployed in establishing whether such a justification exists, and as was confirmed by the House of Lords in *R. v Secretary of State for Work and Pensions, Ex p. Carson*[31] the intensity of this test varies according to the context, including the ground of discrimination in issue. The question of judicial deference, considered under the heading of the "margin of appreciation" at Strasbourg level and as the "discretionary area of judgment" at national level, may also arise.

Four points concerning Art.14 should be noted. First, and most importantly, the overriding focus of the ECtHR's approach to Art.14 is on the issue of justification: whether a distinction has been drawn is very much a preliminary point, with questions about the intention and motive associated with a distinction arising (if they do at all) as part of the court's justification inquiry.[32] As we will see below, this is a very different focus from that found in EU law and domestic statutory provisions. Secondly, while it is clear that an Art.14 claimant must establish that those in an "analogous" or "relevantly similar" situation have been treated more favourably,[33] the House of Lords emphasised in *Carson* – albeit without offering real guidance as to how it should operate— that this was a loose and flexible requirement which was not to be approached in an unduly inflexible fashion (see chapter 2, section IV).[34] This again represents, as we will see, a different approach from that found in judicial treatments of EU law and, to a greater extent, of domestic statutory provisions (and may be a reaction to concerns which have arisen in those contexts). Thirdly, the ECtHR has made clear in respect of the burden of proof that once the claimant has shown a difference of treatment, it is for the respondent gov-

[29] Ibid.

[30] Ibid.

[31] [2005] UKHL 37; as the ECtHR noted in *Timishev v Russia*, app. nos. 55762/00 and 55974/00 and reiterated in *D.H. v Czech Republic*, app. no. 57325/00, November 13, 2007, para.[176] (Grand Chamber), no difference of treatment based exclusively or to a decisive extent on a person's ethnic origin is capable of objective justification in a contemporary democratic society.

[32] Something which has caused Evelyn Ellis to suggest that Art.14 offers a weaker model for discrimination law than that found in EU law: *EU Anti-Discrimination Law* (Oxford: Oxford University Press, 2005), p.112, n.123.

[33] *Van der Mussele v Belgium* (1983) 6 E.H.R.R. 163, 179-180; *D.H. v Czech Republic*, ibid., para.[175] (Grand Chamber).

[34] *R. v Secretary of State for Work and Pensions, Ex p. Carson* [2005] UKHL 37.

ernment to show that the difference was justified.[35] In determining what constitutes prima facie evidence capable of shifting the burden of proof on to the respondent, there are no procedural barriers to the admission of evidence or pre-determined formulae for its assessment; all evidence is freely evaluated. Proof "may follow from the coexistence of sufficiently strong, clear and concordant inferences or of similar unrebutted presumptions of fact . . . the level of persuasion necessary for reaching a particular conclusion and, in this connection, the distribution of the burden of proof are intrinsically linked to the specificity of the facts, the nature of the allegation made and the Convention right at stake."[36] Where events lie wholly or in large part within the exclusive knowledge of the national authorities, the burden of proof may be regarded as lying on them to produce a satisfactory and convincing explanation.[37] Fourthly, where a case falls within its scope, Art.14 may be used in domestic law to secure the reinterpretation of legislation (whether concerned with discrimination or any other subject-matter) under s.3 of the Human Rights Act 1998, remedies against public authorities (judicial review or damages) under s.6 of that Act, or a declaration of incompatibility under s.4.

IV. Direct Discrimination in EU Law

The concept of "discrimination" operates in a number of different contexts in EU law. It is included in areas other discrimination law such as nationality where it is defined as: "the application of different rules to comparable situations or the application of the same rule to different situations."[38] The original concept of direct discrimination in EU law developed in the context of Art.141 (previously Art.119). The more recent Art.13 directives, the Race Equality Directive (RED) and the Employment Equality Directive (EED), adopt a different definition of direct discrimination and they are too recent to have a concrete elaboration of the concept. As Ellis notes, in the context of EU discrimination law the ECJ is likely to apply the Art.141 definition of discrimination in a wider context to sex discrimination and develop a unified definition of discrimination. Moreover, domestic courts have treated "discrimination" as a unified concept in EU law.[39]

In the early case law, there is some reference to the way in which direct discrimination is concerned with direct overt acts whereas indirect discrimination is concerned with hidden forms of discriminatory acts. For example, in *Defrenne v Sabena*, the ECJ stated:

[35] *D.H. v Czech Republic*, ibid., para.[177] (Grand Chamber).
[36] *D.H. v Czech Republic*, ibid., para.[178] (Grand Chamber).
[37] *D.H. v Czech Republic*, ibid., para.[179] (Grand Chamber).
[38] Case C-279/93 *Finanzampt Koln-Alstadt v Schumacker* [1995] E.C.R. I-225, at 259.
[39] E. Ellis, *EC Sex Equality Law* (Oxford: Clarendon Press, 1998) 2nd edn at p.123. Now discussed and updated in E. Ellis, *EU Anti-Discrimination Law* (Oxford: OUP, 2005).

"A distinction must be drawn within the whole area of application of Art 119 between, first, direct and overt discrimination which may be identified solely with the aid of the criteria based on equal work and equal pay referred to by the Article in question and, secondly, indirect and disguised discrimination which an only be identified by reference to more explicit implementing provisions of a Community or national character."[40]

This early identification of direct with overt discrimination was transformed in subsequent case law as the ECJ moved away from this early assimilation of "direct discrimination with overt acts" and "indirect discrimination with disguised acts".[41] This definition of direct discrimination includes unintentional as well as intentional acts of discrimination, which obviously fits in with the original economic rationale for Art.141 of the EC.

This principle was confirmed in *Enderby v Frenchay HA*:

"Forms of direct sex discrimination are quite conceivable without sex being expressly mentioned in the contract of employment, pay scales or collective agreement as the criterion for the higher or lower pay. The conceptual scheme of that category makes it clear that discrimination does not even have to have been intentional."[42]

It is also clear that the EU concept of direct discrimination favours an objective test. In the *Worringham v Lloyds Bank Ltd*. The ECJ confirmed that intention, motivation and the state of mind of the perpetrator of the discriminatory act are not requirements of the test for direct discrimination under Art.141 of the EC.

"Art 119 of the Treaty applies directly to all forms of discrimination which may be identified solely with the aid of the criteria of equal work and equal work referred to by the Article in question, without national or Community measures being required to define them with greater precision in order to permit of their application [...] This is the case where the requirement of pay contributions applies only to men and not to women and the contributions payable by men are paid by the employers in their name by means of an addition to the gross salary the effect of which is to give men higher pay within the meaning of the second paragraph of Article 119 than that received by women engaged in the same work or work of equal value."[43]

Dekker also confirmed this development and that there is no need for an intention to discriminate as a requirement for establishing direct discrimination: "If the employers liability for infringement of the principle of equal

[40] Case 43/75 [1976] E.C.R. 455 at 473.
[41] In *Worringham v Lloyds Bank Ltd* [1981] E.C.R. 767 at 802–3.
[42] Case C-127/92 [1993] E.C.R. I-5535, *per* Lenz AG.
[43] Case 69/80 [1981] E.C.R. 767 at 792.

treatment were made subject to proof of a fault attributable to him and also to there being no ground of exemption recognized by the applicable national law, the practical effect of those principles would be considerably weakened."[44]

Dekker was also significant because it represented a departure from the British approach to pregnancy discrimination. Domestic law required a women to show a male comparator in pregnancy discrimination cases. *Dekker* confirmed that pregnancy discrimination would be direct sex discrimination per se without the need to show a comparator. The move away from a comparator is also a feature of EU discrimination law on harassment. Sexual harassment is defined in the Code of Practice. The fact that EU discrimination law has moved away from the need for a comparator in its treatment of pregnancy and harassment does not, however, alter the basic point that like domestic discrimination law, the concept of direct discrimination in EU law is essentially comparative. A focus on direct discrimination as "less favourable treatment" makes comparison central to the analysis the idea of difference of treatment. Less favourable treatment is established through a comparison with how another similarly situated person of the other sex would be treated. In the area of equal pay the comparator must be real although, as Ellis observes, the words of the legislation do not theoretically rule out a hypothetical comparator.[45] Recent cases have ensured that there is a broader range of potential comparators available in equal pay cases (e.g. predecessors and successors in the workplace).[46] The Equal Treatment Directive uses of wider language to prohibit discrimination in employment matters other than pay.[47] The prohibition in the ETD of "no discrimination whatsoever on grounds of sex either directly or indirectly" introduces the possibility that hypothetical comparators can be permitted. The possibility of the use of hypothetical comparators to establish direct discrimination is now explicitly included in the Race Equality Directive that defines direct discrimination as: "where one person is treated less favourably than another is has been or would be treated in a comparable situation on grounds of racial or ethnic origin."

The key features of EU concepts of direct discrimination—its symmetrical structure that gives equal protection to men and women; majorities and minorities; the focus on the regulation of individual acts of discriminators; the central importance of comparison as the mechanism for identifying discriminatory conduct—are also recurring aspects of direct discrimination in domestic discrimination law.

44 Case 177/88 [1990] E.C.R. I-3941.

45 E. Ellis, *EC Sex Equality Law* (Oxford: Clarendon Press, 1998) 2nd edn at p.149. Ellis qualifies this by noting that the horizontal effect of Art.119 will not extend to the situation of hypothetical comparison, see Case 129/79 *Macarthys Ltd v Smith* [1980] E.C.R. 1275. See E. Ellis, EU Anti-Discrimination Law, (Oxford: OUP, 2005).

46 Ibid.

47 Ibid.

V. Defining Direct Discrimination

The concept of direct discrimination in the main domestic anti-discrimination legislation captures and reflects the idea of "less favourable treatment". However the definitions in the legislation do vary. The key direct discrimination provisions are set out briefly below before we move on to a discussion of the main legal issues. The main focus is on the definition of direct discrimination in the SDA and its analogous provisions in the RRA. There have also been piecemeal amendments to this legislative framework through secondary legislation which has implemented the RED and EED into domestic law. This is discussed in detail in Chapter 2.

The SDA and RRA have analogous definitions of direct discrimination. Both statutes treat direct discrimination as a statuary tort which gives rise to civil law remedies. The main legal elements of direct discrimination reflect the EU definitions and which focus on less favourable treatment. In the SDA 75, for example, s.1(1)(a) confirms that:

"A person discriminates against a woman in any circumstances relevant for the purposes of this Act if—(a) on the ground of her sex he treats her less favourably than he treats or would treat a man."

There are two noteworthy features of the definition of direct discrimination. First, the definition is symmetrical: s.2(1) confirms that the relevant parts of the SDA applies "equally to the treatment of men." Second, the definition requires comparison. Direct sex discrimination is defined by reference to comparison which is defined further in s.5(3) in the following terms:

"A comparison of the cases of persons of different sex or marital status under section 1(1) or 3(1) must be such that the relevant circumstances in the one case are the same, or not materially different, in the other."

These features of direct sex discrimination—symmetry and comparison—are also reflected in the definition of race discrimination in the RRA although there are some differences in language. The core of the definition is less favourable treatment of a person on "racial grounds" (rather than on the grounds of race). Section 1(1)(a) RRA states: "A person discriminates against another in any circumstances relevant for the purposes of any provision of this Act if—(a) on racial grounds he treats that other less favourably than he treats or would treat other persons". Section 3(1) defines "racial grounds" and "racial groups" (relevant for the definition of indirect race discrimination) widely as including any grounds relating to colour, race, nationality or ethnic or national origins. It does not specify that the RRA had or has as its aim the protection of specific racial groups or minorities. Instead, the legal protection of the RRA extends symmetrically to both all such groups: majorities as well as minorities. Like the

SDA direct race discrimination is identified through acts of comparison because s.3(4) RRA confirms that:

"A comparison of the case of a person of a particular racial group with that of a person not of that group under section 1(1) must be such that the relevant circumstances in the one case are the same, or not materially different, in the other."

The DDA defines direct discrimination in s.5(3) as less favourable treatment that is "for a reason which relates to the disabled person's disability." The EqPA also contains prohibitions against discrimination on the grounds of pay between men and women (thereby giving effect to Art.119/141 EC). It functions by deeming that where a woman (or man) does the same work or work of equal value as a man (or woman) in the same employment then she (or he) is entitled to have an equality clause inserted into her (or his) contract of employment. It is also worth noting that s.1(3) of the EqPA permits the justification of direct discrimination by introducing the "genuine material factor" defense.

The Fair Employment and Treatment (Northern Ireland) Order 1998 (FETO 98) prohibits direct discrimination in terms similar to the SDA and RRA. Direct discrimination is defined as a situation where a person "treats that other less favourably than he treats or would treat other persons" (s.3(2) FETO). It is prohibited on the grounds of "religious belief or political opinion" and "victimisation" s.3(1) FETO). Significantly, like the SDA and RRA hypothetical comparators are permitted. Moreover, like the analogous provisions in s.5(3) SDA and s.3(4) RRA, comparison is defined as where "the relevant circumstances in the one case are the same, or not materially different, in the other." (s.3(3) FETO).

One noteworthy feature of the SDA and the RRA is that they extend the scope of prohibited direct discrimination beyond pay and employment. Public goods (education, health and education) as well as private goods and services are covered. It is also worth noting that the definition of race discrimination has recently been extended by the introduction of a positive duty not to discriminate beyond indirect discrimination to cover institutional and structural discrimination. This aspect is discussed in the context of the introduction of positive duties via the Race Relations Amendment Act 2000.

The SDA and the RRA explicitly develop concepts of discrimination in the context of the US Civil Rights Act 1964 (now amended by the Civil Rights Act 1991). This is most obvious in the context of definition of indirect discrimination which is a statutory enactment of the principle developed in the US Supreme Court decision in *Griggs v Duke Power Co.*[48] Although the influence of US law and politics is most obvious in the context of indirect discrimination, the development of the idea of discrimination in the US 14th

[48] (1971) 401 U.S. 424.

Amendment jurisprudence and under Title V11 of the Civil Rights Act 1964 has also influenced the approach to direct discrimination as "less favourable treatment" that makes symmetry of treatment and comparison central to the definition.

Before moving on to a discussion of the concept of direct discrimination it is worth noting two issues: first, that instructions to discriminate fall under the definition of direct discrimination; and second, that direct discrimination also includes prohibitions on victimisation and harassment. The next section discusses instructions to discriminate and victimisation, whilst harassment is discussed in detail in Chapter 8.

A. *Instructions to Discriminate and Victimisation*

The difference in the statutory language between the SDA and RRA may have relevance in the context of instructions to discriminate. In the context of SDA direct discrimination is defined as "on the ground of (her) sex". In the context of RRA 76 direct discrimination is defined as including "on racial grounds". In *Showboat Entertainment Centre Ltd v Owens*[49] the EAT held that "on racial grounds" included not only the race of the victim, but also the racial attitudes of the manager who had ordered an employee to discriminate against another person.

Chapter 2 sets out the main provisions that prohibit discriminatory victimisation. Here, it is worth noting one example of a statutory definition of victimisation.

Race Relations Act, section 2(1)(2)

"A person ('the discriminator') discriminates against another person ('the person victimised') in any circumstances relevant for the purposes of any provision of this Act if he treats the person victimised less favourably than in those circumstances he treats or would treat other persons, and does so by reason that the person victimised has : (a) bought proceedings against the discriminator or any other person under the relevant Act; or (b) given evidence or information in connection with proceedings brought by any person against the discriminator or any other person under the relevant Act; or (c) otherwise done anything under or by reference to in relation to the relevant Act the discriminator or any other person; or (c) alleged that the discriminator or any other person has committed an act which (whether or not the allegation so states) would amount to a contravention of the relevant Act; OR victimisation is also established by reason that the discriminator knows that the person victimised intends to do any of those things, or suspects that the person victimised has done, or intends to do, any of them. The victimisation provisions do not

[49] [1984] I.C.R. 65 (EAT).

apply 'to treatment of a person by reason of any allegation made by him if the allegation was false and not made in good faith' "

The analysis of "less favourable treatment" in the context of victimisation has been interpreted in similar ways to the interpretation of direct discrimination more generally (e.g. as defined in RRA s.1). Issues relating to the choice of comparator, establishing a link between the discriminator's act and the "less favourable treatment" have raised similar problems and they have been treated in a uniform way. For these reasons, key cases under the victimisation provisions are included as part of the general discussion on the concept of direct discrimination. There are a few specific issues that relate to the victimisation provisions. Some early case law had established that some type of acts that were in fact related to the cause of action remained outside the definition of "protected acts". For example, in *Kirby v Manpower Services Commission,*[50] the EAT had found that the applicant's demotion had been caused by his breach of duty of confidentiality to employers in reporting his employers racially discriminatory conduct to the relevant authorities; any employee (including one not involved in a claim under the relevant Act) would have been treated in the same way; and therefore, this was not a protected act for the purposes of victimisation. In *Aziz v Trinity Street Taxis*[51] the approach in *Kirby* was criticised as "absurd" and as contrary to the legislative intent. In *Aziz,* the Court of Appeal found that a comparator to establish whether or not there had been "less favourable treatment" did not need to be someone who had undertaken a protected act. In fact, the Court of Appeal found that the legsislative intent of provisions on victimisation such as RRA, s.2, was to ensure that victims of racial discrimination were not deterred from seeking legal redress. They stated that the *Kirby* approach would be an "absurd result" because it would allow a discriminator to avoid liability for victimisation by arguing that he would have treated all employees in an equally intolerant way. The Court of Appeal focused on the issue of motive and construed RRA, s.2(1) as requiring motive, i.e. that the discriminator (who has victimised) should have a motive that was consciously connected with race relations legislation. More recently, the House of Lords has considered the test for victimisation under SDA, s.4 in *St Helens BC v Derbyshire.*[52] In *St Helens,* a number of catering staff challenged two letters sent out by the council which claimed that continuance of the legal claims against the Council would have a dire consequence for public services (including school meals for children) and stated that it was "important to ensure that all affected staff are fully aware of the longer term employment consequences" of their equal pay claims succeeding. The Court of Appeal had held that there was no unlawful victimisation if the employer's letters were an "honest and reaosonable" attempt to settle the claim. The House of Lords overturned the decision of the Court of

[50] [1980] I. C.R. 420 (EAT).
[51] [1989] 1 Q.B. 463 (Court of Appeal).
[52] [2007] IRLR 540 HL.

Appeal and made clear that victimisation does not contain an "honest and reasonable" test.

Lord Hope summarised the approach in the following terms:

St Helens BC v Derbyshire [2007] UKHL 16

Para.26–para.28: "It is the employee's interest in pursuing the claim that provides the test of what is and what is not 'reasonable'. But the employer who is looking for guidance needs a bit more than that. One can do no more than resort to generalities on such a fact-sensitive issue. However, I think that this much can be said. The employer should reflect on the way he wishes to conduct himself will be seen through the eyes of the employee—how would she be likely to react if she were to be treated in that way? He is entitled to bear in mind that an unjustified sense of grievance cannot amount to 'detriment': Barclays Bank v Kapur and ors (No. 2) [1995] IRLR 87; Shamoon v Chief Constable of the Royal Ulster Constabulary [2003] ICR 337, paras. 35 and 105. But he must also bear in mind that the right of the employee to enforce compliance with the principle of equal treatment is protected by the Directive. So he must avoid doing anything that might make a reasonable employee feel that she is being unduly pressurised to concede her claim. Indirect pressure of the kind that the tribunal found established in this case—fear of public odium, or the reproaches of colleagues—is just as likely to deter an employee from enforcing her claim as a direct threat. Sensitivitiy to the wider effects of what he plans to do will be crucial to the exercise of an informed judgment as to what is reasonable. The question whether the borderline has been crossed is, in the end, a question of fact for the tribunal. It will exercise its judgment, in the way I have suggested, on a consideration of all the evidence. It is not to be criticised if it asks itself, in so many words, whether the employer's conduct was 'honest and reasonable'. On the facts of this case, a finding that the detriment was 'by reason that' the employees were insisting on their claims because the respondents went further than was reasonable in protecting their own interests was inescapable."

The House of Lords stated that the issue of victimisation is determined primarily through an analysis of whether the victim has suffered a detriment, and from the point of view of the alleged victim rather than from the point of view of the discrimination. This does not preclude an employer from undertaking "ordinary steps" and attempts to settle the claim.

In theory, an employer could send a letter pointing out the dire consequences of an equal pay claim or to settle the claim. However, on the facts of this case, the employers had breached the victimisation provisions in the SDA.

What follows is a discussion of the main cases on direct discrimination that give some guidance to the central "mischief" that the legal concept seeks to address. The discussion gives an overview of the main issues that are relevant to the legal definition of direct discrimination, such as the question of whether intention is required and the relevance of "but for" causation. The discussion also relates these issues to the ongoing questions about the role of comparators in definitions of direct discrimination, as well as the consequences this has in generating a symmetrical model of discrimination Law.

At the most basic level a provision a provision such as s.1(1)(a) SDA 75 can challenge sex stereotypes and prejudice. Early cases saw this as being a key function for the concept of direct discrimination. An illustration of the type of conduct that direct discrimination can usefully catch in *Peake v Automotive Products Limited* one of the earliest cases on the meaning of direct discrimination in the SDA.

B. *Historical Developments—Direct Discrimination and Stereotypes*

Peake was one of the first case under the SDA to come before the Court of Appeal. The facts of the case are worth setting out in detail because they illustrate the type of practice that prohibitions on direct discrimination seek to prohibit. In *Peake*, employers of some 3,500 men and 400 women in a factory had for some 30 years operated a "ceasing work" rule by which both men and women workers stopped work at 4.25 pm but the women were allowed to leave their place of work at any time during the five minutes before 4.30 pm when the men left. The rule, which had been approved by the relevant trade unions, was claimed to be in the interest of safety and good administration to prevent women being jostled in the rush for the gates at 4.30 pm After the SDA 1975 came into force, the complainant, a male manual worker, applied to an industrial tribunal for a declaration that the practice was discriminatory against him on the ground of sex within s.1(1)(a) and unlawful under s.6 of the SDA 75. The tribunal dismissed his complaint. On appeal, the Employment Appeal Tribunal held that the practice did involve treating women more "favourably" than the men within s.1(1)(a) and was a "benefit" to the women and a "detriment" to the men within s.6(2)(a) and (b), and ordered that the practice should be altered within 12 months. The complainant appealed to the Court of Appeal.

The Court of Appeal upheld his appeal and held that the rule was not direct discrimination under the SDA 75. The main analysis of direct discrimination was set out in the speeches of Lord Denning M.R. and Shaw L.J. set out below.

Peake v Automotive Products Ltd [1977] I.C.R. 968 (alternative citations [1978] QB 233; 1978] I W.L.R. 853; [1978] I All. E. R. 106)

LORD DENNING M.R.

[p.972]: This is the first case we have had on the Sex Discrimination Act 1975. When it was enacted its principal object was, no doubt, to prevent discrimination against women. But now it is a man who complains. Mr. Peake says that his employers, Automotive Products Ltd., have unlawfully discriminated against him in favour of women. [. . .]

[p.974]: Although the Act applies equally to men as to women, I must say it would be very wrong to my mind if this statute were thought to obliterate the differences between men and women or to do away with the chivalry and courtesy which we expect mankind to give womankind. The natural differences of sex must be regarded even in the interpretation of an Act of Parliament.

[p.975]: Applied to this case it seems to me that, when a working rule is made differentiating between men and women in the interests of safety, there is no discrimination contrary to section 1 (1) (a) of the statute. Instances were put before us in the course of argument, such as a cruise liner which employs both men and women. Would it be wrong to have a regulation "Women and children first"? Or in the case of a factory in case of fire? As soon as such instances are considered, the answer is clear. It is not discrimination for mankind to treat womankind with the courtesy and chivalry which we have been taught to believe is right conduct in our society.

So the appeal tribunal held that the men in this case were discriminated against in this way: benefits were afforded to women which were not afforded to men: the particular benefit being the five minutes that the women leave early. The appeal tribunal said also that the men were subjected to a detriment because they did not get the benefit of that five minutes and had to work five minutes longer. On that ground the appeal tribunal held that this was unlawful discrimination.

[...]

In my opinion, however, there was no unlawful discrimination in this case. It seems to me that arrangements which are made in the interests of safety or in the interests of good administration are not infringements of the law even though they may be more favourable to women than to men: or conversely more favourable to men that to women.

The appeal tribunal were fearful that unless they construed the statute strictly it would open a loophole for evasion. But I think that is too pessimistic a view. There is ample scope for the operation of the Act without trespassing on sensible administrative arrangements. The intention of the Act is to ensure that men and women doing the same work shall have the same opportunities for promotion or transfer or training and the same benefits, loans or fringe benefits, and the like. That can be ensured without going so far as is suggested here.

If this be wrong, and if the Act is to be construed literally, I would say that this discrimination is perfectly harmless. If need be, I would apply the maxim de minimis non curat lex, but to my mind that is quite unnecessary. I cannot think that this is discrimination within the Act, certainly not unlawful discrimination. I think the appeal should be allowed.

SHAW L.J.

[p. 976]: The Sex Discrimination Act 1975 was not, in my judgment, designed to provide a basis for capricious and empty complaints of differentiation between the sexes. Nor was it intended to operate as a statutory abolition of every instinct of chivalry and consideration on the part of men for the opposite sex. The phrase used in all the prohibitions imposed by the Act is "discrimination against" one sex or the other. This, to my mind, involves an element of something which is inherently adverse or hostile to the interests of the persons of the sex which is said to be discriminated against.

[...]

In applying statutory provisions which touch human conduct and relationships in infinite ways, it is vitally important to cling to common sense. Otherwise it may be argued by some troublemaker some day that the provision of separate and different arrangements for hygiene and sanitation constitutes an act of discrimination against the males or the females or both. Some acts or differentiation or discrimination are not adverse to either sex and are not designed so to be. Nor, without surrendering to absurdity, can they be so regarded. The discrimination alleged in this case appears to me to fall within that category. I too would allow the appeal."

The decision in *Peake* was subject to severe criticism by academic commentators who argued that it allowed exactly the stereotypes that the SDA was introduced to challenge.[53] In the subsequent case of *Ministry of Defense v Jeremiah*,[54] Lord Denning M.R. held that the decision in *Peake* could be understood as turning on the *de minimis* principle rather than on the substantive point that the practice in question (allowing women to leave early) did not fall within the definition of direct discrimination under the SDA. *Jeremiah* involved a challenge to a workplace rule that required men rather than women who volunteered for overtime to work in the shop that made colour bursting shells. The employers defended the practice arguing that women did not want to work under these conditions and that they did not therefore provide facilities (showers, etc) for women. In *Jeremiah*, Lord Denning M.R. once again considered the issue of whether "chivalry" could justify this difference along the lines developed in *Peake*. He concluded that:

"Next, the Ministry relies on *Peake v Automotive Products Ltd.* [1978] Q.B. 233. The women there were allowed to go off work five minutes before the men—for reasons of safety to avoid the rush. Turning to that case again, I think we were under a disadvantage, because Mr. Peake appeared in person: and we were not referred to some of the relevant parts of the statute. There were two grounds for the decision. Now on reconsideration, I think the only sound ground was that the discrimination was de minimis. Mr. Lester told us that, on a petition to the Appeal Committee of the House of Lords, they refused leave to appeal for that very reason. They thought that the decision was correct on the de minimis ground. In these circumstances, the other ground (about chivalry and administrative practice) should no longer be relied upon."[55]

At the most basic level direct discrimination targets the wrong of "less favourable treatment" that includes the types of stereotypes that are operating in cases such as *Peake* and *Ministry of Defense v Jeremiah*. More recently, direct discrimination has been defined more widely to include not only explicit and clear forms of unequal treatment, but also more subtle forms of "less favourable" treatment. However, not all instances of less favourable treatment fall within the legal definition of direct discrimination. The central question is when and how is less favourable (unequal) treatment translated into prohibited direct discrimination. The definitions of direct discrimination in EU and domestic discrimination law make this transition from less favourable (unequal) treatment to unlawful direct discrimination using a number of key concepts.

First, the treatment becomes direct discrimination when it can be linked to certain prohibited grounds. The second significant feature of direct discrimination is that it uses comparison. Less favourable (unequal) treatment is

[53] P. Wallington, "Ladies First—How Mr Peake was piqued" [1978] C.L.J. 37.
[54] [1980] Q.B. 87; [1980] I.C.R. 13.
[55] [1980] Q.B. 87 at p.98.

established through comparison between two entities. Although there may be some value in defining direct discrimination without comparison, and this has been possible in the case of pregnancy and harassment, both EC and domestic discrimination law take an equality based approach which has two important consequences: it makes comparison central to a definition of direct discrimination; and second, it is symmetrical, ie, not only women but men, not only majorities but also minorities, are protected by the legislation.

C. *Direct Discrimination as "Less Favourable" Treatment*

The legal definition of direct discrimination as less favourable treatment contains a number of related elements. First, it is important to establish that the less favourable treatement is on the prohibited grounds (e.g. race or sex). Second, the present definition of direct discrimination requires a "comparison" (except in the case of pregnancy discrimination) to establish whether or not there has been less favourable treatment.

1. Direct Discrimination and the grounds of discrimination

As stated, not all discriminatory acts are prohibited by law, and there needs to be a link between the discrimination act and the prohibited grounds of discrimination. There are important inter-related aspects to this search for a "link" between the discrimination and the prohibited ground.[56] This section discusses the second question about the precise nature of the requirement that will link discrimination to the prohibited ground.

The earlier discussion of direct discrimination in EU law highlighted the way in which the early cases on equal pay and equal treatment suggested that there was a need for an explicitly motive or intention to discriminate by introducing the term "overt" as a requirement for direct discrimination. Subsequent case law confirmed that Art.119 (141) EC applies to unintentional direct discrimination. In *Enderby v Frenchay HA* the ECJ stated: "The conceptual scheme of that category (direct sex discrimination) makes it clear that discrimination does not even have to have been intentional."[57] Here it is worth noting that, for example, although in *Dekker* the fact that the motive of the employer (the financial consequence of employing a pregnant woman) was discounted in *Hertz*, the ECJ held that the "fundamental reason" for the employment decision was a factor in establishing whether or not the Directive applied. As Bamforth notes, this line of reasoning and a requirement to

[56] For a discussion that relates these two aspects see J. Gardner, "On the Grounds of Her Sex(uality)" (1998) 18 O.J.L.S. 169.

[57] Case C-127/92 [1993] E.C.R. I–5535, at 5558.

establish the "fundamental reason" for the discriminatory act introduces a focus on the mental element of the discriminatory.[58]

Domestic discrimination law has resolved the issue by moving away from a focus on motive and intention towards the "but for" test. We saw in the discussion of the *Peake* case that Denning L.J. and Shaw L.J. were willing to treat conduct based on "benign motives" and "chivalry" as outside the scope of direct discrimination. In *Peake*, Shaw L.J. stated:

"The Sex Discrimination Act 1975 was not, in my judgment, designed to provide a basis for capricious and empty complaints of differentiation between the sexes. Nor was it intended to operate as a statutory abolition of every instinct of chivalry and consideration on the part of men for the opposite sex. The phrase used in all the prohibitions imposed by the Act is 'discrimination against' one sex or the other. This, to my mind, involves an element of something which is inherently adverse or hostile to the interests of the persons of the sex which is said to be discriminated against."[59]

On this analysis, the mere fact that sex is operating as a reason for the difference in treatment is not sufficient to translate the treatment into legally prohibited sex discrimination: where the difference in treatment is motivated by "good reasons" it will fall outside the SDA. In *Peake*, the focus on "chivalry" could reinforce stereotypes about women being weak. Moreover, as stated earlier, the assumption that direct discrimination is solely or predominantly about stereotypes would necessarily restrict the concept. Nevertheless, there is a sense in which *Peake* raises an issue which remains central to our analysis of the concept: namely, what are the reasons for the action of the discriminatory? As the next discussion suggests, although the courts have moved away from a focus on the intention and motive of the discriminator, the issue of the "reasons" for the discriminatory conduct remain important to an analysis of direct discrimination.

In a series of cases on direct discrimination and victimisation in the SDA and RRA the House of Lords have now refined the legal definition of direct discrimination. The most authoritative statement of the present test was established by the House of Lords in *James v Eastleigh*[60] which confirmed the emerging analysis in the *Birmingham City Council*[61] by establishing the "but for" test for direct discrimination. The issue has also been considered by the House of Lords in *Nagarajan*,[62] Khan[63] and *Shamoom*[64] on victimisation under the RRA.

[58] N. Bamforth, "The Changing Concept of Sex Discrimination", (Nov 1993) 56 M.L.R. 872–890, at 878.

[59] Peake v Automotive Products Ltd. [1977] I.C.R. 968, at p.976.

[60] *James v Eastleigh BC* [1990] I.C.R. 554.

[61] *R v Birmingham CC* Ex p. Equal Opportunities Commission.

[62] *Nagarajan v London Regional Transport* [2000] 1 A.C. 501.

[63] *Chief Constable of West Yorkshire Police v Khan* [2001] 1 W.L.R. 1947.

[64] *Shamoom v Chief Constable of Royal Ulster Constabulary* [2003] I.C.R. 337.

(i) *The "but for" test for direct discrimination*

In *R v Birmingham CC* the issue was discrimination in the criteria for selective state schooling. The allegedly discriminatory practice of the Council was the requirement for a higher standard of entry for girls as compared with boys. The Council argued that their motives for the discrimination were to ensure that there was matched entry for the boys and girls to the grammar school. The House of Lords had to consider the definition of direct discrimination in s.1(1)(a) of the SDA 75. The significance of the *Birmingham CC* case was that it developed this shift away from motive and intention and articulated instead the "but for" test. Lord Goff stated:

> **[p.1194]** "... There is discrimination under the statute if there is less favourable treatment on the ground of sex, in other words if the relevant girl or girls would have received the same treatment as the boys *but for* their sex (emphasis added). The intention or motive of the defendant to discriminate, though it may be relevant so far as remedies are concerned (see section 66(3) of the Act of 1975), is not a necessary condition of liability; it is perfectly possible to envisage cases where the defendant had no such motive, and yet did in fact discriminate on the ground of sex."[65]

This embryonic reference to "but for" crystallised into the present "but for" test in the reasoning of the House of Lords in *James v Eastleigh*.[66] The case involved the claim by a man that he had been discriminated against on the ground of his sex. The rule at issue was that there was free entry to a swimming pool for those who had reached the state retirement age, which was lower for women than it was for men. Mr James, as a 61-year-old man, did not qualify for the free swimming because the statutory retirement age for men was 65 years. If he had been a woman he would have qualified because the statutory retirement age for women was 60 years. Mr James did not qualify for free swimming; whereas his wife did qualify. The reasons for Eastleigh BC's decision were the commendable motives of assisting those who had no wages. The House of Lords overturned the decision of the Court of Appeal and held that there was direct sex discrimination in this case. *James v Eastleigh* is now accepted as the foundation of the contemporary test for direct discrimination. The judgment has also been the subject of some controversy. Lord Browne-Wilkinson has cast doubt on its universal application as a test for direct discrimination in *Nagarajan*; and in a subsequent series of cases on victimisation (*Khan* and *Shamoon*) Lord Nicholls has discussed the test in terms that reinstate the importance of analysing the discriminator's reasoning process, so that some commentators have found it difficult to reconcile the later cases with the decision in *James v Eastleigh*[67]. Therefore, it is worth setting out and discussing the passages in *James v Eastleigh* in some detail.

65 *R v Birmingham CC*, ibid., at para.1194.

66 [1990] I.C.R. 554 (relevant citation used in this discussion). Also [1990] 2 A.C. 751.

67 See the discussion by L. Barmes, "Promoting Diversity and the Definition of Direct Discrimination" (2003) 32 I.L.J. 3 200–213.

First, Lord Bridge considered but rejects the reasoning of Browne-Wilkinson V.C. in the Court of Appeal.

In the Court of Appeal, Browne-Wilkinson V.C. had introduce two principles for interpreting the meaning of direct discrimination: first, the idea that a critical aspect of direct discrimination is that it is concerned with the discriminator's reasons for action; and second, that the definition of direct discrimination in s.1(1)(a) must be conceptually distinct from indirect discrimination which is defined in s.1(1)(b) SDA.

Lord Bridge declined to follow the reasoning of Browne-Wilkinson V.C. and the Court of Appeal. Instead, he explicitly adopted the "but for" analysis that had been previously developed in the *Birmingham CC* case and justifies this in the following terms:

James v Eastleigh [1990] I.C.R. 554

p.567 "The fallacy, with all respect, which underlies and vitiates this reasoning is a failure to recognise that the statutory pensionable age, being fixed at 60 for women and 65 for men, is itself a criterion which directly discriminates between men and women in that it treats women more favourably than men 'on the ground of their sex.' This was readily conceded by Mr. Beloff and is indeed self-evident. It follows inevitably that any other differential treatment of men and women which adopts the same criterion must equally involve discrimination 'on the ground of sex.' [. . .] The expression 'pensionable age' is no more than a convenient shorthand expression which refers to the age of 60 in a woman and to the age of 65 in a man. In considering whether there has been discrimination against a man 'on the ground of his sex' it cannot possibly make any difference whether the alleged discriminator uses the shorthand expression or spells out its full meaning."[68]

Lord Bridge then goes on to explicitly reject the place of any subjective element in the test for direct discrimination by stating:

p.567–568 "The Court of Appeal's attempt to escape from these conclusions lies in construing the phrase 'on the ground of her sex' in section 1(1)(a) as ***568** referring subjectively to the alleged discriminator's 'reason' for doing the act complained of. As already noted, the judgment had earlier identified the council's reason as 'to give benefits to those whose resources would be likely to have been reduced by retirement' and 'to aid the needy, whether male or female.' But to construe the phrase, 'on the ground of her sex' as referring to the alleged discriminator's reason in this sense is directly contrary to a long line of authority confirmed by your Lordships's House in *R. v Birmingham City Council, Ex p. Equal Opportunities Commission* [1989] A.C. 1155."[69]

Lord Bridge was supported by the majority including Lord Goff who reiterated his "but for" test in this context in the terms set out below. It is also

[68] *James v Eastleigh*, ibid., at p.567.
[69] Ibid., at p.567–568.

worth noting that Lord Goff was not persuaded by the argument that the type of situation in this case (the impact of a statutory age for retirement that discriminates between men and women) could be dealt with by indirect discrimination, and that there was a need to maintain conceptual distinction between direct and indirect discrimination. He stated:

[p.577] "In other words, I do not read the words 'on the ground of sex' as necessarily referring only to the reason why the defendant acted as he did, but as embracing cases in which a gender-based criterion is the basis upon which the complainant has been selected for the relevant treatment. Of course, there may be cases where the defendant's reason for his action may bring the case within the subsection, as when the defendant is motivated by an animus against persons of the complainant's sex, or otherwise selects the complainant for the relevant treatment because of his or her sex. But it does not follow that the words 'on the ground of sex' refer only to cases where the defendant's reason for his action is the sex of the complainant; and, in my opinion, the application by the defendant to the complainant of a gender-based criterion which favours the opposite sex is just as much a case of unfavourable treatment on the ground of sex. Such a conclusion seems to me to be consistent with the policy of the Act, which is the active promotion of equal treatment of men and women.

[...]

But the simple fact is that, under section 1(1)(a) of the Act of 1975, which is concerned actively to promote equality of treatment of the two sexes, the adoption for this purpose of a gender-based criterion is unlawful; and the task of the council is to find some other reasonably practical criterion, which does not contravene the Act of 1975, by which it can achieve its laudable purpose.

Finally, I wish briefly to refer to the use, in the present context, of such words as intention, motive, reason and purpose. [...] It follows that, in a legal context, if words such as intention or motive are to be used as a basis for decision, they require the most careful handling, and it also follows that their use in one context may not be a safe guide to their use in another context.

For these reasons, I am reluctant to have to conclude that those who are concerned with the day to day administration of legislation such as the Sex Discrimination Act 1975, who are mainly those who sit on industrial tribunals, should have to grapple with such elusive concepts as these. However, taking the case of direct discrimination under section 1(1)(a) of the Act, I incline to the opinion that, if it were necessary to identify the requisite intention of the defendant, that intention is simply an intention to perform the relevant act of less favourable treatment. Whether or not the treatment is less favourable in the relevant sense, i.e. on the ground of sex, may derive either from the application of a gender-based criterion to the complainant, or from selection by the defendant of the complainant because of his or her sex; but, in either event, it is not saved from constituting unlawful discrimination by the fact that the defendant acted from a benign motive. However, in the majority of cases, I doubt if it is necessary to focus upon the intention or motive of the defendant in this way. This is because, as I see it, cases of direct discrimination under section 1(1)(a) can be considered by asking the simple question: would the complainant have received the same treatment from the defendant but for his or her sex? This simple test possesses the double virtue that, on the one hand, it embraces both the case where the treatment derives from the application of a gender-based criterion, and the case where it derives from the selection of the complainant because of his or her sex; and on the other hand it avoids, in most cases at least, complicated questions relating to concepts such as intention, motive, reason or purpose, and the danger of confusion arising from the misuse of those elusive terms. I have to stress, however, that the 'but for' test is not appropriate for cases of indirect discrimination under section 1(1)(b), because there may be indirect discrimination against persons of one sex under that subsection, although a (proportionately smaller) group of persons of the opposite sex is adversely affected in the same way.

I trust that the foregoing will explain why I expressed myself as I did, I fear too tersely, in *R. v Birmingham CC, Ex p. Equal Opportunities Commission* [1989] A.C. 1155, 1193–1194."

Lord Lowry gave detailed dissent in *James v Eastleigh* with which Lord Griffiths concurred. The dissent is important not only because the final decision in *James v Eastleigh* was a bare majority—with a 3/2 split) but also because of the confusion surrounding the "but for" test in the subsequent victimisation cases i.e. *Nagarajan, Khan* and *Shamoon*. It should be noted that it may be possible to accept the distinctions that Lord Lowry makes between two different approaches to the "but for" test, whilst at the same time rejecting his conclusions that in the *James v Eastleigh* case the "but for" test was not satisfied. In his dissent Lord Lowry makes the following observations of the "but for" test in *Birmingham City Council*.

LORD LOWRY:

[p.579–580] "As Mr. Beloff put it, section 1(1)(a) refers to the activities of the discriminator: the words 'on the ground of his sex' provide the link between the alleged discriminator and his less favourable treatment of another. They introduce a subjective element into the analysis and pose here the question 'Was the sex of the appellant a consideration in the council's decision?' Putting it another way, a 'ground' is a reason, in ordinary speech, for which a person takes a certain course. He knows what he is doing and why he has decided to do it. In the context of section 1(1)(a) the discriminator knows that he is treating the victim less favourably and he also knows the ground on which he is doing so. In no case are the discriminator's thought processes immaterial.

[p.579] In my judgment section 1(1)(a) is looking to the case where, subjectively, the defendant has treated the plaintiff less favourably because of his or her sex. What is relevant is the defendant's reason for doing an act, not the causative effect of the act done by the defendant. As Mr. Towler for the council pointed out, section 1(1) is referring throughout to the activities of the alleged discriminator. In the case of direct discrimination 'a person discriminates against a [man] . . . if on the ground of sex he treats less favourably . . .' Those words indicate that one is looking, not to the causative link between the defendant's behaviour and the detriment to the plaintiff, but to the reason why the defendant treated the plaintiff less favourably. The relevant question is 'did the defendant act on the ground of sex?' not 'did the less favourable treatment result from the defendant's actions?' "

Lord Lowry rejects what he terms the "causative construction" formula as a basis for the "but for" test.. It is strict because it does not require any focus on the discriminator's state of mind or reasons (hence the use of the term objective to refer to this formulation). Lord Lowry dismisses this construction in the following terms:

[p.583] "It can thus be seen that the causative construction not only gets rid of unessential and often irrelevant mental ingredients, such as malice, prejudice, desire and motive, but also dispenses with an essential ingredient, namely, the ground on which the discriminator acts. The appellant's construction relieves the complainant of the need to prove anything except that A has done an act which results in less favourable treatment for

B by reason of B's sex, which reduces to insignificance the words 'on the ground of.' Thus the causative test is too wide and is grammatically unsound, because it necessarily disregards the fact that the less favourable treatment is meted out to the victim *on the ground* of the victim's sex."

Lord Lowry's dissent with the majority, therefore, turns on the fact that the "causative construction" of the "but for" test does not pay sufficient attention to the reasoning process of the discriminator.

(ii) *"But for": causative construction or deliberative reasons*

Bob Watt has argued that the "but for" test in *James v Eastleigh* is "not a test at all" and he has offered a critique of the causative construction version of that test.[70] Did Lord Bridge and Lord Goff mean to adopt the "causative construction" version of the "but for" test? It is perhaps worth noting the precise language used by Lord Bridge, where he states that he is rejecting the requirement for "referring subjectively to the alleged discriminator's 'reason' for doing the act complained of." (p.568) He also asserted that "to construe the phrase 'on the ground of her sex' as referring to the alleged discriminator's reason in this sense is directly contrary to a long line of authority *R. v Birmingham CC, Ex p. Equal Opportunities Commission*". (p.568) These phrases can be construed in two ways. First, that there is no need to focus on the deliberation of the discriminator, so that the "but for" test becomes a purely causal enquiry (*causative construction*). Second, that the "but for" test obviates the need to focus on the discriminator's state of mind with respect to malign motives or intend to discriminate but that there is still an enquiry into whether discrimination based on the prohibited grounds was a factor in the decision-making of the discriminator (*deliberative reasoning*). Although Lord Bridge's analysis has often been read as a strict causative construction test, it is also possible to reconcile his analysis with the deliberative reasoning test. The central issue becomes whether when he refers to the need to exclude "subjectively the alleged discriminator's 'reasons' for doing the act", he means to exclude (a) all deliberative reasons of the discriminator; or (b) only motives and intentions for discrimination. It might also be argued that Lord Goff explicitly excludes reason for action from the "but for" test by stating that "motive, intention, reasons and purpose", and that he is explicitly endorsing a purely "causative construction" of the "but for" test. However, it is noteworthy that Lord Goff states in the passages extracted above that:

"if it were necessary to identify the requisite intention of the defendant, that intention is simply an intention to perform the relevant act of less favourable treatment". (p.577)

It could be argued that this last phrase corresponds to the "deliberative reasoning" that Lord Lowry sees as being essential to establishing that dis-

[70] B. Watt, "Goodbye 'but for', hello 'but why?' (1998) 27 I.L.J. 121.

crimination is on the grounds of sex, race etc. On this reading of the majority in *James v Eastleigh*, the "but for" does not exclude all deliberative reasons of the discriminator. This construction is supported by the subsequent explicit comments of Lord Nicholls in *Nagarajan* where he states:

"Lord Bridge [...] described Lord Goff's test in the Birmingham case as objective and not subjective. In stating that he was excluding as irrelevant the (subjective) reason why the council discriminated directly between men and women. He is not to be taken as saying that the discriminator's state of mind is irrelevant when answering the crucial, anterior question: why did the complainant receive less favourable treatment?"[71]

Although in *Nagarajan*, Lord Steyn did not explicitly endorse this interpretation of Lord Bridge's "but for" test he confirmed that victimisation requires more than just a causal link between the grounds of discrimination (i.e. race, sex and the protected act) and the less favourable treatment. Moreover, it is also significant that Lord Steyn did not find the subjective versus objective distinction helpful and states that the approach he is advocating "postulates that the discriminator's knowledge of the protected act had a subjective impact on his mind."[72]

In her comments on the *Nagarajan* decision Barmes concludes:

"It is clear from both Lord Nicholls' and Lord Steyn's speeches that their comments regarding motive did not refer to the reason for the less favourable treatment, but to the 'reason for the reason'. In other words, they did not treat the reason for the less favourable treatment as irrelevant, but the reason for treating someone less favourably *on grounds of race or sex, or for a protected reason*."[73]

Barmes does not consider the possibility that the "but for" test in *James v Eastleigh* can on one possible reading, be reconciled with Lord Nicholls conclusions in *Nagarajan*. One way of recasting the need for "reasons for the reasons" is that it incorporates the need to analyse the discriminator's reasons, and displays a preference for the "deliberative reasoning" model over the "causative construction" model of the "but for" test.

Nagarajan[74] was part of a trio of House of Lords decisions following *James v Eastleigh* that included *Chief Constable of the West Yorkshire Police v Khan*[75] and *Shamoon v Chief Constable of the Royal Ulster Constabulary*[76]. These cases appear

71 [2000] 1 A.C. 501, at 511.
72 [2000] 1 A.C. 501, at 519–522.
73 L. Barmes, "Promoting Diversity and the Definition of Direct Discrimination" (2003) 32 I.L.J. 3 200, at 205.
74 [2000] 1 A.C. 501
75 [2001] I W.L.R. 1947
76 [2003] I.C.R. 337

to favour a "deliberative reasoning" model for the "but for" test for direct discrimination. Despite some arguments that there is a sufficient distinction between victimisation and s.1(1)(a) direct discrimination to justify divergent legal tests for these two forms of direct discrimination (see for example Lord Hoffman in *Chief Constable of West Yorkshire Police v Khan*),[77] it seems clear from the discussions of the House of Lords in these cases that they will take a unified approach to the definition of "but for" in both contexts. This is clear from the speech of Lord Nicholls in *Nagarajan* who states that section 2 RRA 76 on victimisation should be read in the context of s.1 on direct discrimination[78]. Lord Nicholls states: "The key question under section 2 is the same as under section 1(1)(a): why did the complainant receive less favourable treatment?"[79] The analysis of direct discrimination in these cases suggests that the "but for" test does not obviate the need to consider the discriminator's reasons, i.e. the correct interpretation for the "but for" test is not "causative construction" but is rather "deliberative reasoning".

Chief Constable of the West Yorkshire Police v Khan[80] and *Shamoon v Chief Constable of the Royal Ulster Constabulary* also support the view that the "but for" test for direct discrimination requires analysis of the discriminator's reasons. *Khan* involved a claim of victimisation for refusing (on the basis of legal advice) to give the complainant an employment reference. In his judgment, Lord Nicholls developed the ideas he set out in *Nagarajan* in terms that make it clear that he was rejecting a causative construction model for the "but for" test. The passage is worth setting out in detail:

> Causation is a slippery word, but normally it is used to describe a legal exercise. From the many events leading up to the crucial happening, the court selects one or more of them which the law regards as causative of the happening. Sometimes the court may look for the 'operative' cause, or the 'effective' cause. Sometimes it may apply the 'but for' approach. For the reasons I sought to explain in Nagarajan v London Regional Transport [2001] 1 A.C. 502 510–12, a causation exercise of this type is not required either by s.1(1)(a) or s.2. The phrases 'on racial grounds' and 'by reason that' denote a different exercise: why did the alleged discriminator act as he did? What, consciously or unconsciously, was his reason? Unlike causation, this is a subjective test. Causation is a legal conclusion. The reason why a person acted as he did is a question of fact."[81]

The importance of a factual search for the reason that provides the link

[77] [2001] 1 W.L.R. 1947. Lord Hoffman at p.1955: "There are parallels between the purposes of sections 1 and 2 of the Race Relations Act 1976 (and between the corresponding sections 1 and 4 of the Sex Discrimination Act 1975) [...] but the causal questions that they raise are not identical."

[78] [2000] 1 A.C. 501, 510–511, see also p.512.

[79] [2000] 1 A.C. 510, at p.512.

[80] [2001] I W.L.R. 1947.

[81] [2001] 1 W.L.R. 1947, at 1954.

between the prohibited ground and the less favourable treatment was reiterated by Lord Nicholls in *Shamoon v Chief Constable of the Royal Ulster Constabulary*. He stated:

"Employment tribunals may sometimes be able to avoid arid and confusing disputes about the identification of the appropriate comparator by concentrating primarily on why the claimant was treated as she was. Was it on the proscribed ground which is the foundation of the application? That will call for an examination of all the facts of the case. Or was it for some other reasons?"[82]

"Applying the same reasoning (i.e. as set out by Lord Nicholls in *Khan* above) in the *James* context would surely have resulted in the Council being exonerated, since it was accepted that the subjective reason for the Council's action was the alleviation of pensioner poverty. In effect, in my view, this approach to liability entails a requirement that a motivation to discriminate or victimise be present."[83]

Barmes usefully focuses on the difficulty of formulating a subjective test that requires attention to be paid to to the discriminator's state of mind, but that at the same time distinguishes between different types of reasons. However, it might also be suggested that this is exactly the exercise that is required to give any meaningful sense to the "but for" test and its function in establishing direct discrimination.

James v Eastleigh clearly establishes that motive and intention are not necessary to establish direct discrimination. Yet, at the same time, and as the subsequent victimisation cases make clear, discounting these factors does not mean that the test for liability for direct discrimination is reduced to solely a causal enquiry or a strict liability test. These later cases clearly reject the causal construction "but for" test, in favour of a test that focuses attention on the discriminator's deliberation and reasons. In *James v Eastleigh* a focus on the reason for doing the discriminatory act (introducing statutory pension age, as the determinant for free swimming facilities) was on the grounds of sex because the majority of the Law Lords found that statutory pension age was not a gender neutral criteria. It was, rather, a "marker" for gender discrimination. The subjective part of the analysis that includes the discriminator's reasons was relevant. However, the motive (helping the unwaged) for using this marker was irrelevant.

John Gardner, in his discussion of *James v Eastleigh* and the "but for" test analyses how a discriminator's reasons might be analysed in the context of the "but for" test. He argues that definitions of direct discrimination should focus

82 [2003] I.C.R. 337 at para.11.

83 L. Barmes, "Promoting Diversity and the Definition of Direct Discrimination" (2003) 32 I.L.J. 3 200, at 207.

on the dsicriminator's reasoning. He also argues that this reason-based paradigm for the concept of direct discrimination allows it to perform a distinct function in discrimination law, which is different to other concepts such as indirect discrimination and positive action.

John Gardner On the Ground of Her Sex(uality) (1998) 18 O.J.L.S. 167–187

p.180: "All reasoning contains both major (or operative) premisses and minor (or auxiliary) ones. I reason: (1) I need to be at home at seven; (2) its now only six; (3) the bus sometimes takes as much as an hour; so (4) I'd better leave now. Only (1) is an operative premise, while (2) and (3) are auxiliary, leading to conclusion (4). Premisses (2) and (3) simply supply the information which allows me to derive one injunction to action from another, to work out the means I must use, (4), from the end I must achieve, (1). That 'it's now six' or 'the bus sometimes takes as much as an hour' is motivationally inert by itself, without some premise like (1) to give it some significance in my action. That's what makes these premisses auxiliary. And the issue now is: When some factor figures in the auxiliary premisses of my thinking but not in the operative ones, does it still figure in my thinking in the sense which is relevant for the question we just put to our hypothetical discriminator?

These are both well known problems for discrimination lawyers. The first problem, the problem of incorporation by logical reference, arises most obviously in pregnancy discrimination cases. An employer may say: I didn't sack her because she is a woman, I sacked her because she's pregnant; that she's a woman didn't bother me at all. The law may answer: Sorry, but since only women can become pregnant, sacking her because she's pregnant just is a case of sacking her because, among other things, she's a woman. Being pregnant is a logically sufficient condition of womanhood even though not a logically necessary one, in much the same way as having one's heart ripped out and one's head cut off add up to a logically sufficient condition of death even though not a logically necessary one. So denying that pregnancy discrimination is sex discrimination is just like saying you intended to rip out the heart and cut off the head, but not to kill. One may argue that those who say such things are playing with words, and not offering a serious defense. Meanwhile the second problem, the problem of auxiliary premisses, will be most familiar to watchers of British anti-discrimination law from the case of James v Eastleigh Borough Council, where a local authority attempted to target resources on the less well-off by directing discounts on its leisure facilities to people of pensionable age. Since the statutory pensionable age for men was at the time higher than for women, the authority's initiative had the necessary effect that some women received benefits which men of the same age did not. The problem with which the courts had to grapple was that the sex of those applying for discounts was figuring in the auxiliary rather than operative premisses of the council's reasoning. It was not motivated by sex but only by pensionability, with sex as a (motivationally inert) indicator of pensionability. The reaction of the House of Lords was to broaden out the definition of direct sex discrimination beyond the obvious case in which sex itself is part of the operative premisses. To achieve this broadening out they coined the now widely-used phrases 'but for' test of direct discrimination: but for his sex, other things being equal, would this man have received the discount? [. . .]

p.186: But it should be noted that even the 'but for' test in James v Eastleigh is a test which looks to the discriminator's reasoning. It merely takes a wider view of what counts as the discriminator's reasoning, by including under that heading minor or auxiliary as well as major or operative premisses (together with whatever is built into any of these premisses by logical implication). The majority of the House of Lords was deeply confused about this point in James itself. Lord Bridge said that the 'but for' test was 'objective' rather than 'subjective'; Lord Goff said that it was a test which focused not on the discriminator's reasons but on the discriminator's actions; even Lord Lowry, in his dissenting speech, labeled the 'but for' test as 'causative [. . .] reduc[ing] to insignificance the words "on the grounds of"'. But all these suggestions are seriously misleading. The 'but for' test asks not merely whether the decision complained of affects men differently from women, but also *why* it does so, and the 'why' here cannot but be read as interrogating the discriminator's reasons. There is no other 'causative' process in play but the causative process of the discriminator's reasoning, the list of considerations which affected him in what he did. The only live question is: How should 'reasoning' here be interpreted? I interpreted it narrowly in carrying out the moral paradigm of direct discrimination"

Significantly, in US statutory discrimination law there remains a focus on the discriminator's reasoning. For example, to establish disparate impact under Title VII of the Civil Rights Act 1964 cases, the plaintiff has to prove that the prohibited reason was a substantial and motivating factor in the disputed employment decision. The standard test was set out in *McDonnell Douglas Corp v Green* in terms that make it clear that the focus is on the discriminator's deliberation processes. The case acknowledged that disparate treatment can be established by direct evidence of discrimination such as the statement of an employee that reveals an intention to treat someone differently on the grounds of sex. In addition, in other cases, once the claimant establishes a prima facie case of direct discrimination then the defendant must "articulate some legitimate, non-discriminatory reason for the employee's rejection."[84] If the defendant is able to establish this point then the claimant must establish that the reasons for the discrimination were in fact an excuse or pretext.[85] In the Civil Rights Act 1991, Congress confirmed the importance of focusing on the discriminator's reasons for action. The Act defines disparate treatment as requiring the claimant to prove that a discriminatory reason was a "motivating factor," not that it was a "substantial factor".[86]

2. Mixed Reason Cases

Another issue that cases like *James v Eastleigh* raise is the problem of mixed reasons cases. Once we accept Gardner's argument sex and race can operate at the auxiliary stage of the reasoning process of the discriminator, and a broadening of the range of this analysis, then this widens the range of information and reasons that were operating to influence the decision-making of the discriminator. In those cases where a prohibited ground (e.g. sex) is the only reason influencing the decision-making of the discriminator, this should be sufficient to establish "but for" causation. Where the prohibited ground is

[84] 411 U.S. 792 (1973), at 802.
[85] 411 U.S. 792 (1973), at 802.
[86] US Civil Rights Act 1991, s.706(g)(2)(B), 42 U.S.C. s2000e–5(g)(2)(B) (2000).

entailed in the operative part of the reasoning of the discriminator—is necessarily entailed in the reasoning as in the case of pregnancy—then this may also be sufficient. However, what about cases where the prohibited ground is one of a number of reasons that operate within the discriminator's deliberation? Domestic discrimination law the discriminatory reason need not be the sole reason for the less favourable treatment. In *Owen & Briggs v James*[87] the Court of Appeal considered the issue of whether there can be direct race discrimination. The applicant had been turned down for a job for a number of different reasons. The Industrial Tribunal had found that these reasons were excuses and that race had played a role in the non-appointment of the applicant for the job. In the course of their decision the Court of Appeal upheld the decision of the Industrial Tribunal. Sir David Cairns stated that the Industrial Tribunal was justified in reaching the "the conclusion that an important factor in the refusal to consider the application was the racial reason".[88] Stephenson L.J. agreed with this analysis and also cited with approval the approach of the EAT:

"Having considered all these matters, they came unanimously to the conclusion that one of the important factors in the conduct of the partner was that the applicant was colored. So they found the case made out. If the tribunal finds that a substantial reason for what has happened is that a candidate has not been considered for a post, or has been refused an appointment because of his or her race, then it seems to us that the tribunal is entitled to say that there has been a breach of the legislation."[89]

In *Nagarajan*, commenting on *Owen & Briggs* Lord Steyn concluded:

"the interpretation put forward by the applicant merely requires that a claimant must prove that the principal or at least an important or significant cause of the less favourable treatment is the fact that the alleged discriminator has done a protected act: as to causation, see Owen & Briggs v James [. . .] Counsel were in agreement, and I would accept, that there is realistically no scope for any other interpretation."[90]

The US Civil Rights Act 1991 assigns mixed motive defenses to the remedial stage of a discrimination case. The general remedial section of Title VII now contains a section that allows the defendant to escape liability for compensation upon proof that the defendant "would have taken the same action in the

[87] [1982] I.C.R. 618.
[88] [1982] I.C.R. 618 at 626.
[89] [1982] I.C.R. 618 at 626–627.
[90] [1999] I. C. R. 877, at 893.

absence of the impermissible motivating factor". Significantly, even if the defendant succeeds in establishing this, the court can award remedies such as an injunction or declaration.[91]

D. *Direct Discrimination and "Comparators"*

The definition of discrimination in section the SDA and RRA includes the less favourable treatment by making a comparison with a similarly situated person of the opposite gender or race. The SDA and RRA also include a statutory definition of what this comparison entails. SDA, s.5(3) states that the comparison of persons of different sex required to establish direct discrimination under SDA, s.1 "must be such that the relevant circumstances in the one case are the same, or not materially different, in the other". There are similar provisions in RRA, s.3(4). The requirement for a "comparator" causes significant problems in discrimination law, e.g. in the context of pregnancy discrimination.

In *Shamoon* the House of Lords emphasised that in order to establish direct discrimination and less favourable treatment there was a need to undertake a factual search for the reason that provides the link between the prohibited ground and the less favourable treatment. Lord Nicholls stated:

"Employment tribunals may sometimes be able to avoid arid and confusing disputes about the identification of the appropriate comparator by concentrating primarily on why the claimant was treated as she was. Was it on the proscribed ground which is the foundation of the application?"

We will see that the analysis in *Shamoon* appears to merge the issue of (a) the grounds for discrimination; and (b) the need for a comparator. The factual search for the reason that links the less favourable treatment to the prohibited ground will often involve the use of a comparison. In many cases the issue of whether the less favourable treatment was for the reasons linked to the prohibited ground will be established by examining how a similarly situated person who does not share the characteristic (e.g being male/female; or black/white) has or would be treated. This comparison performs two functions:

(a) it sets the standard of what constitutes the appropriate treatment against which the term "less favourable" is being judged; and

(b) it allows an identification of whether or not the prohibited ground has

[91] US Civil Rights Act 1991, s.706 (g)(2)(B)(i), 42 U.S.C. S 2000e–5(g)(2)(i) (2000). This modifies the decision of the US Supreme Court in *Price Waterhouse v Hopkins* 490 U.S. 228 (1989) that established that the defendant has the burden of production of proof and persuasion in mixed motive cases.

been a reason that has influenced the decision-making of the discriminator.

There is, therefore, an inherent bias towards a comparative analysis which is built into the analysis of less favourable treatment and direct discrimination. As stated in the chapter on theory, equality is a relational concept which encourages the use of comparison to give substance to questions such as "equality for whom" and "equality of what"? In the context of direct discrimination, therefore, it is worth observing that although it is sometimes useful to separate out an analysis of different stages of the legal analysis (e.g. keeping separate the issue of the grounds of discrimination from the need for a comparator) it is also important to understand that in practice there will be a substantial overlap between these issues.

1. *Shamoon*

Shamoon was a case under the Sex Discrimination (Northern Ireland) Order 1976 which is materially the same as the SDA 75. The complainant was removed from her position as an appraiser because of complaints that were made against her. The two male comparators in the case had no complainst made against them. The tribunal had upheld her complaint of discrimination. The Northern Ireland Court of Appeal had upheld the appeal against the Tribunal's decision because they found that the two male comparators were not similarly situated to Ms Shamoon. The House of Lords upheld the decision of the NI Court of Appeal on the basis that were insufficient reasons to justify the tribunals finding of sex discrimination. In reaching this decision, the House of Lords confirmed the need to link less favourable treatment to the protected ground of discrimination.

Lord Nicholls stated:

"This legislation was, and is, highly important. It attempts to remedy various types of social injustice. But an implementation of the legislation that tends to require a more favourable treatment of the protected class than a member of the class could expect if he or she were not a member of that class turns anti-discrimination legislation on its head and brings it into disrepute. A finding of discrimination where no material exists to support the finding tends, in my opinion, to that result."[92]

Lord Nicholls also clarified that comparison is inherent to an analysis of direct discrimination.

[92] [2003] W.L. 270780, at para.119.

Shamoon v Chief Constable of the Royal Ulster Constabulary [2003] WL 270780, paras 108–110

"**108.** First, the statutory definition of what constitutes discrimination involves a comparison: '. . . treats that other less favourably than he treats or would treat other persons'. The comparison is between the treatment of the victim on the one hand and of a comparator on the other hand. The comparator may be actual ('treats') or may be hypothetical ('or would treat') but 'must be such that the relevant circumstances in the one case are the same, or not materially different, in the other' (see Article 7). If there is any material difference between the circumstances of the victim and the circumstances of the comparator, the statutory definition is not being applied. It is possible that, in a particular case, an actual comparator capable of constituting the statutory comparator can be found. But in most cases a suitable actual comparator will not be available and a hypothetical comparator will have to constitute the statutory comparator. In Khan one of the questions was as to the circumstances that should be attributed to the statutory hypothetical comparator. It is important, in my opinion, to recognise that Article 7 is describing the attributes that the Article 3(1) comparator must possess.

109. But, secondly, comparators have a quite separate evidential role to play. Article 7 has nothing to do with this role. It is neither prescribing nor limiting the evidential comparators that may be adduced by either party. The victim who complains of discrimination must satisfy the fact finding tribunal that, on a balance of probabilities, he or she has suffered discrimination falling within the statutory definition. This may be done by placing before the tribunal evidential material from which an inference can be drawn that the victim was treated less favourably than he or she would have been treated if he or she had not been a member of the protected class. Comparators, which for this purpose are bound to be actual comparators, may of course constitute such evidential material. But they are no more than tools which may or may not justify an inference of discrimination on the relevant prohibited ground eg. sex. The usefulness of the tool will, in any particular case, depend upon the extent to which the circumstances relating to the comparator are the same as the circumstances relating to the victim. The more significant the difference or differences the less cogent will be the case for drawing the requisite inference. But the fact that a particular chosen comparator cannot, because of material differences, qualify as the statutory comparator, eg. under Article 7, by no means disqualifies it from an evidential role. It may, in conjunction with other material, justify the tribunal in drawing the inference that the victim was treated less favourably than she would have been treated if she had been the Article 7 comparator.

110. In summary, the comparator required for the purpose of the statutory definition of discrimination must be a comparator in the same position in all material respects as the victim save only that he, or she, is not a member of the protected class. But the comparators that can be of evidential value, sometimes determinative of the case, are not so circumscribed. Their evidential value will, however, be variable and will inevitably be weakened by material differences between the circumstances relating to them and the circumstances of the victim."[93]

However, despite the emphasis on the need for the comparator as part of the statutory requirement to establish direct discrimination, Lord Nicholls also recognised that it is not possible to have a separate and sequential analysis of (a) whether the less favourable treatment is by reason of the claimant's

[93] [2003] W.L. 270780, at paras 108–110.

membership of the protected class; and (b) the comparator requirement. Lord Nicholls recognises this in his observations that:

(para.8) "No doubt there are cases where it is convenient and helpful to adopt this two step approach to what is essentially a single question: did the claimant, on the proscribed ground, receive less favourable treatment than others? But, especially where the identity of the relevant comparator is a matter of dispute, this sequential analysis may give rise to needless problems. Sometimes the less favourable treatment issue cannot be resolved without, at the same time, deciding the reason why issue. The two issues are intertwined."[94]

As stated earlier, in his discussion of the "but for" test in *Shamoon*, Lord Nicholls stated:

(para.11) "Employment tribunals may sometimes be able to avoid arid and confusing disputes about the identification of the appropriate comparator by concentrating primarily on why the claimant was treated as she was. Was it on the proscribed ground which is the foundation of the application? That will call for an examination of all the facts of the case. Or was it for some other reasons?"[95]

This more flexible approach to the need to precisly identify a comparator (even a hypothetical comparator) as a pre-condition to an analysis of discrimination has also been confirmed in recent case law such as *The Law Society v Bahl* where Elias J. suggested that the EAT and tribunals are now taking a more flexible approach to the need for a comparator in their analysis of direct discrimination.[96] This is discussed in more detail in the chapter on individual enforcement. Aileen McColgan has argued that there is a need to re-think the central place given to comparison in discrimination law which was discussed in Chapter 2 in the context of *Carson*.

Nevertheless, despite some possibility for a more flexible approach to comparators, the need for a comparator remains a central part of the definition of direct discrimination. As Lord Nicholls has confirmed in the passages from *Shamoon* cited above, comparison operates in a number of ways: the analysis of less favourable treatment is inherently comparative; comparison is defined and required by statute; and comparison is also relevant in the analysis of evidence.

This focus on symmetry in the concept of direct discrimination can be traced to the historical development of domestic discrimination law. Lester and Bindman state that the main concern with definitions of discrimination in the earlier Race Relations Act 1968 was that the term "less favourable treatment" may in fact introduce the danger of the US style "separate but equal" doctrine that had been so difficult to dislodge in the struggle for civil rights in the US.[97] The main concern during the formulation of the definition of direct dis-

94 [2003] W.L. 270780, at para.8. Also [2003] I.C.R. 337.
95 [2003] I.C.R. 337 at para.11.
96 [2003] I.R.L.R. 640 (EAT).
97 Anthony Lester and Geoffrey Bindman, *Race and Law*, (London: Longman, 1972) at 166.

crimination during this period was to ensure that definitions of equality did not include "unequal treatment". By contrast, modern criticisms of equality have concentrated on the way in which symmetrical concepts of equality which are said to inform the definition of direct discrimination can operate to undermine some of the main goals of discrimination law.

If equality is understood as a relational concept, then central to any question about whether a person has been treated equally are further questions about the relationship of that person to a number of other variables. For example, in order to determine whether there is equality we need to ask the question "equality of what", i.e. what is the particular act or conduct, or good or resources, in relation to which there is a demand for equality. The claim to equality does not in and of itself specify what the appropriate treatment should be or the precise amount of the resource or good (employment, money, etc.) to be redistributed.[98]

Questions about the appropriate choice of comparator inevitably become important in any discussion of equality. On this analysis, the issue of the choice of comparator raises a fundamental point about the ways in which the two entities that are claimed to be equal are similar and difference. Lord Denning makes this general point in *Peake*. He noted the way in which the SDA cannot be taken to climate all differences between men and women and stated:

> **"Page 974** [...]: Although the Act applies equally to men as to women, I must say it would be very wrong to my mind if this statute were thought to obliterate the differences between men and women or to do away with the chivalry and courtesy which we expect mankind to give womankind. The natural differences of sex must be regarded even in the interpretation of an Act of Parliament".[99]

More specifically, s.5(3) of the SDA s.4 of the RRA explicitly introduce into the choice of comparator the issue of equality and difference: comparison must be such that "the relevant circumstances in the one case are the same, or not materially different, in the other".

A number of questions open up for consideration: what are the principles that can guide the choice of a comparator in cases of direct discrimination; in what respects (and according to what values or goods) can it be said that the two entities are "the same" and "not materially different". As the discussion in Chapter 3 suggested, our perception of the values of these acts (e.g. fair procedure) or goods (e.g. education) may change depending on social and historical context and the nature of the good. These aspects add complexity to the choice of a comparator and identifying when two entities are similar or different. There is also a further analytical problem which arises because differences can be either natural or socially constructed.

The other problem raised by the need for a comparator is that it cannot

98 See Peter Westen, "The Empty Concept of Equality"
99 *Peake v Automative Products Ltd* [1977] I.C.R. 968, at p.974.

coherently deal with differences between relevant entities: e.g. men and women; racial majorities and minorities. The act of comparison allows the identification of the other entity provide answers to questions of comparison. In sex discrimination cases, the answers suggest that equality is in relation to men; and the norm or standard for treatment (whether an act or access to goods) is set by whatever norm or standard is available for men. This analysis will require decisions about the appropriate choice of comparator: under what circumstances are men and women alike or different. One possible answer to this question is that there are never any relevant differences between men and women that are relevant for analysis. This would mean that there needs to be a legislative response in all cases where there is a difference in treatment between any man and any woman. Legislation, however, does not seek to eliminate all different treatment between men and women. This does, also, raise an issue for direct discrimination because legal definitions (e.g. s.5(3) SDA; s.3(4) RRA) require that the relevant circumstances in the cases compared are not "materially different". In US terms, this is referred to as men and women need to be "similarly situated". In *Peake*, as we have seen, Denning L.J. refers to "natural difference" between men and women as a justification for applying different work place rules to men and women. Clearly, there will be certain differences between men and women, different races and religious groups, homosexuals and heterosexuals. A key issue in discrimination law is how these differences are identified and analysed.

There is a vast range of criticism of the requirements for a comparator in discrimination law. There are the arguments that make clear the limits of the comparison and symmetry at the heart of direct discrimination by pointing to its inability to cope intelligently with a *natural difference*, such as pregnancy. There are also objections that in discrimination law lead to comparison and symmetry that can be called "*assimilating difference*".[100]

E. *Natural Differences—Pregnancy Discrimination and the Choice of Comparator*

The first example—pregnancy—concerns natural (biological) difference. Domestic discrimination law has struggled to make conceptual sense of how pregnancy discrimination can fit within the paradigm of direct sex discrimination under the SDA. *Turley v Alders Department Stores Ltd.*[101] is a vivid illustration of the problem of choice of comparator in pregnancy discrimination cases. In that case the applicant claimed that she was dismissed on the grounds of pregnancy. The central question was whether—and if so how—dismissal on the grounds of pregnancy could be seen to be less favourable

[100] See for example Sandra Fredman, *Discrimination Law*, (Oxford: OUP, 2002) at pp.95–102. See the discussion in Ch.2 on Katherine O'Donovan: *Sexual Divisions in Law*, (London: Weidenfield and Nicholson, 1985).

[101] [1980] I.C.R. 66.

treatment on the grounds of sex. The EAT focused on the issue of comparison as the key to their analysis of direct discrimination under the SDA. They stated:

"You have to compare like with like. So, in the case of a pregnant woman there is an added difficulty in the application of subsection (1) (of s.1). Suppose that to dismiss her for pregnancy is to dismiss her on the ground of her sex. In order to see if she has been treated less favourably than a man the sense of the section is that you must compare like with like, and you cannot. She is a woman, as the Authorised Version of the Bible accurately puts it, with child, and there is no masculine equivalent."[102]

There was a remedy available to the applicant under s.34 of the Employment Protection Act 1975 which offered a legal remedy for dismissal on the ground of pregnancy without the need to rely on comparison.

The subsequent case of *Hayes v Malleable Working Men's Club*[103] also illustrates the problem in pregnancy discrimination cases. In *Hayes*, unlike *Turly*, the EAT did undertake the task of selecting and constructing a relevant comparator to a pregnant woman. Their solution was stated in the following terms:

"the proper approach is to ask whether pregnancy with its associated consequences is capable of being matched by analogous circumstances such as sickness applying to a man, and if so whether they are closely enough matched to enable a fair comparison to be made between the favourable-ness of treatment accorded to a man in one situation and to a man in the other."[104]

This analogy between a pregnant woman and sick man powerfully illustrates the problem with using comparison. The requirement to identify a comparator in this way fails to take into account the way in which the difference in question here—pregnancy—raises unique issues. The use of a sick man as a comparator for a pregnant woman is demeaning. Moreover, a sick man—unlike a pregnant woman—does not have the concomitant needs for time off for maternity or child care. This issue also illustrates problems with searching for the way in which two entities—men and women; blacks and white—are similar or different. We may be able to agree that the fact of pregnancy itself is a natural difference between men and women: but what other differences follow from this? Are the roles of childrearing also naturally women's role or are they socially constructed? The use of an inappropriate comparator in this context prevents discrimination law from addressing disadvantage caused to women because of pregnancy/maternity and also because of their childcare

[102] [1980] I.C.R. 66 at p.70.
[103] [1985] I.C.R. 703.
[104] [1985] I.C.R. 703, at p.708.

responsibilities. EU law has preferred to abandon the search for a comparator in pregnancy discrimination cases and treats pregnancy as an example of direct sex discrimination.[105] As we see from the pregnancy cases the search for a comparator can be problematic where difference is caused by natural difference. It may also be problematic where socially constructed differences are given weight through their prevalence or the power of hierarchy that supports them (stereotypes about the role of mothers).

Entrenching Social Differences

The second set of arguments that criticise comparison are, most notably, those of feminists, that discrimination law may replicate and entrench exactly those differences and stereotypes that concepts such as direct discrimination are designed to challenge. This objection can be called "*entrenching difference*". The following passage illustrates the main objections to this approach:

Catherine A. MacKinnon: "Difference and Dominance" in *Feminism Unmodified*
Cambridge, Mass.: Havard University Press, 1987

pp.37–38: "I will concede that there are many differences between women and men. I mean can you imagine elevating one half of the population and denigrating the other half and producing a population in which everyone is the same? What the sameness standard fails to notice is that men's differences from women are equal to women's differences from men. There is an *equality* there. Yet the sexes are not socially equal. The difference approach missed the fact that hierarchy of power produces real as well as fantasised differences, differences are also inequalities. [. . .]

Therefore the more unequal society gets, the *less* likely the difference doctrine is to be able to do anything about it, because unequal power creates both the appearance and the reality of sex differences along the same lines as it creates its sex inequalities."

One area in discrimination law where the search for a comparator will be problematic is in cases where the relevant differences between two otherwise potential comparators are themselves caused by either historical or present discrimination. One example of this is equal pay cases where job segregation makes the search for a comparator problematic in exactly those situations where women are most disadvantaged in terms of pay. This problem arises because in some low paid professions which are all female there will simply be no female comparator (the legislation on equal pay does not allow the use of a hypothetical comparator).

The search for a comparator can also cause problems in race discrimination

[105] Case 177/88 *Dekker* [1990] ECR 1–394; and Case C-32/93 *Webb* [1994] E.C.R. I–3567.

cases. The *Dhatt*[106] case also illustrates this point as well rasing a general question about the need for such a strict statutory definition of the form that comparison should take in analysing direct discrimination. In that case a man who was a non-EU Indian national resident in Britain was dismissed from McDonalds (the defendant employer) because he was not able to show that he had the right to work in Britain. The applicant complained that there had been direct race discrimination. He argued that he had been treated less favourably than EU nationals (which he used as the relevant comparator). The industrial tribunal found that the request to provide evidence of the right to work was discriminatory but that the comparison between his status and that of an EU national was not a comparison of like with like as required by s.3(4) RRA. They found that EU nationals required no official sanction to work, whereas non-EU nationals did. This, it was argued, was a "relevant circumstance" under s.3(4) that rendered the applicants case "materially different" from that of his preferred comparators, i.e. EU nationals. The Court of Appeal found that the appropriate comparison was between the applicant and individuals who were neither British nor EU citizens. That is, the difference in nationality was a "relevant circumstance" that was a "material difference" under s.3(4) RRA.

Dhatt is important for the present analysis of the concept of direct discrimination because it illustrates the danger of merging different parts of the conceptual analysis in direct discrimination. Significantly, as McColgan notes,[107] the issue of the immigration and work status of the applicant which concerned the Court of Appeal in *Dhatt* could have been dealt with by s.41 RRA. It provides that an otherwise discriminatory act is not unlawful if it is done in pursuance of or to comply with an Order in Council, and enactment of a Minister of the Crown; or to comply with any condition or requirement (before or after the RRA 76) imposed by a Minister of the Crown. Immigration rules relating to work permits would fall within this defense to direct race discrimination. By treating nationality as part of the analysis of direct discrimination via s.3(4) of the RRA 76, the *Dhatt* case fails to distinguish between two separate levels of enquiry: (a) the issue of choice of comparator; and (b) the issue of whether there is a s.41 RRA defense to direct race discrimination. Merging these two levels of analysis re-introduces the problems caused by the discriminatory consequences of nationality requirements into the definition of direct race discrimination.

Where discrimination is a structural problem the courts need to ensure that the "relevant circumstance" in the choice of comparator does not replicate the exact mischief that is being addressed. Here it is worth noting that by introducing nationality as a relevant circumstance that influences the analysis of

[106] *Dhatt v McDonalds Hamburgers Ltd* [1991] (CA) 1 W.L.R. 527. The *Dhatt* case has been cited and followed in *Ice Hockey Super League Ltd v Henry*, 2001 W.L. 482930 (EAT) which confirmed that the distinction between EC and non EC nationals was a relevant circumstance for the purposes of choice of comparator under s.3(4) RRA 76.

[107] A. McColgan, *Discrimination Law: Text, Cases and Materials*, (Oxford: Hart Publications, 200?) at p.50.

comparison (and choice of comparator) in *Dhatt*, the court is in fact introducing a factor that is (a) included within the definition of "racial grounds" within the RRA, and that is likely therefore (b) to be discriminatory on racial grounds. The possibility that the choice of an inappropriate comparator can reintroduce the exact mischief that direct discrimination is seeking to address is also acknowledged by Staughton L.J. in *Dhatt* who states: "It is true that this approach treats nationality as a relevant circumstance, and that nationality is itself discriminatory in racial terms."[108] A similar example of the risk of merging the comparator and justification parts of the analysis in direct discrimination can be seen in litigation under the HRA: for example, in *A v Secretary of State for the Home Department*, the Home Secretary made an order (under a derogation from ECHR, Art.5) that suspected terrorists who were aliens (non-UK nationals) could be detained without trial. The claimaints argued that the order discriminated against them on the basis of ECHR Art.14. In finding that there was no breach of ECHR, Art.14 the Court of Appeal had treated "right of abode" as a material circumstance and for that reason found that "British suspected terrorists" were not an appropriate comparator. The House of Lords recognised that the appropriate comparator was a British national who was a suspected terrorist and recognised that the Court of Appeal's analysis of the issue was just a way of reintroducing the discriminatory practice into the choice of the comparator. Lord Bingham stated:

"This is, however, to accept the correctness of the Secretary of State's choice of immigration control as a means to address the Al-Qaeda security problem, when the correctness of that choice is the issue to be resolved."[109]

More recently, the House of Lords has considered the issue of comparators in the context of ECHR, Art.14 again in *R (on the application of Carson) v Secretary of State for Work and Pensions*.[110] Aileen McColgan has questioned the focus on comparators in constitutional discrimination law and she has argued that the appropriate weight to comparators should be at the stage of "justification" rather than an earlier analysis of whether or not there has been discrimination.[111], and these issues are discussed in more detail in Chapter 2.

F. *Reform of the Concept of Direct Discrimination*

Justice the law reform body have made a number of suggestions that include a new definition of direct discrimination which takes a more flexible approach

108 *Dhatt*, ibid., at 541.
109 A and Ors [2004] UKHL 56.
110 [2005] UKHL, 37.; [2006] 1 A.C. 173.
111 Aileen McColgan, "Cracking the Comparator Problem: 'Discrimination', 'Equal Treatment' and the Role of Comparisons" (2006) 6 E.H.R.L.R. 650.

towards the protected grounds (allowing claims that combine grounds). This would also reduce the reliance on comparison as an explicit requirement of direct discrimination. They argue:

Justice: Briefing Paper for Discrimination Law Review Multiple Discrimination: How real are the problems and what are the solutions? (London: Justice, November 30, 2006)

"Can effect be given to multiple discrimination in domestic legislation?

The question is: how should domestic legislation give effect to multiple discrimination? We suggest a new definition of prohibited grounds, a new provision dealing with direct and indirect discrimination and the omission of current comparison provisions as well as specific provisions to deal with exceptions such as genuine occupational requirements.

Prohibited ground

We suggest the following definition for "prohibited ground", that is the grounds on which the legislation prohibits discrimination or harassment:

"A prohibited ground" means one or a combination of the following grounds:

- *colour, race, nationality or ethnic or national origins,*
- *sex,*
- *marital status,*
- *gender re-assignment,*
- *disability,*
- *sexual orientation,*
- *religion or belief, or*
- *age.*

This would enable claims to be brought on either single or multiple grounds.

Direct Discrimination

Direct discrimination could then be defined as:

A person directly discriminates against another if, on a prohibited ground a person "A"

a) treats a person "B' less favourably than "A" treats, has treated or would treat other persons, or
b) subjects "B" to a detriment.

Comparisons?

One frequently repeated question is how do you carry out a comparison where it is alleged that a person has suffered multiple discrimination? Indeed the issue of comparison has much vexed those considering these issues.

However we consider that it is much less of an issue than has been supposed. This is because the question who is a correct comparator is a *second* order question following on from the first question: why did the alleged discriminator act (or fail to act) in the way that they did? This was made quite clear by Lord Nicholls in his Opinion in *Shamoon v. Royal Ulster Constabulary*.

In this case he made if clear that if the court or tribunal can answer the second question. then it is clear what would be the treatment for another in a comparable circumstance.

Forensic considerations may include comparisons of course. Treatment of a comparator will often be critical evidence of discrimination, but, we suggest, it should not be an essential element in the definition of discrimination. The employer may point to his or her treatment of others as evidence of his non—discriminatory approach. However, the issue for the court or tribunal will be:

> *Is the apparently non—discriminatory treatment of others forensically relevant, where the complaint is that it was some special combination of grounds—and not a single ground—which was causative of the treatment under scrutiny?*

The answer may be yes or no. It will be for the court or tribunal to assess this.

Existing comparable situation provisions

We suggest that the new equality legislation should not include a provision equivalent to RRA 3(4), SDA 5(3) etc. which imposes a very strict test in the identification of a comparator. In our view such a provision is unnecessary and its inclusion puts too great an emphasis on finding a specific actual, or hypothetical, comparator.

It is worth noting that of all the EC countries that have implemented the equality directives none has a provision equivalent to these provisions of our current discrimination legislation. We submit, therefore, that such a provisions is not required for full implementation of the EC directives.

The wording suggested above does not entirely remove the comparative element because in order to establish 'less favourable treatment' or a 'detriment' a comparative assessment has to be made, and treatment of a comparator will often be relevant evidence of discrimination.''

This proposal would allow a more flexible approach towards protected grounds and comparators in a way that overcomes many of the problems faced by litigants who fall within one protected ground. Moreover, by eliminating the specific statutory requirement for comparators in RRA s.3(4); SDA s.5(3) it would allow courts to take a more flexible approach in cases of multiple discrimination. This is, in some ways, similar to the analysis that is recommended by Lord Nicholls in *Shamoon*. However, it could be argued that the Justice recommendations under-estimate the extent to which comparison is inherent in the analysis of direct discrimination in the present formulation of discrimination law. The Justice recommendations treat comparison as a second stage tier stage. They state in the passage cited above:

''This is because the question who is a correct comparator is a *second* order question following on from the first question: why did the alleged discriminator act (or fail to act) in the way that they did? This was made quite clear by Lord Nicholls in his Opinion in *Shamoon v. Royal Ulster Constabulary*. In this case he made if clear that if the court or tribunal can answer the second question. then it is clear what would be the treatment for another in a comparable circumstance. Forensic considerations may include comparisons of course. Treatment of a comparator will often be critical evidence of discrimination, but, we suggest, it should not be an essential element in the definition of discrimination."

The Justice approach assumes that a focus on establishing "less favourable treatment" will substantially reduce the role of the "comparator" in any definition of direct discrimination. However, this analysis under-estimates the extent to which an analysis of "less favourable treatment" already contains a substantial comparative aspect. An analysis of "less favourable treatment" is in many cases intrinsically a comparative enterprise. As discussed in Chapter 2 in the context of constitutional discrimination law, one way of minimising, rather than eliminating altogether, the detrimental impact of the "comparator" requirement might be to introduce the "comparator" analysis at the "justification" stage.[112]

Some of the problems in the definition of direct discrimination which are caused by the need for comparison can be overcome by statutory reform to RRA s.3(4) and the SDA s.5(3) of the type that is recommended by Justice and by taking a more flexible approach to prohibited grounds. However, as the radical critiques of direct discrimination that were discussed in Ch.2 argue, many of the challenges that are faced by direct discrimination relate to the inherent limits of the concept of equality and the individualistic nature of the concept of discrimination.

VI. Conclusion

The "comparative" nature of discrimination law has been the subject of considerable criticism[113] These criticisms have been discussed in this chapter, and they support the view that comparison is too individualistic and does not take sufficient account of the social context within which individuals find themselves, or of the difficulties involved in extracting individuals from their social context or social groups. On this view, the legal concept of direct discrimination's focus on individuals is an insufficient response to discrimination as a structural problem. It is also sometimes claimed that that a symmetrical concept of discrimination that makes comparison central to an analysis of direct discrimination can in some cases perpetuate the exact harms—of hierarchy and stigma—that discrimination law and policy seek to address. In some areas such as equal pay the search for a comparator can undermine the goal of challenging structural discrimination against women. In other areas,

[112] Aileen McColgan, "Cracking the Comparator Problem; Equal Treatment and the Role of Comparison", (2006) 6 EHRLR 650.

[113] Richard H. Fallon and Paul C. Weiler, "Firefighters v Stotts: Conflicting Models of Racial Justice" (1985) Supreme Court Review 1; see also Christopher McCrudden, "Institutional Discrimination" (1982) 2 OJLS 303.

such as pregnancy discrimination, the 'comparator' requirement has been abandoned (see Chapter 10).

The government's *Discrimination Law Review* (DLR) has recently considered the issue of comparators.[114] It has affirmed its commitment to what it terms the "British" model and the 'comparative' nature of discrimination law.[115] Yet, at the same time, the DLR implicitly recognises the limits of the comparative approach by remaining flexible in some contexts. For example, it proposes the removal of the comparator requirement in cases of discriminatory victimisation. Given that a significant number of discrimination cases are also employment cases, the differential definitions of victimisation are a further source of complexity and confusion, and this change should promote harmonisation[116]

Direct discrimination is therefore an area of real complexity. At a theoretical level, there is intense debate as to the justification for prohibiting direct discrimination and the nature of the wrong at which it is aimed. Concepts of direct discrimination are found in the European Convention, EU law and domestic statutory provisions, and the reconciliation of these concepts, where they differ, can pose problems for national courts. More broadly, issues such as the mental state of the defendant (is it necessary to have shown an intention to discriminate, or a motive for doing so, or is the 'but for' approach sufficient?) and the comparator requirement continue to be debated. Given that direct discrimination touches every area of discrimination law, the question and debates discussed in this chapter are thus relevant throughout the subject.

114 *Discrimination Law Review. A Framework for Fairness: Proposals for a Single Equality Act for Great Britain.* (Department of Communities and Local Government: London, 2007).

115 DLR, p.62, para.10 and para.1.16.

116 DLR, pp. 43–44, para.1.60–1.62.

5

INDIRECT DISCRIMINATION

I. Introduction

Indirect discrimination, often referred to in US legal terminology as "disparate impact" discrimination and in Canadian terminology as "adverse impact", is a key concept in discrimination law. Anti-discrimination legislation, constitutional equality clauses and human rights instruments usually explicitly or implicitly prohibit acts or omissions that result in indirect discrimination. This prohibition of indirect discrimination has considerably expanded the range and scope of discrimination law. It has made it possible to use the law as a tool to challenge certain deeply-rooted social practices that are not at first glance discriminatory, but which in practice impose disadvantages upon particular social groups. For this reason, it could be argued that the prohibition on indirect discrimination is potentially one of the most significant and transformative elements of discrimination law. However, it is also complex, intricate and difficult to understand. The prohibition on indirect discrimination generates endless controversy, dispute and uncertainty. This chapter will not examine each and every aspect of indirect discrimination as the concept is applied by courts and tribunals. Instead, we set out the key elements of indirect discrimination, establishing how the concept is defined, applied and understood. The aim in this chapter is to clarify the basic generic structure of indirect discrimination claims: the specific application of indirect discrimination law across each of the prohibited grounds of discrimination will be examined in more detail in the chapters in Part C detailing with each of these individual grounds. We also consider the possible goals of indirect discrimination law, as well as the conceptual boundaries of indirect discrimination and the limits to its use, effectiveness and application.

II. The Conceptual Basis for Indirect Discrimination

A. What Is Indirect Discrimination?

In straightforward terms, indirect discrimination occurs where the use of an apparently neutral and non-discriminatory way of distinguishing between individuals has a disproportionately negative impact upon members of particular groups, and the use of this method of making distinctions cannot be shown to be necessary and justified in the circumstances. In other words, indirect discrimination occurs where:

(i) a criterion is applied to differentiate between individuals which may not involve direct discrimination, but which

(ii) particularly disadvantages women, or particular ethnic or racial groups, or any other particular group, and

(iii) the use of this criterion cannot be shown to have been appropriate in the particular context at issue.

To give a classic example, giving preferential treatment to full-time employees at the expense of part-time workers may constitute indirect discrimination against women. At first glance, differentiating between full-time and part-time workers appears not to involve any discrimination. In applying this distinction, there is no direct discrimination on any of the standard prohibited grounds of gender, race, sexual orientation, age and so on: there is direct discrimination between the two categories of worker, but not on any of the historically prohibited grounds. However, women are at present much more likely to work part-time than men, partially due to current social patterns that tend to result in women assuming greater child-care responsibilities. As a result, discriminating against part-time workers may have a disproportionately negative impact on female employees. Therefore, the application of an apparently neutral distinction may have a "disparate impact" upon women. If this is the case, then the burden to show that the distinction between part-time and full-time employees is necessary and justified in the circumstances falls upon the employer. If the employer cannot discharge this burden, then indirect discrimination will be held to exist.

Christopher McCrudden has pointed out that the law's focus on indirect discrimination historically accompanied the identification and recognition of a phenomenon known as "institutional discrimination". While direct discrimination no longer turns on proof of prejudiced intention on the part of the respondent, his discussion of "institutional discrimination" in the context of race still helps to explain the differing roles of direct and indirect discrimination as legal concepts.

Christopher McCrudden
"Institutional Discrimination" (1982) 2 OJLS 303

[305-6:] "By the later 1960s...the predominant approach in the United States changed to one which emphasized institutional and structural reasons for exclusion in addition to 'prejudiced discrimination'. Adjectival use of 'institutional' or 'structural' before 'discrimination' or 'racism' became common to describe the exclusion of blacks from housing and employment for whatever reason ... Knowles and Prewit in 1969 termed as 'institutional racism' any situation where 'behaviour has become so well institutionalized that the individual generally does not have to exercise choices to operate in a racist manner. The rules and procedures of the large organization have already prestructured the choice. The individual only has to conform to the operating norms of the organization and the institution will do the discriminating for him' [*Institutional Racism in America* (Prentice Hall, 1969), p.143].

[311:] By the late 1960s there was thus developing a concern that the demonstrably unequal position of the 'immigrant', particularly in the labour market, could not entirely be explained by the largely immigrant status of the minority worker or by 'prejudiced' discrimination ... Studies began to turn up examples where neither prejudiced discrimination nor immigrant disadvantage contributed at all (or only in part) to the disadvantaged status of minority groups. In Britain too 'institutional racism' became a term used to describe such inequalities. As in the United States one example of such discrimination was seen to be the direct effects in the present of past discrimination, leading to minority group workers not even applying for housing or for work at a particular plant ...

[336:] Initially the 1965 and 1968 [U.K.] Race Relations Acts concentrated on a notion of 'direct discrimination' as it later came to be called, i.e. race was made irrelevant for the distribution of certain resources ....

[However] There was a growing awareness of the limited coverage of this definition of discrimination coinciding with an increased awareness of the problems of immigrant disadvantage, urban deprivation, and in particular with the development in Britain of the idea of institutional discrimination. This definition [i.e., of direct discrimination] was regarded as limited for several reasons ... Firstly, it was difficult to establish that it had been breached because [at the time] it required proving that a person had a discriminatory intention. Secondly, this concept of discrimination had little effect on the use of criteria which had the effect of excluding disproportionate numbers of minority groups irrespective of intention. It was limited, for example, in looking at what happened after a black worker came to a factory looking for a job, but ignoring the fact that even if his racial origin was not directly taken into account at the time he applied there was a greater chance that he would lack those attributes which went to make a successful applicant."

The distinction between direct and indirect discrimination is important. Direct discrimination involves differential treatment on the grounds of a "suspect" or "controlled" characteristic, i.e. on the grounds of race, sex, disability or one of the other prohibited grounds. In contrast, indirect discrimination, as indicated above, involves differential treatment on the basis of a "neutral" characteristic, where the application of this differentiating factor will disproportionately affect a particular group. This form of discrimination will only be prohibited if the particular group affected is defined by its possession of a suspect or controlled characteristic, i.e. before indirect discrimination will usually be found to exist, usually the disproportionately disadvantaged group will have to be defined by their age, sexual orientation, gender, religious belief, ethnic or racial origin or any other suspect characteristic.

This means that indirect discrimination is often thought to be primarily concerned with *group disadvantage*: the focus is on prohibiting forms of discrimination that disproportionately disadvantage vulnerable groups. In contrast, it is assumed that direct discrimination tends to be more focused on *individual disadvantage*: the emphasis is on prohibiting the treatment of individuals based on their possession of a suspect characteristic. Nonetheless, Christopher McCrudden in a further extract from the article cited above has suggested that there are important similarities between the two:

"Both take the characteristics of groups into account only insofar as it is necessary to do so in order to allow the individual to compete unhampered by restrictions which effectively keep individuals within groups and which are irrelevant or detrimental to rational decision-making on merit. The concepts are also similar in that they do not assume that one particular pattern of distribution of goods should result from these procedures. Both look to how the distribution was arrived at rather than the outcome."[1]

A further apparent difference is that direct discrimination involves less favourable treatment linked directly to a suspect characteristic, while indirect discrimination involves discrimination against a group that arises as a result of the "fallout" from the application of an apparently non-discriminatory criterion. Many social practices have a disparate impact upon different groups, so indirect discrimination could have a very wide reach. However, social practices that disadvantage particular groups may sometimes be necessary and justified. For example, requiring airline pilots to have excellent eyesight may disadvantage persons in older age groups, but may be necessary to ensure the safety of passengers. Therefore, unlike direct discrimination, which cannot—outside of Art.14 of the European Convention on Human Rights[2]—be justified outside of the specific contexts of age and disability discrimination, practices that would otherwise amount to indirect discrimination can be shown to be *objectively justified* in law. In this way, the potentially vast reach of the prohibition on indirect discrimination, which could cover a very wide range of social practices, is compensated for by the possibility that the use of a practice that has a disparate impact upon a particular group can be objectively justified. For this to happen, EU and national law now require that a criterion or requirement that has a disparate impact upon a particular group needs to be:

(a) applied to achieve a legitimate aim or need;

[1] "Institutional Discrimination" (1982) 2 OJLS 303, 344.

[2] Although note the argument as to whether it may be justified under EU law: see chapter 4.

(b) reasonably linked to the aim sought to be achieved; and

(c) proportionate and necessary in the circumstances, taking into account factors such as the impact on the disadvantaged group, the nature of the legitimate aim or need in question, and the position of the employer or service provider applying the criterion.

This *objective justification* test is a key element of indirect discrimination case law: developed mainly in the case law of the European Court of Justice (ECJ), it is similar to the proportionality test used in other areas of EU law and has overlaps in the case law of the European Court of Human Rights (ECHR).

B. *Justifying the Prohibition on Indirect Discrimination*

Various attempts have been made to provide a solid normative basis for the prohibition of indirect discrimination. John Gardner, for example, has suggested that the legislative prohibition of direct discrimination is based upon standard *corrective* principles, whereby the ban on direct discrimination prevents and compensates for the direct harm inflicted on the fundamental autonomy of individuals by unjustified discriminatory treatment: in contrast, he argues that the prohibition on indirect discrimination is based upon concepts of *distributionist* justice. It ensures that social practices that have an adverse impact on particular disadvantaged groups are prohibited, even if the person applying the rule or practice in question is not directly harming the autonomy of particular individuals.

John Gardner, "Discrimination as Injustice" (1996) 16 OJLS 367

[359-60:] "In committing an act of unlawful [indirect] discrimination I commit no corrective injustice against anyone. There is no previous act of mine, or anyone else's, which by discriminating indirectly I am failing or refusing to make up for. What I do is merely apply to apply an unjustifiable standard which people of one sex or race find it harder to comply with than people of another, to the detriment of someone who is a member of the former sex or race. My failure is fundamentally a geometric failure, a failure to divide up in legally acceptable proportions the opportunities over which I exercise control. It is not an arithmetic failure, a failure to replace some opportunity which I, or indeed some other protagonist, earlier subtracted. Of course it *happens* that in our society someone *did* earlier subtract opportunities from black people and from women. That is why black people and women are now so seriously disadvantaged, particularly in the labour market. It is also why race and gender have developed their special symbolic importance in our public culture, so that discrimination on these grounds now has the powerful social meaning that it does, making the case for thorough legal regulation so unanswerable, even if it has significant economic or social costs. But the key thing is that the primary legal duty not to discriminate indirectly focuses centrally on the relative disadvantage of some applicants *as such* rather than on the past actions which established and maintained their relative disadvantage. For that reason it is essentially a duty of distributive, not corrective, justice."

Gardner justifies this application of distributionist justice on the basis of a liberal concern with individual autonomy: the justification for the ban on indirect discrimination is derived from the core rationale for prohibiting discrimination. In other words, the prohibition on indirect discrimination is secondary and based upon the core principle of discrimination law, the ban on direct discrimination.

John Gardner, "On the Ground of her Sex(uality)" (1998) 18 OJLS 167

[182-3:] "There are various moral arguments, for example, for attending to the discriminatory side-effects of some decisions as well as the discriminatory grounds on which they were reached. These arguments supply the foundation for the secondary paradigm of *indirect* discrimination (or "disparate impact" discrimination) found in today's more sophisticated anti-discrimination statutes. For example: prohibitions on direct discrimination alone typically do rather little to expand the options of those who have been discriminated against in the past, when the world has been so comprehensively organized around their absence. Making progress with the problem may therefore require one not only to control perpetuation of the direct discrimination which was the original source of the problem, but also to add some positive duties to make the options from which those discriminated against were excluded genuinely acceptable and hospitable to them so that they aren't still excluded in effect even though not on purpose. This is where the indirect discrimination paradigm comes in. But it does not replace the original paradigm of direct discrimination, on the moral significance of which, as my remarks have just illustrated, it depends for its own moral force."[3]

Others have questioned these arguments and their focus on liberal individualism. Oran Doyle for example has argued that the moral justification for indirect discrimination should not be seen as a secondary follow-on from the prohibition on direct discrimination, but should instead be seen as justified by reference to substantive equality principles: indirect discrimination for him is an essential tool for combating unjust practices that subordinate disadvantaged groups, and its legitimacy can be derived directly from this important role.[4] Denise Réaume has suggested that the extension of dis-

[3] See also John Gardner, "Liberals and Unlawful Discrimination" (1989) 9 O.J.L.S. 1; "Private Activities and Personal Autonomy: At the Margins of Anti-discrimination Law" in Bob Hepple and Erika Szyszczak (eds), *Discrimination: the Limits of the Law* (Mansell, 1992); "Discrimination as Injustice" (1996) 16 O.J.L.S. 367.

[4] O. Doyle, *Constitutional Equality Law* (Thomson Round Hall, 2004), pp. 212-251: see also O. Doyle, "State of Denial: Equality, Autonomy and Indirect Discrimination" (2007) 27 O.J.L.S. 537.

crimination law to include indirect discrimination is based upon a recognition that that the protection of the human dignity of disadvantaged groups requires the legal regulation of practices that contribute to their subordination.[5]

Irrespective of its precise normative basis, it is clear that the prohibition on indirect discrimination is an essential component part of any discrimination law system (even if it is merged within a broader approach that combines elements of direct and indirect discrimination, as with the "accommodation" approach adopted by the Canadian Supreme Court to interpreting Canadian human rights legislation: see the conclusion to this chapter). Without this prohibition, it would be easy for deliberate discrimination to be camouflaged, by being dressed up in the form of facially neutral requirements. In addition, if indirect discrimination was not prohibited, then most social practices that contribute to the disadvantages faced by women, ethnic minorities and other underprivileged groups would remain outside of the scope of the law.

C. *Griggs v Duke Power and the Emergence of Indirect Discrimination Analysis*

The necessity of including disparate impact analysis within discrimination law was recognised by the US Supreme Court in the famous and ground-breaking case of *Griggs v Duke Power*,[6] where it interpreted the US Civil Rights Act 1964 as extending to disparate impact cases in order to ensure that the Act was capable of achieving its objective of ensuring equality of employment opportunities. In *Griggs*, a power company required all employees applying for jobs within higher-paid departments to score well in two separate aptitude tests and to have a high school graduation certificate. These requirements were not directly related to any particular aspect of the jobs being performed, but had the *de facto* effect of excluding Afro-Americans from the higher-paid posts, as Afro-Americans as a group were less likely to score highly in the particular aptitude tests used and were also less likely to have obtained a high school graduation diploma. In other words, the employer was applying facially-neutral tests (the aptitude tests and the requirement for high school graduation) which had the effect of considerably disadvantaging Afro-Americans. However, the Supreme Court interpreted Title VII of the Civil Rights Act as providing that the application of facially neutral tests that had a disparate impact upon particular racial groups had to be shown to be "reasonably related" to the job or position for which the test is required. In the circumstances, the aptitude tests and high-school certificate requirements were not "reasonably related" to the performance of the jobs in the power station that were at issue, and therefore the employers were in breach of the Act.

[5] Denise Réaume, "Discrimination and Dignity" (2004) Louisiana L. Rev. 1.
[6] (1971) 401 U.S. 424.

Griggs v Duke Power Co. (1971) 401 U.S. 424

BURGER CJ:
[430–431] "The objective of Congress in the enactment of Title VII is plain from the language of the statute. It was to achieve equality of employment opportunities and remove barriers that have operated in the past to favor an identifiable group of white employees over other employees. Under the Act, practices, procedures, or tests neutral on their face, and even neutral in terms of intent, cannot be maintained if they operate to "freeze" the status quo of prior discriminatory employment practices...

Discriminatory preference for any group, minority or majority, is precisely and only what Congress has proscribed. What is required by Congress is the removal of artificial, arbitrary, and unnecessary barriers to employment when the barriers operate invidiously to discriminate on the basis of racial or other impermissible classification.

Congress has now provided that tests or criteria for employment or promotion may not provide equality of opportunity merely in the sense of the fabled offer of milk to the stork and the fox. On the contrary, Congress has now required that the posture and condition of the job-seeker be taken into account. It has—to resort again to the fable—provided that the vessel in which the milk is proffered be one all seekers can use. The Act proscribes not only overt discrimination but also practices that are fair in form, but discriminatory in operation. The touchstone is business necessity. If an employment practice which operates to exclude Negroes cannot be shown to be related to job performance, the practice is prohibited.

On the record before us, neither the high school completion requirement nor the general intelligence test is shown to bear a demonstrable relationship to successful performance of the jobs for which it was used. Both were adopted, as the Court of Appeals noted, without meaningful study of their relationship to job-performance ability...

The Court in *Griggs* therefore set out the key elements of "disparate impact" or indirect discrimination, with Burger C.J. referring to "business necessity" as the required standard of justification.[7] This interpretation of Title VII as extending to disparate impact cases was based upon a purposive interpretation of the legislation: if the Act could not apply to such situations, then its impact would inevitably be blunted.

This recognition by the US Supreme Court of the functional necessity of any discrimination law framework being able to address questions of disparate impact has had a considerable impact. The US law has developed since *Griggs*, and an express cause of action for disparate impact was established in the Civil Rights Act 1991.[8] As the law currently stands in respect of private employers subject to Title VII, the plaintiff bringing a disparate impact case must prove, generally through statistical comparisons, that the practice at issue has a substantial adverse impact on a protected group. If the plaintiff establishes the existence of a disparate impact, the employer must then justify the practice by proving that the challenged practice is "job-related for the

[7] See also *Albemarle Paper Co. ltd. v Moody* 422 U.S. 405 (1975).
[8] 42 U.S.C. § 2000e-2(k)(1)(A) (2000).

position in question and consistent with business necessity."[9] Even if the employer proves business necessity, the plaintiff may still win by showing that the employer has refused to adopt an alternative employment practice which would satisfy the employer's legitimate business needs without having a disparate impact on a protected class.

The necessity of discrimination law frameworks to make provision for controls upon indirect discrimination has also been recognised in the UK and by the EU. The UK government drew upon *Griggs* and the US experience in making explicit provision for a prohibition on indirect discrimination in the Sex Discrimination Act 1975 and the Race Relations Act 1976. The ECJ followed a similar logic in recognising that the Equal Treatment Directive extended to indirect discrimination. Subsequent EU legislation has made express provision requiring the prohibition of indirect discrimination.

Despite its contested conceptual basis, indirect discrimination has therefore become recognised as a necessary and indispensable part of effective discrimination legislation. Its emergence as a key element in the repertoire of discrimination law lies in its practical utility: it can go beyond the more limited range of direct discrimination to attack deeply-rooted and unjustifiable structural forms of discrimination.

However, the underlying conceptual uncertainty has resulted in indirect discrimination and disparate impact analysis tending to occupy an uncertain place within some constitutional law frameworks. In *Washington v Davis*,[10] the US Supreme Court recognised that the disparate impact analysis which it had recently developed in *Griggs* could be applied to cases brought under the equal protection clause of the US Bill of Rights. However, in applying this analysis under the Equal Protection Clause, the Supreme Court held that discriminatory *motive* was required before disparate impact generated by state action would be held to be unlawful. The Court was of the view that "disproportionate impact is not irrelevant, but it is not the sole touchstone of an invidious racial discrimination forbidden by the Constitution". The stricter test applied under the Civil Rights Act 1964 post-*Griggs* was therefore not carried across to the constitutional context: the Court considered that the Equal Protection Clause could not be construed as prohibiting unintentional discrimination.[11]

The approach set out in *Washington v Davis* was subsequently applied in

[9] In *Wards Cove Packing v Atonio* 490 U.S. 642 (1989), the Supreme Court ruled that an employer was only obliged under Title VII of the Civil Rights Act 1964 to produce evidence of the *existence* of a legitimate business justification in response to the applicant making out a prima facie case of disparate impact to escape liability: this was subsequently reversed by Congress in the Civil Rights Act 1991, which established that the burden rested on the employer to demonstrate that any particular practice is job related for the position in question and consistent with business necessity.

[10] 426 U.S. 229 (1976).

[11] For a recent critique of this approach to the Equal Protection Clause, see Richard Primus, "Equal Protection Clause and Disparate Impact: Round Three" (2003) 117 Harvard Law Review 493.

Village of Arlington Heights v Metropolitan Housing Development Corp,[12] with the effect that the Equal Protection Clause has rarely proved to be a happy hunting ground for disparate impact claims: the existence of intent to discriminate can be very difficult to prove. This lack of a firm constitutional basis for disparate impact analysis has arguably seeped into how the US courts have interpreted the civil rights legislation, despite the influence of *Griggs*. Under the Civil Rights Act, compensatory and punitive damages for disparate impact can only be obtained if an intention to discriminate was present.[13] In the context of the US age discrimination legislation, the US Supreme Court recently recognised in *Smith v Jackson* that disparate impact claims could be brought on the basis of age, but exempted situations where the differentiating criteria at issue were "based on reasonable factors other than age."[14] The US courts have also tended to set high evidentiary hurdles before a *prima facie* disparate impact case can be made out, often requiring statistical evidence that is difficult to obtain.[15] They have also been increasingly willing to accept business justification arguments, in particular employer arguments that particular practices or evaluation tests were linked to job performance.[16]

Disparate impact claims have a significant presence in US discrimination law, but their overall impact has tended to be muted and diluted in recent years. What appears to be lacking is a firm constitutional recognition of the central importance of indirect discrimination and disparate impact analysis as a key element in combating inequality. In contrast, indirect discrimination and disparate impact analysis has been more readily accepted in judicial interpretations of constitutional non-discrimination provisions in other jurisdictions, a good example being the case law dealing with s.15(1) of the Canadian Charter of Rights.[17] This openness at the constitutional level has been mirrored in how the Canadian legislative framework has been interpreted and applied to give wide-ranging protection against indirect discrimination.

The status of indirect discrimination analysis is a little less clear in the UK context, where indirect discrimination is a concept found in domestic statutory protections against discrimination and—with differences of formulation—within the case law based upon Art.14 of the European Convention on Human Rights (a relatively recent development) and in EU law.[18] As already discussed

[12] 429 U.S. 252 (1977).

[13] See Title 42 USC 1981, s. 1977A.

[14] 544 U.S. 228 (2005).

[15] See e.g. *New York City Transit Authority v Beazer* 440 U.S. 568 (1979).

[16] See N. DeSario, "Reconceptualizing Meritocracy: The Decline of Disparate Impact Discrimination Law" (2003) 38 Harvard Civil Rights-Civil Liberties Law Review 479.

[17] See chapter 4, section II.

[18] As already discussed in previous chapters, where a case falls within its scope, Art.14 may be used in domestic law to secure the reinterpretation of legislation (whether concerned with discrimination or any other subject-matter) under s.3 of the Human Rights Act 1998, remedies against public authorities (judicial review or damages) under s.6 of that Act, or a declaration of incompatibility under s.4. Where a case falls within the scope of directly effective provisions of EU law, domestic legislation must be read in the light of those provisions and may be "disapplied" for incompatibility.

in chapter 4, in relation to direct discrimination, and in more general terms in chapter 2, the extent to which the notions of indirect discrimination in play at these different "levels"—the Convention, EU law and domestic legislation—are reconcilable is an important problem for national courts, as is the question of how far ECHR and EU law notions of prohibited discrimination operate in a "constitutional" fashion in domestic law. These questions also come to the fore when looking at indirect discrimination. EU law has developed a clear stance on indirect discrimination in the context of gender, which has considerably expanded and strengthened the UK legislative prohibition on indirect discrimination. In contrast, the ECHR case law has been much more tentative. As a result, until very recently, the "constitutional" dimension of indirect discrimination analysis has tended to be manifested through EU legislation and case law rather than via the application of the ECHR. Therefore, in contrast to the approach adopted in the previous chapter, it is necessary to examine the development of disparate analysis approaches within the public law context after an initial examination of the much more developed discrimination law framework, which has absorbed a much clearer and structured approach to indirect discrimination from EU law.

III. The Evolution of Indirect Discrimination in UK and EU Law

The initial tentative steps taken in the 1960s to prohibit forms of race discrimination contained no reference to concepts of indirect discrimination. Similarly, the Equal Pay Act 1970 contained no explicit prohibition on indirect forms of pay inequality *per se*. However, in framing UK race and sex discrimination legislation in the mid 1970s, the then Labour government decided to include an explicit prohibition on indirect discrimination, having examined the *Griggs* decision and concluded that such a ban was essential to ensure effective protection for disadvantaged groups.[19] This resulted in the Sex Discrimination Act 1975 and the Race Relations Act 1976 containing explicit prohibitions on indirect discrimination, imposed upon employers and service providers. Christopher McCrudden has thus noted that the legislature in the 1970s tended to equate the problems of race and sex discrimination, and the definition of indirect discrimination used in the 1975 Act was used as a model for that in the 1976 Act.[20]

[19] See Christopher McCrudden, 'Institutional Discrimination' (1982) 2 O.J.L.S. 303, 335-6, 345-6 (although note the differences between the US and UK approaches noted at 345-65); Anthony Lester, 'Discrimination: What Can Lawyers Learn From History' [1994] P.L. 224.

[20] "Institutional Discrimination", id., 337.

Sex Discrimination Act 1975

S. 1(1)—In any circumstances relevant for the purposes of any provision of this Act, a person discriminates against a woman if—

(b) he applies to her a requirement or condition which he applies or would apply equally to a man but—

(i) which is such that the proportion of women who can comply with it is considerably smaller than the pro-portion of men who can comply with it, and

(ii) which he cannot show to be justifiable irrespective of the sex of the person to whom it is applied, and

(iii) which is to her detriment because she cannot comply with it."

Section 1(1)(b) of the Race Relations Act 1976 made similar provision.

These provisions ensured that indirect discrimination would be prohibited in domestic law. However, they were initially given an often narrow interpretation by domestic courts. For example, the phrase "requirement or condition" was interpreted by the Court of Appeal in the race discrimination case *Perera v Civil Service Commission*[21] as only covering criteria which the complainant *had* to satisfy to get the post in question. If factors were taken into account which were not determinative, then their impact was not caught by the prohibition. In *Perera*, the applicant alleged that the Commissioners had subjected him to indirect discrimination on the grounds of his ethnic origin and nationality, on the basis that various factors were taken into account as "plus" or "minus" factors in assessing his application, including age, British nationality, command of the English language and experience in the UK. As none of these factors were decisive in themselves, they were deemed not to constitute a "requirement or condition" and therefore their disparate impact on recently-arrived migrant groups was not covered by s.1(1)(b) of the RRA.[22] This restriction to the scope of protection still applies to indirect discrimination based on colour or nationality, or forms of indirect discrimination linked to race, ethnic origin or nationality which otherwise falls outside the scope of the Race Equality Directive 2000 (more on this below). As McColgan notes,[23] a similar constrained interpretation was taken when it came to assessing whether an individual had suffered a "detriment", and considerable leeway was given to employers to justify disparate impact in cases such as *Panesar v Nestlé*.[24]

However, the ECJ in interpreting the former Art.119 (now Art.141) of the EC

[21] [1983] I.R.L.R. 166.

[22] See also *Meer v London Borough of Tower Hamlets* [1988] I.R.L.R. 399.

[23] See Aileen McColgan, *Discrimination Law: Text, Cases and Materials* 2nd edn (Oxford: Hart, 2005) pp. 92–105.

[24] [1980] I.C.R. 144.

Treaty, the Equal Treatment Directive 76/207, the Equal Pay Directive 75/117/EC and other EC discrimination legislation has developed an expansive concept of indirect discrimination. This has had a considerable influence on UK law, both through the direct application by UK courts of the ECJ's gender discrimination case law in line with the supremacy of EU law, and the influence of this case law on the application of the prohibition on indirect race discrimination in the RRA, which although until recently not directly controlled by EU law has been heavily influenced by the ECJ's gender discrimination jurisprudence. This has resulted in a gradual strengthening of the controls on indirect discrimination in UK law.

Article 119 (now Art.141) EC established the principle of equal pay for equal work, but contains no reference to indirect discrimination per se. However, Art.2 of the 1976 Equal Treatment Directive opened the door for the ECJ to give effect to the concept of indirect discrimination by its provision that "there shall be no discrimination whatsoever on grounds of sex either directly or indirectly". The Directive thus explicitly prohibits both direct and indirect discrimination, but does not define what is meant by indirect discrimination. In the case of *Jenkins*, the ECJ held that paying a lower hourly wage to part-time employees could constitute indirect sex discrimination, as women were more likely to work part-time: indirect discrimination therefore made its appearance in ECJ case law and in its interpretation of the Equal Pay Directive and Art.119 EC.[25]

In Directive 97/80 on the burden of proof in cases about sex discrimination, Art.2(2) defined, for the first time in EU legislation, what was meant by indirect discrimination. According to the Directive, indirect discrimination exists:

"where an apparently neutral provision, criterion or practice disadvantages a substantially higher proportion of the members of one sex unless that provision, criterion or practice is appropriate and necessary and can be justified by objective factors unrelated to sex."

Subsequently, the major ECJ decision of *Bilka-Kaufhaus*[26] established the test for indirect discrimination in EU law that has now become the template for determining whether indirect discrimination exists in UK law as well. The ECJ in *Bilka* interpreted Art.119's requirement for equality between male and female workers as extending to prohibit indirect discrimination, even in the absence of an express reference to the concept in the text of the EC Treaty. The Court also held that if the plaintiff can produce statistical evidence to demonstrate that significantly more women than men are placed at a disadvantage by a provision which is facially neutral, a presumption of indirect discrimination arises. The burden of proof then shifts to the respondent, who

[25] Case C-96/80, *Jenkins v Kingsgate (Clothing Productions) Ltd* [1981] E.C.R. 911.
[26] C-170/84, [1986] I.R.L.R. 317.

has to justify the use of the provision in question by demonstrating the existence of an objective justification. Therefore, the Court held that Art.119 (now Art.141) EC is infringed where part-time employees are excluded from an occupational pension scheme, if that exclusion affects a far greater number of women than men, unless the exclusion is shown to be based on objectively justified factors. The ECJ was also of the view that the factors cited as giving rise to an objective justification could not be themselves related to or based upon any discrimination on the ground of sex.

Case C-170/84, *Bilka—Kaufhaus GmbH v Karin Weber von Hartz* [1986] E.C.R. 1607

[36] "It is for the national court, which has sole jurisdiction to make findings of fact, to determine whether and to what extent the grounds put forward by an employer to explain the adoption of a pay practice which applies independently of a worker' s sex but in fact affects more women than men may be regarded as objectively justified economic grounds. If the national court finds that the measures chosen by Bilka correspond to a real need on the part of the undertaking, are appropriate with a view to achieving the objectives pursued and are necessary to that end, the fact that the measures affect a far greater number of women than men is not sufficient to show that they constitute an infringement of Article 119.

[37] ... under Article 119 a department store company may justify the adoption of a pay policy excluding part-time workers, irrespective of their sex, from its occupational pension scheme on the ground that it seeks to employ as few part-time workers as possible, where it is found that the means chosen for achieving that objective correspond to a real need on the part of the undertaking, are appropriate with a view to achieving the objective in question and are necessary to that end."

The ECJ in *Danfoss* adopted the same test in interpreting the prohibition of indirect discrimination in the Equal Treatment Directive.[27] The ECJ approach as it developed in the case law gradually began to percolate through into the interpretation by the domestic courts of the indirect discrimination provisions of the SDA and the RRA. This was seen by some as a slow process, with some commentators expressing regular criticism about how the justification test in particular was being applied by the domestic courts.[28] However, gradually the ECJ approach became embedded in domestic law. In *Rainey v Greater Glasgow Health Board*,[29] the House of Lords applied the approach adopted by the ECJ in *Bilka Kaufhaus*, finding that the objective justification test to be applied in domestic law involved an assessment of whether there is a reason for the

[27] C-109/88, [1989] E.C.R. 3199.

[28] See e.g. T. K. Hervey, "Justification for Indirect Sex Discrimination in Employment: European Community and United Kingdom Law Compared" (1991) 40 International and Comparative Law Quarterly 807.

[29] [1987] I.C.R. 129.

difference which is not discriminatory, whether the means selected to achieve the chosen aim corresponds to a real need on the part of the employer, whether the means are appropriate to achieve that aim, and whether they are necessary to achieve that aim. The Lords also held that the same test for indirect discrimination applied in equal pay and sex discrimination claims.

At first, a less strict approach was adopted for race discrimination claims, over which the ECJ did not have jurisdiction prior to the insertion of Art.13 EC. In *Ojutiku & Uburoni v Manpower Services Commission*[30] the Court of Appeal held that it was not essential for an employer in justifying a requirement or condition that had a disparate impact upon particular ethnic groups to prove that its use was essential for the business in question, and appeared to have different views on what standard of justification should be applied. Eveleigh J. suggested that a practice would be justified if an employer "produces reasons for doing something would be acceptable to right-thinking people as sound and tolerable reasons for so doing"[31]: this was a much less onerous standard than that established in *Bilka Kaufhaus*. In contrast, Stephenson L.J. took a more rigorous approach, closer to the approach adopted by the ECJ: the justification test "requires the party applying the discriminatory condition to prove it to be justifiable in all the circumstances on balancing its discriminatory effect against the discriminator's need for it ... that need is what is reasonably needed by the party who applies the condition."[32]

In *Hampson v Department of Education and Science*[33] the Court of Appeal preferred Stephenson L.J.'s approach, stating that tribunals should apply an objective test, balancing the discriminatory effects of the condition in question against the reasonable needs of the person applying the condition: only if the disparate impact could be objectively justified by the reasonable needs could the condition be "justifiable". The Court of Appeal was also of the view that there should be no significant difference between the correct test for whether a requirement or condition was "justifiable" under the RRA and the equal pay and sex discrimination legislation: it therefore indicated that courts and tribunals applying the race discrimination legislation should follow the approach set out by the Lords in *Rainey*, which meant by extension the ECJ approach set out in *Bilka Kaufhaus*.

Therefore, in many respects, domestic law absorbed the ECJ approach. Nonetheless, some differences remained. The ECJ in *Enderby v Frenchay Health Authority*[34] indicated that even if a provision was not a "requirement' or "condition", it could still be held to give rise to indirect sex discrimination under EU law: in other words, it took a different approach from the legislative interpretation adopted by the domestic courts in *Perera* that a claim for indirect discrimination could only be made in respect of a determinative factor. The

[30] [1982] I.C.R. 661.
[31] Ibid., 668.
[32] Ibid., 674.
[33] [1989] I.R.L.R. 69.
[34] [1994] I.C.R. 112.

EAT in *Falkirk Council and others v Whyte and others*[35] held that indirect sex discrimination and equal pay claims could in the wake of *Enderby* be made in respect of non-determinative factors, on the basis that this was necessary to give effect to the requirements of EU law. However, as the same requirement did not apply to race discrimination, the *Perera* approach continued to be applied in race discrimination claims until the implementation of the Race Equality Directive 2000, and still continues to apply as discussed above to cases based on nationality and skin colour. Similarly, the shift in the burden of proof required in indirect sex discrimination cases did not apply in race discrimination claims until the implementation of the 2000 Directive, and still does not in claims based solely on nationality and skin colour. Also, the application of the ECJ case law by domestic courts has not always appeared to adhere closely to the approach of the Court of Justice: in particular, domestic courts and tribunals have not always applied the objective justification test with the same degree of rigour as the ECJ case law indicates is appropriate. However, the gap between UK and EU standards appears to be gradually closing, enhancing protection against indirect discrimination.

IV. The Current Ambit of Indirect Discrimination

As noted above, for the most part, the ECJ approach to indirect discrimination is now applied by domestic courts. The basic approach established in *Bilka Kaufhaus* has also been extended by the Racial Equality Directive 2000/43/EC and the Employment Equality Directive 2000/78/EC to apply across the prohibited grounds of race, sexual orientation, age and religion or belief, albeit now also couched in more precise legislative language. The latter Directive makes special provision for disability, specifying in Art.2(2)(ii) that practices that have a disparate impact upon disabled people can either be objectively justified in accordance with the standard *Bilka Kaufhaus* approach, or can be deemed by national legislation to be acceptable if the employer in question has made reasonable accommodation in line with Art.5 of the Directive (see chapter 14). The UK has made use of this second option in the disability context.

The Directives essentially restate the *Bilka Kaufhaus* standard, but, significantly, require disparate impact that has a "particular disadvantage" upon a relevant group to be justified. This clarification may have important consequences for the future development of indirect discrimination: see below.

[35] [1997] IRLR 560, EAT.

Council Directive 2000/43/EC of 29 June 2000 implementing the principle of equal treatment between persons irrespective of racial or ethnic origin (the "Racial Discrimination Directive")

Article 2

Concept of discrimination

"1. For the purposes of this Directive, the principle of equal treatment shall mean that there shall be no direct or indirect discrimination based on racial or ethnic origin.

2. For the purposes of paragraph 1:

(a) . . . ;

(b) indirect discrimination shall be taken to occur where an apparently neutral provision, criterion or practice would put persons of a racial or ethnic origin at a particular disadvantage compared with other persons, unless that provision, criterion or practice is objectively justified by a legitimate aim and the means of achieving that aim are appropriate and necessary."

Council Directive 2000/78/EC of 27 November 2000 establishing a general framework for equal treatment in employment and occupation (the "Employment Equality Directive")

Article 2

Concept of discrimination

"1. For the purposes of this Directive, the 'principle of equal treatment' shall mean that there shall be no direct or indirect discrimination whatsoever on any of the grounds referred to in Article 1.

2. For the purposes of paragraph 1:

(a) direct discrimination shall be taken to occur where one person is treated less favourably than another is, has been or would be treated in a comparable situation, on any of the grounds referred to in Article 1;

(b) indirect discrimination shall be taken to occur where an apparently neutral provision, criterion or practice would put persons having a particular religion or belief, a particular disability, a particular age, or a particular sexual orientation at a particular disadvantage compared with other persons unless:

(i) that provision, criterion or practice is objectively justified by a legitimate aim and the means of achieving that aim are appropriate and necessary, or

(ii) as regards persons with a particular disability, the employer or any person or organisation to whom this Directive applies, is obliged, under national legislation, to take appropriate measures in line with the principles contained in Article 5 in order to eliminate disadvantages entailed by such provision, criterion or practice."

The revised Equal Treatment Directive 2002/73/EC and the Gender Directive 2004/113/EC also contain express definitions of indirect discrimination, essentially couched in the same terms as that contained in the Race and Employment Equality Directives.

The RRA 1976 (Amendment) Regulations 2003 implemented the Race Equality Directive's provisions in domestic law, introducing a new definition of indirect discrimination for the grounds of race or ethnic or national origins that was presented as complying with the Directive's requirements.

RRA 1976 (Amendment) Regulations 2003

"1(1A) A person also discriminates against another if in any circumstances relevant for the purposes of any provision referred to in subsection (1B) he applies to that other a provision, criterion or practice which he applies or would apply equally to persons not of the same race or ethnic or national origins as that other, but—

(a) which puts or would put persons of the same race or national or ethnic origins as that other at a particular disadvantage when compared with other persons,

(b) which puts that other at that disadvantage, and

(c) which he cannot show to be a proportionate means of achieving a legitimate aim."

Regulation 3(1)(b) of the Employment Equality (Sexual Orientation) and Employment Equality (Religion or Belief) Regulations 2003 implemented the Employment Equality Directive's provisions, with both providing that:

Common Regulation 3(1)(b) of the Employment Equality (Sexual Orientation) and Employment Equality (Religion or Belief) Regulations 2003

"a person ('A') discriminates against another person ('B') if . . . A applies to B a provision, criterion or practice which he applies or would apply equally to persons not of the same sexual orientation/religion or belief as B, but

(i) which puts or would put persons of the same sexual orientation/religion or belief as B at a particular disadvantage when compared with other persons,
(ii) which puts B at that disadvantage, and
(iii) which A cannot show to be a proportionate means of achieving a legitimate aim."

Regulation 3 of the Employment Equality (Age) Regulations 2006 (and the equivalent provisions of the Northern Irish age, race, sexual orientation and religion or belief regulations) use a similar definition. So too does the Employment Equality (Sex Discrimination) Regulations 2005 (and their Northern Ireland equivalent), which implemented the revised Equal Treatment Directive 2002/73 EC, and the proposed Sex Discrimination Act (Amendment) Regulations 2008 which will implement the Gender Directive 2004/113/EC.

As a result of this flurry of legislation, there is now a more or less standard domestic definition of indirect discrimination in those areas covered by the Regulations and applying in the field of employment and occupation for the grounds of race, religion or belief, sexual orientation, age and gender, and to the provision of goods and services and "social advantages" for the grounds of gender and race. This definition is supposed to give domestic effect to the more or less common definition of indirect discrimination contained in the post-2000 Directives. However, it should be noted that the definition of indirect discrimination contained in these UK regulations appears to be an uncomfortable compromise between the wording of the original RRA and the SDA and the wording of the post-2000 Directives. This new common domestic definition of indirect discrimination appears to be narrower in key aspects than the definition given by the Directives.

The definition in the Directives appears to be capable of being applied to group disadvantage which could be anticipated before the provision, criterion or practice was actually applied. The text of the new UK definition does not make this express. (The definition in the Directives applies where a practice put or "would put" a person at a disadvantage: the UK regulations only prohibit provisions that "apply" to disadvantage persons). It could also be argued that the new UK definition is more restrictive by appearing to require evidence that there is a *group* defined by the particular characteristic which is disadvantaged, while under the wording of the Directives, indirect discrimination could potentially occur when only *one person* defined by the particular characteristic was put at a disadvantage. Also, the domestic Regulations define objective justification as requiring that it be shown that the provisions, criteria or practices under attack are "proportionate means of achieving a legitimate aim". In contrast, the Directives define objective justification as requiring that it be demonstrated that the impugned measure is "objectively justified by a legitimate aim and the means of achieving that aim are appropriate and necessary". The apparently demanding requirement in the Directive that the measures be "appropriate and necessary" appears to have been watered down in the Regulations with their diluted reference to "proportionate means". The Regulations also require that an individual claimant show that they were actually put at a disadvantage, while the Directives do not appear to contain this requirement, apparently permitting action to be brought by individuals if they are part of a group that has been subject to discriminatory procedures and other forms of indirect general group disadvantage.[36]

As a consequence inter alia of these apparent deficiencies in the transposition of the definition of indirect discrimination contained in the Directives, the European Commission has sent the UK a "reasoned opinion" arguing that the Directives have not been implemented properly. Enforcement procedures may follow. These concerns may be purely textual. The UK government has for example suggested in the recent Discrimination Law Review that the objective justification test contained in the Regulations ("proportionate means of achieving a legitimate aim") has the same effect as the wording ("appropriate and necessary") in the Directives.[37] However, this is contestable. There are not yet any reported decisions by higher courts and tribunals offering an interpretation of this new definition, but decisions such as *Azmi v Kirklees Metropolitan Council*[38] have seen the employment tribunals adopt a similar approach to the new indirect discrimination statutory test as that applied in *Bilka*. In any case, the requirements of the Directive as interpreted by the ECJ will ultimately control the application and interpretation of the UK regulations.

There also exist further complications in this area. The original RRA definition of indirect discrimination (RRA s.1(1)(b)) continues to apply where the grounds are those of colour or nationality or where the activity in question falls outside the scope of the 2000 Directives. In addition, s.45(3) of the Equality Act 2006 adopts the following definition in prohibiting indirect discrimination on the grounds of religion or belief in the provision of goods,

36 Aileen McColgan, *Discrimination Law: Text, Cases and Materials* 2nd edn (Oxford: Hart, 2005), pp. 99–102.

37 See Discrimination Law Review, *A Framework for Fairness* (London: HMSO, 2007), para.1.42.

38 Employment Tribunal October 19, 2006. This case concerned the dismissal of a Muslim primary teacher who wore a face-veil: her dismissal was upheld on the basis that children in her class had complained that they were having difficulties in understanding her.

facilities and services and public functions, which again lies outside the scope of the Directives[39]:

S. 45(3) Equality Act 2006

[45(3)]"—A person ("A") discriminates against another ("B") for the purposes of this Part if A applies to B a provision, criterion or practice—

(a) which he applies or would apply equally to persons not of B's religion or belief,
(b) which puts persons of B's religion or belief at a disadvantage compared to some or all others (where there is no material difference in the relevant circumstances),
(c) which puts B at a disadvantage compared to some or all persons who are not of his religion or belief (where there is no material difference in the relevant circumstances), and
(d) which A cannot reasonably justify by reference to matters other than B's religion or belief."

A similar definition has been used in reg.3(3) of the Equality Act (Sexual Orientation) Regulations 2007 and the equivalent Northern Irish regulations, which prohibit indirect discrimination on the ground of sexual orientation in the provision of goods, facilities and services and public functions. This new definition could again be considered to be weaker than those used in the 2003 Regulations and the EC Directives, as it refers to an employer being able to "reasonably justify" disparate impact rather than having to show the provision in question to be "a proportionate means of achieving a legitimate aim".

It is not clear why this alternative definition was used, as it now means that domestic law has several different definitions of indirect discrimination, which has the potential to confuse considerable confusion even if the *Bilka Kaufhaus* approach is generally applied. The Discrimination Law Review proposes to standardise all these different definitions, at least as regards the legislation that applies to Britain, and to adopt the basic format used in the 2003 Regulations throughout all the prohibited grounds of discrimination, including retaining references to "particular disadvantage" (the 2006 Act refers just to "disadvantage") and to a "proportionate means of achieving a legitimate aim". This will bring about greater clarity, but may not solve the problem of incompatibility with EU law.

[39] The equivalent Northern Irish legislation, s.3 of the Fair Employment and Treatment (Northern Ireland) Order 1998, defines indirect discrimination in similar terms as the original SDA and RRA.

V. Applying the Definition of Indirect Discrimination

Having established the key elements of indirect discrimination and its development, it is now necessary to break down the indirect discrimination test as set out in the Directives, Regulations and case law into its component parts and see how they are applied.

A. *The Application of a Provision, Criterion or Practice*

The first element required under the new test set out in the post-2000 Directives, Regulations and other domestic legislation (and previously in equal pay and sex discrimination cases that came within EU law) is that an employer or service provider apply a "provision, criterion or practice" which is facially neutral, i.e. which does not involve overt direct discrimination. (As noted above, for cases based on nationality, skin colour or those residual elements of the RRA that lie outside the scope of the 2000 Race Equality Directive, the *Perera* approach still applies: a "requirement or condition" which is determinative will have to be applied before a finding of indirect discrimination can be made out.)

"Provisions, criteria or practices" can be written or unwritten, formal or informal, explicit or implicit. What is required is that some differentiating factor is applied that has an impact upon the complainant. Unless *Perera* still applies, criteria do not have to be essential job requirements to form the basis of an indirect sex discrimination claim. The Equal Opportunities Commission on its website for legal advisers has given the following examples of criteria which have been sufficient for indirect discrimination claims:

Equal Opportunities Commission, Website for Legal Advisers: Legal Framework and Procedure[40]

Examples of job criteria which could potentially be indirect sex discrimination (if not objectively justified) are:

- Age restrictions: *Price v Civil Service Commission* [1978] I.R.L.R. 3, E.A.T.; *Perera v Civil Service Commission (No.2)* [1983] I.R.L.R. 166, C.A.

[40] See *www.eoc-law.org.uk* (last accessed September 5, 2007)—now also available at *http://www.equalityhumanrights.com/en/foradvisers/eoclaw/eoclawenglandwales/legalframeworkandprocedure/pages/default.aspx* (last accessed December 23, 2007).

- Length of service requirement.
- Management and supervisory experience: *Falkirk Council and others v Whyte and others* [1997] I.R.L.R. 560, E.A.T.
- To be of a particular grade before applying for promotion: *Taylor v Commissioners of the Inland Revenue, EAT 498/98 (IDS 649).*
- To be working full-time to be considered for promotion: *Neary v Ladbrookes Casinos Ltd,* ET, EOR DCLD 47.
- To be able to work full-time in the new position.
- Working particular shifts or variable shifts: *Edwards v Derby City Council* [1999] I.C.R. 114 (E.A.T.);
- Height requirements.
- Physical strength requirements (note that tests of physical strength which vary between men and women could constitute direct discrimination: *Allcock v Chief Constable Hampshire Constabulary, ET case no 3101524/97, unreported*).
- A requirement to achieve particular results in certain psychometric tests (note that some psychometric tests could incorporate direct discrimination).
- Mobility requirements: *Meade-Hill and National Union of Civil and Public Servants v British Council* [1995] I.R.L.R. 47
- A requirement to "live in": *Douglas v the National Trust,* ET case no. 2502505/99.
- Having a degree: *Douglas v the National Trust, ET case no. 2502505/99.*
- Being able to contribute to the Research Assessment Exercise: *Mercer v London School of Economics, ET case no. 2201988/98.*
- Not being in a relationship with another police officer: *Chief Constable of the Bedfordshire Constabulary v Graham* [2002] I.R.L.R. 239
- The need to satisfy "vague" promotion procedures: *Watches of Switzerland v Savell* [1983] I.R.L.R. 141, E.A.T.
- the refusal to allow flexible working to suit the employee's childcare or care for an adult in need of care, such as job-share, term-time working, annualised hours, teleworking, compressed hours or self-rostering.
- a change in working hours imposed by the employer
- a provision that employees should be available to work their normal contractual hours without variation: *Dillon v Rentokil UK Limited,* Reading ET Case No. 2700899/01
- a requirement to work overtime

- a contractual obligation or a practice of undertaking long hours
- being placed on rotating shifts: *Hale & Clunie v Wiltshire Healthcare NHS Trust* [1999] DCLD 39
- a refusal to allow a woman to work from home: *Lockwood v Crawley Warren Group Ltd* EAT No 1176/99 DCLD 47
- a requirement to work without set hours but as and when required: *S.Smith v Greyfriars Taverns Ltd Sheffield* ET No 2801894/01 (2002).[41]

It may be unclear whether a criterion has in fact been applied. Again from the E.O.C. Legal Advisers' website, the following are examples of situations where no provision was applied:

- Where a woman does not consider options offered by the employer and/or makes no enquiries about flexible working to suit her childcare, no provision, criterion or practice will have been applied: e.g. *Barancewicz v RAC Motoring Services Birmingham ET 2002 Case no 5200086/01 and 1201690/99.*
- If a woman is invited to let the employer know if she needs more time or has any positive suggestions to make, and she resigns without taking up this opportunity, the tribunal may find that no practice, criterion or provision was applied: e.g. *Hill v Staffordshire Sentinel Newspapers Ltd Shewsbury ET Case No. 2900163/01.* The tribunal found that the employer had not closed their mind to the possibility of some alternative arrangement and there was a very real possibility that some accommodation might have been reached which would have enabled her to continue work consistently with her childcare obligations.
- If the employer has reserved the right to review the claimant's hours with a view to changing the hours—but has not actually done so—then no provision, criterion or practice will have been applied. In *O'Neill v NTL Group Ltd Manchester ET 2403260/01* the tribunal held that it could not take pre-emptive action in respect of potential future acts of discrimination.
- If a woman is asked to work additional hours, says they are inconvenient and is told she does not have to work them, there will be no application of a provision, criterion or practice: e.g. *Wilcockson v Global Video* plc Case No.2406814/97.

In general, the domestic courts have adopted a reasonably broad interpretation of what constitutes a failure to comply with a provision, criterion, practice, requirement or condition. In *Price v Civil Service Commissioners*, the E.A.T.

[41] *http://www.eoc-law.org.uk/default.aspx?page=2799.*

recognised that an artificial approach which treated the claimant as capable of complying if they could conceivably have taken some hypothetical steps to meet the requirement was not appropriate.[42] However, as McColgan suggests, there have been many instances where a less flexible approach was adopted.[43] The fact that the new test for indirect discrimination set out in the Directives and Regulations requires examination of which groups were placed at a "particular disadvantage" by the criterion in question, rather than an examination of who *cannot comply* with the criterion as was the requirement under the old test, may be significant. This apparently small change in definition may encourage courts and tribunals to focus less on assessing in a mechanistic way whether a particular group can comply or not comply with a particular provision or criterion, and concentrate more upon assessing whether a group was in some way particularly disadvantaged by the provision or criterion in question.

B. *Establishing the Existence of "Particular Disadvantage"*

The next stage under the new test for indirect discrimination introduced by the post-2000 Directives is to assess whether the application of a provision, criterion or practice has caused "particular disadvantage" to a relevant group of persons defined with reference to one of the prohibited grounds of discrimination. (This requirement may differ and be narrower in scope from "disadvantage" as required under the Equality Act 2006 for discrimination on the grounds of religion or belief and sexual orientation in the provision of goods, services, education and public functions. It may also differ from the requirements imposed in the residual category of skin colour and nationality cases where the original wording of the RRA still applies: see below.) In other words, a complainant must show from a comparison between a group of persons distinguished by a prohibited ground of discrimination and another group who are in similar or analogous circumstances that the first group has been put at a notably greater disadvantage than the other by the application of the provision, criterion or practice in question. To take the example of an indirect sex discrimination claim, it is necessary to show that the challenged provision, criterion or practice causes a particular disadvantage to a group defined by their sex, when compared to another group of the opposite sex who are in an analogous situation: the comparison will be between men and

42 [1978] I.C.R. 27. See also *Mandla v Dowell Lee* [1983] 2 A.C. 548, where a Sikh pupil alleged indirect race discrimination on the basis that the school uniform policy required him to wear a cap in place of his religiously mandated turban. The fact that the pupil could have taken off his turban in a physical and hypothetical sense was held by the Law Lords not to mean that the pupil could have complied with the requirement to wear a cap and therefore had not been subject to a detriment.

43 Aileen McColgan, *Discrimination Law* 2nd edn (Oxford: Hart, 2005), p.82, citing *Chyoo v Wandsworth Borough Council* [1989] I.C.R. 250.

women in general (if all persons are potentially affected by the application of the criterion in question) or men and women of a particular group whose circumstances are similar.

Before the introduction of the new definitions, complainants under the SDA and the RRA had to show that the provision, criterion or practice in question would be to the detriment of a considerably larger proportion of one group than the other. This usually required the production of statistical evidence. With the new definition, this requirement is relaxed: "particular disadvantage" is required, rather than detriment to a "considerably larger proportion" or the group. This is a potentially very significant shift. While the "old" case law will still remain very relevant, it may be considerably easier with the new definition to establish the existence of "particular disadvantage" than it was previously to show the existence of a "considerably larger" detriment.

In the past, the key initial step was to determine the relevant "pool", who would usually be all the individuals whose circumstances were similar to the affected group. Then the plaintiff would have to identify the proportion of the group defined by the relevant characteristic (their race, sex or whichever discrimination ground was at issue) who were unable to comply with the provision, criterion or practice that was being applied. Then the plaintiff would have to identify the proportion of the others that were outside that specific group but within the common "pool" who were similarly unable to comply with the provision, criterion or practice. A *prima facie* case of indirect discrimination would only be established if the disadvantaged proportion of the first group was "considerably larger" than the disadvantaged proportion of the other group within the common pool. With the new definition, it may be sufficient to show that the group defined by the relevant discrimination ground was in general subject to a "particular disadvantage": a comparison with the others within the pool may often be necessary for evidential purposes to show the existence of a "particular disadvantage" but may no longer be a legal requirement. In addition, as McColgan notes, the new definition should result in less of a focus by courts and tribunals on the proportions of the different groups who can comply with the provision, criterion or practice at issue, and a greater emphasis on the proportions of groups who are actually disadvantaged.[44] Comparing the proportions of different groups who can comply can often result in courts and tribunals overlooking or brushing aside the situation of small proportions of groups who cannot comply: a concentration on ascertaining whether "particular disadvantage" has occurred should encourage a greater focus upon the disadvantaged elements and more sustained intensity of review.

To give an example, let us suppose that the Bar Council of England and Wales introduced a new requirement to the effect that before an individual was called to the Bar, he or she would have to have done six months voluntary

[44] Aileen McColgan, *Discrimination Law* 2nd edn (Oxford: Hart, 2005), pp. 92–97.

work in the UK. This could cause disadvantage to students who were not UK nationals but were attempting to join the English Bar, who would have much less opportunity to undertake such voluntary work in the UK. Under the old definition, a potential plaintiff attempting to allege the existence of indirect discrimination on the grounds of national origin or nationality would first of all identify the relevant pool, who would in this case be all the individuals with the necessary qualifications to be called to the English Bar. Then the plaintiff would have to identify the proportion of non-UK nationals within this pool who could or could not comply with this requirement. They would then have to identify the proportion of UK nationals that could comply with this requirement. All of this evidence might be difficult to gather: even if the plaintiff could collect it all, he or she would have to show that the proportion of non-UK nationals that could not qualify was considerably larger than the proportion of UK students who could. The new definition now requires that the plaintiff show that non-UK students would be subject to a "particular disadvantage": it may be much easier for the plaintiff to show this, as a court or tribunal might be prepared to infer that non-UK students were obviously put at a particular disadvantage when compared to UK nationals by this requirement. Even if some statistical data was required to establish the existence of a particular disadvantage, this data would not be required to show that that non-UK nationals were *considerably* more likely to run foul of the requirement: a distinct pattern of extra disadvantage might be sufficient.

It remains to be seen how this shift in definition will affect the indirect discrimination test as it is applied in practice. Much of the existing case law will probably continue to be very influential. A wider range of evidence may now be capable of being used to establish the existence of a particular disadvantage. However, the use of workplace statistics will still often be crucial, as they are at present. The use of such statistical evidence is relatively common. This information can often be obtained through the use of the questionnaire procedure provided for in the anti-discrimination legislation, whereby written questions to the employer can be asked, with courts and tribunals able to draw negative inferences from an employer's failure to respond. It can be invaluable in identifying the proportions of the relevant groups within the overall pool of affected employees who are placed at a disadvantage.

Common sense assumptions about how one group may be affected by a particular criterion may also be used by courts and tribunals to establish that a particular disadvantage exists, and will in all probability continue to be used under the new test. For example, the Court of Appeal in *London Underground v Edwards (No. 2)* made use of the common sense assumption that for reasons of family commitments women are often less able to work long and inflexible hours than men, and so would usually be put at a disadvantage if they were required to work such hours. In this case, the Court of Appeal and the EAT also decided that they could take into account national statistical patterns that indicated that women had greater primary care responsibility for children than men in general.[45] The Court of Appeal confirmed this approach as correct, and it is expected to be applied across all the grounds covered by the Directives. Analogies may be drawn here with the approaches adopted in the race discrimination cases of *CRE v Dutton*[46] and *Perera v Civil Service Commissioners*,[47] where similar common sense assumptions were applied.

Other rules of thumb can be detected in the existing case law, which again may well carry over to the new test. In *Enderby*,[48] for example, the ECJ held that statistical evidence in equal pay claims must usually cover a sufficient number of people within the affected group so as not just to reflect random or abnormal chance eventualities. (This may be relaxed with the new emphasis on establishing "particular disadvantage" rather than 'considerably larger' detriment.) In *Royal Copenhagen*,[49] the ECJ also was of the view that all persons in the comparator groups who are in comparable situations must be taken into account. If it is not possible to compare two groups within the workplace by statistical evidence, hypothetical comparators can be used to establish the probability of disparate impact.

However, the evidence of "particular disadvantage" must relate to a precise group that is affected by the criterion in question. There is a considerable and complex case law on which groups are the appropriate comparators for the purpose of establishing disadvantage or detriment. Much will depend upon the circumstances of a particular case, and who will be deemed to constitute the relevant "pool" of persons in similar or analogous circumstances. The requirement to point to appropriate pools may be relaxed under the new test, as discussed above, but in practice it may very well remain a key element of proving the existence of indirect discrimination. Case law has established that it will be usually the task of the primary trier of fact to decide on the relevant "pools". It will be difficult to challenge the decision of the primary fact-finders. However, in the Court of Appeal decision of *Allonby v Accrington*,[50] Sedley L.J. said that once the "requirement or condition" being challenged (this case predated the new definition) has been correctly identified by the primary fact-finder, there is likely to be only one comparator pool that will test its effect, which will be a matter of "logic" rather than a pure matter of fact. This means that the decisions of the primary fact-finder may be more open to attack, on the basis that they misapplied the relevant logical approach rather than making an error of fact, which would normally be non-appealable.

In selecting the relevant pool, the comparison will usually be made between two groups who have similar qualifications, perform similar work or hold

[45] [1999] I.R.L.R. 364.
[46] [1989] I.R.L.R. 8.
[47] [1977] I.R.L.R. 291.
[48] Case C-127/92, *Enderby v Frenchay Health Authority* [1993] E.C.R. 1-5535; [1993] I.R.L.R. 591.
[49] C-400/93, *Specialarbejderforbundet i Danmark v Dansk Industri* (the *Royal Copenhagen* case) [1993] E.C.R. I-1275.
[50] [2001] I.R.L.R. 364.

similar jobs. In *Jones v University of Manchester*,[51] the plaintiff was denied a job on the basis that the post was confined to graduates who were between 27 and 35 years of age: she had graduated as a mature student and was 44 years old. She challenged this age limit on the basis that it constituted indirect sex discrimination, as it discriminated against older "mature student" graduates like her and therefore had a disproportionate impact upon women, who made up a greater proportion of older mature student graduates than they did of younger graduates. The plaintiff argued that the relevant pool should be established by reference to all the individuals potentially eligible for the post in question who shared a common characteristic with her and would be directly affected by the age limit in question (in this case, all graduates who had obtained their degrees as mature students who were over a certain age). The Court of Appeal disagreed, finding that the appropriate pool for comparison were all the individuals who possessed all of the required qualifications for the post in question, excluding the age requirement that was the subject of the complaint: in this case, this meant all graduates, not just mature students. In other words, the Court of Appeal ruled that the pool was not established by asking who was in a similar position as the individual plaintiff: the pool was established by reference to all those who were eligible for the post in question and subject to the requirement at issue.

This case shows how the often arcane art of identifying the relevant pool will often be the key issue in an indirect discrimination claim, which may continue to be the case under the new test. In *London Underground v Edwards (No. 1)*, where the plaintiff was challenging new rostering arrangements that involved a shift to longer hours, the Employment Appeals Tribunal held that the relevant pool was the relevant part of the workforce that was affected or potentially affected by the rostering requirement.[52] When national legislation is at issue, often the courts will identify the relevant group as all individuals potentially affected by the measure in question, not just those immediately

[51] [1993] I.R.L.R. 218. In this case, the Court of Appeal gave guidance as to how tribunals should proceed in indirect sex discrimination cases similar to this, having correctly identified the relevant pool. The tribunal should:

1. identify all those men and women who, but for the disputed requirement (*i.e.* the age), would be in a position to qualify for the advertised job;
2. divide that population into those who can comply with the requirement and those who cannot comply;
3. ascertain the number of men and the number of women in each of these two groups and the number of men and women in the pool as a whole;
4. express the proportion of men in the pool who can comply with the requirement as a percentage of the total number of men in the pool. Do the same in relation to the women in the pool;
5. compare the percentage proportion of men who can comply with the requirement with the percentage proportion of women who can comply with it and decide whether that comparison reveals that a considerably smaller proportion of women than men in the pool can comply with the requirement.

[52] [1995] I.R.L.R. 355.

affected at a particular moment in time.[53] The problem with these rules of thumb is that specific forms of structural discrimination may be lost in the application of general pool identification rules:[54] selecting the appropriate pool may involve complex judgments, and unconscious assumptions may easily influence the process. It is certainly a less than satisfactory area of discrimination law, and one that continues to generate considerable problems. It remains to be seen whether the application of the new test will significantly vary the current approaches to showing that disadvantage exists.[55]

Under the old definition, the *Bilka Kaufhaus* formula required—in order to show "considerably larger" detriment—that "a substantially higher proportion" of the disadvantaged group had to be placed at a disadvantage than the comparator group. What exactly constitutes a "substantially higher proportion" has remained unclear, as is what will constitute a "particular disadvantage" under the new definition of indirect discrimination used in the Regulations. In *London Underground v Edwards (No. 2)*, the Court of Appeal indicated that:

- there must be a substantial (and not "marginal") discriminatory effect as between the relevant groups;
- the disparate impact should be inherent in the application of the requirement and not simply a result of unreliable statistics or fortuitous circumstances;
- whether a particular percentage disadvantage is "substantially smaller" in any given case will depend on all the circumstances;
- in indirect sex discrimination cases, it is significant if no man is disadvantaged by the practice.

In *Edwards*, 100 per cent of men could comply with the requirement to work anti-social shifts and 95.2 per cent of women could do so. However, 2,023 men were affected, but only 21 women: due to the nature of the work in question, it was a very male-dominated workforce. Only one woman (the plaintiff) could not comply with the new rostering requirements at issue. However, the Court of Appeal accepted that the Employment Tribunal was right to take into

[53] See e.g. *Rutherford v Secretary of State for Trade and Industry and others (No 2)* [2006] UKHL 19; [2006] I.R.L.R. 19.

[54] For criticism of the *Jones* decision as having done precisely this, see Tamara K. Hervey, "Structural Discrimination Unrecognised: Jones v University of Manchester" (1994) 57 M.L.R. 307.

[55] It should be noted that the indirect discrimination test is concerned with whether a particular group has been subject to disparate *impact* , not whether differences in *treatment* have taken place. The Law Lords in *Barry v Midland Bank* [1999] I.R.L.R. 859 appear to have slipped into an approach that involved the use of comparators to ascertain whether a difference in *treatment* between full-time and part-time workers had occurred, when as McColgan notes, the purpose of the comparator analysis is to ascertain whether disparate *impact* has occurred. See McColgan, *Discrimination Law, ibid.*, pp.84–85.

account the social fact that the effect of the shift pattern (which would require early morning working and considerable variation in hours) would inevitably have a disproportionate impact upon women. The fact therefore that one of the 21 women affected could not comply was sufficient to establish the existence of disparate impact in the circumstances.[56]

Edwards can be welcomed as a judgment that takes a nuanced and contextual approach to determining the existence of disparate impact. A similar approach can be detected in the general approach of the European Court of Justice in equal pay cases to determining whether disparate impact exists. In certain contexts, the ECJ has considered that the existence of statistical evidence showing differences in pay between jobs of equal value, when combined with the presence of additional factors, can lead to an inference of disparate impact that would not otherwise exist in other circumstances. In *Enderby*,[57] the ECJ held that it could be assumed that disparate impact existed where statistical evidence showed that an appreciable difference existed in pay levels between two jobs of equal value, one of which was carried out almost exclusively by women and the other predominantly by men. In *Danfoss*,[58] the Court considered that evidence of differences in pay between jobs of equal value accompanied by a lack of transparency in the pay system could also give rise to an inference of disparate impact: in the *Swedish Ombudsman* case,[59] the Court came to a similar conclusion in respect of differences in pay levels between two jobs of equal value where the lower-paid job was being undertaken by a substantially higher proportion of women than men.

A similar contextual approach can also be detected in the protracted and long-drawn out case of *R v Employment Secretary, Ex p. Seymour Smith*,[60] where judicial review was sought of the statutory requirement for employees to have two years of continuous service of at least sixteen hours a week before protection was available against unfair dismissal, on the grounds that this requirement had an unjustified adverse impact on women. The proportion of men over the relevant time period (1985–1993) that could comply with this requirement ranged from 72 per cent to 77.4 per cent, while the corresponding figure for women was within the range of 63.8 per cent to 68.9 per cent. There was therefore a background context of persistent and consistent gender disparity over seven years, but there was some evidence that the gap between the genders was narrowing over time and uncertainty existed as to whether the statistical gap was sufficient to establish the existence of disparate impact between the genders. The High Court found that there was insufficient evidence of disparate impact, while the Court of Appeal took the opposite view. The House of Lords referred the question of what legal test should determine

[56] See also *Chief Constable of Avon and Somerset v Chew* (EAT 503/00 unreported).
[57] Case C-127/92, *Enderby v Frenchay Health Authority* [1993] E.C.R. 1-5535.
[58] [1989] E.C.R. 3199.
[59] Case C-236/98, *Jämställdhetsombudsmannen v Örebro läns landsting* (the *Swedish Ombudsman* case) [2000] E.C.R. I-2189, [2000] I.R.L.R. 421.
[60] C-167/97, *R v Secretary of State for Employment, Ex p. Seymour-Smith and Perez* [1999] E.C.R. I-623.

whether disparate impact existed to the European Court of Justice. The European Court of Justice's judgment has been criticised as lacking clarity:[61] however, the Court appeared to indicate that disparate impact could be established where (a) a considerably smaller percentage of women than men was able to satisfy the requirement at issue, or (b) the available statistical evidence demonstrated the existence of a less significant but nevertheless distinct gender gap but also that a persistent and relatively constant disparity existed over a long period of time between the proportion of men and women who could satisfy the requirement.

The ECJ in this judgment seemed to suggest that in the absence of a persistent and relatively constant disparity, the statistical difference of approximately 8.5 per cent between the genders in this case would not have been "considerable". The ECJ also appeared to reject the suggestion that evidence of long-term non-random differences between the genders could by itself show the existence of "considerably larger" detriment: specific evidence of disproportionate impact was required. However, even given this cautious approach, the Court's readiness to accept that evidence of persistent disparity could contribute to a finding of disparate impact which would not otherwise have been held to exist shows some sensitivity to background context and the reality of structural discrimination in contemporary societies. In applying this approach in *Seymour-Smith (No. 2)*,[62] the majority of the House of Lords considered that the evidence of constant disparity combined with the statistical evidence of the existence of a distinct gender gap was enough to establish the existence of disparate impact, although the application of the qualifying requirement in question was subsequently found to be objectively justified.

It is likely that much of this broadly contextual approach will be carried over into the case law concerning the new definition. However, problems will inevitably remain. The plaintiff is still under an obligation to show the existence of a "particular disadvantage". Relevant statistical evidence may be difficult to find, and in any case may not reflect the disadvantages and structural discrimination faced by many disadvantaged groups. This contextual approach may need further development if indirect discrimination claims are not to repeatedly fail at the hurdle of establishing differential impact.

C. *Has the Claimant as an Individual Been Put at a Disadvantage?*

Under the new test set out by the 2003 Sexual Orientation and Religion or Belief Regulations, the claimant has to show that they themselves have been

[61] See Catherine Barnard and Bob Hepple, "Indirect Discrimination: Interpreting *Seymour-Smith*" (1999) 58 C.L.J. 399.

[62] [2000] I.R.L.R. 263.

subjected to a disadvantage by the application of the provision or criteria at issue. (Previously, under the SDA and the RRA, the claimant had to show that he or she had been subject to a "detriment".) It would appear that this requirement in the Regulations means that the alleged disadvantage must be tangible and impact more or less directly upon the claimant by operating to deny them a post or entitlement to which they would otherwise be entitled, as was the case previously with the "detriment" requirement: being a member of a group that is subject in general to a particular disadvantage which does not affect the claimant will not be sufficient.[63] However, it is worth noting that the post-2000 Directives do not appear to contain this requirement of individual exposure to disadvantage: it may be the case that the Directives permit an action to be brought if one is simply a member of a group that is subject to disadvantage, without requiring any additional evidence of specific individual impact. This would allow individuals to obtain a remedy for discriminatory procedures that had an unjustified disparate impact upon their particular group, even if they themselves would not have obtained the position or entitlement at issue.[64]

Domestic courts have traditionally adopted a relatively broad interpretation of what qualifies as being subject to a "detriment", which presumably will be carried over to the new test of being subject to "disadvantage"[65]: however, there have been cases when a much more restrictive approach has been adopted.[66] There is no requirement that the disadvantage reach a certain level of severity: it is sufficient that an individual was "subject to" the disadvantage, although obviously the less the damage suffered, the lower will be the sum of any compensation awarded. In practice, this element of indirect discrimination is closely interwoven with the question of whether the claimant was subject to a "provision, criterion or practice" in the first place.

D. *Objective Justification*

As previously noted, even if all the other elements of indirect discrimination are present, the application of a "provision, criterion or practice" that has a disparate impact upon a particular group can still be shown to be objectively justified and thereby escape sanction. The burden of proof shifts to the alleged discriminator to demonstrate the existence of an objective justification, once the other parts of the indirect discrimination claim have been established to

63 See *Coker v Lord Chancellor* [2002] I.C.R. 321.
64 See Aileen McColgan, *Discrimination Law, ibid.*, p.82.
65 See *Price v Civil Service Commissioners* [1978] I.C.R. 27; *Mandla v Dowell Lee* [1983] 2 A.C. 548.
66 *Chyoo v Wandsworth BC* [1989] I.C.R. 250: *Coker v Lord Chancellor* [2002] I.C.R. 321.

exist on the balance of probabilities by the claimant.[67] Much depends upon how rigorously this objective justification test is applied by the courts: if considerable leeway is given to alleged discriminators to justify their actions, then there is a danger that the objective justification defence will turn into a general "escape clause", substantially diluting the impact of the prohibition on indirect discrimination.

We saw in previous sections that the wording of the objective justification standard to be deployed by courts and tribunals varies across the different pieces of primary and secondary legislation dealing with indirect discrimination. The original Sex Discrimination and Race Relations Act simply required that the criterion which is applied be "justifiable" if it was to survive scrutiny. Regulation 97/80, by contrast, talks of the criterion needing to be shown to be appropriate and necessary, using objective factors unrelated to sex. More recently, most of the Regulations introduced post-2003 refer to a criterion needing to be a "proportionate means of achieving a legitimate aim", while the Equality Act 2006 and regulations introduced under its provisions refer to an obligation to "reasonably justify". The post-2000 Directives use the most expansive formulation in play by talking of the criterion needing to be objectively justified by a legitimate aim, with the means of achieving that aim being "appropriate and necessary".

A similar proportionality analysis should logically be used in general by domestic courts when determining whether an apparently indirectly discriminatory provision, criterion or practice is nonetheless justifiable. In the Discrimination Law Review, as discussed above, the UK government has suggested that all these different formulations reflect the same basic concept. However, again as discussed above, there is concern that the domestic legislation makes use of a weaker formula than that applied in EU law, by failing to transplant the phrase "appropriate and necessary", which appears to set a more rigorous standard than "proportionate means" by requiring any measures to be "necessary", not just "proportionate". It remains to be seen what the effect of these varying definitions will be.

The basic test for justification was set out by the European Court of Justice in *Bilka-Kaufhaus GmbH v Weber von Hertz*,[68] a test that the House of Lords indicated in *Rainey v Glasgow Health Board*[69] should be followed by courts and tribunals in applying domestic sex discrimination law (and which subsequently has been applied in race discrimination cases on account of the similar wording of the SDA and RRA justification requirements). Under this test,

[67] See Case 170/84, *Bika-Kaufhaus GmbH v Weber von Hartz* [1986] E.C.R. 1607, [1987] I.C.R. 110, 125, para.31. Case C-33/89, *Kowalska v Freie und Hansestadt Hamburg* [1990] E.C.R.-1 2591, [1992] I.C.R. 29, 35, para.16 and Case C-184/89, *Nimz v Freie und Hansestadt Hamburg* [1991] E.C.R. I-297, 320, para.15.

[68] Case 170/84, [1986] E.C.R. 1607. *Bilka* concerned the application of the objective justification defence in equal pay claims: the subsequent ECJ decision in *Danfoss* [1989] E.C.R. 3199 confirmed that this test should also be applied in indirect discrimination claims arising in respect of "treatment" under the Equal Treatment Directive.

[69] [1987] A.C. 224.

which is likely to continue to be applied under the new Regulations, the alleged discriminator must show that the provision, criterion or practice:

- corresponds to a real need on their part as an employer, and
- is appropriate with a view to meeting that need, and
- is necessary to meet that need.

This *Bilka Kaufhaus* test therefore involves the application of proportionality, as Lord Nicholls recognised in *Barry v Midland Bank*:[70] "In other words, the ground relied upon as justification must be of sufficient importance for a national court to regard this as overriding the disparate impact of the difference in treatment, either in whole or in part."

This basic test has been applied in many cases, including by the Court of Appeal in *Allonby* v. *Accrington and Rossendale College*,[71] the House of Lords in *Hampson v Department of Education and Science*[72] (where it was used in applying the indirect discrimination provisions of the RRA) and recently by the ECJ itself in *Cadman v Health & Safety Executive*.[73] In applying the test in *Bilka*, case law has clarified that courts and tribunals should also take the following steps, as usefully described by the Equal Opportunities Commission:

Equal Opportunities Commission, Website for Legal Advisers: The Legal Test for Justification in Indirect Discrimination Cases[74]

1. **Evaluate critically the justification put forward in the employer.** The tribunal should not simply accept the explanation offered by the employer without any scrutiny. It must conduct some form of critical evaluation into whether the employer's reasons meet the *Bilka* standard by demonstrating a real need for the hours of work required by the employer. In *Allonby* v. *Accrington and Rossendale College* [2001] I.R.L.R. 364, the Court of Appeal said that the facts required at the minimum a critical evaluation of:
whether the employer's reasons demonstrated a real need on the part of the undertaking;
if there was such a need, a consideration of the seriousness of the disproportionate impact of the dismissals policy on women including the claimant; and
an evaluation of whether the real need was sufficient to outweigh the seriousness of the impact.

70 [1999] I.C.R. 859.
71 [2001] I.R.L.R. 364.
72 [1989] I.R.L.R. 629.
73 [2007] I.R.L.R. 969.
74 See www.eoc-law.org.uk (last accessed September 5, 2007)—now also available at *http://www.equalityhumanrights.com/en/foradvisers/eoclaw/eoclawenglandwales/legalframeworkandprocedure/pages/default.aspx* (last accessed December 23, 2007).

2. **Consider whether there was another way to achieve the employer's aim.** For example, if the aim was to maintain continuity of service to clients, could a job share arrangement achieve this? In *Kutz-Bauer v Freie und Hansenstadt Hamburg* [2003] I.R.L.R. 368, the ECJ said that it was necessary "to ascertain, in the light of all the relevant factors and taking into account the possibility of achieving by other means the aims pursued by the provisions in question, whether such aims appear to be unrelated to any discrimination and whether those provisions, as a means to the achievement of certain aims, are capable of advancing those aims".

3. **Balance the employer's need against the discriminatory impact.** The greater the number of women adversely affected by it, and the seriousness of its impact on any individual worker, the harder it will be for the employer to justify the provision, criterion of practice: *London Underground v Edwards (No. 2)* [1999] I.R.L.R. 364. In *Hampson v Department of Education and Science* [1989] I.R.L.R. 629, the House of Lords held that a justification requires an objective balance between the discriminatory effect of the practice, provision or criteria and the reasonable needs of the employer.

4. **Examine whether the employer has taken into account the detriment to the claimant and those in the same position as her.** It is not enough for the employer merely to show that it considered its reasons to be adequate. In *Hale & Clunie v Wiltshire Healthcare NHS Trust*,[75] the ET held that the decision to introduce compulsory rotating shifts for all nursing staff and without any allowance for childcare responsibilities was not justifiable.

A range of factors (not always explicitly articulated in the case law) appear to be important to courts and tribunals in determining whether a policy or practice is justifiable. The Equal Opportunities Commission website for legal advisers proceeds to set out some additional factors that courts and tribunals should or should not take into account in applying the *Bilka* test:

"In the case of *Hardys and Hansons plc v Lax*,[76] the appellant employer argued that it should be granted a margin of discretion in deciding whether to permit a job share and that the employment tribunal should limit itself to considering only whether the decision fell within the range of responses open to a reasonable employer (as for unfair dismissal). The Court of Appeal rejected this argument holding that it is for the tribunal to make its own judgment as to whether the discriminatory practice is justifiable: "The principle of proportionality requires the tribunal to take into account the reasonable needs of the business. But it has to make its own judgment, upon a fair and detailed analysis of the working practices and business considerations involved, as to whether the proposal is reasonably necessary."

It is insufficient for an employer to assert that it has simply followed its normal policy and was unaware of any discriminatory effect. Once it has been shown that a policy, practice or criterion has been adopted, the employer is required to show by means of oral or documentary evidence:

- the importance of the policy, practice or criterion to the employer and why it is necessary for the employer to have it, and
- why it is necessary for the policy to have the particular clause, or for the practice to take the particular form, which disadvantaged the claimant and others, and

[75] (1999) DCLD 39.
[76] [2005] IRLR 668.

- why it was necessary to apply it to the claimant and others in the form or manner which it took.

In *Whiffen v Milham Ford Girls' School* [2001] I.R.L.R. 468, the Court of Appeal said that: "[a]uthorities have stressed the desirability (if not quite necessity) of there being evidence to establish these matters" [and] "[w]hat the employer had to show was that the policy of dismissing fixed-term contract holders first was necessary to meet the employer's needs. The needs were not identified by the employer; the necessity for, as opposed to the commonplace use of, the policy was never considered"...As the ET pointed out in *Manning v Wick Hill Ltd* ET/2300178/02 (unreported), if an employer is to establish a "real need on the part of the undertaking it must do sufficient research and analysis in order to reach a sound conclusion"...

Furthermore, the requirement must not be discriminatory: it must be justified apart from the sex of the worker. An argument that it was justified to pay part-time workers less as this would encourage employers to recruit part-timers would thus be inherently discriminatory."

An employer is free to advance factors to justify the challenged provision, criterion or practice which where not considered at the time the challenged provision, criterion or practice was actually applied. In *British Airways v Starmer*,[77] an employment tribunal allowed British Airways to put forward safety considerations as justification for differential treatment, even though it was accepted that safety considerations had not featured in their initial decision to refuse a female pilot's request to work 50% of her contracted hours. The Court of Appeal approved the decision, finding that the employment tribunal was entitled to take safety into account as a justification, even though this factor was only invoked to justify the decision after it had been made. However, the Court of Appeal nevertheless suggested that such a retrospective justification should be given close and careful scrutiny: in addition, a tribunal would be entitled in certain circumstances to give the retrospective justification less weight, due to its absence from the initial decision-making process.[78]

The use of casual assumptions and automatic stereotyping to justify the application of a provision, criterion or practice, such as structuring an employment policy on part-time work around the generalised assumption that part-time workers are not as committed as full-time workers, will not usually be sufficient to establish the existence of objective justification, at least not without evidence to substantiate the accuracy of these assertions. In the Irish case of *Hill and Stapleton v the Revenue Commissioners*,[79] the length of service of job sharers was treated as half that of full-timers for various employment-related purposes, primarily on the basis of an assumption that employees sharing jobs did not acquire the same levels of experience as full-time employees. The ECJ held that a simple reliance upon this assumption was not sufficient to establish the existence of objective justification, but that it might be

77 [2005] I.R.L.R. 862.

78 See also the ECJ decision in Case C-4/02, *Schönheit v Stadt Frankfurt am Main* [2003] E.C.R. I–12575; [2004] I.R.L.R. 983.

79 Case C-243/95, [1998] E.C.R. 1- 03739; [1998] I.R.L.R. 466.

different if the employer could actually demonstrate that the job sharers were less experienced or less effective.[80] In *Cadman v Health & Safety Executive*, the ECJ held that linking pay to length of service may often be capable of being objectively justified, on the basis that length of service and the ensuing experience it generates often enables a worker to perform better.[81] However, the Court also held that this argument was rebuttable if the claimant provides evidence that is sufficient to raise substantial doubts as to whether using length of service as a criterion in setting pay levels was, in the particular circumstances involved, appropriate to achieve the object of rewarding experience.[82]

A blanket policy which takes no account of individual circumstances may be difficult to justify, especially where no consideration had been given to whether some adjustment could have been made to the "provision, criterion or practice" in question.[83] As noted above, the Court of Appeal was of the view in *Allonby* that there must be some critical evaluation on the part of the alleged discriminator of the justification being offered and its applicability to the claimant's situation.[84] The same logic applies to justification that rests solely upon the aim of avoiding setting a precedent. In *Parry v De Vere Hotels and Leisure Ltd*,[85] an employment tribunal held that the employer's refusal to allow a woman to alter her working hours had been based on employer's fear that it would open the floodgates for women in the future to ask for less and less hours to suit their childcare. This was found not to be an acceptable justification. Similarly, a failure to apply a well-established policy or practice, such as an employer's policy in respect of part-time work or an equal opportunities policy, in a particular case may in certain circumstances lead to a finding that objective justification did not exist, on the basis that no clear non-discriminatory rationale existed for the departure from the normal practice. For example, in *Amos v IPC Magazines*, the ET held that a refusal to allow the claimant to job-share could not be justified in the light of the respondent's significant failures to follow its own maternity policy.[86]

The position becomes a little more complex when we turn to circumstances where alleged discriminators invoke economic and cost factors to justify the existence of disparate impact. As *Rainey* v. *Glasgow Health Board* makes clear,[87] a genuine material difference rooted in extrinsic factors (such as economic

[80] For an example of a situation where evidence did support reliance upon a general assumption, see Case C-25/02, *Rinke v Arztekammer Hamburg* [2003] E.C.R. I–8349, where the ECJ held that a requirement for doctors to do part of their training full time was objectively justified on the basis that in general it would enable doctors to acquire sufficient experience in the various situations likely to arise in general practice.

[81] [2006] EUECJ C-17/05; [2006] I.R.L.R. 969.

[82] See also Case C-148/89, *Nimz v Freie und Hansestadt Hamburg* [1991] E.C.R. I-297.

[83] See e.g. *Smith v Penlan Club*, ET Case 1602995/01. For a failure to consider alternative arrangements in general, see also *Brown v McAlpine and Co Ltd*, EATS/009/05 22.9.05.

[84] [2001] I.R.L.R. 364.

[85] 2005 2101853/04.

[86] Case 2301499/00.

[87] [1987] 1 A.C. 224.

considerations) between two groups may justify what would otherwise constitute indirect discrimination, even if the personal qualities of the two groups are not intrinsically different. In this case, Mrs Rainey, a prosthetist employed by the NHS, claimed equal pay with a male prosthetist, Mr C., who earned over £2,000 a year more than she did. Mrs Rainey and Mr C. had broadly the same qualifications and experience: however, Mr C. had been recruited by the Glasgow Health Board from private practice, where salaries were much higher, and had consequently sought and obtained a higher salary. (The NHS had found it necessary to recruit a number of prosthetists from private practice in order to have sufficient expertise and medical support in this area of health care.) The Law Lords held that it was necessary for the Health Board to pay a higher salary to prosthetists recruited from private practice in order to establish a new prosthetics service and to attract the necessary specialist expertise. Therefore, a genuine material difference rooted in economic factors had therefore been established between Ms Rainey and Mr C., and this served as sufficient objective justification.

A similar approach had been adopted by the ECJ in *Jenkins v Kingsgate Clothing Ltd*,[88] where it held that paying full timers more than part timers in the interests of maximising the use of expensive machinery and encouraging greater productivity could in principle be objectively justified as a genuine and substantive material consideration. Similarly in *Bilka Kaufhaus*, the ECJ considered that a possible objective justification for favouring full time workers over part timers might exist where this would entail "lower ancillary costs and [permit] the use of staff throughout opening hours". Therefore, the existence of material considerations, including concerns about cost and maximising profit, may be a relevant factor in making out the existence of objective justification.

However, in *Kutz-Bauer v Freie und Hansenstadt Hamburg*,[89] the ECJ held that although a Member State may take budgetary considerations into account in deciding the nature and scope of social protection measures which it wished to adopt, cost considerations by themselves could not constitute objective justification for legislative measures that produced differential treatment between men and women. While this decision involved national legislation, the same approach was adopted in respect of private employers in the Irish case of *Hill and Stapleton v The Revenue Commissioners*,[90] where the ECJ held that an employer could not justify adverse impact arising from the design of a job-sharing scheme solely on the ground that avoiding this discrimination would involve increased costs for the employer. This was confirmed in the recent ECJ decision in *Schonheit v Stadt Frankfurt Am Main*,[91] where a part-time worker had received a proportionately smaller pension than her full time equivalent, with the employer justifying this difference in treatment on the basis of lim-

[88] [1981] I.R.L.R. 228.
[89] [2003] I.R.L.R. 368.
[90] [1998] I.R.L.R. 466.
[91] Case C-4/02 [2003] E.C.R. I–12575; [2004] I.R.L.R. 983.

iting public expenditure. The ECJ reiterated that the right to equal pay and non-discrimination could not be frustrated by the state relying on the constraints of public expenditure, and this could not by itself constitute objective justification for differential impact.

Therefore, it appears that cost considerations cannot *solely* serve as objective justification, but when combined with other economic and material considerations may play some role in establishing the existence of justification. The ECJ's concern to prevent cost becoming an easy excuse for justifying the maintenance of indirect discrimination is understandable and very necessary. However, the distinction drawn in the case-law between reliance just on cost considerations and reliance upon wider economic and other material considerations is not particularly clear.

In *Cross v British Airways plc*,[92] the EAT took a very literal approach to the ECJ's position that an employer cannot rely *solely* on cost considerations to justify indirect discrimination, finding that "an employer seeking to justify a discriminatory [provision, criterion or practice] cannot rely solely on considerations of cost. He can however put cost into the balance, together with other justifications if there are any". In *Redcar & Cleveland BC v Bainbridge (No.1)*,[93] the EAT attempted to clarify this position and reconcile *Cross* with *Schonheit*, stating that "we do not think that the case law supports the conclusion that the question of cost should always be irrelevant (para.90)."

However, in *Bainbridge (No. 1)*, the EAT also applied an additional important principle that plays an important role in constraining when economic, cost and other material considerations can justify disparate impact, stating that "We wholly accept that where a benefit is introduced and where costs determine the scope and size of that benefit, as they inevitably will, then it would be unlawful to allocate the benefit on a discriminatory basis . . . if there are cost constraints, they must be allocated in a way which limits any discriminatory impact as much as possible (para.91)." This reflects the position adopted by the ECJ in *Enderby*[94] that "sex-tainted" factors cannot be used to justify disparate impact: in other words, material considerations which are rooted in and stem from underlying patterns of inequality, or which contribute to or reinforce discriminatory treatment, cannot be used to justify disparate impact. In *Enderby*, the ECJ held that the fact that the pay scales at issue had been established via a process of collective bargaining could not constitute objective justification, as the collective bargaining process had been based upon and reinforced existing patterns of gender inequality.

In *Bainbridge* and the recent decision of *Middlesbrough v Suttees*,[95] this well-established principle of excluding "sex-tainted" factors was used to find that certain elements of "pay protection" schemes introduced in the wake of substantial equal pay awards, designed to permit employers to adjust pay

[92] [2005] I.R.L.R. 423.
[93] [2007] I.R.L.R. 91
[94] Case C-127/92, *Enderby v Frenchay Health Authority* [1993] E.C.R. 1-5535.
[95] [2007] UKEAT 0077_07_1707 (July 17, 2007).

scales gradually over time without triggering excessive costs or pay reductions for better-paid male workers, constituted unjustified sex discrimination against certain categories of women workers. These decisions are part of a complex chain of litigation, which will inevitably generate more higher court decisions as to when economic factors, including cost, can be used as objective justification, and when the use of such factors will be prohibited due to their "sex-tainted" nature.

This litigation also demonstrates the complex and difficult nature of indirect discrimination law in general, and the difficult questions it can generate. Many areas of indirect discrimination remain bedeviled by uncertainty, which successive ECJ and domestic court decisions have failed to resolve. In particular, the degree of scrutiny that courts and tribunals should apply in assessing whether objective justification exists remains uncertain. In early cases such as *Panesar v Nestlé Co. Ltd.*,[96] the domestic courts took an "extraordinarily lax" approach to the justification test, in McColgan's words.[97] Subsequent decisions such as *Hampson* saw a more stringent approach applied: however, *Hampson* and subsequent cases used the language of an "objective balance", which has been criticised as falling short of the stricter requirements of the ECJ case-law.[98] The *Allonby* decision saw Sedley L.J. emphasise that the objective justification test required a close analysis of the proportionality and need for the measures at issue, which marks a step closer to the ECJ standard. However, uncertainty appears to persist as to the appropriate standard of review in this area.

However, the broad parameters of the general approach to establishing the existence of indirect discrimination are well-established, as are the general contours of the *Bilka Kaufhaus* test for determining when what would otherwise constitute indirect discrimination can be objectively justified. Thus far, the bulk of the indirect discrimination case-law has been generated in the gender context, with a few significant cases such as *Hampson* and *Mandla* arising in the context of race discrimination. It remains to be seen how this case law will be applied across the other prohibited grounds of discrimination, and in particular in the complex area of religious and age discrimination, where complex issues concerning the wearing of religious symbols, seniority requirements and other controversial "flash points" will be litigated using the language and framework of indirect discrimination.

It also remains to be seen how the wholly unnecessary variation between the different statutory definitions of indirect discrimination will impact upon the development of the case-law, and whether the new "appropriate and necessary" standard established in the post-2000 Directives will result in any significant tightening of the objective justification test. It may help in formulating a clear and coherent approach to indirect discrimination if the essential pur-

[96] [1980] I.C.R. 144

[97] Aileen McColgan, *Discrimination Law, ibid.*, p.105.

[98] See Michael Connolly, "Discrimination Law: Justification, Alternative Measures and Defences Based on Sex" (2001) 30 I.L.J. 311, 313-8.

pose and object of disparate impact analysis is emphasised. As originally recognised in *Griggs*, effective and rigorous controls on indirect discrimination are required to address the structural forms of discrimination that continue to afflict many disadvantaged groups: this social policy goal underpins the development of the ECJ case law and should continue to guide the evolving jurisprudence in this area.

VI. Indirect Discrimination, Public Law and the Human Rights Act 1998

With the gradual extension of anti-discrimination legislation to cover the performance of public functions by public authorities, and the application of domestic and EU indirect discrimination law to national social protection and regulatory measures in cases as such as *Seymour-Smith*, it is apparent that indirect discrimination law will come to play an ever increasing role in regulating the decision-making of public authorities. For example, in *Secretary of State for Defence v Elias*, the exclusion of British subjects interned by the Japanese during World War Two from an *ex-gratia* compensation scheme, unless they had been born in the UK or had a parent or grandparent born there, was held by the Court of Appeal to constitute unjustifiable indirect discrimination on the grounds of national origin, contrary to the RRA 1976.[99]

It remains to be seen how extensive will be the impact of the gradual extension of indirect discrimination controls into the public law realm: indirect discrimination law, and in particular how the objective justification test will be applied when the decisions of public bodies are concerned, generates particular complexities that do not exist to the same degree when it comes to direct and other forms of discrimination. For example, even in the relatively well-established context of EU indirect sex discrimination controls, uncertainty persists as to the degree of scrutiny to be applied to state social protection measures which have a disparate impact on particular groups: Lord Nicholls in *Seymour-Smith* appeared to suggest that the state was entitled to a relatively wide degree of discretion in this area, whereas the ECJ decision in the same case appeared to take a stricter approach.

Considerable uncertainty has also tended to bedevil the development of protection against indirect discrimination through the ECHR, which in turn ensures a lack of clarity about the potential application of the HRA within domestic law to situations where disparate impact is at issue. As we saw in Ch.2, in order to show that there has been a violation of Art.14 ECHR, a claimant must first establish that the subject-matter of the case falls within the ambit of another Convention right, given that Art.14 currently relates, in so far as UK cases are concerned and until the UK accedes to Protocol 12, to the

[99] [2006] EWCA 1293.

enjoyment of other Convention rights (raising questions, for example, about whether discrimination in the context of employment falls within Art.14).[100] The claimant must also establish that they have been discriminated against on one of the grounds listed in Art.14 (namely sex, race, colour, language, religion, political or other opinion, national or social origin, association with a national minority, property and birth) or by reference to one of the judicially-recognised "other statuses" (including sexual orientation). Whether indirect discrimination linked to one or more of these grounds was sufficient to trigger an Art.14 remained uncertain for some time: as we also saw in Ch.2, indirect discrimination was not acknowledged in the Convention case law until comparatively late, in *Thlimmenos v Greece*.[101]

In *Thlimmenos*, the Court of Human Rights seemingly treated Art.14 (when coupled with another Convention right) as prohibiting indirect as well as direct discrimination.[102] On the facts, it was found to be impermissible for the state to apply a blanket rule which precluded *all* persons with serious criminal convictions from qualifying as a chartered accountant, when the rule impacted for no defensible reason on persons of *particular* religious beliefs.[103] *Thlimmenos* thus seems to have established that the Court is prepared to bear disparate impact analysis to bear in its case law. As the Grand Chamber of the ECtHR more recently noted in *D.H. v Czech Republic*, Art.14 no longer prohibits

> "a member State from treating groups differently in order to correct 'factual inequalities' between them; indeed in certain circumstances a failure to attempt to correct inequality through different treatment may in itself give rise to a breach of the Article.... The Court has also accepted that a general policy or measure that has disproportionately prejudicial effects on a particular group may be considered discriminatory notwithstanding that it is not specifically aimed at that group ... and that discrimination potentially contrary to the Convention may result from a *de facto* situation ... ".[104]

One implication of the recognition of indirect discrimination in *Thlimmenos* is that analogous proportionality and justification tests to those used in direct discrimination cases within Art.14 should be employed by the Court in applying disparate impact analysis. If that is so, it would seem likely that similar uncertainties to those seen in the Court's direct discrimination case law will come into play—relating in particular to the closeness of connection with a substantive Convention right which is necessary before an Art.14 claim can

[100] See, e.g., *Belgian Linguistic (No.2)* case (1968) 1 E.H.R.R. 252, para.[9].

[101] (2000) 31 E.H.R.R. 15.

[102] (2000) 31 EHRR 15.

[103] For further discussion of the extension involved, see Judge Luzius Wildhaber, "Protection against Discrimination under the European Convention on Human Rights: A Second-Class Guarantee?" (2002) 2 Baltic Yearbook of International Law 71, 81; Robert Wintemute, "'Within the Ambit': How Big *Is* the 'Gap' in Art.14 ECHR?" [2004] E.H.R.L.R. 366, 377–8; "Filling the Article 14 'Gap': Government Ratification and Judicial Control of Protocol No.12 ECHR" [2004] E.H.R.L.R. 484, 496–9; Aaron Baker, "The Enjoyment of Rights and Freedoms: A New Conception of the 'Ambit' under Art.14 ECHR" (2006) 69 M.L.R. 714, 723–5.

[104] *D.H. v Czech Republic*, app. no. 57325/00, November 13, 2007, para.[175] (Grand Chamber).

be made (and in particular, whether Art.14 has a role to play in employment cases), the intensity with which the Court will conduct proportionality review, and the extent to which the Court regards it as appropriate to defer to national authorities. It also remains unclear as to the extent to which the European Court of Human Rights will draw upon or deviate from the well-developed EU approach in this context. For example, in relation to the application of the justification test, the ECtHR has suggested that discrimination on account of a person's ethnic origin is incapable of justification in a contemporary democratic society[105]: a ringing statement which may potentially give rise to conflict with the justification provisions in EU law and national legislation concerning justifications for indirect discrimination relating to ethnic origin.

Similar questions about the extent to which the ECtHR will draw upon the EU approach also crop up in relation to the question of burden of proof and showing the existence of disparate impact. The rules concerning burden of proof in Art. 14 direct discrimination cases, considered in Ch.4, appear also to apply in ECHR indirect discrimination cases. However, one point of considerable importance is when the ECtHR will consider it permissible to infer the existence of discrimination from empirical evidence relating to the impact of the rule or practice in issue. While the ECtHR's general practice has been to exercise caution in making use of statistics, recent indirect discrimination case law has involved the use of official statistics in establishing that a neutrally formulated rule in fact affects a clearly higher percentage of members of one group than of another, shifting the onus of proof to the respondent national authority to show that the difference was the result of objective factors unrelated to any discrimination.[106] This shift from an initial cautious approach to a much more developed engagement with disparate impact analysis can be illustrated by comparing two cases.

The first, *Hoogendijk v The Netherlands*, concerned an alleged violation of Art.14 coupled with Art.1 of the First Protocol (the right to peaceful enjoyment of possessions).[107] The claimant had been rejected for a disability allowance under national law due to her husband's earnings. The legislation involved a means test which resulted in more married women than men losing a claim to benefits. Although the claim was declared inadmissible, the Court offered some practical guidance as to how indirect discrimination claims would be handled:

105 *D.H. v Czech Republic, ibid.*, para.[176] (Grand Chamber).
106 *D.H. v Czech Republic, ibid.*, para.[180] (Grand Chamber).
107 (2005) 40 E.H.R.R. SE22.

Hoogendijk v The Netherlands (2005) 40 EHRR SE22

... the Court considers that where a general policy or measure has disproportionately prejudicial effects on a particular group, it is not excluded that this may be regarded as discriminatory notwithstanding that it is not specifically aimed at that group....Although statistics in themselves are not automatically sufficient ... the Court considers that where an applicant is able to show, on the basis of undisputed official statistics, the existence of a prima facie indication that a specific rule—although formulated in a neutral manner—in fact affects a clearly higher percentage of women than men, it is for the respondent Government to show that this is the result of objective factors unrelated to any discrimination on grounds of sex. If the onus ... does not shift to the respondent Government, it will be in practice extremely difficult for applicants to prove indirect discrimination.

Having stipulated that the question facing the respondent was whether an objective and reasonable justification could be shown for the measure concerned, the Court accepted rather cursorily that such a justification had been shown here since the means test had been introduced to remove the discriminatory exclusion of married women from the national scheme (following previous litigation to the ECJ) while seeking to keep the costs of the scheme within acceptable limits. Apart from the rather limited explanation here—reinforcing the notion, seen in relation to direct discrimination, that the Court conducts justification exercises rather vaguely—it is interesting to note that the Court accepted cost as a legitimate justification for a *prima facie* discriminatory scheme.

In the second case, *D.H. v Czech Republic*, the Grand Chamber of the Court took a much stronger approach, after an initially very cautious decision by a Chamber of the Court at first instance.[108] The claimants challenged the functioning of the Czech educational system as being indirectly discriminatory against Roma children, given that statistics demonstrated that the proportion of Roma children in special schools for children with learning deficiencies was higher than that of other children (the claim was thus based on Art.14 coupled with Art.2 of the First Protocol (the right to education)). The claim was initially rejected by the Chamber of the Court, which adopted a sceptical tone concerning the use of statistics in indirect discrimination cases.

D.H. v Czech Republic Application No 57325/00

[45] ... The Court points out .. that ... it is not its task to assess the overall social context. Its sole task in the instant case is to examine the individual applications before it and to establish on the basis of the relevant facts whether the reason for the applicants' placement in the special schools was their ethnic or racial origin.

[108] Application No 57325/00, unreported.

> **[46]** In that connection, the Court observes that, if a policy or general measure has disproportionately prejudicial effects on a group of people, the possibility of its being considered discriminatory cannot be ruled out even if it is not specifically aimed or directed at that group. However, statistics are not by themselves sufficient to disclose a practice which could be classified as discriminatory . . .

The Chamber decision resolved the case using the margin of appreciation, emphasising that the margin was just as relevant in indirect as in direct discrimination cases. The power of the margin is particularly evident in how the Court used it to rebut the claimants' argument based on statistics:

> **[46]** . . . With regard to pupils with special needs, the Court . . . wishes to reiterate with regard to the States' margin of appreciation in the education sphere that States cannot be prohibited from setting up different types of school for children with difficulties or implementing special educational programmes to respond to special needs . . .
> **[49]** The Court observes that the rules governing children's placement in special schools do not refer to the pupils' ethnic origin, but pursue the legitimate aim of adapting the educational system to the need and aptitudes or disabilities of the children. Since these are not legal concepts, it is only right that experts in educational psychology should be responsible for identifying them . . .
> **[52]** Thus, while acknowledging that these statistics disclose figures that are worrying and that the general situation in the Czech Republic concerning the education of Roma children is by no means perfect, the Court cannot in the circumstances find that the measures taken against the applicants were discriminatory. Although the applicants may have lacked information about the national education system or found themselves in a climate of mistrust, the concrete evidence before the Court in the present case does not enable it to conclude that the applicants' placement . . . in special schools was the result of racial prejudice . . .

However, the subsequent decision by the Grand Chamber of the Court saw a remarkable reversal of approach.[109] The Grand Chamber considered that statistical evidence such as that at issue in this case could (and did in this case) impose a burden of justification on a Member State. As a result, the Grand Chamber (not without a few strongly worded dissents) found the Czech Republic to be in violation of Art.14: it concluded that the Czech government had failed to demonstrate the existence of objective justification for the patterns of segregation of Roma children within the state education system that the statistical data clearly showed to exist. The Grand Chamber cited leading ECJ, UK and US authority on the issue of statistical evidence, including *Bilka-Kaufhaus*, *Seymour-Smith* and *Griggs*, and was clearly keen to echo the approaches taken by these courts towards the use of statistical data in indirect discrimination cases.

DH is a decision of considerable potential importance. With *Thlimmenos*, it marks the beginning of the development by the ECtHR of what was hitherto lacking in its jurisprudence—a clear and coherent stance on indirect discrimination, which unlocks its potential to address serious rights abuses that

[109] [2007] ECHR 922, November 13, 2007.

take the form of structural discrimination, but which cannot be classified as direct discrimination. The impact of *DH* in future ECHR and domestic human rights cases under the HRA remains to be seen, but with the extension of domestic discrimination legislation to the performance of public functions and the evolving ECJ case law, indirect discrimination is coming to occupy a place in European and domestic public law which hitherto had been largely left vacant.

VII. The Conceptual Boundaries of Indirect Discrimination: "Institutional Discrimination", Positive Duties and Positive Action

We have discussed in this and other chapters the differences between direct and indirect discrimination as legal concepts, alongside the differing social policy goals towards which they seem to have been aimed. The increasing acknowledgement of institutional discrimination as a social evil, which the law of indirect discrimination is to some extent intended to counter, gives rise to a further issue, which we consider here: namely, the extent to which indirect discrimination liability alone can counter institutional discrimination, and what other measures are necessary in order to do so. Closely related to this is a conceptual question, to which there does not appear to be a clear answer, namely where the boundaries lie between direct discrimination, indirect discrimination, positive duties to make reparation for past discrimination, and affirmative action.

An early use of the term "institutional racism" (as a form of institutional discrimination) in an official context in the U.K. can be found in the 1981 Scarman Report into the Brixton riots, in which racial grievances had played a large role.[110] More recently, the Stephen Lawrence Inquiry—which investigated the role of alleged racism in the Metropolitan Police in their handling of a murder investigation—adopted a broader definition of the term, going beyond the notion of 'unwitting' racism employed by Lord Scarman[111]:

The Stephen Lawrence Inquiry: Report of an Inquiry by Sir William MacPherson of Cluny (London: HMSO, 1999), Cm. 4262-I

6.7 In 1981 Lord Scarman's Report into The Brixton Disorders was presented to Parliament. In that seminal report Lord Scarman responded to the suggestion that *"Britain is an institutionally racist society,"* in this way:—

[110] Cmnd 8427, *The Brixton Disorders: Report of an Inquiry by the Rt Hon the Lord Scarman OBE* (London: HMSO, 1981).

[111] See also Christopher McCrudden, "Institutional Discrimination", id., 304.

"If, by [institutionally racist] *it is meant that it* [Britain] *is a society which knowingly, as a matter of policy, discriminates against black people, I reject the allegation. If, however, the suggestion being made is that practices may be adopted by public bodies as well as private individuals which are unwittingly discriminatory against black people, then this is an allegation which deserves serious consideration, and, where proved, swift remedy".* (Para.2.22, p.11—Scarman Report).

6.34 Taking all that we have heard and read into account we grapple with the problem. For the purposes of our Inquiry the concept of institutional racism which we apply consists of:

The collective failure of an organisation to provide an appropriate and professional service to people because of their colour, culture, or ethnic origin. It can be seen or detected in processes, attitudes and behaviour which amount to discrimination through unwitting prejudice, ignorance, thoughtlessness and racist stereotyping which disadvantage minority ethnic people.

It persists because of the failure of the organisation openly and adequately to recognise and address its existence and causes by policy, example and leadership. Without recognition and action to eliminate such racism it can prevail as part of the ethos or culture of the organisation. It is a corrosive disease.

As the Inquiry went on to recognize, the redress of institutional discrimination as a social problem required a strategy going far beyond individual remedies for discrimination, including indirect discrimination. In reality, emphasis had to be placed on altering the culture of powerful bodies such as the police—something which might entail organizational changes—as well as public education concerning racism. This is evident from the following observations:

6.35 As Dr Oakely [a witness] points out [in his evidence], the disease cannot be attacked by the organisation involved in isolation. If such racism infests the police its elimination can only be achieved "by means of a fully developed partnership approach in which the police service works jointly with the minority ethnic communities. How else can mutual confidence and trust be reached?" . . .

6.54 **Racism, institutional or otherwise, is not the prerogative of the Police Service. It is clear that other agencies including for example those dealing with housing and education also suffer from the disease. If racism is to be eradicated there must be specific and co-ordinated action both within the agencies themselves and by society at large, particularly through the educational system, from pre-primary school upwards and onwards.**

If the Stephen Lawrence Inquiry's definition of institutional racism is adopted, therefore, the legal concept of indirect discrimination cannot be seen—at least, considered on its own—as an adequate form of redress, given its emphasis on individual remedies when what is involved is a deep and broad problem of institutional culture and societal values more generally. If we assume, however, that indirect discrimination is but one of a collection of legal (and extra-legal) strategies for countering institutional discrimination—others including, for example, positive action measures or the imposition of positive duties on particular bodies—we must consider how far it is possible cleanly to distinguish between the different strategies (something which might be felt important for the sake of precision, or to demonstrate the legitimacy of a choice to use one type of strategy rather than another).

Two examples demonstrate the real difficulty in making a clean distinction. First, *Thlimmenos v Greece*—which, as noted earlier, is generally treated as a recognition by the Court of Human Rights that indirect as well as direct discrimination is prohibited under Art.14 of the Convention—might on one view illustrate the existence of a slightly unpredictable boundary line between indirect discrimination and positive action. The characterization of the case as one of indirect discrimination arises from the Court's conclusion that a facially neutral rule—"no one with a criminal conviction may become a chartered accountant"—was disproportionate and impermissible since it automatically prevented those who had refused to participate in military service due to their religious faith, thereby securing a criminal conviction, from qualifying to be accountants. However, as Richard Clayton and Hugh Tomlinson have argued, it is also possible to categorise *Thlimmenos* as a complaint about the state's failure to promote positive action,[112] given that the Court emphasized that Art.14 was "violated when States without objective and reasonable justification fail to treat differently persons whose situations are significantly different".[113] On this view, the case might be thought to be saying that different (and more favourable) treatment should be accorded to aspiring chartered accountants who had been convicted of a criminal offence due to their religious faith than to other aspiring accountants with criminal convictions.

Secondly, McCrudden has alluded, in his analysis of institutional discrimination, to the uncertain boundary between indirect discrimination and positive duties or positive action. McCrudden suggests that "fair equality of opportunity"—a policy goal he associates with the redress of institutional discrimination—differs from the "simple non-discrimination principle" which he associates with direct discrimination:

Christopher McCrudden "Institutional Discrimination" (1982) 2 O.J.L.S. 303

[344–5]: . . . in being positive as well as negative in its requirements and in taking into account some of the prior existing disadvantages which black workers bring to the market place. Though phrased negatively, the new meaning of discrimination [i.e., indirect discrimination] sometimes has the effect of requiring employers to do certain things in addition to prohibiting other actions. For example, if, by advertising in a newspaper which is not bought by the majority of potential minority group workers, a considerable number

112 *The Law of Human Rights* (Oxford: OUP, 2000), paras 14.81, 17.91A, 17.115, 17.142.
113 *Ibid.*

of these workers are not even aware of job opportunities, it may be argued that the employer has a positive duty to advertise in those newspapers which do reach the black population. The employer must, if he is not to be in breach of the prohibition, so operate his recruitment and promotions as positively to offset the group related disadvantages which adversely affect the black workers' chances of being hired or promoted.

However, once the nature of the duty imposed shifts from being negative to positive—something the possibility of which must depend upon how expansively the idea of a requirement or condition is defined—it becomes difficult to see where, if anywhere, a boundary can be drawn between indirect discrimination and affirmative action. It seems likely that the location of the relevant boundary—if anywhere—must ultimately turn on our understanding of how the law's social policy goals might most effectively be met.

Going a step further, the Canadian Supreme Court in its decision in *British Columbia (Public Service Employee Relations Commission) v British Columbia Government Service Employees' Union* (the "Meiorin" case)[114] merged direct discrimination and disparate impact analysis under the Canadian human rights legislative framework within a single combined framework, whereby an employer had to demonstrate that a discriminatory practice could not to be accommodated to include the individual complainant without undue hardship. This "reasonable accommodation" approach merges direct discrimination, indirect discrimination and reasonable accommodation of individual needs: it therefore could be said to contain elements of both negative prohibition and positive action, and illustrates again how the current distinctions that exist between the different forms of discrimination may be less solid and substantial than sometimes is assumed to be the case.

VIII. Conclusion

It is clear from this chapter that the definition, conceptual basis and evolution of indirect discrimination as a form of legal liability is closely linked to some of the ten key questions that were identified in Ch.1 as repeatedly surfacing throughout discrimination law. In particular, questions as to "how wide are the protections against discrimination?" and "what justifications may be available for particular types of discrimination?" loom large when we consider indirect discrimination. It is clear that from its initial recognition in *Griggs*, indirect discrimination was conceived of as going beyond direct discrimination, and that one of its social policy goals was to challenge the somewhat amorphous idea of "institutional discrimination". It also seems clear that the case law dealing with, for example, part-time workers and child-care responsibilities has aimed to attack long-standing employment practices which impact adversely on women. Nonetheless, the tests for indirect dis-

[114] [1999] 3 S.C.R. 3,

crimination are extremely complex and arguably not applied consistently by the employment tribunals and courts, undermining the law's potential for success in this area. Serious uncertainties linger, in particular when we consider the place of indirect discrimination within the broader framework of human rights protection. Whether a legal concept as complex as indirect discrimination could ever be sensitive enough to the issues thrown up by the social problem of "institutional discrimination" and the other complex forms of structural discrimination it is designed to tackle is thus a live question. With the gradual expansion of the European Convention on Human Rights into this area, with the recognition that indirect discrimination is prohibited by Art.14, and the ongoing transformation of EU and domestic law in this field, the potential for complexity, uncertainty and potentially unexpected side-effects seems likely to increase.

6

JUSTIFYING POSITIVE ACTION

I. Introduction

Positive action[1] is a concept of great significance in the context of anti-discrimination law. It is closely connected in particular to the third and fourth questions of our set of ten questions about discrimination law: how wide is protection against discrimination, and when might forms of apparent discrimination be justified for policy reasons? How these questions relate to positive action measures tends to generate considerable controversy. Debates about "affirmative action", "positive discrimination" or "preferential treatment" have generated high-profile litigation, divisive political disputation and reams of academic analysis. Yet this controversy has often sowed more confusion than it has provided illumination. In particular, there has been a tendency to overlook the complex range of measures, policies and practices that come within the overall term of "positive action". This has often excessively simplified and distorted the issues that arise when "positive action" is used.

The definition and implementation of positive action raises many of the key ten questions that we identified in chapter 1 as recurring over and over within discrimination law. It is worth therefore returning to first principles and critically examining the conceptual foundations that underpin the use of positive action, and then to look at how these measures have been applied in practice. In this chapter we will focus in particular on some of the conceptual problems that arise when forms of positive action that entail preferential treatment are used in anti-discrimination law. In the next chapter, we examine positive action more generally and discuss some of the key legal and policy issues surrounding the use of positive action in discrimination law.

[1] The term positive action was first introduced by the Home Office guide to the Race Relations Act 1976: see Home Office, *Racial Discrimination: A Guide to the Race Relations Act 1976* (London: Home Office, 1977). The term is also included in two important US anti-discrimination law statutes: Title VII of the Civil Rights Act 1964 where it is used to describe a remedy available to judges as a response to unlawful discrimination; and in Executive Order 11, 246 where it is used to describe "contract compliance", i.e. the obligations of a federal government contractor in a situation where a minority or women workers are underrepresented in the workforce of the contractor. See Christopher McCrudden "Rethinking Positive Action" (1986) 15 I.L.J. 219, at 221.

II. The Limits of "Mainstream" Discrimination Law

To understand the development and rationale underpinning positive action approaches, it is necessary first of all to understand the limits of "mainstream" discrimination law. Eliminating discrimination within the public and private sectors is now accepted as an important goal of public policy. To give effect to this principle, UK and EU discrimination law is designed to prevent the expression or manifestation of particular forms of prejudice. It focuses upon the elimination of differences of treatment which are based upon the prohibited grounds of race, gender, sexual orientation, age, religious belief and disability, usually (but not always, as in the case of pregnancy and disability discrimination) defining discriminatory behaviour by reference to comparator tests. It relies upon individuals bringing civil actions to ensure that the legislation is enforced, and uses retrospective civil sanctions to punish and deter those who might be tempted to break the law.

This approach has achieved some success in altering behaviour and preventing overt forms of discrimination.[2] However, the limitations of this approach have also been widely recognised. Underlying this way of approaching equality issues is the assumption that discriminatory acts are isolated and abnormal events, capable of being solely remedied via the normal individual-based approach of a civil action, just as one would attempt to remedy a normal tortious act. This assumption disregards the evidence that discriminatory attitudes are deeply embedded, often constituting the "norm" upon which many social practices and forms of cultural identity are based, and impact mainly upon disadvantaged groups that often are the least able to make use of individual litigation.[3] Discrimination law relies for its effectiveness upon the willingness and ability of individuals to bring actions and, if necessary, to litigate their cases to a conclusion in the face of considerable

[2] See Bob Hepple, Mary Coussey, and Tufyal Choudhury, *Equality: A New Framework*, Report of the Independent Review of the Enforcement of UK Anti-Discrimination Legislation (Oxford: Hart, 2000), para.1.33 (hereafter referred to as the "Hepple Report"). See also Chris McCrudden, "Theorising European Law", in C. Costello and E. Barry (eds) *Equality in Diversity: The New Equality Directives* (Dublin: Irish Centre for European Law, 2003).

[3] The underlying view of "discrimination as aberration" also distorts how discrimination law is applied and perceived. Victims have to establish that defendants clearly committed acts that come within the narrow and limited definitions of discriminatory acts as recognised by the legislation and case-law, while defendants often strongly contest any attempt to tag them with the stigmata of being "racist" or "sexist", often out of a genuine self-perception that they were in no way culpable. What defendants often will in actuality have failed to do is to take active steps to scrutinise their policies and practices for discriminatory effects, rather than "discriminate" in a positive manner as envisaged in the scheme of the legislation and as commonly understood by non-lawyers. However, as the legislation contains no requirement to take positive steps, litigants have to couch their claim in terms of direct or indirect discrimination: this generates ferocious resistance, lessens their chances of success and often distorts what is actually at issue.

social and financial pressures.[4] If there is a lack of individual complainants willing to bring an action against particular public or private sector bodies, then discrimination law may have very little impact within particular occupations or areas of economic or state activity.[5] In addition, the inevitable difficulty in establishing a clear case under discrimination legislation makes it difficult for individuals, employers and public authorities to identify their legal rights and obligations, which discourages reliance upon equality laws.[6] Even if an action is successful, the available remedies are limited to redressing retrospectively the immediate wrong to the aggrieved individual, and cannot require the modification of discriminatory practice across an organisation.[7]

In addition, where it is applied, the use of the comparator test limits the applicability of discrimination law, encourages assimilation to existing practices, and means that oppressive power relations often remain unchallenged and unaltered.[8] It also encourages a perception that discrimination law is only concerned with the abnormal behaviour of some bigoted individuals, rather than with achieving social transformation.[9] The concept of indirect discrimination is intended to compensate for some of these limitations, by

[4] See Sandra Fredman, *Discrimination Law* (Oxford: OUP, 2001), p.165. See also Sandra Fredman and Erika Szyszczak, 'Interaction of Race and Gender', in B. Hepple and E. Szyszczak, *Discrimination: The Limits of the Law* (London: Mansell, 1992), p.216. This is especially true for cases relating to goods and services, which are heard by the courts and not tribunals, with the result that complainants may more readily be exposed to cost orders. Between December 2, 1996 and July 9, 1998, only nine disability cases concerning access to goods and services were lodged in England and Wales, whereas 2,456 were lodged in employment tribunals in respect of employment-related matters: see Meager *et al.*, "Monitoring the Disability Discrimination Act 1995", Research Report 119 (London, Department of Employment and Education, 1999).

[5] It could be argued that significant areas of the workforce have seen little or no challenge to discriminatory practices, as perhaps exemplified by the treatment of women within some financial sectors of the City of London.

[6] In particular, discrimination law generates costs and complexities due to the perennial interpretation difficulties relating to the need to show the existence of a "requirement" or "practice", the usual requirement to identify a suitable comparator, as well as the uncertain and shifting extent of the justification defence in indirect discrimination. See Chris McCrudden, "Anti-Discrimination Goals and the Legal Process" in N. Glazer and K. Young (eds) *Ethnic Pluralism and Public Policy* (London: Treasury, 1983); Bob Hepple, "Judging Legal Rights" [1983] CLP 71. See also G. Bownes, *Snakes and Ladders: Advice and Support for Discrimination Cases in Wales* (Cardiff: EOC, 2003). The applicant success rate in employment tribunal cases involving race discrimination has been described by the UK Cabinet Office Strategy Unit as "notably low": see UK Cabinet Office Strategy Unit, *Ethnic Minorities and the Labour Market* (London: Cabinet Office, 2002), para.4.56.1, at p.119. At the very least, this demonstrates that a considerable lack of congruity exists between the subjective perceptions of litigants that discriminatory behaviour has occurred and the much more limited types of conduct that are legally deemed to constitute discriminatory acts.

[7] See S. Fredman, *Discrimination Law* (Oxford, OUP, 2001), pp.170–73. The individual enforcement model also sets up a two-party winner-takes-all contest, which is confined in effect to the two parties concerned, leaving no room for best practice group settlements or the input of third parties. For the classic discussion of the limits of adjudication in such circumstances, see A. Chayes, "The Role of the Judge in Public Law Litigation" (1976) 89 Harvard L.R. 1281. The individual decision is supposed to produce an indirect knock-on effect, but this is not always inevitable, especially when a case is settled out-of-court.

[8] See also S. Fredman, *Discrimination Law* (Oxford: OUP, 2001), p.165.

[9] See Nicola Lacey, "From Individual to Group", in B. Hepple and E. Szyszczak, *Discrimination: The Limits of the Law* (London: Mansell, 1992), pp.102–3.

removing obstacles faced by disadvantaged groups. However, its impact is often limited, due to the complexity of applying indirect discrimination rules in practice, and the wide scope often given to the justification defence (see chapter 5).

In general, the problem with discrimination law is that its primary focus is on securing equal treatment for individuals. This emphasis on ensuring sameness of treatment can result in underlying structural or group-related forms of inequality being ignored.[10] Institutional forms of exclusion that cannot be readily classified as "discriminatory" tend to slip beneath the radar of equality and anti-discrimination laws.[11] Structural forms of discrimination, such as negative stereotyping, expectations of conformity to dominant social norms, or a lack of understanding of the specific needs and perspectives of disadvantaged groups, often remain untouched by discrimination law.[12] The findings of the Macpherson Report demonstrated that even the comparatively well-developed race relations legislative framework was having little impact upon the persistence of forms of "institutional racism" in the Metropolitan Police.[13]

Much of the prejudicial treatment faced by disadvantaged groups stems from neglect, lack of understanding of their specific needs, and the failure to take into account their particular circumstances. This neglect is often due to the limited participation of members of these disadvantaged groups in decision-making processes.[14] No obligation exists for employers or service providers to take anticipatory action to alter practices and policies that may disadvantage particular groups, with the exception of the reasonable accommodation obligations imposed by the Disability Discrimination Act, which in any case only arise with respect to the needs of particular individuals.

The concerns with the limits of a model of discrimination law that is solely focused on individual complaints are summarised in the following passage:

[10] See Fredman, *Discrimination Law* (Oxford: OUP, 2001), pp.7–11. See also J. Squires, *Gender in Political Theory* (Cambridge: Polity Press, 1999).

[11] Such practices are often made to appear positively acceptable, as they are outside the legally established definition of discrimination. See N. Lacey, "From Individual to Group", in B. Hepple and E. Szyszczak, *Discrimination: The Limits of the Law* (1992), pp.102–3.

[12] See Fredman, *Discrimination Law*, 22–23. The effect of equality legislation may often be to confine the expression of prejudice within certain tolerated spheres or within "coded" language, rather than to shift social attitudes.

[13] Macpherson et al., *The Stephen Lawrence Inquiry* (1999).

[14] See S. Fredman, *Discrimination Law* (Oxford: OUP, 2001), 22–23. The Hepple Report, para.2.19, regarded, as a basic principle of discrimination law, the need for "opportunities for those directly affected to participate, through information, consultation and engagement in the process of change".

Sandra Fredman and Sarah Spencer, "Beyond Discrimination: It's Time for Enforceable Duties on Public Bodies to Promote Equality Outcomes" [2006] E.H.R.L.R. 598

599–600 "The complaints-led model requires an individual victim to bring a complaint to a court or tribunal to establish a breach of his or her right not to be discriminated against. This has several problematic consequences. First, reliance on an individual complainant to bring an action in court puts excessive strain on the victim in terms of resources and personal energy. This means that many individuals, particularly those in employment cases who are not members of unions, are unable to pursue their claims. The result is that the court's intervention is ad hoc, does not necessarily challenge the worst offenders, and many cases of discrimination go unremedied.

Secondly, the complaints-led model is retrospective. It therefore does not steer policy, either by preventing the adoption of policies with a deterimenal impact on equality, or by requiring bodies consciously to adopt policies which promote equality.

Thirdly, it assumes that fear of litigation or respect for the law will be sufficient to motivate organisations to review their policies or practices. Yet the adversarial nature of claims often means that they are resisted by employers and service providers against whom the complaint is made. Instead of viewing equality as a shared goal, to be achieved co-operatively, addressing discrimination becomes a source of conflict and resistance. There are other policy levers which may be as or more effective as a catalyst for change but discrimination law, in the absence of a duty on the organisation to promote equality, does not bring those levers into play. Finally, the litigation model is individualised, providing remedies to individuals rather than the institutional change which is so often needed.

Proactive models aim to remedy each of the deficiencies of the complaints-led approach. Most important, the initiative lies not with the individual victim of discrimination to make a complaint, but with the employer and service provider. This relieves individual victims of the burden and expense of litigation (although they rightly retain the right to do so), and should deliver the progressive realisation of equality within an acceptable time-frame. It should mean that change is sytematic rather than reliant on ad hoc complaints, and that the institutional and structural causes of inequality can be diagnosed and addressed collectively and institutionally.

The intention is that organisations identify the barriers to equality in their employment and service provision and take steps to address those barriers. In addition, organisations are expected to be forward-looking, ensuring that their mainstream policies do not have a negative impact on women, disabled people and minorities, while framing specific policies to promote equality."

These criticisms of discrimination law are now widely accepted in the academic literature and in policy debates. They could be seen as demonstrating the inevitable limits of what legal norms can achieve by way of social transformation. For example, a sceptic about the possibility of achieving social change through anti-discrimination legislation could argue that if structural forms of group exclusion in contemporary society are to be broken down, reliance will have to be placed upon other types of policy levers and initiatives to bring about change: discrimination law should recognise its limits and confine itself to protecting individuals against certain forms of discrimination.

However, attempts have been made to extend the "classical" framework of equality and anti-discrimination law in an attempt to overcome these inherent limits. Generally, these involve the stretching of the existing fabric of discrimination law to permit or to require the adoption of measures designed to break down or eliminate structural patterns of group exclusion. In other words, attempts have been made to modify the standard focus of discrimination law on individuals facing distinct types of discrimination to accommodate the introduction of a wide range of "positive action" measures.

III. What is "Positive Action"?

Various terms are used to describe types of positive action, such as "affirmative action", "positive discrimination", "employment equity" and so on: McColgan has described these terms as "as politically controversial as they are linguistically indeterminate".[15] The need for conceptual clarity in this context is essential, especially given the confusion, distortions and emotional baggage that inevitably accompany any discussion of this issue.

The term "positive action" can cover a huge variety of policies and initiatives. A common thread is that these measures are usually anticipatory in effect, i.e. designed to remove obstacles to equal participation before an individual is affected, or else are designed to help disadvantaged groups overcome such obstacles. A broad definition of positive action would therefore include all measures which go beyond the prohibition of discrimination and seek by means of positive steps to alter existing social practices so as to eliminate patterns of group exclusion and disadvantage.[16] The term is best understood as extending to any form of proactive action designed to benefit a disadvantaged group, and therefore can cover a huge variety of policies and initiatives. It can extend from the taking of basic steps to eliminate prohibited discrimination to the use of mainstreaming initiatives,[17] the provision of special welfare assistance and preferential treatment in certain employment contexts.[18]

"Positive action" does not automatically involve the use of preferential

[15] A. McColgan *Discrimination Law: Text, Cases and Materials*, 2nd edn (Oxford: Hart Publishing, 2005), p.130.

[16] This broad definition is adopted from C. Bell, A. Hegarty and S. Livingstone, "The Enduring Controversy: Developments on Affirmative Action Law in North America" (1996) *International Journal of Discrimination and the Law* 233, 234.

[17] Considerable uncertainty exists as to what "mainstreaming" actually requires: the word is prone to a variety of interpretation. The basic aim of mainstreaming strategies is to make sure that public authorities identify forms of structural discrimination which may exist within existing systems and structures, and take action to eliminate these discriminatory factors and promote diversity. See below, and Theresa Rees, "Mainstreaming Equality", in S. Watson and L. Doyal (eds) *Engendering Social Policy* (Buckingham: Open University Press, 2000).

[18] For example, eliminating a height requirement, or modifying an assessment process might be necessary to avoid a finding of indirect discrimination, but would also be an effective step in a positive action strategy.

treatment for particular groups, although this strategy might be adopted as a significant part of a wider positive action approach. This point is worth emphasising, as a popular perception exists that positive action automatically equates to the use of forms of preferential treatment. Proponents of positive action approaches frequently argue that the use of otherwise suspect classifications such as ethnicity, gender or age to identify groups who require targeted special assistance is legitimate, as such measures can be necessary to redress patterns of systematic discrimination that particularly affect those groups.[19] However, positive action strategies can take a variety of forms, which may not involve the use of preferential treatment *per se*.[20] Indeed, any well-designed positive action strategy will probably attempt to make use of several different forms of positive action. Also, different strategies may use different forms of action at different times depending upon the nature of the disadvantages at issue and the relevant socio-economic and political context in question.

Examples of positive action could include the following:

- identifying and dismantling discriminatory barriers such as forms of testing or recruitment that unfairly disadvantage particular groups;
- conducting outreach exercises to encourage greater representation in social environments and activities by underrepresented groups;
- increasing workplace diversity by allowing factors such as race, ethnicity or gender to be considered in evaluating qualified candidates for employment and promotion, if permitted;
- introducing special training programs for underrepresented groups; and
- setting targets for managers, administrators or service providers for enhanced diversity to be achieved in recruitment, promotion and service provision.

Within this wide spread of measures, McCrudden has identified five basic core categories of positive action:

[19] See Elizabeth Anderson, "Integration, Affirmative Action and Strict Scrutiny" (2000) 77 N.Y.U.L. Rev. 1195–1271.

[20] Chris McCrudden, "Rethinking Positive Action" (1986) 15(1) I.L.J. 219.

Christopher McCrudden, "Rethinking Positive Action" (1986) 15(1) I.L.J. 219

"What is 'positive action?'

The variety of employer action which fits under the umbrella of 'positive action' is considerable. Five types of action appear to come under the rubric of what positive action *might* include, not in the sense of what is legally permissible, but in the sense of how the term appears to be used in common parlance.

Eradicating discrimination. This conception of positive action is the most commonly used idea of what positive action means in Britain. It involves identifying and replacing discriminatory practices, especially those which have the effect of disadvantaging one group more than another and are not 'justifiable'. A number of examples are well known (word of mouth hiring) and much of the CRE's Code of Practice is devoted to setting out a number of others. . . . There are also likely to be substantial differences between those employers who adopt the spirit of the law and those who merely adhere to its letter. Employers should be encouraged to consider it necessary to review regularly the action taken to eradicate unlawful discrimination, assess the effectiveness of the steps taken, and consider what more needs to be done to achieve the objective. This type of 'positive action' is the only one to have become at all well known, if not well implemented, in Britain.

Facially neutral but purposefully inclusionary policies. Such policies seek to increase the proportion of members of the previously excluded or currently under-represented group (women, racial minorities, Catholics). They do so by using criteria which are facially neutral (in the sense that they do not identify or use group membership as either a necessary or a sufficient condition). Thus, for example, the status of being unemployed or of living in a particular geographical area might be stipulated as a relevant condition in order to be eligible for apprenticeship or entry level employment, with the knowledge that a greater proportion of those who are unemployed or who live in that area are members of the underrepresented group than of the majority group.

Outreach programmes. The remaining elements in what constitutes 'positive action' make direct use of group membership in the allocation of benefits, but otherwise vary considerably among themselves.

Outreach programmes are designed to attract qualified candidates from the previously underrepresented group. They do so in two ways: first, by bringing employment opportunities to the attention of members of the group who might not previously have been aware of them and encouraging them to take up the opportunity to apply when otherwise they might not; second, by providing members of the underrepresented group without the necessary skills or qualifications with training the better to equip them for competing when they do apply. The aim of positive action in this sense is 'to accelerate the process whereby black employees are encouraged to apply for work in which they have been under-represented and, in such circumstances, to help them qualify on merit for appointment and promotion.' . . . Unlike the previous types of programmes this variety of positive action does not use the criterion of membership in the underrepresented group as an immediately relevant condition for identifying who should be informed, encouraged and trained. Unlike the next types of programme, however, the relevance of group membership ceases when the selection stage for the job or the promotion itself is reached.

Preferential treatment in employment. This fourth type of positive action programme, where racial or gender preferences are adopted, involves a plan to reduce the underrepresentation of minorities and women more directly than the third, by introducing what has sometimes been called reverse discrimination in favour of members of those groups at one or more points of the employment relationship such as hiring, promotion and redundancy. Fullinwider's definition of preferential hiring is useful at this point. '[A] black is preferentially hired over a white,' he writes, 'when the black, because he is black, is chosen over at least one better qualified white, where being black is not a job-related qualification.' The differences within this fourth broad type of 'positive action' are considerable. There may be different aspects of the employment relationship covered, with some programmes involving preferences only in hiring while others extend to promotion and redundancy. A second difference relates to whether race or gender is merely a relevant consideration among others (e.g. where minority status is a positive factor to be considered in evaluating the applications of minority applicants) or whether it is the sole consideration (e.g. where a predetermined number of new hires is reserved for qualified minority applicants).

'Redefining merit'. This fifth and last type of positive action differs from the previous four in that it alters substantially the qualifications which are necessary to do the job by including race, gender, or religion as a relevant 'qualification' in order to be able to do the job properly. Group membership is a job-related qualification, rather than an exception to it, as it is in the fourth type. Dworkin has argued that there 'is no combination of abilities and skills and traits that constitutes "merit" in the abstract. ... If a black skin will, as a matter of regrettable fact, enable another doctor to do a different medical job better, then that black skin ... is merit.' Positive action has been defended, for example, as a means of encouraging the recruitment of more social workers from minority groups on the grounds that ' ... there are situations when ... colour alone can sometimes serve as a source of client–worker identification. Sharing a devalued minority group position in society can help communication across West Indian and Asian ethnic barriers'. A similar argument can be applied to the police. However, if race can in some circumstances be treated as an added qualification, it should also be able to be used as an added disqualification."

Positive action strategies can therefore take a variety of forms, often combining elements of several or even all of these different categories. The key issues in designing such a strategy often involve deciding which policies should be utilised in what combination to achieve the greatest effect in the relevant circumstances.

IV. The Legitimacy Debate: When is Positive Action Unfair?

The rights and wrongs of positive action, however defined, have been strongly debated, and so before embarking on a detailed exploration of relevant legal provisions in chapter 7, it is necessary to explore and debate that further. Although some types of positive action within the McCrudden typology set out above will not cause a conceptual problem for discrimination law, others will be problematic and difficult to justify. More specifically, there are two types of cases where positive action measures may apparently conflict with the aims of discrimination law: (i) preferential treatment that involves direct discrimination in favour of particular groups; and (ii) where use of a neutral criterion for a good motive may constitute indirect discrimination because it can disproportionately benefit particular groups. This means that there is a need for some sort of conceptual framework to assess when special treatment directed towards disadvantaged groups is desirable and permissible. The debate on permissible and impermissible positive action has developed in a

US context where affirmative action measures have been categorised as a version of "unjustified classification". In a contrast to this approach, European and domestic discrimination law has tended to classify positive action as a useful concept which is a way of giving "priority" to certain groups in order to reach the goals of discrimination law. In the next section we will examine these two perspectives: of positive action as "unjustified classification"; and positive action as an example of "equality as priority".

The arguments surrounding the ethical and legal legitimacy of these "preferential" forms of positive action have generated considerable debate over the last thirty years. Proponents of such measures argue that preferential treatment may be necessary to correct inherent biases that impact upon disadvantaged groups. The argument is also made that the use of such means is justified by the overall end of enhanced real and substantive equality for all in society: the special treatment of disadvantaged groups compensates for and redresses the persistent inequalities to which they are subject.[21] Opponents question the legitimacy of preferential treatment as a tactic to achieve these gains, on the basis that "suspect" characteristics such as race and gender should not be used to make distinctions even for ameliorative or beneficial purpose. They also question its long-term effectiveness as well as its principled basis. Abrams has critiqued the use of "social engineering" using these "suspect characteristics", questioning the consequences of maintaining the use of racial distinctions with their potentially divisive effect.[22] Other critics have also questioned whether preferential treatment for particular disadvantaged groups will undermine the "merit" principle. Proponents of positive action, on the other hand, argue that while positive action strategies may often involve a widening and re-examination of conventional notions of merit, it need not in any way undermine the quality of job performance or of those who fill posts, if applied properly.[23]

Much of this debate centres around the question of the legitimacy of the use of "suspect" characteristics such as ethnicity and gender to demarcate the beneficiaries of positive action. At first glance, the standard approach of discrimination law is to treat "equal treatment" as an individual right to have decisions that affect the individual taken without reference to particular characteristics such as race, sex and so on. Most derogations from this approach are treated as requiring clear and compelling justification. This has been described as an "anti-classification" approach: it assumes that discrimination law should prioritise the elimination of the use of particular forms

[21] See, e.g. R. Dworkin, *A Matter of Principle* (Cambridge MA: Harvard University Press, 1985); G. Ezorsky, *Racism and Justice: The Case for Affirmative Action* (Ithaca NY: Cornell University Press, 1991).

[22] See M. Abram, "Affirmative Action: Fair Shakers and Social Engineers" (1986) Harvard L.R. 1312–26.

[23] H. J. Holzer and D. Neumark "What Does Affirmative Action Do?" (2000) 53 Industrial and Labour Relations R. 240–66.

of suspect distinctions.[24] From this perspective, the use of forms of positive action that involve preferential or special treatment for groups defined by "suspect" characteristics is controversial, as this appears to violate the principle of equal treatment and make use of these "suspect" classifications, when the law should be concerned with eliminating their use.

V. "Affirmative Action"—The US Debate

This is especially clear in the US debates on forms of positive action that involve some use of preferential treatment, known as "affirmative action". Some forms of affirmative action are permitted by legislation, e.g as a remedial measure under the Civil Rights Act 1964, Title VII; or as part of a contract compliance obligation by a federal government contractor.[25] However, the US constitutional case law illustrates how such positive action measures can generate complex conceptual problems.

There is now a large volume of case law and academic commentary on affirmative action, especially in the US literature. In this section we will focus on the decisions of the United States Supreme Court in the *Bakke* and *Grutter* cases as a point of entry into the discussion about the justification of preferential treatment. *Bakke* confirmed that some types of affirmative action which established preferential treatment on the grounds of race in university admissions could be permissible in US constitutional and statutory discrimination law. This led to a ferocious legal and political debate about the permissibility and place of affirmative action in the US. Almost a quarter of a century later the US Supreme Court in the *Grutter* case confirmed that affirmative actions programmes, narrowly tailored, and with the aim of promoting diversity in the student body, were permissible under US constitutional and statutory discrimination law. The case divided the US Supreme Court: *Grutter* was a 5–4 decision in favour of the permissibility of the affirmative action programme in that case and there is a powerful dissent by four Supreme Court judges (including Chief Justice Rehnquist).

In *Bakke*, in 1978, a scheme by the University of California Medical School to establish a twin track admissions policy that set aside certain places for minority groups was challenged by Bakke who was a white applicant who had been refused a place at the medical school. The Californian Supreme Court had ordered that the medical school should admit Bakke and that the use of "race" as a factor that was used to make admissions decisions was a "suspect" classification and unconstitutional under the Equal Protection Clause. In effect, this meant that Californian universities could not take race into account when

[24] J. Balkin and R. Siegel, "The American Civil Rights Tradition: Anticlassification or Antisubordination?" (2004) 58 Miami L.R. 9.

[25] See Chris McCrudden, "Rethinking Positive Action" (1986) I.L.J. 219, at p.221.

designing their admissions policies. The US Supreme Court held that Bakke should be admitted into the medical school on the basis that the fixed quota scheme in question was excessively rigid. Yet, at the same time, a majority of the US Supreme Court (five out of nine judges) did clearly hold that under limited circumstances race could be taken into account as part of a university admissions scheme, i.e. they held that the Californian Supreme Court was wrong to prohibit as unconstitutional the use of race in all admissions decisions. Out of the five judges in the majority, the plurality (represented by the opinion of Brennan J.) decided the case on the general grounds that affirmative action was permissible as a remedial response to past discrimination. One judge out of the majority, Powell J., agreed that affirmative action programme was permissible but for the different reason that it was justified on the grounds that it promoted a diverse student body.

This division of opinion in *Bakke* left the constitutional justification for affirmative action confused. However, in the recent *Grutter* case, this issue has been resolved. In *Grutter v Bollinger*, the Supreme Court has affirmed the approach adopted by Powell J. in *Bakke* that the justification for affirmative action measures in universities such as those in *Bakke* can be based upon the need for diversity in the student body. The section that follows set out detailed extracts from the *Bakke* and *Grutter* case, thereby presenting the facts and range of arguments that arise in affirmative action cases. *Bakke* is also a useful representative case because it raises issues about the legality of affirmative action in constitutional and statutory discrimination law.

The facts of **Bakke** were as follows. Mr Bakke was a white applicant to the University of California at Davis Medical School (UCD Medical School). The UCD Medical School ran a twin track admissions policy. Eighty four places were subject to a general admissions programme that allocated places according to test scores. Bakke failed to gain admission although he had high test scores. UCD Medical School also ran a special programme called the "task force programme" that related to sixteen places that were set aside for minority students. The UCD Medical School could not establish that Bakke did not have test scores to gain admission for the sixteen places that had been set aside for minority students under the "task force" programme. Bakke commenced a legal action that the UCD Medical School and asked the California state court alleging that the special admissions program operated to exclude him on the basis of his race in violation of (a) the Equal Protection Clause of the Fourteenth Amendment, a provision of the California Constitution, and (b) Title VI of the Civil Rights Act of 1964,. UCD Medical School applied for a declaration that its special admissions program was lawful.

The trial court found that the special program operated as a racial quota, because minority applicants in that program were rated only against one another, and 16 places in the class of 100 were reserved for them. The California Supreme Court, applying a strict-scrutiny standard of the Equal Protection Clause, concluded that the special admissions program was not the least intrusive means of achieving the goals of the admittedly compelling state interests of integrating the medical profession and increasing the number of doctors willing to serve minority patients. They held that UCD's special admissions program violated the Equal Protection Clause. The UCD Medical School applied to the US Supreme Court. The general issue of the constitutionality of affirmative action admissions policies that used race as a category for selection was decided in favour of UCD Medical School. By a majority of five to four (Brennan, White, Marshall and Blackmun JJ., and Powell J. who gave a separate opinion) the US Supreme Court held that the use of "race" as part of an admissions programme to assists minority applicants was not unconstitutional under the Equal Protection Clause. However, as Powell J. considered that the special admissions program was excessively rigid in foreclosing consideration being given to individuals in a similar position to Bakke, Bakke's exclusion was overturned (Powell J. joined with Stevens J., Burger C.J., Stewart and Rehnquist JJ. on this point).

Three different approaches to affirmative action are adopted in this decision. First, there are traditional arguments from the anti-classification approach which treat affirmative action as a form of reverse discrimination. These are summarised in the dissent by Stevens J. in *Bakke* and are discussed below under the title "Affirmative Action as Suspect Classification". Second there are justifications of affirmative action that treat it as a permissible (and in some cases required) remedial response to the problem of discrimination. These are contained in the *Bakke* case and are discussed below under the title "Affirmative Action as a Remedial Response". Third, there are also arguments that justify affirmative action because it can, if designed narrowly and in a narrow range of circumstances, promote the goal of greater diversity. These arguments originate in the opinion of Justice Powell in *Bakke* and they are affirmed and developed in *Grutter v Bollinger*. They are discussed below under the title "Affirmative Action and the Goal of Promoting Diversity".

A. *Affirmative Action is "Reverse Discrimination"*

The "Suspect Classification Approach": "Race cannot be the basis of excluding anyone from participation in a federally funded program." (per Stevens J.)

Four judges of the Supreme Court (Burger C.J. and Stevens, Stewart and Rehnquist JJ.) agreed with the Californian Supreme Court that the exclusion of Bakke from the UCD Medical School special admissions programme was unlawful discrimination, on the basis that the use of his race as a criterion in the admissions process was unlawful in this particular case. In Stevens J.'s opinion, with which the others concurred, the case was treated as an issue between two private litigants rather than as raising more general questions about social policy, racial equality and the permissibility of affirmative action programmes in general. Stevens J. stated that "[T]his is not a class action. The controversy is between two specific litigants. ... It is therefore perfectly clear that the question whether race can ever be used as a factor in an admissions decision is not an issue in this case, and that discussion of that issue is inappropriate." For these four judges, the issue in *Bakke* was simply whether the relevant provisions of Title VI of the Civil Rights Act 1964 prohibited the use of race as a criterion.

This classification of *Bakke* as a private law issue between private bodies is significant: it ensures that the analysis need not give any consideration to the role of the admissions policy as part of a wider programme to deal with discrimination against Afro-Americans as a long standing and structural problem. As we see in the judgment of Brennan J., discussed below, if affirmative action is viewed as a remedial response to past and structural discrimination, the arguments for the constitutional validity of strong "preferential" forms of positive action will be greatly strengthened. However, once Stevens J. and the other three judges in the minority on this issue constructed the UCD admissions scheme as a private law issue that can be resolved by the application of statutory anti-discrimination law, these wider constitutional considerations could be set aside in favour of a narrower approach based upon statutory interpretation.

In applying this approach, the four judges who adopted this view found no grounds for interpreting Title VI to permit the use of race as a criterion, even to benefit disadvantaged groups, and so found UCD Medical School to be in breach of the Civil Rights Act 1964. Section 610 of the 1964 Act provides that "[n]o person in the United States shall, on the ground of race, color, or national origin, be excluded from participation in, be denied the benefits of, or be subjected to discrimination under any program or activity receiving Federal financial assistance." Stevens J. considered that the University, through its special admissions policy, had plainly excluded Bakke from participation in its program of medical education because of his race:

[414–415] " ... The language of the entire section is perfectly clear; the words that follow 'excluded from' do not modify or qualify the explicit outlawing of any exclusion on the stated grounds ... it seems clear that the proponents of Title VI assumed that the Constitution itself required a colorblind standard on the part of government, but that does not mean that the legislation only codifies an existing constitutional prohibition ... since the meaning of the Title VI ban on exclusion is crystal clear: Race cannot be the basis of excluding anyone from participation in a federally funded program."

There are two features that are critical in this analysis. First, it treats "race" as a concept that must be interpreted and understood in the same way irrespective of the motivation or context in which the category is used: i.e. it is used symmetrically, irrespective of motivation or the normative goal. Later in the chapter on race discrimination, we discuss different ways in which the term "race" can be constructed and defined and note that one line of argument suggests that the meaning of the term varies depending on why, where and for what purpose it is being used. However, in Steven J.'s opinion in *Bakke*, the view was taken that both race discrimination (i.e where race is used to deny access to minorities to a benefit) and "reverse" race discrimination (i.e. where race is used to facilitate access of minorities to a benefit) are equivalent. As Richard Posner notes in his commentary on *Bakke*, the use of race in the context of reverse discrimination is a stereotype: "... a favourable one perhaps (like 'Orientals are good at maths')—but a racial stereotype nonetheless—and the 14th Amendment would seem to forbid racial stereotyping even when it is used to confer preference on members of some racial minority".[26] Second, once the issue is construed as a private matter, and race is treated as a "suspect classification", it follows that this type of affirmative action programme is a breach of the individual rights of those who have been discriminated against, i.e in this case Bakke and other students of the advantaged majority group. It is in this sense that this suspect classification analysis concludes that "affirmative action" is prohibited "reverse discrimination."

B. *Affirmative Action as a Remedial Response*

"*Properly construed, therefore, our prior cases unequivocally show that a state government may adopt race-conscious programs if the purpose of such programs is to remove the disparate racial impact its actions might otherwise have and if there is reason to believe that the disparate impact is itself the product of past discrimination, whether its own or that of society at large.*" (Per Brennan, J. in *Bakke*)

Four out of five judges in *Bakke* who found that the affirmative action programme of UCD was permissible under Title VI based their reasoning on the need for race to be taken into account in devising a response to prohibited discrimination. There were two aspects to this line of reasoning: (a) justifications of affirmative action under statutory discrimination law provisions under Title VI of the Civil Rights Act 1964; and (b) constitutional justifications of affirmative action under the US Constitution 14th Amendment Equal Protection Clause. As stated by Brennan J., with whose opinion the other three joined:

BRENNAN J.

[326–344] "Our Nation was founded on the principle that 'all Men are created equal.' Yet candor requires acknowledgment that the Framers of our Constitution, to forge the 13 Colonies into one Nation, openly compromised this principle of equality with its antithesis: slavery. The consequences of this compromise are well known and have aptly been called our promise are well known and have aptly been called our 'American Dilemma.' Still, it is well to recount how recent the time has been, if it has yet come, when the promise of our principles has flowered into the actuality of equal opportunity for all regardless of race or color.

[26] Richard Posner: "The *Bakke* Case: The Future of 'Affirmative Action' " [1979] California L.R. 67, at 177.

. . . Against this background, claims that law must be 'color-blind' or that the datum of race is no longer relevant to public policy must be seen as aspiration rather than as description of reality. This is not to denigrate aspiration; for reality rebukes us that race has too often been used by those who would stigmatize and oppress minorities. Yet we cannot—and, as we shall demonstrate, need not under our Constitution or Title VI, which merely extends the constraints of the Fourteenth Amendment to private parties who receive federal funds—let color blindness become myopia which masks the reality that many 'created equal' have been treated within our lifetimes as inferior both by the law and by their fellow citizens. . . .

In our view, Title VI prohibits only those uses of racial criteria that would violate the Fourteenth Amendment if employed by a State or its agencies; it does not bar the preferential treatment of racial minorities as a means of remedying past societal discrimination to the extent that such action is consistent with the Fourteenth Amendment. The legislative history of Title VI, administrative regulations interpreting the statute, subsequent congressional and executive action, and the prior decisions of this Court compel this conclusion. None of these sources lends support to the proposition that Congress intended to bar all race-conscious efforts to extend the benefits of federally financed programs to minorities who have been historically excluded from the full benefits of American life. . . .

These regulations clearly establish that where there is a need to overcome the effects of past racially discriminatory or exclusionary practices engaged in by a federally funded institution, race-conscious action is not only permitted but required to accomplish the remedial objectives of Title VI."

It is worth noting that the justification for affirmative action in these passages starts with a recognition of the historical legacy of slavery. Brennan J. also noted that although there was no evidence that UCD had engaged in past discrimination, the mere fact that the racial minorities were themselves victims of past discrimination was sufficient to justify affirmative action measures in limited circumstances. Brennan J. went on to address the argument that the racial classification in the UCD affirmative action programme failed the "strict scrutiny" test. He distinguished the UCD classification from those that are designed to stigmatise a particular racial group:

"Nor has anyone suggested that the University's purposes contravene the cardinal principle that racial classifications that stigmatize—because they are drawn on the presumption that one race is inferior to another or because they put the weight of government behind racial hatred and separatism—are invalid without more."

Brennan J. then set out the conditions which limited the permissibility of affirmative action as a remedial response to past discrimination. These included, inter alia:

[359–362] "Instead, a number of considerations—developed in gender-discrimination cases but which carry even more force when applied to racial classifications—lead us to conclude that racial classifications designed to further remedial purposes '"must serve important governmental objectives and must be substantially related to achievement of those objectives. . . . In sum, because of the significant risk that racial classifications established for ostensibly benign purposes can be misused, causing effects not unlike those created by invidious classifications, it is inappropriate to inquire only whether there is any conceivable basis that might sustain such a classification. Instead, to justify such a classification an important and articulated purpose for its use must be shown. In addition, any statute must be stricken that stigmatizes any group or that singles out those least well represented in the political process to bear the brunt of a benign program. Thus, our review under the Fourteenth Amendment should be strict—not '"strict" in theory and fatal in fact,' because it is stigma that causes fatality—but strict and searching nonetheless. Davis' articulated purpose of remedying the effects of past societal discrimination is, under our cases, sufficiently important to justify the use of race-conscious admissions programs where there is a sound basis for concluding that minority underrepresentation is substantial and chronic, and that the handicap of past discrimination is impeding access of minorities to the Medical School."

The split between the "suspect classification" and the "remedial response" approaches in the *Bakke* case (as already noted, four Supreme Court judges joined Stevens J. in the dissent; another four joined the opinion of Brennan J.) left the opinion of Powell J. as the critical judgment. Powell J. considered that the use of race even for beneficial purposes was constitutionally problematic and triggered the application of strict scrutiny by the courts. However, while general arguments such as remedying past injustice would not usually satisfy this standard of scrutiny, the use of race as a criterion in attaining diversity in education could in certain circumstances. Therefore, Powell J. was of the view that race could in some circumstances be used in admission decisions, but that the use of race in this way had to be narrowly tailored to achieve the objective of enhanced diversity. It was this approach that has been applied in the majority in the most recent case, *Grutter*.

C. *Affirmative Action as a Means of Promoting Diversity*

The facts of the **Grutter** case were as follows. In 1992 Michigan Law School adopted a new admissions policy that was designed to balance the need for intellectual ability and the need for diversity of the student body within the limits of the law on affirmative action. The hallmark of that policy was inter alia: to focus on academic ability but the use of 'soft criteria' to promote the goal of a certain type of racial diversity.

The applicant, Barbara Grutter, was a white Michigan resident who applied to the Law School in 1996 with a 3.8 grade point average and 161 LSAT score. The Law School initially placed her on a waiting list, but subsequently rejected her application. In December 1997, Grutter bought an action against the Law School. Grutter claimed that the Michigan Law School policy was unlawful racial discriminated against her, in violation of the Fourteenth Amendment; [and] Title VI of the Civil Rights Act of 1964. Grutter claimed that her application was rejected because the Law School uses race as a 'predominant' factor because it gives applicants who belong to certain minority groups 'a significantly greater chance of admission than students with similar credentials from disfavored racial groups.' Grutter argued that the respondents 'had no compelling interest to justify their use of race in the admissions process.'

Grutter claimed: compensatory and punitive damages, an order requiring the Law School to offer her admission, and an injunction prohibiting the Law School from continuing to discriminate on the basis of race.

A majority of the US Supreme Court in *Grutter* found that the Michigan University Law School Admission policy was not unlawful statutory race discrimination under Title VI, and it was not unconstitutional race discrimination under 14th Amendement Equal Protection Clause. The majority opinion was that of O'Connor J. (joined by Justices Stevens, Souter, Ginsburg, and Breyer) who adopted the reasoning of Powell J. in *Bakke* as the rationale for permitting this form of affirmative action. Four out of the total nine members of the Supreme Court dissented with this judgement: Chief Justice Rehnquist (with whom Scalia, Kennedy, and Thomas JJ. agreed).

The majority of the Supreme Court affirmed the Powell line of reasoning in *Bakke* in a number of key areas, discussed below by reference to the relevant extracts from *Grutter*. In particular, they affirmed (a) that *any* use of a protected characteristic such as race was prima facie problematic for the constitutional right to equal protection and triggered strict judicial scrutiny; (b) the justification for affirmative action programmes was not based on general arguments for the need to remedy past injustice or the instrumental policy goals, e.g the need for minority doctors; and (c) the only justification for affirmative action was the "attainment of a diverse student body". However, in relation to this final point, the majority emphasised that this justification was also subject to strict conditions about the design of the programme *and* that race was one but not the only factor that should be taken into account to maintain this diversity.

(a) That *any* use of a protected characteristic such as race was prima facie problematic for the constitutional right to equal protection and triggered strict judicial scrutiny

JUSTICE O'CONNOR:

[322–323] "Since this Court's splintered decision in *Bakke*, Justice Powell's opinion announcing the judgment of the Court has served as the touchstone for constitutional analysis of race-conscious admissions policies. Public and private universities across the Nation have modeled their own admissions programs on Justice Powell's views on permissible race-conscious policies. . . . We therefore discuss Justice Powell's opinion in some detail.

Justice Powell began by stating that '[t]he guarantee of equal protection cannot mean one thing when applied to one individual and something else when applied to a person of another color. If both are not accorded the same protection, then it is not equal.' . . . In Justice Powell's view, when governmental decisions 'touch upon an individual's race or ethnic background, he is entitled to a judicial determination that the burden he is asked to bear on that basis is precisely tailored to serve a compelling governmental interest.' Under this exacting standard, only one of the interests asserted by the university survived Justice Powell's scrutiny."

Justice O'Connor then went on to endorse the strict scrutiny standard:

O'CONNOR J:

[326–327] "We have held that all racial classifications imposed by government 'must be analyzed by a reviewing court under strict scrutiny.' This means that such classifications are constitutional only if they are narrowly tailored to further compelling governmental interests. 'Absent searching judicial inquiry into the justification for such race-based measures,' we have no way to determine what 'classifications are "benign" or "remedial" and what classifications are in fact motivated by illegitimate notions of racial inferiority or simple racial politics.'

When race-based action is necessary to further a compelling governmental interest, such action does not violate the constitutional guarantee of equal protection so long as the narrow-tailoring requirement is also satisfied.

Context matters when reviewing race-based governmental action under the Equal Protection Clause. . . . Not every decision influenced by race is equally objectionable and strict scrutiny is designed to provide a framework for carefully examining the importance and the sincerity of the reasons advanced by the governmental decisionmaker for the use of race in that particular context. . . ."

(b) the justification for affirmative action programmes was not based on general arguments for the need to remedy past injustice or the instrumental policy goals, e.g. the need for minority doctors;

O'CONNOR J.:

[323–324] "First, Justice Powell rejected an interest in 'reducing the historic deficit of traditionally disfavored minorities in medical schools and in the medical profession' as an unlawful interest in racial balancing. Second, Justice Powell rejected an interest in remedying societal discrimination because such measures would risk placing unnecessary burdens on innocent third parties 'who bear no responsibility for whatever harm the beneficiaries of the special admissions program are thought to have suffered.' Third, Justice Powell rejected an interest in 'increasing the number of physicians who will practice in communities currently underserved,' concluding that even if such an interest could be compelling in some circumstances the program under review was not 'geared to promote that goal.'"

(c) the only justification for affirmative action was the "attainment of a diverse student body"

O'CONNOR J.:

[324–325] "Justice Powell approved the university's use of race to further only one interest: 'the attainment of a diverse student body.' With the important proviso that 'constitutional limitations protecting individual rights may not be disregarded,' Justice Powell grounded his analysis in the academic freedom that 'long has been viewed as a special concern of the First Amendment.' Justice Powell emphasized that nothing less than the '"nation's future depends upon leaders trained through wide exposure" to the ideas and mores of students as diverse as this Nation of many peoples.' . . . In seeking the 'right to select those students who will contribute the most to the "robust exchange of ideas,"' a university seeks 'to achieve a goal that is of paramount importance in the fulfillment of its mission.' Both 'tradition and experience lend support to the view that the contribution of diversity is substantial.'

Justice Powell was, however, careful to emphasize that in his view race 'is only one element in a range of factors a university properly may consider in attaining the goal of a heterogeneous student body.' For Justice Powell, '[i]t is not an interest in simple ethnic diversity, in which a specified percentage of the student body is in effect guaranteed to be members of selected ethnic groups,' that can justify the use of race. Rather, '[t]he diversity that furthers a compelling state interest encompasses a far broader array of qualifications and characteristics of which racial or ethnic origin is but a single though important element.' "

Therefore, applying the Powell J. test in *Bakke* to the facts in this case, the majority in *Grutter* found that the admissions programme was sufficiently narrow in its design to be permissible affirmative action. They affirmed that universities could not use quotas or have a segregated stream of admissions for certain racial groups. The majority also found that relevant factors other than those of promoting racial diversity were sufficiently incorporated into the decision-making of the admissions process, and that there was no substantial harm to non-minority students. In *Grutter*, therefore, the majority concluded that the Michigan Law School's narrowly tailored use of race in admissions was sufficiently tailored to be constitutionally permissible under the Equal Protection Clause.

Four out of five members of the US Supreme Court dissented from the majority decision and the judgment of O'Connor J. in *Grutter v Bollinger*. Rehniquist argued that the scheme was not narrowly tailored. It was, rather, aimed towards a numerical mass of underrepresented students which was an effort to maintain a statistical representation of the application pool from underrepresented students and therefore "a naked effort to achieve racial balancing", analogous to impressible racial quotas. Chief Justice Rehnquist went on to discuss the way in which the Michigan Law School scheme was insufficiently transparent and targeted to meet the conditions for a constitutional affirmative action programme. The Michigan Admission Policy, therefore, failed in the view of the minority to meet the requirement to apply "strict standard" scrutiny under the Equal Protection clause, which should be applied in its full rigour irrespective of issues of "good motive" or the "purported reason" for the racial classification.

VI. Commentaries on *Bakke* and *Grutter*—Justifying Affirmative Action

A. *Liberal Individualism: Affirmative Action as a Breach of Colour Blind Justice*

The opinion of the dissenting minority in *Bakke* and *Grutter* represents the orthodox objection to affirmative action programmes: that they are just another form of direct discrimination under Title VI, involving "suspect classification" and use of race, which is unconstitutional under the US Constitution's Equal Protection Clause. By construing the issue as a private right between individuals this dissent illustrates a powerful critique of affirmative action programmes: that they involve a clash between the goals of the affirmative action programmes of the UCD Medical School and the "right" of Bakke to equality or non-discrimination.

In the previous chapter we noticed the way in which one distinct justification of the anti-discrimination principles uses not just liberalism but procedural liberalism as its foundations: i.e this is a form of liberalism that gives priority to individual rights as the framework within which individuals are left free to pursue their own concept of the good. Procedural liberalism's focus in minority protection is on an "individual right" to be free from discrimination rather than on the substantive outcomes of law and policy for minorities. One consequence of treating the anti-discrimination as an individual right to be free from discrimination is that it generates a "colour blind" approach to equality and discrimination. Moreover, this approach is likely to yield a symmetrical discrimination law that treats all use of racial criteria as a "suspect classification". In many ways, all the positions in *Bakke* and *Grutter* that we have considered accept this dominant paradigm. However, the liberal individualism and "colour blind" approach to affirmative action is most obvious in the dissenting judgments in *Bakke* and *Grutter*. The justification for affirmative action moves away from individual justice and towards pragmatism and social goals of equality and diversity. There is however a principled argument that affirmative action is "suspect classification" and sacrifices individual rights (such as those of Bakke and Grutter) for social goals such as equality and diversity.[27]

However, there also exists a strong critique of liberal individualism that argues that the principle of colour blind justice needs to be applied in a more nuanced way. Glenn Loury for example writes:

[27] See for example, Terry Eastland, *Ending Affirmative Action: The Case For Colorblind Justice* (New York: Basic Books, 1996) p.229.

Glenn C. Loury, *The Anatomy of Racial Inequality* (Cambridge, MA: Harvard University Press, 2002)

pp.151–152: "We have, then, these three domains—implementation, evaluation, and civic construction—giving rise to three classes of public questions: How should we treat individuals? How should we choose the goals to be pursued through our policies? And how much awareness ought we to have of the ways in which the conduct of public business can perpetuate into yet another generation the stigma of race? Liberal individualism seems to militate strongly in favor of 'blindness' in both the first and the second domains. I believe this is wrong on both counts, because it is ahistorical and sociologically naïve. Race blind proceduralism fails, I have suggested, because (among other reasons) it is not closed to moral deviation. And a principled stance of indifference is unacceptable as well, I have argued, because it rules out policies that are almost universally credited as being necessary and proper to combat lingering effects of past racial injustice."

More specifically, the argument from liberal individualism—i.e. that those who suffer a loss of opportunity because of affirmative action programmes (such as Bakke or Grutter) have had their "individual rights" infringed—is considered in more detail by Dworkin below.

"Bakke's Case: Are Quotas Unfair?" and "What Did The Bakke Case Really Decide?" *A Matter of Principle*, (Oxford: Clarendon Press, 1986)

p.298: "If Allan Bakke has a constitutional right so important that the urgent goals of affirmative action for society as a whole must yield, then this must be because affirmative action violates some fundamental principle of political morality. . . . What could that right be? The popular argument frequently made or editorial pages is that Bakke has a right to be judged as an individual rather than as a member of a social group. Or that he has a right, as much as any black man, not to be sacrificed or excluded from any opportunity because of his race alone. . . .

There is no combination of abilities and skills and traits that constitutes 'merit' in the abstract; if quick hands count as 'merit' in the case of a prospective surgeon, this is because quick hands will enable him to serve the public better and for no other reason. If a black skin will, as a matter of regrettable fact, enable another doctor to do a different medical job better, then that black skin is by the same token 'merit' as well. That argument may strike some as dangerous; but only because they confuse its conclusions—that black skin may be a socially useful trait in particular circumstances—with the very different and despicable idea that one race may be inherently more worthy than another. . . ."

On the second point, about whether Bakke had an individual constitutional right to be free from race-based disadvantage, Dworkin has a subtle argument which distinguishes the case of Bakke from other types of racial discrimination on the basis that Bakke is not subject to a racial classification that treats his race as being the object of prejudice and contempt and therefore a special type of public insult. This argument is similar to the justification for discrimination law generally, and race discrimination law in particular, that emphasises the harm of "stigma". Dworkin's argument is that in Bakke's case his race does not fall within the category of a stigma or public insult.

"Every citizen has a constitutional right that he not suffer disadvantage, at least in the competition for any public benefit, because the race or religion or sect or region or other natural or artificial group to which he belongs is the object of prejudice or contempt. That is a fundamentally important constitutional right, and it is that right that was systematically violated for many years by racist exclusions and anti-semitic quotas. Color bars and Jewish quotas were not unfair just because they fixed on qualities beyond individual control. It is true that blacks of Jews do not choose to be blacks or Jews. But it is also true that those who score low in aptitude or admissions tests do not choose their levels of intelligence. . . . Race seems different because exclusions based on race have historically been motivated not by some instrumental calculation, as in the case of intelligence or age or regional distribution or athletic ability, but because of contempt for the excluded race or religion as such. Exclusion by race was in itself an insult, because it was generated by and signaled contempt. . . .

Allan Bakke is being 'sacrificed' because of his race only in a very artificial sense of the word. He is being 'sacrificed' in the same artificial sense because of his level of intelligence, since he would have been accepted if he had been more intelligent. In both cases he is being excluded not by prejudice but because of a rational calculation about the socially most beneficial use of limited resources.

It may now be said that this distinction is too subtle, and that if racial classifications have been and may still be used for malign purposes, then eveyone has a flat right that racial classifications not be used at all. This is the familiar appeal to the lazy virtue of simplicity. . . . If racially conscious admissions policies now offer the only substantial hope for bringing more qualified black and other minority doctors into the profession, then a great loss is suffered if medical schools are not allowed to purse such programmes. We should then be trading away a chance to attack certain and present injustice in order to gain protection we may not need against speculative abuses we have other means to prevent. And such abuses cannot, in any case, be worse than the injustice to which we would then surrender.

There is, of course, no suggestion in that program that Bakke shares in any collective or individual guilt for racial injustice in the United States; or that he is any less entitled to concern or respect than any black student accepted in the programme. He has been disappointed, and he must have the sympathy due that disappointment. . . . Each is disappointed because places in medical school are scarce resources and must be used to provide what the more general society most needs. It is not Bakke's fault that racial justice is now a special need—but he has no right to prevent the most effective measures of securing that justice from being used."

Elizabeth Anderson has similarly criticised the automatic assumption that faithful adherence to the anti-discrimination principle necessarily requires societies to refrain from using "suspect" characteristics and adhere rigidly to the anti-classification principle.[28] She argues that the anti-discrimination principle is based around an objection to the use of "suspect" classifications in a manner that is linked to demeaning assumptions, or where they result in

28 Elizabeth S Anderson, "Integration, Affirmative Action and Strict Scrutiny" (2002) N.Y.U.L. R. 1195.

negative stereotyping or denial of dignity, or overinclusion and/or under-inclusion in particular categories.[29] The use of such characteristics for positive purposes need not be considered to be inherently problematic. She also criticises crude empirical generalisations about the inevitable negative impact of the use of "suspect" characteristics and the confusion of ideals with causes, whereby the ideal of a colour-blind society results in the perception that the problems faced by disadvantaged minorities always stem from the existence of classifications based upon suspect characteristics, rather than from structural disadvantages that require targeted remedial measures. Anderson concludes:

"There is no contradiction ... in using race-conscious means to eradicate the causes of race-based disadvantages. Surgery is often needed to repair knife wounds."[30]

B. *Affirmative Action as an "Exception" In Discrimination Law*

Arguments that seek to justify affirmative action from within the traditional analysis of equality as symmetrical treat affirmative action as a "necessary evil" and an exception that is necessary to achieve a desirable social goals.[31] These are reflected in the two sets of justification that emerge in *Bakke* and *Grutter*. Firstly, Brennan J. in *Bakke* justified the exception as a remedial response. Second, Powell J. in *Bakke*, in his opinion that was applied and developed by Justice O'Connor in *Grutter*, justifies affirmative action as an exception in limited circumstances which is justified because it promotes the goal of diversity.

Both these approaches have some support. In a recent article, Dworkin sets out the shift that has occurred in the United States since the controversy over *Bakke*. He notes that powerful lobbies now support some form of affirmative action and the goal of diversity, e.g. the Bush (Republican) administration, the business and corporate sector and the armed forces who cite racial segregation as one of the problems that they faced during the Vietnam war. He also notes that the justification of "diversity" adopted by the *Grutter* decision is more easy to justify as a forward looking goal that can be justified because it contributes towards the creation of a more just and racially balanced community.

[29] ibid., 1235.
[30] ibid., 1270.
[31] Richard A. Wasserstrom, "Racism, Sexism and Preferential Treatment: An Approach to the Topics" (1977) U.C.L.A.L. R. 581; Alan Wertheimer, "Jobs, Qualifications and Preferences" (1983) 94 *Ethics*, 99.

Ronald Dworkin, "The Court and the Diversity" (2003) 50(8) *New York Review of Books*, May 15, 2003

"... So there is now growing support for the view that affirmative action is of great and general value to the country, because it attacks the economic racial imbalances that have proved so harmful. There is also less apparent support, at least among leading American institutions, for the once-popular view that affirmative action is unfair to white applicants. ... Universities say they are training the nation's and the world's future leaders: if it is best for the nation that its leaders more closely match the diversity of its citizens, then no one is cheated by universities who include that goal among their aims. Of course, they must not act unjustly or in violation of anyone's moral rights. In particular, they must not exclude students out of racial or any other form of prejudice or stereotype. But Michigan's programs do not reflect racial or other prejudices—on the contrary the scholars who choose such programs aim, among other goals, to reduce prejudice in the classroom and in the country.

Even if it is beneficial for universities to use race-sensitive tests in admission, however, and even if no moral principle forbids this, we must still ask whether the Supreme Court's own precedents require it to strike down the University of Michigan's plans. The equal protection clause does not, of course, forbid government to make distinctions or classifications among citizens. But the Supreme Court has ruled over many decades that classifications according to race are inherently 'suspect' and must therefore be subject to a 'strict' scrutiny that imposes the following three tests. Race-sensitive admissions plans must serve some 'compelling' goal, universities must not be able to pursue that goal adequately without them, and they must be 'narrowly tailored' to achieving that goal.

Do racially sensitive admission plans serve a compelling goal? The briefs supporting the University of Michigan cite two different goals as compelling, and it is important to distinguish between them. The first is the social goal that the corporate and military briefs I mentioned emphasize: equipping more minority students for leadership in order to attack damaging racial stratification in politics, business, the professions, and the military. The second is the educational goal of classroom diversity: universities argue that a racially diverse student body helps them to fulfill their most basic pedagogic functions because students with different backgrounds, experiences, and perspectives can contribute to each other's education.

The opponents of the Michigan plan challenge both of these goals, but on different grounds. They say that past Supreme Court decisions rule out the first, social, goal because the Court has repeatedly declared that remedying past socioeconomic injustice cannot count as a compelling goal justifying racial classifications. But this objection confuses two different ideas: the backward-looking claim that affirmative action is justified in order to compensate minority students for past injustice to their race, which the Court has rejected, and the forward-looking claim that it is justified in order to improve society in ways that benefit practically everyone.

Several justices have declared, in past cases, that though an institution may use racial classifications to compensate for its own past discrimination, it may not do so to compensate for discrimination by others or in the community as a whole. It is, in fact, doubtful that affirmative action can ever be justified as compensation, because compensation is a matter of individual, not group, entitlement, and allowing black applicants to have preference now cannot compensate generations of blacks who suffered injustice in the past. But the forward-looking social goal is very different: it justifies sensitivity to race not on the basis of any compensatory theory, but on the pragmatic assumption that securing a better racial balance in positions of prestige and influence benefits the community as a whole. Universities may properly serve that goal through their admissions procedures, just as they may legitimately choose students in order to provide a better balance in the community between corporate and civil rights lawyers, for example, or between specialist and primary care doctors. . . .

But race matters independently of the other background factors with which it may or may not be correlated, for two reasons. First, the experience of a black person in American society is special, and cannot be duplicated by the experience of a white person of similar economic or social background; it is pedagogically important that the perspectives of that distinct experience be available to students of history, politics, and society who would not otherwise encounter it. Second, learning that race is not correlated with stereotypical perspectives—learning, for example, as Justice Stephen Breyer put it during the oral argument, that a black student may be a rich Exeter graduate and a conservative Republican—is itself of educational value, and that lesson about stereotyping may well be best learned from direct experience. It is controversial whether racial diversity in classrooms produces other pedagogical benefits as well, and how far its overall benefits are offset by disadvantages. But in the judgment of the great majority of selective American universities and colleges, the educational benefits of affirmative action outweigh any educational costs.

. . . Of course it is deplorable that America is still plagued by racial inequality so many decades after it committed itself to ending it. It would compound our failure, however, to forbid what so many of our academic, economic, and political leaders, after a quarter-century of reflective experience, think is our best weapon against that inequality. Colorblindness that has no basis in moral principle and helps only to perpetuate racial stratification is worse than pointless.

Our colleges and universities have, on the whole, served the country brilliantly: the US is widely acknowledged to have the best institutions of higher education in the world. They are committed to academic excellence and the common good, and they have, as institutions, no political goals that compete with these aims. They each decide on admissions strategies for themselves, they impose no strategies on other institutions, and they are supervised by courts alert to the slightest evidence of improper motives. It would be foolish not to allow them to do what they think urgent for their students and their country."

In the previous passage, Dworkin ends by citing the institutional independence of universities and colleges as one of the main beneficial outcomes of the *Grutter* case. Richard Epstein also welcomes the *Grutter* decision because it is an example of a "libertarian" approach: it upholds the decision of a private educational institution about the best admissions policy. However, he also criticises the increasing development of fine tuning by the Supreme Court in the context of affirmative action programmes. He comments in particular on the increasing complexity of the remedial provisions under which the affirmative action doctrine in *Bakke* and *Grutter* were developed:

"Title IX started as a modest effort to secure equal opportunity at university level. Its most obvious target were explicit exclusions from programs on accout of sex, all of which were on their way out anyway. . . . The reach of that statute was successively extended until this modest sex-blind provisions became a full scale regulatory regime of inordinate complexity whose equal participation goal swamped countervailing considerations and have placed just about every college program in noncompliance with the basic norm. Just that path would have been traveled if the color-blind norm had applied to academics because the aggressive use of outcome standards would have forced in the name of color-blindness the same kinds of programs on univerisities. . . . As between government programs that force equality and decentralized programs that allow for differences in the instituitonal level, I would take the latter every time even if I believed that many private institutions in question would behave in scandalous ways in their implementation of the diversity ideal. The world is not a perfect place. ... I would rather take my chances on a decentralized system that permits some diversification than to work under a state monopoly in which 'diversity' becomes the one true goal."[32]

Other inherent tensions exist within liberal justifications for affirmative action. Returning to Dworkin's arguments, it should be noted that they echo the judicial reasoning of Brennan J. in *Bakke* that affirmative action is justified as it is a remedy for past discrimination and to promote the goal of equality, and also the argument of Powell J. and the *Grutter* majority that it promotes the goal of diversity. However, if affirmative action is justified from within the paradigm of an approach to equality that treats it as a procedural matter of treating like with like, then these arguments may be difficult to sustain.

Brennan J. and Dworkin distinguish the stigma attached to racial classification in the case of the "pejorative use of race" in the case of slavery or segregation from the different case of the "remedial use of race" in affirmative action. On this analysis, the use of special treatment as part of positive action strategies is sometimes presented as remedial action for existing and persistent forms of disadvantage that discrimination law cannot redress. Often the social objectives sought to be achieved are expressed to be a desire to ensure "diversity" or to compensate for "past injustice", and the importance of these objectives is used to justify a departure from the normal "anti-classification" principle. The approach of Brennan J. and Dworkin de-emphasises discrimination law's traditional concern with prohibiting classification and instead places more emphasis on eliminating the "subordination" of particular groups.

However, this approach is open to critique from within the liberal tradition. "Diversity" as a justification for special treatment for particular groups can open the door for every social group to claim a stake. "Past injustice" claims often fail when a clear link is sought between the past discrimination and the current individuals or groups making the claim, as is accepted in the *Bakke* case itself where there is no evidence that Bakke himself discriminated in his past. It is likely to be the case that those who suffer a disadvantage because of a racial classification in an affirmative action programme will deeply resent this unequal and discriminatory treatment. The fact that Bakke and Grutter litigated is illustrates their resentment and sense that they had been injured. Although affirmative action programmes may not have "stigma" as their main purpose they may indirectly stigmatise the victim. Moreover, as we discuss later in this chapter, they may over a period of time contribute to and entrench new forms of stereotype.

Some alternative arguments used to justify the use of preferential treatment

[32] Richard A. Epstein, "On Same Sex Relationships and Affirmative Action: The Covert Libertarianism of the United States Supreme Court" Northwestern University School of Law, Constitutional Theory Colloquium Series, March 31, 2004 (copy of paper with the author), at pp.44–45.

and other forms of special treatment in positive action strategies suggest that overriding principles are in play, which act as sufficient justification for the departure from the usual norm of "anti-classification". In particular, these arguments are often used to justify the use of such measures where the lack of participation by disadvantaged groups in key social activities may be damaging for the legitimacy and effectiveness of institutions, or contribute to the social exclusion of these groups. The use of preferential or special treatment to break through "glass barriers", alter organisational cultures or to create a "critical mass" of employees from a disadvantaged group within an organisation is often justified by reference to these external and compelling social objectives. So too is the use of such methods to ensure greater diversity within representative institutions, workforces or educational environments. However, these arguments sit uneasily within a paradigm of discrimination law that focuses on equality as a symmetry of "like with like" and treats discrimination as an individual wrong. Dworkin acknowledges this in the passage cited above when he writes:

"It is, in fact, doubtful that affirmative action can ever be justified as compensation, because compensation is a matter of individual, not group, entitlement, and allowing black applicants to have preference now cannot compensate generations of blacks who suffered injustice in the past. But the forward-looking social goal is very different: it justifies sensitivity to race not on the basis of any compensatory theory, but on the *pragmatic* (my emphasis) assumption that securing a better racial balance in positions of prestige and influence benefits the community as a whole."

This line of reasoning moves the analysis towards treating positive action as a limited exception to the principle of non-discrimination. It de-emphasises discrimination law's traditional concern with prohibiting classification and instead places more emphasis on eliminating the "subordination" of particular groups. In the next section we examine a different perspective that accepts the advantages of equality and diversity that are cited in cases such as *Bakke* and *Grutter*, and by Dworkin and others. Yet, at the same time, it adopts a different paradigm to argue that these forms of positive action are a principled requirement of equality and anti-discrimination rather than pragmatic exceptions.

C. *Affirmative Action as a "Requirement" Of Discrimination Law—The Case For "Positive Action"*

All the judgments in *Bakke* and *Grutter*, even those that permit affirmative action, argue from within a symmetrical view of equality and discrimination law. However, the assumption that the "suspect/anti-classification" principle should be the central guiding principle of discrimination law can be questioned. By arguing within the paradigm of an discrimination law approach that accepts the symmetry between the advantaged and disadvantaged, and using a concept of equality as "like with like", this approach may fail to provide a principled justification of positive action as an important part of discrimination law. Moreover, approaches that exceptionally permit affirmative action as necessary to achieve remedial justice or diversity tend to establish the advantaged group as the standard against which injustice is measured, and therefore the norm to which all must comply. This symmetrical approach can struggle to achieve conceptual coherence.

In the previous chapter on justifying discrimination law we examined different definitions of equality and non-discrimination, some of which draw on substantive arguments that accept the need for asymmetry of treatment as a central requirement of the goals of discrimination law. Strong arguments are made that positive action, rather than involving exceptions to the general thrust and direction of the anti-discrimination principle, is actually entirely compatible with a more coherent understanding of equality. This analysis goes further than the argument that affirmative action is justified as an exception because of past discrimination. Rather, it argues that some forms of affirmative action are a *requirement* of the principle of equality, or at least can be seen as advancing the goals of discrimination law and embodying its underlying values.

Peter Westen in a now famous article in the *Harvard Law Review* proclaimed that "equality is an empty idea", devoid of real substantive content. Westen's critique of the value of equality as a substantive moral concept is echoed by others such as J. R. Lucas and Joseph Raz, who note that the term "equality" is often used rhetorically to signify a principle of universal humanity, where the real concern with discrimination law and other normative "equality" instruments is with achieving and giving effect to some other substantive value, such as respect, human dignity or recognition.[33] Some reference to often inchoate ideas of equality seems to be necessary to frame and delineate the scope and limits of discrimination law.[34] However, it is necessary to bear this critique of the inherent uncertainty of the equality principle in mind. It is also important to delineate and distinguish between the different uses of the term equality in discrimination law. By questioning exactly what "harms" the concept of equality is attempting to redress, it may emerge that in some contexts positive action measures involving preferential or special treatment could be entirely compatible with the substantive goals of constitutional and statutory discrimination law.

Derek Parfitt, in his taxonomy of equality, has identified three distinct ways in which equality is used in arguments generally and in the context of dis-

[33] See for example J. R. Lucas, "Against Equality", *Philosophy*, October 1965, XL pp.296–307 and J. Raz, *The Morality of Freedom*, (Oxford: Clarendon Press, 1987) at pp.228. For a recent analysis along similar lines, see Elisa Holmes, "Anti-Discrimination Rights Without Equality", (2005) 68 M.L.R. 2 175–194.

[34] See Colm O'Cinneide, "Fumbling Towards Coherence: The Slow Evolution of Equality Law in England and Wales" (2006) *Northern Ireland Legal Quarterly* 57–102.

crimination law in particular.[35] These be summarised as: (i) strict equality; (ii) instrumental equality; and (iii) equality as priority.

(i) *Strict Equality*: this is the claim that equality is intrinsically a bad thing; and, it is in itself bad if some people are treated differently or have less of any goods *than others*;

(ii) *Instrumental Equality*: this view suggests that although societies should sometimes aim for equality, that is because "equality" is a tool for realising some other moral reason (e.g. as a requirement of justice). On this view, it is not in and of itself bad if some people are treated differently or have less of any goods *than others*;

(iii) *The Priority Principle*: this requires priority to be given to the needs of people who are substantially disadvantaged or worse off.

These categories are not a perfect prism through which we can distinguish and understand the complexity of discrimination law. Nevertheless, presenting a taxonomy of equality encourages greater clarity about the substantive values that underlie equality claims. The choice about which of these concepts of equality is used as the underlying principle for discrimination law will have important consequences. For example, if a preference for strict equality is adopted, then the main concern may be with maintaining a strict "anti-classification" approach. If, on the other hand, the preference is for instrumental equality, then exceptions to the "anti-classification" approach may be more tolerable as necessary to advance primary goals such as reducing the disadvantages faced by particular groups. The priority principle would be only concerned with the absolute disadvantage and exclusion of certain groups, and be much less concerned with maintaining a strict "anti-classification" approach.

The assumption that strict equality has to be the underlying principle of discrimination law can be therefore called into question. There are alternative definitions of equality, which often are much more open to the use of positive action involving preferential or special treatment. These alternative visions of equality are already embedded in case-law and legislative approaches to anti-discrimination norms. The law at present often requires special treatment to be made for particular groups identified by their possession of a "suspect;" characteristic, in order to compensate for disadvantages they might otherwise face. Legislative protection for pregnancy and maternity rights is a classic example of differential treatment which is justified by reference to equality concerns, but which benefits women in particular. The requirement to make reasonable accommodation for disabled persons is another example (see the

[35] Derek Parfitt, "Equality and Priority", in A. Mason (ed.), *Ideals of Equality* (Oxford: Blackwell, 1998).

chapter on disability discrimination). The use of sex, disability and age to determine eligibility for welfare support is commonplace, and the use of ethnicity to define groups in need of special assistance is standard practice in many areas of social policy. The "anti-classification" principle is not a universal principle underpinning all law, and is too simple an approach in its assumption that the "strict equality" principle is the only way of giving effect to equality. Instrumental and priority approaches to equality are already deeply embedded in many areas of law and policy.

It can be argued that (a) positive action can be differentiated from unlawful direct discrimination because it is not intended to stigmatise or harm the individual; and also in a more affirmative sense (b) positive action can be justified by a particular version of equality according to the priority principle. The use of preferential treatment in positive action strategies, on this analysis, is distinct from unlawful direct discrimination because it is not based on the assumption of using race or sex as a factor to disadvantage the disadvantaged groups. In fact, it is the use of race of sex as factors to achieve exactly the opposite result of breaking down patterns of disadvantage, based upon a priority approach to equality, or even an instrumental analysis.[36] The argument can be made that it makes little sense to treat preferential treatment introduced as part of a positive action scheme to combat structural disadvantage as being on a par with unfair discriminatory measures that attack the dignity of disadvantaged groups. The focus on priority is sometimes eclipsed by continuing reference to "equality". As we discussed in the previous chapter, in these contexts the continuing use of equality can be understood as: (a) either a rhetorical use that draws attention to the greater needs of those who deserve priority; or (b) as a way of settling the standard against which the needs of the disadvantaged are evaluated.

Other theories have suggested alternative means of fleshing out and giving substance to the equality principle, which again tend to conceptualise positive action as advancing the content of this principle rather than constituting a departure or exception to its normal rule.

Owen Fiss has argued for the acceptance of an "anti-subordination" approach in place of the "anti-classification" approach: "affirmative action" measures that aim to break down what he describes as "caste" patterns of disadvantage and subordination should under this approach not be treated as discriminatory measures requiring special justification, but rather as special support and remedial measures.[37] Fredman has similarly argued that the use of otherwise suspect classifications to identify groups who require targeted

[36] See J. Gardner, "Liberals and Unlawful Discrimination", O.J.L.S. 9 (1989), 1; reprinted in Christopher McCrudden (ed.), *Anti-Discrimination Law* (Aldershot: Dartmouth, 1991) and J. Gardner, "On the Grounds of Her Sex(uality), O.J.L.S. 18 (1998), 167. See also in the specific context of the use of "motive" in the context of direct discrimination and its relevance to positive action programmes, Lizzie Barmes, " Promoting Diversity and the Definition of Direct Discrimination" 32 I.L.J. 3 200–213.

[37] Owen M Fiss, "Groups and the Equal Protection Clause" (1976) 5 Phil & Pub Aff 107, 126.

special assistance is legitimate, as such measures are redressing patterns of systematic discrimination that especially affect those particular groups. She suggests that such types of positive action can be necessary to break down structural forms of indirect discrimination, and can therefore be conceptualised as a *remedy* for discrimination. She contrasts this "substantive equality" perspective with approaches that emphasise "formal equality", i.e. sameness of treatment and the rejection of distinctions based on suspect grounds. She contends that if excessive reliance is placed upon securing "formal equality", combating discrimination all too often becomes a matter of proving formal guarantees of equal treatment, rather than tailoring specific and effective measures to assist and empower disadvantaged groups and individuals.[38]

Therefore, it could be argued that it can be unhelpful to assume that is automatically problematic for the law to permit the use of a "suspect" characteristic such as gender or race for the purposes of delineating who is to benefit from positive action. A better approach might be to ask whether the use of a suspect classification is linked to the imposition of an unfair, demeaning or unjust burden, or whether it is being used to correct for persisting inequalities. This approach relies to a degree upon instrumental and prioritarian concepts of equality, and has been adopted in several jurisdictions. In South Africa, equality legislation prohibits "unfair discrimination" rather than "discrimination" and defines inequality not in terms of making classifications upon suspect grounds but as constituting a denial of dignity and the imposition of harmful and demeaning burdens upon particular groups. Therefore, positive action that utilises normally suspect classifications such as race but which is ameliorative in nature is not "unfair" and demeaning, and therefore is not classified as problematic, unless it is irrational or applied in a disproportionate manner. Section 15(2) of the Canadian Charter adopts a similar approach, specifically recognising the legitimacy of positive action as an expression of the equality principle.

Others have called for discrimination law to be structured around a central principle of the recognition of "diversity". This argument needs to be distinguished from the analysis in *Bakke* and *Grutter* that justify affirmative action as an exception to the principle of equal treatment as a short term measures to achieve diversity. This "substantial diversity" approach is influenced by the work of Charles Taylor, Iris Marion Young and other proponents of "identity politics", who argue for recognition of the equal worth of the diverse types of social and cultural group identities, and for the accommodation of difference and the elimination of social barriers that exclude particular groups.[39] Under this approach, positive action strategies advance the instrumental and prior-

[38] See Owen M Fiss "Groups and the Equal Protection Clause" in M. Cohen, T. Nagel and T. Scanlon (eds) *Equality and Preferential Treatment* (Princeton NJ: Princeton University Press, 1977) 85.

[39] See I. M. Young, *Democracy and Inclusion*, (Princeton, NJ: Princeton University Press, 2000). See also A. Phillips, *Which Equalities Matter?* (Cambridge: Polity Press, 1999).

itarian goals of attaining greater diversity and acknowledgement of equal worth that are seen as underpinning discrimination law. Therefore, under this approach to interpreting the equality principle, positive action is again viewed not as an exception to the general rule, but rather as an important tool for giving effect to equality.

What unites all of these different approaches to the equality principle is that they reject the "anti-classification" and strict equality approaches as excessively simple, and view positive action as usually constituting an unproblematic acknowledgment of, and tool for redressing, group-based disadvantage. Proponents of these approaches argue that discrimination law should not been understood as always requiring "equal treatment" in the sense of the same treatment: equality can be achieved through different treatment in appropriate circumstances. Equality is to be achieved through different treatment in appropriate circumstances, and the use of positive action is seen as a justified tool for eliminating structural forms of discrimination, to ensure a fairer representation of disadvantaged groups in workplaces and institutions, and to promote full equality of access to goods and services.[40] The previous discussion of direct discrimination set out the distinction between an analysis that does not consider the motives of the perpetrator from an approach that takes the "reasons for discrimination" as central to the concept of discrimination. On the latter approach, there is a clear distinction between unlawful discrimination as a form of stigma which uses race or sex as a "suspect classification"; and positive action which is based on a motive to promote the key goals of discrimination law and equality.[41]

VII. Possible Limits on the Scope of Positive Action

A. *The Risk Of Entrenching Difference*

Even if the use of positive action is accepted, there may still be a need for considerable caution in how it is applied. Allegedly ameliorative measures may nevertheless actually be rooted in stereotypes, paternalism and the denial of genuine equality of regard. Even positive action measures that set out to remedy disadvantage may lack a firm rational basis, or be underinclusive, or

[40] Research has shown in a number of different public and private sector contexts that concentrating upon complying with anti-discrimination norms alone yields limited results: patterns of inequality and exclusion are extremely difficult to break down unless positive action is taken. See H. C. Jain, P. J. Sloane and F. M. Horwitz, *Employment Equity and Affirmative Action: An International Comparison* (London: M.E. Sharpe, 2003); Federal Glass Ceiling Commission, *Good for Business: Making Full Use of the Nation's Human Capital* (Washington D.C.: Printing Office, 1995).

[41] Lizzie Barmes, "Promoting Diversity and the Definition of Direct Discrimination", 32 I.L.J. 3 200–213.

be manipulated to support special interests or cliques, or may unduly penalise others outside of the disadvantaged group in question. There may be a residual interest in discouraging the use of "suspect" characteristics in law and policy in the absence of good reason, in particular to prevent concepts of "group essentialism", the perpetuation and entrenching of racial difference, or allowing patterns of social differentiation to develop and become exacerbated.[42]

Larry Alexander argues that justifications of positive action need to be tempered by an awareness of the risks and limits of its use. The use of positive action generally, and especially in the context of the award of job opportunities by private organisations or important social goods (e.g. housing or education) by the public sector, may entrench and essentialise difference. Moreover, the allocation of valuable opportunities and goods on the basis of group membership may encourage individuals to focus on "group politics" rather than individual productivity or advancement. This in turn may fuel resentment by other groups and encourage conflict on the basis of unequal group status and social hierarchies. The sum of these risks may be to increase conflict on the basis of group difference and entrench negative sterotypes.[43]

Amy Gutman has distinguished between "essentialist" race consciousness which she critiques as treating race as a relevant factor in making fundamental distinctions between the worth of different human beings and "contingent" race consciousness that recognises that race may be used as a basis for discrimination and that taking this into account may be necessary to achieve social justice.[44] This speaks to the need to tailor positive action measures and to scrutinise them for their impact and consequences.[45] The issue of the institutional design of positive action, and how positive action initiatives are applied in different contexts, becomes especially important.

B. *Institutional Balance—Constitutionally Important Public Institutions*

As discussed earlier, Richard Epstein has argued that one advantage of *Grutter* was that it left the power over what constitutes an appropriate admissions policy to the private educational institution (i.e. University of Michigan Law

[42] Anderson makes the point that even if the "separate but equal" doctrine rejected in the seminal US Supreme Court decision in *Brown v Board of Education Education of Topeka* (1954) 347 U.S. 483 delivered genuinely equivalent levels of treatment for blacks and whites, the maintenance of segregated schooling systems would still constitute a denial of fundamental values: see E. Anderson "What is the Point of Equality?" (1999) 109 *Ethics* 287–338

[43] Larry Alexander, "What Makes Wrongful Discrimination Wrong?" (1992–1993) U. Pa. L. R. 154, at 217

[44] See A. Gutman, "Responding to Racial Injustice", in K. A. Appiah and A. Gutman (eds) *Color Conscious* (Princeton NJ: 1996) 355.

[45] S. Fredman, " European Community Discrimination Law: A Critique" (1992) 21 I.L.J. 2 119, at 130

School). Epstein goes on to argue that there are good reasons to have a differential standard to apply between private and public institutions in scrutinising affirmative action programmes. Epstein's solution is that constitutional discrimination law should apply the standard of strict scrutiny in the case of private associations and the less onerous rational basis standard in the case of public institutions. This differential approach recognises a number of important institutional factors in the context of affirmative action and discrimination law. First, it acknowledges that constitutional discrimination law has a function to perform in providing the framework within which the limits of affirmative action programmes are developed and implemented. Second, it recognises that there may be a special and distinct need for public (as opposed to private) institutions to implement affirmative action and positive duty programmes. The inclusion of excluded groups in key public institutions, as well as their influence on the design and delivery of key public goods, may be of particular importance as a social goal.

Moreover, there may be a special symbolic value in public institutions taking a lead in promoting the goals of equality and non-discrimination. This second aspect is given statutory recognition in British law with the introduction and increasing expansion of special duties to promote equality that apply in the public sector. Although the statutory duties to promote equality fall within the category of statutory discrimination law, they can also be understood as requiring some use of positive action by constitutionally important public institutions. These issues are discussed in more detail in the next chapter.

C. *Appropriate Design Of Affirmative Action*

One of the main features of the dissent in *Grutter* was its concern with the inappropriate reach and design of the affirmative action programme introduced by Michigan Law School.

REHNQUIST J:

[386–387] "Finally, I believe that the Law School's program fails strict scrutiny because it is devoid of any reasonably precise time limit on the Law School's use of race in admissions. We have emphasized that we will consider 'the planned duration of the remedy' in determining whether a race-conscious program is constitutional. . . . Our previous cases have required some limit on the duration of programs such as this because discrimination on the basis of race is invidious.

The Court suggests a possible 25-year limitation on the Law School's current program. See *ante*, at 30. Respondents, on the other hand, remain more ambiguous, explaining that 'the Law School of course recognizes that race-conscious programs must have reasonable durational limits, and the Sixth Circuit properly found such a limit in the Law School's resolve to cease considering race when genuine race-neutral alternatives become available.' Brief for Respondents Bollinger et al.

32. These discussions of a time limit are the vaguest of assurances. In truth, they permit the Law School's use of racial preferences on a seemingly permanent basis. Thus, an important component of strict scrutiny—that a program be limited in time—is casually subverted.

The Court, in an unprecedented display of deference under our strict scrutiny analysis, upholds the Law School's program despite its obvious flaws. We have said that when it comes to the use of race, the connection between the ends and the means used to attain them must be precise. But here the flaw is deeper than that; it is not merely a question of 'fit' between ends and means. Here the means actually used are forbidden by the Equal Protection Clause of the Constitution."

As already discussed, the alternative judgments in *Bakke* and *Grutter* provide arguments that challenge a strict approach to affirmative action that deems it to be reverse discrimination. However, the dissent in *Grutter* used a different set of arguments to formulate its concerns: it criticised the Michigan Law School policy as insufficiently targeted and applied too rigidly. Formulating appropriate positive action programmes that do not entrench or essentialise stereotypes is discussed later in this chapter, and it is part of the rationale for the US Supreme Court's insistence that affirmative action programmes can only pass the standards of "strict scrutiny" if they are truly remedial, targeted and temporary measures. The dissent in *Grutter* emphasised this dimension to the Supreme Court's jurisprudence.

However, it is worth observing that Chief Justice Rehnquist's call for a more targeted affirmative action programme in *Grutter* has been questioned. Richard Epstein notes that it would be impractical to ask for a more transparent or targeted programme:

"Chief Justice Rehnquist's analysis, which consists of a wooden recitation of why the University of Michigan College program fails strict scrutiny because of its rigid quality. There is only one thing left for the program to do. Which is to make covert the mass production of decisions that were done above board before hand. There is not the personnel or time to treat thousands of applicants with the care and affection that the Chief Justice wants, and absolutely no reason to think that his approach would lead to better classes. The most determined foe of affirmative action should prefer an affirmative action world in which both rules and case-by-case analysis applied ... they reduce the level of intrigue in individual cases, and they shore up the traditional standards of merit by rejecting any argument that boards and grades are used strictly to advance the position of priveliged white (and Asian) applicants."[46]

The need to focus more clearly on the design of positive action rather than simply permitting wide ranging preferential treatment or preventing it completely is also discussed by Hugh Collins, whose principle of "social inclu-

[46] Richard A. Epstein, "On Same Sex Relationships and Affirmative Action: The Covert Libertarianism of the United States Supreme Court", Northwestern University School of Law, Constitutional Theory Colloquium Series, March 31, 2004.

sion" as the justification for discrimination law provides arguments in support of positive action.

Hugh Collins: "Discrimination, Equality and Social Inclusion" (2003) 66 M.L.R. 16

pp.42–43: "Our earlier review of equality justifications for anti-discrimination laws noted the tension between any kind of different treatment based upon the characteristics of protected groups and the equal treatment principle. This tension has not entirely precluded some forms of positive action, but any measures have been subject to 'strict scrutiny' or a stringent test of 'proportionality'. In the United Kingdom, with the possible exception of Northern Ireland, positive action with respect to the allocation of jobs by quotas or the like has been regarded as too great a violation of the equal treatment principle. Our earlier theoretical discussion suggested that, in order to override the equal treatment principle and to justify different treatment, what is required is a compelling distributive justification. What kind of positive action does the distributive goal of social inclusion mandate?

Positive discrimination for the purpose of social inclusion requires that employers should be sensitive to difference and make reasonable adjustments, in order to enable members of excluded groups to overcome obstructions to their obtaining work suitable for their skills and capability. This duty requires employers to consider amongst many things how the workplace is organised, how jobs are structured, and how the skills and capabilities of the workers could be improved, with a view to the reduction of barriers to employment for excluded groups. We have already considered an example of such a duty of positive discrimination in the duty to make reasonable accommodations under the Disability Discrimination Act 1995.

Social inclusion does not, however, require the employer to adopt quotas to eliminate statistical discrimination, as might be required under a strong egalitarian approach. These quotas are unsatisfactory from the point of view of social inclusion, both because they ignore the question whether the individual worker can achieve 'well-being' from the job, and because they do not address the causes of social exclusion. If the cause of social exclusion is that applicants from a particular excluded group lack the training to perform the job, the solution lies either in the provision of training or the reorganisation of work so that less training is required for some positions. If the cause of social exclusion is that the hours of work render it difficult for the excluded group to conform, the solution lies in a consideration of whether flexibility in hours could be introduced. This duty to make reasonable adjustments in hours of work might apply to our earlier example of job-sharing the position of librarian, or to the case of a religious minority for whom work at a particular time is incompatible with required religious observances."

Although at first sight this concept of positive action as mandated by the social inclusion principle appears to be at odds with current discrimination law, which in general forbids different treatment, a closer inspection of the operation of the law of indirect discrimination reveals that it can approximate to the model suggested by the aim of social inclusion.

In a claim for indirect discrimination, once the indirect discriminatory effect of a hiring rule is revealed by statistical evidence, the employer must justify the rule on business grounds to avoid a successful claim of discrimination. As discussed in the previous chapter, justification standard currently used in cases of indirect sex discrimination is under EU law a test of proportionality, while a slightly weaker test is perhaps applied in domestic law. Notwithstanding these differences in approach, the justification defence as applied in the indirect discrimination context requires the employer to discover and reveal the potential costs of eliminating the hiring rule. Then the court must balance those costs to the employer against the exclusionary impact of the rule. Positive action schemes based upon the social inclusion principle could be seen as involving a similar process of balancing the negative costs of such schemes against their inclusionary potential.

Following this logic, retaining a legal requirement for an objective and proportionate justification to be offered where "suspect" classifications are utilised therefore may make sense. Often, designing positive action programmes on an identity-neutral basis, such as identifying beneficiary groups by reference to socio-economic status or geographical location, will be more appropriate than confining the scope of their application to groups defined in terms of their identity (race, gender, disability, etc.) However, there will be circumstances where it may be desirable to target positive action at particular identity-based groups, as only specifically focused schemes may eliminate the disadvantages to which they are subject. However, in applying any requirement that positive action be objectively justified, it may be important to avoid the automatic assumption that the use of "suspect" grounds can make the use of positive action measures inherently dubious. Proponents of "anti-subordination", "substantive equality" or "social inclusion" approaches would argue that there is nothing inherently objectionable in the use of such forms of positive action, provided that they are clearly linked to the reduction of group disadvantage.

VIII. Conclusion

In the discussion of the specific law and policy on positive action in the next chapter, it becomes clear that different forms of positive action are not only permissible but also in some cases may be required by discrimination law. However, approaches to positive action in European case-law and national anti-discrimination legislation often remain attached to the "anti-classification" approach. The use of preferential or special treatment in positive action strategies often has to be explicitly justified as an exception to the general anti-discrimination principle, and is usually given a very circumscribed scope of application. The case-law of the European Court of Justice does increasingly show a general trend to permit greater use of "suspect" characteristics in positive action strategies. However, the reasoning of the ECJ is often uncertain in these decisions, as it struggles to reconcile this greater tolerance of the use of such positive action strategies with its formal adherence to the "anti-classification" principle. Similarly, UK national legislation remains firmly wedded to an "anti-classification" approach, even though this approach continues to generate inconsistencies, and makes the application of clearly-justified positive action measures unnecessarily complex and uncertain. The debates about which form of equality should have priority remain fiercely contested: the "anti-classification"/strict/formal equality approach retains considerable support for its clarity and rejection of distinctions, notwithstanding the well-developed academic critique of some of its assumptions.

Concepts of positive action can be found in a wide range of instruments: international law; constitutional and human rights law; European Union law; and domestic statutory instruments. We now proceed to discuss these concepts in the next chapter. In addition, there are non-legal techniques which act as a form of positive action. These are discussed in the final part of the book in the chapter on non-legal responses to discrimination.

7

IMPLEMENTING POSITIVE ACTION

I. Introduction

The previous chapter explored theoretical questions about the concept of positive action: why has it emerged as a necessary concept and regulatory technique in discrimination law; what are the different types of positive action; is positive action a version of unlawful discrimination or a requirement of the goal of equality and non-discrimination. In this chapter we move on to consider the practical issues surrounding positive action in discrimination law: why is there a need for positive action alongside developed concepts of direct and indirect discrimination? How should we design effective positive action measures? What are the specific examples of positive action in international, constitutional and human rights, EU and domestic sources of discrimination law? These questions link back to many of the key questions we set out in chapter 1, especially the ninth question (what remedies are available?) and the tenth (how far should solutions be sought outside the law?).

II. Where Positive Action is Used

It should be noted that many forms of positive action have been deployed at different times, and their use often predates the introduction of discrimination law in certain contexts. The use of some forms of employment quotas and "set-aside" places for disabled persons dates back to the aftermath of the Second World War in many European states and the USA (see the chapter on disability discrimination)).[1] Other forms of positive action measures were introduced initially in the USA in the late 1960s and early 1970s to remedy the wide-spread segregation of the Afro-American community. Many of these "affirmative action" measures, such as altering recruitment criteria to elim-

[1] For an account of disability quotas see Lisa Waddington, "Reassessing the Employment of People with Disabilities in Europe From Quotas to Anti-Discrimination Laws" (1996) 18 *Comparative Labour L.R.* 62.

inate factors that directly contributed to racial disparities, were originally introduced to comply with court orders following a finding of indirect discrimination, or "consent decrees" agreed by employers with the US Department of Justice to avoid litigation.[2]

Other forms of positive action, such as the use of preferential treatment to benefit particular disadvantaged groups in undergraduate admission decisions to university faculties, or the use of similar measures in the US army, have stemmed from the desire to ensure greater diversity and to combat segregation. The use of positive action measures in the US was therefore part and parcel of the post-1960s desegregation drive, with the underlying rationale for their use tending now to shift from this initial impulse towards an emphasis on securing diversity and fair representation in key institutions. Despite ongoing political controversy about the use of preferential treatment, the strength of support in the US for the use of a range of positive action measures can be seen in the briefs submitted to the US Supreme Court in the affirmative action case of *Grutter* from bodies such as the US Army and leading business corporations (see the previous chapter).

Therefore, positive action in the US has a comparatively long history, has almost from the outset of the civil rights movement been seen as an integral and necessary part of policy and legal responses to segregation, and tends to involve both the imposition of compulsory measures as part of court-sanctioned remedial steps in the wake of discrimination and the use of voluntary measures by a range of public and private bodies. However, the extent to which such positive action measures should involve the use of preferential treatment remains a persistent source of legal and political controversy, despite the widespread acceptance of its use, as already discussed.

Within the EU, there is a wide diversity of approaches to the use of positive action. Differences exist not alone between different member states,[3] but also within member states in respect of the types of positive action permitted across the different equality grounds, or even in respect of a particular equality ground. Certain very general cross-European trends can be detected. Greater latitude is usually permitted for positive action to benefit disabled persons than for other grounds, including the use of quotas and "set-aside" posts for disabled individuals, which is a legacy of the initial use of quotas in the post-war period.[4] In contrast, positive action in the ethnic/race context is much less developed, and in particular wide resistance exists to the use of any forms of

[2] For example, the US Justice Department under the Violent Crime Control and Law Enforcement Act 1994 may enter into consent decrees with municipal police departments alleged to engage in a "pattern or practice" of conduct that infringes upon the civil rights of its persons as afforded by federal state and local laws. See 42 U.S.C. 14141 (Su IV 1998).

[3] See the discussion on the divergences in the approaches of member states to identity-based redistributive policies in D. Caruso, "Limits of the Classic Method: Positive Action in the European Union After the New Equality Directives" (2003) 44 Harvard International L.J. 331.

[4] For an account of the use of quotas for disabled persons, and the problems inherent in such schemes, see L. Waddington, "Reassessing the Employment of People with Disabilities in Europe: From Quotas to Anti-Discrimination Laws", 18 Comparative Labour L.R. (1996) 62.

preferential treatment in this context. In the age context, widespread uncertainty and lack of analysis exists as to the extent to which positive action on the grounds of age is desirable.[5] In general, the use of "mainstreaming" initiatives designed to identify and modify policies and practices that disadvantage particular groups appears to be less controversial and more acceptable than other "harder" forms of positive action.

Generally, EC law permits, rather than requires, the use of certain forms of positive action (see below). Thus what form positive action takes is dictated at Member State, rather than Community, level. In certain EU Member States, positive action is imposed by federal or state legislation on state bodies, rather than the private sector. For example, many German states have introduced strong positive action measures in the context of gender equality, which have generated much of the ECJ case-law on positive action (see below). The impetus for these measures came from an influential report which advocated that the German public service should become a "model" of employment equality.[6] The UK makes use of positive duties to steer public authorities towards the adoption of certain forms of positive action measures (see below).

Certain states also impose certain obligations upon a combination of public and private bodies. In several Scandinavian countries, certain requirements to ensure a fair representation of women upon state and private sector corporate boards have been introduced. In France, a failure to ensure a fair representation of both sexes on party lists can result in the sanction of loss of state funding, and a variety of measures have been introduced in other European states to either permit or require political parties to take positive action measures in selecting female candidates.[7] In Northern Ireland, a set of fair employment duties are imposed upon all private and public sector bodies above a certain size, and the Hepple Report in 2000 argued very strongly for the imposition of affirmative action requirements upon private bodies in Britain, suggesting that the imposition of statutory requirements was essential to drive forward change.[8] (See below.)

Positive action may also be court-imposed upon individual employers, as has been the case in the US (see above). In the Republic of Ireland, the Irish Equality Tribunal and Labour Court have powers under the Employment Equality Act 1998 ("EEA") and Equal Status Act 2000 ("ESA") to make orders for discriminating bodies to undertake a specified course of remedial action, as well as traditional remedies in damages.[9] Private employers may also be required to adopt positive action measures, often in particular where they

[5] See C. O'Cinneide, *Age Discrimination and European Law* (Brussels: European Commission, 2005), 38–41.

[6] N. Colneric "Making Equality Law More Effective Lessons From the German Experience" (1996) 3 Cardozo Women's L.J. 229. See also D. Schiek, "Sex Equality after *Kalanke* and *Marschall*" (1998) E.L.J. 148.

[7] See Colm O'Cinneide and Meg Russell, "Positive Action to Promote Women in Politics: Some European Comparisons" (2003) 53 International Comparative L.Q. 587–614.

[8] See the Hepple Report, para.337.

[9] s.82(e) EEA and s.27(1)(b) of the ESA.

wish to tender for public sector contracts. In the US in 1961, President Kennedy introduced this form of positive action, requiring government contractors not only to abstain from unlawful discrimination, but also to increase the numbers of racial minorities on the workforces. Later amended to cover the grounds of sex and religion and embodied in Executive Order 11246, these requirements are enforced by the Office of Federal Contract Compliance Programs. Their scope is broad, applying to about 300,000 contractors, employing about 40 per cent of the US workforce (see the chapter on collective remedies).[10]

This form of positive action has also been applied (in various forms) in Canada,[11] Australia,[12] and South Africa.[13] In the EC context, public procurement has tended to be strictly regulated in a manner which generally precludes or deters the use of social criteria in public sector tendering by public authorities in member states, but recent modifications to the public procurement rules have opened up the possibility of new attempts to utilise "contract compliance" measures to bring about the greater use of positive action measures by private bodies (see again the chapter on collective remedies).[14] Private and public sector bodies may also voluntarily introduce positive action programmes, which may be encouraged by government policy, or by trade unions, community groups, NGOs and other voluntary sector bodies. These can take a wide variety of forms and can vary considerably in terms of their underlying justifications, their objectives and their design.

A. *Designing Effective Positive Action Strategies*

From a policy perspective, the advantage of positive action mechanisms is that they compensate for the limitations of discrimination law which have been discussed above: they are potentially useful tools to break down structural patterns of exclusion and disadvantage. Devising a coherent and effective set of positive action strategies can however be a challenge.[15] Often, positive

[10] See further B. Hepple, M. Coussey and T. Choudhury, *Equality: A New Framework Report of the Independent Review of the Enforcement of UK Anti-Discrimination Legislation* (Oxford: Hart Publishing 2000) 65 (the "Hepple Report").

[11] Employment Equity Act 1995.

[12] Equal Opportunity for Women in the Workplace Act 1999, amending and consolidating the Affirmative Action (Equal Employment Opportunity for Women) Act 1986.

[13] Employment Equity Act 1998.

[14] See Hepple Report, paras 374–377, pp.84–85; C. O'Cinneide, *Taking Equal Opportunities Seriously* (London: Equality and Diversity Forum, 2003), Pt VIII.

[15] See H. Gleckman, et al, "Race in the Workplace Is Affirmative Action Working?" *Business Week* July 8, 1991, 50–63. See also G. Stephanopoulos, et al, *Affirmative Action Review Report to the President* (Washington DC: White House 1995), Pts 3 and 4.

action measures may be introduced as tokenistic gestures, or without adequate resources and support, or substitute for real and meaningful action.[16] They may also prove underproductive if they generate a backlash or perpetuate stereotypes. Positive action mechanisms can also be abused to favour distinct sub-groups or particular "client" groups.

There is no fixed formula for automatic success—different measures have very different impact in different contexts.[17] The variety and diversity of disadvantaged groups has to be taken into account. Different groups may be exposed to different levels of prejudice and different types of stereotyping assumptions. For a positive action strategy to be effective, it should be designed for the particular environment within which it will be applied, and have clear justifications, goals and targets.

Comparative experience has repeatedly shown that clarity as to why securing adequate levels of disadvantaged group representation throughout various public and private sectors is important.[18] Without such clarity, attempts to frame good recruitment policies often become mired in uncertainty and lack of focus, and the priority initially given to securing adequate representation tends to slip and be displaced by other concerns.[19] Repeated experience in the UK, US and elsewhere has shown that the intent and goals of such measures can often be misunderstood and misinterpreted as "special treatment" or "political correctness".[20] Lack of clarity tends to generate fear and suspicion, but where the case for positive action measures is made well, a more accepting environment is often created.[21] Experience from Canada, the Netherlands, the USA, Australia, the UK and elsewhere has shown that the success of positive action policies often depends upon the depth and width of understanding of how such polices work, as well as their ultimate purpose.[22]

Repeated experience has also shown that attempts to develop positive action in recruitment have tended to flounder on a lack of sustained focus, or of internal institutional support. Clear targets and goals are usually necessary for positive action programmes to have any real impact, and also have an important symbolic value.[23] It is also be necessary to have strong enforcement

[16] See C. Agocs, "Systemic Discrimination in Employment Mapping the Issue and the Policy Responses" in C. Agocs, et al, *Workplace Equality International Perspectives on Legislation Policy and Practice* (London Kluwer 2002).

[17] J. Wrench and T. Modood, "The Effectiveness of Employment Equality Policies in Relation to Immigrants and Ethnic Minorities in the UK", Report commissioned by the International Labour Office International Migration Papers 38 (Geneva: I.L.O., 2000).

[18] See the essays in C. Agocs (ed), *Workplace Equality International Perspectives on Legislation Policy and Practice* (London: Kluwer, 2003).

[19] ibid.

[20] M. Frase-Blunt, "Thwarting the Diversity Backlash Develop an Inclusive Plan that Highlights the Bottom-line Effect and Benefits to all Employees (2003) 48 HR Magazine 6 137–138 141–144.

[21] See the US Federal Glass Ceiling Commission, *A Solid Investment Making Full Use of the Nation's Human Capital* (Washington DC: Printing Office, 1995).

[22] See the essays in Agocs, et al, above.

[23] See J. E. Kellough, *Federal Equal Opportunity Policy and Numerical Goals and Timetables* (New York: Praeger, 1989). See also J. S. Leonard, "What Promises are Worth: The Impact of Affirmative Action Goals" (1985) 20 J. of Human Resources 1 3–20.

mechanisms to ensure compliance with positive action policies, and to have sufficient legal or political support for these initiatives. "Contract compliance" mechanisms, for example, have generated very positive results when linked to strong enforcement mechanisms and backed by sufficient political will, as in Northern Ireland: in the Netherlands, in contrast, the imposition of positive duties upon private businesses lacked sufficient enforcement controls or political support and so proved ineffective.[24] Contract compliance and supply side measures are discussed in more detail in the chapter on collective remedies. Here it is worth emphasising that these policy responses are also important examples of positive action to supplement individual litigation.

In the next part of this chapter, we set out and discuss positive action in a number of different forms of discrimination law and policy: international instruments; the comparative experience from the US, Canada and Europe; and the domestic British and Northern Irish law and policy. This should provide some sense of the potential scope and range of positive action measures, and how they interact with the standards set by international human rights law and national discrimination legislation.

III. International and Comparative Approaches

A. *International Human Rights Law*

The recognition of equality as a central element of human dignity is a "dominant and recurring theme of international law"[25], and is enshrined in two complementary and linked principles that are present in the Universal Declaration of Human Rights ("UDHR"), International Covenant on Civil and Political Rights ("ICCPR") and the International Covenant on Economic, Social and Cultural Rights ("ICESCR")—a positive right to equality, and a negative right to freedom from discrimination.[26] Respect for equality as a principle or norm composed of these twin rights is also embedded in the Convention on the Elimination of Racial Discrimination ("CERD") and the Convention on the Elimination of Discrimination Against Women ("CEDAW"), as well (in diluted form) in the European Convention on Human Rights.

[24] See C. O'Cinneide, *Taking Equal Opportunities Seriously* (London Equality and Diversity Forum 2003), ch.4.

[25] See A. Bayefsky, "The Principle of Equality and Non-Discrimination in International Law" (1990) 11 Human Rights L.J. 1, p.2.

[26] See Art.1 and 2 UDHR, Art.2(1) ICCPR and Art.2(2) ICESCR; see also O'Hare, "Equality and Affirmative Action in International Human Rights Law and its Relevance to the European Union (2000) 4 International J. of Discrimination and the Law 3, 10. O'Hare also argues that these two complementary principles have become part of customary international law, citing inter alia Judge Tanaka's opinion in the *South West Africa Case*: see O'Hare, p.11.

Ramcharan has emphasised that the (relatively vague) equality principle as recognised in international human rights law does not preclude states making legitimate distinctions between those subject to its authority that are based upon objective and proportionate criteria[27]: it does however preclude discriminatory treatment based upon "arbitrary, invidious or unjustified distinction[s]".[28] While recognising the importance of treating individuals in similar situations in a similar manner when appropriate, international human rights law clearly recognises the principle that different treatment may be necessary to secure de facto equality or to achieve justice.[29] Therefore, giving real and substantive effect to the principle of equality may involve differential or special treatment for a disadvantaged group to assist in redressing social and historical patterns of unequal treatment.

Article 26 of the ICCPR provides that "[a]ll persons are equal before the law" and that States Parties "shall ... guarantee to all persons equal and effective protection against discrimination on any ground such as race ...": this equality guarantee is also reinforced by Art.2 of the Covenant. In its General Comment 18, the Human Rights Committee (HRC) charged with interpreting the Covenant has provided authoritative recognition that "[not] every differentiation of treatment will constitute discrimination, if the criteria for such differentiation are reasonable and objective and if the aim is to achieve a purpose which is legitimate under the Covenant."[30] At para.10, the HRC recognised the need for positive action:

> "[T]he principle of equality sometimes requires States to take affirmative action in order to diminish or eliminate conditions which cause or help to perpetuate discrimination prohibited by the Covenant. For example, in a State where the general conditions of a certain part of the population prevent or impair their enjoyment of human rights, the State should take specific action to correct those conditions. Such action may involve granting for a time to the part of the population concerned certain preferential treatment in specific matters as compared with the rest of the population. However, as long as such action is needed to correct discrimination in fact, it is a case of legitimate differentiation under the Covenant."

Similarly, in its General Comment 4, the Committee noted that:

> "The principle of equality sometimes requires States parties to take affirmative action in order to diminish or eliminate conditions which cause or help to perpetuate discrimination prohibited by the Covenant. [...] Such action may involve granting for a time ... certain preferential treatment in specific matters..."

[27] See also *Broeks v The Netherlands*, Comm. 267/1987, Doc. A/43/40 (1988).

[28] W. McKean *Equality and Discrimination Under International Law* (Oxford: Clarendon, 1983), pp.185–6: see also O'Hare, p.12.

[29] See the Inter-American Court in *Fourth Advisory Opinion on the Costa Rican Constitution*, para.57, available in (1984) 5 Human Rights L.J. 161, 172. See also the decisions of the Permanent Court of International Justice in the cases of *German Settlers in Poland* Series B No.6 (1923), p.24 and *Minority Schools in Albania* Series A/B, No.64, April 6, 1935 (Advisory Opinion), p.19.

[30] General Comment 18, para.13, at 28 (1994).

General Comment No.4 thereby makes it clear that positive action is permissible, but it also stated that the obligation in the ICCPR to secure equality of treatment can take positive form.[31]

The HRC in General Comment 27 gave some indication of when this obligation would apply, by recognising Roma communities as among the most disadvantaged in the contemporary world and calling upon States to adopt positive action measures on behalf of the Roma in a number of fields, including education, public and private employment, public contracting and the media. The HRC in its individual complaint decisions and comments on country reports has also consistently supported preferential treatment for disadvantaged groups in education, the public service, or other positions. It has upheld preferential treatment policies even when other individuals have felt discriminated against them by them. In *Stalla Costa v Uruguay*[32] the applicant complained that preference was given to certain public officials in getting admitted to the public service, who had previously been unfairly dismissed on ideological or political grounds. The HRC considered that in the light of the previous discrimination suffered by those individuals, the measure was held to be permissible affirmative action.[33]

Article 4(1) of the Convention on the Elimination of All Forms of Discrimination Against Women expressly shields positive action programs, exempting them from the definition of discrimination: it states that:

> "Adoption by States Parties of temporary special measures aimed at accelerating de facto equality for men and women shall not be considered discrimination as defined in the present Convention, but shall in no way entail as a consequence the maintenance of unequal or separate standards; these measures shall be discontinued when the objectives of equality of opportunity and treatment have been achieved."

The same article also provides that "special measures ... aimed at protecting maternity shall not be considered discriminatory." In line with these provisions, the Commission on the Status of Women has called upon national governments to make use of temporary and special measures in line with Art.4(1) where necessary to alleviate the effects of past discrimination: the Commission suggested that international law clearly recognises that "without temporary measures to alter [discriminatory] structures, movement towards significant societal objectives ... will be unjustifiably slowed."

As with the ICCPR, this permissive approach is also supplemented by

[31] In General Comment 23 the HRC recognised that (in para.6.2) that: "positive measures by states may also be necessary to protect the identity of a minority and the rights of its members to enjoy and develop their culture and language and to practice their religion, in community with other members of the groups."

[32] No.198/1995, ICCPR.

[33] The HRC has also approved the use of quotas in several of its country reports. For example, in its concluding observations on India, it approved a constitutional amendment in India that reserves one third of seats in elected local bodies for women and also approved the practice of reserving elected positions for members of certain tribes and castes. See UN Doc. CCPR/C/79/Add.81, para.10.

provisions that indicate that positive action of some form may actually be required in particular circumstances. Articles 2(e) and 3 of CEDAW impose a strong positive obligation upon signatory states to take active steps to secure equality for both sexes, with Art.3 requiring states to "take in all fields ... all appropriate measures ... to ensure the full development and advancement of women". Article 5(1) CEDAW illustrates the breath of this requirement, with its obligation upon states to "modify the social and cultural patterns of conduct of men and women, with a view to achieving the end of prejudices ... and all other practices which are based on the idea of the inferiority ... of either of the sexes or on the stereotyped roles for men and women." Article 7 of CEDAW makes clear that such "temporary special measures" may be used to secure equality of political representation:

"States Parties shall take all appropriate measures to eliminate discrimination against women in the political and public life of the country and, in particular, shall ensure to women, on equal terms with men, the right ... to vote in all elections and public referenda and to be eligible for election to all publicly elected bodies ..."[34]

In its General Comments, the Women's Committee has argued that positive action measures may be necessary to give full effect to the provisions of CEDAW. In its General Comment on Temporary Special Measures, the Committee emphasised that temporary and proportionate positive action measures were needed to promote *de facto* equality between the sexes[35], and General Comment No.23 called for such measures to be introduced to encourage parity of participation in public life.[36]

CERD, as with CEDAW, authorises by its express terms affirmative action programs to redress past wrongs. While the treaty's general provisions outlaw all forms of racial discrimination, certain "special measures" are expressly excluded from the definition of proscribed racial discrimination.[37] As the Convention states in Article 1(4):

"Special measures taken for the sole purpose of securing adequate advancement of certain racial or ethnic groups or individuals requiring such protection as may be necessary in order to ensure such groups or individuals equal enjoyment or exercise of human rights and fundamental freedoms shall not be deemed racial discrimination, provided, however, that such measures do not, as a consequence, lead to the maintenance of separate rights for different racial groups and that they shall not be continued after the objectives for which they were taken have been achieved."

[34] The insertion of the "sunset clause" into the UK Sex Discrimination (Election Candidates) Act which permits preferential treatment in favour of female candidates, proving for its expiry after 14 years unless renewed by Parliament, was a direct result of a desire to comply with the "temporary special measures" requirement in Art.4 of the Convention for the Elimination of Discrimination Against Women, the equivalent of Art.2 of CERD.

[35] General Comment No.5, UN Doc. A/43/38 (1988).

[36] General Comment No.23 of January 13, 1997, para.15.

[37] See P. Justesen, "Equality for Ethnic Minorities—International and Danish Perspectives" (2003) 10 *International Journal on Minority and Group Rights* 1 1.

Notably, this caveat appears in the Convention's very first article, even before the document's direct prohibitions of race discrimination. Significantly, and again paralleling CEDAW, Art.2(2) of CERD also provides that states "shall ... take ... special and concrete measures to ensure the adequate development and protection of certain racial groups ...", and "to bring to an end, by all appropriate means, racial discrimination ..."[38] This positive obligation is unequivocal in requiring special measures when appropriate and necessary: however, as with CEDAW, Art.2(2) also provides that positive action steps are to be taken only "when the circumstances so warrant", and again are to be proportionate in nature and time limited: "these measures shall in no case entail ... the maintenance of unequal and separate rights for different racial groups after the objectives for which were taken have been achieved".[39]

So again, CERD both permits and possibly requires the introduction of positive action measures in certain circumstances, if such measures are temporary, targeted and proportionate in scope. The Committee of the Elimination of Racial Discrimination addresses the issue of positive action regularly in its concluding observations to State reports, and has called in several circumstances for temporary special measures to be introduced as part of States parties' obligations under the Convention.[40] The Committee has also been explicit in arguing that the adoption of affirmative action measures where necessary is an *obligation* under Art.2(2) of CERD.[41]

Other international instruments and bodies have adopted similar positions. The ILO Discrimination (Employment and Occupation) Convention (No.111) classifies special measures for those needing special assistance as falling outside the definition of discrimination. A series of UN policy documents have also adopted similar views, such as The Mexico Declaration on the Equality of Women and the 1995 Copenhagen Declaration. The additional protocol to the European Social Charter permits the use of special measures to reverse de facto inequalities. The protection of minority rights may also involve the taking positive action. The HRC's General Comment No.27 supports this position, as has the UN Special Rapporteur on Minorities.[42]

Therefore, there is a broad consensus that international human rights law should be interpreted as permitting the use of temporary and proportionate positive action measures, and even imposes certain obligations to utilise such

[38] See also Art.2(d) CERD, where State parties are required "to bring to an end, by all appropriate means ... racial discrimination by any persons, groups or organisations."

[39] Article 2(2).

[40] See, for instance, A/51/18 (September 30, 1996) at 503, where CERD recommended that the government of Namibia adopt affirmative action measures "to overcome vestiges of the past that still hamper the possibilities for black people, including vulnerable groups among them" in areas of education and employment. See also A/53/18 (September 10, 1998), at 434, where CERD welcomed the Government of Nepal's affirmative action programmes for "less developed groups", but requested information on the results of those programmes.

[41] Committee on the Elimination of Racial Discrimination, *Concluding Observations: United States of America*, 14/08/2001, UN Doc. A/56/18, para.399.

[42] Capotorti, *Study on the Rights of Persons Belonging to Ethnic, Religious and Linguistic Minorities* (New York: UN, 1991). See also O'Hare, above, 17–18.

measures where appropriate and necessary. All these are useful indicators that a broad range of positive action measures will be permitted, subject to the temporary and proportionate requirement. Positive action is therefore seen as a remedy rather than as an inherently discriminatory act requiring special justification: however, its use is subject to the basic requirement that all forms of positive action utilised by states are to be reasonable, objective and proportionate in their design and execution.

Justesen has suggested that such measures may be necessary when the disadvantaged group in question requires the protection and aid of the state to attain the full and equal enjoyment of human rights[43]: she has also suggested that such measures must be introduced for the benefit of genuinely disadvantaged groups, must be directed towards achieving de facto equality, must be necessary and proportionate to achieve this aim, and should be time-limited.[44] Within this general scheme, states are given considerable latitude as to what (if any) positive action measures may be necessary and proportionate.

International human rights instruments may also impose *positive obligations* upon states to take positive action in certain circumstances to secure meaningful and real equality for disadvantaged groups.[45] Certain human rights instruments, in particular the CERD, appear to impose positive obligations to take certain forms of positive action: however, the extent to which the introduction of positive action measures may therefore be *required* to comply with international human rights obligations remains unclear.

International obligations therefore require states to guarantee equal treatment for all, but permit the use of proportionate and temporary measures to achieve this goal. This would indicate that preferential treatment measures if introduced need to be time-limited, proportionate and demonstrated to be necessary and fairly implemented. It is noteworthy that the Patten Report adopted a similar approach, and imposed a ten-year time limit on their quota scheme for the Police Service for Northern Ireland.[46] The UK Joint Select Committee on Human Rights was of the opinion that the UK Sex Discrimination (Election Candidates) Act 2002, which permits political parties to give preference to female candidates, met the requirement of proportionality, by virtue of its "sunset clause", its purely permissive character, the specific and defined scope of the legislation, and the continuing ability of the Equal Opportunities Commission to scrutinise the positive action measures used by the parties. This again reflects the basic approach of international human rights law to positive action measures.

[43] P. Justesen, "Special Measures and Affirmative Action—Genuine Equality Strategies", p.5: see also T. Meron, "The Meaning and Reach of the International Convention on the Elimination of all Forms of Racial Discrimination" (1985) 79 American Journal of International Law 287, 308.

[44] Justesen, p.5.

[45] See O'Hare, 18–20.

[46] See the *Patten Report*, 14.11.

B. *US and Canadian Approaches to Positive Action*

In the previous chapter we examined the justification of affirmative action in US constitutional law with an analysis of key cases such as *Bakke* and *Grutter*, as well as critical commentary of the role of affirmative action in the US context. One feature of the US experience that is mentioned in the case law and by commentators is that the history of slavery in the US creates a special context for the introduction of positive action measures. Comparative analysis in this context needs to be sensitive to these differences. However, a comparison of the US and Canadian material with British and European approaches to positive action also reveals similar issues, e.g. the need to place limits on positive action in the context of employment in the US are developed in ways that are similar to the development of positive action in EU discrimination law.

1. Canada

Turning for a moment to a comparative perspective, Canada has employed forms of "employment equity" after federal experiments with voluntary employment equity in the late 1970's proved unsuccessful. The Canadian Charter of Rights and Freedoms[47] explicitly permits affirmative action programs: Section 15 of the Charter provides that:

"(1) Every individual is equal before and under the law and has the right to the equal protection and equal benefit of the law without discrimination and, in particular, without discrimination based on race, national or ethnic origin, colour, religion, sex, age or mental or physical disability.

Affirmative action programs

(2) Subsection (1) does not preclude any law, program or activity that has as its object the amelioration of conditions of disadvantaged individuals or groups including those that are disadvantaged because of race, national or ethnic origin, colour, religion, sex, age or mental or physical disability."

Thus, the Charter permits the implementation of programs that are designed to ameliorate conditions of disadvantage. In other words, though affirmative action programs are reviewable under s.15(1), s.15(2) does not provide for a defence *per se*. Rather, it merely indicates that programs designed to ameliorate the position of disadvantaged groups or individuals in society are linked with the very purposes of s.15(1) equality rights. This was made clear in the following extract from the Canadian Supreme Court decision in *Lovelace v Ontario*:

[47] Enacted as Sch.B to the *Canada Act 1982* (UK) 1982, c.11. (Hereafter "Charter").

Lovelace v Ontario, Supreme Court of Canada [2000] 1 S.C.R. 950

JUSTICE FRANK LACOBUCCI

[93] "... This Court has not defined the scope or content of s. 15(2) of the Charter, at least not as a substantive or independently applicable subsection of s. 15. However, s. 15(2) has played an important role in the evolution of s. 15 jurisprudence. In particular, s. 15(2) provides a basis for the firm recognition that the equality right is to be understood in substantive rather than formalistic terms (see Andrews v. Law Society of British Columbia ... Having accepted the substantive approach, the Court has interpreted s. 15(1) not only to prevent discrimination but also to play a role in promoting the amelioration of the conditions of disadvantaged persons. [...]

104 In this regard, Edward M. Iacobucci [Justice Iacobucci's son, a law professor at the University of Toronto] stated, in "Antidiscrimination and Affirmative Action Policies: Economic Efficiency and the Constitution" (1998), 36 Osgoode Hall L.J. 293, at p. 326:

"The debate is whether section 15(2) informs the interpretation of section 15(1), which if true indicates that while section 15(2) is not absolutely necessary to establishing equality rights, it is important in determining the scope of the equality rights set out in section 15(1). Under this view, section 15(2) admittedly does not set out any new rights, but it is not redundant."

He goes on to say that the preferred view is recognizing s. 15(2) as an interpretive aid to s. 15(1), since taking the exemptive approach means that affirmative action programs are construed as somehow conflicting with the purpose of s. 15(1). [...]

105 The plain meaning of the language in these subsections is consistent with the view that s. 15(2) is confirmatory and supplementary to s. 15(1). In this respect, it is clear that the s. 15(2) phrase "does not preclude" cannot be understood as language of defence or exemption. Rather, this language indicates that the normal reading of s. 15(1) includes the kind of special program under review in this appeal. Indeed, Walter S. Tarnopolsky noted that the drafters of s. 15 added s. 15(2) out of "excessive caution", intending to bolster the substantive equality approach in s. 15(1), since, at the time the Charter was being drafted, there was a worry that affirmative action programs would be over-turned on the basis of reverse discrimination ... In short, s. 15(2) is referenced to the s. 15(1) subsection and there is no language of exemption; on its face s. 15(2) describes the scope of the s. 15(1) equality right [...]

108 In summary, at this stage of the jurisprudence, I see s. 15(2) as confirmatory of s. 15(1) and, in that respect, claimants arguing equality claims in the future should first be directed to s. 15(1) since that subsection can embrace ameliorative programs of the kind that are contemplated by s. 15(2). By doing that one can ensure that the program is subject to the full scrutiny of the discrimination analysis, as well as the possibility of a s. 1 review. However, as already stated, we may well wish to reconsider this matter at a future time in the context of another case."

Generally speaking, both provincial and federal human rights codes in Canada also permit the use of employment equity measures.[48] For example, in Ontario, employment equity programs have been deemed permissible so long as they do not "disproportionately harm the interests of non-protected persons."[49] Human rights tribunals often have the statutory jurisdiction to order the

[48] See, for example, s.16(1) of the *Canadian Human Rights Act*, RSC 1990 C H-6; as an example of similar provincial provisions, see s.14(2) of the *Ontario Human Rights Code* RSO 1990, Ch19.

[49] *Roberts v Ontario* (1994), 117 D.L.R. (4th) 297, especially at 303 & 306, (Ont CA); see also *Tomen v OTF (No 4)* (1994), 20 CHRR D/257 (Ont Bd Inq).

implementation of fairly sweeping employment equity programs, where such are viewed as necessary to remedy particular instances of systemic discrimination. One notable example of such an order was at issue in *CNR v Canada (Human Rights Commission)*,[50] in which the employer's workforce included only 0.7 per cent of women in "blue-collar" positions in a particular region and 13 per cent in Canada as a whole, compared with a female representation rate in such jobs of 40.7 per cent across Canada and 39 per cent in Quebec. The Supreme Court of Canada upheld an order of the federal Human Rights Tribunal that required the employer to hire at least one woman for every four non-traditional vacancies until women occupied 13 per cent of such positions.

2. US Law and Policy

Positive or "affirmative action" in the US is mired in legal and political controversy, as noted in the previous chapter. Nonetheless, several important lessons may be drawn. First, US experience shows that much positive action is necessary in response to undo the consequences of large-scale systemic discrimination. Secondly, and relatedly however, the US jurisprudence shows the disadvantages of conceiving of positive action in purely remedial terms. It has tended to require the identification of particular perpetrators and victims of past discrimination before employers may engage in affirmative action, which has limited its range and focus. Outside the employment context in contrast, US courts have begun to accept forward-looking rationales for positive action. Thirdly, the US application of strict and intermediate scrutiny to race and gender-based affirmative action respectively provides a useful contrast with the ECJ's approach. It allows us to see the issues on which the ECJ has been quite flexible, such as accepting current group-based disadvantage affecting women and where the ECJ is quite strict, such as requiring strict adherence to merit at the hiring stage.

C. *The US Experience with Affirmative Action*

1. Introduction

The term "affirmative action" in the US context is used to cover any measure within the broad definition of positive action adopted in this chapter. However, as discussed in the previous chapter, political and legal debates about "affirmative action" tend to focus overwhelmingly on the use of preferential treatment and merit redefinition strategies to assist disadvantaged groups and to reduce the lingering after-effects of segregation. The use of these strategies is relatively common, but has generated a considerable amount of litigation. A

[50] [1987] 1 S.C.R. 1114 (hereafter CNR).

distinction has to be made between the impact of constitutional and statutory controls in this area, and between ameliorative measures introduced in the wake of a finding of discrimination or as part of an agreed remedial strategy, and other forms of affirmative action.

2. Constitutional Controls

The Equal Protection Clauses of the US Constitution binds federal and state authorities, as well as receipts of state funding (by an indirect route), with the clauses of the 5th and 14th Amendments applying respectively.[51] Any use of race as a classification by a federal or state authority has to satisfy the very exacting justification standard of "strict scrutiny".[52] Gender is another form of "suspect" classification, but gender-based classifications are subject to the less exacting standard of "intermediate scrutiny".[53] Distinctions based on other grounds such as age and disability discrimination usually face a lower standard of "rationality" review.[54] Under "strict scrutiny" review, there must be a compelling government interest at stake, and the means employed in the measure in question must be "narrowly tailored" to suit the compelling objective sought to be achieved. Under the "intermediate scrutiny" standard, the purpose must be important, and the means substantially related. The "rationality standard" just requires the measure to be founded on a rational basis.

Some of the initial early decisions concerning the constitutionality of state affirmative action on the grounds of race, such as *University of California v Bakke*[55] and *Fullilove v Klutznick*[56] left some uncertainty about the appropriate standard of review when "benign" measures were at issue, that is motivated by the desire to ameliorate segregation or social disadvantage. Since *Croson*,[57] strict scrutiny has been established as the applicable standard for racially-based affirmative action that involves preferential treatment, except for voluntary private programmes (see below).[58] In *Croson*, the Supreme Court struck down state measures to give preference to minority-owned firms in awarding certain municipal construction contracts, as the measures in question could not be shown to be sufficiently justified and narrowly-tailored on the evidence available.

51 Title VI of the Civil Rights Act applies if affirmative action is practiced by state or private recipients of federal funds. However *Regents of the University of California v Bakke* 438 U.S. 265 (1978) clarified that the requirements of Title VI are the same as those for the 14th Amendment, so now there are just two standards, Title VII and the 14th Amendment.

52 *Brown v Board of Education of Topeka* (1954) 347 U.S. 483.

53 *Craig v Boren* (1976) 429 U.S. 190.

54 See *Massachusetts Board of Retirement et al v Murgia* 427 U.S. 307 (SC) (age); See M. Weber, Disability and the Law of Welfare: a Post-integrationist Examination" 2000 U. Ill. L. Rev. 889 for disability.

55 Above, n 2.

56 448 U.S. 448 (1980).

57 488 U.S. 469 (1989).

58 *United Steelworkers of American v Weber* 443 U.S. 193 (1979).

Initially, strict scrutiny was not applied to Federal programmes, but this was changed by *Adarand*[59] in 1995. Strict scrutiny will often be a very difficult hurdle to overcome for affirmative action programmes, but its application can vary in intensity, with O'Connor J in *Adarand* emphasising that strict scrutiny need not be inevitably fatal in practice. In the *Paradise* case,[60] the Supreme Court clarified that court-imposed affirmative action measures to redress past discrimination or segregation was permitted under the Equal Protection Clause. In this case, an "accelerated" promotion quota had been imposed as a remedy, whereby the ratio of black employees to whites was to exceed the ratio of qualified blacks to qualified whites in the workforce, until the percentage of blacks in higher positions equaled the percentage of qualified blacks in the relevant workforce. The Court considered that in light of the "pervasive, systematic and obstinate discriminatory" exclusion of Afro-Americans, the measure withstood strict scrutiny, as there was no realistic "race-neutral" alternative remedial measures available, the quota was flexible in that it could be waived if there was a lack of qualified minorities as well as being temporary and time-limited, it was reasonable in requiring a relationship between the goal/quota and numerical representation of minorities in the qualified labor pool and it minimised the burden on innocent third parties.

However, the case-law does establish that affirmative action measures designed to address overall social disadvantage will not be usually justified in the absence of a specific pattern of under-representation linked to past disadvantage or segregation. In *Wygant*,[61] preferential treatment for Afro-Americans in selecting employees for redundancy was held to be unconstitutional, as no specific disadvantage faced by this group had been identified and the penalty on the third-parties disadvantaged by the preferential treatment was too great.

As previously discussed, the focus on seeing affirmative action as largely remedial in nature has limited its impact, especially as the US courts have tended to require evidence of actual discrimination in the past, as in *Wygant* (although this does not apply to voluntary private sector programmes: see *Johnson* below.) In practice, this may be difficult to prove. These constraints have resulted in advocates of strong affirmative action measures to seek alternative rationales for its use, such as preventing future disadvantage or securing greater diversity.[62] In *Sheet Metal Workers*, the Court appeared to accept the dismantling of "prior patterns of employment discrimination and to prevent discrimination in the future" as a suitable aim.[63] In *Metro Broadcasting Inc v FCC*,[64] the Supreme Court recognised "broadcast diversity" as an

[59] 515 US 200 (1995).
[60] *United States v Paradise* 480 U.S. 149 (1987).
[61] *Wygant v Jackson Board of Education* 476 U.S. 267 (1986).
[62] See in particular Elizabeth S Anderson "Integration, Affirmative Action and Strict Scrutiny" (2002) N.Y.U.L. Rev.1195.
[63] at 474.
[64] 497 US 547, 567 (5th Cir 1996)

important aim of government policy. As already discussed previously, in *Bakke*[65] a majority of the Supreme Court upheld the use of race as a "plus" factor in admissions, although they condemned the particular system of "set-aside" quota places in use at the state university in question. Different judges identified different acceptable rationales for affirmative action. Justice Powell focused on the desirability of enhancing educational diversity, while other judges appeared willing to accept affirmative action to remedy wider patterns of social disadvantages. This rationale was rejected in *Wygent*, as noted above, but the most recent Supreme Court decision in *Grutter v Bollinger*[66] saw the Court upholding the University of Michigan Law School's affirmative action programmes on the ground that it met the compelling state interest of educational diversity and enhanced integration in education establishments (once again, see the previous chapter). Justice O'Connor suggested that "effective participation by members of all racial and ethnic groups in the civic life of our Nation is essential if the dream of one Nation, indivisible, is to be realized",[67] and that "the path to leadership [must] be visibly open to talented and qualified individuals of every race and ethnicity". The programme in question was held to meet the requirements of strict scrutiny, as it was be narrowly tailored with individualised examination of each applicant, with race being one of several different considerations used in the assessment process. In contrast, an undergraduate admissions system under review in *Gratz*[68] was deemed to be too "mechanical" for failing to take into account "all factors that may contribute to student body diversity."[69]

In *Weber*, the Kaiser company had agreed with the steelworkers union that they would introduce a training scheme for "crafts work" in which there would appointment according to "general seniority scheme" (open to all) but where in addition there would be some preferential treatment of black workers who were severely underrepresented in "crafts work". Weber applied for the training scheme. He was insufficiently senior to gain a place according to the "general seniority scheme" but he was more senior than the employee who was appointed under the special scheme for black workers. Weber sued Kaiser claiming that their scheme was unlawful racial discrimination under Title VII of the Civil Rights Act 1964. This was solely a case of the statutory legality of the training scheme under Title VII rather than its costitutional legality under the Equal Protecition Clause. Five Justices of the Supreme Court (Brennan, Marshall, White, Stewart and Blackmun) held that Title VII did not prohibit training plans of this type. Burger and Rhenquist J.J. dissented.

[65] 438 U.S. 265 (1978).
[66] 539 U.S. 306 (2003).
[67] ibid.
[68] *Gratz v Bollinger* 539 U.S. 244 (2003).
[69] ibid. at 288.

3. Affirmative action practiced by private or public employers and unions

Affirmative action practiced by private or public employers and unions is subject to review under the anti-discrimination provisions of Title VII of the Civil Rights Act of 1964. Private bodies are generally given wider discretion in adopting positive action measures, especially when these measures were adopted to compensate for or to remove discriminatory practices or patterns of segregation and exclusion, as recognized by the Supreme Court in the key Title VII decision of *Weber*.[70] In this decision, Blackmun J.'s concurring opinion recognised that the use of race as a tool for identifying the group in need of special assistance was necessary to undo past discrimination, and that Title VII had to be interpreted so as to permit such remedial affirmative action.

Many affirmative action plans were in fact introduced as part of remedial action to preempt or respond to the threat of legal action on the grounds of "disparate impact" or indirect discrimination. Even if a private affirmative action measure was introduced as part of a "consent" agreement with the US Justice Department or in response to government pressure, such plans are regarded as "voluntary" and therefore need only be justified under the looser *Weber* standard. *Sheet Metal Workers v EEOC*[71] clarified that not only could employers and unions voluntarily adopt affirmative action to undo the legacy of past discrimination, but that the courts were permitted under Title VII to impose such programmes.

Private affirmative action programmes must in general be directed towards the remedying of past discrimination, which can however be satisfied by evidence of wide social patterns of disadvantage, unlike the normal approach for state and federal bodies. In *Johnson v Transportation Agency*[72] the Court upheld the legality under Title VII of a gender-based affirmative action plan adopted to remedy a pattern of gender segregation in transportation jobs, even where there was no specific discrimination on the part of the employer. The programme met each of the legal requirements necessary: the male and female candidate had to be qualified for the position, there had been female under-representation, the use of preferential treatment was to be temporary and time-limited, and did not create an absolute bar to the promotion of male candidates. In *Johnson* factors such as, inter alia, the case by case nature of the approach, the minimal intrusion into the legitimate expectations of all employees and the short term nature of the temporary nature of the affirmative action programme contributed to the decision that it was lawful under Title VII. The temporary nature of the program, in particular, allowed it to be classified as a contingent race conscious policy rather than a use of race as suspect classification that carries the risk of essentialising racial difference (see the discussion of Gutman earlier). A subsequent case, *Taxman*, illustrates the types of fact situations under which an affirmative action will overstep the

[70] *United Steelworkers of American v Weber* 443 U.S. 193 (1979).
[71] 478 U.S. 421 (1986).
[72] 480 U.S. 616 (1987).

mark and be found to be unlawful Title VII discrimination. The following extracts include a detailed discussion of cases such as *Bakke, Weber* and *Johnson*. In *Taxman*, the Board of Education of Piscataway introduced an affirmative action scheme that made race a factor in selecting which of two equally qualified employees to lay off. Title VII permits an employer with a racially balanced work force to grant a non-remedial racial preference in order to promote "racial diversity". However, in this case the US Court of Appeal held the affirmative action plan to be in breach of Title VII (the case was settled before it could be heard by the US Supreme Court). In addition, the court made the following observations:

Taxman v Board of Education of Piscataway, 91 f. 3d 1547 (1996) US Court of Appeals for the Third Circuit

MANSMANN, Circuit Judge.

"In relevant part, Title VII makes it unlawful for an employer 'to discriminate against any individual with respect to his compensation, terms, conditions, or privileges of employment' or 'to limit, segregate, or classify his employees ... in any way which would deprive or tend to deprive any individual of employment opportunities or otherwise affect his status as an employee' on the basis of 'race, color, religion, sex, or national origin.' 42 U.S.C. § 2000e–2(a). For a time, the Supreme Court construed this language as absolutely prohibiting discrimination in employment, neither requiring nor permitting any preference for any group. [...]

In 1979, however, the Court interpreted the statute's 'antidiscriminatory strategy' in a 'fundamentally different way', id. at 644, holding in the seminal case of United Steelworkers v. Weber, 433 U.S. 193 (1979), that Title VII's prohibition against racial discrimination does not condemn all voluntary race-conscious affirmative action plans. [...]

The significance of this second corrective purpose cannot be overstated. It is only because Title VII was written to eradicate not only discrimination per se but the consequences of prior discrimination as well, that racial preferences in the form of affirmative action can co-exist with the Act's antidiscrimination mandate.

Thus, based on our analysis of Title VII's two goals, we are convinced that unless an affirmative action plan has a remedial purpose, it cannot be said to mirror the purposes of the statute, and, therefore, cannot satisfy the first prong of the Weber test. [...]

We turn next to the second prong of the Weber analysis. This second prong requires that we determine whether the Board's policy 'unnecessarily trammel[s] ... [nonminority] interests. [...]' Weber, 433 U.S. at 208. Under this requirement, too, the Board's policy is deficient. [...]

Moreover, both Weber and Johnson unequivocally provide that valid affirmative action plans are "temporary" measures that seek to "'attain'", not "maintain" a "permanent racial ... balance." Johnson, 480 U.S. at 639–40. See Weber, 433 U.S. at 208. The Board's policy, adopted in 1975, is an established fixture of unlimited duration, to be resurrected from time to time whenever the Board believes that the ratio between Blacks and Whites in any Piscataway School is skewed. On this basis alone, the policy contravenes Weber's teaching. [...]

Finally, we are convinced that the harm imposed upon a nonminority employee by the loss of his or her job is so substantial and the cost so severe that the Board's goal of racial diversity, even if legitimate under Title VII, may not be pursued in this particular fashion. This is especially true where, as here, the nonminority employee is tenured. In Weber and Johnson, when considering whether nonminorities were unduly encumbered by affirmative action, the Court found it significant that they retained their employment. Weber, 433 U.S. at 208 (observing that the plan did not require the discharge of nonminority workers); Johnson, 480 U.S. at 638 (observing that the nonminority employee who was not promoted nonetheless kept his job). We, therefore, adopt the plurality's pronouncement in Wygant that "[w]hile hiring goals impose a diffuse burden, often foreclosing only one of several opportunities, layoffs impose the entire burden of achieving racial equality on particular individuals, often resulting in serious disruption of their lives. That burden is too intrusive." [Wygant, 476 U.S. at 283 (footnote omitted)]

In *Taxman*, the court found that the affirmative action plan overstepped the limits on lawful affirmative action in employment cases. The court noted that there was no evidence that the affirmative action was in response to past discrimination, i.e. that it was remedial. Moreover, and significantly, the US Court of Appeals distinguished the *Bakke* case which concerned diversity in the student body through affirmative action in admissions from this case which involved affirmative action in employment. The court in *Taxman* also refuses to apply the "role model" theory as the basis for extending the limits of permissible affirmative action in employment (Title VII) cases (see discussion of the *Wygant* case below). The court also found that the on-going nature of the affirmative action plan (i.e. it was not temporary and did not have a time limit) was problematic. Finally, the court found that in this case the affirmative action plan would result in the lost of a job of a particular employee rather than being diffuse amongst the whole workforce. This was too high a burden on the "non-minority" employees which made this impermissible affirmative action.

Many of these criteria for permissible "affirmative action" in employment cases under Title VII are similar to the limits placed on permissible positive action in employment by the ECJ in EC sex discrimination law (discussed below). The US Disability Discrimination Act does not prohibit positive action on the grounds of disability, similar to the UK legislation which was based on the US Act. The US age discrimination legislation only prohibits discrimination against those forty years old or older, so much of age-based positive action will not be affected by the legislation, although positive action that could distinguish between particular age groups over the age of forty might be affected. Even under strict scrutiny, departures from "appointing the best" are permitted. In *Johnson*, the programme allowed the employer to hire anyone among the top seven candidates.

In the US generally, when quotas are discussed, it is assumed that these may entail appointing women who are less qualified than at least some of the male applicants. For example in *Danskine v Miami Dade Fire Department*,[73] the appointment process was altered for women, so that they did not have to go through any random selection, and were automatically advanced to the later

[73] 253 F 3d 1288 (11th Cir 2001).

stages. The US gender caselaw is stricter than the EC in this respect. It does not allow generalised assumptions of women's disadvantage, and requires greater evidence than simply a less than 50 per cent representation in the workforce. It requires programmes to provide evidence of discrimination based on the available female workforce, and detailed statistical evidence is required to demonstrate this. Gender-based programmes require "sufficient probative evidence" while race-based one require "a strong basis in evidence". In contrast, where employees are laid off, such as in *Wygant*,[74] this is seen as having a greater adverse impact. Also in assessing this limb, courts check whether the level of quota set is appropriate. This is also well-illustrated in *Danskine*, where unsuccessful male applicants challenged the fire department's imposition of a 36 per cent quota for women in hiring. The quota was based on the general female population (52 per cent), reduced by 30 per cent in order to take account of the fact that not all women would either want or be able to become firefighters. The Court stated that the employer was not permitted to rely on the general population figure when setting a quota, but rather must look at the available female workforce for the position in question.

D. *The European Convention on Human Rights*

The European Convention on Human Rights (ECHR) appears to confer a reasonably similar degree of latitude, but its implications for positive action measures in general remains uncertain, principally due to the lack of a comprehensive case-law by the European Court of Human Rights on the scope of the equality right in the Convention in general. The ECHR in its current form contains a limited prohibition in Art.14 on discriminatory treatment in the enjoyment of other Convention rights: this non-discrimination right is "parastic" upon other Convention rights and falls short of the full equality principle recognised in other international instruments. However, in applying this slightly stunted non-discrimination right, the Strasbourg court has left room for the application by signatory states of positive action measures.

In particular, as with the other international human rights bodies, the European Court of Human Rights has held that differential treatment in relation to the enjoyment of rights is not unlawful under Art.14, if there is an objective and reasonable justification for the difference in treatment, and positive action can be regarded as a justified form of differential treatment. In the *Belgian Linguistics* case, the Strasbourg court made clear that positive action is not incompatible with Art.14, finding that "certain legal inequalities tend only to correct factual inequalities".[75] Similarly, in *Lindsay v UK*, tax advan-

[74] *Wygant* 476 U.S. 267 (1986).
[75] *Belgian Linguistics* [1967] 1 E.H.R.R. 241.

tages for married women were held not to be contrary to Art.14 as it had objective of encouraging married women back to work.[76]

However, the European Court of Human Rights also requires any measures adopted to be proportionate to the legitimate aim to be achieved. Positive action rules must therefore "strike a fair balance between the protection of the interests of the community and respect for the rights and freedoms safeguarded by the Convention. Therefore, positive action to compensate for existing disadvantages appears to be permissible under the Convention, if it satisfies the proportionality test that requires such action to be rationally linked to the desired objective, necessary and proportionate to the objective sought to be achieved.[77] Recital 3 to the Preamble of the new Protocol 12 to the ECHR (which the UK has not as yet signed or ratified) reiterates the importance of positive action:

"Reaffirming that the principle of non-discrimination does not prevent States Parties from taking measures in order to promote full and effective equality, provided that there is an objective and reasonable justification for those measures."

The extent to which positive action may be required under the Convention in certain circumstances is much less certain. Article 14 of the ECHR provides that the enjoyment of the rights and freedoms in the Convention "shall be secured" without discrimination. As this language replicates the language of other Conventions articles in its use of "shall", this wording emphasises that states may have positive obligations under Art.14, as well as negative obligations to refrain from discriminatory acts. The European Court of Human Rights made this point in *Belgian Linguistics*:

"...it cannot be concluded ... that the State has no positive obligation to ensure respect for such a right ... the word "secured" implies the existence of obligations upon the Contracting States to take action and not simply a duty to abstain from action."[78]

Recent cases have reinforced the nature of the positive obligations on states under Art.14. In *Thlimmenos v Greece*, the European Court of Human Rights held that discrimination might arise if states "without objective and reasonable justification fail to treat differently persons whose situations are significantly different."[79] In addition, other Convention rights have been interpreted by the Court as imposing certain positive obligations upon states to provide special treatment in appropriate circumstances. For example, in

[76] No.11089/84, 49 DR 181.
[77] See *Belgian Linguistics*, 1 E.H.R.R. 241.
[78] [1967] 1 E.H.R.R. 241 at para.3.
[79] No.34369/97, 06/04/2000. See also the judgment of the ECtHR in *Nachova v Bulgaria*, Nos 43577/98 and 43579/98, 28/02/2004.

Connors v UK, the Court held that the UK could be obliged to provide special facilities for members of the travelling community to order to uphold their right to home and family life. The scope of these positive obligations remains uncertain: however, there may be circumstances where some forms of positive action may be required, as with the other human rights instruments.[80]

E. *EU Discrimination Law*

The term "positive action" is not defined in EU law and policy has a wide ranging meaning: it includes permissible legal positive action; but it also includes a range of measures to promote substantive equality, e.g. mainstreaming, recommendations and guides. This part of the chapter deals with the legal issues raised by "positive action" and the case law of the ECJ which defines the scope of lawful positive action. Subsequent sections of the chapter deal with the wider policy mainstreaming measures, recommendations and guides overcome the under-representation of women and minorities and promote substantive equality. The main legal provisions are Art.3 of the new amended Equal Treatment Directive 2006 (previously in ETD Art.2). The new provisions are set out below.

EC Treaty, Art.141(4)

"With a view to ensuring full equality in practice between men and women in working life, the principle of equal treatment shall not prevent any Member State from maintaining or adopting measures providing for specific advantages in order to make it easier for the underrepresented sex to pursue a vocational activity or to prevent or compensate for disadvantages in professional careers."

Directive 2006/54/EC of the European Parliament and of the Council of 5 July 2006 on the implementation of the principle of equal opportunities and equal treatment of men and women in matters of employment and occupation (recast), Art.3

Positive Action

"Member States may maintain or adopt measures within the meaning of Article 141(4) of the Treaty with a view to ensuring full equality in practice between men and women in working life."

[80] For an analysis of the scope of positive obligations under the ECHR in general, see A. Mowbray, *Positive Obligations* (Hart: Oxford, 2004).

Former Amended Equal Treatment Directive, Art.2(8) (Directive 2002/73)

"Member States may maintain or adopt measures within the meaning of Article 141(4) of the [EC] Treaty with a view to ensuring full equality in practice between men and women."

Former Equal Treatment Directive, Art.2(4) (Directive 76/207)

"This Directive shall be without prejudice to measures to promote equal opportunity for men and women, in particular by removing existing inequalities which affect women's opportunities in the areas referred to in Article 1(1) [especially employment and vocational training]."

Employment Equality Directive, Art.7(1)

Positive Action

"With a view to ensuring full equality in practice, the principle of equal treatment shall not prevent any Member State from maintaining or adopting specific measures to prevent or compensate for disadvantages linked to any of the grounds referred to in Article 1."

Race Equaity Directive, Art.5

Positive Action

"With a view to ensuring full equality in practice, the principle of equal treatment shall not prevent any Member State from maintaining or adopting specific measures to prevent or compensate for disadvantages linked to racial or ethnic origin."

EU Constitutional Treaty—Equality Between Women and Men Art.23(2) (not in force)

"Equality between women and men must be ensured in all areas, including employment, work and pay.

> The principle of equality shall not prevent the maintenance or adoption of measures providing for specific advantages in favour of the under-represented sex."

The language of the Race Equality Directive and the Employment Equality Directive in relation to positive action is more permissive than that used in the Equal Treatment Directives. RED Art.5 states that "With a view to ensuring full equality in practice, the principle of equal treatment shall not prevent any Member State from maintaining or adopting specific measures to prevent or compensate for disadvantages linked to racial or ethnic origin. The provisions are similar in the EED (although there may be some differences in the way in which positive action is applied in the context of disability discrimination). This suggests that the ECJ may develop a consistent analysis of positive action across EU discrimination law.[81]

Ultimately, however, the approach taken by the ECJ to the interpretation of the EC Equality Directives determines what scope for positive action is permitted within the Union. As McCrudden has argued, trace elements of a variety of different theoretical approaches to equality can be detected in the case law of the ECJ, with a strong residue of affection for the "equality as sameness" approach.[82] The ECJ therefore appears to oscillate between approaches rooted in formal equality, and others that are based to some degree on substantial, instrumental or prioritarian approaches to equality:[83] this oscillation can cause real conceptual problems.

The scope of permissible positive action in EC law has been developed in a line of ECJ decisions which are discussed below: *Marschall; Abrahamson; Fogelquist and Badeck.* These cases followed the decision in the *Kalanke*[84] case in which the ECJ conceptualised positive action as a "derogation" from the principle of equal treatment and therefore to be interpreted narrowly. As argued in the previous chapter, this analysis can be questioned because it is possible to argue that, rather than being a derogation from the principle of non-discrimination and equality, in some cases "equality as priority" will not only permit but require positive action to fulfill the goals of discrimination law.

The ECJ cases that have followed *Kalanke* are more compatible with this different interpretation of positive action. However, they all still stop short of permitting affirmative action meaures of the type that are permissible in limited circumstances in US discrimination law.

81 Evelyn Ellis, *EC Anti-Discrimination Law* (Oxford: Oxford University Press, 2005) at pp.312–313.

82 C. McCrudden, "Theorising European Law", p.36.

83 Mark Bell has argued that a "patchwork of models" of equality has developed within EU equality law and policy, made up of three main strands: the standard discrimination approach, a newer attachment to substantive equality, and a desire to manage diversity. See M. Bell, "The Right to Equality and Non-Discrimination", in T. Hervey and J. Kenner (eds.) *Economic and Social Rights under the EC Charter of Fundamental Rights: A Legal Perspective* (Oxford: Hart Publishing, 2003), 91. See also G. More, "Equal Treatment of the Sexes in European Community Law: What Does 'Equal' Mean?", 1 *Feminist Legal Studies* (1993), 45.

84 *Kalanke v Freie Hansestadt Bremen* [1995] E.C.R. I-3051. See also discussion of the case and positive action in EC discrimination law in Evelyn Ellis, *EC Anti-Discrimination Law* (Oxford: Oxford University Press, 2005) pp.297–313

Case C-409/95, *Marschall v Land Nordrhein Westfalen* [1987] E.C.R. I–6363

"22. According to Article 2(4), the Directive is to 'be without prejudice to measures to promote equal opportunity for men and women, in particular by removing existing inequalities which affect women's opportunities in the areas referred to in Article 1(1)'.

23. In paragraph 16 of its judgment in [Case C-450/93 Kalanke v Freie Hansestadt Bremen [1995] ECR I-3051], the Court held that a national rule which provides that, where equally qualified men and women are candidates for the same promotion in fields where there are fewer women than men at the level of the relevant post, women are automatically to be given priority, involves discrimination on grounds of sex.

24. However, unlike the provisions in question in Kalanke, the provision in question in this case contains a clause ("Öffnungsklausel", hereinafter "saving clause") to the effect that women are not to be given priority in promotion if reasons specific to an individual male candidate tilt the balance in his favour.

25. It is therefore necessary to consider whether a national rule containing such a clause is designed to promote equality of opportunity between men and women within the meaning of Article 2(4) of the Directive.

26. Article 2(4) is specifically and exclusively designed to authorize measures which, although discriminatory in appearance, are in fact intended to eliminate or reduce actual instances of inequality which may exist in the reality of social life...

27. It thus authorizes national measures relating to access to employment, including promotion, which give a specific advantage to women with a view to improving their ability to compete on the labour market and to pursue a career on an equal footing with men (Kalanke, paragraph 19).

28. As the Council stated in the third recital in the preamble to Recommendation 84/635/EEC of 13 December 1984 on the promotion of positive action for women (OJ 1984 L 331, p. 34), "existing legal provisions on equal treatment, which are designed to afford rights to individuals, are inadequate for the elimination of all existing inequalities unless parallel action is taken by governments, both sides of industry and other bodies concerned, to counteract the prejudicial effects on women in employment which arise from social attitudes, behaviour and structures" (Kalanke, paragraph 20).

29. As the Land and several governments have pointed out, it appears that even where male and female candidates are equally qualified, male candidates tend to be promoted in preference to female candidates particularly because of prejudices and stereotypes concerning the role and capacities of women in working life and the fear, for example, that women will interrupt their careers more frequently, that owing to household and family duties they will be less flexible in their working hours, or that they will be absent from work more frequently because of pregnancy, childbirth and breastfeeding.

30. For these reasons, the mere fact that a male candidate and a female candidate are equally qualified does not mean that they have the same chances.

31. It follows that a national rule in terms of which, subject to the application of the saving clause, female candidates for promotion who are equally as qualified as the male candidates are to be treated preferentially in sectors where they are under-represented may fall within the scope of Article 2(4) if such a rule may counteract the prejudicial effects on female candidates of the attitudes and behaviour described above and thus reduce actual instances of inequality which may exist in the real world.

32. However, since Article 2(4) constitutes a derogation from an individual right laid down by the Directive, such a national measure specifically favouring female candidates cannot guarantee absolute and unconditional priority for women in the event of a promotion without going beyond the limits of the exception laid down in that provision...

[Kalanke, paragraphs 22, 23: "22. National rules which guarantee women absolute and unconditional priority for appointment or promotion go beyond promoting equal opportunities and overstep the limits of the exception in Article 2(4) of the Directive. 23. Furthermore, in so far as it seeks to achieve equal representation of men and women in all grades and levels within a department, such a system substitutes for equality of opportunity as envisaged in Article 2(4) the result which is only arrived at by providing such equality of opportunity."]

33. Unlike the rules at issue in Kalanke, a national rule which ... contains a saving clause does not exceed those limits if, in each individual case, it provides for male candidates who are equally as qualified as the female candidates a guarantee that the candidatures will be the subject of an objective assessment which will take account of all criteria specific to the individual candidates and will override the priority accorded to female candidates where one or more of those criteria tilts the balance in favour of the male candidate. In this respect, however, it should be remembered that those criteria must not be such as to discriminate against female candidates.

34. It is for the national court to determine whether those conditions are fulfilled on the basis of an examination of the scope of the provision in question as it has been applied by the Land."

Case C-407/98, *Abrahamsson v Fogelqvist* [2000] E.C.R. I–5539

"**45.** In contrast to the national legislation on positive discrimination examined by the Court in its Kalanke, Marschall and Badeck judgments, the national legislation at issue in the main proceedings enables preference to be given to a candidate of the under-represented sex who, although sufficiently qualified, does not possess qualifications equal to those of other candidates of the opposite sex.

46. As a rule, a procedure for the selection of candidates for a post involves assessment of their qualifications by reference to the requirements of the vacant post or of the duties to be performed.

47. In paragraphs 31 and 32 of Badeck, cited above, the Court held that it is legitimate for the purposes of that assessment for certain positive and negative criteria to be taken into account which, although formulated in terms which are neutral as regards sex and thus capable of benefiting men too, in general favour women. Thus, it may be decided that seniority, age and the date of last promotion are to be taken into account only in so far as they are of importance for the suitability, qualifications and professional capability of candidates. Similarly, it may be prescribed that the family status or income of the partner is immaterial and that part-time work, leave and delays in completing training as a result of looking after children or dependants in need of care must not have a negative effect.

48. The clear aim of such criteria is to achieve substantive, rather than formal, equality by reducing de facto inequalities which may arise in society and, thus, in accordance with Article 141(4) EC, to prevent or compensate for disadvantages in the professional career of persons belonging to the under-represented sex.

49. It is important to emphasise in that connection that the application of criteria such as those mentioned in paragraph 47 above must be transparent and amenable to review in order to obviate any arbitrary assessment of the qualifications of candidates.

50. As regards the selection procedure at issue in the main proceedings, it does not appear from the relevant Swedish legislation that assessment of the qualifications of candidates by reference to the requirements of the vacant post is based on clear and unambiguous criteria such as to prevent or compensate for disadvantages in the professional career of members of the under-represented sex.

51. On the contrary, under that legislation, a candidate for a public post belonging to the under-represented sex and possessing sufficient qualifications for that post must be chosen in preference to a candidate of the opposite sex who would otherwise have been appointed, where that measure is necessary for a candidate belonging to the under-represented sex to be appointed.

52. It follows that the legislation at issue in the main proceedings automatically grants preference to candidates belonging to the under-represented sex, provided that they are sufficiently qualified, subject only to the proviso that the difference between the merits of the candidates of each sex is not so great as to result in a breach of the requirement of objectivity in making appointments.

53. The scope and effect of that condition cannot be precisely determined, with the result that the selection of a candidate from among those who are sufficiently qualified is ultimately based on the mere fact of belonging to the under-represented sex, and that this is so even if the merits of the candidate so selected are inferior to those of a candidate of the opposite sex. Moreover, candidatures are not subjected to an objective assessment taking account of the specific personal situations of all the candidates. It follows that such a method of selection is not such as to be permitted by Article 2(4) of the Directive.

54. In those circumstances, it is necessary to determine whether legislation such as that at issue in the main proceedings is justified by Article 141(4) EC.

55. In that connection, it is enough to point out that, even though Article 141(4) EC allows the Member States to maintain or adopt measures providing for special advantages intended to prevent or compensate for disadvantages in professional careers in order to ensure full equality between men and women in professional life, it cannot be inferred from this that it allows a selection method of the kind at issue in the main proceedings which appears, on any view, to be disproportionate to the aim pursued."

To place these decisions in context, it is necessary to return to *Kalanke*, where a regulation of the Bremen state government giving automatic priority to a woman over an equally qualified man in recruitment to state government posts where women were under-represented, was challenged as incompatible with EC law's prohibition on sex discrimination.[85] Advocate General Tesauro stated that the priority given to women was "only too obviously … discrimination on the grounds of sex" and that positive action "conflicts with the principle of equality in the formal sense". In other words, Tesauro A.G. considered that exceptions to the formal "anti-classification" principle had to be clearly and compellingly justified. Article 2(4) of the Equal Treatment Directive provides that "this Directive shall be without prejudice to measures to promote equal opportunity for men and women, in particular by removing existing inequalities which affect women's opportunities …" as a derogation from the principle of equal treatment in Art.2(1): Tesauro A.G. considered that with all derogations from the principle of equal treatment, this exception had to be given a narrow and limited interpretation. He was of the view that the rule in question did not fall within the scope of the exception in Art.4(2), as it went beyond the provision of equal opportunities by providing for automatic priority for women and thus fell foul of the ban on direct discrimination on the grounds of sex.

In the final judgment, the ECJ in a brief and somewhat opaque judgment

[85] Case C-450/93 *Kalanke v Freie Hansestadt Bremen* [1995] ECR I-3051.

agreed that the exception in Art.2(4) was a derogation from the principle of equal treatment and that, despite the fact that the case involved a "soft" rather than "hard" quote and that it was designed to over women's disadvantage caused by past inequities, the rule in question fell outside the scope of permissible positive action. This judgment indicated a firm attachment to an "anti-classification" approach and a preference for the strict or formal equality approach. Tesauro A.G.'s analysis seems to find no difficulty with forms of positive action that involved action with regard to vocational guidance and training with the objective of reducing the causual factors for discrimination. It also apparently sees no problem with positive action measures that aim to alter work practices and childcare arrangements to achieve more equal opportunities for women. However, compensatory measures giving automatic preference to disadvantaged groups, as at stake in *Kalanke,* were regarded as overstepping the limits of what was permissible under EC law.

The decision in *Kalanke,* in giving preference to an "anti-classification" approach, was followed by substantial criticism by academics and attempts at clarification by the Commission.[86] There has been a gradual yet definite re-positioning by the Court since this decision.[87] In *Marschall,*[88] the ECJ refined its approach in the extract above by distinguishing the rule in *Kalanke* from the approach to be applied to the rule at stake in this case, which was another German state law giving priority to women in recruitment to the state government service where they were underrepresented, but only where the men and women candidates affected had been individually assessed and found to have equivalent qualifications. This nuanced "saving clause" was held to ensure that there was no guarantee of unconditional priority to women, and therefore the principle of strict equality recognised in *Kalanke* was held not to have been breached. This more permissive approach was also adopted in *Badeck,* where considerable scope for positive action, including preferential treatment, was permitted at initial stages of recruitment prior to the actual hiring decision, including the reservation of places at interview for a disadvantaged group.[89] This more permissive approach was also preferred in the most recent case of *Lommers* where the ECJ upheld the compatibility with Art.2(1) and Art.2(4) of the Equal Treatment Directive of a child care scheme which prioritised women, under a scheme to tackle the under-representation

[86] The Commission proposed an amendment to the Equal Treatment Directive along the following lines: "Possible measures shall include the giving of preference, as regards access to employment or promotion, to a member of the under represented sex, provided that such measures do not preclude the assessment of the particular circumstances of an individual case." This amendment was subsequently rejected. See COM (96) 88 final, and (97/C 30/19) OJ C.30/57 January 30, 1997.

[87] Case 450/93 *Kalanke v Bremen* [1995] E.C.R. I-3051. See C. Tobler, "Positive Action under the Revised Second Equal Treatment Directive", in AFFA and EWLA (ed.) *L'égalité entre femmes et hommes et la vie profesionnelle; Le point sur les développements actuels en Europe* (Paris: Dalloz, 2003) 59–92 for an excellent analysis of this gradual shift in position.

[88] Case C-409/95, *Helmut Marschall v Land Nordrhein Westfalen* [1987] E.C.R. I-6363

[89] Case C-158/97, *Badeck v Landesanwalt beim Staatsgerichtshof des Landes Hessen* [1999] E.C.R. I-1875

of women, in a situation "characterised by a proven insufficiency of proper, affordable child-care facilities".[90]

At first sight these ECJ cases are difficult to reconcile. At present there is a tendency in the case law to conceptualise positive action as a derogation from the principle of equal treatment and the fundamental right to non-discrimination. The analysis tends to be constructed around a confrontation between two forms of equality: formal and substantial equality. Some of the confusion surrounding the legitimacy of positive action is linked to the use of the formal versus the substantive equality analysis without any further differentiation of the work that the concept of equality is doing in these different contexts. There remains an underlying tension in the cases between the idea of equality and non-discrimination on the one hand (described as formal equality) and the permissibility of positive action now given constitutional status by the EU Charter (described as substantive equality) which suggests that rather than performing a role as a derogation from the principle of equality it is in fact part of the constitutional vision of the EU. The relevant provision states:

Art.23(2) EU Charter of Fundamental Rights—Equality Between Women and Men

"Equality between women and men must be ensured in all areas, including employment, work and pay.

The principle of equality shall not prevent the maintenance or adoption of measures providing for specific advantages in favour of the under-represented sex."

These provisions attempt to establish that positive action should be conceptualised as an element of ensuring equality of opportunity rather than as an exception to that principle, and have the effect of establishing that positive action is permissible when used to compensate for specific disadvantages faced by particular groups and is capable of being objectively justified. The inclusion of positive action as part of the sections on equality in the Charter of Fundamental Rights and Freedoms confirms the increasing recognition that (a) EC concepts of equality generate constitutional and statutory forms of discrimination law; and (b) positive action is now a well established category of the EC concept of equality. This acceptance of positive action is also reflected and also encouraged the Court's loosening of its position in *Marschall*[91] and *Badeck*.[92] Subsequent to these decisions and following the approach set out in Art.141(4), the ECJ appears to have evolved a new proportionality approach,

[90] Case C-476/99, *Lommers* [2002] E.C.R. I-2891.
[91] Case 409/95 *Marschall v Land Nordrhein-Westfalen* [1997] E.C.R. I-6363.
[92] Case 158/97 *Badeck v Hessischer Ministerpresident* [2000] E.C.R. I-1875.

to the effect that preferential treatment on the grounds of gender to compensate for past disadvantages is permissible when used to distinguish between similarly qualified candidates, provided that an opportunity for individual merit assessment is always available, and that the measure can be deemed to be objectively justifiable.[93]

The new shift towards a greater embrace of the substantive equality approach can be seen in *Schnorbus*,[94] where the Court gave considerable leeway in applying the justification test to positive action measures which were neutral on their face but could constitute indirect discrimination. In this case, a rule giving those who had undergone national service priority in admission to legal training was held not to violate the principle of equal treatment, even though only men could benefit as only men underwent national service. However, the ECJ were of the view that the purpose of the rule was to compensate for a disadvantage and that considerable scope should be given to such compensatory measures. In *Briheche*,[95] the Court adopted the language of substantive equality, recognising that considerable scope should be granted for measures designed to remedy disadvantage against women: however, in this case, the exception of certain categories of women from an upper age-limit on recruitment to the civil service to compensate for their adoption of family responsibilities violated the provisions of the Equal Treatment Directive, as similar exemptions were not available for men in a similar position. In *Lommers*, the ECJ upheld the compatibility with Art.2(1) and Art.2(4) of the Equal Treatment Directive of a child care scheme which prioritised women, under a scheme to tackle the under-representation of women, in a situation "characterised by a proven insufficiency of proper, affordable child-care facilities."[96]

Notwithstanding this welcome shift in position, and despite the views of Koukoulis-Spiliotopoulos that the "apple of discord" initially produced by *Kalanke* is now a thing of the past,[97] problems remain. The ghost of *Kalanke* still haunts the Court's case-law. In both the *Abrahamssohn* decision,[98] and that of the EFTA Court in *EFTA Surveillance Authority v Norway*,[99] it was held that in the gender context, forms of positive action that give automatic preference to members of disadvantaged groups will still not survive challenge. In *Abrahamssohn*, extracted above, [100] the Swedish rule in question allowed the under-represented sex to be appointed in preference to another where the "difference in merits of the candidates was not so great as to breach the requirements of

[93] See *Badeck* [2000] E.C.R. I-1875.

[94] Case 79/99 *Julia Schnorbus v Land Hessen* [2000] E.C.R. I-10997.

[95] Case 319/03 *Briheche v Ministre de l'Intérieur* [2004] E.C.R. I–8807.

[96] Case C-476/99, *Lommers* [2002] E.C.R. I–2891.

[97] Sophia Koukoulis-Spiliotopoulos, *From Formal to Substantive Gender Equality: The Proposed Amendment of Directive 76/207 Comments and Suggestions*, (Brussels: Bruylant, 2001). Athens 2001 58.

[98] Case 407/98, *Abrahamsson and Andersson v Fogelqvist* [2000] E.C.R. I-5539.

[99] Case E-1/02, January 24, 2003. See the annotation on this case by C. Tobler, 41 Common Market L.R. (2004), 245–260.

[100] Case C–407/98, *Abrahamsson v Fogelqvist* [2000] E.C.R. I–5539.

objectivity." The ECJ found that this clearly fell outside the terms of permissible positive action in Art.2(4) of the Equal Treatment Directive. The Court did consider that Art.141(4) inserted by the Treaty of Amsterdam could cover this type of action, but that on the facts of the case this selection method was disproportionate to the aim pursued and therefore it was not justified. Once again, the Court re-iterated its commitment to the strict equality approach and the "anti-classification" principle: the use of gender as a "suspect" characteristic to distinguish at a point of final decision-making between individuals was not permitted, notwithstanding the greater scope given to positive action in general by Art.141(4).

It must be questionable whether a similar approach will be applied across all the different equality grounds under the Framework Equality and Race Directives, given for example the widely accepted use of reserved "set-aside" places for disabled persons. The gender approach adopted in *Kalanke* and *Abrahamsson* does not appear capable of being applied across all these "new" grounds, and disability in particular, where special treatment for disabled persons is commonplace. However, if this approach will not be applied across all the grounds, when will it be applied, and to which grounds? In addition, the lack of definition of what exactly constitutes an automatic preference ensures that the *Abrahamssohn* test remains ambiguous and uncertain, especially when reserved places at the initial interview stage are permitted by virtue of *Badeck*. This lack of clarity can have a "chilling-effect" on the use of any form of preferential treatment or merit re-definition in member states: any measure that strays anywhere near giving an "automatic" preference may be vulnerable to challenge.

Also, it remains uncertain whether the Court has worked out a consistent and rigorous conceptual framework to provide a backbone for its Court's rhetorical commitment to a substantive equality approach. At present, even with the new proportionality approach, the ECJ views positive action involving preferential treatment of any type as a derogation from the principle of equal treatment and the fundamental right to non-discrimination. Therefore, it is not surprising that even cases such as *Marschall, Badeck, Abrahamsson* and *Lommers* have confirmed that it is available under strict circumstances, i.e. (i) they are genuine measures designed to compensate for career disadvantage and (ii) they are based on transparent and objectively justified criteria.

Despite the more permissive approach to positive action in these post-*Kalanke* cases, there remains an underlying tension in the cases between the maintenance by the Court of a strong attachment to the "anti-classification"/ strict equality approach on the one hand (described as "formal equality" in the literature), and the enhanced permissibility of positive action recognised by the Court in some of these decisions (especially in *Schnorbus* and *Lommers* where indirect discrimination is at issue) and in various Treaty sources and the text of the EU Charter. There has been only a limited shift towards an "anti-subordination" or "substantial equality" approach, but the ECJ at present seems caught in an uncertain "no man's land" between the different approaches.

Given these persisting problems, Caruso has argued that in the ethnicity/race context, a preferential approach would be for the Court to classify group identity-based positive action measures as coming within the category of member state welfare provision, and therefore outside the competency of the Court to review.[101] Caruso's argument is attractive, as this would grant leeway to member states to develop their own context-specific positive action approaches. However, it is very questionable whether this approach could or should be adopted across all the equality grounds. Paul Skidmore has warned that the general exception for security and welfare measures contained in Art.2(5) of the Framework Directive and the religious ethos exception in Art.4(2) could be used to justify unfairly discriminatory practices under a cloak of positive action.[102]

Even in the ethnicity/race context, if the Court had no capacity to review positive action measures at all, this could leave room for member states to maintain some questionable practices. Even positive action measures designed to remedy disadvantage may lack any real rational basis, or be distorted to benefit special interests, or may excessively penalise non-members of the beneficiary groups. There may also be circumstances where the use of particular forms of group classification may encourage "group essentialism",[103] stereotyping or patterns of social segregation.[104] In *Lommers*, special measures which provided extra childcare facilities only to women were upheld, even though these measures could be criticised as serving to reinforce traditional gender roles by solely making provision for *women* with child-care responsibilities.[105] This reinforces the point made above that positive action measures can reinforce stereotypical assumptions even with the best of underlying intentions.

In general, the European Court of Justice needs to clarify its approach, and develop a reasonably rigorous conceptual approach to positive action that is more consistent and well-founded in principle than its current oscillation between formal and substantive equality approaches. A strong case exists for the adoption of an approach that allows greater leeway for national positive action measures that adopt a more substantive/"anti-subordination"

101 D. Caruso, "Limits of the Classic Method: Positive Action in the European Union After the New Equality Directives" (2003) 44 Harvard International L.J. 331.

102 See P. Skidmore, "The EC Framework Directive on Equal Treatment in Employment: Towards a Comprehensive Community Anti-Discrimination Policy?", 30 Industrial L.J. (2001) 1, 126–132, 129–30.

103 See A. Guttman, "Responding to Racial Injustice", in K. A. Appiah and A. Guttman (eds.) *Color Conscious* (Princeton NJ: 1996), 355.

104 For a discussion of how "quota" measures designed to assist disabled persons often proved to be stereotyping and to reinforce segregation, see L. Waddington, "Reassessing the Employment of People with Disabilities in Europe: From Quotas to Anti-Discrimination Laws", 18 Comparative Labour L.R. (1996) 62.

105 See the contrasting decision in Case 312/86, *Commission v France* [1986] E.C.R. I-6316; see also the excellent analysis by Cathryn Costello in "Positive Action", in C. Costello and E. Barry (eds.) *Equality in Diversity: The New Equality Directives* (Dublin: Irish Centre for European Law, 2003), 177–212.

emphasis, given the wide diversity of views and approaches in this area across the various member states. The ECJ's current approach is perhaps too restrictive in its adherence to a strict equality approach. In addition, the risk remains that the lack of clarity at the level of EC law will continue to seriously hinder the development of comprehensive and effective positive action measures at national level. In the absence of such a shift, the other option is for the EU to strengthen its support for substantive equality through its procurement and mainstreaming provisions, and also through the use of investment and supply side measures that assist women and minorities in EU member states.

F. *EU Public Procurement Law*

Another area of EU law with considerable implications for the development of positive action is public procurement law. Space does not permit a detailed analysis of this area at this stage (see the chapter on collective remedies), but uncertainty has been allowed to persist in the regime of EC public procurement law as to the extent to which public authorities in the various member states can use "contract compliance" measures to ensure that the private firms supplying them with goods and services have implemented, and are continuing to implement, appropriate measures to promote greater equality of opportunity. Potentially greater scope for equality-based measures has been opened up by the *Helsinki Concordia Bus* decision,[106] where the ECJ recognised that a public authority could factor environmental and other "social" considerations into their contracting process. Recent legislative reforms to the framework of Public Procurement Directives have clarified to a degree the scope for social considerations available in public procurement.[107] This is valuable, as EC legislation in this area has consistently lacked real clarity as to when the introduction of such contract compliance requirements are compatible with EC law.[108] This uncertainty has acted as a deterrent to public authorities in nation states attempting making use of such measures.[109] The new legislative provisions may open up space for national authorities to introduce contract compliance initiatives with greater freedom, thereby

[106] Case 513–99, [2002] E.C.R. I-7213.

[107] Directives 2004/17/EC and 2004/18/EC.

[108] See the critique of the initial legislative proposals by the NGO network, Coalition for Green and Social Procurement, at *http://www.solidar.org/english/pdf/PPCoalitionEN.doc* (last accessed October 5, 2005). See also C. Tobler, "Encore: 'Women's Clauses' in Public Procurement under Community Law", 25 European L.R. 6 [2000], 618–631; Rambøll Management, *Study of the Use of Equality and Diversity Considerations in Public Procurement: Final Report* (Brussels: European Commission, 2003).

[109] The Hepple Report, paras 3.71–3.73, pp.83–84. The implications for equality initiatives of this lack of clarity have often been overlooked or marginalised in framing and wording the relevant Directives—a classic example of a failure to mainstream (see below).

ensuring greater leeway in developing positive action strategies. However, see further analysis on this point in the collective remedies chapter.

IV. Positive Action in the UK

A. *Introduction*

EU law is significant in that it ultimately controls the scope available for member states to introduce positive action measures. However, the member states can choose to introduce their own strategies: there is no explicit obligation in EC law to introduce positive action measures, although there may be a possibility that a positive obligation to introduce some basic positive action measures may arise from the provisions of the Equality Directives. The UK has traditionally shown a preference in case-law and legislation for the "anti-classification"/formal equality approach. However, in recent years, public policy in the UK has increasingly made use of a variety of positive action strategies. These strategies have aimed, via the introduction of new legislative obligations and policy incentives, to encourage proactive action on the part of public authorities and employers to identify and eliminate discriminatory policies and practices, and to ensure greater integration and equality of opportunity for disadvantaged groups. To an extent, these public policy steps have been mirrored in changing private sector employment practices, which increasingly embrace "diversity management" strategies.[110]

These public and private sector positive action strategies have mainly been designed to eradicate discrimination, implement targeted inclusionary policies and establish outreach programmes, with some attempts being made to encourage a redefinition of merit. There has been a widespread acceptance of the appropriateness of substantive equality approaches, and a cautious and piecemeal shift away from reliance upon the formal equality approach that had characterised UK equality strategies until recently. However, with significant exceptions in the context of Northern Ireland, selection of parliamentary candidates on the basis of gender and disability rights, UK equality legislation and public policy has continued to reject the use of preferential treatment, on the basis that it constitutes "reverse discrimination" and might trigger harmful backlash.

[110] See L. Barmes, "Promoting Diversity and the Definition of Direct Discrimination" (2003) 32 I.L.J. 3 200; see also L. Barmes with S. Ashtiany, *Diversity in the City: Initiatives in Investment Banks in the UK* (London: Nabarro Nathanson, 2003); L. Barmes and S. Ashtiany, "The Diversity Approach to Achieving Equality: Potential and Pitfalls" (2003) 32 Industrial L.J. 3. See also J. Wrench, "Managing Diversity, Fighting Racism or Combating Discrimination? A Critical Exploration", paper delivered at Council of Europe and European Commission Research Seminar *Re-situating Culture—Reflections on Diversity, Racism, Gender and Identity*, Budapest, June 2003.

The absence of a written constitution in the UK means that legal questions as to the scope of permissive positive action are determined by reference to the statutory framework and the requirements of the ECHR and EU. If particular forms of positive action are not prohibited by legislation, then public and private bodies are able to implement these steps without restraint. This permitted local authorities in the 1980s to introduce a series of contract compliance and mainstreaming measures designed to promote equality of opportunity for ethnic minorities, women and disabled persons. However, "Best Value" controls introduced by the Conservative government in the mid to late 1980s subjected local and central public authority to much tighter statutory constraints, which closed off many of the avenues that had previously been open to positive action initiatives. The scope for contract compliance measures in UK law still remains uncertain, which generates a chilling effect that discourages public authorities from adopting such initiatives (see the chapter on collective remedies).[111] However, recent legislation, in particular the introduction of the positive duties (see below), has however begun to open the door for the re-introduction of new and large-scale positive action initiatives. The private sector has remained less constrained, and many businesses have in recent years adopted various diversity management strategies, often on an *ad hoc* basis.

Both the public and private sectors are of course also subject to the UK's anti-discrimination legislation, which reduces to an extent their scope of manoeuvre in the sphere of positive action. The various anti-discrimination statutes, with the significant exception of the Disability Discrimination Act 1995 (discussed below) adopt a symmetrical and formal model of equality. All forms of differentiation on the basis of gender and race are prohibited in the SDA 75 and RRA 76, subject to specific genuine occupational requirement exceptions and the odd positive action exemption, detailed below: a similar approach is adopted in the regulations implementing the Employment Equality Directive in respect of sexual orientation and religious discrimination.

Generally what is the scope of preferential treatment in (a) direct discrimination and (b) indirect discrimination?

The test adopted by the House of Lords in *Eastleigh BC v James*[112] to determine if discrimination has taken place is based around the question whether a difference of treatment would have occurred "but for" the sex, race, sexual orientation or religion of the person affected. This test is purely causative: it disregards the motive or intent underlying the difference in treatment, and in particular does not involve an analysis of whether disadvantage or a denial of dignity is underpinning the act of differentiation. While functionally useful from one perspective, as it obviates the need for employment tribunals and

[111] See P.E. Morris, "Legal Regulation of Contract Compliance: An Anglo-American Comparison" (1987) 19 Anglo-American L.R. 87–144.

[112] [1990] 2 A.C. 751.

courts to assess intent and thereby makes it easier to litigate claims of negative discrimination, the "but for" test as currently applied treats differences of treatment designed to achieve ameliorative or compensatory goals in a identical manner as differences based upon stereotyping or prejudice.[113] A clear preference therefore exists for the "anti-classification"/formal approach to equality.

Barmes has argued that an alternative, more nuanced approach to the "but for" test is possible within the parameters of existing precedent and the legislative framework, and has suggested that this fresh approach should be applied so as to permit a much greater range of positive action initiatives.[114] However, given the current interpretation and application of the legislation, positive action based on equality grounds will fall foul of the anti-discrimination controls and the "but for" test, unless it comes within the scope of a statutory exception, or else falls outside the scope of discrimination law.

The scope of application of positive action measures varies considerably across the different equality grounds.

1. Race/Ethnic Origin

The RRA 76 in general prohibits any unequal treatment on grounds of race, ethnic or national origin and nationality, which applies to measures designed to give preferential treatment an underrepresented racial or ethnic group as it would to measures designed to discriminate against that group.[115] Private and public sector bodies are subject to the same controls: no real distinctions are made between them, with the exception of the positive duty that is imposed upon public authorities (see below). The exceptions to this general prohibition of preferential treatment are very limited.

Sections 37 and 38 of the RRA 76 allow the provision of access to facilities or training to persons from a particular racial or ethnic group, or the encouragement of members of that group to hold certain posts, to do certain types of work, or to join an organisation, where there exists clear under-representation of that group in a particular workforce, defined as when there have been no persons or a "comparatively small" proportion of that particular racial or ethnic group doing that particular work in the last twelve months in the specific workforce in question or in the "normal recruitment area" for that workforce. Sections 37 and 38 therefore appear permit mentoring, monitoring and outreach initiatives to encourage candidates or new members from ethnic minorities, as this would constitute special training and encouragement for members of ethnic minority groups. However, any measures that gave auto-

[113] See *ACAS v Taylor* EAT/788/97.

[114] See L. Barmes, "Promoting Diversity and the Definition of Direct Discrimination" (2003) 32 I.L.J. 3 200.

[115] H. Slater, "Making a Positive Difference: A Legal Guide to Positive Action", Equal Opportunities R., No.111, November 2002, p.12–17.

matic preferment or substantial advantages to minority candidates over and above special "training and encouragement" remain contrary to the RRA 76.

There is a possibility that the scope of ss.37 and 38 might be capable of supporting a wider meaning that set out here: but in the absence of any judicial decisions supporting this possibility, it appears unlikely that these provisions can by themselves support any form of preferential action.[116] In *Hughes v Hackney LBC*[117], an industrial tribunal gave a narrow interpretation to s.38, ruling that a local authority could not rely upon under-representation in a workforce as compared to the population of the borough in question, but rather had to demonstrate under-representation as compared to the "normal recruiting area", which proved fatal to the measure in question. In addition, the tribunal ruled that s.38 did not permit the restructuring of job opportunities (in this case, the creation of special apprenticeships) but was confined to the provision of training for existing posts.

Section 35 of the 1976 Act permits the provision of facilities or services in the form of education, welfare, training and ancillary benefits if necessary to meet the special needs of particular racial groups. However, in *Hughes v Hackney LBC*[118], access to facilities was held not to extend to the provision of job opportunities, therefore confirming that s.35 could not be used as a foundation for preferential treatment or reserved places ("set-asides") in the employment context.[119] A similar decision was taken in *Lambeth LBC v Commission for Racial Equality*,[120] where the need to provide housing services to particular ethnic groups was held not to justify a requirement that a particular post only be filled by members of a specified set of ethnic groups.

Therefore, no form of positive action can utilise someone's race, national origin, nationality or ethnicity as a preferential factor except within the scope of the very narrow exceptions permitted by the legislation. However, this does not prevent initiatives designed to identify and eliminate forms of direct, indirect or institutional discrimination, or outreach programmes and other steps to encourage greater participation by ethnic minorities. There is a very uncertain dividing line between encouragement and preferential treatment, which has not been clarified by case-law. In recent years, many public and

[116] The Sex Discrimination (Electoral Candidates) 2002 permits preferential treatment in the selection of parliamentary candidates, but this is confined to gender. See C. O'Cinneide and M. Russell, "Positive Action to Promote Women in Politics: Some European Comparisons" (2003) International Comparative Law Quarterly 587–614. See also R. Ali and C. O'Cinneide, *Our House? Race and Representation in British Politics* (London: Institute for Public Policy Research, 2002).

[117] ET, February 6, 1986, unreported.

[118] ET, February 6, 1986, unreported.

[119] In Spring 2004, the Arnolfini Gallery in Bristol advertised a fellowship for a Senior Curator, which was open only to Black, Asian and Caribbean applicants. This triggered hostile media coverage and resulted in complaints to the Commission for Racial Equality, even though the advertisement stated that the Gallery was taking positive action to tackle the under-representation of these groups among senior curators. On the CRE's advice, the Gallery withdrew the advertisement and reconsidered the criteria for the post. See R. Karim, "Take Care While Being Positive" (2004) *CRE Connections*, Winter 2004.

[120] [1990] I.R.L.R. 231.

private sector positive action initiatives have used target mechanisms to monitor and encourage greater ethnic minority participation and take-up of services.

These strategies have had some success, and have contributed greatly to a culture change where the use of such positive action initiatives is generally welcomed and normalised. However, the lack of a clear-cut distinction between encouragement and preferential treatment (which may be impossible to identify in reality) and the absence of a wider positive action exception in the legislation means that many such initiative sexist in a "grey area" of legal uncertainty.[121] It can be argued that these initiatives do not produce automatic outcomes in favour of disadvantaged groups, meaning that the "but for" test is not triggered and therefore no violation of the legislation is made out: however, the formal symmetry approach around which the legislation was originally framed still generates inevitable uncertainty about any measure that directly or indirectly utilises the ethnic origin of an individual at any stage of formulating a policy or practice.

2. Gender

A similar position applies in the private and public sectors in the gender context. The SDA 75 similarly only permits preferential treatment or the targeting of benefits at women in tightly circumscribed situations, or where other legislation (for example social security regulations) permits such action. Section 47 of the SDA 75 permits training and "encouragement" for members of one sex only in respect of "particular work", where that sex has been under-represented, defined in similar terms as in ss.37 and 38 of the RRA 76 with the exception that under-representation in the particular workforce or throughout the whole of Great Britain can be sufficient to permit special measures,[122], or where persons are in "special need of training by reason of their "discharging domestic or family responsibilities to the exclusion of full-time regular employment. Section 48 permits employers to provide similar "training and encouragement" measures for employees of only one sex where that sex is "under-represented" in that particular workplace. Both sections resemble ss.37 and 38 of the RRA 76, with the exception of the inclusion of the domestic responsibilities trigger, and there has been no case-law on the definition of "under-representation" in ss.47 and 48, or on the specific definition of training and encouragement.

121 See Lizzie Barmes, "Promoting Diversity and the Definition of Direct Discrimination" (2003) 32 I.L.J. 3 200.

122 This permits the introduction of training and encouragement measures directed towards members of a single ethnic group if there is a national pattern of under-representation, even if in the particular workplace or geographical area that ethnic group is not "under-represented" at present. This provision varies from the RRA due to the fact that under-representation of ethnic groups across Britain may be very difficult to demonstrate and would be an excessively restrictive threshold requirement, given the concentration of ethnic minorities in particular areas of Britain.

Section 49 permits very limited positive action by trade unions, employer organisations and professional bodies in selecting elected representative bodies to reserve seats specifically for members of one sex to "secure a reasonable minimum number" on that body. Section 33 in turn permits political parties to any special provision for persons of one sex only in the constitution, organisation or administration of the political party. This provision was at the heart of the successful challenge brought against the Labour Party's policy of introducing all-women shortlists in particular Westminster constituencies before the 1997 election. In *Jepson and Dyas-Elliot v The Labour Party*[123], the complainants argued that candidate selection by political parties was subject to Pt II of the SDA 75, which applies to "employment", and that the all-women shortlist policy therefore constituted sex discrimination as it favoured one sex over the other. The Labour Party argued in contrast that parliamentary candidates could not be covered by s.13 of the Act, because candidates could not be said to be "employed" by the party: it also argued that preferential treatment in favour of women in candidate selection was entirely lawful, by virtue of s.33 of the SDA 75, as the selection of candidates formed part of its "constitution, organisation or administration". The tribunal held that, in selecting candidates, a political party should be considered as a body granting a qualification, and as a consequence, it concluded that Labour's all-women shortlists constituted unlawful discrimination contrary to s.13. It then also concluded that the selection of candidates did not fall within s.33, which it interpreted in relatively narrow terms to relate to the internal order of a political party only.[124]

Jepson v Labour Party [1998] I.R.L.R. 116

"We can see no difficulty in bringing Members of Parliament within that wide coverage. They are not, we readily accept, in employment as defined in s 82 but they are engaged in an occupation which involves public service and for which they receive remuneration from public funds. It is immaterial so far as s 13 is concerned that a person seeking to be considered for approval as an official candidate for a major political party has further hurdles to overcome before he or she can achieve a position as a Member of Parliament. He has to be actually selected as the candidate in competition with others and then gain

[123] *Jepson and Dyas-Elliot v The Labour Party*, [1996] I.R.L.R. 116 ET. For a more detailed discussion of the case see H. Davis, "All-Women Shortlists in the Labour Party", P.L., 207–214 (1995), and R. Ali and C. O'Cinneide, *Our House? Race and Representation in British Politics*, 53–54 (Institute of Public Policy Research: 2002).

[124] The all-women shortlist policy was dropped by the party at this point. It was suggested that there should be an appeal to a higher court, but no such appeal was made. This was partly done to preserve the position of those already selected by virtue of all-women shortlists, as industrial tribunal decisions are only binding in respect of the individual case considered. See Meg Russell, *Women's Representation in UK politics: What can be done within the law?* (London: The Constitution Unit, July 2001).

the approval of the electorate at an election. However, in that sense he is in no different position from a person denied approval by a body under s 13, who does not as yet have any particular work to do and who would need selection by others before obtaining such work. [...]

We are not satisfied that s 29 of the Act applies at all to this situation. We agree with Mr Goudie that Parts II and III of the Act should be regarded if possible as mutually exclusive and that it would be absurd to have something lawful under one part and unlawful under the other. Where we differ from him, however, is that s 29 is clearly intended to cover situations where persons or bodies provide goods, facilities and services to the public, that is to say what may broadly be described as 'trade' or matters similar thereto. It is an ingenious but fallacious argument to bring the matter we are considering into the ambit of s 29 although we can understand why Mr Goudie has endeavoured to do this because he believes it provides a defence for the respondents under s 33. Whatever be the correct interpretation of the ambit of s 33 we are unable to accept that s 29 should take precedence over s 13. [...]

We certainly reject there being any justification for this positive discrimination arising from Article 2(4) of the Equal Treatment Directive as submitted by Mr Goudie. That would have to be in the context of the Equal Treatment Directive applying directly in the first place which it clearly does not since the respondents are not emanations of the State (although as we have seen we can refer to the Directive as assisting the construction of the national law).

In any event such a total block on one sex as occurs here cannot have been the intention in that Article, a view which we regard as fully endorsed by the decision of the European Court in the Kalanke case.

We conclude therefore that the complaints of both applicants that they have been unlawfully discriminated against on the grounds of their sex are well-founded and the tribunal makes a declaration to that effect."

Several selection methods were subsequently used to attempt to circumvent the *Jepson* decision, which provided highly successful in the devolved elections in Scotland and Wales but rested upon an uncertain legal basis.[125] However, the UK government considered that the uncertain status of positive action measures under national and EC law meant that the use of such measures as an *ad* hoc response to the Jepson decision could not be sustained.[126] The Sex

[125] The "zipping and twinning" systems used by Labour in the devolved elections were not tested in the courts or employment tribunals, despite talk of legal challenge. The result of the elections produced Labour parliamentary groups containing 54 per cent women in Wales and 50 per cent women in Scotland. Similarly, the Liberal Democrats constructed a selection system for the European elections of 1999 (run, for the first time, under a proportional list system) whereby the list of candidates in each region placed men and women in alternate positions. This too was threatened with legal challenge which did not materialise, and the party went on to elect five male and five female MEPs. These strategies are discussed in M. Russell, *Women's Representation in UK Politics*. For the parliamentary debates, see *House of Commons Hansard*, 2 March 1998, col.787–797 for Wales and 31 March 1998, col.1134–1146 for Scotland. For a fuller discussion of the selection process for the Scottish Parliament and Welsh Assembly, see M. Russell, F. Mackay and L. McAllister "Women's Representation in the Scottish Parliament and National Assembly for Wales: Party Dynamics for Achieving Critical Mass", *Journal of Legislative Studies*.

[126] The *Guardian* reported that a leaked cabinet committee minute from the Lord Chancellor argued that the proposed amendments would not remove the possibility of a challenge under the EC Equal Treatment Directive. See *Guardian*, March 3, 1998, "Why Irvine sent Dewar plan to boost women in Scottish Parliament back to drawing board". These concerns were reiterated by ministers in debate—see HC Deb. Vol.309, c.1143–1146.

Discrimination (Election Candidates) Act 2002 was therefore introduced, amending the SDA 75 to ensure that its prohibition of discrimination does not make unlawful any arrangements made by a registered political party which "are adopted for the purpose of reducing inequality in the numbers of men and women elected, as candidates of the party, to be members of the body concerned".[127] It applies to selection of candidates at all levels of government, including local government, Scottish Parliament, Welsh Assembly and Northern Ireland Assembly[128] elections, the House of Commons and elections to the European Parliament. By immunising positive action by political parties from discrimination law, the Act places the process of selecting political candidates in a special category. This recognises the importance of securing equal representation in the political process of both sexes, and goes further in allowing special measures to achieve this than is permitted with respect to employment or other fields covered by the SDA 75.

Sex Discrimination (Election Candidates) Act 2002

"The Act inserts the following new section into the Sex Discrimination Act 1975, which will expire at the end of 2015, unless extended by an executive order:

s.42A (1) Nothing in Parts II to IV shall—

(a) be construed as affecting arrangements to which this section applies, or

(b) render unlawful anything done in accordance with such arrangements.

(2) This section applies to arrangments made by a registered political party which—

(a) regulate the selection of the party's candidates in a relevant election, and

(b) are adopted for the purpose of reducing inequality in the numbers of men and women elected, as candidates of the party, to be members of the body concerned.

(3) The following elections are relevant elections for the purposes of this section—

(a) parliamentary elections;

(b) elections to the European Parliament;

(c) elections to the Scottish Parliament;

127 See C. O'Cinneide and M. Russell, "Positive Action to Promote Women in Politics: Some European Comparisons" (2003) International Comparative L.Q. 587–614.

128 Legislation relating to equal opportunities covers England Scotland and Wales only under the devolution settlement, with responsibility for equal opportunities in Northern Ireland being devolved to the Belfast Assembly. The Act however extends the exemption to Northern Ireland, by inserting an equivalent new article to that inserted in the SDA 75 in the Sex Discrimination (Northern Ireland) Order 1976 (SI 1976/1042).

(d) elections to the National Assembly for Wales;

(e) local government elections..."

The Act does restrict the exemption in a number of ways. Political parties can only take action to reduce inequality amongst their own representatives: hence if one party had a low proportion of women MPs, another could not decide to give extra preference to female candidates in order to balance the membership of the House of Commons as a whole. The Act also includes a "sunset clause", which provides for it to expire at the end of 2015 unless an order, approved by Parliament, is made to the contrary. The stated rationale for this time-limit was based upon the requirements of international human rights law, in particular Art.4 of the CEDAW which permits "temporary special measures".

A key element of the Act is its permissive nature: it allows parties to take positive action, but does not oblige them to do so, unlike the similar French legislation. It is thus at the discretion of individual political parties whether and how they want to use their new freedom. However, this exemption remains with the training and encouragement exceptions the major areas of permissible preferential treatment permitted by the bulk of UK anti-discrimination legislation, and they are rarely utilised. Other positive action initiatives are used in both the public and private sectors, but they are noticeably less developed and systematic than those developed in the race context. At present such initiatives usually consist of mainstreaming and gender diversity strategies, although the introduction of a gender positive duty on public authorities was introduced by the Equalities Act 2006, ss.84–85 introduce a general and specific duty on public authorities to eliminate unlawful sex discrimination and harassment and promote gender equality. The Gender Equality Duty will be in force by April 2007. The Equal Opportunities Commission has drafted a final version of the Code of Practice (there will be a separate code for Scotland) which provides guidance to public authorities on how to implement the general and specific duty. The Code of Practice has been laid before Parliament.[129]

3. Disability

Unlike the other UK anti-discrimination statutes, the DDA 95 is not based upon a symmetric model of equality, but rather is designed to protect disabled persons against discrimination. Therefore, only persons with disabilities can benefit from the asymmetrical nature of the Act, and consequently it is not unlawful to accord preferential treatment to disabled persons without providing the same treatment for the non-disabled. This means that the full range of positive action measures can generally be utilised in the disability context, including all forms of preferential treatment and direct targeting of resource to

[129] See *www.eoc.org* for a copy of the final draft of the code of practice (accessed December 30, 2006).

the disabled. Other legislative provisions reflect this approach: the Disability Rights Commission Act 1999 explicitly requires that 50 per cent of the Commission's board of commissioners must have a disability, and s.10 of the DDA 95 permits "supported employment" and charitable support to be directed towards particular groups of disabled persons, i.e. permits distinctions can be drawn between different groups of disabled people. The DDA 2005 has imposed a positive duty to promote equality of opportunity for disabled persons upon public authorities and those "exercising public functions", an uncertain category whose definition will be borrowed from the HRA 1998.[130]

The one exception to this general principle of freedom of action in the scope of positive action for disabled persons is s.7 of the Local Government and Housing Act 1989, which requires all local authority employees to be appointed "on merit". Section 7(2) of the Act had originally provided for an exemption to this general requirement linked to the provisions of the Disabled Persons (Employment) Act 1944, which required that 3 per cent of local authority employees should be registered as disabled: however, this quota arrangement, which was rarely if ever enforced and attracted little support from disability rights activists concerned about its "tokenistic" impact, was repealed by the DDA.[131] Section 7 now therefore appears to prevent any deviation from "merit" based decisions in local authority employment and to confine positive action in this area firmly within the constraints of conventional merit-based approaches.

However, as the Disability Rights Commission have commented, the requirement in the DDA to make "reasonable accommodation" where necessary does inherently require a reassessment of "merit" requirements for any given post, and for the particular qualities, abilities and talents of a disabled person to be taken into account and given due consideration in determining what will constitute reasonable accommodation.[132] In *Archibald v Fife*, the Law Lords held that the duty imposed by the DDA on employers to make reasonable accommodation could require employers to give disabled persons preferential treatment where necessary to give effect to this duty (in this case, to exempt them from competitive interview requirements for particular posts).[133] A positive duty to promote equality in relation to disability discrimination has now been introduced by the Equality Act 2006.

130 See C. O'Cinneide, "A New Generation of Equality Legislation? Positive Duties and Disability Rights", in A. Lawson and C. Gooding, *Disability Rights in Europe* (Oxford: Hart, 2005).

131 s.70(4) and Sch.6 of the DDA 1995; see also I. Cunningham and P. James, "The DDA—An Early Response from Employers" (1989) 29 Industrial Relations J. 304.

132 See *Code of Practice for the Elimination of Discrimination in the Field of Employment Against Disabled Persons* (London: HMSO, 1996), para.4.66. See also M. Connolly, *Townshend-Smith on Discrimination Law: Text, Cases and Materials* (London: Cavendish, 2004), 573.

133 [2004] UKHL 32.

4. Religion and Belief, Sexual Orientation and Age

The UK has given effect to the Framework Equality Directive by the introduction of the sexual orientation and religious discrimination regulations in 2003. The only areas where preferential treatment on these grounds is permitted are where being of a particular sexual orientation or religion constitutes a genuine occupational requirement or is necessary to preserve the ethos of a religious establishment, in line with the contents of the Framework Directive.

Interestingly, many public authorities have begun to implement equality mainstreaming policies which include a focus on eliminating barriers to participation based upon sexual orientation and religious belief, as well as introducing outreach and consultation schemes. Developing such equality mainstreaming policies, which have a parallel in private sector diversity strategies, has raised issues of how intersectional approaches can and should be incorporated. Tentative attempts to develop an appropriate strategy have begun in the public sector:[134] the establishment of a single unified Commission for Equality and Human Rights is viewed by the UK government as an essential step in encouraging the development of adequate intersectional approaches.[135]

In relation to religious discrimination there is an issue (discussed in a later chapter) of an overlap between discrimination on the grounds of race, religion and culture which gives rise to cultural racism. In this context, the introduction of positive action measures in relation to race discrimination, and to promote racial minorities, can be applied flexibly to ensure that there are no arbitrary distinctions in the protection offered and those who are the intersection of race, culture and religion are covered. This flexible approach to the overlap between race, religion and culture is also highlighted in the recent Department of Works and Pensions study on positive action which concludes:

Dr Ravinder Singh Dhami, Professor Judith Squires and Professor Tariq Modood, *Developing Positive Action Policies: Learning from the Experiences of Europe and North America*, Research Report No.406 Department for Works and Pensions

pp.119–121: "[. . .]

- **Religion.** Positive action programmes should consider both religious and ethnic minority equality measures.

[134] See the *Equality Standard for Local Government* (London: Employers' Organisation for Local Government), available at *http://www.lg-employers.gov.uk/diversity/equality/index.html*.

[135] See *Fairness for All: A New Commission for Equality and Human Rights* White Paper Cmnd. 6185 (London: Dept for Trade and Industry, May 2004).

The evidence from this research has shown that there can be clear benefits from a programme of positive action. Existing policy approaches have been limited in redressing ethnic penalties. In our view, a government committed to eradicating social exclusion can legitimately and confidently engage with an advanced programme of positive action, which includes contract compliance. The implementation of such a policy would send the right signal both to the intended beneficiaries and to those organisations and individuals that continue to deny ethnic groups and visible minorities their full part in the economic and social life of the country. As it is over four decades since the first Race Relations Act, and given that ethnic inequality continues to be a part of the social fabric of our country, the time is now right for such a step."

The Employment Equality (Age Discrimination) Regulations 2006 only permit positive action for disadvantaged age groups in training and encouragement, similar to the provisions in the sex and race discrimination legislation. However, as direct age discrimination legislation can be justified, and substantial exceptions exists to the scope of the legislation, certain forms of positive treatment for particular age groups will be protected from legal challenge by these provisions (see the Age Discrimination chapter).

5. The Limits of Permissive Positive Action

Many private and public sector organisations have in recent years adopted various forms of diversity management strategies. Such strategies aim to ensure a more "diverse" workforce, and are intended to mainstream good diversity practice into business decision-making and practices, and in particular into human resources policy.[136] They make use of a range of positive action strategies, which are designed to encourage more applicants for employment or promotion from under-represented groups.[137] However, as Barmes and Ashtiany have argued, many of these strategies exist in a legal grey zone.[138]

The "but for" test adopted by the House of Lords in *Eastleigh BC v James*[139] to determine if direct discrimination has taken place does not involve an analysis of whether disadvantage or a denial of dignity is underpinning the act of differentiation.[140] As noted above, preferential treatment will therefore fall foul of anti-discrimination controls, unless it comes within a statutory exception.

136 See R. Thomas, "From Affirmative Action to Affirming Diversity" (1990) 68 Harvard Business R. 107–117.

137 For a discussion of the strengths and problems of "diversity management" strategies, see L. Barmes with S. Ashtiany, "The Diversity Approach to Achieving Equality: Potential and Pitfalls" (2003) 32 Industrial Law Journal 274–96; J. Wrench, "Diversity Management Can Be Bad For You" (2005) 46 *Race and Class* 3 73–84.

138 ibid.

139 [1990] 2 A.C. 751.

140 See *ACAS v Taylor* EAT/788/97. Lizzie Barmes has argued that recent decisions may have begun to adopt a greater focus on the intent behind the use of suspect classifications, and therefore that there may be a move away from the strict application of the *James* "but for" test. However, as she notes, this trend is not clear, and may be confined to victimisation cases. See L. Barmes, "Promoting Diversity and the Definition of Direct Discrimination" (2003) 32 I.L.J. 3 200.

However, very few exceptions have been permitted, as again discussed above. The ones that do exist have been given narrow interpretations by courts and tribunals, and appear to be very circumscribed in scope.[141] In particular, the scope of the "training" and "encouragement" positive action exceptions in the existing legislation is not clear.

Article 7 of the Employment Equality Directive allows Member States to adopt measures to prevent or compensate for disadvantages linked to any of the grounds covered by the Directive.[142] However, in implementing these Directives, the government elected not to take advantage of this permitted scope for positive action.[143] The major exception is the Disability Discrimination Act, which does not adopt a symmetrical model of equality and permits preferential treatment for disabled persons.[144] However, with this and the other narrow exceptions, forms of preferential treatment that fall outside the scope of the statutory exceptions will constitute direct discrimination and therefore are illegal.

Therefore, any diversity programmes that could be interpreted as benefiting a member of a disadvantaged group may run the risk of falling outside the scope of these exceptions, and therefore of being in violation of the legislation.[145] Barmes suggests that this uncertainty generates a "chilling effect" that can deter the use of such diversity strategies, and renders some of the positive action policies used by employers potentially vulnerable to challenge.[146] It is certainly true that any attempts to use any form of preferential treatment to compensate for disadvantage or to create a "critical mass" of employees or managers from under-represented groups will fall foul of the legislation. So do will the use by public authorities of even minor forms of preferential treatment designed to enhance equality of opportunity, notwithstanding the existence of the positive public sector duties (see below).

Academic critics of the adherence to the formal equality approach argue that the current restrictions are incoherent, as they deprive policymakers of a

[141] See e.g. *Hughes v Hackney LBC*, Employment Tribunal Feb 6, 1986, unreported; *Lambeth LBC v Commission for Racial Equality* [1990] I.R.L.R. 231. See H. Slater, "Making a Positive Difference: A Legal Guide to Positive Action" (2002) 111 Equal Opportunities R., November 2002, 12–17.

[142] Art.5 of the Race Directive contains a similar provision.

[143] See *Equality and Diversity: Coming Of Age* (2005), Pt 4.2. The draft Age Regulations make provision for exceptions for training and encouragement of under-represented age groups, similar to the narrow exceptions contained in the SDA and RRA.

[144] See S. Fredman, "Disability Equality: A Challenge the Existing Anti-Discrimination Paradigm?", in A. Lawson and C. Gooding, *Disability Rights in Europe* (Oxford: Hart, 2005) 199–218.

[145] See L Barmes, "Promoting Diversity and the Definition of Direct Discrimination" (2003) 32 I.L.J. 3 200. Similar problems apply in Ireland: see C. Costello, "Positive Action", in C. Costello and E. Barry (eds.) *Equality in Diversity: The New Equality Directives* (2003) 177–212, especially at 199–206.

[146] Barmes, ibid. The CRE has been obliged recently to offer more guidance for employers in this area: see R. Karim, "Take Care When Being Positive", *Connections*, Winter 2004.

potentially valuable tool for addressing group disadvantage.[147] However, successive UK governments have adhered to his approach and set their face against the use of preferential treatment in Britain.[148] The difficulty with this approach is that while in the abstract, it may be possible to distinguish preferential treatment from other types of positive action, this is increasingly proving difficult to do in practice, given the range of diversity strategies that are now commonplace. There is an uncertain borderline between preferential treatment and strong encouragement for disadvantaged groups, and the law at present is not providing clear or coherent boundary lines.

There is also a clear lack of clear principle underlying the current set of exceptions, and an overall lack of clarity in the legislation. For example, the Sex Discrimination (Election Candidates) Act 2002 permits political parties to take positive action, including the use of preferential treatment, to reduce inequalities on the grounds of gender in candidate numbers.[149] The introduction of this exception has not been followed by other new exceptions. But why is preferential treatment permissible in selecting political candidates and not in other areas? The answer is not apparent. Greater clarity and coherence are required, and some loosening-up of the current restrictions on the use of preferential treatment (and thereby other forms of positive action) appears to be on the agenda of the Discrimination Law Review.[150]

[147] S. Fredman, "Reversing Discrimination" (1997) 113 L.Q.R. 575; B. Parekh, "A Case for Positive Discrimination", in B. Hepple and E. Szyszczak (eds.) *Discrimination: The Limits of the Law* (1992). Trevor Phillips, chair of the CRE, has called for the suspension of restrictions on preferential treatment to ensure that more ethnic minority recruits join the police: see P. Butler and S. Salman, "Police 'Should Favour Black Recruits'", *The Guardian: Society*, March 17, 2004. There were media reports that the UK government was toying with this suggestion: see BBC News, "Police Plan to Boost Ethnic Ranks", available at *http://news.bbc.co.uk/2/hi/uk_news/3634085.stm* (accessed November 15, 2005. See also S. Fredman, "Reversing Discrimination" (1997) 113 L.Q.R. 575; B. Parekh, "A Case for Positive Discrimination", in B. Hepple and E. Szyszczak (eds.) *Discrimination: The Limits of the Law* (1992).

[148] In contrast, successive UK governments have been less concerned about the use of forms of preferential treatment in Northern Ireland, such as the introduction of the "Patten quota" for recruitment to the Police Service for Northern Ireland, and the leeway given to positive action to address group under-representation by the employment equity legislation. Again, Northern Ireland is seen as a "special case". See *A New Beginning: Policing in Northern Ireland*, The Report of the Independent Commission on Policing for Northern Ireland (1999).

[149] See C. O'Cinneide and M. Russell, "Positive Action to Promote Women in Politics Some European Comparisons" (2003) I.C.L.Q. 587–614.

[150] Even if British law is clarified, the case-law of the European Court of Justice on positive action may still generate uncertainty. It is still not clear how much freedom the ECJ will permit to member states in using special measures to combat disadvantages across the different equality grounds. However, at present, EC law is more permissible and flexible than British law when it comes to positive action: see C. Costello, "Positive Action", in C. Costello and E. Barry (eds.) *Equality in Diversity: The New Equality Directives* (2003), 177–212; C. Tobler, "Positive Action under the Revised Second Equal Treatment Directive", in AFFA and EWLA (ed.) *L'égalité entre femmes et hommes et la vie profesionnelle; Le point sur les développements actuels en Europe* (2003) 59–92.

V. Northern Ireland

Special affirmative action provisions exist in the Northern Irish legislation, in the context of religious discrimination. The Fair Employment Act 1989 imposes a set of mandatory positive duties upon private and public sector employees with ten or more employees to monitor and review their employment polices, and to take "affirmative action" if such monitoring indicates that either of the two major communities are not enjoying fair participation in employment. The definition of what qualifies as affirmative action prohibits preferential treatment, except where it involves targeted training in a particular area or at a particular class of persons in order to help fit persons from under-represented groups for employment, or the encouragement of applications for employment or training from persons from the under-represented group, or the negotiation of an agreed redundancy scheme in order to preserve gains made by persons from the under-represented group, or to prevent disproportionate losses of such persons. In 1998, a further legislative development protected direct recruitment from the unemployed from charges of direct or indirect discrimination, given that Catholics at that time were approximately two and a half times more likely be unemployed than Protestants.

Therefore, the Northern Irish legislation goes further in permitting positive action, while still mainly relying upon duty-based reviews and monitoring, with some room for training and encouragement linked preferential treatment strategies and the special exemptions available in the redundancy and direct recruitment from the unemployed contexts. The Northern Irish measures have had considerable and well-documented success[151]: in fact, the emphasis on setting and meeting transparently defined targets has generated better results than virtually any other set of positive action approaches.[152] However, as with the positive duties in Britain, a notable grey area does exist as to the degree to which meeting targets can be factored into employment decisions that do not fall within the specific preferential treatment exceptions.

In addition, the Police (Northern Ireland) Act 2000 now implements the quota system proposed by the Patten Report, requiring that for the next ten years, 50 per cent of all recruits into the new police service will have to be from the Catholic community. This is a dramatic use of preferential treatment, based upon the detailed analysis contained in the Patten Report, which emphasised the particular importance of securing fair representation in the Northern Irish Police Service and the proportionate need to achieve a balanced intake within a short time-frame. The ten year time limit was again introduced to conform with international human rights law requirements.

[151] See C. McCrudden, R. Ford, and A. Heath, "Legal Regulation of Affirmative Action in Northern Ireland: An Empirical Assessment" (2004) 24 O.J.L.S. 3 363–415.

[152] See H. C. Jain, P. J. Sloane and F. M. Horwitz, *Employment Equity and Affirmative Action: An International Comparison* (London: M.E. Sharpe, 2003).

VI. Mainstreaming, Diversity Management and Positive Duties

The public and private sectors are subject to the same basic statutory requirements under the anti-discrimination legislation, and are treated identically for the purposes of required affirmative action measures under the Northern Irish legislation. However, both sectors adopt quite different positive action strategies in practice, and the introduction of mainstreaming and positive duties in the public sector has meant that considerable divergences are beginning to open up between both sectors.

The narrow scope of the positive action exemptions in the legislation (with the significant exception of the disability legislation) has meant that the range of positive action measures that have been adopted in the public sector in the UK have tended to involve initiatives that fall short of making actual differentiation between individuals on the basis of an equality ground. Instead, the focus has been on utilising mechanisms that aim to identify and eliminate discriminatory polices or practices, to expand the levels of participation of disadvantaged groups, and to target resources and support to disadvantaged groups within the constraints of existing statutory frameworks.[153]

Moves towards responding to the limits of existing anti-discrimination legislation have generally in the EU and elsewhere taken the form of the piecemeal adoption by the public sector of various forms of diversity strategies or "mainstreaming" policies. Considerable divergence exists as to what "mainstreaming" in the context of equality actually entails: the word is prone to a variety of interpretation.[154] It has been defined by the Council of Europe in the gender context as the incorporation of a gender equality perspective in all policies at all levels and at all stages by the actors normally involved in policy making.[155]

McCrudden has identified two main components of effective mainstreaming: impact assessment, concentrating on the impact of policies on disadvantaged groups, and the participation of these groups in decision-making processes.[156] Rees also emphasises the importance of due regard for the individual, representative structures and adequate institutional and financial support structures.[157] Mainstreaming as a strategy has attracted support from the UN, the EU, Commonwealth Secretariat, ILO and OECD in recent years,

[153] See C. O'Cinneide, "Making Use of Positive Equality Duties: The UK Experience", in C. Costello and E. Barry (eds) *Equality in Diversity: The New Equality Directives* (Dublin: Irish Centre for European Law, 2003), 75–99; O'Cinneide, *Taking Equal Opportunities Seriously: The Extension of Positive Duties to Promote Equality* (London: Equality and Diversity Forum/Equal Opportunities Commission, December 2003).

[154] See T. Rees, *Mainstreaming Equality in the European Union* (London: Routledge, 1998).

[155] See *Gender Mainstreaming: Conceptual Framework, Methodology and Presentation of Good Practices*, Final Report of Activities of the Group of Specialists on Mainstreaming (EG-S-MS (98), (Strasbourg: Council of Europe 1998 May).

[156] C. McCrudden, "Mainstreaming Equality in the Governance of Northern Ireland" (1999) 22 Fordham International L.J. 4 22.

[157] See Rees, *op cit*.

and has been presented as the solution to the problems identified here with the existing anti-discrimination model.[158]

Almost all of the EU states, as well as the EU institutions, have implemented gender mainstreaming programmes of varying degrees of effectiveness and ambition.[159] In these countries, gender mainstreaming is usually based around what Sue Nott has described as the "expert-bureaucratic" model, where specialist units with gender expertise within the government structure push internally for the incorporation of gender perspectives all at levels of public sector decision-making.[160] Other forms of equality mainstreaming are much less well developed, and in many member states, mainstreaming initiatives remain patchy at best. There have been some limited attempts to mainstream disability issues into EU law and policy,[161] but no comprehensive cross-ground programme of equality mainstreaming.[162] This reflects the similar position in the bulk of the member states.

Mainstreaming does clearly have great potential for encouraging a greater focus upon the need to develop positive action strategies. However, a major problem with mainstreaming policies is that they are "soft law" initiatives. This means that the implementation of effective mainstreaming often only happens when all the necessary ingredients of political good-will, organisational capacity, sustained leadership and expert advice are in place.[163] Rees

[158] UN Fourth World Conference on Women (1995) *Global Platform for Action—Beijing*. New York; United Nations Publishing. See also S. Razavi and C. Miller, "Gender Mainstreaming: A Study of Efforts by the UNDP, the World Bank and the ILO to Institutionalise Gender Issues", Occasional Paper No.4, UN Fourth World Conference on Women, 1995. For a very comprehensive account of mainstreaming initiatives and best practice, see F. Mackay and K. Bilton, *Learning From Experience: Lessons in Mainstreaming Equal Opportunities* (Edinburgh: Scottish Executive Social Research, 2003), available at *www.institute-of-governance.org/index.html* (last accessed October 15, 2003).

[159] See Final Report of Activities of the Group of Specialists on Mainstreaming, *Gender Mainstreaming: Conceptual Framework, Methodology and Presentation of Good Practices*, EG-S-MS (98), (Strasbourg: Council of Europe, May 1998); F. Mackay and K. Bilton, *Learning From Experience: Lessons in Mainstreaming Equal Opportunities* (Edinburgh: Scottish Executive Social Research, 2003).

[160] S. Nott, "Accentuating the Positive: Alternative Strategies for Promoting Gender Equality" in F. Beveridge, S. Nott, and K. Stephen (eds.) *Making Women Count: Integrating Gender into Law and Policy-making* (Aldershot: Ashgate, 2000). See also T. Donaghy, "Mainstreaming: Northern Ireland's Participative-Democratic Approach", 32 Policy and Politics (2004) 49.

[161] Shaw, "Mainstreaming Equality and Diversity", 264.

[162] See J. Shaw, *Mainstreaming Equality in European Union Law and Policy-Making* (Brussels: European Network Against Racism, 2004). Shaw suggests that Article III-118 of the Constitutional Treaty could open the door to the development of a comprehensive mainstreaming programme, especially if read with the equality provisions of the Charter of Fundamental Rights and other provisions of the Constitutional Treaty. see also M. Bell, "Equality and European Union Constitution", 33 I.L.J. (2004) 242–260.

[163] For example, criticism has been expressed that gender equality considerations have been noticeably absent from the development of the European Employment Strategy. See J. Rubery, "Gender Mainstreaming and Gender Equality in the EU: The Impact of the EU Employment Strategy", 33 *Industrial Relations Journal* (2002) 500; J. Rubery, *et al*, "Gender Equality Still on the European Agenda—But For How Long?", 34 Industrial Relations Journal (2003) 477–97; J. Rubery, *et al*, "The Ups and Downs of European Gender Equality Policy", 35 Industrial Relations Journal (2004) 603.

suggests that many mainstreaming initiatives across Europe have been under-resourced, an emphasis on procedure and "tick-boxing" at the expense of outcomes has been prevalent, and sustaining attention and support for mainstreaming has proved difficult.[164] This reflects a recurring experience in discrimination law: pious equality initiatives have little or no real impact without strong enforcement provisions and a clear set of legal requirements that compel action.[165]

In the UK public sector, mainstreaming initiatives introduced in the mid 1990s aimed to ensure that the needs of disadvantaged groups were factored in to public authority decision-making, resource allocation and employment strategies.[166] Mainstreaming has been used in Britain since the early 1990s to encourage the implementation of transformative equality strategies in the public sector.[167] However, the effectiveness of mainstreaming mechanisms has proved mixed: positive developments in Scotland and Wales have not always been paralleled in England.[168] Sue Nott has argued that the lack of any clear role for the new CEHR in promoting effective mainstreaming represents a serious wasted opportunity.[169] Despite its considerable promise, mainstreaming has only really taken root in Wales and Scotland, where fertile political soil exists for it to put down roots: in the perhaps more hostile political climate of England, results have been less good.[170]

This has prompted the introduction of a series of legally binding positive duties upon public authorities since 1998. Positive duties are designed to provide a firm statutory backbone to mainstreaming initiatives, and their basic objectives are threefold: to make public authorities give due consideration as to how their policies and practices might impact upon the aim of achieving greater equality of opportunity across all of their field of activity; to establish the promotion of equality of opportunity as a core objective for the public sector; and to ensure that disadvantaged groups are consulted and their views incorporated in the decision-making process.[171] In discharging this duty, public authorities have to assess the impact that their employment practices,

164 ibid.

165 See C. McCrudden, "Equality" in C.J. Harvey (ed.), *Human Rights, Equality and Democratic Renewal in Northern Ireland* (Oxford: Hart, 2001) for a comprehensive discussion of these limitations in the Northern Irish context.

166 See C. O'Cinneide, *Taking Equal Opportunities Seriously: The Extension of Positive Duties to Promote Equality*, Part II. For the use of (often ineffective) mainstreaming in Northern Ireland, see C. McCrudden, "Equality" in C. Harvey (ed.), *Human Rights, Equality and Democratic Renewal In Northern Ireland*, (Oxford: Hart, 2001).

167 See M. Pollack and E. Hafner-Burton, "Mainstreaming Gender in the European Union" (2000) 7 J. of European Public Policy 3, 432–457; T. Rees, *Mainstreaming Equality in the European Union* (1998); S. Nott, "Mainstreaming Equal Opportunities: Succeeding Where All Else Has Failed?" in A. Morris and T. O'Donnell (eds.) *Feminist Perspectives on Employment Law* (1999) 203.

168 See S. Nott, "Securing Mainstreaming in a Hostile Political Environment" [2005] 8 International J. of Discrimination and the Law 1 121.

169 See S. Nott, "Securing Mainstreaming in a Hostile Political Environment".

170 ibid.

171 The Hepple Report, 1990: para.3.9, p.60: see also C. McCrudden, "Equality" in C. Harvey (ed.), *Human Rights, Equality and Democratic Renewal In Northern Ireland*, (Oxford: Hart, 2001).

delivery of public services and policies in general are having upon the goal of promoting equality of opportunity. If they identify the existence of a negative impact in some area of their activities, or consider that they are taking inadequate steps in the performance of their functions to break down structural forms of discrimination, then appropriate steps should be taken to remedy this failure. Consultation with affected groups should also form a central part of this assessment process.[172]

The single most extensive positive duty imposed in the UK is that provided for by s.75 of the Northern Ireland Act 1998, which imposes a duty on specified public authorities to have "due regard to the need to promote equality of opportunity" across all the equality grounds, including disability, age, sexual orientation and also political belief, in carrying out their public functions.[173] A wide range of Northern Irish public authorities are subject to the legislation, with some important exceptions.[174] The accompanying specific steps which authorities subject to the duty are required to implement are set out in Sch.9 of the Act, which requires these authorities to prepare an "Equality Scheme", setting out the equality impact assessments (EQIAs), monitoring, consultation, training and publicity arrangements that the authority intends to take to implement the duty. The enforcement mechanism provided for by the s.75 duty requires all equality schemes to be submitted for approval to the Northern Ireland Equality Commission. If dissatisfied with a scheme, the Commission can refer the authority in question to the Secretary of State for Northern Ireland, who can impose an alternative scheme if necessary. The Commission can also investigate the extent of compliance with the duty or with a specific scheme, as well as investigate complaints about non-compliance from individuals.

General equality duties have also been imposed on many of the new UK devolved and regional authorities. Section 120 of the Government of Wales Act 1998 imposes a single general duty on the Assembly to ensure that its business and functions are conducted with due regard to the principle of equality of opportunity for all people.[175] Section 33 of the Greater London Authority Act 1999 imposes a similar set of duties upon the Greater London Authority (GLA) to make appropriate arrangements with regard to the principle that there should be equality of opportunity for all. The Scottish Parliament in contrast is not subjected to an equality duty, but under The Scotland Act 1998, Sch.5, Pt II, L.2 is given the power itself to impose duties on any office-holder in the

[172] The Hepple Report, 1990: para.3.11, at p.60; O'Cinneide, *Taking Equal Opportunities Seriously: The Extension of Positive Duties to Promote Equality* (London: Equality and Diversity Forum/ Equal Opportunities Commission, 2003), Pt III.

[173] See C. McCrudden, "The Equal Opportunity Duty in the Northern Ireland Act 1998: An Analysis", in *Equal Rights and Human Rights—Their Role in Peace Building* 11–23 (Belfast: Committee on the Administration of Justice, 1999).

[174] R. D. Osborne, "Progressing the Equality Agenda in Northern Ireland" (2003) 32 J. of Social Policy 2 339–360, 348.

[175] P. Chaney and R. Fevre, *An Absolute Duty: Equal Opportunities and the National Assembly for Wales* (Cardiff: Equal Opportunities Commission, 2002).

Scottish Administration or any Scottish public authority subject to the control of the Scottish Parliament to "make arrangements to ensure that their functions are carried out with due regard to the need to meet the equal opportunity requirements". This power has been used to impose equality duties on relevant local authorities in relation to housing and other local government functions.[176]

These Welsh, GLA and Scottish duties all lack specific monitoring and publication requirements, and also lack strong enforcement arrangements: judicial review and auditing mechanisms remain the nominal enforcement tools, and no formal role is given to the equality commissions. Comprehensive positive duties comparable to the Northern Irish duty have only been imposed so far across Britain as a whole in respect of race, gender and disability.[177] In the wake of the Macpherson Report, and following political pressure from the CRE and ethnic minority organisations, a much stronger positive race equality duty was imposed on listed public authorities in the Race Relations (Amendment) Act 2000. This considerably extended the largely ineffective duty originally imposed upon local authorities by s.71 of the RRA 76 to promote equality of opportunity.[178] The 2000 Act imposes a general positive duty on an extensive list of specific public authorities listed in Sch.1A of the Act to pay "due regard" to a) the need to eliminate racial discrimination and the complementary positive obligations to b) promote equality of opportunity and c) good relations between people of different ethnic groups.

The general duty is supplemented by specific duties imposed by the Home Secretary on particular categories of listed public authorities, including obligations to prepare "race equality schemes", to monitor on ethnic lines the composition of the staff and the ethnic make-up of the pool of applicants for posts, promotion and training, and, in the case of particular education authorities, to monitor patterns of educational attainment and involvement in disciplinary processes. The primary enforcement responsibility for these specific duties is conferred upon the Commission for Racial Equality (CRE). The DDA 2005 introduces a similar duty in respect of disability equality, which came into force in October 2006, and a gender duty structured along the same lines has been introduced in the Equality Act 2006, which came into force in April 2007.[179]

[176] O'Cinneide, *Taking Equal Opportunities* Seriously, Pt V, pp.58–59.

[177] The race duty had its origins in the limited duty imposed by s.71 of the Race Relations Act 1976 on local authorities to make "appropriate arrangements" to eliminate unlawful discrimination and to promote equality of opportunity and good relations between persons of different racial groups. However, in the absence of any real enforcement mechanism or specific monitoring and reporting requirements, the duty was very limited in impact, thus constituting a cautionary tale for all positive duties: see O'Cinneide, *Taking Equal Opportunities Seriously*, Pt IV.

[178] See C. McCrudden, "Equality and Non-Discrimination", paras 11.189–11.191, pp.663–4.

[179] The new Commission for Equalities and Human Rights can investigate whether public authorities are complying with all the positive equality duties (including the general duties), and to issue a compliance notice requiring the public authority to take steps to implement any of the duties (including the general duty) if necessary. If a compliance notice is in its turn not complied with, the Commission can seek an enforcement order from a court.

To ensure that the duties are not ignored or sidelined, the relevant equality commissions (through special investigatory and enforcement powers), audit bodies (such as the Audit Commission, the inspectorates and other regulatory agencies) and the courts (via the uncertain and expensive route of judicial review) are given roles in enforcing compliance. In addition, specific duties are usually imposed in tandem with the general duty, generally via the introduction of statutory instruments by the relevant Secretary of State.

These specific duties are supposed to ensure that public authorities adequately formulate and publicise their methods of complying with the duty, and carry out the necessary monitoring, consultation and data collection that is required to meaningfully assess the impact of their policies and practices. What this mechanism is not intended to do is to prescribe fixed and definite types of positive action, or a set of socio-economic entitlements, or the delivery of particular services: instead, the duties are supposed to "steer" how other duties and functions are performed and public powers are exercised.

The positive duties are nevertheless an ambitious attempt to make equality issues a core concern for public authorities, and through this to encourage the transformation of existing practices.[180]

The duties are however limited in certain important respects. The duties are supposed to "steer" how other duties and functions are performed: equality concerns are to be given their due proportionate weight in decision-making.[181] However, this by itself gives little guidance as to how important promoting equality of opportunity should be, or when equality considerations can be overridden by other policy considerations, or what constitutes promoting equality of opportunity in the first place.[182] Once again, the lack of underlying agreement on what equality principles should govern public policy generates an inevitable lack of clarity: positive duties may encourage an analysis of what steps should be taken to promote equality, but do not specify what vision of equality should be applied.

Adherence to the duties could also just take the form of "process compliance", where authorities treat the duty as merely involving complying with a set of bureaucratic "tick-box" requirements. Verloo has suggested that

180 Some of the tools of "new public management", such as auditing mechanisms, monitoring requirements, and a steering duty, are combined together with neo-republican and democratic-participative aspirations within the positive duty mechanism. See O'Cinneide, "Positive Duties and Gender Equality". The potential impact of these duties has lead to calls for their scope to be extended beyond the equality context to the full range of human rights. See G. McKeever and F. Ni Aoláin, "Thinking Globally, Acting Locally: Enforcing Socio-Economic Rights in Northern Ireland" [2004] E.H.R.L.R. 158. For a more sceptical perspective, see C. McCrudden, "Mainstreaming Human Rights", in C. Harvey (ed.) *Human Rights in the Community: Rights as Agents for Change* (2005).

181 Fredman, *Discrimination Law*, 180.

182 In an important judgment in *R(Elias) v Secretary of State for Defence* [2005] I.R.L.R. 788, Elias J. held that a failure to consider whether a particular policy raised issues relating to racial equality, or to assess whether any adverse impact was possible, or to consider what steps might be necessary to eliminate any negative impact, would breach the duty. This gives some "teeth" to the duty, but does not clarify how an authority is to balance competing considerations.

mainstreaming has to "resonate" with the existing assumptions, rhetoric and practices within which public authorities work.[183] This could equally also apply to positive duties. There is therefore a danger that the duties may become no more than a technocratic tool in policymaking, which can be readily co-opted to maintain existing practices.[184]

The following passage makes clear some of the ways in which the development of a "proactive model" and the positive duty to promote equality has been hampered by imprecise goals and legal drafting that has creating a insufficiently strong legal requirement to promote equality. Moreover, as the discussion illustrates, rather than just being a remedial response, enforceable equality duties raise fundamental questions about the meaning of equality and the goals of discrimination law.

Sandra Fredman and Sarah Spencer
"Beyond Discrimination: It's Time for Enforceable Duties on Public Bodies to Promote Equality Outcomes" [2006] E.H.R.L.R. 598

600: "There are thus many advantages to the proactive model. However, the United Kingdom has found that formulating a statutory duty to promote equality has raised its own challenges. Requiring public bodies to be proactive in delivering equality goals has t take account of their other statutory responsibilities and competing demands for resources, leaving the authority room to set its own agenda. Priorities in delivering equality can, moreover, only be set when current inequality in employment and across service areas have been identified—requiring a strong evidence base, consultation and transparency.

A proactive duty requires guidance to the authority on the range of equality goals it is expected to reach and means to achieve them: the action needed will differ on race, disability or sexual orientation, for instance, in differing circumstances. Furthermore, in the absence of an individual complainant, there is a need to find appropriate monitoring and compliance mechanisms to ensure that the required changes take place.

Weak Duty

The statutory duty instituted in Northern Ireland and in Britain respond to these challenges in specific ways. With hindsight, the drafting was not optimal if the intention was that authorities should review the evidence, idenfity barriers to equality and take appropriate action. Most significantly, the authority is only required by law to "pay due regard" to the need to promote equality; that is, to give proper consideration to the need to act. "Due regard" leaves the authority to decide, having taken that need into account along with its other priorities, whether to take any action at all.

[183] M. Verloo, "Another Velvet Revolution? Gender Mainstreaming and the Politics of Implementation", *IWM Working Paper*, no.5/2001 (2001), 9–10; available at: *http://www.iwm.at/publ-wp/wp-01–05.pdf* (last accessed October 5, 2005).

[184] See also N. Lacey, "Legislation Against Sex Discrimination: Questions from a Feminist Perspective" (1987) 14 J. Law and Society 411–21.

Narrow Equality Goal

Secondly, while moving beyond the elimination of unlawful discrimination, the law refers to the goal as "to promote equality of opportunity", without further definition. This is both vague and limited. In principle, equality of opportunity is a broader concept than the formal version of equality, equal treatment found in the EU equality directives, which requires only that similarly situated people be treated equally. Recognising that the same treatment might perpetuate disadvantage by failing to address existing discrimination and disadvantage, equal opportunity aims to equalise the starting point. But the legislation fails to make clear what equal opportunities would entail and to what extent this principle permits different treatment.

Equal opportunities can have a range of meanings. At its narrowest it requires the removal of a barriers at the demand side. This may open the doors to excluded groups, but does not mean that they have the resources to progress through the open doors. [. . .] A broader understanding of equal opportunities would require that resources be provided to ake sure that members of diadvantaged groups can make use of new opportunities (authors note, e.g training, child care or transport may be needed).

Nor does the concept of equal opportunities easily cover sine if what we might call the *qualitative* measures of inequality, including denial of dignity and self-respect—perhaps the most important dimensions of equality for elderly people or psychiatric patients in care for instance, or for gay pupils facing bullying at school. Nor does it cover the equal right to participate, whether in the workforce or society more generally."

The authors go on to identify that monitoring outcomes which has been such a key focus of the public equality duty, and which remains an important policy lever, can also have some disadvantages.

"The importance of monitoring results means that there can in practice be a focus on assessing equality outcomes for groups, rather than measuring opportunities. However, while 'equality of outcomes' can be a meaningful goal for disadvantaged groups in some contexts, (for example, average attainment of ethnic minorities or immigrant children at school, or proportionate representation of women in the boardroom), it can mask inequality within groups (the over-representation of Chinese pupils among high achievers masking the underachievement of another minority for instance). A focus on outcomes also reinforces the emphasis on quantitative measures to the exclusion of the qualitative dimensions of equality to which we have referred; and finally is not applicable as a measurement for individuals, who have differing priorities: an individual who has a genuine opportunity to participate may nevertheless choose not to take it."

Fredman and Spencer also go on to identify a third limitation on existing duties which they argue arises from the relationship between the two tiers of duties, i.e. between the general duty and the specific duty to promote equality. The general duty is: (a) only enforceable through judicial review which is costly and therefore out of the range of action of most individuals and organisations; and (b) weakly framed as requiring "to have due regard" to the need to promote equality. This pushes the burden of enforcement back on individuals and introduces the problems of the individual discrimination law model discussed above. They also criticise the specific duty which they argue merely requires the framing of a race equality duty which is a requirement to make arrangements rather than an active duty to carry out the arrangements.

Moreover, the requirement of larger employers to monitor under-representation in employment, use of services and service outcomes is, the authors argue, at risk of becoming a goal in itself rather than fulfilling the function of triggering reform and an appropriate response.

Fredman and Spencer also argue that the introduction of the race equality duty has not achieved its promise or potential. They identify the weaknesses discussed above as part of the reason for this under-performance of the postive duties, and they argue that the positive duty has too often been focused on procedures and paperwork rather than genuine institutional change. They cite a recent assessment of this policy lever by the Women and Equality Unit in their report "Advancing Equality for Men and Women: Government proposals to introduce a public sector duty to promote gender equality" which concluded that the race duty is "overly bureaucratic, process-driven and resource intensive"[185] However, Fredman and Spencer conclude that these difficulties with the race equality duty can be overcome, and cite the strengthened versions of the positive duty in the areas of disability and gender as an example of how this can be achieved. For example, the disability duty is more specific in the equality goals that it sets itself: it requires public authorities to have due regard to the need to eliminate harassment, promote positive attitudes towards disabled people and to encourage participation by disabled people in public life.

The duties are therefore far from being an ideal mechanism for ensuring the adoption of anti-subordination approaches on the part of public authorities. However, their existence enables the equality commissions to investigate the failure of public authorities to take positive steps to eliminate discrimination and promote equality of opportunity.[186] In addition, the duties have considerable symbolic and educative potential, and can serve as useful "pressure points" to demand greater focus upon equality issues from public authorities: authorities can be called to account for how they have complied with the duty, and pressed to demonstrate progress.

The existence of the duty can also enable public authorities to take proactive measures designed to promote equality of opportunity. In the past, the absence of a specific duty to promote equality of opportunity has meant that public authorities have often lacked a clear statutory authority for

[185] Sandra Fredman and Sarah Spencer: "Beyond Discrimination: It's Time for Enforceable Duties on Public Bodies to Promote Equality Outcome [2006] E.H.R.L.R. 598, at p.602.

[186] The important decision of the Northern Ireland High Court in *The Matter of an Application by Peter Neill for Judicial Review* [2005] N.I.Q.B. 66 confirmed that the Equality Commission for Northern Ireland (ECNI) had the power under its investigatory function conferred by the s.75 duty to find that the positive equality duty had not been sufficiently complied with by the Northern Ireland Office in considering the equality impact of its decision to extend the legislation permitting the issuing of ASBO orders to Northern Ireland.

implementing equality policies.[187] The introduction of positive duties now partially overcomes this problem. The duties will also have an impact upon how authorities perform *other* statutory duties: they can justify the placing of considerable weight on equality considerations in deciding how to perform other duties and functions. Moreover, as argued in the Fredman and Spencer passage above, there is a need to reconsider the meaning of equality of opportunity to ensure that substantive issues of dignity (e.g. the treatment of the old) and participation (e.g. involvement in the workforce) are included within the discussion of the positive duty to promote equality. Fredman and Spencer also propose ways of strengthening the positive duty which are considered below.

A. *Strengthening the Positive Duties*

Two of the key ways in which the positive duties can be strengthened is (a) to be more clear about the equality goals that they are there to enhance; and once this is achieved this enables (b) a shift from the present focus on "due regard" and process to more action based/goal orientated duties.

In relation to (a) the equality goals, many of the arguments in the previous chapter outline the need to deepen our understanding of the goals of discrimination law. Therefore, a view of equality as the treatment of "like with like" needs to be supplemented by a focus on substantive equality that includes a focus on remedying social exclusion and also redressing harms to dignity such as violence, harassment and degrading treatment. Moreover, a more sophisticated understanding of equality of opportunity in this context requires a recognition that in some cases there is a justification of differential treatment and the accommodation of difference, i.e. where there is a pressing need for the accommodation of a difference that is a crucial part of an individual's positive identity and self-respect. This shift in definition will also facilitate the increased participation of groups that have been discriminated against in the decisions that affect their lives: this active participation can serve the important goals of ensuring that policy is accurately responsive to the needs of individuals and it will also ensure that positive duties are not seen to be patronising and negating the autonomy of the individual whom they are designed to benefit. In this way, one of the political goals of the positive duty is to facilitate participation of marginalised group in mainstream institutions.

187 See P. E. Morris, "Legal Regulation of Contract Compliance: An Anglo-American Comparison" (1991) 19 Anglo-American L.R. 87–144, especially at 93–103. The s.71 duty on local authorities to promote race equality, while limited in impact, did give local authorities some legal basis for funding race equality councils and some scope for the insertion of race equality clauses into procurement contracts: *ibid.* 93–121. However, the extent and enabling impact of this remained very uncertain: see *Wheeler v Leicester CC* [1985] 1 A.C. 1054 and *R v Lewisham LBC, ex p. Shell (UK) Ltd* [1988] 1 All E.R. 938.

Fredman and Spencer have emphasied many of the points discussed above. They give special emphasis to (b), the need to shift positive duties from a passive to a more active duty. They suggest that this tranformation can be achieved by following the model of other jurisdictions such as South Africa which require a public authority to take positive steps towards the actual realisation of the duty. Fredman and Spencer argue:

"Adapting this to the equality field, we propose the following duty for public bodies in Europe:

> 'A public authority shall, in carrying out its functions, take such steps as are necessary and proportionate to eliminate discrimination and to achieve the progressive realisation of equality (as defined).'

This comprises of the following elements:

- It is *action-based*. It requires the public body to take steps to eliminate discrimination and achieve equality, rather than just paying due regard to the need to do so.
- It is *goal-orientated*. Instead of a vague notion of equality of opportunity, it specifies the equality goals to which the body is directing its actions: to eliminate unlawful discrimination and to achieve equality (defined as redressing disadvantage, equal respect, accommodation and affirmation and equal participation).
- It is *progressive*: the public body does not need to achieve the goals immediately, but it must take immediate action to make progress towards the goals. It is dynamic, requiring ongoing action.
- It requires action from the authority which is *necessary* and *proportionate*. This means that the authority can set its own priorities, within available resources and in the context of competing aims. Its decisions on priorities must be measured against the standard of proportionality and necessity: a clear and strict standard. The body need not do everything at once, but it must base its priorities on evidence and consultation. Where steps to achieve equality are not taken, or are taken too slowly, the body must be able to show that this was because it was pursuing other legitimate aims; and that those aims could not be achieved in an alternative way which was compatible with furthering the equality agenda. This is a well-known standard, found in anti-discrimination law, human rights law, and the law of judicial review, and provides an appropriate balance between autonomy and obligation."

By formulating the general duty in these terms Fredman and Spencer seek to balance two competing principles: autonomy for public authorities to set their own priorities; and the need for the harmonisation of standards to ensure equality for minorities and protected groups such as women. Moreover, the principle of proportionality ensures that the specific needs of smaller (and perhaps poorer) public authorities are taken into account when setting a standard.

Fredman and Spencer conclude that these changes are a realistic and feasible way of ensuring that the public duty to promote equality becomes a more effective policy response. They state:

"The model we have proposed requires action, but leaves the authority with autonomy in deciding what the necessary steps should be. As the requirement is proportional, it can be imposed on the smallest public body as well as those employing thousands of staff. It keeps the procedural requirements to the minimum necessary to ensure a level of consistency in approach across authorities, that they consult before acting, and that there is transparency on both the evidence uncovered and the action taken. The requirements are clear, facilitating enforcement action should encouragement and guidance fail. Finally, in providing a multi-dimensional definition of equality goals, it enables the authority to identify the goal that is most appropriate in each circumstance."

However, the introduction of a comprehensive scheme of positive duties will not be enough in itself to establish an adequate equality and anti-discrimination framework for the British public sector. Positive duties can orient how public authorities exercise their powers and functions within the existing statutory framework, but cannot overcome or modify statutory restrictions on what public authorities can do, or resolve debates about core issues of principle. Finally, their effect is confined to the public sector: the shrinking sphere of public authority activity means that the impact of the duties is confined to this narrowing sphere.[188]

The duties are increasingly becoming the major vehicle for positive action initiatives within the UK public sector. However, the constraints imposed by discrimination law remain: action to remedy identified disadvantages or to promote equality of opportunity cannot fall foul of the prohibition on preferential treatment. This means that the application of the duties can often result in serious gaps being identified in how resources are allocated to disadvantaged groups or in employment rates, but public authorities cannot go further than identifying the problem, setting targets to attempt to remedy it, and utilising outreach, inclusionary and promotional strategies to close the gaps in question. Sometimes this may be sufficient, if this approach is applied with enthusiasm and precision: but sometimes it will not result in a solution. There is therefore a need to consider other policy levers that can enable the public sector to pursue equality goals and mainstreaming, considered in the section below.

VII. Positive Action and the Private Sector

In the private sector, positive action approaches have generally taken the form of diversity management techniques, whereby internal support and advice is given to employees from under-represented groups, outreach programmes aim to encourage a wider diversity of staff, and company policies and prac-

[188] However, the duties apply to all functions of public authorities, including those that they choose to contract out: the responsibility for complying with the duty requirements remains with the authority, which means that the duties may have some impact even in areas marked by extensive contracting-out of service delivery and other functions. See O'Cinneide, *Taking Equal Opportunities Seriously*, Pt V. See also CRE, *Statutory Code of Practice on the Duty to Promote Race Equality* (2002).

tices are overhauled to reduce any discriminatory impact.[189] Questions have been raised about the effectiveness of diversity management, its actual impact and the level of commitment given to implementing these strategies: there is clearly a wide range of divergence across the private sector as to the extent to which diversity management is proving successful,[190] but in certain areas there have been notable shifts in the level of ethnic minority and female under-representation. Concerns have also been expressed that when such strategies are implemented with real enthusiasm, the limits on positive action imposed by the current legislative framework artificially constraints what can be done in practice:[191] see above.

The potential of positive duties is not confined to the public sector.[192] They can also be applied to the private sector, in the form of legislative duties requiring proactive action on the part of private employers with a sufficiently sizeable workforce to eliminate discrimination. This approach has been adopted with some success in Canada.[193] In Northern Ireland, the Fair Employment Act 1989 (FEA) as extended and modified by the Fair Employment and Treatment (Northern Ireland) Order 1998 (FETO) imposed a positive duty on employers to take measures to ensure fair proportions of Catholics and Protestants in their workforce.[194] These duties have had considerable and well-documented success, due partially to the strength of the accompanying enforcement mechanisms.[195] The Hepple Report recommended that positive duties be imposed upon British employers to take measures to promote equality of opportunity in their employment practices.[196]

[189] See R. Kandola and J. Fullerton, *Diversity in Action: Managing the Mosaic* (Institute of Personnel and Development, 1998).

[190] See the Hepple Report, para.1.39, p.16, citing data from the ESRC Data Archive at the University of Essex.

[191] See L. Barmes with S. Ashtiany, *Diversity in the City: Initiatives in Investment Banks in the UK* (London: Nabarro Nathanson, 2003); L. Barmes and S. Ashtiany, "The Diversity Approach to Achieving Equality: Potential and Pitfalls" (2003) 32 Industrial L.J. 3.

[192] See the *Hepple Report*, para.3.3, pp.56–57.

[193] See H.C. Jain, P.J. Sloane and F.M. Horwitz, *Employment Equity and Affirmative Action: An International Comparison* (London: M.E. Sharpe, 2003), 22–27.

[194] See C. McCrudden, "The Evolution of the Fair Employment (Northern Ireland) Act 1989 in Parliament" in R.J. Cormack and R.D. Osborne (eds.), *Discrimination and Public Policy in Northern Ireland* (Oxford, OUP, 1991).

[195] See C. McCrudden, R. Ford and A. Heath, "Legal Regulation of Affirmative Action in Northern Ireland An Empirical Assessment" (2004) 24 O.J.L.S. 3, 363–415. For a contrasting examination of the lack of success of Dutch attempts to place duties upon private bodies, without introducing an effective enforcement mechanism, see F.J. Glastra and others, "Between Public Controversy and Market Initiative: The Politics of Employment Equity and Diversity in the Netherlands", in C Agocs (ed.), *Workplace Equality: International Perspectives on Legislation, Policy and Practice* (London, Kluwer, 2003), Ch.8.

[196] The Hepple Report suggested that employers should be required to undertake a three-year periodic review of employment procedures, and, in the event of the discovery of significant under-representation of particular groups, obligated to take reasonable remedial action by means of an employment equity plan. See the Hepple Report, para 3.37. Employers with 10 or more employees would also be required to carry out a similar three-yearly periodic pay audit and take appropriate action via a pay equity scheme where discrepancies were identified. See paras 3.41–3.50.

Another possible reform could involve the introduction of a cross-ground set of "reasonable accommodation" requirements into British discrimination law. Disability discrimination legislation imposes an obligation to take special measures to facilitate the needs of disabled persons in accessing services and in employment: this legislative obligation to take positive measures is capable of being transplanted to other equality grounds. Canadian anti-discrimination legislation, for example, extends the requirement to make "reasonable accommodation" across all the recognised equality grounds, meaning that employers and service providers have to accommodate reasonable requests for part-time work, time-off related to religious holidays and other special provisions related to the needs of disadvantaged groups.[197]

The "reasonable accommodation" requirement is essential in the disability context, and has worked well when applied in Canada across all the other equality grounds: there appears to be no reason why a similar approach could not be adopted in the UK. The imposition of such a statutory requirement would have certain advantages the "reasonableness" requirement retains an element of flexibility in its application, the onus is on the employer or service provider to accommodate difference, and the need for appropriate special provision is built into the legislative framework. Difficulties arise with the width often given to the defence of justification, whereby a failure to make accommodation can be justified on the grounds of unreasonable cost: experience from the disability context shows that considerable latitude is often given to employers' perceptions of what is reasonable and what is not.

In addition, reasonable accommodation involves the making of exceptions to the norm to accommodate special needs, often only required in response to active requests: employers and service providers are not required to scrutinise their policies and practices in the absence of requests,[198] nor are they obliged to assess their "normal" practices. In the context of disability rights, there is considerable debate as to whether reasonable accommodation is bets classed as a form of positive action or as a remedy for discrimination: the latter view is probably more valid in the disability context (see the chapter on disability discrimination), and possibly across other equality grounds as well. However, imposing reasonable accommodation requirements could serve as an effective mechanism to encourage the greater use of positive action approaches.

Contract compliance mechanisms, whereby public authorities require contractors to introduce rigorous equal opportunity policies, could also be very effective tools to require private contractors seeking public tenders to adopt

[197] For the Canadian approach, see *British Columbia (Public Service Employee Relations Comm) v B.C.G.E.U.* (1999) 35 C.H.R.R. D/257 and *British Columbia (Superintendent of Motor Vehicles) v British Columbia (Council of Human Rights)* (1999), 36 C.H.R.R. D/129; *Central Okanagan School Dist. No.23 v Renaud* (1992), 16 C.H.R.R. D/425 (S.C.C.).

[198] Thus under the Canadian legislation, if an employee does not communicate a need for reasonable accommodation, the employer may be absolved of its legal duty to accommodate: see *Williams v Elty Publications Ltd,* (1992), 20 C.H.R.R. D/52 (BCCHR).

positive action initiatives and these are discussed in the chapter on collective remedies.[199]

VIII. The Conceptual and Political Debate—Justifying Positive Action

In general, UK policy remains committed to avoiding preferential treatment strategies, on the alleged basis that they damage merit requirements and can result in "reverse discrimination". However, the exceptions introduced in Northern Ireland, and in Britain in respect of parliamentary candidates, indicate a greater recent willingness to utilise such approaches, and in particular where broad political support for the necessity of such measures exists. In both circumstances, the failure to break down systemic patterns of disadvantage over a considerable period of time was cited as the justification for such "exceptional" measures.

However, the principal thrust of positive action strategies in the UK remains the use of positive duties to drive forward change in the public sector, and the encouragement of diversity strategies in the private sector. Whether this strategy will generate long-term results and how it will impact upon the private sector remains unclear: the grey area between the use of such duties and preferential treatment approaches also remains unclear. The justification for the use of such strategies remains the need to ensure social inclusion of disadvantaged groups, to encourage greater participation and "community cohesion", and to remedy patterns of indirect and institutional discrimination.[200] Historical disadvantage is not cited as a justification, principally due to the reality that ethnic minorities are in the main recent arrivals in the UK, and questions of historical injustice and to whom any remedial action is owed remain controversial and unsettled. Often, the emphasis on remedying current disadvantage means that positive action initiatives on the grounds of disability and race in particular are often linked to new anti-poverty approaches, and attempts are being made to encourage the combination of such strategies within common frameworks. However, the recognition does exist that while such approaches may parallel and complement each other, a specific focus on the equality grounds remains necessary.

What selection methods are adopted in determining positive action strategies has often depended upon a perception of what is politically possible. A political fear that the use of preferential treatment will prove unpopular has resulted in its comparative under-utilisation: the positive duties may be seen as an attempt to achieve some of the benefits of preferential strategies via an indirect route. Northern Ireland is seen as a special case, and the use of far-

199 See C. McCrudden, "Using Public Procurement to Achieve Social Outcomes" (2004) 28 Natural Resources Forum 4 257–267.

200 See H. Collins, (2004) 66 M.L.R. 16.

reaching affirmative action measures do not attract significant political hostility or even comment in Britain: hence the comparative ease with which Westminster governments have been prepared to introduce quite stringent requirements upon both the public and private sectors there. The considerably more advanced nature of race-based positive action strategies is also due to political considerations: race issues have a high political profile in the UK, while other equality issues, in particular those related to gender, have a much lower profile.

Another pressing political consideration is the desire to avoid the imposition of "excessive regulation" upon the private sector, with Northern Ireland again being the significant exception. This desire has resulted in the side-lining of the Hepple Report's recommendation that positive duties be applied to the private sector, and has resulted in little political or legal pressure for private sector bodies to adopt positive action. It is worth noting that the use of diversity management strategies—which are in themselves often problematic and under-resourced—in the private sector has been often driven by US businesses transplanting such strategies from their home environment. The increased use of contract compliance schemes, now made easier to introduce by virtue of the positive duties, has been proposed as a potential method for encouraging greater use of positive action in the private sector.[201] It remains to be seen whether proves to be a realistic prospect.

IX. Conclusion

Rees has called for the use in equality law and policy of what she describes as a combination of "tinkering", "tailoring" and "transforming" approaches: the use of equal treatment laws to prohibit unjust forms of unequal treatment, the introduction of targeted measures to help disadvantaged groups overcome obstacles to full equality of participation, and the implementation of "mainstreaming" strategies to identify how existing systems and structures create patterns of structural discrimination and "altering or redesigning them as appropriate".[202] At present, the lack of clarity as to the permissible scope of positive action, and the lack of meaningful implementation of mainstreaming initiatives all mean that the "tailoring" and "transforming" approaches remain chronically underdeveloped at both national and EU level.

Proponents of prioritarian or substantive approaches to equality argue that there is a pressing need for greater scope to be given to positive action measures, greater clarity in legislation and the case-law, and reinforcement of mainstreaming initiatives by the use of positive duty and reasonable accom-

[201] Hepple Report, paras 3.74–3.77, pp.84–85. See also UK Cabinet Office Strategy Unit, *Ethnic Minorities and the Labour Market*, (London: Cabinet Office, 2003).

[202] T. Rees, "The Politics of 'Mainstreaming' Gender Equality", in E. Breitenbach and others (eds), *The Changing Politics of Gender Equality in Britain* (Basingstoke: Palgrave, 2002) 45, 46–48.

modation requirements. There has been a gradual shift in both UK and EC law towards this approach in recent years. But both legal systems remain largely wedded to the "anti-classification" approach. Even if this were to change, interesting questions remain. How to measure the extent to which different groups are disadvantaged, and how to determine what positive action measures might be necessary and appropriate to redress this disadvantage? Is there a danger that other forms of disadvantage such as socio-economic status will be overlooked in the focus upon race, gender, disability and the other grounds of disadvantage recognised in the anti-discrimination legislation? Does positive action serve to reinforce divisive group identities and perpetuate inter-group tensions? Does it encourage claims of victim status, engendering a cycle of assertions of group disadvantage that can become self-fulfilling prophecies?

What is clear is that well-designed positive action strategies can be potentially very effective. Recent US positive action initiatives are summed up in the following passage:

Dr Ravinder Singh Dhami, Professor Judith Squires and Professor Tariq Modood, *Developing Positive Action Policies: Learning from the Experiences of Europe and North America*, Research Report No.406
Department for Works and Pensions

p.5: [. . .] there are currently four main types of affirmative action (in the US): that required by **federal contractors**; required by **government agencies; court-ordered and voluntary**. Affirmative action is required in at least 35 states and the District of Columbia. Executive orders or statutes apply to all state agencies, state universities, state contractors and subcontractors. Court-Odered Affirmative Action is ordered by Federal Courts under the Equal Employment Opportunity Act (1972), which is an amendment to Title VII of the Civil Rights Act. This power applies where a firm is found guilty of discriminaiton and is required by the court to adopt affirmative action. Voluntary affirmative action covers voluntary activities by employers. Survey data suggests that many more employers engage in some form of voluntary affirmative action than are required to do so by executive orders or the courts (Section 5.2).

The experiences of the USA suggest firstly that preferential treatment for unqualified individuals does not carry popular support and can therefore be counter-productive but that there is also **legal, popular and corporate support** for affirmative action policies that promote diversity in a non-mechanistic manner. Secondly, that **contract compliance** is the most effective instrument for promoting positive action in employment and particularly well suited to changing key employers' practices with minimum pain and resistance. Thirdly, that successful employment equity programmes need to pay attention to both **demand and supply-side** issues. The importance of securing an adequate supply of suitably qualified and trained individuals means that employment policies need to be attentive to educational equity. Fourthly, that a **continual review** of positive programmes in relation to effectiveness, business efficiency and fairness may be useful for the acceptance and effectiveness of the programmes" (Section 5.3)

These conclusions about the US experience of positive action confirm the potential usefulness of positive action strategies. However, EC and UK law have not always built on the full potential of positive action.

The Discrimination Law Review (DLR) has recently considered whether more use should be made of positive action in UK discrimination law and policy. The Review explicitly identifies the need to tackle "tackle disadvantage" through positive action. Greater use of the positive duty mechanism and more freedom for public and private bodies to make use of 'balancing measures' (the Review's term for positive action) are presented as the key to make the law effective. The DLR is emphatic that discrimination law has a central role in this context: "The law underpins our approach to equality, providing a framework against which everyone can assess whether an approach is the right one. The law is the key to achieving a society in which all people can fulfil their potential, not held back by unnecessary barriers to equality of opportunity".[203]

In relation to positive action, the DLR vision is to create a more flexible "legal space" for private organisations who are "seeking to make progress towards their goals of tackling under-representation and disadvantage to be able to use a wider range of voluntary balancing measures".[204] However, the Review expresses concern about the slow rate of progress towards giving everyone in society an "equal chance of participation". As a result, it suggests that steps should be taken to permit employers, public authorities and other organisations greater scope to take "proportionate" positive action to benefit under-represented groups, provided that such action is based on a "sound analysis of the issues' and does not "inadvertently introduce new and unjustifiable inequality or disadvantage". The specific proposals set out in the consultation paper are as follows:

(a) to consider whether to adopt wider balancing measures to allow employers and others to make more rapid progress towards redressing under-representation (paras 4.44 to 4.47);

(b) to allow all protected groups to benefit from measures to meet particular needs in relation to education, training and welfare or other benefits (para.4.48);

(c) to give the Commission for Equality and Human Rights a role in issuing clear practical guidance and Codes of Practice, but not in approving positive action programmes (paras 4.49 to 4.51);

(d) to continue and/or broaden if necessary the scope of permitted

203 Department for Communities and Local Government, *A Framework for Fairness: Proposals for a Single Equality Bill for Great Britain* (the Discrimination Law Review) (DCLG: London, June 2007), para.2.2, p.60.

204 Department for Communities and Local Government, *A Framework for Fairness: Proposals for a Single Equality Bill for Great Britain* (the Discrimination Law Review) (DCLG: London, June 2007), para.4.47, p.75.

voluntary positive action in the selection of candidates by political parties (paras 4.52 to 4.57).

To give a little more detail on these proposals, the Review suggests that the existing provisions in discrimination law that permit some limited positive action in training, education and ancillary areas appear to be of excessively limited scope and to lack clarity (paras 4.36–4.38). As a result, it proposes that greater scope should be opened up for employers, service providers, public authorities and other organisations to take positive action measures if they wish to help address disadvantage. The Review does not propose to set out in detail in legislation the "balancing measures" that will be able to be taken, but instead it proposes to clarify the "purposes" for which such measures can be taken. In para.4.46 of the Review, it is stated that:

"As a general principle, we propose that balancing measures should be permitted to prevent or compensate for disadvantage or to meet special needs linked to the protected ground. Any balancing measures would always have to be:

- necessary,
- proportionate, and
- time-limited."

Examples given include the provision of free sight-tests and prescriptions for older people, or provision for special health needs of particular ethnic minorities (para.4.47). "Positive discrimination" in the sense of measures such as inflexible quotas, will remain prohibited (para.4.44). The Review considers that it would be an excessive burden to require the CEHR to approve the use of such schemes, but considered that the Commission should play a role in providing guidance (paras 4.49–4.51).

Whilst clear guidance by the CEHR would be useful, the more significant issue is that the DLR has failed to take this opportunity to create the optimal conditions for the appropriate use of positive action in the private sector. What is lacking is an over-arching vision of how behavioural and organisational change will take place. The DLR assumes that once the private sector understands what constitutes permissible positive action, there will automatically be willing compliance. However, even if an organisation is committed to diversity, the DLR proposes no coherent framework within which the organisation can identify its precise "internal problem" as a first step towards designing and adopting balancing measures.

One vision for the private sector would be to mirror the "duty" approach taken in the public sector with its focus on participation, evidence gathering and designing solutions "within the organisation". However, the DLR rejects private sector duties to promote equality (DLR, para.6.13) and the Northern Ireland model of a statutory requirement for some employers to monitor their workforce (DLR, para.6.11). Instead, the DLR suggests that existing reporting requirements under the Companies Act 2006 could be extended to include information about the company's employees and social issues (DLR, para.6.12). This light touch 'equality check tool' provides some evidential basis for employers who are already committed to the goals of non-discrimination and diversity. This system does not, however, contain any incentives for individuals and organisations for whom "equality" and "diversity" are not a priority.

The DLR also could perhaps have strengthened its proposals by supporting periodic reviews of employment practices, which are agreed and conducted in consultation with employees and representative trade unions.[205] The DLR's reluctance to introduce a strongly enforceable private sector duty or follow the Northern Ireland model of reporting and enforcement (DLR, para.6.11) is perhaps understandable because of the larger scale of the private sector in Britain. The precise details of how periodic reviews should be enforced could have been left as an issue for consultation; and a "lighter touch" regulatory scheme may well be more appropriate for the British context. The main point, however, is that the DLR could build on the wide support for "diversity" that it claims exists in the private sector. To this end, the DLR could perhaps have thought more imaginatively and explicitly consulted on developing a framework for employers, employees and trade unions to work together to (i) gather base line evidence of employment practices; and then to act on this information by (ii) jointly drawing up an employment equity plan which could include "balancing measures". This process would have been more likely to result in the optimal use of balancing measures than the option (which the DLR rejects) of giving the CEHR a role in approving positive action plans (see para.4.51). However, once again, it seems if the use of positive action in the UK will be kept tightly reined in.

[205] B. Hepple, M.Coussey, T. Choudhry, 2000, Recommendation 28.

8

HARASSMENT, HATE CRIMES AND HATE SPEECH

I. Introduction

Previous chapters have addressed the core concepts that enable the legal regulation of discrimination. In this chapter we examine discriminatory harassment, hate crimes and hate speech. The law has provided a range of techniques to protect individuals from the harm of harassment. Criminal and civil law prohibitions on assault and battery, as well as the law on defamation and privacy, have fulfilled this function. The recognition of harassment as a form of discrimination has been more recent. The original impetus to regulate harassment using discrimination law came from feminist scholars, such as Catherine Mackinnon, who argued that sexual harassment was a patriarchal practice that caused harm to working women. More recently, harassment has been included within definitions of discrimination in constitutional, EU and statutory discrimination law for a number of grounds (e.g. gender, race, religion, sexual orientation, disability) and in a range of areas (e.g. employment, public services, private goods and services). This chapter also examines the legal regulation of hate crimes and hate speech. Like harassment, the regulation of hate crimes and hate speech is justified as necessary to protect individual autonomy, dignity and personality. Unlike harassment which is now a well established concept within discrimination law, the use of legal regulation to tackle hate crimes and hate speech has been controversial. Part I of this chapter examines the theory and law relating to discriminatory harassment. Part II discusses the increasing use of the criminal law to regulate the problem of "hate crimes" (also discussed in the chapter on race discrimination). Part III considers the controversy about whether there should be legal regulation of hate speech which raises distinct issues because of constitutional protection for freedom of speech.

Although these three topics—harassment, hate crimes and hate speech—are discussed separately, they raise some common themes. All three areas can be justified as examples of legal regulation that perform an "expressive function" and thereby validate the central message of discrimination law.[1] In addition,

[1] For a discussion of the "expressive function" of harassment see Richard Mullender, "Racial Harassment, Sexual Harassment and the Expressive Function of Law, (1998) 61 M.L.R. 2 236.

harassment, hate crimes and hate speech regulation can also be justified in accordance with the liberal harm principle by citing specific mental and psychological harms.[2] These harms can be represented as individual because they are ways on interfering with the well being and autonomy of individuals.[3] Moreover, and significantly, some commentators also argue that there is a collective element because the harm is caused through acts which stigmatise the membership of an individual in social groups from which they derive their personal identity. An additional collective element in the analysis is introduced by those who argue that harassment, hate crimes and hate speech harm members of a group, as well the specific individual who has been the immediate target for the act in any particular instance.[4] Finally, and following on from the analysis of groups, theorists also argue that by harming vulnerable social groups, harassment, hate crimes and hate speech undermine social cohesion and the value of living in a free and equal society for all citizens.[5]

There are also practical reasons why these three issues, overlap and can be usefully discussed within one chapter. Harassment is both recognised as a form of discrimination, and also one way in which hate crimes can be committed; hate speech raises independent issues, and at the same time sexist speech in the workplace can sometimes be regulated as a form of discriminatory harassment.

II. Harassment

Conduct that constitutes harassment is, of course, subject to the normal criminal and civil law. In particular, civil law causes of action such as assault and battery, intentional infliction of distress, harassment, defamation and invasion of privacy may be available in cases where an individual has been the

[2] For the harm of sexual harassment, see for example, Catherine A. MacKinnon and Riva B. Siegel, (eds), Directions in Sexual Harassment Law, New Haven, USA: Yale University Press, 2004, especially Pt II. See also S. Virdee, Racial Violence and Harassment (London: Policy Studies Institute 1995) Ch. 4 which discusses the effects and constraints on the lifestyles of ethnic minorities caused by the fear of racial violence and harassment. See also the discussion of the psychological effects of this type of conduct in Joan C. Weiss "Ethnoviolence: Impact Upon and Response of Victims and the Community", in Robert J. Kelley (ed.), Bias Crime: American Law Enforcement and Legal Responses (Chicago: University of Illinois, 1993).

[3] See the relationship between the value of autonomy and the need to have the psychological well-being to be able to exercise choice see Thomas E. Hill Jr., *Autonomy and Self-Respect*, (Cambridge: Cambridge University Press, 1991) Ch.4.

[4] The arguments concerning the psychological harm to individuals, the harm to the social group and harm to society are very usefully summarised in Fredrick Lawrence, *Punishing Hate: Bias Crimes Under American Law* (Cambridge, MA: Harvard University Press, 1999)

[5] For a principled argument of the way in which acts which target social groups who are marginalised can undermine their right to political equality in a liberal democracy see Andrew Altman, "The Democratic Legitimacy of Bias Crime Laws: Public Reason and the Political Process, (2001) 20(2) Law and Philosophy (C. H. Wellman, special editor) 141–173.

subject of harassment by words or conduct. Harassment and bullying in the workplace are particular problems which have been defined by ACAS in the following terms:

ACAS Advice leaflet—Bullying and harassment at work: guidance for employees (available at *www.acas.org/uk* accessed July 10, 2007)

"What are bullying and harassment?

These terms are used interchangeably by most people, and many definitions include bullying as a form of harassment.

Harassment, in general terms is: unwanted conduct affecting the dignity of men and women in the workplace. It may be related to age, sex, race, disability, religion, nationality or any personal characteristic of the individual, and may be persistent or an isolated incident. The key is that the actions or comments are viewed as demeaning and unacceptable to the recipient.

Bullying may be characterised as: offensive, intimidating, malicious or insulting behaviour, an abuse or misuse of power through means intended to undermine, humiliate, denigrate or injure the recipient.

Bullying or harassment may be by an individual against an individual (perhaps by someone in a position of authority such as a manager or supervisor) or involve groups of people. It may be obvious or it may be insidious. Whatever form it takes, it is unwarranted and unwelcome to the individual.

Examples of bullying/harassing behaviour include:

- spreading malicious rumours, or insulting someone by word or behaviour (particularly on the grounds of age, race, sex, disability, sexual orientation and religion or belief)
- copying memos that are critical about someone to others who do not need to know
- ridiculing or demeaning someone—picking on them or setting them up to fail
- exclusion or victimisation
- unfair treatment
- overbearing supervision or other misuse of power or position
- unwelcome sexual advances—touching, standing too close, the display of offensive materials
- making threats or comments about job security without foundation
- deliberately undermining a competent worker by overloading and constant criticism
- preventing individuals progressing by intentionally blocking promotion or training opportunities.

Bullying and harassment are not necessarily face to face. They may also occur in written communications, email, phone, and automatic supervision methods such as computer recording of downtime from work or the number of calls handled if these are not applied to all workers.

Bullying and harassment make someone feel anxious and humiliated. Feelings of anger and frustration at being unable to cope may be triggered. Some people may try to retaliate in some way. Others may become frightened and demotivated. Stress, loss of self-confidence and self-esteem caused by harassment or bullying can lead to job insecurity, illness, absence from work, and even resignation. Almost always job performance is affected and relations in the workplace suffer."

The ACAS definition relates to the general problems of harassment and bullying in the workplace. This chapter, however, is concerned with the more specfic issue of when harassment and bullying can be said to be discriminatory harassment.

Early empirical research in the EU had confirmed that women's experience of sexual harassment in the workplace does not involve isolated phenomena but is a more systemic problem.[6] The Third European Survey on Working Conditions, based on 21, 500 face to face interviews with workers throughout the EU, indicated that: two per cent (three million) workers are subjected to physical violence from people in the workplace[7]; four per cent (six million) workers are subjected to physical violence from people outside their workplace; two per cent (three million) workers are subjected to sexual harasssment; and nine per cent (13 million) workers are subjected to intimidation and bullying.[8] The first findings from the Fifth European Survey on Working Conditions (carried out in 2005) confirms that bullying and harassment remain a problem. Two forms of harssment were identified in this survey: general harassment and/or bullying; and sexual harassment (defined as unwanted sexual attention). The Fifth Survey indicates: around one in twenty (five per cent) of EU Workers have been subjected to violence or harassment; women are more subjected to bullying and harassment (six per cent) than men (four per cent) and younger women are at the highest risk (eight per cent).[9]

Recent research confirms that sexual harassment is also a persistent problem at a domestic level. Research for the Equal Opportunities Commission (EOC), "*Sexual Harassment in the Workplace*" (2007) summarised the extent of the problem.[10] Despites difficulties in collating data, the research confirms that sexual harassment is an ongoing problem in the workplace: of all the com-

[6] Michael Rubenstein, The Dignity of Women at Work, (Commission of the European Communities, 1988).

[7] "Framework Agreement on Harassment and Violence at Work", European Social Dialogue, Published by Europa April 26, 2007 (available at *www.europa.eu*—accessed July 10, 2007)

[8] "Violence at Work in the European Union: Recent Findings", published by European Foundation for the Improvement of Living and Working Conditions (Dublin, Ireland: December, 2000)

[9] "Fourth European Working Conditions Survey", published by European Foundation for the Improvement of Living and Working Conditions (Dublin, Ireland: December, 2005) at p.36.

[10] Carrie Hunt, et al, "Sexual Harassment in the Workplace: A Literature Review", EOC Working Paper Series No.59 (EOC: London, 2007)

pensation awards made for sex discrimination in tribunals in 2005, about 18 per cent were for sexual harassment; a police survey in 1993 found that nearly all the policewomen participating in the survey had experienced some form of sexual harassment from policemen; and a TUC survey of women delegates in 1999 found that 27 per cent of women had experienced sexual harassment in the workplace.[11] The most comprehensive recent research on unfair treatment at work carried out by the Department of Trade and Industry in 2005 included a question on sexual harassment and also confirms the extent of the problem. The survey involved face to face interviews carried out in the British workplace between November 2005 and January 2006. The results confirmed that: less than one in every hundred (0.9 per cent) of employees had experienced sexual harassment in the last two years; women had a higher incidence of experiencing sexual harassment (1.1 per cent) than men (0.7 per cent); of British employees who reported sexual harassment, 59 per cent were women; employees with a disability, or a long term illness, were more likely to have experienced sexual harassment than employees without a disability; men were more likely to report sexual harassment than women; and private sector employees were more likely to report sexual harassment than those in the public sector.

The EOC "Sexual Harassment in the Workplace" (2007) report confirmed high levels of sexual harassment in the police force. A recent investigation by the EOC has also revealed a recurring structural problem of sexual harassment of women serving in the armed forces. In June 2005, the Secretary of State for Defence conceded that there was "significant sexual harassment" in the armed forces.[12] The EOC had received 2,390 complaints in one year and launched an investigation. The Ministry of Defence agreed an action plan with the EOC on tackling the problem, and this halted the investigation. One Nimrod pilot had been subjected to sexist comments which were dismissed internally as part of the "maritime tradition".[13]

A recent report of the TUC's "Rooting Out Racism" hotline confirms that racial harassment (including verbal abuse on the grounds of race and religion) at work also remains a problem.[14] In the area of sexual orientation, there is evidence of specific forms of harassment that target gay and lesbian workers. Early studies by Stonewall (1993) and the TUC (1999) had already confirmed high levels of discrimination on the grounds of sexual orientation. A recent study by the Wales TUC in 2007 has confirmed that gay and lesbian workers also suffer high levels of discriminatory harassment. The TUC survey of gay and lesbian workers found that one third of respondents reported harassment

[11] *Ibid.*

[12] Equal Opportunities Commission Annual Reports and Accounts, 2005–2006 (London: EOC, 2005) (available at *www.eoc.org.uk*).

[13] See report, "Armed forces admit sex harassment", Thursday 23 June 2005 at *www.news.bbc.-co.uk* (accessed July 10, 2007).

[14] Report of the TUC's "Rooting Out Racism" Hotline: Exposing Racism at Work, Published by the TUC's Campaigns and Communications Dept, TUC Congress House: London, 1998). Available at *www.tuc.org.uk* (accessed July 10, 2007).

because of their sexual orientation.[15] The survey also found that there was a more significant problem in the private sector, and recommended working with employers on putting into place effective anti-harassment policies and improving training.

There is also evidence of discriminatory harassment when individuals are receiving public services. The Commission for Racial Equality has noted that racial harassment is a serious problem in the primary health care sector and has urged health care providers (such as GPs and Community Health Councils) to tackle the problem.[16] In education, the problems of discriminatory bullying and harassment of school children is of particular concern, given that it indicates the formation of discriminatory attitudes by perpetrators at a young age, and also because the victims are young and vulnerable. Stonewall has recorded high levels of bullying and harassment of students on the ground of sexual orientation in education.[17] There are also high levels of racist bullying at school which are recorded and reported by school according to the Local Education Authority.[18] This confirms earlier reports by the CRE of racial harassment in schools.[19] Although the evidence as collected relates to racist bullying, some of the recorded incidents reveal that some forms of this bullying, especially after September 11, 2001, are targeting visible religious minorities, e.g. young Muslim school girls in Nottingham who wear a headscarf.[20] Disability harassment in school is also a potential problem, although it is difficult to collect data. In the US context, Mark Weber has commented that there is a social problem of harassment of school children who suffer from disabilities which takes the form of "abuse by teachers or toleration of peer harssment" of the pupils. Weber comments that disability harassmsent has not been prioritised with the same heightened awareness as sexual or racial harassment.[21]

[15] "Gay workers need support against harassment", (2007) 166 Equal Opportunities Review, (IRS: London, 2007).

[16] See the CRE's Primary Health Care Service Code of Practice at *www.cre.gov.uk/gdpract/health_care_cop_harass.html* (accessed on July 10, 2007)

[17] "The School Report: The Experience of Young Gay People in Britain's Schools", London: Stonewall, 2007.

[18] A collection of relevant reports of LEA's from key areas are collected for the Channel 4 report "Why am I being picked upon" (at *www.channel4.com/news/articles/society/education/*) (accessed on July 10, 2007).

[19] For examples of low level harassment see Learning in Terror: A survey of racial harassment in schools and colleges in England, Scotland and Wales, 1985–1987 (Commission for Racial Equality: London). Where there is more than one incident of harassment, such low level harassment can now be dealt with under the Protection from Harassment Act 1997 which provides for criminal sanctions, as well as a remedy in tort for damages or an injunction.

[20] See fn18 above and the incidents reported by a young Muslim school girls, Yasmeen al Ameen, who reports harassment including language such as "you are a suicide bomber".

[21] Mark. C. Weber, "Disability Harassment in the Public Schools", (2002) 43(3) William and Mary L.R. 1081.

A. *Legal Regulation of Discriminatory Harassment*

Although the historical origins of sexual harassment as a form of recognised discrimination lie in the US, there is increasing recognition that this an international problem. A large number of jurisdictions (including the EU) have prioritised the legal regulation of this problem.[22]

The regulation of discriminatory harassment through international human rights law is recent. As Christine Chinkin notes, issues such as sexual harassment have received less attention at the international level than other forms of violence against women, reproductive rights and crimes committed against women involved in armed conflict. One of the difficulties of internationalising these issues is that in the global context the situations within which harassment takes place vary and it is not limited to the workplace. Moreover, the international context increases the diversity of working conditions and locations. This makes it difficult to develop international norms despite the fact that the undervaluation of women's work, and poor regulation of their working conditions, makes women especially vulnerable to gendered forms of exploitation and violence.

One context in which there has been success is developing an international response to the problem of discriminatory harassment is the work of the International Labour Organisation (ILO). The ILO Committee of Experts has recognised that sexual harassment is a form of discrimination under ILO Convention No.111, which is concerned with the promotion of equality of opportunity in public and private employment.[23] The original Convention for the Elimination of Discrimination Against Women (CEDAW) provisions did not contain a specific provision concerning sexual harassment. However, subsequent changes via General Recommendations No.19 on Violence Against Women (paras 17 and 18) include a link between equality for women and the need to address the problem of sexual harassment. This has been addressed by the Special Rapporteur on Violence Against Women, who has said that states should treat sexual harassment seriously because of the way in which it degrades women.[24] Article 8 of the ECHR provides a right to privacy which may also be a source of protection for individuals against harassment in the form of invasive questions about personal life.

The development of a specific cause of action for discriminatory harassment emerged out of a concern with the sexual harassment of working women.

[22] For an international, global and comparative perspective see Kathrin S. Zippel, The Politics of Sexual Harasment: A Comparative Study of the United States, the European Union, and Germany (Cambridge: Cambridge University Press, 2006)

[23] Christine Chinkin, "Sexual Harassment: An International Human Rights Perspective", in Catherine A. MacKinnon and Riva B. Siegel, (eds.), Directions in Sexual Harassment Law, New Haven, USA: Yale University Press, 2004, at p.659.

[24] Christine Chinkin, "Sexual Harassment: An International Human Rights Perspective", in Catherine A. MacKinnon and Riva B. Siegel, (eds), Directions in Sexual Harassment Law, New Haven, USA: Yale University Press, 2004, at pp.664–665.

Catherine MacKinnon's book *Sexual Harassment of Working Women* (1979) developed an argument that presented sexual harassment as a patriachal practice that is both an outcome of, and contributes to, the structural inequality of women. She argues that women are sexually harassed by men because of the social meaning that is assigned to female sexuality: for example, women's social roles are largely assigned by their sexuality; women are assumed to be sexually available for men; and sexual harassment is an expression of male sex roles concerning women which are often coercive.

Catherine MacKinnon, *Sexual Harassment of Working Women: A Case of Sex Discrimination*, (New Haven: Yale University Press, 1979) (Chapter 2)

"Women work 'as women'. The American workplace and work force are divided according to gender. Compared with men, women's participation in the paid labour force is characterized by horizontal segregation, vertical stratification and income inequality. Women tend to be employed in occupations that are considered 'for women', to be men's subordinates on the job, and to be paid less than men both on the average and for the same work.

Sexual harassment on the job occurs in this material context and is directly related to it. Horizontal segregation means that most women perform the jobs they do because of their gender, with the element of sexuality pervasively implicit. Women who work at 'men's jobs' are exceptions. By virtue of the segregation of most women into women's jobs, such women are residually defined as 'tokens'. So even women who are exceptional among their sex remian defined on the job according to gender, with sexuality a part of that definition. Vertical stratification means that women tend to be in low-ranking positions, dependent upon the approval and good will of male superordiantes for hiring, retention, and advancement. Being at the mercy of male superiors adds direct economic clout to male sexual demands. Low pay is an index to the foregoing two dimensions. It also deprives women of material security and independence which could help make resistance to unreasonable job pressures practical.

This is not to suggest that sexual harassment alone explains these characteristics of women's position in the labour force. But very little is known about the day-to-day processes by which women's disadvantaged work status is attained This chapter takes the view that the sexual harassment of women can occur largely because women occupy inferior job positions and job roles; at the same time, sexual harassment works to keep women in such positions. Sexual harassment, then, uses and helps create women's structurally inferior status."

Seven years after MacKinnon and other feminist advocates developed their theoretical arguments, the US Supreme Court recognised that harassment could also be a form of discrimination. In *Meritor Savings Bank v Vinson*[25] it was unanimously held that where a supervisor in a workplace harasses a subordinate because of the subordinate's sex, that supervisor "discriminates" on

[25] 477 U. S. 57 (1986).

the basis of sex. In *Meritor*, the Supreme Court suggested that sexual harassment could take two forms: first, an economic *quid pro quo*; or second, a practice that creates a hostile working environment.

Despite some progress at the international level, the main sources for the legal regulation of discriminatory harsasment are national. As discussed above, US case law under Title VII accepted that sexual harassment was a form of sex discrimination under federal discrimination law.[26] Canadian case law has followed a similar line of reasoning. In *Janzen v Platy Enterprises Ltd* the Canadian Supreme Court confirmed that sexual harassment was a form of sex discrimination. In that case, Chief Justice Dickson used the language of discrimination to discuss harassment. However, and significantly, rather than focusing on equality and comparison, he also framed the problem in the following terms as a harm to the autonomy and dignity of the victim. He said:

> "Sexual harassment is a demeaning practice, one that constitutes a profound affront to the dignity of the employees forced to endure it. By requiring an employee to content with unwelcome sexual actions or explicit sexual demands, sexual harassment in the workplace attacks the dignity and self-respect of the victim both as an employee and as a human being."[27]

In the British context, it has been recognised that sexual harassment can constitute sex discrimination under the Sex Discrimination Act 1975 (SDA 75). Although the domestic case law on sexual harassment is complex, early cases including *Strathclyde Regional Council v Porcelli* (discussed below), where Scotland's Court of Session found that sexual harassment could in certain circumstances be direct sex discrimination in breach of s.1(1)(a) of the SDA 75. In *Porcelli*, the key concept that transformed harassment into discriminatory harassment against a woman was where it was akin to a "sexual sword": i.e. it was a particular kind of harassment (the judgment uses the word "weapon") that would not have been used on an equally disliked man.[28] Subsequent case law has developed this idea and often veers between two approaches: first, using a comparator-based equality analysis (approach) which treats harassment as a form of discrimination since it is less favourable treatment "because of sex"; and second, deeming harassment to be a form of discrimination (an associative approach) which focuses on the specific way in which it subordinates and harms women or members of minorities.

EU law has tended towards the second associative approach. The distinction between the two has recently been recognised by the High Court, which has held that the domestic definition of sexual harassmsent (which uses the "comparative approach") is narrower than the EU definition (using the 'associative approach); and that the Employment Equality (Sex Discrimina-

[26] *Meritor Savings Bank v Venison* 477 U. S. 57 (1986).
[27] *Janzen v Platy* (1989) 1 S.C.R. 1284.
[28] See *Strathclyde Regional Council v Porcelli* [1986] I.C.R. 564.

tion) Regulations, which use the 'comparative approach' to defining sexual harassment, did not properly implement the Equal Treatment Directive in relation to provisions on sexual harassment.[29] This decision and the new legal regime on discriminatory harassment following EU law changes are discussed below. First, however, it is necessary to examine the developments in domestic discrimination law that, like the US and Canadian case law, led to the recognition of sexual harassment as a form of sex discrimination.

Domestic case law recognised sexual harassment as a form of sex discrimination before the regulation of the issue by EU discrimination law. The early recognition of sexual harassment as a form of sex discrimination under the Sex Discrimination Act was in *Strathclyde Regional Council v Porcelli*, a Scottish case.

Strathclyde Regional Council v Porcelli [1986] I.C.R. 564
Scotland Court of Session: First Division, IH (1 Div)
Lord President (Lord Emslie), Lord Grieve and Lord Brand

The applicant was one of three laboratory technicians employed at a school. The other technicians were male who undertook acts of sexual harrassment against her. She argued that this constituted unlawful sex discrimination contrary to sections 1(1)(a) and 6(2)(b) of the Sex Discrimination Act 1975. An industrial tribunal found that she had been discriminated against by the two male laboratory technicians but the tribunal concluded that, although their conduct subjected the applicant to a detriment, they would have treated a male colleague whom they disliked just as unpleasantly so that it could not be said that the employers through the two male technicians had treated her less favourably than they would have treated a man within the meaning of section 1(1)(a) of the Act. The applicant appealed. The EAT allowed the appeal, and this decision in favour of the applicant's claim was upheld by the Scottish Court of Sessions.

Lord Emslie (President) (pp.569–70): After some initial hesitation which I freely confess I have come to be of opinion that for the reasons advanced by the Dean of Faculty for the applicant the submissions for the employers fall to be rejected. Section 1(1)(a) is concerned with 'treatment' and not with the motive or objective of the person responsible for it. Although in some cases it will be obvious that there is a sex related purpose in the mind of a person who indulges in unwanted and objectionable sexual overtures to a woman or exposes her to offensive sexual jokes or observations that is not this case. But it does not follow that because the campaign pursued against the applicant as a whole had no sex related motive or objective, the treatment of the applicant by Coles [one of the male technicians], which was of the nature of 'sexual harrassment' is not to be regarded as

[29] *Equal Opportunities Commission v Secretary of State for Trade and Industry*, High Court, Queen's Bench Division, Administrative Court March 12, 2007, [2007] 2 C.M.L.R. 49.

having been 'on the ground of her sex' within the meaning of section 1(1)(a). In my opinion this particular part of the campaign was plainly adopted against the applicant because she was a woman. It was a particular kind of weapon, based upon the sex of the victim, which, as the industrial tribunal recognised would not have been used against an equally disliked man. Indeed, I do not understand from the reasons of the industrial tribunal that they were not entirely satisfied upon that matter, and they were in my opinion well entitled to be so satisfied upon a proper interpretation of section 1(1)(a). As I read their reasons the decision against the applicant, which they reached with evident regret, proceeded only upon their view that Coles and Reid [the male technicians] would have treated an equally disliked male colleague just an unfavourably as they had treated the applicant. It is at this point, in my opinion, that their decision is vulnerable.

The industrial tribunal reached their decision by finding that Coles' and Reid's treatment of an equally disliked male colleague would have been just as unpleasant. Where they went wrong, however, was in failing to notice that a material part of the campaign against the applicant consisted of sexual harrassment, a particularly degrading and unacceptable form of treatment which it must be taken to have been the intention of Parliament to restrain. From their reasons it is to be understood that they were satisfied that this form of treatment—sexual harrassment in any form—would not have figured in a campaign by Coles and Reid directed against a man. In this situation the treatment of the applicant fell to be seen as very different in a material respect from that which would have been inflicted on a male colleague, regardless of equality of overall unpleasantness, and that being so it appears to me that upon a proper application of section 1(1)(a) the industrial tribunal ought to have asked themselves whether in that respect the applicant had been treated by Coles (on the ground of her sex) 'less favourably' than he would have treated a man with whom her position fell to be compared. Had they asked themselves that question it is impossible to believe that they would not have answered it in the affirmative."

Porcelli was a significant case because it established the principle that sexual harassment could be actionable as unlawful sex discrimination under the SDA. The reasons why sexual harassment was a form of sex discrimination were not, however, made clear. Lord Emslie did recognise that in some cases there will be a clear sexual motive in the form of "unwanted and objectionable sexual overtures". In addition, he also recognised that other cases could fall within the definition of sexual harassment: e.g. those cases where sex is used as a particular kind of "weapon" (or what Lord Grieve refers to as a "sexual sword") which "would not have been used against an equally disliked man". In Lord Emslie's analysis the reason that sexual harassment is a form of sex discrimination is because it is conduct that is "on the ground of her sex", i.e. he argued within the paradigm of the "comparator-based" approach. This justification of sexual harassment as a form of sex discrimination within the comparator-based approach also underlies the reasonsing of Lord Grieve who explicitly states:

"**Lord Grieve (p.574):** In so saying however I am not to be taken as agreeing with the reasoning of the appeal tribunal. They concentrated, in my respectful opinion, wrongly, on a consideration of what they called 'sexual harrassment' a phrase which finds no place in the Act of 1975.

In approaching the construction of sections 1(1)(a), 5(3) and 6(2)(b), it is imperative to keep in mind one of the main purposes of the Act of 1975, which is to prevent persons in employment being discriminated against on the ground of their sex, that is to say being treated less favourably than they would have been had it not been for their sex. The treatment must first be identified and, if necessary, analysed, if it is not clear that it, or any part of it, is sexually orientated. In making the comparison between the treatment accorded to a woman and that accorded to a man in a similar position as required by section 5(3) (in a case where such a direct comparison is possible) if it appears that that accorded to the man is infinitely more cruel than that accorded to the woman (assuming her to be the complainer) that does not answer the question which the provisions of section 1(1)(a) require to be answered. The reason for that is that while the treatment accorded to the woman may be less cruel than that accorded to the man, it may still have been meted out to her on the ground of her sex, and therefore be 'less favourable' in terms of section 1(1)(a)."

This approach was followed in subsequent cases such as *Institu Cleaning Co Ltd v Head* which involved a single act of sexual harassment[30] and where remarks of a derogatory nature which were sexual and aimed at a woman were distinguished from generally derogatory remarks aimed at a man. The principle was also extended to cases of racial harassment. In *Burton and Rhule v De Vere Hotels*,[31] black waitresses who were subjected to racialised sexual abuse by the performer and clients at a dinner were found to have a cause of action against their employer for racial discrimination under the Race Relations Act 1976 (RRA) 76, s.1. Moreover, in *Burton* it was held that the employer's control over the situation meant that they should have attended to, and addressed, the risk that their employees (the black waitresses) would be subjected to the racial harassment which was in breach of the RRA. Consequently, it was found that the employee waitresses had a cause of action for unlawful race discrimination against their employers.

These cases established the principle that overtly sexual comments could be the basis for unlawful sex discrimination. Lord Grieve was explicit that the basis of the claim was sex discrimination rather than sexual harassment. However, they did not make clear the justification for recognising sexual harassment as a form of sex discrimination. They recognised that sex was used as a distinct form of weapon against women and yet, at the same time, the structure of the SDA 75 required them to place their analysis within the paradigm of a comparator-based appproach. The tension between this approach and the associative approach recognises sexual harassment as a gender specific practice (discussed above, which was never explicitly resolved). The shift in favour of the associative approach is reflected in *British Telecoms Plc v Williams*[32] which treated sexual harassment as a gender specific practice that does not require a male comparator or an enquiry into whether a person of the other sex would have been treated in the same way. However, subsequent cases reaffirmed the balance in favour of the comparator-based approach. More specifically, cases also raised issues relating to whether sexual

[30] *Bracebridge Engineering Ltd v Darby* [1990] I.R.L.R. 3, the EAT also confirmed that a single act could be sufficient to constitute sexual harassment which was unlawful sex discrimination.

[31] *Burton and Rhule v De Vere Hotels* [1997] I.C.R. 1.

[32] [1997] I.R.L.R. 668.

orientation discrimination could be a form of sexual harassment. Therefore, they raise in its most acute form the critique of the comparator-based approach that was made by Katherine Franke and Katherine Abrams (above), who argue that its analysis fails to take into account the true "mischief" of harassment, i.e. discriminatory harassment is a harm not because it is less favourable treatment but because it reflects, and reinforces, patterns of subordination. In the case of sexual harassment, this subordination will take a specific form of forcing gender stereotypes on to individuals, which can be enforced against both heterosexuals and also gays and lesbians. *Smith v Gardner Merchant* illustrates the way in which harassment of gays and lesbians raises a distinct challenge for the comparator-based analysis of discriminatory harassment generally, and sexual harassment in particular. For practical purposes, the challenge has been largely resolved given that EU and domestic law now prohibits, in certain contexts, sexual orientation harassment in its own right. However, cases such as *Smith* continue to highlight the conceptual problems posed by the comparator-based approach. If defined as as an aspect of gender inequality it is difficult to see how harassment of a gay man could be sexual harassment. However, if (following Franke and Abrams) it is defined as a form of stereotypical subordination, it becomes easier to see that the harassment of a gay man could be a reflection of, and an enforcement of, stereotypical gender norms which force the subordination of men and women, homosexuals and heterosexuals.

In *Smith v Gardner Merchant*, the applicant, a male homosexual, was the subject of a complaint to his employers by a fellow employee who was female and who complained that he had been abusive and threatening towards her. He denied the allegation and claimed that the female complainant disliked him because he was a gay man and that she had constantly made offensive remarks about his being gay, including statements to the effect that he probably had all sorts of diseases and that gay people who spread AIDS should be put on an island. The general manager investigated the complaint and dismissed the applicant on the ground of gross misconduct. The applicant complained that he had been subjected to unlawful sex discrimination contrary to section 1(1)(a) and section 6(2)(b) of the SDA 75 in that: (a) the female complainant's allegations would not have been made against a gay woman, and (b) in conducting the disciplinary process and in making the decision to dismiss the applicant rather than the female complainant the employers had treated the applicant less favourably than they had treated her. The industrial tribunal held that they could not entertain such a claim under SDA, but the Court of Appeal instead considered whether a comparator was needed—cases of sexual harassment under the SDA. It concluded on the facts that there was no claim for sexual harassment in this case. On the issue of the need for a comparator in sexual harassment cases, Ward L.J. stressed that:

Smith v Gardner Merchant Ltd [1999] I.C.R. 134 Court of Appeal, CA (Civ Div) Beldam and Ward L.JJ. and Sir Christopher Slade

WARD L.J.

p.144: "(2) As the language of section 1(1)(a) makes clear, the comparison can be made with the way the employer has in fact treated a woman or the way in which the employer would hypothetically treat a woman. [. . .] To subject a person to sexual harassment is to subject them to: 'a particularly degrading and unacceptable form of treatment which it must have been the intention of Parliament to restrain' (per the Lord President, Lord Emslie, in Porcelli v. Strathclyde Regional Council [1986] I.C.R. 564, 569H. In a passage to which I must later refer again, Morison J. said in British Telecommunications Plc. v. Williams [1997] I.R.L.R. 668, 669: 'Discrimination on the grounds of sex can take many forms. Sexual harassment is a particular form. Sexual harassment can best be defined as unwanted conduct of a sexual nature, or other conduct based on sex affecting the dignity of women and men at work. To affect a person's dignity on the grounds of sex will, as with other forms of sexual harassment, cause a detriment to that person. Thus, proof of sexual harassment, of whatever form, will satisfy the criterion . . . : see Porcelli v. Strathclyde Regional Council.'

Sexual harassment constitutes 'detriment' because, as the Lord President, Lord Emslie, explained in Porcelli's case, at p. 568F, relying on Brandon L.J. in Ministry of Defence v. Jeremiah [1980] I.C.R. 13, 26, 'detriment' simply means 'disadvantage' in its statutory context. [. . .]

To found a claim based on section 6(2)(b), it is, however, not enough only to show that there was some detriment: the applicant must go further and establish that the discrimination predicated by section 6(2)(b) was discrimination within the meaning of section 1(1)(a). It was on this premise that the Court of Session proceeded in Porcelli's case [1986] I.C.R. 564 and on this basis that they took issue with the Employment Appeal Tribunal which had seemed simply to have asked itself, 'Has there been sexual harassment?' As the Lord President, Lord Emslie, stated in Porcelli's case, at pp. 568–569:" Although it is necessary for a woman seeking to found a claim upon section 6(2)(b) of the Act to establish that her employer had discriminated against her by dismissing her or subjecting her to some other detriment it is accepted by the employers for the purposes of this appeal, that if the applicant . . . was discriminated against within the meaning of section 1(1)(a) she was subjected to a detriment within the meaning of section 6(2)(b). ... In the result, accordingly, the critical issues in the appeal required attention to be concentrated upon the decision of the industrial tribunal in so far as it bore to deal with the matter of discrimination within the meaning of section 1(1)(a) ... as it applies to the facts of this case, section 1(1)(a) gives rise to two questions: (first) was the applicant subjected by [her fellow employees] to treatment on the grounds of her sex (i.e. because she was a woman) and (second) if so, was she treated less favourably than the man with whom she falls to be compared would have been treated by these [fellow employees.]"

I have added the emphasis to show the dependence of section 6(2)(b) on section 1(1)(a). [. . .]

(pp.146–151): Conclusions

1 The industrial tribunal and the appeal tribunal were, therefore, correct to conclude that there is a difference between discrimination on the ground of sex and discrimination on the ground of sexual orientation and that a person's sexual orientation is not an aspect of his or her sex.

2 The reasoning that followed was along these lines, largely, I suspect, dictated by the way the preliminary issue suggested itself to the industrial tribunal and was framed by them: (a) the applicant's case was that he was discriminated against because he was gay;

(b) the industrial tribunal assumed he was harassed and suffered less favourable treatment by reason of his sexual orientation; (c) the appeal tribunal indeed found [1996] I.C.R. 790, 795A that: "The campaign alleged to have been adopted against the applicant was not because he was a man, but because he was a homosexual;" (d) because discrimination on the ground of homosexuality is discrimination on the ground of sexual orientation and thus not discrimination on the ground of sex it followed that: (i) "The applicant's claim of discrimination on the grounds of his sexual orientation is not within the jurisdiction of the tribunal:" per the industrial tribunal; and (ii) "we do not have to examine the question whether a comparator must be found, let alone whether such a comparator would be a heterosexual or a homosexual woman:" per the appeal tribunal, at p. 794G. It needed all the persistence and eloquence Ms Cox could muster before I began to see even a possibility that that logic could be faulted, but she has persuaded me.

3 The error lies in the conclusion, which was virtually a conclusion of cadit quaestio, when, as I now see it, the right question had not been addressed. The right question framed in terms of section 1(1)(a) is whether the applicant, a man, had been less favourably treated than his employers treated or would have treated a woman. By focusing on the applicant's homosexuality, the drift of the argument pushes one almost ineluctably—as I myself was carried along—to ask the wrong question: was he discriminated against because he was a man (sex) or because he was a homosexual (sexual orientation)? In concentrating on that, one falls into the error that one does not make the comparison which the statute requires namely between his position as a man, and the comparative position of a woman. The fault in the argument is that it precludes consideration of a vital question, namely whether or not discrimination against him based upon his homosexuality may not also be discrimination against him as a man. I am grateful to Ms Cox for withstanding a fairly hostile judicial barrage and for opening my eyes to errors made by the tribunal.

It is upon that further reflection that I have come to the conclusion that the task imposed on the tribunal by section 1(1)(a) read with section 5(3) is to ascertain: (a) what, as a matter of fact, was the treatment received by the employee; (b) was he treated less favourably than the woman with whom he falls to be compared; and (c) would he have been so treated but for his sex?"

Ward L.J. went on to dismiss an argument which suggested by analogy with discrimination on the ground of pregnancy, that no comparator was necessary. He also dismissed the argument that the appropriate comparator in this case was a hetereosexual male. Nonetheless, Ward L.J. reaffirmed in strong terms the need for a comparator-based approach in sexual harassment cases:

(pp.147–85): "A different argument for avoiding the necessity to look for a comparator of the opposite sex may arise in connection with allegations of sexual harassment. The argument is taken from the judgment of Morison J. in the appeal tribunal in British Telecommunications Plc. v. Williams [1997] I.R.L.R. 668, 669 developing the passage already cited from:

> 'To affect a person's dignity on the grounds of sex will, as with other forms of sexual harassment, cause a detriment to that person. Thus, proof of sexual harassment, of whatever form, will satisfy the criterion. Because the conduct which constitutes sexual harassment is itself gender-specific, there is no necessity to look for a male comparator. Indeed, it would be no defence to a complaint of sexual harassment that a person of the other sex would have been similarly so treated: see Porcelli v. Strathclyde Regional Council [1986] I.C.R. 564.'

The judgments of the President of the Employment Appeal Tribunal always command respect but I regret I do not fully agree with what fell from him on this occasion. I agree that the kind of conduct which constitutes sexual harassment can be, indeed usually is, gender-specific. It was in Porcelli's case [1986] I.C.R. 564. The abuse to which the applicant was subjected was being shown a screw nail and asked if she wanted a screw and being shown a penis-shaped glass rod holder and asked if she had use for it. It was this sort of behaviour which ineluctably compelled the conclusion:

> 'In my opinion this particular part of the campaign was plainly adopted against the applicant because she was a woman. It was a particular kind of weapon, based upon the sex of the victim, which, as the industrial tribunal recognised, would not have been used against an equally disliked man:'

per the Lord President, at p.569E, with my emphasis added.

> "If any [of the weapons used against the complainer] could be identified as what I called 'a sexual sword,' and it was clear that the wound it inflicted was more than a mere scratch, the conclusion must be that the sword had been unsheathed and used because the victim was a woman:" per Lord Grieve at p. 573 G.

These are conclusions of fact. Why I disagree with the observations of Morison J. is that he seems to elevate a conclusion of fact—usually, in the context of the case, an absolutely inevitable conclusion of fact—into a principle of law. Picking up the emphasis I added to his judgment, it is not the case that because the abusive conduct is gender-specific that there is no necessity to look for a male comparator; but it is rather the case that, if it is gender-specific, if it is sex-based, then, in the nature of the harassment, it is almost certainly bound as a matter of fact to be less favourable treatment as between the sexes. The male employee would never have been subjected to the indignity of being asked if he wanted a screw or had use of the phallic rod holder. Thus, in those circumstances, there is no need for a comparator simply because res ipsa loquitur.

However, once the discrimination is not "based on stereotypical assumptions as to gender characteristics" to borrow Simon Brown L.J.'s words in Ex parte Smith [1996] I.C.R. 740, 767A—then the matter is no longer straightforward. The case will be different when it is not a "gender-based criterion [which] is the basis upon which the complainant has been selected for the relevant treatment," in the words of Lord Goff in James v. Eastleigh Borough Council [1990] I.C.R. 554, 574F. As soon as the premise that the campaign is sex/gender-based is called in question, then, as Porcelli's case established, the proper questions are those imposed by the disciplines of sections 1(1)(a), 5(3) and 6(2)(b). When the harassment is, as is alleged here, the taunting of a male homosexual with the scorn of his being gay, of his being a risk to the spreading of disease and with the wish that gay people, by implication, like him, should be banished to a remote island, then it is not immediately apparent that the harassment is based on sex as opposed to sexual orientation. It may be easy to conclude, as the tribunal did, that the applicant was being differently treated from a comparable man who was not homosexual and that but for his homosexuality this would not have happened. But that is not the inquiry directed by the Act of 1975. The proper questions are whether he is being treated differently from a woman in comparable circumstances (section 1(1)(a) read with section 5(3)), and, if so, was this differential treatment on the ground of sex (within section 1(1)(a)). The search for the appropriate comparator was a necessary one in this case."

Sir Christopher Slade also affirmed the use of the comparator-based approach in sexual harassment cases:

pp.153–4: "Sexual harassment is not as such specifically provided for in the Act of 1975 and in my judgment gives rise to no points of legal principle different from any other claim made in reliance on section 6(2)(b) of the Act. If it is to give rise to a claim in the present case at all, it will not be enough for the applicant to show that, by reason of such harassment, he has been subjected to 'detriment' within the meaning of section 6(2)(b). He will also have to show that the subjection to such detriment constituted discrimination within the meaning of section 1(1)(a). While section 1(1)(a) will oblige him to satisfy the tribunal that Ms Touhy treated him less favourably on the ground of his sex than she would have treated a woman, section 5(3) will require that in effecting such comparison the tribunal shall compare like with like: see Bain v. Bowles [1991] I.R.L.R. 356, 358, per Dillon L.J.

In my judgment the only proper way for the tribunal to compare like with like will be to compare the treatment which Ms Touhy directed to the applicant with the treatment she would have directed to a female homosexual. If the facts were to show that she had a rooted aversion to homosexuals of either sex and that she would have subjected a female homosexual to the like harassment, the applicant's claim under this head would inevitably fail because no discrimination under section 1(1)(a) would have been established. In my judgment the applicant's only hope of success under this head will lie in satisfying the tribunal that the harassment occurred because he was a man with a particular relevant personal characteristic rather than a woman with the same relevant characteristic. The relevant characteristic in the present case happens to be homosexuality. It might have been some form of physical disability (e.g. blindness) or lack of an educational qualification (e.g. a university degree), in which case similar principles would in my judgment have fallen to be applied. I do not for my part see how the industrial tribunal can be expected to reach the right answer in regard to the first head of complaint unless the question which it asks itself includes a reference to such a highly relevant characteristic of the applicant.

I should add that neither the decision in Grant's case [1998] I.C.R. 449 nor any other authority cited to us, in my judgment, precludes the possibility of a valid claim under section 1(1)(a) of the Act of 1975 arising from discrimination against homosexuals of one sex in circumstances when it would not have been directed against homosexuals of the other sex."

Both the judgments in the Court of Appeal make clear the central importance of the comparator-based analysis. Ward L.J.'s states that in some cases there may be an impression that the basis for the cause of action is gender specific harassment rather than "less favourable treatment".

"[. . .] it is not the case that because the abusive conduct is gender-specific that there is no necessity to look for a male comparator; but it is rather the case that, if it is gender-specific, if it is sex-based, then, in the nature of the harassment, it is almost certainly bound as a matter of fact to be less favourable treatment as between the sexes. The male employee would never have been subjected to the indignity of being asked if he wanted a screw or had use of the phallic rod holder. Thus, in those circumstances, there is no need for a comparator simply because res ipsa loquitur."

According to this analysis, the actual basis why the sexual harassment is unlawful, and falls within the SDA, is because it is "less favourable treatment". Subsequent cases have accepted the need for a comparator-based approach whilst, at the same time, recognising that there will be a category of cases where the harassment is so clearly less favourable treatment on the grounds of sex or race that there is no need for explicit evidence that a person of another sex or race would be treated more favourably.

In *Sidhu v Aerospace Composite Technology Ltd*[33], for example, the allegation related to racial harassment under the RRA. Peter Gibson L.J. concluded that there was clearly a need for comparison for the racial harassment to qualify as unlawful racial discrimination under RRA 76, s.1(1)(a). He acknowledged that in some cases there was no need for a comparison, because race-specific conduct was involved and this was self-evidently less favourable treatment on the ground of race.

"But in certain cases the comparison need not be demonstrated by evidence as to how a comparator was or would be treated, because the very action complained of is in itself less favourable treatment on sexual or racial grounds. Thus in a sex discrimination case, if it can be shown that the less favourable treatment meted out to a woman was only because she was a woman, it follows that the woman was treated less favourably than a man (*Porcelli v Strathclyde Regional Council* [1986] ICR 564). In the jargon of employment lawyers that conduct is gender-specific. So also, if a person is harassed or abused because of his race, that conduct is race-specific and it is not necessary to show that a person of another race would be treated more favourably (*Burton v De Vere Hotels Ltd* [1997] ICR 1). In the present case the finding of a racial attack by Mr Smith is a finding of race-specific conduct."

The reaffirmation in *Smith v Gardner Merchant* of the comparator-based approach perhaps illustrates the force of the arguments of Katherine Franke and Kathryn Abrahams that such an approach ignores the way in which gender stereotypes can subordinate both men and women, and both hetero-sexuals and homosexuals. Nonetheless, the use of the comparator-based approach has now been affirmed by the House of Lords in *Pearce v Governing Body of Mayfield Secondary School*. Pearce has also narrowed the circumstances in which an employer can be held liable for acts of discriminatory harass-ment.[34] The House of Lords in Pearce disapproved of the decision in *Burton*[35] which had established that an employer "subjects" an employee to the det-riment of racial harassment if he causes or permits the racial harassment to occur in circumstances in which he can "control" whether or not the harass-ment takes place. Having disapproved of this "control" test in *Burton*, the House of Lords went on to find that even if the claimant had been subjected to sexual harassment in the present case, the school could not be held responsible for the conduct of the pupils.

33 *Sidhu v Aerospace Composite Technology Ltd* [2001] I. C. R., CA (Peter Gibson, Brooke, Robert Walker, L.JJ.) (paras 29–39).

34 See *Canniffe v East Riding of Yorkshire Council* [2000] I.R.L.R. 555 (EAT) for the application of section 41 SDA in relation to the vicarious liability of employers for the acts of employees. The EAT rules that an employer does not satisfy the defence for liability for sexual harassment merely by showing that there was nothing it could have done to stop the harassment from occurring. In order to satisfy the statutory defence, an employer must show positively that it took such steps as were reasonably practicable. Reported at (2000) 93 (EOR), Published IRS, London, September 1, 2000.

35 *Burton v De Vere Hotels Ltd* [1997] I.C.R. 1, EAT

Pearce, like *Smith v Gardner Merchant* (involving a gay male barman), was another case of harassment which focused on the sexual orientation of the victim (this time a lesbian female teacher).

The claimant was a lesbian who was employed in an inner city comprehensive school where the pupils subjected her to a sustained campaign of taunts, abuse and harassment by reference to her sexual orientation. This included verbal abuse using words such as "lezzie" and "dyke". She complained to an employment tribunal that she had been unlawfully discriminated against on the ground of her sex pursuant to section 1(1)(a) of the SDA 75 in that her employers had failed to prevent the pupils from harassing her. The tribunal dismissed her complaint on the ground that there was no evidence that a hypothetical homosexual male teacher would have been treated more favourably than the applicant either by the pupils or the school. The claimant argued that the use of gender specific language as the means of harassment was sufficient to constitute "less favourable treatment" and allow her to claim unlawful sex discrimination under the SDA 75. The Employment Appeal Tribunal and the Court of Appeal dismissed her appeals by the applicant. The House of Lords upheld the decision of the Court of Appeal. The case focused on the way in which the "comparator" requirement should be understood.

Pearce v Governing Body of Mayfield Secondary School (and Macdonald v Ministry of Defence) [2003] UKHL 34, House of Lords (Lord Nicholls, Lord Hope, Lord Hobhouse, Lord Scott and Lord Rodger)

LORD NICHOLLS

(para.14).: Ms Pearce advanced her claim on an alternative basis. She was subjected to a campaign of gender specific harassment. She was vilified in terms which would not have been used against a man. This, it was submitted, is capable of amounting to less favourable treatment on the ground of her sex without the need to identify a male comparator and regardless of the reason for the campaign. [. . .]

para.15: The starting point here is to note that the expression "sexual harassment" is ambiguous. The adjective "sexual" may describe the form of the harassment; for instance, verbal abuse in explicitly sexual terms. Or it may be descriptive of the reason for the harassment; for instance, if a male employee makes office life difficult for a female employee because he does not wish to share his office with a woman. It is only in the latter sense that, although not as such prohibited by the Sex Discrimination Act 1975, sexual harassment may nevertheless be within the scope of the Act as less favourable treatment accorded on the ground of sex. A claim under the Act cannot get off the ground unless the claimant can show she was harassed because she was a woman. A male employee may make office life difficult for a female employee, not because she is a woman, but because he objects to having anyone else in his office. He would be equally unwelcoming to a male employee. Harassment of a woman in these circumstances would not be sex discrimination.

para.16: In some cases there are suggestions of a different approach. It has been suggested that if the form of the harassment is sexual, that of itself constitutes less favourable treatment on the ground of sex. When the gender of the victim dictates the form of the harassment, that of itself, it is said, indicates the reason for the harassment, namely, it is on the ground of the sex of the victim. Degrading treatment of this nature differs materially from unpleasant treatment inflicted on an equally disliked male colleague, regardless of equality of overall unpleasantness: see Lord President Emslie in *Porcelli v Strathclyde Regional Council* [1986] I.C.R. 564, 568–570. Because the form of the harassment is gender specific, there is no need to look for a male comparator. It would be no defence to a complaint of sexual harassment that a person of the opposite sex would have been similarly treated: see Morison J in *British Telecommunications plc v Williams* [1997] IRLR 668, 669.

para.17: In agreement with Ward LJ in *Smith v Gardner Merchant Ltd* [1999] I.C.R. 134, 147–148, I respectfully think some of these observations go too far. They cannot be reconciled with the language or the scheme of the statute. The fact that the harassment is gender specific in form cannot be regarded as of itself establishing conclusively that the reason for the harassment is gender based: "on the ground of her sex." It will certainly point in that direction. But this does not dispense with the need for the tribunal of fact to be satisfied that the reason why the victim was being harassed was her sex. The gender specific form of the harassment will be evidence, whose weight will depend on the circumstances, that the reason for the harassment was the sex of the victim. In some circumstances the inference may readily be drawn that the reason for the harassment was gender based. A male employee who subjects a female colleague to persistent, unwelcome sexual overtures may readily be inferred to be doing so on the ground of her sex.

para.18: In the case of Ms Pearce the abuse was in homophobic terms: "lezzie", "lemon", "lesbian shit" and the like. The natural inference to be drawn from this form of abuse is that the reason for this treatment was Ms Pearce's sexual orientation, not her sex. Further, as the employment tribunal noted, Ms Pearce did not put forward any evidence or argument that a male homosexual teacher would have been treated any differently either by the pupils or by the school. This being so, Ms Pearce did not establish that the harassment was on the ground of her sex. Her appeal on this second ground also must fail.

[. . .]

LORD HOPE:

"Sexual harassment

para.92: The key to a proper understanding [of *Porcelli*] is to be found in the fact that Lord President Emslie has identified sexual harassment as a particular form of treatment which was to be distinguished from other forms of unpleasantness. Having done so the application of the comparator test became a formality, because the tribunal's findings indicated that this form of treatment would not have featured in a campaign against a man. But I do not think that he is to be taken as laying down any principle. What he was doing, as he explained at p 568D, was examining the question whether the tribunal had correctly applied the provisions of section 1(1)(a) to the facts which it found proved. Lord Brand's observation at p 576 that, if a form of unfavourable treatment is meted out to a woman to which a man would not have been vulnerable, she has been discriminated against within the meaning of section 1(1)(a) reads as if he understood this to be a point of principle. A similar observation is to be found in the opinion of Lord Grieve at p 574G, where he suggests that treatment meted out to a woman on the ground of her sex, although less cruel than that accorded to the man, would fall to be regarded as less favourable treatment simply because it was sexually orientated. But that is not how the case appears to have been decided by the Lord President.

para.93: In my opinion Morison J read too much into *Porcelli* when he said in *British Telecommunications plc v Williams* [1997] I.R.L.R. 668, 669, para 8 that it would be no defence to a complaint of sexual harassment that a person of the other sex would have been similarly so treated. It was precisely because the tribunal's reasons showed that they were satisfied that sexual harassment in any form would not have been used in a campaign which Coles and Reid directed against a man that Lord President Emslie felt able to say that if they had asked themselves whether Mrs Porcelli had been treated less favourably than a man they would have been bound to answer the question in the affirmative. In so far as Lord Grieve and Lord Brand may be taken to have been suggesting that this was not a relevant question where the harassment is sexually orientated, I would disapprove of their observations. I respectfully agree with the way Ward LJ dealt with *Porcelli* in *Smith v Gardner Merchant Ltd* [1999] I.C.R. 137, 147–148. As he said, the conclusions in that case were conclusions of fact and Morison J was wrong to elevate them into a principle of law.

para.94: There is no escape, then, from the need to resort to a comparison. The words 'less favourable treatment' in section 1(1)(a) render this inevitable. It may be that the conduct complained of is so specific to the claimant's gender that there is no need to do more than to ask the question, to which the answer may well be, as Ward LJ put in *Smith v Gardner Merchant Ltd* [1999] I.C.R. 137, 148, res ipsa loquitur; Deakin and Morris, *Labour Law* 3rd ed (2001) p 598, note 6. But that conclusion may be more easily drawn in cases of sexual harassment which do not involve any homophobic element than in cases such as those of Mr Macdonald and Ms Pearce where the context for the abuse is the abuser's belief that the victim is a homosexual. This is because those who abuse homosexuals tend to pick on them not because of their gender but because they are homosexual. The form which the abuse takes may well be specific to the gender of the person who is being abused, but this is because the terminology which is used to describe homosexuals and the acts which they can perform with each other tend to vary according to the gender of those who are involved in this relationship. That is not to exclude the possibility that an abuser may treat a woman who is a homosexual less favourably than he would treat a male homosexual. That may indeed happen, and an employment tribunal must always be alert to this possibility. But whether this is so will be a question of fact in each case.

para.95: The facts as found by the employment tribunal in the cases of Mr Macdonald and Ms Pearce leave no room for doubt on this issue. In Mr Macdonald's case the finding is that the interview would have been no less intrusive if it had been a female homosexual officer who was being interviewed. In Ms Pearce's case the finding is that the pupils would not have treated a hypothetical homosexual male teacher more favourably. On these findings they were not discriminated against on the ground of their sex."

The majority approach is to be found in the decisions of Lord Nicholls and Lord Hope who both re-affirmed the comparator-based approach, whilst not departing from the position (established since *Porcelli*) that domestic law recognises sexual harassment as a form of sex discrimination under the SDA. Lord Hobhouse formally concurred with the judgment of Lord Nicholls of Birkenhead. Nevertheless, he also said: "I also agree specifically that *Porcelli v Strathclyde Regional Council* [1986] ICR 564, *British Telecommunications plc v Williams* [1997] IRLR 668, *Burton v de Vere Hotels Ltd* [1997] ICR 1 and *Go Kidz Go Ltd v Bourdouane* (unreported) 10 September 1996 should be disapproved". Lord Rodger was most vocal in disapproving of the approach in *Porcelli*. This analysis now needs to be reconsidered in the light of the decision in *EOC v*

Secretary of State for Trade and Industry,[36] which is discussed below, which held that the comparator-based approach is not sufficient to give effect to EU law which "deems" harassment to be a form of discrimination. Lord Nicholls in *Pearce* acknowledged that this would be relevant to the definition of sexual harassment, and that this would require a shift from the focus on "comparison" towards an approach that "deems" sexual harassment to be a form of sex discrimination:

para.20: "As with sexual orientation, so with sexual harassment, the law is in the process of being changed. Here again, however, this change in the law will come too late to assist the appellants. The Equal Treatment Directive (Council Directive 76/207/EEC) has recently been amended by Council Directive 2002/73/EC of 23 September 2002 (OJ 20002, L269, p 15). In article 2(2) of the Equal Treatment Directive as amended, sexual harassment is specifically identified by reference to the form of the harassment and is, as such, prohibited. Sexual harassment is defined as 'any form of unwanted verbal, non-verbal or physical conduct of a sexual nature' having 'the purpose or effect of violating the dignity of a person, in particular when creating an intimidating, hostile, degrading, humiliating or offensive environment'. *Sexual harassment, as so described, is deemed to be discrimination on the grounds of sex. Thus sexual harassment is treated as an independent, free-standing ground of complaint. (author's emphasis)*. Member states are required to give effect to the amendments to the Equal Treatment Directive by 5 October 2005".[37]

Nevertheless, the comparator-based approach, confirmed in *Pearce* will still apply in those areas of the SDA 75 and RRA 76 which are not covered by EU discrimination law. Therefore, the narrowing of the definition of harassment through the insistence on the use of the comparator-based approach will have a significant influence on the protection from discriminatory harassment.

The adoption of a non-comparative approach to harassment is discussed in more detail below. Here it is worth examining the way in which harasssment can be justified as a form of discrimination without relying on the need for comparisons. One important point is whether the comparator-based approach is a coherent basis on which to justify the recognition of harassment as a form of discrimination. The *Porcelli* case held that sexual harassment was a form of direct sex discrimination because, in that case, sex was used as a weapon: i.e. that this was treatment that fell within the "but for" the sex of the woman analysis of direct sex discrimination. In subsequent cases the need for a male comparator that is inherent in this approach became both more clear, and more problematic, until the recognition in *Sidhu* that there should be a more flexible approach to the need for a comparator.

There are, however, certain limits to the use of the comparator-based approach and the "but for" test. As Katherine Franke has argued,[38] the assumption that underlies this approach is that men sexually harass women as an expression of their heterosexuality. In MacKinnon's analysis, this expres-

[36] [2007] I.R.L.R. 327.

[37] *Pearce v Governing Body of Mayfield Secondary School* and *Macdonald v Ministry of Defence* [2003] UKHL 34, at para.20.

[38] Katherine Franke, "What's Wrong With Sexual Harassment?" (1977) 49 Stan. L. Rev. 691.

sion of their hetereosexuality as a form of sexual harassment of women is part of the social meaning that deems that women are sexual objects and are sexually available for men. This analysis tends to makes the issue of "sexual attraction" a core part of the determination of the "but for" test: i.e. the harasser's sexual attraction for the woman as a member of the opposite sex, or the fact that he finds her sexually attractive, is of significance. Franke argues that this makes the "sexual orientation" of the harasser important because it assumes that he or she harasses members of the class of people whom he or she finds sexually attractive. This has a number of consequences. It encourages the equation of sexual harassment with sexual desire; it also obscures the way in which sexual harassment is a form of exercising power and dominance.

As Franke argues, the "but for" test makes issues of sexual desire central to sexual harassment. Franke also argues against a "gender" subordination approach that focuses solely on sexual harassment as something that men do to women. Franke wants to include a wider notion of sexism within her definition of sexual harassment. One advantage may be that this approach gives more scope for female agency. The assumption that the proper response to sexual harassment is to foreclose on all sexualised behaviour fails to distinguish between different forms of sexual conduct. The focus on subordination makes it easier to distinguish between welcome and unwelcome sexual conduct in the workplace by focusing more precisely on the mischief in issue. The "harm" of this conduct is that it is used as a form of exercising power, dominance and discipline to enforce gender stereotypes. This definition extends the problem of discriminatory harassment beyond what men do to women. It defines the problem of gender stereotypes in a much wider context: as the policing of stereotypical roles of masculinity for men; as well as the enforcement of stereotypical roles of femininity on women. This explains the overlap and continuity between the harassment of women on the one hand, and gays and lesbians on the other. Kathryn Abrams has summarised this view of sexual harassment as conduct that is:

"either a form of gender discrimination against women—derision of some of the qualitities that make women targets of sexual harassment—or a form of gender discrimination against men that disciplines not the group but a distinct subset for abandoning the qualities associated with men for the more socially stigmatised characteristics associated with women."[39]

The shift away from comparators also allows a greater focus on the precise ways in which harassment can cause harm to its victims. One feature of the harm of harassment generally, and sexual harassment in particular, is that it has a social and collective aspect: it reflects, and perpetuates, patterns of subordination directed against women, racial groups, gays and lesbians and

[39] Kathryn Abrams, quoted in Katherine Franke, "What's Wrong With Sexual Harassment?" (1977) 49 Stan. L. Rev. 691, at p.761, n. 373 and 218.

the disabled. On this analysis, the wrong of harassment is that it is a specific harm to an individual's autonomy and personality, because it interferes with their pyschological well being and their choices and desires. In the context of sexual harassment, Robin West has argued that this move away from comparator-based analysis and towards the harm allows a greater focus on the problem of "unwelcome sex". West concludes that:

"Unwelcome sex—including consensual but unwelcome sexual intercourse in the home and in marriage, unwelcome sexual attention and behaviours in schools and at work, and unwelcome sexual hassling on the street is a unique but foundational harm to a person's pyschic integrity, or put differently, a unique harm to personhood, particularly as personhood is understood, constructed, reflected, and expected in a liberal society."[40]

The focus on the harm that harassement causes to individual personality, and its role in keeping in place patterns of subordination, has a number of other advantages. It allows issues of overlap between different forms of dominance to be addressed: not only the dominance of men over women, but also the way in which both men and women can be victims. As Abrams argues, this explains why in some cases discriminatory harassment will be concerned not only with how men harass women, but also with how men may harass other men who do not adhere to prevalent gender norms. In addition, a more generally framed subordination approach can address the problems where there is intersectionality and a complex range of reasons for harassment. This can occur in cases where there is an overlap between harassment on the grounds of gender and sexual orientation; gender and race; gender and disability, and other forms of intersectionality. By shifting the definition of discriminatory harassment towards a more general theory of power and dominance, it is possible to open up the analysis to intersectional discrimination and also to provide a way of justifying the use of discrimination law to regulate other harms such as racial, disability and sexual orientation harassment.

A recent domestic case illustrates how a wider formulation of sexual harassment as a form of power and dominance may operate. In *Houlden v Ian Fairden*,[41] the Employment Tribunal found that there had been sexual harassment because the employer's conduct sought to control and humiliate the woman, not because he was sexually attracted to her. In *Houlden*, the woman employee worked in the accounts department. The male respondent who took over the department used language such as "top dog" and the "main man" to describe himself. He also adopted bullying and controlling behaviour towards the female employee: including swearing and belittling her in front of custo-

[40] Robin West, "Unwelcome Sex" in Catherine A. MacKinnon and Riva B. Siegel, (eds), *Directions in Sexual Harassment Law*, New Haven, USA: Yale University Press, 2004, at p.140.

[41] *Houlden v Ian Fairburn t/a Foxhall Plant & Tool Hire*, see discussion by Tina McKevitt, (2007) 161 Equal Opportunities R. March 2006; case No.2601288/05.

mers and staff; and subjecting her to verbal and physical sexual harassment. The ET upheld the complaint for sexual harassment. They found that sexual harassment was not a predominat motivation for the respondent's behaviour, but that he "used the claimant's sexual vulnerability as a method for controlling her. Significantly, this method was not, and never would have been, used towards a male employee". The ET also held that the non-sexual verbal bullying "was part and parcel of the same controlling, humiliating conduct."

A further analytical problem with the comparator-based and "but for" approach to defining sexual harassment is the inability of this method to deal with the complexities of intersectional discrimination. This is discussed by Sarah Hannett in the passage below:

Sarah Hannett, "Equality at the Intersections" (2003) 23 O.J.L.S., 65–86

pp.78: "For Pearce, discriminated against on the basis of her sexual orientation and her sex, anti-discrimination law provided no remedy. She could not find a ground of anti-discrimination law to fit her story. Yet, more than that, the failure of the law to proscribe discrimination on the grounds of sexual orientation appeared to colour the court's decision not to find her discriminated against on the basis of her sex. Her intersectionality fuelled her failure to gain protetion: it was precisely because she is both a woman and a lesbian that her claim failed. The reasoning in *Pearce* focues on the claimant's lesbianism to conclude that the remarks made against her, although sexual in nature, constituted harassment on the basis of sexual orientation rather than sex discrimination. But the Court of Appeal could equally have concentrated on the gender of the claimant, with a potentially different outcome. Following the decisions in *Strathclyde Regional Council v Porcelli* and *Institu Cleaning Co Ltd v Heads*, comments of an overtly sexual nature made to a woman may form the basis of a sex discrimination claim, whether or not they would also have been made to a man. The comments made in *Pearce* were unequivocally sexual in nature, referring to intimate sexual acts and sexual choices. An argument can be made then, that Pearce was excluded from the ambit of sex discrimination only because she was a lesbian, and that a hetereosexual woman would have been protected from the adverse treatment she suffered. The Court of Appeal considered this argument, but concluded that a comparator was still needed in cases of sexual harassment. Hale LJ commented 'the critical distinction between sexual harassment cases and others is that the disliked woman is being subjected to abuse of a sexual nature whereas an equally disliked man would be subject to a different sort of abuse. This is a difference of treatment based on sex."

As the final quote by Hale L.J. suggests, the use of the comparator-based paradigm, and "but for" approach to sexual harassment, means that this is a limited version of sexual harassment. An alternative formulation that focuses on the way in which sexual harassment is a practice which allows the exercise of power and dominance to enforce gender stereotypes would have allowed the claimant in *Pearce* to argue that irrespective of her sexual orientation, she was the victim of sexual harassment because she was subjected to treatment that was based on sexual stereotyping. On this analysis, comments of a sexual nature which are aimed at a lesbian woman, to police gender stereotypes, could potentially fall within the mischief of sexual harassment irrespective of how the perpetrator would have treated a man.

Another example of where the comparator-based and "but for sex" approach to sexual harassment fails is where there is an intersection between gender and race. For example, in *Burton v De Vere Hotels*[42], technically a racial harassment case (discussed above), the language used by the harassers included comments that referred to "black women" being good at certain sexual acts. The women who were harassed could claim that these comments drew on stereotypes about them as women; and in addition because of their race. It is not, therefore, sufficient to label this conduct as either sexual or racial harassment. The harassment was based on "racialised gender stereotypes". A theory that defines the harm of sexual harassment only around the pole of gender may miss the way in which the presence of both race and gender tranforms the nature of the harassment. As Kimberle Crenshaw has argued, the way in which black women are sexualised is distinct: it draws on stereotypes not just about women or blacks; it also draws on historically specific stereotypes about black women as sexually available that are founded in the institutional practices of slavery and colonialism.[43]

Once the mischief of sexual harassment is framed in terms of power and dominance, which are aimed at policing and enforcing gender stereotypes, it is also possible to see a continuity between the harm of sexual harassment and other forms of discriminatory harassment. In EU and domestic discrimination law, harassment on the grounds of race, religion, sexual orientation, disability and age is now prohibited in employment, as well as in some other areas such as public services and the provision of private goods and services. These developments mean that sexual harassment is no longer the only relevant issue for discrimination law. Formulating the harm of sexual harassment in terms of power and dominance, based on structural stereotypes, has an advantage because this is a theme that also explains why other forms of harassment should be regulated. Placing harassment as a form of discrimination in this more general paradigm, rather than limiting it to arguments about patriachy, also allows justifications for prohibiting discriminating harassment, to connect with theoretical justifications for discrimination law such as autonomy, dignity and respect. It is also possible, following Iris Marion Young's analysis of discrimination as a form of group oppression, to

[42] *Burton and Rhule v De Vere Hotels* [1997] I.C.R. 1. For a discussion of the "expressive function" of hraassment see Richard Mullender, "Racial Harassment, Sexual Harassment and the Expressive Funciton of Law, (1998) 61(2) M.L.R. 236.

[43] Kimberle Crenshaw, "Whose Story Is It Anyway? Feminist and Anti-Racist Appropriations of Anita Hill" in Toni Morrison (ed.) *Race-ing Justice, Engendering Power*, (Pantheon, Canada, 1992). See also the discussion of slavery as including the harm of sexual harassment in Adrienne D. Davis, "Slavery and the Roots of Sexual Harassment", in Catherine A. MacKinnon and Riva B. Siegel, (eds), *Directions in Sexual Harassment Law* (New Haven, USA: Yale University Press, 2004).

formulate this concern with harassment as an attempt to prevent systematic discrimination against certain social groups. On this analysis, the concept of discriminatory harassment has both collective and individual aspects. First, discriminatory harassment can be delineated as power and dominance that arises out of, and perpetuates, stereotypes about a group. In addition, perpetuating and maintaining these patterns of dominance is also serious harm to the personality, autonomy and dignity of individuals who are members of those groups. The risk with an approach that uses general categories of dignity, power and dominance to analyse all forms of discriminatory harassment is that the gender equality arguments may become marginalised. There are, however, advantages for women in formulating arguments in these terms because, as Kathrin Zippel notes, the concept of dignity resonates better than sex discrimination with individual women's understandings of the experience of sexual harassment, particularly in Europe, where treating men and women the same goes against the cherished notions of "gender difference". On this view, violated human dignity, sexual autonomy, and integrity capture what happens to women when they feel that someone has overstepped a boundary or intruded into their emotional or physical space.[44]

These justificatory arguments provide a possible basis for delineating a concept of discriminatory harassment that includes, but is not limited to, sexual harassment. The way that this concept manifests itself in particular contexts will vary, these conceptions of discriminatory harassment will, however, diverge from each other depending on factors such as the ground of discrimination and the context in which the treatment occurs. Therefore, whereas sexual harassment will focus on stereotypes about appropriate gender characteristics, e.g. the sexual availability of women. Racial harassment, on the other hand, may draw on different types of structural stereotypes such as the belief in the inferiority of certain racial or cultural groups. Similar issues arise for other types of harassment (e.g. sexual orientation, religion, disability) which draw on the distinct nature of prejudice in these areas.

There is now widespread law, specific to the EU to tackle the problems of discriminatory harassment in the workplace. Michael Rubenstein, who undertook the original EU law research on sexual harassment, had recommended the creation of a special directive on sexual harassment which would have treated this form of discriminatory harassment as a distinct problem. He focused on preventing sexual harassment from occuring or recurring in the workplace.[45] However, the EU has used the existing structure of discrimination law to address the problem of discriminatory harassment. Sexual harassment is deemed to be a form of prohibited discrimination, and this is made clear in the new Equal Treatment Directive. This is supplemented by "soft law". A Council of Ministers resolution in May 1990 on the protection of the

[44] Kathrin S. Zippel, *The Politics of Sexual Harasment: A Comparative Study of the United States, the European Union, and Germany* (Cambridge: Cambridge University Press, 2006) at p.220.
[45] Michael Rubenstein, *The Dignity of Women at Work*, (Commision of the European Communities, 1988).

dignity of women and men at work dealt with sexual harassment, and set the foundations for a subsequent Commission Recommendation and Code of Practice in 1992 (92/131/EC). The Code of Practice has been cited as a specific source of useful guidance in sexual harassment cases in Employment Tribunals.[46] It defined sexual harassment as including a number of aspects: unwanted conduct of a sexual nature, or other conduct based on sex affecting the dignity of women and men at work, which includes physical, verbal and non verbal conduct; the recipient's rejection of or submission to the conduct is used explicitly or implicitly as a basis for a decision affecting their job, promotion, training, salary, or any other employment decision; and conduct that creates an intimidating, hostile, or humiliating working environment for the recipient may also be sexual harassment. The Code of Practice also made clear that the conduct of superiors or colleagues is unacceptable if it is unwanted, unreasonable and offensive to the recipient. This definition of sexual harassment was significant for a number of reasons: it focused on issues of power rather than sexual attraction or desire; it included "quid pro quo" sexual harassment where refusal by the recipient of the sexual conduct was used as a detriment in job selection or promotion; it included the creation of a hostile working environment; and it focused on the perspective of the recipient of the conduct (rather than the intention of the perpetrator) to establish whether the conduct was unreasonable, unacceptable and unwanted. Moreover, the Code of Practice suggested that employers should put into place procedures and remedies to tackle sexual harassment as misconduct: including statements that sexual harassment would not be tolerated. Significantly, it also included suggestions that there should be training for all staff, including managers and supervisors. Therefore, the Code of Practice provided both reactive policies and protective deterrent measures to prevent the problem of sexual harassment in the workplace. Subsequent reporting-back procedures confirmed that few countries had put into place measures to combat sexual harassment.[47] Since then, the amended Equal Treatment Directive has now specified that sexual harassment will be deemed to be a form of sex discrimination. This replicates the method of the Race Equality Directive and Employment Equality Directive which deem harassment on the grounds prohibited under, and within the scope of, those directives, to fall within the definition of discrimination.

The Equal Treatment Directive 2006/54/EC ETD 2006 is entitled "On the implementation of equal opportunities and equal treatment of men and women in matters of employment and occupation (recast)". This consolidates seven directives on gender equality issues. It contains a provison on harassment in Art.2 which includes a general definition of harassment and a specific

46 *Wadman v Carpenter Farrer Partnership* [1993] I.R.L.R. 374 EAT, reported at (1993) 50 EOR, published by IRS, London, July 1, 1993.

47 Evelyn Ellis, *EC Sex Equality Law*, 2nd edn., (Oxford: Clarendon Press, 1998) at p.219. See the summary of this discussion in Evelyn Ellis, *EU Anti-discrimination Law*, (Oxford: Clarendon Press, 2005).

definition of sexual harassment which is deemed to fall within the definition of discrimination. Article 2(1)(c) defines harassment as: "harassment: where unwanted conduct *related to the sex of a person* occurs with the purpose or effect of violating the dignity of a person, and of creating an intimidating, hostile, degrading, humiliating or offensive environment." This formulation, especially the use of the phrase "related to the sex of a person" replicates the EU wide definition for harassment on other grounds, e.g. race, religion, sexual orientation, and disability found in the Race Equality and Employment Equality Directives (see further Chapter 2). The ETD 2006 also introduces a second definition of harassment in Art.2(1)(d) as:

"sexual harassment: where any form of unwanted verbal, non-verbal or physical conduct of a sexual nature occurs with the purpose or effect of violating the dignity of a person, in particular when creating an intimidating, hostile, degrading, humilitating or offensive environment."

The implementation of EU discrimination law provisions into domestic discrimination law has taken place through the use of secondary legislation. This has been a complex process which has created a myriad of different definitions of discrimination across numerous statutory provisions. The wording of the Race Equality Directive (which is replicated in the Employment Equality Directive in relation to the other prohibited grounds) states at Art.2(3):

"Harassment shall be deemed to be discrimination within the meaning of paragraph 1 [defining prohibited discrimination], when an unwanted conduct related to racial or ethnic origin takes place with the purpose or effect of violating the dignity of a person and of creating an intimidating, hostile, degrading, humiliating or offensive environment. In this context, the concept of harassment may be defined in accordance with the national laws and practice of the member states."

There are a number of noteworthy features of the new definition of harassment that relates to race, religion, sexual orientation, disability and age. First, it specifically deems harassment to be a form of discrimination without requiring the use of equality arguments or the identification of a comparator. Second, it uses the language of "dignity" of the individual rather than unequal treatment to justify the concern with harassment. These features make this EU wide definition of harassment distinct from the earlier domestic case law which recognises sexual harassment as a form of sex discrimination, and uses the term "less favourable treatment" thereby introducing the need for a comparator. This contrast between the established domestic discriminatory law focus on equality and the new EU definition which focuses on harm to the individual dignity of the victim is significant. It generates a significant difference between the domestic "comparative" approach and an emering EU "associative" approach to harassment.

This difference became especially significant because of domestic incorporation of EU discrimination law has used the phrase "on the grounds of" rather than "relates to" in the context of the prohibited grounds, e.g. race, sex and religion. For example, the implementation of the definition of racial harassment in the Race Equality Directive into British law was via the Race Relations Act (Amendment) Regulations 2003[48]. These regulations introduced a new definition of "harassment" into the RRA 76 (s.3A) which now states:

"A person subjects another to harassment in any circumstances relevant for the purposes of any provision referred to in section 1(1B) where, *on grounds of race or ethnic or national origins*, he engages in unwanted conduct which has the purpose or effect of—(a) violating that other person's dignity, or (b) creating an intimidating, hostile, degrading, humiliating or offensive environment for him." (author's emphasis).

The EOC has recently successfully challenged the implementation of the Equal Treatment Directive (2002/73) (which preceded the new consolidated Equal Treatment Directive (2006/54)) into domestic law via the Employment Equality (Sex Discrimination) Regulations 2005. In *EOC v Secretary of State for Trade and Industry*, the EOC challenged a number of provisions, including those relating to pregnancy. It argued that the Employment Equality (Sex Discrimination) Regulations did not properly implement EU law in relation to provisions on sexual harassment and pregnancy discrimination.[49] The High Court accepted the central claim of the EOC that the new s.4A(1) introduced into the SDA the use of the words "on the ground of her sex" which impermissibly imported the issue of causation not required or allowed for in the wording of the Directive. Instead, it was held, that ETD 2006 provided a more generous (associative) definition than that introduced into domestic law given that it had introduced a causative factor into the definition of sexual harassment. Therefore, the Directive provided more generous protection from sexual harassment than that provided by domestic discrimination law. This in turn had implications for the way in which the test for sexual harassment and issues of third party liability would be construed.

The government has now confirmed that changes to sex discrimination legislation, reflecting the High Court decision, will be introduced.[50]

EOC v Secretary of State for Trade and Industry confirms that the EU-wide definition of harassment uses an associative approach through its language that the harassment must "relate to" the protected characteristic (e.g. sex or race). This is distinct from the comparator-based approach which uses the stricter test that the harassment must be "on the grounds of" the protected

[48] SI 2003/1626.

[49] *Equal Opportunities Commission v Secretary of State for Trade and Industry*, High Court, Queen's Bench Division, Administrative Court March 12, 2007, *Equal Opportunities Commission v Secretary of State for Trade and Industry* [2007] I.R.L.R. 327 HC.

[50] (2007) EOR Upfront, published by IRS, June 5, 2006.

characteristic. The case confirms that where domestic discrimination law has used the narrower comparator-based approach and the words "on the grounds of", it will have failed to properly implement the EU protection against discriminatory harassment into domestic law. This has wide ranging implications for all the present domestic law provisions that have used the comparative approach to give protection against discriminatory harassment in the areas of gender, race, religion and sexual orientation and age, and which use the formulation "on the grounds of".

In the context of disability, the definition of harassment in the Employment Equality Directive was implemented into domestic law using a different formulation. The Disability Discrimination Act (Amendment) Regulations 2003 introduced a definition of harassment into the Disability Discrimination Act 1995 (DDA 95) 1995. This new s.3B of the DDA 95 defines harassment as:

"a person subjects a disabled person to harsassment where for a reason *which relates to the disabled person's disability, (author's emphasis)* he engages in unwanted conduct which has the purpose or effect of—(a) violating the disabled person's dignity, or (b) creating an intimidating, hostile, degrading, humiliating or offensive environment for him."

The use of the formulation "relates to" rather than "on the grounds of" disability suggests that this definition of disability harassment will fall within the wider associative approach required by EU discrimination law.

In two recent cases the EAT has referred to the new provisons of racial harassment which have been introduced to give effect to the Racial Equality Directive in domestic law, i.e. RRA 76, s.3A (inserted by RRA (Amendment) Regulations 2003, Reg.5). In *Wandsworth NHS Primary Care Trust v Ms A K Obonyo*[51], the Employment Appeals Tribunal held that the new racial harassment provision of RRA 76, s.3A did not require a comparative exercise.

In a subsequent case, *Ms P Gravell v London Borough of Bexley (EAT)*[52] in 2007, Peter Clarke J., again confirmed that there was no need for a comparator in the case of racial harassment. In *Gravell*, Peter Clarke J. also commented that the disapproval of *Burton* by the House of Lords in *Pearce* did not preclude a claim by an individual that the comments of a third party had created a "racialised" and racially hostile environment that consituted racial harassment. Peter Clarke J. noted that the Chief Executive had a long-standing policy not to challenge racist comments or behaviour by customers. He distinguished the nature of the enquiry in cases where racial harassment is argued as a part of racial discrimination under RRA 76, s.1, from the new provision on racial harassment in RRA 76, s.3A. He concluded that in relation to s.3A:

[51] *Wandsworth NHS Trust Primary Care Trust v Ms A K Obonyo*, EAT [2006] W.L. 2150169 (at the Tribunal on May 11, 2006; and July 14, 2006).

[52] *Ms P Gravell v London Borough of Bexley* (EAT), [2007] W.L. 1243146, (at the Tribunal March 2, 2007)

"The case which the Claimant wishes to advance is that the Respondent's policy of not challenging racist behaviour by clients is capable of itself of having the effect of creating an offensive environment for her. That, if established on the facts, is capable in my judgment of falling within s.3A RRA. In short, the Chairman fell into error in concluding that the opinions of their Lordships in Pearce, dealing with a different statutory provision applied in Burton, had the effect in law of rendering this part of her claim without reasonable prospect of success."[53]

Given the interpretation of the new provision of racial harassment (as not requiring a comparator-based approach despite the fact that it uses the formulation on the "grounds of race"), there is a possibility that a similar approach will be followed in relation to the other definitions of discriminatory harassment (e.g. on the grounds of religion or sexual orientation) that have been introduced by secondary legislation to comply with EU discrimination law. The provisions use the "on the grounds of" formulation.

The existing comparator-based approach to discriminatory harassment is also relevant in those areas not covered by EU discrimination law. This now includes measures which prohibit discriminatory harassment in the provision of public services on the grounds of:

(1) race (race equality duty in the Race Relations Amendment Act 2000);

(2) gender (gender equality duty introduced in Equality Act 2006, s.84 inserts s.76A into the SDA);

(3) disability (disability equality duty introduced by the Disability Discrimination Act 2005, s.3 which inserts s.49A(1)(b) into the Disability Discrimination Act 1995).

The Sexual Orientation Regulations 2003 make provision for sexual orientation harassment in the context of employment harassment being defined as conduct violating the victim's dignity, or creating an intimidating, hostile, degrading, humiliating, or offensive environment for them (if having regard to all the circumstances should reasonably be considered as having this effect) (Regs 5(1) and 5(2)). The Equality Act 2006 permits the Secretary of State to make regulations governing sexual orientation-related harassment more broadly including in relation to advertisements.

Section 8 of the Equality Act also gives the new Commission for Equality and Human Rights (CEHR) a general duty to exercise its powers to eliminate unlawful harassment. The inclusion of "prohibition of harassment" in the public duty, and as a general duty for the CEHR, suggests an increasing awareness that the problem of discriminatory harassment needs to be

[53] *ibid.* at para.[20].

addressed through proactive measures before the harassment has taken place, rather than through legal remedies afterwards.

Remedies for discriminatory harssment, including claims for injury to feelings and aggravated damages, are discussed in further detail in Chapter 16. As that discussion illustrates, there has been a willingness on the part of Employment Tribunals to make substantial awards in cases of discriminatory harassment, including awards for aggravated damages. However, this focus on damages is essentially reactive and does not address the problem of preventing sexual harassment. As the Rubenstein Report (discussed above) confirms, one of the key issues in addressing problems of discriminatory harassment is to prevent the harm from taking place rather than focusing solely on providing a remedy for those who have already been the victims of discriminatory harassment. Under the Rubenstein proposals:

"it would become a duty of every employer to take reasonably practicable steps to maintain a work-place free of the risk to employees of sexual harassment, and employers would be liable for any unlawful sexual harassment committed by their employees at the work-place unless they could show that reasonably practicable steps had been taken to prevent harassment. In addition, the Commission would be deputed to publish a Code of Practice giving guidance on reasonably practicable steps to prevent and deal with sexual harassment at work."[54]

As mentioned above, Rubenstein advocated the introduction of a distinct directive on sexual harassment that would include a requirement to introduce preventative strategies. This has not taken place. However, in a series of recent cases, Employment Tribunals have been willing to find that the failure to take reasonable steps, especially where these are in breach of the employers own code of practice on discriminatory harassment, can be the basis of a claim for damages against employers.

For example, in *Yamaguchi v (1) Orlean Invest Services Ltd (2) Kotronius*[55] an employer had failed to take disciplinary action against a manager in accordance with its own harassment policy despite the fact that he had knowledge of the manager's behaviour towards female staff. The Employment Tribunal found that the employer could not rely on the fact that he had taken reasonable steps to protect the female employee from harassment. Significantly, the ET also found that the fact that although the manager (harasser) and the female employee (victim) had a social relationship, this did not prevent the possibility of the manager's act constituting harassment. Finally, *Yamaguchi* is also significant because it confirms that employers will need to take adequate steps to investigate allegations of harassment. In some cases, penalising an

[54] Evelyn Ellis, EC Sex Equality Law, 2nd Edition, (Oxford: Clarendon Press, 1998) at p.217.

[55] *Yamaguchi v (1) Orlean Invest Services Ltd (2) Kotronius* [2006] ET/2201404/05, reported at Tina McKevitt, Case Digest: Sexual Harassment, (2007) 161 EOR, published by IRS, London, February 1, 2007.

employee for making allegations of sexual harassment, or for pursuing a claim, can also constitute victimisation under the SDA.[56]

The development of proactive policies to address the problems of harassment within the workplace before it develops into litigation have been developed in the private and public sector. For example, large organisations such as London Underground often in conjunction with trade unions, have developed policies for ensuring "zero tolerance" of harassment in an attempt to transform workplace culture[57]. Following an investigation by the Equal Opportunities Commission in 2003 into allegations of widespread sexual harassment of female employees, Royal Mail developed a comprehensive dignity at work strategy which included fast track complaints procedure, specialist investigators, a free helpline and retraining of staff.[58] More recently, public authorities have recognised the high financial (as well as personal) costs in allowing a workplace culture of harassment to turn into incidents of harassment generally, including discriminatory harassment. Councils like Brent have, therefore, have introduced pro-active policies and informal procedures that prioritise and speed up dealing with allegations of harassmsent.[59]

III. Hate Crimes

Section II has focused on the way in which certain acts of harassment can be categorised as "discriminatory harassment" where they reflect, or entrench, stereotypes that subordinate individuals who are members of a protected group. To this extent, discriminatory harassment reflects many of the concerns of discrimination law: a concern with ensuring autonomy and dignity for individuals who are members of protected groups; and a concern with the goal of equality. The topic of hate crimes raises similar issues because it concerns a class of criminal acts (e.g. assault or property damage) which are categorised as hate crimes (e.g. racially aggravated assault or racially aggravated property damage) because the victim is a member of a protected group.

The problem of criminal acts that target members of minority groups is well established. The US and British experience confirms that the early forms of discrimination law were a response to violent racism and often used the

[56] *Andrews v (1) Oxleas NHS Trust (2) Mohoboob* [2006] ET/2305176/05 & ET/2301426/06 (1 report); *Boporan v (1) Jaguar Sports and Social Club (2) Woods* [2006] ET/1302506/04 & ET/1306744/04 (1 report), reported at Tina McKevitt, Case Digest: Sexual Harassment, (2007) 161 EOR, published by IRS, London, February 1, 2007.

[57] See for example the anti-harassment policies of London Underground called the "Ending Harassment" programme which won the "Opportunity Now" public sector prize in 2002, discussed by Carol Foster, "London Underground; Ending Harassment", (2003) 118 EOR, published by IRS, London, June 1, 2003.

[58] Carol Foster, "Royal Mail: Delivering Dignity at Work", (2004) 132 EOR, published by IRS, London, August 1, 2004.

[59] Kate Godwin, "Bullying and Harassment at Work", (2007) 162, published by IRS, London, March 1, 2007.

criminal law. For example, the early British race relations legislation used criminal law and included a specific criminal for incitement to racial hatred. More recently, there is also concern with racism within the criminal justice system, both in relation to policing violent racism and also in relation to the treatment of minorities during all stages of the criminal justice process. The emergence of "hate crime" statutes has, however, been a more recent phenomenon. It raises an interesting question about whether there is any, and if so what, role for the criminal law in addressing some of the key goals of discrimination law. The later discussion of hate speech confirms that the early use of the criminal law to regulate racism in Britain included privisons to criminalise incitement to racial hatred. More recently, the criminal law has been used to address the problem of criminal offences that target members of groups who are protected by discrimination law. The resulting hate crime statutues are now a common feature of many jurisdictions including the US, Canada and Britain. There are also versions of hate crimes legislation in many European Union member states where specific criminal penalties are in place for acts such as "grave desecration". Hate crimes raise issues of constitutional significance because of their potential impact on constitutionally protected speech; and they are also controversial in liberal democracies because some theorists argue that they breach the liberal requirement of neutrality. Although crimes such as domestic violence against women and rape are rarely placed within this category, it is also possible to anaylse these as "hate crimes" against women. Domestic violence predominantly targets women for abuse and violence within the private sphere; and rape is a crime whose victims are almost exclusively women. The specific issues of crimes that predominantly target or cause harm to women are dealt with in chapter 10 concerning sex discrimination.

This section focuses on the increasing use of the criminal law to address problems of racism and other forms of prejudice. It starts with a brief overview of the social problem of hate crimes, before moving on to summarise different legal responses to this problem in a number of jurisdictions. It also includes a discussion of the legitimacy of hate crimes legislation in liberal democracies.

A. *International Perspectives on Hate Crimes*

The UN Convention on the Elimination of Racial Discrimination (CERD) provides a general international law obligation to address the problems of racism with a reporting procedure: it requires states to refrain from racial discrimination; and to take preventative measures (which may include the use of the criminal law) to prevent racial discrimination. More specifically, the Office for Democratic Institutions and Human Right (ODHR) which is part of the Organisation for Co-operation and Security in Europe (OSCE) has also prioritised the problem of hate crimes through a series of reports and initiatives. The ODIHR defines hate crimes in the following terms:

> "(A) Any criminal offence, including offences against persons or property, where the victim, premises, or target of the offence are selected because of their real or perceived connection, attachment, affiliation, support, or membership of a group as defined in Part B.
> (B) A group may be based upon a characteristic common to its members, such as real or perceived race, national or ethnic origin, language, colour, religion, sex, age, mental or physical disability, sexual orientation, or other similar factor."

This working definition takes national differences into account, such as differences in legislation, resources, approach and needs, and thus allows each state to amend the definition as it sees fit.[60]

B. *US and Canadian Hate Crimes Legislation*

The introduction of hate crimes provisions in the criminal code, and the statistical monitoring of hate crimes incidents, has now become a common feature in the US and Canada. In the US, for example, an increasing number of state legislatures responded to the rising incidents of racially motivated crime by introducing "hate crimes" legislation.[61] These statutes frequently take the form of prohibiting crimes committed against racial groups, and also on the disabled, gays and lesbians. These "hate crimes" statutes use penalty enhancement to increase the sentence for basic criminal offences that were either (a) motivated by racial "animus" or (b) discriminatory on the grounds of race, sexual orientation or disability. Commentators point to the potential for a conflict between these US "hate crimes" statutes and the constitutionally protected right to free speech. This issue was considered in *RAV v St Paul*,[62] where the US Supreme Court found that a municipal state ordinance in St Paul, Minnesota, that criminalised the use of racist symbols was facially invalid as a breach of the First Amendment protection of free speech. This called into question whether the strategy of using hate crimes legislation was compatible with the constitutional right to free speech. However, in *Wisconsin v Mitchell*,[63] the US Supreme Court affirmed that if drafted in a sufficiently narrow way, hate crimes legislation was compatible with the constitutional right to free speech.

60 Set out at *www.osce.org/* (accessed July 10, 2007).
61 See Ian Loveland, "Hate Crimes and the First Amendment" [1994] P.L. 174.
62 *RAV v St Paul* (1992) 120 L. Ed. 2d 305.
63 *Wisconsin v Mitchell* (1994) 124 L. Ed. 2d 436.

C. *European Perspectives on Hate Crimes*

There have been increasing legal mechanisms to address the problems of hate crimes generally, and racially aggravated crimes in particular at European level. For example, the Council of Europe introduced an "Additional Protocol to the Convention on cybercrime, concerning the criminalisation of acts of a racist and xenophobic nature committed through computer systems"[64] which supplements national hate crimes legislation by facilitating co-ordinated action to address the problem of hate crimes in cyber space. Furthermore, the European Monitoring Centre on Racism EUMC (whose work will now continue through the EU Ageny for Fundamental Rights)[65] records hate crimes in EU member states, as well as setting out "good practice" in the policing of racist crimes. High profile attacks on visible minorities in EU member states, as well as the banning of a gay pride march in Russia, has led the European Parliament to issue a resolution on tackling the increase in xeonophobic and homophobic violence in Europe.[66] There has also been some political progress towards addressing the problem of hate crimes at an EU wide level. A proposal for introducing a Framework Decision on combating racism and xenophobia has been in place since 2001[67]. This Framework Decision would include minimum harmonisation across the following areas (on grounds which include race, national origin and also religion): criminal liability for disseminating racist and xenophobic statements; public incitement to violence and hatred; and gross triviliasation of genocide out of racist or xenophobic motives. It also specifically contains penalty enhancement provisions which follow US and British hate crimes legislation: i.e. provisions which provides that racist or xenophobic motives are to be considered as an aggravating factor which may be taken into account by the courts in fixing penalties. The proposed Framework Decision also states that Member States are still obliged to respect fundamental freedoms and can set a threshold significance for criminal liability, which are both measures designed to safeguard freedom of speech.[68] As mentioned, these EU wide initiatives supplement the work of the Council of Europe on addressing the problem of hate crimes committed on cyber space. However, the Framework Decision has not yet been adopted by the Council, raising questions as to the level of official EU commitment to it.

64 European Treaty Series No.189. Opened for signature January 28, 2003; entry into force March 1, 2006.

65 See for example the following reports of the EUMC: "Policing Racist Crime and Violence", EUMC: Vienna, 2005; "Racist Violence in 15 EU Member States", EUMC: Vienna, 2005.

66 "European Parliament Resolution on the increase in racist and homophobic incidents in Europe". Text adopted Thursday June 15, 2006. Text adopted P6_TA(2006)0273.

67 Proposal for a Council Framework Decision on combating racism and xenophobia. Official Journal C 075 E, (26/03/2002) P. 0269–0273. (28/11/2001). COM/2001/0664 final—CNS 2001/0270 28/11/2001.

68 For details of the political agreement of the EU Justice Ministers see: Press Release 8364.07 (Press 77), Council of the European Union, 2794th Council Meeting, Luxembourg April 19–20, 2007.

D. *Domestic Perspectives on Hate Crimes*

Hate crime legislation was introduced at national level in the Crime and Disorder Act 1998 (CDA 98). The CDA has used the technique racial aggravation to regulate serious hate crimes, i.e. if basic offences are committed with "racial hostility" they attract a more substantial penalty. The basic offences include: grievous and actual bodily harm; property damage; public order offences; and harassment.[69] This form of racially aggravated criminal offences has subsequently been extended to cover crimes committed with animus (hostility) against religious minorities (see the Anti-Terrorism, Crime and Security Act 2005, Pt 5) which follow the structure of racially aggravated offences in the CDA 98. There is also now a general requirement to increase sentences to take into account aggravation related to hostility based on race, religion and sexual orientation (see Criminal Justice Act 2003, s.145)[70] and disability (see Criminal Justice Act 2003, s.146). The next section introduces a discussion of racist crime as a background to this legislation.

1. Background to Race Hate Crimes Legislation in Britain[71]

The introduction of racially aggravated offences in Pt II of the Crime and Disorder Act 1998 represented a major shift in the state response to violence and harassment of minorities in the United Kingdom (UK).[72] It came at a time when "racial violence" was being increasingly recognised as a persistent social problem. High profile incidents such as the Stephen Lawrence inquiry have also ensured that the debate about the relationship between racial violence, crime and law enforcement agencies in the United Kingdom have taken on greater urgency.[73] Previous governments resisted pressure to introduce a specific criminal offence of racial violence and harassment. In 1994, the then Home Secretary, Michael Howard, summarised this standpoint in setting out the government's objection to the Home Affairs Committee's call to introduce such an offence in its report on Racial Attacks and Harrassment: "All violent

69 For a full discussion of these provisions see Maleiha Malik, Racist Crime, (1999) 62(3) M.L.R. 409–424.

70 For discussion of homophobic (and other) forms of hate crimes see Gail Mason, "Being Hated: Stranger or Familiar" in Social & Legal Studies, Vol.14, No.4, 585–605 (2005)

71 For a detailed discussion of these issues see the full article on which this section is based, Maleiha Malik, "Racist Crime", (1998) 62 (3) M.L.R. 409–424.

72 For the most recent figures on the incidence of racial violence and harassment see "Ethnicity and Victimisation: Findings From the 1996 British Crime Survey, Home Office Statistical Bulletin Issue 6/ 98, Research and Statistics Directorate (Government Statistical Service, April 3, 1998).

73 See The Stephen Lawrence Enquiry: Report of an Enquiry by Sir William Macpherson of Cluny (London: Home Office, February 1999).

crimes, regardless of motivation, can already be dealt with properly under existing legislation''.[74] In a sharp contrast to this approach, the Labour Party's 1997 election manifesto stated that ''Britain is a multiracial and multicultural society. All of its members must have the protection of the law. We will create a new offence of racial harassment and a new crime of racially motivated violence to protect ethnic minorities from intimidation.''[75]

The introduction of racially aggravated offences meant that the UK was in line with the strategy of other members of the EU and the USA, as discussed above. Some individual member states of the EU also have amended and supplemented their existing criminal law provisions in order to respond to the distinct form that racism has taken in those countries. The Criminal Code in France, which came into force on 1 March 1994, amended and supplemented existing provisions on racism. In relation to the offence of desecration of graves, heavier penalties are now incurred when these offences are racially motivated.[76] The German government introduced legislation to extend criminal liability for neo-Nazi, racist and xenophobic attacks.[77]

Issues of motivation and racial hostility are the key to establishing when there is ''racial aggravation'' for the purposes of the domestic hate crimes legislation. Delineating the meaning of these terms is essential for understanding the role and limits of criminal liability for racist conduct. There are also pragmatic and institutional reasons for prioritising this task. Law enforcement agencies have stressed that their ability to deal with racist crime depends in large part on ensuring that they are presented with precise and clear definitions of what constitutes ''racially motivated conduct''. Definitions also need to draw upon and reflect not only those ideas which find support amongst the victim's (minority) and wider community, but they must also remain sensitive to the beliefs and perceptions which prevail amongst perpetrators and their communities.[78]

[74] The Government Reply to the Third Report From the Home Affairs Committee Session 1993–94 HC 71 (1994), Cmnd. 2684. See HC Deb Vol. 235 Col. 32 January 11, 1994, for Michael Howard's rejection of the Committee's proposals. There were a number of attempts to introduce legislation. See HC Deb Vol.215 Col. 850 December 9, 1992 for the attempt by Mr David Winnick to make racial violence and harassment a specific criminal offence. See also HL Deb Vol. 556 Cols 1646–67 July 12, 1994 for proposals by Lord Irving of Lairg to introduce a new offence of racially motivated violence; and *ibid.*, Cols 1682–1699 for Baroness Flather's suggestion for statutory recognition of racial motivation as an aggravating factor in sentencing.

[75] *New Labour: because Britain deserves better*, Labour Party Manifesto 1997, (London: Labour Party, 1997) 23.

[76] See Art.225–17 of the new Criminal Code 1994. This followed the desecration of Jewish graves in a cemetery in Carpentras in 1990 (*The Times*, August 15, 1990). For a discussion of these changes see European Commission against Racism and Intolerance (ECRI), ''Legal measures to combat racism and intolerance in the member States of the Council of Europe'', Strasbourg, March 21, 1996.

[77] The Verbrechensbekampfungsgestz of October 28, 1994 which came into force on December 1, 1994 (BGB1.I 1994, 3186). See Human Rights Watch/Helsinki, *Germany for Germans: Xenophobia and Racist Violence in Germany* (New York: Human Rights Watch, 1995).

[78] E Burney and G. Rose, Racist Offences: How is the Law Working?: The implementation of the legislation of racially aggravated offences in the Crime and Disorder Act 1998. (London: Home Office Research Development and Statistics Directorate 2002).

The racially aggravated offences represent an interesting development in the use of the criminal law to protect minorities in the UK. Since the enactment of the RRA, with its treatment of discriminatory conduct in specified contexts as a statutory tort, the civil law has been adopted as the appropriate paradigm for addressing minority rights issues. The dominance of this model makes it inevitable that the debate on racist crime is conducted in the shadow of discrimination law. However, any easy assimilation of discrimination law concepts into the law on racially motivated crime is impossible. Although discrimination law can provide some useful resources for analysis, there are good reasons to keep the issue of racially motivated crime distinct from the more general problems of "racism" which the RRA and other related legislation seeks to address. The term "racial aggravation" in the CDA 98 should be developed as an autonomous concept by relating it to the underlying problems of racial violence and harassment in the community, rather than through the automatic application of existing discrimination law concepts. Such a strategy has the benefit of ensuring greater clarity and certainty, which is especially important in the context of racist crime. In addition, it is more likely to find support in the wider community, and especially the perpetrator's community, whose co-operation is necessary for ensuring successful enforcement. Defining racial hostility in a way which attends to the causes and contexts within which racist crimes occur in the community is more likely to ensure that the most culpable forms of racist conduct are regulated by the criminal law, whilst at the same time ensuring that the Government's aims of promoting a "multi-racial and multicultural Britain" are realised by the legislation.[79]

2. Violence and harassment against ethnic minorities

Public concern with racial violence and harassment is not new. Throughout the 1980s policy makers became increasingly aware of the importance of this issue. The action of the Home Office in 1981 which led to the commissioning of the first official study of racial attacks and harassment[80] was prompted by the lobbying of groups such as Joint Committee against Racialism (JCAR) whose influential report was presented to the Home Secretary in February 1981. Since this date government agencies have kept a record of these types of incidents and sought to develop appropriate policy responses. The reason for the renewed interest in this social problem is partly the increasing recognition of the gravity of the harm caused by racially aggravated crime to individuals, their communities and to the wider public interest. In addition, the view that racially motivated violence and harassment is a peripheral rather than substantial problem can no longer be sustained in the light of increasingly sophisticated and widely available quantitative data which confirms the exact opposite. Moreover, the assumption that such conduct is ad hoc is being

[79] See M. Malik, Racist Crime, *ibid.*
[80] HC Deb Vol.998 Col.393 February 5, 1981.

increasingly challenged by evidence which suggests that racist crime in the UK is often the end-product of organised and planned "political" activity.[81]

In quantitative terms, the Home Office has listed the most recent figures on hate crimes as follows:

Home Office: Keeping Crime Down—Hate Crimes
http://www.homeoffice.gov.uk/crime-victims/reducing-crime/hate-crime
(accessed on December 10, 2005)

"Facts and Figures. Nationally, the police recorded 50,000 racially or religiously motivated hate crimes last year. The British Crime Survey, which is based on interviews with a wide sample of people and picks up crimes that are not reported to police, indicated that there were 260,000 such offences last year.

The Metropolitan Police alone reported 11,799 incidents of racist and religious hate crime and 1,359 incidents of homophobic hate crime in the 12 months to January 2006.

However, the police estimate that most racist and religious hate crime, and as much as 90% of homophobic crime, goes unreported (source: Hate Crime: Delivering a Quality Service) because victims are too frightened or embarrassed to let someone know."

Under-reporting of incidents and problems with co-operation between victims of racist crime and law enforcement agencies will be a substantial barrier to the success of the new offences, and are bound to remain among the most controversial areas in the debate on regulating racist crime. The categorisation of a crime as "racial" and prosecution for the new offences will depend on co-operation between the victims of the crime and the police. The pressing need to develop an appropriate institutional framework for dealing with racially aggravated offences was noted by Baroness Amos, who argued that:

"the success of this legislation will rest on the consistency and priority afforded it by key agencies—particularly the police, the Crown Prosecution Service and local authorities. We shall need to ensure that mechanisms are put in place to enable us to judge how well those agencies are doing. This is particularly the case in the light of the findings of the Police Complaints Authority investigation into the death of Stephen Lawrence ... The results of the investigation show how under-performance and a low priority can lead to the mishandling of cases, and it shows how such failures undermine public

[81] See Human Rights Watch, *Racist Violence in the United Kingdom* (Human Rights Watch, USA, 1997) 13–20. See also Satnam Virdee, *Racial Violence and Harassment* (London: Policy Studies Institute, 1995) Introduction, which discusses the relationship between racist crime and organised political activity. More recently it was disclosed that membership of the far-right group Combat 18 included some soldiers from Britain's elite regiments: *The Independent* March 8, 1999.

confidence—particularly the confidence of ethnic minority communities in the justice system.''[82]

The continued interest in the relationship between the police and racist crime, sustained by the Stephen Lawrence case, led to the then Home Secretary (Jack Straw) setting out a number of new initiatives aimed at improving the relationship between the police and ethnic minorities which is discussed in more detail in chapter 12, concerning race discrimination.

Quantitative data, although useful for understanding the extent of racist crime, is not a good guide to analysing the causes of racial violence and harassment. The lack of detailed qualitative research in this area has been noted by a number of commentators, who point out that the focus on the incidence of racial violence and harassment fails to take into account the way in which a more dynamic analysis is appropriate. Identifying the causes of this type of harm requires an understanding of the social relationships between all the actors; the continuity across threats, intimidation and violence; repeated victimisation; and the way in which this behaviour is underpinned by intricate inter-relationships between different communities. Although there is clearly a complex set of motivating factors which underpin this type of conduct there is one set of relationships which is especially important to consider if criminalising racist conduct is adopted as part of a general strategy to promote tolerance and non-discrimination towards minorities. Sibbit's research on the perpetrators of racial violence and harassment analyses the interplay between perpetrators and the wider community. In her case studies of the perpetrators of racial violence she concludes that:

''Based on existing evidence and evidence from two case study areas, it paints a picture which suggests that the perpetrators of the most violent racist assaults do not act in a social vacuum. They carry out their assaults in areas in which all age groups across the local community share common attitudes to ethnic minorities, where people regularly express these views to each other . . .

[82] HL Deb Vol.584 Col.585 December 16, 1997. For an anecdotal example of ''underreporting'' of racially motivated incidents to the police see the comments of Kirit Gordhandas, a police officer with over ten years experience. He comments on how incidents of racially motivated violence were kept down in one police station in West Yorkshire: ''I was sent to a racially motivated incident and after taking details I returned to the station to complete the racially motivated crime incident book. I was told the book was kept under lock and key so that forms could not be submitted. It was explained to me that this was a way of ensuring that no one submitted such an incident form—thus there were no racially motivated incidents within the division''. See ''When Colour is a Crime'', *The Independent on Sunday*, February 21, 1999, which also discusses the issue of ''institutional racism'' in the police force. There have also been a number of comments from senior ranking members of the police force which support the view that racism within the police force is a wide ranging and serious problem. See for example the comments of Dr Robin Oakley, an independent consultant to the police on race, who stated that the problem is not confined to a ''few rotten apples'' *The Independent*, August 3, 1998. See also the comments of the Commissioner of the Metropolitan Police, Sir Paul Condon, who stated: ''Is there racism in the police force? Yes, there is. Is it more than a few bad apples? Yes, it is''. *The Times*, February 2, 1999.

regularly engage in the verbal abuse and intimidation of ethnic minorities ... There therefore appears to be a critical, mutually supportive relationship between the individual perpetrator and the wider community."[83]

Sibbit identifies three ways in which the individual perpetrator is linked to the community: the attitudes of the wider community help to shape the views of individual perpetrators; the actions of extremely violent perpetrators serve as markers by which other perpetrators are able to judge that their own abusive and intimidatory actions are relatively harmless; and the perpetrator serves the wider community in a vicarious manner by taking their collective views and acting them out. The research makes clear that any strategy for dealing with racial violence and harassment will need to focus on not only the individual conduct of the perpetrator, but also the relationship between this conduct and the wider community which may support and articulate the beliefs which underpin racist crime.

A number of other conclusions are noteworthy. Sibbit suggests that any attempt to reduce or prevent racial violence and harassment needs to distinguish between three sets of strategies: first, identification and effective action against perpetrators; second, identifying potential perpetrators and the development of effective strategies to prevent them becoming actual perpetrators; and finally, the development of a range of strategies for consistently addressing the perpetrator community's general attitudes towards ethnic minorities. Sibbit notes that there is a significant role for non-legal agencies with responsibility for tackling racism within perpetrator communities. She concludes that it is in this area of work that there may be some cause for optimism. A number of examples discovered in the case studies—and elsewhere—have demonstrated that individuals within perpetrator communities and perpetrators themselves have, on occasions, transcended (or side-stepped) the local tendency to see others in purely racial terms. It is where there has been space for individual relationships to develop that—even within a seemingly rigid perpetrator community—relations have been able to cross apparent boundaries of ethnicity.[84]

3. Legal regulation of racial hostility

Traditionally offences involving racial hatred have been characterised as "public order" problems in the United Kingdom. An offence of "incitement to commit racial hatred" was introduced by the Race Relations Act 1965 by means of an amendment to the Public Order Act 1936. Its goals have always uncomfortably straddled the objectives of public order on the one hand and non-discrimination as reflected in the RRA 76 on the other. The Public Order

[83] Rae Sibbit, *The Perpetrators of Racial Harassment and Racial Violence*, Home Office Research Study. 176 (London: Home Office, 1997), 11–18. See too Chs 4 and 5.

[84] Rae Sibbit, *The Perpetrators of Racial Harassment and Racial Violence*, Home Office Research Study 176 (London: Home Office, 1997), 11–18. See too Chs 4 and 5.

Act 1986 reformed the offence of incitement to racial hatred, as well as introducing a new offence of possession of racially inflammatory material and causing harassment, harm and distress.[85] The government has built on "sentence enhancement" for racially aggravated crimes as its preferred strategy for dealing with racial violence and harassment, thereby following the practice preferred in a number of American state legislatures such as the state of Wisconsin in *Wisconsin v Mitchell*.[86] Under ss 29–32 of the Crime and Disorder Act 1998, where the prosecution can prove that the relevant "basic offence" was "racially aggravated", there is a mandatory requirement to add to the existing range of the sentence through additional fines and periods of imprisonment which are specified in the Act. This sentence enhancement means that the basic offence is transformed into a "racially aggravated offence". The "basic offences" include: common assault; assault occasioning actual body harm and malicious wounding under the Offences against the Person Act 1861; criminal damage; offences under the Public Order Act 1986 and offences under the Protection from Harassment Act 1997.[87]

Judicial sentencing discretion, which allows a judge to take into account "racial motivation" as a factor in determining the final sentence, has been an effective weapon in dealing with racially motivated crime. In this way, even before the introduction of the racially aggravated offences under the Act there was some potential for dealing with racially motivated crime by imposing a more severe sentence. The case of *R v Ribbans, R v Duggan, R v Ridley*[88] affirmed this principle in the strongest terms. Following that case, where racial motivation was proved the court was required to take such motivation into account at the sentencing stage as an aggravating feature. Lord Chief Justice Taylor stated that:

"We take the view that it is perfectly possible for the court to deal with any offence of violence which has a proven racial element in it, in a way which

[85] See too the Football (Offences) Act 1991, s.3 which makes it an offence to take part in racist chanting at a designated football match.

[86] The provision of the Wisconsin criminal code which passed the scrutiny of the Supreme Court in *Wisconsin v Mitchell* (1993) 508 U.S. 47 as compatible with the accused's First Amendment free speech rights is a good example. The relevant provision enhances the maximum penalty for an offence whenever the defendant "intentionally selects the person against whom the crime ... is committed ... because of the race, religion, colour, disability, sexual orientation, national origin or ancestry of that person".

[87] The full details are as follows. Racially aggravated assaults (Crime and Disorder Act 1998, s.29): basic offence is an offence under the Offences against the Persons Act 1861, s.20 (malicious wounding or grievous bodily harm); or s.47 (actual bodily harm), or common assault; racially aggravated criminal damage (Crime and Disorder Act 1998, s.30): basic offence is an offence under the Criminal Damage Act 1971 s.1(1) (destroying or damaging property belonging to another); racially aggravated public order (Crime and Disorder Act 1998, s.31): basic offence is an offence under s.4 (fear or provocation of violence), s.4A (intentional harassment, alarm or distress) or s.5 (harassment, alarm or distress) of the Public Order Act 1986. Racially aggravated harassment (Crime and Disorder Act, s.32): basic offence is an offence under the Protection from Harassment Act 1997, s.2 (offence of harassment) or s.4 (putting people in fear of violence).

[88] (1995) Cr. App. R. (S) 698.

makes clear that that aspect invests the offence with added gravity and therefore must be regarded as an aggravating feature".

However, this did not end the argument in favour of specific legislation to deal with racial violence and harassment. In particular, in the *Corbett* case,[89], the court refused to give detailed guidance on the extent to which racial motivation aggravated the offence, suggesting that it should be treated as one of a number of different factors taken into the balance rather than a factor which has special weight during the sentencing process.

Section 82 of the Act gives statutory effect to the decision in *R. v Ribbans* and applies to all offences other than those deemed to be basic offences in Pt II of the Act. Where there is evidence of racial aggravation as part of the offence, the judge is required to consider this and impose a higher sentence within the maximum available. In addition, s.82(2) makes it clear that it will be stated in open court that the offence is racially motivated, thereby ensuring that the rhetorical power of sentence enhancement is conveyed to the victims, perpetrators and the community.

Section 28 of the Act sets out the test which is to be applied in determining whether an offence listed under ss 29 to 32 (the basic offences) is racially aggravated. It is also the test which the court applies in considering an increase in sentence for offences other than those under ss 29–32 (see s.82). Section 28 introduces a test for what is "racially aggravated", which uses two sets of definitions. First, s.28(1)(a) states that there is racial aggravation where "at the time of committing the offence, or immediately before or after doing so, the offender demonstrates towards the victim of the offence hostility based on the victim's membership (or presumed membership) of a racial group". Second, s.28(1)(b) adds to this meaning by confirming that racial aggravation is also established where "the offence is motivated (wholly or partly) by hostility towards members of a racial group based on their membership of that group". In addition, s.28(3)(a) states that it is immaterial that the offender's hostility is also based on either "the fact or presumption that any person or group of persons belongs to any religious group" or any factor not mentioned in that paragraph. This last provision confirms that "racial hostility" need not be the sole motivation for commission of the basic offence.

4. The coverage of racially aggravated offences

Before moving on to consider the definition of racial aggravation in s.28 of the Act, it is worth noting the potential problems with the coverage of the racially aggravated offences. The explanatory provision in s.28(2) confirms that "membership", in relation to a racial group, includes association with members of that group and "presumed" means presumed by the offender. Section 28(4) sets out the definition of the term "racial group". It means "a group of

[89] (1996) 2 Cr. App. R.(S) 336. For comment see [1996] Crim. L.R. 525; 39 [1983] 2 A.C. 548.

persons defined by reference to race, colour, nationality (including citizenship) or ethnic or national origins". This is the same as the definition of "racial group" in s.3(1) of the RRA 76, in relation to which the term "racial" was given an extended meaning by the House of Lords in *Mandla v Dowell Lee* (see Chapter 12). In this way, discrimination law has provided concepts which have been explicitly "borrowed" for the purposes of defining racially aggravated offences. This was also the preferred strategy for defining "racial group" for the purpose of the criminal offence of incitement to racial hatred in Pt III of the Public Order Act 1986.

However, the strategy of using the RRA 76 as the alpha and omega for the legal regulation of violence and harassment against vulnerable minority groups is not ideal. Most obviously, it replicates the anomalies of *Mandla*[90] and the domestic definition of "race". In addition, it fails to take into account the compound and overlapping nature of the characteristics of relevant minorities which in turn provoke hostility.[91]

However, there are likely to be problems with such a piecemeal and arbitrary approach to an issue as critical as the coverage of the racially aggravated offences. Home Office research supports the view that terms such as Asian are too crude to capture the diversity of factors which will be relevant to understanding the motivation of the offender and the feelings of the victim. The racial offence is seen to be more serious than the basic offence because of the additional harm to the individual and the group. By forcing an attack motivated by one type of individual characteristic (such as religion) into the category of "ethnicity" or "culture", there is the danger of trying to fit a square peg into a round hole. The individual victim and the relevant community group will not feel that the harm they have suffered has been recognised by the law. Given that attacks against ethnic minorities are often a prelude to more serious and widespread racial tensions, it is important that the new offences are perceived as an adequate response to grievances, thereby alleviating the fears and resentment of individuals and groups. In this context, failing to ensure that the definition of the harm suffered by victims (individuals and groups) correlates with legal definitions and remedies may have a detrimental impact on good race relations.

5. Racial hostility

Section 28 of the Act makes it clear that it is the presence of "racial hostility" that is the key triggering device which transforms the basic offences into the racially aggravated offences: assault (s.29); criminal damage (s.30); public order offences (s.31) and harassment (s.31). How do the racially aggravated

[90] See *Mandla v Dowell Lee* [1983] 1 All E.R. 1062.

[91] See also *Labour Research* (October 1991) Vol. 80, No. 10, 15 which concluded that there had been an increase in the levels of racial violence specifically targeting Muslims during the Gulf War. See also Mason and Palmer, *Queer Bashing—A National Survey of Hate Crimes Against Lesbians and Gay Men* (London: Stonewall, 1993).

offences relate to the underlying basic offences? The new offences shift issues concerning the motivation of the perpetrator, which are characteristically reserved for sentencing, back into the definition of the racially aggravated offence. The main focus for any justification for these offences will be on the greater culpability of the perpetrator who acts out of "racial hostility". However, this emphasis on fault should not obscure the fact that the racially aggravated offences are not merely an instance of the same harm (of the basic offences) being carried out in a certain serious way (with racial aggravation). The new racially aggravated offences are aimed at conduct which causes a harm of a qualitatively different type to that caused by the basic offences. Delineating with greater precision the nature of this harm should be a high priority for those analysing racially aggravated offences, thereby enabling a more principled development of the new offences. Here, it is worth noting that this project will have to focus on the harm of racially aggravated offences at a number of different levels. At an individual level, where a victim is targeted because of a characteristic such as race, this is an additional harm of a greater and of a more serious order than a "normal" incident of violence and harassment. In addition, the harm to the victim's community which is said to experience the harm of "racial hostility" in a vicarious way is also relevant.[92] Finally, racist crime has the potential to undermine the state interest in good race relations, and it is this last goal which is cited by the government as its main justification for prioritising violence and harassment against "ethnic minorities" as part of its aim to promote multiculturalism.

There is a clear and obvious relationship between the racially aggravated offences and the justification for discrimination law generally, and the RRA 76 in particular. Both are based on the same idea: that acts and conduct which express contempt for members of a minority on the basis of their group characteristic are a serious harm. Those seeking to understand the racially aggravated offences can therefore usefully draw on the substantial body of analysis of the justifications for discrimination law considered in Chapter 3. However, the continuity between the two areas of law also poses dangers. As stated, not only the additional harm but also the greater fault of the perpetrator provides the justification for differentiating between the "ordinary" basic offences and the more heinous racially aggravated offences. There are a number of stages which need to be kept separate in analysing the state of mind of a perpetrator of the racially aggravated offences. It needs to be established that they had the mens rea which is required to complete the commission of the basic offence, for example intention or recklessness in the case of racially aggravated assaults under s.29 of the Act. In addition, the prosecution needs to

[92] See Satnam Virdee, *Racial Violence and Harassment* (London: Policy Studies Institute 1995) Ch. 4 which discusses the effects and constraints on the lifestyles of ethnic minorities caused by the fear of racial violence and harassment. See also the discussion of the psychological effects of this type of conduct in Joan C. Weiss "Ethnoviolence: Impact Upon and Response of Victims and the Community", in Robert J. Kelley (ed.), *Bias Crime: American Law Enforcement and Legal Responses* (Chicago: University of Illinois, 1993).

prove beyond reasonable doubt that (a) "at the time of committing the offence, or immediately before or after doing so, the offender demonstrates towards the victim of the offence hostility based on the victim's membership (or presumed membership) of a racial group" or (b) the offence is "motivated (wholly or partly) by hostility towards members of a racial group based on their membership of that group". How should the requirement for "racial hostility" be construed in this context?

It is at this stage that it is tempting to borrow from the developed concepts of direct (and to a lesser degree indirect) discrimination. Such an inquiry encourages analysing racist conduct by examining its impact on the victim and the community. The focus is on whether from the perspective of the victim or the wider community there is evidence which demonstrates the racial hostility or motivation of the perpetrator. If "racial hostility" is being understood from the perspective of the victim or the community, then any further inquiry about the state of mind of the perpetrator will be irrelevant. Such an approach would be consistent with the interpretation of direct discrimination under the SDA 75 and the RRA 76, which has shifted from a test which focuses on the subjective intention of the discriminator to one which is more objective (see chapters 2 and 4).[93]

Although this move towards a more objective, results-focused approach to the concept of discrimination has not been unproblematic in discrimination law, it does demonstrate an increasing tendency on the part of the courts to adopt a strong response to the problems of discrimination in the civil law. Is a similarly trenchant and results-focused model appropriate in the context of criminalising racist conduct? It might be argued that such a model would be inappropriate, and that objective proof of discrimination along these lines is an insufficient guide to the presence of racial hostility and motivation as required by s.28 of the Act. For example, where a perpetrator of one of the basic offences has selected the victim "because of her race", this can be cited as evidence of racial hostility. Rather than being an anonymous act of random selection of the victim, the fact that the victim has been chosen because of membership of a racial group will reveal hatred. However, discriminatory selection arguably should not be taken as conclusive proof of racial motivation in this context. An offender may choose to attack a member of a racial group—such as an Asian woman—because (rather like the choice of a victim because of his or her age or disability) she is less likely to respond and resist. In this example of discriminatory selection on the ground of race, the motivation may itself be based on prejudices that Asian women are more passive and less likely to resort to anger or retaliation. However, this type of motivation should arguably not of itself and automatically be sufficient to translate the basic offence into the racially aggravated offence.

Stereotyping is not synonymous with the racial hostility which is required

[93] *R. v Birmingham C.C., ex p Equal Opportunities Commission* [1989] 1 A.C. 1155; *James v Eastleigh B.C.* [1990] 2 A.C. 751.

by s.28 of the Act. Civil discrimination law may legitimately be concerned with the regulation of the manifestations of unconscious stereotypes, but for the purposes of the criminal law the perpetrator must have been subjectively aware that his conduct was the manifestation of racial hatred.[94] An act based on stereotyping does not express or convey the idea that the victim is held in contempt because of membership of a particular racial group. In employer-related discrimination law, the reasons for the discriminator selecting the victim "because of" membership of a racial group may be irrelevant; even if benign they will be caught by the definition of discrimination under the RRA 76. However, in the context of racist crime, there needs to be an attribution of moral culpability to the perpetrator to justify the greater seriousness and higher penalties of the racially aggravated offences. Racial hostility is required, and makes these crimes more heinous, not because it indicates the type of faulty or inflexible generalisation towards an individual which characterises racial stereotyping, but rather because it is evidence of a conscious animus which is deliberately directed towards an individual because of his or her membership of a protected group. On this view, discriminatory selection of a victim should not therefore be sufficient to prove such animus as the essential element which transforms the basic offence into the racially aggravated offence. Therefore, although the RRA 76 and the 1998 Act will often overlap, discriminatory selection of a victim may often fall outside the definition of racial hostility under s.28 of the 1998 Act. In such circumstances, it may be more appropriate to use strategies other than the criminal law to challenge attitudes and stereotypes within the perpetrator communities and in the media and wider public culture.

Subjectivism is especially important in these contexts in the light of evidence which suggests that racist attitudes and conduct are prevalent within the perpetrator community and are often automatically assimilated and articulated. Sibbit has noted that racial harassment and violence occurs in communities where "people of all ages, including very young children and older adults, regularly engage in verbal abuse and intimidation of ethnic minorities".[95] In this context it is not difficult to envisage a scenario of negligent racist conduct which should not lead to criminal liability for the racially aggravated offences. A perpetrator may merely "parrot" and repeat a racist term in the course of carrying out an attack, or use an offensive sign or means of carrying out an attack without being aware of the full implications of the use of such symbols. For example, criminal damage may be caused by a perpetrator in a whole range of ways. What if the perpetrator uses language

[94] See Andrew Ashworth: *Principles of Criminal Law*, (Oxford: Clarendon, 1995) 83–85.

[95] Rae Sibbit: *The Perpetrators of Racial Harassment and Racial Violence*, Home Office Research Study 176 (London: Home Office, 1997), 11–18. at p.100 Ch.4 "Constructing a profile of perpetrators" which confirms that many of those who articulate racist views are young and with low educational qualifications. Recent Home Office Studies confirm that the perpetrators of low level racial harassment are often found to be children between four and ten. The Home Office is looking into the use of the Child Safety Order and Parenting Order to prevent acts of harassment by children: *The Independent on Sunday* June 21, 1998.

("Wogs Out") or a symbol (a swastika) which objectively and according to its interpretation by the victim and the community is evidence of racial hostility? In these circumstances, if this conduct is being judged according to its impact on the community or by an objective test then this is a clear case of racial hostility. If a subjective standard is used the prosecution needs to show that the perpetrator intended or was knowingly reckless as to the use of this language or these symbols. As a practical matter, the use of such obviously racist language and symbols will be the strongest evidence that there is such subjective racial hostility, but there may be instances where the use of racist language may be coincidental or serve another function. Hare cites examples of instances where the use of racist language may be coincidental or serve the function of identifying the victim rather than a conscious insult which demonstrates racial hostility and deliberately singles out the victim for contempt. This point becomes clearer by focusing on the use of more subtle means which could be construed as a demonstration of racial hostility, for example, if a perpetrator accidentally used pig meat to attack a Jewish person, or alcohol to attack a Bangladeshi person, or cow's leather to attack someone who is Indian. In these cases, from an objective reasonableness test, or using the "impact on the victim or community" criteria, this will undoubtedly be an instance where there is a demonstration of racial hostility. However, this is exactly the type of case where the application of subjective criteria will provide the perpetrator with an opportunity to argue that his use of this mode for the attack (although it may be negligent conduct) was not a demonstration of his or her racial hostility.

In this context it could be argued that there is no necessity for such "correspondence" between the perpetrator's state of mind and the harm; that there is no need for the intention or recklessness to be related to the particular harm of racial hostility. The fact that the perpetrator has carried out the basic offence, and has done so in a way which could be taken as evidence of racial hostility, means that he or she exposes himself or herself to the risk that he or she will be liable for the more serious racially aggravated offence. Such a response is especially tempting in the context of racially aggravated crime where proving racial hostility is notoriously difficult, and where these difficulties have led some commentators in the USA to argue that less stringent standards of proof are necessary if the criminal law is to be successful in addressing the problems of racist crime.[96]

Although this may be justified in the context of other criminal law provisions, there are good arguments to avoid such an approach to racially aggravated offences. Any policy of criminalising racist conduct has to perform a delicate balancing exercise. On the one hand, it has to express the idea that acts which express contempt for individuals on the grounds of their mem-

[96] John Gardner, "Rationality and the Rule of Law in Offences Against the Person" (1994) C.L.J. 502. For a discussion of the American debate on shifting the burden of proof in hate crimes cases see J. Morsch, "The Problem of Motive in Hate Crimes: The Argument Against Presumptions of Racial Motivation" (1991) 82 J. Crim. L. and Criminology 659.

bership of an ethnic group are a serious harm which justifies the strongest action. However, this aim has to take into account the perceptions of communities which are most likely to be affected by the legislation. Although always an important constraint, it is particularly important that the racially aggravated offences should reflect attitudes and meanings which are likely to find support in the wider community, and especially the communities where racist crime occurs.

Research suggests that within these communities there exists a continuum between "acceptable" racist views and stereotypes and the violent behaviour of the perpetrators of serious racist crime.[97] In relation to the most serious cases, the criminal law serves an important specific function which goes beyond its impact on the individual perpetrator, the victim and community interests. Criminalising the most serious forms of racist conduct sends a clear message to potential perpetrators and supporters within the perpetrator community, many of whom set their own standards of acceptable "racist conduct" by using more serious attacks as a benchmark, that these types of acts are heinous and will lead to additional criminal sanctions.

Yet paradoxically, prevailing racist attitudes also set important constraints on the use of the criminal law in these contexts. The success of any policy against racial violence and harassment needs to stay attentive to the attitudes and beliefs of perpetrator communities where racist attitudes prevail. Legal definitions and strategies must draw on and reflect distinctions which make sense and have meaning for the social actors. In this context, the insistence on subjectivism ensures that only the most serious forms of racist conduct, which are without doubt an expression of conscious racial hatred and not just prejudice or discriminatory attitudes, are regulated by the criminal law. This is more likely to reflect distinctions which make sense to the relevant parties within the perpetrator communities: that those who commit acts of violence and harassment of minorities out of a deliberate and conscious hatred based on their membership of a racial group deserve to be penalised by the criminal law. Of course, this does not mean that other forms of racist conduct are acceptable or that legal and policy responses other than the use of the criminal law should not be actively adopted.

Ensuring a high degree of willing compliance and co-operation with the policy underlying the new racially aggravated offences is also important from the perspective of victims and their communities. Where there is a wide divergence between concepts and definitions which are developed in the law and those which are used in communities, it is likely that there will be a build up of resentment and a "backlash" against minorities who may be viewed as enjoying an "unfair advantage" under the criminal law. The fact that ethnic minorities are concentrated in the lowest income groups in the economy means that they will have to share and compete for scarce public goods (local

[97] Rae Sibbit, *The Perpetrators of Racial Harassment and Racial Violence*, Home Office Research Study 176 (London: Home Office, 1997), at Ch.3.

housing, schools and other public facilities) with potential perpetrators on a daily basis.[98] These individuals have to continue to function and co-exist in communities where racist attitudes prevail and where the perpetrators of racist crime often have wide support. Any policy of singling out certain groups for special protection under the criminal law which fails to attend to the views which prevail in these social contexts is likely to place at risk exactly those individuals and communities which racially aggravated offences seek to protect.

E. *Assessment of Hate Crimes Law and Policy*

There are arguments that the criminal law has no substantial role to play in addressing the most extreme consequences of racism.[99] There are also reservations about the theoretical justification of hate crimes legislation in liberal democracies. It is a mistake, however, to over-estimate the criminal law's role. Any strategy which is too ambitious and which seeks to be tough on racism by extending the definition of racist crime too far is likely to undermine the interests of those whom it seeks to protect. The use of the criminal law should be reserved for the most serious and culpable instances of racist conduct. Other strategies, including the civil law and non-legal measures which require public funding are available for those situations which fall outside this narrow category. It can thus be argued that clear and meaningful distinctions need to be drawn and maintained between the behaviour of those who undertake criminal acts motivated by conscious racial hatred on the one hand, and those who are potential perpetrators or passive supporters. The government's aim of protecting ethnic minorities from intimidation and promoting multiculturalism requires a nuanced and complex strategy. The introduction of racially aggravated offences can make a contribution towards this goal, but it cannot be a substitute for it. In the context of hate crimes, rather than focusing on the quantity of prosecutions, it is also critically important to focus on qualitative issues: such as the perception of victims; minority communities; the wider community; and wider questions of relations between different communities. In this context, research on hate crimes has focused on reform and improvement across the whole criminal justice system and relating to the whole range of treatment of hate crimes: e.g. from reporting, to recording and provision of counselling, through to prosecution and sentencing. Issues relating to the reporting of incidents and the criminal justice system have been considered in a recent Home Office report by Maria Docking and Rachel

[98] See Modood, *Ethnic Minorities in Britain: Diversity and Disadvantage*, (London: Policy Studies Institute, 1997).

[99] For the view that criminal statutory regulation does not have a significant role in regulating racist behaviour see F. Brennan, "Racially Motivated Crime: the Response of the Criminal Justice System" [1999] Crim. L.R. 17.

Tuffin which also proposes concrete reforms which can improve the way in which agencies such as the police and the Crime Prosecution Service handle racist incidents. These would include better training for the police; better co-ordination between the police, local authorities and other agencies in relation to reporting of incidents and common data bases; the Home Office possibly providing guidance on reporting, and the Department of Education and Skills could possibly take lead responsibility on monitoring and recording racist incidents at schools. In addition, the Docking and Tuffin report emphasises the importance of prevention: it recommends work by the Probation Service to challenge the beliefs and attitudes of racist offenders; and the use of Citizenship education by the Department of Education and Skills to educate children about other cultures.[100] These preventative measures are especially important given the evidence that many offenders who commit hate crimes are young and that non-legal policy interventions can be effective in challenging the racist attitudes of individual perpetrators (and the perpetrator communities) which underpin hate crimes.[101] Docking and Tuffin also emphasise the importance of ensuring that hate crimes are prosecuted in a way that ensures that there is positive publicity (through keeping all parties informed and through contact with the local media) about the offence. Failed prosecutions could have the perverse effect of weakening the confidence of ethnic minority communities in hate crimes legislation. Proposals to increase the quality of prosecutions, and to strengthen the law on hate crimes, were also advanced by Burney and Rose, who suggested that there is a need to provide more guidance to prosecutors and the courts. The Burney and Rose report also emphasised the need for clearer guidance and definition of the term "racial animus" that converts basic offences into hate crimes.[102]

In the recent House of Lords decision in *R. v Rogers*[103] on the hate crimes (racially aggravated crime) provisions in the CDA 98 the issue was whether the words "bloody foreigner" and "get back to your own country" can transform the offence of abuse under the Public Order Act 1986 into a racially aggravated abuse contrary to CDA 98, s.31(1)(a). The House of Lords found that these words could be sufficient to show that conduct fell within the meaning of the word "racial". In the course of the judgment, Baroness Hale also commented on the issues of motivation and animus that translates the basic criminal offence into the racially aggravated offence. She stated that there were advantages in keeping the basic and the racially (or religiously) aggravated offence distinct and to leave this issue to fact-finders:

[100] Maria Docking and Rachel Tuffin, Racist Incidents: Progress Since the Lawrence Inquiry, Home Office Online Report 42/05, at pp. 49–50, (accessed December 10, 2006).

[101] *The Perpetrators of Racial Harassment*, by Rae Sibbitt (London: Home Office, 1997).

[102] Elizabeth Burney and Gerry Rose, "Racist Offences—how is the law working?", Home Office Research Study 244, (London: Home Office Research, Development and Statistics Directorate, July 2002).

[103] *R v Rogers* [2007] UKHL 8.

R v Rogers [2007] UKHL 8

"**[16]**: The late Sir John Smith, commenting on *Pal*, was critical of what he saw as a further complication of our already over-complex law of offences against the person in order to meet a problem which could equally well be met by sentencing guidelines. But as Mr Perry has pointed out, there is an advantage for the accused in differentiating between the basic and the aggravated offence. The fact finders, whether a jury or magistrates, have then to decide whether the offence was indeed racially or religiously aggravated. If they decide that it was not, then the offender should be sentenced on that basis. If the offence is not covered by these provisions, it is for the sentencer to decide whether it was racially aggravated and, if it was, to treat this as an aggravating factor in sentencing (Criminal Justice Act 2003, section 145).

[17]: The Court of Appeal in this case [2005] EWCA Crim 2863, [2006] 1 WLR 962, para 24, expressed some concern that

> '[t]he very width of the meaning of racial group for the purposes of section 28(4) gives rise to a danger that charges of aggravated offences may be brought where vulgar abuse has included racial epithets that did not, when all the relevant circumstances are considered, indicate hostility to the race in question.'

If that is what the evidence suggests, of course, the normal criteria for bringing proceedings would not be met. There is no reason for the Crown Prosecution Service to be any more hesitant about charging these offences, if they are properly supported by the available evidence, than about any other."

F. *Justifications for having Hate Crimes legislation*

The hesitance and reservations expressed in the Burney and Rose report, and certain cases, about the need to investigate the issues of "racial motivation" and "racial animus" as an essential part of the analysis that tranforms the basic criminal offence into a hate crime is also echoed in the work of some writers who question the legitimacy of hate crimes legislation in a liberal democracy. In Chapter 3 we discussed the different versions of liberalism that are used to justify discrimination law. That chapter also set out other arguments that are used to regulate forms of inequality and discrimination. These theories can generate arguments both for and against hate crimes. For example, neutrality based liberals such as Heidi Hurd argue that by criminalisng "ideas", hate crimes legislation breaches the requirement about neutrality in relation to individual conceptions of morality (the good) which is one of the fundamental requirements of a liberal democracy. In Chapter 3, we also considered the theories of writers such as Iris Marion Young who argue that targetting an individual for violence because of their membership of a group is one aspect of group oppression which can also be used to justify discrimination law. The arguments concerning the rights of vulnerable and protected groups is developed by Andrew Altman in the context of hate crimes, to argue that hate crimes legislation can be justified as a requirement of political liberalism. In this section we consider the arguments of Heidi Hurd and Andrew Altman and discuss (a) whether there is any justification for introducing hate crimes legislation in a liberal democracy; and also (b) to what extent hate crimes legislation fits into the general structure of, and promotes, the goals of discrimination law.

A number of writers have challenged the legitimacy of hate crimes legislation on the basis that it breaches core liberal principles. Jacobs and Potter argue that the term "hate crimes" introduces "identity politics" into the criminal law.[104] This, they argue, is inappropriate because it makes the criminal law a focus for struggles between groups, e.g. on the basis of race, gender, sexuality and religion. Potter and Jacobs also suggest that, by extenuating difference, hate crimes legislation may exacerbate rather than contribute towards addressing problems of inequality.

Heidi Hurd is representative of a number of liberal writers who argue that hate crimes legislation (even where it is narrowly drafted as in the Wisconsin criminal code, an issue in *Wisconsin v Mitchell* (see above)) is a fundamental deviation from the liberal requirement of neutrality. Hurd's main argument is that the justifications for hate crimes legislation are empirically, morally or conceptually suspect. She considers the main justifications that are often given for hate crimes legislation. First, in relation to the "wrongdoing thesis" which states that the harms perpetrated by offenders of hate crimes (e.g. psychiatric harms to the victims; fear to the victim's community; the threat to social order). Hurd argues that neither social science evidence, nor conceptual and moral consistency, justify the blanket sentence enhancements that are entailed by existing hate crimes legislation. Second, in relation to the "expressivist" thesis that hate crimes are a form of disrespect for victim communities and that a greater sentence in these cases reflects a legitimate denunciation of this lack of respect, Hurd notes that it is impossible to read a true stable message into the act of "hate crime". The final set of justifications that Hurd considers rely on the "greater culpability" of the perpetrator: that hate constitutes a unique "bad" mental state that justifies the higher sentence. Hurd argued that this is a serious deviation from a liberal system of criminal law which should focus on the wrongful act rather than the wrongful character of the perpetrator. In relation to the "greater culpability" and "worse character argument" Hurd states:

"In as much as hate/bias crime legislation in particular, and motivationally-oriented legislation in general, ultimately punishes persons for standing traits of character, it is best explained and justified by what is often called a 'character theory of criminal law'—a theory that takes the proper goals of the criminal law to be the punishment of vice and/or the cultivation of virtue. In

104 James B. Jacobs and Kimerley Potter, *Criminal Law and Identity Politics*, New York, USA: Oxford University Press, 2000).

as much as these are distinctly illiberal goals, those who advocate hate/bias crime legislation, or who are persuaded to generalize the sort of inquiry that it permits, cannot simultaneously count themselves political liberals."[105]

Hurd also challenges "greater culpability arguments" by noting that:

"As such, none, as yet, (of the theories) provide the necessary theoretical legitimacy for this politically popular form of criminal legislation. While little could be more important than breaking down the barriers of racism, chauvinism, bigotry, and homophobia, it is incumbent upon the state to restrict its means to those that can be justified by our best theory of criminal law [...] the case remains to be made out that hate/bias crime legislation can be so justified."[106]

Hurd concludes that:

"Perhaps the law is too effective a tool for accomplishing personal improvement to deny its use to those who can show that such evils as racism, sexism and homophobia, and other forms of hatred and bias can be reduced without significant costs to aspects of character that we value. But the burden remains on those who would operate on people's personalities with the state's most powerful instrument to assure us that they will excise only what is diseased".[107]

Dan Kahan has replied to Hurd's main claim that in liberal democracies the criminal law does not, or should not, punish "motive" and "character"; and that this provides an argument against hate crimes legislation. Kahan notes that a number of criminal law provisions already punish motive. He cites the law on self-defence, and the distinction between the law of assault and the law of rape. Kahan notes that there are examples in the criminal law that take into account motive and values, i.e. offenses where if the offender can show that he values the rights things, in the right way and amount, the criminal law exonerates him or mitigates his penalty. Kahan argues that the key focus of hate crimes legislation should be on the question of whether hate crimes legislation express values (i.e. the need to challenge bigotry and prejudice; or the need to promote goals such as equality) that can be endorsed. Kahan's response to liberals such as Hurd is that "what the opponents of hate crimes can't persuasively argue, however, is that hate crime laws are a bad idea

105 Heidi M. Hurd, and Michael S. Moore, "Punishing Hatred and Prejudice", Illinois Public Law and Legal Theory Research Papers Series, Research Paper No.3–17, November 18, 2003 at p.112.

106 Heidi M. Hurd, and Michael S. Moore, "Punishing Hatred and Prejudice", Illinois Public Law and Legal Theory Research Papers Series, Research Paper No.3–17, November 18, 2003.

107 Hedi M. Hurd, "Why Liberals Should Hate 'Hate Crimes Legislation' in (2001) 220 Law and Philosophy (C. H. Wellman, special editor) 215–232, at p.232.

because they take values into account in a way that the rest of the law does not."[108] Kahan goes on to conclude that one of the reasons that it is more difficult to justify hate crimes legislation is because it represents values that are emerging rather than established. Unlike the existing structure of criminal law which reflects established values, hate crimes legislation reflects "new" progressive values. Kahan concludes that the existing criminal law stacks "the rhetorical deck of the law in favor of traditionally heirarchical social norms and against progressive egalitarian ones."[109]

Andrew Altman, like Dan Kahan, has also argued in favour of hate crimes legislation, and he has done so within the explicitly liberal paradigm of John Rawls' theory of political liberalism. More specifically, Altman argues that hate crimes legislation can be justified as a requirement of liberal "public reason". His argument is similar to those of writers such as Fredrick Lawrence who argue that hate crimes legislation is essential to ensure the "equal" standing of minorities.[110] However, Altman's argument is distinct because he argues that hate crimes create a special kind of harm that should concern liberals. Altman states:

"the focal point should be that the harm of bias crime has a distributional impact that implicates the principle of equal citizenship: the harm threatens to undermine that principle. Such is the sort of harm that, from the perspective of public reason, can provide sufficient normative clout to justify even laws involving the stigmatization of certain political values and beliefs. And it is the sort of harm that can explain why antidiscrimination laws are publicly reasonable: such laws stigmatize but they are crucial in preventing the kind of harm that perpetuates or creates second-class status for certain social groups."[111]

Altman's justification is especially relevant in the context of hate crimes laws that are increasingly starting to replicate, and mirror, the social groups who are protected by employer-related discrimination law, e.g. not just race, but also sexual orientation, religion and disability. For example, as noted earlier, although the original hate crimes legislation in Britain focused on race (the CDA 98), there has been subsequent protection granted to religion (Anti-Terrorism, Crime and Security Act 2005) and also now statutory penalty enhancement in the areas of sexual orientation and disability (Criminal Justice Act 2003).

[108] Dan M. Kahan, "Two Liberal Fallacies in the Hate Crimes Debate", in (2001) 20(2) Law and Philosophy (C. H. Wellman, special editor), 175–193, at p.183.

[109] Dan M. Kahan, "Two Liberal Fallacies in the Hate Crimes Debate", in (2001) 20(2) Law and Philosophy (C. H. Wellman, special editor), 175–193. at p.190.

[110] Fredrick Lawrence, *Punishing Hate: Bias Crimes Under American Law* (Cambridge, MA: Harvard University Press, 1999).

[111] Andrew Altman, "The Democratic Legitimacy of Bias Crime Laws: Public Reason and the Political Process", (2001) 20(2) Law and philosophy (C. H. Wellman, special editor), 141–173, at p.164.

IV. Hate Speech

It is possible for the legal regulation of harassment and hate crimes to have an impact on the value of free speech. These conflicts between the normative goals of discrimination law on the one hand, and the constitutional protection accorded to free speech can arise in a number of areas. As *RAV v St Paul,* discussed above, illustrates, if hate crimes legislation is too broad it can pose a risk (in the US context) to constitutionally protected free speech.[112] The prospect that hate crimes legislation could potentially "chill" the speech of individuals more generally was considered in *Wisconsin v Mitchell,* but it was dismissed by Rehnquish C. J. as "too speculative".[113] In the context of harassment, certain speech in the workplace can constitute discriminatory harassment, and is restricted by discrimination law.[114] In the areas of hate crimes and discriminatory harassment, the nature of the harm that is caused by speech, as well as the context within which speech takes place, provide a justification for resolving any potential conflict in favour of the goals of discrimination law. This argument relies, in part, on distinguishing these spheres of speech (used in the commission of a criminal offence or in the workplace) from more general public discourse in a liberal democracy.

In the case of discriminatory harassment in the workplace, for example, it might be argued that (a) there are legitimate limits that can be placed on speech because employees do not have the power to be able to escape from an unduly hostile environment; and (b) democratic arguments to allow free discussion of ideas are less urgent. This suggests that certain types of speech in the workplace, e.g. sexist speech, can be limited.[115] It can also be argued that a liberal democracy can legitimately give priority to allowing vulnerable minorities to ensure that they have access to key social and economic goods (such as employment and also public services). This can be facilitated by prohibiting discriminatory harassment in contexts where there is a risk of the abuse of public and private power that may harm women and minorities through certain types of speech and acts.[116]

Arguments that justify giving weight to the goals of non-discrimination in the context of hate crimes and harassment do not, however, apply easily in the wider public sphere, in which free speech is considered to be a cornerstone of

[112] For a discussion of the free speech implicaitons of hate crimes legislation in the British context see Maleiha Malik, Analysis of the Crime and Disorder Act 1998 [1999] 10(1) K.C.L.J 126.

[113] *Wisconsin v Mitchell* (1993) 124 L. Ed. 436.

[114] For a discussion of sexual harassment and free speech see Catherine A. MacKinnon and Riva B. Siegel, (eds), Directions in Sexual Harassment Law, New Haven, USA: Yale University Press, 2004, Part V.

[115] For a discussion of the difficulties of regualting sexist speech see Marcy Strauss, "Sexist Speech in the Workplace", (1990) 25 Harv. C. R. C. L. L. Rev. 1

[116] Robert Post, "Sexual Harassment and the First Amendment", in Catherine A. MacKinnon and Riva B. Siegel, (eds.), Directions in Sexual Harassment Law (New Haven, USA: Yale University Press, 2004) Part V.

liberal democracy and has greatest weight. This section is concerned with the issue of speech in this wider public context. Within this context, it has been argued that speech that targets individuals because of their membership of protected social groups is a form of "hate speech" that can be regulated.

A. *Hate Speech Regulation*

1. International, US and Canadian Law

ICCPR Article 20

"1. Any propaganda for war shall be prohibited by law.
2. Any advocacy of national, racial or religious hatred that constitutes incitement to discrimination, hostility or violence shall be prohibited by law."

The International Convention on the Elimination of All Forms of Racial Discrimination (1966) contains a provison that deals with racial hatred. CERD states in s.4:

International Convention on the Elimination of All Forms of Racial Discrimination
Adopted and opened for signature and ratification by General Assembly resolution 2106 (XX) of December 21, 1965
(entry into force January 4, 1969, in accordance with Article 19)

Article 4

"States Parties condemn all propaganda and all organizations which are based on ideas or theories of superiority of one race or group of persons of one colour or ethnic origin, or which attempt to justify or promote racial hatred and discrimination in any form, and undertake to adopt immediate and positive measures designed to eradicate all incitement to, or acts of, such discrimination and, to this end, with due regard to the principles embodied in the Universal Declaration of Human Rights and the rights expressly set forth in article 5 of this Convention, inter alia:

(a) Shall declare an offence punishable by law all dissemination of ideas based on racial superiority or hatred, incitement to racial discrimination, as well as all acts of violence or incitement to such acts against any race or group of persons of another colour or ethnic origin, and also the provision of any assistance to racist activities, including the financing thereof;

(b) Shall declare illegal and prohibit organizations, and also organized and all other propaganda activities, which promote and incite racial discrimination, and shall recognize participation in such organizations or activities as an offence punishable by law;

(c) Shall not permit public authorities or public institutions, national or local, to promote or incite racial discrimination."

The UN's observations on the United Kingdom's compliance with CERD, art.4, and the Government response, have been summarised by the Joint Committee on Human Rights in its 2004–5 Report concerning CERD. The report highlights a number of important points about this international legal standard:

(a) The Concluding Observations re-stated the UN Committee's view that the UK's interpretation of Article 4 was unduly restrictive, and stressed that the Article 4 obligation was a mandatory one (para 86);

(b) The Minister argued before the Committee that there would be no advantage to race relations, community cohesion or race equality in removing the interpretative declaration to Article 4 and taking steps to criminalise racist ideas and organisations. The Government also confirmed that their priority was to ensure prosecutions under incitement provisions rather than pursue criminalisation of organisations (see para. 91 and 92);

(c) in relation to incitement to religious hatred "the UN Committee expressed its concern in the Concluding Observations at the recent increase in anti-Islamic attacks, and recommended the criminalisation of offences motivated by religious hatred against immigrant communities."[117] (para.93)

In the US a strict approach is taken to the criminalising of hate speech generally, including racist speech. Hate crimes legislation was recognised as permissible under the US constitutional protection of free speech because its potential impact on speech was felt to be "speculative". However, in relation to "hate speech", as opposed to "hate crimes", the US approach comes down in favour of the free speech principle. This is illustrated by *RAV v St Paul*, which permitted the burning of a cross (a racist symbol of the far right KKK group). Perhaps the most dramatic and clear illustration of the US first amendment protection for hate speech is the *Skokie* case, in which it was held that the US National Socialist Party (a far right Nazi group) had the right to march and parade through Jewish areas of the town of Skokie whilst wearing uniforms that displayed the swastika.[118]

The Canadian Supreme Court has taken a different approach to the rela-

[117] Joint Committee On Human Rights—Fourteenth Report of Session of 2004–2005 on "The Convention on the Elimination of Racial Discrimination", HL 88/HC 471 (Session 2004–05).

[118] *National Socialist Party v Skokie*, 432 U.S. 43 (1977).

tionship between hate speech and the goals of discrimination law. In *Keegstra*, a secondary school teacher had made anti-semitic statements in classes in breach of the Canadian Criminal Code (Criminal Code, s.319 prohibits the wilful promotion of hatred against identifiable groups).[119] The Canadian Supreme Court unanimously found that "hate speech" falls within the definitions of protected free speech: Dickson C.J. stated that

> "It must be emphasized that the protection of extreme statements, even where they attack those principles underlying the freedom of expression, is not completely divorced from s.2(b) (freedom of expression provison) of the Charter [. . .] the protection of communications virulently unsupportive of free expression values may be necessary in order to ensure that expression more compatible with these values is never justifiably limited."[120]

Nevertheless, the majority found that hate speech restrictions in the criminal code were a reasonable limit on free speech. It is worth noting that this analysis and justification did not rely on s.15 (equality) and s.27 (multiculuralism) of the Canadian Charter i.e. rights to equality, non-discrimination and tolerance for minorities were not used to interpret and limit the scope of the s.2(b) freedom of expression provision of the Charter. Rather, the majority relied on the provision of s.1 of the Canadian Charter which guarantees rights and freedoms but also states that these can only be proscribed by law as can be demonstrably justified in a free and democratic society. On the facts of *Keegstra*, the majority in the Canadian Supreme Court found that the provisions in the Criminal Code met the tests of reasonableness and proportionality, and they were not overbroad. Significantly, the majority held that the effects of the restriction on hate speech were not so deleterious in their result that they undermined the constitutional right to free speech. The Canadian Supreme Court focused on the fact that the "expressive activity" of hate speech was a special category which did not contribute to the promotion of the key values of free speech, such as quest for truth, promotion of individual self-development or fostering a vibrant democracy.[121]

The justification in *Keegstra* for treating hate speech as a "special category" within the generical class of constitutionally protected speech is similar to the European Court of Human Rights analysis of the issue, i.e. hate speech falls within constitutionally protected speech under Art.10 of the ECHR, but can (subject to the legal tests of necessity and proportionality) be justified by a legimate exception under Art.10(2). In *Lingens v Austria* the Court held that speech which shocks of offends is protected free speech.[122] Two Eur. Ct. H.R. cases—*Jersild v Denmark*[123] and *Otto-Preminger Institu v Austria*[124]—illustrate this point, although they also modify the Court's approach towards hate

[119] *R v Keegstra* [1990] 3 S. C. R. 697.
[120] *R v Keegstra* [1990] 3 S. C. R. 697, 765.
[121] *R v Keegstra* [1990] 3 S. C. R. 697, (see opinion of Dickson C. J.)
[122] *Lingens v Austria* [1986[E. H. R. R. 103.
[123] Series A, No.298-A
[124] Series A, No.295-A

speech. The facts of *Jersild* are especially important because they shed light on the potential use of Art.10 of the ECHR to prohibit hate speech, and the legality of incitement to racial hatred legislation in Britain. In *Jersild*, during the course of a television interview, some young men made racist comments. The young men were convicted for incitement to racial hatred. In addition, the journalist who interviewed them was convicted of aiding and abetting them. The Court found that there was a breach of Art.10 ECHR, but did so in a way that does not render all incitement to racial hatred legislation in breach of the ECHR. They found that the statements of the young men did not enjoy the protection of Art.10 and could be prosecuted as hate speech. However, they also found that the conviction of the journalist was not permissible under Art.10 because (a) it had a non-racist context and purpose, rather than being a means for the propagating of racism; and (b) the punishment of a journalist under these contexts would hamper the public function of the press to discuss matters of public interest in a democratic society.

Therefore, it seems clear from the discussion in *Jersild* that an appropriately drafted statute which targets the actual perpetrators of hate speech will not necessarily breach ECHR Art.10. The European Court of Human Rights has gone even further in *Otto-Preminger*.[125] On the facts, a religious group in Austria had started a prosecution (at the request of the Roman Catholic Church) of a film that was potentially offensive to Christians. The Austrian court had allowed the conviction and ordered the seizure and forfeiture of the film. The majority of the Eur. Ct. H.R. found that the Austrian authorities had acted within their "margin of appreciation" under Art.10(2) and "to ensure religious peace [. . .] and to prevent that some people should feel the object of attacks on their religious beliefs in an unwarranted and offensive manner."[126] The Court accepted that there should be criticism of religion but also stated that "the manner in which religious beliefs and doctrines are opposed or denied is a matter which may engage the responsibility of the State [. . .]"; the Court then went on to cite a "chilling effect" justification for restricting speech in these contexts and stated that "in extreme cases the effect of particular methods of opposing or denying religious beliefs can be such as to inhibit those who hold such beliefs from exercising their freedom to hold and express them".[127] Finally, the Court concluded that a state may "legitimately consider it necessary to take measures aimed at repressing certain forms of conduct, including the imparting of information and ideas, judged incompatible with the respect of freedom of thought, conscience and religion of others".

In *Otto-Preminger*, the Court drew on a number of justifications, including the argument that certain types of hate speech are a special category that can be prohibited because of their impact on the social (racial or religious) groups that are its targets. In addition, the Court also gave a special status to religious

125 *Otto-Preminger v Austria* (1995) 19 E. H. R. R. 34.
126 *ibid.*, paras 52–56.
127 *ibid.*, paras 47–48.

belief as a special category which deserves protection. It refers to states being left a margin of appreciation in relation to speech which is directed at the religious *feelings* of others. In so far as the European Court of Human Rights is analysing the harm of hate speech in terms of the harm to the "religious feelings" of individuals or religious groups rather than speech that is likely to incite group hated, the *Otto-Preminger* case is protecting offences such as blasphemy. In *Choudhry v UK* the Eur Comm. H. R. has held that there is no obligation on a state to extend protection from blasphemy to minority religions.[128] This has been confirmed by the European Court of Human Rights in *Wingrove v UK*[129] which held that there was no breach of Art.10 when the British Board of Film Classification refused a classification for a film (with the consequence that it could not sold or put on public display) which depicted sexually explicit scenes of Christ and St Theresa of Avila.

Before moving on to a discussion of "incitment to hatred" as a form of regulating hate speech, it is important to recognise that blasphemy and "incitement" are two very different ways of addressing the problem of hate speech. Blasphemy has been a well established criminal offence in domestic law. As the refusal to grant a classification to the film in *Wingrove*, and the successful criminal prosecution in *R. v Lemon* confirms, the offence has been used to prohibit films that offend Christian sentiment. *Choudhry v UK* (which had gone to the Eur.Comm. H. R. on appeal from a decision of the Divisional Court in *R. v Chief Metropolitan Magistrate Ex p. Choudhry*[130]) which held that Muslims were not protected under the domestic criminal law on blasphemy. The case had arisen out of the Salman Rushdie controversy which had led many Muslims to argue in favour of protecting their "religious sentiment" from vilification and offence. The result suggests unequal protection of religious groups.

Despite the often easy assimilation between blasphemy and hate speech provisions (such as incitement to racial hatred), it is important to keep them distinct. As David Nash has noted, an essential feature of blasphemy is that it is based on a relationship with the sacred.[131] Therefore blasphemy law's purpose is to protect religious belief and sentiment from attack, and the victim who is offered protection is the person who holds that religious belief. This is different to the offence of incitement to racial or religious hatred, which is aimed at preventing hatred against those who hold a certain belief (rather than safeguarding religious sentiment). Moreover, as Helen Fenwick and Gavin Phillipson note, the relevant target audience of blasphemy and incitement to hatred are different: whereas blasphemy seeks to protect the sacred beliefs of

[128] Choudhry v UK (Case No.17439/90) (1991) H. R. L. J. 172. See also discussion of this anomoly in the ECHR approach to blasphemy in Robert Wintemute, "Blasphemy and Incitement to Hatred under the Convention" (1995–96) 6 K.C.L.J. 143.

[129] (Application No.17419/90) Judgment of November 25, 1996, R.J.D. 1996-V; 24 E.H.R.R.

[130] [1991] 1 Q.B. 429.

[131] David Nash, *Blasphemy in the Christian World: A History*, (Oxford: Oxford University Press, 2007).

religious individuals; incitement, seeks to regulate hate speech that is aimed not at the believer but rather at *others*. Fenwick and Phillipson analyse the underlying rationale for the two offences as addressing very different issues: incitement to hatred legislation is aimed at preserving harmony in a diverse (multiethnic and multifaith) society; whereas blasphemy protects certain sacred beliefs from critical comment, satire and ridicule. They conclude that the law relating to blasphemy should be repealed.[132] Robert Post has also stated that blasphemy laws lead to a loss of democratic legitimacy in the liberal state:

''With respect to those who do not share the religious beliefs protected by particular blasphemy laws, and who are therefore expelled from public discourse, the state is rendered heternomous. The state loses democratic legitimacy with respect to those who do not believe in the truths protected by a law of blasphemy. This loss of democratic legitimacy may be acceptable if a state does not aspire democratically to govern those of differing religious beliefs. But most modern states define their jurisdiction in terms of geographical territory that includes persons of many different religious beliefs. To the extent that democratic legitimacy is important with respect to persons who do not share the beliefs enshrined in a state's law, any such loss of democratic legitimacy should be unacceptable.''[133]

2. ''Incitement to Hatred—the British Experience''

There has been a criminal offence of incitement to racial hatred since the early race relations legislation (Race Relations Act 1965, s.6). This was introduced against a background of increased post-war immigration from the Commonwealth, and the prospect of the rise of a far right political movement and later Powellism.[134] Here, it is worth observing that this recurring theme of race as a ''public order'' problem, rather than a concern with the rights of dignities of minorities, provided the background for the early regulation of racist speech. This concern with public order is reflected in the language and context of the early incitement offence which, as commentators have noted, shared a lineage with the earlier common law offences of sedition and mischief which also focused on (i) intention; (ii) raising discontent amongst those *to whom the speech*

[132] Helen Fenwick and Gavin Phillipson, *Media Freedom under the Human Rights Act* (Oxford: Oxford University Press, 2006) Ch.9.

[133] Robert Post, ''Religion and Freedom of Speech: Portraits of Muhammad'' (2007) 14(1) Constellations 72.

[134] For discussion see Anthony Lester and Geoffrey Bindman, *Race and Law*, (Penguin: Harmondsworth, 1972), especially pp.344–360 and pp.417–418.

is addressed; and (iii) promoting hostility between different *classes* of such subjects.[135] The current offence of incitement to racial hatred draws on these roots and is now explicitly placed within the context of public order (Public Order Act 1986, Pt III, ss.17–23). There have been very few prosecutions under these provisions. Under the original legislation it was essential that the incitement to hatred was within the territorial boundaries of Britain. This jurisdictional limiting condition was removed by the Anti-terrorism, Crime and Security 2001 which states at s.37 that "In section 17 of the Public Order Act 1986 (c.64) (racial hatred defined by reference to a group of persons in Great Britain) omit the words 'Great Britain'". The removal of this jurisdictional limit has meant that it has been possible to prosecute those who have called for the killing of members of a racial group outside Britain. Incitement to religious hatred is prohibited under the Public Order (Northern Ireland) Order 1987, although there have not been a significant number of prosecutions under this provision.[136]

A central issue in understanding the protection afforded by the current incitement to racial hatred provisions has been the range of groups who are protected (an example of what was described in chapters 1 and 2 as the first key question of discrimination law). The Public Order Act 1986 provisions on incitement to racial hatred have replicated the definition of "racial group" that was developed in *Mandla v Dowell Lee*.[137] One consequence is that they have also replicated the anomolies of that definition, in that it covers ethnic religious minorities (e.g. Jews and Sikhs) but not non-ethnic religious minorities (e.g. Rastafarians and Muslims).[138] Despite the application of this anomoly, there is also case law that suggests that anti-Muslim incitement could still fall within the definition of "racial hatred" under the current legislation.[139]

The European analysis of the overlap between racial and religious hatred confirms this approach. In *Norwood v DPP* a man displayed a sign in his shop window which stated "Islam out of Britain—Protect the British People", and a symbol of the cresent and star with a prohibition sign. He was prosecuted under the Public Order Act 1986, s.5 which criminalises:

135 Ivan Hare, "Crosses, Crescents and Sacred Cows: Criminalising Incitement to Religious Hatred", [2006] P.L. 521–538. Hare notes this overlap and cites Stephen's definition of sedition which states "an intention [...] to raise discontent or disaffection amongst Her Majesty's subjects, or to promote feelings of ill-will and hostility between different classes of such subjects."

136 See Theresa Murphy, "Incitement to Hatred: Lessons from Northern Ireland", in S. Coliver (ed.), *Sriking a Balance: Hate Speech, Freedom of Expression and Non-Discrimination* (Essex: Art.19, 1992).

137 *Mandla v Dowell Lee* [1983] 2 A. C. 548.

138 See analysis of the anti-Muslim politics of the BNP in Kay Goodall, "Incitement to Religious Hatred: All Talk and No Substance" (2007) 70(1) M.L.R. 89–113, at p.94.

139 See Kay Goodall, "Incitement to Religious Hatred: All Talk and No Substance" (2007) 70(1) M.L.R. 89–113, at pp.96–98.

"any writing, sign or other visible representation which is threatening, abusive or insulting, within the hearing or sight of a person likely to be caused harassment, alarm, distress thereby."

He was also charged with the religously aggravated version of the POA 85, s.5 offence with is contained in the Crime and Disorder Act 1998. The man's appeal from conviction to the High Court was not allowed, as the Court found that the restriction on speech did not breach the HRA or ECHR freedom of speech provisions.[140] He appealed to the European Court of Human Rights which found that there had been no breach of the Art.10 ECHR free speech provision. The Court held that there was a legitimate interest in protecting religious groups from this type of "hate speech", and to promote the ECHR values of tolerance, social peace and non-discrimination.[141] This approach fits in with the general trend of using the criminal law to address the most serious forms of hate speech, as illustrated by the recommendation of a recent opinion of the Parliamentary Assembly of the Council of Europe which has endorsed this strategy.[142] Significantly, the recommendations also emphasised that blasphemy should not be criminalised.

The government's response to the challenge of prejudice and hatred against Muslims was to extend the incitement to racial hatred provisions to religion. To this end, it introduced the Racial and Religious Hatred Bill in June 2005[143] which sought to add hatred on the ground of religion to the existing racial incitement provisions. There was, however, a significant media and political campaign against the Bill, which has been described by Fenwick and Phillipson as "ill informed."[144] Parliament approved the amended version and passed the Racial and Religious Hatred Act 2006, which created a new Pt 3A of the Public Order Act 1986 containing the offence of incitement to religious hatred.

The government's acceptance of the amendments to this Bill (the new Pt 3A) meant that it is now in a different form to the provisions on incitement to racial hatred. The assessment of whether this is a welcome development have been mixed. Kay Goodall argues that: "The legislative history in Britain and Northern Ireland suggests that the new part 3A will be almost unenforceable. Without a confession it will be very difficult to prove the purposive intention. [...] The Lords have pruned this statute so hard they have left it a stump".[145] Ivan Hare on the other hand argues that there are important freedom of speech

140 *Norwood v DPP* (2003) W.L. 21491815.

141 *Norwood v UK* (2004) 40 E.H.R.R. SE111.

142 "Blasphemy, religious insults and hate speech against persons on the grounds of their religion Opinion", Committee on Legal Affairs and Human Rights Rapporteur: Mr Jaume BARTUMEU CASSANY, Andorra, Socialist Group, Doc. 11319, June 25, 2007, see paras 7–8.

143 Bill 11, 54/1 introduced to the House of Common on June 9, 2005.

144 Helen Fenwick and Gavin Phillipson, *Media Freedom under the Human Rights Act* (Oxford: OUP, 2006) Chapter 9.

145 Kay Goodall, "Incitement to Religious Hatred: All Talk and No Substance" (2007) 70(1) M.L.R. 89–113, at p.113.

concerns that justify either no legislation or very narrow legislation in drafting incitement to religious hatred provisions. He cites the fact that race and religion are different; and also that once hate speech is extended to religion this will let in claims to protection by numerous other groups. Hare concludes that "the UK already has ample general criminal law provisions to deal with incitement to hatred and any public order consequences which may follow from it and therefore has no need of further restrictions which are certain to make us less free and are likely to prove to be counter-productive [. . .] Perhaps then, the only merit of the proposal is that it may provoke further reflection on the desirability of the existing prohibition on incitement to hatred on racial grounds."[146] This final point reinforces the views of those, like Eric Heinze, who argue that existing hate crimes legislation favours some powerful groups (and viewpoints) over others, and that the only consistent principled approach is to abolish all hate speech statutes.[147]

B. *Non-Legal Responses to Hate Speech—Cultural Policy and Media Regulation*

A focus on the use of the criminal law to protect minorities, especially given the controversial British debates on incitement to racial and religious hatred legislation, can obscure an analysis of whether or not the use of the criminal law is an appropriate or sufficient response in the context of hate speech. As stated earlier, there are very few prosecutions under these criminal provisions. There is also increasing concern that the structural lack of power of minorities that motivates the introduction of hate speech regulation also affects the way in which hate speech legislation is prosecuted, i.e. that provisions such as incitement to racial and religious hatred are used more frequently to criminalise the speech of minorities rather than protect them from hate speech. This may be especially true in the case of the speech of religious minorities on issues such as the rights of women or gays. This assymmetry of power, and risk of disproportionately criminalising minorities, suggests that incitement provisions offer some limited protection, whilst at the same time arguably reducing the rights of these minorities to exercise freedom of speech.[148]

There are, also, arguments in support of the view that free speech rather than the restriction of speech is a key value for minorities. David Richards, for example, argues that the American scepticism about allowing group based harms (such as hate speech) to justify restrictions on constitutionally protected free speech cannot be fully explained in terms of its concern for democracy. Richards argues that there is an additional factor that explains the US

146 Ivan Hare, "Crosses, Crescents and Sacred Cows: Criminalising Incitement to Religious Hatred", [2006] P.L. 521–538.

147 Eric Heinze, "Viewpoint Absolutism and Hate Speech" (2006) 69(4) M.L.R. 543.

148 Helen Fenwick and Gavin Phillipson, *Media Freedom and the Human Rights Act* (Oxford: Oxford University Press, 2006), Ch.9.

approach. On this analysis, free speech is a critical constitutional and legal tool for minorities who have suffered injustice: to criticise and challenge dehumanising stereotypes. Richards argues that it also "empowers the legitimacy and integrity of the politics of identity in the reasonable understanding and remedy of structural injustice of group and national identity whose political power has rested on invisibility and unspeakability of such injustice."[149] This approach enables a focus on the strucutural disadvantage of minorities who are the targets of hate speech; but it also suggests that the appropriate response to hate speech minorities is not criminalisation but rather enabling more speech by minorities. This shifts the argument from strategies of law towards non-legal strategies of cultural policies that create the capacity in minorities to respond to hate speech through developing what Richards calls a "personal moral voice":

"it is because such voice is personal (not based on the state's judgment of group based harms) that has the moral authority and integrity that it has in addressing the terms of structural injustice."[150]

It can, therefore, be argued that the key goals of discrimination law are better secured by allowing minorities to develop a "personal voice" and to give them more opportunities for speech. This is also compatible with the liberal free speech principle because although a liberal state cannot easily interfere with free speech it can legitimately prioritise a concern with the autonomy and well being of individuals who are victims of hate speech. It can also legitimately use investment and cultural policy, to develop the capacity of minorities to respond to hate speech. In order to do this, there may be a need for some regulation, although this need not be legal (especially not criminal law) regulation. It is significant that incitement to racial or religious hatred targets the most extreme forms of speech. Whilst these are serious forms of hate speech, it is also the case that there is prejudice and stereotyping in the mainstream media which, in many cases, will have a more widespread influence. Prejudice and stereotypes in the mainstream media may in fact be more pernicious because these views and representations are "normalised" and "presented as the ordinary truth about the world in which we live". This is one of the issues in the debate about pornography (which can be analysed as a form of hate speech against women). The use of media regulation may therefore be a more successful way of addressing this "normalised" source of hate speech. For example, clause 13 of the Press Complaints Commission Code of Practice which deals with discriminatory speech states that:

149 David A. J. Richards, *Free Speech and the Politics of Identity*, (Oxford: Oxford University Press, 1999) at p.237.

150 David A. J. Richards, *Free Speech and the Politics of Identity*, (Oxford: Oxford University Press, 1999) at p.242.

"(i) the press must avoid prejudicial or pejorative references to an individual's race, colour, religion, gender, sexual orientationor to physical or mental illness or disability; (ii) Details of an individual's race, colour, religion, sexual orientation, physical or mental illness or disability must be avoided unless genuinely relevant to the story."

A greater use of this provision, and the use of third party support to support individual litigants through the use of the CEHR, may allow the creation of a public sphere that is more conducive to allowing the pariticipation of minorities in public debate.[151]

V. Conclusion

This chapter has charted the legal and policy issues surrounding the increased regulation of harassment, hate crimes and hate speech. In relation to harassment, there is now a consensus that it is legitimate for the law to prohibit discriminatory harassment. Such a prohibition is thus found in EU and domestic discrimination law, and applies to all grounds of prohibited discrimination (e.g. race, sex, and sexual orientation) and in relation to most of the areas falling within the scope of discrimination law (most consistently, employment). There is also increasing focus on putting into place preventative procedures in the workplace, introducing a duty on employers to protect workers against discriminatory harassment, bullying and violence.[152] The treatment of "hate crimes" and "hate speech" also reveals an increasing use of the criminal law to pursue the goals of discrimination law.

These developments implicate various of the key questions of discrimination law discussed in Chapters 1 and 2. All the measures considered, this chapter raises the question of "who is preferred?" and "when are they protected". Furthermore, the use of criminal law to regulate hate speech raises the issue of clashes between the right not to be discriminated against and the protected rights (in the case of free speech). Due to this clash, there may be good arguments for using other legal strategies such as cultural policy, which do not risk clashing with fundamental values such as free speech in pursuit of the values associated with discrimination law.

151 For a discussion of these issues in the context of media freedom see Jacob Rowbottom, "Media Freedom and Political Debate in the Digital Era", (2006) 69(4) M.L.R. 489–513.

152 See, for example, the text of EU Framework Agreement on Harassment and Violence at Work, signed April 26, 2007; see Michael Rosenstein, *EU Framework Agreement on Harassment and Violence at Work* (2007) 169 E.O.R. 24.

9

MULTIPLE DISCRIMINATION, INTERSECTIONALITY AND CONFLICTS OF RIGHTS

I. INTRODUCTION

The expansion of the prohibited grounds of discrimination, especially in EU and domestic law makes the issue of the relationship between these "protected characteristics" especially important. Moreover, the creation of a single equality commission, the Commission on Equality and Human Rights, means that there is an opportunity to address some of the issues raised by multiple discrimination. Wherever there is more than one possible ground of discrimination[1] there is complexity in a case. However, it is worth separating out the way in which different prohibited grounds of discrimination may interact with each other. There are also significant causes of discrimination (e.g. poverty) that operate simultaneously with prohibited grounds such as race or gender that are often ignored in a "single axis" approach to discrimination law. In particular, an analysis of protected groups as homogenous entities ignores the fact that not all individual members of relevant groups share the same social position: for example, individual members of racial groups, or women, are divided from each other by social differences such as income and education. The facts of a case may reveal that there is more than one possible ground on which discrimination has occurred. For example, a woman may be discriminated against because she is also African; or a disabled person may also be discriminated against because of his or her sexual orientation. There are many combinations of the prohibited grounds on which the discrimination has occurred that can be present in the same case. Where it is quite clear that the relevant ground is *either* sex or race, disability or sexual orientation, the case will be straightforward. However, even in cases where there seems to be only one ground, the fact that there are a number of potential and overlapping prohibited grounds may be relevant. It may be that a single ground is identified because a strategic choice has been made to choose one over the other

[1] The Equal Opportunities Commission published a summary of cases where Industrial Tribunals have considered issues of multiple discrimination, see *http://www.eoc.org.uk/Default.aspx?page=15655*. These are discussed in more detail below.

ground for evidentiary reasons. In such cases, a certain legal framework can provide an incentive to prefer one ground over another, e.g. a lower burden of proof for sex rather than race, or a more generous definition of indirect discrimination for disability rather than sexual orientation, may explain the choice of that single ground as the cause of action.

In other cases, there may be facts that suggest that there has been compounded discrimination, i.e. that discrimination on more than one ground has taken place. In these cases, there is a tendency to treat the presence of more than one ground of discrimination as a quantitative matter, i.e. it "adds" to the nature of the discrimination. So, if there are two grounds the quantity is doubled and if there are three grounds it is trebled. This approach can be called *additive discrimination*. It is argued that this fails to take into account the qualititative change that might occur where there is the presence of more than one ground of discrimination. This qualitative transformation in the nature of the discrimination experienced may take place in a number of ways. First, the fact that an African woman has experienced discrimination cannot just be distinguished into two characteristics: sex and race. It could be argued that the presence of both these categories transforms both sex and race as grounds. Therefore, an African woman experiences discrimination as a woman in a way that is distinct from other women who are not African. She also experiences discrimination as an African in a way that is distinct from other Africans who are not women. We can call this *intersectional discrimination*.

Before moving on to a discussion of intersectional discrimination, it is important to identify a further way of expressing the relationship between the different prohibited grounds: in some cases, it may be impossible to reconcile the claims of one group to non-discrimination on a prohibited ground (e.g. sex) and the claims of another group that is also relying on a right in discrimination law on a different prohibited ground (e.g. religion). Discrimination law has specifically recognised that there may be such conflicts and made exceptions for these situations by creating specific exclusions (e.g. where appointment of ministers of religion is not covered by the prohibition on sex discrimination in employment). This category can be called *conflicts of grounds* and is discussed in Pt II of this chapter.

II. Multiple Discrimination

Commentators, such as Sarah Hannett[2] have highlighted the importance of addressing this issue "multiple discrimination". Yet, at the same time, the existing structure and concepts of discrimination law has been criticised as

[2] Sarah Hannett, "Equality at the Intersections: The Legislative and Judicial Failure to Tackle Multiple Discrimination" (2003) 23 O.J.L.S. 65.

framed around a "single axis" which is ill suited to respond to the challenge of multiple discrimination.

A. *"Single Axis" Discrimination Law—the critique*

Kimberle Crenshaw criticises the "single axis" of discrimination law which is concerned with ensuring what she categorises as procedural fairness, i.e. a result that would be reached "but for" the effects of race and sex. She argues that this single-axis framework of discrimination law cannot deal with the complex relationship between categories, such as race and gender, that contribute to the substantive problems of disadvantage and discrimination. The structure of liberal discrimination law, with its focus on symmetry and comparison is—on this view—inhospitable to claims of multiple discrimination. The need for a "hypothetical comparator" often focuses on one narrow point of comparison and fails either to (a) examine confluence or relationships with other protected grounds; or (b) recognise the context in which the conditions for multiple discrimination and its resulting structural disadvantage operate.

According to Crenshaw, "single axis" discrimination law results in the exclusion, marginalisation or distortion of the experiences of those individuals who are subordinate and have less power. Single axis discrimination law defines prohibited grounds in discreet and additive categories: as sex or race or sexual orientation. Where there is more than one prohibited ground, there can be a claim for sex *and/or* race *and/or* sexual orientation. This single axis structure has no room for an analysis that treats the relationship between these grounds as being more closely related, so that the presence of sex and race leads to a new ground such as African women; or the presence of race and sexual orientation results in the ground of African lesbian. Moreover, this single axis approach to discrimination law and the prohibited grounds is based on a reductionist view that cannot respond to the problems of intersectionality.

More specifically, there are at least three ways in which it could be argued "single axis" discrimination law is unable to address problems of multiple discrimination generally and intersectionality in particular.

First, it assumes that claimants can be categorised according to one dominant social ground such as race or sex. In earlier chapters we examined the critique of discrimination law which questions its focus on symmetry and comparison. This approach, it is argued, gives priority to the viewpoint of those with greater power: i.e the norm against which treatment is evaluated is provided by standards such as "men" or the majority "white" or "heterosexual". This critique of discrimination law is also relevant in understanding the reasons that discrimination law finds it difficult to address problems of multiple and intersectional discrimination. The "background" norm means that certain dominant social norms and social identities become the entrenched and neutral (and almost "invisible") background against which protected characteristics are analysed and applied. The choices of which grounds are recognised within discrimination law, how these grounds are defined and how individuals are categorised within and between these different grounds all takes place within this paradigm. Where a particular group does not fit into the predominant social norm or social identity it will find it difficult to fit into this paradigm, with the consequence that its experiences may be excluded, distorted or marginalised. Moreover, definitions of the prohibited grounds themselves may be influenced by the "background norm" and issues of social power. Nitya Iyer[3] has argued that the fact that comparison is so important in discrimination law will mean that the definition of the established prohibited ground, and the identification of difference, will tend to be filtered through the normative standard of those in power. For example, in the context of race discrimination, out of all the substantive characteristics that a racial or ethnic minority may have, the one that becomes predominant for discrimination law is the one characteristic which emerges from a comparison with the dominant group, i.e. they are not white. Characteristics such as these then become entrenched and an "identifier" for the whole group: they become wholly constitutive of that group's social identity within discrimination law, irrespective of the reality of differences within that group on the basis of gender, sexuality or class, etc. In this way, discrimination law essentialises and homogenises social groups according to normative standards that reflect the social norm and social identity of those who have greater power. The dilemma for those with less social power is that in order to bring themselves within the protection of discriminaton law they have to fit within these categories. This forces them to adopt the protected characerisitics that they confront despite the fact that they may not fit into these categories in an easy way.

Second, a single axis approach often construes a prohibited ground in a essentialist fashion, a fixed category that is beyond renegotiation or reconstruction. This essentialist approach also means that one (of a number) of ways of defining the relevant social characteristic is used as way of defining the experience of the whole group. As Angela Harris has noted, this essentialism also entrenches the viewpoint of those who have greater power.[4] In the context of gender, for example, it may lead to a neglect of certain groups within the category "women", e.g. ethnic minority women whose experience of discrimination will be significantly different (in terms of causes and structural factors) to those of majority women. In the context of intersectional discrimination, not only will outsiders to a group seek to define the boundaries of acceptable conduct that define that social group, but dominant insiders in a group may seek the police norms of behaviour. As Kathryn Abrams has observed, the phenomenon of "disciplinary harassment" ensures that those

[3] Nitya Iyer, "Categorical Denials: Equality Rights and the Shaping of Social Identity" (1993–1994) 19 Queen's L. J. 179, at 188–191.

[4] Angela P. Harris, "Race and Essentialism in Feminist Legal Theory" (1989–90) 42 Stan. L. R. 581.

who are biological members of a protected group (e.g. men) may seek to control—and where there is transgression to discipline—those such as gays, bisexuals or transexuals who "attempt to escape from the social characteristics ascribed to their groups."[5] This tendency towards essentialism also means that all group members are treated as sharing the same qualities irrespective of the fact that there may be important differences between them either (a) because of other social characteristics such as race, class or sexual orienation; or (b) because the way in which the same characteristic, e.g. gender or race, manifests itself in their lives is different to the "norm".

This essentialising and homogenising tendency of the single axis appraoch is summarised by Iyer in the following passage:

Nitya Iyer,
"Categorical Denials: Equality Rights and the Shaping of Social Identity" (1993–1994) 19 Queen's L. J. 179, at 193

"Since it is assumed that everyone in a particular pocket has no other relevant characteristics, it is not possible to articulate differences between those within a pocket—differences with respect to other social characteristics and even with respect to the social characteristic under discussion. If Joel and Claire are both 'white' then differences of age and gender between them disappear, as does the fact that one is Jewish (arguably a racial characteristic in that anti-semitism is considered to be race discrimination) and one is not. This has disturbing implications. For example, when a claimant wins an anti-discrimination case, the law assumes that the remedy is appropriate for all members in the group; differences among those within the group (or pocket) which might make the remedy unhelpful, or even harmful for some, are not perceived."

Third, a single axis framework for discrimination law seals off this ground from other related and overlapping protected grounds. Moreover, this atomistic method isolates each of the grounds from each other rather than encouraging an analysis that explores their relationship, overlap and interconnectedness. Iyer summarises this tendency in the following terms:

Nitya Iyer,
"Categorical Denials: Equality Rights and the Shaping of Social Identity" (1993–1994) 19 Queen's L. J. 179, at 192–193.

"At least two sets of problems arise from this model of anti-discrimination law. The first arises from the fact that each pocket is isolated from the others. That is, it is assumed that it

[5] Kathryn Abrams, "Title VII and the Complex Female Subject", (1993–1994) 92 Mich. L. Rev. 2479, at 2533.

is possible and appropriate in the context of redressing relations of inequality to consider the social characteristics each pocket represents in isolation. Although it is useful to maintain analytic distinctions between race and gender and all of the other grounds, I believe that it is rarely, if ever, possible to arrive at socially just outcomes by treating rights claimants as if they *are* one (and only one) particular social characteristic. Further, because pockets are isolated, the definition of the characteristic each represents is similarly isolated and static. The definition of the characteristic is what, in the dominant group's view (necessarily a perspective external to those in the pocket) the meaning of that characteristic is, what it considers to be the 'difference' from the dominant social identity. As categorizer, I choose what I see as different about Gwen and what that means. Regardless of how she would describe her racialization, I can decide that she is white and, by extension, what 'whiteness' is. Therefore, there is no guarantee that someone whose subjective experience of adverse treatment corresponds to the label on one or more pockets will actually succeed in her or his claim. The claim will fail unless the claimant's experience of discrimination can be made to accord with how the dominant group imagines discrimination on the basis of a given characteristic. [...]"

All three critiques of "single axis" discrimination reinforce the conclusion that this approach to categorising the subjects of discrimination law can cause distortion. The failure of categories in discrimination law, especially in the context of multiple discrimination, is not just a technical problem of legal concepts. For those individuals who suffer double discrimination, single axis discrimination law makes it difficult for them to use existing categories to advance their claims. In the context of the intersection of gender and race the consequences of such failure are profound. The structure of discrimination law enables those in positions of power within the category "gender" to maintain their social and economic advantages; and it asks those who are most marginalised and vulnerable within that category (e.g. ethnic minority women) to bear the burden for advancing this model of gender discrimination. Moreover, the homogeous treatment of grounds of discrimination, that forces minority women into the position of arguing all their experiences of discrimination at the intersection of race and gender as "race" discrimination, prevents them from developing a distinct personal identity, consciousness and politics which is distinct from that of men within their racial groups. This seriously hampers their ability to challenge sex discrimination within their own racial, cultural and religious communities. Finally, the failures of single axis discrimination law also have significant political and constitutional implications for minority social groups because as Judy Scales-Trent argues, "Naming oneself, defining oneself and thereby taking the power to define out of the hands of those who wield that power over you, is an important act of empowerment."[6]

Before moving on to consider the general arguments about multiple discrimination, it is worth re-iterating that the presence of more than one prohibited ground in a case can cause real difficulties for the courts. The previous theoretical analysis of the issues is important precisely because we need a better understanding of the real fact situations where multiple discrimination

[6] Judy Scales-Trent, "Black Women and the Constitution: Finding Our Place, Asserting Our Rights" (1989)24 Harv. C.R.C.L.L. Rev. 9, at 43.

claims arise. So far they do so in a significant number of cases in Employment Tribunals. While the literature on multiple discrimination (including that discussed in this chapter) tends to focus on the conflict between role and gender, and the position of ethnic minority women, it is important to recognise that multiple discrimination issues can arise in a wide range of factual contexts across the whole range of prohibited grounds: sex, race, disability, religion, sexual orientation and age. An understanding of the way in which these factors relate to each other, and also relate to the social context in which discrimination occurs and is experienced, is therefore essential. One difficulty in relation to these emerging types of multiple discrimination is the availability of statistics. Nevertheless, as the prohibited grounds of discrimination expand the need for quantitative work and the collection of statistics to understand the issue becomes more important. It is also important to undertake qualitative work on multiple discrimination in areas including but not limited to the overlap between race and gender. In an important qualitative study of multiple discrimination, the Joint Equality and Human Rights Forum (JEHR Forum) bought together human rights and equality bodies in Britain Ireland and Northern Ireland to examine the issue of multiple identities. The resulting publication, "*Rethinking Identity: The Challenge of Diversity*"[7] deals not only with ethnic minority women but also multiple groups such as gay, lesbian and bisexual (LGB) disabled persons. There are very few statistics on the number of peole who would fall into this category but a conservative estimate puts the number of LGB disabled persons in Britain at about 255,000[8]. This confirms that there are important issues of inequality, discrimination and exclusion experienced by those who have multiple identities and are members of multiple minority groups. The qualitative studies in *Rethinking Identity* confirm that issues of multiple identity and multiple discrimination are also of critical importance to, inter alia, disabled minority ethnic people or lesbian, gay or bisexual people who suffer from a disability. The report emphasises a number of essential aspects: the importance of a focus on identity to a person's sense of self; the complexity and fluidity of identity; the need for attitudinal and systemic change within institutions; and the need to raise awareness on issues that relate to multiple identity groups.

Multiple discrimination can occur across the range of identities that are protected in discrimination law. Nevertheless, and as stated, the interface between race and gender has given rise to considerable discussion. There is increasing recognition of the structural difficulties faced by ethnic minority women in employment, and questions about why sex discrimination law and policy is failing to deal with this inequality. Another factor that makes the issue of multiple discrimination, especially in relation to sex and race in

[7] "*Rethinking Identity: The Challenge of Diversity*", (Katherine Zappone (ed.), Commissioned by the Joint Equality and Human Rights Forum, June 2003.

[8] See Michael Brothers, "It's Not Just About Ramps and Braille: Disability and Sexual Orientation", in "Rethinking Identity: The Challenge of Diversity"' (Katherine Zappone (ed.), Commissioned by the Joint Equality and Human Rights Forum, June 2003, at p.51.

employment, of particular urgency is the increasing evidence of the concentration of ethnic minority women in low paid work. The EU has recently recognised the need to widen its concern with the rights of women by also considering the distinct needs of minority women.[9] Recent evidence which confirms this trend is summarised by the Equal Opportunities Commission:

Statement Of The Equal Opportunities Commission:
"New eoc research shows bigger challenges in the workplace for ethnic minority women"
April 7, 2006 *http://www.eoc.org.uk*

"On the eve of the TUC Black Workers conference, the Equal Opportunities Commission has published early findings from its ongoing investigation into ethnic minority women at work, which shows that:

- Pakistani women face a pay gap at least 10 percentage points higher than that of white women, whilst the pay gap for Bangladeshi women is at least 5 percentage points higher. A quarter of Pakistani and Bangladeshi women work in wholesale and retail, where the median pay for sales assistants, for example, is £5.15 per hour, £4.61 less per hour than average earnings for women working full time.
- Working Black Caribbean women are 8 percentage points more likely to have a degree than white women. Yet only 9% of Black Caribbean women are managers/ senior managers, compared to 11% of white women. Job segregation is more of an issue too: almost a third of all Black Caribbean women work in health and social work, compared to less than a fifth of white women.

Ahead of the TUC Black Workers conference, the EOC and TUC are releasing a joint statement calling for renewed urgency to deal with the persistent inequality facing ethnic minority women in the workplace.

Jenny Watson, Chair of the Equal Opportunities Commission, said:

"The Women and Work Commission has reminded us again of the continuing pay gap that women face. But it is particularly disturbing that this gap is larger for Pakistani and Bangladeshi women than for white women and that they, and Black Caribbean women, also face higher levels of job segregation and fewer opportunities to progress to more senior positions." [...]

The EOC's investigation has shown that, for example, ethnic minority women surveyed by the EOC were three times more likely than white women to be asked at job interviews about their plans for marriage and children—a violation of the Sex Discrimination Act. And one in five Pakistani and Bangladeshi women, over 90% of whom are Muslim, said they had often experienced negative attitudes towards religious dress at work."

[9] The EU European Women's Lobby (EWL) has recently held consultations and discussions on this issue. See the conclusions and recommendations: EWL: Equal Rights, Equal Voices, Migrant Women in the EU, Brussels 19–21, January 2006 (available at *www.womenlobby.org*, accessed March 13, 2007).

The final paragraph of this statement illustrates in the most dramatic way how multiple discrimination claims may arise. The experiences of Pakistani and Bangladeshi women can be categorised as discrimination based on sex, race and religion. For example, there is increasing evidence that although young Pakistani Muslim women are doing well in school, they are being held back in job markets and employment. The EOC cites questions by employers about their intimate private relationships which may be indicative of prejudices and assumptions that their marriage patterns and personal relationships will make them unreliable employers. The EOC study states that: "One in six young Pakistani women is often asked at job interviews about plans for marriage and children, or the attitude of a husband or partner towards her going to work. One in eight young Bangladeshi and black African-Caribbean women face similar questions about their private lives, compared with one in 17 white women."[10] Legal and policy responses that merely target on an undifferentiated analysis of gender will fail to capture the full nature of the harm experienced by these women. Moreover, a focus on the explicit prohibited grounds of discrimination may also miss the differences of social class and education that differentiate some ethnic minority women from others. The Equal Pay Act focuses on comparisons between men and women and is not well suited to address the complexity of overlaps of gender and race (and socio-economic differences in each category) that combine to create pay disparaties between men and women, or majority women and ethnic minority women.

Existing concepts and institutional arrangements in discrimination law are not ideally placed to address problems of multiple discrimination. There is increasing recognition that a more sophisticated approach to categories such as "sex" and "race" is required in order to deal with the claims of ethnic minority women. Recent employment or industrial tribunal cases summarised by the Equal Opportunities Commission illustrate the increasing sophistication in responding to multiple discrimination claims by ethnic minority women.[11]

[10] John Carvel, Muslim girls surge ahead at school but held back at work, *The Guardian*, Thursday September 7, 2006

[11] For a more qualitative and analytical discussion of the intersection of gender, race and religion (including interviews with women)see Fauzia Ahmad, Tariq Madood, Stephen Lissenburgh, *South Asian Women and Employment in Britain: The Interaction of Gender and Ethnicity* (London: Policy Studies Institute, 2003).

EOC case summaries on race and sex cases—multiple discrimination *http://www.eoc.org.uk*

"Listed below are a number of case decisions concerning sex and race discrimination to illustrate the way that tribunals deal with the issues. The decisions are helpful in informing any negotiations you may have with an employer about your treatment, whether it is likely to be unlawful, and in preparing your employment tribunal case.

Mrs C Mackie v G & N Car Sales Ltd t/a Britannia Motor Co. Case: 1806128/03

Mrs. M, a book-keeper/assistant accountant, claimed that she was unfairly dismissed because of being a woman of Indian origin. During her 5 months of employment she was told by a colleague that the three company directors, who were also of Indian origin, did not approve of Asian women working for the company and the only reason they allowed themselves to take on Mrs M. was because she was married to a Scotsman.

Following a visit from the directors' father, who normally lived in India, Mrs M. was told that she was being dismissed. She asked for the reason but was not given one. She was later told by letter that there was no obligation to provide her with a reason given her short period of employment, though at the hearing the company came up with a reason.

The tribunal found that Mrs M. had been subjected to less favourable treatment by being dismissed and then being denied a reason. In coming to their decision the tribunal considered a hypothetical comparator of a male with identical qualities to Mrs M. but of a racial origin other than Indian. They found that a comparator would not have been dismissed in the same circumstances. *The tribunal was not convinced by the company's evidence and found that Mrs M. was not treated less favourably because she was a woman nor simply because she was Indian, but because she was an Indian woman.* [emphasis added]

Mrs M. had not been employed for one year and therefore could not claim unfair dismissal, however her claim of sex and race discrimination was successful.

Miss A Rawat v Kirkless Metropolitan Council (1) Mr Singh (2) Mr G Harker(3) Ms J Lancaster(4) Mr S Laher(5) Case No.1804500/98

Miss R. claimed that she had been subjected to detrimental treatment on the grounds of her sex and race as an Asian Muslim woman by her manager, an Asian male; that when she complained the investigation into her grievance was biased; that subsequent report findings were flawed; and that she was victimised as a result of her complaints.

Miss R. claimed that her manager would not relate to her professionally because she was an Asian woman, and did not respect her rights as an employee. In contrast, he had a good rapport with a white woman who job shared with Miss R.

Miss R. claimed that when she complained about her treatment she was then victimised by a closing of ranks around her manager and an unfavourable change in the way that she was treated by her colleagues. She also felt that the grievance meetings were not conducted impartially, instead of being treated as the aggrieved party she was made to justify her allegations, more like a disciplinary, and her manager was not similarly dealt with.

The respondents denied the claims and said they had carried out an investigation into her claims of race discrimination, which was thorough and fair.

The tribunal found that Miss R. had been discriminated against on the grounds of her sex and/or race.

[...]

Mrs S Ali v (1) North East Centre for Diversity & Racial Equality (2) Jamiel Bux Case No.2504529/03

Mrs A, a finance officer, claimed that she had been treated less favourably on the grounds of her race and sex when she suffered humiliating treatment by Mr B. in front of her colleagues and her family. She received demands that she cook for Mr B., received unjustified complaints about her work, and was required to be involved in dubious financial arrangements.

The tribunal described as extraordinary, Mr B's insistence that Mrs A. attend at his house with her family for work-related issues and found it to be harassment on grounds of sex and race. The tribunal made the same finding in relation to an incident when Mrs A. sought advice from a male colleague regarding her banking duties and became so upset by Mr B's reaction that she needed to attend hospital and never returned to work at the centre.

The tribunal found that the treatment of Mrs A. amounted to harassment on the grounds of sex and race and was the result of a perception of Mrs A. as being *compliant because she was a Pakistani Muslim woman who had been brought up in Pakistan. Mr B. decided that he could manipulate her. The tribunal considered that Mr B. would not have made the same demands of a white female employee nor of Muslim female employees who had been brought up in Britain* [emphasis added]. He would not have acted in the same way towards the men employed."

In some cases, there are fact situations that could be construed as either sex and/or race/nationality discrimination. In *Mrs D Webley v Gefco (UK) Limited*, reported by the Equal Opportunities Commission, the applicant Mrs Webley argued both nationality discrimination and sex discrimination. After hearing the evidence the Tribunal found that there had been nationality discrimination but that there had been no sex discrimination.

Mrs D Webley v Gefco (UK) Limited Case No. 2203901/00 (cited in EOC case summaries *http://www.eoc.org.uk*)

"Mrs W, a human resources manager, claimed less favourable treatment by reason of her race or nationality when a part of her job was assigned to a male French national (Mr R) who did not have the relevant experience or training. She claimed that she was treated less favourably on grounds of sex by both the conduct of the General Manager towards her and by the imposition of a male French national as a member of staff. She claimed that there was a strong emphasis on recruiting more French people from the Gefco's holding company. Mrs W. resigned as a result.

The Tribunal held that Gefco unlawfully discriminated against Mrs W. on the grounds of her race in that Mrs W. suffered detriment because part of her job was taken away. Mr R. did not have the credentials to do the job. The Tribunal was satisfied that had he been English he would not have been appointed to the job.

The Tribunal found that Gefco did not unlawfully discriminate against Mrs Webley on the grounds of her sex. Whilst the General Manager was casual and perhaps thoughtless in his dealings with her this was not on the basis of her gender. Mrs W. succeeded in her claim of unfair dismissal on this ground."

B. *Additive Discrimination*

Cases where two types of discrimination can be argued as alternatives can be distinguished from cases of additive discrimination where the presence of two prohibited grounds increases the quantitative nature of the experience of discrimination and is a double burden. *Nwoke v Government Legal Service & Civil Service*,[12] discussed by Sarah Hannet, provides an example of additive discrimination. Nwoke was a Nigerian born woman who applied for a job in the Government Legal Service. The evidence established that: (a) white applicants for the post were ranked higher, even if they possessed a lower class of degree; (b) white women were less likely to be appointed than men; and (c) even if white women were appointed, they received a lower salary than men. Moreover, the only person on a temporary contract who was not appointed to the permenant post was a black woman. Nwoke successfully claimed for both race and sex discrimination. There was "additive" double discrimination in this case because *Nwoke* suffered from two types of prejudice and disadvantage in employment: as a woman and as someone who was black.

C. *Multiple Discrimination in International law*

The issue of multiple discrimination also arises, and has been discussed, in the context of international human rights and equality law. In fact, there will be an increased likelihood of multiple discrimination at the international level, where differences within and across different grounds of discrimination will be more likely because of a greater diversity of culture, ethnicity and religion.

The *Sandra Lovelace* case,[13] which is discussed in more detail in the section on conflict of grounds below, illustrates the way in which two international human rights norms can overlap. *Lovelace* concerned Art.26 ICCPR right to non-discrimination on the ground of sex as well as the group's collective right to cultural life under Art.27 ICCPR. *Lovelace* also illustrates the specific challenge of addressing multiple discrimination at the international level: Lovelace's claims was for sex discrimination; but at the same time she was asserting her right from within her racial and cultural group as a member of an indigenous people. Two sources of non-discrimination were overlapping and apparently in conflict in this case.

International human rights equality norms also raise issues of additive and intersectional discrimination. Kimberele Crenshaw discusses this issue in a

[12] (1996) 28 EOR 6. See discussion, and cited in Sarah Hannet, "Equality at the Intersection" (2003) 23 O.J.L.S. 65, at 69.

[13] *Sandra Lovelace v Canada*, Communication No.R. 6/24, U. N. Doc. Supp. No.40 (A/36/40) at 166 (1981).

background paper on the intersection of race and sex discrimination in the context of international human rights law. Crenshaw makes the point that there has been greater mainstreaming of sex discrimination norms in international human rights documents, such as the Convention on Elimination of Discrimination Against Women, than there has been of international human rights norms in the field of race discrimination. This has, she argues, marginalised the experiences of minority women. Clearly, the issue of variation within the category "women" will be exacerbated at the international level: differences of race, culture and religion will significantly increase once there is a move from a domestic to an international context. Crenshaw also notes that men can suffer from intersectional discrimination: for example, African Caribbean men are the targets for lynching on the grounds of both their gender and race. She also goes on to argue that these problems of intersectional discrimination (which are at their most tragic and acute in the context of armed conflict, rape and other forms of violence that targets women) are also relevant in the distribution of political, social and economic goods to women.

Crenshaw's analysis applies the conceptual categories that she has developed in the context of US discrimination law to international human rights law. In the context of international human rights law, the issue is not the coverage of the legal norms because there are comprehensive conventions that cover protected grounds such as race, gender, religion and disadvantage. Instead there is a need for some interpretative link between the different legal norms and prohibited grounds that gives sense to the way in which individuals experience discrimination and disadvantage in a complex way. Crenshaw argues for the development of a new "International Protocol" to address the problem of intersectional discrimination in international law:

Background Paper for the Expert Meeting on the Gender-Related Aspects of Race Discrimination November 21–24, 2000, Zagreb, Croatia

World Conference Against Racism Selected Documents and Links (*http://www.wicej.addr.com/wcar_docs/index.html*) Durban, South Africa 31 August–7 September 2001

"It is important to recognize that although prevailing conventions and laws have sometimes been narrowly interpreted to capture only discrimination or disempowerment that occurs along a single axis of power, such cramped interpretations contravene the explicit scope of conventions, laws and declarations which are intended to protect individuals from race and gender based denial of rights. Thus, to the extent that CERD is intended to protect individuals from race discrimination, the rights protected therein encompass all aspects of race discrimination, including those aspects that effect women and men differently. The same interpretation applies to gender discrimination: the rights guaranteed by CEDAW encompass the full range of race-related experiences of gender discrimination.

While no additional articulation of basic principles is necessary to create rights and protections against intersectional discrimination, it would be useful to develop interpretive protocols to break existing interpretations and practices that diminish the rights of victims of intersectional subordination."

Crenshaw also notes that there is evidence from UN agencies that women migrants face double discrimination, based on both gender and other grounds such as race or religion.[14] Crenshaw's analysis is developed in the specific context of gender and race but it could apply to other international non-discrimination norms, governing for example religion and disability. Crenshaw's international protocol on multiple discrimination could include and provide guidance on, inter alia, contextual analysis and information-gathering and developing methods to uncover intersectional discrimination. Such a protocol could make clear that race and gender are not fixed and constant markers; and it could compensate for what Crenshaw describes as the uneven development of international law in the field of sexism rather than racism, as well as the North/South Divide. The recommendations that Crenshaw makes for a new protocol are interpretative and practical measures designed to enable greater interaction between existing international non-discrimination norms in instruments such as CEDAW and CERD rather than the creation of new norms. These measures include, inter alia: the creation of incentives for data collection by states to identify those such as minority women who are at risk of intersectional discrimination; the introduction of cross-referenced interpretative guidance such as Recommendation 25 of CERD which states that "the Committee will endeavor in its work to take into account gender factors or issues which may be interlinked with racial discrimination"; encouraging national bodies and legal systems to introduce effective strategies and remedies against intersectional discrimination; and increasing the capacity of those who are marginalised to participate in human rights discourse.[15]

[14] Maxine Frith, "Women migrants 'suffer double discrimination', *The Independent*, September 7, 2006.

[15] See discussion in "BACKGROUND PAPER for the EXPERT MEETING on the Gender Related Aspects of Race Discrimination", November 21–24, 2000, Zagreb, Croatia. Document available at: World Conference Against Racism, Durban, South Africa 31 August–7 September 2001, *http://www.wicej.addr.com/wcar_docs/index.html* (accessed on 23 August 2006).

III. Intersectional Discrimination

A. *What is Intersectional Discrimination?*

The concept of intersectional discrimination can be applied to a number of different prohibited grounds. It has been developed in detail in the context of the intersection between race and sex discrimination. It is argued that where there is an overlap between prohibited grounds, there is also a complex relationship that can lead to a quanitative change (additive discrimination) and also a qualitative change (intersectional discrimination). Kimberle Crenshaw, for example, sets out the main characteristics of intersectional discrimination.

Crenshaw identifies this tendency in discrimination law which she concludes is a "procedural approach" in which race and sex only become important when they operate explicitly and interfere with what are considered to be neutral decisions.[16]

Kimberle Crenshaw, "Demarginalising the Intersection of Race and Sex: A Black Feminist Critique of Antidiscrimination Doctrine, Feminist Theory and Antiracist Politics" (1989) U. Chi. Legal F. 139

p.140: "I want to suggest further that this single-axis framework erases Black women in the conceptualization, identification and remediation of race and sex discrimination by limiting inequiry to the experiences of otherwise-priveleged members of the group. In other words, in race discrimination cases, the focus on race and class priveleged women.

This focus on the most privileged group members marginalizes those who are multiply burdened and obscures claims that cannot be understood as resulting from discrete sources of discrimination. I suggest further that this focus on otherwise privileged group members creates a distorted analysis of racism and sexism because the operative conceptions of race and sex become grounded in experiences that actually represent only a subset of a much more complex phenomenon. [. . .]

I argue that Black women are sometimes excluded from feminist theory and antiracist policy discourse because both are predicated on a discrete set of experiences that often does not accurately reflect the interaction of race and gender. These problems of exclusion cannot be solved simply by including Black women within an already established analytical structure. Because the intersectional experience is greater than the sum of racism and sexism, any analysis that does not take intersectionality into account cannot sufficiently address the particular manner in which Black women are subordinated. Thus for feminist theory and antiracist policy discourse to embrace the experiences and concerns of Black

[16] Kimberle Crenshaw, "Demarginalising the Intersection of Race and Sex: A Black Feminist Critique of Antidiscrimination Doctrine, Feminist Theory and Antiracist Politics (1989) U, Chi. Legal F. 139, at 151.

women, the entire framework that has been used as a basis for translating 'women's experience' or 'Black experience' into concrete policy demands must be rethought and recast.

p.149: I am suggesting that Black women can experience discrimination in ways that are both similar to and different from those experienced by white women and Black men. Black women sometimes experience discrimination in ways similar to white women's experiences; sometimes they share very similar experiences with Black men. Yet often they experience double-discrimination—the combined effects of practices which discriminate on the basis of race, and on the basis of sex. And sometimes they experience discrimination as Black women—not the sum or race and sex but as Black women."

As the Crenshaw passage indicates, there are a number of ways in which the single axis approach of discrimination law and the failure to construct adequate categories can be problematic. In some cases the experiences of those who are at the intersection of grounds will be erased, distorted or marginalised. Iyer summarises this dilemma in a dramatic way in the following passage:

Nitya Iyer, "Categorical Denials: Equality Rights and the Shaping of Social Identity" (1993–1994) 19 Queen's L. J. 179, at 192.

"In order to succeed in an anti-discrimination law claim in law, an individual or group must first convince a decision-maker, who is usually a member of the dominant social group, that the individual or group belongs in a pocket. This means that the claimant must present a carciature of the individual or group's social identity, distorting the individual and communal experience of a social characteristic (one that is historically specific and contingent, and which interacts in complex ways with other characteristics), into a static and oversimplified image of the claimant's 'difference'. In this cartoon drawn from the perspective of the categorizer not from that of the subject of the categorization, one social characteristic assumes gigantic proportions while other aspects of social identity are rendered indistinguishable from the background norm. If this distortion is accepted by the court, the claimant can then go on to show a causal link between this image and the harm suffered."

In other cases, there will need to be a more complex analysis. Once we accept that the co-existence of more than one ground of discrimination can lead to a qualitiative as well as quantitative change a number of further questions arise. How does this qualitative change occur? Does it render the new form of intersectional discrimination unique (i.e. is the experience of ethnic minority women unique?) or is it similar and related in form to the established category of discrimination (i.e. it is similar to race or sex discrimination)? What is the relationship between those practices that are intersectional as compared with those that target just one group? Is intersectional discrimination hierarchically worse than other forms of discrimination? As the analysis on intersectional discrimination matures these questions can be explored with greater sophistication. Distortion, misrepresentation and exclusion may be caused because existing categories (the prohibited grounds of discrimination) are over-inclusive or underexclusive of the reality of discrimination as experienced by the victim. These defects will sometimes be difficult to distinguish, and they may overlap in some cases. Nevertheless, this distinction provides one way of understanding the way in which intersectional discrimination operates in relation to individuals.

B. *Overinclusive Categories—the problem of misrepresentation and distortion*

A prohibited ground of discrimination can be said to be overinclusive where it fails adequately to reflect the fact that some of those who fall within that category is more likely to experience discrimination either (a) quantitatively, i.e. they suffer a greater amount of discrimination; or (b) qualitatively, i.e. they have a different experience of the way in which discrimination is suffered. An example of the way in which a prohibited ground may be overinclusive is provided by analysing the case of ethnic minority women.

A useful illustration of the possible overinclusiveness of race as a single issue category is seen in *Burton and Rhule v De Vere Hotels*,[17] also discussed in Ch.8. In *Burton* two young black waitresses were employed to serve at tables at the respondent's hotel at a dinner where the comedian Bernard Manning was the main speaker. During the course of the evening, Manning made jokes about the sexuality of black men and women including statements, inter alia, that black women were good at certain sexual acts. Guests at the dinner also made sexist and racist comments: one guest tried to put his arms around one of the waitresses whilst making sexually offensive comments to her; another guest asked the waitresses what "a black vagina taste[s] like?" The claimants successfully brought a claim for racial harassment under the Race Relations Act 1976 (RRA). It was recognised that they could have also brought a claim for sexual harassment under the Sex Discrimination Act 1975 (SDA). However, this choice of racial harassment or sexual harassment (i.e. an addititive approach to the discrimination) fails to capture the way in which this is a case of intersectional discrimination. Both race and sex were used simultaneously and they cannot be separated. The language used by the discriminators reproduces general stereotypes about all women, but it is also distinctive in its use of stereotypes about the sexuality of black women (and, in some of the

[17] *Burton and Rhule v De Vere Hotels* [1997] 1 I. C. R. 1. Intersectional discrimination is a common problem in harassment cases involving both sex and race. For example of Canadian cases see *Cuff v Gypsy Restaurant and Abi-ad* (1987) 8 C. H. R. R. D/3972, (Ontario Board of Inquiry); *Olarte v DeFillippis and Commodore Business Machines Ltd* (1983), 4 C. H.R.R. D/1705 (Ontario Board of Inquiry). Discussed in "An Intersectional Approach to Discrimination: Addressing Multiple Grounds in Human Rights Cases", (Canada: Ontario Human Rights Commission Discussion Paper, 2001).

comments, black men). This is an example of stereotypes about the sexuality of women that are based on more than just their race: both gender and race are operating simultaneously to produce the problem. The use of either the race and/or sex formulation fails to capture the distinctive way in which harassment has functioned in this context. The use of race as the relevant category is overinclusive. It excludes the fact that the way that the language used targets the victims as "women". The role of gender in creating the harassment is obscured and subsumed within the category race.

Burton involves a problem of intersectional discrimination because the category "gender" or "race" is being used to express the whole of the discrimination issue without any acknowledgement that these categories need to be refined to express the "qualitative change" that occurs when they co-exist. Of course, in many cases factors that are not prohibited grounds in discrimination law, such as class, may also be a relevant cause. Later in the chapter we discuss the way in which a move away from a single axis approach to discrimination law may take variables into account. Here it is worth reiterating that the full range of the problem that is produced (through the simultaneous of impact of gender and race) is not taken into account by the single axis approach to discrimination law.

C. *Underinclusive categories*

We have seen a single prohibited ground may be overinclusive. It could dominate the whole of the analysis of discrimination or subsume other relevant prohibited grounds that are operating to create the discrimination. There is, therefore, a risk that the true nature of the discrimination will not properly be analysed and appropriate remedies will not be developed. Another type intersectional discrimination operates in a related way: mainly where a category such as gender is underinclusive.

Unlike overinclusive categories, which create distortion by subsuming the discrimination into one general ground (e.g. gender) underinclusive categories create distortion by failing to take into account relevant information. Kimberle Crenshaw distinguishes this type of intersectional discrimination because it is particularly relevant to groups who are likely to be subordinated through multiple discrimination, e.g minority women. Crenshaw states that:

"A gender analysis may be under-inclusive when a subset of women who are subordinated experience a problem, in part because they are women, but it is not seen as a gendered problem because it is not the experience of women from the dominant groups. A more common site of under-inclusion occurs where there are gender distinctions among men and women within racial or ethnic groups. Often it seems that if a condition or problem is specific to women within a racial or ethnic group, and by its nature unlikely to happen to men, its identification as a problem of race or ethnic subordination is compromised. Here the problem is that the gendered dimension of a problem renders it invisible as a matter of race or ethnicity. The reverse, however, is rarely the case; usually race discrimination that functionally targets men does warrant inclusion into the category of race discrimination even though women may not be equally effected by it"[18]

It will sometimes be difficult to distinguish between overinclusive and underinclusive forms of intersectional discrimination, and there may sometimes be an overlap between the concepts. Nevertheless, it is important to notice that the distinguishing feature of underinclusive intersectional discrimination will be that it is likely to occur in two ways. First, discrimination may involve an established category but in a way that renders invisible or marginalises the experience of some members of that group (marginalisation within a protected group). Second, and more seriously, underinclusive intersectional discrimination may occur because there is a failure to provide a category which is able to reflect the harm as experienced by the victim (exclusion from a protected group). Examples of marginalisation include cases where claims of discrimination and harassment by lesbian women have been deemed to fall outside the category "sex". Examples of exclusion include those cases where there are gender distinctions between men and women in a racial or ethnic group that are experienced by minority women as sex discrimination *within* that group, but these are not treated as sex discrimination because the category "sex" reflects the viewpoint of majority women.

D. *Marginalisation and Exclusion*

In some cases of intersectional discrimination, the fact that protected categories of discrimination law are underinclusive may mean that an individual who has suffered from discrimination does not have protection because he or she may fall between relevant prohibited grounds. They may be unable to bring themselves within any of the available protected characteristics. At first sight, it may be assumed that those systems of discrimination law where there is a strong constitutional framework, and which have a more flexible approach to the definition of which grounds are prohibited, will be better equipped to deal with multiple discrmination. However, the decision of the Supreme Court of Canada in *Canada v Mossop*[19] illustrates that this is not always the case. In *Mossop*, the claimant was a translator who worked for the Secretary of State. His collective agreement in employment provided for one day of bereavement leave from work in relation to the death of a member of the family. Mossop claimed this day of bereavement leave when his same sex partner's father

[18] Kimberle Crenshaw, "Background Paper for the Expert Meeting on the Gender-Related Aspects of Race Discrimination, November 21–24, Zagreb Croatia. Document filed at following source: World Conference Against Racism, Durban 31 August–7 September, Selected Documents and Links at *http://www.wicej.addr.com/wcar docs/index.html* (accessed on August 20, 2006).

[19] *Canada (Attorney-General) v Mossop* [1993] 1 S.C.R. 554.

died. His application was denied on the basis that because the bereavement related to his partner's father, and his partner was of the same sex, this situation was not covered by the provisions for bereavement leave in the collective agreement. Mossop bought an action under the Canadian Human Rights Act (CHRA) section 3 and argued that this denial of leave constituted discrimination on the grounds of family status. CHRA, s.3 states:

"For all purposes of this Act, race, national or ethnic origin, colour, religion, age, sex, marital status, family status, disability and conviction for which pardon has been granted are prohibited grounds of discrimination."

Significantly, sexual orienation is not included in the list of prohibited grounds. Therefore, Mossop was forced to rely on the protected ground of family status. The tribunal at first instance decided in favour of Mossop. On appeal by the Attorney General to the Supreme Court of Canada, the majority held that Mossop could not bring himself within the category of "family status". What is interesting about this conclusion is that it confirms the way in which a single axis approach to the prohibited grounds gives preference to dominant forms of social identity, even within a discrimination law regime that defines prohibited grounds in an open textured way. The Canadian Supreme Court assumed that the only manifestation of Mossop's social identity as a gay man was in the context of sexual orientation: it did not permit an analysis of his social identity as a gay man that manifested itself in the context of family relationships. Therefore, the inevitable consequence of this analysis was that the only protected ground in which Mossop could have fit his claim was sexual orientation. There was no possibility for him to argue that one way in which his identity as a gay man manifested itself was in his same-sex relationship[20], and therefore he had experienced discrimination not because of his sexual orientation, but rather because of his family status. The protected characteristic "family status" was defined from the perspective of hetereosexual family forms (the dominant social norm that acts as the "neutral background" against which the protected category is defined). All issues of difference within family forms were excluded from the analysis and relegated to the category "sexual orientation". Therefore, Mossop would have had a claim under the Canadian Charter, Section 15 which prohibits discrimination on the ground of sexual orientation, but he could not claim that the discrimination was on the basis of family status.

The dissenting judgment of L'Heureux-Dube J., in *Mossop*, recognised the need to move away from a focus on a single ground. She stated that:

"categories of discrimination can overlap and [. . .] individuals may suffer historical exclusion on the basis of both race and gender, age and physical handicap, or some other combination. The situation of individuals who confront multiple grounds of disadvantage

[20] *Canada (Attorney-General) v Mossop* [1993] 1 S.C.R. 55, 645–646.

is particularly complex. Categorizing such discrimination as primarly racially orientated, or primarily gender-oriented, misconceives the reality of the discrimination as it is experienced by individuals [. . .]. There are situations where a person suffers discrimination on more than one ground, but where only form of discrimination is a prohibited ground. When faced with such situations, one should be cautious not to characterise the discrimination so as to deprive the person of any protection [. . .] One should not lightly allow characterization which excludes those from the scope of the Act who should legitimately be included"[21]

This approach was reiterated by L'Heureux-Dube J. in the *Egan* case, where she stressed that categories of discrimination were likely to overlap.[22]

An example of intersectional discrimination in the European Court of Human Rights is the *Leyla Sahin* case.[23] Sahin was a Turkish medical student who argued that a prohibition on wearing the headscarf whilst a student at a Turkish medical school was a breach of her rights under the European Convention on Human Rights. The European Court of Human Rights found that there was no breach of Sahin's right to freedom of religion (ECHR, Art.9(1)) because of the margin of appreciation afforded to Turkey under ECHR, Art.9(2). In some ways cases such as *Sahin,* and other dress code cases, illustrate the problems of the misrepresentation and distortion of the nature of the discrimination experienced by minority women. The category of religion (or race) in these cases is being used to subsume the category gender, and it is therefore an example of an "overinclusive" category. However, these cases can also be understood as an example of the marginalisation that minority women may experience because a concept such as gender or sex is underinclusive. Leyla Sahin's right was constructed as being the right to religion under Art.9. The choice of Art.9 as the appropriate legal basis for the claim is significant. However, this analysis of her choice to wear a headscarf as an aspect of her "religion" was given precedence over an analysis that had constructed the right as either an aspect of race or gender. The failure to argue that the prohibition on wearing a headscarf is a form of gender discrimination is of particular interest here. It is significant that only women would seek to assert the right to wear a headscarf. Yet, this link between gender and the practice of wearing the headscarf is eclipsed by the preference given to Art.9. Religion becomes the paradigm and explanation for the practice of wearing the headscarf. The interaction of religion with gender is rendered invisible by this choice of a single causal explanation. In fact, the judgment in Sahin goes even further. Rather than avoiding the issue of gender altogether, it constructs a conflict of rights, i.e. some of the arguments in favour of prohibition on headscarves are constructed as a response to a practice of gender discrimination.[24] Therefore, the multiple sources of discrimination in a case such as *Sahin* are translated into legal analysis in a way that either ignores the issue

[21] *Canada (Attorney-General) v Mossop* [1993] 1 S.C.R. 55, 645–646.
[22] *Egan v Canada* [1995] 2 S.C.R. 513.
[23] Case C-44774/98, *Leyla Sahin v Turkey,* E. Ct. H.R., decision of November 10, 2005.
[24] Case C-42393/98, *Dahlab v Switzerland* E. Ct. H.R., decision of February 15, 2001.

of gender that is specific to Sahin as a Turkish Muslim woman or translates a case of multiple discrimination into a case involving a conflict of grounds. In this particular case such an analysis renders invisible the fact that Sahin had experienced gender discrimination in a way that was specific to her personal characteristics and choices. Moreover, and significantly, one result of the restriction on headscarves could be indirect sex discrimination against large numbers of Turkish women in their access to education. Neither of these consequences of the ban find prominence in the decision of the European Court of Human Rights. In this way, the intersectional nature of the claim obscures the nature of the experience of individual and structural discrimination. The *Sahin* case is an example of the problem that occurs in cases where there is an overlap of race, religion and gender. The concept of gender in this case is not seen to be the relevant prohibited ground because the practice of headscarves gives rise to a "problem" that is experienced by minority women and not by the dominant group, whose experiences define the category "women". In *Sahin* there is a recognition that minority women can be marginalised in these types of cases by the dissenting judge Tulkens J. whose analysis seeks to recognise the diversity within the viewpoint of women. Tulkens J. states:

"Wearing the headscarf has no single meaning; it is a practise that is engaged in for a variety of reasons. It does not necessarily symbolise the submission of women to men and there are those who maintain that, in certain cases, it can even be a means of emancipating women. What is lacking in this debate is the opinion of women, both those who wear the headscarf and those who choose not to."[25]

In domestic discrimination law, cases on dress codes of ethnic minority women also illustrate the problem of intersectional discrimination. In two cases, ethnic minority women who challenged employer dress codes on the grounds of race, culture or religion both chose to frame their case within the RRA rather than the SDA. In *Kingston & Richmond AHA v Kaur*,[26] a claim of a woman to wear trousers because she was a Sikh was argued as a race discrimination case (although the claim was dismissed because the dress code requirements were found to be justified). In *Malik v Bertram Personnel Group*,[27] a Muslim woman challenged an employer dress code and argued that she should be allowed to wear trousers at work. Her claim was argued and upheld as race discrimination. She did not argue sex discrimination.

Indirect discrimination claims that require a single axis approach, without allowing the relationship between relevant prohibited grounds to be explored, can also be problematic. In establishing "disproportionality", the analysis

[25] *ibid.* Tulkens J., paras 11–12.
[26] *Kingston & Richmond AHA v Kaur* [1981] I.C.R. 631.
[27] (1991) 7 E.O.R. 5.

must focus on the number of those in the relevant pool who can comply with the criteria, provision or practice in issue in the case. The definition of the relevant pool is critical. This problem becomes most clear in areas where, for example, a small minority within the general category "women" have distinct characteristics not shared by the wider majority of women. In *Kaur* and *Malik* the fact that ethnic minority women are more likely to work full time was relevant. Another example is distinctive dress codes which raises the issue of the treatment of smaller minorities of women. A Sikh or Muslim woman may adopt a distinctive form of dress in the workplace, such as a headcovering, as part of a racial, cultural or religious practice. The claim for indirect discrimination will use pools of comparison either under the RRA or the SDA: i.e. the pool will be a comparison of Asians and non-Asians who can comply; or women and men who can comply. However, at a theoretical level it can be argued that many Asian men and women could comply with the requirement; and also that a majority of women (most of whom will not need to cover their heads) can comply with the requirement. This analysis ignores the way in which even where a requirement or condition does not disproportionately effect Asians or women, it may have a significant and disproportionate impact on Asians who are women.[28] Moreover, as Sarah Hannett notes, the focus of equal pay legislation on pay disparaties caused by sex, without any inquiry about the influence of factors such as race and disability, exacerbates the problems of those who suffer discrimination and disadvantage on multiple grounds. Although it is possible to challenge pay discrimination using the RRA and DDA, the structure of the legislation is such that bringing a number of "additive" claims is difficult, and exploring the inter-relationship between all the grounds that may contribute to intersectional discrimination is impossible.[29]

Similar difficulties in the context of sexual orientation are evident in statutory discrimination law. Discrimination on the ground of sexual orientation is now prohibited in its own right, but earlier sex discrimination claims have been unsuccessful. For example, where a lesbian woman has experienced discrimination a question arises as to whether or not she can bring herself within the protected category "sex" and "woman". If these categories are defined from the viewpoint of established majorities they are likely to reflect the view of hetereosexual women and may exclude lesbians. The case law confirms the resistance of courts to arguments that the categories "sex" and "women" should include lesbians. Two cases that are discussed in other chapters illustrate this problem.

First, in *Grant v South West Trains Ltd*,[30] a lesbian worker was unable to claim employment benefits for her same sex partner which were deemed to be

[28] See discussion of these cases and issues by Sarah Hannett, "Equality at the Intersections: The Legislative and Judicial Failure to Tackle Multiple Discrimination (2003) 23 O.J.L.S. 65.

[29] See Sarah Hannett, "Equality at the Intersections: The Legislative and Judicial Failure to Tackle Multiple Discrimination" (2003) 23 O.J.L.S. 65, at 77.

[30] *Grant v South West Trains*, Case C–249/96 [1998] E. C. R. I–621 (E.C.J.).

available to a "spouse" of an employer. She argued that this constitued sex discrimination in EU discrimination law. The European Court of Justice had previously held in *P v S*[31] that the principle of equal treatment on the ground of sex extended to a person undergoing gender reassignment. However, in *Grant* the ECJ refused to extend this to cover discrimination experienced by a woman, who was a lesbian, on the ground of her same sex relationship. By using a comparison with a male worker in a same sex relationship, the ECJ found that the rule applied in the same way to men and women. The ECJ was also influenced by the fact that the Art.13 EC directives on prohibition of employment discrimination on the ground of sexual orientation would in the future provide lesbian workers such as Grant a remedy. However, the existence of specific legislation dealing with sexual orientation does not fully answer the question of why the term "sex" should exclude the viewpoint of those within the category "women" who have a different sexual orientation to the majority. At a practical level, there are critical differences between the degree of protection granted on the ground of sex (which is comprehensive and extends to equal pay) as compared with sexual orientation (which is usually limited to employment and training). Once the analysis is framed in this way, the "underexclusion" of the protected ground "sex" becomes more clear.

This "underexclusion" is also clear in the *Pearce v Mayfield*[32] decision of the House of Lords, discussed in Chapter 8. In *Pearce*, the applicant was a teacher at Mayfield Secondary School. She was a lesbian and suffered homophobic abuse by pupils at the school, including the use of words such as "dyke", "lesbian shit", "lemon", "lezzie" or "lez". At the time of her claim there was no specific legislation that prohibited discrimination on the ground of sexual orientation. Pearce claimed sex discrimination, arguing that the school failed to take effective action to protect her. An employment tribunal dismissed her claim. It found that the detrimental treatment was on the ground of sexual orientation rather than sex. There could only be discrimination if a hypothetical male homosexual teacher would have been treated differently from Ms Pearce, which was not the case. The Court of Appeal upheld this decision and held that the word "sex" in the SDA does not cover sexual orienation. The House of Lords confirmed the decision and reasoning of the Court of Appeal. They held that in the context of s.1 of the SDA "sex" means gender and does not include sexual orientation. Thus harassment on the grounds of sexual orientation does not of itself amount to discrimination on the grounds of sex for the purposes of the SDA. Significantly, Ms Pearce did seek to bring her claim as a lesbian within the category gender in an explicit way. Instead she argued that the treatment she had suffered was "gender specific" less favourable treatment on the ground of her sex. There was, therefore, no need for comparison with the way in which a man would have been treated. In

31 Case C–13/94 [1996] E.C.R. 1–2143.
32 *Pearce v Governing Body of Mayfield School* [2003] I.R.L.R. 512 (HL).

response to this argument, the House of Lords held that there was a need for a comparator. More importantly, in the context of intersectional discrimination, they found that the treatment was on the ground of her sexual orientation and not her gender.

IV. Addressing Multiple Discrimination

Analysis of multiple discrimination needs to focus on conceptual, remedial and institutional factors. In some cases of multiple discrimination—such as additive discrimination—a remedial response which allows greater flexibility in bringing alternative claims may be sufficient. As we have seen, a single axis approach to discrimination excludes, marginalises or distorts the experiences of those who fall within more than one of the prohibited grounds of discrimination, e.g. ethnic minority women who suffer both racism and sexism. The concept of multiple discrimination allows us to identify the cases where there will be a double burden and additive discrimination.

It is more difficult to formulate an adequate response to cases of intersectional discrimination, where two or more grounds of discrimination have resulted in a qualitative change or increase in the experience of discrimination. It is also difficult to maintain a clear distinction between additive discrimination as a quantitative increase in discrimination, and intersectional discrimination as a qualitative increase in discrimination. Where an individual falls within more than one protected group of discrimination they will be more vulnerable to the experience of discrimination than those who only experience discrimination in one way. For example, woman A may experience sex discrimination but no other form of discrimination. Woman B may experience exactly the same type of sex discrimination, but in addition she may also suffer race discrimination. Additive discrimination suggests that this is a doubling of the harm and a clearly "quantitative" increase. However, one consequence of double discrimination, and the increased vulnerability of woman B because of her membership of not just one but two protected groups, is that she experiences the same incident of sex discrimination in a more acute way. This heightened vulnerability of some groups was recognised by the Canadian Supreme Court in the *Egan* case where L'Heureux-Dube J. observed that:

"No one would dispute that two identical projectiles, thrown at the same speed, may nonetheless leave a different scar on two different types of surfaces. Similarly, groups that are more socially vulnerable will experience the adverse effects of a legislative distinction more vividly than if the same distinction were directed at a group which is not similarly socially vulnerable".[33]

[33] *Egan v Canada* [1995] 2 S.C.R. 513 (Supreme Ct, Canada) at p.553.

Distinctions within discrimination law between direct discrimination, indirect discrimination and positive action will also be relevant in developing conceptual and remedial responses to multiple discrimination. It may be possible to undertake a more wide ranging "holistic" approach to intersectional discrimination where there is a explicit direct discrimination because this can be isolated and easily identified. However, if such an approach is made available in the context of indirect discrimination there may be risks of manipulation of statistics to establish disproportionate impact in a way which will encourage a "volley of claims." This is not to say that there should not be a more sophisticated approach to indirect discrimination where there is an overlap between different prohibited grounds, but rather that there need to be checks and guarantees to ensure that such risks do not materialise or are minimised.[34]

A. *Multiple Discrimination as a New "Analogous Ground"*

Remedial and institutional reform, and the imaginative use of positive action, can make a substantial contribution towards addressing multiple discrimination. Recent developments in Canadian constitutional discrimination law suggest that it is possible to address the challenge raised by multiple discrimination at a conceptual level. In *Law v Canada*[35] the Canadian Supreme Court accepted that grounds of discrimination that were intersectional could be argued as "newly postulated analogous grounds" under s.15(1) of the Charter.[36] This shows a more flexible approach towards multiple discrimination, and those fact situations where a complex range of factors operate to create disadvantage and discrimination. In *Corbiere v Canada*[37] this new approach was applied to recognise aborigiality-residence as a new analogous ground of discrimination. In *Corbiere*, L'Heureux-Dube J. noted that interpreting s.15 in the context of a claim to a new analogous protected ground requires the legal analysers to:

"be flexible enough to adapt to stereotyping, prejudice or denials of human dignity and worth that might occur in specific ways for specific groups of people, to recognize that personal characteristics may overlap or intersect (such as race, band membership, and place of residence in this case) and to reflect changing social phenomenon or new or different forms of stereotyping or prejudice."[38]

[34] Elaine W. Shoben, "Compound Discrimination: The Interaction of Race and Sex in Employment Discrimination" (1980) 55 N. Y. U. L. Rev. 793.
[35] *Law v Canada* [1999] 1 S. C. R. 497.
[36] *ibid.*, at p.554–555.
[37] *Corbiere v Canada* [1999] 2 S. C. R. 203.
[38] *ibid.*, at 253.

B. *Multiple Discrmination—US Title VII "sex plus" analysis*

Flexibility in defining the prohibited grounds of discrimination can also be in statutory anti-discrimination law. US case law under Title VII of the Civil Rights Act 1964 illustrates that a single axis discrimination can give way to an analysis that recognises that grounds of discrimination can operate in an additive and intersectional way. This "sex plus" analysis—which allows the use of "sex" plus one other factor as the basis for a discrimination claims—was developed by the US courts in *Jeffries v Harris County Community Action Association*[39]. This was an important development because it marked a departure from the decision of the US employment courts in *DeGraffenreid v General Motors Assemply Division*[40] which rejected the argument that "*black* women" are a special category protected by discrimination law as compared with just "women", and also rejected an analysis that merged and recognised the overlap between different grounds of discrimination. *Jefferies* permitted a sex-plus analysis in a case of multiple discrimination involving a black woman. The court acknowledged and gave a remedy for intersectional discrimination because discrimination can "exist even in the absence of discrimination against black men or white women".[41] The important point of statutory interpretation that *Jefferies* endorsed was that prohibiting employment discrimination under Title VII on *any or all* the enumerated prohibited grounds also provided a justification for treating a combination of this grounds that caused intersectional discrimination. Further, the court held that the legislature's rejection of the word *solely* to modify the word *sex* suggested that Congress did not intend to leave black women without a remedy against discrimination directed particularly at them.

As Kathryn Abrams has noted[42], although the *Jefferies* decision endorsed a "sex plus" analysis, it did not provide sufficient guidance on how such an analysis should apply. It therefore failed to provide a useful definition of intersectional discrimination. This left open a number of questions, e.g. how does intersectional discrimination which is "sex plus" relate to sex discrimination which is based on "sex" alone? Confusion about the way in which the different protected characteristics could interact to produce a new category have led to a judicial retreat from the *Jefferies* "sex plus" approach in multiple discrimination cases. In *Judge v Marsh*, the court held that employment decisions that targeted black women specifically fall within the definition of prohibited discrimination, but the court also restricted the scope of the "sex plus" doctrine to sex plus *only* one other characteristic. The court stated:

[39] *Jeffries v Harris County Community Action Association* 615 F 2d 1025 (5th Cir 1980)
[40] 413 F Supp 142 (ED Mo 1976)
[41] *Jeffries v Harris County Community Action Association* 615 F 2d 1025 (5th Cir 1980), at 1032.
[42] Kathryn Abrams, "Title VII and the Complex Female Subject", (1993–1994) 92 Mich. L. Rev. 2479, at 2497.

"The difficulty with this ["sex plus"] position is that it turns employment discrimination into a many-headed Hydra, impossible to contain within Title VII prohibition. Following the *Jeffries* rationale to its extreme, protected subgroups could exist for every possible combination of race, color, sex, national origin and religion. It is questionable whether an employer could make an employment decision under such a regime without incurring a volley of discrimination charges. For this reason, the *Jefferies* analysis is appropriately limited to employment decisions based on one protected, immutable trait or fundamental right, which are directed against individuals sharing a second protected, immutable characteristic. The benefits of Title VII thus will not be splintered beyond use and recognition; nor will they be constricted and unable to reach discrimination based on the existing unlawful criteria".[43]

The *Judge v Marsh* decision is a significant limit on the *Jefferies* approach to statutory interpretation of the different grounds of discrimination in the Civil Rights Act: that approach treated the different grounds as related and a part of a cohesive strategy to tackle discrimination. The fear of multiple "hydra like" claims and the emergence of sub groups illustrates the limits of the "sex plus" approach to tackling multiple discrimination. These are legitimate concerns, especially in the context of indirect discrimination where the fragmentation of "disproportionate impact" analysis into ever smaller categories may lead to a large volume of claims against employers. However, as Elaine Shoben argues, procedural safeguards on limiting the way in which statistics are used could be introduced to prevent unfairness to employers.[44] Shoben also acknowledges that outside the sex plus one other category (she addresses sex plus race) there are difficulties when indirect discrimination claims are "compounded" for more than two characteristics:

"Title VII should not be interpreted to prohibit disparate impact against groups formed by the interaction of more than two characteristics, such a young black Catholic men. Overt discrimination against such groups should be prohibited, but policy dictates that disparate impact analysis should not be applied: it would subject defendents to numerous suits and virtually unlimited liability while enhancing the possibility of unjustifiable applications of statistical proof."[45]

For these reasons, "sex plus" analysis can deal with some issues of intersectional discrimination for vulnerable groups such as ethnic minority women. However, it seems unable to move discrimination law from its single axis focus: towards the recognition of complex identities and overlapping grounds

[43] *Jeffries v Harris County Community Action Association* 615 F 2d 1025 (5th Cir 1980), at 1032.

[44] Elaine W. Shoben, "Compound Discrimination: The Interaction of Race and Sex in Employment Discrimination" (1980) 55 N. Y. U. L. Rev. 793, at 835.

[45] Elaine W. Shoben, "Compound Discrimination: The Interaction of Race and Sex in Employment Discrimination" (1980) 55 N. Y. U. L. Rev. 793, at 835.

of discrimination; or towards an analysis of how intersectional discrimination operates within and across groups; or towards a more realistic response to the complex ways in which those who are victims of multiple grounds of discrimination are constructed, excluded or marginalised by the law.

C. *Reforms to EU and Domestic Discrimination Law*

The expansion of the grounds of prohibited discrimination in EU discrimination law makes issues of multiple discrimination especially important in a European context. Although EU discrimination law does not contain any specific provisions on how to resolve problems of multiple discrimination,[46] (additive discrimination, intersectionality or a conflict of rights) it does contain general guidance that suggesting that equal treatment should be treated as a cohesive principle across the different prohibited grounds, e.g. gender, race, religion and sexual orientation. The case law of the ECJ has conceptualised "equal treatment" in provisions such as Art.14 of the Treaty as a general and fundamental right in general terms.[47] There is a specific recognition of the risk of multiple discrimination faced by women who are also racial or ethnic minorities in the Race Equality Directive (RED), with similar provisions in the Employment Equality Directive. For example, Recital 14 of the RED states:

"In implementing the principle of equal treatment irrespective of racial or ethnic origin, the Community should, in accordance with Article 3(2) of the EC Treaty, aim to eliminate inequalities, and to promote equality between men and women, especially since women are often the victims of multiple discrimination."

As Sandra Fredman argues, one way to overcome the problems of multiple discrimination at the EU level would be to move towards a more open list of prohibited grounds which allows greater flexiblity and choice to complainants who fall into more than one. Making the scope of the directives similar across the different grounds would also reduce the incentive to bring the claim within one ground rather than the other: e.g. other grounds could be prohibited in all the same types of spheres as race (e.g. education).[48] EU policy responses are also increasingly focusing on the intersection between gender

46 S. Fredman, "Double Trouble: Multiple Discrimination in EU Law", European Anti-Discrimination L. R., p.13–18, see *http://ec.europa.eu/employment_social/equality2007/aims_en.htm* (accessed November 2006). See also Mieke Verloo, "Multiple Inequalities, Intersectionality and the European Union" (2006) (13) European J. of Women's Studies 211–228.

47 See for example the discussion of "equality" as a fundamental right in *P v S and Cornwall CC* Case-13/94 [1996] E.C.R. I-2143.

48 S. Fredman, Double Trouble: Multiple Discrimination in EU Law, in (October 200) Vol.2 European Anti-Discrimination L. R., p.13–18, see *http://ec.europa.eu/employment_social/equality2007/aims_en.htm* (accessed November 2006).

and race, e.g. through the mainstreaming and lobbying work of the European Women's Lobby.[49] As EU discrimination Law develops, it is likely that the issue of multiple discrimination, intersectionality and the conflicts between different protected grounds will become an increasingly important issue.

As well as the conceptual changes discussed above, there are a number of other reforms that could facilitate a shift from a single axis to a more complex model in EU and domestic discrimination law. Justice has proposals to reform the definitions and structures of existing discrimination law in a way which would facilitate claims in cases where there is multiple or intersectional discrimination. Their proposal is to allow an open list of prohibited grounds that would allow individuals to bring a claim for direct and indirect discrimination by citing more than one ground of discrimination, e.g. race and gender. The reform also suggests a modification to justifications for discrimination and the "Genuine Occupational Requirements", so that justifications for multiple discrimination would have to show that *each* of the different grounds had been justified (similar to the German legislation). Justice also recommend that proposed new legislation should not contain RRA s.3(4) and SDA s.5(3), which require comparators to be "similarly situated". Finally, Justice suggest that a purpose clause could provide a guide to a consistent and principled approach in multiple discrimination cases.[50]

These proposals would make it easier to bring cases based on multiple discrimination. However, many of the problems with discrimination law which result in its inability to accommodate the difference of complex subjects relates to structural problems such as its individualistic focus. The shift away from requiring comparators to be "similarly situated" in RRA s.3(4), and SDA s.5(3), will not overcome the problem of the choice for a comparator altogether and it is likely that there will remain a bias against those victims of discrimination who identify themselves by reference to a number of different protected grounds. Moreover, although the Justice reform proposals will assist those who have claims for "multiple discrimination", they will also raise difficulties where more than one claim (e.g. race and gender) is raised in the same cause of action. More specifically, the potential for a conflict between different grounds of discrimination (e.g. religion and gender/sexual orientation) is likely to increase.

[49] The EU European Women's Lobby (EWL) has recently held consultations and discussions on this issue. See the conclusions and recommendations: EWL: Equal Rights, Equal Voices, Migrant Women in the EU, Brussels 19–21, January 2006 (available at *www.womenlobby.org*, accessed March 13, 2007).

[50] Justice Briefing Paper for Discrimination Law Review: "Multiple Discrimination: How real are the problems and what are the solutions?" (London: Justice, November 30, 2006).

D. *Remedial and Institutional Reforms*

In many cases, remedial arrangments that allow a more sophisticated treatment of multiple claims, pleadings and other procedural changes can ensure that those who suffer a quantiative increase in harm caused by additive discrimination are fully compensated. A more detailed and sophisticated definition of what constitutes harm in discrimination cases, and how this is exacerbated in cases of multiple discrimination is also required. In Part D we discuss the principles for the award of remedies in discrimination cases. There is very little guidance on how remedies can be designed to reflect the quantitative and qualitative increase in discrimination in multiple discrimination cases. Where there is evidence of multiple discrimination, or where the experience of discrimination has been heightened because of the victim's special vulnerability as a member of a number of protected groups, there may be an argument for the award of an extra sum either to (a) represent the greater harm suffered by this particular victim of discrimination; or (b) act as a deterrent or punitive measure against a perpetrator who it can be shown has chosen an especially vulnerable victims.

The development of a single equality legislative framework that eliminates anomalies of proof and definition between the prohibited grounds of discrimination can encourage coherence and fairness in multiple discrimination cases, by reducing the incentive to prefer one ground over another, or to force a choice between two grounds. Moreover, institutional reform such as the move towards a single enforcement commission—the Commission on Equality and Human Rights—can also assist those who have suffered discrimination on more than one ground. A single non-discrimination statute covering all prohibited grounds,[51] and a single commission in the form of the CEHR, should provide a conceptual, remedial and institutional structure that is more hospitable to those who suffer from multiple discrimination. This structure should allow coherence between different types of legal claims; reduce incentives (e.g. differences in burden of proof and compensation) to drop one type of claim in favour of another; and offer a coherent and flexible response to conflicts and overlap between different prohibited grounds. It should also permit consistent advice, training and support in multiple discrimination cases. It is partly for these reasons that bodies that are especially concerned with multiple discrimination, such as the Equal Opportunities Commission specifically mentioned that one of its key challenges is to

[51] See the discussion and arguments for the harmonisation of discrimination law into a single equlity act in Bob Hepple, Anthony Lester, Dinah Rose and Rabinder Singh, Improving Equality Law: The Options, (March 1997: Justice and the Runnymead Trust, London). See also the discussion of a single equality act and single equality commission in Robert Wintemute, "Time for a Single Anti-Discrimination Act (and Commission) (1997) 26(3) I. L. J. at 259.

explain how sex discrimination is related to other forms of discrimination, have welcomed the CEHR.[52]

E. *Positive Action as a response to multiple discrimination*

The use of positive action, and in particular the positive public duty to promote equality also provides a range of flexible measures to address multiple discrimination and structural disadvantage. If single axis discrimination law provides protected categories that give an advantage to those individuals within these groups who have greater social power, it is likely that discrimination law will operate in a way that benefits these groups. The use of positive action measures, such as affirmative action or public duties to promote equality, can restore the balance by allowing those who are especially vulnerable and socially excluded to be specifically targetted through proactive and specially designed programmes.

V. Conflicts of Rights

A. *General Introduction to the problem*

Beyond the problems of multiple, additive and intersectional discrimination, there is a further, more intractable, challenge that emerges where there are more than one protected ground of discrimination that co-exist within the same fact situation. This is the problem of a conflict of rights, which is a version of the sixth key question of discrimination law that we identified in Chapters 1 and 2—"what happens when protection from discrimination clashes with other rights or values conflict between different grounds of discrimination?" In Chapter 8 we discussed the possible conflicts that arise when two sets of norms or rights clash, e.g. where non-discrimination conflicts with another individual right such as freedom of speech or freedom of association. In this section, we examine the issue of conflicts within and between different grounds of non-discrimination. As the prohibited grounds in discrimination law proliferate there is a greater likelihood that such conflicts will emerge.

52 In their response to the Government White Paper on the creation of the CEHR the EOC argued that one of its main concerns, and reasons for supporting the single equality commission, was the fact that the causes of sex discrimination are increasingly complex and require work to be done across the different strands of anti-discrimination law. See EOC Response to the Government White Paper on the CEHR, "Fairness for All: a new Commission for Equality and Human Rights), London: EOC, August 6, 2004, text available *www.eoc.org* (accessed on August 24, 2006).

Any combination of the prohibited grounds may produce the relevant conflict. For example, it may be that a group based upon race, ethnicity or religion includes practices that are themselves discriminatory towards women, the disabled or gays and lesbians. In these circumstances, the protection of one of the grounds may entail discrimination against an individual on some other ground. Two of the most prominent and controversial conflicts are (a) the conflict between race, culture, religion and gender; and (b) the conflict between religion and sexual orientation. In the next section we explore some of the issues concerning "conflicts between grounds" in these two specific contexts.

There is a hierachy between different grounds of discrimination in provisions such as the US 14th Amendment Equal Protection jurisprudence. In general, any deviation from the principle of equal protection on the grounds of sex/gender requires close scrutiny and justification. In statutes which prohibit discrimination there are specific exceptions to sex discrimination law: genuine occupational qualification/requirement provisions; and specific exceptions for areas such as employment in the armed services. SDA s.19 specifically addresses the conflict between gender and religion, as discussed in Chapter 2. In the context of sexual orientation, there are broader grounds for developing exceptions. As we see in the section below, the potential conflict between religion and sexual orientation is specifically resolved in domestic law by including a mechanism for allowing organised religions and religious organisations some scope to discriminate on the grounds of sexual orientation.

B. *Feminism v Multiculturalism*

The recent concern with cultural pluralism, the rights of culture and "multiculturalism" reflects, in part, an increasing globalisaton and pluralisation of Western democractic societies. There are two aspects to this debate about cultural pluralism. At one level, there is a factual claim: that social changes in Western liberal democracies have led to the emergence of diverse races, cultures and religious groups. At another level, there is a normative claim: that it is a good thing that there is diversity; that such diversity should be preserved or encouraged; and that a liberal commitment to equality and autonomy requires support for the communal and collective contexts in which individuals exercise choice. This second normative argument in favour of cultural autonomy and cultural pluralism has been increasingly used to justify a commitment to non-discrimination in the context of racial, cultural and religious minorities.

Some writers such as Will Kymlicka and Charles Taylor have argued that limited recognition is required as part of the necessary context within which individuals can exercise meaningful choice; and that the recognition of certain key aspects of culture and religion in the public sphere is essential to the well being and autonomy of a person.[53] The claim that culture and multiculturalism are an important requirement of the liberal commitment to individual freedom is not without its critics. Brian Barry, for example, has launched a trenchant critique of multiculturalim from within the paradigm of liberal equality.[54] More specifically, Barry argues against the accommodation of the needs of cultural minorities that is entailed in policies of multiculturalism. Some minorities argued for a limited accommodation of racial, cultural or religious practices through "rule exemptions". Cases such as that of the Muslim schoolgirl arguing that she should be able to wear an extensive veil (*Shabina Begum*) or the case of the Sikh school boy who sought to carry a kirpan (a symbolic religious dagger) to his school in Canada (the *Multani* case) are examples of rule exemption claims by cultural minorities.[55] Barry argues that, in general, there should be a preference for universal rules, although he concedes that in some cases (such as the *Mandla v Lee* situation of the young Sikh boy seeking permission to wear a turban to school) there can be an exception to the rule.(n.43)[56]

Despite the normative questions about the pros and cons of cultural pluralism or multiculturalism, the social reality of an increasing diversity of race, culture and religion ensures that complex fact situtations in which minorities argue for the accommodation of minority practices and needs keep arising. Prominent cases that we have examined—the *Shabina Begum* case in Britain; the *Leyla Sahin* case in the European Court of Human Rights; and *Multani* in the Canadian Supreme Court—are all a reminder of this phenomenon.

C. *"Is Multiculturalism Bad for Women?"*

The thesis that "multiculturalism is bad for women" was most forcefully articulated by Susan Moller Okin.[57] Her main argument was that an inherent part of traditional cultures, and especially religions, is that they are misogynist and sexist. She therefore argued that liberal theories and policies that encourage the state to "accommodate" the practices of these minority cultures invariably introduced a risk of harm to women and young girls. Case law confirms that there is such a risk. In the discussion that follows we examine some of the cases where these conflicts have arisen in discrimination law. It is

[53] See Will Kymlicka, "Introduction" in Will Kymlicka (ed.), *The Rights of Minority Cultures*, (Oxford: Oxford University Press, 1995); Charles Taylor, *Multiculturalism and the Politics of Recognition*, (Princeton, NJ: Princeton University Press, 1994)

[54] Brian Barry, Culture & Equality: An Egalitarian Critique of Multiculturalism (Polity Press: London, 2003).

[55] *R. (on the application of Shabina Begum) v Headteacher and Governor of Denbigh School* [2006] UKHL 15: *Multani v Commission Scolaire Margherite-Bourgeoys* [2006] SCC 6.

[56] Brian Barry, *Culture & Equality: An Egalitarian Critique of Multiculturalism* (Polity Press: London, 2003, at p.62.

[57] S. Okin (1998) "Feminism and Multiculturalism" 108 Ethics 661.

also worth observing that this conflict between gender equality and multi-culturalism can also arise in other areas. The "Sexual and Cultural" Research Project at the London School of Economics sets out the considerable number of British cases where there is a conflict between gender equality on the one hand and cultural, racial or religious equality on the other[58] A number of the cases relate to forced marriage or violence against women. The cases on forced marriages arise not only in criminal law proceedings, but also in wardship proceedings in the family courts and petitions for the annulment of marriages. Other cases relate to divorce or the dissolution of marriages. Problems about the status and suitability of traditional norms have also arisen in the regulation of divorce where the parties (often members of religious minorities) have chosen to submit to foreign jurisdictions in preference to English law. Difficult questions also arise in cases involving the upbringing of children where that child or its parents are from a traditional culture or religion. The possibility that traditional practices may cause harm to young girls makes this a particularly important issue for law and policy relating to children. Young girls are vulnerable to harmful traditional practices within their cultures for two reasons: because of their sex and also because of their age.[59] Of course, parents are rightly concerned about the environment in which their children are raised, but can they impose practices on their young female members that may cause these children harm? John Eekelaar has discussed this issue and concluded:

"Perhaps we should acknowledge that, at least normally, (that is outside cases of persecution), communities may have no specific interests *as communities*. Their individual members most certainly do, and this includes the interest in passing on their culture to their children. But that interest is limited, and it is limited first and foremost by the interests of the communities' own children."[60]

The claims of cultural minorities vary, but one recurring theme has been the claim for control over, or the right to, separate family law tribunals that can govern civil law disputes for minorities. The recent experience of Canada is a good example of the way in which claims of traditional minorities have moved beyond abstract political demands to become a legal reality. Ontario's Arbitration Act 1991 which allowed the use of alternative dispute resolution procedures to resolve personal disputes in areas as diverse as wills, inheritance, marriage, remarriage, and spousal support.[61] This legislation allowed indivi-

[58] See project on Women and Cultural Diversity: A Digest of Cases at *http://webdb.lse.uk/gender* (accessed on May 20, 2005).

[59] Susan Moller Okin makes the point that leaving young girls to be raised in a culture which does not respect their autonomy can cause them harm even—and especially—where these young girls internalise the values of the culture. S. Okin (1998) "Feminism and Multi-culturalism" 108 Ethics 661.

[60] J. Eekelaar, (2004) "Children between cultures" 18 Intl. J. of Law, Policy and the Family 178, at p.191.

[61] For a summary of relevant primary and secondary sources see the bibliography at *www.attorneygeneral.jus.gov.on.ca/english/about/pubs/boyd/bibliography.pdf*.

duals to resolve civil disputes within their own faith community, providing all affected parties give their consent to the process and the outcomes respect Canadian law and human rights codes. The use of separate tribunals is a real, rather than a theoretical possibility, in Ontario where groups from religious minorities such as Jews and Muslims have indicated their preference for resort to traditional religious justice to resolve family law disputes.[62]

It is understandable why traditional minorities will choose to focus on private relationships and family law when they make claims for accommodation. Areas such as family law govern some of the most private and intimate aspects of who we are, and they relate to our personal identity in the most profound way. It therefore seems appropriate to allow citizens in a liberal democracy to reach an agreement about the rules that will govern these aspects of their life. The problem for those concerned with gender equality becomes most acute when there are claims by not only men but also women from traditional cultures that they prefer traditional legal rules to govern their private disputes. If all persons, and women, freely choose to be governed by a traditional justice system—the argument goes—then there seem to be no conclusive reasons why the state should not respect these choices. This is—at first sight—an attractive argument. However, feminist theory suggests a need to be vigilant about the automatic acceptance of claims of the "free choice of women" without asking further questions about context: "which women"; "when"; "how"; "under what personal, social, economic or political conditions?". Once we undertake this more detailed analysis it becomes clear that the argument moves too swiftly from "free choice of minority women" to a separate system of family law. Most significantly, such a quick analysis may pay insufficient attention to the myriad of ways in which granting control over definitions of relationships and membership of communities to a traditional culture or religion has the potential for causing harm to vulnerable group members, e.g. women and young girls, and also less powerful minorities within groups (such as the disabled, gay, lesbian and bi-sexual persons).

Some of these issues become clear in cases where there has been a conflict between gender equality and the rights to culture and religion, One such case is *Lovelace v Canada*,[63] a decision of the United Nations Human Rights Committee. In *Lovelace* the proceedings were initiated by an individual Canadian citizen—Sandra Lovelace—using the individual complaints procedure established by the Optional Protocol to the International Covenant on Civil and

[62] See report in *The Forward*, January 14, 2004: "In a move that is angering Jewish feminists, B'nai Brith Canada is supporting the demands of conservative Muslims in the province of Ontario who wish to have the right to use private arbitration based on Islamic law for the resolution of their marital, custody and inheritance disputes. A report prepared for the Ontario Ministry of the Attorney General recommended last month that family arbitration based on Islamic law be permitted, but regulated, under the province's Arbitration Act. But both Muslim women's groups and Jewish feminists are opposed, fearing that vulnerable female immigrants will be coerced into submitting to Islamic arbitration." Cited in The Pluralism Project. See: *www.pluralism.org/news/*.

[63] U.N. Doc. Supp. No.40 (A136140) at 166 (1981).

Political Rights. Although *Lovelace* is concerned with territorial residence as an aspect of a right to culture we can generalise and see the way in which conflicts between sex and race/religious discrimination legislation raises issues about membership of cultural and religious groups that may have practices that are discriminatory towards women.

In *Lovelace*, The applicant Sandra Lovelace had lost her legal status as one of Canada's tribal people as a result of her marriage to a non-Indian, given the operation of s.12(1) (b) of the Indian Act R.S.C. 1970 which stated that: "The following persons are not entitled to be registered [as Indians], namely [...] a woman who has married a person who is not an Indian." Lovelace claimed that this was a violation of the rights set out in Arts 2(1), 3, 23(1) and (4), 26 and 27 of the International Covenant on Civil and Political Rights. Article 26 of the ICCPR is the guarantee to equality (see Chapter 2). "In those States in which ethnic, religious or linguistic minorities exist, persons belonging to such minorities shall not be denied the right, in community with the other members of their group, to enjoy their own culture, to profess and practice their own religion, or to use their own language." The key issue was whether Sandra Lovelace, because she was denied the legal right to reside in the tribal area of the group, had by that fact also been denied the right guaranteed by Art.27 to persons belonging to minorities, to enjoy their culture and to use their own language in community with other members of their group. There were a number of other issues, but at the heart of the case and the Committee's reasoning, is an analysis of how to read a group right such as Art.27 in the light of individual rights to non-discrimination such as Art.26.

The key passages in the decision of the Committee are in paras 15–18:

***Sandra Lovelace v Canada*, Communication No. R. 6/24, U. N. Doc. Supp. No.40 (A/36/40) at 166 (1981)**

"The Committee recognises the need to define the category of persons entitled to live on a reserve, for such purposes as those explained by the Government regarding the protection of its resources and preservation of the identity of its people. However, the obligations which the Government has since undertaken under the Covenant must also be taken into account. [...] In this respect, the Committee is of the view that statutory restrictions affecting the right to residence on a reserve of a person belonging to the minority concerned, must have both a reasonable and objective justification and be consistent with the other provisions of the Covenant, read as a whole. Article 27 must be construed and applied in the light of the other provisions mentioned above, [...] and also the provisions against discrimination, such as articles 2, 3 and 26, as the case may be. It is not necessary, however, to determine in any general manner which restrictions may be justified under the Covenant, in particular as a result of marriage, because the circumstances are special in the present case. [...] Whatever may be the merits of the Indian Act in other respects, it does not seem to the Committee that to deny Sandra Lovelace the right to reside on the reserve is reasonable, or necessary to preserve the identity of the tribe. The Committee therefore concludes that to prevent her recognition as belonging to the band is an unjustifiable denial of her rights under article 27 of the Covenant, *read in the context of the other provisions referred to*. [emphasis added]. [. . .] The Committee's finding of a lack of reasonable justification for the interference with Sandra Lovelace's rights under Article 27 of the Covenant also makes it unnecessary, as suggested above (para 12), to examine the general provisions against discrimination (articles 2, 3 and 26) in the context of the present case."

Lovelace illustrates, in stark terms, the choices that a legal system and court confront when faced with a situation where there is a conflict between the rights of an individual woman to non-discrimination on the ground of sex (her right under Art.26) and the claims of a cultural minority to preserve their identity as a viable cultural group (the right under Art.27). One interpretation of this conflict suggest that because Art.27 safeguards the value of membership of a cultural group, it is solely a matter for that group to determine issues such as group membership and the content of all the practices within that group. According to this analysis an individual such as Sandra Lovelace who challenges some, although not all, of the practices of a cultural group is treated as an outsider and a "cultural dissenter". On this analysis the power to define membership of the group and its practices rests solely with the group itself and the "cultural survival of the group" in its present form is given priority.

A second interpretation focuses on the individual, and confirms that the reason for our concern with the value of membership of a cultural group is its importance to the autonomy and well being of *the individual*. This analysis does not treat provisions such as Art.27 as purely group rights but rather treats the group aspect as an instrumental means of promoting the rights and well being of individuals. On this second analysis, someone who disagrees with an aspect of the group practices is treated as an insider and a "cultural reformer" or "social critic" of the group and its practices. Individuals within the group have some influence over membership and the internal practices of the group, and the focus is on "cultural adaptation of the group."[64] The Committee in the *Lovelace* case preferred the second strategy of treating Sandra Lovelace as a cultural reformer within her group. Most significantly, the Committee preferred its own definition of cultural membership over that of the group (Art.12 of Canada's Indian Act 1970).

A feminist analysis of conflicts such as the one in *Lovelace* encourages us to undertake a deeper explanation of social practices to reveal the distinct impact that they have on women. This should immediately alert us to the more subtle reasons why women have become a focus for traditional groups concerned with the preservation and transmission of their culture or religion. Women are always at the forefront of attempts to recreate collective identity because they reproduce and socialize future members of the group. Therefore, controlling with whom and on what terms they should undertake their childbearing and

[64] For a discussion of the "cultural survival" and "cultural dissent" models see Madhavi Sunder: "Cultural Dissent" (2001) Standford L. R. 495.

childrearing functions becomes an issue not only for individual women, their partners and families but also for the wider community. From this perspective, it becomes a critical matter that women should enter into their most intimate relationships and functions in a way that preserves the membership boundaries and identity of the whole community. For all these reasons the control of women—especially in areas such as sexuality, marriage, divorce and in relation to their children—is a recurring feature of traditional cultural and religious communities. Women are also often given the status of passing on the particular collective history of the tradition and its social, cultural and religious norms to the next generation. Women become a public symbol of the group as a whole. This explains why traditional communities focus on family law when they demand accommodation. These groups draw on multiculturalism in support of their political claims: they insist that they, rather than the liberal State, should have exclusive jurisdiction in these key areas.

Simply citing multiculturalism in defence of these claims by traditional groups cannot, however, be the end of the matter for discrimination law. One of the most powerful arguments for multiculturalism is that there are power hierarchies between minority groups, majorities and the State that should be re-negotiated. However, this recognition of external hierarchies should signpost the fact that there are also power hierarchies within groups. These internal inequalities of power may cause vulnerable individuals, such as women, to bear a disproportionate burden of any policy of accommodation of cultural or religious practices. The resulting costs can include entering into a marriage without the right to divorce; inadequate financial compensation in the case of divorce; giving up the right to custody over children; restriction on the right to education, employment or participation in the public sphere; and giving up the right to control over their bodies and reproduction.

It is often argued that many women choose to remain members of a group despite the fact that traditional rules and practices undermine their interests. "They have a right to exit but they freely choose to remain" is the response to any challenge.[65] But this right to exit argument is not a realistic solution to the problem of oppression within groups. It offers an *ad hoc* and extreme option to what is often a systematic and structural problem within traditional cultures and religions. It puts the burden of resolving these conflicts on individual women and relieves the state (which has conceded jurisdiction in this area to the group) of responsibility for the protection of the fundamental rights of its

[65] The right to exit argument is defended by C. Kukathas, "Are there any cultural rights" in W. Kymlicka (ed.), *The Rights of Minority Cultures* (Oxford: Oxford University Press, 1995). For the opposite view, see L. Green, "Internal Minorities and their rights", in W. Kymlicka (ed.), *The Rights of Minority Cultures, ibid*. In the particular context of women's right in minority cultures see Ayelet Shachar, *Multicultural Jurisdictions: Cultural Differences and Women's Rights*, (Cambridge: Cambridge University Press, 2001).

citizens. Most significantly, the right to exit argument suggests that an individual woman at risk from a harmful practice should be the one to abandon her group membership, her family and community.[66] The complexity of the choices that women face in these circumstances makes it more likely that they will continue to consent to practices despite the fact that they experience harm. This internalisation of harmful practices is exactly what exacerbates women's vulnerability in these contexts. Feminist theory thus suggests that women can develop a false understanding of their own best interests; and that consciousness raising is an important task for those concerned with the defence of the rights of women.[67] In the "multiculturalism and minority women" debate, the stark fact is that emotional attachment, economic circumstances and sometimes religious commitment makes the "right to exit" not only an unrealistic but also a tragic choice for many women from minority communities.[68]

There will be significant diversity in the response of minority women who are faced with harmful practices within their own communities. Discrimination law needs to be careful to avoid the error of assuming that "minority women" are a monolithic group. In this context, it is worth noting that not only does the category "women" need to be opened up to differences in race, culture and religion, but we also need to recognize variety *within* the category "women". This method is more likely to ensure that analysis does not distort the choices of minority women. Theory must also be alert to the fact that although women's membership of a cultural or religious group may provide a useful marker of their preferences, it cannot be allowed to pre-determine the complex possibilities for belief and action available to them. In the face of oppressive practices within their group some women will choose to leave altogether. Such women should presumably be assisted if they make this decision and exercise their "right to exit". These are not, however, the hard cases. It is much more difficult to know how to respond to those women

66 Ayelet Shachar, *Multicultural Jurisdictions: Cultural Differences and Women's Rights*, (Cambridge: Cambridge University Press, 2001, Chapter 3). For a critique of the right to exit argument in the specific context of minority women see Susan Moller Okin, "Feminism and Multiculturalism" (108) Ethics 661.

67 For a discussion of the case for, and some scepticism about, consciousness raising in feminist theory see Carol Smart, "*Feminism and the Power of Law*", (London: Routledge, 1989) at p.80. A classic exposition of consciousness raising is to be found in the work of the late Andrea Dworkin see for example *Pornography: Men Possessing Women* (London: The Women's Room, 1983). Feminist theory that draws on methods from psychoanalysis understandably gives great status to consciousness raising as a useful method for theory and practice. Luce Irigaray and Julia Kristeva's work are examples of this; see C. Duchen, *Feminism in France* (London: Routledge, 1986).

68 The LSE Gender Institute's Project Grant Report on the Nuffield *Sexual and Cultural Equality: Conflicts and Tensions* states in the context of forced marriage: "The UK initiatives have focused very heavily on exit, and more specifically, on assisting individuals forced into marriage with an overseas partner [...] our research suggests that exit only works up to a point. It leaves to many individuals with what they perceive as no choice, for when the choice is between rejecting an unwanted marriage partner or being rejected by one's family (and as many experience it, then having to abandon one's cultural identity), the costs are set impossibly high."

(probably the majority) who choose to remain "insiders" within cultures and religions which do not always give them power, safeguard their interests or allow them full participation as equals. This is perhaps one of the most perplexing aspects of the behaviour of minority women that confuses contemporary feminists. There is rarely one right answer to such complicated personal choices. Some women may choose to remain silent despite the injustice in their communities. Others may seek to challenge the dominance of certain "interpretations" of their traditions that are a source of their oppression.

Of course all women will immediately recognise that collective units such as the family can often oppress women. Feminists are familiar with the argument that vesting rights in the family does not safeguard the interests of women and that the grant individual civil and political rights to women has been an invaluable strategy in challenging oppression.[69] Yet, at the same time, there is considerable agreement that the understandable status of individual rights needs to be offset against the importance of group membership (in a family and wider community) for minority women which is a critical aspect of their self-definition.[70] However this analysis need not collapse into a zero sum game between individual and group rights. One of the great errors of some forms of multiculturalism is the assumption of essentialism of groups: the claim that it is possible to identify one fixed definition of a tradition or culture or religion or family. Any complex group contains not just one but a plurality of ideas and arguments. Some of these voices are backed by existing power structures whilst others are relatively silent and do not have access to public space.[71] It should not surprise us to learn that very often those who purport to speak on behalf of traditional cultures or families do not represent the interests of women.

This conflict is not just a quarrel between minority women and their communities. It is also of vital concern for discrimination law, the state and outsiders who are not members of these communities. Questions about how minority women should respond to harmful practices within their own groups, and how other women can support them in this struggle, will also be of critical concern to feminism. If complex traditional groups contain within them a plurality of ideas and arguments, then women who are insiders within these groups have some space for resistance against the dominant inter-

[69] See for example Susan Moller Okin's comment that: "In spite of the supposedly individual premises of the liberal tradition, John Stewart Mill was the first of its members to assert that the interests of women were by no means automatically upheld by the male heads of the families to which they belonged, and that therefore women, as individuals, should have independent political and legal rights.", see Susan Moller Okin, *Women in Western Political Thought*, (Princeton, NJ: Princeton University Press) at p.282

[70] See W. Kymlicka (ed.), *The Rights of Minority Cultures* (Oxford: Oxford University Press, 1995), p.7. See also Maleiha Malik, "Faith and the State of Jurisprudence" in Sionaidh Douglas-Scott, Peter Oliver and Victor Tadros, (eds), *Faith in Law: Essays in Legal Theory*, (Oxford: Hart Publishing, 2000).

[71] For a discussion of some of these issues see Martha Nussbaum, *Sex and Social Justice* (Oxford: Oxford University Press, 1999), especially pp.8–10.

pretations of the groups' practices. This struggle bypasses the tragic choices involved in "exit" from the group. It is also exactly the sphere in which minority women can and should expect support—intellectual, political and practical—from other women. A sensitive understanding of the concerns of minority women can assist in this delicate task of political advocacy. Once we move beyond the assumption that "exit" is the only legitimate response of minority women who face injustice within their communities then it becomes clear that the challenge is to strike a balance between showing solidarity for minority women whilst at the same time maintaining a critical perspective. This less extreme response would accept that partial recognition of a traditional group does not require the wholesale uncritical acceptance of all its practices.

Here, it is important to stress that clarity and articulacy about these foundations are invaluable assets for minority women themselves. In fact, one of the most significant contributions that outsiders can make is to "hold the line" by using key principles such as autonomy as the basis for a detailed and constructive critique of traditional communities and their family practices. Insiders, minority women, can turn to this critique as a precious source of information and ideas. It is likely to be a strongly held belief amongst minority women that their tradition contains within it the resources to allow them to challenge injustice and oppression within their own communities and families. However, this belief should not prevent them from appropriating legitimate arguments from outside their own tradition; using the experience of Western feminism and other political movements as a source of ideas and experience; and making demands for dignity by citing successful examples of women from other traditions. Western feminism has made an outstanding contribution towards securing dignity for women. It also has an understandable and healthy skepticism about traditional group practices particularly.

There are other arguments against an "all or nothing" approach. Insisting that all traditional groups are misogynistic and patriarchal—whether or not this is true—will cause us to miss those areas in which there is internal resistance to the oppression of women. This is likely to put minority women on the defensive by reintroducing the stark dilemma of "your rights or your culture". Multiculturalism draws its strength from the idea that membership and public recognition of a cultural or religious group can be a source of individual well being.[72] In addition to this point of principle, there is also a strategic argument against such a wholesale rejection of traditional practices. Vehement and indiscriminate attacks on traditional practices, through the use of criminal or discrimination law, may make a community group defensive thereby weakening the position of minority women in their attempts to launch an internal challenge to harmful practices. It is essential that minority women are given an opportunity to formulate a criticism of their practices from within

[72] Charles Taylor, *Multiculturalism and the Politics of Recognition* (Princeton NJ: Princeton University Press, 1992)

their own tradition. Minority women have the potential to be the most effective and devastating social critics of the traditional practices that harm them. Their knowledge and experience—and ability to speak the language of the group—gives them an authority that cannot be replicated by outsiders. This analysis also reinforces the point that discrimination law needs give priority to understanding and accommodating minority women. Taken together with the previous argument that "outsiders" can offer an invaluable critique of social practices this analysis supports the view that there is a need for discrimination law to protect women against practices that may cause them harm.

D. *Conflicts of Rights: Religion and Sexual Orientation*

Although conflicts involving racial, cultural and religious groups tend to come up most often in the context of the rights of women, this issue also has wider implications for other prohibited grounds of discrimination. For example, the questions in *Lovelace* over who is a member of a cultural group, how their rights should be constructed, and how conflicts should be resolved also arose in a case which illustrates the conflicts that arise in the context of sexual orienation discrimination.

In *Boy Scouts of America v Dale*[73] the applicant James Dale was a former boy scout who had remained a volunteer for the organisation after entering college. He had been a member of the boy scouts movement for over twelve years during which time the had earned twenty five badges of honour and other commendations. In 1990 after the Boy Scouts movement became aware that Dale was the head of his college's gay student group, the local leader of his boy scouts movement wrote to tell him that his membership was revoked because the Boy Scouts movement prohibits membership by gays. Dale sued the Boy Scouts movement under New Jersey state discrimination law which prohibits discrimination on the grounds of sexual orienation in accessing public accommodation. The New Jersey law stated that:

"all persons shall have the opportunity [. . .] to obtain all the accommodations, advantages, facilities, and privileges of any place of public accommodation [. . .] without discrimination because of [. . .] sexual orientation."

The New Jersey (State) Supreme Court found that the Boy Scouts did fall within the public accommodation sphere of the discrimination law statute. Therefore, prima facie, the Boy Scouts had discriminated against Dale on the ground of sexual orientation. However, the Boy Scouts had a claim that the statute breached their First Amendment right to freedom of association. On this point, the New Jersey Supreme Court found that the "ethos" of the Boy

[73] *Boy Scouts of America v Dale* 530 U.S. 640.

Scouts Movement was diverse: some within the movement opposed homosexuality; whilst others were opposed to discrimination on the grounds of freedom of association. The New Jersey court also found that the belief that homosexuality was immoral was not a core aspect of the associational beliefs, or "ethos", of the Boy Scouts movement. Therefore, they granted a judgment in favour of Dale and concluded that this decision, and the New Jersey non-discrimination provision, did not violate the Boy Scouts' First Amendment right to freedom of association.

On appeal, the US Supreme Court overturned the decision of the New Jersey Supreme Court and found in favour of the Boy Scouts. A bare majority (expressed in the opinion of Relinquist C.J.) found that the New Jersey anti-discriminaton provision had violated the Boy Scouts' First Amendment right to freedom of association. They used the test of whether the non-discrimination provision (the public accommodation statute) would be a "serious burden" to the ideas of the organisation and the ability of the association to express its message. The majority found that the Boy Scouts movement does have an "official position" that is anti-gay, and they deferred to this official position for the purposes of constructing the First Amendment right to freedom of association.[74] The majority also accepted the *Boy Scouts'* conclusion that the presence of Dale would interfere with their ability to maintain this aspect of their beliefs and expressive message. In contrast to the views of the majority, there was a powerful dissent (expressed in the opinion of Stevens J. and Souter J.) that used a different test for examining the conflict between the discrimination law (public accommodation) provision that prohibited sexual orientation discrimination and the First Amendment right to freedom of association of the Boy Scouts. This dissenting view argued that before the conflict could be resolved in favour of the right to free association of the group it should be found that "at a minimum, a group seeking to prevail over a non-discrimination law must adhere to a clear and unequivocal view."[75]

The *Dale v Boy Scouts* case raised the issue of a conflict between sexual orientation discrimination and a constitutional right to freedom of association. As Chapter 13 on religion makes clear, the fact that one of the prohibited grounds of discrimination—religion—is also in many jurisdictions an independently protected constitutional right through constitutional provisions on freedom of religion is another potential source of conflict. If we distinguished between "religion" as an aspect of the right to freedom of religion and "religion" as an aspect of the right to non-discrimination, the first use of religion as "freedom" constructs it as an aspect of the constitutional right to certain key freedoms; the second use of religion constructs it as part of the constitutional right to non-discrimination. However, the constitutional right to non-discrimination is increasingly being extended to a wider range of protected groups. There is, therefore, an increasing possibility of a conflict

[74] *Boy Scouts of America v Dale* 530 U.S. 640.
[75] *Boy Scouts of America v Dale* 530 U.S. 640, at 676 and 686.

between the right to freedom of religion and the right to non-discrimination. This is especially likely in the context of traditional religions, many of whom have ideas and practices that discriminate on the grounds of gender or sexual orientation. One example of exactly such a clash is the *Trinity Western University v British Columbia College Teachers* case in the Canadian Supreme Court.[76]

Trinity Western University (TWU) was a private institution associated with the Evangelical Free Church of Canada. TWU had a teacher training course and applied to the BC College of Teachers (BCCT) for permission to assume full responsibility for teacher training in part to give a Christian view of the world. BCCT refused, citing as its reason that it was contrary to public policy to approve a teacher training programe offered by a private institution which appears to follow discriminatory practices. BCCT's concern was that TWU Community Standards applicable to all staff embodied discrimination against homosexuals. The majority found that BCCT did not require public universities with teacher training programmes to screen out applicants with homophobic views.

In her dissent, Heureux-Dube J. disagreed with the majority and found that decision of BCCT was (a) within their jurisdiction and (b) should be upheld. It is significant that this dissent relied on *Bob Jones University v US* where the US Supreme Court stated that sexual orientation discrimination in education violates deeply and widely accepted views of elementary justice.[77] This dissent also raises questions about how conflicts of rights should be resolved as between the public and private sphere, and whether there should there be a difference in the standards of non-discrimination to be applied to private as opposed to public bodies?

E. *Conflicts in EU and Domestic Discrimination Law*

The potential for a conflict between religion and sexual orientation is a particular risk in the context of religious associations and organisations. At EU level the Employment Equality Directive, which prohibits sexual orientation discrimination in employment and training, explicitly deals with this conflict. It introduces a narrow range of categories in which the right to freedom of association of a group will take precedence over the right to non-discrimination on the ground of sexual orientation in employment and training. This narrow exception is available only for (a) organised religions; and (b) religious organisations. Analogous if differently worded exceptions are found at national level in the Employment Equality (Sexual Orientation) Regulations 2003. The exact details of these exceptions are set out and discussed in detail in

[76] *Trinity Western University v British Columbia College Teachers* [2001] 1 SCR 772.
[77] *Bob Jones University v United States* 461 U.S. 574 (1983).

Chapters 11 and 13. For the moment it is useful simply to note that what is significant is that the conflicting rights to non-discrimination on the grounds of religion and sexual orientation are both accorded the same form: the same definitions of discrimination are used to protect both religion and sexual orientation. It is also significant that non-discrimination on the ground of religion is not formulated as a group right. The "group" or "collective" aspect of the right is partially achieved through the exceptions and justifications. The Sexual Orientation Regulations which are specified in both EU and domestic provisions are returned to in Chapter 11.

VI. Conclusions

The problems posed by "multiple discrimination" cases raise a fundamental issue of "who is protected?", the first question of discrimination law that we identified in Chapters 1 and 2. The overlap between different prohibited grounds of discrimination, as well as the "single axis" focus of discrimination law, can operate to exclude or marginalise exactly those individuals who have the greatest need of the protection of discrimination law. The co-existence of a number of different prohibited grounds also raises the intractable problem of "conflicts of rights", e.g. where there is a clash between the rights to non-discrimination on the bases of religion and gender or religion and sexual orientation. In these cases, it can be difficult to develop a coherent analysis from within discrimination law.

In dealing with multiple discrimination, the government's *Discrimination Law Review* (*DLR*) has missed an opportunity to take a more flexible approach to comparators.[78] Multiple discrimination may result from an "overlap" where an individual falls into more than one protected ground, e.g. race and sex. It also raises the possibility that an individual who is at the "intersection" of a number of different protected grounds, e.g. race and sex, may experience discrimination in ways that cannot be captured by a choosing between the existing grounds, as in *Burton and Rhule v De Vere Hotels* (considered above). Harmonising discrimination law following the introduction of disability, religion, sexual orientation and age as prohibited grounds of discrimination will inevitably increase the risk of overlaps and intersections. The *DLR* concludes that "We do not have any evidence that in practice people are losing or failing to bring cases because they involve more than one protected ground".[79] A more constructive analysis would have been to focus on the precise additional problems faced by individuals once they have commenced proceedings. It would then have become clear that there are problems in the domestic

[78] *Discrimination Law Review. A Framework for Fairness: Proposals for a Single Equality Act for Great Britain* (Department of Communities and Local Government: London, 2007).
[79] *DLR*, para.123.

approach, which requires that each prohibited ground is considered independently and separately.[80]

The *DLR* could have considered a number of responses to the problem of multiple discrimination without abandoning the British comparative model or adopting the solution of "new analogous grounds" developed by the Canadian Supreme Court.[81] Most importantly, the *DLR* could have proposed that multiple comparisons be allowed, using a provision which stated that "a discriminatory practice includes a practice based on one or more prohibited grounds of discrimination or on the effect of a combination of prohibited grounds".[82] The *DLR* could also have proposed removing the additional statutory requirement for a comparator to be similarly situated (see, e.g., RRA s.3(4) and SDA s. 5(3)). In this way, comparison would remain relevant to establish "less favourable treatment" but the victim of multiple discrimination would be saved the additional burden of establishing precisely the same factual characteristics as the comparator. A more imaginative use of remedies could also assist victims. Evidence of multiple discrimination could trigger the award of extra damages to represent the greater harm suffered by the victim of discrimination, or to act as a deterrent or punitive measure against a perpetrator who has chosen an especially vulnerable person. Specially designed positive action measures could also assist individuals who fall within a number of prohibited grounds, especially where there is evidence that multiple discrimination has resulted in structural disadvantage, e.g. in the case of ethnic minority women in employment.[83]

80 Sarah Hannett, "Equality at the Intersections: The Legislative and Judicial Failure to Tackle Multiple Discrimination" (2003) 23 O.J.L.S. 65.

81 *Law v Canada* [1999] I S. C. R. 497; *Corbiere v Canada* [1999] 2 S. C. R. 203.

82 Justice, "Multiple Discrimination: How real are the problems and what are the solutions?" (London: Justice, November 2006).

83 "Moving On Up" (London: EOC, Spring 2007).

PART C

PROHIBITED GROUNDS WITHIN DISCRIMINATION LAW

10

SEX DISCRIMINATION

I. Introduction

The prohibition of discrimination against women is a well established category in international, constitutional and statutory discrimination law. Moreover, the concern with eradicating sexism and women's subordination often covers a wider sphere than the usual scope of discrimination law, and often includes a concern with practices which specifically cause harm to women, e.g. pornography or rape. The main focus of this chapter is on discrimination in pay and employment. However, the chapter also goes on to discuss issues relating to unequal distribution of political power, as well as violence, harassment and the representation of women.

The discussion over the meaning of the term "sex" as an essential category, that is distinct from "gender" as a social construct, is also developed in this chapter. The issue of whether the term "sex" can also be extended to include gays and lesbians—which was raised in cases such as *P v S* and *Grant v South West Trains*[1]—is discussed in Chapter 11 concerning sexual orientation and gender identity discrimination. The present chapter focuses on sex discrimination, arising from the social construction of gender which leads to harmful stereotypes and discrimination against women. This chapter focuses on discrimination in employment. It also includes an analysis of sex discrimination in other spheres such as politics and of women's experiences as victims of violence. Before moving on to a discussion of these isssues, however, the chapter starts with a discussion of "feminism", which provides many of the main theoretical justifications for the legal regulation of discrimination against women.

[1] Case C-13/94 *P v S and Cornwall CC* [1996] E. C. R. I-2143; Case C-249/96 *Grant v South Western Trains* [1998] I. R. L. R. 165.

II. Accommodating Difference: Feminism and Discrimination Law

Feminism is a wide ranging term that has come to represent different types of philosophical position. It is, nevertheless, possible to identify some common themes that run through these wide ranging theories. There are two particular feminist concerns that are especially relevant to an understanding and evaluation of the role and effectiveness of discrimination law in eradicating sex discrimination. First, there is the feminist insight that the "private/public" dichotomy within liberal discrimination law maintains women's subordination. Second, there is also the feminist concern about the damaging consequences of formal equality. Moreover, a significant challenge to equality of opportunity has come from feminists who argue that this concept is insufficiently radical and ignores important and relevant differences between men and women . In the passage that follows, these two themes are set out in the context of how the category "woman" and "women's difference" can and should be analysed within the law.

Katherine O'Donovan, *Sexual Divisions in Law* (London: Weidenfeld and Nicolson, 1985)

pp.16–18: "The focus on the social construction of women's difference from men had an immediate consequence in terms of law. Feminists and liberals were agreed in questioning differential treatment of women and men in legislation. In particular, in the United States, a whole series of challenges to gender-based legislative classifications took place. [. . .] The aim was to eliminate women's differences as a source of subordination so far as possible by opening up the public sphere and assimilating women to men. But in their alliance with liberal reformers feminists seemed to forget that element of the analysis of difference that identified the private sphere as the location of women's oppression.

With the focus on sexual division came the celebration of women's difference. The woman-centred analysis which developed from the mid-1970s studied women's culture, held up by some as a model for all persons. This meant an examination of mothering, of women's virtues, of female sexuality, of female experience as values for the culture as a whole, and a critique of masculinity. Celebrating women's difference as a source of strength rather than of oppression became an accepted mode of analysis. Important and perhaps even essential though this stage in the development of feminist theory was, it seemed to lose contact with the major early feminist dissection of the myths surrounding gender.

There is a curious similarity between the positions of feminist theorists of the 1960s and early 1970s who focused on eliminating women's differences and those from the mid-1970s onwards who celebrated difference. Both streams accepted the dichotomy between public and private. The first group favoured eliminating the differences between women and men, but not necessarily the division between private and public. The second group celebrated women's private existence.

Yet there is within feminist analysis a slogan 'the personal is political' which emphasises the falsity of the public/private dichotomy. Male hegemony has been identified as a continuum in relations between the sexes in all spheres. In the private arena, according to this analysis, relations of domination and subordination are masked by the ideology of love. In the public economic and cultural factors hide the reality. Gender relationships are power relationships.

This account of the feminist critique of the private thus far is a resume of radical feminist thought since the mid-1960s. There is also within feminist theory a marxian analysis which places class alongside gender in its account of women's oppression. [. . .]

Recently a series of questions about the state have been raised by the feminist lawyer Catharine MacKinnon. Pointing out that feminism has a theory of power but not theory of the state, she argues that the 'state's formal norms recapitulate the male point of view on the level of design'. Her view is that the liberal state's claim to objectivity rests on its allocation of public matters to itself to be treated objectively, and of private matters to civil society to be treated subjectively. 'But feminist consciousness has exploded the private . . . To see the personal as political means to see the private as public.' MacKinnon criticises both marxism and liberalism for transcending the private and for failing to confront male power and its expression in state and law."

Katherine O'Donovan and Erika Szyszczak, *Equality and Sex Discrimination Law* (Oxford: Blackwell Ltd., 1988)

p.7.: The question of whether equality is viewed as competition between women and men starting from the same point, or as a pluralistic recognition of different qualities and needs, is fundamental to theories of sex equality. The first approach, of an equal starting point, may fulfil the criteria defined for equality of opportunity. But it does rest on the twin assumptions that women do start from the same point as men; or that if not, they can do so. The starting point is, as it were, open to all. Differences between women and men are ignored. That women might find it difficult or impossible to get to the starting point is overlooked. This version of equality can be criticised as a procrustean bed into which the sleepers must be fitted through cutting or stretching. If the model for whom the competition (or bed) is designed is male then women may find it difficult to fit. They may be forced to accept a starting point and a competition which does not suit them. Their qualities and needs may be overlooked. Economic and social institutions, willing to admit women under a policy of equality, will not necessarily adapt to accommodate them. These institutions may regard their admission of women as more than sufficient to fulfil equality requirements.

If treatment as an equal implies respect for others, avoidance of stereotypes and viewing the world from another's point of view, then pluralism goes further than equal treatment. For it allows for differences in persons, their situations, their needs. It requires "an effort at identification" in the way we treat others. In this guise equality does not mean giving or receiving the same treatment, but rather giving or receiving equal concern. Each person is then taken account of in her particular environment. [. . .]

One scholar would take the view that this examination of varying definitions of equality is pointless. Peter Westen states that treating people equally (alike) where they are similarly situated is the Aristotelian notion of justice. Yet there is a difficulty with the standard of measurement to be applied. "The ideas of equality and inequality relate the consequences of applying one standard as opposed to another, but the ideas do not themselves specify particular standards of measurement." Westen argues that concepts of equality and inequality are prescriptively empty, in that they do not specify the norms of measurement.

"They are formal relationships among persons that depend on a variable prescriptive standard that must be filled in to give them actual content. That is what philosophers mean in saying that, prescriptively, the idea of equality is 'formal'. This is illustrated by an example of workers A, B and C who work identical hours. C has greater seniority than A and B. A has greater skill than B and C. B is older than A and C. The question is whether they are equal for wage purposes. The answer depends on the standard that governs wages: is it according to hours, seniority, skill or age? Thus the prescriptive rule for wages determines their equality or inequality.

Although we may not go as far as Westen in the rejection of conceptions of equality as empty, his example does illustrate the centrality of the standard against which persons are to be measured. This is taken up also by Catherine MacKinnon. She suggests that existing inequalities should be taken into account in law-making and application. Her proposal is that in considering legal standards, a distinction should be made as to whether (a) a given standard is equally premised between women and men but unequally applied; (b) unequally premised but equally applied; or (c) equally premised and equally applied to an existing social inequality. Earlier, MacKinnon had argued that the focus in equal protection law should not be on whether the sexes are similarly or dissimilarly situated; nor on "differences"; nor on whether differences are "arbitrary" rather than "rational"; but on inequality. The courts should consider whether legal treatment results in systematic disadvantage because of membership of a particular group. In the area of sex discrimination the "only question for litigation is whether the policy or practice in question integrally contributes to the maintenance of an underclass or a deprived position because of gender status". [. . .]

It is pertinent to ask whether MacKinnon has disposed of the "the difference approach" in her focus on inequality. It seems rather that her proposal links inequality and difference. It allows in some pluralist ideas of equality by admitting that not everyone starts from the same position, or is similarly circumstanced. It gets away from equal treatment which limits itself to a comparison of treatment. Pluralism goes further than equal treatment because it allows the dissimilarities between the sexes to enter in. A focus on inequality puts differential treatment to the forefront. This is a deeper approach which enables the standpoint or perspective of those, unequal in social reality, to emerge. But instead of women's difference from men being a signal for unequal treatment to follow, as it has done in the past, it would be a sign for suspicion of the existing inequality, whether it existed in law, its application, or because of extraneous factors.

What MacKinnon's scheme for inquiry into inequalities highlights is that existing approaches of equal treatment or equal standard assume that women and men can be taken to be the same. This takes no account of inequalities and differences, whether they be of social, economic or biological origin. But it is an open question whether the differences approach is entirely avoided by a focus on inequality. Feminist analysis argues that differences should not be made the justification for unequal treatment. But differences, where they exist in biology or socioeconomic structures, cannot be ignored. The problem remains that, just as courts have justified differential treatment on grounds that women and men are not similarly circumstanced, so too may they justify inequality.

Like other radical critiques, feminists challenge the liberal state's claim to neutrality and its failure to address the reality of oppression and domination. Feminists also highlight the distinction between biological sex on the one hand, and the expectation and roles which are associated with the social and cultural construction of gender. The distinction between these two concepts—sex and gender—has had a significant impact on sex discrimination law. Arguments concerning "biological" and natural differences between men and women, as well as social and economic differences, have led feminists to disagree about the foundations of discrimination law. MacKinnon, for example, argues that analysis should focus on disadvantage rather than comparison on the basis of equality or difference between men and women. Mackinnon has developed a feminist response to the liberal equality of opportunity standard which uses the usual contrast between equality and difference as the essential organising idea. Like other radical critiques of liberalism (e.g. Iris Marion Young) feminists argue that abstract liberal concepts of equality fail to recognise the real differences (political, social and economic) caused by patriarchy. These differences mean that men and women cannot compete for, and have access to, goods in a similar way. The application of the principle "like with like" in this context fails to alleviate women's disadvantage. Within feminist theory, there is an ongoing debate about whether the differences between men and women are "essential" or the product of "social construction".

This debate has implications for discrimination law because the way in which a definition of discrimination is applied in a practical context (such as pregnancy, child care or sexual harassment) depends on understanding the goal which women are seeking. Although feminists such as Mackinnon or Littleton[2] have argued that there is a need to move away from equality towards the recognition of difference, some modern feminist writers have challenged their acceptance of the equality—difference dichotomy. For example, Drucilla Cornell's work uses of the idea of "double movement"—which builds on the technique of "double writing" introduced by Jacques Derrida—as a critique of more orthodox concepts in feminist writing.[3] Cornell challenges the value of certain binaries: e.g. either women and men are equal or different; either essentialism (the claim that similarities or differences are determined by their essences) or constructivism (the claim that things have no knowable essence and are therefore historically or discursively constructed) is true. Cornell argues that to use these binaries is to argue from within, rather

[2] For analysis, see Bahadid, Burke, et al (eds.). *Feminist Collections: A Philosophical Exchange.*

[3] See Jacque Derrida: Positions (Chicago, USA: Chicago University Press, 1981). Derrida uses this technique in the following way. In Positions he argues for a general strategy of deconstruction. The first stage is the overturning where the existing binary opposition man/woman is overturned. Thus, the hierarchy is challenged by showing that the hierarchically superior could not exist without the inferior turn, i.e. that it is marked by the trace of the other. Second, is a movement outside this phase which is still determined by the existing deconstructed system. We do this by through the emergence of a new concept that cannot be, and could never be within the deconstructed system. This concept is new, resistant and challenging without ever emerging as a third term. Thus, in relation to this second phase he writes: "we must also mark the interval between inversion, which brings low what was high, and the irruptive emergence of a new 'concept', a concept that could no longer be, and never could be, included in the previous regime . . . resisting and disorganising it, without ever constituting a third term" (pp. 42–43).

than to challenge, modern patriarchy's values.[4] Criticism of equality of opportunity and the preference for concepts which "accommodate difference" are also relevant to issues of race, religious and multiculturalism. The feminist challenge to the private/public dichotomy also provides an argument for extending scope of discrimination law beyond public goods and employment to include spheres such as the home (domestic violence issues) and private speech (pornography). These issues are discussed below and have also been discussed in Chapter 8.

III. Women's Inequality—the Past

Patriarchy has resulted in structural inequalities, and stereotypes about women, that continue to have consequences in the present period. Classical and early modern conceptions of the role of women produced inequality in the distribution of social, economic and political power, as well as perpetuating stereotypes about the natural role of women and the "feminine".[5] The modern enlightenment ideas of "freedom and equality", and the liberal social contract, did not eliminate these gender inequalities because it was assumed that a "free equal citizen" did not include women. There has been a slow process of eliminating the most invidious forms of gender inequality: most significantly, through allowing married women to have individual juridical personality and the right to own property; through the extension of the right to equal participation in political and public life; and the elimination of inequalities in employment and welfare provision.[6] Yet, at the same time, despite the fulfilment of the promise of formal equality for women, there has been slow progress in obtaining concrete results in the form of social, economic and political equality. Some of the reasons for this have been explored in the chapter on theory, and in the O'Donovan extract above, that set out the feminist critique of a liberal model of discrimination law which, through its focus on formal equality and the public-private distinction, is not able to deal with the structural causes that result in women's inequality. For these reasons, as the next section sets out, the present reality is that women are disadvantaged in key areas of social, economic and political life, in areas such as the workplace, in

[4] For examples of double movement feminism see the work of Drucilla Cornell and Judith Butler. See also an overview of the ideas in her essay Cornell, "What is Ethical Feminism?" in Benhabib, Butler, et al. (ed.): *Feminist Contentions: A Philosophical Exchange* (London: Routledge, 1995). See also the work of Judith Butler, *Bodies that Matter: On the Discursive Limits of "Sex"*, (London: Routledge, 1993).

[5] For a general overview see Susan Moller Okin, *Women in Western Political Thought*, (NJ, USA: Princeton University Press, 1979). See also Roger Just, *Women in Athenian Law and Life* (Routeledge: London, 1979); Jane F Gardner, Women in Roman Law and Society (Routeledge: London,1986); Martin van Gelderen and Quentin Skinner. Republicanism: A Shared European Heritage, Vol.II (Cambridge: Cambridge University Press, 2002), see Vol.II, Pt II, The Place of Women in the Republic.

[6] Sandra Fredman, *Women and the Law* (Oxford: Clarendon Press, 1997).

politics and in the private sphere. Although social security and welfare law and policy are not the main focus of this book, it is also important to note that discrimination in the access to welfare benefits, as well as discriminatory tax regimes, have in the past, and continue, to act as constraints to women's social, economic and political equality.

IV. Women's Inequality—the Present

Atlhough the primary focus of this chapter is on EU and domestic sex discrimination law, it is also important to put the issue of women's inequality in a more international context. There are substantial legal and policy initiatives to address this issue at the international level. Moreover, the consequences of an increasing move towards globalisation of the world economy have, as Valentine Moghadem[7] argues, a "gendered" aspect. The concern about the increasing feminisation of global poverty has led to the specific inclusion of gender equality as "Target 3" of the Millenium Development Goals to eliminate gender disparity in primary and secondary education by 2005, and to all levels of education no later than 2015. It has also been argued that gender should be mainstreamed across all the Millenium Development goals, and within international development targets.[8]

There are a number of legal and policy initiatives to address gender equality at the international level.[9] The key international law obligations are contained in Art.26 of the International Covenant on Civil and Political Rights which states in Art.2(1) that all persons are entitled to be free from discrimination on the ground of sex. There is also a specific provision on women's equality called the Convention on the Elimination of All Forms of Discrimination Against Women (CEDAW) that was adopted by the UN General Assembly in 1979. CEDAW creates obligations on contracting states to, inter alia: incorporate the principle of equality of men and women in their legal system; abolish all discriminatory laws and adopt appropriate ones prohibiting discrimination against women; establish tribunals and other public institutions to ensure the effective protection of women against discrimination; and ensure elimination of all acts of discrimination against women by persons, organisations or enterprises. There is also legal regulation of sex discrimination in key human rights and constitutional provisions: Art.14 of the ECHR includes a prohibition against gender based discrimination in the enjoyment of ECHR rights; the US

[7] Valentine M. Mogahdem, *Globalising Women: Transnational Feminist Networks* (Maryland, US: The John Hopkins University Press, 2005).

[8] See the report of the UNDP, "Millenium Development Goals: National Reports, A Look Through a Gender Lense", UNDP Publication, May 2003, available at *www.undp.org* (accessed August 2007).

[9] Hilary Charlesworth & Christine Chinkin, *The Boundaries of International Law: A Feminist Analysis* (Manchester Univesity Press, 2000).

14th Amendment and Canadian Charter prohibits sex discrimination; and the EU Charter of Fundamental Rights (Arts 21–23) contains a provision that explicitly prohibts sex discrimination as well as permitting positive action on the grounds of gender. Prohibitions on direct and indirect sex discrimination extend beyond the employment context. There are international standards which prohibit discrimination against women. For example, the International Covenant on Civil and Political Rights states:

Article 24

"1. Every child shall have, without any discrimination as to race, colour, sex, language, religion, national or social origin, property or birth, the right to such measures of protection as are required by his status as a minor, on the part of his family, society and the State.

2. Every child shall be registered immediately after birth and shall have a name.

3. Every child has the right to acquire a nationality."

In the US (the 14th Amendment Equal Protection clause) and in Canada (s.15 of the Charter) also ensures constitutional protection against sex discrimination. The US Supreme Court has held that sex-based classification is unconstitutional unless it can be shown to serve "an important governmental objective and be substantially related to the achievement of those objectives".[10] The ECHR also provides explicit protection through Art.14, as discussed in Chapter 2.

EU sex discrimination law has focused on pay and employment. The original treaty provision regulated sex discrimination in pay through an equal pay provision which states at Art.141 (previously Art.119) the principle of equal pay for equal work between men and women (and this is extended to work of equal value through the Equal Pay Directive). Subsequent EU sex discrimination law has introduced directives in the areas of part time work, pensions, pregnancy and maternity and sexual harassment. More recently, this legislation has been consolidated into one directive that brings together the following seven directives into one text:

- Directive 75/117/EC on the application of the principle of equal pay for men and women;
- Directive 76/207/EC on equal treatment for men and women as regards access to employment;
- Directive 2002/73/EC, amending Directive 76/207/EC, on equal treat-

[10] *Craig v Boren* 429 U.S. 190 (1976), see p.197.

ment for men and women as regards employment, vocational training and promotion and working conditions;

- Directive 86/378/EC on equal treatment for men and women in occupational social security schemes;
- Directive 96/97/EC, amending Directive 86/378/EC, on the implementation of the principle of equal treatment for men and women in occupational social security schemes;
- Directive 97/80/EC on the burden of proof in cases of discrimination based on sex; and
- Directive 98/52/EC on the extension of Directive 97/80/EC to the UK.

The new consolidated Equal Treatment Directive is Directive 2006/54/EC of the European Parliament and of the Council of July 5, 2006 on the implementation of the principle of equal opportunities and equal treatment of men and women in matters of employment and occupation.

In the EU context, the focus of EU sex discrmination law on equal pay and workplace issues is clear from the provisions of Art.141 and from the equal pay and equal treatment legislation (e.g. directives on part-time workers). However, EU sex discrimination law is also expanding its scope with provisions to prohibit sex discrimination in the provision of goods and services (see Council Directive 2004/113/EC of December 13, 2004). Moreover, the EU is developing action plans to combat violence against women and children in a wider range of contexts (e.g. through its initiatives on tackling the problem of the trafficking of women).[11]

In the domestic context, the Equal Pay Act and the SDA 75 provide detailed coverage of sex discrimination in the areas of pay and employment. The SDA 75 also already covers goods and services, housing and education, although there is very little case law in these areas. There were important early non-employment cases, such as *Gill and Coote v El Vino*[12] where a bar refused to serve a woman customer. This case raised issues about sex discrimination in the provision of goods and services (SDA 75, s.29). Nevertheless, the majority of the cases under the SDA 75 have related to employment. Significantly, in the domestic context, the Equality Act 2006 has extended the public sector duty to promote gender equality. These provisions were discussed in Chapter 2 and are referred to again below.

At the European and domestic level, there is evidence of continuing inequality in women's access to political, social and economic goods. A recent

[11] See for example, Decision No.779/2007/EC of the European Parliament and of the Council of June 20, 2007 establishing for the period 2007–2013 a specific programme to prevent and combat violence against children, young people and women and to protect victims and groups at risk (Daphne III programme) as part of the General Programme "Fundamental Rights and Justice".

[12] *Gill and Coote v El Vino* [1983] 1 All E.R. 398.

summary of the position of women in the EU member states is provided by the the European Women's Lobby.[13] The EWL has summarised the relevant facts and figures concering women in Europe in the following statistical overview:

"Facts and figures about the situation of women in Europe"
Published by European Women's Lobby
http:www.womenslobby.org (accessed July 2007)

"1. WOMEN AND POVERTY

At-risk-of-poverty rate after social transfers in EU member states and acceding countries in 2001:

- Women: 16%
- Men: 14%

2. WOMEN AND HEALTH

Percentages of adult population with HIV (15–49 years of age): Eastern Europe and Central Asia—

- 1995: 28% women; 72% men
- 2002: 33% women; 67% men
- 2004: 34% women; 66% men

3. WOMEN AND THE ECONOMY

Gender pay gap (average gross hourly earning of women as a percentage of men's): 15 old EU Member States—

- 1995: 17%
- 2001: 16%

Unemployment rates (EU-15)—

	Women	Men
• 1994:	12.7%	9.9%
• 2000:	9.7%	7.0%
• 2001:	8.7%	6.4%

13 "A Statistical View of Life of Women and Men in the EU25", Eurostat News Release, March 6, 2006, (Eurostat Press Office: Luxembourg, 2006).

Long-term unemployment rates, i.e. 12 months or more (EU-15)—

	Women	Men
• 1994:	6.3%	4.6%
• 2000:	4.5%	3.1%

Part-time employment (EU-wide)—

- 33% of women in employment are working part-time
- 6% of men in employment are working part-time

4. WOMEN AND DECISIONMAKING

Representation of women in the European Parliament:

- 1995: 26.8%
- 2004: 30.3% women

Representation of women in national Parliaments:

15 old EU Member States—

- 1996: 14.8%
- 2004: 25.9%

25 Member States and accessing countries—

- 2004: 20.1%

Managers (15 EU Member States)[8]:

- 1995: 30% women
- 2002: 30% women

5. VIOLENCE AGAINST WOMEN

Rape

Reported numbers of rape in 2001:

- England and Wales: 9743 cases;
- Germany: 7891 cases.

Trafficking in women: Approximately 500,000 women are annually trafficked into Western Europe.

Domestic violence

- In the EU 1 in 5 women experience violence by their intimate male partner. 95 % of all acts of VAW take place within the home.
- 6 women die every month in France as a result of domestic violence, in the UK: 8 women every month, in Finland: 27 per year.

Sexual harassment

Between 40 and 50% of female employees have experienced some form of sexual harassment or unwanted sexual behaviour in the workplace.

Violence experienced by women in prostitution

- The average age of women entering into prostitution is 13 or 14; there is no evidence to suggest that this age is decreasing.
- Data provided by the British Medical Journal on the experience of client violence against women prostitutes indicates that 93% of women had an experience of client violence.
- Around 80% of women in prostitution have been sexually abused in their childhood.''

As the previous statistics illustrate, there is still considerable disparity between men and women in the distribution of resources and employment. Women are at higher risk of poverty; the pay gap has increased in recent years; and women are more likely to be unemployed or concentrated in part time work. There is also under-representation of women in political life. Women also experience violence and harmful practices, in the form of death, domestic violence and rape.

This overall picture of disadvantage at a European level is replicated in the domestic context. The recent summary of statistics on the position of women that has been published by the Equal Opportunities Commission in its final ''Gender Agenda'' and ''Gender Equality Index'', which summarised the state of women and gender equality in Britain,[14] concluded that:

''The way we live our lives has transformed dramatically in the last 30 years. New parents expect to share the upbringing of their children and both women and men want to work more flexibly and provide more support for older relatives. But life around us has not caught up and we are living with the consequences of an unfinished social revolution. We are still faced with many workplaces, institutions and services designed for an age when women stayed at home. In other areas of modern life, inequality underpins life and death issues.''

[14] See two publications: ''Gender Agenda'' and ''Gender Equality Index'' (London: Equal Opportunities Commission, 2007), (available at *www.gender-agenda.co.uk*).

The EOC has set five priorities which it argues must be continued by the new equalities body (the CEHR) which has responsibilty for gender equality: closing the income gap between men and women; giving better support to families; sharing power equally and modernising public services; and providing equal access to justice and safety.

The EOC has identified a number of gaps that face women in Britain. In the areas of employment, pay and work it noted that there was ongoing gender segregation on occupations. The "part-time pay gap" will take 25 years to close; and the "full-time pay gap" will take 20 years, in a system that now pays women 38 per cent less per hour than men for working part time and 17 per cent for full-timers. The EOC also noted that 45 per cent of pregnant women experience "tangible discrimination". Mothers spend 12 per cent more time than fathers looking after children; and the "chores gap" is worsening, with women spending an average 180 minutes a day on housework, against 101 minutes for men.

In the remaining parts of this chapter, we examine the way in which discrimination law has addressed, and can continue to address, the core objectives of gender equality. Section V deals with issues of pay, workplace and preganancy discrimination. Section VI discusses how law and policy can give support to more family friendly policies in the workplace. Section VII is an analysis of how the new gender equality duty, and other policies, can make public services more responsive to the needs of women. Section VIII considers issues of safety, and the way in which some forms of rape, domestic violence and sexual harassment, as well as hate speech and pornography, specifically target women. Finally, section IX considers the ways in which law and policy can ensure that political power is shared more equally between men and women.

V. The Workplace: Equal Pay, discriminatory practices, and pregnancy discrimination

A. *Past and Present Context of Women's Inequality in Work*

As the previous section makes clear, women remain disadvantaged in their access to social and political goods despite the removal of formal discrimination against them. This persistent disadvantage becomes clear in a comparison of a number of indicators: for example, the "pay" and "pensions" gap that is highlighted by the EOC gender index. These gaps highlight the inequality of women's renumeration for formal work. In addition, it is also worth highlighting that certain types of work that women undertake—such as domestic work or informal care giving—are not renumerated or acknowledged as justifying renumeration through formal labour markets.[15]

There are a number of explanations for the persistent form of women's social and economic disadvantage, despite the introduction of formal equality in pay and employment. One aspect is, as discussed, the relationship between women's role as economic actors and their private and social roles as care-givers. This "dual aspect" of women's lives has an impact on their economic productivity in a way that is not true for men, i.e. women undertake a range of activities in the private lives as care givers which is not recognised or renumerated. As Fredman concludes, "the key to a proper understanding of women's work is to consider paid and unpaid work simultaneously".[16] In section VI of this chapter, we consider the role of law and policy in making it easier for women to combine paid and unpaid work in a more just and equitible way. In this section, we consider the issues of equal pay, as well as sex and pregnancy discrimination in employment.

The social and economic factors which lead to the "undervaluation" of women's work are an important context for understanding the role of discrimination law in tackling sex discrimination in pay and in the workplace. The undervaluation of women's work cannot be attributed solely to "one off" individual acts of discrimination but is, rather, an ongoing process "which is shaped by the actions of employers, governments, trade unions and other social actors".[17] This issue can be related back to the harm of exploitation, which was one of the "faces of oppression" which were identified as part of Iris Marion Young's analysis of "discrimination as oppression". The next extract summarises some of the key factors that contribute towards unequal outcomes in pay and in the working conditions between women and men.

Damian Grimshaw and Jill Ruberry
Undervaluing Women's Work
EOC Working Paper Series No.53
Equal Opportunities Commission: Manchester, Spring 2007

pp.v–x: "The undervaluation of women's work is a thread which links together the three causes of the gender pay gap: occupational segregation, discrimination and women's unequal share of family responsibilities. Undervaluation, which is defined in the report as

15 See the discussion of the "chores gap" by the EOC Gender Index. See also the discussion of re-evaluating the role of the care giver, and gender equality models, in Nancy Fraser, "Gender, Equity and the Welfare State: A Postindustrial Thought Experiment" in Seyla Benhabib (ed.), *Democracy and Difference: Contesting the Boundaries of the Political* (NJ, USA: Princeton University Press, 1996).

16 Sandra Fredman, *Women and the Law*, (Oxford; Clarendon Press, 1997), at p.98.

17 Damian Grimshaw and Jill Ruberry, Undervaluing Women's Work, EOC Working Paper Series No.53, Equal Opportunities Commission: Manchester, Spring 2007, at page x.

a higher quality of labour for a given wage, is nevertheless being overlooked within current policy debates and proposals. [. . .]

Definitional Issues

Women face two main risks of undervaluation—that they will be paid less than men for the same effiicency within the same job and that they will be employed in jobs or occupations which are themselves undervalued.

The consequences of undervaluation is that employers have access to a *higher quality of labour for a given wage*. The employee may offer a higher level of effort, skill or commitment for a given wage level, or the job itself may require a higher level of effort or skill than might be reasonably expected at that wage level. In addition, women's potential may be underutilised.

Main Findings

Understanding how pay is determined

Economic perspectives

For economists, pay is primarily related to productivity. Evidence of lower returns to women's productive characteristics suggests undervaluation. In practical terms, this means that women will receive lower rewards from investing in education or from their own work experience. But despite such evidence, some studies claim that women must in fact be less committed workers or be willing to trade off pay for higher job satisfaction.

Some economic theories do allow for unequal outcomes under the following conditions.

- Trade unions push up wages in protected segments and thereby crowd displaced workers (mainly women) into unprotected segmentes and lower wages
- Social norms divide jobs into those appropriate for men and those appropriate for women, again pushing women into a smaller, more overcrowded, lower paid and technologically stagnant segment.
- Wages are held down by too powerful employers; again, women may be affected to a greater extent than men.
- Some employers, or even other workers, exercise a "taste for discrimination"
- Gender is used as a screening device in recruitment and pay decisions on the grounds that it is too costly to acquire accurate information on the potential productivity of employees.

Sociological, psychological, industrial relations and management perspectives. Five main dimensions are discussed within the literature.

- Low valuation of the productive activity—women are concentrated in lower paying firms in the secondary labour market.
- Low valuation and visibility of skill and status—women's work is often constructed as low skilled and their skills are not recognised in classification or grading schemes.
- Low valuation associated with high job satisfaction—women are low paid because they are expected to derive greater satisfaction from their work or to have lower expectation of rewards from work.

- Low valuation of women's work associated with perceptions of women as second income earners—women are expected to work for "pin money" or "extras".
- Low valuation of embedded in payments systems—low valuation occurs through the construction of pay hierarchies, the choice of wage comparators, the structure, design and implementation of payment systems.

A dynamic and integrated approach

Pay serves multiple roles and functions. It reflects compromises between competing pressures, with different outcomes in different institutional, social and economic contexts. Pay is not simply to be explained by productivity. A corrollary of this approach is that these institutional arrangements and their impact will change over time and context."

There are two particular issues that Grimshaw and Ruberry identify (set out below) which are of particular relevance in the context of discrmination law: the social construction of value, and payment systems. The legal regulation of sex discrimination—through sex discrimination and equal pay legislation—seeks to overcome and replace both stereotypes about women. At the same time, equal pay legislation which concerns job markets and pay systems is a targetted response to the structural (individual and collective) problems of job segregation and pay inequity. The relevance of the social construction of women's work and payment systems to the undervaluation of women's work is summarised by Grimshaw and Ruberry in the following discussion:

The social construction of value

Segregation makes it much more difficult to compare the relative skills or contributions of women and men directly. Segregation may disguise the influence of gender on wage differentials between sectors and organisations and on pay and grading hierarchies within firms. These influences can be summarised as follows.

- *Visibility*—women's skills are often simply not visible, since pay and grading structures are still often based on male-type skills
- *Valuation*—women's skills may not be valued, since pay and grading structures are stil often based on male-type skills.
- *Vocation*—women's skills are often treated as "natural", deriving from women's essences as mothers and carers, and are considered to provide opportunities for high levels of job satisfaction that justify the provision of low pay.
- *Value added*—women are more likely than men to be found in low value added or labour intensive occupations.
- *Varianace*—women's lives follow a different pattern to men's. This variance from a male norm promotes the notion that women's work (e.g. part time work) occupies a separate sphere that is non commensurate with that of men.

Payment systems

Women's pay may be lower than men's if there is no job grading system in place; if there are separate systems related to different kinds of jobs; and if the system does not reflect the kind of skills found in women's as well as men's jobs.

Starting salaries and individualised pay increments tend to be lower for women than for men. Men appear both more able or willing to engage in individual bargaining and to use external pay offers to boost pay.

Some women are less able than men to gain access to higher level jobs, as they face higher progression bars or are less able to meet them. Even if promoted, they may receive initial or continued pay rises.

Performance pay acts to maintain or exaggerate undervaluation by being more common in, and providing higher rewards in, male dominated occupations; by being based on discretion; and by being based on variable, subjective, or male-biased, criteria of assessment.

Non-pay elements of the reward package tend to be higher, the higher the pay, and do not provide compensation for lower pay.

Pay systems are often based on rewarding the male model of continuity of employment and long hours of work."

These structural problems identified by Grimshaw and Rubery are becoming translated into the reality of a persistent "gender pay gap" and undervaluation of women's work. The EOC Gender Index confirms that women continue to earn less than men in paid work. Despite thirty years of sex discrimination laws at the EU and domestic level, women who work full time earn 17 per cent less than men; women who work part time earn 38 per cent less per hour than men; and women graduates still earn less than men who have the same qualifications.[18] The EOC summarises the main reasons for this research as occupational segregation, the penalty that women face when they become mothers and the difficulties that they have in combining paid work as employees and unpaid work as care givers. Occupational segregation occurs when certain forms of employment have been, and continue to be, "no go" areas for women; or when certain processes within the same category of work are divided into "men's work" and "women's work".[19] In addition, women were also barred from training for, and undertaking, certain types of professional work such as medicine or law, and women were specifically excluded from holding certain posts in the civil service. The result of this structural job segregation continues in the present, as women are concentrated in forms of work, which are also often non-unionised and in smaller firms, which entrenches low pay. As a study of occupational segregation in 2004 reveals, "for every 10% greater the proportion of men in the workforce, the greater the increase of wages by 1.3%, *even after other factors are taken into account*."[20] Research also confirms that the "gender wage gap" is primarily explained by

[18] See EOC "Gender Equality Index" (London: Equal Opportunities Commission, 2007), (available at *www.gender-agenda.co.uk*; and also EOC, "Britain's Competitive Edge: Women, Unlocking the Potential" (EOC: London, October 2004).

[19] Sandra Fredman, *Women and the Law* (Oxford; Clarendon Press, 1997), at p.111.

[20] EOC, "Britain's Competitive Edge: Women, Unlocking the Potential" (EOC: London, October 2004), at p.2, quoting EOC commissioned research by Olsen and Walby).

the lesser value (measured as renumeration for human capital) which is attributed to women's jobs.[21] Occupational segregation is a particularly important point in the context of evaluating sex discrimination law, especially the legal regulation of pay discrimination, because of the importance of the use of "comparators" in a determination of whether there has been unlawful sex discrimination in the areas of pay and terms and conditions of employment.

As Fredman notes, this combination of factors meant that women have been locked into a vicious cycle of low pay and job segregation. This cycle produced and sustained other factors which contributed to women's low pay and socio-economic disadvantage: trade unions did not prioritise organisation in those industries that were dominated by women; education and training which allowed mobility across segregated job markets was not available for women, who were also hampered by stereotypes about what constituted appropriate work for "female" subjects.[22]

Moreover, as Fredman argues, the recent potential for progress towards women's equality in the area of pay and conditions in the workplace through the increasing legal regulation of sex discrimination has been undercut by a parallel development of a move towards greater neo-liberal policies which have resulted in demands for "greater flexibility" in the labour market. This "flexibility" has resulted in a greater use of part time low paid labour, much of which has been filled by women, and in particular ethnic minority women. Economic progress by women has, therefore, not been evenly distributed across all racial, social or economic groups. There has, as Fredman notes, been an increasing fragmentation of which women have benefitted from the increased opportunities and protection afforded to women through sex discrimination law:

"Demands by employers for flexible working have facilitated the entry of large numbers of women into the paid labour force, but only on exploitative terms. The picture is one of greater polarisation between the few successful women and the remainder, rather than of a general upward trend."[23]

There are also, as Fredman notes, and as recent ECO research confirms, significant and additional disadvantages faced by ethnic minority women who face discrimination on multiple grounds such as gender *plus* race and religion.[24] EOC research of March 2007 on ethnic minority women summarised five specific barriers that they face as: *Participation*—Bangladeshi and Pakistani

[21] For specialist literature on this subject see: S Horrell, et al, "Unequal Jobs for Unequal Pay" (1990) 20 Industrial Relations J. 177; P Sloane, "The Gender Wage Differential" in A. Scott, *Gender Segregation and Social Change: Men and Women in the Changing Labour Markets* (Oxford: Oxford University Press, 1994). See also the application of this literature in the context of equal pay law in Aileen McColgan, *Just Wages for Women*, (Oxford: Oxford University Press, 1997).

[22] Sandra Fredman, *Women and the Law*, (Oxford; Clarendon Press, 1997), at Chs 3 and 4.

[23] Sandra Fredman, *Women and the Law*, (Oxford; Clarendon Press, 1997), at p.176.

[24] Sandra Fredman, *Women and the Law* (Oxford; Clarendon Press, 1997), at p.147. See also EOC report "Moving On Up: Ethnic Minority Women at Work, (EOC: London, March 2007).

women have the lowest rates of participation in the labour market of any group in Britain; *Unemployment*—Bangladeshi, Pakistani and Black Caribbean women are more likely to be unemployed than white British women; *Progression*—Bangladeshi, Pakistani and Black Caribbean women continue to be under represented in senior level jobs; *Pay*—Pakistani and Bangladeshi women face a bigger pay gap than white women; *Occupational Segregation*—Ethnic minority women are clustered in a narrow range of workplaces, jobs, sectors and local labour markets.

B. *Sex Discrimination Law—Equal Pay Legislation and Pay Equity*

As stated above, the persistence of women's disadvantage in the area of paid work, and their concentration in low paid sectors, has been an ongoing concern. Legislation to address the problem of sex discrimination in the area of pay dates back to the post war era (1951) and the ILO Convention on Equal Pay which states:

ILO Equal Remuneration Convention, 1951 (No.100)—articles 2.1 and 3.3:

Article 2

1. Each member shall, by means appropriate to the methods in operation for determining rates of remuneration, promote and, in so far as is consistent with such methods, ensure the application to all workers of the principle of equal remuneration for men and women workers of work of equal value.

Article 3

3. Differential rates between workers which correspond, without regard to sex, to differences, as determined by such objective appraisal, in the work to be performed shall not be considered as being contrary to the principle of equal remuneration for men and women workers for work of equal value.

In the US, the Equal Pay Act 1963, which is enforced by the US Equal Employment Opportunity Commission, prohibits sex based wage discrimination. More significantly, initiatives in Canada have developed a more detailed system for tackling the problem of equal pay. The Ontario Pay Equity Act 1990, for example, assigns a role to trade unions in the pay equity process, or the use of low pay commissions, may be preferable to the exclusive reliance on individual litigation.

C. EU and Domestic Equal Pay Legisaltion

In the domestic context, the most important developments in the area of equal pay legislation have taken place through a complex interaction between EU and domestic law. This has led to the development of a complex body of case law which has been set out, and discussed, in specialist publications on the subject.[25] The following section gives an over-view of the main issues in EU and domestic equal pay legislation and case law, and relates them more generally to the issues concerning women's inequality discussed in this chapter, and to the issues about discrimination law.

The main EU source for equal pay legislation is Art.141 (formerly Art.119) of the EC Treaty; and the main source of domestic equal pay law is the Equal Pay Act 1970. The original Art.119 of the EC Treaty stated that "Each Member State shall ensure that the principle of equal pay for male and female workers for equal work or work of equal value is applied". The context in which this provision was introduced was that the French and German model of social policy included a high level of interference in wages, which were an indirect additional cost for employers. Article 119 was an outcome of the success of the French delegation's arguments, during the negotiation of the Treaty, that there should be a policy of harmonising indirect social costs which arose from protective legislation, thereby protecting French industry from the "social dumping" which could arise if other member states did not meet the same standards of social protection as the French system.[26] Since then, however, social policy has taken on a more prominent, and less instrumental role, in EU discrimination law. A number of EC institutions—the Commission, Council and Parliament—have taken a lead in developing strong initiatives to address the problem of sex discrimination. These have included, for example: Social Action programmes; an "Advisory Committee on Equal Opportunities for Women and Men"; the establishment of the European Women's Lobby and policies of positive action and mainstreaming for women. Particularly significant has been the role the European Parliament, which contains a large number of women Members of European Parliament, who have established a strong and influential Standing Committee on Women's Rights providing a lead for European Union action on gender equality.[27] There has also been legal and judicial recognition of the importance of gender equality as a key aspect of social policy[28]. In *Defrenne v Sabena*, the ECJ stated that Art.141 (formerly Art.119) was "part of the social objectives of the Community, which is not

[25] See for example Aileen McColgan, *Just Wages for Women*, (Oxford: Clarendon Press, 1997); and Evelyn Ellis, *EC Sex Equality Law*, 2nd Edition, (Clarendon Press: Oxford, 1998).

[26] Evelyn Ellis, EC Sex Equality Law, 2nd Edition, (Oxford: Clarendon Press, 1998) at pp.59–60. See the updated discussion in Evelyn Ellis, *EU Anti-Discrimination Law* (Oxford: Clarendon Press, 2005).

[27] Evelyn Ellis, *EC Sex Equality Law*, 2nd Edition, (Oxford: Clarendon Press, 1998) at pp.60–61.

[28] *Defrenne v Sabena* (No.2), Case 43/75 [1976] E.C.R. 455.

merely an economic union, but is at the same time intended, by common action, to ensure social progress and seek the constant improvement of the living and working conditions of their peoples".[29] In the second *Defrenne v Sabena* case,[30] the ECJ confirmed as a general principle that the Art.141 equal pay provisions had "horizontal direct effect": they can be enforced against private employers as well as the State. The full extent of the "horizontal direct effect" of Art.141 remains, however, unclear.[31] The ECJ also stated that non-discrimination on the ground of sex is one of the fundamental human rights of the EU legal order: "The Court has repeatedly stated that respect for fundamental personal human rights is one of the general principles of Community law, the observence of which it has a duty to ensure. There can be no doubt that the elimination of discrimination based on sex forms part of those fundamental rights."[32] More recently, the ECJ has recognised in the *P v S* decision that gender equality, and discrimination law, are part of the EU commitment to individual human rights.[33] However, the limits of the extension of the principle of sex discrimination to protect the full range of gender equality is illustrated by the refusal to grant equal rights to a same sex partner in *Grant v South West Trains,*[34] which is discussed in more detail in Chapter 11.

The Art.141 definition contained in the original EC Treaty was broad and widely defined (especially in comparison to the Equal Pay Act 1970), and therefore required further elaboration in the form of the Equal Pay Directive of 1975 which made clear that EC law requires non-discrimination on the grounds of sex for both equal work and work of equal value. The increasing "social policy" and "individual human rights" aspects of gender equality in the EU culminated in a substantial extention of the scope of EC sex discrimination law beyond pay to cover a range of other related areas such as employment, training and social security. This extention took place through the passing of a Council resolution which required a social action programme which prioritised action for achieving equality between men and women in employment, vocational training, working conditions and including pay.[35] The Equal Pay Directive of 1975 ensured that this principle was implemented, and extended, in the context of pay. This Council initiative also led to the introduction of the Equal Treatment Directive in 1976 which covered the other non-pay related areas including social security. The original ETD was also followed by a number of other directives which extended and specified the areas of EC

29 *Defrenne v Sabena* (No.2), Case 43/75 [1976] E.C.R. 455, at 471.

30 *Defrenne v Sabena* (No.2) Case 43/75 [1976] E.C.R. 455.

31 See the discussion by Evelyn Ellis, *EU Anti-Discrimination Law*, (Oxford: Clarendon Press, 2005) at pp.182–187.

32 *Defrenne v Sabena* (No.3) Case 149/77 [1978] E.C.R. 1365, at 1378.

33 Case C-13/94 *P v S and Cornwall CC* [1996] E. C. R. I-2143.

34 Case C-249/96 *Grant v South Western Trains* [1998] I. R. L. R. 165.

35 For background to these developments, see Evelyn Ellis, *EC Sex Equality Law*, 2nd Edition, (Oxford: Clarendon Press, 1998) at p.190. See updated discussion in Evelyn Ellis, *EU Anti-Disrimination Law* (Oxford: Clarendon Press, 2005).

sex discrimination law. The ETD, and subsequent directives, have now been recast and consolidated into one consolidated single text.

The Equal Pay Act, on the other hand, contains very specific provisions to address the problems of sex discrimination in pay. As Fredman argues in the following passages, the EqPA was original formulated to address a narrow type of sex discrimination in pay, and despite the subsequent extention of the concept of "like work" by the EAT, these inherent origins limited the ability of domestic equal pay legislation to address the structural problems of women's low pay.

Sandra Fredman, *"Women and the Law"*
Oxford: Clarendon Press, 1999

pp.226–227: "The aims of the Equal Pay Act were initially highly circumscribed, the idea being to eliminate the widespread practice of separate pay scales for men and women doing the same work. Hence the core of the Act as originally formulated gave a woman the right to claim equal pay which a man employed by the same employer in only two situations: if she and he were doing "like work"; or if their work has been rated as equivalent under an employer-initiated job evaluation study. "Like work" is defined as work of the same or broadly similar nature. To its credit, the EAT, aware of employers' attempts to disguise continuing pay discrimination, was adept at recognising work as "alike" where it was clear that differences in name or job description had been introduced to maintain the existing pay differential between previously "male" and "female" jobs. The second head, "work rated as equivalent", extends beyond like work but is limited to situations in which the employer has initiated dramatic, but its impact was soon exhausted. As noted above, the effect of these provisions was initially dramatic, but its impact was soon exhausted. Progress could only be made if the comparison was extended beyond like work. [. . .]

The Act contains two crucial restrictions. First, although the claimant is free to choose her own male comparator, the scope of the comparison is limited to a man simultaneously employed by the same employer at the same establishment, or one at which common terms and conditions are observed. Secondly, even if a relevant comparison has been established, it is still open to the employer to argue that the difference in pay was genuinely due to a material factor other than the difference in sex. If a claim is successful, an equality clause is implied into the woman's contract, and any term in her contract which is less favourable than her comparator's is modified so as not to be less favourable. The tribunal may award up to two year's arrears of pay and damages for breach of an equality clause. The proceedings instituted by the woman to an employment tribunal within six months of the termination of the woman's employment."

The differences in coverage and definition between EU discrimination law definitions of equal pay (and Art.141 and related directives) and the EqPA mean that in some cases where the EqPA does not cover an issue such as "pay" or where there is a failure to provide a relevant "comparator", it will be more favourable for a claimant to rely on EU law where it has direct effect and enjoys supremacy over domestic law. Some of these differences between the

Art.141 and EqPA protections have now been reduced by the introduction of the Equal Pay (Amendment) Regulations of 1983, which have amended the EqPA to allow for "equal value" claims.

Although this chapter does not give a comprehensive account of equal pay legislation at the EU or domestic level, there are a number of key issues to consider in the context of equal pay claims. These include, first, a consideration of the procedural mechanism through which a right to equal pay is made available to claimants. Second, we discuss: the concept of discrimination contained within the legislation; the definition of pay; definitions of like work, work of equal value and work rated as equal value; and choice of comparators. Finally, we consider the ability of employers to defend an equal pay claim and reform of equal pay law.

1. Procedural Mechanisms of Equal Pay Claims

In relation to the EqPA, there are a number of pre-requisites that a claimant must establish for a successful claim. The way in which the claim operates is through the introduction of an implied term—an equality clause—into the individual woman's contract of employment (EqPA, s.1(2)). Therefore, if there are terms in the woman's contract which are less favourable than those of a man (chosen as the comparator), the woman's contactual term is modified so that it is not less favourable; or if the man (chosen as the comparator) benefits from terms that are not included in the woman's contract, then the woman's contract is amended so that it does include that term. Conceptually, therefore, the legislation operates by altering the woman's contract of employment where there is evidence of a difference between contractual terms of employment between her and a comparable man. The conceptual issues, and the issue of choice of comparator, are discussed below. Here it is worth observing that the complexity in bringing equal pay claims can act as a substantial disadvantage for individual women claimants. There has been support by the trade unions for using this mechanism to defend better pay and conditions for women with the result that there were a significant number of high profile equal pay cases in the 1980s. However, it remains difficult to bring a case in an employment tribunal where there is very little access to legal aid or specialist legal advice. The equality commissions—previously the EOC and now the CEHR—do have the power to assist with claims, and ACAS also have a role in providing advice and conciliation services. The recent changes with allow the appointment of specialist panels in equal pay cases, and the introduction of time limits and procedures that allow better case management, do alleviate some of these challenges for claimants.[36] Practical difficulties, combined with the complexity of bringing an equal pay claim, are alleviated by a more flexible approach to the "burden of proof" in equal pay cases. EU law,

[36] See Employment Tribunals (Constitutions and Rules of Procedure Amendment) Regulations 2004.

for example, has taken a more flexible attitude towards the proof of discrimination which allows women to establish a prima facie case, e.g. by establishing that the average pay of women was lower than that of men; or by showing a pay disparity between men and women without in addition showing that this had been the result of a particular requirement or condition.[37]

These procedural difficulties, and the problems of proof of discrimination in pay, also reflect a more fundamental problem with the use of individual litigation to address the structural problems of pay inequity. As stated earlier, the entrenched nature of labour market segregation, as well as the associated and related problems of lack of training and marginal working, are "structural" problems rather than one-off acts of discrimination by employers. The use of an individual litigation model to address what are collective, and deeply entrenched, forms of social and economic organisation is problematic. This focus on individual litigation is reinforced by the conceptual structure of the EqPA, which atomises pay structures by requiring a narrow range of comparisons, and which ignores the inter-related nature of pay structures both within industries, and across the public and the private sector. Reforms which are able to address these collective dimensions, such as the Ontario Pay Equity Act, which assigns a role to trade unions in the pay equity process, or the use of low pay commissions, may be preferable to the exclusive reliance on individual litigation.

2. Conceptual issues

The early interpretations of Art.141 confirmed that both direct and indirect discrimination were prohibited, although the early definitions of indirect discrimination were not clear. In cases such as *Defrenne v Sabena*[38] the ECJ developed the idea that the concept of discrimination in Art.119 would include indirect as well as direct discrimination. Later cases, however, confusingly equated indirect discrimination with "disguised" as opposed to direct "overt" discrimination.[39] Subsequent case law has confirmed that the concept of indirect discrimination (emerging from US and domestic discrimination law) is included within the definition of discrimination in Art.119. This was confirmed in *Jenkins v Kingsgate*[40] and also in the *Bilka Kaufhaus* case.[41] Moreover, the concept of direct discrimination in Art.141 does not have to be "inten-

[37] See discussion by Sandra Fredman, *Women and the Law*, (Oxford; Clarendon Press, 1997), at page 252, and the ECJ line of reasoning developed in *Danfoss* Case C-109/88 [1989] IRLR 532 and *Enderby v Frenchay HA* Case C-127/92 [1993] I.R.L.R. 591 (ECJ).

[38] *Defrenne v Sabena* Case 43/75 [1976] E.C.R. 455.

[39] *Burton v British Railways Board* Case 19/81 [1982] E.C.R. 555.

[40] Case 96/80 [1981] E.C.R. 911.

[41] Case 170/84 [1986] E.C.R. 1607. See also *Rinner Kuhn v FWW* Case 171/88 [1989] E.C.R. 2743.

tional'' direct or indirect discrimination.[42] The *Bilka Kaufhaus* case also set the qualification that indirect pay discrimination may be permitted under Art.141 if it was ''justified'' which is discussed below.

While the EqPA leaves open the precise definition of pay, Art.141 gives pay a very wide meaning to include ''the ordinary basic or minimum wage the worker receives, directly or indirectly, in respect of his employment from his employer'' (Art.141(2)), and this has been held to apply to ''perks'' of the job such as concessionary rail travel[43] It also extends widely to all forms of payment made because of the link between an employer and employee, e.g. expatriation allowances[44] or a Christmas bonus.[45] In *Barber v Guardian Royal Exchange Assurance Group* the ECJ confirmed that Art.141 also covers occupational pensions (which are not pure social security schemes) which the ECJ has held can constitute consideration paid by the employer to the worker; and it also covers redundancy payments.[46] This extension of the principle of equal pay to pensions has led to the introduction of specific directives to address the problem of sex discrimination in pensions and occupational social security schemes.[47]

3. Definition of like work, work of equal value, and work rated as equal value

Earlier case law on definitions of ''like work'' under the EqPA took a narrow approach which focused on specific distinctions between the work that was being categorised as ''like''.[48] The Court of Appeal, however, confirmed in *Shields v E Coomes (Holdings) Ltd*[49] that trivial differences were not relevant in establishing whether there was ''like work'' for the purposes of the EqPA and held that ''this principle of 'equal value' is so important that you should ignore differences between two jobs which are 'not of practical importance'.'' The employer should not be able to avoid the principle by introducing comparatively small differences in ''job content'' between men and women; nor by giving the work a different ''job description''. The EqPA also allows comparisons between women and men where there is work that is ''rated as equivalent''. This equivalence is established via a job evaluation scheme (JES). In *Springboard Sunderland Trust v Robson* the EAT held that the JES needed to be examined in its entirety to establish whether the two jobs compared could be

[42] See *Enderby v Frenchay HA* Case C-127/92 [1993] E.C.R. I-5535. For a detailed discussion see Evelyn Ellis, *EC Sex Equality Law*, 2nd ed. (Oxford: Clarendon Press, 1998) at p.116, now also Evelyn Ellis, *EU Anti-Discrimation Law* (Oxford: Clarendon Press, 2005).

[43] *Garland v British Rail* Case 43/75 [1976] E.C.R. 455.

[44] *Sabbatini v European Parliament* Case 32/71 [1972] E.C.R. 345.

[45] *Lewen v Denda* Case C-333/97 [1999] E.C.R. I-7243.

[46] *Barber v Guardian Royal Exchange Assurance Group* Case C-262/88, [1990] E.C.R. I–1889.

[47] See Occupational Social Security Directive, Dir 86/378, OJ [1986] L225/40. See Evelyn Ellis, *EU Anti-Discrimination Law* (Oxford: Clarendon Press, 2005) at Ch.5.

[48] See, for example, *Eaton Ltd v Nuttal* [1977] I.C.R. 272, and the discussion in Aileen McColgan, *Discrimination Law: Text, Cases and Materials* (Oxford: Hart Publications, 2005) at p.426.

[49] *Shields v E Coomes (Holdings) Ltd* [1978] I.C.R. 1159.

rated as equivalent. Moreover, the House of Lords has held that for the purposes of the EqPA, the JES takes effect as soon as it has been completed, rather than when it has been put into effect through the new grading scheme.[50]

The introduction of the Equal Pay Directive (now incorporated into the recast Equal Treatment Directive 2006) clarified the fact that equal pay included "work of equal value" (Art.1(1); and it also introduced the possibility of a wider interpretation of the "comparator" and the term "discrimination" (e.g. to also include indirect discrimination).[51] These developments had already been developed by the more flexible attitude of the ECJ to definitions of "like work" and work of equal value, and it has justified this more permissive attitude by reference to the "protective nature" of this non-discrimination measure. In *Defrenne v Sabena*, the ECJ summarised this principle as:

"The principle of equal pay contained in Article 119 may be relied upon before the national courts and [...] these courts have a duty to ensure the protection of the rights which this provision vests in individuals, in particular as regards those types of discrimination arising directly from legislative provisions or collective labour agreements, as well as in cases in which men an d women receive unequal pay for work of equal work which is carried out in the same establishment or service, whether public or private."[52]

This last sentence confirms that Art.141 permits a much more wideranging use of comparators across time periods (i.e. not contemporaneously) and across different workplace establishments (i.e. not necessarily in the same workplace). This is wider than the domestic EqPA paradigm, as discussed below.

4. Choice of comparators

The structural nature of segregation in the labour market makes it difficult to reduce the issue to one of a contrast between one man and one woman. This causes problems, as discussed, in designing appropriate procedures and remedies to bring an action. This also causes problems in establishing whether there has been like work or work of equal value, especially in the context of the choice of comparators to establish this equivalence. One common theme in this book has been that a symmetrical model of discrimination law, and the requirement of an atomistic individual comparison between men and women, is not an appropriate conceptual framework to address the collective challenge of structural disadvantage. This problem also recurs in the context of equal pay claims. In this context, the search for a comparator (the "male" norm) often hampers the goals of combating sex discrimination in employment. In

50 *O'Brien v Sim-Chem Ltd* [1980] I.R.L.R. 151.
51 See Evelyn Ellis, *EU Anti-Discrimination Law* (Oxford: Clarendon Press, 2005), pp.190–207.
52 *Defrenne v Sabena* Case 43/75 [1976] 455, at p.476.

the next section we examine the way in which the comparative approach and use of a male norm may be inappropriate to accommodate women's needs in the context of pregnancy, as well as part-time and flexible work which is necessary to accommodate their roles as carers. In the context of equal pay, the search for a comparator is often a futile exercise in pursuing the goal of pay equity and justice for women workers, because structrual job segregation means that there is often no equivalent man in the same establishment doing "like work" or "work of equal value". In order to address the entrenched problems of job segregation, the equal pay regime would need to allow comparisons across firms and across industries to "reach" those areas where men are employed and earn higher wages. One way of doing this would be through the imaginative use of "cross establishment comprison" or "hypothetical comparison". However, as we see in the next discussion, there has been resistance to allowing women to use these wider range of comparisons to make claims for equal pay.

5. "Cross Establishment" and "Hypothetical" Comparison

Initially it was assumed that the male comparator had to be in the same establishment with a comparison in other establishments in limited circumstances, for example, where the employer was the same or associated entity or where there were common term and conditions of employment between the comparators.[53] Subsequent decisions of the ECJ in *Macarthys Ltd v Smith (No.2)*[54] case, however, have made it clear that Art.141 permits comparators to a man who was employed prior to the woman's employment (i.e. not contemporaneously) but who did work of equal value. This principle of allowing comparisons, without a requirement for contemporaneous employment between the woman and male compartor, has been recognised by the *Court of Appeal in Diocese of Hallam Trustees v Connaughton*,[55] where the EAT allowed a claimant to rely on a male successor as the relevant comparator in an equal pay case. The individualistic approach to Art.141 undermines the ability of the legal mechanisms to address the precise features that lock women into a cycle of job segregation and low pay. It does not, for example, address the reality of the inter-connectedness of pay. There is some limited scope in EqPA, s.1(6) for allowing comparison across firms, but this is constrained by requirements that the employer must be the same or associated, and that there must be common terms and conditions. The wider interpretation of comparison allowing cross employer comparisons in Art.141, was also confirmed in *Defrenne v Sabena* where the ECJ held that it was possible to draw comparisons between work at one firm and work carried out in the same range of establishments, whether

[53] See the following cases for a more flexible approach to cross establishment comparisons: *Leverton v Clwyd* [1989] I.R.L.R. 28 (HL); *British Coal v Smith* [1996] I.R.L.R. 404 (HL).

[54] *Macarthys Ltd v Smith (No.2)* Case C-129/79 [1980] E.C.R. 1275.

[55] *Diocese of Hallam Trustees v Connaughton* [1996] I.R.L.R. 505.

public or private, rather than with one specified employer.[56] This approach has been followed by the EAT, which has held that the wider Art.141 interpretation displaces the narrower EqPA, s.1 (6) requirement for the comparison to be limited to "assocated employers".[57]

The ECJ also clarified its position on cross-establishment comparison under Art.141 equal pay claims in a series of other cases. In *Lawrence v Regent Office Care Ltd* the women were a group of public sector workers whose jobs were tranferred into the private sector with the consequence of a deterioration in their pay and working conditions. The women sought to compare their pay (for their work in the private sector) with that of men who were still in the public sector (who were doing work that was rated as equivalent value). The EAT dismissed the claims of the women claimants. Morrison J. citing the ECJ case law in *Defrenne v Sabena*, justified the refusal to give a wide definition to the requirement for work carried out in the same establishment or servie under Art.141 by noting that:

"Such a construction would be likely to create a substantial economic effect of the sort which, no doubt, the Court had in mind in the *Defrenne* case and which would need 'legislation'. Further, without such legislation, a wide interpretation would deny the respondent any effective opportunity for a defence of justification. Again, no doubt the ECJ had in mind the need for progressive implementation of any industry-wide application, with proper safeguards built in to accommodate some kind of a justification defence."[58]

The ECJ endorsed this narrow interpretation by relying on the idea of a need for the "individual responsibility" of an employer for creating the pay inequity or discrimination, reflecting once again the use of an individualistic model of equal pay to address structural problems in pay structures. In *Lawrence*, the ECJ followed the line of reasoning developed in *Defrenne*, and stated that there was no reason of principle why Art.141 should be limited to factual situations where men and women were employed by the same employer. Nevertheless, the ECJ was not prepared to go so far as to allow the claim of the women in *Lawrence* who were seeking to make a comparison between the private and public sphere for work that had been rated as being of "equivalent value". In justifying their decision, the ECJ stated: "However, where, as in the main proceedings here, the differences identified in the pay conditions of workers performing equal work or work of equal value cannot be attributed to a single source, there is no body which is responsible for the inequality and which could restore equal treatment. Such a situation does not come within the scope of Art.141(1) EC. The work and pay of those workers cannot therefore be compared on the basis of that provision. In view of all the

[56] *Defrenne v Sabena (No.2)* Case C–Case 43/75 [1976] 455.
[57] *Scullard v Knowles & Southern Regional Council for Education & Training* [1996] I.C.R. 399 (EAT).
[58] *Lawrence v Regent Office Care Ltd* [1999] I.C.R. 654.

foregoing, the answer to the first question must be that a situation such as that in the main proceedings, in which the differences identified in the pay conditions of workers of different sex performing equal work or work of equal value cannot be attributed to a single source, does not come within the scope of Art.141(1).''[59]

The ''single source'' test was confirmed by the ECJ in *Allonby v Accrington Rossendale College*.[60] In *Allonby*, the complainant was a woman who was a part time hourly paid lecturer who had been employed for over five years on a series of one-year contracts. In 1996, Ms Allonby's employment was terminated and she was told that she would have to provide her future services through an employment agency (ELS) as a self-employed person. The proportion of fees that Ms Allonby would be paid in the agreement with ELS would be lower than those previously paid by Accrigton College. Ms Allonby made a claim for equal pay under Art.114 and used the pro-rata rate paid to full time male lecturers at Accrington College as her comparator. The ECJ confirmed the single source test, which requires the comparator to be at an establishment which can be clearly identified as responsible for the inequality, and which can re-establish pay equity.

The ''single source'' test, and the limits to wider cross establishment comparisons, are particularly problematic in the context of pay equity in the public sector, which is also significant because of the large number of women who are employed in public services. The use of Compulsory Competitive Tendering resulted in the ''contracting out'' of public services to outside commerical enterprises. In the 1980s, the way in which firms were able to present themselves as ''most competitive'' was through a reduction in labour costs. This had an impact for pay equity between men and women because large numbers workers in the public sector, and especially women, were made redundant and re-employed as workers in the private sector for lower wages.[61] In some cases, the local authorities had to bid for the services which meant that they often cut wages to ensure that their bid was competitive as illustrated by the *Ratcliffe v North Yorkshire CC* (which is also discussed in the context of defences to equal pay claims). In *Ratcliffe*, the local council cut the pay of its women workers who were ''dinner ladies'' to compete with outside tendering for that service function. The women won their claim under the EqPA as the House of Lords held that the local council was required to pay the women according to its internal pay structure which permitted them to make an equal pay claim. Although the individual women won their claim, this left the local council at a competitive disadvantage in relation to private contractors. The case illustrates the difficulty of segmenting different types of work and leaving different pay structures in place: across industries, between the public and private sector and especially where there is sub-contracting of work. In order to make a

[59] *Lawrence v Regent Office Care Ltd* Case C-320/00 [2002] E.C.R. I-7325.
[60] *Allonby v Accrington and Rossendale College* Case C-256/01, [2004] I.R.L.R. 224.
[61] Aileen McColgan, *Discrimination Law*, 2nd ed., (Oxford: Hart Publications, 2005) at p.436–437.

realistic change for wages for this type of work, which has large number of women workers there would need to be parallel pay equity standards and structure in the private sector which is taking over service provision. As discussed in Chapter 17 (on collective remedies), this would require a stronger and more enforceable regime of "contract compliance" and conditions imposed on private firms that bid for "public procurement" to meet minimum standards of pay and working conditions for women (and other workers) who are tranferred from the public to the private sector. The risk that contracting out jobs may undermine the core aims of equal pay legislation was recognised by Geelhoed A.G. in the *Allonby* case.[62] Despite the recognition that contracting out could have this impact on women's pay equality, Geelhoed A.G. suggested that the solution for this problem had to come through legislation rather than the judicial development of EU sex discrimination law.[63]

Some protection against a deterioration in pay and conditions on the transfer of an undertaking between different employers is provided by the Transfer of Undertakings Regulations (TUPE)[64] which give effect to the EC Acquired Rights Directive[65]. This ensures that the rights, powers, duties and liabilities of workers are transferred between the original (pre-transfer) and final (post-transfer) employer.

The development of cross establishment comparators by the ECJ has extended the EqPA test. It is, however, significant that although the ECJ in *Macarthys* allowed comparators with men who were employed before (or after) in the same establishment, it did not allow hypothetical comparison across an industry which, as we have seen, may be necessary to address the complex and related nature of pay discrimination against women. In *Macarthys,* the ECJ concluded that such a "hypothetical comparison" would require a wide ranging comparative study that fell outside the scope of Art.141, and that required explicit guidance from the EU. They concluded that a "hypothetical comparison" would imply: "comparative studies of entire branches of industry and therefore requires, as a prerequisite, the elaboration by the Community and national legislative bodies of criteria of assessment. From that it follows that, in cases of actual discrimination falling within the scope of the direct application of Art.141, comparisons are confined to parallels which may be drawn on the basis of concrete appraisals of the work actually performed by employees of different sex within the same establishment or service."[66] The use of the hypothetical male comparator is permissible under the SDA and the Equal Treatment Directive which allows a more wide ranging application of the concept of "less favourable treatment." The US has made use of a more wide ranging concept of "comparison" that includes the scenario of what an

[62] *Allonby v Accrington and Rossendale College* Case C-256/01 [2004] I.R.L.R. 224.

[63] For a discussion of this point see Sandra Fredman, "Marginalising Equal Pay Laws" (2004) 33 Industrial L. J. 281.

[64] Tranfer of Undertakings (Protection of Employment) Regulations (SI) 1981.

[65] Directive 77/187 EC.

[66] *Macarthys Ltd v Smith (No.2),* Case C-129/79 [1980] E.C.R. 1275, at 1289–1290.

employer would have paid to the woman *had she been a man*.[67] "Pay" is now included within the Equal Treatment Directive, and also within the scope of the constitutional requirement for gender equality in the Charter of Fundamental Rights of the EU (Arts 21 and 23) and the Equal Treatment Directive. Moreover, all these provisions are now consolidated along with the Equal Pay Directive in the new recast Equal Treatment 2006/54. This suggests that future development of the definition of male comparator under the Art.141 equal pay law (and consequently the domestic EqPA regime) should be harmonised with the test for the comparator under the other parts of EU and domestic sex discrimination law which (as we see below) take a more flexible approach to the requirement for a comparator.

An individualistic approach, which does not allow cross establishment or hypothetical compators, ignores the inter-related collective and structural causes of women's low pay. This legal approach also does not address the fact that pay equity for women needs to take into account issue of pay across different firms: most significantly, because the ability of one employer to pay a higher wage to women is dependent on a similar adjustment by the firms competitors to ensure that they do not obtain a competitive advantage through "social dumping" (and undercutting wages for women). This individualistic approach has also not taken into account the importance of relating the legal regime of equal pay claims to the reality of collective bargaining structures, which are an important form of protecting fair wages and working conditions.[68]

6. Defence to an Equal Pay Claim

It is possible for employers to defend an equal pay claim under Art.141 and the EqPA. Although Art.141 does not contain any express provisions for a defence to an equal pay claim. Case law has (as we see below in cases such as *Bilka-Kaufhaus* and *Enderby v Frenchay HA*) established that it is open for an employer to rely on the defence of "justification" in relation to a claim of indirect discrimination under Art.141.

The EqPA contains an explicit provision that allows for a defence by employers. EqPA, s.1(3) states:

> "An equality clause [. . .] shall not operate in relation to a variation between the woman's contract and the man's contract if the employer proves that the variation is genuinely due to a material factor which is not the difference of sex and that factor—
>
> (a) in the case of an equality clause falling within subsection (2)(a) or (b) above, must be a material difference between the woman's case and the man's; and;

[67] See County of Washington, *Oregan v Gunther* 425 U.S. 161 (1981), discussed in David Pannick, *Sex Discrimination Law* (Oxford: Oxford University Press, 1985), pp.94–96.

[68] Sandra Fredman, *Women and the Law* (Oxford; Clarendon Press, 1997) at pp.251–251.

(b) in the case of an equality clause falling within subsection (2)(c) above, may be such a material difference."

This provision, and the term "material difference", has been interpreted in *Rainey v Greater Glasgow Health Board*[69] to include factors such as, inter alia: personal skills, experience, training; and also a difference which is connected with economic factors and business efficiency relevant to the employer's business.[70] *Rainey* follows the ECJ approach in *Jenkins v Kingsgate* and *Bilka Kaufhaus* (discussed below) of allowing "market forces" to be included within the category of "material difference", which can in turn justify an equal pay claim. This widens the interpretation in *Clay Cross v Fletcher* where the Court of Appeal stated that an employer's defence that included "market forces" was not a material difference. In *Clay Cross*, the "market forces" defence was that the employer had to pay the comparator man the higher salary because that was the market wage; and that the higher salary paid to the man was necessary to attract him to the job. Lord Denning dismissed this argument in *Clay Cross* in clear terms, stating that: "the tribunal is not to have regard to any extrinsic forces which have led to the man being paid more. [...] Nor can the employer avoid his obligations by giving the reasons why he submitted to the extrinsic forces."[71] In *Rainey*, the House of Lords held that this was an "unduly restrictive" interpretation of EqPA. The approach in *Rainey*, however, underestimates the risk of the "material factors" defence replicating exactly those stereotypes and forms of sex discrimination that the equal pay legislation is designed to remove. Lord Denning analysis in *Clay Cross* recognised this risk which he stated could render the equal pay legislation into a "dead letter".[72] The risk that "market forces" will replicate and reflect exactly the underlying causes of pay inequity between men and women is a particular risk because, as stated earlier, the problems of women's low pay arises in large part from the operation of market forces themselves which past discrimination and present segregation in labour markets. For example, standard forms of setting pay such as "red circling", valuing certain job types over others or collective bargaining structures will sometimes be founded on sex discrimination. It is, therefore, especially important that the employer's defence under EqPA, s.1(3), and under Art.141, does not permit the employer to merely cite existing pay setting practices as a sufficient justification and a "material factor" that justifies the difference in pay between women and men. In particular, once a job has passed the first stage of an equal pay claim and been found to be either

[69] *Rainey v Greater Glasgow Health Board* [1987] 1 A.C. 224.
[70] *Rainey v Greater Glasgow Health Board* [1987] 1 A.C. 224.
[71] *Clay Cross (Quarry Services) Ltd v Fletcher* [1979] I.C.R. 47.
[72] See also Lord Denning's comments in *Shields v E Coombes (Holdings) Ltd* [1978] I.C.R. 1159 (CA).

equal or of equal value, it should not be possible to claim that a difference in the "value" of the job is a material difference which can operate as a defence to an equal pay claim.[73] This makes it especially important for there to be judicial scrutiny of the reasons that employers are relying on the "material difference" which justifies the difference in pay between women and male comparators doing the same work or work of equal value.

The House of Lords decision in *Rainey* was after, and applied, the ECJ's test for the "justifiability" defence under Art.141 which allows market forces to be included within the category of "objectively justified grounds". *Jenkins v Kingsgate* first introduced the idea that employer's business needs were a relevant factor in the context of an indirect discrimination claim under Art.141.[74] In *Bilka-Kaufhaus v Weber*, the ECJ confirmed that it is open to employers to jutify Art.141 by establishing that the disparity in pay can be justified by employers. In *Bilka*, the ECJ found that disparities in pay can be justified where they are part of a "real need", are appropriate to achieve the objective to be pursued and are necessary to that end.[75] This test has subequently also been applied beyond the "business needs" of private employers to also cover state legislation and policy, and to legislation.[76] As we saw in the chapter on indirect discrimination, and as discussed in more detail below in the context of the test for justifiability for indirect discrimination in the context of the Equal Treatment Directive and part time workers, in cases such as Seymour Smith, this focus on necessity and proportionality has become part of the test of justification of indirect discrimination under Art.141.

The ECJ has shown a willingness to scrutinise the reasons put forward as part of the justifiability defence under Art.141, and to ensure that the introduction of market forces and business necessity into the defence does not undermine the goals of Art.141. In *Nimz*, for example, the ECJ had to consider the discriminatory impact of a collective agreement which reclassified jobs on to a higher earnning grade on the basis of length of service for almost full time work (they required longer length of service for part time workers who were predominantly women). The employer relied on the business necessity argument as a defence, and argued that the rule was justified because full time workers acquired skills quicker than part timers. The ECJ dismissed this argument and held that there was a need for a closer scrutiny of these argu-

[73] See cases where the EAT has found that a difference in the "value of the job" can be a "material factor" providing a defence to an equal pay claim, despite the fact that the jobs between the woman and male comparator were found to be of equal value: *Davies v McCartneys* [1989] I.C.R. 705, EAT; *Christie v John E Haith Ltd* [2003] I.R.L.R. 670, EAT; discussed at Aileen McColgan, *Discrimination Law: Text, Cases and Material* (Hart Publishing: Oxford, 2005) at p.449.

[74] *Jenkins v Kingsgate* [1981] I.R.L.R. 228 (ECJ).

[75] *Bilka Kaufhaus GmbH v Weber Von Hartz* Case 170/84 [1986] E.C.R. 1607.

[76] *Rinner-Kuhn v FWW Spezial-Gebaudereinigung GmbH* Case 171/88 [1989] E.C.R. 2743.

ments, stating that "such considerations, in so far as they are no more than generalizations about certain categories of workers, do not make it possible to identify criteria which are both objective and unrelated to any discrimination on grounds of sex".[77]

This more robust scrutiny is also illustrated by the willingness of the ECJ to not allow whole categories of pay mechanisms—such as red circling, seniority and collective bargaining—to be cited as part of the business necessity test by employers. In *Enderby v Frenchay* the EAT had held that the fact that a pay structure had been developed as a result of collective bargaining processes that had been conducted separately between two professional groups of workers—one predominantly women and other predominantly men—was not of itself a sufficient objective justificaiton under Art.141. This approach of allowing collective bargaining processes to be treated as an employer defence reflected earlier EAT decisions.[78] The ECJ has, however, developed a different approach. In its decision in *Enderby v Frenchay*, the ECJ specifically did not follow this EAT line of reasoning. They made it clear that the objective justification also had to scrutinise the practice that was being cited as "business necessity" in more detail: it had to be proportionate; and once the employee had established that there was sex discrimination under Art.141, the onus shifted on to the employer to establish that the discriminatory measure was objectively justified by factors that did not themselves include sex discrimination.[79] The *Enderby* emphasis—on requiring a more detailed scrutiny of the employer's justification of the discrimination, proportionality and shifting the onus of proof on to employers—reflects the earlier ECJ decision in the *Danfoss* case.[80] This line of reasoning confirms that under Art.141 there is a need to undertake a more detailed analysis of the employer's defence. This requires employers to explain the sex discrimination in pay in detail rather than in general terms by citing a pay practice such as seniority or collective bargaining. Significantly, the application of the test of proportionality means that the reasons that are provided by the employer need to be sufficiently weighty to over-ride the impact of the pay discrimination on women. The application of this line of reasoning in the domestic context has, however, not been a straighforward matter. In the House of Lords in *Strathclyde Regional Council v Wallace*, Lord Browne-Wilkinson stated that:

"Provided that there is no element of sexual discrimination, the employer establishes a sub-s(3) [EqPA s.1(3)] defence by identifying the factors which he

[77] *Nimz v v Freie und Hansestadt Hamburg* Case C-184/89 [1991] E.C.R. I-297. See also *Hill and Stapleton v Revenue Commissioners* Case C-243/95 [1998] E.C.R. I-3739, where the ECJ held that an employer could not justify a discriminatory job sharing scheme solely on the basis of economic costs. See discussion Evelyn Ellis, *EU Anti-Discrimination Law* (Clarendon Press: Oxford, 2005) p.173.

[78] *Reed Packaging Ltd v Boozer* [1988] I.C.R. 391.

[79] *Enderby v Frenchay HA* Case C-127/92 [1993] E.C.R. I–5535.

[80] *Handels-OG Kontorfunkionaernes Forbund I Danmark v Dansk Arbejdsgiver-forening (acting for Danfoss)* Case 109/88 [1989] E.C.R. 3199.

alleges have caused the disparity, proving that those factors are genuine and proving further that they were causally relevant to the disparity in pay complained of [...]".[81]

However, this approach did not emphasise the need for a detailed scrutiny, as in the *Danfoss* case, of the reasons put forward by the employer to distinguish between those that are "objectively justified" and those that may themselves be tainted by sex discrimination. A higher level of scrutiny of the employers reasons and justification under Art.1(3) was required by Lord Nicholls in *Glasgow CC v Marshall*.[82] The case involved seven men and a man who were employed by at a special school in Scotland. The comparators used in the case who were teachers of the opposite sex who were paid under a different pay structure negotiated by different instituitons. The tribunal had allowed the claim because they found that the employers were not able to justify the difference in pay under the EqPA, s.1(3) defence by reference to anything other than "historical factors". Lord Nicholls disapproved of this approach and found against the claimants. He observed that it was "curious" that a sex discrimination case claims by women and by a man all succeed. This, however, assumes that there historical forms of discrimination that have resulted in job segregation will exclude all men, rather than recognising that there can forms of practices that have a disproportionate impact on women's pay, and jobs where women are concentrated, but which can also sometimes include male employees. This assumes that the EqPA is focused on sex discrimination rather than inequity in pay. Moreover, Lord Nicholls also went on to doubt that in order to discharge the burden under s.1(3) that in this case the reason for the differences in pay between the two groups of workers were the different regimes for negotiating pay scales. He concluded that this was the reason for the difference and that no-one had argued that this was not a genuine explanation, nor that this distinction was itself tainted by sex discrimination. Lord Nicholls did not, however, scrutinise the historical context in which this difference had arisen to see if the cause for the difference in pay between the two pay scales arose from factors such as job segregation or historic discrimination against women workers. This ahistorical approach to the employer's defence, which allows employers to cite the present pay scales as the "reason for the difference" without a further analysis about how these have emerged, will often mean that the causes of pay inequity will fall outside the reach of equal pay legislation.

Lord Nicholls concluded that the employer's defence requires that:

"the employer must satisfy the tribunal on several matters. First, that the proffered explanation, or reason, is genuine, and not a sham or pretence. Second, that the less favourable treatment is due to this reason. The factor relied upon must be the cause of the disparity. In this regard, and in this sense, the factor must be a 'material factor', that is, a

[81] *Strathclyde Regional Council v Wallace* [1998] I.C.R. 205.
[82] *Glasgow Corp v Marshall* [2000] I.C.R. 196.

significant and relevant factor. Third, that the reason is not 'the difference of sex'. This phrase is apt to embrace any form of sex discrimination, whether direct or indirect. Fourth, that the factor relied upon is or, in a case within s.1(2)I, may be a 'material' difference, that is, a significant and relevant difference, between the woman's case and the man's case."

One particular issue has been whether and at what stage the "burden of proof" shifts to the employer in equal pay cases. *Enderby* and *Danfoss* support the proposition that once the complainant has made out a case of sex discrimination under Art.141, it is for the employer to establish that they have a valid defence to justify the discrimination and difference in pay. In *Barry v Midland Bank Plc* the House of Lords had followed a similar analysis and confirmed that once the woman complainant had established a case of sex discrimination, it was for the bank to objectively justify the difference in treatment.[83] However, in *Nelson v Carillion Services Ltd*,[84] the Court of Appeal held that the burden of proof remains on the complainant throughout the case. In *Nelson* the CA held that the tests for burden of proof in "indirect discrimination" for the EqPA, the SDA and Art.141 should be interpreted in the same way. However, the Court went on to hold that:

"It would be bizarre to require an applicant to establish her prima facie case of indirect discrimination for the purposes of establishing that a term of her contract 'is less favourable treatment' but not when her case of indirect discrimination is advanced to counter the employer's explanation for her less favourable term, an explanation which is apparently genuine and attributable to reasons other than sex."

The CA in *Nelson* concluded that "merely to raise 'a credible suggestion' that, were the relevant (valid and significant) statistics provided, these might establish disproportionate impact is not sufficient for the applicant's purposes and imposes no further burden of explanation upon the employer.". Given the recognition by the CA that the EqPA, SDA and Art.141 should be harmonised, and the need to follow the authority of the ECJ in *Enderby, Danfoss,* and the House of Lords in the *Barry* decision, it would seem appropriate to read the CA decision in *Nelson* as making a narrow point that the complainant must establish that there has been a breach of Art.141 or the EqPA resulting in sex discrimination. The burden of proof in relation to establishing sex discrimination is on the complainant. Where, as in *Parliamentary Commissioner v Fernandez*[85], there is no sex discrimination it cannot be said that there is any burden of proof on the employer to justify the difference in pay. However, as the ECJ has made clear, once sex discrimination has been established, it is then for the employer to "defend" his claim by proving that there are objective

[83] *Barry v Midland Bank Plc* [1999] 859.
[84] *Nelson v Carillion Services Ltd* [2003] I.C.R. 1256.
[85] *Parliamentary Commissioner for Administration v Fernandez* (EAT) [2004] I.R.L.R. 22.

justifiable reasons which mean that he is not liable. This interpretation of *Nelson* would also be consistent with the decision of the House of Lords in *Strathclyde Regional Council v Wallace* (already discussed) where Lord Browne-Wilkinson concluded that: "There is no question of the employer having to 'justify' (in the *Bilka* sense) all disparities of pay. Provided that there is no element of sexual discrimination, the employer establishes a subs(3) [EqPA s.1(3)] defence by identifying the factors which he alleges have caused the disparity, proving that those factors are genuine and proving further that they were causally relevant to the disparity in pay complained of [...]."[86]

This approach would also be consistent with the analysis of Lord Nicholls in the *Glasgow City Council* case, where he concluded that: "If there is any evidence of sex discrimination, such as evidence that the difference in pay has a disparately adverse impact on women, the employer will be called upon to satisfy the tribunal that the difference in pay is objectively justifiable. But if the employer proves the absence of sex discrimination he is not obliged to justify the pay disparity."[87]

7. Reform

Substantive reform of the equal pay law and policy is one way of overcoming some of the problems with a model of discrimination law that relies on individual litigation to address structural problems of women's low pay. One possibility for reform is to encourage the use of equal pay reviews (EPR) by employers. Recent EOC research confirms that EPRs reduce pay gaps over a period of time; and also, that EPRs are more prevalent in the public rather than the private sector.[88] It is, therefore, especially unfortunate that the Women and Work Commission Report—*Shaping a Fairer Future (2006)*—has failed to recommend the introduction of mandatory pay audits to force private sector employers to comply with equal pay legislation, to mirror the equality reviews carried out in the public sector.[89] The Ontario Pay Equity Act 1987 places a positive duty on employers to establish and maintain compensatory practices that ensure pay equity. This approach, however, still uses the individual bargaining unit and work unit as its paradigm. There has been a move towards a more collective model in Australia where the use of centralised wage fixing has led to the improvement in women's wages. This approach also overcomes some of the weakness of the individual models, although it has been criticised as a model which has not been comprehensively applied to tackle structural job segregation and women's low pay.[90]

86 *Strathclyde Regional Council v Wallace* [1998] I.C.R. 205.
87 *Per* Lord Nicholls in *Glasgow Corp v Marshall* [2000] I.C.R. 196.
88 "Equal Pay Reviews", *Research Findings* (EOC: Manchester, 2005).
89 "Commission Rejects Mandatory Equal Pay Reviews" (2006) 151 EOR (IRS: London, published April 1, 2006).
90 For a discusson of reform of equal pay law and policy, and the Ontario and Australian models, see Sandra Fredman, *Women and the Law* (Oxford: Oxford University Press, 1997) at pp.272–281.

Some of the difficulties that have been discussed with the use of discrimination law as the mechanism for addressing the problems of pay inequity have led to arguments that it may be more effective to use non-legal techniques for addressing the issue. A minimum wage strategy, for example, would set substantive standards of just wages, thereby raising the wages of women to an absolutely fair level rather than requiring a comparison with a man. This shift from requiring a male comparator towards setting an absolute standard for what is a fair wage for women would represent a shift in the concept of equality: from the use of equality as an intrinsically or instrumentally important marker, to the use of equality as a substitute for giving priority to women because of their absolutely worse position as wage earners. Grimshaw and Ruberry note that:

"Women have been the main beneficiaries of the National Minimum Wage since its introduction in 1999, but it has not transformed the conditons underpinning the undervaluation of their work. There has been a major clustering of women workers around the minimum wage and few employers have introduced new training provision, or redesigned jobs."[91]

VI. The Coverage of Sex Discrimination Law

EU and domestic sex discrimination law provides extensive protection against direct and indirect sex discrimination. As stated earlier, the large number of directives relevant to sex discrimination (e.g. in the areas of equal pay, equal treatment and the burden of proof) have now been consolidated into one Equal Treatment Directive (Directive 2006/54/EC of the European Parliament and of the Council of July 5, 2006 on the implementation of the principle of equal opportunities and equal treatment of men and women in matters of employment and occupation). In addition, it is also worth noting that a number of other directives are relevant to the discussion that follows: especially, the Pregnancy Directive (Directive 92/85); and the Directive on Parental Leave (Directive 96/34). Moreover, because women are concentrated in part-time and fixed term work, the following directives are of particular relevance in this context: the Directive on Part-Time Work (Directive 97/81); the Directive on Fixed Term Employees (Directive 99/70). The Directive on Equal Treatment of the Self-Employed is also of relevance to EU protection against sex discrimination.[92] The EU has also now moved beyond its focus on pay and employment with the prohibition of sex discrimination in the provision of goods and services (Council Directive 2004/113/EC of 13 December 2004)

[91] Damian Grimshaw and Jill Ruberry, *Undervaluing Women's Work*, EOC Working Paper Series No.53, Equal Opportunities Commission: Manchester, Spring 2007, at p.xi.

[92] For a full discussion of these provisions see Evelyn Ellis, *EU Anti-Discrimination Law* (Oxford: Oxford University Press, 2005) at pp.241–253.

In the domestic context, the SDA prohibits direct and indirect discrimination on the ground of sex. It also permits some positive action measures which are discussed in detail in Chapters 6 and 7. Prohibitions on direct and indirect sex discrimination extend beyond the employment context. The SDA also covers goods and services, housing and education. Early cases, such as *Gill and Coote v El Vino*[93] where a bar refused to serve a woman customer raised issues about sex discrimination in the provision of goods and services (SDA, s.29), but there are very few cases in this area. The main focus of the following discussion is therefore on employment and workplace issues. There is also a discussion relating to the gender equality duty, violence and women's participation in the public sphere in later sections. There are also significant exceptions to the coverage of sex discrimination law which are discussed in the next section.

As stated the SDA has a scope that extends to a wide range of areas: employment (SDA, Pt II) and goods and services in the public or private sphere (Pt III). There are, however, specific exceptions to the coverage of the SDA in these areas. In the context of employment, there is a general exception of "genuine occupational qualification" (GOQ) which is set out in SDA, s.7. However, the SDA definition of a GOQ is narrower and more specific than the general definition contained in the Equal Treatment Directive (ETD) which ensures a greater degree of protection against sex discrimination in domestic discrimination law. SDA, s.7(2) makes clear that being a man is a GOQ for a job only in limited circumstances: where the essential nature of the job calls for a man for reasons of physiology, or in a dramatic performance, and where the essential nature of the job would be materially different if carried out by a woman (s.7(2)(a)); where the job needs to be held by a man to preserve decency because of physical contact to which women may reasonably object or where men may object to contact with women because they are in a state of undress or using sanitary conditions where[94]; the job is likely to involve working or living in a private home (s.7(2)(c)). In addition, SDA, s.7 introduces a GOQ exception in two further specific cases: where the nature of the establishment (e.g. prison or hospital) requires special care, supervision or attention in an all male environment (s.7(2)(d)); and where the holder of the job provides individuals with personal services promoting their welfare or education, or similar personal services, and these services can most effectively be provided by a man (s.7(2)(e)).

The SDA also contains specific provisions relating to gender and employment in religious institutions. Where there is a provision that is otherwise discriminatory, namely a requirement to be of a particular sex or a requirement not to be undergoing or to have undergone gender reassignment, SDA,

[93] *Gill and Coote v El Vino* [1983] 1 All E.R. 398.

[94] This was considered in *Sisley v Brittania Security Systems Ltd* [1983] I.R.L.R. 404 where it was held that women working on rotating shifts (supplied with beds for rest periods) would often remove uniforms when sleeping and that it was not reasonable to provide separate facilities. Therefore, the employer was allowed to rely on the GOQ defence to this form of sex discrimination.

s.19 introduces an exception from the prohibition on sex discrimination in the case of employment for the purposes of organised religion: where the requirement is applied to (a) comply with the doctrines of religion; and (b) because of the nature of the employment and the context in which it is carried out, so as to avoid conflicting with the strongly-held religious convictions of a significant number of the religion's followers.

Another specific exception to the scope of the SDA is the armed services. There is a specific national security exception in SDA, s.52(1) which provides that the SDA does not render unlawful acts done for the purpose of safeguarding national security. Moreover, although relevant parts of the legislation apply to "service in the armed forces, as they apply to employment by a private person" it is made clear that "nothing in this Act shall render unlawful an act done for the purpose of ensuring the combat effectiveness of the armed forces" (see SDA, s. 85). Issues relating to national security and the armed forces have arisen in a number of ECJ decisions which have clarified the scope of the ETD; the meaning of "genuine occupations requirements"; and the relationship between the tests for exceptions in domestic (genuine occupational qualifications) and EU sex discrimination law (genuine occupational requirements). In *Johnstone v Chief Constable of the Royal Ulster Constabulary*,[95] the ECJ considered the Northern Ireland equivalent of the national security exception in SDA, s.52(1). The Court rejected the argument of the UK government that the ETD did not cover national security issues, although it accepted that that it was for the national court to determine whether the principle of proportionality in had been observed. Significantly, the ECJ stressed that the exceptions in ETD, Art.2 were a derogation from an important individual right to non-discrimination and they had to be construed strictly. This approach was confirmed in the later case of *Sirdar v Secretary of State for Defence*[96] which concerned a woman who challenged the rule that only men could serve in the combat units of the marines. Her claim was under SDA, s.85(4). The UK government argued that decisions concerning the armed forces fell outside the scope of the ETD. The ECJ confirmed, as it had in *Johnstone*, that the case fell within the scope of the ETD. Moreover, it also confirmed that the exception in ETD Art.2 had to be interpreted strictly; and that member states should review the exception to ensure that the derogation should be maintained in the light of social developments. The ECJ concluded that:

"That principle requires that derogations remain within the limits of what is appropriate and necessary in order to achieve the aim in view and requires the principle of equal treatment to be reconciled as far as possible with the requirements of public security which determine the context in which the activities in question are to be performed. [...] The question is therefore

[95] *Johnstone v Chief Constable of the Royal Ulster Constabulary* Case C-222/84 [1986] E.C.R. 1651.
[96] *Sirdar v Secretary of State for Defence* Case C-273/97 [1999] E.C.R. I-07403.

whether, in the circumstances of the present case, the measures taken by the national authorities, in the exercise of the discretion which they are recognised to enjoy, do in fact have the purpose of guaranteeing public security and whether they are appropriate and necessary to achieve that aim"[97]

There are also exceptions in the context of non-employment sex discrimination. One significant exception is the provision in SDA, s.45. This permits exceptions from the SDA in relation to annuities, life assurance policies, accident insurance policies or similar maters concerning risk assessment and actuarial evidence. This provision has been criticised because it uses "sex" and a general group of "women" as a marker for making assumptions about risk more generally. This means that individual women who may not fall within that risk group are subject to a detriment (e.g. a higher insurance permimum) irrespective of their actual attributes. The directive on equal treatment between men and women in the provision of goods and services (Council Directive 2004/113/EC of December 13, 2004) limits the ability of member states to exempt sex based discrimination in insurance and actuarial evidence through Art.5 which introduces special reporting and monitoring provisions relating to data on all exceptions that are used after December 31, 2007. The Discrimination Law Review has indicated that they intend to amend the existing insurance exemption in SDA, s.45 to comply with the terms of this directive.[98]

The previous discussion has concentrated on the way in which discrimination can lock women into a cycle of job segregation and low pay, which is difficult to address through discrimination law. This pattern arises from a range of factors, e.g. historic stereotypes about women's roles as well as lack of education and training. One recurring factor which is a cause of structural sex discrimination is that the workplace is designed to reflect male patterns of work which cannot easily accommodate the distinct needs of women. This raises the question of the equality–difference debate. In the next section we explore these issues in the context of two distinct areas: pregnancy discrimination and indirect discrimination.

97 *Sirdar v Secretary of State for Defence* Case C-273/97 [1999] E.C.R. I-07403. The ECJ has confirmed that the ETD extends to decisions in the organisations of armed forces, see *Kriel v Germany* Case C-285/98 [2000] E.C.R. I-69. The ECJ has also recognised, however, that the decision by the German government to reserve military service only for men was a choice that fell within their discretion, see *Dory v Germany* Case C-186/01[2003] E.C.R. I-02479.

98 *Discrimination Law Review 2007* (London: Department of Communities and Local Government, 2007) at p.180, para.B.20–B.22.

VII. Accommodating Women in the Workplace—Pregnancy Discrimination

The structural problems which lead to the undervaluing of women's work, pay inequity and the inability to accommodate female work patterns are also relevant when women become pregnant and take time off or return to work after maternity leave. As Grimshaw and Ruberry's research confirms:

"Mothers and women returners are particularly at risk of undervaluation, both because of childcare constraints and because of interruption to their careers. This is not associated with motherhood per se, but with the low pay and status of part time jobs that they may be forced into accepting."[99]

A survey of the experiences of pregnant women suggests that although large numbers of pregnant women had experienced discrimination or poor employer practices during pregnancy, maternity or return to work periods, very few of them considered using discrimination law. One in eight women stated that their treatment and workplace experiences during these periods had caused them to consider leaving work altogether.

Lorna Adams, Fiona McAndres and Mark Winterbotham *Pregnancy Discrimination at Work: A Survey of Women* EOC Working Paper Series No.24 (EOC: Manchester, Winter 2004/2005), pp.71–74

Conclusions

"The research suggests that it is only a minority of mothers with young children who have not encountered any form of discrimination, workplace unpleasantness or poor employer practice either while they were pregnant, while on maternity leave or on their return to work. Three quarters have had a problem in at least one of these areas.

Occupation

The proportion of women experiencing tangible discrimination is comparable across all occupational categories at between two-fifths and a half, although slightly higher among both managers and those employed in elementary roles than in other occupations. However, within this definition, the likelihood to have experienced specific types of treatment varies:

[99] Damian Grimshaw and Jill Ruberry, *Undervaluing Women's Work*, EOC Working Paper Series No.53 (Equal Opportunities Commission: Manchester, Spring 2007) at p.viii.

- Managers were particularly likely to experience discrimination leading to financial loss. They were also more likely to experience dispute over the type of work that they were entitled to take up on their return. Those who returned to work for the same employer after having their child were more likely than average to consider that they were treated worse than prior to their pregnancy (13 per cent)
- Employees in sales and customer services were twice as likely as average to be dismissed, made redundant or treated so badly that they felt they had to leave their job. Women working in these positions who returned to work for the same employer were also more likely than average to consider that they were treated worse on their return than before they informed their employer that they were pregnant.
- Those working in manual roles were more likely to have been encouraged to start maternity leave or signed off sick before they were ready to do so.
- Workers in elementary roles were slightly more likely than average to encounter dispute about whether they were entitled to return to work after maternity leave (although this still only affected a minority—eight per cent) [. . .]

Action taken

It was relatively uncommon for women to take action on the back of discriminatory or inappropriate behaviour by their employer. In some cases it seems that this resulted from an assumption that the treatment they received was not serious enough to warrant action. Two-thirds (67%) of women interviewed stated that they did not take any action because they did not feel that they had experienced any problems. Even among those who did feel that they had encountered problems, over half (55 per cent) either took no action, or only took informal action such as discussing the matter with family, friends or work colleagues. [. . .] Compared with the small number (three per cent) of those who actually approached an employment tribunal, the proportion of women considering doing so was relatively large (17 per cent). This would seem to indicate that women often find the process of approaching a tribunal daunting.

Attachment to work

There is some evidence from the research to suggest that poor treatment by employers impacts on the attachment that women feel to the labour market. For example, the proportion of those who considered that their employer was very or quite supportive during their pregnancy who had returned to work was higher than those who found their employer was unsupportive (77 per cent compared with 63 per cent).

In addition, the proportion of women who were not working who stated that the reason for this was because they could not find an appropriate job, was higher among those who experienced tangible discrimination than among those who had not (24 per cent compared with 14 per cent). This would seem to indicate that the treatment that these women received during their pregnancy has impacted on what they consider to be an appropriate work environment for the mother of a young child.

Of the relatively small proportion who had initially returned to work but had subsequently left, the most common reason for leaving work (mentioned by 22 per cent) was that the job did not have the right hours (which suggests a lack of flexibility on the behalf of employers) while a further 13 per cent stated that they were treated so badly that they felt they had to leave.

Finally, one in eight of those who were working at the time of the interview stated that the way in which they had been treated during their pregnancy, maternity leave or on their return to work had made them consider leaving work altogether. This increased to a fifth of those who had experienced tangible discrimination."

This empirical research concerning the experiences of pregnant women suggests that despite the prohibition of pregnancy discrimination, and the increasing focus on better maternity leave and return to work conditions, pregnant women face considerable difficulities in the workplace. Some of the reasons for this have been discussed earlier: stereotypes about the role of women; past discriminatory practices; and structural problems that mean that the workplace is designed around male patterns of work. There is also evidence that employers are influenced by specific stereotypes about women of childbearing age, pregnancy and women as mothers. Reseach confirms that women's family responsibilities are one of the primary concerns employers had about women workers: "Forty two per cent of ... employers, without prompting from interviewers, brought up images of motherhood and family when asked to talk about women. Employers often made these characterisations of women as mothers without empirical knowledge of their actual family situations."[100]

1. The Legal Response to Pregnancy and Maternity

Although domestic law on pregnancy discrimination has since developed in line with EU sex discrimination law, it is important to examine the difficulty that the SDA concepts of discrimination initially had in responding to the issues of pregnancy and maternity. Some of these points have already been discussed in the analysis of direct discrmination in Chapter 4 because they reveal a conceptual problem concerning the identity of the appropriate "comparator". In the US context, there has been explicit legislation to address this problem, given that the Civil Rights Act 1964 Title VII, which prohibits sex discrimination, was specifically amended in 1978 to prohibit discrimination on the ground of pregnancy in terms that obviate the need for a pregnant woman to find a "similarly situated" male comparator.

The treatment of pregnancy might therefore be seen to raise a core dilemma in sex discrimination law, discussed at the start of this chapter, about the tension between the public and private spheres, and equality and difference. Sandra Fredman notes that:

"Traditional assumptions that pregnancy and maternity belonged to the home, or the 'private sphere', are increasingly challenged by the great increase in women working in the market-place, or 'public sphere'. Indeed, the pregnant worker forces the law to confront the traditional divisions between pubic and private. [...] In facing this challenge, however, legislatures and courts have become ensnared in another of the dichotomies which bedevil analysis of women's rights: that between equality and difference. Most anti-discrimina-

[100] Kennelly (1999) cited at p.51 in Sara Davis, Fiona Neathey, Jo Reagan and Rebecca Wilson, *Pregnancy Discrimination at Work: A Qualitative Study*, EOC Working Paper No.23 (EOC: Manchester, 2004/5).

tion legislation follows a well-trodden path: those who are equal deserve equal treatment, and, conversely, those who differ may be treated differently. [...] clearly a woman is different from a man when she is pregnant, but how significant is this difference, and what legal consequences should follow from it?"[101]

3. The SDA 75 Response to Pregnancy Discrimination—the search for a "male comparator"

This section focuses on the conceptual problems which arose when the SDA definition of direct discrimination was originally applied to pregnancy. The issue of comparison arises in two contexts which are problematic: first, comparison is relevant to establishing discrimination as part of the concept of "less favourable treatment", secondly, SDA, s.5(3) requires that the comparators must be similarly situated.

Pregnancy initially caused problems because tribunals found it difficult to make a comparison in this context. In *Reany v Kanda Jean Products*, a tribunal held that because a man could not become pregnant it was impossible to compare a pregnant woman to a man.[102] This line of reasoning was also applied by the EAT in *Turley v Allders Department Stores Ltd*. In *Turley*, the applicant's complaint was that she was unfairly dismissed because of pregnancy. The central issue was whether dismissal on the grounds of pregnancy was less favourable treatment on the ground of sex and therefore capable of being sex discrimination. The EAT dismissed the applicant's claim citing the following reasons:

"You are to look at men and women, and see that they are not treated equally simply because they are men and women. You have to compare like with like. So, in the case of a pregnant woman there is an added difficulty in the application of subsection (1)(of s.1). Suppose that to dismiss her for pregnancy is to dismiss her on the ground of her sex. In order to see if she has been treated less favourably than a man the sense of the section is that you must compare like with like, and you cannot. When she is pregnant a women is no longer just a woman. She is a woman, as the Authorised Version of the Bible accurately puts it, with child, and there is no masculine equivalent."[103] (*per* Justice Bristow)

The difficulty here is that sex discrimination, as conceptualised in the SDA, requires a symmetrical approach where the comparison with a "man" is the key criterion which provides the basis for evaluating the treatment in issue,

[101] Sandra Fredman, "A Difference with Distinction: Pregnancy and Parenthood Reassessed" (1994) 110 L.Q.R. 106.

[102] *Reany v Kanda Jean Products* [1978[I.R.L.R. 427.

[103] *Turley v Allders Department Store* [1980] I.C.R. 66, at p.70.

arguably resulting in the application of a normative "male" standard which it is assumed should apply "universally", including to all women.

The dissenting judgment in *Turley* is worth noting because it reveals an alternative way of conceptualising the issue of pregnancy in the context of discrimination law. It states:

"The case under the direct discrimination provision is a simple one. Pregnancy is a medical condition. It is a condition which applies only to women. It is a condition which will lead to a request for time off from work for the confinement. A man is in a similar circumstance who is employed by the same employer and who in the course of the year will require time off for a hernia operation, to have his tonsils removed, or for other medical conditions. The employer must not discriminate by applying different and less favourable criteria to the pregnant woman than to the man requiring time off. That is 'like for like' comparison, not one between women who are pregnant and men who cannot become pregnant."[104]

On this analysis, pregnancy does not find an equivalent with a male comparator, but it is analogised with the male norm using the analogy of illness as a way of ensuring equal treatment. The problem with this analysis, however, is that the analogy breaks down when the issue of the consequences of pregnancy are analysed. So, for example, male illnesses that are used as the basis of comparison with pregnancy, e.g. a hernia, do not give rise to other issues that are relevant for equal treatment in the workplace, such as maternity leave or child care responsibilities. Futhermore, it could be thought demeaning and unfair to compare pregnancy—a healthy and socially valuable condition—with illness.

The minority approach from *Turley* was preferred in *Hayes v Malleable Men's Working Club and Institute*[105], where the comparison of a pregnant woman with an ill man was used to allow a woman who had been dismissed on the ground of pregnancy (but who could not claim unfair dismissal protection because of lack of a qualifying period) to bring a claim for sex discrimination under the SDA.

In neither case, however, did the courts consider an alternative way of conceptualising the issue which would treat pregnancy as sex discrimination because it is a characteristic or condition that is uniquely associated with women. This approach has long been associated in the US with Title VII of the Civil Rights Act, in relation to which it has been held that the statute is aimed at all sex stereotypes and "discrimination is not to be tolerated under the guise of physical properties possessed by one sex."[106] This approach requires an analysis of the reason for the disadvantageous treatment of women, and where

104 *Turley v Allders Department Store* [1980] I.C.R. 66, at p.71.
105 *Hayes v Malleable Working Men's Club* [1985] I.C.R. 703.
106 *Sprogis v United Air Lines* [444 F 2d 1194 (1971).

this is related to a factor that is uniquely associated with their sex, can fall within the category "sex discrimination". The advantage of this approach is that it moves away from inappropriate comparisons of "pregnancy" with illness. These inappropriate comparisons cannot take into account the way in which pregnancy, maternity leave and childcare responsibilities raise wider challenges for accommodating women in the workplace.

The ECJ has played a crucial role in recognising that discrimination due to pregnancy is per se sex discrimination, in case law under the Equal Treatment Directive 76/207 (now Directive 2006/54/EC). This approach moves away from the requirement for a "male comparator". In this sense, EU sex discrimination law has developed an approach to pregnancy which, like its approach to sexual harassment, treats pregnancy discrimination as a distinct form of harm to women, the move away from the use of a "male comparator" is also reflected in the approach of EU sex discrimination law towards maternity. In *Boyle v Equal Opportunities Commission*, the ECJ (and Advocate General Colomer) have explicitly rejected the comparison between a man on sick leave and a woman on maternity leave.[107]

The domestic approach to pregnancy, as reflected in the cases discussed above, shows a slow evolution away from the use of the comparator-based paradigm. The catalyst for the final break from this comparative approach came in the decision of the House of Lords in *Webb v EMO (Air Cargo) (No.2)* which responded to developments in EU law. The main case in which the ECJ laid the foundation for its approach to pregnancy was *Dekker*. In this case, the applicant applied for a job as an instructor at the defendant's establishment which was a training centre. She made it clear that she was three months pregnant. She was rated as the most suitable candidate for the job by the appointments committee. However, the defendant did not appoint her citing the reason that they would not be able to recover the money paid to her as benefit during her maternity leave, and that they would therefore suffer a financial loss. The Dutch Supreme Court asked for a preliminary reference from the ECJ about whether this constituted a breach of the Equal Treatment Directive. The ECJ held that this was sex discrimination in breach of the ETD, and in developing its reasons relied on a different analysis to that of the "male comparator" that was preferred in the UK domestic case law.

Dekker v Stichting Vormingscentrum voor Jong Volwassenen (ECJ) Case C-177/88, [1990] E.C.R. I-3941

[12]: [. . .] it should be noted that only women can be refused employment on grounds of pregnancy and such a refusal therefore constitutes direct discrimination on grounds of

[107] *Boyle v Equal Opportunities Commission Case* C-411/96 [1988] ECR I-6401

sex. A refusal of employment on account of the financial consequences of absence due to pregnancy must be regarded as based, essentially, on the fact of pregnancy. Such discrimination cannot be justified on grounds relating to the financial loss which an employer who employed a pregnant woman would suffer for the duration of her maternity leave [...]

[17]: It should be stressed that the reply to the question whether the refusal to employ a woman constitutes direct or indirect discrimination depends on the reason for that refusal. If that reason is to be found in the fact that the person concerned is pregnant, then the decision is directly linked to the sex of the candidate. In those circumstances the absence of male candidates cannot affect the answer to the first question.

The *Dekker* reasoning is significant because it confirms that pregancy discrimination is a form of unlawful sex discrimination without the need to establish comparison with a man, i.e. it is "less favourable treatment" per se without the need to undertake a comparison with a similarly situated man who cannot work for medical reasons. There is no need to search for a comparator in these cases because only women can become pregnant. In *Hertz*[108] this principle was extended beyond pregnancy to cover the whole of the relevant period of maternity leave. However, the ECJ also held in *Hertz* that after the period of maternity, leave the woman would be required to rely on the "male comparator" analysis, so that she would have to find an ill man to establish less favourable treatment under the ETD. It is also significant that in *Dekker* the ECJ considered, but was not influenced by, the fact that the employer would have to bear the costs which resulted from employing a pregnant worker. The issue of the distribution of the costs of accommodating women who are pregnant has, by contrast, been an issue in some of the post-*Dekker* case law.

The *Dekker* reasoning was extended in *Webb v EMO Air Cargo (UK) Ltd*, where the ECJ ruled, on a reference from the House of Lords, that the dismissal of a woman who was employed on an indefinite contract but who had been taken on to replace a worker who was on maternity leave, was contrary to the requirements of the Equal Treatment Directive (Council Directive 76/207):

Webb v EMO Air Cargo (UK) Ltd (ECJ)
Case C-32/93 [1994] E.C.R. I-3567

[21]: In view of the harmful effects which the risk of dismissal may have on the physical and mental state of women who are pregnant, have recently given birth or are breastfeeding, including the particularly serious risk that pregnant women may be prompted voluntarily to terminate their pregnancy, the Community legislature subsequently provided, pursuant to Article 10 of Council Directive 92/85 on the introduction of measures to

108 *Handels-og Kontrofunktionaerenes Forbund I Danmark v Dansk Arbejdsgiverforenin* [1990] E.C.R. I-3879

encourage improvements in the safety and health at work of pregnant workers and workers who have recently given birth or are breastfeeding, by prohibiting dismissal during the period from the beginning of their pregnancy to the end of their maternity leave.

[22]: Furthermore, Article 10 of the Directive 92/85 provides that there is to be no exception to, or derogation from, the prohibition on the dismissal of pregnant women during that period, save in exceptional cases not connected with their condition.

[23]: The question submitted by the House of Lords, which concerns Directive 76/207, must take account of that general context.

[24]: First, in response to the House of Lords inquiry, there can be no question of comparing the situation of a woman who finds herself incapable, by reason of pregnancy discovered very shortly after the conclusion of the employment contract, of performing the task for which she was recruited with that of a man similarly incapable for medical or other reasons.

[25]: As Mrs Webb rightly argues, pregnancy is not in any way comparable with a pathological condition, and even less so with unavailability for work on non-medical grounds, both of which are situations that may justify the dismissal of a woman without discriminating on grounds of sex. Moreover, in *Hertz* [. . .] the Court drew a clear distinction between pregnancy and illness, even where the illness is attributable to pregnancy but manifests itself during the period of maternity leave. As the Court pointed out, in paragraph 16, there is not reason to distinguish such an illness from any other illness.

[26]: Furthermore, contrary to the submission of the United Kingdom, dismissal of a woman recruited for an indefinite period cannot be justified on grounds related to her inability to fulfil a fundamental condition of her employment contract. The availability of an employee is necessarily, for the employer, a precondition for the proper performance of the employment contract. However, the protection afforded by Community law to a woman during her pregnancy and after childbirth cannot be dependent on whether her presence at work during maternity is essential to the proper functioning of the undertaking in which she is employed. Any contrary interpretation would render ineffective the provisions of the Directive. In circumstances such as those of Mrs Webb, termination of a contract for an indefinite period on grounds of the woman's pregnancy cannot be justified by the fact that she is prevented, on a purely temporary basis, from performing the work for which she has been engaged: see *Habermann-Beltermann*.

When the case returned to the House of Lords, Lord Keith, with whom the other members of the House agreed, applied the ECJ ruling and confirmed that dismissal due to pregnancy was a breach of the SDA without a make comparator being needed. However, it is worth noting that ECJ had stressed the fact that the woman employee in *Webb* was employed on an indefinite (rather than fixed term) contract. Lord Keith built this distinction into his analysis and stated:

"It does not necessarily follow that pregnancy would be a relevant circumstance in the situation where the woman is denied employment for a fixed term in the future during the whole of which her pregnancy would make her unavailable for work, nor in the situation where after engagement for such a period the discovery of her pregnancy leads to cancellation of the engagement."[109]

[109] *Webb v EMO Air Cargo (UK) Ltd* [1994] I.C.R. 1021.

The House of Lords therefore left open the issue of whether a woman employed for a fixed term period, and whose pregnancy would make her unavailable for work during the whole of that period, could bring a claim .

These developments seem to reflect a move towards an approach that focuses on ensuring that pregnancy and maternity are not used as the basis for creating a "disadvantage" for women. In the Canadian context, this was also the preferred approach in the analysis of pregnancy by the Canadian Supreme Court in *Brooks v Canada Safeway Ltd*, where it treated pregnancy as a discreet issue that could potentially be the source of disadvantage for women rather than an issue about equality with a "male comparator".[110] Moreover, in *Brooks* the Canadian Supreme Court showed a willingness to understand that pregnancy, maternity and child care perform wider social functions for the whole of society that need to be acknowledged.[111]

Nevertheless, there are limits (as the House of Lords treatment of *Webb* suggests) to the extent to which the ECJ and domestic courts will make allowance for pregnancy-related illness. Although *Hertz* was concerned with issues of illness after the period of pregnancy and maternity, it did open up the possibility of arguing that a woman who was dismissed for taking time off due to illness (in circumstances where a man would also have been dismissed) would not be able to rely on the protective principle established in *Dekker*. This was the line of reasoning adopted in the *Larsson* decision where the ECJ held:

"a woman is not protected under the Directive against dismissal on grounds of periods of absence due to an illness originating in pregnancy [...] as male and female workers are equally exposed to illness, the Directive does not concern illnesses attributable to pregnancy or confinement. The principle of equal treatment enshrined in the Directive does not, therefore, preclude account being taken of a woman's absence from work between the beginning of her pregnancy and the beginning of her maternity leave when calculating the period providing grounds for her dismissal under national law."[112]

The *Larsson* decision would have seriously weakened the protection to women in the workplace during their period of pregnancy and maternity. The ECJ very quickly moved away from the *Larsson* analysis in *Brown v Rentokil Ltd* where it held that:

"where a woman is absent owing to illness resulting from pregnancy or childbirth, and that illness arose during pregnancy and persisted during and

[110] *Brooks v Canada Safeway Ltd* (1989) I S.C.R. 1219.

[111] *Brooks v Canada Safeway Ltd* (1989) I S.C.R. 1219, at p.1237. See also the discussion of the way in which modern liberal approaches treat women's childbearing functions as a purely "private matter" as compared with classical approaches that recognised its wider contribution to society, Sybil A. Schwarzenbach, "On Civic Friendship" (October 1996) 107 (1) Ethics 97–128, at p.102.

[112] *Handels-og Kontrofunktionaerenes Forbund I (acting on behalf of Helle Elisabeth Larsson) v Dansk Hanel & Service, acting on behalf of Fotex Supermarked A/S* [1997] E.C.R. I-2757.Case C-400/95,

after maternity leave, her absence not only during maternity leave but also during the period extending from the start of her pregnancy to the start of her maternity leave cannot be taken into account during computation of the period justifying her dismissal under national law. As to her absence after maternity leave, this may be taken into account under the same conditions as a man's absence, of the same duration, through incapacity for work."[113]

The issue of how much of the cost for accommodating pregnancy and maternity should be borne by the employer was also relevant in cases such as *Webb* which distinguished between the nature of the protection where women were employed in full time (indefinite) contracts as compared with fixed term contracts. As we saw, the ECJ reasoning opened up the possibility that protection against pregnancy discrimination may vary depending on the nature of the contract, i.e. whether it was for an indefinite term or a fixed term. One justification for making this distinction would be that in the case of a fixed term contract the grant of full benefits to a woman for the whole of the period of that contract may mean that she performs none of the work for which she is employed. Nevertheless, the ECJ has more recently confirmed that protection from pregnancy discrimination covers both indefinite and fixed term contracts. In *Tele Danmark A/S v HK* the ECJ held that the duration of an employment contract is always uncertain; and, moreover, the ETD and Pregnancy Directives do not distinguish between the types of contracts, suggesting that they did not intend to offer lesser protection to women on fixed term contracts. In *Tele Danmark* the ECJ stated:

"Since the dismissal of a worker on account of pregnancy constitutes direct discrimination on grounds of sex, whatever the nature and extent of the economic loss incurred by the employer as a result of her absence because of pregnancy, whether the contract of employment was concluded for a fixed or an indefinite period has no bearing on the discriminatory character of the dismissal. In either case the employee's inability to perform her contract of employment is due to pregnancy. Moreover, the duration of an employment relationship is a particularly uncertain element of the relationship, in that, even if the worker is recruited under a fixed-term contract, such a relationship may be for a longer or shorter period, and is moreover liable to be renewed or extended. Finally, Directives 76/207 and 92/85 do not make any distinction, as regards the scope of the principle of equal treatment for men and women, according to the duration of the employment relationship in question."[114]

113 *Brown v Rentokill Ltd* Case C-394/96 [1998] E.C.R. I-4185.

114 *Tele Danmark A/S v Handels-og Kontorfunktionaerenes Forbund I Danmark (HK)* Case C-109/00 [2001] ECR I-6993, at 7025. This clarified the position, and any uncertainty about whether the national court had discretion to find that non-renewal of a fixed term contract fell outside the scope of prohibited pregnancy discrimination, in the following case: *Jimenez Melgar v Ayuntamiento de Los Barrios Case* C-438 /99, [2001] ECR I-6915.

3. The Pregnancy Directive, Directive 92/85

Protection against discrimination due to pregnancy is now offered by the Pregnancy Directive, Directive 92/85.[115] Although the ECJ has taken a robust approach to protecting pregnant women as workers, its case law did not regulate national systems of substantive benefits available to women who are pregnant and on maternity leave. The Pregnancy Directive now covers workers who are pregnant, who have recently given birth or who are breastfeeding. It contains provisions (Art.3) that safeguard the health and safety of women during pregnancy, e.g. against chemical hazards, and against nightwork (Art.7). Article 8 ensures that protected workers who fall within the scope of the Pregnancy Directive are given fourteen weeks continuous maternity leave before and/or after birth, including at least two weeks compulsory maternity leave in accordance with national legislation. Article 10 provides that Member States must protect women against dismissal during this period (except in exceptional cases not connected with pregnancy). Article 11 protects accrual of occupational pension rights and annual leave. In *Lewen v Denda*,[116] it has been held that this provision is subject to a narrower construction than "pay" under the equal pay legislation, so that, a Christmas bonus was held not to be "pay" for the purposes of the Pregnancy Directive.

An alternative approach would have been to ensure that women are not disadvantaged in pay terms the fact of pregnancy—an approach preferred in *CNAVTS v Thibault*, where the ECJ held that a woman had the right to an annual assessment (which may be basis for her promotion) despite the fact that she was pregnant and on maternity leave.[117] One criticism of the Pregnancy Directive is that although it has created a system of substantive rights for pregnant women which do not depend on comparison with other workers, it may paradoxically have created a system which treats women as "dependent mothers" within the realm of social protection rather than productive workers.[118] Pregnancy/motherhood is treated as "unproductive" rather than a valuable activity.[119] Moreover, even in relation to the specific rights protected by the Pregnancy Directive, the complexity of the notice period, as well as requirements for precise compliance with notification periods, have tended to work to the disadvantage of pregnant workers.[120] Grace James's research confirms that pregnant women still face considerable hurdles ranging from the extreme (abuse and harassment) to the denial of long term job opportunities

[115] Pregnancy Directive, Directive 92/85, O.J. (1992) L 348/1.
[116] *Lewen v Denda* Case C-333/97 [1999] E.C.R. I-7243.
[117] *CNAVTS v Thibault* Case C-136/95 [1998] E.C.R. I-2011, [1998] I.R.L.R. 399.
[118] See M. Wynn, "Pregnancy Discrimination: Equality, Protection or Reconciliation?" (1999) 62 M.L.R. 435.
[119] Sybil A. Schwarzenbach, "On Civic Friendship" (October 1996) 107 (1) Ethics 97–128, at p.102.
[120] For a discussion of some of these problems see Sandra Fredman, *Women and the Law* (Clarendon Press: Oxford, 1989) at p.202; Evelyn Ellis, Parents and Employment [1986] 15 I.L.J. 97.

and training. Moreover, the ability to claim and enforce rights through the tribunals is fraught with difficulties.[121]

4. Statutory Protection for Pregnancy and Maternity in the UK

Various additional specific statutory safeguards for pregnant women now exist at national level. Amendments to the SDA now include an explicit prohibition on adverse treatment on the ground of pregnancy or maternity leave (SDA, s.3A). It is now unlawful sex discrimination to treat a woman, during her period of pregnancy and until the end of the maternity leave period (or two weeks after the pregnancy ends if she is not entitled to ordinary maternity leave), less favourably than she would be treated had she not become pregnant, or had she not exercised or sought to exercise her statutory right to maternity leave (or were she now doing so or seeking to do so). Other statutory provisions that provide protection for pregnant women include the Employment Rights Act 1996 (ERA 96) and the Maternal and Parental Leave Regulations 1999 (MPLR 99), which provide protection from dismissal and detriment. This protection is available where the principal reason for the dismissal or detriment for a protected reason which includes, inter alia: the employee's pregnancy (MPLR, Reg.19); the fact that the employee sought to take time off for parental leave (ERA 96, s.47); or that the employee sought to exercise the right to flexible working (ERA 96, s.47). There are also Health and Safety provisions which safeguard pregnant women (The Management of Health and Safety at Work Regulations)[122] relating to risk assessments and the safety of pregnant employees. As discussed below, one of the main sources of disadvantage for women is poverty in their retirement, and lack of access to secure pension facilities. Therefore, it is especially important that protection is offered to pregnant women, through the provisions of the Social Security Act 1989, Sch.5, which ensure that employment related schemes for pensions and other related pensions comply with the principle of equal treatment, given the Act's specific inclusion of equal treatment in relation to pregnancy and maternity (s.5(1)).

VIII. Female Patterns of Work and Sex Discrimination

In this section, we examine the extent to which the concepts of direct and indirect discrimination provide solutions to the specific problems faced by pregnant women. As we shall see, indirect discrimination can sometimes be useful, but the ability to "justify" indirect discrimination by relying on existing

[121] Grace James, *Pregnancy Discrimination at Work: A Review*, EOC Working Paper No.14, EOC: Manchester, 2004, pp.44–45.
[122] The Management of Health and Safety at Work Regulations SI No.3242.

business needs limits the extent to which indirect discrimination as a legal concept can achieve the wider re-structuring of patterns of work necessary to accommodate women.

It is sometimes argued that the increasing demand for more "flexible" work in recent years provides an opportunity for women to negotiate terms and conditions of work that can accommodate their distinct needs. However, flexibility of work that has allowed part time work and job sharing has often been designed to meet the needs of employers rather than women. EOC research has confirmed this ongoing structural barrier and concluded that flexible working patterns were structured to suit the operational needs of employers and often remain very "inflexible" from the point of view of women and their families.[123] On this view, flexible patterns of work in fact suit employers' needs (a large factor being savings in costs that arise from flexibility) rather than representing a response to women's needs for work that can accommodate their family responsibilities. The consequence is that women with family responsibilities either do not enter the workforce, or when they do they are concentrated in part time work (which fits in with their family life). This type of work is often low paid, lacks long term job security and also does not have significant potential for development, training or promotion.[124] Some of these issues are discussed in the passage below.

Damian Grimshaw and Jill Rubery
Undervaluing Women's Work
EOC Working Paper Series No. 53
(Equal Opportunities Commission: Manchester, Spring 2007)

pp.v–x: "Outsourcing of work formerly undertaken in-house creates new risks, especially for the lower paid and more vulnerable groups of workers. Cost competition among suppliers exerts downwards pressures on pay; reduces job security; increases the use of temporary contracts; and flattens and fragments job ladders. This is because outsourcing may weaken collective representation; lead to a worsening of employment policy and practice; and result in an intensification of work to meet performance targets specified in contracts for services.

New organisational forms bring new inequalities. "Networked" organisations may exploit women's capacities for "relational work", while delayered structures may constrain women's career development by removing rungs from traditional job ladders. Multi-employer coordination of activities may make legal comparisons of pay between colleagues impossible because they are tied to different employers.

Trade unions' power in shaping labour market conditions has weakened considerably and, in key sectors, of women's employment, weak unionisation has failed to halt a steady decline in relative average pay.

New technologies have multiple effects on the valuation of jobs, with managerial dis-

[123] A. Coyle, *Women and Organisational Change* (EOC Research Discussion Series: London, 1995).
[124] Sandra Fredman, *Women and the Law* (Oxford; Clarendon Press, 1997), at p.153.

cretion having an important influence on the impact they make. Studies of new call centre workplaces suggest that traditional sex typing of jobs continues in new ways, while low skill jobs are created through unbundling of job tasks following the adoption of new technologies.

Both part-time work, and part-time workers are often undervalued. This is because:

- part time work is often undervalued work;
- many part time workers enjoy little control over their working hours;
- women in part-time work experience a persistently large pay gap;
- work for many part-time workers has intensified, often through the manipulation of scheduling by employers to avoid paid breaks; and
- female part-time workers have weak career opportunities and face constraints in transferring to full-time jobs.

[...] The conditions that underpin the undervaluation of women's work are not only restricted to traditional areas of "women's work", but may follow women as they move into new job areas traditionally sex typed as "men's work". [...] In line with earlier research for the US, there is evidence that in the UK, feminisation was linked with pay decline.

A. *Direct Sex Discrimination*

The direct discrimination provisions of the SDA have served, and continue to serve, an important function in protecting against certain forms of prejudice against women. The focus of the discussion concerning pregnancy on accommodating difference to advance the interests of women may obscure the fact that in the past assumptions about "women's difference" and femininity were used to exclude women from "men's work", and also more generally from political, social and economic life. In *Peake v Automative Products Ltd*, for example, the Court of Appeal considered a concession by an employer that women workers could leave work five minutes before men. The tribunal had held that this was direct sex discrimination against men. The Court of Appeal reversed this, and Lord Denning stated that:

"it would be very wrong to my mind if this statute were thought to obliterate the differences between men and women or to do away with the differences and courtesy which we must expect mankind to give womankind. The natural differences of sex must be regarded even in the interpretation of an Act of Parliament."[125]

In *Ministry of Defence v Jerimiah*,[126] the employer did not require women to do especially dirty and onerous work. By contrast with *Peake*, the Court of Appeal

125 *Peake v Automative Products Ltd* [1977] I.C.R. 968, at 973.

126 *Ministry of Defence v Jerimiah* [1980] I.C.R. 13.

held that this was sex discirmination against men and explained the *Peake* case as a decision based on the *de minimis* nature of the discrimination. In *Gill and Coote v El Vino*,[127] a bar owner who refused to serve women at the bar sought to argue that the women did not suffer a "detriment" because they could obtain drinks at their tables. The Court of Appeal dismissed this argument and held that this conduct was direct sex discrimination in the provision of goods and services. This analysis was applied in the employment context in *Brennan v Dewhurst*, which confirmed that direct discrimination was per se unlawful under the SDA and did not require a further proof of detriment.[128] As Chapter 4 discussed, direct discrimination has now moved to an analysis of unfavourable treatment rather than a predominant focus on stereotypes.

B. *Indirect Sex Discrimination*

Although the legal concept of indirect discrimination has been applied to challenge structural problems, it is worth noting that precisely delineated legislative change can often also have a significant influence on re-structuring working practices that disadvantage women. For example, the introduction of specific EU directives in areas such as Part Time Work,[129] Fixed Term Employees[130] and Equal Treatment of the Self Employed,[131] might be thought to help promote the accommodation of women by identifying precisely those areas (e.g. part-time work) in which they face structural barriers.[132]

As we saw in Chapter 5, the concept of indirect discrimination was developed by the US Supreme Court in its interpretation of Civil Rights Act 1964 Title VII in *Griggs v Duke Power Company*.[133] Indirect discrimination is a particularly helpful concept in the context of sex discrimination because it allows a shift of focus from individual acts towards altering systemic structures and practices (which have emerged through long standing stereotypes and prejudice against women) which impact on women as a group. EU sex discrimination law has had a significant impact on the definition of indirect discrimination in domestic law. As in the cases of equal pay and pregnancy, EU sex discrimination law has provided a catalyst for extending relevant definitions and their application at domestic level.

The old definitions of indirect sex discrimination originate in SDA 75 s.1. They have three main aspects: (1) *a requirement or condition*; (2) *disparate (or disproportionate) impact*; and (3) *justification by the employer*. The old definition

[127] *Gill and Coote v El Vino* [1983] 1 All E.R. 398.
[128] *Brennan v Dewhurst* [1984] I.C.R. 52.
[129] Part Time Work Directive, Directive 97/81, O.J. [1998] L14/9.
[130] Directive on Fixed Term Employees Directive 1999/70, O.J. [1999] L175/43.
[131] Directive on Equal Treatment of the Self Employed Directive 86/613, O.J. [1986] L359/56.
[132] For a detailed discussion see Evelyn Ellis, *EU Anti-Discrimination Law* (Clarendon Press: Oxford, 2005) at pp.246–253.
[133] *Griggs v Duke Power* 401 U.S. 424 (1971).

applies in the context of those areas (non-employment related) which are not covered by EU discrimination law. The areas covered by EU sex discrimination law are employment, goods and services (the latter via the new Goods and Services Directive which has now been implemented into domestic law). This "new" definition of indirect sex discrimination was introduced via an amendment to the SDA 75 and states in s.1(2) that a person (indirectly) discriminates against a woman if:

"he applies to her a provision, criterion or practice which he applies or would apply equally to a man, but—

(i) which puts or would women at a particular disadvantage when compared with men,
(ii) which puts her at that disadvantage, and
(iii) which he cannot show to be a proportionate means of achieving a legitimate aim".

One significant difference between these definitions is that the "new" EU discrimination law definition permits a test for indirect discrimination based on contingent harm. This will allow the concept of indirect discrimination to catch practices that produce an adverse impact on (or disparate treatment of) a group before these materialise into harm. It will also catch practices which do cause adverse impact but which are difficult to prove through statistics. In the discussion which follows, the old definition of indirect sex discrimination is generally used, and where relevant the implications of the introduction of the new definition are also considered.

1. "Requirement or Condition"

One of the early difficulties which courts faced was the degree of flexibility that should be used in defining the SDA, s.1 term "requirement or condition". This issue is now less important because the EU definition of indirect discrimination, which applies, inter alia, to employment related sex discrimination, uses the different formulation of "provision, criterion or practice". In the past, there was a flexible approach to this issue which opened up the prospect of using the concept of indirect discrimination to challenge the structural and "institutional" barriers that are created by historical and entrenched forms of discrimination against women. A number of structural barriers faced by women have been deemed to fall within the term "requirement or condition", even if the barrier is not precisely defined or delineated, or if the practice is a result of custom: e.g. requirements concerning part-time work[134]; or seniority based on age limits.[135] This flexibility was critical to allowing the concept of indirect discrimination to perform the function of tranforming the workplace

134 *Meeks v National Union of Agricultural and Allied Workers* [1976] I.R.L.R. 98, although the claim failed for different reasons. *Home Office v Holmes* [1984] I.R.L.R. 299.

135 *Price v Civil Service Commission (No.2)* [1978] I.R.L.R. 3.

to accommodate the needs of women, against a background in which British industrial relations as Lawrence Lustgarten notes, was based on informal rather than formal workplace rules and practices:

"This is a key point, for the characteristic preference in British industrial relations for shared understandings, custom and informal methods of settling disputes rather than formal agreements and precise interpretations, would make discrimination laws a nullity if they could be applied only to formally proclaimed rules."[136]

However, there have also been more restrictive and problematical decisions about what constitutes a "requirement or conditon". For example, one consequence of the *Perera v Civil Service Commission & The Department of Customs & Excise*[137] decision was to limit the scope of the interpretation of "requirement or condition". In *Perera* the applicant was challenging requirements for communication in English which he claimed indirectly discriminated against him on the grounds of nationality and colour. More specifically, *Clymo v Wandsworth London Borough of Transport Council*[138] is an example of an unimaginative approach to the interpretation of the term "requirement or condition". In *Clymo*, the woman applicant had made a request to her employers to move from full time work to reduced working hours after the birth of her child. The EAT held that "full time work" was not a prohibited "requirement or condition". Rather, it was part of the fundamental nature of the job, which in turn provided the structure within which managerial discretion was exercised. Moreover, in *Brook v London Borough of Haringay* the EAT also interpreted "requirement or conditon" in narrow terms, finding that redundancy selection which was made from one particular trade (which had larger numbers of women) did not constitute the use of a "requirement or condition".[139] This line of reasoning has been disapproved by the Court of Appeal in *Allonby v Accrington & Rossendale College*[140] where Sedley L.J. stated that:

"It is for the applicant to identify the requirement or condition which she seeks to impugn. These words are not terms of art: they are overlapping concepts and are not to be narrowly construed [...] If the applicant can realistically identify a requirement or condition capable of supporting her case [...] it adds nothing to the point that her employer can with equal cogency derive from the facts a different and unobjectionable requirement or condition."[141]

136 Lawrence Lustgarten, *Legal Control of Racial Discrimination* (London and Basingstoke, Macmillan, 1980) at p.43.
137 *Perera v The Civil Service Commission & The Department of Customs & Excise* [1983] I.C.R. 428.
138 *Clymo v Wandsworth LBC* [1989] I.C.R. 250.
139 *Brook v London Borough of Haringey* [1992] I.R.L.R. 478. See also the problematic analysis of the House of Lords in an equal pay case, *Barry v Midland Bank* [1999] I.C.R. 859. See discussion by Aileen McColgan, *Discrimination Law: Text, Cases and Materials* (Oxford: Hart Publishing, 2005) at p.84.
140 *Allonby v Accrington & Rossendale College* [2001] I.R.L.R. 364.
141 *Allonby v Accrington & Rossendale College* [2001] I.R.L.R. 364, para.12.

The proposals by the government's Discrimination Law Review in 2007 that a proposed non-discrimination statute covering all prohibited grounds of discrimination should harmonise the definition of indirect discrimination on all grounds and in all spheres to the EU definition of "provision, criterion or practice" (involving a "particular disadvantage" to the claimant) should reduce the impact of the SDA definition of "requirement or condition".[142]

2. Disparate (Disproportionate) Impact

(i) *Detriment*

Before moving on to consider the way in which "disparate impact" is defined in the context of indirect sex discrimination, it is worth noting that a restrictive reading of the requirement of detriment has been problematic. The domestic definition of indirect discrimination requiring the court to consider whether the claimant "can comply" with the requirement or condition. This is different to the EU discrimination law definition which focuses on the impact of the "provision, criterion or provision" on the claimant. The introduction of this part of the domestic definition was justified as a way of ensuring that the definition of indirect discrimination was related to an indentifiable victim: as the responsible minister stated, "there must be a particular victim of indirect discrimination, and she must, for obvious reasons, be one of the women who are unable to qualify for the benefits."[143] This provision could have restricted the ability of women to use the concept of indirect discrimination to challenge informal, but structural, sources of disadvantage in the workplace.[144] The development and application of the provision was, however, flexible. In *Price v Civil Service Commission*, the EAT held that "it should not be said that a person 'can' do something merely because it is theoretically possible for him to do so: it is necessary to see whether he can do so in practice".[145] This approach was adopted and endorsed in the context of indirect race discrimination in *Mandla v Dowell Lee*.[146] One particular difficulty which remains, however, is the operation of stereotypes which suggest that women cannot "comply" with full time working practices because of their obligations as mothers: exactly the type of structural problem that sex discrimination law seeks to challenge. In

142 *Discrimination Law Review* (London: Department for Government and Local Government, June 2007) at p.39, para.1.37.

143 *Per* Mr John Fraser, Under Secretary of State for Employment, 893 HC 1491–2 (June 18, 1975)

144 See *Turner v Labour Party* [1987] I.R.L.R. 101 where the Court of Appeal used a restrictive interpretation of "can comply" to find that a woman could not challenge a pension scheme becaue the conditions for benefit were at a future date.

145 *Price v Civil Service Commission* [1987] I.R.L.R. 101.

146 *Mandla v Dowell Lee* [1983] 2 A.C. 548.

cases where the claim is that there is a general sexist (or racist) atmosphere which creates a hostile working environment it may also be difficult to show that there is a precise detriment to an individual.[147] The "can comply" requirement might also be criticised on the basis that practices that are discriminatory in the workplace should be challenged, even without the additional hurdle that they are causing specific detriment to an individual woman, because individual discrimination cases perform the important public function of promoting gender equality.

(ii) *Disparate Impact*

At the heart of the concept of indirect discrimination is the idea that discrimination can occur through the imposition of a facially-neutral rule which has a differential impact on individuals from one particular group, either because of a particular characteristic that makes them different; or because of a past history of prejudice; or because they have lacked the power to define the way in which norms in employment or other spheres are defined. Within the analysis of indirect discrimination, therefore, the idea that the same practice is having a disproportionate impact on one particular group is critical. Moreover, to be unlawful indirect discrimination the relevant disproportionate impact needs to be on a group that is "protected" within discrimination law.

This idea is reflected in different ways in the "old" and EU law-based definitions of indirect discrimination. The "old" SDA definition is much more focused on comparisons and issues of "how" to establish disproportionate impact. Consequently, the case law reflects a complex range of analyses of "pools of comparison" and the use of "statistics". The newer definition, introduced to ensure compliance with EU discrimination law, focuses on the whether "the provision, criterion or practice puts or would put at a particular disadvantage" as compared with men. This can be established without resort to detailed statistics, and the definition also focuses on preventative issues by including the term "would put" at a particular disadvantage. However, both definitions require a comparison (between the impact of the practice on women as compared with men). This, in turn, means that it is important to ask questions about the nature of the "relevant circumstances" which establish that a comparison can be made. Moreover, there is a need to establish how to determine whether there has been a particular disadvantage, and whether there is disparate impact.

The predominant focus of the "old" domestic test on proof of disparate impact is reflected in the case law on indirect sex discrimination. The use of statistics and "pools of comparison" in this context performs two key functions. First, it determines who are the relevant comparators, which is also

[147] See for example cases on sexual and racial harassment: on sexual harassment *Porcelli v Strathclyde Regional Council* [1986] I.C.R. 564; on racial harassment *De Souza v Automobile Association* [1986] I.R.L.R. 103.

subject to the additional requirement that the comparator should share the same "relevant circumstances" as the claimant (SDA, s.5(3). Second, the "pools of comparison" permit some assessment of what constitutes, and whether there is, a considerably smaller proportion who can comply with the requirement or condition from the protected group.

As we have seen in earlier chapters, the use of a "comparative" model can often be problematic and undermine the realisation of the underlying goals of discrimination law. This is well demonstrated by the problems caused by the courts' early attempts to use a male comparator in pregnancy discrimination cases. This problem is also evident in some of the indirect discrimination case law concerning "pools of comparison". In *Kidd v DRG (UK) Ltd*,[148] for example, the approach to the pool of comparison left in place the advantaged position of full time work in relation to part time work. In *Kidd*, the issue was complex because it concerned a collective agreement that would enable part time workers to be the first ones to be made redundant. On the issue of the pools of comparison, the EAT held that issues relating to the construction of the relevant "pool of comparison" were matters of fact, and confirmed that there was a need for a narrow formulation of "comparison" so that all the relevant circumstances between the pools of comparison were similar (as required by the additional comparator requirement of the SDA, s.5(3)). In *Kidd*, this meant that the EAT ignored the fact that many women are unable to work full time, and went on to find that there was not indirect sex discrimination. Despite case law discussed below, which indicates a willingness to take a more flexible approach towards comparators, there is sometimes a tendency to require a strict similarity between the pools of comparison. This strict approach which is also encouraged by the specific requirement for the comparators to share relevant characteristics (SDA, s.5(3). In *Jones v University of Manchester*,[149] the challenge was to the requirement of an age band of twenty-seven to thirty-five for a post as careers advisor. The applicant argued this was indirect discrimination because there were fewer women who could comply with this requirement. The tribunal held in her favour using a pool of comparison of men and women who had obtained degrees at the age of twenty five years or over. The Court of Appeal upheld the decision, preferring to use a comparison of all men and women who are within the age range and graduates with the relevant experience. The CA specifically cited SDA, s.5(3), which they said justified this analysis because it requires comparisons between men and women to be such that the relevant "circumstances" are the same.

The issue of part time work raises the problem that the "pool of comparison" may itself reflect (or be tainted by) the structural discrimination that is the mischief which the concept of sex discrimination seeks to address. A more flexible approach might avoid this problem. One example of a more flexible approach can be found in *R v Secretary of State for Education Ex p. Schaffter*, a

[148] *Kidd v DRG (UK) Ltd* [1985] I.C.R. 405.
[149] *Jones v University of Manchester* [1993] I.C.R. 474.

case concerning the availability of education grants. Schiemann J. ensured that the pool of comparison accommodated the larger number of *unmarried* women who were lone parents with children, who were less able to comply with the conditions of education grants that were available for lone parents who were married which included similar proportions of men and women. Through the creative use of the concept of indirect sex discrimination, the court was able to ensure that a key benefit relating to education and training was available to single mothers who were at greater risk of social and economic exclusion.[150]

The more flexible approach towards pools of comparison is also reflected in recent domestic discrimination law cases, and it is also preferred in EU sex discrimination law. In the domestic context, the move away from a strict focus on statistics was confirmed by the House of Lords in *Barry v Midland Bank Plc* which concerned a claim that a serverance payment scheme discriminated against part time workers (and indirectly against women). In *Barry*, the Court of Appeal had held that the claimant did not provide sufficient evidence of the impact of the scheme on part-time women workers. The House of Lords, however, took a more flexible approach. Lord Nicholls held that:

"In the present case, the figures needed to make these comparisons are not available. The Court of Appeal considered this fatal to the claim, although the court was reluctant to decide the appeal on this ground. [...] I consider that, although unsatisfactory, the figures available are sufficient to enable an inference to be drawn that, in the Midland Bank as elsewhere, a disproportionately high percentage of key part-time employees are women".[151]

This more flexible approach to statistics and comparison was also developed in *London Underground v Edwards*[152] which illustrates the willingness of domestic tribunals to apply the concept of indirect discrimination to challenge structural forms of sex discrimination. In *London Underground*, the applicant was a female train driver. She challenged a change in the allocation of shift work which meant that it would be more difficult for her as a woman (and a lone parent) to fulfil her child care responsibilities. She showed that a considerably smaller proportion of women as compared with men would be able to comply with the new shift arrangements.

As domestic law illustrates, despite some restrictive decisions, there is also a trend towards allowing a flexible and purposive approach to comparison to establish disparate impact in indirect sex discrimination cases. The movement towards this approach, however, was confirmed through the influence of EU

150 *R v Secretary of State for Education Ex p. Schaffter* [1987] I.R.L.R. 53.
151 *Barry v Midland Bank Plc* [1999] I.C.R. 859.
152 *London Underground v Edwards* [1999] I.C.R. 494.

sex discrimination law. As stated earlier, the definition of indirect discrimination in EU discrimination law permits for "contingency" and has less focus on statistics. This should, in principle, permit a more flexible approach to comparisons.[153]

In *Seymour Smith*, the ECJ was specifically asked for its opinion on the "degree" of disparate impact that is required to establish that there has been indirect discrimination. In its opinion, it emphasised that there must be a considerably smaller percentage of women rather than men. The ECJ also confirmed that the issue for the national court to ascertain whether there was such a "considerably smaller percentage" and:

"that situation would be evidence of apparent sex discrimination unless the disputed rule were justified by objective factors unrelated to any discrimination based on sex. That would also be the case if the statistical evidence revealed a lesser but persistent and relatively constant disparity over a long period between men and women who satisfy the requirements of two years' employment. If would, however, be for the national court to determine the conclusions to be drawn from such statistics. It is also for the national court to assess whether the statistics concering the situation of the workforce are valid and can be taken into account, that is to say, whether they cover enough individuals, whether they illustrate purely fortuitous or short-term phenomenon, and whether, in general, they appear to be significant."[154]

The ECJ also stated that national courts could take into account statistics available at the point in time when the impugned practice was adopted but also statistics compiled subsequently and which are likely to provide an indication of the practice's impact on men and women. In relation to the appropriate moment at which to judge the impact of the rule, the ECJ concluded that:

"The requirements of Community law must be complied with at all relevant times, whether that is the time when the measure is adopted, when it is implemented or when it is applied to the case in point."

This confirms the general approach of the ECJ of not specifying or demanding detailed proof of disparate impact.[155]

The determination of what constitutes "considerably smaller" in the national context has not, however, been a straightforward matter. In *Seymour Smith*, the House of Lords applied the analysis of the ECJ's preliminary ruling

[153] For a discussion of this issue and of some narrower interpretations of comparison see Evelyn Ellis, *EU Anti-Discrimination Law* (Clarendon Press: Oxford, 2005), at p.95. See *Gruber v Silhouette International Schmied GmbH & Co KG* Case C-249/97 ECR I–5295. At domestic level, see *R. v Secretary of State for Employment Ex p. EOC* [1994] I.R.L.R. 176.

[154] *R v Secretary of State for Employment Ex p. Seymour Smith* Case C-167/97 [1999] E.C.R. I–00623.

[155] *Notle v Landesversicherungsanstalt Hannover* Case C-317/93 [1995] E.C.R. I-4625.

to find that there was disparate impact although they went on to find that the indirect discrimination in the case was justified. For the majority, Lord Nicholls stated that the period over which the statistical disparity occurred was relevant:

"A considerable disparity can be more readily established if the statistical evidence covers a long period and the figures show a persistent and relatively constant disparity. In such a case a lesser statistical disparity may suffice to show that the disparity is considerable than if the statistics covered only a short period or if they present an uneven picture".[156]

Moreover, in early decisions domestic courts have shown a willingness to interpret the requirement that a "considerably smaller" proportion of women can comply in a way that reflects the central purposes of the concept of indirect sex discrimination. In *London Underground v Edwards*, the woman applicant was challenging a decision to change the rota which would have a particularly detrimental impact on women like her who were lone mothers with child care responsibilities. The pool of comparison was taken to be the number of women train-drivers like her (who were lone mothers) who could comply with the rota as compared with men train drivers. If the pool of comparison had been all women train drivers in that establishment the figure would not have been as great and it was significant that she was the only woman who could not comply (because other women train drivers did not have the same personal childcare responsibilities as her). The Court of Appeal, however, took a flexible approach and noted that it was common knowledge that women were more likely to be single parents with childcare responsibilities than men. The Court of Appeal (*per* Potter L.J.) noted that the aspects of the indirect discrimination provisions that require showing that a considerably smaller proportion of women can comply (SDA 75, s.1(b)) had two functions:

"The first is to prescribe as the threshold for intervention a situation in which there exists a substantial and not merely marginal discriminatory effect between men and women, so that it can be clearly demonstrated that a prima facie case of discrimination exists, sufficient to require the employer to justify the application of the condition or requirement in question: see paragraph (ii). The second is to ensure that a tribunal charged with deciding whether or not the requirement is discriminatory may be confident that its disparate impact is inherent in the application of the requirement or condition and is not simply the product of unreliable statistics or fortuitous circumstances. [...] In many respects no doubt, it would be useful to lay down in relation to s1(1)(b) a rule of thumb or to draw a line defining the margin within, or threshold beyond which, in relation to a small percentage differences, the lower percentage should not reasonably be regarded as 'considerably smaller'. However, it does

[156] *R v Secretary of State for Employment Ex p. Seymour Smith & Perez (No.2)* [2000] I.C.R. 244.

not seem to me appropriate to do so. For the various reasons in this judgment and because of the wide field and variety of situations in which the provisions of the section are to be applied, the circumstances and arguments before the adjudicating tribunal are bound to differ as to what in a particular case amounts to a proportion which is 'considerably smaller' for the purposes of determing the discriminatory or potentially discriminatory nature of a particular requirement or condition."[157]

This last point, about not prescribing what constitutes considerably smaller in indirect discrimination cases, is especially important because it indicates the needs (a) to stay flexible in the way in which the test is applied; as well as (b) to take a purposive approach to the impact of employment practices on women, as in the case of *London Underground v Edwards* itself. An additional feature of this analysis is that it raises the question of "from whose viewpoint" the issue of a considerably smaller proportion is to be determined, i.e. is the question "can a significantly greater number of men comply", or is the question "are a significantly larger number of women disadvantaged". In *Rutherford v Towncircle*, Lord Justice Mummery that this difference of viewpoint was significant:

"[...] concentrating on the proportion of men and women in the workforce who are disadvantaged because they cannot comply with the disputed requirement, can produce seriously misleading results, as in the simple case of a requirement with which 99.5 per cent of men can comply and 99 per cent of women can comply. If the focus is then shifted to the proportions of men and women who cannot comply (i.e. 1 per cent of women and 0.5 per cent of men) the result would be that twice as many women as men cannot comply with the requirement. That would not be a sound or sensible basis for holding that the disputed requirement, with which the vast majority of both men and women can comply, had a disparate impact on women."[158]

This focus on disproportionality as a core feature of indirect discrimination is also clear from *Coker & Osamor v Lord Chancellor & Lord Chancellor's Department*.[159] The applicants (who fell within the category "women" and "African Carribean") challenged the decision by the Lord Chancellor to make a public appointment from among his circle of friends (which was predominantly white and male) which they said was a form of indirect discrimination. The Court of Appeal dismissed the decision of the tribunal and found that there was no basis for finding that the number of women who could comply with the requirement (circle of friends and aquaintainces of the Lord Chancellor) was considerably smaller. Lord Phillips held that:

157 *London Underground v Edwards* [1999] I.C.R. 494, per Potter L.J.
158 *Rutherford v Towncircle Ltd (No.2)* [2005] I.R.L.R. ICR 119.
159 *Coker & Osamor v Lord Chancellor & Lord Chancellor's Department* [2002] I.C.R. 321.

"The test of indirect discrimination focuses on the effect that the requirement objected to has on the pool of potential candidates. It can only have a discriminatory effect within the two statutes if a significant proportion of the pool are able to satisfy the requirement. Only in that situation will it be possible for the requirement to have a disproportionate effect on the men and the women, or the racial groups, which form the pool. Where the requirement excludes almost the entirety of the pool it cannot constitute indirect discrimination within the statutes. For this reason, making an appointment from within the circle of family, friends and personal acquaintainces is seldom likely to constitute indirect discrimination. Those known to the employer are likely to represent a minute proportion of those who would otherwise be qualified to fill the post. If the above proposition will be true in most cases of appointments made on the basis of personal acquaintainceship, it was certainly true of the appointment of Mr Hart by the Lord Chancellor. [...] However many other persons there may have been who were potential candidates, whatever the proportions of men and women or racial groups in the pool, the requirement excluded the lot of them, except Mr Hart. Plainly it can have had no *disproportionate* effect on different groupings within the pool."[160]

This approach, however, gives a great deal of weight to the issue of disproportionality, rather than treating the issue of difference in the ability of men and women to comply with a practice to be a guide to identifying the structural barriers that cause women's exclusion and disadvantage. The use of the "new" definition of indirect discrimination with a greater focus on "particular disadvantage", rather than statistical disparity, could usefully shift the analysis in the domestic context towards something more purposive. From this alternative perspective of ensuring women's accommodation in the workplace, the relevance of even a small number of women who cannot comply (1 per cent), despite the fact that large numbers of women are able to comply, is that it alerts the tribunal that the practice that is being challenged is an entrenched type of practice which has an impact on a particularly vulnerable and socially excluded category of women.

3. Justification of Indirect Discrimination

A key feature of the concept of indirect discrimination is that it can be justified. The extent to which indirect discrimination can be used to challenge structural sex discrimination or provide a framework for the accommodation of women will depend on the way in which the justifiability issue is construed.

One key issue in analysing the concept of justification is to ask why it has been introduced within the definition of indirect discrimination. One way of understanding the concept is that it allows employers to rely on those reasons that are intrinsically job related and yet, at the same time, provide a way for

160 *Coker & Osamor v Lord Chancellor & Lord Chancellor's Department* [2002] I.C.R. 321.

challenging sexist stereotypes and practices within the structure of industries and the workplace. *Holmes v Home Office,*[161] illustrates how this process can work. In *Holmes* the practice that was being challenged was the "full time work only" rule in the Home Office which was applied to deny a mother returning to work after the birth of a child the flexibility of part time work. The industrial tribunal and EAT both analysed the issue in a way that focuses on whether the "full time only" rule was necessary in the context of the relevant job. They were influenced by evidence that part time work can have the benefits of facilitating the retention of staff and increasing efficiency; and they noted the fact that the Home Office had not undertaken any analysis of whether part time work would be feasible in their organisation.

This approach, however, raises the issue of the extent to which discrimination law can and should interfere with managerial discretion in terms of how employers should organise the workplace. Early domestic case law adopted a strict interpretation of justification in SDA 75, s.1 by equating it with "necessity" and making it clear that "business convenience" was not sufficient.[162] However, a concern with ensuring that employers have the discretion to remain "competetive" in the face of commercial realities is reflected in *Kidd v DRG (UK) Ltd,*[163] where the issue was whether part time workers (who were disproportionately more likely to be women) could be made redundant before full time workers. In *Kidd,* the Industrial Tribunal allowed the employer to justify this preference for full time work in relation to redundancy selection. The EAT upheld the decision and stated that it was indicative of a realistic approach required under modern business conditions: "under the competitive conditions of modern industry small advantages of that kind, though singly they be of little account, can cumulatively make a crucial difference between success or failure in attracting or maintaining orders."[164] In *Ojutiku v Manpower Services Commission,*[165] a case under the RRA, the Court of Appeal moved further away from a strict "necessity" test by accepting that "reasonableness" would be sufficient to justify indirect race discrimination.

The risk that permitting such a wide margin to managerial discretion can undermine the goals of indirect sex discrimination legislation was recognised in *Clarke and Powell v Eley (IMI Kynoch) Ltd* where Browne-Wilkinson J. noted that the concept of justifiability required the tribunal to make value judgments, and that there was likely to be great variation in relation to this issue between different tribunals:

"To decide whether some action is 'justifiable' requires a value judgment to be made. On emotive matters such as racial or sex discrimination there is no generally accepted view as to the comparative importance of eliminating

161 *Holmes v Home Office* [1984] I.R.L.R. 299.
162 *Steel v Union of Post Office Workers* [1977] I.R.L.R. 288.
163 *Kidd v DRG (UK) Ltd* [1985] I.C.R. 405.
164 *Kidd v DRG (UK) Ltd* [1985] I.C.R. 405, at 425.
165 *Ojitku v Manpower Services Commission* [1982] I.C.R. 661.

discriminatory practices on the one hand as against, for example, the profitability of a business on the other. In these circumstances, to leave the matter within the unfettered decision of the many Industrial Tribunals throughout the country, each reflecting their own approach to the relative importance of these matters, seems to us likely to lead to widely differing decisions being reached."[166]

The risk of wide-ranging and varying value judgments about how to restructure employment practices to accommodate women suggests that, in some cases, there may be a need for a more precise legislative solution. In the case of a practice such as part-time work, for example, there may be a need for more systematic restructuring which is not dependent on a general legal concept such as indirect sex discrimination. EU sex discrimination law has taken this approach by introducing specific directives which regulate discrimination against part-time workers. These are discussed below.

EU discrimination law now forms the context within which the concept of "justifiability" in indirect discrimination is developed. In the early ECJ cases the concept of justifiability under Art.141 (formerly Art.119) and the Equal Treatment Directive stressed that "objective reasons" would be the focus of the analysis.[167] More recent case law has narrowed the range of discretion and the reasons that will justify indirect sex discrimination. In equal pay cases, as we saw earlier, it is open to employers to argue that pay discrimination is justified because of the operation of grounds other than sex. There has been an analogous development in indirect sex discrimination law with a focus on explaining that the discriminatory impact of a practice is for some "objectively justified" reason. The ECJ has developed a stricter test for justifiability in this context and has shown a willingness to scrutinise the discretion of the employer. One of the key ways in which the ECJ has developed the framework for their definition of justifiability is through the concept of "proportionality". In *Bilka-Kaufhaus*, the ECJ made it clear that the issue of justifiability is a matter for the national court. Yet, at the same time, it introduced the idea that justifiability requires a focus on objectively justified factors which are not not themselves related to discrimination:

"It falls to the national court, which has sole jurisdiction to make findings of fact, to determine whether and to what extent the grounds put forward by an employer to explain the adoption of a pay practice which applies independently of a worker's sex, but in fact affects more women than men may be regarded as objectively justified. If the national court finds that the measures chosen by Bilka correspond to a real need on the part of the undertaking, are appropriate with a view to achieving the objectives pursued, and are necessary to that end, the fact that the measures affect a far greater number of women

166 *Clarke and Powell v Eley (IMI Kynoch) Ltd* [1982] I.R.L.R. 482.
167 *Jenkins v Kingsgate (Clothing Productions) Ltd* Case 96/80 [1981] E.C.R. I-5483.

than men is not sufficient to show that they constitute an infringement of Article 119."[168]

The shift in the ECJ approach to justifiability influenced the willingness of the domestic courts to use a test of "objective balance" between the discriminatory effect of the condition and the reasonable needs of the employer.[169] Some domestic tribunals continued to leave in place practices which created barriers for women in employment[170]: such as inflexibility in rearranging work; and age limits which had a discriminatory impact on women as compared with men.[171] Some domestic tribunals have shown a willingness to scrutinise the reasons given by employers to justify indirect discrimination. In *London Underground v Edwards*, discussed earlier, the practice was a shift towards a working rota which had a disproportionate impact on single mothers like the applicant. In the final hearing of the issue, the EAT considered whether London Underground could have accommodated the applicant. They stated that:

"In the first place, employers should recognise the need to take a reasonably flexible attitude to accommodationg the particular needs of their employees. In a case such as this, had it been obvious that London Underground could have accommodated Ms Edwards' needs, without any difficulty or expense, there might have been a case for alleging direct discrimination. Changing the roster in a way which they must have appreciated would cause her a detriment might have justifiably led to an inference that they had treated her less well than they would have treated male train operators who had been in a similar position. In other words, the more clear it is that the employers unreasonably failed to show flexibility in their employment practices, the more willing the tribunal should be to make a finding of unlawful discrimination [...]"[172]

Subsequent ECJ decisions have developed on these central ideas that justifiability requires "objective" factors which are "necessary" and "proportionate". The ECJ has held that a policy by the state that is indirectly discriminating on the ground of sex can only be justified if it can be shown that it corresponds to an objectively necessary response to the relevant problem, and that it is appropriate and necessary to achieve this goal. These ideas

168 *Bilka Kaufhaus GMBH v Weber Von Hartz* Case 170/84 [1986] E.C.R. 1607, at pp. 1628.

169 *Hampson v Department of Education and Science* [1989] I.C.R. 179.

170 *Briggs v North Eastern Education and Library Board* [1990] I.R.L.R. 181, where the NI Court of Appeal upheld as justified the refusal of a school to rearrange coaching duties from after school to lunchtime which would have allowed her to retain an employment benefit.

171 *Bullock v Alice Ottley School* [1993] I.C.R. 138 where the Court of Appeal found that a later retirement age of 65 years for gardners (who were predominantly men) as compared with 60 for domestic workers (who were predomiantly women) was justified. See also *University of Manchester v Jones* [1993] I.C.R. 474 where the Court of Appeal upheld as justified a decision by University of Manchester to impose a maximum age limit of 35 years for an appointment which had a disproportionate impact on women.

172 *London Underground v Edwards (No 2)* [1997] I.R.L.R. 157.

crystallised into a clear principle in *R v Secretary of State for Employment Ex p. Seymour-Smith*.[173] In *Seymour Smith*, women employees challenged legislation on unfair dismissal which introduced a two year continuous employment requirement before a worker could rely on unfair dismissal protection. The women argued that this was indirect see discrimination. The House of Lords requested a preliminary ruling from the ECJ. The ECJ made it clear that social policy was a matter for national member states but they provided guidance on the test for justifiability in cases of indirect sex discrimination:

"It is for the Member State, as the author of the allegedly discriminatory rule, to show that the said rule reflects a legitimate aim of its social policy, that that aim is unrelated to any discrimination [...] However, although social policy is essentially a matter for the Member States under Community law as it stands, the fact remains that the margin of discretion available to the Member States in that connection cannot have the effect of frustrating the implementation of a fundamental principle of Community law such as that of equal pay for men and women. Mere generalisations concerning the capacity of a specific measure to encourage recruitment are not enough to show that the aim of the disputed rule is unrelated to any discrimination based on sex nor to provide evidence on the basis of which it could reasonably be considered that the means chosen were suitable for achieving that aim."[174]

The formulation of a test of justifiability, with its focus on legitimacy, necessity and proportionality is a more strict analysis than that developed by domestic courts. It suggests a need for an analysis that takes into account a number of factors:

(i) that there is a legitimate aim for the indirectly discriminatory practice;

(ii) that the indirectly discriminatory means chosen are suitable to attain that objective; and

(iii) that the means chosen are themselves necessary to attain that objective, and that there are no reasonable alternatives to attain the objective which would not be discriminatory.

Moreover, as the recent application of this test by the ECJ has made clear, indirect discrimination must be justified by objective reasons that are not themselves related to (tainted by) sex discrimination.[175]

In *Seymour Smith*, the House of Lords applied this guide to the test of justifiability. They found that the two year continuous employment rule was justified and that the Court of Appeal had not given a sufficient margin of

[173] Case C-167/97 [1999] E.C.R. I-623.
[174] Case C-167/97 [1999] E.C.R. I-623, at p.686.
[175] *Kutz Bauer v Freir und Hansestadt Hamburg* Case C-187/00 [2003] E.C.R. I-02741.

appreciation to the state which allowed it to formulate appropriate social policies. Moreover, the House of Lords also applied the ECJ test in a way that made clear that although the government has a margin of appreciation it is also under an obligation to show that the choice of a measure that is indirectly discriminatory is reasonable. Lord Nicholls recognised the need for practicalities of government to be borne in mind but also noted that:

"The requirements of Community law must be complied with at all relevant times. A measure may satisfy Community law when adopted, because at that stage the minister was reasonably entitled to consider the measure as a suitable means for achieving a legitimate aim. But experience of the working of the measure may tell a different story. In course of time the measure may be found to be unsuited for its intended purpose. The benefits hoped for may not materialise. Then the retention in force of a measure having a disparately adverse impact on women may no longer be objectively justifiable. In such a case a measure, lawful when adopted, may become unlawful.

Accordingly, if the government introduces a measure which proves to have a disparately adverse impact on women, the government is under a duty to take reasonable steps to monitor the working of the measure. The government must review the position periodically. The greater the disparity of impact, the greater the diligence which can reasonably be expected of the government. Depending on the circumstances, the government may become obliged to repeal or replace the unsuccessful measure."[176]

Lord Nicholls' observation that: "the greater the disparity of impact, the greater the diligence which can reasonably be expected of the government" raises a further question about the relationship between the extent of the sex discrimination caused by the indirectly discriminatory rule and the standard of the justifiability test. Lord Nicholls' comments suggest that one consequence of applying the ECJ test of proportionality is that the greater the discriminatory impact the higher the required standard of justification. In *Allonby v Accrington and Rossingdale College* (discussed in the context of equal pay earlier) the Court of Appeal also commented on the "justifiability test" developed by the House of Lords in *Seymour Smith*. They held that there needs to be a degree of scrutiny of the claim that the discriminatory condition is justifiable:

"Once a finding of a condition having a disparate and adverse impact on women had been made, what was required was at the minimum a critical evaluation of whether the college's reasons demonstrated real need to dismiss the applicant; if there was such a need, consideration of the seriousness of the disparate impact of the dismissal on women including the applicant; and an evaluation of whether the former were sufficient to outweigh the latter. There

[176] *R v Secretary of State for Employment, Ex p. Seymour-Smith & Perez (No.2)* [2000] I.C.R. 244.

is no sign of this process in the tribunal's extended reasons. In particular, there is no recognition that if the aim of dismissal was itself discriminatory (as the applicant contended it was, since it was to deny part-time workers, a predominantly female group, benefits which Parliament had legislated to give them) it could never afford justification."[177]

There are now proposals under the government's *Discrimination Law Review* (DLR)[178] to harmonise the test of "objective justification" across all the grounds of indirect discrimination. The DLR's proposals seek to harmonise definitions of indirect discrimination to EU standards ("provision criterion or practice" and "particular disadvantage") across all the prohibited grounds will ensure simplification and efficiency. Unfortunately, the new test would not adopt the precise words of the directive, which stipulate that a measure must be "objectively justified by a legitimate aim and the means of achieving that aim are appropriate and necessary". Instead, the DLR "translates" this test into a domestic formula that requires "a proportionate means of achieving a legitimate aim"[179] There is already a complex body of case law on "justification" in EU law and under Art.14 of the European Convention on Human Rights (see Chapters 2, 4 and 5). Having different tests for "objective justification" in EU and domestic discrimination law adds additional and unnecessary complexity. There is already a risk, as critical commentary on the interpretation of the "justifiability" requirement in cases such as *Allonby* makes clear, that domestic law on "justifiability" will be less rigorous than EU discrimination law.[180] Moreover, although the word "proportionate" is likely to capture most relevant factors, a potential conflict may be created between EU and domestic definitions of "objective justification". This is a risky strategy at a time when the European Commission has sent the UK formal requests requiring full implementation of the Race Equality Directive (RED), and specifically cites differences in the domestic and RED definition of indirect discrimination as the basis for potential infringement proceedings.[181]

177 *Allonby v Accrington and Rossingdale College* [2001] I.C.R. 1189.

178 *Discrimination Law Review* (London: Department for Government and Local Government, June 2007)

179 *Discrimination Law Review* (London: Department for Government and Local Government, June 2007, p.37–41.

180 M. Connolly, "Discrimination Law: Justification, Alternative Measures and Defences Based on Sex" (2001) 30 I.L.J. 311.

181 The European Commission has already sent formal requests to the UK requiring full implementation of the Race Equality Directive citing the definition of indirect race discrimination in UK law as one of the issues for consideration, see "EC Infringement Proceedings" (2007) 168 EOR 5.

C. *Family Friendly Policies for Women and Men*

1. Providing Support for Families

One of the recurring issues in the previous discussions has concerned the way in which women's responsibilities for children are not accommodated in the workplace and private sphere: either at the stage of their needs during pregnancy and maternity; or in accommodating their needs for work practices that are sufficiently flexible to allow them to combine work with child care. The issue of accommodating the needs of parents is not, however, limited to women. Both women and men have responsibilities for parenting and a need for "family friendly" policies. In fact, one stereotype that often operates against women is that they are uniquely or solely responsible for child care. As the following passage makes clear, the issue of how women are accommodated on their return to work after they have had children is critical to their participation in employment.

Lorna Adams, Fiona McAndres and Mark Winterbotham Pregnancy Discrimination at Work: A Survey of Women EOC Working Paper Series No. 24 (EOC: Manchester, Winter 2004/2005)

p.74: "Of the relatively small proportion (of pregnant women interviewed) who had initially returned to work but had subsequently left, the most common reason for leaving work (mentioned by 22 per cent) was that the job did not have the right hours (which suggests a lack of flexibility on the behalf of employers) while a further 13 per cent stated that they were treated so badly that they felt they had to leave."

Sara Davis, Fiona Neathey, Jo Reagan and Rebecca Wilson, Pregnancy Discrimination at Work: A Qualitative Study, EOC Working Paper No.23, (EOC: Manchester, 2004/5)

Not returning to work

pp.57–59: "The Parents' Demand for Childcare survey (Woodland et al. 2002) also researched reasons given by women who had chosen not to return to work. The most common reason reported was a lack of work with suitable hours (cited by 28 per cent) followed closely by demands of the job (20 per cent). Other reasons identified by fewer respondents included the potential loss of benefits, a lack of suitable qualifications and an inability to work due to illness/disability.

The survey also found that 24 per cent of families reported not being able to find suitable childcare when needed. National shortages of affordable and high quality childcare are well documented and have attracted considerable attention from the Government in recent years. High profile initiatives such as the introduction of the childcare element of the Working Families Tax Credit and documents such as the Inter-departmental Childcare Review (2002) and the recently published 10 year Strategy on Childcare (2004) have backed up the Government's commitment to improve and increase the availability of high quality childcare.

Aside from the difficulties of accessing childcare, a study by Bevan et al. (1999) reported data from the TUC (1996) which identified adverse career effects resulting from lack of childcare. The research showed that 35 per cent of working mothers said a lack of suitable childcare had made it harder to work extra hours and found that 19 per cent of working mothers had been forced to take a career break due to the lack of childcare facilities. Reinforcing some employers perception (see above), 14 per cent reported that lack of suitable childcare had made them appear less reliable and available for work, while a similar proportion had been prevented from seeking promotion."

This analysis goes on to note that not all the reasons that lead to mothers and fathers not using child care can be attributed to employers or inflexible work practices. For example:

"The 10 year strategy on Childcare reinforced that in addition to the availability of childcare, there are clearly other influential factors which have a largebearing on the decision about whether to return to work."

Almost half of the parents surveyed felt that there was not enough child care in their local area. However, findings from the survey suggest that a lack of suitable provision was not the most significant reason why parents were not using child care services. Parents who did not use child care were most likely to say that they preferred to care for their children themselves. However, the study did find that that were certain factors and policy levers that are within the control of employers and the government.

"Factors which are within the remit of the employer, such as the effective administration of the career break; the general attitude of the employer; knowing other women/role models who had successfully managed a career break and subsequent return; are all seen as less important. However, the authors note that although these factors did not rank in the top reasons, they were nevertheless very significant for a considerable per centage of the sample. [. . .]"

The authors also draw attention to the following points:

Perceived disadvantages of flexible working

"Recent research for the DTI (2004) amongst 1001 employees in the IT sector examined the attitudes around work-life balance and flexible working from the perspective of employees. Although 84 per cent believed that flexible working should be available to all employees, the research revealed that many employees felt that this might come at a cost. Almost three-quarters of respondents agreed that moving to a part-time or flexible career will harm your promotional prospects (74 per cent). And almost as many agreed that there are fewer promotional opportunities available to part time workers (72 per cent). The image of part-time work being the domain of women workers persists with 81 per cent of respondents agreeing that flexible or part-time work is usually taken up by women (despite a general belief that it should be equally available to men and women."

Finally, they suggest the following:

Sara Davis, Fiona Neathey, Jo Reagan and Rebecca Wilson, p.60.

Implications of combining work and family life

"Research for the DTI (2004) into attitudes surrounding work-life balance, referred to what is called the "uneasy truce between work and home". Key findings from this include:

- 50 per cent agreeing that they do not get involved with their family as much as they would like;
- 53 per cent agreeing that it is difficult to get involved in school activities
- 49 per cent agreeing that they miss out on their children's development.

The research notes that although female respondents to the survey tended to rate these factors higher than their male counterparts, there is still a strong feeling that fathers are missing out. This suggests that:

> . . . these issues are no longer the preserve of women in the labour market and that a significant proportion of the male labour force in the IT sector are becoming uncomfortable with some of the costs of working long hours and without fully fledged flexibility (DTI 2004)."

2. The Role of Fathers

The issue of work life balance, and the accommodation of the needs of parents (mothers and fathers) is an issue that is increasingly of concern to men as well as women. Recent research has confirmed the importance of the role of fathers to the well being of children, as well as of the parents themselves. Moreover, once the issues of sex and gender are distinguished it becomes more clear that men can also be the victims of stereotypes arising from the social construction of masculinity and assumptions about their approriate "natural" roles. These essentialised stereotypes can, therefore, reduce the autonomy and choices of men who may want to give priority to spending time with their family and children, rather than conforming to assumptions about male patterns of work.

Discrimination law and policy responses are increasingly seeking to respond to this new challenge, as discussed below. In the EU, despite the availability of a right to parental leave, research suggests that fathers are not exercising this right for a number of reasons including, inter alia: lack of knowledge about rights; fears about the impact of taking leave on their carreer prospects; and assumptions that women should have the primary role in parental responsibilities.[182] Recent research by the EOC *Fathers and the Modern Family*, for example, confirms the importance of fathers to the well being of children, and it also confirms that fathers feel that they do not spend enough time with their children.[183]

Fathers and the Modern Family,
(EOC Research, EOC: Manchester, 2007)
(available at *www.eoc.org.uk*)

Dads at Work

Most fathers are in paid work and their earnings are crucial to the family. Many share responsibility for earning with their partner, the patterns of employment often change after the birth of the baby, when mothers may reduce their working hours or withdraw from employment leaving the father as the sole earner. So fathers' breadwinner role becomes more important at a time when they want to spend more time with their young children (Thomspon et al., 2006). Fathers, like mothers, may experience tension in balancing their work and family.

Most fathers were working their their child was 9–10 monts old:

- 91 per cent of fathers were employed and of these, 85 per cent full-time
- A higher proportion of Pakistani (22 percent) and Indian (20 per cent) of fathers were self-employed than those of other ethnicities (16 per cent overall)
- 9 per cent of fathers were not in paid work, rising to 19 per cent of Pakistani and 22 per cent of Bangladeshi fathers. Fewer than 1 per cent had never had a paid job.

Fathers were crucial in keeping their family out of poverty. Having a low household income was strongly tied to a lack of employment, so where the father was not in work this had a huge effect on the family finances. [...]

The "breadwinner dad, stay at home mum" model is increasingly a thing of the past. There was a considerable movement in couples' employment when they had a young child and fathers were more likely to be the sole partner earner than before the child's birth.

The assumption that "flexible working patterns" will be a panacea for fathers is not, therefore, a straightforward matter for law or social policy. The degree of freedom for men to spend time with children will depend on issues such as their socio-economic class. Moreover, if the role of fathers is crucial in lifting children out of poverty, it is essential that men are in paid work, which for

[182] European Attitudes to Parental Leave, European Opinion Research Group, Special Ethnobarometer Project, (Brussels: European Opinion Research Group (EEIG), 2004)

[183] *Fathers and the Modern Family*, (EOC Research, EOC: Manchester, 2007) (available at *www.eoc.org.uk*)

men in in lower occupational groups may involve long hours away from their families and children.

"[. . .] Flexibility at work

It was widely accepted that mothers will make use of flexible working arrangements to combine their roles as carers and workers. But it is still less accepted for fathers to do so. Their access to flexible working arrangments depends heavily on their social-economic status and the type of work they do.

There is a marked divide between "have and have-not" families. Fathers in higher occupational groups are more likely to have access to longer paternity leave, for their statutory pay entitlement to be topped up by their employer and to be offered certain types of flexible working than other fathers are."

3. Legal and Social Policy Responses

There are a number of legal responses that seek to address the problems of work-life balance, and to give all parents (including men) the right to time off work to enable them to enjoy a suitable balance. We have already discussed the provisions which protect the rights of mothers: legal and policy measures which prohibit pregnancy discrimination, as well as safeguarding the right to maternity leave and a reasonable amount of time off (see ERA, s.57A). In addition, there are legal provisions at the EU and domestic level which enable women and men to take time off as part of their right to "parental leave". At the EU level, the Directive on Parental Leave is an important form of legal regulation that aims to enable a better family-work balance for men and women. The Parental Leave Directive[184] enacted a framework agreement of 14 December 1995 under the Protocol on Social Policy. The United Kingdom opted out of the agreement initially, but did opt in subsequently, and the legal provision was extended to the UK a few years later.

The Parental Leave Directive stresses the importance of reconciling work and family as part of the promotion of equal opportunities for men and women. This approach recognises that women's equality is dependent on challenging gender stereotypes that force men into patterns of work and that do not allow them to spend more time on their roles as fathers. It introduces a right to parental leave for at least three months to all workers on the birth or adoption of a child. Member States are also required to protect workers from dismissal on the ground of seeking or taking parental leave. When parental leave ends, the worker has the right to return to the same job or, if that is not possible, to an equivalent or similar job. In addition to parental leave, the Directive entitles workers to time off work "on grounds of force majeure" for urgent family reasons, sickness, or an accident which makes the presence of the worker at home indispensible.

[184] Parental Leave Directive, Directive 96/34, OJ [1996] L145/4; amended and extended to apply to the UK by Directive 97/75, OJ [1998] L10/24. See discussion by Evelyn Ellis, *EU Anti Discrimination Law* (Oxford: Clarendon Press, 2005).

The Parental Leave Directive has been implemented in the UK through the Parental Leave and Maternity Regulations 1999[185] (Parental Leave Regulations). The Parental Leave Regs (Pt III) introduce a right to three months' unpaid parental leave in the first five years' of the child's life. There is a one year qualification period. After the parental leave, the employee has the right to return to work on equivalent or no less favourable terms, and to not suffer a detriment (Pt IV). The enforcement of the parental leave rights is by "workforce agreements"; or in the absence of such an agreement through a system of advance notice and written requests.

The Parental Leave Regulations have been criticised as being an insufficient protection for women and men who want a better work-life balance, and want to devote more time to their children when they are young. The legal mechanism has been criticised as inadequate for a number of reasons: it allows employers to postpone parental leave; it adopts a five year rather than eight year cut off period; and it applies only to employees with a one year qualification period.[186]

As discussed above, one of the key issues for parents is the ability to negotiate more flexible working patterns of work. Moreover, as the EU and domestic research confirms, there are at present barriers that prevent women and men negotiating flexible patterns of work. For women, flexible work often means low paid work or work that has no prospect of promotion or training. For men, there is a fear that flexible work will prevent long term career development. In the light of these deep-rooted problems there needs to be a clearly defined legal right as well as social policy to create a structure to allow parents to negotiate flexible working conditions. For these reasons, it is significant that the Parental Leave Regulations are supplemented by a legal regime which allow parents to request flexible work. Amendments which introduce a new s.80F to the Employment Rights Act 1996 were introduced by the Employment Act 2002. This provides for a right to request flexible work rather than a right to be granted more flexible work. Therefore, the right is exercised through a series of requests by employees, that are followed by a procedure to consider the request by the employer: for a child under the age of six (eighteen if disabled) an employee can request a variation in hours, timing or place of work, submitted through established forms and procedures. Once the employee has made a request for flexible work, the employer and employee meet to discuss the request. The employer can reject the request for flexible working on a number of grounds, including inter alia: cost; detrimental effects on ability to meet consumer demand or quality; inability to organise work amongst staff or recruit extra staff; or planned structural changes. The employee has a right to receive reasons for the employer's decision, as well as a right to appeal to a tribunal on the basis of an error of

[185] The Maternity and Parental Leave, etc. Regulations 1999, Statutory Instrument 1999 No. 3312.

[186] See Aileen McColgan, *Discrimination Law: Text, Cases and Materials* (Hart Publishing: Oxford, 2005) at p.507.

procedure or in the facts, but cannot request a reconsideration of the substantive reasons for the employer's decision.[187]

The Department of Trade and Industry's *Third Work Life Balance Survey* conducted in 2006 suggests that there is support for this regime of requesting flexible working time. The survey found high levels of employee satisfaction with flexible working arrangements since 2003. Employees were positive about their own experiences; most had at least one flexible working arrangement available to them, the most common flexible arrangements including flexi time and working from home. The findings of the survey that relate to the legal right to request flexible work are summarised below:

Huyla Hooker, Fiona Neathey, Jo Casebourne and Miranda Munro The Third Work Life Balance Employees Survey: Executive Summary (Employment Relations Series No.58 DTI: London, 2006)

"Take-up of flexible working arrangements

Those employees who said that a particular work arrangement would be available to them if they needed it were also asked if they currently worked, or had worked, in any of these ways in the last 12 months with their current employer. Nearly half (49 per cent) of employees who had flexitime avaiable to them made use of that arrangement, and over four in ten (44 per cent) who were able to work regularly from home did so. In addition, nearly two-fifths of those who said that the arrangement was available to them worked part-time (38 per cent); and over a third of employees who were able to do so (36 per cent) worked term-time only.

Take-up of the other flexible working arrangements was lower, with around a quarter working annualised hours (27 per cent) or a compressed working week (24 per cent); under one fifth (18 per cent) taking advantage of opportunities to work reduced hours for a limited period; and just over one in ten (12 per cent) taking up job sharing opportunities. There was little change in the proportions of all employees taking up flexible working arrangements since WLB2 (the second survey). [. . .]

Take-up of the right to request flexible working

Employees were asked if they were aware of the right for some employees to request flexible working introduced in April 2003; over half (56 per cent) said that they were aware of the new right. They were also asked whether over the last two years they had approached their current employer to make a request to change how they regularly work for a sustained period of time. In all, 17 per cent of employees had made such a request (the same proportion as in LW2B [the second survey]). Female employees (22 per cent) were more likely than male employees (14 per cent) to have requested to work flexibly over the last two years.

When asked about the nature of their requests, 30 per cent of employees who had asked to change their working arrangements did so to reduce their hours of work or to

[187] See cases discussed in Aileen McColgan, *Discrimination Law: Text, Cases and Materials* (Hart Publishing: Oxford, 2005) at p.509.

work part-time (compared to 29 per cent in LWB2). A quarter (25 per cent) had asked to change "when I work including the number of days that I work" (compared to 23 per cent in LWB2). Eleven per cent of employees making a request to work flexitime (13 per cent in WLB2) and ten per cent had requested some time off or additional leave arrangements (eight per cent in WLB2)."

Despite changes to the legal regime to allow more flexible work practices for parents, a survey of recent cases highlights the difficulties still faced by those who request time off or home working to accommodate their child care responsibilities. As the survey established, women are much more likely than men to request flexible working time. Moreover, recent research by the TUC, including a survey of tribunal decisions relating to the legal right to request flexible working arrangements (requests by women and men), suggests that tribunals take a "narrow approach" to the application of the regulations. In a number of cases, employment tribunals have been resistant toward allowing men to make applications for more flexible work patterns.[188] Clearly, the present arrangements under the ERA, s.80F right to request flexible work give employers a wide range of justifications for refusing requests; and they do not give Employment Tribunals substantial powers to interfere with the decisions of employers. Nevertheless, the application of a range of legal concepts and measures within sex discrimination law (e.g. concepts of indirect discrimination, as well as the provisions on part time work, parental leave and flexible working) are available. These can be combined with the imaginative use of remedial provisions (such as detailed recommendations that respond to the child care needs of parents) to encourage changes in the workplace and work patterns that facilitate a better balance between the needs of employers and workers who are parents. This analysis can also be applied beyond parents to all those who have care responsibilities. This use of discrimination law concepts and remedies to facilitate better working arrangements is illustrated by the Employment Tribunal's decision in *Orok v Shepherds Bush Housing Association*:

[188] TUC, "More Time for Families: Tackling the Long Hours Crisis in UK workplaces", discussed, along with the relevant cases, in Aileen McColgan, *Discrimination Law: Text, Cases and Materials* (Hart Publishing: Oxford, 2005) at p.512.

Orok v Shepherds Bush Housing Association Ltd
May 17, 2006; Case No. 3306338/05.
Reported in (2007) 165 Equal Opportunities Review, published by IRS on June 1, 2007

"£13,364 for refusal to allow homeworking

A Watford employment tribunal (Chair: K Monaghan) holds in *Orok v Shepherds Bush Housing Association Ltd* that an employer indirectly discriminated against and victimised an employee who requested homeworking. It awarded £10,000 for injury to feelings.

Facts

Ms Orok commenced full-time employment with the housing association as a financial accountant in October 1998, working a 35-hour week, Monday to Friday, at one of its offices. The housing association's homeworking protocol (HWP) provided for homeworking in certain circumstances, excluding childcare needs. One employee, Annette Hunter, worked at home one day a week under an agreed arrangement that fell outside the HWP because it was to facilitate her childcare.

On her doctor's recommendation, Ms Orok worked at home during her pregnancy for two to three days per week from February 2004 until the start of her maternity leave in June 2004. The situation did not appear to give rise to any insurmountable problems and Ms Orok wished to continue the arrangement on her return to work.

By the time she returned in February 2005 she had filed a tribunal complaint against the respondent alleging sex discrimination in relation to an increment and bonus during maternity leave. Her request for homeworking was refused, although her employer had previously suggested that it could be dealt with relatively informally "rather like Annette". Ms Orok was instructed to work full time at the office, despite childcare problems. Alternatively, she was told she could relinquish her line management responsibilities and work only four days a week.

Ms Orok's line manager told her that all flexibility previously given would be withdrawn unless she withdrew "the pending issues". She continued to work, but issued tribunal proceedings.

Findings

The only issue in dispute in relation to indirect sex discrimination was whether or not the respondent could justify its insistence on full-time work at the office. Upholding the claim, the tribunal found that the respondent's reasons were either not genuine or were fairly insubstantial. On the facts, these duties could have been adequately dealt with when Ms Orok was in the office and/or by telephone and/or email.

The tribunal noted that Ms Hunter was permitted to work at home to accommodate childcare needs and was given a trial period. It held that the respondent's refusal of Ms Orok's request was causally connected to her previous tribunal claim and amounted to victimisation.

Remedies

Injury to feelings

The tribunal had regard to the fact that Ms Orok had to continue to work full time away from home when she had a young child to care for. She was subjected to intrusive questioning about her childcare arrangements and certain assumptions were made; for example, that working longer hours on some days would be too stressful for her as a new mother. The tribunal awarded £10,000 including an unspecified element of aggravated damages, plus interest of £657.69.

Childcare costs

These were increased because Ms Orok had to pay other carers to look after her baby when her usual childminder was unavailable. Over 44 weeks these costs came to £2,640 plus interest of £67.01.

Recommendation

The tribunal recommended that within 14 days of its judgment Ms Orok be allowed to work from home for two days a week and that the arrangement be reviewed at the end of 2007 when she expected that her youngest child would start attending a nursery."

As well as the use of law, social policy can also contribute towards "family friendly" policies for women and men. However, there are recurring barriers to this type of restructuring and change: gender stereotypes about men and women; and past practices that entrench work patterns and job segregation. An additional barrier is provided by conceptions of the role of the family which treat women's family responsibilities as a "private matter" beyond the regulation of the state, and the care of children to be purely a matter for the private nuclear family. Alternative conceptions acknowlege that the care of children is a matter of supreme importance for the whole political community. Such views treat reproduction and childrearing as an ethical activity which is aimed at creating core relationships of *philia* (relational goods) and as being just as valuable as forms of economic and paid production. A good example is provided by the following passage:

Sybil A. Schwarzenbach, "On Civic Friendship" (October 1996) 107 (1) Ethics 97–128

p.102: "The biological sense of "reproduction" is the one most familiar to us all. It refers to those biological processes whereby we reproduce another member of the species (processes such as menstruation, production of semen, pregnancy, etc.). With the ethical sense of reproduction, by contrast, I intend all those rational activities (thinking about particular others and their needs, caring for them, cooking their meals, etc.) which go toward reproducing a particular set of relationships between persons over time—in the best sense, my thesis runs, relations of philia. These activities are clearly "ethical" because we here have to do with activities which involve choice and which are fundamentally imbued with reason or logos. But such activities are also "political"; they aim at reproducing the best relations conceived now within the context of a polis—whether in the so-called private or civic domain. In order to clarify this ethical notion of reproduction, I shall contrast it with that of "production". My goal is to show that what I am calling ethical, reproductive activity—in contrast to productive activity—falls under Aristotle's category of praxis or "moral action". Moreover, it is at least as important and fundamental an activity as production."

As Sandra Fredman has observed, real change requires a mix of law and state intervention in the form of social policy, and also a recognition that good child care, and the well being of children are a matter of importance to the whole community.

Sandra Fredman, *Women and Law* (Oxford; Clarendon Press, 1997)

pp.415–416: "Real change requires far more radical intervention, in which legal forms are complemented by wide ranging social measures opening the door to balanced participation by women in paid work and facilitating balanced partcipation by men in family work. Such measures require changes in working-time for both men and women, a high level of child-care provision, and parental leave for both parents at sustainable levels of pay. Nor should these measures impose legal obligations on individual employers alone. It is crucial that they be seen as a community responsibility spearheaded and resourced by the state: to burden individual employers is similarly counterproductive if it acts as a disincentive to employ women with actual or potential family responsibilities."

The low take up of the right to request flexible working arrangements by fathers makes it especially important to consider ways of allowing fathers to be be able to spend more time on parenting. Employer discrimination against men (fathers) who make requests for flexible working arguably needs to be addressed explicitly. In addition, this legal right can be supplemented by social policy measures such as greater financial support to enable low paid fathers to take full advantage of paternity leave; recognition by, and health and child care services of the need for both mothers and fathers to be involved and consulted about their children."

IX. "Sharing Power Equally and Modernising Public Services"—political representation and the "gender equality duty"

In its Gender Index the Equal Opportunities Commission has noted that there is a "power gap" in Parliament, where only 20 per cent of MPs are women. At the current rate, it will take 195 years for this to close and 65 years to achieve a gender balance in the boardrooms of the top companies listed in the FTSE 100 index. There is also a "pensions gap" that leaves retired women with 40 per cent less income than male contemporaries; this gap could take 45 years to close.[189] The Sex Discrimination (Election of Candidates) Act 2002 allows a special form of positive aciton (e.g. women only short lists) which were discussed in chapter 7. The introduction of a "gender equality duty" in the Equality Act 2006, which came into force in April 2007, places a duty on public bodies to promote gender equality.

It is also worth noting, building on our discussion of harassment, hate crimes and hate speech in chapter 8, that in the areas of crime and safety, the EOC also noted that women were five times more likely than men to feel unsafe when walking alone in their area after dark. This concern with levels of violence against women is reinforced by statistics that confirm that women continue to be at risk of domestic violence and rape. The total number of sexual offences recorded by police in England and Wales, in the year ending March 2006, was 62,081, although it is unclear to what extent this reflects an increase in reporting. This is very similar to the previous annual figures of 62,084 and it is a 17 per cent rise since the year 2003–2004.[190]

The EOC also noted two important areas in which men face discrimination: a "crime gap" where men are more likely to be victims of crime than women (e.g. in 2006, 13 per cent of young men were victims of violent crime, compared with seven per cent of young women); and a "health gap" in which men aged 16–44 are less than half as likely as women to consult their GP, resulting in later diagnosis of serious illnesses.[191]

In addition, issues relating to the representation and images of women in the wider public sphere are also relevant to the existence of discriminatory stereotypes about women. In this context some commentators have argued that pornography is a form of sexual discrimination because it reinforces stereotypes about women which, in turn, reinforce a patriachal society.[192] This raises the same issues that arise in the context of prohitions on hate speech (e.g. incitement to racial hatred) about the appropriate balance between free speech and intervention to disrupt forms of speech and representation that may create stereotypes about women or minorities.[193]

[189] EOC "Gender Agenda" and "Gender Equality Index" (London: Equal Opportunities Commission, 2007) (available at *www.gender-agenda.co.uk*).

[190] Alison Walker, Chris Kershaw and Sian Nicholas, "Crime in England and Wales 2005/2006", (London: RDS, Home Office, 2006). For summary of government response see *http://www.homeoffice.gov.uk/crime-victims/reducing-crime/sexual-offences/*.

[191] See EOC "Gender Agenda" and "Gender Equality Index", above.

[192] Catherine MacKinnon, "Not a Moral Issue" in Feminsim Unmodified: Discourses on Life and Law (Mass, USA: Harvard University Press, 1987)

[193] Susan Easton, "Pornography as Incitement to Sexual Hatred" (1995) I Feminist Legal Studies, pp.89–1040.

X. Conclusion

This chapter has discussed some of the key discrimination-related problems faced by women in employment, as well as broader concerns relating to the family and child care. Many of these problems are associated with a long history of prejudice or gender stereotyping, and with the existence of entrenched structural disadvantage. As the Equal Opportunities Commission's final "Gender Agenda" and "Gender Index" confirmed, women continue to face inequality in their access to key political, economic and social goods.[194] The ability of discrimination law to address these problems is limited for a number of reasons. First, it tends to echo the long-standing view of the family as a "private" realm within which legal regulation is impermissible, thereby failing to redress inequality within the family structure (a predominant cause of women's disadvantage). Moreover, the requirement for a "comparator" continues to pose a problem in sex discrimination law. This was true in the past in relation to pregnancy, although EU discrimination law has ensured that most of the problems relating to pregnancy have now been addressed, and it continues to cause difficulty in equal pay cases.

The government's *Discrimination Law Review* has advocated the reform of equal pay law so as to ensure that it is more "simple" and "effective".[195] However, most of its proposals focus on procedure rather than the "comparator" problem. The nature of women's work means that they are often concentrated in segregated forms of employment where the search for a male comparator is futile. Challenging pay discrimination therefore requires a more flexible and purposive approach towards the need for a "comparator", reaching across establishments, sectors and industries.[196] However, the DLR has concluded that the use of a "hypothetical comparator" in equal pay cases would not yield any benefits in practice, and cites the inability of claimants to provide tribunals with evidence of the pay and conditions of a hypothetical comparator as a particular problem.[197] In reality, the word "hypothetical" is misleading in this context. There are a number of ways in which, despite the lack of an actual comparator, a woman could provide evidence relating to her employer's pay practices from which discrimination could be inferred. Moreover, women in the public sector may be able to point to a man in the private sector who is not an "actual comparator" but who is doing equivalent work. Given the recent EOC research (cited earlier in the chapter) confirming that despite four decades of equal pay legislation, the "part-time pay gap"

[194] See EOC, *Gender Equality Index* (London: Equal Opportunities Commission, 2007), available at *www.gender-agenda.co.uk*; and also EOC, *Britain's Competitive Edge: Women, Unlocking the Potential* (EOC: London, October 2004).

[195] *Discrimination Law Review. A Framework for Fairness* (Department of Communities and Local Government: London, 2007), para.3.21.

[196] Damian Grimshaw and Jill Ruberry, *Undervaluing Women's Work*, EOC Working Paper Series No.53 (Manchester: EOC, Spring 2007).

[197] DLR, paras 3.25–3.29.

affecting women will take a further 25 years to close and the "full-time pay gap" 20 years, and that women earn 38 per cent less per hour than men for working part-time and 17 per cent less for full-time work,[198] it seems unlikely that the DLR's recommendations will radically improve the effectiveness of the law: what is instead needed is more substantive change, including a more flexible approach to comparators.

The other major barrier to women's participation in the workforce is the penalty they suffer because they are so frequently the primary carers within their families. Some of the recent proposals on "family friendly policies" (discussed earlier in the chapter) may assist women in achieving a better work-life balance without being penalised for their care responsibilities, although the evidence suggests that these policies have so far had a limited impact.[199] One way to strengthen such policies might be by introducing an enforceable right to non-discrimination on the ground of one's parenting or caring responsibilities. Significantly, the DLR rejects this proposal as a piece of unnecessary legal regulation "cutting across the balance of existing provisions"[200]: thereby leaving open the question of how discrimination law and policy can assist women in combining paid work with their private family responsibilities.

198 EOC, *The Gender Agenda* (London: EOC, Spring 2007).

199 Grace James, "Enjoy Your Leave, But 'Keep in Touch': Help to Maintain Parent/Workplace Relationships" (2007) 36 I.L.J. 313.

200 DLR, para.8.20.

11

SEXUAL ORIENTATION AND GENDER IDENTITY DISCRIMINATION

I. Introduction

Until quite recently, discrimination on the basis of sexual orientation and gender identity was not only permitted in most western societies, but actively encouraged by the law. Private homosexual acts were decriminalised (and then only in restricted circumstances) in England and Wales in 1967,[1] and it took until as late as 2003 for the US Supreme Court to rule, as it did in *Lawrence v Texas*, that it was an unconstitutional denial of due process to criminalise consenting sexual activity between adult males or adult females.[2] Discrimination on the basis of sexual orientation is now prohibited under EU law (and hence in the legal systems of the member states, including the UK) in employment and related situations, and in relation to the enjoyment of Convention rights under Art.14 of the European Convention on Human Rights. Furthermore, same-sex partnership rights have increasingly been recognised—whether as a result of legislative initiatives or due to constitutional litigation—in a number of constitutional democracies, including the UK Nonetheless, violent attacks on lesbians, gay men, transsexuals and transgendered persons remain common, even in countries which officially prohibit discrimination on the basis of sexual orientation and gender identity, and certain religions continue to claim an entitlement to treat such people unfavourably, at least in so far as they refuse to agree not to engage in consensual

[1] Sexual Offences Act 1967. Partial decriminalisation came later in Scotland (via the Criminal Justice (Scotland) Act 1980, s.80) and Northern Ireland (via the Homosexual Offences (Northern Ireland) Order 1982, following the ruling of the European Court of Human Rights in *Dudgeon v United Kingdom* (1981) 4 E.H.R.R. 149). For an important historical survey, see Stephen Jeffery-Poulter, *Peers, Queers and Commons: The Struggle for Gay Law Reform from 1950 to the Present* (London: Routledge, 1991).

[2] (2003) 539 U.S. 558; 123 S. Ct. 2472.

sexual activity.[3] In consequence, this area provides an interesting and important case study of the development of the law (from explicit hostility towards relevant sexual minority groups through to prima facie acceptance that discrimination on the basis of sexual orientation and gender identity is generally unacceptable[4]), of the responsiveness of discrimination law to changes in social attitudes, of the roles of European Convention and EU law within domestic law, and of the simultaneous relevance of criminal law, public law and private law in one area of the discrimination law field.

Controversies concerning the boundaries of and bases for anti-discrimination protections in relation to discrimination due to sexual orientation and gender identity are also of significance. In relation to boundaries, the acceptance that sexual orientation and gender identity discrimination is unacceptable has been sufficiently recent that many practices still exist—often strongly defended by moral conservatives—that might be described as being discriminatory in at least an indirect sense. Perhaps the most contentious examples relate to the "traditional" definition of civil marriages as involving only partners of the opposite birth sex, and to issues bearing on the availability of broader partnership and family rights for same-sex couples (including rights relating to parenting and the adoption of children). It is sometimes said that it is one thing to have discrimination laws to protect sexual minorities, but quite another to advocate the opening of marriage to encompass (or the creation of civil partnership rights to include) same-sex couples. Related to this is the difficult question of when rights to freedom of religious belief or practice should take priority over freedom from sexual orientation discrimination, and vice versa. It is due to the balance between these two, sometimes competing, interests that many protections against sexual orientation discrimination are only of a prima facie character. This ties back to the difficult constitutional/political question, discussed in Chapter 1, of how far it is appropriate for discrimination *law* to go in countering socially hostile attitudes or expression, and how far it can successfully work to counter attitudes of deep-seated hostility.

In relation to the bases for anti-discrimination protections, three key issues arise. First, sexual orientation and gender identity discrimination is an area in which some conservative thinkers have openly sought to *justify* the existence of discrimination in the law. It therefore becomes especially important for those concerned to justify the existence of discrimination laws to frame coherent philosophical and constitutional arguments for their position. Secondly, there has been considerable debate about the exact philosophical basis

[3] For horrific examples (from both countries which do and do not prohibit sexual orientation discrimination), see Amnesty International's Report *Crimes of Hate, Conspiracy of Silence: Torture and Ill-treatment Based on Sexual Identity* (2001) (the Amnesty International Reports) *Broken Bodies, Shattered Minds: Torture and Ill-treatment of Women* (2001) and *It's In Our Hands: Stop Violence Against Women* (2004). These and other examples are discussed in the essays by Nicholas Bamforth, Judith Butler and Alan Sinfield in Nicholas Bamforth (ed.), *Sex Rights: The Oxford Amnesty Lectures 2002* (Oxford: Oxford University Press, 2005).

[4] See, e.g. Stephen Cretney, *Same Sex Relationships: From "Odious Crime" to "Gay Marriage"* (Oxford: Oxford University Press, 2006).

or bases for anti-discrimination protections, and about which constitutional or ordinary legal ground or grounds should be used to prohibit discrimination on the basis of sexual orientation and gender identity: arguments based on equality and autonomy/dignity are particularly popular. Thirdly, there has been debate in many jurisdictions about whether sexual orientation and gender identity discrimination is also—or is best seen as an example of—sex discrimination, given that hostility towards sexual minority groups is often associated with assumptions about "appropriate" gender roles (for example, that it is "appropriate" for a man to have sex with a woman but not for a woman to do so, and appropriate for a woman to have sex with a man but not for a man to do so, or that it is "appropriate" for a woman to dress in a "feminine" way but not for a man to do so). If it is correct to associate sexual orientation discrimination with sex discrimination (or even to bring it within its remit) it may be necessary to broaden our understanding of sex discrimination.

It is also important to remember that the evolution of the law in this area has involved three connected strands in England and Wales. Most visible are developments encouraged or mandated by the UK's membership of the European Convention on Human Rights and the EU (which constitute the first two strands). Articles 8, 12 and 14 of the Convention have generated case law concerning the criminal prohibition of consenting sexual activity between persons of the same sex, dismissal from military employment due to a person's sexual orientation, discrimination on the basis of sexual orientation more generally, certain aspects of partnership and family rights for same-sex couples, and whether those who have undergone gender reassignment may alter the official record of their birth sex. EU law now prohibits discrimination in employment and the position of goods and services due to sexual orientation or gender identity, but the European Court of Justice's stance concerning the rights of same-sex partners to claim employment-related benefits has been distinctly cautious. The Convention and EU law are, as we saw in Chapter 2, highly important for national courts. In particular, all national legislation must, so far as is possible, be read in the light of relevant Convention and EU case law, and may be disapplied for incompatibility with directly effective EU law (a national court is limited, under s.4 of the Human Rights Act 1998, to making a declaration of incompatibility in the case of national legislation which contravenes Convention rights). The Gender Recognition Act 2004 is thus a national-level response to the Court of Human Rights' decision in *Goodwin v United Kingdom*,[5] while the Employment Equality (Sexual Orientation) Regulations 2003 were passed to give effect to the sexual orientation-related requirements of the Employment Equality Directive. However, the development of the law at national level has also been associated with the emergence of a more liberal social climate within the UK, and important developments such as the creation of the institution of civil partnership for

[5] (2002) 35 E.H.R.R. 447.

same-sex couples (in the Civil Partnership Act 2004) or the extension of protections against sexual orientation discrimination to the provision and receipt of goods, facilities and services as well as within employment, appear to be home-grown ideas rather than things emanating from the Convention or EU law (although relevant measures are still subject to interpretation, etc., in the light of the Convention and/or EU law). Changes at a purely "domestic" level, prompted by national level policy concerns, thus constitute the third strand. We examine the content of national law, as influenced by the European Convention on Human Rights and by EU law, in detail below. For the moment, it should be observed that discrimination on the basis of sexual orientation and gender identity has implications for an extremely wide range of areas—including, but not confined to, the criminal law, employment law, housing law, family law and public law.

In the first section, we explore some general arguments about the way in which many western legal systems moved (or began to move), in the late twentieth century, from treating lesbians, gay men and transgendered and transsexual persons in an actively unfavourable way, towards prohibiting discrimination and even, in some cases, recognising partnership and family-related rights. In the second section, we explore the meaning of the terms "sexual orientation" and "gender identity", and in the third section we examine the constitutional dimensions of this heading of discrimination (building on the analysis in chapter 1). In Section V, we explore the case law of the European Court of Human Rights, and in Section VI the legislation and case law of the European Union. This allows us, in Section VII, to analyse the present state of domestic law in further detail. Finally, in Sections VIII and IX, we consider two distinct issues: clashes between claims to freedom from sexual orientation- and gender identity-based discrimination and the arguments of some religious groups to be free, due to their beliefs, from relevant obligations not to discriminate; and the question whether sexual orientation- and gender identity-related discrimination is also a form of sex discrimination.

II. The Development of the Law

As Mark Bell has suggested, "Discrimination against lesbians and gay men has a long history, but the construction of their maltreatment as *discrimination*, and therefore unacceptable behaviour, is more recent."[6] Robert Wintemute explains the development of the law (in western Europe) from the starting point that it is a "practical reality" that:

[6] *Anti-Discrimination Law and the European Union* (Oxford: Oxford University Press, 2002), p.89.

Robert Wintemute, "From 'Sex Rights' to 'Love Rights': Partnership Rights as Human Rights", Ch.6 in Nicholas Bamforth (ed.), *Sex Rights: the Oxford Amnesty Lectures 2002* (Oxford: Oxford University Press, 2005)

pp.187–191: "... a non-discrimination principle will be taken seriously only once it has been well established in cases where the discrimination causes substantial, tangible harm.

This progression from greater material harms to lesser material harms to symbolic harms may be found in other areas. Legal responses to race discrimination began with the abolition of slavery and the extension of the franchise, before turning to segregation and unequal opportunities in education, employment and housing. By the time separate drinking fountains or beaches for whites and blacks in the USA and South Africa were being challenged, no one could claim that an important human rights principle was not at issue because these facilities were 'trivial'. Similarly, the law had to address the denial of contract and property rights to married women and of the vote to all women, before it could turn to the question of equal access to jobs and services....

A similar progression may be seen with regard to sexual orientation and gender identity discrimination. The first stage requires that certain 'Basic Rights' be respected: the right not to be killed or arrested or imprisoned without legal authority, the right not to be tortured, the right to a fair trial, and the rights to freedom of expression, assembly and association. Without these fundamental protections, it is impossible for lesbian, gay, bisexual and transgendered (LGBT) individuals to form non-governmental organizations and campaign for legal reforms, or even to meet publicly. We take these 'basic rights' for granted in industrialized democracies, but throughout much of the world they are non-existent or only sporadically protected....

Once 'basic rights' are in place, LGBT individuals can turn to the second stage, 'sex rights' [...] a broad reading of 'sex rights' could capture virtually all sexual orientation and gender identity discrimination, including claims to partnership rights. However, for the sake of my argument, I will read 'sex rights' narrowly as focusing on discrimination against LGBT *individuals* because of their actual or presumed same-sex sexual activity or their undergoing gender reassignment (which discrimination ranges from criminalization of same-sex sexual activity or nonrecognition of gender reassignment to the denial of employment, housing or parental rights), and as excluding the 'love rights' of same-sex *partners* (the denial of rights or benefits or recognition to any factually or legally same-sex partner an LGBT individual may have, including employment, housing and parental rights the partner derives through his or her relationship with the individual). Defined this way, the battle for 'sex rights' for LGBT individuals in the forty-five Council of Europe countries has largely been won, at least in the realm of legal principles as opposed to the practical enforcement of these principles, and putting aside sexual freedom issues that are shared by heterosexual and LGBT individuals....

Starting from a position in Western Europe in 1970 of enjoying 'basic rights' but few 'sex rights', LGBT individuals have over the past three decades gradually persuaded legislatures and courts across Europe to provide much greater, if not yet complete, protection of their 'sex rights'. As a result, the new legislative and judicial battleground is what I will call partnership rights or 'love rights': legal recognition and equal treatment of the relationships between LGBT individuals and their partners. The progression from the second stage of 'sex rights' to the third stage of 'love rights' requires a society to acknowledge that there is more to the lives of LGBT individuals than a search for sexual pleasure, or a need to change their physical appearance and dress. Rather, they have the same human capacity as heterosexual and non-transsexual individuals to fall in love with another person, to establish a long-term emotional and physical relationship with them, and potentially to want to raise children with them. When they choose to do so, they will often want the same opportunities as heterosexual individuals to be treated as a 'couple', as 'spouses', as 'partners', as 'parents', as a 'family'."

It is important not to regard the development of the law as following a completely systematic pattern in every jurisdiction, however. As Kees Waaldijk has noted, the enactment of s.28 of the Local Government Act 1988—since repealed, but which, when in force, made it unlawful for local authorities to "promote" homosexuality as a "pretended family relationship"—hardly fitted, at the time of its enactment, with the notion that the UK was engaged in a smooth journey from decriminalisation of homosexual acts through to the general liberalisation of the law in this area.[7] Nonetheless, it is clear that the past fifty years has generally witnessed (blips such as s.28 aside) an enormous liberalisation in the legal and social treatment of sexual minorities. This point is neatly captured by Stephen Cretney:

Stephen Cretney
Same-Sex Relationships: From "Odious Crime" to "Gay Marriage"
(Oxford: Oxford University Press, 2006)

pp.1–2: "In 1953 no fewer than 2,267 men were prosecuted for indictable homosexual offences. The accused was sentenced to imprisonment in as many as half of those cases in which the 'offence' had been committed in private with a consenting adult. But whatever the sentence, each and every prosecution (as Wildeblood put it) implied the 'downfall and perhaps the ruin' of a human being. And it was not only those prosecuted to conviction who could be, and were, ruined. Some, confronted with exposure, succumbed to blackmail and thereby bought an uneasy freedom. There were those who, unable to bear the disgrace of exposure and the shame of imprisonment, preferred to kill themselves.

Today it seems difficult to believe that this ever happened. Even in the 1950s the perceptive observer might reasonably have thought that the laws which sent more than a thousand men to prison each year would probably not survive into the twenty-first century. But who could have foreseen that, fifty years on, in 2004, the United Kingdom Parliament would in the name of 'equality and social justice' [the words of Jacqui Smith MP, then Deputy Minister for Woman and Equality] pass an Act (the Civil Partnership Act) which was intended to acknowledge same sex relationships as analogous to heterosexual relationships, and to recognize the 'legitimacy of the claim' that they be 'accorded equal respect with heterosexual relationships' and placed 'firmly in the civil sphere of our national life'? And there was overwhelming all-party (albeit not unanimous) support for the Act which permits same sex couples to acquire legal rights and subject themselves to legal duties similar to those of a married couple and aims to remove the 'practical difficulties' such couples faced. In little more than fifty years, behaviour regarded as *criminal* (that is to say, so wrong that it is properly the business of the state to pursue the perpetrator and impose

[7] Kees Waaldijk, "Taking same-sex partnerships seriously—European perspectives as British perspectives?" [2003] I.F.L. 84.

penal sanctions intended in part to mark society's disapproval of what he has done) has been moved not merely into the neutral zone in which the state leaves it to the individual to make decisions but into the zone in which the state, by creating supporting legal or administrative structures, recognizes and approves the conduct in question"

Nonetheless, it is important to remember that powerful social hostility continues to be expressed towards lesbians, gay men, transsexuals and transgendered persons. Social persecution remains widespread in the United States even today, as was powerfully illustrated by Amnesty International's 2001 Report *Crimes of Hate, Conspiracy of Silence: Torture and Ill-treatment Based on Sexual Identity*—which makes the telling point, by reference to practical examples in the USA, that laws which "institutionaliz[e] discrimination [...] can act as an official incitement to violence against LGBT people in the community as a whole, whether in custody, in prison, on the street or in the home"[8] Anti-gay violence also remains a reality in Britain, with widespread speculation that a 24-year-old man beaten to death on Clapham Common in October 2005 was the victim of a "queer-bashing" attack.[9] As Alan Duncan MP noted during the House of Commons second reading debate on the Civil Partnership Bill in October 2004,

"There is a long way to go in eroding the homophobia that still exists in certain places in Britain today. Gay people still face many barriers to full acceptance, but eliminating discrimination from our laws is an essential first step to eliminating discrimination from our hearts and minds."[10]

The presence of continuing hostility helps explain why sexual orientation and gender identity, as prohibited grounds of discrimination, tend more frequently than most grounds to run up against arguments that the competing rights of others—for example, to exercise religious convictions which disapprove of same-sex sexual relations—should take priority.

III. Scope of the Law's Concern

There is a degree of definitional ambiguity about the ambit of discrimination on the basis of sexual orientation and gender identity. Two broad issues are

8 (Amnesty International, 2001), p.14; more generally, see pp.13–18 (for longer discussion, see Nicholas Bamforth, "Introduction", in Nicholas Bamforth (ed.), *Sex Rights: The Oxford Amnesty Lectures 2002*.

9 See, in particular, Matthew Parris's powerful analysis "Is queer-bashing just the tip of an iceberg of homophobia?", *The Times*, October 29, 2005, p.21; and the editorial comment "Murder on the Common: Yob culture claims another innocent victim", *The Times*, October 18, 2005, p.21. For discussion of earlier widely-reported homophobic attacks, see HC Deb., November 9, 2004, Cols.735 (Angela Eagle MP) and 796 (Jacqui Smith MP).

10 HC Deb., October 12, 2004, Col.190; note also Robert Key MP at Col.207, David Borrow MP at Col.209.

important here. The first is how we define the terms "sexual orientation" and "gender identity". The second is how we understand the idea of discrimination on the basis of sexual orientation or gender identity, something which entails consideration of the areas and subject-matters which fall within the scope of such discrimination.

Turning to the first, definitional issue, it is important to understand the differences and overlaps between the notions of sexual orientation and gender identity. Robert Wintemute has defined an individual's sexual orientation in terms of their emotional/sexual attraction and/or emotional/sexual conduct,[11] and uses this definition to draw a conceptual analogy between religion and sexual orientation as grounds of discrimination.[12]

Robert Wintemute
Sexual Orientation and Human Rights: The United States Constitution, the European Convention, and the Canadian Charter (Oxford: Clarendon Press, 1995)

pp.6–8: "[The term 'sexual orientation'] describes a complex phenomenon and has several senses, making its meaning uncertain . . . But there are two main senses that are, in my view, most relevant for legal analysis. Used in (a) the *first sense*, a person's *sexual orientation* indicates whether, in deciding with whom to engage in 'emotional-sexual conduct', they are emotionally or sexually attracted to persons of the opposite sex (i.e. they are 'heterosexual'), persons of both sexes (i.e. they are 'bisexual'), or persons of the same sex (i.e. they are 'gay', if they are male, or 'lesbian', if they are female). This sense is applied to a person's *attraction*, without regard to their actual conduct . . . whether they perceive their attraction as unchosen or not. . . .

By '*emotional-sexual conduct*', I mean any kind of activity or relationship involving two (or more) persons that has, or could be perceived as having, both emotional and sexual aspects or a purely sexual aspect, including private sexual activity, public displays of affection, and the formation of 'couple relationships' [. . .] sexual orientation [. . .] involves the expression of emotions and the formation of emotional relationships, i.e. it is about love as well as sex. . . .

Used in (b) the *second sense*, a person's '*sexual orientation*' indicates whether the emotional-sexual conduct in which they actually choose to engage is with persons of the opposite sex (i.e. they are 'heterosexual'), persons of both sexes (i.e. they are 'bisexual'), or persons of the same sex (i.e. they are 'gay' or 'lesbian'). This sense is applied to a person's *conduct*, without regard to the direction of their attraction. [. . .]

There are, of course, *additional senses* in which '*sexual orientation*' can be used. Any statement that a specific person is heterosexual, bisexual, gay, or lesbian could refer to (a) the direction of the person's attraction, (b) the direction of their conduct (taken as a whole), (c) the direction of a specific instance of their conduct, or (d) their 'identity' (i.e. whether

[11] While speculation persists as to the "cause" (if any) of personal sexual orientation, little turns on the point in philosophical terms: Nicholas Bamforth, *Sexuality, Morals and Justice* (London: Cassell, 1997), pp.203–6.

[12] See, more broadly, David A.J. Richards, *Identity and the Case for Gay Rights: Race, Gender, Religion as Analogies* (Chicago: University of Chicago Press 1999).

they consider that the direction of their emotional-sexual attraction or conduct serves in part to define them both as a unique individual and as part of a group or community of similar individuals). The addition of (c) and (d) further complicates the analysis, because there is [. . .] no necessary consistency among the four senses. For example, a married man who has just engaged in sexual activity with another man, does so frequently, and is primarily attracted to men, but considers himself heterosexual and frequently engages in sexual activity with his wife, might be gay under (a) or (c), bisexual under (b), and heterosexual under (d). . . .

p.9: . . . it is essential that a fully developed concept of 'sexual orientation' includes both emotional-sexual attraction and emotional-sexual conduct resulting from emotional-sexual attraction. Such a broad concept of sexual orientation is similar to a concept of 'religion' that includes both religious beliefs and religious practices that are motivated by religious beliefs."

Wintemute distinguishes sexual orientation and gender identity in the following way:

Robert Wintemute
"Sexual Orientation and Gender Identity", Ch.10 of Colin Harvey (ed.), *Human Rights in the Community: Rights as Agents of Change* (Oxford: Hart, 2005)

p.176: "The concept of 'sexual orientation' is used to classify individuals as heterosexual, bisexual, lesbian or gay, whereas (one sense of) the concept of 'gender identity' is used to classify individuals as non-transsexual or transsexual. An individual can be a member of the majority with respect to one of these characteristics, both or neither: most individuals are heterosexual and non-transsexual, but some are LGB [lesbian, gay or bisexual] and non-transsexual, some are heterosexual and transsexual, and some are LGB and transsexual."[13]

Unfortunately, current legislation lacks the sophistication of Wintemute's definition. Section 35 of the Equality Act 2006, which allows Regulations to be made governing sexual orientation discrimination (see Section VII below), defines sexual orientation in a circular fashion: " 'sexual orientation' means an individual's sexual orientation towards- (a) persons of the same sex as him or her, (b) persons of the opposite sex, or (c) both."

Turning to the second issue—the meaning of discrimination on the basis of sexual orientation or gender identity—Wintemute suggests that discrimination on the basis of sexual orientation:

[13] See also *Sexual Orientation and Human Rights*, p.12.

***Sexual Orientation and Human Rights: The United States Constitution, the European Convention, and the Canadian Charter* (Oxford: Clarendon Press, 1995)**

p.10: "[C]an easily be described by using the terminology associated with Great Britain's Sex Discrimination Act 1975 and Race Relations Act 1976 (section 1(1) of both Acts). One person may discriminate *directly* against another person either because of the sexual orientation (as direction of attraction or of conduct as a whole) of the other person, or because of the sexual orientation of a specific instance of emotional-sexual conduct in which the other person has engaged. This will involve treating the other person less favourably than persons of another sexual orientation, or than persons who have engaged in a specific instance of emotional-sexual conduct of another sexual orientation. One person may also discriminate *indirectly* against another person by applying a neutral requirement (other than being of a particular sexual orientation) with which a disproportionate number of persons of the other person's sexual orientation are unable to comply, and which cannot be justified."

Discrimination against a person on the basis of their gender identity might, by analogy, be divided into direct and indirect varieties. Using the direct/indirect distinction, the criminal prohibition of sexual acts between persons of the same sex, or penalisation of other expressions of same sex affection, would thus involve prima facie direct discrimination on the basis of sexual orientation, as would the dismissal of an employee because he or she was lesbian or gay and/or had engaged in sexual activity with a person of the same sex. The dismissal of an employee because he or she had undergone gender reassignment or was seeking to do so would constitute prima facie direct discrimination on the basis of gender identity. In a society where marriage was confined to persons of opposite sexes, a rule that "only married couples" may adopt children would constitute prima facie indirect discrimination on the basis of sexual orientation. As we shall see below, most instances of direct discrimination in the criminal law have now disappeared from domestic law in the UK. Discrimination (direct and indirect) in employment and the provision of goods, facilities and services, or any context involving Convention rights, has been prohibited, as has harassment on the basis of a person's sexual orientation or gender identity. While persons who have undergone gender reassignment may now be legally categorised according to their reassigned gender, thus enabling them to marry, there has been considerable argument about how far the institution of civil partnership for same-sex couples is akin to marriage.[14]

Two further points are also important at this general, definitional level. The first is that, while discrimination on the bases of sexual orientation and gender identity are technically separable in the way just described, they are also

[14] For the one attempt legally to define direct and indirect discrimination on the basis of sexual orientation, see the Equality Act (Gender Reassignment) Regulations 2007, reg.3, discussed in Section VI below.

strongly linked in so far as lesbians, bisexuals, gays, transvestites and transgendered persons are all perceived as challenging social expectations arising from gender stereotypes concerning "appropriate" male and female roles: as Wintemute notes, the positions of both groups "involve what the majority sees as disturbing departures from traditional sex roles (e.g., in the case of a gay man, wishing to marry another man, or in the case of a transsexual woman who was born male, wishing to have her penis surgically removed)."[15] In several jurisdictions, the link between sexuality minority groups and gender stereotypes has given rise to the argument that sexual orientation and gender identity discrimination are forms of sex discrimination and should be prohibited as such.

The second point is that, as Wintemute notes, it is important to separate discussion of discrimination on the basis of sexual orientation (or gender identity) from more general questions of sexual freedom:

Sexual Orientation and Human Rights: The United States Constitution, the European Convention, and the Canadian Charter (Oxford: Clarendon Press, 1995)

p.11: "... many general issues of 'sexuality' (i.e. a person's capacity to engage in emotional-sexual conduct and every aspect of their exercise of that capacity) or 'sexual freedom' may not involve any discrimination on the ground of sexual orientation. Thus, the law's treatment of such issues as paedophilia, incest, prostitution, pornography, sado-masochism or polygamy may interfere with sexual freedom or constitute prima facie discrimination on other grounds. ... But it does not raise an issue of sexual orientation discrimination, provided that all such conduct (or expression) is treated in the same way, whether it is opposite-sex or same-sex, or involves persons who are heterosexual, bisexual, gay or lesbian."

Analytically, and in terms of the case law, this distinction is important: arguments for general sexual freedom are indeed of a different character from arguments against discrimination. Nonetheless, despite the examples Wintemute uses, it is important to remember that restrictions traditionally imposed on same-sex sexual activity and relationships, or people's ability to change sex, directly implicate the issue of sexual freedom and have always done so. Historically, the issue of "discrimination" has only been recognised since lesbians and gay men were recognised as a discernible social group, and there remain many situations in which restrictions of the type Wintemute describes are applied with particular emphasis towards lesbians and gay men. In practice, issues of discrimination and general sexual freedom may therefore be

[15] "Sexual Orientation and Gender Identity", *ibid.* at p.176.

hard to disentangle: a point which becomes particularly clear from the case law of the European Convention and the United States.

IV. Sexual Orientation Discrimination, Gender Identity Discrimination and Constitutional Litigation

In recent years, cases concerning sexual orientation and gender identity discrimination have reached the highest courts in the UK, the EU, under the European Convention on Human Rights, and in the USA (both federally and at state level), Canada and South Africa. Such cases have raised important questions concerning the ambit of (as appropriate) constitutional or other legal protections against prohibited forms of discrimination, and concerning the respective powers of courts and legislatures in prohibiting discrimination—powerfully highlighting the constitutional dimensions of discrimination law. Arguments of principle, concerning human rights, play a particularly strong role—arguments concerning equality and dignity being especially popular.[16] The following passage traces the use of such arguments in litigation concerning same-sex partnerships; they could equally, however, be used to advance any claim against sexual orientation discrimination or gender identity discrimination.

[16] Respect for privacy is a popular constitutional argument when litigants challenge criminal prohibitions on consenting same-sex sexual activity (see, e.g. *Lawrence v Texas* (2003) 123 S.Ct. 2472). However, it is harder to use such arguments when arguing for the legal recognition of same-sex partnerships, or for protections against discrimination in the workplace: as Baroness Hale has argued extra-judicially, "to regard homosexual relationships as a narrow privacy issue is to deny to them the full enjoyment [of legal rights] which other relationships take for granted". "Homosexual Rights" (2004) 16 C.F.L.Q. 125, 127. Privacy may in any event turn out to rest on deeper values. In *Lawrence v Texas,* while the majority judgment—delivered by Justice Kennedy—was couched in the language of the right to respect for privacy, human dignity also appears: he talks of the adverse effect on the "dignity of the persons charged" of a sodomy offense (*ibid.*, 2482), and makes clear that lesbian and gay persons are entitled to respect for their private lives: "The State cannot demean their existence or control their destiny by making their private sexual conduct a crime." (*ibid.*, 2484). In *Goodridge v Department of Public Health* (2003) 798 N.E. 2d 941, Marshall C.J. interpreted *Lawrence* thus: "There, the [Supreme] Court affirmed that the core concept of common human dignity protected by the Fourteenth Amendment to the United states Constitution precludes government intrusion into the deeply personal realms of consensual adult expressions of intimacy and one's choice of an intimate partner" (*ibid.*, 948). See also *National Coalition for Gay and Lesbian Equality v Minister of Justice* (1999 (1) S.A.6), paras 31 (Ackermann J.), 115, 116, 120 (Sachs J.).

Nicholas Bamforth
"Same-sex Partnerships: Some Comparative Constitutional Lessons" [2007] EHRLR 47

pp.54–56: "Claims for legal protections for lesbians and gays have tended—since the mid-1980s—to be expressed in the language of equality. Broadly speaking, equality arguments maintain that lesbians and gay men should not, because of their sexual orientation, be treated any less favourably than heterosexuals since the two groups are of equal moral worth, and in consequence that same-sex partnerships deserve analogous, similar or identical (as appropriate) legal protection to that granted to heterosexual partnerships. There are many recent examples of such arguments being used in the U.K. In the House of Commons Second and Third Reading debates for the Civil Partnership Bill, Jacqui Smith MP—then Deputy Minister for Women and Equality—explained the proposals as a 'sign of the Government's commitment to social justice and equality', as being 'about equality', and as marking 'an important stage on the progress towards equality for lesbian and gay people'. In *Ghaidan*, [v. Godin-Mendoza], Baroness Hale stressed that: 'a guarantee of equal treatment is [. . .] essential to democracy. Democracy is founded on the principle that each individual has equal value.' [para [132]] The popularity of equality arguments was also made clear by Lord Hoffmann, when he stated in *R. v Secretary of State for Work and Pensions, ex p. Carson* that 'The principle that everyone is entitled to equal treatment by the state, that like cases should be treated alike and different cases should be treated differently, will be found, in one form or another, in most human rights instruments and written constitutions. They vary only in the generality with which the principle is expressed.' [para [10]] Furthermore, equality arguments have frequently been relied upon in Canadian and South African cases.

Equality arguments have a simple, crystal clear moral appeal. Who, after all, wants to be labelled a supporter of inequality? Nonetheless, as the cases show, equality—while a popular and powerful argument—is best seen as relying upon a deeper, underpinning justification for protecting same-sex partnership rights: namely human dignity or autonomy. My main reason for saying this is that equality arguments depend—at least, when dealing with same-sex partnerships—on comparisons. As such, if they are to be of real use as justificatory arguments, they beg the prior question of why the things being compared are morally valuable. One merely needs to state the proposition—same-sex couples deserve equal treatment to opposite sex-couples because they are morally equal—to see its circularity. It is therefore the deeper argument that, as a matter of logic, explains *why* same-sex and opposite-sex couples deserve equal treatment, and in turn offers the *real* foundation for claims to same-sex partnership rights. Autonomy or dignity arguments suggest that sexual and emotional desires—including, as Baroness Hale powerfully demonstrated in *Ghaidan*—feelings, aspirations, and behaviour, are of central importance for human beings. For most people, participation in a happy sexual and emotional relationship is a central aspect of their well-being, or something which they aspire to have as such an aspect. Provided that a relationship is based on consent, it is—from this perspective—highly unjust for the law to penalise it or to refuse to provide it with an adequate level of support. It is at this stage in the dignity argument that equality becomes relevant. For we can clearly say that, in circumstances of existing inequality, one sensible way to measure the level of protection that should be offered is by comparison with already protected heterosexual relationships.

The dependence of equality arguments on a defense of deeper values is clearer still in practice. For example, Jacqui Smith M.P., after framing her argument in favour of the Civil Partnership Bill in terms of equality, went on to suggest that the proposals were a 'historic step on what has been a long journey to respect and dignity for lesbians and gay men in Britain. [The Bill] is a natural progression in our vision to build an inclusive society'.

Equality was, in other words, elided into an argument concerning respect, dignity and social inclusiveness. Furthermore, in *Ghaidan*, after making her equality-related statement, Baroness Hale went on to stress that equal treatment was essential to democracy and that 'Democracy is founded on the principle that each individual has equal value. Treating some as automatically having less value than others not only causes pain and distress to that person but also violates his or her dignity as a human being. The essence of the Convention, as has often been said, is respect for human dignity and human freedom . . .' [*Ghaidan v Godin-Mendoza* (2004) UKHL 30, para.[132].] Her analysis, having started with equality, thus turned into an assertion of the requirements of human dignity, dignity being found—in this context—in legal respect for intimate relationships. And, in the *Carson* case, having talked about the importance of equal treatment, Lord Hoffmann went on to associate the wrong involved in cases of discrimination with a 'denial of respect' for people as individuals [*R. v Secretary of State for Work and Pensions* ex p. Carson [2005] UKHL 37, para.[18].] Sachs J's reasoning in *Minister of Home Affairs v Fourie* confirms the dependence of equality on deeper values. The Constitutional Court's decision that the existing South African common and statutory law of marriage unconstitutionally failed to treat gays and lesbians equally was based in large part on the constitutional guarantee of equality. However, Sachs J. emphasised how the denial of equality constituted 'discrimination . . . at a deeply intimate level of human existence and relationality.' [[2006] ISA 524, para.[50].] Furthermore, throughout his judgment he tied the notion of equality to the idea of dignity and sometimes to fairness, as well as tolerance and mutual respect."[17]

Cases concerning sexual orientation discrimination and gender identity discrimination have also highlighted in vivid form the "constitutional" question of how far it is appropriate for courts to recognise new forms of prohibited discrimination (where they are allowed to do so), and how far this task should be left to legislatures (see further Chapters 1 and 2).

"Same-Sex Partnerships: Some Comparative Constitutional Lessons"

pp.56–58: "Analogous constitutional arguments concerning the appropriate role of courts—as opposed to that of legislatures—have been voiced in each of the jurisdictions I have been discussing, despite the formal differences between the national constitutions involved. At stake here is a straightforward question: namely whether, if same-sex partnerships are to be granted legal recognition and protection, it is more appropriate for the legislature or the courts to do so (or to take the lead in doing so) in the jurisdiction concerned.

This question has been particularly important in the U.S.A., where one of the most bitter issues in political debate—at least, for opponents of same-sex partnership rights—has been the perception that such rights are emerging through the courts without the voices of elected legislators being heard. Part of the rhetoric used by those campaigning for an amendment to the federal U.S. constitution so as to block same-sex marriage has thus been that this would be an expression of the 'will of the people' in the face of an 'elite of liberal judges' who want to defy that will. The argument about the 'place' of courts was also used with particular vehemence by the dissenters in *Goodridge*, echoing the dissents of Scalia J. and Thomas J. on the issue of decriminalization—at federal Supreme Court

[17] *ibid.*, para.[60].

level—in *Lawrence*. In *Goodridge*, Marshall C.J. sought to justify the Massachusetts Supreme Judicial Court's decision as an exercise of its proper constitutional function: 'The Massachusetts Constitution requires that legislation meet certain criteria and not extend beyond certain limits. It is the function of courts to determine whether these criteria are met and whether these limits are exceeded. . . . To label the court's role as usurping that of the Legislature . . . is to misunderstand the nature and purpose of judicial review [of legislation]. We owe great deference to the Legislature to decide social and policy issues, but it is the traditional and settled role of courts to decide constitutional issues.'[18] Despite the vehemence of some of the dissenting judgments, it might be said that even here the Court was in fact being somewhat deferential to the state legislature, given that it allowed it time to rectify the impugned legislation instead of striking that legislation down immediately (as it could have done). A similar strategy is evident in South Africa: emphasizing the importance of separation of powers and *in spite* of the strong normative importance that he had attached to the recognition of same-sex marriage, Sachs J. agreed in *Fourie* to postpone for a year the Constitutional Court's declaration of invalidity concerning the Marriage Act 1961's exclusion of same-sex couples, so as to give the legislature time to produce a constitutionally satisfactory solution. And one might almost argue that, in Canada, a mirror image process has been taking place: that one reason for the federal government's reference of its proposed same-sex marriage legislation to the Supreme Court was in effect—given its narrow Parliamentary majority at the time—to pass a difficult decision about a socially contentious issue to a nationally respected institution that had long accepted responsibility for adjudicating upon the more sensitive aspects of citizens' constitutional rights unhindered by concerns about Parliamentary majorities or future general elections."

The constitutional dimensions of discrimination law discussed in Chapter 1 could be said to be well-illustrated by the combination of arguments of constitutional principle in many of the cases concerning sexual orientation and gender identity discrimination, and the disputes to which these cases have given rise about the proper role of courts in protecting against such discrimination.[19]

V. The European Convention on Human Rights and the Human Rights Act 1998

Issues concerned with sexual orientation and gender identity have been litigated before the European Court of Human Rights under Art.8 (the right to respect for private family life), Art.14 (the right to be free from discrimination) and Art.12 (the right to marry). In this section, we consider relevant Court of Human Rights and domestic case law (arising under the Human Rights Act

[18] *ibid.*, 966.

[19] For explicitly constitutional treatments of sexual orientation discrimination, see William N. Eskridge, *GayLaw: Challenging the Apartheid of the Closet* (Cambridge: Harvard University Press, 1999) and *Equality Practice: Civil Unions and the Future of Gay Rights* (New York: Routledge, 2002); Andrew Koppelman, *Antidiscrimination Law and Social Equality* (New Haven: Yale University Press, 1996); David A.J. Richards, *Women, Gays and the Constitution* (Chicago: Chicago University Press, 1998); Robert Wintemute, *Sexual Orientation and Human Rights*; *ibid.*

1998). As we will see, the reach of the Convention has been wide: while the earliest sexual orientation cases concerned national laws prohibiting same-sex sexual relations, the Court has gone on to deal with public employment in the military and with issues connected with partnership rights. However, due to the presence of the margin of appreciation (see Chapter 2) and disputes about the boundaries of Art.8, recent case law has arguably been inconsistent. The margin has also played a key role in cases dealing with gender identity, to the extent that the Court has reversed its position due to a reinterpretation of the margin's demands.[20] The Strasbourg case law will be relevant to our discussion in s.6 of legislative developments at national level. For one thing, the Gender Recognition Act 2004 was clearly a response to the House of Lords' declaration of incompatibility concerning existing legislation in *Bellinger v Bellinger*, and to that extent it is directly prompted by the Convention.[21] The Civil Partnership Act 2004 (CPA), by contrast, was presented as a domestic initiative and was not associated with any accompanying Strasbourg-level (or domestic) litigation. Convention rights are nonetheless important to the CPA in the context of statutory interpretation.

A. *Articles 8 and 14*[22]

European Convention on Human Rights, Article 8

"(1) Everyone has the right to respect for his private and family life, his home and his correspondence.

(2) There shall be no interference by a public authority with the exercise of this right except such as is in accordance with the law and is necessary in a democratic society in the interests of national security, public safety or the economic well-being of the country, for the prevention of disorder or crime, for the protection of health or morals, or for the protection of the rights and freedoms of others."

European Convention on Human Rights, Article 14

"The enjoyment of the rights and freedoms set forth in this Convention shall be secured without discrimination on any ground such as sex, colour, language, religion, political or other opinion, national or social origin, association with a national minority, property, birth or other status."

[20] See *Goodwin v United Kingdom* [2002] 35 E.H.R.R. 447.

[21] [2003] UKHL 21.

[22] The argument in this section builds upon Nicholas Bamforth, "'The benefits of marriage in all but name?' Same-sex couples and the Civil Partnership Act 2004" (2007) 19 C.F.L.Q. 133. For general analysis, see also Helen Toner, *Partnership Rights, Free Movement and EU Law* (Oxford: Hart, 2004), Ch.3; Robert Wintemute, "Strasbourg to the Rescue? Same-Sex Partners and Parents under the Convention", Ch.40 in Robert Wintemute & Mads Andenaes (eds.), *Legal Recognition of Same-Sex Partnerships: A Study of National, European and International Law* (Oxford: Hart, 2001).

The Court's first key decision concerning sexual orientation was *Dudgeon v United Kingdom*,[23] in which it was held that the continuing existence in Northern Ireland of laws which criminalised sexual acts between consenting adult males violated the right to respect for private life under Art.8 (the first limb of the Article) and were not justifiable in terms of Art.8(2). Although some of the Court's views now seem old-fashioned, they deserve to be considered in detail given that they provide the foundation for much of the Court's analysis in later cases. Crucially, *Dudgeon* established that "particularly serious reasons" were needed to justify a restriction on sexual privacy. However, the decision also generated uncertainty given its emphasis on the "margin of appreciation" and its treatment of the relationship between Arts 8 and 14.

The Court was clear that the impugned legislation constituted "a continuing interference with the applicant's right to respect for his private life (which includes his sexual life) within the meaning of Article 8(1)" given that in his "personal circumstances ... the very existence of this legislation continuously and directly affects his private life [...] either he respects the law and refrains from engaging—even in private with consenting male partners—in prohibited sexual acts to which he is disposed by reason of his homosexual tendencies, or he commits such acts and thereby becomes liable to criminal prosecution".[24] The Court noted that:

> **[49]** "... some degree of regulation of male homosexual conduct ... by means of the criminal law can be justified as 'necessary in a democratic society'. The overall function served by the criminal law in this field is, in the words of the Wolfenden report ... 'to preserve public order and decency [and] to protect the citizen from what is offensive or injurious'. Furthermore, this necessity for some degree of control may even extend to consensual acts committed in private, notably where there is [a] call—to quote the Wolfenden report once more—'to provide sufficient safeguards against exploitation and corruption of others, particularly those who are specially vulnerable because they are young, weak in body or mind, inexperienced, or in a state of special physical, official or economic dependence'. ... It being accepted that some form of legislation is 'necessary' to protect particular sections of society as well as the moral ethos of society as a whole, the question in the present case is whether the contested provisions of the law of Northern Ireland and their enforcement remain within the bounds of what, in a democratic society, may be regarded as necessary in order to accomplish those aims."

The Court then drew upon *Handyside v United Kingdom* (concerning Art.10) to make clear that the concept of "necessity" implied that a "pressing social

[23] (1982) 4 E.H.R.R. 149.
[24] para.[41].

need" needed to be shown for the interference in question,[25] and also stressed that "the notion of 'necessity' is linked to that of a 'democratic society' ... two hallmarks of which are tolerance and broadmindedness".[26] National authorities could make the initial assessment of whether a "pressing social need" existed, retaining a margin of appreciation but subject to review by the Court.[27] While state judgments concerning morals attracted a margin of appreciation, "not only the nature of the aim of the restriction but also the nature of the activities involved will affect the scope of the margin of appreciation. The present case concerns a most intimate aspect of private life. Accordingly, there must exist particularly serious reasons before interferences on the part of the public authorities can be legitimate" within Art.8(2).[28]

On the facts, the Court accepted that the national authorities could legitimately take into account the conservative moral climate which then existed in Northern Ireland, and that the national government had sought to reach a balanced judgment in good faith.[29] However, it noted that by comparison "with the era when [the] legislation was enacted, there is now a better understanding, and in consequence an increased tolerance, of homosexual behaviour to the extent that in the great majority of the member States of the Council of Europe it is no longer considered to be necessary or appropriate to treat homosexual practices of the kind now in question as in themselves a matter to which the sanctions of the criminal law should be applied" and that no evidence had been produced to show that the national authorities' general failure to enforce the law in relation to sexual acts between consenting adults aged over 21 had been injurious to moral standards in Northern Ireland or that there had been a public demand for stricter enforcement of the law.[30] It could not therefore be shown that there was a "pressing social need" for criminalisation, no sufficient justification having been provided by the risk of harm to vulnerable sections of society or adverse effects on the public. In relation to proportionality, such justifications as existed for retaining the law were outweighed by the detrimental effects which the very existence of the legislation could have on the life of a gay man such as the claimant. The fact that "members of the public who regard homosexuality as immoral may be shocked, offended or disturbed by the commission by others of private homosexual acts" was not enough "on its own" to warrant "the application of penal sanctions when it is consenting adults alone who are involved."[31] The Court also took care to stress, however, that its conclusions applied only to the criminalisation of sexual behaviour between men over twenty-one. By con-

[25] paras [51] and [52], drawing on *Handyside v United Kingdom* (1976) 1 E.H.R.R. 737, paras [48] and [49].
[26] para.[53].
[27] paras [51] and [52], drawing on *Handyside v United Kingdom* (1976) 1 E.H.R.R. 737, paras [48] and [49].
[28] para.[52].
[29] paras [57] and [59].
[30] para.[60].
[31] para.[60]; see also para.[61].

trast, it fell "in the first instance to the national authorities to decide on the appropriate safeguards of this kind required for the defence of morals in their society and, in particular, to fix the age under which young people should have the protection of the criminal law", that age potentially being different for heterosexual and homosexual acts.[32] Finally, the Court did not consider it necessary to assess the compatibility of the Northern Irish laws with Art.14 (on the basis that they were discriminatory) as well as with Art.8, suggesting that an Art.14-based argument would effectively amount to the same compliant seen from a different angle.[33]

While reaffirming its decision in *Dudgeon*,[34] the Court has gone further in later cases. The *Dudgeon* reasoning, including the need for particularly serious reasons, was used in *Smith and Grady v United Kingdom* to find that sufficiently convincing and weighty reasons had not been offered to justify a policy of automatically discharging from military service those who were found to be lesbian or gay, nor the sustained and intrusive investigations into the claimants' sexual lives which had taken place prior to their discharge.[35] The Court also found, as in *Dudgeon*, that the claimants' Art.14-based argument amounted "in effect to the same complaint, albeit seen from a different angle".[36] Meanwhile, in *ADT v United Kingdom*, the Court found that insufficient reasons had been offered to justify the criminalisation of sexual activity involving more than two men in a private home, national authorities having only a "narrow margin of appreciation" in such a case.[37] In *L and V v Austria*, the Court went still more clearly beyond *Dudgeon*, acknowledging the existence of "an ever growing European consensus to apply equal ages of consent for heterosexual, lesbian and homosexual relations" and finding that insufficiently weighty reasons had been offered to justify the existence of a law which singled-out for punishment homosexual activity involving males aged under eighteen.[38] The Court implied that the emerging consensus gave rise to a relatively narrow margin of appreciation concerning ages of consent, a con-

[32] para.[62]; see also paras [66] and [68].

[33] paras [69] and [70].

[34] In relation to criminal prohibition of consenting same-sex sexual activity, see *Norris v Ireland* (1989) 13 E.H.R.R. 186; *Modinos v Cyprus* (1993) 16 E.H.R.R. 485.

[35] (1999) 29 E.H.R.R. 493; see also *Lustig-Prean and Beckett v United Kingdom* (1999) 29 E.H.R.R. 548. The Court cited and then applied the *Dudgeon* reasoning at paras [87]–[112].

[36] para.[115].

[37] (2001) 31 E.H.R.R. 33, para.[38]. Note, however, the contrast with *Laskey, Jaggard and Brown v United Kingdom* (1997) 24 E.H.R.R. 39, involving sado-masochistic group sexual activity, causing the Court to accept in *ADT* that "at some point, sexual activities can be carried out in such a manner that State interference may be justified, either as not amounting to an interference with the right to respect for private life, or as being justified for the protection, for example, of health or morals" (para.[37]).

[38] Unreported, January 9, 2003, para.[50]; this was a case based on Art.8 coupled with Art.14, rather than Art.8 considered alone. See also *Sutherland v United Kingdom* (1997) 24 E.H.R.R. 22.

clusion reached more openly by the former Commission on Human Rights in *Sutherland v United Kingdom*.[39]

Article 14, coupled with Art.8, also now plays an important role. In *Salgueiro da Silva Mouta v Portugal*, the Court accepted that where a difference of treatment in relation to the enjoyment of another Convention right was based upon the claimant's sexual orientation, it violated Art.14 in the absence of an objective and reasonable justification (in other words, if there was no legitimate aim or reasonable relationship of proportionality between the means employed and the aim being pursued).[40] As such, the defendant state's refusal to award custody of a child to a gay parent because of that parent's sexual orientation could not—without more—survive Art.14 scrutiny. This position was seemingly strengthened in *Karner v Austria*, where the Court stressed that "differences based on sexual orientation require *particularly serious reasons* by way of justification"[41] and that states had only a narrow margin of appreciation in relation to such differences in treatment.[42] Indeed, the Court made clear that, where the surviving partner in a same-sex couple was excluded from a right, contained in national legislation, to succeed to the tenancy of the property in which the couple had lived, the state was obliged specifically to show that it was necessary, in order to achieve the Convention-approved aim pursued by the legislation, to exclude same-sex couples from the protection offered by national law.[43] Nonetheless, a certain measure of ambiguity persists given that the Court accepted that the aim invoked by the state in this case—namely, the "protection of the family *in the traditional sense*"—was "in principle, a weighty and legitimate reason which might justify a difference in treatment" in appropriate circumstances,[44] and that its reasons for holding that a sufficient justification had not been advanced on the facts were only cursorily stated.[45] Furthermore, *Salgueiro* and *Karner* are not easy to reconcile with the Court's contemporaneous decision in *Frette v France*, where it was described as "quite natural" that the "national authorities ... should enjoy a wide margin of appreciation when they are asked to make rulings" about the suitability of a single gay man—by contrast with a single heterosexual—to adopt a child.[46] The Court suggested that in *this* context, "delicate" issues were involved, that there was little common ground among the signatory states, and that the law appeared to be in a transitional stage when it came to adoption: empirical observations that provide no principled basis for explaining why

[39] *L and V*, paras [49]–[50]; *Sutherland*, para.[57]. For early analysis of the margin of appreciation and the significance of consensus within Convention States in relation to ages of consent, see Laurence R. Helfer, "Finding a Consensus on Equality: the Homosexual Age of Consent and the European Convention on Human Rights" (1990) 65 N.Y.U. L. Rev. 1044.

[40] (2001) 31 E.H.R.R. 47, paras [26]–[36]; *Frette v France* (2002) 38 E.H.R.R. 21, para.[32].

[41] (2003) 38 E.H.R.R. 24, para.[37] (emphasis added).

[42] *ibid.*, para.[41].

[43] *ibid.*, para.[41].

[44] *ibid.*, para.[40] (emphasis added).

[45] *ibid.*, paras [41]–[42].

[46] *Frette v France*, (2002) 38 E.H.R.R. 21, para.[41]. On the facts, this clearly involved a difference of treatment based upon sexual orientation: see paras [32]–[33].

adoption should be treated in such a different fashion from child custody, or—in the absence of further explanation—from the right to succeed to property.[47]

Two further complications affect the Art.8 and 14 case law concerning sexual orientation (whether Art.8 is pleaded on its own or in conjunction with Art.14). The first relates to the fact that for the moment, Art.14 prohibits only discrimination in the enjoyment of other Convention rights (although, if the UK signs Protocol 12 to the Convention, discrimination in any context will be prohibited) and must be pleaded in conjunction with another right.[48] As we saw above, the Court has sometimes deemed it sufficient to rule that a restriction unjustifiably violates Art.8, finding that arguments based on Art.14 do not raise a separate issue.[49] However, in other cases—without real explanation of the distinction—the Court's main focus has been on the discriminatory aspect of the restriction in issue, Art.14 forming the *basis* for its judgment.[50] The sexual orientation cases might therefore be thought to illustrate the broader uncertainty, considered in Chapter 2, concerning the relationship between Art.14 and the substantive Convention right(s) to which it is tied in any given case.[51] A related difficulty concerns discrimination in employment. It has been argued that employment, or at least access to employment, lies outside the permissible scope of any claim based on Art.14 given that it does not fall within the scope of other, substantive Convention rights.[52] As noted in ch.2, however, this argument may in fact be too broad. The Court accepted in *Smith* that Art.8 precludes dismissal from military employment, and rejected the claimants' Art.14 argument *not* because employment was deemed to fall outside the scope of either Article, but because it raised the same point as their Art.8 argument.[53] Furthermore, Robert Wintemute has argued that the cases should be interpreted not as requiring the denial of an opportunity falling within the ambit of a substantive right in order for a claim to fall within Art.14 (thus excluding employment), but

[47] *ibid.*, paras [41]–[42]. In their joint partly dissenting opinion in *Frette*, para.[1], Judges Bratza, Fuhrmann and Tulkens place reliance—in seeking to explain the difference between the cases—on the distinction between a gay man seeking to adopt a child of which he is not the biological father, and a gay man seeking custody of an existing child of which he is: a distinction which is arguably not clear-cut; however, the judges went on (correctly) to doubt the Court's treatment of the margin of appreciation: para.[2(c)].

[48] For discussion of the present position, see Richard Clayton and Hugh Tomlinson, *The Law of Human Rights* (Oxford: Oxford University Press, 2000), paras 17.86 to 17.88.

[49] *Dudgeon v United Kingdom*, paras [67]–[70]; *Smith and Grady v United Kingdom*, paras [115]–[116]; *Lustig-Prean and Beckett v United Kingdom*, paras [108]–[109]; *ADT v United Kingdom*, para.[41].

[50] *Frette v France*, paras [30]–[33]; *Karner v Austria*, paras [32]–[33]. This uncertainty will not be alleviated by the provisions of Protocol 12 to the Convention (to which the United Kingdom is not a signatory) which allow Art.14 to be relied upon regardless of whether another Convention right is also in issue.

[51] See, generally, Judge Luzius Wildhaber, "Protection against Discrimination under the European Convention on Human Rights—A Second-Class Guarantee?" (2002) 2 Baltic Yearbook of International L. 71, especially 78–9.

[52] See Judge Luzius Wildhaber, 73 (access to employment); Stephen Livingstone, "Article 14 and the prevention of discrimination in the European Convention on Human Rights" [1997] E.H.R.L.R. 25, 26 (provision of employment).

[53] *Smith and Grady v United Kingdom, ibid.*; *Lustig-Preen and Beckett v United Kingdom, ibid.*

merely as requiring that the ground on which the decision to deny the opportunity was based does so (thus including discrimination in employment, at least in relation to certain "sensitive" or "ordinary" grounds).[54] And, while the exclusion of private employment from either Article is perhaps encouraged by the fact that the only permissible defendants before the Strasbourg Court are national authorities, courts are not confined by this restriction at national level.[55]

The second complication relates to the ambit of the second, respect for family life limb of Art.8 (the second limb of the Article)[56]. The Court concluded in *Estevez v Spain* that "long-term homosexual relationships between two men do not fall within the scope of the right to respect for family life" and that "despite the growing tendency in a number of European States towards the legal and judicial recognition of stable *de facto* partnerships between homosexuals, this is, given the existence of little common ground" an area in which signatory states "still enjoy a wide margin of appreciation".[57] In consequence, same-sex couples did not enjoy family rights when claiming social security entitlements under Spanish law. This seems hard to reconcile with the later decision in *Karner* in which, as we have seen, it was held to be a violation of Art.14, coupled with Art.8, for the surviving partner in a same-sex relationship to be denied the right to succeed—where a heterosexual partner could do so—to the tenancy of property the partners had shared. *Estevez* does not explain how the one scenario can cleanly be separated from the other. The Court's partnership rights decisions may thus be thought to illustrate long-standing criticisms made of the Court's Art.8 case law: namely that it lacks conceptual unity[58] and that the operation of the "margin of appreciation" is hard to predict.[59]

54 "'Within the Ambit': How Big *Is* the 'Gap' in Article 14 European Convention on Human Rights?" [2004] E.H.R.L.R. 366, 369–378; Wintemute relies for authority on *Thlimmenos v Greece* (2000) 31 E.H.R.R. 15, paras [41]–[42].

55 For an obvious Art.8 case at national level involving only private parties, see *Ghaidan v Godin-Mendoza* [2004] UKHL 30, [2004] 2 A.C. 557.

56 For analysis of the Strasbourg case law concerning same-sex couples up to 2001, see Robert Wintemute, "Strasbourg to the Rescue? Same-Sex Partners and Parents Under the European Convention", Ch.40 in Robert Wintemute and Mads Andenaes (eds.), *Legal Recognition of Same-sex Partnerships: A Study of National, European and International Law* (Oxford: Hart, 2001).

57 May 10, 2001.

58 Compare David Feldman, "The Developing Scope of Article 8 of the European Convention on Human Rights" [1997] E.H.R.L.R. 265 and Colin Warbrick, "The Structure of Article 8" [1998] E.H.R.L.R. 32.

59 See, e.g., the material discussed by Richard Clayton & Hugh Tomlinson, *The Law of Human Rights*, paras 6.50–6.53. A further, normative criticism of *Estevez* might be that when the decision is coupled with earlier cases, the Court might seem to be saying that lesbians and gay men may secure Convention protection when it comes to sexual activity or matters related to their *private lives as individuals* (for example, against prosecution for private sexual activity), but not when their deeper emotional and *familial* relationships are directly in issue.

B. *Articles 8 and 14 in domestic law: the uncertain relationship between the* Ghaidan *and* M. *cases*

The uncertainties concerning Arts 8 and 14 at Strasbourg level have been reflected in the two key authorities at national level, namely the House of Lords' decisions in *Ghaidan v Godin-Mendoza*[60] and *Secretary of State for Work and Pensions v M.*[61] While the subject-matters of both cases now fall within the Civil Partnership Act 2004 and would be dealt with using that act,[62] they provide a useful illustration of the House of Lords' commitment to the principle of non-discrimination, as well as providing a useful background when considering whether the CPA is compatible with relevant Convention rights (see further below).

Ghaidan concerned Sch.1 to the Rent Act 1977 (as amended), which allowed the surviving partner in an unmarried heterosexual relationship to succeed, on the death of the other partner, to the protected tenancy of the property in which they had lived "as husband and wife", but made no reference to same-sex partners. The claimant sought, on the death of his male partner, to succeed to the protected tenancy of the flat in which they had lived in a long-term relationship. Lord Nicholls noted (citing *Frette*) that a difference in legal treatment based upon sexual orientation was unacceptable under Article 14 unless "good reason exists".[63] While protection of the traditional family unit may, as accepted in *Karner*, be "an important and legitimate aim" and a "cogent reason justifying differential treatment", this was only in "certain contexts" and in deciding whether its use was appropriate it was important to identify the *element* of the traditional family that the legislation in issue sought to protect[64]—suggesting that use of the justification must be tightly controlled. Similarly, Baroness Hale stressed that "sexual orientation is one of the grounds covered by [A]rticle 14 on which, like race and sex, a difference in treatment is particularly suspect", and that justifications advanced for differences in treatment "require careful scrutiny".[65] She thus argued that what was "really meant by the 'protection' of the traditional family"—when used as a justification—"is the encouragement of people to form traditional families and the discouragement of people from forming others", and that it did not protect the traditional family to grant it a benefit denied to those who could not or would not become such a family.[66] There may be legitimate reasons to

[60] [2004] UKHL 30.

[61] [2006] UKHL 11.

[62] Note Lord Walker's suggestion in *M.*, para [38], about the difference of outcome under the CPA

[63] [2004] UKHL 30 para.[9]. The other Law Lords agreed with Lord Nicholls and Baroness Hale concerning Art.14: see paras [37] (Lord Steyn), [55] (Lord Millett), and [103], [127] and [128] (Lord Rodger).

[64] para.[16]; see also Baroness Hale at para.[138].

[65] para.[136].

[66] para.[143].

encourage people to marry and to discourage them from living together without marrying, but these did not justify legislation which encouraged heterosexual unmarried relationships but discouraged same-sex ones,[67] the aim of "discouraging homosexual relationships" being inconsistent with respect for private life under Art.8.[68] Lord Nicholls also discussed the "discretionary area of judgment" (see Chapter 2), and suggested that arguments based upon it led nowhere in this context. While a court would be less ready to reach a different conclusion from Parliament about the meaning of legislation in an area like housing policy, where Parliament had to strike a balance between the interests of landlords and tenants, if—within such an area—the alleged breach of Art.14 involved "differential treatment based on grounds such as ... sexual orientation" the court would still "scrutinise with intensity any reasons said to constitute justification. The reasons must be cogent if such differential treatment is to be justified."[69]

Ghaidan clearly establishes that legislation must—within the limits imposed by s.3(1) of the HRA—(see Chapter 2) be interpreted so as to preclude discrimination on the basis of sexual orientation wherever the Strasbourg case law so requires, a position reinforced by the House of Lords' stipulation in *R. v Secretary of State for Work and Pensions, Ex p. Carson* that some of grounds of discrimination precluded by Art.14—including sexual orientation—were more sensitive than others and placed a stronger burden of justification on the respondent.[70] However, *Ghaidan* left unaddressed the difficulties in the Strasbourg case law: since it was accepted that Art.8 was engaged,[71] their Lordships did not discuss whether the claimant's family life had been interfered with, nor how the definition of family life should be understood, and Baroness Hale associated the illegitimacy of discouraging same-sex relationships with the *private life* limb of Art.8.

The meaning of "family life" was addressed in *M*, which concerned the basis on which child maintenance payments were calculated under the Child Support Act 1991 and accompanying secondary legislation. The claimant argued that a parent who now lived with a same-sex partner was assessed less generously than a parent who lived with an opposite-sex partner, and that this difference fell foul of Art.14 coupled with the "family life" limb of Art.8.[72] The majority judgments placed considerable weight on the Strasbourg "margin of

67 para.[143].
68 para.[143], citing *Dudgeon v United Kingdom, ibid.*
69 para.[19].
70 [2005] UKHL 37, paras [15]–[17] (Lord Hoffmann), [55], [57]–[58], [89] (Lord Walker). Lords Nicholls, Rodger and Carswell (paras [1], [42] and [92]) agreed with both judgments. Lord Hoffmann suggested that discrimination on a sensitive ground could not be justified merely by appeal to a "utilitarian" value such as the general public interest (para.[16]), while Lord Walker—echoing the Strasbourg Court—asserted that "very weighty reasons" would be needed. Lord Walker describes the sensitive grounds, by analogy with US 14th Amendment jurisprudence, as "suspect categories" (para.[58]), although his assertion (at para.[55]) that sexual orientation constitutes such a category in US law is, with respect, an over-simplification.
71 See Lord Nicholls, paras [11]–[12], Baroness Hale, para.[135].
72 See Lord Walker at para.[60].

appreciation" and four of the five judgments differed about how the Strasbourg Court would now interpret "family life".[73] Turning first to the ambit of "family life", Lord Nicholls was confident that the *Estevez* exclusion of same-sex couples from this limb of Art.8 still applied,[74] and asserted that since signatory states enjoyed a wide margin of appreciation in this area, "[f]or the time being the respect accorded" to same-sex relationships was a matter for them.[75] Art.14 was thus not engaged.[76] Lord Mance also invoked *Estevez* and the wide "margin",[77] but was far less categorical in that he linked the existence of the wide "margin" to the time period "very shortly before the period relevant to the present appeal".[78] While the claimant's same-sex relationship did not fall within the ambit of family life *at that time*,[79] Lord Mance had "little doubt" that were a similar question to arise based on contemporary circumstances, it "could well be regarded, in both Strasbourg and the United Kingdom, as involving family life for the purposes of [A]rticle 8."[80]

By contrast, Lord Walker (with whom Lord Bingham agreed[81]) was more ambiguous. As a general matter, after noting the somewhat open-ended nature of Art.8 and the fact that the ambits of the "private life" and "family life" limbs seemed to have been extended in some cases, he suggested that "private life" limb hinged on a failure to show *respect* for the claimant,[82] and to be invoked, the "family life" limb required a very close connection with family life.[83] In reviewing the relevant Strasbourg case law,[84] Lord Walker noted *Estevez*[85] but did not rely upon it, and was willing to *assume* that the claimant and her female partner, taken together with their children from previous marriages, counted as a family for Art.8 purposes.[86] However, he did not believe that the 1991 Act was closely enough connected with family life to bring Art.8 (and in consequence Art.14) into play. Baroness Hale, who dis-

[73] Also significant are their Lordships' observations on how to evaluate whether complained of discrimination falls within the ambit of another Convention right, thus bringing Art.14 into play: compare Lord Nicholls, paras [10]–[14], Lord Walker, paras [56]–[63], [82]–[84], Baroness Hale, paras [105]–[106], [111], Lord Mance, para.[124]; for more general discussion of this question, see Robert Wintemute, "'Within the Ambit': How Big *Is* the 'Gap' in Article 14 European Convention on Human Rights?" [2004] E.H.R.L.R. 366, Aaron Baker, "The Enjoyment of Rights and Freedoms: A New Conception of the 'Ambit' under Article 14 ECHR" (2006) 69 M.L.R. 714.

[74] paras [24], [25], [28].

[75] para.[26]; note also the assertion at para.[28] that *Karner* adds nothing to the issue.

[76] para.[34].

[77] paras [133] and [134] (citing *Frette*).

[78] para.[133].

[79] para.[155].

[80] para.[152].

[81] paras [1], [4]–[6].

[82] para.[83]; Lord Walker characterized the criminalization of consensual sexual activity (as in *Dudgeon*) or humiliating dismissal from the armed forces after an intrusive investigation (as in *Smith*) as examples of failures to show respect.

[83] para.[84].

[84] paras [64]–[84]. Note the discussion of *Frette* and *Karner* at paras [78] and [79].

[85] para.[75].

[86] para.[87].

sented, was clear that the case fell within the scope of family life. She argued that *Karner* demonstrated the existence of a narrow margin of appreciation in Art.14 cases involving discrimination on the basis of sexual orientation,[87] and accepted (by implication) the logical implication of *Salgueiro* when she stated that while the Strasbourg Court had:

"not yet recognised that the relationship between two adult homosexuals amounts to family life.... I know of no case in which it has recognised that the relationship between two adult unmarried heterosexuals amounts to family life. Family life has so far been confined to the relationships between married couples and between parents or other relatives and carers and their children. This includes the relationship between a [...] [gay] [...] parent and his children and between a same sex couple and the children of their family."[88]

Finally, when testing whether the 1991 Act's provisions could be justified (she held that they could not), Baroness Hale reiterated a point she made in *Ghadian* by noting that while *Karner* treats the protection of the traditional family as a weighty aim, it had to be shown that the exclusion of same sex couples from a particular benefit was necessary to achieve *that* aim:

"No one has yet explained how failing to recognise the relationships of people whose sexual orientation means that they are unable or strongly unwilling to marry is necessary for the purpose of protecting or encouraging the marriage of people who are quite capable of marrying if they wish to do so."[89]

The four majority judgments relied heavily upon the margin of appreciation. Lord Nicholls, after stating that the current "margin" in this area was a wide one, nonetheless went on to accept that in the light of the fast-developing state of the law on same-sex partnerships, there would come a time when a sufficiently developed consensus emerged in Convention states, enabling the Strasbourg Court to remove that "margin" and recognise that *Estevez* had been overtaken.[90] Lord Walker, by contrast, emphasized that the width of the "margin" was already changing.[91] He thus accepted that "No right-minded person would now say that discrimination against homosexuals was ever justifiable", but stressed that this was "by today's standards" and that in past centuries a same-sex couple would have faced severe social and legal sanctions.[92] Prior to the coming into force of the CPA, it was therefore within the United Kingdom's "margin" to determine whether to treat a same-sex couple

[87] para.[102].
[88] para.[112].
[89] para.[113]; note, more generally, paras [113]–[117], echoing *Ghaidan*, paras [138]–[143].
[90] paras [30], [34].
[91] paras [91]–[96]; this follows from Lord Walker's discussion of the Court of Appeal's treatment of the "margin": para.[85].
[92] para.[95].

as a family unit or as two individuals for social security purposes.[93] In similar vein, but without openly mentioning the margin, Lord Bingham suggested that a new consensus about same-sex partnerships had been formed with the CPA, and that a litigant could properly complain if a discriminatory regime was to be established today; however, it would be unrealistic to condemn a regime established in 1991.[94] Lord Mance also stressed that "any Court considering the current scope of [A]rticle 8(1) would take most careful account" of the continuing social and legal changes in Convention states in the past five years, and that the position today was quite different from that in play when the facts of the case arose.[95]

We discuss in Section VII the relevance of the House of Lords' analysis of the margin of appreciation in *M.* for any argument concerning the compatibility with the Convention of the distinction between marriage and civil partnership established in domestic law by the CPA. For the moment, it is sufficient to note that *M.* leaves domestic case law in an ambiguous position concerning the application of the family life limb of Art.8 to same-sex couples. This will remain important on an on-going basis given that s.3(1) of the Human Rights Act 1998 requires that legislation, including the CPA, be interpreted in the light of Convention rights so far as this is possible.

C. *Articles 12 and 14*

European Convention on Human Rights, Art.12

(1). Men and women of full age, without any limitation due to race, nationality or religion, have the right to marry and found a family. They are entitled to equal rights as to marriage, during marriage and at its dissolution.

Article 12 stipulates that *men and women* of marriageable age have the right to marry and found a family *according to the national laws* governing the exercise of such a right. Although the boundaries of the definition of "family" are, as we saw in relation to Art.8, open to dispute, the very drafting of Art.12 identifies marriage with persons of opposite sexes rather than of the same sex.[96] In addition, the Article's reference to "national laws" appears to leave it to the signatory states to formulate rules governing capacity to marry, an area in which states enjoy a wide margin of appreciation.[97] Richard Clayton and Hugh Tomlinson also suggest, by reference to the Strasbourg case law, that

93 para.[96].

94 para.[6].

95 para.[152]. For more general discussion of the importance of timing, see paras [152]–[156].

96 See, at national level, Baroness Hale in *Ghaidan v Godin-Mendoza*, para.[138]. The dissenting opinion of Mr Schermers in relation to the Commission Decision in *W v United Kingdom* (1989) 63 D.R. 34, 48 is not a strong counter-example.

97 Clayton & Tomlinson, *The Law of Human Rights, ibid.* para.13.73.

Art.12 "means that the Convention confers preferential status to the traditional marriage. Married couples are, therefore, not treated as being in an analogous position with unmarried couples in relation to their right to found a family or where complaints of discrimination are made concerning differential tax regimes or differences in their parental rights".[98]

The Strasbourg level Art.12 case law has, however, involved significant developments in the area of gender identity discrimination. Departing from a stream of previous cases, the Court of Human Rights recognized in *Goodwin v United Kingdom* that post-operative transsexuals may invoke Art.12 to challenge national laws which deny them the right to marry a person of the sex opposite to their reassigned sex,[99] a development which carries with it the right to have one's physical sex post-gender reassignment recognised as one's "official" sex for legal purposes. In *Bellinger v Bellinger*, the House of Lords relied on *Goodwin* when ruling that s.11(c) of the Matrimonial Causes Act 1973, which restricted the right to marry in national law to men and women defined as such according to the sex registered on their birth certificate, was incompatible with the Convention.[100] *Goodwin* appears to have turned on the margin of appreciation: in its earlier case law concerning gender identity, the Court had found that transsexuals did not enjoy the protection of Art.12 when it came to marriage, and pointed to the lack of consensus among signatory states and the fact that a wide margin of appreciation was open to them.[101] It was only after changes in the national laws of many Convention signatory states that the Court reversed its stance in *Goodwin*. Furthermore, the Court stressed in *Goodwin* that Art.12 protects the right of *men and women* to marry[102]—suggesting that the inclusion of post-operative transsexuals within its scope reflects the fact that the parties *are now of* opposite sexes, rather than any broader attempt by the Court to deconstruct traditional notions of "male" and "female".

These points might suggest that Art.12, considered alone, may not at present offer much support for arguments that Convention states are obliged to recognise same-sex marriage. *Goodwin* suggests that Art.12 tends to follow trends at national level relating to the right to marriage, rather than to lead the way. Furthermore, while an Art.14 claim may be allied to Art.12, there have been very few practical examples of this happening at Strasbourg level: in *B and L v United Kingdom*, for example, the Court asserted in two paragraphs that the applicant's claim based on Art.14 coupled with Art.12 raised no separate issues to their argument based on Art.12 considered alone.[103] We return to this issue below when considering civil partnership in domestic law.

98 *ibid.*, para.13.71.
99 (2002) 35 EHRR 447, paras 100 to 104.
100 [2003] UKHL 21.
101 *Rees v United Kingdom* (1986) 9 EHRR 56; *Cossey v United Kingdom* (1990) 13 E.H.R.R. 622; and *Sheffield and Horsham v United Kingdom* (1998) 27 E.H.R.R. 163.
102 para.98.
103 September 13, 2005, paras 42–3.

D. *Conclusion*

It is clear that the Strasbourg case law has developed significantly, beginning with the criminal prohibition of consenting sexual activity and moving into the field of same-sex partnership rights, while recognising the right of those who have undergone gender reassignment to be registered with their reassigned sex despite its earlier refusal to do so. Nonetheless, the case law contains many uncertainties: not least, those relating to the family life limb of Art.8, the boundary between private life and family life within that Article, and the relationship between Arts 8 and 14. Furthermore, the role of the margin of appreciation makes it particularly difficult to determine how the case law is likely to develop in future.[104] Nonetheless, its influence on national law (most recently through the Human Rights Act 1998) cannot be denied. As we shall see below, despite its uncertainties, the Strasbourg case law is important to any interpretation of significant national legislation such as the Civil Partnership Act 2004.

VI. The European Union

EU Law has a narrower application than the European Convention, focusing to date on sexual orientation- and gender identity-based discrimination in the employment context.

Article 13 EC, which entered into force via the Treaty of Amsterdam in 1999, allows European Community institutions to legislate to combat discrimination based on (among other grounds) sexual orientation, and the Employment Equality Directive (Directive 2000/78/EC), adopted to give effect to that Article (Art.13 EC being thought to lack direct effect in its own right[105]), precludes direct and indirect discrimination on the ground of sexual orientation, as well as harassment and the victimisation of complainants. This Directive is confined to discrimination in the context of employment (see Chapter 2) and its drafting raises several significant questions about the ambit of the protections which it offers. An important additional question is raised by pre-existing EU case law. Prior to the passage of the Directive, a trio of cases—*P v S and Cornwall CC*,[106] *Grant v South-West Trains*[107] and *D and Sweden v Council*[108]—had established that discrimination on the basis of gender identity *was* a form of impermissible sex discrimination (contrary to the Equal Treatment Directive/

[104] See Robert Wintemute, "Strasbourg to the Rescue? Same-Sex Partners and Parents Under the European Convention", *ibid.*

[105] Mark Bell, *Anti-Discrimination Law and the European Union*, p.125.

[106] Case C-13/94, [1996] E.C.R. I-2143.

[107] Case C-249/96, [1998] E.C.R. I-621.

[108] Cases C-122/99P and C-125/99P, [2001] ECR I-4139.

Art.141 EC) but that discrimination on the basis of sexual orientation, including the denial of employment benefits to the same-sex partner of a company's or an EU institution's employee (within the scope of the EU Staff Regulations), was not. Since sexual orientation-related cases can now be litigated using the European Equality Directive, the significance of *Grant*—as Mark Bell has put it—might seem at first sight to be that it is "historically interesting, but not so important in the long run".[109] In fact, however, dicta from these cases may remain (depending, in part, on one's reading of the Court's later decision in *KB v National Health Service Pensions Agency and Secretary of State for Health*[110]) relevant when considering the possible application of the Employment Equality Directive in cases concerning employment-related benefits granted to the same-sex partners of employees, and—perhaps more significantly—in relation to obstacles posed by the denial of partnership-related benefits to employees or service-providers with same-sex partners who wish to travel to take up employment (or provide services) in other EU member states. The provisions of the European Equality Directive have been given effect in national law under the Employment Equality (Sexual Orientation) Regulations 2003, which are considered below. By considering the role of and questions posed by the European Equality Directive at a "purely" European level in this section, we can establish—given the supremacy of EU law and the principle of direct effect (see Chapter 2)—a framework for considering the questions which are likely to be faced by national courts. A useful starting point, before considering the European Equality Directive, is to examine *P, Grant, D and KB* in further detail.[111]

A. The background case law: *P. v S., Grant, D. v Council* and *K.B.*

In *P v S and Cornwall CC*, the dismissal of a transsexual employee who was about to undergo gender reassignment—an example of direct discrimination due to gender identity—was found to constitute impermissible sex discrimination contrary to the Equal Treatment Directive. Tesauro A. G. suggested that the Community law principle of equality meant that "connotations

[109] *Anti-Discrimination Law and the European Union*, p.110. The relationship between sex discrimination, sexual orientation discrimination and gender identity discrimination is considered in Section IX below.

[110] Case C-117/01, [2004] E.C.R.-I [541].

[111] See, generally, Evelyn Ellis, *EU Anti-Discrimination Law* (Oxford: Oxford University Press, 2005), pp.25–8; Catherine Barnard, *EC Employment Law* (Oxford: Oxford University Press, 3rd edn., 2006), pp.384–6; Takis Tridimas, *The General Principles of EU Law* (Oxford: Oxford University Press, 2nd edn., 2006), pp.104–111; Catherine Barnard, "*P.* v *S.*: Kite Flying or a New Constitutional Approach?", Ch. IV in Alan Dashwood and Siofra O'Leary (eds.), *The Principle of Equal Treatment in EC Law* (London: Sweet & Maxwell, 1997); Mark Bell, *Anti-Discrimination Law and the European Union*, pp. 97–120; Robert Wintemute, "Recognising New Kinds of Direct Sex Discrimination: Transsexualism, Sexual Orientation and Dress Codes" (1997) 60 M.L.R. 334; Nicholas Bamforth, "Sexual Orientation Discrimination after *Grant v South-west Trains*" (2000) 63 M.L.R. 694.

relating to sex and/or sexual identity cannot be in any way relevant" in assessing an employee's suitability for continued employment.[112] In turn, the Court of Justice asserted in its judgment that the Directive's scope could not be confined "simply to discrimination based on the fact that a person is of one sex or the other sex. In view of its purpose and the nature of the rights which it seeks to safeguard, the scope of the Directive is also to apply to discrimination arising, as in this case, from the gender reassignment of the person concerned",[113] such discrimination being based "essentially if not exclusively, on the sex of the person concerned".[114] Dismissal of such a person was thus contrary to Art. 5(1) of the Directive unless it could be justified under Art. 5(1), a conclusion which would in logic seem also to apply to a refusal to apply someone who has undergone or is about to undergo gender reassignment.

While the "essentially if not exclusively" formulation in *P* appears at first sight broad enough to bring instances of direct sexual orientation discrimination within the ambit of prohibited sex discrimination, the Court adopted a narrower view in *Grant* and *D*. In *Grant*, the defendant employer refused to grant an employment-related benefit to the long-term same-sex partner of the claimant, an employee, despite granting the benefit to long-term opposite sex partners of employees including the claimant's predecessor in post. The claimant, relying on *P*, challenged the refusal as an instance of direct sex discrimination contrary to Art.141 EC (which guarantees equal pay, regardless of sex, for equal work or work of equal value) or Directive 75/117 (the Equal Pay Directive), given that the only difference between her predecessor and herself was one of sex: her predecessor was a man with a female partner, whereas she was a woman.[115] While Advocate General Elmer accepted the claimant's arguments in his Opinion, the Court reached the opposite conclusion.

Case C-249/96, *Grant v South-west Trains Ltd* [1998] E.C.R. I-621

[25] "... it should be observed that the regulations of the undertaking in which Ms Grant works provide for travel concessions for the worker, for the worker's "spouse", that is, the person to whom he or she is married and from whom he or she is not legally separated, or the person of the opposite sex with whom he or she has had a "meaningful" relationship for at least two years, and for the children, dependent members of the family, and surviving spouse of the worker.

[26] The refusal to allow Ms Grant the concessions is based on the fact that she does not satisfy the conditions prescribed in those regulations, more particularly on the fact that she does not live with a "spouse" or a person of the opposite sex with whom she has had a "meaningful" relationship for at least two years.

112 *P v S and Cornwall, ibid.*, Advocate-General's Opinion, para.[19].
113 para.[20].
114 para.[21].
115 The Court accepted that the benefit in question constituted pay: para.[14].

> **[27]** That condition, the effect of which is that the worker must live in a stable relationship with a person of the opposite sex in order to benefit from the travel concessions, is, like the other alternative conditions prescribed in the undertaking's regulations, applied regardless of the sex of the worker concerned. Thus travel concessions are refused to a male worker if he is living with a person of the same sex, just as they are to a female worker if she is living with a person of the same sex.
> **[28]** Since the condition imposed by the undertaking's regulations applies in the same way to female and male workers, it cannot be regarded as constituting discrimination directly based on sex."

As a broader matter, the Court also asked itself whether Community law nonetheless "requires that stable relationships between two persons of the same sex should be regarded by all employers as equivalent to marriages or stable relationships outside marriage between two persons of opposite sex".[116] Its answer was in the negative. The laws of the Member States did not generally treat same-sex relationships as equivalent to marriage,[117] the Commission on Human Rights (then still in existence) did not treat stable same-sex relationships as falling within the scope of family life as protected by Art.8 of the Convention,[118] while the Court of Human Rights (which at the time had not yet decided *Goodwin v United Kingdom*) had interpreted the right to marry, protected by Art.12, as "applying only to the traditional marriage between two persons of opposite biological sex".[119] The Court of Justice thus concluded that:

> **[35]** "... in the present state of the law within the Community, stable relationships between two persons of the same sex are not regarded as equivalent to marriages or stable relationships outside marriage between persons of opposite sex. Consequently, an employer is not required by Community law to treat the situation of a person who has a stable relationship with a partner of the same sex as equivalent to that of a person who is married to or has a stable relationship outside marriage with a partner of the opposite sex.
> **[36]** In those circumstances, it is for the legislature alone to adopt, if appropriate, measures which may affect that position."

The Court was clear, albeit without offering any explanation, that its conclusion in *P* that dismissal due to gender reassignment was based "essentially if not exclusively" on sex was limited to cases of gender reassignment and did not apply to differences of treatment based on a person's sexual orientation.[120] *Grant* thus established, albeit without clear explanation, a distinction between the Court's apparently sympathetic treatment of gender identity-related discrimination in employment, and its much more cautious—if not conservative—attitude to claims relating to sexual orientation and/or partnership rights. This caution might well be reflected in the Court's curious use of Convention case law, in so far as it invoked decisions concerning the definition

116 paras [24], [29].
117 para.[32].
118 para.[33].
119 para.[34]. This assertion was based on the Court's judgments in *Rees v United Kingdom* (1986) 9 E.H.R.R. 56 and *Cossey v United Kingdom* (1990) 13 E.H.R.R. 622.
120 para.[42].

of marriage when what was at issue in *Grant* was an employment benefit that was available to cohabiting partners *as well as* those who were married. To associate the case with the very definition of marriage was unnecessary, and had the effect of raising the stakes in a way which is unhelpful to litigants faced with hostile national laws. Furthermore, the Court of Human Rights decisions cited—*Rees* and *Cossey*—both concerned the right of *transsexuals* to marry: in other words, a gender identity-question rather than (as the Court of Justice characterised it in *Grant*) the "separate" question of the right of lesbians and gay men.

A similarly cautious attitude was evident in *D*, where the claimant, a Community official who had entered into a registered same-sex partnership in his home country (Sweden), argued that he was entitled to the household allowance granted to married officials under Annex VII to the Staff Regulations of Officials of the European Communities. The Court began by drawing a distinction between the claimant in *Grant*, who had not been in a *formally* recognised partnership, and the claimant in *D*, who was—a move which might be felt, given that the Court then found against the claimant, to highlight the totality of its exclusion of same-sex couples from the protections offered to others.

Cases C-122/99P and C-125/99P, *D and Sweden v Council* [2001] E.C.R. I-4139

[33] "... the question whether the concepts of marriage and registered partnership should be treated as distinct or equivalent for the purposes of interpreting the Staff Regulations has not until now been resolved by the Court of Justice. As the appellants contend, a stable relationship between partners of the same sex which has only a *de facto* existence, as was the case in *Grant* ... is not necessarily equivalent to a registered partnership under a statutory arrangement, which, as between the persons concerned and as regards third parties, has effects in law akin to those of marriage since it is intended to be comparable.

[34] It is not in question that, according to the definition generally accepted by the Member States, the term 'marriage' means a union between two persons of the opposite sex.

[35] It is equally true that since 1989 an increasing number of Member States have introduced, alongside marriage, statutory arrangements granting legal recognition to various forms of union between partners of the same sex or of the opposite sex and conferring on such unions certain effects which, both between the partners and as regards third parties, are the same as or comparable to those of marriage.

[36] It is clear, however, that apart from their great diversity, such arrangements for registering relationships between couples not previously recognised in law are regarded in the Member States concerned as being distinct from marriage.

[37] In such circumstances the Community judicature cannot interpret the Staff Regulations in such a way that legal situations distinct from marriage are treated in the same way as marriage. The intention of the Community legislature was to grant entitlement to the household allowance under Article 1(2)(a) of Annex VII to the Staff Regulations only to married couples.

[38] Only the legislature can, where appropriate, adopt measures to alter that situation, for example by amending the provisions of the Staff Regulations. . . .

[39] It follows that the fact that, in a limited number of Member States, a registered partnership is assimilated, although incompletely, to marriage cannot have the consequence that, by mere interpretation, persons whose legal status is distinct from that of marriage can be covered by the term 'married official as used in the Staff Regulations.''

As should be clear from *Grant* and *D*, the Court placed considerable weight on what it perceived to be the consensus among the Member States. We return below to how far this consensus might have shifted in favour of same-sex partnership rights in the years since both cases were decided. Even if the consensus has shifted, however, these cases (perhaps particularly *D*, given that the claimant's relationship was registered in national law) raise the broader question of whether the Court of Justice would ever be willing to grant protection to same-sex couples going beyond the text of what was clearly included within EU legislation—an issue which remains just as relevant after the passage of the Employment Equality Directive as it was before. The Court of Justice also rejected on the facts the claimant's argument based on Art.8 of the Convention,[121] but without going so far as the Court of First instance, which ruled—erroneously, it should be noted, given the Art.8 case law discussed in the previous section—that same sex partnerships fell outside the right to respect to private life protected by Art.8.[122]

In *KB*, the Court had to consider whether an employer's refusal to accept that the female-to-male transsexual partner of a female employee could be nominated to receive benefits as a ''widower'' under an employment pension scheme constituted sex discrimination contrary to Art.141 EC and Directive 75/117 (the Equal Pay Directive). As such, the case appeared directly to confront the Court with the apparent tension between its willingness to prohibit gender identity-related discrimination in *P v S* and its more cautious, if not conservative, attitude to partnership rights in *Grant* and *D*. This point is clear from the arguments advanced by the parties. On the one hand, the claimant presented two arguments based on *P v S*: first, that her partner's exclusion from the scheme was due solely to the fact that he had undergone gender reassignment, contravening *P v S* presumably as an instance of direct sex discrimination;[123] and secondly, that the requirement that a beneficiary

121 paras [58]–[61]. The claimant argued, perhaps rather tenuously, that the transmission of incorrect information concerning his marital status (i.e. that he was unmarried rather than, as according to national law, married) violated his Article 8 right to family life, same-sex partnerships falling within that part of Art.8.

122 para.[14].

123 paras [17]–[18]. The Court accepted at para [27], following Case C-262/88, *Barber* [1990] E.C.R. I-1889, para.[28], Case C-351/00, Case C-109/91, *Ten Oever* [1993] E.C.R. I-4879, paras [12] and [13], and Case C-379/99, *Menauer* [2001] E.C.R. I-7275, para.[18], and *Niemi* [2002] ECR I-7007, para.[40], that a survivor's pension paid under an occupational pension scheme constituted pay within the meaning of Art.141 EC and Directive 75/117.

under the scheme be *married* to an employee constituted indirect sex discrimination since, as the case arose prior to the Gender Recognition Act 2004, the marriage requirement could never be met by a heterosexual couple one of whose members had undergone gender reassignment surgery (by contrast with a heterosexual couple neither of whose members had done so).[124] On the other hand, the national government argued that the exclusion of the claimant's partner turned on the fact that the two were not married, and that the reason for their unmarried state (i.e. that national law prevented them from marrying) was, by analogy with *Grant* and *D*, irrelevant.[125] The Commission, intervening, sought to go still further. It argued first that *P v S* could be distinguished since the unfavourable treatment in that case had arisen directly from the claimant's gender reassignment, whereas in the present case it was a step further removed, arising from the definition of marriage in national law; and secondly, that *Grant* implicitly recognised that the definition of marriage fell within the scope of family law, which was reserved to the Member States.[126]

The Court's judgment looks a little like an attempt to juggle between these competing perspectives. The reasoning can be divided into four stages. First, the Court appeared to echo the national government and the Commission by applying *Grant* and *D* and emphasising the importance of deference to the Community legislature and national courts in relation to partnership rights.

Case C-117/01, *KB v National Health Service Pensions Agency, Secretary of State for Health* [2004] E.C.R. I-

[28] "The decision to restrict certain benefits to married couples while excluding all persons who live together without being married is either a matter for the legislature to decide or a matter for the national courts as to the interpretation of domestic legal rules, and individuals cannot claim that there is discrimination on grounds of sex, prohibited by Community law (see, as regards the powers of the Community legislature, *D. v Council*, paras [37] and [38]).

[29] In this instance, such a requirement cannot be regarded *per se* as discriminatory on grounds of sex and, accordingly, as contrary to Article 141 EC or Directive 75/117, since for the purposes of awarding the survivor's pension it is irrelevant whether the claimant is a man or a woman."

However, the Court appeared secondly to recognize the force of the claimant's indirect discrimination argument:

[30] "... in a situation such as that before the national court, there is inequality of

124 para.[19].
125 paras [20] and [21].
126 paras [22] to [24].

treatment which, although it does not directly undermine enjoyment of a right protected by Community law, affects one of the conditions for the grant of that right . . . the inequality of treatment does not relate to the award of a widower's pension but to a necessary precondition for the grant of such a pension: namely, the capacity to marry.

[31] In the United Kingdom, by comparison with a heterosexual couple where neither partner's identity is the result of gender reassignment surgery and the couple are therefore able to marry and, as the case may be, have the benefit of a survivor's pension which forms part of the pay of one of them, a couple such as [the claimant and her partner] are quite unable to satisfy the marriage requirement, as laid down by the [employer's] Pension Scheme for the purpose of the award of a survivor's pension."

The Court also noted that the "fact that it is impossible for them to marry" was due to the definition of marriage in force in national law at the time when the case arose, and the operation of the register of births and deaths at that point.[127]

The third stage of the Court's reasoning is possibly the most significant. For it used the Court of Human Rights' decision in *Goodwin* (discussed in the previous section) to suggest that a decision in favour of the claimant was in principle possible.

[33] "The European Court of Human Rights has held [in *Goodwin*] that the fact that it is impossible for a transsexual to marry a person of the sex to which he or she belonged prior to gender reassignment surgery, which arises because, for the purposes of the registers of civil status, they belong to the same sex (United Kingdom legislation not admitting of legal recognition of transsexuals' new identity), was a breach of their right to marry under Article 12 of the ECHR . . .

[34] Legislation, such as that at issue in the main proceedings, which, in breach of the ECHR, prevents a couple such as [the claimant and her partner] from fulfilling the marriage requirement which must be met for one of them to be able to benefit from part of the pay of the other must be regarded as being, in principle, incompatible with the requirements of Article 141 EC."

However, despite this strong assertion, the Court fourthly brought the Commission's argument about the jurisdiction of national law over marriage back into play and asserted that the matter was ultimately one for national courts to determine.

[35] "Since it is for the Member States to determine the conditions under which legal recognition is given to the change of gender of a [transsexual] person . . .—as the European Court of Human Rights has accepted (*Goodwin v United Kingdom* . . .)—it is for the national court to determine whether in a case such as that in the main proceedings a person in [the claimant's] situation can rely on Article 141 EC in order to gain recognition of her right to nominate her partner as the beneficiary of a survivor's pension.

[36] It follows from the foregoing that Article 141 EC, in principle, precludes legislation, such as that at issue before the national court, which, in breach of the ECHR, prevents a couple such as [the claimant and her partner] from fulfilling the marriage requirement which must be met for one of them to be able to benefit from part of the pay of the other. It is for the national court to determine whether in a case such as that in the main pro-

[127] para.[32].

ceedings a person in [the claimant's] situation can rely on Article 141 EC in order to gain recognition of her right to nominate her partner as the beneficiary of a survivor's pension."

Within the United Kingdom, a situation such as that in *KB* would now be covered by the Gender Recognition Act 2004 (see section below). However, three aspects of the case are interesting for present purposes. The first is what looks to be the Court's fence-sitting approach, captured in the simultaneous presence of the statements beginning "It follows from ... in principle" and "It is for the national court to determine ..." in the paragraph just cited. The paragraph clearly goes beyond the position that partnership rights are *solely* reserved to national courts (otherwise, the words "in principle" would make no sense), while simultaneously urging national courts to keep cases concerning partnership issues at national level ("It is for the national courts to determine ..."). Secondly, the Court relied on the changing Convention case law as a way of showing that the "consensus" concerning the partnership rights of transsexuals among sources of authority on which it could rely had become more liberal, thus allowing it to make its "in principle" statement and avoid rejecting the claimant's arguments outright. Thirdly, despite avoiding the need to make an overt choice between the liberal attitude of *P v S* and the caution of *Grant* and *D*, and despite the Court's co-opting arguments from both sides in its decision, the judgment in *KB* implies that the distinction between gender identity and sexual orientation remains firmly entrenched in the Court of Justice's case law. Furthermore, the reliance placed on the Strasbourg Court's decision in *Goodwin* arguably suggests that any "softening" of approach in claims concerning employment benefits for same-sex partners (including in cases brought under the Employment Equality Directive) might require—given that *Goodwin* involved a reversal of the Strasbourg Court's previous position concerning the ability of transsexuals to be registered with their reassigned sex, and in consequence to marry—a Strasbourg decision of equivalent clarity in favour of same-sex partnership rights. Having said this, however, since it was the pre-*Goodwin* case law concerning gender identity which the Court of Justice employed in *Grant* when discussing same-sex partnerships, it is perhaps also arguable that the shift of position at Strasbourg level in *Goodwin* should itself have a knock-on effect in the Court of Justice in relation to same-sex partnership rights.

B. *The Employment Equality Directive*

Gender identity discrimination continues to be dealt with, under Community law, as an instance of sex discrimination—whether in relation to equal pay or equal treatment. However, direct discrimination, indirect discrimination, harassment and instructions to discriminate on the basis of a person's sexual orientation are now precluded under the Employment Equality Directive.[128]

[128] Arts 2(1) to 2(4); for general discussion of these provisions, see Ch.2.

The Employment Equality Directive's prohibition applies to "all persons, as regards both the public and private sectors", and does so in relation to conditions for access to employment, self-employment or occupation, including selection criteria and recruitment conditions, including promotion; access to vocational guidance and training and retraining, including practical work experience; employment and working conditions, including dismissals and pay; and membership of and involvement in workers' or employers' organisations, or any organisation whose members carry on a particular profession, including benefits provided by such organisations.[129] However, the Directive does not apply to payments made by state schemes, including social security or social protection schemes,[130] does not cover differences of treatment based on nationality,[131] and according to Art.2(5) is "without prejudice to measures laid down by national law which, in a democratic society, are necessary for public security, for the maintenance of public order and the prevention of criminal offences, for the protection of health and for the protection of the rights and freedoms of others". According to Art.4(1), member states may also provide that a difference of treatment based on sexual orientation is not discriminatory where, "by reason of the nature of the particular occupational activities concerned or of the context in which they are carried out, such a characteristic constitutes a genuine and determining occupational requirement, provided that the objective is legitimate and the requirement is proportionate". More specifically, Art.4(2), considered in detail below, allows for certain exceptions where the employer is a church or other organisation based on religion or belief. As with the other grounds of discrimination precluded under the Employment Equality Directive, member states may engage in positive action to prevent or compensate for material disadvantages linked to sexual orientation,[132] and the Directive's standard burden of proof and anti-victimisation provisions apply in cases of sexual orientation discrimination.[133]

We considered some of the general questions posed by the drafting of the Directive, as well as its treatment of direct discrimination, indirect discrimination and harassment, and the operation of the proportionality and genuine occupational requirement standards, in Ch.2. In addition to questions arising under these headings, Mark Bell has raised four concerns which relate specifically to the Directive's treatment of sexual orientation.[134] The first relates to the burden of proof. As we have noted, the Employment Equality Directive's general burden of proof standard applies in sexual orientation cases. However,

[129] Art.3.

[130] Art.3(3). See also Recital 13: "This Directive does not apply ... to any kind of payment by the State aimed at providing access to employment or maintaining employment".

[131] Art.3(2).

[132] Art.7(1).

[133] Arts 10 and 11, respectively.

[134] See also Paul Skidmore, "The EC Framework Directive on Equal Treatment in Employment: towards a comprehensive Community anti-discrimination policy?" (2001) 30 I.L.J. 126.

Mark Bell
***Anti-Discrimination Law and the European Union* (Oxford: Oxford University Press, 2002)**

p.115 "the Employment Equality Directive, Recital 31, adds that 'it is not for the respondent to prove that the plaintiff adheres to a particular religion or belief, has a particular disability, is of a particular age or has a particular sexual orientation'. This suggests that there may be situations where individuals are required to 'prove' their sexual orientation. This is quite disturbing as it creates an obvious conflict with privacy rights and it could deter many individuals from litigating. A better view would be that sexual orientation discrimination occurs where the employer or any other person discriminates on the basis of an assumption regarding a person's sexual orientation. For example, an employer might refuse to employ a man because he or she thinks that the man in question is gay. For discrimination law, it seems irrelevant whether the man actually is gay or not; in either case, he has suffered discrimination based on (perceived) sexual orientation and the detriment is no less real. The Employment Equality Directive does not explicitly deal with the issue, but Article 2(1) states that any discrimination 'whatsoever' on grounds of sexual orientation is prohibited. This formulation appears sufficiently broad to include discrimination based on perceived sexual orientation."

If Bell's argument is correct, then the text of the Directive may provide an answer to the burden of proof concern.

Bell's second concern relates to the "without prejudice" provision in Art.2(5), which appears to draw on the wording of the European Convention on Human Rights. Bell notes that:

Mark Bell
***Anti-Discrimination Law and the European Union* (Oxford: Oxford University Press, 2002)**

pp.115–16 "This provision was only inserted in[to] the Directive late in its negotiation and its intended purpose is not immediately apparent. From the perspective of sexual orientation, it may be aimed at reassuring national law makers (and the general public) that a ban on sexual orientation discrimination cannot be interpreted as according protection to paedophiles or other persons engaging in unlawful sexual behaviour. However, the breadth of the exception raises the possibility of an extended application. For example, it is conceivable that certain Member States might attempt to rely on this provision to defend restrictions on the expression of homosexuality within the armed forces. The scope of Article 2(5) will be ultimately a matter for the Court of Justice to determine, but it introduces an unwelcome area of ambiguity."

A third concern voiced by Bell relates to Art.4(2)'s treatment of the relationship between discrimination on the basis of religion or belief and discrimination on the basis of sexual orientation. The potential for conflict between these two grounds of prohibited discrimination has already become an issue in national law, and we explore it further below and in ch.9. To understand Bell's argument concerning the Directive, it is necessary to set out the wording of Art.4(2).

Employment Equality Directive, Art.4(2)

"Member States may maintain national legislation in force at the date of adoption of this Directive or provide for future legislation incorporating national practices existing at the date of adoption of this Directive pursuant to which, in the case of occupational activities within churches and other public or private organisations the ethos of which is based on religion or belief, a difference of treatment based on a person's religion or belief shall not constitute discrimination where, by reason of the nature of these activities or of the context in which they are carried out, a person's religion or belief constitute a genuine, legitimate and justified occupational requirement, having regard to the organisation's ethos. This difference of treatment shall be implemented taking account of Member States' constitutional provisions and principles, as well as the general principles of Community law, and should not justify discrimination on another ground.

Provided that its provisions are otherwise complied with, this Directive shall thus not prejudice the right of churches and other public or private organisations, the ethos of which is based on religion or belief, acting in conformity with national constitutions and laws, to require individuals working for them to act in good faith and with loyalty to the organisation's ethos."

Bell observes that:

Mark Bell
Anti-Discrimination Law and the European Union (Oxford: Oxford University Press, 2002)

pp.117–8 "[Article 4(2)] was the subject of intense debate during the negotiation of the Directive, with an active campaign by certain religious lobby groups to have an open-ended exception for religious organisations, or even the deletion of sexual orientation and religion from the Directive altogether. The terms of this exception shifted considerably during the legislative process, and the final text is a complex and cumbersome compromise. Essentially there are three key elements. First, it is important to note that it is not, strictly speaking, an exception to the ban on sexual orientation discrimination. In fact, this is an exception to the prohibition on discrimination on the grounds of religion or belief, and Article 4(2) expressly states that it 'should not justify discrimination on another ground'. At the same time, the reluctance of certain organisations with a religious ethos to employ lesbians and gay men is one of the key reasons why this provision is present in the Directive, and therefore it would be naïve to ignore the connections between the two issues. The Directive does not, however, permit a religious organisation to simply (and overtly) exclude all lesbians and gay men from access to employment.

Second, where it is already permitted in national law or practice, religious organisations will continue to be able to take into account religion or belief in making recruitment decisions, but only if this is necessary to maintain the ethos of the organisation. In deciding whether or not such a difference in treatment is necessary, regard must be had to the specific occupation in question. For example, in selecting a teacher for a religious school, it will be easy to justify taking the religion of a candidate into account if the position in question is a religious education teacher. In contrast, if the position was in, say, maths or chemistry, then the school would need to establish more closely why the teacher needs to share the religion of the organisation. If all teachers were required to undertake certain religious activities—such as prayers with a class at the start of the day or religious counselling with a teacher's individual year group of students—then this might be sufficient to justify religion being a relevant characteristic of teachers in general.

Finally, in respect of existing employees, religious bodies can 'require individuals working for them to act in good faith and with loyalty to the organisation's ethos', although this is subject to compliance with the other provisions of the Directive. The extent of these 'good faith' obligations is not explained elsewhere in the Directive and as this position resulted from an amendment late in the negotiations, there is no other source to account for its meaning. A delicate issue would be the degree to which a religious organisation could require a lesbian or gay employee to keep secret their sexual orientation, or alternatively to refrain from making statements contrary to the official teaching of the religion in question on homosexuality.

The intersection of rights to religious freedom and equal treatment is one of the most difficult areas of the Directive to negotiate. The provisions of the Directive provide some guidance, but equally leave much to be determined by the courts based on the facts of any specific dispute. Both parties to such a case will evidently take the view that their own fundamental right should 'trump' that of the other. However, as the spirit of the Directive indicates, a careful balancing act will be necessary on a case-by-case basis."

A fouth concern relates to marital benefits. Given that this concern was voiced prior to the passage of the Civil Partnership Act 2004, its exact impact now depends upon the extent to which the European Court of Justice might consider that civil partnership is analogous to marriage.

Mark Bell
***Anti-Discrimination Law and the European Union* (Oxford: Oxford University Press, 2002)**

pp.116–7: "As demonstrated by *Grant* and *D v Council*, benefits provided by employers in respect of the members of an individual worker's family are frequently a source of discrimination against lesbian and gay workers. This discrimination takes mainly two forms; denial of benefits to unmarried partners irrespective of sex (*D v Council*), and denial of benefits specifically to same-sex couples (*Grant*). The latter is the most straightforward to challenge as it is direct discrimination on the basis of sexual orientation and the Directive prohibits this. Nonetheless, in many cases—like *D. v Council*—benefits are limited to married couples, thereby creating indirect discrimination on the ground of sexual orientation as lesbians and gay men are placed at a particular disadvantage because they are unable to marry their partners (with the exception of [countries which permit same-sex marriage]).

Although indirectly discriminatory measures are also prohibited by the Directive, they can be 'objectively justified' where there is 'a legitimate aim and the means of achieving that aim are appropriate and necessary'. In respect of benefits available only to married couples, the Member States have strongly indicated that these are to be regarded as objectively justified. Recital 22 in the preamble states 'this Directive is without prejudice to national laws on marital status and the benefits dependent thereon'. As part of the preamble, this is not binding on the Court of Justice. Nonetheless, it is unlikely the Court would disregard such a clear direction in the Directive, especially in the light of its general caution in matters pertaining to marriage and the family.[135]"

We can thus see that, at face value, the [Employment Equality Directive] represents a large step forward in the protection of individuals from sexual orientation discrimination under EU law. However, this statement is subject to qualification in light of the four points raised by Bell. Furthermore, the Directive is silent on the issue of employment-related rights for the same-sex partners of employees, and it seems likely that the influence of *Grant* and *D.* may continue to be felt, given the generality of some of the statements about partnership rights in those cases, in future litigation concerning this issue. It is to this issue which we now turn.

C. *Partnership rights, the Employment Equality Directive, and Freedom of Movement*

As Mark Bell has noted:

"the heated debates over whether sexual orientation could be squeezed within the framework of gender discrimination laws could be expected to fade now that specific and separate protection against sexual orientation discrimination exists in Community law."[136]

Nonetheless, Bell suggests that *Grant* remains significant for reasons. First, it confirms the separation in EU law between sex and sexual orientation discrimination: an issue which we consider in Section IX below. Second, the decision could be said, by highlighting the absence of protection for lesbians and gay men under EU law, to have "reinforced the reasons why legislation implementing EC Treaty, Art.13 was essential."[137] Thirdly, and crucially for present purposes, Bell argues that *Grant* laid the foundation for Mischo A.G.'s and the Court's hostility to the claimant's arguments in *D and Sweden v Council*. In *D*, the Advocate-General suggested that same-sex and opposite-sex partnerships were not equivalent within EU law, there being differences "in nature" between same-sex and opposite-sex couples.[138] The European Court of Justice rejected such a sweeping approach, stressing that, by contrast with the claimant in *Grant*, the claimant in *D* had a partnership which was legally recognised under the national law of their home member state. The Court

[135] See also pp. 185–6.

[136] *Anti-Discrimination Law and the European Union*, p.110.

[137] Mark Bell, *Anti-Discrimination Law and the European Union*, p.111.

[138] Cases C-122/99P and C-125/99P, *D and Sweden v Council* [2001] E.C.R. I-4319, para.[87]; see also para.[86]. See generally, Mark Bell, pp.111–2.

nonetheless concluded that, due to the diversity of laws at member state level, the situation of an official with a registered partnership under national law was not the same as that of a married official within the Staff Regulations.[139] Bell uses this to suggest that, while the Court's approach might change as legal recognition of same-sex partnerships becomes more widespread at national level:

"[t]he blindness of the EU Courts to same-sex partnerships appears to be an institutional legacy of *Grant* ... This conservatism must be borne in mind when analysing the possibilities under the "[Employment Equality]" Directive and how the Court of Justice can be expected to interpret areas of ambiguity."[140]

Quite apart from the Court's interpretive attitude to the Directive in general, it must also be remembered that for so long as *D* remains good law, the Community courts would appear to be excluding themselves as a general matter from making discrimination-related assessments of the rights granted to same-sex couples in contrast within opposite-sex couples.

These issues are important in relation to the rights of same-sex partners in EU law more broadly. For there has been considerable argument to the extent that bars on national (or EU-level) recognition of legal rights for same-sex partners constitute an impermissible obstacle to the free movement of an employee, self-employed person or service-provider who wishes to travel from a member state where legal recognition is granted to same-sex couples, to a state where this is not the case. Article 12 EU-based arguments of this type have been powerfully developed by Elspeth Guild and Helen Toner, but have yet to be tested.[141] An obstacle which this otherwise promising argument might face, however, is the hint in *D* that, even outside the context of employment discrimination, same-sex partners are not entitled to equal treatment with opposite-sex partners under EU law.

D. *Conclusion*

In conclusion, we can see that EU law is relevant to sexual orientation and gender identity discrimination in a number of ways. First, gender identity discrimination employment and the provision of goods and services constitutes a form of impermissible sex discrimination. Secondly, direct and indirect sexual orientation discrimination in employment, as well as harass-

139 *D and Sweden v Council*, para [33], [50]–[51].

140 *Anti-Discrimination Law and the European Union*, p.112.

141 Elspeth Guild, "Free Movement and Same-Sex Relationships: Existing EC Law and Article 13 EC", Ch.38 in Robert Wintemute and Mads Andenas (eds.), *Legal Recognition of Same-sex Partnerships, ibid.*; Helen Toner, *Partnership Rights, Free Movement, and EU Law* (Oxford: Hart, 2004).

ment and victimisation, are now precluded under the Employment Equality Directive. Thirdly, however, the provisions of the Directive contain exceptions and ambiguities, especially in relation to justifications for what would otherwise constitute sexual orientation discrimination. Fourthly, pre-existing Court of Justice dicta concerning the entitlements of same-sex partners of employees to employment-related partnership benefits suggest that, while there may be room for argument to be developed before the Court of Justice in this area based upon freedom of movement, clear limits might be placed on the ambit of the Employment Equality Directive by the Court of Justice in relation to partnership rights. Given the rules concerning direct effect and the obligation of national courts to interpret national law in the light of directives, these issues are likely to be of some significance to national courts as well as the European Court of Justice.

VII. Developments in National Law

In section 1, we highlighted the enormous extent to which there has been change at national level in the law's treatment of direct and indirect discrimination on the basis of sexual orientation and gender identity. This point can be further highlighted if we contrast the legal position today—to be discussed in the present section—with that which prevailed even fifteen years ago. As Robert Wintemute has noted:

Robert Wintemute
"Sexual Orientation and Gender Identity", Ch.10 in Colin Harvey (ed.), *Human Rights in the Community: Rights as Agents for Change* (Oxford: Hart Publishing, 2005)

pp.176–7: "Looking back to 1993, very little had been done to ensure equal rights and obligations for LGBT individuals in England and Wales. Although sexual activity between men had been legal since 1967, the age of consent to male-male sexual activity was 21 vs. 16 for male-female or female-female sexual activity, sexual activity involving three or more men was illegal, the armed forces actively excluded LGBT personnel, there was no legislation prohibiting discrimination based on sexual orientation or gender identity in employment, and the infamous Section 28 of the Local Government Act 1998 prohibited 'promot[ing] the teaching ... of the acceptability of homosexuality as a pretended family relationship'. In the case of LGB individuals who formed same-sex partnerships, they could not marry, were denied the rights and obligations of married and unmarried different-sex partners (including succession to the tenancy of a local authority house or flat), and could not adopt each other's children or adopt unrelated children jointly (which was also the case for unmarried different-sex partners).

As for transsexual individuals, they could not have the sex on their birth certificates changed after gender reassignment. If they were heterosexual after gender reassignment, they could not marry a person of the sex opposite to their (non-recognised) reassigned sex or (in the case of transsexual men) be treated as the fathers of their non-transsexual female partners' children by donor insemination. However, if they were LGB after gender reassignment, they *could* marry a person of the same sex as their (non-recognised) reassigned sex and (in the case of transsexual women) be treated as the fathers of their non-transsexual female partners' children by donor insemination. Thus, unlike heterosexual transsexual individuals, LGB transsexual individuals were better off *not* having their gender reassignments recognised, as long as sexual orientation discrimination in relation to marriage and donor insemination persisted."

Some of the recent developments at national level—concerning in particular employment and discrimination on the basis of gender identity—have been prompted by the developments at European Convention or E.U. level discussed in the two preceding sections. However, other developments, in particular the creation of the institution of civil partnership for same-sex couples, have been the product of initiatives purely at national level. We consider five areas in this section. The first, very briefly, is the criminal law, which has moved towards a position of equal treatment when dealing with the sexual behaviour of gay men. A proposal has also been made to prohibit incitement to hatred on the basis of sexual orientation. Such developments involve a combination of domestic initiatives and Convention decisions. Secondly, we consider discrimination in employment, which is now prohibited in the case of sexual orientation under the Employment Equality (Sexual Orientation) Regulations 2003 (Parliament's response to the Employment Equality Directive) and in the case of gender reassignment under the Sex Discrimination (Gender Recognition) Regulations 1999. It will also be noted that, in so far as Convention rights are relevant in the context of public or private employment, legislation must (so far as it is possible) be interpreted so as to preclude such discrimination. Thirdly, we consider the prohibition on discrimination in relation to the provision of goods, facilities and services. Fourthly, we explore other obligations imposed on public authorities not to discriminate on the basis of sexual orientation and gender identity. Fifthly, we explore family and partnership rights. In the case of sexual orientation, these are now covered by the Civil Partnership Act 2004 and associated legislation. The CPA was very much presented as a domestic initiative, and indeed its compatibility with Strasbourg case law, in relation to same sex partners, remains to be tested beyond High Court level. Nonetheless, the Strasbourg case law, and its interpretation at domestic level in cases such as *Ghaidan* and *M.*, remains important for statutory interpretation. We also consider, under this geading, the Gender Recognition Act 2004, which is a Parliamentary response to the Strasbourg case law dealing with gender identity, and in particular to the House of Lords' decision in *Bellinger v Bellinger*.[142]

One general point to note at the outset is the emphasis placed by the House

[142] [2003] UKHL 21.

of Lords in *Ghaidan v Godin-Mendoza* and *R. v Secretary of State for Work and Pensions, ex p. Carson* (see Section V above) on the point that some of the grounds of discrimination precluded by Article 14—including sexual orientation—were more sensitive than others and placed a stronger burden of justification on the respondent.[143] Given that Convention rights may be invoked in cases involving statutory interpretation (under s.3 of the Human Rights Act 1998), interpretation of the common law, and actions against public authorities (under s.6 of the Human Rights Act 1998), this stronger burden of justification will apply in cases involving sexual orientation and Convention rights.

A. *Criminal law*

As Robert Wintemute suggests, "Since 1993, discrimination against same-sex sexual activity in the formulation (as opposed to the enforcement) of the criminal law has gradually been eliminated".[144] Via a series of measures, the age of consent for same-sex sexual activity between men has been reduced from twenty-one to sixteen (the age applicable to heterosexual and lesbian intercourse).[145] Furthermore, the restrictive "in private" condition found in earlier legislation, whereby two men—but not any other combination of persons—could be guilty of a criminal offence if they had sex in a place on which others might stumble, disappeared with the repeal in 2003 of earlier sexual offences legislation.[146] There is now no specific statutory prohibition on those aged sixteen or over, whatever their number or sexes, engaging in consenting

[143] [2005] UKHL 37, paras [15]–[17] (Lord Hoffmann), [55], [57]–[58], [89] (Lord Walker). Lords Nicholls, Rodger and Carswell (*ibid.*, paras [1], [42] and [92]) agreed with both judgments. Lord Hoffmann suggested that discrimination on a sensitive ground could not be justified merely by appeal to a "utilitarian" value such as the general public interest (para [16]), while Lord Walker—echoing the Strasbourg Court—asserted that "very weighty reasons" would be needed. Lord Walker describes the sensitive grounds, by analogy with US 14th Amendment jurisprudence, as "suspect categories" (para.[58]), although his assertion (at para.[55]) that sexual orientation constitutes such a category in U.S. law is, with respect, an over-simplification.

[144] "Sexual Orientation and Gender Identity", *ibid.*, p.177.

[145] See the Sexual Offences (Amendment) Act 2000, s.1 (reduction to sixteen), now superseded by the Sexual Offences Act 2003, ss.1, 2, 9, 10, 13. The earlier reduction to eighteen was made in the Criminal Justice and Public Order Act 1994, ss.143 and 145. The 2000 Act followed the conclusion of the then Commission on Human Rights in *Sutherland v United Kingdom* that unequal ages of consent contravened Articles 8 and 14 of the Convention. In addition, s.146 of the 1994 Act decriminalised consenting homosexual activity in the armed forces (although dismissal from military employment was not prohibited until after the European Court of Human Rights' decisions in *Smith and Grady v United Kingdom* and *Lustig-Preen and Beckett v United Kingdom*.

[146] The legislation followed a Consultation Document issued by the Home Office, entitled *Setting the Boundaries: Reforming the Law on Sex Offences* (London: Home Office, 2000), *http://www.homeoffice.gov.uk/documents/vol1main.pdf*.

sexual activity with each another.[147] However, s.71 of the Sexual Offences Act 2003 makes it an offence to have sex in a public lavatory. While the offence is neutral with regard to the sexes of the defendants, it remains an open question whether, given past history, police practice will be targeted more at same-sex male than at male-female couplings.[148] In addition, the old common law offences of conspiracy to corrupt public morals and conspiracy to outrage public decency, previously targeted at gay men expressing affection for one another in public, remain in force,[149] although it seems unlikely, given the Court of Human Rights' recent case law concerning Articles 8 and 14 of the Convention (discussed in Section V), that these offences could nowadays be interpreted so widely – or, arguably, as even applicable given national courts' duties under ss.3 and 6 of the Human Rights Act 1998. As Wintemute suggests, the "1986 conviction of two men for 'insulting behaviour', consisting of kissing and cuddling at a bus stop at 1.55 am, should no longer be possible".[150] Finally, while the permissibility or otherwise of consenting sado-masochistic sexual activity might seem to be an issue of sexual freedom rather than one of discrimination on the basis of sexual orientation, it should be noted that sado-masochistic sexual activity is a criminal offence when conducted between men (a position supported by the Court of Human Rights),[151] but not when conducted between opposite-sex partners who are married to one another.[152]

Although the social climate in the United Kingdom has undoubtedly become more liberal in the past ten years, lesbians and gay men remains all-too-frequent victims of physical violence and threatening language.[153] The Criminal Justice Act 2003 sought partly to counter this by requiring courts to treat as an aggravating factor when sentencing an offender the fact that they demonstrated hostility towards the victim based on the latter's actual or presumed sexual orientation, or that the offence was wholly or partly motivated by hostility towards persons of a particular sexual orientation.[154] Nonetheless, as Robert Wintemute notes, this only corresponds to "part of" the legislation dealing with religious and racial hatred, since it does not create

[147] See Sch.7 of the Sexual Offences Act 2003 for the repeal of earlier legislation. [on "privacy", see the cases cited in *SMJ* ch.2].

[148] Wintemute characterises the offence as "equalising down": "Sexual Orientation and Gender Identity", *ibid.*, p.179.

[149] See, e.g., *Masterson v Holden* [1986] 3 All ER 39.

[150] "Sexual Orientation and Gender Identity", pp.179–80.

[151] *R. v Brown* [1994] 1 A.C. 212; *Jaggard, Laskey and Brown v United Kingdom* (1997) 24 E.H.R.R. 39.

[152] *R. v Wilson* [1997] Q.B. 47.

[153] For general analysis, see the websites of GALOP (the Gay London Policing Group): *http://www.galop.org.uk/*, and Stonewall: *http://www.stonewall.org.uk/*. The apparently homophobic murder of Jody Dobrowski on Clapham Common in October 2005 has generated much comment: see, in particular, Matthew Parris, "Is queer-bashing just the tip of an iceberg of homophobia?", *The Times*, October 29th 2005, p.21 and the editorial comment "Murder on the Common: Yob culture claims another innocent victim", *The Times*, October 18th 2005, p.21. For discussion of earlier widely-reported homophobic attacks, see *Hansard*, HC Deb., 9th November 2004, Cols.735 (Angela Eagle MP) and 796 (Jacqui Smith MP).

[154] Criminal Justice Act 2003, s.146.

any specific offences aggravated by reference to sexual orientation.[155] However, Jack Straw MP, Secretary of State for Justice, announced on 8th October 2007 that the Criminal Justice and Immigration Bill currently before Parliament would be amended "to extend the offence of incitement to racial hatred to cover hatred against persons on the basis of their sexuality."[156] The Secretary of State suggested that "It is a measure of how far we have come as a society in the last 10 years that we are all now appalled by hatred and invective directed against gay people, and it is now time for the law to recognise the feeling of the public" and that "Homophobic abuse, lyrics and literature are every bit as abhorrent to those concerned as material inciting hatred based on race or religion, and have no place in olur communities."[157] Assuming that the amended is Bill is passed, it will not however tackle crimes based upon hostility to a person due to their gender reassignment. It remains to be seen how far the law is successful in challenging social hostility directed at sexual minority groups.

B. *Employment*

Discrimination in employment on the basis of gender identity and sexual orientation is now covered by secondary legislation created to give effect, respectively, to the decision in *P. v S. and Cornwall County Council*[158] and the Employment Equality Directive. Furthermore, when applying the Human Rights Act 1998, courts are obliged to read national legislation in the light of Convention case law concerning the impermissibility of sexual orientation discrimination under Arts 8 and/or 14 (see Section IV), the key example in the employment context relating to military employment.[159] The employment case law therefore highlights the potential for overlap between anti-discrimination protections which have their origins in EU law and those deriving from Convention rights: an issue first considered in Chapter 2 in relation to *Chief Constable of the West Yorkshire Police v A (No. 2)*, a case dealing with discrimination on the basis of gender identity.[160] Potential problems also arise for the courts in determining the limits of the protection offered by relevant secondary legislation (partly reflecting the questions raised about the coverage of the Employment Equality Directive in section VI) and by Arts 8 and 14 (reflecting the questions raised in Section IV). In this section, we deal first with

155 "Sexual Orientation and Gender Identity", *ibid*., p.180.

156 *Hansard*, HC Deb., 8th October 2007, col.67. See also the Ministry of Justice's announcement at See *http://www.justice.gov.uk/news/newsrelease081007a.htm*.

157 *Hansard*, HC Deb., 8th October 2007, col.67.

158 *ibid*.

159 See *Smith and Grady v United Kingdom; Lustig-Preen and Beckett v United Kingdom, ibid*.

160 [2004] UKHL 21; [2005] 1 A.C. 51.

employment discrimination on the basis of gender identity, before moving on to consider discrimination based on a person's sexual orientation.[161]

The Sex Discrimination (Gender Reassignment) Regulations 1999, passed in response to *P. v S. and Cornwall C.C.*, insert a new s.2A into the Sex Discrimination Act 1975 so as to specify that discrimination due to the fact that a person "intends to undergo, is undergoing or has undergone gender reassignment" (section 2A(1)), constitutes unlawful sex discrimination in the range of circumstances covered by the 1975 Act (employment and the provision of goods, facilities and services, etc.).[162] Section 2A(3) makes clear that a person is also treated less favourably than others if, in making arrangements for that person's absence from work to undergo gender reassignment, they are treated less favourably than they would be if their absence was due to sickness or injury, or treated less favourably than they would be if their absence was due to some other cause and it is reasonable, having regard to the circumstances, for them to be treated no less favourably. Sections 6 and 8 of the 1975 Act are amended so that gender identity-related discrimination in relation to pay falls under the 1975 Act rather than under the Equal Pay Act 1970.[163] Section 29 is amended to cover discrimination due to gender identity in respect of goods, facilities or services relating to vocational training.

The 1975 Act was also amended so as to deal with genuine occupational qualifications. A new section 7A makes clear that discrimination falling within s.2A is not unlawful if "(a) in relation to the employment in question—(i) being a man is a genuine occupational qualification for the job, or (ii) being a woman is a genuine occupational qualification for the job, and (b) the employer can show that the treatment is reasonable in view of the circumstances described in the relevant paragraph of s.7(2) and any other relevant circumstances."[164] Section 7B was also inserted to create supplementary exceptions relating to gender reassignment. Section 7B(2) makes clear that there is a supplementary genuine occupational qualification for a job only if:

"(a) the job involves the holder of the job being liable to be called upon to perform intimate physical searches pursuant to statutory powers;

(b) the job is likely to involve the holder of the job doing his work, or living, in a private home and needs to be held otherwise than by a person who is undergoing or has undergone gender reassignment,

[161] We return in Section IX to the question whether sexual orientation discrimination in employment can also be considered a form of sex discrimination.

[162] See *Chessington World of Adventures Ltd v Reed* [1998] I.C.R. 97, in which the Employment Appeal Tribunal suggested that the unamended Sex Discrimination Act could be interpreted to preclude gender identity discrimination. See also *Chief Constable of West Yorkshire Police v A (No. 2)*, [2004] UKHL 21, for analysis of how national law is to be interpreted in the light of changing E.U. and Convention interpretations.

[163] The legislation also covers partnerships and principal/agent relationships.

[164] Note also the Gender Recognition Act 2004, Sch.6, para.2, which amends s.7A to make provision for the legal consequences of gender reassignment (see also paras 4 and 5).

because objection might reasonably be taken to allowing to such a person—

(i) the degree of physical or social contact with a person living in the home, or

(ii) the knowledge of intimate details of such a person's life, which is likely, because of the nature or circumstances of the job or of the home, to be allowed to, or available to, the holder of the job;

(c) the nature or location of the establishment makes it impracticable for the holder of the job to live elsewhere than in premises provided by the employer, and—

(i) the only such premises which are available for persons holding that kind of job are such that reasonable objection could be taken, for the purpose of preserving decency and privacy, to the holder of the job sharing accommodation and facilities with either sex whilst undergoing gender reassignment, and

(ii) it is not reasonable to expect the employer either to equip those premises with suitable accommodation or to make alternative arrangements; or

(d) the holder of the job provides vulnerable individuals with personal services promoting their welfare, or similar personal services, and in the reasonable view of the employer those services cannot be effectively provided by a person whilst that person is undergoing gender reassignment."

According to s.7B(3), paragraphs (c) and (d) of s.7B(2) apply only to discrimination against a person who intends to undergo gender reassignment or is doing so.[165]

Finally, a special exception was created for religion. The non-discrimination provisions of s.2A do not apply, according to s.19 (as amended):

"(3) … to employment for purposes of an organised religion where the employment is limited to persons who are not undergoing and have not undergone gender reassignment, if the limitation is imposed to comply with the doctrines of the religion or avoid offending the religious susceptibilities of a significant number of its followers.

[or]

(4) … to an authorisation or qualification … for purposes of an organised religion where the authorisation or qualification is limited to persons who are not undergoing and have not undergone gender reassignment, if the limitation

[165] The provisions governing genuine occupational qualifications in ss 9 and 11 of the 1975 Act (dealing with contract workers and partnerships) are similarly amended.

is imposed to comply with the doctrines of the religion or avoid offending the religious susceptibilities of a significant number of its followers."

The scope of the religion exception has not been the subject of litigation in relation to gender reassignment, but a similar exception is included in the Regulations governing sexual orientation discrimination and has been analysed in detail in *R. (AMICUS) v Secretary of State for Trade and Industry*.[166] We discuss this case below.

It should also be noted that issues of gender identity discrimination must be resolved by courts in the light of the requirements of both EU law and the Convention. As discussed in Chapter 2, the question arose in *Chief Constable of West Yorkshire Police v A (No. 2)* whether, in a challenge to the failure to accept the application of a post-operative transsexual to join the police, relevant provisions of domestic law should be interpreted in the light of EU law and in turn in the light of Convention rights. The issue was only relevant in *A (No. 2)* because the two bodies of "European" law had not been consistent at the time the facts of the case arose.[167] The House of Lords was able to avoid the overlap problem in *A (No.2)* due to the interpretation it placed on *Goodwin v United Kingdom* (see Section V): that is, as a decision with purely prospective effect only due to the weight placed on the margin of appreciation by the Strasbourg Court,[168] making it an inappropriate decision to use in the interpretation of national and EU measures as they applied when the facts of *A (No.2)* arose. However, this merely serves to highlight the possibility—also relevant in sexual orientation cases—that in situations where there is a *relevant* divergence between EU and Convention case law, domestic courts will need to find a solution. This point is reinforced by the emphasis placed by Lord Bingham and Baroness Hale on the common values shared by EU law and the Convention. Lord Bingham suggested that the "importance of the Convention in this appeal derives not from the decision in *Goodwin* but from the part which the Convention has played in shaping the current European understanding of what fundamental human rights require and mean."[169] Meanwhile, Baroness Hale stressed that the "human rights values which led to" the *Goodwin* decision "also underpin the EC legislation", that is, the Equal Treatment Directive.[170]

Direct and indirect discrimination, harassment and victimisation in employment based on a person's sexual orientation are now policed by the Employment Equality (Sexual Orientation) Regulations 2003, implemented in

166 [1994] EWHC 869 (Admin) 2007 I.C.R. 1176.

167 The case involved a refusal to appoint a post-operative transsexual because, being still legally classified as of her birth sex, she would have been unable to conduct intimate searches of either male or female suspects. The birth sex problem has been removed by the Gender Recognition Act 2004, although s.7B(2)(a) of the Sex Discrimination Act 1975 (inserted under the 1999 Regulations) would still apply to intimate searches.

168 *ibid.*

169 Para [13].

170 Para [54].

response to the Employment Equality Directive. The three central provisions of the Regulations establish obligations not to discriminate, victimise or harass a person due to their sexual orientation.

Employment Equality (Sexual Orientation) Regulations 2003

Discrimination on grounds of sexual orientation

3.—(1) For the purposes of these Regulations, a person ("A") discriminates against another person ("B") if—

(a) on grounds of sexual orientation, A treats B less favourably than he treats or would treat other persons; or

(b) A applies to B a provision, criterion or practice which he applies or would apply equally to persons not of the same sexual orientation as B, but—

(i) which puts or would put persons of the same sexual orientation as B at a particular disadvantage when compared with other persons,
(ii) which puts B at that disadvantage, and
(iii) which A cannot show to be a proportionate means of achieving a legitimate aim.

(2) A comparison of B's case with that of another person under paragraph (1) must be such that the relevant circumstances in the one case are the same, or not materially different, in the other.

Discrimination by way of victimisation

4.—(1) For the purposes of these Regulations, a person ("A") discriminates against another person ("B") if he treats B less favourably than he treats or would treat other persons in the same circumstances, and does so by reason that B has—

(a) brought proceedings against A or any other person under these Regulations;

(b) given evidence or information in connection with proceedings brought by any person against A or any other person under these Regulations;

(c) otherwise done anything under or by reference to these Regulations in relation to A or any other person; or

(d) alleged that A or any other person has committed an act which (whether or not the allegation so states) would amount to a contravention of these Regulations,

or by reason that A knows that B intends to do any of those things, or suspects that B has done or intends to do any of them.

(2) Paragraph (1) does not apply to treatment of B by reason of any allegation made by him, or evidence or information given by him, if the allegation, evidence or information was false and not made (or, as the case may be, given) in good faith.

Harassment on grounds of sexual orientation

5.—(1) For the purposes of these Regulations, a person ("A") subjects another person ("B") to harassment where, on grounds of sexual orientation, A engages in unwanted conduct which has the purpose or effect of—

(a) violating B's dignity; or

(b) creating an intimidating, hostile, degrading, humiliating or offensive environment for B.

(2) Conduct shall be regarded as having the effect specified in paragraph (1)(a) or (b) only if, having regard to all the circumstances, including in particular the perception of B, it should reasonably be considered as having that effect.

As reg.6 makes clear, the obligation not to discriminate applies to arrangements made for determining who should be offered employment, the terms on which employment is offered and refusals or deliberate failures to offer employment; the terms of existing employees, opportunities offered for promotion, transfer, training or other benefits, refusals or deliberate failures to afford such opportunities, and dismissals or other detriments; and renders it unlawful for an employer to harass an employee or someone who applies for employment. Regulation 8 extends these protections to contract workers. Subsequent Regulations apply the obligation not to discriminate in a variety of contexts: to oil fields and ships (reg.9); to appointment (but not election) to office, the term "office" excluding political office-holders (reg.10); to arrangements governing the holding of the office of police constable (reg.11); to barristers (reg.12); to partnerships (reg.14); to trade organizations (reg.15); to bodies providing professional or trade qualifications (reg.16); to providers of vocational training (reg.17); to employment agencies (reg.18); to the relevant Secretary of State when providing statutory facilities for employment and training (reg.19); and to institutions of further and higher education (reg20). Regulation 36 makes clear as a general matter that, as well as applying to private persons, the Regulations apply to acts done by or for a Minister of the Crown or government department and to service in the armed forces.[171] Schedule 4 deals with the validity of contracts, collective agreements and rules of undertakings. Part V deals with enforcement and remedies, as well as the burden of proof.

The ambit of liability is extended by Regs 22 and 23. Regulation 22 makes an employer liable for the actions of employees done in the course of their employment, and principals for the actions of agents acting with their express or implied authority (in each case, the employee or agent remains liable as well). Liability extends to an employer whether or not the allegedly discriminatory actions were carried out with their knowledge or approval, but it is a defence for the employer to show that they took such steps as were

[171] Note the qualification in reg.23(4). Regulations 37 and 38 cover House of Commons and House of Lords staff.

reasonably practicable to prevent the employee from doing the act concerned, or from doing acts of that description in the course of their employment. Regulation 23 makes it unlawful to knowingly aid another person to do an act which is unlawful under the Regulations. However, reg.23(3) makes it clear that a person does not knowingly aid another for these purposes if they act in reliance on a statement made to them by the other person that, due to a provision of the Regulations, the aided act would not be unlawful, provided that it is reasonable for them to rely on the statement concerned.

Regulation 26 allows for positive action. We discuss positive action as a general matter in Chapters 6 and 7. For present purposes, it is sufficient to note that the obligation not to discriminate on the basis of sexual orientation does not render unlawful any act done in or in connection with (i) affording to persons of a particular sexual orientation access to facilities for training which would help fit them for particular work, or (ii) encouraging persons of a particular sexual orientation to take advantage of opportunities for doing particular work, provided that, in both cases, it reasonably appears that the act prevents or compensates for disadvantages linked to sexual orientation which are suffered by persons of that sexual orientation doing that work or likely to take up that work. Analogous exemptions apply to trade organisations in relation to training and similar facilities and in encouraging only persons of a particular sexual orientation to become members.

The most obviously contentious aspects of the Regulations relate to the complete exemptions from their scope and to the ambit of genuine occupational qualifications. Dealing first with exemptions, reg.24 makes clear that the Regulations do not "render unlawful an act done for the purpose of safeguarding national security, if the doing of the act was justified by that purpose", while reg.25 stipulates that they do not "render unlawful anything which prevents or restricts access to a benefit by reference to marital status". As we will see below, reg.25 has since been amended by the Equality Act (Sexual Orientation) Regulations 2007 so as to make provision for civil partnerships. Turning to genuine occupational qualifications, reg.7(2) makes clear that the non-discrimination obligation established in regs 3 and 6 does not apply where:

"having regard to the nature of the employment or the context in which it is carried out—

(a) being of a particular sexual orientation is a genuine and determining occupational requirement;
(b) it is proportionate to apply that requirement in the particular case; and
(c) either—
    (i) the person to whom that requirement is applied does not meet it, or
    (ii) the employer is not satisfied, and in all the circumstances it is reasonable for him not to be satisfied, that that person meets it,

and this paragraph applies whether or not the employment is for purposes of an organised religion."

Regulation 7(3) goes somewhat further in relation specifically to organised religion, allowing for a genuine occupational qualification to apply where[172]:

"(a) the employment is for purposes of an organised religion;
(b) the employer applies a requirement related to sexual orientation—
  (i) so as to comply with the doctrines of the religion, or
  (ii) because of the nature of the employment and the context in which it is carried out, so as to avoid conflicting with the strongly held religious convictions of a significant number of the religion's followers; and
(c) either—
  (i) the person to whom that requirement is applied does not meet it, or
  (ii) the employer is not satisfied, and in all the circumstances it is reasonable for him not to be satisfied, that that person meets it."

In a comprehensive survey of cases brought under the Regulations, commissioned by the T.U.C. and funded by the (then) Department of Trade and Industry, Barry Fitzpatrick concludes that "there has [. . .] been a preponderance of direct discrimination cases but many cases have been direct discrimination and harassment cases. On the other hand, there have not yet been any decided indirect discrimination cases on sexual orientation discrimination."[173] Under the direct discrimination heading, "there has been a willingness on the part of tribunals to find in favour of LGB claimants, particularly if they have corroborating evidence. Most of these cases have been direct discrimination/harassment cases. In the most high-profile direct discrimination case, *Lewis*, the complainant had limited success at the tribunal stage but this was overturned at the EAT [. . .] *Lewis* shows that 'underlying suspicions' e.g. in relation to homophobic phone calls and alleged homophobic remarks made by some parties, may not convince a tribunal that an organisation is engaging in sexual orientation direct discrimination. So also the tribunal was unwilling to interfere where an employer chooses to believe a straight person, admittedly corroborated by another, rather than a gay man facing serious allegations."[174] Fitzpatrick also notes that issues connected with the "purported distinction between sexual orientation and sexual practices" (discussed in relation to the Framework Directive in Section VI) have not yet

[172] See also reg.16(3).
[173] "Sexual orientation and religion or belief cases" (London: Trades Union Congress, 2007), available at *http://www.tuc.org.uk/equality/tuc-13485-f0.cfm*, para.6.1.
[174] *ibid.*, para.6.3.1. *Lewis v HSBC Bank*, EAT/0346/06/RN, 19 December 2006.

emerged in domestic cases, but may yet do so in future.[175] Fitzpatrick suggests that:

"There has been a range of successful sexual orientation harassment cases. However they have all been examples of 'crude' harassment with the possible exception of *Gaman*, in which the tribunal took a robust approach towards the line between 'banter' and unlawful harassment.... We did not encounter cases in which there was detailed consideration of the component elements of an 'unacceptable' environment in the harassment definition. In most cases, the tribunal concluded that the harassment was both 'purpose-based' and 'effects-based'. By and large, sexual orientation harassment allegations have been sympathetically treated by tribunals."[176]

Four cases deserve particular mention. First, the defintion of "on grounds of sexual orientation" in reg.3 was analysed in *Lacey v The University of Ulster*.[177] Here, it was accepted that the coverage of the Regulation was not restricted to the fact of the complainant's sexual orientation, so that failure to employ an applicant for an academic post due to their expressed research interest in homosexuality could, if proven, constitute discrimination "on grounds of sexual orientation". Secondly, a particularly "high profile sexual orientation discrimination case", to quote Fitzpatrick,[178] has been *XY v AB Bank*, in which the claimant challenged his dismissal by the bank following reports by two members of staff that he had allegedly exposed himself in the bank's gym facilities.[179] The proceedings at the Employment Tribunal and Employment Appeal Tribunal stages mainly concerned the adequacy of the bank's internal disciplinary investigation, and the claimant ultimately lost. As Fitzpatrick notes, however, the case demonstrates the importance of ensuring that internal disciplinary proceedings are conducted without any taint of discrimination: "Employers and trade union representatives should be acutely aware of potential homophobic undercurrents in the workplace so that, if disciplinary matters arise in relation to LGB workers, there is no taint of discrimination in the treatment of them".[180] It shoud also be noted that the case turned in part on the issue of which comparator it was appropriate for the claimant to compare his position with—a general problem in discrimination law (see chapter 2), which may arguably come to prove important on a general basis at national level in relation to sexual orientation discrimination.

The third and fourth cases—*R. (AMICUS) v Secretary of State for Trade and Industry*[181] and *Reaney v Hereford Diocesan Board of Finance*[182]—concern the

[175] *ibid.*, para.6.3.1.
[176] *ibid.*, para.6.4.1. *Gorman v Vickery*, case no, 1400100/06. 1400246/06 August 2006.
[177] Case Ref 970/05, February 2007.
[178] *ibid.*, para.3.2.1.5.
[179] Case No 3200440/2005 (5056/98) May 2006,
[180] *ibid.*, para.3.2.1.5.
[181] [2004] EWHC 860 (Admin), [2007] ICR 1176.
[182] Case No: 1602844/2006.

religious genuine occupational qualifications provided for under reg.7. The *AMICUS* case involved a challenge to the compatibility of regs 7(2) and 7(3) with the Framework Directive and Arts 8 and 14 of the Convention (we also explore the Convention arguments in Section VIII, given that they focus on the balance to be struck between the right to non-discrimination and the competing right to freedom of religion). After making an important general observation about the nature of the right not to be discriminated against on the ground of sexual orientation, Richards J. went on to explore regs 7(2) and 7(3) in turn, finding that each was compatible.

R. (AMICUS) v Secretary of State for Trade and Industry [1994] EWHC 869 (Admin), [2007] I.C.R. 1176

RICHARDS J.:

[31]: "The right not to be discriminated against on grounds of sexual orientation is not [...] an absolute right. Much of this case is concerned with the striking of the balance between that right and other interests. In the case of regulation 7(2) the interests in issue are those of employers for whom being of a particular sexual orientation is a genuine and determining occupational requirement. There may, for example, be an occupational requirement for a homosexual (as for certain posts in gay or lesbian organisations) or an occupational requirement for a heterosexual (as for certain religious posts). It is in relation to employment for purposes of an organised religion, however, that issues of particular sensitivity and difficulty may arise. That is why reg.7(3) seeks to make specific additional provision in relation to employment for such purposes.

Regulation 7(2): compatibility with the Directive

[67]: Regulation 7(2), read with regulation 7(1), contains an exception in respect of discrimination where sexual orientation is a genuine and determining occupational requirement. It is intended to implement article 4(1) of the Directive.

[68]: It is common ground that a derogation in respect of occupational requirements is permitted by article 4(1) of the Directive, and there are important respects in which regulation 7(2) is accepted to be an appropriate form of derogation: in particular, by providing that proportionality is to be assessed on a case by case basis (in contrast to the approach adopted in regulation 7(3)). The Amicus claimants contend, however, that it is defective and incompatible with the Directive in two respects: (i) it does not include a provision that the discriminatory requirement must meet a legitimate objective; and (ii) the exception applies not only where a person does not in fact meet the requirement as to sexual orientation but also, by virtue of regulation 7(2)(c)(ii), where the employer is reasonably not satisfied that the person meets it...

[69]: The first ground, concerning legitimate objective, is based on the absence from regulation 7(2) of language corresponding to the express proviso in article 4(1) that "the objective is legitimate"...

[70]: For my part, I accept the submissions for the Secretary of State that the concept is indeed implicit and that express reference to a legitimate objective is unnecessary. The exception applies only where being of a particular sexual orientation is "a genuine and determining occupational requirement" and it is "proportionate" to apply that requirement in the particular case. If the exception can apply only where the requirement is *genuine* and *determining*, it is difficult to see how the objective could be anything other than legitimate. Moreover, it is inherent in the test of proportionality that the exception must serve a legitimate aim. Nor has anyone suggested any factual scenario in which it could sensibly be argued that, in the absence of an express reference to a legitimate objective, regulation 7(2) could be relied on in pursuit of a non-legitimate objective.

[71]: It is true that article 4(1) itself contains the same language of "a genuine and determining occupational requirement" which must be "proportionate", yet makes additional reference to the need for a legitimate objective. It does not follow, however, that the reference to a legitimate objective adds anything of substance. If it does add something, then I see no difficulty in the national court implying a corresponding substantive requirement in pursuance of its duty to interpret the Regulations purposively so as to ensure compliance with the Community obligation.

[73]: The claimants contend [...] that [regulation 7(2)(c)(ii)] is objectionable for a number of reasons....

[80]: ...In my judgment regulation 7(2)(c)(ii) has a sensible rationale. In those cases where being of a particular sexual orientation is a genuine and determining occupational requirement, it cannot be right that an employer, having asked the plainly permissible initial question whether a person meets that requirement, is bound in all circumstances to accept at face value the answer given or is precluded from forming his own assessment if no answer is given. At the same time the provision limits the risk of unduly intrusive inquiry. If the employer is not satisfied that the person meets the requirement, and if it is reasonable in all the circumstances for him to do so, the employer can decline to employ the person without having to make the same degree of inquiry as might be called for if it were necessary to gather sufficient evidence by way of proof of sexual orientation to meet a potential complaint of unlawful discrimination.

[81]: The requirement of reasonableness ensures that decisions cannot lawfully be based on mere assumptions or social stereotyping...

[82]: Nor do I accept the claimants' argument that any form of inquiry beyond the initial question whether a person meets the requirement would amount to unlawful harassment or to breach of article 8 of the Convention. It is certainly true that particularly intrusive inquiries could give rise to such breaches, but that possibility exists independently of regulation 7(2)(c)(ii). In my view the provision serves to reduce rather than to increase the risk.

[83]: That still leaves the question whether the provision comes within the terms of the derogation in article 4(1) of the Directive. In my view the derogation, which refers to a difference of treatment "based on a characteristic related to" sexual orientation, is wide enough to cover it, even allowing for the need to construe derogations strictly (see e.g. Johnston v. Chief Constable of the Royal Ulster Constabulary [1986] ECR 1651 at para [36] of the judgment). Equally I see nothing in the policy of the Directive that calls for so restrictive a construction as to preclude a provision of this kind.

[84]: I should make clear that, whilst I accept that the general prohibition on discrimination in article 2 is intended to apply to discrimination on grounds of perceived as well as actual sexual orientation, I do not think that the same reasoning can automatically be applied to the power to derogate in article 4(1). Article 2 confers protection in respect of a fundamental right and should be given a broad construction. On the other hand, a derogation from such protection should in principle be given a narrow construction. Nevertheless, as I have indicated, the derogation in article 4(1) is in my view apt to cover regulation 7(2)(c)(ii).

Regulation 7(3): compatibility with the Directive

[114]: In relation to regulation 7(3), as in relation to regulation 7(2), in general I accept the submissions for the Secretary of State.

[115]: The main question, as it seems to me, concerns the scope of the exception. ... I think it clear from the Parliamentary material that the exception was intended to be very narrow; and in my view it is, on its proper construction, very narrow. It has to be construed strictly since it is a derogation from the principle of equal treatment; and it has to be construed purposively so as to ensure, so far as possible, compatibility with the Directive. When its terms are considered in the light of those interpretative principles, they can be seen to afford an exception only in very limited circumstances.

[116]: The fact that the exception applies, by regulation 7(3)(a), only to employment "for purposes of an organised religion" is an important initial limitation [...] that is a narrower expression than "for purposes of a religious organisation", or the expression "where an employer has an ethos based on religion or belief", as used in the corresponding regulations relating to discrimination on grounds of religion or belief. I also accept [...] that employment as a teacher in a faith school is likely to be "for purposes of a religious organisation" but not "for purposes of an organised religion".

[117]: The conditions in regulation 7(3)(b) impose very real additional limitations. In my view the condition in regulation 7(3)(b)(i), that the employer must apply the requirement "so as to comply with the doctrines of the religion", is to be read not as a subjective test concerning the motivation of the employer, but as an objective test whereby it must be shown that employment of a person not meeting the requirement would be incompatible with the doctrines of the religion. That is very narrow in scope. Admittedly the alternative in regulation 7(3)(b)(ii) is wider; but even that is hemmed about by restrictive language. The condition must be applied "because of the nature of the employment and the context in which it is carried out"—which requires careful examination of the precise nature of the employment—"so as to avoid conflicting with the strongly held religious convictions of a significant number of the religion's followers". Again this is in my view an objective, not subjective, test. Further, the conflict to be avoided is with *religious convictions*, which must be *strongly held;* and they must be the convictions of a *significant number* of the religion's followers. This is going to be a very far from easy test to satisfy in practice.

[118]: The fact that reference is made to "a significant number" rather than to all or the majority of a religion's followers not only reflects the desirability of avoiding detailed statistical analysis ... but also ensures that proper account is taken of the existence of differing bodies of opinion even within an organised religion. Sexual orientation is a matter on which some followers of a religion may hold stronger religious convictions than others. In my view it is legitimate to allow for the possibility of applying a relevant requirement even if the convictions in question are held only by a significant minority of followers.

[119]: One further point I should deal with in connection with regulation 7(3)(b) concerns its opening words, which refer to an employer applying "a requirement related to sexual orientation". Those words may in one way make the provision wider in scope than the regulation 7(2), where the relevant occupational requirement is expressed in terms of "being of a particular sexual orientation". I note that the choice of wording in regulation 7(3) was deliberate, so as to accommodate the concerns of some Churches about certain forms of sexual *behaviour* rather than sexuality as such. In my view the wording is apt to cover the point, and it may have been prudent to use such wording in order to avoid argument about the scope of the expression "being of a particular sexual orientation". I do not consider, however, that the point has a material effect on the present analysis. The protection against discrimination on grounds of sexual orientation relates as much to the manifestation of that orientation in the form of sexual behaviour as it does to sexuality as such. I have already mentioned this when looking generally at the fundamental rights in issue in this case. The wording of the derogation in article 4(1) of the Directive, which refers to a difference of treatment "which is based on a characteristic related to" sexual orientation, is wide enough to embrace a difference of treatment based on sexual behaviour related to sexual orientation.

[120]: The conditions in regulation 7(3)(c), that either (i) the person does not meet the requirement or (ii) the employer is not satisfied, and in all the circumstances it is reasonable for him not to be satisfied, that the person meets the requirement, are the same as in regulation 7(2)(c) and do not need to be considered separately. . . .

[122]: Looking at regulation 7(3) as a whole . . . I take the view that the exception is a lawful implementation of article 4(1) of the Directive.

[123]: The exception involves a legislative striking of the balance between competing rights. It was done deliberately in this way so as to reduce the issues that would have to be determined by courts or tribunals in such a sensitive field. As a matter of principle, that was a course properly open to the legislature. ... Regulation 7(3) [. . .] lays down the specific conditions that have to be met and thereby avoids the need for the court or tribunal to consider some of the issues that might otherwise arise on a case by case basis under regulation 7(2). But in no way does it remove effective access to the court or tribunal, which will still have an important role in determining whether the conditions laid down are met. The fact that this may still take the court or tribunal into difficult areas does not invalidate the motivation of reducing the issues to be determined. The value of cutting down the issues is illustrated by the debate raised before me about the theological validity of the interveners' religious beliefs, a matter which I have concluded is inappropriate for determination by the court.

[124]: The conditions laid down must themselves, of course, comply with article 4(1) of the Directive. As to that, I think it clear that a requirement meeting the conditions pursues a legitimate aim. In addition, should it be necessary, I would rely here on . . . the protection of religious rights and freedoms as a justification for interference with rights under article 8 of the Convention. I reject the submission . . . that a restriction on employment by reference to the religious convictions of followers of a religion cannot pursue a legitimate aim. As to proportionality, the balance struck in this sensitive and difficult area is in my view an appropriate one. If regulation 7(3) had the wide scope that the claimants attribute to it, the issue of proportionality would be one of real concern. But the view that I take about the narrow scope of the provision also leads me to the conclusion that it complies with the test of proportionality. For the same reason, and subject to the point [. . .] about its application to sexual *behaviour* as well as sexuality as such, I do not think that the exception in regulation 7(3) is likely to apply in practice in a wider range of circumstances than would fall within the exception in regulation 7(2), though the difference in legislative approach in relation to the two exceptions leads to some differences in the issues to be determined by a court or tribunal when considering whether the exceptions apply.

[127]: For the reasons given above I hold that regulation 7(3) is compatible with the Directive."[183]

Richards J. also dismissed the claimant's arguments that regs 7(2) and 7(3) contravened either Art.8 or Art.14 of the European Convention. Richards J. was clear, first, that there was no violation of Art.8. The issue of justification under Art.8(2), *if it arose at all*, would involve much the same issues as those already considered in the context of the compatibility of the Regulations with the Directive. For the reasons given in that context (see above), Richards J. considered that the Regulations would meet a legitimate aim and be proportionate, thus meeting the requirements of Art.8(2).[184] In fact, however, he did not believe that the issue of justification arose at all, given that he did not think that the Regulations in fact interfered with rights under Art.8(1): instead, the Regulations "add to existing rights. The [Regulation 7] exceptions of which complaint is made limit the scope of what is added, but do not interfere with any rights".[185] Furthermore, a claim based on Art.14 coupled with Article 8

[183] See also paras [129] to [135] on the compatibility of Regulation 20(3) with the Directive.
[184] *ibid.*, para.[187].
[185] *ibid.*, para.[189].

could not succeed since the Regulations did not "produce any difference of treatment in the enjoyment of rights falling within the ambit of the Convention; they simply confer certain rights not to be discriminated against".[186] It should be noted, however, that since the conclusion concerning Art.14 rested on a combination of the "*Michalak* criteria", later discredited by the House of Lords in *Carson*, and the conclusion that same-sex and married couples were not in analogous situations for comparison purposes when determining whether discrimination contrary to Art.14 had occurred[187]—a position arguably since displaced, at least for some same-sex couples, by the Civil Partnership Act 2004—it is unclear whether similar reasoning could be used today.

AMICUS involved a challenge to the general compatibility of the Regulations with the Directive. By contrast, *Reaney v Hereford Diocesan Board of Finance* provides a useful illustration of how arguments based on reg.7(3) are likely to be handled on their facts.[188] A Church of England Diocesan Bishop had refused to employ the claimant, a gay man, as a Diocesan Youth Officer on the basis that he was not convinced by the claimant's assurance that he would remain celibate (in line with Church policy) for so long as he held the post. In dismissing the Church's attempt to rely upon reg.7(3), the Employment Tribunal suggested that as a general matter, "[t]he provisions of Regulation 7 should be narrowly construed being a derogation from the principle of equal treatment".[189] Furthermore, the Tribunal subjected the Church's arguments to close scrutiny, being concerned to test whether there was a specific justification—rather than an argument rooted in generality—for the failure to employ the claimant.

The Tribunal divided its handling of reg.7(3) into three questions. The first question, given the drafting of part (a) of reg.7(3), was whether the employment fell within the scope of the Regulation as being for the purposes of an organised religion. The Employment Tribunal suggested that it was necessary to consider—by reference to the job application, job description and associated documents—specifically what the post involved. The Tribunal held that the post fell within reg.7(3). The organised religion in issue was that of the Church of England. The key roles of the post-holder were to represent the Diocese to local authorities and other secular bodies and to co-ordinate, encourage and promote church youth organisations. The post was closely bound up with the Bishop as Head of the Diocese, and with putting into effect the priorities of the Bishop and the Church. The Tribunal noted that the post-holder "would be in one of the small number of jobs which would be closely associated with the promotion of the Church [. . .] [and] [. . .] would have been promoting religion

186 *ibid.*, para.[199]; as paras [194]–[198] reveal, this conclusion was based on the now discredited "*Michalak* criteria": one assumes, however, that the result would not be different even following the discrediting in *ex p. Carson*.

187 *ibid.*, para.[199].

188 *ibid.*

189 para.[100]. Note also the Tribunal's treatment of the Convention argument at [97].

in the way in which it has been suggested the regulations are meant to encompass".[190] The second question, given part (b) of reg.7(3), was whether a requirement related to sexual orientation had been applied so as to comply with the doctrines of the religion or to avoid, given the nature of the employment and the context in which it was carried out, conflicting with the strongly-held religious convictions of a significant number of the religion's followers. The Tribunal accepted that since the current pastoral position of the Church of England was that sexual behaviour outside of marriage, whether homosexual or heterosexual, did not live up to the ideals of the Christian faith, the Diocesan Bishop's requirement that the claimant declare that he had made a commitment to abstaining from sexual behaviour was in accordance with the doctrines of the Church of England.[191] The third question, given part (c) of reg.7(3), was whether the person to whom the requirement had been applied did not meet it, or whether the employer was not satisfied, and in all the circumstances it was reasonable for them not to be satisfied, that the person met it. The Tribunal held that the claimant met the requirement: his past relationship had ended some months before and he was committed to working in the Church in full compliance with the requirement of not entering into a sexual relationship. Given the language of the Regulations, the further question whether it was nonetheless reasonable for the Bishop not to be satisfied that the claimant met the requirement needed to be answered by reference to the present circumstances, and on the facts no good reason had been shown. Even if it was, contrary to the Tribunal's view, correct to look to future rather than present circumstances, there were no good reasons for disbelieving the claimant's assurances concerning his intention to remain celibate for so long as he held the job. It was certainly not reasonable to employ any notion that a person whose relationship had recently come to an end could not be relied upon to state a future intention because of the present fragility of their state of mind [192]

A further significant aspect of *AMICUS* at the time the case was decided was Richards J's. treatment of reg.25 and his expansive view of the European Court of Justice's position concerning same-sex couples and EU sex discrimination law in *Grant v South-west Trains*,[193] *D. and Sweden v Council*[194] and *KB v Secretary of State for Health*.[195] One of the claimants had argued that reg.25, which exempted benefits consequent upon marital status from the general prohibition on sexual orientation discrimination contained in the Regulations, contravened the rule in Art.3(1)(c) of the Employment Equality Directive that discrimination in relation to pay was prohibited (such benefits constituting a form of pay). Richards J. held that recital (22) of the Directive, which stated

[190] para.[102].
[191] para.[103].
[192] *ibid.*, paras [105]–[108].
[193] *ibid.*
[194] *ibid.*
[195] *ibid.*

that the Directive was "without prejudice to national laws on marital status and the benefits dependent thereon" indicated a clear legislative intention to limit the Directive in the fashion also employed by reg.25, thus destroying any argument that the latter contravened the former.[196] As a fall-back, he also accepted, relying on *Grant*, *D and Sweden* and *KB*, that the exclusion contained in reg.25 did not involve direct discrimination contrary to the Directive since the ground of the difference in treatment was marriage, not sexual orientation, and the "consistent approach of the ECJ, up to and including [...] *KB*, has been to hold that married partners are not in a comparable position to same-sex partners".[197] In addition, it did not involve indirect discrimination since married and unmarried couples are not in a materially similar situation. If this last conclusion was wrong, Richards J. was happy to accept that the maintenance of a difference of treatment between married and unmarried couples with regard to access to benefits could be objectively justified and did not for this reason give rise to unlawful discrimination.[198]

Parliament's direct response to this aspect of the *AMICUS* decision was to insert a new reg.3(3) into the Regulations at the same time as it passed the Civil Partnership 2004.[199] Regulation 3(3) stipulates that:

> "For the purposes of paragraph (2) [the definition of discrimination], in a comparison of B's case with that of another person the fact that one of the persons (whether or not B) is a civil partner while the other is married shall not be treated as a material difference between their respective circumstances."

The new reg.3(3) enables a civil partner who is treated less favourably than a married person in similar circumstances to bring a claim for sexual orientation discrimination, given that marital status no longer—contrary to the *AMICUS* interpretation—counts as a material difference. In addition, s.251 of the Civil Partnership Act 2004 extends the protection of married persons against discrimination in employment under s.3 of the Sex Discrimination Act 1975 to civil partners. Discrimination on the basis of civil partnership status, like discrimination on the basis of marital status, is thus now also a form of unlawful sex discrimination. It therefore seems correct to say that reg.3(3) and s.251 of the 2004 Act in combination allow employers to favour married couples and civil partners over unmarried and unregistered couples in relation to partnership-related employment benefits.[200]

196 *ibid.*, paras [156]–[160].
197 *ibid.*, para.[164].
198 *ibid.*, paras [165]–[171].
199 For comment, see Mark Bell, "Employment law consequences of the Civil Partnership Act 2004" (2006) ILJ 179.
200 Mark Harper, Martin Downs, Katharine Landells and Gerald Wilson, *Civil Partnership: The New Law* (Bristol: Jordan Publishing, 2005), paras 7.49 and 8.61–8.63. See also *AMICUS*, *ibid.*, para.[170].

C. *Goods, facilities and services*

Section 81 of the Equality Act 2006 entitles Regulations to be made covering discrimination or harassment on the ground of sexual orientation. According to s.81(3), such Regulations may define discrimination and harassment, make provision for enforcement (including by the criminal law, in relation to the validity and revision of contracts, in relation to discriminatory advertisements, and concerning instructing or causing discrimination or harassment) and provide for exceptions. One such set of Regulations is the Equality Act (Sexual Orientation) Regulations 2007, which extend the obligation not to discriminate beyond employment—thereby extending a wider range of protection in domestic law than that required under the Employment Equality Directive. One of the major concerns of the Regulations is with the provision of goods, facilities and services. Unlike the 2003 Regulations, the 2007 Regulations also take care to provide definitions of direct and indirect discrimination.

Equality Act (Sexual Orientation) Regulations 2007

Discrimination on grounds of sexual orientation

3.—(1) For the purposes of these Regulations, a person ("A") discriminates against another ("B") if, on grounds of the sexual orientation of B or any other person except A, A treats B less favourably than he treats or would treat others (in cases where there is no material difference in the relevant circumstances).

(2) In paragraph (1) a reference to a person's sexual orientation includes a reference to a sexual orientation which he is thought to have.

(3) For the purposes of these Regulations, a person ("A") discriminates against another ("B") if A applies to B a provision, criterion or practice—

(a) which he applies or would apply equally to persons not of B's sexual orientation,

(b) which puts persons of B's sexual orientation at a disadvantage compared to some or all others (where there is no material difference in the relevant circumstances),

(c) which puts B at a disadvantage compared to some or all persons who are not of his sexual orientation (where there is no material difference in the relevant circumstances), and

(d) which A cannot reasonably justify by reference to matters other than B's sexual orientation.

(4) For the purposes of paragraphs (1) and (3), the fact that one of the persons (whether or not B) is a civil partner while the other is married shall not be treated as a material difference in the relevant circumstances....

Goods, facilities and services

4.—(1) It is unlawful for a person ("A") concerned with the provision to the public or a section of the public of goods, facilities or services to discriminate against a person ("B") who seeks to obtain or to use those goods, facilities or services—

(a) by refusing to provide B with goods, facilities or services,

(b) by refusing to provide B with goods, facilities or services of a quality which is the same as or similar to the quality of goods, facilities or services that A normally provides to—
  (i) the public, or
  (ii) a section of the public to which B belongs,

(c) by refusing to provide B with goods, facilities or services in a manner which is the same as or similar to that in which A normally provides goods, facilities or services to—
  (i) the public, or
  (ii) a section of the public to which B belongs, or

(d) by refusing to provide B with goods, facilities or services on terms which are the same as or similar to the terms on which A normally provides goods, facilities or services to—
  (i) the public, or
  (ii) a section of the public to which B belongs.

(2) Paragraph (1) applies, in particular, to—

(a) access to and use of a place which the public are permitted to enter,

(b) accommodation in a hotel, boarding house or similar establishment,

(c) facilities by way of banking or insurance or for grants, loans, credit or finance,

(d) facilities for entertainment, recreation or refreshment,

(e) facilities for transport or travel, and

(f) the services of a profession or trade.

(4) For the purposes of paragraph (1) it is immaterial whether or not a person charges for the provision of goods, facilities or services.

Premises

5.—(1) It is unlawful for a person to discriminate against another—

(a) in the terms on which he offers to dispose of premises to him,

(b) by refusing to dispose of premises to him, or

(c) in connection with a list of persons requiring premises.

(2) It is unlawful for a person managing premises to discriminate against an occupier—

(a) in the manner in which he provides access to a benefit or facility,

(b) by refusing access to a benefit or facility,

(c) by evicting him, or

(d) by subjecting him to any other detriment.

(3) It is unlawful for a person to discriminate against another by refusing permission for the disposal of premises to him.[201]

Subsequent Regulations apply to discriminatory practices (reg.9), discriminatory advertisements (reg.10), instructing or causing discrimination (reg.11), and associations of 25 or more people which are not trade associations (reg.16). The Regulations cover actions of the police constables (reg.32), bind the Crown, including actions done by or on behalf of ministers and government departments (reg.33), and apply to British vessels and aircraft (reg.34). Regulation 26 renders void contract provisions which contravene the Regulations. The ambit of liability is extended by regs 29 and 30. Regulation 30 effectively reproduces Regulation 22 of the 2003 Regulations in its definition of the liability of employers and principals as well as employees and agents. Regulation 29 makes it unlawful to knowingly help another person to do an act which is unlawful under the Regulations: a slightly different formulation from that used in reg.23 of the 2003 Regulations.

As a matter of logic, there can be no such thing as a genuine occupational qualification in Regulations dealing with goods, facilities and services, but the 2007 Regulations contain analogous exemptions for religious organisations to those seen in the 2003 Regulations, as well as additional exemptions for "sensitive" areas where it is felt that the obligation not to discriminate should not be absolute. Four groups are discernible.[202] First, reg.13 appears to be concerned with the welfare of sexual minorities. It stipulates that the Regulations do not make it unlawful to do anything to meet special needs for education, training or welfare on the ground of a person's sexual orientation. regs 17 and 18 are concerned with the provision of facilities for persons of particular sexual orientations, but without reg.13's clear implicit focus on sexual minority groups. Regulation 17 thus exempts any association the main object of which is to enable the benefits of membership (whatever they may be) to be enjoyed by persons of a particular sexual orientation, while reg.18 stipulates that the Regulations do not make it unlawful to provide benefits only to persons of a particular sexual orientation if this is done in pursuance of a charitable instrument and the restriction to persons of that sexual orientation is imposed by reason of or on the grounds of the provisions of the charitable instrument. A second set of exceptions deal with the home. Regulation 6 seems concerned to prevent the obligation not to discriminate from intruding upon domestic space. It thus sets up a series of exemptions to the requirements of regs 4 and 5, in particular where people take children, elderly people or those requiring a special degree of care and attention into their homes (where they

201 In reg.2, an act is deemed to include a deliberate omission.

202 Note also the exemption in reg.12 for things done under the authority of an Act of Parliament (see also reg.4(3)) and reg.25, concerning national security.

or their near relatives live) and treat them as a member of their family. Thirdly, regs 27 and 28 cover situations of perceived risk. Regulation 27 stipulates that it is not unlawful to treat a person less favourably on the ground of sexual orientation in relation to an annuity, life insurance policy, or similar matter involving the assessment of risk, where the treatment is by reference to actuarial or other data from a source on which it is reasonable to rely, and is reasonable having regard to that data and any other relevant factors. Regulation 28 states that blood donation services may not discriminate, but that it is permissible to do so if a refusal to accept blood is based on a risk assessment which is reasonable by reference to recognised scientific data.

The fourth, and doubtless most contentious, set of exemptions relates to organizations of a particular religion or belief, and fostering agencies with a religious affiliation. Since these provisions are likely to generate *AMICUS*-style litigation (albeit without reference to any background EU instrument), they are worth setting out in detail:

Organisations relating to religion or belief

14.—(1) Subject to paragraphs (2) and (8) this regulation applies to an organisation the purpose of which is—

(a) to practise a religion or belief,

(b) to advance a religion or belief,

(c) to teach the practice or principles of a religion or belief,

(d) to enable persons of a religion or belief to receive any benefit, or to engage in any activity, within the framework of that religion or belief.

(3) Nothing in these Regulations shall make it unlawful for an organisation to which this regulation applies, or for anyone acting on behalf of or under the auspices of an organisation to which this regulation applies—

(a) to restrict membership of the organisation,

(b) to restrict participation in activities undertaken by the organisation or on its behalf or under its auspices,

(c) to restrict the provision of goods, facilities or services in the course of activities undertaken by the organisation or on its behalf or under its auspices, or

(d) to restrict the use or disposal of premises owned or controlled by the organisation,

in respect of a person on the ground of his sexual orientation.

(4) Nothing in these Regulations shall make it unlawful for a minister [of religion]—

(a) to restrict participation in activities carried on in the performance of his functions in connection with or in respect of an organisation to which this regulation relates, or

(b) to restrict the provision of goods, facilities or services in the course of activities carried on in the performance of his functions in connection with or in respect of an organisation to which this regulation relates,

in respect of a person on the ground of his sexual orientation.

(5) Paragraphs (3) and (4) permit a restriction only if imposed—

(a) if it is necessary to comply with the doctrine of the organisation; or

(b) so as to avoid conflicting with the strongly held religious convictions of a significant number of the religion's followers.

(8) This regulation does not apply where an organisation of the kind referred to in paragraph (1) or any person acting on its behalf or under its auspices—

(a) makes provision of a kind referred to in regulation 4, or

(b) exercises a function of a kind referred to in regulation 8, on behalf of a public authority under the terms of a contract for provision of that kind between that authority and an organisation referred to in paragraph (1) or, if different, the person making that provision.

Adoption and fostering agencies

15.—(1) Paragraph (2) applies to a voluntary adoption agency or fostering agency that—

(a) is an organisation of the kind referred to in regulation 14(1), or

(b) acts on behalf of or under the auspices of such an organisation.

(2) Subject to paragraph (3), during the period from the commencement of these Regulations until 31st December 2008, nothing in these Regulations shall make it unlawful for such a voluntary adoption agency or fostering agency to restrict the provision of its services or facilities to a person on the grounds of his sexual orientation.

(3) If such a voluntary adoption agency or fostering agency restricts the provision of those services or facilities as mentioned in paragraph (2), it must at the same time refer the person seeking them to another person who the agency believes provides similar services or facilities to persons of his sexual orientation.

(4) Paragraph (2) permits a restriction only if imposed—

(a) if it is necessary to comply with the doctrine of the organisation, or

(b) so as to avoid conflicting with the strongly held religious convictions of a significant number of the religion's followers.

D. *Obligations on public authorities*

Regulation 8(1) of the Equality Act (Sexual Orientation) Regulations 2007 moves beyond the 2003 Regulations by imposing a *general* duty on public authorities not to discriminate on the ground of sexual orientation,[203] and a similarly broad duty is imposed on educational establishments (including local educational authorities) under reg.7. The regulation 8 duty is not, how-

[203] See regs 7(1) and 8(1). Regulation 8(2) stipulates that a "public authority" includes any person who has functions of a public nature (so long as they are not exempted by Sch.1), while "function" means function of a public nature (so long as it is not exempted by Sch.1).

ever, universal: for Sch.1 exempts certain public authorities and functions from its scope.[204] This duty sits alongside that implicitly imposed by s.6 of the Human Rights Act 1998, which obliges public authorities to act in accordance with Convention rights save where primary legislation dictates otherwise: a provision which applies the non-discrimination obligations recognised in the Arts 8 and 14 case law whenever s.6 applies.

Section 29 of the Local Government Act 1988, which infamously prohibited local authorities from "intentionally promot[ing] homosexuality" or "promot[ing] the teaching [. . .] of the acceptability of homosexuality as a pretended family relationship" was repealed in 2003.[205] While this clearly amounted to a victory against direct discrimination on the basis of sexual orientation, Robert Wintemute has questioned how suitable the replacement position is. Section 403(1A) of the Education Act 1996, inserted by section 148 of the Learning and Skills Act 2000, requires the Secretary of State for Education to issue guidance covering the sex education of pupils at maintained schools, the guidance being designed to ensure that pupils learn the nature of marriage and its importance for family life and the bringing up of children. Wintemute notes that "The resulting *Sex and Relationship Education Guidance* states that '[t]here shall be no direct promotion of sexual orientation' (except presumably for the promotion of different-sex marriage as the ideal form of family life). The absence of a reference to 'homosexuality' appears to be an improvement on section 29. However, many people read 'sexual orientation' as meaning same-sex sexual orientation, because they do not see heterosexual individuals as having a sexual orientation. So it is possible that the harmful effects of section 29, and the hopelessly vague word 'promote', have been transferred from the statute book to the statutory guidance".[206]

E. *Relationships and family life*

This is clearly the area in which the most significant change, measured both in terms of quantity and social importance, has been seen in national law in recent years. As Stephen Cretney's discussion, cited in section 1, makes clear, the notion that the law would come to recognise same-sex partnerships and allow same-sex couples to acquire custody of children would have seemed an

204 Sch.1 exempts from the application of reg.8 the House of Commons, the House of Lords, authorities of either House, the Security Service, the Secret Intelligence Service, Government Communications Headquarters, or a part of the armed forces which is, in accordance with a requirement of the Secretary of State, assisting the Government Communications Headquarters. Functions which are exempted include the exercise of a judicial function or matters connected with it, preparing, passing (or making), confirming, approving or considering an enactment, the making of an instrument by a Minister of the Crown under an enactment, or a decision not to institute or continue criminal proceedings.

205 Local Government Act 2003, s.127(2) and Sch.8.

206 "Sexual Orientation and Gender Identity", *ibid.*, p.188.

impossibility, fifty years ago. Yet this is what has happened with the Civil Partnership 2004 and previous legislation concerning children (although it remains an open question how far civil partnership differs from marriage and whether the latter should be opened up to same-sex couples). Furthermore, the Gender Recognition Act 2004 allows those who have undergone gender reassignment to be registered with their reassigned sex, thus enabling them to enter into marriages or civil partnerships.

1. The Gender Recognition Act 2004

The 2004 Act was effectively enacted in response to the Court of Human Rights' decision in *Goodwin v United Kingdom* (see Section V above).[207] In the light of *Goodwin*, the House of Lords decided in *Bellinger v Bellinger* to issue a declaration of incompatibility concerning s.11(c) of the Matrimonial Causes Act 1973 in so far as it prevented a person who had undergone gender reassignment from marrying.[208] The 2004 sets out to remedy this deficiency, and to make provision for the consequences of gender reassignment in a wide range of areas. Sections 1 to 5 focus on the procedures for acquiring legal recognition of gender reassignment, while other sections tend to concentrate on the legal consequences (including in relation to marriage).

Gender Recognition Act 2004

1 Applications

(1) A person of either gender who is aged at least 18 may make an application for a gender recognition certificate on the basis of—

(a) living in the other gender, or

(b) having changed gender under the law of a country or territory outside the United Kingdom.

(2) In this Act "the acquired gender", in relation to a person by whom an application under subsection (1) is or has been made, means—

(a) in the case of an application under paragraph (a) of that subsection, the gender in which the person is living, or

(b) in the case of an application under paragraph (b) of that subsection, the gender to which the person has changed under the law of the country or territory concerned.

207 *ibid.*
208 [2003] UKHL 21.

(3) An application under subsection (1) is to be determined by a Gender Recognition Panel.[209] . . .

2 Determination of applications

(1) In the case of an application under section 1(1)(a), the Panel must grant the application if satisfied that the applicant—

(a) has or has had gender dysphoria,

(b) has lived in the acquired gender throughout the period of two years ending with the date on which the application is made,

(c) intends to continue to live in the acquired gender until death, and

(d) complies with the requirements imposed by and under section 3.

(2) In the case of an application under section 1(1)(b), the Panel must grant the application if satisfied—

(a) that the country or territory under the law of which the applicant has changed gender is an approved country or territory, and

(b) that the applicant complies with the requirements imposed by and under section 3.

(3) The Panel must reject an application under section 1(1) if not required by subsection (1) or (2) to grant it. . . .

3 Evidence

(1) An application under section 1(1)(a) must include either—

(a) a report made by a registered medical practitioner practising in the field of gender dysphoria and a report made by another registered medical practitioner (who may, but need not, practise in that field), or

(b) a report made by a chartered psychologist practising in that field and a report made by a registered medical practitioner (who may, but need not, practise in that field).

(2) But subsection (1) is not complied with unless a report required by that subsection and made by—

(a) a registered medical practitioner, or

(b) a chartered psychologist,

practising in the field of gender dysphoria includes details of the diagnosis of the applicant's gender dysphoria.

(3) And subsection (1) is not complied with in a case where—

(a) the applicant has undergone or is undergoing treatment for the purpose of modifying sexual characteristics, or

(b) treatment for that purpose has been prescribed or planned for the applicant,

[209] The operation of which is governed by Sch.1.

unless at least one of the reports required by that subsection includes details of it.

(4) An application under section 1(1)(a) must also include a statutory declaration by the applicant that the applicant meets the conditions in section 2(1)(b) and (c).

(5) An application under section 1(1)(b) must include evidence that the applicant has changed gender under the law of an approved country or territory.

(6) Any application under section 1(1) must include—

(a) a statutory declaration as to whether or not the applicant is married or a civil partner,

(b) any other information or evidence required by an order made by the Secretary of State, and

(c) any other information or evidence which the Panel which is to determine the application may require, and may include any other information or evidence which the applicant wishes to include. . . .

(8) If the Panel which is to determine the application requires information or evidence under subsection (6)(c) it must give reasons for doing so.

4 Successful applications

(1) If a Gender Recognition Panel grants an application under section 1(1) it must issue a gender recognition certificate to the applicant.

(2) Unless the applicant is married or a civil partner, the certificate is to be a full gender recognition certificate.

(3) If the applicant is married or a civil partner, the certificate is to be an interim gender recognition certificate. . . .[210]

5 Issue of full certificates where applicant has been married[211]

(1) A court which—

(a) makes absolute a decree of nullity granted on the ground that an interim gender recognition certificate has been issued to a party to the marriage, or

(b) (in Scotland) grants a decree of divorce on that ground,

must, on doing so, issue a full gender recognition certificate to that party and send a copy to the Secretary of State.

(2) If an interim gender recognition certificate has been issued to a person and either—

(a) the person's marriage is dissolved or annulled (otherwise than on the ground mentioned in subsection (1)) in proceedings instituted during the period of six months beginning with the day on which it was issued, or

(b) the person's spouse dies within that period,

the person may make an application for a full gender recognition certificate at any time within the period specified in subsection (3) (unless the person is again married or is a civil partner).

210 Sch.2 governs interim certificates.

211 Note also s.5A governing the issuing of a full certificate where the applicant has been a civil partner.

(3) That period is the period of six months beginning with the day on which the marriage is dissolved or annulled or the death occurs.

(4) An application under subsection (2) must include evidence of the dissolution or annulment of the marriage and the date on which proceedings for it were instituted, or of the death of the spouse and the date on which it occurred.

(5) An application under subsection (2) is to be determined by a Gender Recognition Panel.

(6) The Panel—

(a) must grant the application if satisfied that the applicant is neither married nor a civil partner, and

(b) otherwise must reject it.

(7) If the Panel grants the application it must issue a full gender recognition certificate to the applicant.

9 General

(1) Where a full gender recognition certificate is issued to a person, the person's gender becomes for all purposes the acquired gender (so that, if the acquired gender is the male gender, the person's sex becomes that of a man and, if it is the female gender, the person's sex becomes that of a woman).

(2) Subsection (1) does not affect things done, or events occurring, before the certificate is issued; but it does operate for the interpretation of enactments passed, and instruments and other documents made, before the certificate is issued (as well as those passed or made afterwards). . . .

10 Registration

(1) Where there is a UK birth register entry in relation to a person to whom a full gender recognition certificate is issued, the Secretary of State must send a copy of the certificate to the appropriate Registrar General.

(2) In this Act "UK birth register entry", in relation to a person to whom a full gender recognition certificate is issued, means—

(a) an entry of which a certified copy is kept by a Registrar General, or

(b) an entry in a register so kept,

containing a record of the person's birth or adoption (or, if there would otherwise be more than one, the most recent). . . .[212]

12 Parenthood

The fact that a person's gender has become the acquired gender under this Act does not affect the status of the person as the father or mother of a child.

In addition, s.6 makes provision for errors in certificates, s.8 allows for appeals to the High Court against the refusal of a certificate, s.13 and Sch.5 govern social security benefits and pensions, and s.15 governs succession. Centrally to

[212] See also Sch.3.

the scheme of the Act, section 11 allows an unmarried individual whose gender has been reassigned to contract an (opposite-sex) civil marriage after a full gender recognition certificate has been issued (see also schedule 4).

2. The Civil Partnership Act 2004

This section summarizes some of the main features of civil partnership, and analyses the extent to which it is a similar institution to heterosexual marriage by focusing on the drafting of the Civil Partnership Act 2004 ("C.P.A."), the government's and legislature's justifications for establishing civil partnership as a distinct institution, relevant House of Lords' *dicta* from *Ghaidan* and *M* and the High Court's decision in *Wilkinson v Kitzinger*.[213]

Ministers in the House of Commons and House of Lords, together with the Department of Trade and Industry's pre-legislative Consultation Paper *Civil Partnership: A framework for the legal recognition of same-sex couples*, explained the case for civil partnership legislation in terms of the promotion of equality and stability.[214] According to the Consultation Paper, civil partnership registration "would be an important equality measure for same-sex couples in England and Wales"[215] and would provide "a framework whereby same-sex couples could acknowledge their mutual responsibilities", thereby encouraging "more stable family life".[216] In the House of Commons Second and Third Reading debates, Jacqui Smith MP, then Deputy Minister for Women and Equality, explained the legislation as a "sign of the Government's commitment to social justice and equality",[217] as being "about equality",[218] and as marking "an important stage on the progress towards equality for lesbian and gay people".[219] The Bill was also concerned to underpin "the importance of stable and committed same-sex relationships", and marked "a major step in helping [same-sex] couples gain greater social acceptance of their partnership and overcome the distressing consequences for many people of their legal invisibility".[220] Same-sex couples who registered as civil partners would gain

213 [2006] E.W.H.C. 2022 (Fam.), [2007] I.F.L.R. 296. This section draws upon Nicholas Bamforth, "'The benefits of marriage in all but name?' Same-sex couples and the Civil Partnership Act 2004" (2007) 19 C.F.L.Q. 013.

214 Although equality may, on analysis, break down to deeper arguments based upon dignity and autonomy: see further Nicholas Bamforth, "Same-Sex Partnerships and Arguments of Justice", in Robert Wintemute and Mads Andenaes (eds.), *Legal Recognition of Same-Sex Partnerships* (Oxford: Hart, 2001), and "The role of philosophical and constitutional arguments in the same-sex marriage debate: a response to John Murphy" (2005) 17 C.F.L.Q. 165. It is also interesting to note that in the House of Lords Second Reading debate for the Civil Partnership Bill, Baroness Scotland (leading for the government) suggested that the Bill signalled that same-sex couples "should be treated with fairness and dignity" (HL Deb., April 22, 2004, col.392).

215 (DTI, Women and Equality Unit, 2003), para.1.2; see also para.2.6.

216 *ibid.*, para.1.2; see also para.2.1.

217 H.C. Deb., October 12, 2004, Col.174.

218 Col.176; see also cols. 177–8.

219 HC Deb., November 9, 2004, Col.796.

220 HC Deb., October 12, 2004, col. 174; see also Baroness Scotland, HL Deb., 22nd April 2004, cols. 387, 392.

greater "security in life",[221] legally-speaking, given that registration would overcome the adverse consequences of invisibility in all areas where spousal status is crucial for opposite-sex partners: for example, succession rights to the matrimonial home, next-of-kin status in the event of emergency medical care and death, coverage by "standard" insurance policies and pension rights, and so on. In similar vein, Baroness Scotland stressed during the House of Lords Second Reading debate that the Bill was "seeking to give people an opportunity to recognise the stability" of committed same-sex relationships,[222] and that it had been introduced "for reasons of social justice and equality".[223]

A civil partnership is defined in s.1(1) of the CPA as "a relationship between two people of the same sex ... which is formed when they register as civil partners of each other" or when their relationship was registered overseas but falls within the ambit of Pt 5 (ss.212 to 218). Part 2 governs civil partnerships in England and Wales, with c.1 of that Part (ss.2 to 36) dealing with their formation, and c.2 (ss.37 to 64) with dissolution and nullity.[224] That the CPA is a lengthy and complex piece of legislation (it contains a total of two hundred and sixty-four sections and thirty schedules) is unsurprising.[225] For one thing, civil partnership provides a completely new legal status that will affect every area of the shared lives of those same-sex couples who register. Apart from making detailed provision for the formation and termination of civil partnerships, the CPA has implications for the law's treatment of parents (biological, step- and adoptive), children and other family members, and for the holding of property by same-sex couples. For another, it establishes and lays down rules governing the operation of civil partnerships in all parts of the United Kingdom, rather than just one of its three component jurisdictions.

A civil partnership is registered when two people sign a civil partnership document in the presence of a registrar and two witnesses.[226] The procedures for registration are generally analogous to those that apply to civil marriages (there are thus waiting periods, rules governing objections,[227] and special procedures applicable where one party is house-bound,[228] detained in a hospital or prison[229] or terminally ill[230]) or else perform an equivalent function (for

221 HC Deb., October 12, 2004, col. 175.
222 HL Deb., April 22, 2004, col.392.
223 HL Deb., April 22, 2004, col.430; see also HL Deb., May 10, 2004, cols.GC46, GC48.
224 CPA, Pt 3 deals with Scotland and Pt 4 with Northern Ireland. This article focuses on the law in England and Wales. For general discussion of formation and dissolution, see Harper, et al, Ch.4.
225 For a summary of the Bill's Parliamentary history, see Mark Harper, Martin Downs, Katharine Landells and Gerald Wilson, *Civil Partnership—The New Law* (Bristol: Jordan Publishing, 2005), paras 3.30 to 3.40 (hereafter "Harper, et al").
226 CPA, s.2; the technical meaning of a civil partnership document is set out in s.7.
227 CPA, ss.8 to 17; the comparable marriage procedures are usefully summarized in Stephen Cretney, Judith Masson & Rebecca Bailey-Harris, *Principles of Family Law* (London: Sweet & Maxwell, 7th edn., 2003), Ch.1 (hereafter "Cretney, Masson & Bailey-Harris").
228 CPA, s.18; compare Marriage Act 1983, s.1.
229 CPA, ;s.19; compare Marriage Act 1983, s.1.
230 CPA, ss.21 to 27; this is known as the "special procedure". Compare the Marriage (Registrar-General's Licence) Act 1970.

example, the requirement that non-religious *premises* be used for civil partnership registration[231] has the same practical effect as the prohibition on the use of religious *services* at marriages in registry offices and on "approved premises"[232]). However, some technical differences remain. First, in certain detailed respects the CPA procedures reflect the updated scheme for civil marriage contemplated in the government's Consultation Paper *Civil Registration: Delivering Vital Change*,[233] rather than the procedures applicable to marriage when the Act came into force.[234] Secondly, as Baroness Scotland (who led for the government in the House of Lords) stressed during the Bill's passage, whereas a marriage is formed with the exchange of vows during the ceremony, so that the formal registration records an event which has *already* occurred, in a civil partnership it is the act of registration that marks the formation of the relationship regardless of any words previously exchanged.[235]

The provisions governing eligibility to form a civil partnership would appear to be similar to or the logical counterpart of those governing marriage. Section 3 stipulates that two people may not register if they are not of the same sex (the counterpart to the requirement that parties to a marriage not be of the same sex[236]), if either is already a civil partner or married (echoing the prohibition of bigamy in marriage[237]), if either is under sixteen (echoing the position in relation to marriage[238]), or if the partners are within what are called the prohibited degrees of relationship. The prohibited degrees are set out in Pt 1 of Sch.1, "absolute prohibitions" paralleling the prohibited degrees of consanguinity in marriage and "qualified prohibitions" the prohibited degrees of affinity.[239] Two people are absolutely prohibited from forming a civil partnership if one is the child or parent (whether biological, adoptive or formerly

[231] CPA, s.6.

[232] Marriage Act 1949, ss.45 and 46B. Of course, there is nothing to stop a couple who have been married at a registry office or on "approved premises", or who have become civil partners on non-religious premises, from having a later religious celebration elsewhere: see Paul Mallender and Jane Rayson, *The Civil Partnership Act 2004: A Practical Guide* (Cambridge: Cambridge University Press, 2005), para.4.2.2 (hereafter "Mallender and Rayson").

[233] (January 2003). For detailed discussion of the analogies, see Harper, et al, paras 4.12 to 4.34.

[234] For discussion of which, see Cretney, Masson & Bailey-Harris, Ch.1. It was originally envisaged that the new scheme for marriage could be introduced by order under s.1 of the Regulatory Reform Act 2001, but it has since been accepted that primary legislation will be needed. For discussion, see the General Register Office Consultation Paper *Registration Modernisation* (November 2005), especially Annex 1; also *Registration Modernisation: Outcome of Consultation* (May 2006). Once the new scheme is enacted, the Chancellor of the Exchequer will be able to use CPA, s.35 to assimilate by order civil partnership procedures with the revised procedures for marriage.

[235] HL Deb., June 24, 2004, Col. 1359; this point is broadly reflected in the drafting of s.2.

[236] Matrimonial Causes Act 1973, s.11(c), *Hyde v Hyde* (1866) L.R. 1 P. & D. 130, 133 (Lord Penzance); for discussion, see Cretney, Masson & Bailey-Harris, para.2–021.

[237] Cretney, Masson & Bailey-Harris, para.2–022.

[238] For discussion, see Cretney, Masson & Bailey-Harris, paras 2–017 & 2–018. Permission must be granted by an appropriate person (usually the parent or guardian) where a person aged under eighteen wishes to enter into a civil partnership (see ss.4, 52(1) and Sch.2), again echoing the position in relation to marriage: Cretney, Masson & Bailey-Harris, paras 1–007 to 1–010.

[239] These are governed by the Marriage Acts 1949 to 1986: for discussion, see Cretney, Masson & Bailey-Harris, paras 2–007 to 2–016.

adoptive), parent's sibling, grandparent, grandchild, sibling, or sibling's child of the other.[240] The qualified prohibitions fall into two groups. First, a partnership may not be formed—unless both parties are twenty-one or over and the younger was never, before the age of eighteen, a "child of the family"[241] in relation to the older—if one is the child of a former civil partner or former spouse of the other, a former civil partner or former spouse of a parent or grandparent of the other, or a grandchild of a former civil partner or former spouse of the other.[242] Secondly, unless both intending partners are twenty-one or over, a person may not form a civil partnership with a parent of someone they have previously been married to or the civil partner of, unless that person and their other parent are dead; nor with the parent of their former civil partner or spouse unless the former civil partner or spouse and their other parent are dead.[243]

Courts tended until comparatively recently to be troubled by the presence of lesbians or gay men as would-be adopters.[244] However, the Adoption and Children Act 2002 allowed for adoption orders to be applied for on the same basis by same-sex *and* opposite-sex couples who were living together in an "enduring family relationship",[245] prompting some authors to suggest that it was "arguable that the real breakthrough" in relation to the recognition of same-sex partnerships occurred at this stage[246]: by making analogous provision for same-sex couples, the 2002 Act "removed from the debate one of the most contentious arguments of all, that if lesbians and gay men were allowed to enter civil partnerships should they not also be allowed to adopt children?".[247] In relation to adoption, the role of the CPA is thus to include civil partners within the provisions of the 2002 Act, allowing for the same assessment criteria to apply to married, unmarried, partnered and un-partnered couples,[248] as well as amending related statutory provisions to include civil partners.[249] The CPA also amends the Children Act 1989 so as to place a civil

[240] CPA, Sch.1, para.1.

[241] That is, someone who lived in the same household and was treated by the older person as a child of the family.

[242] CPA, Sch.1, para.2. Paras 4 to 8 set out the special procedures applicable in such cases.

[243] CPA, Sch.1, para 3. Paragraph 9 sets out the special procedure applicable in such cases

[244] Or as biological parents in child custody cases. See, generally, *Re D* [1977] A.C. 603; *Re P* (1983) 4 F.L.R. 401; *B v B* (1991) 1 F.L.R. 402. Even if a parent's sexuality was not automatically determinative of the outcome, courts repeatedly expressed their concern about the possibility of "corruption" or "stigmatization".

[245] Adoption and Children Act 2002, ss.49, 50, 144(4). This Act followed the adoption of a more sympathetic judicial treatment of same-sex partnerships: see *Re W* (1997) 2 F.L.R. 406 and *G v F* (1998) 2 F.L.R. 799.

[246] Harper *et al., ibid.*, para.1.8.

[247] *ibid.*, para 1.9; see also para 6.3 ("relatively uncontroversial").

[248] CPA, s.79; for general discussion of adoption, see Cretney, Masson & Bailey-Harris, Ch.23.

[249] For the amended provisions, see Adoption and Children Act 2002, ss.21 (placement orders), 47 and 51 (conditions for making adoption orders), 64, 74(1), 79 and 81.

partner in an analogous position to an opposite-sex step-parent when it comes to acquiring parental responsibility for the biological child(ren) of their partner,[250] and on the same footing as the married in relation to a "child of the family" under the 1989 Act[251] and when it comes to applying for a residence or contact order.[252] When it comes to financial provision for children where a relationship ends, civil partners are to be treated as parents on the same basis as the married.[253] Furthermore, the concept of a "relative" of a child in the 1989 Act is expanded so as to include relatives by virtue of a civil partnership,[254] and the earlier Act's guardianship provisions are amended so as to treat civil partners and married couples in the same fashion where one partner has appointed the other as guardian (in the event of their death) of a child for which they have parental responsibility and the relationship is dissolved or annulled.[255]

The comprehensive nature of the CPA is reflected in the fact that it makes provision for civil partners in just about all other areas in which provision is made for married couples. Civil partners are thus inserted into the Wills Act 1837,[256] the Administration of Estates Act 1925,[257] the Intestates' Estates Act 1952,[258] the Births and Deaths Registration Act 1953,[259] the Family Provision Act 1966,[260] the Inheritance (Provision for Family and Dependants) Act 1975,[261] the Fatal Accidents Act 1976,[262] the Enduring Powers of Attorney Act 1985,[263] and into rules relating to the giving of evidence by a spouse,[264] to tenancies,[265] to pensions,[266] to insolvency,[267] to the definition of consideration in relation to real property,[268] and to social security, child support and tax credits[269]—to cite but a few examples.[270] Perhaps ironically, given the emphasis placed upon it

250 They may do so by agreement with their partner (the biological parent), or with both parents if responsibility is shared, or by court order: CPA, s.75(2), amending Children Act 1989, s.4A. For general discussion of parental responsibility, see Cretney, Masson & Bailey-Harris, paras 18–101 to 18–049; for discussion of the 2004 Act, see Paul Mallendar and Jane Rayson, para.8.2.
251 CPA, s.75(3), amending Children Act 1989, s.105(1); for discussion, see Paul Mallendar and Jane Rayson, para.8.3.
252 CPA, s.77, amending Children Act 1989, s.10(5).
253 CPA, s.78, amending Children Act 1989, Sch.1.
254 CPA, s.75(4), amending Children Act 1989, s.105(1).
255 CPA, s.76, amending Children Act 1989, s.6.
256 CPA, Sch.4, paras 1–5.
257 CPA, Sch.4, paras 7–12.
258 CPA, Sch.4, para.13.
259 CPA, Sch.27, para.19.
260 CPA, Sch.4, para.14.
261 CPA, Sch.4, paras 15–27.
262 CPA, s.83.
263 CPA, Sch.27, paras 106–8.
264 CPA, s.84 and Sch.27.
265 CPA, Sch.8, following *Ghaidan, ibid.*
266 CPA, Sch.24.
267 CPA, Sch.27, paras 112–122.
268 CPA, Sch.7.
269 CPA, Sch.24.
270 As Baroness Hale noted in *M, ibid.*, paras [100] & [101], these changes are not always to the financial advantage of those who register as civil partners.

during the CPA's passage through Parliament, the Act does not itself make provision for inheritance tax (and other similar forms of tax): instead, s.103 of the Finance Act 2005 allows for differences of treatment between civil partners and spouses to be corrected by secondary legislation.

The procedures governing the ending of civil partnerships are set out in c.2, of Pt 2. As s.37 makes clear, a court[271] may make a "dissolution order" where a civil partnership has broken down irretrievably; a "nullity order" annulling a partnership which is void or voidable; or a "presumption of death order" dissolving a partnership on the ground that one partner is presumed to be dead. All three types of order are in the first instance conditional and may not be made final before six weeks have elapsed.[272] Subsequent sections make more detailed provision for each type of order. First, s.44 stipulates that a dissolution order must be made where the court is satisfied—provided that it is not also satisfied that the relationship has *not* broken down irretrievably—that the applicant cannot, by reason of the respondent's behaviour, reasonably be expected to live with them; and/or that the parties had lived apart for a continuous period of at least two years immediately before the order was applied for and the respondent consents to the order; and/or that the parties had lived apart for a continuous period of at least five years immediately before the order was applied for; and/or that the respondent had deserted the applicant for a continuous period of at least two years before the order was applied for.[273] An application for a dissolution order may not be made before a year has elapsed from the date on which the partnership was formed.[274] (Provisions also exist for situations falling short of the termination of civil partnerships: a court must make a "separation order"[275] where it is satisfied that one or more of the evidential bases for establishing irretrievable breakdown set out in s.44 exists, although it is irrelevant—by contrast with an application for a dissolution order—whether the relationship *had* in fact broken down irretrievably.[276]) Secondly, a civil partnership is either void or voidable, leading to a nullity order, in situations governed respectively by ss.49 and 50. Section 49 declares a partnership to be void if the partners were not eligible to register, by reference to the criteria set out in s.3, at the time that they did so; or if the procedural requirements concerning the giving of notice, the issuing of the civil partnership document, the place of registration, or the presence of an approved registrar, were not complied with and the parties

[271] CPA ss.37(4) and (5), 58–61 and 219–224 define which courts have jurisdiction in the circumstances covered.

[272] CPA ss.37(2) and 38(1). Note also ss.39 and 40 concerning the intervention in a case of the Queen's Proctor.

[273] Further details and qualifications are specified in CPA, ss.45 to 48.

[274] CPA, s.41(1). See also ss.42 and 43, dealing with attempts to reconcile and consideration by the court of agreements between the parties concerning the outcome of dissolution or separation proceedings.

[275] CPA, s.37(1)(d).

[276] Note also the distinction between the requirement that one (or more) of the bases "exists" (CPA s.56(1)) in the case of a separation order and that the court is "satisfied" of such existence (ss.44 (4) and (5)) in the case of a dissolution order.

were aware of this at the time of registration. According to s.50, the partnership is voidable[277] (subject to a series of constraints imposed by s.51 relating to the conduct of the applicant for the nullity order and the timing of the proceedings) where either party did not validly consent to its formation, or was suffering from a sufficiently serious mental disorder, or was pregnant by a person other than the intended civil partner,[278] or was the subject of an interim gender recognition certificate under the Gender Recognition Act 2004, or where their gender had become their acquired gender in terms of that Act (both the latter scenarios run contrary to the requirement that civil partners be legally of the same sex[279]). Thirdly, presumption of death orders are governed by s.55, which makes clear that a court may make such an order on an application by a civil partner if it is satisfied that there are reasonable grounds for supposing the other partner to be dead, the other partner's absence for a period of seven years or more—when coupled with the applicant having had no reason to believe them to be alive within that period—being evidence, until the contrary is proved, of their death.

The procedures for terminating a civil partnership (or for separation) would in general seem—as with those governing formation—to be similar to those governing marriage. As Paul Mallender and Jane Rayson put it:

"The orders that the court can make are very similar to those made ... on the breakdown of a marriage, and divorce practitioners will readily recognise the language and concepts".[280]

With the exception of adultery (see below), the evidential bases that apply in the case of a dissolution order parallel those which apply, under s.1(2) of the Matrimonial Causes Act 1973, when establishing the irretrievable breakdown of a marriage.[281] As with marriage, a year is needed before dissolution can occur, helping Mark Harper and others to conclude that a dissolution order seems intended to be the civil partnership equivalent of a divorce.[282] The order's conditionality would seem, furthermore, to parallel the workings of

[277] With the consequence, according to CPA, s.37(3), that the partnership is annulled from the time of the nullity order but is not void *ab initio*. The void/voidable distinction is explained by Lord Greene M.R., in the context of marriage, in *De Reneville v De Reneville* [1948] 1 All E.R. 56, 60.

[278] Harper, et al rightly criticise this requirement, at para.4.52, as being otiose in most situations given that civil partners must be of the same sex. The requirement could nonetheless turn out to be *genuinely problematical* in terms of its results: for example, where a long-standing, deeply committed lesbian couple wish to become civil partners in order to publicly express their commitment to founding a family, shortly before one of them—who is pregnant having been artificially inseminated with the full support of the other—gives birth.

[279] For practical illustrations of the types of situation that will be covered by these provisions, see Paul Mallendar and Jane Ryson, *ibid.*, para.11.2.3.

[280] *ibid.*, para.10.1.

[281] See further Mallender and Rayson, paras 10.5 to 10.15, in which it is assumed (at paras 10.5 and 10.6) that divorce case law will be applicable in the context of the dissolution of civil partnerships.

[282] ibid., para.4.47.

the *decree nisi* within marriage,[283] while nullity orders generally appear to be grantable in equivalent situations to those in which a marriage would be found to be void or voidable.[284] Presumption of death orders have been argued to mirror the power conferred on courts by s.19(3) of the Matrimonial Causes Act 1973 in the context of divorce,[285] and an analogous argument can be made about the similarity between separation orders and the provisions applicable to marriage under s.17 of the 1973 Act.[286]

Nonetheless, there are two slightly curious differences between ending a marriage and a civil partnership. First, adultery is (so long as the applicant finds it intolerable to live with the respondent) a basis for establishing an irretrievable breakdown in the case of marriage, but not in the context of civil partnership.[287] This difference has been explained on the basis that "adultery" is, as a concept, defined in such a way as to be confined to the arena of heterosexual marriage, in that it involves partial or complete penetration of a woman by a man, neither party being married to the other and at least one of the two being married to someone else.[288] Nonetheless, this might be thought unduly formalistic: for whatever the sex of the parties, the law is seeking to deal in this area with the consequences of sexual infidelity within a relationship, and one might imagine—given that other aspects of the law governing marriage have been adapted to cover same-sex relationships—that a more flexibly phrased but directly analogous concept to adultery could have been included within the legislation. Paul Mallender and Jane Rayson seek to minimise the significance of this omission when they suggest that "the failure of imagination of the draftsman (or his disinclination) ought not to create any real difficulty, as it is highly likely that sexual intercourse, or even acts falling short of that, with someone, whether of the same or different gender, will persuade a court that the respondent [in divorce/dissolution proceedings] has thereby behaved in such a way that the applicant cannot reasonably be expected to live with" them.[289] This will doubtless be the case in practice, even if those who claim that civil partnership is the *exact* legal equivalent of marriage are compelled—in order to defend the logic of their position—to argue for marriage to be brought into line with civil partnerships, with adultery being removed as a cause of breakdown in the case of marriage and the focus shifted to unfaithfulness as an unreasonable form of behaviour. Secondly, a civil partnership may not—unlike a marriage—be ended for non-

283 Mallender and Rayson, para.10.1.

284 Compare Mallender and Rayson, ch.11 (civil partnerships) and Cretney, Masson & Bailey-Harris, paras 2–002 to 2–050 (marriage).

285 Mallender and Rayson, para.11.4.

286 For analysis of those provisions, see further Cretney, Masson & Bailey-Harris, Ch.12.

287 In the context of marriage, see Matrimonial Causes Act 1973, s.1(2)(a); Cretney, Masson & Bailey-Harris, Ch.11.

288 Harper, et al, para.4.48.

289 Mallender and Rayson, para.10.3. Harper, et al make a similar suggestion: see para.4.48.

consummation or venereal disease.[290] Other than the marginally greater difficulty of defining non-consummation in the case of a same-sex relationship, and the distaste doubtless felt by Parliamentarians about specifying the various forms of sexual infection that are transmissible through sexual activities of different types, no obvious reason has been offered for these drafting differences.[291] As with adultery, the practical importance may well be small: nonetheless, those who argue that marriage and civil partnership are *exact* equivalents will doubtless be keen for them to be eliminated.

The provisions concerning property and financial relief where a civil partnership breaks down are complex but largely mirror the rules which apply to marriage. In relation to property, the Act includes civil partners within Pt IV of the Family Law Act 1996, so that they are treated on the same basis as married couples when it comes to occupation of the home they inhabited.[292] Courts are thus entitled (depending on each civil partner's interests in or relating to the property) to issue occupation orders in relation to the "civil partnership home". "Matrimonial home rights", a key aspect of the 1996 Act regime, are re-designated "home rights" and extended so as to include civil partners, as are non-molestation orders.[293] Schedule 5 of the CPA makes provision for corresponding financial relief to that provided for "in connection with marriages by Pt 2 of the Matrimonial Causes Act 1973."[294] Mark Harper and others regard the presence of this declaration as "important" since it "gives the clearest indication possible that the purpose of the civil partnership regime is to extend all of those rights and responsibilities invoked by a marriage ... at least as regards ancillary relief".[295] Schedule 5 allows a court to make a series of orders which are analogous to those available under the 1973 Act.[296] Part 1 governs the making of periodical payments or the payment of a lump sum or sums to a civil partner, to any person for the benefit of a child of the family, or to a child of the family, if a dissolution, nullity or separation order is made or at any time afterwards. Part 2 allows for property adjustment; Pt 3 governs sale of property orders; and Pt 4 governs pension sharing orders. Part 5 then sets out the factors that a court must have regard to when making any of these orders, beginning—according to paragraph 20—with all the circumstances of the case and giving "first consideration" to the welfare of any child of the

290 In the case of non-consummation, see HL Deb., November 17, 2004, Col.1479 (Baroness Scotland).

291 The silence of Harper, et al—*ibid.*, para.4.52—is visible. For discussion of the position in relation to marriage, compare Cretney, Masson & Bailey-Harris, paras 2–022 to 2–037, where difficulties relating to the requirement of consummation are usefully outlined.

292 For discussion of the 1996 Act, see Cretney, Masson & Bailey-Harris, paras 6–005 to 6–010 and 10–005 to 10–025; for more detailed analysis of the effects of the 2004 Act, see Paul Mallender and Jane Rayson, ch.13, Mark Harper, et al, paras 8.8 to 8.15.

293 CPA, Sch.9. Note also ss.65 to 68 concerning other orders relating to property.

294 CPA, s.72(1).

295 *ibid.*, para.5.8.

296 For discussion of the 1973 Act, see Cretney, Masson & Bailey-Harris, paras 14–009 to 14–108. For detailed analysis of the 2004 Act's intervention, see Paul Mallender and Jane Rayson, Ch.14, Mark Harper, et al, ch.5.

family who has not reached eighteen. Paragraphs 21 and 22 provide more detailed lists of particular factors to be taken into account, both generally and when exercising powers in relation to children. The lists include factors relating to income, earning capacity and assets; financial needs, obligations and responsibilities; physical or mental disability; and family arrangements more broadly. It has been suggested that the general factors are likely to be interpreted as they are in Matrimonial Causes Act case law, with the possible difference that pre-conceptions concerning gender roles in a relationship may be difficult to carry over to civil partnerships.[297]

Viewed in the round, the drafting of the CPA therefore seems to suggest that most of the differences between civil partnership and marriage are relatively minor.[298] Paul Mallender and Jane Rayson note that:

"Although it is not marriage, civil partnership is in truth very close to that institution ... Many of its provisions are taken directly, word for word, from the statutes that regulate heterosexual married life and many of the amendments to existing legislation are achieved by inserting after 'spouse' the words 'or civil partner'. The vast array of amendments to existing legislation ensure that partners who are in a civil partnership are put on a similar footing to a couple who have married heterosexually with the result that, although the proponents of the legislation assiduously avoided the phrase, something very like 'gay marriage' has been created by this Act."[299]

This is reinforced by Baroness Scotland's assertion, at the Bill's House of Lords Report Stage, that the formation of a civil partnership would—like that of a marriage—involve a change of status rather than being a merely contractual matter.[300]

How far civil partnership is similar to—or distinct from—marriage was a central issue in the political debate preceding and surrounding the passage of the CPA. The Consultation Paper *Civil Partnership: A framework for the legal recognition of same-sex couples* was clear that it was quite distinct from any proposal to introduce same-sex marriage, for which the government had no plans,[301] and that opposite-sex couples retained the separate option of

[297] Mark Harper, et al, para.5.19.

[298] Note also the powers of amendment granted to the government by CPA, ss.259 and 260.

[299] Paul Mallender & Jane Rayson, para.1.2. Mark Harper, et al reach the perhaps stronger conclusion (echoed in comments made throughout their book) that the Act "applies most of the legal incidences of marriage to civil partnership. The policy of the Act is that civil partners should be treated equally to spouses wherever possible and that any differences from marriage must be objectively justifiable": para.8.99. The "objectively justifiable" aspect of this interpretation may attribute an overly schematic approach to the legislature.

[300] HL Deb., June 24, 2004, Cols 1361–2. See also Harper, et al, pp.40–1. In relation marriage going beyond contract, see P.M. North & J.J. Fawcett, *Cheshire and North's Private International Law* (Oxford: Oxford University Press, 13th edn., 2004), p.704.

[301] *ibid.*, para.1.3; see also *Responses to Civil Partnership: A framework for the legal recognition of same-sex couples* (DTI, Women and Equality Unit, 2003), para.3.4.

marriage.[302] Baroness Scotland stressed that the legislation would not "undermine or weaken the importance of marriage and we do not propose to open civil partnership to opposite-sex couples. Civil partnership is aimed at same-sex couples who cannot marry."[303] The distinction between marriage and civil partnership was repeatedly emphasised by the Bill's supporters in both the Commons and the Lords.[304] Nonetheless, the somewhat blurry nature of the distinction is clear from Jacqui Smith MP's acknowledgement, when speaking for the government in the Commons, that "in the vast majority of cases ... those people who enter into a civil partnership" would "receive the same rights and take on the same responsibilities as those that we expect of those who enter into civil marriage"[305] and that civil partnership provided "the same opportunity for same-sex couples to gain legal recognition of their relationship as currently exists for opposite-sex couples through the route of marriage."[306]

When one considers the provisions of the CPA in the light of these observations, it might well be concluded that the idea of civil partnership involves something of a tension: on the one hand, civil partners enjoy—and were intended by the legislature to enjoy—just about all of the legal benefits, and to be burdened with all the relevant legal responsibilities, of marriage; yet on the other hand, civil partnership is, and was intended by the legislature to be, a distinct institution from marriage. This point is also reflected in relevant House of Lords dicta in *Ghaidan* and *M*. In her dissenting judgment in *M*, Baroness Hale emphasised the similarities between civil partnership and marriage in terms of benefits and responsibilities, observing that the Act "grants to same sex couples the same legal recognition that the law grants to opposite sex couples. It allows them to contract into a formal status with virtually identical legal consequences to those of marriage".[307] In similar vein, Lord Mance stated that it gave them "expressly the same rights as opposite sex couples".[308] Lord Millett emphasised the apparent tension rather more bluntly in his dissenting judgment in *Ghaidan*, where he stated that "Persons cannot be or be treated as married to each other or live together as husband and wife unless they are of the opposite sex", but that the Act did not attempt to "do

302 *Civil Partnership: A framework*, paras 2.6–2.8; *Responses to Civil Partnership*, para.3.6.

303 HL Deb., April 22, 2004, Col.388 and May 10, 2004, Col.GC31. Note also the repeated emphasis on the opt-in nature of civil partnership: *Civil Partnership: A framework*, paras 2.2 and 2.3; H.C. Deb., October 12, 2004, Col.179 (Jacqui Smith MP); HL Deb., April 22 2004, Cols 392, 431 & 432 (Baroness Scotland); HL Deb., May 10, 2004, Col. GC40 (Baroness Scotland).

304 See, e.g., HC Deb., October 12, 2004, Cols 185 & 186 (Alan Duncan MP), 200 (Angela Eagle MP); HC Deb., November 9, 2004, Col.737 (Angela Eagle MP); HL Deb., May 10, 2004, Col.GC41 (Baroness Scotland); HL Deb., November 17, 2004, Col.1477 (Baroness Scotland).

305 H.C. Deb., October 12, 2004, Col.177.

306 H.C. Deb., October 12, 2004, Col.179. The point also emerges with real force in a marvellously equivocal passage in the commentary on the Act by Mark Harper, et al, para.4.4: "The truth of the matter from a legal perspective is that civil partnership to all intents and purposes is civil marriage in all but name. It is nonetheless a different institution from civil marriage. The effective legal differences between civil partnership and civil marriage are few."

307 para.[99]; see also paras [100]–[101], and her judgment in *Ghaidan* at para.[140].

308 para.[123].

anything as silly as to treat same sex relationships as marriages, whether legal or de facto. It pays them the respect to which they are entitled by treating them as conceptually different but entitled to equality of treatment".[309] Sir Mark Potter P. suggested, similarly, in *Wilkinson v Kitzinger* that the CPA grants "statutory recognition of a status and relationship closely modelled upon that of marriage" and "made available to civil partners essentially every material right and responsibility presently arising from marriage, with the exception of the form of ceremony and the actual name and status of marriage."[310]

These uncertainties suggest that it is difficult to gauge with confidence the prospects of success of any challenge to the marriage/civil partnership distinction, resting on the argument that marriage should be open to same-sex couples, before the Strasbourg Court or domestically.

Two further factors reinforce this: the first relates to the margin of appreciation, and the second to the limits of the courts' interpretive powers under section 3(1) of the Human Rights Act 1998. The margin of appreciation was discussed at length by the House of Lords in *M.* in relation to secondary legislation created under the Child Support Act 1991. However, their Lordships also speculated about how the margin might be applied in the context of a Convention-based challenge to contemporary legislation which appeared to draw a distinction based upon sexual orientation. Lords Bingham, Walker and Mance appeared to agree that the margin of appreciation had changed since the secondary legislation at issue in *M* was created: Lord Mance thus stated that a case brought before a domestic court in the wake of the C.P.A. would now be likely to establish that a same-sex couple fell within the ambit of "family life" within Art.8 of the Convention, and Lord Bingham's and Lord Walker's judgments fit comfortably with this possibility (as does Baroness Hale's). This does not tell us whether the marriage/civil partnership distinction would be found to fall foul of Art.8, either alone or (more likely) coupled with Art.14 if it was found to treat same-sex couples less favourably than marriage, but three points emerging from the judgments suggest that the distinction might well survive judicial scrutiny. First, both Lord Walker (supported by Lord Bingham) and Baroness Hale placed emphasis on the presence of the claimant's and her partner's *children* when discussing the nature of the relationship in *M. M.* tells us nothing about how a couple *without* children might be categorized, and—as Baroness Hale noted—the Strasbourg Court has yet to address this issue (Lord Mance noted that the institutions of Convention states are free to offer more generous protection to same-sex couples than that granted under the uniform interpretation of Art.8 adopted by the Strasbourg Court,[311] a point which might assist a litigant before a domestic court). Secondly, Baroness Hale's analysis of the limits of the "protection of the traditional family" justification for less favourable treatment of

[309] para.[82]; Lord Millett also stresses what he regards as the inherently opposite-sex nature of marriage at paras [78]–[81], [92], [97]–[98].

[310] n.1 above, para.[49]; see also paras [20], [50], [88].

[311] Paras [135]–[136].

same-sex couples, advanced in both *Ghaidan* and *M.*, appears—when referring to those "unable" to enter into marriage—to assume that marriage is, by definition, an institution designed for persons of the opposite sex. Thirdly, and perhaps most significantly, Lords Walker and Bingham placed considerable emphasis on the importance of respecting the legislature's assessments *at the time when the legislation in issue was passed* (hence their dismissal of "today's standards" when assessing past legislation, and Lord Bingham's invocation of a post-1994 consensus). If this reasoning was to be applied to the marriage/civil partnership distinction, it could fairly easily be concluded that the legislature's policy choice to create a separate institution of civil partnership in 2004 represented—not least given the careful consultation involved before the legislative process—the "consensus" at the time, rendering irrelevant any later views ("today's standards"). Lord Mance's observation (made in relation to the 1991 social security provisions in *M.*) that the United Kingdom could not be criticised for changing its laws *gradually* over a period so as to reflect changes in attitudes, could also be applied with equal force in defence of Parliament's decision to establish civil partnership as a formally separate institution from marriage, rather than immediately incorporating same-sex couples within the existing institution.[312]

However, there may be two problems with this third point. First, Lord Bingham's and Lord Walker's position seems inconsistent with Lord Nicholls' assertion in *Ghaidan* that under the HRA, the compatibility of legislation with Convention rights "falls to be assessed when the issue arises for determination, not as at the date when the legislation was enacted or came into force."[313] Secondly, their position appears to misunderstand the nature of the "margin of appreciation" and to overlook the discretionary area of judgment. In so far as the "margin" focuses on the existence of a consensus, it is concerned with the position that generally prevails in *Convention signatory states*—not the consensus of contemporary opinion within an *individual* Convention state, which appears to be Lord Bingham's understanding (while Lord Walker is not as explicit on this point, his references to the margin certainly invoke the position in Britain at the start of the 1990s).[314] Indeed, Lord Bingham's view would severely restrict the role of courts under the HRA: for, if applied literally, it would mean that so long as legislation is compatible with prevailing social understandings (or perhaps merely public opinion) at the time of its

312 para.[155].

313 *Ghaidan.*, para.[23]. Given that Lord Nicholls suggested in *M.*—unlike Lords Bingham and Walker—that the margin had yet to change but might do so *in the future*, his own judgments are not inconsistent. Furthermore, Lords Bingham and Walker are not endorsing the approach adopted in Lord Millett's dissenting judgment in *Ghaidan*: the issue in *M.* was *whether* the legislation was incompatible with Convention rights; by the time Lord Millett stressed the importance of giving effect to Parliament's intentions at the time when the Rent Act was drafted and amended, he had *accepted* that the Act's provisions were incompatible, and was concerned only with whether s.3 could be used to remove that incompatibility (*Ghaidan*, paras [78], [81], [83]–[95], [99]).

314 If their view was correct, then it is plain that *Dudgeon ibid.* would not have been decided as it was.

passage, it will fall within the margin. Furthermore, since the margin applies to the Strasbourg Court's role *as an international court*: it is not designed to be used within domestic law in assessing the freedom of action open to institutions such as Parliament. That task is performed by the "discretionary area", which is mentioned only by Lord Mance, and even then merely as part of his discussion of the "margin" rather than as a principle which serves a distinct purpose.[315]

Turning to the limits of the courts' interpretive powers (the second issue mentioned above) it is also unclear, if a breach of one or more of Arts 8, 12 or 14 was established, whether the wording of either the CPA or the Matrimonial Causes Act 1973 could be reinterpreted, using s.3(1) of the HRA, so as to remove any incompatibility. As we saw in Chapter 2, the limits of s.3(1) remain ambiguous, but it does at least seem clear—not least from *Ghaidan*—that courts are not prepared to use it to permit "amendment" of legislation rather than just reinterpretation, or in a way that is inconsistent with a fundamental feature or the underlying thrust of the legislation in issue.[316] Given that Parliament deliberately chose to create parallel but separate schemes of civil partnership and marriage, it might therefore be argued that reinterpretation would be impermissible. If this was so, a declaration of incompatibility would doubtless be issued under s.4, leaving the claimant to take the matter to Strasbourg.

The only case to have arisen before national courts, to date, concerning the CPA and the rights of same-sex couples, has been *Wilkinson v Kitzinger*. The claimant in *Wilkinson* relied on Arts 8, 12 and 14 in order to ask the High Court either to reinterpret s.11(c) of the Matrimonial Causes Act 1973 and ss.1(1) and 212 to 218 of the CPA, pursuant to s.3(1) of the HRA, so as to recognise her Canadian same-sex marriage as a marriage rather than a civil partnership, or to issue a declaration of incompatibility concerning those provisions. Sir Mark Potter P. found that Art.8 was not engaged, whether considered alone or in conjunction with Art.14, that Art.12 had not been breached when considered alone, and that although there was a *prima facie* violation of Art.12 when considered in conjunction with Art.14, the violation was justifiable.

In relation to Art.8 considered alone, Sir Mark noted that while intimate relationships (same-sex or opposite-sex) fell within the scope of the private life limb and that sexual orientation was a most intimate part of a person's private life,[317] *M* recognised that the family life limb did not at present extend to childless same-sex couples.[318] He also suggested that *M* signified the recognition of a broader limit to the ambit of Art.8, laying particular emphasis on

315 Paras [137]—[138].

316 *ibid.*, especially paras [33] Lord Nicholls, [122] Lord Rodger. For analysis, compare Danny Nicol, "Statutory interpretation and human rights after *Anderson*" [2004] P.L. 274; Aileen Kavanagh, "Statutory interpretation and human rights after *Anderson:* a more contextual approach" [2004] P.L. 537 and 'Unlocking the Human Rights Act: The "Radical Approach to Section 3(1) Revisited" [2005] E.H.R.L.R. 259.

317 paras [68]–[69].

318 para.[75].

Lord Walker's suggestion that arguments under the private life limb had to turn on a failure to show *respect*.[319] This interpretation of Art.8 was to form a central plank in Sir Mark's later dismissal of the claimant's Art.8-based argument. For he suggested that Parliament had neither intruded upon the private life of loving and monogamous same-sex couples, nor interfered with the respect due to them, "by declining to recognise a same-sex partnership as a marriage in legislation [the CPA] the purpose and thrust of which is to enhance their rights".[320] Furthermore, the Convention "living instrument" principle (whereby Convention rights must be interpreted in the light of contemporary circumstances[321]) could not be used to bring controversial issues which are matters of "political, social, and economic valuation" within the scope of the Convention, and signatory states are not required to establish particular forms of institution to cover particular relationships, especially in controversial areas.[322] Civil partnerships afforded equivalent legal rights to marriage, and by withholding the actual title and status of marriage there had been no interference with same-sex couples' right to respect for private life of the type involved in criminalising their sexual activity or otherwise threatening their home lives.[323] The claim thus fell outside the ambit of Art.8 considered alone.

In relation to Art.12 considered alone, Sir Mark noted that read in a "straightforward manner", the Article "refers to the right to 'marry' in the traditional sense (namely as a marriage between a man and a woman)."[324] Despite the Strasbourg Court's acceptance in *Goodwin* that the Art.12 right of a post-operative transsexual woman who was precluded from marrying a man had been breached, that decision turned on the re-assigned gender of the claimant as a *woman* wishing to marry a *man*[325] and could not be used as a basis for employing the "living instrument" principle to reinterpret Art.12 more broadly when to do so would—as here—have the effect of bringing within the Convention "issues which are plainly outside its contemplation".[326] While there had been a general move towards granting legal recognition to same-sex relationships across Europe, there was not yet a Europe-wide consensus concerning same-sex marriage, by which the Convention could be seen as having brought same-sex relationships within the definition of marriage. It would not therefore be appropriate to expand Art.12 by interpreting it as supporting a right to same-sex marriage.[327]

319 paras [76]–[80].
320 para.[85]
321 For discussion, see Clayton & Tomlinson, *The Law of Human Rights*, *ibid.*, paras 6.23–6.27.
322 para.[86]. Note, more broadly, the interpretation of Art.8 as being confined to non-intervention: paras [86]–[87].
323 para.[88].
324 para.[55], relying upon *Rees v United Kingdom*, *ibid.*, para.49; *Cossey v United Kingdom*, *ibid.*, 642; and *Sheffield and Horsham v United Kingdom*, para.66.
325 para.[61], relying on *Goodwin v United Kingdom* (2002) 35 E.H.R.R. 447, paras 100 to 104.
326 para.[62], relying on *Johnston v Ireland* (1986) 9 E.H.R.R. 203, para.53.
327 paras [63]–[67].

The claimant also argued that that the CPA's failure to accord same-sex couples the status and title of marriage, together with its categorisation of a foreign same-sex marriage as a civil partnership, violated Art.14 when considered in conjunction with Arts 8 and 12. In order to develop this argument, the claimant had to show that the case fell within the ambit of one of these substantive Articles.[328] Sir Mark Potter echoed his reasoning concerning Art.8 considered alone by stating that the claimant's personal or sexual autonomy had not been interfered with, nor had she been regulated by the criminal law, threatened or humiliated. There was thus no breach of the "private life" limb of Art.8. Neither did the matter fall within the "family life" limb, given that the Convention had yet to recognise a childless same-sex relationship as family life. Even if that was not the case, the withholding of the title of marriage did not in practice impair the essence of a couple's family life.[329]

However, the position in relation to Art.12 coupled with Art.14 was rather different. Sir Mark employed a broad view of Art.12, accepting for present purposes that its core values were concerned with the limitations placed on the rights of an individual to marry the partner of their choice, *rather than* just with restrictions placed on the right of opposite-sex couples to marry. While Parliament had no positive obligation to take steps to redress the social disadvantages faced by same-sex partners, by passing the CPA and providing for the recognition of a foreign same-sex marriage only as a civil partnership, the facts of the case were brought within the ambit of Art.12 for the purposes of Art.14 analysis (a possibly rather surprising argument given the paucity of examples, at Strasbourg level, of the use of these two Articles together).[330] The difference of treatment in this case (same-sex partners in a Canadian marriage being treated as civil partners under domestic law, when opposite-sex partners would be treated as married) was, Sir Mark ruled, based upon sexual orientation,[331] raising the question whether it served a legitimate aim and constituted a proportionate response. Sir Mark was clear that the difference could be justified. There was a legitimate aim, in the form of the protection of the traditional family, as identified in *Karner*.[332] In addition, the difference was proportionate to that aim. The majority of people or governments in Europe regarded marriage as a valuable institution not only for encouraging monogamy but also for "the procreation of children and their development and nurture in a family unit (or 'nuclear family') in which both maternal and paternal influences are available in respect of their nurture and upbringing."[333] By long-standing definition and acceptance, marriage was "a formal relationship between a man and a woman, primarily (though not exclusively) with

[328] For the court's analysis of the "within the ambit" issue, see paras [89]–[95].
[329] para.[107].
[330] para.[110].
[331] para.[115].
[332] para.[116].
[333] para.[118].

the aim of producing and rearing children".[334] This idea was not based on discrimination against those who wished instead to form same-sex unions.[335] Stable same-sex unions were not inferior, and the CPA did not categorise them as such:

> "Parliament has not called partnerships between persons of the same sex marriage, not because they are considered inferior to the institution of marriage but because, as a matter of objective fact and common understanding, as well as under the present definition of marriage in English law, and by recognition in European jurisprudence, they are indeed different."[336]

Effectively, Parliament had decided to accord "formal recognition to relationships between same sex couples which have all the features and characteristics of marriage save for the ability to procreate children" while "preserving and supporting the concept and institution of marriage as a union between persons of opposite sex or gender".[337] The CPA accorded same-sex partners "effectively all the rights, responsibilities, benefits and advantages of civil marriage save the name", removing "the legal, social and economic disadvantages suffered by homosexuals who wish to join stable long-term relationships."[338] While the marriage/civil partnership distinction discriminated against same-sex partners, it had a legitimate aim, was reasonable and proportionate, and fell within the margin of appreciation open to Convention states.

It may well be fair to say that the result in *Wilkinson* is comprehensible, given the present state of the Strasbourg jurisprudence concerning Arts 8, 12 and 14, and in particular the role of the margin of appreciation (as discussed in the previous section). Nonetheless, there are four important problems with Sir Mark Potter's reasoning. First, Sir Mark fails to face up to the consequences of Lord Nicholls' and Baroness Hale's discussions in *Ghaidan* of the significance of procreation to the legal protection of marriage, and of Baroness Hale's powerful arguments about the nature of committed same-sex partnerships more broadly. In relation to procreation, Lord Nicholls stressed in *Ghaidan* that the possibility of parenthood or the presence of children in the home was *not* a precondition of succession to a tenancy under the Rent Act 1977, and could not be used to supply a legitimate reason in terms of Art.14 for distinguishing between same-sex and opposite-sex couples.[339] While this argument was made in the context of succession to property, Lord Nicholls emphasised the point that protection of the traditional family depended for its force as a justification for differences of treatment *upon the context*, and should not automatically be

334 para.[120].
335 para.[119].
336 para.[121].
337 para.[122].
338 para.[122].
339 paras [16]–[17].

associated with procreation. This being so, Sir Mark Potter's reasoning concerning procreation and marriage may be somewhat over-broad. Sir Mark also ignores the importance of two of Baroness Hale's reasons in *Ghaidan* for concluding that procreation could not be considered a relevant difference between same-sex and opposite-sex couples, for Art.14 purposes, in relation to succession to property. Baroness Hale stressed first that:

"the capacity to bear or beget children has never been a pre-requisite of a valid marriage in English law ... Even the capacity to consummate the marriage only matters if one of the parties thinks it matters: if they are both content the marriage is valid. A marriage, let alone a relationship analogous to marriage, can exist without either the presence or the possibility of children from that relationship."[340]

And secondly, that:

"if the couple are bringing up children together, it is unlikely to matter whether or not they are the biological children of both parties. Both married and unmarried couples, both homosexual and heterosexual, may bring up children together."[341]

Both points provide powerful counter-arguments to Sir Mark's equation of marriage with the sexual reproduction of children.

Sir Mark Potter's comments also beg the question, which he did not address, of why marriage *should* be associated, as a normative matter, so strongly with procreation. His tying of marriage so closely to procreation seemingly overlooks Baroness Hale's powerful and important comments in *Ghaidan* about the nature of same-sex relationships: they can, she stressed, "have exactly the same qualities of intimacy, stability and inter-dependence that heterosexual relationships do".[342] Furthermore:

"Homosexual couples can have exactly the same sort of inter-dependent couple relationship as heterosexuals can. Sexual 'orientation' defines the sort of person with whom one wishes to have sexual relations. It requires another person to express itself [...] most human beings eventually want [...] love. And with love they often want not only the warmth but also the sense of belonging to one another which is the essence of being a couple. And many couples also come to want the stability and permanence which go with sharing a home and a life together, with or without the children who for many people go to make a family. In this, people of homosexual orientation are no different from people of heterosexual orientation."[343]

[340] para [141]; note also para [144] on practical arrangements for home life.
[341] para.[141].
[342] para.[139].
[343] para [142].

Secondly, given the rather ambiguous nature of some of the reasoning in *M.*, it is not clear how far Sir Mark Potter's analysis of that decision is correct. In stating that same-sex couples had not been accepted as falling within the scope of "family life", Sir Mark rightly drew attention to the importance placed by Lord Walker (supported by Lord Bingham) and Baroness Hale on the presence of children—a point that, as noted earlier, might be likely to count against a childless couple. Nonetheless, given that Lord Walker (supported by Lord Bingham) was willing to assume that the claimant and her partner fell *within* the scope of "family life", and that Baroness Hale asserted that they *did so*, it may be that Sir Mark went too far in reading *M.* as ruling definitively against the possibility that same-sex couples could count as families. It is also unclear whether his interpretation of a legitimate aim, when testing whether the legislation could be justified, is compatible with Baroness Hale's approach (supported by Lords Steyn, Millett and Rodger) in *Ghaidan*. As we have seen, Baroness Hale stressed that a measure did not serve to protect the traditional family merely by denying a benefit to those who could not form such a family. It is not immediately apparent how the denial of the title "marriage" to a same-sex couple who wished to register their partnership could actually *promote* the traditional family, and Sir Mark Potter's judgment offers no guidance.[344]

Thirdly, Sir Mark Potter seemingly echoes the confusion in *M.* between the discretionary area of judgment and the margin of appreciation, given that he talks of the marriage/civil partnership distinction as falling within the "margin"[345]—an assessment that only the Strasbourg Court is qualified to make. Any reference to deference should, instead, have looked to the "discretionary area". Although Sir Mark did not analyse the "margin" further, by emphasizing *Parliament's* role in legislating to accord particular legal, social and economic benefits to same-sex couples, his judgment perhaps provides some indication as to how a court which considered the discretionary area and the CPA in detail might assess the issue.

Fourthly, Sir Mark's treatment of the claimant's argument based on the symbolism of the marriage/civil partnership distinction was surprisingly brief. The claimant took care to detail her views on this point,[346] yet beyond noting that she and her partner would feel downgraded by being labelled civil partners rather than a married couple, and that they would feel hurt, frustration, humiliation and outrage, Sir Mark merely went on to say that such feelings were not shared by a substantial number of couples who were civil partners, and were not enough to show that the distinction was unjustifiably discriminatory, given the CPA's aims.[347] Given the importance that the symbolic effect of a measure may have where individuals feel themselves to be the victims of discrimination, it is perhaps regrettable that Sir Mark did not

344 See, e.g., para.[119].
345 para.[122].
346 paras [5]–[10].
347 paras [116]–[117].

attempt to consider the issue in more detail. It would be surprising if it did not play a role in future litigation concerning the marriage/civil partnership distinction.

We have seen in this section that by creating the institution of civil partnership, the government and Parliament were apparently keen to eradicate an important example of direct discrimination on the basis of sexual orientation: namely, the law's failure to recognise and support stable same-sex partnerships. As we have also seen, however, there remains considerable room for argument—despite the High Court's decision in *Wilkinson v Kitzinger*—about whether the creation of a separate institution from marriage for same-sex couples is itself a form of impermissible discrimination.

VIII. Hostility and Conflicting Non-discrimination Claims

Sexual minorities face on-going problems of harassment and hostility in employment and in other contexts, and claims concerning freedom from sexual orientation and gender identity discrimination are frequently met with counter-arguments associated with the right of an employer to act on a religious belief in not employing or in dismissing a lesbian, a gay man, or a transgendered or transsexual person. Such arguments have been considered in legal systems around the world[348]

Nicholas Bamforth
"Same-sex Partnerships: Some Comparative Constitutional Lessons" [2007] EHRLR 47

pp.63–65 "...it is however necessary to think about one possible limit to partnership claims, which becomes particularly visible once we categorise them as being of a constitutional nature: namely, how much weight they should have when faced with competing claims, not least to respect for the sentiments of religious believers who are convinced that marriage should be restricted to heterosexual couples.[349] Some extremely helpful guidance has been offered here by Sachs J. in the [South African] *Fourie* case. In an open and democratic society, he suggested, 'there must be mutually respectful co-existence between the secular and the sacred. The function of the Court is to recognise the sphere which each inhabits, not to force the one into the sphere of the other. Provided there is no prejudice to the fundamental rights of any person or group, the law will legitimately acknowledge a

[348] See, in general, Anya Palmer, "Less Equal than Others: A Survey of Lesbians and Gay Men at Work" (London: Stonewall, 1993); the Amnesty International Reports, discussed in Nicholas Bamforth, "Introduction" in Nicholas Bamforth (ed.), *Sex Rights: The Oxford Amnesty Lectures 2002* (Oxford: Oxford University Press, 2005).

[349] A further issue at this point—albeit one that is beyond the scope of the present article—is what role (if any) religious arguments may play in constitutional debate or litigation.

diversity of strongly-held opinions on matters of great public controversy.'[350] Furthermore, 'The hallmark of an open and democratic society is its capacity to accommodate and manage difference[s] of intensely-held views and lifestyles in a reasonable and fair manner.'[351] The South African Constitutional Court thus acknowledged that while for 'millions in all walks of life, religion provides support and nurture and a framework for individual and social stability and growth' and that religious belief 'has the capacity to awaken concepts of self-worth and human dignity' and 'affects the believer's view of society and founds a distinction between right and wrong',[352] it is one thing to allow religious believers freely to express their faith-driven views—and presumably, in applying them, to deny same-sex couples any *religious* celebration of their union—but quite another to use those beliefs as a basis for interpreting the *constitutional* rights of lesbians and gays, including the constitutional right to have their partnerships recognized by the state. Sachs J's 'separate spheres' analysis must, I think, be right. Claims for same-sex partnership rights are claims to state recognition of partnerships, not religious recognition.

While the Civil Partnership Act makes comprehensive provision for the rights of same-sex couples who register their partnership in the U.K., it nonetheless falls to be interpreted—like any other statute—in the light of Convention rights. It is therefore to be hoped that there is room for a similar approach to be used when domestic courts are required to draw a proportionate balance between competing Convention rights, including the right to religion.[353] There have already been hints that this is likely to be so. In *R. v Secretary of State for Education and Employment, ex p. Williamson*, in which a religious institution sought to rely on the Article 9 right to freedom of thought, conscience and belief to justify the infliction of corporal punishment in a religious school, Lord Nicholls was clear that 'In a civilised society individuals respect each other's beliefs'[354] and that 'in a pluralist society a balance has to be held between freedom to practise one's own beliefs and the interests of others affected by those practices'.[355] Also important here are Baroness Hale's sensitive comments in *R. (on the application of Begum) v Headteacher and Governors of Denbigh High School* about the need to prevent religious fundamentalism from undermining individual rights, while remaining sensitive to people's deeply-held religious beliefs.[356] Baroness Hale accepted that in principle, a woman could make an autonomous choice to wear restrictive religious dress: 'If a woman freely chooses to adopt a way of life for herself, it is not for others, including other women who have chosen differently, to criticise or prevent her. ... The sight of a woman in full purdah may offend some people, and especially those western feminists who believe that it is a symbol of her oppression, but that could not be a good reason for prohibiting her from wearing it'.[357] However, 'it must be the woman's choice, not something imposed upon her by others'.[358] Baroness Hale acknowledged the view that sometimes dress requirements are imposed 'as much for political and social as for religious reasons',[359] and—citing the Parekh Report on *The Future of Multi-Ethnic Britain*—'may be used to legitimise power structures rather than to promote ethical principles, and may foster bigotry, sectarianism and fundamentalism. Notoriously, religion often accepts and gives its blessing to gender inequalities.'[360] Baroness Hale thus acknowledged (and disapproved of the fact that): 'strict dress codes

350 *ibid.*, para.[94].
351 *ibid.*, para.[95].
352 *ibid.*, para.[89].
353 See also the Supreme Court of Canada's approach in *Trinity Western University v British Columbia College of Teachers* [2001] 1 SCR 772.
354 [2005] UKHL 15, para [15].
355 *ibid.*, para.[17].
356 [2006] UKHL 15.
357 *ibid.*, para.[96].
358 *ibid.*, para.[95].
359 *ibid.*, para.[95].
360 (Runnymede Trust, 2000), pp.236–7, para.17.3.

may be imposed upon women, not for their own sake, but to serve the ends of others. Hence they may be denied equal freedom to choose for themselves. They may also be denied equal treatment. A dress code which requires women to conceal all but their face and hands, while leaving men much freer to decide what they will wear, does not treat them equally [. . .] the assumption may be that women will play their part in the private domestic sphere while men will play theirs in the public world'.[361] The type of balance which Baroness Hale is trying to strike—between respect for religious beliefs and the autonomy of women—will clearly often require very careful interrogation of the competing claims. But this is surely valuable and important when claims to religious freedom can have adverse implications for other (and others') fundamental rights—particularly, given the traditional male domination of organised religions, of the rights of women (heterosexual or lesbian) and gay men. It is therefore to be hoped that the views of Sachs J. and Baroness Hale are widely followed."

We consider these issues from the standpoint of religious discrimination and other competing non-discrimination or human rights claims in Chapters 9 and 13. From the standpoint of sexual orientation discrimination, it is sufficient to note that a conflict between freedom from that head of discrimination and freedom of religion has, to date, arisen most directly in domestic law in *R. (AMICUS) v Secretary of State for Trade and Industry*,[362] discussed in Section VII. A central issue in *AMICUS* was the compatibility with the Employment Equality Directive and Arts 8 and 14 of the Convention of the genuine occupational qualifications established in regs 7(2) and 7(3) of the Employment Equality (Sexual Orientation) Regulations 2003. Regulation 7(2) is applicable to employment by a religious organisation (but also by other types of organisation), while reg.7(3) has as its specific focus employment by a religious organisation. As Richards J. noted, the arguments put forward by the religious organisations which intervened in the case were based on the Convention Art.9 right to freedom of thought, conscience and religion and s.13 of the Human Rights Act 1998, which stipulates that if a court's determination might affect the exercise by a religious organisation of its Art.9 right, the court must have particular regard to the importance of that right. Richards J. noted that "whilst there is a need to have specific regard to the rights protected by Art.9, s.13 of the 1998 Act does not give greater weight to those rights than they would otherwise enjoy under the Convention. But they are in any event important rights",[363] and that the Convention case law supports the organizational autonomy and essential values of a religion. In terms of regs 7(2) and 7(3), the submissions for the interveners served to emphasise "the need to strike a balance. Religion is an area where the principle of non-discrimination on grounds of sexual orientation may conflict very obviously with other important rights which are themselves recognised by the Convention and by the Directive",[364] the key question being whether the Regulations struck the right balance between the rights to non-discrimination and of religion. As

361 *ibid.*, para.[95].
362 *ibid.*
363 *ibid.*, para.[41].
364 para.[44].

noted in Section VII, Richards J. found on the facts that regs 7(2) and 7(3) were compatible with Articles 8 and 14. Given Richards J.'s observations about s.13 of the Human Rights Act 1998, it will be interesting to see whether a "balanced" approach of this type is attempted in later cases. For the moment, the potential for conflict between the right not to be discriminated against on the ground of sexual orientation, and the right not to be discriminated against on the ground of religion, remains one of the most difficult issues in this area of discrimination law.

IX. Is Sexual Orientation or Gender Identity Discrimination also Sex Discrimination?

As we saw in Section VI, when dealing with EU law, it is sometimes argued that discrimination on the basis of sexual orientation or gender identity also constitutes a form of sex discrimination. In practical terms, this argument is not of much importance when discrimination on the basis of sexual orientation or gender identity is prohibited in similar terms to discrimination on the basis of biological sex. As Robert Wintemute observes, the "sex discrimination argument assumes greater importance in the context of a statutory prohibition of discrimination with a closed list of prohibited grounds to which courts are not free to add ... than in the context of a constitutional prohibition of discrimination with an open-ended list (or no list) of prohibited grounds. In the constitutional context, judicial recognition of 'sexual orientation' as a separate prohibited ground can make the sex discrimination argument unnecessary (if sex does not trigger stricter judicial scrutiny than sexual orientation). However, in the statutory context, judges generally do not have this option."[365] Furthermore, "[I]n jurisdictions where there is comprehensive (not limited to employment) legislation against discrimination based on sexual orientation ... there is no need for the sex discrimination argument. It is only worth preserving ... as a reminder of the connection between sexual orientation discrimination against lesbian, gay and bisexual individuals, and sex discrimination against women." Wintemute nonetheless stresses, however, that "most jurisdictions ... are not as lucky. ... They often have comprehensive legislation on sex discrimination, but no legislation, or no comprehensive legislation, on sexual orientation discrimination. In those jurisdictions, the sex discrimination argument has a future."[366]

The sex discrimination argument is not important merely for tactical reasons, however. For, whether or not sexual orientation and gender identity-related discrimination are prohibited in their own right, the question whether they

365 "Sex Discrimination in *MacDonald* and *Pearce*: Why the Law Lords Chose the Wrong Comparators" (2003) 14 K.C.L.J. 267, 268.

366 "Sex Discrimination in *MacDonald* and *Pearce*", *ibid.*, 280.

also constitute sex discrimination can tell us a lot about how sex discrimination is understood.

Nicholas Bamforth
"Sexual Orientation Discrimination after *Grant* v *South-West Trains*" (2000) 63 M.L.R. 694

p.701: "Although the question whether sexual orientation discrimination may also be prohibited as unlawful sex discrimination usually arises for a tactical reason, it is nonetheless of great conceptual importance for our understanding of the nature of sex discrimination law. For ... if sexual orientation discrimination *is* also sex discrimination, then the latter concept prohibits not only discrimination on the basis of a person's sex-related physical characteristics (that is, the fact that they are physically female or physically male) but extends to encompass discrimination on the basis of *sex-related gender rôles*—potentially warranting the prohibition of any adverse treatment based on the fact that a person behaves in a way which is generally considered "inappropriate" for their sex (in this context, the notion that it is "appropriate" for women to have sexual relations with men but "inappropriate" for men to do so, and "appropriate" for men to have sexual relations with women but "inappropriate" for women to do so)."

pp.703–6: "[...] we must first establish that there is a sound conceptual basis for arguing that sexual orientation discrimination also counts as sex discrimination. One argument—advanced by David Pannick QC and Robert Wintemute ... focuses on the structure of the legal concept of direct sex discrimination, and for this reason can be labelled the "analytical argument". Wintemute suggests that because an individual's sexual orientation can only be defined by reference to their sex, distinctions based on sexual orientation *necessarily* also involve distinctions based on the sexes of the individuals concerned. The basis for categorising a man as gay is that he is attracted to men, in the same way that the basis for categorising a woman as heterosexual is that she is attracted to men. So, where a man is penalised for being attracted to men or for having a male partner but a woman is not, the only difference between the two is their sex. Sexual orientation can be seen as an extra or alternative basis for the differential treatment, but this should not be allowed to hide the fact that straightforward sex discrimination is taking place: for the man and the woman have been treated differently although the circumstances applicable to both are the same—that is, they are both attracted to men or have a male partner.[367] Pannick expresses the point well:

> "Suppose the employer dismisses a male homosexual from employment because he has a rule that he will employ neither men nor women who have sexual preferences for persons of their own sex. The complainant can argue that this is sex discrimination because if two employees—one male, and one female—are romantically or sexually attracted to the same actual or hypothetical male non-employee, the employer treats the male employee less favourably on the ground of his sex than he treats the female employee. ... The employer who has said that a sexual relationship with Mr X is conduct permissible in a female employee but conduct impermissible in a male employee has clearly differentiated in treatment of male and female employees. The differentiation is

[367] R. Wintemute, *Sexual Orientation and Human Rights*, pp.344–348.

on the ground of sex: women may have relationships with Mr X and retain their jobs; if men have such relationships they will be sacked."[368]

[...] Marc Fajer has [...] suggested that the analytical argument merely amounts to the literal assertion that the employer has taken the sex of the parties into account—an assertion which is too simple and stark to have much chance of success in court.[369] In fairness, Fajer's suggestion is probably too blunt. For ... judicial recognition that sexual orientation discrimination is also sex discrimination requires the courts to take a clear conceptual stand by acknowledging that sex discrimination is broad enough to encompass differential treatment based on sex-related gender rôles as well as the fact that a person is of a particular physical sex. Once this acknowledgement is made, it becomes possible to see why it might be conceptually appropriate to compare the employer's treatment of a gay man with their treatment of a heterosexual woman instead of a lesbian—for the sex of a person's actual or desired sexual partner is something about which strong social norms concerning gender identity (relating, more precisely, to the appropriate sexual behaviour of a person of *a particular sex*) do exist. In consequence, the real shortcoming of the analytical argument is not that it is literal *per se*—rather, it is that it requires a conceptual shift in the law's understanding of the nature of sex discrimination (as a social phenomenon as much as anything else), but fails to present anything beyond abstract logic to lend appeal to such a shift.[370]

It is therefore necessary to find an appealing justification, relating to the social rôle of sex discrimination law, for making the conceptual shift. One such justification—which can be labelled the "social argument"—can be found in the writings of Andrew Koppelman[371] and Cass Sunstein.[372] Koppelman concurs with the analytical argument, but goes on to suggest that laws which discriminate against lesbians and gays "rest upon a normative stereotype: the bald conviction that certain behaviour—for example, sex with women—is appropriate for members of one sex, but not for members of the other sex".[373] At the heart of Koppelman's and Sunstein's analysis lies a comparison between contemporary laws which penalise same-sex sexual acts and relationships and the decision in *Loving* v *Virginia*, where the US Supreme Court ruled that state laws prohibiting inter-racial marriages violated the Equal Protection Clause of the Fourteenth Amendment to the U.S. Constitution.[374] In *Loving*, the State of Virginia had tried to defend the disputed statutes by arguing that they affected white and black participants in an inter-racial marriage equally and did not involve racial discrimination—for just as blacks were prohibited from marrying whites, whites were prohibited from marrying blacks. Warren CJ dismissed this argument, stating that "There can be no question but that Virginia's miscegenation statutes rest solely upon distinctions drawn according to race. The statutes proscribe generally accepted conduct if engaged in by members of different races. ... The fact that Virginia prohibits only inter-racial marriages involving white persons demonstrates that the racial classifications must stand on their own justification, as measures designed to maintain White Supremacy."[375]

368 D. Pannick, Sex Discrimination Law (Oxford: Clarendon Press, 1985), pp.201–203.

369 "Can Two Real Men Eat Quiche Together? Storytelling, Gender-Role Stereotypes, and Legal Protection for Lesbians and Gay Men" (1992) 46 University of Miami L. Rev. 511, 634.

370 See also Andrew Koppelman's analogous argument in "Three Arguments for Gay Rights" (1997) 95 Michigan L. Rev. 1636, 1661–1662. For an example of institutional considerations preventing a court from making such a shift, see *Macauley v Massachusetts Commission Against Discrimination* (1979) 397 NE 2d 670, 671 (Supreme Judicial Court of Massachusetts).

371 Principally in A. Koppelman, "Why Discrimination Against Lesbians and Gay Men is Sex Discrimination" (1994) 69 N.Y.U. LRev 197.

372 "Homosexuality and the Constitution" (1994) 70 Indiana L.J. 1.

373 A. Koppelman, "Why Discrimination Against Lesbians and Gay Men is Sex Discrimination", 219.

374 (1967) 388 U.S. 1.

375 "Homosexuality and the Constitution" (1994) 70 Indiana L.J. 1, 11.

By identifying the real social function of the statutes as being the maintenance of white supremacy over blacks, the Court was able to rule that the statutes had no legitimate purpose and violated the Equal Protection Clause—even if they appeared at first glance to apply equally to both groups.[376] However, the Court was able to reach this conclusion only by discounting outward appearances and switching the focus of analysis to the true social function of the statutes. As Sunstein points out, while the ban on inter-racial marriages involved formal equality between blacks and whites, when "[v]iewed in context—in light of its actual motivations and its actual effects", it was "part of a system of racial caste."[377]

Koppelman engages in an analogous recategorisation of laws which penalise or prohibit same-sex sexual relations and relationships.[378] He suggests that, "It should be clear from ordinary experience that the stigmatization of the homosexual has something to do with the homosexual's supposed deviance from traditional sex roles", according to which men (traditionally assigned to the socially "superior" rôle) would pair off with women (traditionally assigned to the "inferior" role).[379] For social conservatives, same-sex sexual relations pose a direct threat to this "natural" order—in just the same way as inter-racial sexual acts were once penalised since they challenged social perceptions of "appropriate" racial hierarchies.[380] Sunstein thus argues that legal prohibition of same-sex marriages can be seen as "part of the social and legal insistence on 'two kinds'"—male and female—an insistence which mandates fixed gender categories and sex-rôle stereotyping.[381] Koppelman in turn maintains that by reinforcing traditional social categorisations, laws which prohibit same-sex sexual acts or penalise lesbians and gays more broadly will "implicitly stigmatize women, and ... reinforce the hierarchy of men over women."[382] Just like laws prohibiting inter-racial marriage, "their purpose is to support a regime of caste that locks some people into inferior social positions at birth."[383]... As Koppelman points out, if bars on inter-racial marriage are to be seen as inherently defined by reference to the races of those involved,[384] adverse treatment of same-sex sexual acts or relationships must equally be defined by reference to the sexes of those involved—for only a person who is female would be penalised for having a sexual relationship with a woman.[385] This analysis of the social rôle of law thus enables Koppelman and Sunstein to conclude that just as inter-racial couples are no longer placed at a legal disadvantage by comparison with same-race couples, same-sex couples should not be placed at a disadvantage by comparison with opposite-sex couples."[386]

376 "Homosexuality and the Constitution" (1994) 70 Indiana LJ 1, 9, 11, 12.

377 C. Sunstein, *ibid.*, 18. See also A. Koppelman, "Why Discrimination Against Lesbians and Gay Men is Sex Discrimination", 223.

378 A. Koppelman, "Why Discrimination Against Lesbians and Gay Men is Sex Discrimination", 222–223. See also Koppelman's "The Miscegenation Analogy: Sodomy Law as Sex Discrimination" (1988) 98 Yale L.J. 145.

379 A. Koppelman, "Why Discrimination Against Lesbians and Gay Men is Sex Discrimination", 234.

380 A. Koppelman, "Why Discrimination Against Lesbians and Gay Men is Sex Discrimination", 234–257.

381 C. Sunstein, 21.

382 A. Koppelman, "Why Discrimination Against Lesbians and Gay Men is Sex Discrimination", 256–257.

383 A. Koppelman, "The Miscegenation Analogy: Sodomy Law as Sex Discrimination" (1988) 98 Yale L.J. 145, 147.

384 In *McLaughlin v Florida* (1964) 379 U.S. 184.

385 A. Koppelman, "The Miscegenation Analogy: Sodomy Law as Sex Discrimination" (1988) 98 Yale L.J. 145, 149–51, 162–163.

386 A. Koppelman, "Why Discrimination Against Lesbians and Gay Men is Sex Discrimination", 284.

As we saw in Section VI, the European Court of Justice has been hostile to the argument that sexual orientation discrimination also counts as a form of sex discrimination, but accepts that discrimination on the basis of gender identity does so. National law takes a similar position, given that the Sexual Orientation (Gender Reassignment) Regulations 1999 cateogise discrimination based on gender reassignment as impermissible sex discrimination, while the Employment Equality (Sexual Orientation) Regulations 2003, s.81 of the Equality Act 2006 and the Equality Act (Sexual Orientation) Regulations 2007 prohibit sexual orientation discrimination in its own right. In *Macdonald v Advocate General for Scotland/Pearce v Governing Body of Mayfield School*, a case which arose before the passage of the Regulations and which therefore had to be brought under the Sex Discrimination Act 1975, the House of Lords was clear that harassment and discrimination due to sexual orientation did not constitute impermissible sex discrimination, and rejected what was described in the extract as the "analytical argument" by holding that the appropriate comparator for a gay man who claimed to have been discriminated against on the ground of sex was a lesbian, not a heterosexual woman.[387] Lord Hope rejected Robert Wintemute's argument (a version of the "analytical argument") that a comparison between a gay man and a lesbian in a sex discrimination claim changes "not only the sex of the man, but also the sex of his partner . . . for a valid sex discrimination analysis, the comparison must change only the sex of the complaining individual, and must hold all other circumstances constant. Otherwise a change in some circumstance (such as the complaining individual's qualifications, their choice of job or the sex of their partner) could hide the sex discrimination. If an employer refused to hire a woman with the required university degree, her comparator would not be a man without the required university degree . . . If a man wanting to be a nurse challenged a rule that only women could be nurses and only men could be doctors, his comparator would not be a woman wanting to be a doctor . . . If the sex of the man [with a male partner or attracted to men] is changed, but the sex of his [actual or desired] male partner is held constant, the man's comparator is a woman with [or desiring] a male partner and the direct sex discrimination is clear."[388] However, Lord Hope objected to Wintemute's argument for the reason that it changes "not only . . . the sex of the complaining individual. It changes his sexual orientation too. The woman with whom his case is compared is a woman with a different sexual orientation from his. She is attracted to persons of the opposite sex, while he is attracted to persons of the same sex".[389] This, according to Lord Hope, "is to break the rule

387 [2003] UKHL 34.

388 Robert Wintemute, "Recognising New Kinds of Direct Sex Discrimination: Transexualism, Sexual Orientation and Dress Codes" (1997) 60 M.L.R. 332, 347–8.

389 para.[70].

which [Wintemute] himself has recognised, namely that for a valid sex discrimination analysis the comparison must change only the sex of the complaining individual."[390]

The argument that sexual orientation discrimination also constitutes a form of sex discrimination thus seems to have been rejected in domestic law. Nonetheless, national law arguably remains ambiguous given that gender identity discrimination continues, due to the Gender Reassignment Regulations, to constitute sex discrimination. Although the distinction might no longer matter much in practice, given the general prohibition of sexual orientation discrimination in its own right, it might be said to leave the law in an analytically uncertain position.[391] Furthermore, while the House of Lords rejected what has been dubbed the "analytical argument" in *Macdonald*, no argument has yet been provided to counter the "social argument", described in the extract above, that sexual orientation discrimination is in practice also a form of sex discrimination.

X. Conclusion

We have seen in this chapter that direct and indirect discrimination on the grounds of sexual orientation and gender identity are now generally prohibited in employment and the provision of goods, facilities and services. Active hostility towards members of sexual minority groups has generally been removed from the criminal law, and public authorities are generally obliged not to discriminate on these headings. Meanwhile, transsexuals can now reassign their sex for legal purposes, and partners of the same sex can acquire an almost identical legal status to marriage by registering as civil partners. Nonetheless, civil marriage remains confined to opposite-sex partners, and claims are made by religious groups to practice their beliefs in a way which might involve discrimination against lesbians and gay men.

Sexual orientation and gender identity discrimination might be thought to illustrate in particularly vivid form two key themes in contemporary discrimination law. The first relates to the constitutional dimensions of the subject. In jurisdictions around the world, litigation concerning sexual orientation discrimination, and in particular the rights of same-sex partners, has provided a very clear illustration of the constitutional law dimensions of antidiscrimination claims, both through the arguments used and through debates concerning the proper role of courts. Within England and Wales, more specifically, the constitutional dimensions have been strongly illustrated by the

390 para.[70]. See, more generally, paras [63]–[85] and Lord Nicholls at paras [6]–[9], Lord Hobhouse at paras [105] and [109], Lord Scott at paras [113] to [119], and Lord Rodger at paras [146] to [176].

391 See Robert Wintemute, "Sex Discrimination in *Macdonald* and *Pearce*: Why the Law Lords Chose the Wrong Comparators", 274–281.

sometimes complementary, sometimes contrasting, roles of the European Courts of Justice and Human Rights. Sexual orientation and gender identity discrimination thus provide an illustration *par excellence* of the "multi-layered" nature of discrimination law (discussed in Chapter 2). The second key theme relates to the range of subject-matters falling within the scope of discrimination law. Any study of sexual orientation or gender identity discrimination would be radically incomplete if it failed to move outside the workplace and consider topics such as partnership rights, the legal recognition of gender reassignment, and so forth. If the law criminalises consenting same-sex sexual acts, or refuses to recognise the gender reassignment of a transsexual, this might constitute an even more direct and immediate assault upon the dignity or equality of that person than would dismissal from employment or bullying at work. Nonetheless, all these forms of hurt are locatable on the same scale, being tied as they are to a person's gender identity or sexual orientation. We cannot, in consequence, treat discrimination in the workplace as any more than one example—albeit an important one—of the types of social ill which discrimination law, broadly understood, works to redress in the areas of sexual orientation and gender identity.

12

RACE DISCRIMINATION

I. Introduction

Race is a well established prohibited ground in discrimination law. The precise meaning of "race", however, is highly constested as social science scholarship increasingly challenges essentialist and biological definitions of the term. Racialisation—the process which can result in discrimination against a social group—can lead to harm to minorities. This process of racialisation can target groups on the grounds of physical characteristics such as colour or appearance; or it may focus on other external visible signs of appearance or dress; and in some cases it can be linked to other social indicators such as culture or socio-economic status. This raises the prospect of an overlap between the criteria that are relevant when defining race as a category within discrimination law: so that, there is often an overlap between factors such as appearance, ethnic origin, language, culture and religion. In this chapter we focus on the factors that have been traditionally been associated with "race": e.g. colour, ethnic origin, nationality and language. We also deal with forms of "cultural racism" that arise when new social groups are racialised into minorities, and new forms of "racism" emerge. In Chapter 13, we focus on religious minorities which can also be targets of "cultural racism" but who are often also able to claim rights to religious freedom.

The sources of the legal regulation of race discrimination are scattered throughout international, regional and domestic provisions. Moreover, a wide spectrum of legal and non-legal techniques are used: e.g. direct and indirect discrimination; positive action; mainstreaming measures and contract compliance. Earlier chapters have explored some of the issues that are relevant to race discrimination law. In this chapter we examine the concept of race more closely, before moving on to consider the legal provisions that prohibit race discrimination. The chapter focuses on domestic race discrimination legislation but it also deals with international provisions on race discrimination as well as giving an overview of the increasing importance of EU law.

The main part of this chapter is an analysis of the protected ground of race that triggers an action for race discrimination. The discussion takes up a number of ways of analysing "race": e.g. theoretical treatment of the concept of "race"; and the historical and contemporary significance of race in law and policy. It then relates these issues to the legal regulation of race discrimination, e.g. the RRA and the emerging body of EU race discrimination law, e.g. the Race Equality Directive.

Before moving on to that discussion, it is important to understand the areas in which race discrimination in prohibited. This requires us to ask a number of questions: how are concepts such as direct and indirect discrimination and positive action applied in the context of race discrimination; and how is race defined for the purposes of legal regulation. As the following discussion makes clear, race discrimination law is not a homogenous field: there are a wide range of sources of law (e.g. international, EU, European Convention and statutory provisions); there are many different techniques for legal regulation (direct and indirect discrimination, positive action, and the criminal law). There are also a diverse range of spheres of activity in which race discrimination is regulated (e.g. in the access to civil and political rights; employment; criminal law and justice). Although "race" is now one of a number of prohibited grounds of discrimination, it is worth noting that racism has a distinct history and contemporary context.

A. *The Harm of Racism*

Discrimination law is increasingly expanding the grounds on which individuals can claim protection, and it is moving towards greater harmonisation between these different grounds. Moreover, analysis of ethnic minorities tends to be more concerned with "diversity" rather than "racial equality". Nevertheless, it is worth emphasising the special status of "race" as a prohibited ground. In Chapter 3 we discussed the different justifications for discrimination law: these related, for example, to equality of opportunity; to autonomy and dignity; and to social exclusion and oppression. These theoretical arguments about discrimination law take a special form in the context of race discrimination.

Unlike other grounds of discrimination, racism is linked with deep rooted political injustice and economic exploitation: through slavery, colonialism and more recently its association with apartheid in South Africa. These types of discrimination are unique because they are not just individual acts of a private actor: these are systematic and instituionalised forms of racism that are supported by the state. This means that arguments about "stigma", autonomy and dignity are especially relevant to capture the harm of racism. Moreover, the systematic nature of economic exploitation of racial groups through slavery (especially in the United States) and colonialism (in Europe) makes arguments about structural disadvantage and distributive justice especially relevant. Theories of discrimination law that take up the issue of structural disadvantage, such as Hugh Collins' focus on "social exclusion" or Iris Marion Young's theory of group injustice through "oppression", are more likely to provide a model (both descriptive and normative) which captures the special harm of racism in Western democracies. Young, for example, emphasises the socio-economic harms of marginalisation and exploitation to forms of group oppression such as racism. Young's other two categories—violence and cultural alienation—are also useful in this context. The fact that an individual may be targetted because of their membership of a racial group (hate crimes), and the increasing use of criminal law to regulate this type harm, means that the assumption that race discrimination legislation is solely a "civil law" matter needs to be re-examined. Moreover, there is increasing recognition that the exclusion or misrepresentation of racial groups in the public sphere is also a form of harm. Two particular harms are associated with this form of "cultural alienation". First, it is argued that adverse public perceptions create and sustain private prejudice that can manifest itself in hate crimes or unlawful racial discrimination. Second, the importance of the "politics of recognition" emphasises that the exclusion or distortion of an individual's group identity in the public sphere can have a detrimental impact on the autonomy and well being of an individual.

In examining race discrimination law and policy it is also especially relevant to recall the critique of Critical Race Theory which applies the methods and analysis of Critical Legal Studies to "race". This theoretical background, considered in Chapter 3, is especially relevant to a discussion and evaluation of the legal regulation of racial discrimination. The chief proponents of Critical Race Theory make a number of claims about discrimination law's ability to respond to racism. These include, inter alia: arguments against the essentialist construction of race; positioning the problem of racism in structural factors other than the indivdual acts of "racist" perpetrators; a critique of the way in which legal concepts are applied in a formalist way that undermines the goals of fighting racism; a focus on the way in which "power" determines the ability and willingness of legal and political institutions to respond to racism; and finally the need to recognise that race frequently interacts with other categories (such as gender) and in forms and multiple intersectional discrimination.[1]

This chapter focuses on domestic law. However, it also uses comparison with international, US and European approaches to explore the subject. Issues of race are considered in their historical, social and political context. There a number of key questions that are at the core of the discussion: how should we define race; how does the process of racialisation operate to create new categories of groups that are "racialised"; or how can discrimination law and

[1] Derrick A. Bell, "Remembrance of Racism Past: The Civil Rights Decline", in Hill & J. E Jones (eds.) *Race in America: The Struggle for Equality*, pp.73–82 (Madison, USA: University of Wisconsin Press, 1993); Kimberele W. Crenshaw, "Race Reform, Retrenchment: Transformation and Legitimation in Anti-Discrimination Law" (1988) 101 Harvard L. R. 1331–1387.; Richard Delgado "Legal Storytelling: Storytelling for Oppositionists and Others: A Plea for Narrative", in R. Delgado (ed.) *Critical Race Theory: The Cutting Edge*. (Philadelphia, US: Temple University Press, 1995); Kimberle Crenshaw, "Demarginalising the Intersection of Race and Sex: A Black Feminist Critique of Antidiscrimination Doctrine", Feminist Theory and Antiracist Politics (1989) U. Chi. Legal F. 139.

policy intervene to prevent, disrupt or reduce the various harms caused by processes of racialisation?

II. Sources of Race Discrimination Law

Historically, the role of race as a prohibited ground of discrimination was particularly significant (for reasons outlined above). One consequence of this is that race discrimination is prohibited in a wide range of contexts and using a diverse range of legal and non-legal instruments. Although race discrimination is now specifically prohibited in many constitutional and domestic law instruments, any discussion of "race" needs to be understood in the wider context of minority protection. Three phases can be discerned within this disparate attempt to regulate the treatment of racial, ethnic, national and also religous minorities (religion is discussed more fully in Chapter 13). In the first phase of "toleration", the guarantee of individual human rights such as freedom of speech and association ensured a framework within which minorities could manifest their particular difference in the private sphere, whilst having equal rights as citizens in the public sphere. This policy meant that, in effect, prejudice against minorities was left unregulated in certain key areas such as employment and education, thereby hampering minority access in these spheres. In the second, "non-discrimination", phase there was some limited recognition of minority differences in the public sphere, with the guarantee of non-discrimination in areas such as employment and education. Finally, and more recently, there has been a call for a more wide ranging recognition of minorities in the public sphere with a call for the "accommodation of differences" and "multiculturalism".[2] What has resulted is a complex body of law and policy to address the issue of minority protection. Each of these three techniques—individual human rights; non-discrimination; and demands for "recognition" and "accommodation"—have influenced law and policy in this area.

A. *International and Comparative Regulation of Race Discrimination*

Part of the history of the protection of racial, ethnic and national minorities relates to international law norms: e.g. the minorities treaties of the League of Nations and the international human rights order created after World War II via the United Nations. Two particular international law instruments provide the framework for minority protection: Art.26 and Art.27 of the International

[2] Joseph Raz, "Multiculturalism", in *Ethics in the Public Domain*, (Clarendon Press: Oxford, 1994) at pp.172–173.

Covenant on Civil and Political Rights. These are supplemented by the Covenant for the Elimination of Racial Discrimination.

International human rights law and constitutional provisions in a number of jurisdictions give priority to regulating race as a prohibited ground of discrimination. Article 26 of the ICCPR is an example of a general non-discrimination clause:

"All persons are equal before the law and are entitled without any discrimination to the equal protection of the law. In this respect, the law shall prohibit any discrimination and guarantee to all persons equal and effective protection against discrimination on any ground such as *race, colour,* sex, language, *religion,* political or other opinion, *national or social origin,* property, birth or status." (emphasis added).

Article 27 ICCPR creates a positive obligation to preserve the collective aspects of the rights of minorities, i.e the entitlement of minorities: "[...] not to be denied the right, in community with the other members of their group, to enjoy their culture, to profess and practise their own religion, or to use their language." The Convention on the Elimination of Racial Discrimination (1969) prioritise the fight against racism and has a supervisory and reporting mechanism to hold the contracting member states to account. CERD defines race discrimination in the following terms:

Article 1

"1. In this Convention, the term "racial discrimination" shall mean any distinction, exclusion, restriction or preference based on race, colour, descent, or national or ethnic origin which has the purpose or effect of nullifying or impairing the recognition, enjoyment or exercise, on an equal footing, of human rights and fundamental freedoms in the political, economic, social, cultural or any other field of public life.

2. This Convention shall not apply to distinctions, exclusions, restrictions or preferences made by a State Party to this Convention between citizens and non-citizens.

3. Nothing in this Convention may be interpreted as affecting in any way the legal provisions of States Parties concerning nationality, citizenship or naturalization, provided that such provisions do not discriminate against any particular nationality.

4. Special measures taken for the sole purpose of securing adequate advancement of certain racial or ethnic groups or individuals requiring such protection as may be necessary in order to ensure such groups or individuals equal enjoyment or exercise of human rights and fundamental freedoms shall not be deemed racial discrimination, provided, however, that such measures do not, as a consequence, lead to the maintenance of separate rights for different racial groups and that they shall not be continued after the objectives for which they were taken have been achieved."

The CERD definition of race discrimination is significant for a number of reasons. It includes nationality discrimination but at the same time, like the Race Equality Directive and domestic legislation, it allows wide ranging exceptions for immigration rules. It also recognises the need for positive action measures but specifies that different treatment should not lead to permanent separate treatment or segregation.

The committee which supervises CERD has recently made the following observations about the UK: that the RRA does not provide comprehensive coverage; that incidents of "deaths in custody" are disproportionately high for certain ethnic groups; and that increasing tensions around issues of asylum are leading to tensions with host communities and are a risk to the well being of established minority communities.[3]

There is increasing concern that issues of race and gender need to be linked. Crenshaw, for example, argues that there is a need for an additional protocol to provide guidance on how racism affects women in a way that is distinct and exacerbates their experience of discrimination.[4]

B. *US, Canadian and South African Perspectives*

Some constitutional guarantees, such as Art.20 of the New Zealand Bill of Rights and Art.33(1) of the South African constitution go beyond the prohibition of race discrimination and protect language and culture through constitutional norms. The history of apartheid obviously makes racism a special type of problem in South Africa. This is addressed in the South African Constitution which includes a commitment to fight racism (along with sexism) in the preamble, and a general non-discrimination clause in s.9 which includes race as one of the prohibited grounds of discrimination. The Canadian Charter also has a non-discrimination clause in s.15 that includes race as a protected ground. The distinct issues of minority protection that have arisen in Canada have focused on the rights of indigenous minorities and language rights for French speakers in Quebec. The Supreme Court of Canada has recognised aboriginal rights in a number of their decisions[5] and there are special provisions to protect French speaking communities. Canadian state legislation also regulates race discrimination in areas such as employment and provision of goods and services.

The history of slavery gives a special status to racism as a source of "stigma" in the US. This historical context ensures that race gets the highest level of protection under the Equal Protection Clause of the Fourteenth Amendment US Constititution: "No State shall [...] deny to any person within its jur-

[3] For an overview of these issues see Karon Monaghan, Max du Plessis Tajinder Malhi, *Race, Religion and Ethnicity Discrimination, A JUSTICE Report* (Jonathan Cooper (ed.), (London: Justice 2003) at p.41.

[4] Kimberle Crenshaw, "Background Paper for the Expert Meeting on the Gender-Related Aspects of Race Discrimination, November 21–24, Zagreb Croatia. Document filed at following source: World Conference Against Racism, Durban August 31—September 7, Selected Documents and Links at *http://www.wicej.addr.com/wcar docs/index.html* (accessed on August 20, 2006).

[5] *R. v Sparrow* [1990] 1 S.C.R. 1075; *Delgamuukw v British Columbia* [1997] 3 S.C.R. 1010.

isdiction the equal protection of the laws." Despite the abolition of slavery and the introduction of the Equal Protection Clause, the "separate but equal" doctrine was deemed to be constitutional until the famous case of *Brown v Board of Education* in 1954.[6] Before *Brown v Board of Education,* the US Supreme Court in *Plessey v Ferguson*[7] upheld a law that required racial segregation. Following protests by the powerful civil rights movement which provided the political impetus for challenging segregation, *Brown* established that segregated schools, and the "separate but equal doctrine", were a breach of the Equal Protection Clause.

The US Supreme Court has developed a hierarchical review of "suspect classificiations" under the Equal Protection Clause that gives the highest status to race: the use of race as a suspect classification requires the strictest scrutiny, as compared with other grounds such as gender or disability. As early as 1944, *Korematsu v United States* established the principle that "All legal restrictions which challenge the civil rights of a single group are immediately suspect."[8] This was applied in the context of race in *Brown* and developed in subsequent cases such as *Cleburne* where the US Supreme Court stated that racial classifications were "subjected to strict scrutiny and will be sustained only if they are suitably tailored to serve a compelling state interest".[9] *Cleburne* is also important because it makes clear what is distinctive about race as a ground for discrimination: i.e. race is especially prone to be a source of stigmatisation of a particular social group. Therefore, in *Cleburne* the US Supreme Court concluded that racial classification is "so seldom relevant to achievement of any legitimate interest that laws grounded in such considerations are deemed to reflect prejudice and antipathy—a view that those in the burdened class are not as worthy or deserving as others."[10] The special status of race as stigma also provides further justification for the argument that racism is a special, and more serious, form of discrimination.[11] Direct race discrimination will be covered by the prohibition on the use of race as a "suspect classification". However, the US Supreme Court has specifically limited claims for indirect discrimination under the Equal Protection Clause to those cases where there is "intention" to discriminate.[12] This significantly limits the *Griggs* doctrine of "disparate impact" in the context of constitutional discrimination law.[13] Indirect race discrimination in the private sphere is addressed because US statutory discrimination law regulates, through Title VII of the Civil Rights

[6] *Brown v Board of Eduction* (1954) 347 U.S. 483.
[7] *Plessey v Ferguson* 163 U.S. 538.
[8] *Korematsu v United States* (1944) 323 U.S. 214, at p.216.
[9] *City of Cleburne v Cleburne Living Centre* (1985) 432 U.S. 440.
[10] *City of Cleburne v Cleburne Living Centre* (1985) 432 U.S. 440.
[11] For a detailed discussion of the stigma theory in the context of US constitutional law see Andrew Koppelman, *Antidiscrimination Law and Social Equality* (New Haven, US: Yale University Press, 1996) at Chs 1–3.
[12] *Washington v Davis* (1976) 426 U.S. 229.
[13] *Washington v Davis* (1976) 426 U.S. 229.

Act 1964, indirect race discrimination in the areas of employment and provision of goods and services.

US discrimination law on race is also significant because it treats the right to equality for racial minorities as a political right in a liberal democracy. Although the analysis treats "stigma" as a key justification for the prohibition of racial discrimination, the US Supreme Court has also cited economic exploitation, social exclusion and structural disadvantge as justifications for the special priority that is given to the fight against race discrimination. In this way, the stigma caused through discrimination is linked to a failure of process and democracy because, as the Supreme Court confirmed in *Carolene Products*:

"prejudice against discrete and insular minorities may be a special condition, which tends seriously to curtail the operation of those political processes ordinarily to be relied upon to protect minorities, and which may call for a correspondingly more searching judicial enquiry."[14]

Kenneth Karst argues that the substantive core of the Equal Protection Clause is "a principle of equal citizenship, which presumptively guarantees to each individual the right to be treated by the organized society as a respected, responsible and participating member".[15] Karst also observes that "The relationship between stigma and inequality is also clear: while not all inequalities stigmatize, the essence of any stigma lies in the fact that the affected individual is regarded as an unequal in some respect. A society devoted to the idea of equal citizenship, then, will repudiate those inequalities that impose stigma of case and thus "belie the principle that people are of equal ultimate worth".[16] Clearly this US analysis is influenced by the political context of slavery and institutionalised inequality that excluded African Americans from all including political participation.[17]

C. *The European Convention on Human Rights*

The ECHR prohibits race discrimination in the enjoyment of convention rights under Art.14, ECHR. Indeed, the jurisprudence of the European Court of Human Rights (Eur.Ct.H.R.) has given special protection to the right to non-discrimination on the ground of race under Art.14 ECHR.[18] Similarly, the Eur.Ct.H.R. stated that race discrimination is given a special priority in the

14 *US v Carolene Products* 304 U.S. 144, 152 at n.4 (1938).

15 Kenneth L. Karst, "The Supreme Court, 1976 Term—Foreword: Equal Citizenship Under the Fourteenth Amendment," (1977) 91 Harvard L. Rev. 1, at 4.

16 Kenneth L. Karst, "The Supreme Court, 1976 Term—Foreword: Equal Citizenship Under the Fourteenth Amendment," (1977) 91 Harvard L. Rev. 1, at 6.

17 F. Michelman, The Supreme Court, 1968 Term,—Foreward: On Protecting the Poor Through the Fourteenth Amendment (1969) 83 Harvard L. Rev. 7.

18 *R. v Secretary of State for Work and Pensions, Ex p. Carson* [2005] UKHL 37.

application of Art.14, ECHR. In *Chapman v United Kingdom*,[19] the Court applied the indirect discrimination analysis developed in *Thlimmenos v Greece*[20] in the context of race discrimination. Although on the facts of the case they found there had been no indirect racial discrimination under Art.14, ECHR (taken in conjunction with an Art.8 claim concerning the right to family life). The applicant in *Chapman* claimed the UK planning laws had denied her access to land that she could use for her mobile home and thereby live her traditional lifestyle according to her ethnic identity as a gypsy. The Eur.Ct.H.R. found that the Art.8 right to family life, could be used to protect minorities such as the Roma and, significantly, to protect her "ability to maintain her identity as a Gypsy and to lead her private her private and family life *in accordance with that tradition* (emphasis added)".[21] The majority found that there was no indirect discrimination because "the Court does not find, in the circumstances of this case, any lack of objective and reasonable justification for the measures taken against the appliant." (para.129). The minority opinion in *Chapman* affirmed *Thlimmenos* as well as suggesting that: "Our view Art.8 of the Convention imposes a positive obligation on the authorities to ensrue that Gypsies have a practical and effective opportuniy to enjoy their right to respect for their home, and their private and family life, in accordance with their traditional lifestyle, is not a startling innovation." (para.9 of the dissenting judgment).

Nachova v Bulgaria[22] concerned the Roma minorities in Bulgaria. The case concerned the unlawful killing in 1996 of the applicant's relatives (the victims were two men who were conscripts in the army) by a military policeman who had tried to arrest them. The victims were previously arrested for repeated absence from the army without leave. The army officers were officially advised to use "all necessary force" to arrest the two men. The autopsy found that the two victims were shot at a long distance; that there had been warning shots; and that they had been shot because they had not surrendered. For these, and other reasons, the military authorities had refused to prosecute the military officers. An eyewitness had claimed that he had been near the area, and he had asked to remove his young grandson from the area of the conflict but one of the officers had pointed a gun at him and said "You damn Gypsies!". The Applicants alleged that there had been:

[19] Case 27238/95, *Chapman v UK*, Eur.Ct.H.R., decision of January 18, 2001.

[20] (2001) 31 E.H.R.R. 15.

[21] In *Chapman v UK* the European Court of Human Rights found that a UK planning scheme that refused a Roma woman to live on a site in her caravan, and issues relating to the positioning of her caravan, could affect her "ability to maintain her identity as a Gypsy and to lead her private and family life in accordance with that tradition." And that the "applicant's right to respect for her private life, family life and home is in issue in the present case." (paras: 73–74) although found that the interferance was "necessary in a democratic society".

[22] Cases 43577/98 and 43579/98 *Nachova v Bulgaria*, European Court of Human Rights, decision of February 26, 2004.

(1) a breach of Art.2 ECHR (right to life) as a result of the deficient law and practice in Bulgaria that allows the lethal use of force even where this is not necessary;

(2) a failure to conduct an effective investigation into the deaths which constituted a violation of Art.2 and Art.13 (right to effective remedy) ECHR; and

(3) a breach of Art.14 in conjunction with Art.2 on the basis that prejudice and hostile attitudes towards people of Roma origin had played a decisive role in the events leading up to the shootings and the fact that no meaningful investigation was carried out.

The European Court of Human Rights unanimously found that there had been:

(1) a violation of Art.2 ECHR concerning the shooting of the applicant's relatives (the two victims);

(2) a violation of Art.2 ECHR concerning the lack of an effective investigation into the deaths of the victims (there was no need to examine the issue of the Art.2 ECHR breach separately from the Art.13 ECHR right to an effective remedy); and

(3) taken together with Art.2 ECHR, there had been a breach of Art.14 ECHR concerning the lack of an investigation into whether discriminatory attitudes played a role in the shootings.

Nachova is significant because it introduces ideas about racism in the criminal justice process into an analysis of the Art.14, ECHR right to non-discrimination. The Eur.Ct.H.R. emphasised the importance of the fight against racism and of minorities maintaining confidence in the ability of authorities to protect them from racist violence. For these reasons, wherever there is a suspicion that a violent act has been committed with a racist attitude, it is especially important that there is an investigation that is conducted with vigour and impartiality. Moreover, the Eur.Ct.H.R. stated that the proper implementation of the right to life under Art.2, ECHR requires that the State should be able to implement its positive obligations irrepsective of the victim's racial or ethnic origin. This obligation is especially significant where the violent act (or death) is caused by the State's agents. Treating racist cases in the same ways as other cases ignores the special status of "racism" as destructive of fundamental rights. A failure to make these critical distinctions may constitute unjustifiable treatment under Art.14, ECHR so that the state may be required to make distinctions in law and practice between a case of death caused by excessive killing and a racist killing. The use of racist language requires full and thorough investigation. Significantly, the Eur.Ct.H.R. also echoed *Thlimmenos* in recognising the role of indirect discrimination and positive action in

Art.14. They stated that there could be recognition that a State measure may be found to be discriminatory where it is not aimed at a particular group, but where it has a disproportionate impact on one particular group (indirect discrimination in *Nachova*). Finally, the Eur.Ct.H.R. confirmed that where the State (as in this case) had disregarded evidence of discrimination in the course of an investigation, this could be the basis for drawing a negative inference of a breach of Art.14.[23]

The *Nachova* decision, and this approach of the Eur.Ct.H.R. cases of racial discrimination, has been affirmed in a case involving discrimination on entry to a region by Russian.

Cases 55762/00 and 55974/00, *Timishev v Russia* [2005] E.C.H.R. 858

[54]: Turning to the circumstances of the present case, the Court notes that the Kabardino-Balkarian senior police officer ordered traffic police officers not to admit "Chechens". As, in the Government's submission, a person's ethnic origin is not listed anywhere in Russian identity documents, the order barred the passage not only of any person who actually was of Chechen ethnicity, but also of those who were merely perceived as belonging to that ethnic group. It has not been claimed that representatives of other ethnic groups were subject to similar restrictions ... In the Court's view, this represented a clear inequality of treatment in the enjoyment of the right to liberty of movement on account of one's ethnic origin.

[55]: Ethnicity and race are related and overlapping concepts. Whereas the notion of race is rooted in the idea of biological classification of human beings into subspecies according to morphological features such as skin colour or facial characteristics, ethnicity has its origin in the idea of societal groups marked by common nationality, tribal affiliation, religious faith, shared language, or cultural and traditional origins and backgrounds.

[56]: A differential treatment of persons in relevant, similar situations, without an objective and reasonable justification, constitutes discrimination (see *Willis v. the United Kingdom*, no. 36042/97, § 48, ECHR 2002–IV). Discrimination on account of one's actual or perceived ethnicity is a form of racial discrimination (see the definitions adopted by the United Nations and the European Commission against Racism and Intolerance, paragraphs 33 and 34 above). Racial discrimination is a particularly invidious kind of discrimination and, in view of its perilous consequences, requires from the authorities special vigilance and a vigorous reaction. It is for this reason that the authorities must use all available means to combat racism, thereby reinforcing democracy's vision of a society in which diversity is not perceived as a threat but as a source of enrichment (see *Nachova and Others*, cited above, § 145).

[57]: Once the applicant has shown that there has been a difference in treatment, it is then for the respondent Government to show that the difference in treatment could be justified (see, for example, *Chassagnou*, cited above, §§ 91–92). The Court has already established that the Government's allegation that the applicant had attempted to obtain priority treatment was not sustainable on the facts of the case (see paragraphs 42–43

[23] Cases 43577/98 and 43579/98, *Nachova v Bulgaria*, European Court of Human Rights, decision of February 26, 2004.

above). Accordingly, the applicant was in the same situation as other persons wishing to cross the administrative border into Kabardino-Balkaria.

[58]: The Government did not offer any justification for the difference in treatment between persons of Chechen and non-Chechen ethnic origin in the enjoyment of their right to liberty of movement. In any event, the Court considers that no difference in treatment which is based exclusively or to a decisive extent on a person's ethnic origin is capable of being objectively justified in a contemporary democratic society built on the principles of pluralism and respect for different cultures.

[59]: In conclusion, since the applicant's right to liberty of movement was restricted solely on the ground of his ethnic origin, that difference in treatment constituted racial discrimination within the meaning of Article 14 of the Convention.

There has therefore been a violation of Article 14 taken in conjunction with Article 2 of Protocol No. 4

More recently, the Eur.Ct.H.R. has considered the disproportionate allocation of Roma children to special schools for children with mental deficiencies, where the curriculum was inferior to that in mainstream education. In this context the court's acceptance of the principle of indirect race discrimination as a part of Art.14 made use of statistical evidence to find that there was a presumption of indirect race discrimination.[24] The Council of Europe structure for minority protection also includes special treaties to safeguard the rights of minorities, e.g. the Framework Convention for the Protection of National Minorities (1995) and the European Charter for Regional or Minority Languages (1992) which are set out in the later discussion on racism and national minorities.

D. *EU and Domestic Race Relations Law*

In the European Union, the fight against racism is increasingly being given priority. The Race Equality Directive grants protection against race discrimination in a wide range of spheres (e.g. social goods, education, etc.) rather than just employment and training. Moreover, as Chapter 7 notes on positive action in Part B sets out, the EU has special programmes to tackle racism and xenophobia, and also to mainstream racial equality.

In the context of EU law it is worth distinguishing between two aspects. First, issues of race may arise when there is movement between EU member states of individuals who are nationals of EU states. We can call this movement intra EU migration, which is a goal of provisions such as the free movement of persons. This type of migration is regulated by the concept of nationality discrimination. Second, there is also migration into the EU of individuals who are not nationals of an EU member state (third country nations). This can be called inter-EU migration. In a pattern similar to that in

[24] Case 57325/00, *DH v The Czech Republic*, European Court of Human Rights, Grand Chamber, decision of November 13, 2007.

Britain, significant increases in inter-EU migration took place in the 1960s and 1970s. The original EC treaty did not give much attention to inter-EU migration. Commentators have pointed to a number of factors that explain why policies aimed at non-national immigrants were not priority: these include, inter alia, an assumption that immigrant labour from outside the EU would be a temporary phenomenon; and the lack of a legal model of anti-racism legislation at a national level.[25] Some commentators have also argued that the marked contrast between EU policies in the area of race as compared with sex discrimination can be explained by the fact that EU Member States were "anxious to make migrant workers less welcome in order to reserve jobs for ther own nationals, who had the inestimable bargaining advantage of possessing votes in that state which they could cast against the government if they felt aggrieved."[26] Increasing concern about the economic and social consequences of immigration during periods of recession started to influence EU policy in the 1970s. Both issues are especially relevant because, as we see later in the chapter, they mirror the factors that motivated the emergence of the legal regulation of race discrimination in Britain in the late 1960s and 1970s. The response of the EU was to use "soft" rather than "hard" law to deal with problems of racism: there were a number of social action programmes that focused on these twin issues of co-ordination of immigration on the one hand, and integration of migrants on the other. There were also the seeds of a more principled approach via the European Social Charter which specifically includes equal treatment of men and women (Art.16), as well as detailed provisions such as rights for women in relation to pregnancy (Art.8), as "Fundamental Social Right of Workers". The European Social Charter also includes a general non-discrimination norm in Art.E:

"The enjoyment of the rights set forth in this Charter shall be secured without discrimination on any ground such as race, colour, sex, language, religion, political or other opinion, national extraction or social origin, health, association with a national minority, birth or other status." The Appendix to the European Social Charter provides a basic justification defence and states that "differential treatment based on an objective and reasonable justification shall not be deemed discriminatory."

More recently, there has been a shift in EU policy which explicitly takes a more principled approach to combating racism. This approach reached its zenith in the use of constitutional norms to regulate race discrimination in the Charter of Fundamental Rights and the introduction of the Race Equality Directive under Art.13 EC. Both legal provisions are significant and they mark a

25 Mark Bell, *Anti-Discrimination Law and the European Union*, (Oxford: Oxford University Press, 2002), pp.55–56.

26 S. George, *Politics and Policy in the European Community* (Oxford: Oxford University Press, 1991) at 208, cited in Mark Bell, *Anti-Discrimination Law and the European Union*, (Oxford: Oxford University Press, 2002), pp.55–56.

recognition of an emerging body of principle and law to regulate racism in the EU. The EU Charter now provides a general non-discrimination norm similar to that in constitutional provisions such as the US 14th Amendment or the Canadian Charter which explicitly cover race discrimination. However, as we saw in Chapter 2, there are significant limits to the competence of the EU in this area. Most significantly, Art.53 makes clear that the Charter has a limited jurisdiction.

In addition to the Charter's general non-discrimination clause there is also more specific legislation against race discrimination such as the Race Equality Directive (RED) introduced under Art.13 EC. The RED prohibits race discrimination in a wide range of areas: employment and training; goods and services; education; social protection and social advantages. The Directive prohibits direct and indirect discrimination, as well as harassment. It permits positive action and it also requires the establishment of administrative agencies to combat race discrimination along the lines of the British model (e.g. the Commission for Racial Equality). However, despite this substantial level of legal regulation there remain important limits to the RED. Most importantly, Art.13 includes the words "within the limits of the powers conferred by the Community". Although the exact nature of these limits has not been established, it is clear that they will act as significant limiting criteria to the scope of application of this provision. For example, areas such as the criminal law and health policy may not be covered by the RED.[27]

Despite these limits, the RED gives a relatively wide range of protections against race discrimination: its scope extends beyond the categories of employment and vocational training that are covered by the Employment Equality Directive. However, there remains an important difference between race and gender discrimination provisions under Art.141 of the EC Treaty. The scope of EU sex discrimination law extends further than race and other categories in relation to areas such as pay and part time work. However, there is more extensive protection of race in the areas of social advantages. Moreover, the EU has special action programmes for race similar to those for gender equality. For example, the EU established a European Year Against Racism[28] and established a special centre (the European Monitoring Centre for Racism and Xenophobia) to monitor and combat racism in the EU.[29]

Generally, the RED follows a structure which replicates domestic race relations legislation. Direct discrimination, indirect discrimination and harassment are prohibited in areas such as employment and in the delivery of public and private services. The remedial structure, as with domestic race

[27] See Mark Bell, *Anti-Discrimination Law and the European Union*, (Oxford: OUP, 2002), pp.130–133.

[28] Commission, "Communication from the Commission on racism, xenophobia and anti-semitism and Proposal for a Council Decision designating 1997 European Year against Racism". COM (95) 653.

[29] Reg. 1035/97 establishing a European Monitoring Centre for Racism and Xenophobia [1997] O.J. L. 151, Art.2. Now incorporated into the work of the EU Fundamental Rights Agency.

relations legislation, includes individual remedies for damages and can include collective remedies via the action of enforcement agencies. Limited positive action programmes are permitted. This similarity between the RED and existing domestic race relations legislation meant that the transposition of the EU legislation into domestic law did not require a new statutory instrument as for religion, sexual orientation and age. However, there were some significant changes that were necessary. For example, there was a need to change the definition of indirect discrimination through the Race Relations Act 1976 (Amendment) Regulations 2003. The piecemeal approach to these changes meant that there is now an anomalous situation whereby the definition of indirect discrimination in those categories mentioned under the RED is different from that used in categories covered by the RRA but not the RED. These points are explored in more detail in Chapter 2.

III. Domestic Race Discrimination Law: The Historical, Social and Political Context

Chapter 3 confirmed that an understanding of discrimination law requires attention to be paid to the way in which concepts have developed, but that these need to be placed in their social, historical and political context. In this section we examine the background context to legal regulation of race discrimination in domestic law.

A. *History of Migrants to Britain*

Britain is historically a state with considerable ethnic and national variation. The well established presence of national, linguistic, racial and religious minorities challenges the idea of Britain as a single racially homogenous state. The movement towards the formation of a unitary state of "Britain" was a complex process. The unification of Wales with England ensured that English law, the Anglican Church and the English language were given precdence in Wales. The Act of Union which created Great Britain linked the physical geography of Scotland to that of England and Wales and formed one political community. This political community ensured rule by a single legislature and one established Church. This physical and political unity, however, did not eliminate diversity. Great Britain includes, inter alia, the union of a number of distinct geographical, cultural and political entities: the union between England, Scotland and Wales. In addition, Great Britain has always been a mixed racial and religious population. Jews are Britain's oldest racial and religious minority, whose earliest presence dates back to the Norman times in the eleventh century.[30] There have been Black and Minority Ethnic communities in Britain from the earliest time periods which includes the importation of African slaves and servants from the sixteenth century onwards. There have also been Roma populations in Great Britain from as early as the sixteenth century[31], and evidence of Muslim settlements in Britain under the Tudors and Stewarts (fifteenth and sixteenth centuries).[32]

Until the large scale Irish and Jewish immigration to Britain in the nineteenth century, and inward migration from the former colonies in the twentieth century, British immigrant populations were small compared with the total population. Any analysis of what it means to be a "minority" in Britain would need to be preceded by some discussion of what it means to be British. A definition of the essence of what it means to be British is not, however, straightforward. Matthew Arnold, for example, notes the way in which three "essences" account for what it means to be British: "the Germanic genius, the Celtic genuis, the Norman genius."[33] The presence of "Celts" in Britain challenges the idea that Britain was a racially and culturally homogenous society before more recent immigration. The recognition of Celts as a national minority also highlights the fact that have always been "indigenous" British minorities with specific political claims such as language rights (Welsh) and devolution (Scots). This historical context is significant because it emphasises the importance of exploring the continuities between the principles that underlie the rights of national minorities and the more contemporary demands for equality by recent migrants (racial, cultural and religious groups). Both sets of claims highlight the importance of recognising group identity as an aspect of well being, (see further Chapter 3) in the context of recent debate about "multiculturalism" and the accommodation of difference. This continuity is also recognised within domestic discrimination law which acknowledges that discrimination against the Irish[34], and also against indigenous minorities such as the Welsh and Scottish people, is prohibited discrimination under the RRA[35]. Jews have had a presence in Britain since the eleventh century. They were initially present but expelled from Britain in 1290 and then later readmitted by Cromwell in 1656. The Roma (sometimes also called gypsies or travellers) have also had a presence in Britain from about the sixteenth century. Both sets of minorities were tolerated rather than welcomed. Jews faced legal obstacles through such indirect devices as the need to swear a Christian oath to hold public office.[36] The Roma faced repressive legislation

[30] For an overview see Sebastian Poulter, *Ethnicity, Law and Human Rights: The English Experience* (Oxford: Clarendon Press, 1998), Introduction, at pp.3–4.
[31] J. Okley, *The Traveller-Gypsies* (Cambridge: Cambridge University Press).
[32] N. Mattar, *Islam in Britain*, (Cambridge: Cambridge University Press, 1998).
[33] Matthew Arnold, *On the Study of Celtic Literature and on Translating Homer* (New York: Macmillan, 1883), p.87.
[34] *Post Office v O'Driscoll*, unreported, April 9, 1992, EAT.
[35] See Aileen McColgan, *Discrimination Law: Text, Cases and Materials* (Oxford: Hart, 2005) at pp.540–548.
[36] Sandra Fredman, *Discrimination Law* (Oxford: Clarendon Press, 2002) at 37.

aimed at expelling them and making their lifestyle more difficult. In the case of the Roma this trend has continued into the contemporary period leading to "an explicitly assimilationist policy, using the criminal law to repress the nomadic tradition of gypsies."[37] The treatment of Roma has also had an increasing European dimension with the enlargement of the EU to countries with a history of discrimination against this group. The EU policy towards the Roma (defined as "a group of people who speak the Romani tongue and/or share a common ethnic identity, culture and history") includes policies of integration and the monitoring of their treatment by the European Monitoring Centre on Racism and Xenophobia.[38]

We now explore the treatment of various specific issues relating to racial diversity in the UK.

1. The British Response to Slavery

The slave trade is an interesting example of the way in which Britain's colonial history impacted on race discrimination law in the domestic context. During the era of slavery, officially confined to the colonies, the courts had sought to distinguish between the legitimacy of slavery *in the colonies* and the principle of the freedom of the individual in relation to slavery *in Britain* as Lester and Bindman suggest: "The courts resolved the difficulty by treating slavery as a relationship created under local colonial law, and enforcing that relationship as a matter of colonial rather than domestic English law".[39] This is an interesting example of a theme that recurs throughout discussions of the relationship between race and law in the contemporary period: i.e. the effort to maintain a strict separation between the international context and the domestic context of racism. The abolitionist movement challenged this dichotomy. Subsequent legislation to abolish slavery in the colonies is an early example of the universalising of the principle that race discrimination is a moral wrong.[40] Yet, subsequent developments suggested that race remained an important factor in the treament of minorities within the domestic context. Slavery provided Britain with contact with non-white others; whilst the abolitionist movement provided an example of how political action could challenge injustice or racism and also how such action was often based on a mixed range of motivations.

[37] *ibid.*, at 39.

[38] For a discussion of this issue see for example "EU support for Roma communities in Central and Eastern Europe", (First published in May 2002), available at *http://www.europa.eu.int* (accessed on November 10, 2005).

[39] Anthony Lester and Geoffrey Bindman, *Race and Law* (London: Longman, 1972) at p.29.

[40] *ibid.*, at Ch.1.

2. Irish Immigration to Britain

The Irish and Jews in Britain were not distinguishable in terms of their skin colour. However, both these groups were racialised as "culturally" different. To this extent the racialisation process by which these groups were constructed as the "other" can be expressed as "cultural racism" rather than "colour racism". There was a longstanding tradition of Irish migration to Britain dating back to the eighteenth and early nineteenth centuries. During this time the cause of the migration can be traced to the increasing British demands for labour caused by increasing and rapid economic expansion.[41] The outbreak of the potato famine of 1845, and the resulting starvation, intensified this pre-existing pattern of migration leading to a large increase in the number of Irish immigrants in Britain. The main settlements of the Irish communities were in London and Lancashire, with smaller communities in the West Midlands and Yorkshire. In Scotland, the main settlements of the Irish community were in the west especially near Glasgow. This pattern led to distinct communities who could be identified on the basis of cultural and religious differences.[42] What is significant about this substantial immigration into Britain is that it was not accompanied by either calls for, or a State response of, regulation. Part of the explanation may be that there were a number of legal and political settlements through which there was already a connection between the Irish and the British State. The Act of Union 1800 had incorporated Ireland into the UK which meant that the people of Ireland were already granted status as British subjects. This link was loosened through the establishment of the Irish Republic in 1922 and after Ireland left the Commonwealth in 1947. However, despite these changes the Irish remained free to enter, settle, work and vote in Britain.[43] Although there were no popular demands to regulate Irish immigration, there was a hostile response against the Irish by some sections of the British public. There was also well established anti-Irish stereotypes in British culture: the Irish were racialised as inferior by reference to "biological difference" and because of their Catholicism. There were also acts of violence towards Irish immigrants. Significantly, middle class Victorian attitudes included the belief that there was a wide racial and cultural gap between the English and the Irish.[44] This early construction of the "essence" of English values, and its difference from "Irish" values, is significant in considering later responses to immigration by Jews and other minorities.[45]

[41] R. Miles, *Racism and Migrant Labour* (London: Routledge, 1982) at pp.120–150.

[42] John Solomos, *Race and Racism in Britain*, 3rd ed., (Hampshire: Palgrave Macmillan, 2003) at pp.38–40.

[43] John Solomos, *Race and Racism in Britain*, 3rd ed., (Hampshire: Palgrave Macmillan, 2003) at pp.38–38.

[44] John Solomos, *Race and Racism in Britain*, 3rd ed., (Hampshire: Palgrave Macmillan, 2003) at pp.36–40.

[45] *ibid.*, at pp.39.

3. Jewish Immigration to Britain

The historical lessons of the political and legal responses to Jewish immigration are especially important for an understanding of racism. The migration of large numbers of Irish people to Britian did not give rise to calls for immigration controls and legal regulation. In a sharp contrast to this, the arrival of large numbers of Jewish immigrants who were fleeing from persecution in Eastern Europe in the late Victorian and early Edwardian period led to a very different political response. This migration led to the assertion of "England for the English" by a wide spectrum of the British public, including conservatives and trade unionists.[46] According to one commentator on political anti-semitism, the presence of Jews in the 1880s and 1890s became associated with domestic issues such as unemployment and poverty, as well as foreign policy issues such as anti-colonial struggles.[47] Despite the small numbers of Jews compared to Irish migrants, there were calls for the state to restrict Jewish immigration. The perception of social problems associated with Jewish immigration in the East End of London led to trade union support for immigration control (resolutions were passed by the Trade Union Congress in 1892, 1894 and 1895).[48] Jews were concentrated in the worst sections of "sweated" labour and were accused of undercutting local labour conditions.[49] There was political agitation in the East End by the British Brothers League to end Jewish immigration, as well as support in Parliament for state regulation of immigration.[50] With the election of a Conservative government in 1895, the political stage was set for the introduction of legislation in the form of the Aliens Order 1905. Subsequently, more detailed legislation appeared in the form of the Aliens Restriction Act 1914. This legislation gave the government wide ranging powers to control immigration through the use of prerogative powers e.g. Orders in Council. These powers were justified as essential for national security during a time of war. The legislation allowed the government to decide who could enter and be deported as well as allowing restrictions on where they lived and travelled. After the First World War this was not fully repealed but was rather amended and developed. The Aliens Order 1920 allowed immigration officials to refuse entry to an alien who it considered was unable to provide for his or her own support. It also gave wider powers to deal with those aliens who evaded immigration control. It was within this legislative and political paradigm that Britain responded to the plight of the growing numbers of Jewish refugees who fled from Nazi Germany in the 1930s. The government justified its restrictive approach to the entry of refugees from fascism by asserting that Britain's large population and high unem-

[46] G. Lebzelter, *Political Anti-Semitism in England* (Basingstoke: Macmillan, 1982) at p.90.
[47] *ibid.*, at p.120.
[48] J. A. Garrard, *The English and Immigration 1880–1914* (Oxford: OUP) at 71 and 174.
[49] Sandra Fredman, *Discrimination Law* (Oxford: Clarendon Press, 2002) at 37.
[50] B. Gainer, *The Alien Invasion: The Origins of the Aliens Act 1905* (London: Heinemann, 1972).

ployment made it an unsuitable host country.[51] Commentators have attributed the failure to act decisively to help Jewish refugees during this period to widespread anti-Semitism in British society.[52] Anti-semitism continues to be a phenomenon in Britain[53] and in the EU context[54].

An understanding of attitudes towards Jewish immigration are particularly important in understanding contemporary attitudes towards race relations law and policy. The fact of increasing Jewish immigration, with the resulting political resistance, introduced "race into politics". It also introduced what was to become an ongoing and symbiotic relationship between calls for immigration and race relations. Irish and Jewish immigration focused on cultural and religious differences. The immigration in the mid-1950s into Britain of large numbers of African-Carribean and Asian workers from the former colonies built on these historical attitudes, and also introduced a new set of challenges. These new immigrants were not white. Rather, they were clearly distinguishable from the majority population because of their colour which could be used as the basis for ongoing differences in treatment. The models of assimilation that could be applied to Irish and Jewish migrants were not appropriate to take into account differences that were based on colour. This new form of immigration also raised further questions that we consider later in the chapter. For example, how does colour and ethnically marked difference translate into discrimination and disadvantage in contemporary Britain? What is the appropriate state response—through law and policy—to this challenge?

4. Commonwealth Citizens

There were ethnic minorities (e.g. Asian, African, African-Carribean and Chinese persons) in Britain before the mid-twentieth century. However, it was not until immigration from the former colonies in the 1950s that significant numbers of migrant groups became clearly distinguishable on the grounds of their colour. This period provides the immediate context for the introduction of contemporary race relations legislation. However, earlier examples of migration remain important because they reveal some of the recurring themes that are relevant in understanding modern race discrimination legislation. During the 1950s, immigration by ethnic minorities was by British subjects who were Commonwealth citizens who had a well established link with the UK. These migrants were workers (and their descendents) from India, Africa and the Carribean, these territories had been colonised by the British. These

[51] A. Sherman, Island Refuge: Britain and Refugees from the Third Reich, (London: Paul Elek, 1973) at 259.

[52] T. Kushner, *The Holocaust and the Liberal Imagination: A Social and Cultural History* (Oxford: Blackwell, 1994).

[53] "A Very Light Sleeper—The Persistance and Dangers of Antisemitism" (Runnymede Trust: London, 1997).

[54] EUMC Report: Manifestations of Antisemitism in the EU 2002–2003, (EUMC: Vienna, 2003). This was the largest ever study of anti-semitism in Europe.

historic links gave these individuals a right to entry to the UK by virtue of common membership of the British commonwealth. The need for labour for the post-war British economy provided the demand which attracted them to Britain. Earlier patterns of Jewish immigration had led to a political reaction in the form of calls for immigration controls. This pattern was repeated in the 1950s as discussed in the following passage by John Solomos:

John Solomos, "From Equal Opportunity to Anti-Racism: Racial Inequality and the Limits of Reform", Policy Paper in Ethnic Relations No.17 Centre for Research in Ethnic Relations, Warwick: University of Warwick, 1989.

Historical Context

"From the 1950s, the question of what to do to counter racial discrimination emerged as a major dilemma in debates about immigration and "race relations". Even in the early stages of black migration there was an awareness that in the longer term the question of racial discrimination was likely to become a volatile political issue (Solomos, 1989). In the early stages of post-war black migration political debates about "race" were centred upon the question of immigration controls, leading to the introduction in 1962 of the Commonwealth Immigration Act which sought to control the flow of black migrants into Britain. However, an underlying concern even at this stage was the question of the future of "racial relations" in British society. The notion that the arrival of too many "black" migrants would lead to "problems" in relation to housing, employment and social services was already widely articulated . . .

Two dimensions of these "problems" were usually distinguished. First, the negative response of the majority white population to the competition of black workers in the labour and housing markets. Second, the frustration of black workers who felt themselves excluded from equal participation in British society by the development of the "colour bar" in the labour and housing markets, along with related processes of discrimination. Both these issues were perceived as potential sources of conflict which the government had to manage and control.

The first attempts to deal with the potential for racial conflict and to tackle racial discrimination can be traced back to the 1960s, and took two basic forms. The first involved the setting up of welfare agencies to deal with the "problems" faced by black migrants and to help white communities to understand the migrants. The second stage of the policy response began with the passage of the 1965 and 1968 Race Relations Acts, and was premised on the notion that the state should attempt to ban discrimination on the basis of race, colour or ethnic origin though legal sanctions and public regulatory agencies charged with the task of promoting greater equality of opportunity . . .

This dual strategy was clearly articulated by the Labour Government's 1965 White Paper on Immigration from the Commonwealth, but it has its origins in the debates of the 1950s and the period leading up to the 1962 Commonwealth Immigrants Act. The notion that immigration was essentially an issue of "race" was consistent with the view that: (a) the growing number of black citizens resident in the UK was either actually or potentially the source of social problems and conflicts, and (b) that it was necessary for the state to introduce measures to promote the "integration" of immigrants into the wider society and its fundamental institutions . . ."

The principles that underlay the early state response to post Second World War immigration laid the foundations for subsequent race relations policy. Three particular principles were relevant:

(a) the assumption that the increase in immigration could lead to social and political problems;

(b) the linking of immigration controls with good race relations;

(c) the need for the integration of minorities.

These three factors are related in important ways. The rationale for linking the principles is that there was an inextricable link between immigration controls, public order and integration. Rather than focusing on the extension of rights of citizenship to the new minorities, there was instead a focus on achieving and managing "good race relations".

5. The Political, Social and Economic Context

During the 1960s, there was an increasing recognition of the disadvantaged social and economic position of the new migrants. Home Secretary Roy Jenkins' speech in 1966 illustrates some of these themes. Commenting on the justified expectations of second and third generation immigrants Jenkins observed:

"And if we allow their expectations to be disappointed we shall both be wasting scarce skills and talents, and building up vast troubles for ourselves in the future. In the next decade this, to my mind, will become the real core of the problem."[55]

Linked to the issue of immigration was the political context of race in the 1960s and especially the rise of Powellism. In 1968, Enoch Powell made his famous "River of Tiber" speech in which he set out his prediction that the new wave of immigration would be the cause of serious social unrest in Britain. Powell was, not surprisingly, opposed to the extension of race relations legislation via the Race Relations Act 1968 (RRA 68). Significantly, the rise of "Powellism" provided an incentive to tackle the problems of race relations within mainstream politics. One response to Powellism was to take "race out of politics" by accepting that (a) there was a need to tackle immigration, and (b) that there should be a stable and orderly integration of migrants. This is in sharp contrast to the treatment of race in the US context, where the Civil Rights Act was introduced after a wide ranging political struggle that involved alliances between African Amercians and other American citizen. Unlike the British

[55] See Anthony Lester and Geoffrey Bindman, *Race and Law* (London: Longman, 1972) at 84.

focus on taking "race out of politics", the US civil rights movement was the outcome of deep rooted social and political concerns.

It is not surprising that employers were opposed to the legal regulation of race discrimination in employment, as envisaged by the RRA 68. More surprising is the clear objection of the trade union movement to this legislation. This resistance can be explained, in part, by a suspicion of relying on the legal regulation of collective bargaining, and a preference for voluntarism. Both sides of industry gradually moved to accept that there might be some role for legislation in this area. Political support for an extension of legislation to employment and housing was also provided by changes on the left. The Labour Party's working party on race relations reported to the Labour Party Annual Conference in 1967, and unanimously voted to extend the RRA 65 to the main areas of racial discrimination such as employment and housing. This reflected the increasing interest and research on race issues on the left of British politics.[56]

This grass roots support for race relations legislation within the Labour Party was accompanied by effective political leadership. Significantly, Roy Jenkins had made some strong public statements in support of a principled approach to race relations and the need for equality of opportunity. Lester and Bindman summarise Jenkins' contribution in the following terms:

"[...] the brief period in which Roy Jenkins was Home Secretary was of decisive importance. Unlike many of his political contemporaries, he was sensitive to the pressing international imperatives of the second half of this century, which have made equality of opportunity a requirement for a civilised modern society. Jenkins's personal qualities of skilful and determined leadership have often been stressed by commentators on these events; but what mattered was his awareness of the need to achieve racial equality. What was crucial was Roy Jenkins's perception, as a liberal, reforming Home Secretary, that in the moral and political climate of the twentieth centruy, no civilised society could permit the growth of racial injustice."[57]

6. Race and Immigration

Legislative action on immigration and race relations followed on from these debates in the 1950s and 1960s. What is particularly striking about the legislative activity around issues of race is that it was accompanied by legislative action on immigration. The three key statutes on race discrimination were the RRA 65, the RRA 68 and the RRA 76. At each stage the political and legal debate about the legal regulation of race relations was accompanied by a simultaneous debate about legislation on immigration to control the entry of

[56] Phillip N. Sooben, *The Origins of the Race Relations Act*, Centre for Research in Ethnic Relations, Research Paper No.12, Warwick, 1990.

[57] Anthony Lester and Geoffrey Bindman, *Race and Law* (London: Longman, 1972) at 149.

people (mainly aimed at those from the former colonies/the commonwealth) into Britain. This public debate led to the Commonwealth Immigrants Act 1962, the Commonwealth Immigrants Act 1968 and Immigration Act 1971. Together, this immigration legislation reversed the previous definition of a British subject which had included those who were colonial subjects in the former colonies. Understanding the link between race relations and immigration remains important because of the contemporary discussions about asylum. Later discussions in this chapter suggest that asylum seekers are increasingly being racialised as a social group.

The connection between the regulation of immigration and issues of race has been mentioned in the context of Jewish immigration. The connection of immigration to race relations continued and became more intense in the context of post-war migration from the former Commonwealth. The government's White Paper on Immigration from the Commonwealth in 1965 gave official recognition to the need for a controlled immigration policy on the one hand, and the problems of the integration and community cohesion issues of migrants already lawfully resident in Britain.[58] Immigration also played a critical role in the period just before the introduction of the RRA 68. In 1967 there were an increasing number of UK citizens of Asian origin who were leaving Kenya as a result of Kenyan "Africanisation" programmes. The Commonwealth Immigration Act 1968 was introduced which restricted the right to UK citizenship for subjects in the former colonies. The Kenyan Asian "crisis", and the resulting immigration legislation which severely restricted the the citizenship rights of mainly ethnic minority British nationals, was at the forefront of discussions just as the RRA 68 was being prepared as a Bill for discussion.

The White Paper on Racial Discrimination that preceded the Race Relations Act 1976 recognised that immigration was a key issue in promoting good race relations. One example of this link between immigration and race relations is the speech made by Roy Hattersley in a debate on immigration in March 1976 where, after recalling his earlier opposition to the immigration control, he said that:

> "the Labour Party of that time should have supported it [...] I now believe that there are social as well as economic arguments [for limiting Commonwealth immigration], and I believe that unrestricted immigration can only produce additional problems, additional suffering and additional hardship unless some kind of limitation is imposed and continued."[59]

Despite the intimate connection between race and immigration prior to the RRA 76, there was an increasing awareness amongst activists and progressives that race was an independent sphere of policy, i.e. racial equality (like gender

[58] Cmnd. 2739, August 1965.

[59] Anthony Lester and Geoffrey Bindman, *Race and Law* (London: Longman, 1972) at 120.

equality) was part of a "principled" response by a modern liberal state rather than an aspect of immigration control.[60] Nevertheless, debates about immigration continued to provide a powerful backdrop for race relations and discrimination law reform. The debates in the 1960s were also taking place against the backdrop of the civil rights movement in the US and an awareness that social problems relating to immigration could give rise to "racial tension" and violence on the American model.[61] The US experience also influenced a number of progressive campaigners such as Geoffrey Bindman and Anthony Lester, as well as Roy Jenkins, who provided political leadership on race issue throughout 1969 and the early 70s. While "progressive" opinion found increasing support with all political parties, the Labour Party, and especially Roy Jenkins, was increasingly concerned with race relations as an important liberal principle that should guide policy in this area.

B. *Race and the Emerging Discrimination Law*

The main legislation that emerged from these discussions in the 1960s and 70s was the Race Relations Act 1976 (RRA). However, the RRA 65 and 68 remain significant because they paved the way for this model of discrimination law in important respects. They set up special bodies (e.g the Race Relations Board under the RRA 65 and the Community Relations Board under the RRA 68) to deal with the problems faced by immigrants (mainly concerned with housing and social welfare). They also had the function of educating the general public about the wider issues of "race relations", which can be seen to be part of a general strategy to avoid the confrontation between racial groups that characterised the US experience of the civil rights movement. These developments are significant because they mark the start of the use of specialised administrative bodies rather than government departments to deal with race relations, which laid the foundations for the eventual establishment of the Commission for Racial Equality.

A historical analysis of the period that immediately preceded the RRA of 1976 (RRA) remains important for understanding the legislation. It is worth identifying a number of recurring themes that had an influence on the RRA, although it is also worth emphasising that it is impossible to discern which of these factors was a significant cause. Rather than seeking to identify cause and effect with precision, this section sets out the background and some of the recurring factors that influenced the RRA. Some can be identified as a causal factor (e.g. the increasing evidence of actual discrimination against minorities

60 Erik Bleich, *Race Politics in Britain and France* (Cambridge: Cambridge University Press, 2003) at 91.

61 John Solomos, *From Equal Opportunity to Anti-Racism: Racial Inequality* and the Limits of Reform, Policy Paper in Ethnic Relations No.17, Centre for Research in Ethnic Relations, Warwick: University of Warwick, 1989.

such as the PEP report), whilst others are relevant as an important influence on the form and content of the legislation (e.g the comparison with US legislation in the late 1960s).

The move away from criminal law regulation between the RRA 65 and RRA 68, which eventually culminated in the preference for a civil law paradigm for the RRA, is significant. The RRA 65 had placed great emphasis on race discrimination in the public sphere where it could become a catalyst for more serious public order problems. Hence, priority was given to the introduction of a criminal offence of incitement to racial hatred which is now included in domestic public order legislation.[62] Sir Frank Soskice emphasised this point in the Second Reading that preceded the RRA 65. He stated that this legislation was:

"[...] concerned with public order. Overt acts of discrimination in public places, intensely wounding to the feelings of those against whom these acts are practised, perhaps in the presence of many onlookers, breed the ill will which, as the accumulative result of several such actions over a period, may disturb the peace."[63]

This was a classic example of the use of the criminal law to preserve the peace, that justified the legal regulation of race discrimination as part of this overall strategy.

During the period between 1965 and 1968 there were developments that complicated this initial justification for race relations legislation. Was there, as a matter of empirial fact, discrimination against these new migrants that justified legal regulation? During this period it increasingly became clear that the answer to this question was clearly "yes". First, increasing research confirmed high levels of race discrimination in areas such as employment, housing and education. The most comprehensive treatment of the extent of actual discrimination in Britain in the period preceding the RRR was carried out in the report of an independent research organisation called Political and Economic Planning (PEP) which published its report in 1967. The PEP report was based on interviews with white and non-white immigrants, and these were compared with a series of "situation tests" carried out in six towns. In these tests, a number of people of different races applied for the same positions in employment, housing and commercial services. The different individuals were: a black West Indian applicant; a white immigrant of Hungarian origin; and a white Englishman. In each test, the three applicants claimed equivalent occupational qualifications or housing requirements. The PEP report confirmed that:

[62] Public Order Act 1986.

[63] Anthony Lester and Geoffrey Bindman, *Race and Law* (London: Longman, 1972) at 114.

"the groups who were most physically distinct in colour and racial features from English experienced the greatest discrimination, [...] The Report illustrated how the processes of racial discrimination tended to push or keep immigrants in poorer housing and lower status jobs, reinforcing stereotypes and preventing integration."[64]

Moreover, the PEP report confirmed that racial discrimination would, if left unregulated, be a growing rather than a stable problem. If discrimination was linked to colour then the passage of time and the transformation of certain migrant communities into an indigenous population would not solve the problems associated with racial discrimination. The PEP report also suggested that one of the causes of discrimination was the perception that others (e.g. white customers) would react badly to employees of other racial groups. Thus, part of the analysis suggested that people practiced discrimination against their own better judgment or wishes. This analysis represented a shift from the model employed by RRA 1965 which had focused on issues of racism in the public sphere as a threat to public order, and had emphasised a criminal law response to incitement to racial hatred. According to Bindman and Lester, the argument in the 1965–1968 period increasingly acknowledged that one of the causes of discrimination was prejudice by proxy rather than personal bigotry. Criminal law regulation of the most pernicious forms of racism in public, for example by criminalising incitement to racial hatred, would not eliminate this source of race discrimination. The ongoing problem of discrimination that would face second and third generation immigrants, became an increasingly important issue in the pre-1976 period, as reflected in the White Paper that preceded the RRA 76.

C. *The US Experience and Influence on Discrimination Law in Great Britain*

Throughout the 1960s, the political conflict and violence associated with civil rights struggles in the US formed the backdrop for a discussion of race and immigration in Britian. Moreover, US models of discrimination law had a more direct influence on the form and content of domestic discrimination law. The US experience had a number of very specific influences on the RRA of 1976. Roy Jenkins' visit to the US in 1974, as well as the influence of US law on policy advisers such as Geoffrey Bindman and Anthony Lester, had a number of critical influences on the legal framework of the RRA of 1976. First, the development of a more extensive definition of discrimination which included "indirect" discrimination as developed by the US Supreme Court in *Griggs v Duke Power*[65] was explictly imported from the US. Second, this shift away from

[64] Anthony Lester and Geoffrey Bindman, *Race and Law* (London: Longman, 1972) at 83.
[65] (1971) 401 U.S. 424.

formal equality towards a more sophisticated understanding of equality and discrimination paved the way for overcoming initial resistance towards endorsement of the earliest examples of positive aciton in British discrimination law.[66] Roy Jenkins summed up his new attitude in comments on positive action measures in the SDA 75 in the following terms:

"I believe that we should not be so blindly loyal to the principle of formal equality as to ignore the actual and practical inequlities between the sexes still less to prohibit positive action to help men and women to compete on genuinely equal terms and to overcome an undesirable historical link."[67]

The choice of the civil model, rather than the criminal law paradigm by the Street Committee, was based on the Ives Quinn Act first introduced in New York in 1945 which had introduced the idea of a special administrative machinery to deal with problems of discrimination. The subsequent prevalence of the idea of discrimination commissions in the form of the Race Relations Board, and subsequently the Equal Opportunities Commission and Commission for Racial Equality, were also modelled on the US type administrative bodies. Street Committee advocated this paradigm.

What is less clear from discussions during this period, is an appreciation of the limits of the comparison with the US and doubts about the easy transfer of discrimination law concepts between jurisdictions. There were, and are, important differences between the US experience and the British situation. For example, in the US context a long history of slavery and segregation of African Americans, as well as a political context that made the demand for inclusion and an end to segregation the main focus, ensured the symmetrical nature of the Civil Rights Act 1964. Therefore, non-discrimination defined in a symmetrical way ensures that both blacks and whites, or men and women, can rely on the legislation in exactly the same terms. There is no recognition that discrimination law can have a role to play in allowing minorities to advance their goals, whilst at the same time recognising important differences (whether of economic position or culture) between them.

D. *The Choice of Civil Law*

It is against this background that the legal regulation of race discrimination, in the form with which we are familiar, was introduced. In 1967 the Street Report set out the legislative choices open to Parliament. It emphasised that the scope

[66] Phillip N. Sooben, "The Origins of the Race Relations Act", Research Paper in Ethnic Relations, No.12, Centre for Research in Ethnic Relations, September 1990 at pp.38–39.

[67] Hansard, Vol.889, Col.514, cited in Phillip N. Sooben, "The Origins of the Race Relations Act", Research Paper in Ethnic Relations, No.12, Centre for Research in Ethnic Relations, September 1990 at p.39.

of the law had to be wide enough to cover the most damaging forms of racial discrimination, e.g. in employment and public services. It also introduced an exception where racial discrimination occurred in relationships that were so personal and intimate that legal intervention was likely to be ineffective or politically and socially unacceptable. Using the previous terminology, it deliberately excluded discrimination in personal contact. Crucially, the Street Report advocated the use of the civil rather than the criminal law, justifiying this decision by referring to the disadvantages of the criminal process. This point is important because, as discussed later, the mechanism used to regulate racial discrimination has an important symbolic value. If discrimination is to be treated as morally reprehensible act, and a moral wrong which causes substantial harm to the individual victim, then the criminal law would seem to be the appropriate form for regulation. The Street Report, however, recommended a move away from the use of the criminal law, explaining its preference for the use of a civil law model for the following reasons:

Anthony Lester and Geoffrey Bindman, *Race and Law* (London: Longman, 1972)

p.100: "This preference for administrative rather than criminal enforcement was partly based on their conclusion that criminal proceedings would be much less likely to be brought. They also referred to several other disadvantages of the criminal process.

For example, in view of the obvious difficulties of obtaining evidence of racial discrimination, it would often be impossible to satisfy the criminal burden of proof beyond reasonable doubt, whereas it would be practicable to satisfy the civil standard of proof on the balance of probabilities. Criminal proceedings would be brought by the police or a public prosecuting authority, neither of which would be especially skilled in problems of race relations. Cases would be tried summarily by magistrates or on indictment by a jury; the former would often lack the necessary time or expertise, especially when dealing with the complexities of employment and housing; the latter might sympathise more with the accused, than with the victim of his crime. On the other hand, an administrative agency would have specialist skills; proceedings in civil courts would conveniently explore the complex issues involved in allegations of unlawful discrimination; and the courts could be assisted in their adjudication by lay experts in the fields of employment, housing and commerce, and race relations. Criminal proceedings would generate wide publicity in a punitive context, which might cast the discriminator in the role of a martyr rather than a law breaker. And perhaps most importantly of all, the punishment of the wrongdoer, by fine or imprisonment, would not provide any remedy for the wrong suffered by his victim."

This move from a criminal to a civil law paradigm paved the way for the introduction of a model of discrimination law, that treats discrimination as a statutory tort giving rise to a claim for individual damages. It is worth noting that other European countries chose a different approach. France, for example, introduced legislation to prohibit race discrimination in 1972 which was broad and comprehensive, but which used criminal rather than civil law sanctions.[68] This point is important in the context of race discrimination legislation for a number of reasons. As we discussed in the context of direct discrimination (see Chapter 4), there remains an important question about the nature of the wrong which justifies direct discrimination. Is it a moral wrong of the type that indicates a morally culpable state of mind on the part of the discriminator (an approach which arguably resembles that of the criminal law, with its focus on *mens rea*); or should we focus on the harm done to the victim of discrimination? Also, the increasing use of law to penalise hate crimes and certain forms of hate speech raises the question of the optimal balance between civil and criminal law in the legal regulation of racism.

In the 1960s there was also a heightened awareness of the ongoing and structural nature of immigrant disadvantage that required more substantial remedies than the mediation of the Race Relations Boards. The PEP report in 1974 confirmed that there was discrimination operating in employment and housing. They also confirmed the weaknesses of the system of complaints based legislation of the RRA 68.[69] By the 1970s the RRA 68 focus on conciliation was widely recognised as an insufficient response to the entrenched problems of race discrimination.

E. *The Political Context before the RRA of 1976*

The crucial factors which were influenced race relations legislation between 1965 and 1968 became more intense in the immediate period preceding the RRA of 1976. There was an increasing recognition of the limits of the RRA 68, as well as an increasing political recognition, confirmed by the PEP report, that the RRA 68 was an insufficient legal response to the problems of racial discrimination. The House of Commons Select Committee on Race Relations and Immigration, which had been set up in 1968, had reported on racial equality in spheres such as housing, immigration and policing. In 1975 it was given special responsibility for (a) review of the work of the RRA 68 and the Race Relations Board; and (b) the admission to the UK of Commonwealth citizens. The Select Committee gathered evidence and made a number of recommendations. Amongst its recommendations was the proposal that existing legislation needed to be strengthended with powers of enforcement that would match those introduced in the context of sex discrimination. A number of aspects of the report provide important background to the RRA of 1976:

[68] Erik Bleich, *Race Politics in Britain and France* (Cambridge: Cambridge University Press, 2003) Chs 5–7.

[69] D. J. Smith, *Racial Disadvantage in Employment*, (London: Political and Economic Planning, 1974)

- The Committee concluded that "The crucial failure has been not to define the nature of the Government concern with race relations, not to clarify the objectives of policy and not to assess the scope and limits of potential Government intervention;[70]
- The Committee felt that the Home Secretary and the Home Office were too passive in their treatment of race relations issues in the domestic context as compared with immigration issues[71].
- The Committee recommended monitoring generally, and especially, for the Civil Service. It also suggested that forms of contract compliance could be a commitment in the public sector which would encourage a positive response in the private sector."

F. *Relationship between SDA 75 and RRA 76—the Gender Analogy*

A number of additional political factors assisted in paving the way towards the comprehensive legal regime of the RRA. First, there was the precedent established by the introduction of the SDA. Since 1973 the Labour Party had commited itself to equality of opportunity in the fields of race and sex. This led to White Papers in both fields: *Equality for Women* in 1974; and the *White Paper on Racial Discrimination* in 1975. Roy Jenkins, who was Home Secretary during this period, treated both these areas of discrimination as related. Jenkins stated: "Sex and race discrimination will be dealt with separately at this stage, but my ultimate aim is to harmonise, and possibly to amalgamate, the powers and procedures for dealing with both forms of discrimination."[72] The relationship between these two grounds of discrimination helps explain why the legislature proceeded to enact discreet statutes on different grounds. The White Paper *Equality for Women* had accepted that although there were similarities between sex and race discrimination, they were not identical in nature or effect.[73] Interestingly, the difficulty of maintaining a distinction between different grounds of discrimination (race, sex and religion, etc.), which is a part of contemporary discussions on the Single Equality Act, was first mentioned by Quintin Hogg during the Committee stage of the Race Relations Bill 1968. As early as the 1960s Hogg had already argued that the definition of discrimination should be extended to other grounds, such as language and religion.[74] This suggestion was dismissed, but it is an early example of the

70 (Select Cttee., Vol III, 1975, at 160); Phillip N. Sooben, "The Origins of the Race Relations Act", Centre for Research in Ethnic Relations, Research Paper No.12, at 23–24.

71 Phillip N. Sooben, "The Origins of the Race Relations Act", Centre for Research in Ethnic Relations, Research Paper No.12, at 23–24.

72 Hansard, Vol.877, Col 1298.

73 Phillip N. Sooben, "The Origins of the Race Relations Act", Centre for Research in Ethnic Relations, Research Paper No.12, at 32.

74 Anthony Lester and Geoffrey Bindman, *Race and Law* (London: Longman, 1972) at 137.

momentum of discrimination law towards expansion beyond sex and race as prohibited grounds of discrimination. However, there were powerful political reasons for a sequential approach to sex and race discrimination. Despite some overlap, the campaigns for race and sex equality were organised as distinct political movements. There were tactical reasons why Parliament was likely to be less resistant to sex rather than race discrimination legislation.[75] The SDA of 1975 helped to prepare and "soften" the ground for the subsequent introduction of the RRA of 1976: it created a legal and political atmosphere in which the legislation seemed to be logical and acceptable.[76]

G. *The White Paper on Racial Discrimination*

There are also a number of dominant themes in the White Paper on Racial Discrimination that need to be explored in order to understand the domestic background to the introduction of the RRA and to an understand domestic discrimination law.[77] It is worth examining the precise language of the White Paper, which reveals the state of mind and intentions of politicians and policy makers as well as their ambitions for the RRA. First, within the first few paragraphs of the White Paper the relationship between domestic race relations legislation and immigration is given priority (para.3). It then goes on to highlight the importance of understanding that there was a need for a long term strategy to deal with the "inter-locking problems of immigration, cultural difference, racial disadvantage and discrimination" (para.22); and states that "legislation is the essential pre-condition for an effective policy to combat the problems experienced by the coloured minority groups and to promote equality of opportunity and treatment. It is a necessary pre-condition for dealing with explicit discriminatory actions or accumulated disadvantages." (para.23). It is also noteworthy that although the White Paper gives priority to legal regulation, it also acknowledges the importance of non-legal responses to the problem of racial discrimination:

"Legislation is capable of dealing not only with discriminatory acts but with patterns of discrimination, particularly with patterns which, because of the effects of past discrimination, may not any longer involve explicit acts of discrimination. Legislation, however, is not, and can never be, a sufficient condition for effective progress towards equality of opportunity. A wide range of administrative and voluntary measures are needed to give practical effect to the objectives of the law" (para.25).

75 Phillip N. Sooben, "The Origins of the Race Relations Act", Centre for Research in Ethnic Relations, Research Paper No.12.
76 *ibid.*, at 33.
77 Cmnd.6234 (London: HMSO 1975).

Therefore the White Paper on Racial Discrimination took a view on the tenth question of discrimination law that we identified in Chapter 1, i.e. "How far should we look outside the law for solutions?". It is assumed that the use of legislation to regulate discrimination was intended to be supplemented by policies that were intended to include supply side investment to over come the problem of racial disadvantage. The White Paper states emphatically that:

"The Government recognises that what is here proposed for a further attack on discrimination will need to be supplemented by a more comprehensive strategy for dealing with the related and at least equally important problem of disadvantage. Such a strategy has major public expenditure implications, including a reassessment of priorities within existing programmes." (para.6).

The ambitions of the White Paper to use both legal regulation, as well as extra-legal measures and supply side investment to deal with racial discrimination and wider disadvantage were, however, thwarted by the economic and political conditions which immediately followed the introduction of the RRA. The 1970s fiscal crisis set serious financial constraints on the ability of central and local government to to undertake a wide ranging investiment programme to supplement the RRA.[78]

H. *Contemporary Issues*

As we have noted, the US experience has had a significant influence on the development of contemporary domestic discrimination law. In the area of race discrimination, the use of the British model as a paradigm in the Race Equality Directive has now ensured that this influence extends throughout the EU member states. This model has a number of key features: the focus on symmetrical protection for both majorities and minorities; the importance of comparison as to establishing discrimination; the choice of a civil law model that uses private law to promote a goal associated with human rights; and the use of individual remedies supplemented by adminstrative support to enforce these rights.

It is also noteworthy that concerns about public order and immigration are a constant theme in the run up to the introduction of the RRA. The introduction of the Race Relations Amendment Act 2000, which was a response to the murder of a black teenager Stephen Lawrence, also followed this pattern. The Macpherson inquiry, which subsequently implicated the police and their procedures in the failure to prosecute for this murder, provided the impetus for regualting institutional racism in Britain. The most recent positioning of the

[78] Phillip N. Sooben, "The Origins of the Race Relations Act", Research Paper in Ethnic Relations, No.12, Centre for Research in Ethnic Relations, September 1990 at p.56.

Government response to racial equality uses the paradigm of "community cohesion", that has developed out of an analysis of the riots in northern British cities in the spring and early summer of 2001.[79] This once again suggests a reactive approach to race relations legislation as a response to public order concerns rather than as an important part of the framework of rights for individuals in a liberal democracy. The Equality Act 2006 continues the focus on social exclusion and includes powers for the newly formed Commission for Equality and Human Rights to promote good relations between different groups. This is an echo of the recurring pattern whereby the treatment of ethnic minorities requires the managing of good "race relations" between groups rather than a focus on the individual rights of citizens. However, the CEHR also links the issues of race relations with those of human rights. There is, therefore, an opportunity for the CEHR to develop a more cohesive and principled approach to the legal regulation of racism.

Despite the substantial period of time since the introduction of the RRA, the contemporary situation of racial minorities suggests that the pattern of disadvantage in key areas (identified by the PEP reports and the White Paper in 1975) has not disappeared or even been substantially reduced for some groups. Substantial differences within the category "new immigrants" in terms of qualifications, education and socio-economic circumstances will make it increasingly important to examine differences within the various immigrant groups.[80] Recent research confirms a pattern of disadvantage amongst ethnic minorities in a range of areas including employment, housing and education.[81] The issue of race and the public sector has also become increasingly relevant as a legal issue since the introduction of the RRAmnd Act 2000. In this area, the government's own research suggests that: (a) many public services have a differential and adverse impact on ethnic minorities as compared with the majority population; and (b) there is a continuing perception of a problem with racial prejudice and a different appreciation of public services by minorities as compared with the majority population.[82]

Before going on to consider these issues, which are of relevance to the civil race discrimination law, it is worth mentioning some of the contemporary issues which are relevant to criminal law regulation of race discrimination such as the racially aggravated hate crimes and incitement to racial hatred. In Britain, there has been an increase in recording and reporting of the offences which agencies take to be a positive sign indicating increasing levels of confidence that the police will take racially aggravated crime seriously.[83] The EU

[79] Community Cohesion: A Report of the Independent Review Team, Chaired by Ted Cantle (Home Office: London, December 2001).

[80] Sarah Kayambi, *Beyond Black and White: Mapping New Immigrant Communities* (IPPR: London, 2005).

[81] Modood, T.R. Berthod et. al, *Ethnic Minorities in Britain: Diversity and Disadvantage*, The Fourth National Survy of Ethnic Minorities, (Policy Studies Institute: London, 1997).

[82] "Race Equality in Public Services", HMSO, February 2001, at p.87.

[83] Maria Docking and Rachel Tuffin, "Racist Incidents: Progress Since the Stephen Lawrence Inquiry" (London: Home Office, 2005) at p.8.

context also continues to be relevant. There is some evidence to suggest an increase in the levels of violent racism incidents in the EU. The European Union Monitoring Centre on Racism and Xenophobia confirmed that racist crime continued to be a problem across EU member states, and it also identified that ethnic minorities are marginalised in areas such as employment and education, and that the Roma in particular were especially disadvantaged in the area of housing.[84]

Most recently, research by the EUMC on anti-Muslim violence in the immediate aftermath of the July 7, 2005 London bombings has confirmed that "The EUMC finds that the strong and united stand taken by the UK Government, police and community leaders, including Muslim community representatives, in condemning both the bombings and any retaliation, has played a major part in preventing an anti-Muslim backlash. This joint action was decisive in countering a short-term upsurge in anti-Muslim incidents in the immediate aftermath of the bombings. Such incidents have now dropped back to levels before the bomb attacks".[85]

I. *Social Exclusion*

The two extracts below illustrate the contemporary socio-economic position of ethnic minorities. The first extract is the "Ethnic Minorities and The Labour Market: Final Report" from the report of the Strategy Unit at Downing Street:

"Key Points From Ethnic Minorities and The Labour Market: Final report of the Strategy Unit Cabinet Office: London, March, 2003)

- Ethnic minorities currently make up 8 per cent of the UK population. Between 1999 and 2009 they will account for half the growth in the working-age population.
- Making the best use of their energy and talent will be a major challenge for Government and employers, as well as for ethnic minorities themselves.
- Currently, there are wide variations in the labour market achievements of different ethnic minority groups.
- Indians and Chinese are, on average, doing well, and often out-performing Whites in schools and in the labour market. Their success shows that there are no insuperable barriers to successful economic and social integration.
- However, other groups are doing less well. Pakistanis, Bangladeshis and Black Caribbeans experience, on average, significantly higher unemployment and lower earnings than Whites. This brings not only economic costs but also potential threats

[84] "Racism and Xenophobia in the EU Member States: Trends, Development and Good Practice", EUMC, Annual Report 2003/4, Pt 2. Available at *http://eumc.eu.int/eumc/material/pub/* (accessed November 10, 2005).

[85] EUMC Report: The impact of July 7, 2005 London bomb attacks on Muslim Communities in the EU, Vienna: EUMC, November 10, 2005. Available at *http://eumc.eu.int/eumc/material/pub/* (accessed on November 17, 2005)

to social cohesion. Improving performance in schools and in the labour market for these groups is a major priority for Government.

- Significantly, the evidence in this report shows that all ethnic minority groups—even those enjoying relative success, such as the Indians and Chinese—are not doing as well as they should be, given their education and other characteristics. Government needs to establish a new framework for action.
- [...]

On average, ethnic minorities are disadvantaged in the labour market relative to their White counterparts

Employment rates amongst almost all ethnic minority groups are lower than those of the White population. With the important exception of Indians, earnings and progression in work are also persistently lower. Critically, these gaps are not closing.

However, this hides enormous variations: the old picture of White success and ethnic minority underachievement is now out of date

Over the last three decades, some ethnic minorities in the UK have done very well. On the measures of employment, earnings and progression within work, there is a clear pattern of Indians on a par with, or outperforming, not just other ethnic minorities, but often Whites as well. This pattern is also reflected in educational achievement, strengthening chances of long-term labour market success.

Nonetheless, all ethnic minorities, including these "successful" groups, are not doing as well as they could be

There are important and worrying disparities in the labour market performance of ethnic minorities and Whites that are not attributable to different levels of education and skills. The persistence of workplace discrimination is an important reason for this. Limited access to job and social networks is also critical, and subtle in its impact.

Failure to make the most of the potential of ethnic minorities has an impact on the UK's economic performance

With ethnic minorities set to account for more than half of the growth of the working population over the next decade, failure to tackle the problems of labour market underachievement will have increasingly serious economic consequences.

Low employment rates for particular ethnic minority groups hold back economic growth, particularly in the context of full employment and skills shortages. For example, if the employment rates of Pakistanis matched those of their Indian counterparts, the proportion of male and female workers in this group would rise by 24 and 136 per cent respectively, an increase of some 96,000 people in work. Similarly, if the employment rates of the Black, Pakistani and Bangladeshi groups matched those of their Indian counterparts, the British workforce would grow by over 180,000 people.

Labour market disadvantage also has potential social costs. Lack of achievement in the labour market feeds social exclusion, damaging relations between ethnic groups in Britain and putting social cohesion at risk.

However, the nature and extent of this disadvantage varies widely, between and within different ethnic minority groups

The position of ethnic minorities is now much more complex than in previous decades, going back to the 1960s. There are significant differences, for example, between the different Asian groups, with Indians having higher employment rates and occupational achievement than Pakistanis and Bangladeshis, as well as much higher participation rates amongst women. The patterns of disadvantage amongst the Black population are different again. Whilst there are only small differences in average pay and occupational achievement between the Black African group and Whites, the Black Caribbean group is significantly disadvantaged in comparison.

Distinctions within ethnic minority groups also shape outcomes in the labour market.

Gender, generation and geography play key roles. In the case of gender, many Asian groups are characterised by low participation rates among women, something that is reversed in the case of the Black Caribbean population. First-generation immigrants among ethnic minorities often do less well in the labour market than their children. Finally, settlement patterns that have taken some groups to certain parts of the country, for example, heavy Pakistani concentrations in the Midlands and the North, have also influenced employment outcomes.

The reasons for labour market disadvantage are no less varied

There is no single cause of this pattern of labour market disadvantage. The class backgrounds of different ethnic minorities, culture and family patterns all play a part. Educational underachievement is both a symptom of these factors and an important cause factor in its own right. The proportion of pupils who get five or more GCSE grades at A*-C is much lower amongst Black, Pakistani and Bangladeshi pupils, especially boys, than amongst Whites—although Indian attainment at GCSE level is actually higher than the White population. However, even when differences in educational attainment are accounted for, ethnic minorities still experience significant labour market disadvantages.

In general, ethnic minorities, including Indians, do not get the jobs that their qualification levels justify.

There are various reasons for this. In some cases, ethnic minority groups are concentrated in areas of deprivation. These areas contain barriers, such as poor public transport and isolation in areas with high proportions of workless households, that may disproportionately affect ethnic minorities.

However, there is also strong evidence that discrimination plays a significant role. Whilst equal opportunities legislation has had some success in combating overt discrimination and harassment, indirect discrimination, where policies or practices have the inadvertent result of systematically disadvantaging ethnic minorities, remains a problem."

The report confirms that despite the existence of race relations legislation, there is a significant problem of ethnic minority disadvantage. However, it is significant that the report confirms the complexity of this issue. For example, although overt acts of discrimination are seen to play a part in the social problem, there is a more complex range of reasons for ethnic minority disadvantage in the labour force. Moreover, the report confirms that the undifferentiated use of the term "ethnic minority" or "race" to analyse the problem fails to capture a number of key factors: e.g that culture and class are also contributory factors and that within the term ethnic minority some groups (e.g. Indian and Chinese are doing well) as compared with other (Bangladeshi and Pakistani):

"The overall picture for the majority of ethnic minority groups is a positive one [...] Children of Afro-Carribean parents are doing very well, as are children of working-class Indians, who are leading all other groups in moving into professional jobs. But for the children of Pakistani and Bangladeshi parents it is quite a different matter. They can be subject to extreme deprivation, are often living in some of the poorest parts of the country, and are in danger of being left behind."[86]

[86] Dr Lucinda Platt, commenting on the recent findings of research by the Joseph Rowntree Foundation, in *The Independent*, Monday, November 14, 2005.

This pattern of disadvantage of ethnic minorities group is also reflected in other social indicators such as deprivation and child poverty as the following extract confirms[87]:

Memorandum submitted by Dr Lucinda Platt (CP 31) to Written Evidence Submitted to the Select Committee on Work and Pensions[88] "Child Poverty in the UK, second report of session 2003–04, Vol.2, Written Evidence, House of Commons Papers 2003–04, 85–II.

SUMMARY

"I. This submission focuses on child poverty among minority ethnic groups. Poverty among children from minority ethnic groups is greater than overall child poverty. Over half of black African children and over two-thirds of Pakistani or Bangladeshi children are in poverty compared with under a third of white children. The differences in poverty rates between children from different ethnic groups are cause for grave concern.

II. Worklessness is a major cause of poverty in households with children. Unemployment rates are much higher than the average for Caribbeans, black Africans, Bangladeshis and Pakistanis and above average for Indians. In addition, economic activity rates are very low for Bangladeshi and Pakistani women. They are also low for Bangladeshi and Pakistani men.

III. For children from some minority ethnic groups income may be a poor measure of well-being. For example, Caribbeans are more likely than the rest of the population to make remissions to relatives abroad. They are also more likely to suffer from debt and financial anxiety. There is also evidence that some of the poorest minority groups, notably Bangladeshis, cluster around the poverty line. This makes a single poverty line particularly arbitrary.

IV. Minority ethnic groups are found to be relatively disadvantaged when measures of material deprivation are used. This is so even when comparing similar income levels. This suggests the impacts of long-term poverty and limited assets within groups. Measures of material deprivation may therefore give greater insight into the poverty of minority ethnic groups. On the other hand, deprivation measures can be quite crude. They and "consensual" measures of poverty or social exclusion may not be sensitive to different cultural practices.

V. Many children from minority groups tend to spend an extended period in education. This can be both "catching up" for qualifications not gained in school and gaining further qualifications. This should result in positive future labour market outcomes. However, it also has immediate implications for the probability of poverty among those remaining in education and for their siblings. In addition, "catching up" maybe be regarded as a necessary response to failures in schooling; and the enhanced achievement of further and higher qualifications may be compensatory for a labour market in which minority groups

[87] Full copy of this memorandum is attached to the end of this chapter.

[88] "Child Poverty in the UK, second report of session 2003–04, Vol.2, Written Evidence, House of Commons Papers 2003–04, 85–II. This report can be obtained via the official web site of the House of Commons, at *http://www.parliament.the-stationery-office.co.uk/pa/cm200304/cmselect/cmworpen/85/85we54.htm* (accessed November 10, 2005).

need to be more highly qualified than the majority to obtain an equivalent probability of employment.

VI. Both the duration and timing of poverty in childhood have been shown to be critical to their impact on children's outcomes. In addition, an extended period of poverty in childhood is damaging for children's experience of childhood itself. There would seem to be variations in duration of poverty by ethnic group, though research findings in this area are currently limited.

VII. Social security impacts on ethnic groups in different ways. For example a high proportion of the incomes of Bangladeshis and Pakistanis derives from means-tested benefits, which makes their welfare highly sensitive to the delivery and value of such benefits. Some changes, such as the equalisation of income support rates for all children under the age of 19 has been of particular benefit to such groups. However, the structure, coverage and delivery of the social security system may disproportionately disbenefit particular groups. The social security system should be evaluated for its differential impact on those from different ethnic groups.

VIII. Minority groups tend to be geographically concentrated; and there is a tendency for minority group concentrations to occur in deprived areas. Children growing up in such areas benefit from neighbourhood-based initiatives, such as the New Deal for Communities. However, given that neighbourhoods contain individuals with different degrees of deprivation and from different ethnic groups, the initiatives may not impact on the most deprived inhabitants to the degree envisaged. Differences within areas as well as between areas need to be taken account of. [Footnotes ommitted but they can be accessed via the original document]"

More recently, the results of the Joseph Rowntree Foundation research on ethnic minorities in the labour force confirms that despite an improvement in their position in the labour market between 1991 and 2001, people from those social groups continued to suffer from higher rates of unemployment than white people, and that substantial disadvantage remained in access to jobs and in earnnings in employment. The main results of that survey[89] are:

- only 20 per cent of Bangladeshis, 30 per cent of Pakistanis and 40 per cent of black Africans of working age are in full time work (compared with over 50 per cent of white British people of working age)
- even with a degree, Pakistani and Bangladeshi men are less likely to be employed than someone who is white with the same types of qualifications;
- despite the rapid growth in the number of Pakistani and Bangladeshi women going to university, they suffer high unemployment and are much less likely than Indian or white British women to be in professional or managerial jobs;
- the problem is not confined to the first generation. British-born people from ethnic minority backgrounds, especially Indian, black, Pakistani and Bangladeshi groups, are less likely to get jobs than their white equivalents; and

89 The results of the survey (which amalgamates four research projects) are summarised at "Ethnic minorities in the labour market", (2007) 165 EOR 19, published by IRS June 1, 2007.

- while poverty levels among white British people are the same whether they live in London or elsewhere in the UK, rates among ethnic minority groups are far worse for those living in London.

It is worth noting that the fact that ethnic minorities are marginal groups in areas such as housing and education, it also suggests that they will be disproportionate users of public services, particularly social security. This, once again, makes the issue of the legal regulation of discrimination in the delivery of public services via the Race Relations Amendment Act 2000 a key issue.

The Platt Memorandum confirms that ethnic minorities are geographically concentrated, especially in deprived areas. However, it also suggests that supply-side measures that target investment in these areas may be a particularly useful policy response. Such investment-led initiatives may be able to deliver some of the goals of discrimination law in the context of ethnic minorities without developing increasingly expansive definitions of unlawful discrimination which seek control the behaviour of employers. Following riots in the Northern towns in the summer of 2006, the government introduced the concept of "community cohesion" as a key goals of its policy response towards ethnic minority groups. A number of report (such as the Cantle report) and government responses examined the issues of community (social) cohesion and integration and proposed solutions in areas such as education and housing.[90] The problem has sometimes been represented as one of the segregation of minorities from the mainstream of British society and culture. However, the concentration of minority groups could be said to fall short of segregation, and some commentators argue that it is a feature of ethnic minority life in Britain. The following summary of the issues explores some of these points:

Professor Ceri Peach, Centre for the Environment, Oxford University Letter to *The Guardian*, September 28, 2005.

"[. . .] there is not a single ward in Britain in which the population is 100% minority-ethnic population. Tracts of 90 to 100% are common in the US. The proportion of individual minority-ethnic groups in 2001 living in wards in Britain where they form as much as 50% of

[90] The key policy document was "Community Cohesion: A Report of the Independent Review Team, Chaired by Ted Cantle" (also called the Cantle Report), December 2001. See also the Home Office policy response set out in "Improving Opportunity, Strenghtening Society: The Government's Strategy to increase racial equality and community cohesion", (London: Home Office, 2005); See also the report of the Office of the Deputy Prime Minister (ODPM) which sets out the response of the Government to the House of Commons ODPM Select Committee to its report on social cohesion of May 14, 2004 (and also contains a summary of the recommendations of the ODPM Select Committee report of May 14, 2004), (2004) HC Cmnd. 2684, presented by the Deputy Prime Minister to the House of Commons on July 2004).

the population is 22%. There are several wards where, if one aggregates all minority-ethnic populations together, they form the majority. However, 78% of the minority-ethnic population do not live in such wards. In Chicago in 2000, on the other hand, the average African-American lived in a neighbourhood which was 78% black. The average minority person in Leicester (the comparator city cited in the article) lives in a ward in which minorities form 54% of the population. The Index of Segregation (IS), which is commonly used, measures the percentage of a minority population which would have to change its location in order to replicate the distribution of the rest of the population of a city. It has a range from 0 (no segregation) to 100 (total segregation). Between 1991 and 2001 these measures indicate decreasing or stable degrees of segregation in English cities. Leicester is the only city in which one of these indices rose between 1991 and 2001 (the Caribbean IS rose from 30 to 39)"

A recent report into the issue by Dr Ludi Simpson of the University of Manchester confirmed this trend towards integration. It also confirmed the importance of poverty, access to housing and education rather than geography as key contributors to social exclusion. The researchers compared data from the 1991 and 2001 censuses, and analysed the change in different ethnic groups in 8,850 electoral wards in England and Wales. They found that the number of mixed neighbourhoods or wards—where at least 10 per cent are from an ethnic minority—increased from 964 to 1,070 in the decade, and predicts that by 2010 the number will rise to 1,300.

The author of the study, Ludi Simpson concludes:

"The common myth is that the growth of the ethnic minority population is due to immigration. That's not true—it is more due to the growth of [ethnic minority] people born in Britain. ... Segregation does not cause social exclusion."

There were 118 neighbourhoods where all non-white groups together were greater than half, and he found there was no ward where white people were less than 10 per cent of the population. "The idea of no-go areas or apartheid does not stand up," he said.

Dr Simpson also said his study suggests factors such as poverty have to be taken into account more than racial tension. In short, where people live is not as big a factor as some people are claiming. "The research shows that geography is not the issue," Dr Simpson said. "Social conditions on the ground such as poverty and equal access to housing and the jobs markets for all groups are more important factors."[91]

In a recent article on racial segregation, Dr Simpson concludes that the fear that certain minorities are "sleep walking their way into segregation" is a "false label". After undertaking an analysis of recent data for the South Asian population, Simpson concludes:

"Thus, the positive message from this analysis is that segregation is not the problem it is perceived to be. Social policy for localities is better informed by a sociological and historical understanding of the class, housing, employment and educational dynamics of neighbourhood residential change. There are many positive aspects of communities that are strenghtened by their historical common culture, which need to be recognised. At the

[91] *The Guardian*, Tuesday, November 15, 2005

same time, the racially motivated barriers to movement and integration need to be dismantled and the structural causes of sustained poor inner-city neighbourhoods addressed."[92]

Simpson goes on to identify the difficulties in using the word "race" as a marker in social policy research without reinforcing essentialist views of race and wrongly attributing social change to racial integration. He concludes:

"Through racially conscious language and research directed at myth-busting and highlighting discrimination both individual and institutional, investigators play a part in making a just society in which racial differences no longer identify cumulative discrimination but one aspect of social description."[93]

Arguments that ethnic minorities need to do more to integrate took on particular importance after the July 7, 2005 bombings in London.[94] It was argued that the Muslim community need to do more to "integrate" into Britain and a new body was launched to encourage "integration"[95]

IV. The Legal Regulation of Racism

As the previous history of the RRA confirms, there were distinct reasons for the legislature's concern with the discriminatory treatment of ethnic minorities and racism that motivated the priority given to legal regulation. The main legal provisions that now regulate race discrimination in Britain are civil law statutes. The RRA as amended by the Race Relations Act 1976 (Amendment) Regulations[96] (which were introduced to ensure compliance with the Race Equality Directive) and the Race Relations Amendment Act 2000. Domestic discrimination law allows some positive action programmes and establishes an administrative agency for promoting racial equality. There are also criminal law measures that address some of the most severe forms of racism. The Crime and Disorder Act 1998 creates a category of criminal offence dealing with

92 Ludi Simpson, "Statistics of Racial Segregation: Measures, Evidence and Policy", (2004) 41 Urban Studies 3 661–681, at 679.
93 *ibid.*
94 Ruth Kelly launched a Commission on Integration and Social Cohesion on August 24, 2006. Speech by Ruth Kelly MP at the launch of the new Commission on Integration and Cohesion on August 24, 2006 (available at *http://www.communities.gov.uk/index.asp?id=1502280*).
95 There was also incidents such as the issue of full facial veiling becoming a focus for the construction of visible Muslim women as "separate". For a discussion of these issues see Jack Straw, "I felt Uneasy Talking to Someone I Could Not See" the letter of the Right Honourable Jack Straw MP which raised the issue of full facial veils, *The Guradian* published on October 6, 2006 at *http://www.guardian.co.uk/commentisfree/story/0,,1889081,00.html* (accessed on October 20, 2006). For media commentary: in favour of Jack Straw see Yasmin Alibhai Brown, "Its not illiberal for liberal socieites to disapprove of the veil", *Time Europe Magazine*, October 16, 2006; against Jack Straw see Madeleine Bunting, "Jack Straw has unleashed a storm of prejudice and intensified division", *The Guardian*, Monday, October 9, 2006.
96 UK SI 2003/1626.

racially aggravated crimes. There is also criminal law legislation in the area of racist speech in the form of incitement to racial hatred legislation.

A key, and controversial question, for domestic race discrimination law has been "what is a race?" Needless to say, the issue of who falls within the definition of the protected ground "race" is a key issue for any legal regulation of race discrimination and it raises the first question of discrimination law, "who is protected?" (see further Chapter 1). We have seen that a number of British minorities experienced persecution and discrimination, but the reasons for this treatment varied. One central challenge for race discrimination law is to develop a legal response that is general and applies to all "racial" minorities. Yet, at the same time, this approach must take into account the social, historical and political variation in the causes of the oppression of British minorities.

A. *The Grounds of Discrimination under the Race Relations Act 1976*

The previous sections have emphasised a number of themes that are relevant to understanding the development of race relations legislation in Britain. These themes include the fact that this legislation was seen as pursuing a number of objectives: community cohesion and stablity for majorities and minorities; alleviating the social and economic disadvantage of minorities; and a more principled treatment of individuals from minority groups. In the next section we suggest that any legal definition of race needs to pay attention to the social and historical context in which the term is being used, rather than assuming that it is a biological or essential category that is fixed in time and place. On this analysis, race is a system of ideas rather than a biological or essential category. Therefore, the mere citing or presence of race within a certain context does not, in and of itself, determine the way in which we should classify that situation. We need further detailed analysis of how and in what context race is being used to understand how race discrimination in the private sphere, as well as its deeper more structural roots, can be addressed. Concepts such as direct and indirect discrimination, as well as policies of positive action, will need to be adapted to take into distinct features of race as a ground of discrimination. We also discuss the legal definition of race in the RRA. The main analysis of these issues arises in the context of the definition of "race" in cases such as *Mandla v Dowell Lee*. Under the RRA, not only race but also "national origin" is a prohibited ground of discrimination. This is discussed in more detail below, and it is worth noting that in R. *(on the application of Elias) v Secretary of State for Defence*[97] the Court of Appeal has held that national origin is to be given a limited interpretation: so that "place of birth" is

[97] [2006] I.R.L.R. 934 CA.

not identical to "national origins" and therefore not inextricably linked to race as a prohibited ground of discrimination.

Before moving on to consider the legal definition of "race", it is also worth noting that the RRA includes the term on "racial grounds" as a prohibited ground of discrimination. The term on "racial grounds" has given rise to specific issues which we consider below before the discussion of the *Mandla* interpretation of "race" under the RRA. It has been interpreted to include a wide range of conduct: not only discriminatory treatment in hiring, but also other "racist acts" and intructions to be racist, have been deemed to fall within the RRA. In *Showboat Entertainment Centre Ltd v Owens*[98] an employer in an amusement centre had instructed an employee to exclude young black men from the centre. The employee was dismissed when he refused to comply with the instructions to exclude the young black men. The EAT found that RRA, s.1(1)(a) covers race discrimination against someone other the claimant, i.e. in this case the race discrimination against the young black men who were excluded from the amusement centre. Therefore, the coverage of race discrimination is extended to include not only discriminatory conduct against an employee but also instructions to discriminate. In a recent case, *Redfearn v Serco Ltd (t/a West Yorkshire Transport Service)*,[99] the Court of Appeal overturned the decision of the EAT who had held that the term "racial grounds" could also include the dismissal of a bus driver because he was a British National Party election candidate. Mr Redfearn was working for Serco Ltd as a driver for Bradford's majority Asian passenger population when he stood as a BNP candidate in local elections. He was sacked after Serco was advised that continuing to employ him would compromise the health and safety of its employees and passengers, cause anxiety to the public and jeopardise the company's reputation and its contract with the local authority. Mr Redfearn could not claim unfair dismissal as he had less than one year's service. Instead, he claimed that his dismissal was less favourable treatment "on racial grounds" contrary to the RRA, because the dismissal was "on the ground of the Asian race and ethnic origin of the people [Serco] transported". Following *Showboat Entertainment* the EAT had held that the term on "racial grounds" could also cover this type of dismissal. The Court of Appeal overturned this decision and rejected Mr Redfearn's argument that, because only white people are allowed to join the BNP, he was treated less favourably because he was white and therefore because of his race. They also emphasised that the policy objectives of the RRA were to protect racial minorities. Therefore, although the legislation was symmetrical, the term "racial grounds" should not be expanded to protect workers who undertake acts that are in clear breach of these policy objectives, i.e. that promote race discrimination against individuals.

Redfearn v Serco Ltd also raises the related point of whether membership of

98 *Showboat Entertainment Ltd v Owen* [1984] I.C.R. 65.

99 *Redfearn v Serco Ltd (t/a West Yorkshire Transport Service)* [2006] EWCA Civ 659 [2006] I.R.L.R. 623

the British National Party can be classified as a "belief" under the new Employment Equality (Religion or Belief) Regulations 2003. In *Baggs* an Employment Tribunal found that the British National Party was a political party that was not protected as a "philosophical belief" under Reg.2 of the Religion and Belief Regs. The Tribunal found that "belief", in this context, needs to be similar to religious belief. For this reason the BNP fell outside the definition.[100] *Redfearn* was followed in *HM Prison Service v Potter*, a recent case involving discrimination against a BNP activist. However, in this case the Court of Appeal distinguished *Redfearn* on the basis that the Prison Service was applying its policy solely against white organisations.

HM Prison Service v Potter EAT/0457/06 (1 report) Equal Opportunities Review 166 1/7/2007 (IRS)

In *HM Prison Service v Potter* (14 November 2006), the EAT upheld the decision of a tribunal chairman not to strike out a claim by a BNP activist that he was discriminated against on grounds of race when he was turned down for employment by the prison service, in accordance with a policy precluding the appointment or employment of individuals who are members of any political organisation with a racist philosophy, or those with racist aims, principles or policies.

Mr Potter claimed that although this policy was ostensibly neutral, in fact it was being applied only to white organisations. The EAT dismissed the prison service's argument that, in light of the judgment of the Court of Appeal in *Redfearn v Serco* [2006] IRLR 623, there was no possibility of the claim succeeding. Mr Justice Elias noted that the claimant's argument "is not on all fours with *Redfearn*. *Redfearn* establishes that it is not direct discrimination on grounds of race to discriminate against somebody because they are a BNP member. Here discrimination arises from the different treatment that is afforded to white racist organisations as opposed to members of racist organisations which are non-white."

B. *The Concept of Race*

How should we define "race" as the prohibited ground within discrimination law? This is a central and vexed question in domestic race discrimination law. There is often a pre-theoretical confidence that "race" is an unproblematic term. A cursory glance at the long-standing controversies about race confirms that this confidence is misplaced. Once the conceptual problem of defining race is acknowledged explicitly, it becomes easier to understand why courts have also struggled with legal definitions of "race" and "racial groups". Domestic discrimination law has had problems with this issue since the House

[100] *Baggs v Dr FDA Fudge* (Chair, AC Tickle), March 24 2005, case no: 1400114/05, reported (Oct 2005) 157 Equal Opportunities Review 31–32.

of Lords decision in *Mandla v Dowell Lee*,[101] which gave an extended definition to race in the context of the RRA. EU discrimination will also have to find a solution to this challenge, because the Race Equality Directive now prohibits race discrimination in a wide range of contexts such as employment, housing and education.

1. Essentialist Concepts of Race

One important distinction in discussions about race is between "essentialist" and "social constructivist" models. As stated in chapter 3, one of the main features of Critical Race Theory is its insistence on treating race as a "constructed" rather than "biological" concept. Essentialist concepts of race, by contrast, are founded on the assumption that race is a "natural" concept or that it can be explained through science. There are a number of variants of this approach. One is the biological concepts of race that focus on the physical and psychological natures of the different races to exemplify the "distinctions that nature has made"[102] This emphasis on physical traits gained support from Darwinism, and ideas of evolution, that supported the assumption that variations in human beings could be explained in biological and evolutionary terms. This biological concept of "race" often develops into arguments of "racialism": i.e. that racial difference is an indicator for a wider range of differences in inherited characteristics such as intelligence, psychology or in some cases morality.[103]

The challenge to biological or evolutionary concepts of race comes from a number of sources. One key argument against this mode of analysis is that it fails to provide a link or "theory of inheritance" of racial characteristics across different generations. In fact, these more "essentialist" views of race start to break down once modern theories of inheritance, that make clear the complex interaction between genes and environment, are taken into account.[104] Biological racism influences contemporary debates, and sometimes collapses into, modern theories of "race" that seek to objectify race concepts and attribute essential characteristics to racial groups. This trend towards essentialism, as well as its repudiation, is discussed in the following extract.

[101] [1983] 2 A.C. 548
[102] K. A. Appiah and A. Gutmann, *Color Conscious: The Political Morality of Race* (NJ,US: Princeton University Press, 1996) at p.49.
[103] *ibid.*, at pp.54–61.
[104] K. A. Appiah and A. Gutmann, *Color Conscious: The Political Morality of Race* (NJ, US: Princeton University Press, 1996) at pp.72–74.

Howard Winant: "Theoretical Status of the Concept of Race" in Les Black and John Solomos (eds), *Theories of Race and Racism: A Reader* (London: Routledge, 2000)

pp.184–5: "Of course, the biologistic racial theories of the past do this: here I am thinking of such precursors of fascism as Gobineau and Chamberlain [. . .] of the eugenicists such as Lothrop Stoddard and Madison Grant [. . .] and of the "founding fathers" of scientific racism such as Aggassiz, Broca, Terman, and Yerkes [. . .]. Indeed, an extensive legacy of this sort of thinking extends right up to the present. Stephen Jay Could makes devastating critiques of such views.

But much liberal and even radical social science, though firmly committed to a social as opposed to biological interpretation of race, nevertheless also slips into a kind of objectivism about racial identity and racial meaning. This is because race is afforded an easy and unproblematic coherence all too frequently. Thus to select only prominent examples, Daniel Moynihan, William Julius Wilson. Milton Gordon, and many other mainstream thinkers theorize race in terms that downplay its flexibility and historically contingent character. Even those major thinkers, whose explicit rejection of biologistic forms of racial theory would be unquestioned, fall prey to a kind of creeping objectivism of race. For in their analysis a modal explanatory approach emerges as follows: socio-political circumstances change over historical time, racially defined groups adapt or fail to adapt to these changes, achieving mobility or remaining mired in poverty, and so on. In this logic there is no reconceptualization of group identities, of the constantly shifting parameters through which race is thought aboutm group interests are assigned, statutses signfied, agency is attained, and roles are performed.

Contemporary racial theory, then, is often "objectivistic" about its fundamental category. Although abstractly acknowledged to be a sociohistorical construct, race in practice is often treated as an objective fact: one simply is one's race; in the contemporary United States, if we discard euphemisms, we have five color-based categories: black, white, brown, yellow and red.

This is problematic, indeed ridiculous, in numerous ways. Nobody really belongs in these boxes; they are patently absurd reductions of human variation. But even accepting the nebulous "rules" of racial classification—"hypodescent," and so forth—many people do not fit in anywhere: into what category should we place Turks, for example? People of mixed race? South Asians? Objectivist treatments, lacking a critique of the *constructed* character of racial meanings, also clash with experimental dimensions of the issue. If one does not "act" black, or white, or whatever, that is just deviance from the norm. There is in these approaches an insufficient appreciation of the *performative* aspect of race, as postmodernists might call it.

To summarize the critique of this "race as objective condition" approach, then, it fails on three counts: First, it cannot grasp the processual and relational character of racial identity and racial meaning. Second, it denies the historicity and social comprehensiveness of the race concept. And third, it cannot account for the way actors, both individual and collective, have to manage incoherent and conflictual racial meanings and identities in everyday life. It has no concept, in short, of what Omi and I have labelled *racial formation*."

2. Constructivist Concepts of Race

If race is not an objective essential category, then a number of key questions open up for further inquiry: how and through what processes has the concept of race (and racial identity) been constructed in the context of discrimination law? If race is a social and historical construct, then is it still a viable category for law and politics? Finally we also need to ask how the concept of "race" (a) relates to other categories that are relevant for discrimination law such as gender, sexual orientation, religion etc.; and (b) relates to other socially constructed but relevant categories such as class or nationality?

Before turning to these issues, we also need to identify the different social processes that construct, and generate, concepts of race. There are a number of different aspects to this process. Winant, whose work has also been discussed in the critique of essentialist concepts of race, has a postive theory about the process of racial formation. Winant argues that a theory of racial formation can:

"steer between the Scylla of 'race as illusion' and the Charybdis of 'racial objectivism' [...] Such a theoretical foundation, too, must be explicitly historicist: it must recognize the importance of historical context and contingency in the framing of racial categories and the social construction of racially defined experiences. [...] I suggest three conditions for such a theory:—It must apply to contemporary *political* relationships.—It must apply in an increasingly *global* context.—It must apply across *historical time*."[105]

Other commentators have focused on the way in which race as a category emerges out of processes of social cognition. On this analysis race is used as a perceptual category that allows people to sort out information and navigate their way through an uncertain social world. The concept of "race" allows them to form broad categories and generalisations about those individuals with whom they interact but about whom they have insufficient information.

This is a point made by Glenn C. Loury, who goes on to make some key observations about the use of race as the basis for social cognition:

"First, whether 'race' is a part of the calculation or not, classifying human subjects in this general way is a universal practice, one that lies at the root of all social-cognitive behaviour. There can only be the question of how, not whether, human agents will classify those subjects to their actions. Second, at this level of generality, the normative status of even a race-based classification cannot be definitively assessed absent some considerations of the purposes on

[105] Howard Winant: "Theoretical Status of the Concept of Race", In Les Black and John Solomos (eds), *Theories of Race and Racism: A Reader* (London: Routledge, 2000) at p.185. In relation to politics note that as the binary of racial antogonism becomes more complex and decentred the political deployment of the concept of race comes to signal qualitatively new types of political domination as well as new types of opposition, *cf.* challenging racism through new forms of individual and political identity and associations/Nation of Islam.

behalf of which the classifying act has been undertaken. That is, the simple fact that a person classified others (or herself, for that matter) in terms of 'race' is in itself neither a good nor a bad thing. Normative judgments must, at the very least, entail some analysis of the goals of classifying agents."[106]

Loury's second point is critically important in the context of race discrimination law. For example, a critical distinction between unlawful race discrimination and affirmative (or positive) action for racial minorities will depend on the ability to distinguish between the reasons for the racial classification in the two different cases. Here it is worth emphasising that the use of race as a way of sorting out social information is a cognitive not a normative act: the fact of the use of racial classification is not in and of itself a morally dubious act.

Loury goes on to argue that the concept of race has three characteristics:

(a) it enables ease of identification of other persons;

(b) it is relatively immutable; and

(c) it acts as a form of social signification.

Loury's general point is not that anything turns on biological markings as such. What is important is that in a particular historical and social context, differences that can be attributed to race are easy to identify and perform a social or political function. Most importantly, Loury emphasises that race is produced through specific cultural and historic processes.[107] It is also worth noticing an internal tension within this argument. On the one hand, race is seen to be a constructed concept; but on the other hand, it is something that is easily identifiable as a marker for social differentiation and signification. This analysis has implications for both the subject and the object. For the subject (the classifier) this process allows the classification of information in ways that are not always explicit. For the object (the person who has been classified), the process also has an impact because it means that these individuals understand and identify themselves as *being raced*. This is a recurring tension in the work of all those who argue against essentialist views of race and in favour of treating race as a social construct. On the one hand, many writers such as Paul Gilroy argue that we need a critical account of race as a system of ideas that can be fluid and that can also be challenged.[108] Generally, there is a recognition that race operates to allow for self and identity formation.

This contrast, between the objectification of race as an essential category and the claim that race is purely a social construct, also maps on to current debates that draw on post-modern approaches to race. Some aspects of this debate

[106] Glenn C. Loury, *The Anatomy of Racial Inequality*, (Cambs, Mass: Harvard Univesity Press, 2002) at p.19.

[107] *ibid.*, at p.21.

[108] P. Gilroy. *The Black Atlantic: Modernity and Double Conciousness* (London: Verso, 1993).

have been considered in Chapter 3. Here, it is worth making the point that there is a vast range of influential work on post-modernism and race. Much of this writing draws on the work of Foucault whose concepts of "power" and "discourse" have provided a rich source of material for the analysis of race and processes of racialisation. Foucoult's stance is anti-essentialist and therefore comfortably fits in with the contemporary scepticism about essentialist concepts of race. Foucault's main concern is to highlight the way in which individual subjects are socially constructed: i.e. their sense of self is produced, and evolves out of, various concepts, modes of seeing and self-understandings that are made available to them in society. Foucault refers to these "sources" and "materials" as discourses. Human subjects are discursively formed, and they are the product of specific historical practices. This analysis is sceptical about an ahistorical or essential notion of the self or race as the starting point for analysis. Foucault's further insight is that power should be understood in terms that are wider than a "juridical" notion. He argues that we need an analysis of power that goes beyond the idea that power is held by one person and denied to another. Instead, Foucault's analysis of power is more complex: he sees power as something that is diffusely distributed throughout social relations and that is constitutive of such relations. The application of this analysis of power to race discrimination is significant. It means that the focus of attention has to move beyond the operation of the state and government, and the employment relationship, to include other "sites" for the operation of power such as social relationships and social spaces (e.g. the media and civic society)[109]. Some of these issues are relevant in the analysis of positive action and institutional discrimination, as well as non-legal responses to the problems of race discrimination.

Once we move away from biological and essentialist concepts of race, the link between race and ethnicity on the one hand, and ethnic and racial groups on the other is weakened. Rogers Brubaker has made this point by arguing that it is possible to recognise the validity of ethnicity without falling prey to the error of attributing a reality to ethnic groups. Brubaker states:

"Ethnicity, race and nation should be conceptualized not as substances or things or entities or organisms or collective individuals—as the imagery of discrete, concrete, tangible, bounded, and enduring 'groups' encourages us to do—but rather in relational, processual, dynamic, eventful, and disaggregated terms. This means thinking of ethnicity, race and nation not in terms of substantial groups or entities but in terms of *practical categories, cultural idioms, cognitive schemas, discursive frames, organizational routines, institutional forms, political projects, and contingent events*. It means thinking of ethnicization, racialization and nationalization as political, social, cultural, and psychological processes. And it means taking as a basic analytical category not the 'group' as

[109] B. Carter, *Realism and Racism: Concepts of Race in Sociological Research*, (London: Routledge, 2000).

an entity but groupness as a contextually fluctuating conceptual variable."[110]

At the same time as denying the essential reality of ethnic groups, Brubaker recognises that groups can become important to the formation of ethnicity, race and nations. He argues that "groupness" can perform this function especially in the context of particular events that act as a catalyst to the awakening and formation of identity.[111] This analysis treats the emergence of certain groups as a social, cultural and political project that is aimed at transforming certain categories—such as ethnicity, race or nationality—into increasing levels of "groupness" for a particular purpose. This process of crystallisation of certain types of experiences of the world using the language of race, ethnicty and nationhood is, therefore, seen as an act of social definition. The process, and resulting definitions, are open to different types of interpretation rather than being the "true" social reality.

C. *The Legal Definition of Race—Mandla v Dowell Lee*

As stated earlier, the key case for defining race for the purposes of the RRA 76 is *Mandla v Dowell Lee*.[112] In this section, we discuss the legal analysis of race and racial group as developed in this line of cases. In *Mandla*, the claimants were a Sikh father and son who in accordance with their Sikh beliefs both wore turbans. The defendants were the headmaster and school who refused to admit the son as a student because the claimants would not agree to the son cutting off his hair and to stop wearing a turban as part of the requirements of the school uniform. The claimants bought an action for a declaration that the defendents had committed an unlawful act against them under the RRA. The judge at first instance dismissed the action on the grounds that Sikhs were not a racial group within the meaning of the RRA. The Court of Appeal dismissed the claimants' appeal against the decision. The House of Lords overturned the decision of the Court of Appeal. The main speeches were given by Lord Fraser and Lord Templeman, with whose speeches the other members of the House of Lords (Lords Brandon, Edmund Davies and Roskill) agreed. Significantly, these three members of the House of Lords agreed with the speeches of both Lord Fraser and Lord Templeman. This consensus suggests that there is no significant difference between the approaches of Lord Fraser and Lord Templeman. Yet, this seeming consensus does not acknowledge subtle but important differences in the tests for "race" and "racial group" under s.1 and s.3(1) of the RRA. In the discussion that follows, the speeches of Lord Fraser and Lord Templeman are treated separately to illustrate these differences. This

110 Rogers Brubaker: "Ethnicity without groups" in S. May, T. Madood and J. Squires, *Ethnicity, Nationalism and Minority Rights* (Cambridge: Cambridge University Press, 2004) at p.54.
111 *ibid.*
112 [1983] 2 A.C. 548

discussion suggests that there is a contrast between the two approaches. Lord Templeman takes a more "essentialist" view of race whereas Lord Fraser's analysis can be understood as part of a "social construction" approach to defining the concept.

1. Lord Templeman: Race as an "essential" concept

(p.569): "I agree with the Court of Appeal that in this context ethnic origins have a good deal in common with the concept of race, just as a group defined by reference to national origins may be different from a group defined by reference to nationality. In my opinion, for the purposes of the Race Relations Act a group of persons defined by reference to ethnic origins must possess some of the characteristics of a race, namely group descent, a group of geographical origin and a group history. The evidence shows that the Sikhs satisfy these tests. They are more than a religious sect, they are almost a race and almost a nation."

2. Lord Fraser: Race as "socially constructed"

(p.561): "[...] My Lords, I recognise that "ethnic" conveys a flavour of race but it cannot, in my opinion, have been used in the Act of 1976 in a strictly racial or biological sense. For one thing, it would be absurd to suppose that Parliament can have intended that membership of a particular racial group should depend upon scientific proof that a person possessed the relevant distinctive biological characteristics (assuming that such characteristics exist). The practical difficulties of such proof would be prohibitive, and it is clear that Parliament must have used the word in some more popular sense. [...] Moreover, "racial" is not a term of art, either legal or, I surmise, scientific. I apprehend that anthropologists would dispute how far the word "race" is biological at all relevant to the species amusingly called homo sapiens.

(p.562): [...] that (the RRA 76) Act is not concerned at all with discrimination on religious grounds. Similarly, it cannot have been used to mean simply any "racial or other group." [...] In my opinion the term "ethnic" still retains a racial flavour but it is used nowadays in an extended sense to include other characeristics which may be commonly thought of as being associated with common racial origin.

For a group to constitute an ethnic group in the sense of the Act of 1976, it must, in my opinion, regard itself, and be regarded by others, as a distinct community by virtue of certain characteristics. Some of these characteristics are essential; others are not essential but one or more of them will commonly be found and will help to distinguish the group from the surrounding community. The conditions which appear to me to essential are these: (1) a long shared history, of which the group is conscious as distinguishing it from other groups, and the memory of which it keeps alive; (1) a cultural tradition of its own, including family and social customs and manners, often but not necessarily associated with religious observance. In addition to these two essential characteristics the following characteristics are, in my opinion, relevant; (3) either a common geographical origin, or descent from a small number of common ancestors; (4) a common language, not necessarily peculiar to the group; (5) a common literature peculiar to the group; (6) a common religion different from that of neighbouring groups or from the general community surrounding it; (7) being a minority or being an oppressed or a dominant group within a larger community, for example a conquered people (say, the inhabitants of England shortly after the Norman conquest) and their conquerors might both be ethnic groups.

A group defined by reference to enough of these characteristics would be capable of including converts, for example, persons who marry into the group, and of excluding apostates. Provided a person who joins the group feels himself or herself to be a member of it, and is accepted by other members, then he is, for the purposes of the Act, a member. That appears to be consistent with the words at the end of section 3(1): "references to a person's racial group refer to any racial group into which he falls". In my opinion, it is possible for a person to fall into a particular racial grop either by birth or be adherence, and it makes no difference, so far as the Act of 1976 is concerned, by which route he finds his way into the group. . . .

[after citing the *King-Ansell v Police* [1979] New Zealand Court of Appeal case approvingly, Lord Fraser went on to observe:]

(p.563–564): Richardson J said at p. 542: "The real test is whether the individuals or the group regard themselves and are regarded by others in the community as having a particular historical identity in terms of their colour or their racial, national or ethnic origins. That must be based on a belief shared by members of the group."

And the same learned judge said, at p. 543: "a group is identifiable in terms of its ethnic origins if it is a segment of the population distinguished from others by a sufficient combination of shared customs, beliefs, traditions and characteristics derived from a common or presumed common past, even if not drawn from what in biological terms is a common racial stock. It is that combination which gives them an historically determined social identity in their own eyes and in the eyes of those outside the group. They have a distinct social identity based not simply on group cohesion and solidarity but also on their belief as to their historical antecedents." My Lords, that last passage sums up in a way upon which I could not hope to improve the views which I have been endeavouring to express."

One clear difference between the speeches of Lord Templeman and Lord Fraser lies in the emphasis that they give to the "essential characteristics" that allow us to identify a person according to ethnic origin. This distinction is noted by H. Benyon and N. Love who argue that there are important distinctions between Lord Fraser and Lord Templeman's approach:

H. Benyon and N. Love, "Mandla and the Meaning of 'Racial Group' (1984) 100 L.Q.R. 120.

pp.121–3: "A very cursory reading of *Mandla* might suggest that Lord Fraser gave the leading speech, which Lord Templeman merely repeated in abbreviated form. But closer inspection reveals important discrepencies between the two speeches. They both regard a sense of history (a "long shared history" (Lord Fraser) or a "group history" (Lord Templeman) as an essential characteristic of a group of persons defined by reference to ethnic origin. But there the similarity ends. The second of Lord Fraser's two essential characteristics (i.e a "cultural tradition" etc.) and the last of four of his five relevant characteristics (i.e "language", "literature", "religion" and "oppressed or dominant group") do not feature in Lord Templeman's definition at all; whilst Lord Templeman's two other essential characteristics (i.e "group descent" and "group of geographical origin") only appear in Lord Fraser's speech in the alternative, as the first of his five non-essential but relevant characteristics. This creates a difficulty in identifying the ratio of the case, in view of the fact that the remaining Law Lords concurred in both speeches. Is the true ratio to be found in Lord Fraser's speech, in Lord Templeman's speech, or perhaps in both? [. . .] Can such a consenus be found if conditions which Lord Templeman states "must" exist ("group descent" and "geographical origin") Lord Fraser merely regards as "relevant"? Surely not. There is surely a crucial difference between "must" and "may", of between a necessary condition and a contingent characteristic, even if, as will be shortly shown, other aspects of Lord Fraser's speech suggest that in other respects he attahced little importance to the distinction he was here at pains to draw. So, at the very least, even if (a dubious point) Lord Fraser and Lord Templeman concurred in requiring a "cultural tradition" as well as a "group history" (lengthy or otherwise) they did not concur as to whether or not "group descent" and "geographical origin" were essentially (Lord Templeman) or merely relevant (Lord Fraser). [The authors go on to consider how to apply Lord Fraser's characteristics to groups such as the Royal Family or the working class.]

One response to this might be that although both the Royal Family and the working class possess Lord Fraser's characteristics, they are not "defined by reference to" them. They are instead probably "defined by reference to" consanguinity or affinity with a reigning monarch, and occupation, respectively. A perfectly sensible response, indeed, but not one open to anyone supporting Lord Fraser's interpretation of the Act, since he himself [...] did not use "defined by reference to" in this limiting sense. So, another possible response might be that, however distinctive the family and social customs of the Royal Family and the working classes, they do not amount to a "cultural tradition", but only to a "sub-cultural" tradition. But if so, the infinite regress towards which that tends is another argument against Lord Fraser's interpretation. The law should try, if it can, to offer clearer criteria for recognising what practices might be unlawfully discriminatory, and on that ground Lord Templeman's formulation is possibly preferable to Lord Fraser's—irrespective of any greater narrowness it may possess."

Benyon and Love argue in favour of Lord Templeman's analysis because it provides a more stable and certain criteria. However, the flexibility of Lord Fraser's analysis is exactly what makes it a more attractive formulation if one accepts that it is preferable to have a view of race as a socially constructed rather than essential or biologically fixed category. Fraser's flexible approach could well be thought to be preferable. Lord Fraser's analysis contains seven criteria. The only fixed categories over which the individual may not have control is a common geographical origin. All the other criteria (even language) are characteristics which can be adopted by an individual as a matter of choice, albeit also subject to group contexts such as community and culture. Belonging to a minority or an oppressed group is more problematic, although this really depends on the prior question of whether or not the individual is a member of the group. This emphasis on characteristics that are a matter of choice very naturally leads on to Lord Fraser's conclusion that his test is able to include converts. Moreover, it is this emphasis on membership of an ethnic group as being a matter of beliefs and choice, rather than biological or racial origin, that is the key distinction between Lord Fraser's and Lord Templeman's analysis. Lord Fraser's adoption on the passages in the judgment of Richardson J. in the *King-Ansell v Police* case is significant because these passages adopt a view of ethnicity that emphasises belief and ideas rather than fixed essences and biology:

"The real test is whether the individuals or the group regard themselves and are regarded by others in the community as having a particular historical identity in terms of their colour or their racial, national or ethnic origins. That must be based on a belief shared by members of the group [and] a group is identifiable in terms of its ethnic origins if it is a segment of the population distinguished from others by a sufficient combination of shared customs, beliefs, traditions and characteristics derived from a common or presumed common past, even if not drawn from what in biological terms is a common racial stock. It is that combination which gives them an historically determined social identity in their own eyes and in the eyes of those outside the group. They have a distinct social identity based not simply on group cohesion and solidarity *but also on their belief [emphasis added]* as to their historical antecedents."[113]

Lord Fraser's focus on choice is in marked contrast to Lord Templeman's comments that emphasise group descent, geographical origin and group history, as well as emphasising physical characteristics such as colour, physique and common anscestry. Lord Templeman's more biological and essential approach to ethnicity (as an aspect of race) is illustrated in the following statement:

"In my opinion, for the purposes of the Race Relations Act a group of persons defined by reference to ethnic origins must possess some of the characteristics of a race, namely group descent, a group of geographical origin and a group history. The evidence shows that the Sikhs satisfy these tests. They are more than a religious sect, they are almost a race and almost a nation. As a race, the Sikhs share a common colour, and a common physique based on common ancestors [. . .].[114]

This distinction between Lord Fraser's and Lord Templeman's speeches is significant because it highlights the different ways in which a statute such as the RRA can regulate race discrimination. Lord Templeman's essentialist approach to race draws on biological concepts of race and emphasises colour. Lord Fraser's emphasis on ideas is more compatible with the view of commentators such as Loury, Gilroy and Appiah who see race as a concept that can be constructed, and that is comprised of ideas rather than biology. This analysis of race may also be more relevant for a modern conception of race discrimination. As the numbers of new migrants to Britain diminishes, the link between race and non-negotiable ethnic origins or historical links becomes weaker. For second and third generation British ethnic minorities, having a common origin and common history become less significant than the fact that certain individuals choose to adopt beliefs or join with others. Individuals and social groups see themselves as part of a common tradition through choice. Of course, the fact that prevailing racism in society will mark out these indivi-

[113] *Mandla v Dowell Lee* [1983] 2 A.C. 548, at 565.
[114] *ibid.*

duals as "raced" irrespective of their choice is also significant to the analysis. In this context, it becomes more meaningful to speak about individuals choosing to associate with others. They form social groups that are, or become, distinct from the majority. As Rogers Brubaker argues, these changes mean that we have to recognise the importance of "groupness" (the fact that as a matter of social reality individuals have chosen to form social groups) without attributing immutable characteristics to groups.[115] Moreover, there is evidence to suggest that there are increasing rates of cross racial marriage, and this development will invariably challenge the possibility of defining race along biological and essential lines altogether.[116]

On this view, and following Lord Fraser's test, it is possible for the legal definition of race to give a central role to individual choice and agency. A number of agents are involved in the social construction of race and ethnicity. The individual subject can make a choice about criteria such as the beliefs, culture, language and literature by which he or she chooses to identity themselves. However, as Lord Fraser's test illustrates, this individual and private choice also has a public and social aspect. Individual beliefs and aspects of personal identity need a public culture within which to operate. As Appiah notes, the individual aspects of ethnic identity as a choice of identity need to be tempered by a realisation that such identities can only be sustained because of the availability of certain beliefs and traditions that are sustained within a wider group: "[. . .] ethnic identities characteristically have cultural distinctions as one of their primary marks. That is why it is so easy to conflate them (i.e. *conflate identity and culture*). Ethnic identities are created in families and community life. These—along with mass-mediated culture, the school and the college—are, for most of us, the central sites of the social transmission of culture. Distinct practices, ideas, norms go with each ethnicity in part because people want to be ethnically distinct: because many people want the sense of solidarity that comes from being unlike others. With ethnicity in modern society, it is often the distinct identity that comes first, and the cultural distinction that is created and maintained because of it—not the other way round. The distinctive cutlures of ethnic and religious identities matter not simply because of their contents, but also as markers of those identities."[117]

On this analysis, race and ethnicity become important because of the role that they play in ensuring that there is an adequate range of choices available for individuals out of which to construct a meaningful identity. Moreover, the fact that race and ethnicity have been, and remain, such an important source of inequality, disadvantage and injustice make them especially relevant. It is this

115 Rogers Brubaker, "Ethnicity without groups" in S. May, T. Modood and J. Squires, *Ethnicity, Nationalism and Minority Rights* (Cambridge: Cambridge University Press, 2004).

116 Sandra Fredman, *Discrimination Law* (Oxford: Clarendon Press, 2002) at 52.

117 K. Anthony Appiah, "Race, Culture, Identity" in K. A. Appiah and A. Gutmann, *Color Conscious: The Political Morality of Race* (NJ,US: Princeton University Press, 1996) at p.89. See also Seyla Benhabib's argument against conflating the policits of recognition with the politics of identity: Seyla Benhabib, *The Claims of Culture: Equality and Diversity in the Global Era* (Princeton N.J.: Princeton University Press, 2002).

feature of entrenched disadvantage and social exclusion that would distinguish a cultural and ethnic group such as Rastafarians or Asians, from the example of the "royal family" used by Benyon and Love in the earlier passage. This focus on social exclusion becomes more explicit in those jurisdictions that have a constitutional prohibition of race discrimination. For example, in the US one of the justifications for the constitutional prohibition of race discrimination in the 14th Amendment to the US Constitution draws on the fact that "prejudice against discrete and insular minorities may be a special condition, which tends seriously to curtail the operation of those political processes ordinarily to be relied upon to protect minorities, and which may call for a correspondingly more searching judicial inquiry."[118] Racial identities relate in crucial ways to the exercise of social and political power. The preference for a private civil law model for regulating race discrimination in Britain obscures the fact that the social, political and economic exclusion of a minority group are relevant facts in any legal definition of "race".

The formation of a racial identity by an individual, therefore, has a number of complex features. It can be understood as an aspect of individual choice which depends on the wider public sphere. Moreover, this choice can reflect a reactive/negative aspect but also a more postive/affirmative narrative. The reactive/negative impetus for identification along these lines can be seen to be a reaction to the use of criteria (such as colour or culture) as the basis for stigma or negative stereotypes. Experience of this type of stigmatisation or discrimination can cause an individual to develop a heightened reactive awareness of these "race" criteria. On the other hand, the same criteria (colour or culture) may provide individuals with an affirmative and contructive narrative: they may choose to identify with these criteria as well as accepting the underlying beliefs and practices that support them. Discrimination law has a critical function to play in preventing the use of negative stereotypes that can cause harm to individuals. It may also have a role to play in allowing a more positive source of ideas about race and ethnicity to be available in the public sphere: thereby enabling individuals to construct a more constructive process of identify formation, and self-identification.

D. *Applying* Mandla: Dutton *and the protection of Roma (gypsies)*

A comparison of two Court of Appeal cases highlights the choices that are open to courts in applying the *Mandla* rule: *Commission for Racial Equality v Dutton*[119] and *Crown Suppliers v Dawkins*[120]. *Dutton* raised the issue of whether

[118] *Carolene Products* (1938) 304 U.S. 144, 152, n.4. See also Kenneth L. Karst, "The Supreme Court, 1976 Term—Foreword: Equal Citizenship Under the Fourteenth Amendment," (1977) 91 Harv L. Rev. 1, at 4.

[119] [1989] Q.B. 783.

[120] [1993] I. C. R. 517.

gypsies (travellers) could be held to be a racial group for the purposes of s.3(1) of the RRA. At first instance, the County Court judge had dismissed an action for an injunction against the defendant pub owner who had placed the sign "no travellers" at his pub. The Commission for Racial Equality had brought the action for an injunction based on the argument that the sign referred to gypsies and was evidence that the defendant would discriminate against them. The judge dismissed the action holding that (a) "travellers" was not synonymous with "gypsies" and (b) that gypsies were not a racial group under s.3(1) of the RRA. The Court of Appeal held that the Roma (referred to as gypsies in the case law) could be a racial group for the purposes of s.3(1) and that, accordingly, a sign that stated "no travellers" was capable of being indirect race discrimination. In his judgment Nicholls L.J. applied the *Mandla* test. Taylor L.J. and Stocker L.J agreed with this, although Stocker L.J. expressed some reservation about applying the concept of "ethnic group" to the Roma (gypsies) in a definitive way. He cited the passages from the speech of Lord Fraser (discussed above) that adopt and cite with approval the judgment of Richardson J. in *King-Ansell v Police*. The trial judge had found that gypsies lacked some of the other important criteria in Lord Fraser's test such as a common literature or religion.

Nicholls L.J. set out Lord Fraser's summary of the criteria to be applied, and acknowledged that the Roma (gypsies) satisfy many of the criteria that are set out in Lord Fraser's guideline (e.g. common origin and customs). Nicholls L.J. summarised his views as follows:

"I am unable to agree with his [the trial judge's] conclusion on what have been called the Mandla conditions when applied, not to the larger, amorphous group of 'travellers' or 'gipsies', colloquially so-called, but to 'gipsies' in the primary, narrower sense of that word. On the evidence it is clear that such gipsies are a minority, with a long-shared history and a common geographical origin. [. . .] They do not have a common religion, nor a peculiar, common literature of their own, but they have a repertoire of folktales and music passed on from one generation to the next. No doubt, after all the centuries which have passed since the first gipsies left the Punjab, gipsies are no longer derived from what, in biological terms, is a common racial stock, but that of itself does not prevent them from being a racial group as widely defined in the Act."[121]

Nicholls L.J. then went on to apply the *Mandla* conditions to what he considered to be the most difficult aspect of the case: i.e. whether the Roma (gypsies) now so assimilated that they had lost their separate, group identity in a way that suggested that they were no longer a community recognisable by ethnic origins within the meaning of the RRA 76. In order to address this crucial question Nicholls L.J. applied the formula set out by Richardson J. in *King-Ansell* and adopted by Lord Fraser in *Mandla*. Nicholls L. J. asked:

[121] [1989] Q.B. 783 at 800–801.

"Have gipsies now lost their separate, group identity, so that they are no longer a community recognisable by ethnic origins within the meaning of the Act? The judge held that they had. This is a finding of fact. Nevertheless, with respect to the judge, I do not think that there was before him any evidence justifying his conclusion that gipsies have been absorbed into a larger group, if by that he means that substantially all gipsies have been so absorbed. The fact that some have been so absorbed and are indistinguishable from any ordinary member of the public is not sufficient in itself to establish loss of what Richardson J., in *King-Ansell v Police* [1979] 2 N. Z. L. R. 531, 543 referred to as "an historically determined social identity in [the group's] own eyes and in the eyes of those outside the group. There was some evidence to the contrary from Mr Mercer, on whose testimony the judge expressed no adverse comment. He gave evidence that 'we know who are members of our community' and that 'we know we are different'. In my view the evidence was sufficient to establish that, despite their long presence in England, gipsies have not merged wholly in the population, as have Saxons and the Danes, and altogether lost their separate identity. They, or many of them, have retained a separateness, a self-awareness, of still being gipsies."[122]

Nicholls L.J.'s approach places emphasis on certain aspects of the *Mandla* test. First, it adopts Lord Fraser's analysis as the appropriate method for defining "racial group". Taylor L.J. also places emphasis on Lord Fraser's analysis, although Stocker L.J. also refers to Lord Templeman's judgment[123]. Second, it recognises that biology is not determinative of the test for a racial group. It also, therefore, avoids giving the test in *Mandla* the gloss of essentialism that, it was argued earlier, is a feature of Lord Templeman's approach. Third, it adopts a flexible approach towards the criteria set out in Lord Fraser's analysis: although gypsies fulfill some of the criteria in the test and not others, they can nevertheless still fall within the concept of a racial group. Fourth, Nicholls L.J. places great emphasis, as Lord Fraser did in *Mandla*, on the test of Richardson J. in *King-Ansell*. This analysis, consequently gives great weight to the issue of whether the social group themselves, as well as the wider community, recognise the Roma (gypsies) as a differentiated and visible social group. According to this approach, the criterion focuses on the *subjective perception* of current social groups rather than the application of clear cut objective criteria. Factual evidence to indicate current social attitudes also plays a relevant role in this analysis. This analysis also coheres with sociological and anthropological approaches to ethnicity, which increasingly verify that essentialist approaches to ethnicity are less useful than a focus on the social processes which produce ethnic groups. For example, the work of the anthropologist Frederik Barth confirms the need to concentrate on the processes which produce, reproduce and organise the boundaries between dif-

[122] *ibid.*, at 801.
[123] *ibid.*, at 809.

ferent ethnic groups.[124] This is a process of identification and differentiation by (a) those within the relevant ethnic group; and also (b) those in the wider community with whom they have contact. On this analysis, cultural difference is relevant not because of its unchanging essence but rather because it allows differentiation of certain social groups and ethnic identification by its members. Moreover, these groups do not exist in isolation: they arise out of, and depend for their recognition on, interaction with other groups and the wider community. In relation to the Roma (gypsies) there are a number of compelling reasons to categorise them as a racial group under the RRA: they have been present in Britain since the sixteenth century; although they may share a common colour, language and some aspects of culture, to the majority they also have certain distinct practices and lifestyles that allow them and others to mark them out as a distinct social group; these differences have been, and are, a source of detriment for the Roma as a group; and the detriment suffered includes discriminatory state policy in areas such as planning law.[125] These are also reasons for the recognition and special protection of the Roma throughout Europe (evidence as recent as 2006 confirms that there remains persecution and violence against the Roma in contemporary Europe)[126]

E. *Dawkins and non-ethnic religious minorities*

Nicholls L.J. analysis in *Dutton* can be contrasted with *Crown Suppliers v Dawkins* a Court of Appeal decision that applied the *Mandla*[127] test to the issue of whether Rastafarians were a racial group under the RRA. In *Dawkins* the applicant was a Rastafarian who wore his hair in dreadlocks. He was refused employment as a van driver by a government agency when he indicated that he would not be willing to cut his hair. The Industrial Tribunal found that there was considerable evidence to support the view that Rastafarians were a racial group under s.3(1) of the RRA: they had a distinct cultural tradition; a common language; common geographical origin and a long shared history dating from 1930, of which the group was conscious and which distinguished them from other African-Carribean groups. The Industrial Tribunal found that Rastafarians were a racial group and upheld the applicant's complaint. The EAT allowed an appeal from this decision citing the decisions of Lord Fraser and Lord Templeman in *Mandla*:

124 Frederik Barth (ed.), *Ethnic Groups and Boundaries: The Social Organisation of Cultural Difference* (Waveland, 1998).

125 See discussion in S. Fredman, *Discrimination Law*, (Oxford: Clarendon Press, 2002) at pp.38–39.

126 Ian Traynor, "Violence and persecution follow the Roma across Europe", Ian Traynor reporting from Ambrus, Slovenia, The Guardian, Monday, November 27, 2006

127 [1993] I. C. R. 517 at 524 (Court of Appeal).

"Lord Templeman held that the Sikhs qualified as a group defined by ethnic origin because they constitute a separate and distinct community derived from racial characteristics. But in our judgment, Rastafarians cannot be so described. This is in our view insufficient to distinguish them from the rest of the Afro-Carribean community so as to render them a separate group defined by reference to ethnic origins. They are a religious sect and no more. In any event returning to Lord Fraser's test, we are unable to agree with the majority of the industrial tribunal that Rastafarians have a long shared history. It cannot reasonably be said that a movement which goes back for only 60 years, i.e. within the living memory of many people, can claim to be long in existence. Its history, in the judgment of the majority, is insufficiently sustained. The fact that the movement has maintained itself and still exists is insufficient. We have no hesitation in disagreeing with the conclusion of the majority of the tribunal on this point, because first we do not regard it as a finding of fact, and secondly, even if it were, we would regard it as a finding which no reasonable tribunal could make, and therefore perverse. So far as Lord Fraser's second essential test is concerned, that of a cultural tradition of its own, our view is that Rastafarians are a group with very little structure, no apparent organisation and having customs and practices which have evolved in a somewhat haphazard way. Nevertheless, notwithstanding these reservations and placing them in the context of a formerly enslaved people striving for an identity, there may be a sufficient cultural tradition to satisfy the test, and we are not prepared to disagree with the finding of the tribunal on this point."[128]

Crown Suppliers v Dawkins [1993] I.C.R. 517 at 528–530

In the Court of Appeal, Neill L.J. confirmed the decision of the EAT in *Dawkins*. He replied to counsel Mr Riza's argument that there are important distincitions between the approach of Lord Fraser and Lord Templeman by stating that, in his view, there was little distinction between the two tests in *Mandla*:

"Mr Riza further argued that in addition to the suggested inconsistency of the approaches of Lord Fraser and Lord Templeman, Lord Fraser was guilty of further inconsistency in that having set out his seven conditions or characteristics he then accepted as a satisfactory test the formula expounded by Richardson J. in *King-Ansell v. Police* [1979] 2 N.Z.L.R. 531, 543. With all due respect to Mr Riza it seems to me that in making these criticisms he falls into the error of equating the language used in speeches or judgments with that of a statute. In giving reasons for a decision a judge seeks to explain the basis on which he has reached his conclusion. The speech or judgment has to read as a whole. It is very often possible to find one passage in a judgment which, because different language is used,

[128] [1991] I.C.R. 583 at 593 (EAT).

gives a slightly different impression or has a slightly different nuance when compared with another passage. For my part, however, I cannot detect any real differences in substance between what Lord Fraser said and what Lord Templeman said. Both of them stressed that the words 'ethnic origins' had to be construed in the light of the fact that they occurred as part of the definition of 'a racial group'. Lord Fraser said that the word 'ethnic' still retained a racial flavour. Lord Templeman at p. 397, agreed that in the context ethnic origins had a good deal in common with the concept of race. [. . .]

It is clear that Rastafarians have certain identifiable characteristics. They have a strong cultural tradition which includes a distinctive form of music known as reggae music [. . .] In speaking about Rastafarians in this context I am referring to the core group, because I am satisfied that a core group can exist even though not all the adherents of the group could, if considered separately, satisfy any of the relevant tests. It is at this stage that one has to take account of both the racial flavour of the word 'ethnic' and Lord Fraser's requirement of a long shared history. Lord Meston submitted that if one compared Rastafarians with the rest of the Jamaican community in England, or indeed with the rest of the Afro-Carribean community in this country, there was nothing to set them aside as a separate ethnic group. They are a separate group but not a separate group defined by reference to their ethnic origins. I see no answer to this submission. Mr Whitmore quite rightly stressed that this case is concerned with identity. The question is: have the Rastafarians a separate *ethnic* identity? Do they stand apart by reason of *their* history from other Jamaicans? In my judgment it is not enough for Rastafarians now to look back to a past when their ancestors, in common with other peoples in the Caribbean, were taken there from Africa. They were not a separate group then. The *shared* history of Rastafarians goes back only 60 years or so. One can understand and admire the deep affection which Rastafarians feel for Africa and their longing for it as their real home. But, as Mr. Riza recognises, the court is concerned with the language of the statute. In the light of the guidance given by the House of Lords in *Mandla (Sewa Singh) v. Dowell Lee* [1983] I. C. R. 385, I am unable to say that they are a separate racial grop. I would dismiss the appeal."[129]

It is worth noting the marked difference in analysis between the decisions in *Dutton* and *Dawkins*. As noted above, Nicholls L.J. in *Dutton* develops an approach that prefers the speech of Lord Fraser and especially those passages that adopt the analysis of Richardson J. This more nuanced analysis leads to a flexible approach to race that adopts the perspective of the subject, and the relevant minority and majority community practices, as the determinant of whether there is a sufficiently distinct ethnic identity which deserves protection under the RRA. In contrast to this, Neill L.J. in *Dawkins* treats the test in *Mandla* as linking ethnicity back to race and applies an "objective" test as to whether or not the group can be said to be an ethnic group, i.e. do Rastafarians, as an objective matter, have a sufficiently long history to be classified as a racial group? In *Dawkins,* this last question is answered in the negative despite the fact that as a matter of evidence the tribunal found that there was such evidence and, moreover, Rastafarians regard themselves as distinct from the general Afro-Caribbean community. The question of whether differences of self-perception in the private identity of Rastafarians have translated into a sufficiently distinct and delineated cultural practice was answered in the

[129] [1993] I. C. R. 517 at 528–530.

negative because 60 years was deemed to be insufficient time using an objective and absolute standard.

As we have stated biology and physical appearance are not in themselves, and should not be, the determining criteria of "race" or "racial group" in discrimination law. Clearly, some limits to this process are necessary: not all differences of private identity that have a public aspect can be recognised under the RRA. These limits can be formulated by referring back to the justifications for treating race as a prohibited ground within discrimination law: i.e the way in which "race" is used as a way of stigmatising individuals and groups by "racialising" key difference; and the resulting socio-economic injustice and oppression of these individuals and groups. A useful definition of race has to be able to perform a number of functions: it has to have the ability to pick out individuals on the basis of a discernable characteristic; to assign individuals to a group; to give emphasis to those criteria that are used to stigmatise and that reflect pejorative or negative assumptions based on the individual's membership of that group; and to protect social groups which are at risk of becoming socially excluded. It would be impractical to have a purely "subjective" definition of race. Nevertheless, it is possible to adopt an approach that is more flexible and draws on factual evidence whilst at the same time giving weight to the self-perception of individuals and their communities about their own sources of identity. Rastafarians are a visible and distinct group who have publicly visible differences as compared with other members of the Caribbean community. These differences can be the basis for negative stereotypes held by others; but exactly the same features can also be the basis on which Rastafarians construct their own positive private (and group) identity. Therefore, it is possible for Rastafarians to develop, as they have done, a distinct private identity that is sustained within a distinct community. The analysis in *Dutton* fails to recognise these complexities. A Rastafarian may well object that dreadlocks are more relevant than colour from his or her perspective; and that discrimination on the basis of this difference (rather than colour) is experienced by Rastafarians as a more grievous harm. This approach is especially relevant if we consider the precise ways in which "race" ideas can operate to stigmatise different groups and the longer timescale within which processes of racialisation take place. As the discussion in the next session suggests, discrimination against national minorities, Jews and colour discrimination all fall within the RRA, although they are not strictly about visible "colour" difference. Essentialist and fixed meanings of the "race" in cases such *Dutton*, however, make it more difficult for discrimination law to respond to emerging forms of racism. It is interesting to note, Rastafarianism has recently been held to fall within the scope of the Employment Equality (Religion and Belief) Regulations as a philosophical belief similar to a religion.[130]

The *Mandla* test already covers many of the key minorities who were

[130] *Harris v JFL Automotive Ltd and Matrix Consultancy UK Ltd* (Jan 2008) 172 E.O.R. 22, EAT.

assumed to acquire protection from racial discrimination in the 1970s and 1980s, and who continue to be at risk in the contemporary period. Minorities who were identified as being at risk of racial violence, persecution and disadvantage include, inter alia: Jews and Sikhs; African and African-Carribean groups; the Roma; Chinese, Indians, Bangladeshi and Pakistani groups. These are all "minority" groups. As we have previously discussed, domestic discrimination law operates symmetrically and protects both men and women; ethnic majorities and ethnic minorities. In the next section, we discuss those national minorities who are often assumed to be "British", but who nevertheless can become "minoritised" or "racialised" because of differences of language or culture from the majority norm. These national minorities, such as the Irish, Welsh and Scots, can also be protected by the RRA although as the following section illustrates there remain some gap for linguistic minorities such as Welsh speakers.

F. *Race, National Origins and Language: English, Irish, Scots and Welsh*

As stated earlier, and as noted in the discussion of what it means to be British by Matthew Arnold, there have been persistent questions about the status of groups such as the Irish or Celts within Great Britain. The fact that the term racial group in the RRA was primarily aimed at the new immigrants from the former colonies often obscures any discussion of its relevance for minorities who were in Britain in the pre-1945 period. We have already mentioned that Jews are covered by the RRA. Moreover, religious minorities in Northern Ireland (Catholics) are covered by religious discrimination legislation in Norther Ireland and the new prohibitions on religious discrimination in employment, training and provision of private services. The position of Irish minorities as an ethnic rather than religious group and the indigenous Celtic minorities is more complex.

As we saw earlier in the *Dhatt* case, and as discussed below, nationality discrimination and immigration issues are a significant exception to the general principle of non-discrimination on the ground of race. The distinction between national origin and nationality is critical in this analysis. In EU discrimination law there is a significant difference in the legal analysis of nationality and other forms of discrimination. Moreover, both EU law and the domestic legislation treat nationality and immigration issues as a significant exception to the general prohibition on race discrimination: the Race Equality Directive contains a specific exception for nationality and immigration issues (see RED, Art.3(2)). Under the RRA national origin rather than nationality discrimination is prohibited, and under the RRAmnd Act (2000) immigration and nationality issues are a significant exception to the coverage of the legislation. This has concrete practical effects and, as we see below, permits discriminatory treatment of refugees and non-nationals who are increasingly "racialised" in Britain and the EU.

It is clear that the "English" can rely on the term "national origin" to fall within s.3(1) of the RRA 76[131] and to argue that they are a protected group. The issue of non-English minorities in Britiain who share many of the ethnic, cultural and religious characteristics of the majority in Britain but who are, nevertheless, able to point to differences that have become a source for disadvantage, detriment and discriminatory treatment is more problematic. The Irish, Scots and Welsh all fall into this category. As discussed earlier, there was substantial immigration from Ireland in the late nineteenth century which led to a proliferation of sterotypes and prejudice against the Irish. In addition, recent surveys confirms that people from the Irish Republic still top the list of people living in Britain but born abroad, with nearly 500,000 residents.[132] Evidence of anti-Irish discrimination was confirmed in "The Irish in Britain" a 1997 report of the Commission for Racial Equality.[133] This report (a) confirmed that there are serious stereotypes about the Irish which give rise to discrimination; and (b) sets out the cases which confirm that Employment Tribunals have recognised "Irish" as a race under the RRA in decisions such as *O'Driscoll v Post Office*.[134] *Northern Joint Police Board v Power*[135] recognised that the Scots and English could be distinguished: before the Act of Union they were separated by geography, language, names, legal systems, churches and education systems. Therefore, it was intelligible to speak about the Scots being a distinct "race" or "racial group" for the purposes of the RRA. The decision in *Power* is significant: by distinguishing between nationality and national origin the EAT was able to ensure that national minorities such as Scots and Welsh were included as protected "races", whilst at the same time excluding nationality and immigration issues from the scope of the RRA. In all these contexts it is important to emphasise the increasing complexity of defining categories such as "Scot" and "Welsh". The principles of multiple and intersectional discrimination will also be relevant where these categories intersect with other grounds such as religion or gender.[136]

Devolution of political power to the regions (and in particular to Scotland,

131 *BBC Scotland v Souter* 2001 S.C. 458.

132 Alan Travis, "Migrant Map of UK reveals surprises", *The Guardian*, Thursday September 8, 2005. Quoting from the Insitute of Public Policy Research study *Black and White Britian*.

133 "The Irish in Britain", Report of the Commission for Racial Equality, (Commission for Racial Equality: London, June 1997).

134 Cited in "The Irish in Britain", Report of the Commission for Racial Equality, (Commission for Racial Equality: London, June 1997) at p.4.

135 *Northern Joint Police Board v Power* [1997] I.R. L.R. 610, (EAT).

136 See for example the ESRC research project on "Devolution and Constitutional Change" which includes projects on the intersection between Scottish national identity and other categories such as gender, ethnicity and religion, *see www.devolution.ac.uk* (accessed on August 20, 2006). For academic literature see for example Catherine Bromley (ed.), John Curtice (ed.), David McCrone (ed.), Alison Park (ed.), *Has Devolution Delivered?* (Edinburgh: Edinburgh University Press, 2006) and Asifa M. Hussain and William L. Miller, *Multicultural Nationalism* (Oxford: Oxford University Press, 2006).

Wales and Northern Ireland) is likely to facilitate calls for differentiation within the term "British". Moreover, if group membership is important to the well-being of individuals, then this is true for the majority as well as for the minority. This "reciprocal" form of multiculturalism requires respect for majorities and national minorities as well as for newly formed groups of ethnic minorities.[137] This provides a powerful argument for ensuring that historically established social groups (such as the English, Irish, Welsh and Scots) are recognised and protected by the RRA. By recognising national origin (e.g. being Scottish or English) as a protected characteristic under the RRA the reasoning in cases such as *Power* or *Souter* can be seen to endorse this more "reciprocal" form of multiculturalism.

The distinct nature of the Celts, and the status of the Welsh language, are common themes in discussion of the term "British". Matthew Arnold, as stated earlier, lamented the loss of the language and culture associated with the Celts when he attended a celebration of Celtic literature. However, the issue is complicated by the fact that not all those who would be defined as Welsh in fact speak the Welsh language. In *Gwynedd County Council v Jones* the EAT declined to apply the *Mandla* test to the Welsh and concluded that the Welsh speaking community was a distinct racial group under the RRA: the language criteria in *Mandla* could not without more be sufficient to constitute a racial group.[138] W Macleod, in his criticism of the decision in *Gwynned v Jones*, argues that regional languages such as Welsh should be recognised under the RRA 76. The present approach in *Jones* ignores the way in which linguistic differences can lead to differences within groups such as Welsh and Scottish; and also the way in which language can be a source of discrimination and disadvantage. In this respect, the position in domestic discrimination law towards minority languages is in stark contrast to the priority given in other systems of minority protection to language as as a critical feature of a minority group and as a potential basis for race discrimination. Language claims in Quebec are, and have been, some of the most salient sources for claims to equality and non-discrimination in Canada. Moreover, the European Court of Human Rights has recognised the importance of language to minorities.[139] The domestic approach tends to ignore the intrinsic link between language and other factors such as culture, literature and other key aspects of individual identity. Macleod concludes:

"The autochthonous language communities are at the margins of British life, typically ignored by politicians, scholars and activists focused on the urban centre. Their relationship to the RRA 76 has rarely been considered, partially because such a connection is

[137] For a more detailed discussion of this more "reciprocal" form of multiculturalism see Maleiha Malik, "Minority Protection and the Human Rights Act" in Tom Campbell et al (eds), *Sceptical Approaches to the Human Rights Act* (Oxford: Oxford University Press, 2001).

[138] [1986] I.C.R. 833.

[139] Belgian Linguistics Case (1968) 1 E.H.R.R. 252. See also Council of Europe treaties and initiatives on the protection of minority languages, e.g. European Charter for Regional or Minority Languages (1992).

not an intuitive one, especially among those for whom the autochthonous language communities do not register on the horizon. Nevertheless, there are significant and interesting issues at stake. An awareness of the RRA can work a range of positive outcomes for the autochthonous language communities, either by granting them formal recognition or by taking their needs into account and considering ways in which language promotion policies can be advanced in the employment field."[140]

One recent development which sought to remedy the inequalities faced by regional linguistic minorities was the proposals to strengthen the support for Gaelic via public broadcasting. In 1999 the Scottish Office established a Task Force chaired by Alasdair Milne to examine the future of Gaelic broadcasting. The Milne Task Force proposed the establishment of a Gaelic Broadcasting Authority to oversee the establishment of a Gaelic television service, initially available through digital satellite, as a free-to-air public service. The Milne Task Force Report highlighted the benefits to the Gaelic language and to the economy of Gaelic-speaking areas of Scotland from such a service.[141] Milne's conclusions were: (a) Gaelic is one of the key historic minority languages in Britain; (b) there is significant discrimination against Gaelic in public broadcasting as compared with other regional languages; (c) such discrimination represents a breach of national interest, social justice and cultural diversity. Milne recommended that "Our report identifies the need for specific allocation of broadcasting spectrum; for a guaranteed funding formula to encompass the delivery of a modern, quality service under the supervision of a Gaelic Broadcasting Authority; and for arrangements to be secured in law through the new broadcasting legislation".

The subsequent Communications Act (2003) has the powers to put Alasdair Milne's recommendations into practice through the establishment of the Gaelic Media Service. However, despite the clear conclusions of the Milne Task Force, very little has been done to give any real effect to its central recommendations. Modest financial support for Gaelic Media Services has been made but the ambition of providing for the needs of the Gaelic community, via a dedicated television channel, has not been realised. Milne concluded that a dedicated Gaelic television channel with established funding would be a "a major contribution towards the future well-being of the language and culture". The British government accepted a legal obligation to preserve indigenous minority languages when it became a signatory to the Council of Europe Charter for Regional or Minority Languages, but, as the failure to implement Milne's recommendations confirm, it has failed to translate this commitment into a practical reality for its national minorities, such as the Scots and the Welsh.

[140] W. McLeod, "Autochthonous language communities and the Race Relations Act" (1998) 1 Web Journal of Current Legal Issues.

[141] Gaelic Broadcasting Taskforce Report, 1999 (henceforth cited as the Milne Taskforce) *http://www.scotland.gov.uk/* (accessed on November 10, 2004).

V. Evolving Forms of Racism

In the previous analysis of *Mandla* and its application in cases such as *Dutton* and *Dawkins*, we discussed the processes through which distinct social groups can emerge over a period of time. We also discussed the way in which the self perception of individuals, as well as the existence of sufficient distinguishing markers which enable others to identify members of distinct social groups, can act as a guide to whether a particular social group can be recognised under the RRA as a protected "racial group". A number of groups such as gypsies/travellers and also non-ethnic religious minorities, may fall within this category. There are two evolving forms of racialisation that are especially significant. First, there is the increasing phenomenon of "cultural racism" that operates at the boundaries between established categories of race, religion and culture. Rastafarians and other cultural groups, as well as non-ethnic religious minorities, are an example of this category. Second, there is the treatement of asylum seekers and refugees. Once we accept that race and racism are socially constructed rather than essentialist concepts, it becomes easier to accept that new forms of racism can emerge as a result of social change. Racism, on this analysis, refers to a process rather than a present state of affairs: i.e. specific forms of racism can emerge out of changing social, economic and political contexts.[142]

In this way, the process of racialisation can enable new ideas about race to enter the existing system. In some cases, these new ideas may overlap with existing ideas about race; whilst in other cases they may displace established categories. Once racialisation is treated as an ongoing process it also becomes important to investigate the way in which legal regulation and the priority given to one criterion (e.g. colour) may lead to a shift in the form of racism rather than its elimination. So, for example, although discrimination on the ground of colour or ethnicity may be unlawful, similar practices may still operate in relation to other types of social group. In deciding whether a new "criterion" should be recognised as the source of the racialisation of a group, e.g being a refugee, there are a number of questions that need to be asked. These include, inter alia: (a) does the criterion allow ease of identification of the individual; (b) does the criterion rely on a relatively stable characteristic or "difference" which allows the group to be distinguished from other social groups; and (c) what is the social significance of this attribution. This analysis pays greater attention to the precise ways in which "difference" becomes significant and is deployed within a process of racialisation. Difference can sometimes operate as a foundation and justification for knowledge, and as a means of normalising some forms of knowledge; and also simultaneously

142 See for example, Howard Winant: "Theoretical Status of the Concept of Race", In Les Black and John Solomos (eds), *Theories of Race and Racism: A Reader* (London: Routledge, 2000); Glenn Loury, *The Anatomy of Racial Inequality* (Cambs, Mass: Harvard Univesity Press, 2002); and Ron Mallon: "Race: Normative, Not Metaphysical or Semantic" (2006) 116 Ethics 525 at 550–551.

pathologises other forms of knowledge and ways of being. David Theo Goldberg has commented on this relationship between racialised difference and knowledge. He observes:

"This phenomenon has no doubt been facilitated by the definitive importance of difference in modernity's development of knowledge. [...] Racial knowledge consists ex hypothesi in the making of difference; it is in a sense and praadoxically the assumption and paradigmatic establishment of difference. An epistemology so basically driven by difference will 'naturally' find racialised thinking comfortable; it will (uncritically) come to assume racial knowledge as given."[143]

As the Goldberg quote makes clear, "knowledge" is taken to racialise difference; and also to make this racialised difference appear to be the natural and neutral truth about the social world. This tendency makes it especially important to be vigilant about the fact that not only well established minorities but also newer social groups will be at risk of being "racialised". The key point is that this process of racialisation can continue to evolve as a way of dividing individuals into groups on the basis of a social difference; and this process also allows racism to function as the basis for detrimental treatment or withholding respect. This process of "racialisation" has, inter alia, two significant aspects. First, racialisation occurs when individuals and groups draw on certain evolving ideas about race in their interpretation of other individuals, groups and the social world. Second, it can also reflect and influence structural changes: as social practices and social institutions increasingly start to reflect and operate on the basis of these new race ideas.[144]

Therefore, "racialisation" as a process can operate to create new social groups which may require protection under race discrimination law. The role of "monopolistic observers" (i.e. those with considerable power in sending out signals that influence public perceptions about social facts) such as the state and the media play a key role in this process of racialisation. As Glenn Loury has argued, the classification of an individual as a member of a group can, and does, have normative consequences. In some cases those who classify individuals into groups, for example the state/public bodies and the media, may have a greater power to influence social attitudes than private individuals. This makes it especially important that the state, its representatives and public institutions are not involved in processes of racialisation which can exacerbate racism. This provides some of the justifications for the special duties that legislation such as the Race Relations Amendment Act (2000) places on public bodies. In addition, it is also worth considering the considerable benefits of

143 David Theo Goldberg, "Racial Knowledge", In Les Black and John Solomos (eds), *Theories of Race and Racism: A Reader* (London: Routledge, 2000).

144 Bob Carter, *Realism and Racism: Concepts of Race in Sociological Research* (Routledge: London, 2000) at p.90–91.

using public campaigns in the media to disrupt racialisation processes before they harden into racist ideas and attitudes.

A. *"Racial Equality", Cultural Racism and Diversity*

In this section we explore the way in which the *Mandla* test can be applied to social groups that are distinct because of an overlapping set of factors: ethnicity, colour, culture and religion. *Mandla* concerned a Sikh boy and affirmed that where there was an overlap between ethnicity and religion the RRA would apply. Therefore, groups such as Sikhs and Jews[145] would clearly be covered. *Dawkins* confirmed, however, that this latitude and extended definition of race would not cover non-ethnic religious minorities. Not only smaller Christian minorities but also all those religions that were not able to show some link with the factors set out in *Mandla* would, therefore, fall outside the defintion of race. In *Dawkins* itself this extended to Rastafarians and subsequent case law has confirmed that this also applies to Muslims. Specific issues relating to religious discrimination are dealt with in Chapter 13. Here it is worth noting that this approach creates a sharp dichotomy between race, ethnicity and culture on the one hand, and religion on the other. In these circumstances, it may be appropriate to use a term such as *"racial equality"* to capture the wider range of criteria that are relevant for analysis and which overlap: race, ethnicity, religion, culture, national origin, and language. Once we move away from essentialist notions of race arguments towards a more complex definition of this type, this conclusion becomes difficult to resist. The fact that there may be a substantial overlap between these categories and that it is difficult to separate out grounds such as race, culture and religion makes it problematic to use such distinctions in a strict way as the basis for the allocation of important rights and protection in discrimination law and policy. A provision which includes both race and religion in its list of prohibited grounds bypasses this problem.[146] For example, Title VII of the Civil Rights Act lists the prohibited grounds as "race, color, religion, sex or national origin"; and s.15 of the Canadian Charter that has a more expansive list of prohibited grounds including race and religion. The boundaries between race, culture and religion (and ethnic and non-ethnic religious minorities) have also become more fluid in the government's strategy for dealing with racial equality and community cohesion. This current strategy acknowledges the way in which diversity is becoming more complex, and the overlap between race, religion and a range of cultures are becoming aspects of the more broad category

[145] *Seide v Gillette Industries Ltd* [1980] I.R.L.R. 427 (EAT).
[146] Now codified in s.703(m), 42 U.S. C., para.2000e–2(m) (2000).

"racial equality".[147] Domestic discrimination law, however, fails to recognise the continuity between race, culture and religion as overlapping criteria in a more general process of racialisation. Moreover, the present structure of the law exacerbates problems because there are different levels of protection relating to race as compared with religion. The distinction between ethnic and non-ethnic religious minorities creates a situation in which some religious minorities (Sikhs and Jews) are covered by the full protection of race discrimination legislation whereas others (Rastafarians and Muslims) are not. This difference may have serious consequences for litigants. Where there is an overlap between race (narrowly defined under *Mandla*) and religion there could be a claim for indirect race discrimination. For example, a Rastafarian could bring a claim for indirect discrimination because a particular requirement or condition has a disproportionate impact on African-Carribean workers. However, there are disadvantages to such a strategy. Most obviously, it is far easier to establish direct rather than indirect discrimination. Moreover, where the majority of the workforce is not of the same racial group as a particular individual who has suffered racism as a result of an overlapping set of factors such as race, culture and religion, it may be difficult to establish that a recognised legal category of discrimination is in play. For example, in an international context in which terrorism, violence and Islam are often conflated. There is also increasing evidence of prejudice against individuals because they are Muslims rather than because they are Asian, Pakistani or Bangladeshi.[148] This anti-Muslim prejudice can be seen to operate in an overlapping way which draws on a range of characteristics: race, religion and culture. Anti-Muslim prejudice has been described as a form of "cultural racism"[149] and it is discussed in more detail below. Moreover, if we accept that race is a set of ideas and a process rather than something linked to biology or colour then the term "racism" can be legitimately applied to this type of discrimination.

This problem has been partially addressed by the introduction of legislation prohibiting religious discrimination in employment and training. However, the difference in the treatment of ethnic and non-ethnic religious minorities remains significant. Race still has more extensive coverage than religion in areas such as the RRAmnd Act 2000 and in the availability of non-legal

[147] "Improving Opportunity: The Government's strategy to increase racial equality and community cohesion", (Home Office: London, 2005) available at *http://www.homeoffice.gov.uk* (accessed November 10, 2005).

[148] See for example the results of the latest survey on prejudice against social groups in contemporary Britain. The survey confirms that the highest levels of prejudice are against (a) Muslims and (b) gays and lesbians. See Dominic Abrams and Diane M. Houston, "Equality, Diversity and Prejudice in Britain", Report for the Cabinet Office Equalities Review 2006, Centre for the Study of Group Processes, (Kent: University of Kent, 2006).

[149] Tariq Madood, *Multicultural Politics: Racism, Ethnicity and Muslims in Britain* (Edinburgh University Press, 2005) at Ch.1.

mainstreaming measures, for example in the civil service.[150] This anomaly creates a potential source of tension between different minorities who enjoy differential levels of protection, and also between the state and non-ethnic religious minorities who feel that they are not being fully protected recognised in the public sphere. On the other hand, it could be argued that there are distinct features of religion that make it a distinct ground of protection. Despite the overlap between race and religion the separation of these two concepts can be justified because religious discrimination takes a distinct form. These issues are discussed further in Chapter 13. Here, it is worth observing that there will be many cases where there is a significant overlap between the prohibited grounds, and in these cases distinguishing between race, culture and religion may cause difficulties. The difficulty of isolating religion from race and culture is also confirmed by observations in the Fourth National Survey of Ethnic Minorities which states "Religion is perhaps the key area where the minority groups manifest a cultural dynamic which is at least partly at odds with native British trend"[151]

1. Cultural Racism

One way in which the overlap between race, culture and religion can be intelligently understood is by recognising the distinct nature of "cultural racism". The increasing recognition of the socially constructed nature of race, and the increasing assertiveness of the demands of minority cultures for recognition, have led some commentators to argue that racism needs to be applied in a wider context to include the concept of "cultural racism".[152] This shift in analysis is important because it may assist in filling some of the gaps left over by existing legal interpretations of the term race. For example, once the wider defintion of race is adopted to include cultures which can change over a period of time, it becomes easier to argue that the emergence of "racial groups" within discrimination law is a dynamic process. Groups, such as Rastafarians who are a sub-group with a more recent history, can more easily bring themselves within this analysis. As a general matter, both race and religion overlap to form distinct cultural practices and groups. There is a complex overlap between these different factors, so that they cannot be reduced to either colour, ethnicity or nationality (in the case of race) or aspects of belief and religious practice (in the case of religion). Commentators have argued that increased contemporary migration (rather than merely a history of past immigration and the presence of established immigrant groups) makes

[150] For a list of policies on diversity in the Civil Service which use the category "black and minority ethnic" as the protected group see *http://www.civilservice.gov.uk/diversity/* (accessed on November 10, 2006)

[151] T. Modood, R. Berthod, et al, *Ethnic Minorities in Britain: Diversity and Disadvantage, The Fourth National Survy of Ethnic Minorities* (Policy Studies Institute: London, 1997).

[152] See for example T. Modood, *Multicultural Politics: Racism, Ethnicity and Muslims in Britain* (Edinburgh: Edinburgh University Press, 2005), especially Chs 1–2.

cultural diversity a critical issue for discrimination law.[153] It is also significant that, as well as containing provisions on non-discrimination, the EU Charter of Fundamental Rights affirms that "The Union shall respect cultural, religious and linguistic diversity." (Art.22).[154]

There is no easy solution to defining "what is culture". One way of approaching a definition of culture is to take a purely external and descriptive approach. This would outline some key markers that allow the identification of a group of practices as a particular culture: for example, inter alia, the rules passed on by one generation to another; pooled learning of a group; and learned behaviour. This descriptive approach, however, fails to capture the significance of culture from the perspective of an insider. One leading anthropologist, Clifford Geertz, makes the following observations in support of an analysis of culture that takes up some aspects of its "significance" for insiders:

Clifford Geertz, *The Interpretation of Cultures* London (Fontana Press, 1993)

pp.4–11: "The concept of culture I espouse [. . .] is essentially a semiotic one. Believing, with Max Weber, that man is an animal suspended in webs of significance he himself has spun, I take culture to be those webs, and the analysis of it to be therefore not an experimental science in search of law but an interpretative one in search of meaning. It is explication I am after, construing social expressions on their surface enigmatical. [. . .]"

This issue has taken on special importance because of the contemporary concern with multiculturalism as both an empirical statement (i.e. about the fact that contemporary societies are composed of a diversity of cultures) and a normative statement (i.e. that liberal democracies should adopt multiculturalism as their preferred ethical and political response to this social fact).[155] It is worth noting that, as the Geertz passage indicates, there is no magical or fixed meaning to social groups and practices that is amenable to being defined as a "culture".

One consequence of accepting that the definition of race under the RRA may also include culture, is that the protection of cultures can lead to a conflict with some of the central goals of discrimination law. One commentator discusses this issue in the following terms:

153 Satvinder Juss, "Free Movement and the World Order", (2004) 16 International J. of Refugee L., 3 289–335, at pp.332–335.

154 See also for example the South African Constitution 1996 which protects cultural, religious and linguistic communities, s.33(1).

155 For selected readings on multiculturalism see C. Taylor, *Multiculturalism* (Princeton University Press: Princeton, N.J. 1995); and W. Kymlicka (ed.), *The Rights of Minority Cultures* (Oxford: Oxford University Press, 1995)).

Seyla Benhabib, The Claims of Culture: Equality and Diversity in the Global Era (Princeton University Press: Princeton, N.J., 2003)

p.3–4: "Whether in politics or in policy, in courts or in the media, one assumes that each human group "has" some kind of "culture" and that the boundaries between these groups and the contours of their cultures are specifiable and relatively easy to depict. Above all, we are told, it is good to preserve and protect such cultural differences. Conservatives argue that cultures should be preserved in order to keep groups separate, because cultural hybridity generates conflict and instablity: they hope to avoid the "clash of civilisations" by reinforcing political alliances that closely follow cultural-identity rifts [...], lest attempts to bridge these rifts produce hybridity and confusion. Progressives, by contrast, claim that cultures should be preserved in order to rectify patterns of domination and symbolic injury involving the misrecognition and oppression of some cultures by others.

Whether conservative or progressive, such attempts share faulty epistemic premises: (1) that cultures are clearly delineable wholes; (2) that cultures are congruent with population groups and that a noncontroversial description of the culture of a human group is possible; and (3) that even if cultures and groups do not stand in one-to-one correspondence, even if there is more than one culture within a human group and more than one group that may possess the same cultural traits, this poses no important problems for politics or policy. These assumptions form what I will call the "reductionist sociology of culture". In the words of Terence Turner, such a view "risks essentialising the idea of culture as the property of an ethnic group or race; it risks reifying cultures as separate entities by overemphasizing their boundedness and distinctness; it risks overemphasizing the internal homogeneity of cultures in terms that potentially legitimize repressive demands for communal conformity; and by treating cultures as badges of group identity, it tends to fetishize them in ways that puts them beyond the reach of critical analysis".

The use of discrimination law to protect culture also raises the spectre of a conflict between different grounds of discrimination. This is a particular risk in cases where the culture defines itself by reference to illiberal and discriminatory practices: e.g. the culture does not grant equal rights to women or excludes members on the ground of their sexual orientation. This "conflict of rights" issue is discussed in more detail in Chapter 9. Nevertheless, it remains important to examine the role of culture in producing racism, as well as discussing how discrimination law should respond to "cultural racism". It is worth first setting out a definition of cultural racism and then examining the way in which the process of cultural racism may operate against a social group.

Tariq Modood
Multicultural Politics
USA: University of Minnesota Press, 2005

pp.38–39: "Having anything but a European physical appearance may be enough in contemporary European societies to make one a possible object of racist treatment (not that only European socieites can be racists . . .). But such phenotypical racism can also be the foundation for a more complex form of racism. I am not, however, arguing that wherever there is biological racism there must be cultural racism too, or that cultural exclusionism occurs only in the context of racism or should be relabeled as "racism". Ethnic hierarchies and religious discrimination, for example, can and do exist in all-white or all-black societies—in societies where groups are not differentiated by physical appearance. My argument is that racialised groups that have distinctive cultural identities or a community life identified as "alien", will suffer an additional dimension of discrimination and prejudice. The hostility against the non-white minority is likely to be particularly sharp if the minority is sufficiently numerous to reproduce itself as a community and has a distinctive and cohesive value system that can be perceived as an alternative, and a possible challenge, to the norm. It is particularly important to recognise that racism constitutes opposition to, discrimination against, not just individuals but, above all, communities or groups. Racism normally makes a linkage between a difference in physical appearance and a (perceived) difference in group attitudes and behavior. In contemporary settings the linkage is not usually crudely genetic or biological but is likely to rest on history, social structure, group normative values, and cultures. The causal linkage is unlikely to be perceived as scientific or determining but as probabalisitc and therefore allowing exceptions. [. . .] Cultural racism is likely to be particularly aggressive against those minority communities that want to maintain, and not just defensively, some of the basic elements of their culture or religion and if, far from denying their difference (beyond the colour of their skin), they want to assert this difference in public and demand that they be respected just as they are. [. . .]

pp.44–45 There may be only a contingent, matter-of-fact connection between color prejudice and cultural prejudice, true for only certain times and places; nevertheless, when the two kinds of exculsionism and oppression come together, we have a distinctive phenomenon worthy of its name and conceptualization. In this conceptualization, far from obscuring racism we learn something about it: contrary to just about everybody who writes about racism, including those who emphasise the specificities of different kinds of racisms and their articulations with nation, gender, class, and so on [. . .] contemporary British racism is not dependent on any (even unstated) form of biological determinism. True, there is always some reference to differences in physical appearances and/or legacy of the racism of earlier centuries, but the reference is not necessarily to a deep biology; minor phenotypical differences are all that is required to mark out racial groups, to stereotype them, and to treat them accordingly. Being able to pick out individuals on the basis of their physical appearance and to assign them to a racial group may be an essential aspect of the definition of racism, but physical appearance stands as a marker for race, not the explanation of a group's behavior. Racists impute inferiority, undesirability, distinctive behavioral traits, and so on to a group distinguished by their appearance, but this does not imply an assumption on their part that the behavioral qualities are produced by biology rather than by history, culure, upbringing, or by certain norms or their absence. In the extreme case, cultural racism, as I have argued, does not necessarily hinge on color racism, merely color racism *at the point* of cultural racism."

A strict distinction between race, religion and culture also under-estimates the extent to which certain ideas can operate simultaneously within different categories (such as race, culture and religion) and yet, at the same time, still racialise individuals and groups in a similar way. Moreover, race as a process can lead to the transfer of ideas from previously racialised groups to new racialised groups. One important historical precedent for current processes of racialisation of minorities is the treatment of Jews in England who are one of earliest racial and religious minority in Britian. As Didi Herman has noted this precedent is critical in understand the way in which processes of racialisation of minorities are tranferred rather than extinguished. Herman writes:

"However, given Jews were amongst the earliest 'raced' peoples in England, there is a debt that all contemporary racialisation processes owe to these earlier ones that has remained largely unexplored, and that is not adequately accounted for in work that roots 'race' or 'strangers' or 'alterity and difference' in imperial and colonial projects."[156]

It is noteworthy, for example, that a recurrent stereotype about Jews in the period 1910–1940 in the East End of London was their alleged attachment to a religious text (the Old Testament) and foreign law (the Talmud) which would result in their following "barbaric customs" about diet, slaughter of animals and with regard to the status and treatment of women. Didi Herman notes that:

"in relation to Jews and Jewishness, understandings of race were also complicated by a traditional Christian ideology identifying Jews as the 'people' of the 'Old Testament'."[157]

Similar processes and trends can be observed in the context of Muslim minorities today, especially after the incidents of September 11, 2001 and July 7, 2005: namely assumptions that Muslims in Britains are necessarily

[156] See Didi Herman, "An Unfortunate Coincidence": Jews and Jewishness in 20th century English Judicial Discourse." (2006) 33 Journal of Law and Society 2, 277–301.
[157] *ibid.*, at p.284.

unassimilable as a group because of their religious attachment to a scriptural text (the Quran) and foreign law (the Shariah).[158]

Pnina Webner has argued that there are three specific tropes that are deployed in the contemporary racialisation of Muslims. First, they are racialised like other "colonised persons" as disobedient slaves when they resist the power of the majority. Second, like some minorities such as the Chinese and Jews, Webner argues that Muslims are sometimes treated as an "enemy within" whose difference remains hidden but can emerge at times of conflict. Finally, Muslims are treated as a distinctly aggressive "other" whenever they emerge into the public sphere to claim rights for accommodation of difference as "visible" Muslims. Webner concludes that in relation to Muslims:

"He [the Muslim] is a figure constructed by fearful elites, which may nevertheless legitimise far cruder forms of biological racism. Anti-fundamentalist images provide these racists with a legitimising discourse against Muslims, [...] What we have, then, uniquely in the case of the representations of contemporary Islam in the media and the public sphere, is an oppositional hegemonic bloc which includes intellectual elites as well as 'real' violent racists."[159]

Webner also writes that "these prejudices about Islam can also recur in discussions about, and in defense of, secularism in liberal democracies"[160] It is worth emphasising this last point because it maps on to a long established construction of Islam as a threat to Western civilisation, which can also be found in medieval discussions. The writer of a study on the representation of Islam in the West, Norman Daniels, has noted that these medieval tropes about Islam from the past continue to haunt Europeans in the present. Daniels concludes that:

158 The representation of this issue in the press is especially significant. There are different ways in which the issue of "religious law" can be presented in the mainstream media. See for examples headlines in a number of newspapers during this period including *The Sunday Telegraph* of February 24, 2006, "Poll reveals 40% of Muslims want sharia law in UK". That analysis fails to distinguish between those legal principles within the shariah which are entirely compatible with existing British law and liberal democracy (e.g. laws of contract, wills, family law and some aspects of the criminal law) and those that are incompatible such as criminal sentencing. A more complex treatment of this issue can be found in *The Guardian*, "British Muslims want Islamic law and prayers at work" by Alan Travis and Madeleine Bunting, Tuesday, November 30, 2004. That commentary makes clear that although Muslims want to be governed by the shariah where it does not contradict British law, they also want integration into mainstream British society: "Muslims in Britain want greater recognition of their faith with the introduction of Islamic law for civil cases and time off for prayers during the working day, but are equally committed to greater participation in British life. A special Guardian/ICM poll based on a survey of 500 British Muslims found that a clear majority want Islamic law introduced into this country in civil cases relating to their own community. Some 61% wanted Islamic courts—operating on sharia principles—"so long as the penalties did not contravene British law".

159 Pnina Webner, "Islamophobia: Incitement to Religious Hatred—Legislating for a New Fear" 21(1) (February 2005) Anthropology Today 5–9.

160 *ibid.*, at p.8.

"Most recently we have seen the application of still newer methods by men of a particular mental or scholastic discipline, such brilliantly effective scholars as Maxine Rodinson and Jacques Berquem both writing in the shadow of colonialism, conscious of it and sensitive to Muslim feeling. [...] Although I personally believe in the 'scientific' historical ideal of objectivity, I think it certain that it has been infiltrated by subjective ideas of cultural, political and social prejudice. [...] For us the chief lesson may be that 'scientific methodology' never did truly escape from its bundle of inherited prejudices of all kinds."[161]

2. The Retreat from Multiculturalism

It now seems apparent that in Britain on response to the July 7 London bombings by British-born extremists was a "retreat from multiculturism", something which was also evident in[162] the debate about the full facial veil in Britain in October 2007.[163] Although leading politicians and public figures are now leading the field as critics of multiculturalism and reviving the debate

[161] Norman Daniel, *Islam and the West: The Making of an Image* (Oneworld Publications: Oxford, 1993) at p.324.

[162] See Tariq Modood's summary of the post July 7 critique of British multiculturalism in his article "Remaking Multiculturalism after 7/7" Opendemocracy, October 29, 2005: "To take just four examples from a waterfall of commentary over the last ten-to-twelve weeks:

- William Pfaff states that "these British bombers are a consequence of a misguided and catastrophic pursuit of multiculturalism" ("A monster of our own making", *Observer* August 21, 2005)
- Gilles Kepel observes that the bombers "were the children of Britain's own multicultural society" and that the bombings have "smashed" the implicit social consensus that produced multiculturalism "to smithereens" ("Europe's answer to Londonistan", openDemocracy, 24 August 2005)
- Martin Wolf concludes that multiculturalism's departure from the core political values that must underpin Britain's community "is dangerous because it destroys political community ... (and) demeaning because it devalues citizenship. In this sense, at least, multiculturalism must be discarded as nonsense" ("When multiculturalism is a nonsense", *Financial Times*, 31 August 2005)
- Trevor Phillips questions, in the context of a speech concerned with "a society ... becoming more divided by race and religion", an "'anything goes' multiculturalism ... which leads to deeper division and inequality ... In recent years we've focused far too much on the 'multi' and not enough on the common culture." ("After 7/7: Sleepwalking to segregation", Commission for Racial Equality, September 22, 2005).

Even those who don't directly regard multiculturalism as the cause of the bombings tend to believe that we need to review the concept, often concluding that it needs to be replaced by "integration". Indeed, this current of thinking predates 7/7 (and, for that matter, 9/11); it became prominent with David Blunkett's arrival at Britain's Home Office in June 2001 and his response to the riots in some northern English cities in the early summer that year"

[163] For a discussion of these issues see Jack Straw, "I felt Uneasy Talking to Someone I Could Not See" the letter of the Right Honourable Jack Straw M. P. which raised the issue of full facial veils, *The Guardian* published on October 6, 2006 at *http://www.guardian.co.uk/commentisfree/story/01889081,00.html* (accessed on October 20, 2006). For media commentary: in favour of Jack Straw see Yasmin Alibhai Brown, "Its not illiberal for liberal socieites to disapprove of the veil", *Time Europe Magazine*, October 16, 2006; against Jack Straw see Madeleine Bunting, "Jack Straw has unleashed a storm of prejudice and intensified division", *The Guardian*, Monday October 9, 2006.

about "Britishness" as a bulwark against security risks, two public thinkers in this field have by contrast suggested that the appropriate State response to the new security risks from extremism therefore is more rather than less multiculturalism and its liberal pluralist variants. Modood concludes that:

"Ideological and violent extremism is indeed undermining the conditions and hopes for multiculturalism but, contrary to the multiculturalism blamers, this extremism has nothing to do with the promotion of multiculturalism but is coming into the domestic arena from the international. The government having created extremism through its foreign policies, by blaming multiculturalism and the Muslims community for the crisis, is losing one sure resource that is necessary for a long-term victory over domestic terrorism: namely, the full active 'on-side co-operation' of the Muslim communities."[164]

On the issue of replacing diversity with a more homogenous public culture John Gray also concludes:

"The attempt to create a liberal monoculture, which many commentators have urged, founders on the fact of diversity. The fantasy of a morally cohesive society has inspired some of the worst types of repression. It is ironic that a panicky reaction against the idea of multiculturalism should have engendered a liberal variant of this dream. The reality is that we cannot hope to share many of our fundamental values. But we can still rub along together, if we can relearn the habit of tolerance."[165]

A further point is that an approach that treats "religion" as an essential category and focuses on individual religious discrimination risks creating "communalism" through law and social policy. It is argued that the priority given to certain characteristics, e.g. a religion, within law and the public sphere tends to "freeze" these categories. This process of "reification" of religion puts the category beyond critical discussion and re-negotiation by insiders and also outsiders to the religious group. In the context of race, treating race as an idea rather than a biological category may be one way of avoiding this trap. In the context of religion, similarly, a focus on social construction rather than essentialism can be an advantage. It means that the secular liberal concern with ensuring that religion does not become immune from criticism can be addressed. This alternative way of analysing religion within discrimination law avoids essentialising and reifying differences. This issue is discussed in more detail in the next chapter on religion.

This focus does not treat "religious identity" as a fixed category deserving legal protection and recognition per se. Rather, the key issue can be refor-

164 Tariq Modood, *Multiculturalism* (Cambridge: Policy Press, 2007), p.139.

165 John Gray, "Islam rejects the liberal consensus: the best we can hope for is tolerance", The Spectator, February 17, 2007.

mulated to focus on how the category "religion" is used to discriminate against individuals or disadvantage them in their access to key goods or social contexts.

This last point is also important because research suggests that problems faced by religious groups, especially minority religions, extend beyond employment, which is now regulated, and also include discrimination in accessing important public services such as education and health care.[166] One example of a gap in service provision which may result from a failure to recognise religion as a factor in addition to race arises in the case of those who are ethnic minorities within a religious group. This fact situation may, for example, arise where there are groups of converts to a non-ethnic religion such as Rastafarianism or Islam. On this view, what may therefore be required is a more expansive definition of racial equality that includes various emerging forms of racism. With this aim in mind Tariq Modood argues that:

Tariq Modood
Multicultural Politics
USA: University of Minnesota Press, 2005

pp.38–39, 42–45: "There is in racial discrimination and color racism quite clearly commonality of circumstances among people who are not white. It is partly what gives sense to the term "ethnic minorities" and to suggest for a "rainbow coalition" [. . .]. The question is not whether coalitional antiracism is desirable, but of what kind. My personal preference and commitment is for a plural politics that does not privilege color identities. We must accept what is important to people, and *we must be evenhanded between the different identity formations*. Political blackness is an important constituent of this pluarlism, but it can't be the overarching basis of unity. [. . .] A new public philosophy of racial equality and pluralism must aspire to bring into harmony the pluarlism and hybridity that exists on the ground, not to pit it against itself by insisting that some modes of collectivity trump all others. That was the error of British anti-racism of the 1980s."

Modood therefore suggests that it is possible to place emerging forms of prejudice within existing paradigms of racism, whilst acknowledging that these new emering forms of racism will be distinct in some ways. That new forms of racism are emerging is clear from the preliminary findings of Home Office Citizenship survey which confirms that 90 per cent of people agree that increased discrimination against Muslims is a problem: "almost anyone who named any group as experiencing more religious prejudice today was think-

[166] See Paul Weller, Alice Feldman and Kingsley Purdam, *Religious Discrimination in England and Wales*, (Home Office Research Study 220, Home Office Research, Development and Statistics Directorate, February 2001), at Chs 3–11.

ing about religious prejudice towards Muslims".[167] This perception is also confirmed more concretely in a Report for the Cabinet Office Equalities Review which concludes, inter alia that people are more likely to feel "hostile prejudice" towards Muslims; people feel least constrained about admitting prejudice about Muslims (and gays, lesbians and women); Muslims and Arabs are least likely to be assumed to fit in with the values of being "British"; Muslims are likely to be perceived as "cold, 'competing for resources'; Muslims are also more likely to evoke the emotional reactions of 'fear' and 'anger' rather than 'pity or envy'.[168]

B. *Asylum Seekers and Refugees*

The case of asylum seekers and refugees is another important example of racialisation. Historically, as we have seen immigration provided an important background to discussions of race in Britain especially in the post-World War II period. This concern with immigration continues to overlap with contemporary race discrimination legislation. Furthermore, the EU is increasingly involved with regulating asylum through law and policy.[169] In the EU context, asylum-seekers are dealt with, for example, indirectly through EU policy towards third country nationals (i.e., non-EU citizens) who are within the EU for the purposes of employment or family reunion or as refugees. In this section we consider in further detail issues posed for discrimination law by the law's treatment of asylum-seekers and refugees.

1. Nationality Discrimination

Nationality discrimination will have a clear impact on groups such as asylum seekers and refugees in so far as distinctions on the basis of nationality are permitted, state law and policy aimed at regulating asylum and immigration, raise the spectre of the racialisation of those who are perceived to be asylum seekers, refugees and immigrants.

EU law uses the distinction between EU nationals and third country nationals as an established category for analysis. Article 3(2) of the Race Equality Directive contains a specific exception for different treatment on the ground of nationality:

[167] Sarah Kitchen, Juliet Michaelson, Natasha Wood, "2005 Citizenship Survey: Race and Faith Topic Report", Department for Communities and Local Government' (DCLG), (London: DCLG Publications, June 2006).

[168] Dominic Abrams and Diane M. Houston, "Equality, Diversity and Prejudice in Britain: Results from the 2005 National Survey", Report for the Cabinet Office Equalities Review 2006, pp.11–16 (University of Kent: Centre for the Study of Group Processes, 2006).

[169] S. Arditti, R. Lewis and C. Manchip, *From Rome to The Hague: European Union Policy Making on Asylum* (IPPR: London, 2005).

"This Directive does not cover difference of treatment based on nationality and is without prejudice to provisions and conditions relating to the entry into and residence of third country nationals and stateless persons on the territory of Member States, and to any treatment which arises from the legal status of the third-country nationals and stateless persons concerned."

In domestic discrimination law in *Dhatt*, for example, discussed in the previous chapter in direct discrimination, the Court of Appeal held that distinctions between EU and non-EU nationals in employment were not race discrimination within RRA.[170] More specifically, the CA held that nationality was a "material difference" under s.3(4) RRA. This makes it permissible for nationality to be used as a criterion for distinguishing between individuals in a wide range of contexts even where this distinction would result in indirect race discrimination. Section 19D of the RRA explicitly excludes certain immigration and nationality functions from the duty on public bodies that was introduced by the RRAmnd 2000.[171] This exemption is subject to a monitoring provision, which is an interesting example of the way in which the possibility of the arbitrary abuse of exceptions can be minimised through administrative scrutiny. The Secretary of State can appoint an individual to monitor the operation of the exception in s.19D of the RRA. This monitoring function includes consideration of the likely effect on the operation of the exception and making an annual report to the Secretary of State that is laid before each House of Parliament.

2. Section 8 Asylum and Immigration Act 1996

Nationality is recognised as a valid ground for distinction, and it is also an important exception to the coverage of race discrimination legislation in both the EU and the UK in a number of additional ways. In the context of employment, s.8 of the Asylum and Immigration Act 1996[172] makes it an offence (resulting in a fine) to employ a person subject to immigration control where the individual has not been granted leave to enter or remain in the UK, and does not have valid or subsisting leave or is subject to a condition precluding employment. Employers have a defence in cases where they can show that they have complied with the requirements (e.g. in relation to documentary evidence of the employees's employment eligibility) which are specified by order of the Secretary of State, see ss.8(2) and 8(2)(A). The Immigration (Restriction on Employment Order) 2004[173] specifies some of the details of these conditions and the types of documents (e.g. UK passports; EC identity papers; work documents with National Insurance numbers along with

[170] [1991] I.C.R. 238 (CA).
[171] Section 19D RRA 76
[172] Asylum and Immigration Act 1996, C.49.
[173] SI 2004/755.

birth certificates) that fall within the s.8(2) defence. This provision was the subject of substantial criticism by academic commentators, the Commission for Racial Equality and the Better Regulation Taskforce. These critics argued that the provision would force employers to perform an immigration control function.[174] The government's response was to reiterate the importance of dealing with illegal working: "Experience suggests that Section 8 can be a valuable tool if targeted against unscrupulous or exploitative employers. Having looked very carefully at the way in which it is operating in practice, the Government has decided to retain s.8 to test its effectiveness in dealing with those who are engaging in systematic abuse. The proposals at cl.18 of the Immigration and Asylum Bill for a Statutory Code of Practice will increase safeguards against discrimination."[175] The Government introduced a Code of Practice (after consultation with the CRE) to address some of the concerns about the potentially discriminatory impact of s.8.[176] This sets out guidance as to how employers could comply with their s.8 duty whilst at the same time avoiding discrimination against employees. A breach of the Code of Practice can be taken into account in an action under the RRA. The Code of Practice's guidance focuses on integrating the need to check the eligibility for employment of the candidate and the need to check documents with good recruitment and interviewing practices more generally. The guidance includes, inter alia, advice that employers need only to keep copies of one of the specified documents rather than asking questions about immigration status in order to rely on the s.8(2) defence (para.23); and should ask for documents from all candidates in a uniform manner rather than selecting just one candidate for a request for documents (para.25).

Despite the safeguards introduced by the Code of Pratice, the CRE has argued that s.8 has encouraged race discrimination in employment:

[174] See for example B. Ryan, "Employer Enforcement of Immigration; Law after Section Eight of the Asylum and Immigration Act 1996" (1997) 26 Industrial L.J. 136–148; The Better Regulation Taskforce recommended repeal of s.8 in its review of anti-discrimination law, see Better Regulation Taskforce: Anti-Discrimination Law, at p.28, *http://www.brtf.gov.uk/docs/pdf/anti-disc.pdf* (accessed on November 10, 2005).

[175] Government Response to the Better Regulation Taskforce: Anti-Discrimination Law by Jack Cunningham on July 14, 1999, at *http://www.brtf.gov.uk/responses_new/antidiscriminationresponse.asp* (accessed on November 10, 2005).

[176] The Immigration (Restrictions on Employment) (Code of Practice) Order 2001 (SI 2001/1436).

Identity Cards Bill: CRE Briefing
House of Commons: Committee Stage
20 January 2005[177]

para.12: "In the UK context, the Commission has repeatedly expressed its concern that section 8 of the Asylum and Immigration Act 1996 might be causing discrimination inadvertently because employers, concerned only to employ staff with the right to work, were favouring EU nationals against non EU nationals, regardless of their right to work. These concerns are based on enquiries and complaints received by the Commission. For example:

- An employer queried whether she could continue to employ a Jamaican security guard who had been taken on 4 months before s.8 came into force, although he had been in the UK for 32 years and had produced a NI number and he still held a Jamaican passport.
- An agency employing temporary staff was unwilling to accept the NI number of a Bangladeshi and refused employment.
- A nursing agency persistently pursued Black African staff for unnecessary documentation."

The conclusions of the CRE about the link between s.8 and racial discrimination raise a key issue about the overlap between discrimination on the grounds of race and the increasing racialisation of refugees by the state through its law and policy on asylum and immigration. If it is argued that racism is now dependent on fixed definitions of racial groups, and that social change can also alter definitions of racisms, then the increasing racialisation of refugees might be said to have a number of features. At one level there is, as with non-ethnic religious minorities, an overlap between older and new categories of race. The established categories of colour, ethnicity, nationality and culture, which are the basis for racial discrimination, can also be applied to asylum seekers as a group, given that they can often be differentiated using these criteria by others and by themselves.[178] Very many asylum seekers and refugees will be easily identifiable because of characteristics such as their race, ethnicity, culture and national origin. This is borne out by the evidence relating to the countries of origin of these individuals. The ten main countries of origin of asylum seekers to Britain in the third quarter of 2004 were: Iran, China, Somalia, Zimbabwe, Iraq, Pakistan, Pakistan, Eriteria, India, Afghanistan and Sudan. There is also some evidence to support the conclusion that attitudes to asylum seekers and refugees are partly driven by established forms of racism: there is, for example, an increasing tendency for issues of asylum and racism to overlap in discussions; and an increasing use of racist language in discussions about asylum seekers.[179]

177 *http://www.cre.gov.uk/id_cards.doc* (accessed on November 10, 2005).
178 Sarah Kayambi, *Asylum in the UK: An IPPR Fact File* (IPPR: London, 2005), pp.10–12.
179 Miranda Lewis, *Asylum: Understanding Public Atttitudes* (IPPR: London, 2005) at p.40.

Emerging "race" ideas that stigmatise asylum seekers and refugees as a distinct group draw on two sets of assumptions: first, their association with crime; and second, that they are heavy users of economic resources. Crime is frequently cited as a reason to feel intimated by asylum seekers despite the absence of a clear empirical connection. There is also an increasing tendency to associate asylum seekers, and especially Muslims, with terrorism.[180]

Miranda Lewis, Asylum: Understanding Public Attitudes Institute for Public Policy Research, London 2005.

p.39: "Crime is another fear. Many white participants admitted to feeling afraid of visible minority ethnic groups. East European immigrants in particular were believed to be linked to prostitution and drugs. Some people felt that minority groups act in a deliberately threatening manner in order to intimidate others.

> *"When you have ethnic groups, the way they carry themselves, its threatening, they do it deliberately."* Male, ABC1, 25 to 50, Birmingham.

Others felt that the presence of non-white groups was in itself threatening. Increased global insecurity exacerbated this and Muslims, in particular, were associated with terrorism. In reality, very few participants mentioned personal experience of crime and none had been the victim of a crime committed by an asylum seeker. However, most were convinced that asylum seekers are heavily implicated in crime.

> *"Most of them have got a knife or blade. They're brought up different to us. These Muslims, you can't keep having them, who's to know these asylum seekers aren't terrorists?"* Male, C2DE, 25 to 50, Norwich.

Levels of recorded crime varied significantly between the areas where the research took place, and local concerns about crime informed fears about asylum seekers and crime. The local media played an important role in this. For example, in Birmingham there has been extensive coverage of various crimes (largely driven by offences) believed to be committed by asylum seekers. Participants from Birmingham frequently refer to these."

The assumption that asylum seekers and refugees cause economic and social problems may also result in prejudice and stereotypes. It is, for example, assumed that asylum seekers and refugees cause a negative economic impact; that they cause problems such as lack of affordable housing, pressure on health services and unemployment; and that they receive special benefits and preferential treatment. It is difficult when considering the racialisation of asylum seekers, to try to separate fact from perception.

[180] Miranda Lewis, *Asylum: Understanding Public Atttitudes* (IPPR: London, 2005) at p.39.

"There is considerable public concern about the impact of asylum seekers on access to resources. Expressing fears about economic competition allowed some people to justify racial prejudice in apparently rational terms. However many others were genuinely fearful of losing hard-won resources. [. . .] While the impact of asylum seekers upon these resources is hugely exaggerated in the public mind, inevitably there are actual impacts. The lack of honest discussion about this, together with the perceived inability of the elite to deal with the needs of vulnerable communities, has increased a deep well of public resentment. [. . .] Resentment over asylum seekers accessing services and jobs is exacerbated by a widely held belief that they, and other minority groups, are given preferential treatment and better benefits. Asylum seekers are widely believed to receive better welfare benefits than the white British-born population and to access the welfare system with greater ease."[181–182]

Government policy towards asylum seekers may well have reinforced this link by making access to state welfare benefits (and their withdrawal) conditional on compliance with asylum and immigration rules. The children's charity Barnardos has expressed concern that some government policies on asylum and immigration may breach the Children Act 1989 and the Human Rights Act 1998 (particularly the Convention Art.8 right to respect for private and family life).[183] There are concerns about the legal regime for the regulation of asylum encouraging racism against refugees. There are also, as Lewis notes in the passage above, genuine concerns about the allocation of scarce resources to asylum seekers and refugees. This suggests the need for open discussion to challenge misconceptions. There are also other policy initiatives that can be used to prevent or slow the racialisation of asylum seekers and refugees. Government could take a lead in a number of areas: discussing and affirming its international obligations to refugees; openly refuting inaccurate media accounts; taking political leadership concerning the rights of asylum seekers; and implementing policies for the stable integration of refugees through preparing local communities for new arrivals. Local government also has a key role to play in the integration of refugees with local communities, ensuring that accurate information about the economic resources available to refugees is made available to counteract misconceptions. Given the clear link between the treatment of asylum seekers and refugees and race discrimination, organisations such as the CEHR and trade unions also need to campaign around this

[181–182] Miranda Lewis, *Asylum: Understanding Public Atttitudes*, (IPPR: London, 2005) at p.27.

[183] Barnardo's Report: "The End of the Road: Families and Section 9 of the Asylum and Immigration (Treatement of Claimants) Act 2004 (available at *http://www.barnardos.org.uk/resources/research*, accessed November 10, 2004).

issue.[184] The media also have a special role to play in taking a more responsible role in its coverage of asylum and immigration issues.[185]

VI. Regulating Race Discrimination

We now turn to another question: what are the legal concepts that are available to intervene into process of racialisation to prevent, disrupt or reduce their impact on victims?

In the previous section we identified two themes particularly associated with responses to processes of racialisation. First, that the method for understanding race that is of most use in discrimination law and policy is one that treats race as a socially constructed concept, rather than as an essential biological category. Second, that it is important to identify how the idea of race is being used, i.e. what matters about the normative significance of race is how, and for what purpose, such a classification is made. As Ron Mallon concludes, what is normative about race as a concept is "how, when and where we decide to talk about it" and what really matters is "what [...] we want our racial concepts, terms and practices to do?"[186]

A. *If Race is Socially Constructed, is it still a Valid Category for Law and Policy?*

Even if race is understood as a socially constructed concept, it remains a relevant and crucial category for legal and political analysis. This point is made by Glenn Loury, who states that:

"'Race' is all about embodied social signification. In this sense, it is a *social truth* that race is quite real, despite what may be the *biologic—taxonomic truth* of the claim that there are no races. Recognizing this social truth is critical to the project of tackling race discrimination and achieving the aim of racial equality. For the social meaning imputed to race-symbols have had the profound, enduring, and all-too-real consequences—consequences due not to any race-dependent biological processes but rather to a sytem of race-dependent

[184] For a recent discussion of these issues see Miranda Lewis, Asylum: Understanding Public Attitudes, London: IPPR, 2005 at pp.49–58.

[185] Roy Greenslade, Seeking Scapegoats: The Coverage of Asylum in the UK Press, (London: IPPR, May 2005).

[186] Ron Mallon: "Race: Normative, Not Metaphysical or Semantic" (2006) 116 Ethics 525 at 550–551.

meanings, habitual social-significations, that can be more difficult to 'move' than that proverbial, all- too-material mountain."[187]

Loury's argument appears to be that ideas about race are a form of error in the social cognition of some individuals, which can lead to racial stereotypes or racial stigma coming into play and causing harm. In fact, Loury argues that his main focus is on social meanings rather than attitudes:

"specifically the meanings conveyed by race-related public actions and events. I am also invoking what might be called the 'etiquette of public discourse' or, [...] the 'boundaries of legitimacy' that constrain politicians when they formulate and justify the policies they advocate. I have in mind the unexamined beliefs that influence how the citizens understand and interpret the images they glean from the larger social world".[188]

Once race is seen as a system of ideas and as a social construct, rather than a biological concept, it is easier to analyse the treatment of "race ideas" in practice. "Race ideas" are used in different ways or contexts. In some cases, "race" is understood in terms of physical appearance and is involved in discrimination based on colour. In other cases, the subjects of exclusion or discrimination may be constructed as a racial group using categories such as "asylum-seeker" or "non-citizen". A non-biological approach to the term "race" can therefore include within the category of "race" groups such as refugees, as well as non-ethnic religious minorities who often straddle prohibited grounds of discrimination such as race and religion.

In the previous section, we saw how the social construction of "race" allows us to understand how some social groups become "racialised" over a period of time. This analysis also allows us to make distinctions between different uses of "race" in decision-making. For example, the goals of domestic race relations legislation are often presented as "community cohesion" or the more principled treatment of individuals. These goals are too general to provide a useful guide to how discrimination law should respond to the vast range of situations where "race ideas" are in play. Therefore, we need to ask further questions about how "race" operates. On the one hand, where an employer refuses to hire workers on the basis that their membership of a particular racial group makes them more likely to be dishonest, a conception of race is being used unjustly to demean the workers concerned, and the employer's refusal constitutes a paradigm example of morally reprehensible racial discrimination. On the other hand, the category "race" sometimes by contrast plays a useful role in devising workable solutions to problems of disadvantage. It can, for example, provide a basis (when tied to a suitable justification for legal inter-

[187] Glenn C. Loury, *The Anatomy of Racial Inequality* (Cambs, Mass: Harvard Univesity Press, 2002) at pp.58 and 70.

[188] *ibid.*, at p.71.

vention) for the use of positive action to promote training for members of racial groups which are not adequately represented in particular sectors of employment. In both situations, "race ideas" are involved at a foundational level: even though this is in a demeaning sense in the first situation, and in order to promote autonomy and respect in the second.

If race is understood as a socially constructed rather than a biological concept, its social meaning therefore varies depending on the context. Given this variety, it is important to examine the precise ways in which "race ideas" can cause harm, as well the optimal role for race discrimination law and policy. More specifically, we need to ask various further questions about the legal regulation of racism and racial disadvantage. For example, should there be, and if so at what stage, intervention through race discrimination law in a given situation? What form should this intervention take? What, if anything, is the role for extra-legal policy responses?

B. *Legal Regulation:*

1. Race in the public sphere

One of the reasons that race received special scrutiny under US and ECHR[189] discrimination provisions has been to prevent the social exclusion of discreet groups. These are "negative aspects" associated with the way in which racist attitudes can create feelings of exclusion. There is a also a more "positive" aspect of this debate which is about whether, and how, there can be a positive narrative for minorities in a nation state. A recurring feature of discussions about minorities in Britain has been the issue of "national belonging". In relation to new migrants, a related issue has been that those who are distinct on how the grounds of criteria such as colour, race, ethnicity, religion or culture can feel a sense of belonging to the political community. Traditional strategies of conservative nationalism that defined national belonging by reference to criteria such as race, common history or colour are arguably no longer a viable way of generating a "sense of belonging", because these criteria will necessarily exclude large number of citizens. It is increasingly argued that a sense of political community can be generated by ensuring that all citizens, and especially minorities, can identify with key national and legal institutions. In this context, there is an important role for discrimination law and policy in a number of respects. The following extract highlights some of these connections, especially in the context of race discrimination issues:

[189] Cases 43577/98 and 43579/98, *Nachova v Bulgaria*, decision of February 26, 2004, European Court of Human Rights.

Andrew Mason
"Political Community, Liberal Nationalism and the Ethics of Assimilation" (1999) 109 Ethics 261–286

"There are, in general, two related factors which can make it hard to achieve or sustain a widespread sense of belonging to a polity in the face of cultural diversity. First, when one or more of the culturally defined groups within it has suffered a history of oppression or unfair treatment in which the state is implicated. Groups in such a position are likely to find it difficult to identify with public institutions and practices if in the past they played a role in their oppression or unfair treatment, even if those institutions have now been reformed. Second, when the particular character of public institutions reflects the dominant culture. In these circumstances, it will be hard for those who are part of other cultural communities to feel at home in the polity, and in some cases their lack of a sense of belonging to it can lead them to demand to be allowed to secede. But neither of these general obstacles to a widespread sense of belonging provides grounds for assimilation policies, designed to promote a shared national identity. Instead they underline the importance of various forms of public recognition, and policies of accommodation, which I have described, and which do not aim at assimilation.

Conclusion

The main aim of this article has been to make plausible the idea that the various benefits which are thought to flow from a shared national identity, such as stability and a politics of the common good, might be secured by a sense of belonging to the polity in the absence of such an identity; and that even when the citizens of a liberal polity possess a sense of belonging together, it may be their sense of belonging to the polity which is the most important factor in explaining its stability and endurance.

Let me conclude by noting the obvious point that the problem of cultivating a sense of belonging has many dimensions to it: for example, those who are homeless or unemployed are likely to lack a sense of belonging to the polity even if they share the culture of a dominant group. My focus, however, has been the particular difficulties associated with fostering a sense of belonging that are created by the coexistence of cultural diversity of cultural communities. These difficulties can't be insulated from others: insofar as some cultural communities are constituted by members of particular races or ethnic groups who have been discriminated against, and perhaps continue to suffer discrimination, then it is unlikely to be cultural difference understood in isolation which makes it hard for them to feel they belong."

It might well be argued that accommodation of difference will require a reciprocal relationship, in which minorities will need to make compromises about some aspects of their culture given that not all of their demands can be accommodated within the public sphere, especially in the case of minorities whose values conflict with those which characterise a liberal state.[190] As public instititutions start to accommodate the most pressing needs of minorities, this will necessarily lead to a redistribution of social, economic and political power from majorities towards minority groups. Nevertheless, the fact that some social groups are in a permenant minority means that they will have diffi-

[190] For a discussion of the limits of accommodation see Sebastian Poulter, *Ethnicity, Law and Human Rights: The English Experience* (Oxford: Clarendon Press, 1998) at pp.22–37.

culties advancing their claims through political processes. However, there are advantages to the discussion of "accomodation of difference" issues through representative institutions because it allows majorities and minorities to reach a mutually agreed compromise without feeling that it has been forced on them by judicial decision. Moreover, representative institutions perform an invaluable function by involving a wide range of citizens in discussions about the appropriate needs of minorities and the wider public interest. In this way, points of conflicts between minorities and majorities can in fact be a catalyst towards public debate, participatory democarcy and the generation of a deeper identification of both minorities and majorities with the compromises required in "accommodation of differences".[191]

More specifically, a number of public institutions have started to devise policies that facilitate this process. There have also been arguments made about the inclusion of minorities in the political process.[192] In addition, the police force has made attempts to increase recruitment of ethnic minorities, especially since the Stephen Lawrence Inquiry: the Home Secretary's Action Plan gave priority to this issue, stating that its main aim was to restore "trust and confidence" in the police force and the criminal justice system. However, there are recurring problems especially with high profile allegations that there is a "racist culture" in the police force, which undermine these initiatives.[193] The Commissioner for the Metropolitan Police has conceded that there are difficulties with ethnic minority recruitment.[194]The government has recently reiterated its commitment to increasing diversity in the police force, as the following extract confirms:

House of Commons April 24, 2006
Hansard, Volume 445, Part No.139
Column 857WPolice (Ethnic Minorities)

Mr. Holloway: "To ask the Secretary of State for the Home Department what steps he is taking to increase the number of recruits from ethnic minorities into the police; whether a target has been set for the Metropolitan Police Service; and whether this target has been broken down by (a) ethnic and (b) other minority groups.

Hazel Blears: It remains the Government's policy that the composition of the police workforce should reflect the communities which it serves. The Police Service continues to

191 For a detailed discussion of these issues see Maleiha Malik, "Minority Protection and Human Rights" in Tom Campbell et al (eds), *Sceptical Essays on Human Rights* (Oxford: Clarendon Press, 2001).

192 See Rushanara Ali and Colm O'Cinneide, Our House? Race and Representation in British Politics, (IPPR: London 2002)

193 See for example Kamal Ahmad and Martin Bright, "New Storm Hits Police Over 'Racist Culture', *The Observer*, November 2, 2003.

194 Jason Benntto, "New Police Chief May Adopt Quota System for Ethnic Minority Recruits" (interview with Sir Ian Blair), *The Independent*, February 9, 2005.

make progress against the Home Secretary's recruitment targets for 2009, and all forces are committed to recruit from minority ethnic groups in proportion to, or at a level above, their representation in the local economically active population. Performance against this objective is a key performance indicator in the Policing Performance Assessment Framework.

The Home Office is working with the Police Service to accelerate the pace of change. The measures currently in hand include promoting the use of outreach workers in police forces, engagement with student faith societies and black students' unions to encourage applications from minority ethnic graduates and measures to increase minority ethnic applications to the High Potential Development Scheme. The Home Office has developed in collaboration with force recruitment departments materials aimed at increasing recruitment from minority ethnic groups, including multi-lingual recruitment material, a toolkit providing best practice guidance for familiarisation events and a video to familiarise applicants with police assessment and selection procedures.

In 1999, two per cent of police officers were from minority ethnic communities, the latest available figures show that at 31 March 2005 black and minority ethnic police officers made up 3.5 per cent. of total officer strength and that minority ethnic representation across the Service as a whole, including special constables and police staff, stood at 4.6 per cent.

The Home Secretary's Employment Targets which were published in 1999 set the Metropolitan Police a target of 25 per cent. ethnic minority representation within the force to be achieved by 2009. The latest available figures show that as at 31 March 2005; 7 per cent. of police officers (an increase from 3.3 per cent. in 1999), 20.8 per cent. of special constables (an increase from 13.9 per cent. in 1999) and 21.9 per cent. of police staff (an increase from 14.6 per cent. in 1999) within the Metropolitan Police were from ethnic minorities. The target set for the Metropolitan Police is based solely on ethnicity."

Similar priority has been given to increasing diversity in the judiciary, the army and the civil service. These types of initiative serve a key function: they ensure that minority concerns are able to enter the policy agenda of relevant organisations which are also then able to respond to minority needs. Also, minorities who see their members represented in public institutions will find it easier to identify with those institutions. This last point does not mean that there should necessarity be a shift towards "politics of presence" whereby it is assumed that only those from a certain racial group can represent the interests of that group. Rather, as Anne Phillips reiterates in her defence of the "politics of ideas", a balance could be struck between recognising that the focus of public representation should be on ideas and policies, and the notion that in some cases the presence of members of minorities can be a useful and creative vehicle for generating debate about appropriate substantive ideas and policies.[195] These arguments also justify the monitoring requirements of the Race Relations Amendment Act 2000 discussed in earlier chapters, which encourage the inclusion of minority representation in public sector employment.

A more complex approach to ensuring that minorities are full participants in the public sector is taken in government initiatives which use the full spectrum of policy levers: e.g ethnic monitoring; targets; equality goals; people's panels and performance indicators. A good example of this is the Home Office

[195] Anne Phillips, *The Politics of Presence* (Oxford: Oxford University Press, 1995) at 150–152.

initiative "Race Equality in Public Services" that sets out the goals and targets for key public organisations such as the criminal justice system, the prison services and the armed forces.[196] This type of approach is also able to use evidence from projects such as the Citizenship Survey which tracks the attitudes and feelings of minority groups in relation to key public services. The preliminary findings from The Citizenship Survey for 2005 suggest that there has been increase in the confidence that Black and Minority Ethnic (BME) groups have in key public service such as the criminal justice system, the police, education and housing.[197]

2. Criminal Law

The most serious forms of racism, namely those that cause the most serious harm to the victim, and those that are indicative of the most serious moral culpability and state of mind of the perpetrator, tend to be addressed via the criminal law. Concepts such as individual responsibility and causation become central when the criminal law is used to regulate race discrimination. The act of the individual, rather than achieving the goal of racial equality, takes on greater significance. Yet, at the same time, criminal law regulation of the most serious forms of racism is also part of the wider social goal: it can be understood as a choice of one amongst a range of legal techniques that are useful. Although civil law is the predominant choice for regulating race discrimination, it is significant that criminal law measures have recently been introduced to address some of its most invidious forms. There are two key areas in which the criminal law is used to regulate racism: hate speech and hate crimes. Significantly, the Crime and Disorder Act 1999 introduced racially aggravated offences that make the commission of certain criminal law offences (such as offences against the person and property and harassment) subject to a higher criminal penalty where these offences are committed with racial hostility.[198] Incitement to racial hatred has also been regulated via the Public Order Act. These are discussed in more detail in Chapter 8.

Hate crimes legislation is also now a well established feature of US and domestic criminal law, and this is also discussed in more detail in the chapter in Part B. The House of Lords continues to scruntinise EU proposals and has noted the difficulties in agreeing definitions, as well as the way in which criminal liability for racist speech needs to be balanced against concerns about freedom of speech.[199] Nonetheless, there has finally been political agreement at

196 "Race Equality in Public Services" (Home Office, London: Home Office, 2001).

197 Rachel Murphy, Elaine Wedlock and Jenny King, "Early Findings from the Home Office Citizenship Survey (2nd Edition), Home Office, On-line Report 49/05, (Home Office: London, 2005).

198 For a full discussion of these provisions see Maleiha Malik, "Racist Crime" (1999) 62(3) M.L.R. 409–424.

199 "The Proposed Framework Decision on Racism and Xenophobia—An Update" (2002–2003) House of Lords, 32nd Report, Select Committee on the EU, HL Paper 136.

EU level with the agreement of the EU Ministers of Justice in 2007 to implement a Framework Decision on combatting racism and xenophobia.[200]

There is a related issue of race discrimination in policing and criminal justice. The events surrounding the murder of Stephen Lawrence and police investigation, the subsequent Macpherson Enquiry report and the recommendations of the Home Secretary's Action Plan all gave priority to the reform of policing and the criminal justice system to prevent and eliminate race discrimination.[201] These recommendations include, inter alia: detailed reforms (with lead responsibility given to the Home Office and the police authorities) to restore trust and confidence in policing; and proposals for the Department of Education to introduce reform of education (via the national curriculum) aimed at valuing cultural diversity and preventing racism.[202]

3. Civil Law—Direct and Indirect Discrimination

The concept of direct discrimination has been discussed in Part B of the book. Here it is worth simply mentioning that in the context of race, the prohibition of direct race discrimination applies in the context of employment, provision of goods and services, education and housing. Racial harassment and victimisation are also prohibited, and instructions to discriminate fall within the defintion of direct race discrimination.

Indirect discrimination discussed in Chapters 2 and 5 raises difficult issues in the context of race discrimination. The need to establish the application of a "requirement and condition" in order to bring a claim under the RRA has been problematic. *Perera v Civil Service Commission & The Department of Customs & Excise*[203] limited the interpretation of a "requirement or condition", in an apparently inflexible way. Moreover, there may be difficulties in deciding which "racial group" is relevant as a comparator for the purpose of legislation and statistical comparison to establish disproportionality.[204] The problems

200 Proposal for a Council Framework Decision on combating racism and xenophobia. Official Journal C 075 E, 26/03/2002 P. 0269–0273. 28/11/2001. COM/2001/0664 final—CNS 2001/027028/11/2001. 52001PC0664.

201 Stephen Lawrence Inquiry: Home Secretary's Action Plan, available at *http://police.homeoffice.gov.uk/news-and-publications/publication/community-policing/* (accessed November 10, 2006).

202 For further discussion of race issues in the context of criminal justice and policing see Ben Bowling, *Racism, crime and justice* (London: Longman Criminology Series (with Coretta Phillips)) (2002) and *Violent Racism: Victimisation Policing and Social Context*, Clarendon Studies in Criminology (Oxford: Oxford University Press, 1998).

203 *Perera v The Civil Service Commission & The Department of Customs & Excise* [1983] I.C.R. 428.

204 In *British Medical Association v Chaudhary* [2007] I.R.L.R. 800, the Court of Appeal considered the issue of pools of comparison in an indirect race discrimination case. The case concerned an Asian doctor who was seeking the advice of the BMA about the racially discriminatory impact of a criterion for selection to a specialist post in the NHS. The Court of Appeal found that there was no disproportionate impact or indirect discrimination where the appropriate pool of comparison consisted of all members who wanted the advice and support of the BMA in relation to race discrimination claims, where no one member of the pool could comply with the conditions and criteria set by the BMA for such claims.

with using the concept of race, as well as the overlap between race, culture and religion, will also be problematic in this context. In some cases, for example, those involving converts into a particular religion or mixed race children, it will be impossible to delineate the precise racial group which is relevant to the analysis. In addition, there may be problems where there is variety within a racial group in terms of practices, e.g. where there are minorities within minorities. There are also distinct problems of multiple discrimination, intersectionaltiy and conflicts of rights, especially in the context of women (see further Chapter 9).

Significantly, "accommodation of difference" and rule exemption claims will be especially relevant in the context of indirect race discrimination. This issue is discussed in more detail in the next chapter where it is related to the discussion about religious discrimination and multiculturalism. Here it is worth observing that allowing a challenge to seemingly neutral rules and practices that have a disproportionate impact on minorities opens up the possibility of allowing rule exemption claims, i.e. allowing an exception from a general rule to accommodate the distinct needs of a member of a minority. Examples of rule exemption claims for racial groups may include, inter alia: claims by Sikhs in relation to "no turban" rules in schools, factories and in relation to motorcycles or health and safety at work; and claims by rastafarians in relation to a "no dreadlocks" rule.

One of the key issues in the context of indirect race discrimination will be the judicial interepretation of the "justifiability", "business necessity" or "proportionality" test. In *Panesar v Nestle Co Ltd* the Court of Appeal[205] had to consider the impact of a "no beard" rule on Sikh employees at a chocolate factory. They held that the employer had justified the rule which indirectly discriminated against Sikhs because it was required for "health and safety" reasons without any further analysis of whether there were alternative ways of achieving the "health and safety" objectives which would not have resulted in the exclusion of Sikhs. In *Ojutiku v Manpower Services Commission*,[206] a case under the RRA, the Court of Appeal moved further away from a strict "necessity" test by accepting that "reasonableness would be sufficient to justify indirect race discrimination. The practice that was challenged in *Ojutiku* was the requirement that candidates for student bursaries should have management experience, something which had a disproportionate impact on West African applicants. Lord Justice Eveleigh stated that:

"For myself, it would be enough simply to ask myself: is it justifiable? But if I have to give some explanation of my understanding of that word, I would turn to a dictionary definition which says 'to adduce adequate grounds for'; and it seems to me that if a person produces reasons for doing something, which

[205] *Panesar v Nestle Co Ltd* [1980] I.C.R. 144.
[206] *Ojitku v Manpower Services Commission* [1982] I.C.R. 661.

would be acceptable to right-thinking people as sound and tolerable reasons for so doing, then he has justified his conduct."[207]

The interpretation of "justifiability" by domestic courts has been developed in a number of cases.[208] The introduction of the Race Equality Direct means that indirect race discrimination must now be interpreted in the context of EU discrimination law which has a stricter test for "justifiability". The *Discrimination Law Review*[209] proposal to harmonise definitions of indirect discrimination to EU standards (of "provision criterion or practice" and "particular disadvantage") across all the prohibited grounds will ensure simplification and efficiency.[210] As discussed in the context of indirect sex discrimination, in Chapter 10, this reform is complemented by proposals to harmonise the test for "objective justification" in indirect discrimination cases. Unfortunately, the new test does not adopt the precise words in the EU directive which states "objectively justified by a legitimate aim and that the means of achieving that aim are appropriate and necessary".

4. Race Discrimination by Public Bodies

The arguments (considered above) about racialisation and the emergence of racial stereotypes in the private employment sector also apply, but arguably with greater force, to public bodies. For such bodies have even greater power to influence the creation of stereotypes than private actors, given their role and power in society. In short they can create "facts" about race. In Chapters 6 and 7 on positive action we saw that this justifies the different approach to regulating racial discrimination by the state or public bodies, as compared with that by private bodies or individuals. For example, in relation to public bodies there is a wider definition of "race discrimination" to include "institutional forms of discrimination" or remedial provisions that go beyond individual damages and include a positive duty to promote race equality (for example, in the Race Relations Amendment Act 2000).

5. Race and Positive (Affirmative) Action

Important legal and political issues follow from a recognition of the way in which race is constructed to produce stereotype and stigma for example, notions (such as race) race which are socially constructed and give rise to stereotypes can often seem to reflect the "natural" order of our social life

[207] *Ojitku v Manpower Services Commission* [1982] I.C.R. 661, at pp.667–8.

[208] In *Board of Governors of St Matthias Church of England School v Crizzle* [1993] I.C.R. 401 the EAT found that the restriction of a headteacher post to communicant Christians was justified although it was indirect discrimination against individuals such as the applicant who was Asian.

[209] *Discrimination Law Review* (London: Department for Government and Local Government, June 2007).

[210] *ibid.*, pp.37–41.

thereby reinforcing present social meanings. The fact that members of a racial group are concentrated in the lowest education indicator could—on this view—be seen to be indicative of their "essential" or "natural" lack of intelligence as compared with other groups. Such an analysis might well, however, miss the historical context within which the situation has arisen. Social interaction and human development can be influenced systematically by stereotypes and stigma giving rise to recurring patterns of structural injustice which cannot be fully addressed by the regulation of individual discriminatory acts in the present. In this context, some argue that positive action is essential to tackle structural discrimination (for discussion of which, see also Chapter 5, 6 and 7) but others object that this is itself discriminatory. As we saw, the mere fact of using race for classification purposes need not say anything about the normative significance of the classification. What matters about the normative significance of race is how, and for what purpose, such a classification is made. As Ron Mallon concludes in his race survey of the concept of race, what is normative about race as a concept is "how, when and where we decide to talk about it" and what really matters is "what do we want our racial concepts, terms and practices to do?"[211] One consequence of this approach to "race" which recognises that its normative meaning shifts depends on context is that it opens up the way to argue that there is a distinction between "racial discrimination" that uses race as the basis for differential treatment and stigma and "positive action on the basis of race" that is introduced to alleviate the problems of racism. This argument was discussed in detail in the chapter on justifying positive action in Part A of the book.

In the light of the available data concerning the social exclusion of ethnic minorities, and the disadvantages faced in education and employment, there may be a need to consider the contribution of appropriately designed positive action policies. In the view of recent researchers in the extract that follows, a combination of positive action policies and contract compliance can play an important role in reducing the "penalty" faced by minorities (racial and religious) in employment:

[211] Ron Mallon: "Race: Normative, Not Metaphysical or Semantic" (2006) 116 Ethics 525 at 550–551.

Dr Ravinder Singh Dhami, Professor Judith Squires and Professor Tariq Modood
Developing Positive Action Policies: Learning from the Experiences of Europe and North America Research Report No.406 (London: Department for Works and Pensions, 2006), pp.119–121

"*General Summary*

- Cheung and Heath conclude their cross-national comparative research into ethnic penalties with the following statement: "We did not intend this study to lead to specific policy recommendations. But one implication of our broadly pessimistic conclusion is that policy interventions will be needed to bring the reality of our liberal democracies closer to their professed ideals of equality of opportunity" (Cheung and Heath forthcoming). They suggested that this could take the form of the affirmative action legislation that has perhaps reduced ethno-religoius disadvantage in Northern Ireland. On the basis of our research, we would affirm their sense that affirmative action policies are needed. We would suggest that they might indeed take the form of the Northern Ireland legislation discussed in the report. We further suggest that these affirmative action policies might usefully take the form of the contract compliance policies adopted in the US and Canada at a federal level, and the covenant adopted in the Netherlands.
- **Political will.** The introduction of proactive equality instruments accompanied by the political will to bring about social change can have an observable impact on employment equality. But political will is needed to implement postive action effectively.
- **Liberal democratic rationale.** The rationale for the policies should appeal to an over-arching liberal democratic culture and respect for diversity and should be able to win broad support both amongst the targeted groups and their citizens rather than specific arguments based on group privelege.
- **Economic rationale.** The rationale for these policies should also embrace the business case for employment equity.
- **Public relations.** This rationale needs to be clearly articulated in a coherent communications strategy.
- **Statistical data.** Detailed statistical data is needed to pinpoint which group require positive action and to evaluate the impact of programmes that incorporate targets or timetables for such groups in quantiative terms.
- **Contract compliance.** The experience from the USA and, to a lesser extent, Canada suggests that contract compliance is an effective positive action policy, changing key employers' practices with minimum pain and resistance and resulting in improved employment and retention rates amongst large corporations.
- **Covenants.** The experience of the Netherlands suggests that small-scale direct approach adopted for the covenants that facilitate co-ordination between employers with vacancies and labour exchanges with access to ethnic minority job seekers can increase ethnic minority employment rates.
- **Enforcement mechanisms.** In addition to being clearly and coherently explained and defended, positive action policies need to be backed up by robust enforcement

mechanisms if employers are to comply. These should entail mandatory goal-setting and vigorous enforcement, including sanctions, by government.

- **Availability index.** The experience from the USA suggests that the creation of availabilities indices is an important mechanism for establishing who is qualified and potentially available for work.
- **Overseer.** The experiences of the USA and Canada suggest that the creation of an institution responsible for overseeing contract compliance programmes is crucial for the effective implementation of the policy.
- **Resources.** The implementation of a contract compliance programme needs to be well resourced.
- **Bureaucracy-light.** The policies also need to be bureaucracy-light if employers are to embrace the scheme with any degree of enthusiasm. Too much red-tape risks alienating employers. However, the production of statistical data and regular programme reviews are needed.
- **Review.** Positive action programmes should be regularly reviewed in relation to effectiveness, business efficiency and fairness.
- **Supply-side.** Ethnic minority education and job skills levels need to be addressed.
- **Religion.** Positive action programmes should consider both religious and ethnic minority equality measures.

The evidence from this research has shown that there can be clear benefits from a programme of positive action. Exisiting policy approaches have been limited in redressing ethnic penalties. In our view, a government committed to eradicating social exclusion can legitimately and confidently engage with an advanced programme of positive action, which includes contract compliance. The implementation of such a policy would send the right signal both to the intended beneficiaries and to those organisations and individuals that continue to deny ethnic groups and visible minorities their full part in the economic and social life of the country. As it is over four decades since the first Race Relations Act, and given that ethnic inequality continues to be a part of the social fabric of our country, the time is now right for such a step."

C. *Extra-Legal Intervention*

Extra-legal remedies also play an important role in combatting discrimination. Because of the significant difference between the social-economic position of racial minorities as compared with other protected groups, the use of supply side investment can be especially significant as a means of allowing structural problems of social exclusion, deprivation and disadvantage to be tackled in s systematic way. This type of investment prevents the development of entrenched disadvantage for certain social groups that may be difficult to tackle using individual litigation. In this way, preventative strategies can be successful in intervening in the process of racialisation before racist attitudes manifest themselves as prejudice, discrimination or criminal acts that can cause substantial harm. Reform of the education syllabus may also be important. For example, the Home Secretary's Action Plan following the Stephen Lawrence enquiry Recommendations for the reform was aimed at valuing cultural diversity and preventing racism. In addition, there are ways of building the self-esteem of children from minority groups by ensuring that the school curriculum reflects their personal experience, e.g. through foreign language teaching or geography classes that draw on the background of pupils.[212] Even in the case of hate crimes, there is evidence that preventative strategies can disrupt the process whereby racism in the wider "perpetrator community" is manifested as an individual crime, as illustrated by the work of Rae Sibbit.[213] It is worth examining in more detail the process that translates an error in cognition relating to race into a stereotype or basis for stigma. Social cognition depends on one's environment and relationships with others. One aspect of this is what Loury calls self-confirming stereotypes: it is by acting on the stereotypes over a period of time that individuals set into motion a series of events that have the effect of reinforcing their initial error of judgment. The qualities needed to question the stereotype include a willingness to stay open-minded and question the initial cognition. This last point is critical: we can interpret data and our social experience in a way that leaves our use of "race" in our analysis obscure even from ourselves. One solution to racism in personal attitudes are schemes such as the "Unity" community scheme instituted by Peterborough County Council which encouraged young people who were involved in racist violence to explore how much they had in common through personal interaction and contact. The details of the scheme, and the consequent personal tranformation of the two young men involved is set out in the article below:

How two racists faced each other in court, then shunned prejudice to become friends
Jonathan Brown, *The Independent*, London: September 9, 2006

"As teenage gang leaders Shaahid Latif and Ricki Elliot spent years fighting each other. The only thing they had in common was mutual hatred and the two young men, who hail from opposite sides of Peterborough's ethnic divide, eventually ended up in court.

Today, however, the once-sworn enemies are firm friends. Rather than scuffling in the city's shopping centre, or trading insults at nightclubs, they are more likely to be found chatting together about R "n" B or helping other young people turn their back on the prejudice which blighted their early lives.

"I was racist and so were they," says Ricki, 18, who hails from the white working class area of Raventhorpe. "I would say things like 'Paki, curry-muncher', he would say things

212 Stephen Lawrence Inquiry: Home Secretary's Action Plan, available at *http://police.-homeoffice.gov.uk/news-and-publications/publication/community-policing/* (accessed November 10, 2006).

213 Rae Sibbit, "The Perpetrators of Racial Violence and Racial Harassment" (1997) Home Office Research Study 176.

like 'White bastard', it just went on. We were racist to each other. It started off with fighting about certain causes and then ended up with gangs and then a big court case."

Shaahid, from Gladstone, the predominately Asian neighbourhood on the other side of the dual carriageway that divides the communities, remembers how the two youngsters would regularly clash. "Sometimes you would look at a person and know you don't like them. It was like there was any excuse to start up," he recalls. "I would look at him, there would be a few words exchanged like 'Who are you looking at?' or 'What's it got to do with you?' We were both really childish I think."

The tension eventually came to a head when Ricki was injured in a hammer attack. He accused Shaahid of taking part in the attack, although the young Asian was later acquitted.

At this point salvation was at hand in the guise of Peterborough City Council's pioneering Unity scheme. The two were sent away together to train as youth workers and discovered—much to their initial horror and surprise—that they actually liked each other.

"We were told we had to get along and we had to set an example," says Ricki. "We ended up sharing a hotel room, listening to music and talking all night. I learnt how to dance like him and, because I'm such a fussy eater, I found I preferred halal meat."

"You don't feel comfortable with someone because you don't know them," agrees Shaahid. "We found we had much more in common than we had differences."

The Unity scheme was established in Peterborough in the wake of the high-profile murder of Ross Parker, 17, who was stabbed to death with a foot-long hunting knife by three Asian men in what the trial judge at Cambridge Crown Court described as a "racist killing". Anxiety had been mounting in the area following the outbreak of racial tension in Bradford and Oldham in 2001, and some feared that Peterborough could be next.

The events of 11 September 2001 exacerbated the situation. While there had been an average of 190 complaints of racial harassment each year before the attacks, this soared to 340 in the 12 months afterwards.

Youth workers observed the conflict between the white youths of Westwood and Raventhorpe and the third-generation Pakistani youngsters of Gladstone, was getting worse. "These were working-class lads facing the same problems but living in parallel worlds," explains Javed Ahmed, manager at Peterborough Youth service.

"They have the same problems with friendships and family dynamics, issues of unemployment and training. They support the same football teams and listen to the same music."

The programme recruited young people to take part in the scheme, leaders with "street cred" among their peers, who had been involved in racially aggravated incidents. The idea was to get them to celebrate not their diversity, but their unity.

Mr Ahmed said what they discovered were young people desperately looking for a way out of the spiral of violence. "I have learned that racism isn't needed," says Ricki. "Hate is baggage and you shouldn't carry it around. If it hadn't been for this scheme I probably would have been in hospital or worse prison."

Shaahid believes he has turned a corner too. Having been excluded from school for fighting, and spending some time in prison, he believes his problem was violence rather than racism. He has now returned to college and is studying for a diploma that will give him access to a business degree.

"Two years ago I wasn't in school and I was on the wrong path to life," he says. "I would only use racism under certain circumstances, when I was pushed to the limits. Now I am educated, I know about different cultures and different religions. I feel comfortable with everyone. We have Portuguese, Polish, Pakistani, Indian and Italian in this city now. I believe that is a good thing. My job now is to tell the kids who are younger than me that violence is a dead end."

The role of the trade union movement in assisting its members and in preventing discrimination, harassment and victimisation at work is also critical. The TUC has been actively involved in the anti-racist movement and in developing a sophisticated response to discrimination issues. The TUC has published a number of publications which cover this area and now include a subtantial guide to equality law.[214] It also undertakes educational and training work for members.[215]

Extra-legal intervention to address the problems of its disadvantage afflicting ethnic minorities can also take the form of proactive (supply side) policies that take into account the need to formulate appropriate stances at the earliest planning and design stage. Policies that could be considered are summarised in a recent Joseph Rowntree report on ethnic minority disadvantage in the labour market as:

"Full diversity among different ethnic groups needs to be considered when setting targets for employment policy and when formulating policies aimed at individual groups (which include):

- Diversity among different ethnic groups needs to be considered when setting targets for employment policy and when formulating policies aimed at individual groups;
- Groups facing the greatest disadvantage should be encouraged to increase their investment in education;
- Although the links between religion and employment are complex, there may be scope for policy initiatives in this area, such as employment agencies working with religious organisation.
- Targeted policies may boost employment in deprived areas.
- The quality as well as the quantity of self-employment among people from ethnic minorities should be monitored; and
- More intervention may be needed to combat persistent, widespread discrimination in the labour market.[216]

Legal and extra-legal responses should also include ethnic minority equality targets in the public sector agreements across different departments. The establishment of an Ethnic Minorities Advisory Group which steers the work of an Ethnic Minorities Task Force has allowed the development of an overarching policy response. The recent work of the Task Force has also concentrated on a city strategy to ensure distribution of work opportunities, public procurement, outreach and employer engagement. It has also focused on using development funding, such as deprived area funding, to target disadvantage in areas where there is a particularly high level of ethnic minority disadvantage, e.g. tackling high rates of unemployment and child poverty in

214 TUC Guide To Employment Law (TUC: London, 2005).

215 See full details at *http:///www.tuc.org.uk* (accessed on November 10, 2005).

216 "Ethnic minorities in the labour market", (2007) 165 EOR 22, published by IRS June 1, 2007.

the East End.[217] There is some evidence that the use of these types of legal and extra-legal responses is having an impact, with indication of improvements in rates of economic inactivity and household poverty.[218]

VII. The Limits of Race Discrimination Law

In this section, we consider the various limits recognised to the application of protections against discrimination. Such limits have a variety of jusitifications.

A. *Race discrimination and Privacy*

Exceptions to the RRA originally included small partnerships and private households: all of which are areas in which the value of privacy could be said to have taken precedence over the principle of non-discrimination on the grounds of race. This reflected the aim in the White Paper to exclude certain types of private and intimate relationships from legal regualtion: "The Bill [i.e. RRA] will include provisions to ensure that it does not apply to personal and intimate relationships".[219] This preference in the White Paper can also be justified as a matter of principle: these relationships can be understood as being "direction sensitive", because they rely on a degree of spontaniety and self-expression that makes them an inappropriate subject matter for legal regulation even if they breach the principle of non-discrimination on the ground of race.[220] These exceptions have now been removed to comply with the EU Race Equality Directive. One exceptions that remains permits racial preferences in the choice of personal carers: i.e. where "the holder of the job provides persons of that racial group with personal services promoting their welfare, and those services can most effectively be provided by a person of that racial group (s.5(2)(d) of the RRA[221]). Recognition of a "privacy" barrier is one of the main sources of criticism of liberal discrimination law by radical critics.[222] Such critics would argue that discrimination arises through positive relationships which can be regulated at law: i.e. through contract, e.g. in

[217] For a summary see "Improving Opportunity, Strengthening Society: Two years on—a progress report on the Government's Strategy for race equality and community cohesion" (Dept for Communities and Local Government: London, August 2007) at pp.27–29.

[218] "Improving Opportunity, Strengthening Society: Two years on—a progress report on the Government's Strategy for race equality and community cohesion" (Dept for Communities and Local Government: London, August 2007) at pp.9–11.

[219] White Paper, *ibid.*, para 59.

[220] John Gardner, "Private Activities and Personal Autonomy", in B. Hepple and E. M. Szyszczak (eds), *Discrimination: The Limits of the Law* (Mansell: London, 1992).

[221] *Lambeth LBC v CRE* [1990] I.C.R. 768.

[222] John Gardner, "Private Activities and Personal Autonomy", in B. Hepple and E. M. Szyszczak (eds), *Discrimination: The Limits of the Law* (Mansell: London, 1992).

employment relationships. However, it can also arise through discrimination through contact between private individuals who choose not to interact with certain types of individuals: i.e. social networks, private clubs and dinner parties. In many respects this discrimination in contact remains outside the realms of legal regulation. Yet, at the same time, it can be a significant cause of stereotypes and stigma.

B. *Other Exceptions to Race Discrimination*

One wholesale exception in the RRA is for discrimination linked to nationality and the immigration function. There are also a number of other specific exceptions permitted under the RRA. For example, there is a special exception for sports and competitions, so that nothing will "render unlawful any act whereby a person discriminates against another on the basis of that other's nationality or place of birth or the length of time for which he has been resident in a particular area or place" (s.39 RRA). In addition, the RRA does not apply to acts done under statutory authority (s.41); these include for example exceptions for national security (s.42 RRA); acts done under ministerial authority (s.42 RRA); acts done to safeguard national security (s.42 RRA); and rules specified that restrict employment in the service of the Crown or any public body (s.75(5)).

It is worth examining the impact of the Race Equality Directive on the RRA. The Government response to implementing the Race Equality Directive was to introduce the Race Relations Act 1976 (Amendment) Regulations 2003 (RRA Regs 2003). The initial consultation document specified that there was a need for "light touch" regulation in this field which translated into minimal changes to the RRA. One consequence of the light touch regulation is that rather than a comprehensive reform of the RRA to ensure compliance, there has been piecemeal change to ensure minimal compliance with the Race Equality Directive. The term "race or ethnic or national" origin is used in the new amendments such as s.1A and s.4A, which contrasts with the term "colour, race, nationality or ethnic or national origins" used in other parts of the RRA (e.g. s.1 of the RRA). This leaves a potential gap in the coverage of these two sets of provisions.

The addition of a new definition of indirect discrimination in s.1A of the RRA ensures compliance with the Race Equality Directive by specifying a new sets of criteria for establishing indirect discrimination; and explicitly including the grounds covered by the Race Equality Directive, e.g. social security; health care; any other form of social protection; and any form of social advantage are covered by the RRA. The new definition of indirect discrimination in these areas is specified as where a person:

"applies to that other a provision, criterion or practice which he applies or would apply equally to persons not of the same race or ethnic or national origins as that other, but- (a) which puts or would put persons of the same race or ethnic or national origins as that other at a particular disadvantage when compared with other persons; (b) which puts that other at that disadvantage, and (c) which he cannot show to be a proportionate means of achieving a legitimate aim."

The new definition of "Genuine Occupational Requirement" (GOR) introduced in s.4A of the RRA, operates to create a dual regime in relation to lawful exceptions to race discrimination under the RRA. In some cases, it applies in relation to employment, applications for promotion, transfer or training in employment; and dismissal from employment and there is a new regime. This provision introduces a new test which ensures compliance with the Race Equality Directive. It sets out the following requirements:

"having regard to the nature of the employment or the context in which it is carried out- (a) being of a particular race or of particular ethnic or national origins is a genuine and determining occupational requirement; (b) it is proportionate to apply that requirement in the particular case; and (c) either- (i) the person to whom that requirement is applied does not meet it, or (ii) the employer is not satisfied, and in all the circumstances it is reasonable for him not to be satisfied, that that person meets it. In this way the twin concepts of 'proportionality' in judging the legitimacy of the requirement and 'reasonableness' in determining whether there has been compliance are the guide to whether the defence applies."

In all remaining areas the established test for Genuine Occupational Qualifications (GOQ) set out in s.5 of the RRA applies. This specifies the conditions for the application of the GOQ defence as:

"Section 5(2):

(a) the job involves participation in a dramatic performance or other entertainment in a capacity for which a person of that racial group is required for reasons of authenticity; or
(b) the job involves participation as an artist's or photographic model in the production of a work of art, visual image or sequence of visual images for which a person of that racial group is required for reasons of authenticity; or
(c) the job involves working in a place where food or drink is (for payment or not) provided to and consumed by members of the public or a section of the public in a particular setting for which, in that job, a person of that racial group is required for reasons of authenticity; or
(d) the holder of the job provides persons of that racial group with per-

> sonal services promoting their welfare, and those services can most effectively be provided by a person of that racial group.

A comparison between the tests for GOR in s.4A and s.5 RRA is instructive. The broad general principles of "proportionality" and "reasonableness" in s.4A can be contrasted with the narrow and specific details of the exact circumstances in which the GOR defence is available in s.5. We have already noted that s.5(2)(d) can be justified, as a matter of principle, as an example of the operation of the privacy barrier: i.e. a circumstance where the principle of non-discrimination on the grounds of race has to make a concession to the personal autonomy and choice of the individual. The other three examples can be justified as examples where race is operating as a legitimate reason because it allows authenticity in artistic expression.

A comparison of these two provisions also suggests that s.4A may apply as a wider defence, which justifies a more extensive range of permissible racial discrimination than that specified under s.5. McColgan notes that a number of factors support this view: s.4A covers dismissal as well as appointment; its wide definitions and tests of "proportionality" and "employer's satisfaction and reasonableness" (without specifying the exact factual circumstances) may permit the defence to be available in circumstances not available under s.5; and it applies to the context of the job rather than the job itself. This last point is especially important because it leaves open the possibility that the s.4A GOR defence may be available in a wider range of circumstances: e.g. does the cook in an Chinese restaurant need to be Chinese as well as the waiter serving in the front of the restaurant; does the manager or accountant of a care home for Indians need to be Indian as well as the actual carer? McColgan also notes that the gap in coverage between discrimination on the grounds of "race or ethnic or national origin" as specfied in s.4A and the wider range of "colour, race, nationality or ethnic or national origins" covered by s.5 exacerbates the risk of some forms of discrimination being more easily justified as a GOR. This would be a breach of the principle of non-regression (a reduction in the level of protection offered by a Member State in domestic law in the course of the implementation of EC law) as required by s.6 of the Race Equality Directive.[223]

VIII. Conclusion

It has been one of the more long-standing concerns of discrimination law to offer protection against race discrimination. International, EU, European Convention and domestic law (as well as the constitutional provisions in force in the USA, Canada and other democracies) thus contain extensive regulation

[223] See Aileen McColgan, *Discrimination Law: Text, Cases and Materials* (Oxford: Hart Publications, 2005).

of race discrimination. The goal of reducing the social exclusion of some racial minorities has also led to extensive positive action and supply-side measures. Yet despite these legal and social policy initiatives, the problems of racial discrimination and social inequality remain deeply entrenched.[224] The proposals in the *Discrimination Law Review* for reform of positive action (categorised as balancing measures), together with further development of permissible targetted public procurement measures, may assist in developing a better range of measures to tackle race discrimination.[225] However, as Singh Dhami, Squires and Modood argue, certain enabling conditions need to be put into place before these measures can properly assist in the task of tackling the deeply entrenched social exclusion of some racial groups.[226] These conditions include, inter alia: appropriate political will and leadership; strong enforcement mechanisms; supply-side investment in the training and education of young people; and regular reviews of positive action schemes. Future policies to address race discrimination and deeper patterns of structural racial inequality will need to focus on achieving an optimal balance between the use of individual discrimination law remedies and more sophisticated forms of positive action and extra-legal measures.

IX. Appendix on Poverty within Ethnic Minority Communities

Memorandum submitted by Dr Lucinda Platt (CP 31) to Written Evidence Submitted to the Select Committee on Work and Pensions[227]

"Child Poverty in the UK", second report of session 2003–04, Vol. 2, Written Evidence, House of Commons Papers 2003–04, 85-II

EVIDENCE

Extent of poverty among minority ethnic groups

"1. Poverty among children differs with ethnic group. While rates of poverty among children are higher than those among all individuals for all groups, the actual rates vary such that over 90% of Pakistani and Bangladeshi children are found in the bottom two-fifths of the income distribution compared to 50% of children overall. In relation to the

[224] *Equalities Review* (London: Cabinet Office, 2007).

[225] *Discrimination Law Review. A Framework for Fairness: Proposals for a Single Equality Act for Great Britain* (Department of Communities and Local Government: London, 2007).

[226] Ravinder Singh Dhami, Judith Squires and Tariq Modood, "Developing Positive Action Policies: Learning from the Experience of Europe and North America", Research Report No. 406 (London: DWP, 2006) at pp.119–121.

[227] This report can be obtained via the official web site of the House of Commons, at *http://www.parliament.the-stationery-office.co.uk/pa/cm200304/cmselect/cmworpen/85/85we54.htm* (accessed November 10, 2005).

60% of the median poverty line, around three quarters of Pakistani and Bangladeshi children are in poverty by this measure, along with over 60% of black African children and roughly 45 and 40% of Indian and Caribbean children respectively. This compares with around 30% of white children being in this position. The very high rates of poverty among children from minority ethnic groups are a cause for grave concern.

2. Demographic factors mean that children from minority ethnic groups are making up an increasing proportion of the child population. According to the 2001 Census 15% of children in England and Wales were from a minority ethnic group (compared with 9% of the total population). This share is set to increase such that by 2010 one in five schoolchildren will be from a minority group background. To the extent that their relative risks of poverty remain higher than those of the majority, this raises concerns about the possibility of achieving the government's targets to reduce child poverty.

3. In addition, to the extent that disadvantage is intergenerationally transmitted, minority ethnic groups, particularly the poorest minority groups, such as Bangladeshis, Pakistanis and black Africans, risk being consigned to long-term positions of economic marginality. The relative success of Bangladeshi children in receipt of free school meals, along with the noted achievement of the Chinese and Indian ethnic groups indicate that such a bleak outcome cannot be assumed. Nevertheless, children from minority ethnic groups face a range of obstacles to future success as well as higher risks of poverty in the present. These include the apparent failure of the education system in relation to Caribbean children.

4. A related issue in consideration of future prospects is the ownership of assets which can be transmitted between generations and impact on future welfare or provide protection against risks. In the population as a whole, only 28% were without any savings but this increased to 54% among black groups and 60% among Pakistanis and Bangladeshis. Housing can also be seen as an asset with potential to be realised by future generations, and there is also substantial inequality here. Bangladeshis have the lowest proportion of any group in owner occupation, with Caribbeans also have rates of owner occupation below the average. While rates of owner occupation among Pakistanis approach the average, the poor quality of much of this housing has been noted. Consideration should then be given to the possibilities for children to protect themselves against future risks as well as to their current situation.

5. Large families have been highlighted as a particularly vulnerable type of household. The proportion of large households is much higher among Pakistanis and Bangladeshis, making them more susceptible to poverty. In such instances, both pay (discussed in Paragraph 10), and the rates of social security benefits (discussed in Paragraph 20) are pertinent. On the other hand, the high rates of lone parenthood among Caribbean families has been shown to be associated with greater risks of poverty among children from this minority group. Though Caribbean lone mothers are more likely to be in employment than other lone mothers, there remain substantial proportions of them in receipt of income support.

Employment, Unemployment and Economic Activity

6. Worklessness is a major cause of poverty in households with children. Unemployment rates are much higher than the average for Caribbeans, black Africans, Bangladeshis and Pakistanis and above average for Indians. The Department for Work and Pensions PSA target to reduce such employment differentials is to be welcomed, but is proving hard to achieve. Local labour markets where minority groups are concentrated may form part of the explanation. For example, inner London has high unemployment rates, and black Africans are very heavily concentrated in inner London, as are, to a slightly lower degree, Caribbeans and Bangladeshis. However, the unemployment rates of black Africans in inner London are still double those of inner London white groups.

7. Another issue relevant to unemployment rates is the effectiveness of New Deals for minority group participants. Parity of outcomes across ethnic groups is welcomed as now being a specified aim of the programmes. This can be seen as a result of outcome statistics revealing variation by ethnic group.

8. Discrimination in the Labour Market will also impact on the employment probabilities of parents and therefore on the poverty of their children. The Race Relations Amendment Act 2000 has substantially strengthened race relations legislation, especially in its positive requirements on public bodies. However, private employers are not subject to such duties to monitor their activities. Given extensive evidence of an "ethnic penalty" in employment, the strength of discrimination law is clearly an issue for the poverty of minority ethnic group children.

9. In addition, economic activity rates are very low for Bangladeshi and Pakistani women. This is particularly the case for Bangladeshi and Pakistani women with families. But they are also low for Bangladeshi and Pakistani men. This means that overall employment rates among these two groups are lower even than the unemployment figures indicate. With such high levels of inactivity, households are limited in the number of potential workers available and therefore in the possibilities of avoiding poverty through work, especially in large households.

10. Levels of pay are also an issue for minority groups. Ethnic minority groups were identified by the Low Pay Commission as being one of the groups likely to be benefited by a minimum wage; and while the introduction of the minimum wage seems to have had some positive effects, it is not at such a level to necessarily raise working families out of poverty. Strong levels of occupational segregation in low-paid occupations raise challenges to reducing poverty in households in employment. For example half of working Bangladeshi men are employed in the restaurant sector and one in eight Pakistani men are either driving cabs or working as chauffeurs. Tax credits may offer possibilities for increasing the incomes of families in with low paid employment or where the prospects of employment are in low-paid sectors—but it may also raise problems for minority ethnic groups (see Paragraphs 21–23). [...]

Length of childhood

16. Many children from minority groups tend to spend an extended period in education. This can be both "catching up" for qualifications not gained in school and gaining further qualifications. This should result in positive future labour market outcomes. However, it also has immediate implications for the probability of poverty among those remaining in education and for their siblings. In addition, "catching up" maybe be regarded as a necessary response to failures in schooling; and the enhanced achievement of further and higher qualifications may be compensatory for a labour market in which minority groups need to be more highly qualified than the majority to obtain an equivalent probability of employment.

17. The rolling out of the Educational Maintenance Allowance is a promising development in this respect, a development which may well benefit minority group members from poorer families and support them in their educational choices. However, approaches to schooling and developments in higher education are not necessarily moving in the direction of greater equality of opportunity. And we already know that the experience of higher education is not equitable across minority ethnic groups. The welfare of children and young people as they are completing their education and the opportunities for the future provided by that education therefore both deserve attention.

18. Moreover, the experience of children from minority ethnic groups cannot be divorced from wider labour market inequalities, both those experienced by their parents and those which they are at risk of experiencing themselves.

Duration and timing of poverty

19. Both the duration and timing of poverty in childhood have been shown to be critical to their impact on children's outcomes. In addition, an extended period of poverty in childhood is damaging for children's experience of childhood itself. There would seem to be variations in duration of poverty by ethnic group, though research findings in this area are currently limited. We need to have a greater understanding of the length of time children from different ethnic groups spend in poverty and how that relates to their outcomes.

The role of social security

20. Social security impacts on ethnic groups in different ways. For example a high proportion of the incomes of Bangladeshis and Pakistanis derives from means-tested benefits, which makes their welfare highly sensitive to the delivery and value of such benefits. Some changes, such as the equalisation of income support rates for all children under the age of 19 will have been of particular benefit to such groups.

21. However, the structure, coverage and delivery of the social security system may disproportionately disbenefit particular groups. For example the greater reliance on means-tested benefits may result in greater stigma and lower take-up; the interaction between immigration and social security, and differences in checks or implementation has produced mistrust as well as unjustified refusals; the complexity of claiming processes may be particularly difficult for those whose first language is not English; and claiming in-work benefits is particularly difficult for the self-employed, who are much more highly represented among minority ethnic groups. Moreover, some of the poorest children from minority ethnic groups may be living in families that are not entitled to means-tested support.

22. The nature of benefits claimed and the ease or difficulty of claiming them for people in different circumstances will therefore be important for the extent to which poverty among minority ethnic group children is alleviated by the social security system. It is too early to know what the impact of a change to tax credits for in-work benefits has been. The greater generosity of tax credits should benefit those minority group families on low pay—or unable to move into work through low pay. However, there may be issues of take-up and responsiveness of the system.

23. In addition, tax credits interact with the housing benefit system in such a way that those with high rents will gain less benefit from the credit. This is a particular issue for London which has high housing costs; and certain minority groups—black Africans, Caribbeans, Bangladeshis—are heavily concentrated in London, as, to a lesser extent, are Indians and Chinese.

24. The social security system therefore has the potential for alleviating some of the poverty experienced by children from minority ethnic groups; however, it also has the potential for not benefiting them equally with other children. The social security system should therefore be evaluated for its differential impact on those from different ethnic groups. We need to know more about take-up of benefit by different ethnic groups and a clearer understanding of the impact on minority group families of changes in the structure and delivery of benefits.

Geographical variation and concentration

25. Minority groups tend to be geographically concentrated; though this is more the case for some groups than others, with Bangladeshis being the most concentrated and Chinese being the most dispersed. Geographical concentration of minority groups may bring benefits; but when concentration coincides with highly deprived areas, or when it is the

potentially more disadvantaged members of the group who are concentrated, then the benefits may not be so evident. In addition, concentrations of minority ethnic group families in deprived areas may have long-term consequences for future generations of the groups.

26. There is a tendency for minority group concentrations to occur in deprived areas. There is increasing recognition of the particular issues that face multiply deprived areas and their residents, with the establishment of the Neighbourhood Renewal Unit and an array of programmes to tackle area-based issues, including Action Zones and the New Deal for Communities. Children growing up in areas of such targeted areas are therefore likely to benefit from them; and the New Deal for Communities explicitly incorporates recognition of an ethnic dimension. However, even the most deprived neighbourhoods contain individuals with different degrees of deprivation, and these can be seen to vary additionally by ethnic groups.

27. The history of urban programmes has been ambiguous and has not necessarily indicated that it is those individuals who are the most vulnerable who benefit most directly from area-based interventions. It is therefore important that area-based programmes can be shown to be effective in their targeting. It is also important to recognise and take account of differences within areas as well as differences between areas."

13

RELIGIOUS DISCRIMINATION

I. Introduction

The idea that there should be "freedom of religion" has a long standing history in most liberal democratic countries. First, it is associated with classical ideas of toleration. Individual freedoms relating to speech, association as well as religion provide an overarching framework within wihich individuals may, within limits, live according to their own beliefs within the private sphere. This idea of religious "tolerance" has more recently given way to a second strategy that has incorporated religion into discrimination law by treating it as a prohibited ground in distinct spheres such as employment. There is also a third development in the form of a tendency to challenge the private-public dichotomy by arguing that freedom, equality and non-discrimination require that certain types of religious claim should be increasingly "accommodated" within the public sphere. The first claim of tolerance can be said to be a negative/private obligation. The second of non-discrimination moves towards a more public standard, i.e. prohibitions on direct discrimination in key public areas such as employment and education; and in some cases the requirement to make changes to existing practices and undertake positive action to eliminate indirect and institutional discrimination. Finally, the third strategy might be seen as a call for "accommodaton of difference", i.e. policies that encourage cultural pluralism and multiculturalism.

In relation to religious discrimination a number of conceptual distinctions need to be kept in mind in order to avoid confusion. There are two legal foundations of obligation not to discriminate on the ground of religion. One is the long standing demand for religious tolerance which is represented in constitutional or quasi-constitutional guarantees of freedom of religion, e.g. Art.9 of the ECHR; the Free Exercise Clause of the US Constitution; and Art.2 of the Canadian Charter. This normative standard can be called "freedom of religion" or religious freedom". The second foundation is the emerging body of law that includes religion as a prohibited ground of discrimination, such as the Employment Equality Directive and the Employment Equality (Religion and Belief) Regulations 2003. These types of provision give effect to a normative commitment to "non-discrimination on the ground of religion and belief". Although there will be an important relationship between norms that protect "religious freedom" and those that protect "non-discrimination on the ground of religion and belief" there will also be important differences between these two sources of protection for religion. For example, it may be problematic to extend provisions that guarantee "religious freedom" to cases where there are demands for the accommodation of religious difference requiring significant reallocation of resources or social power. In the *Copsey WBB Devon Clays* case, domestic judges showed a great reluctance to apply an expansive definition of the right to religious freedom under Art.9 ECHR as the basis for safeguarding against religious discrimination in the workplace.[1] These limits on the use of European Convention arguments suggest that statutory discrimination law may be a more useful form of protection for religion in certain specified spheres such as employment. Statutory discrimination law that limits the material scope of the principle of non-discrimination to specific and narrow spheres (e.g. employment and training), may therefore, be more responsive to accommodating the most pressing needs of religious minorities in the workplace than wide ranging constitutional or human rights provisions such as Art.9 or Art.14 of the ECHR.

Religion, unlike grounds such as gender or disability, raises distinct challenges for liberal democracies and discrimination law. Claims by traditional religious groups, e.g. for the public accommodation of their private religious identity, cause special difficulties. These types of claim challenge the traditional, secular, liberal commitment to a distinction between the public and private sphere, whereby the individual right to freedom of religion is guaranteed in the private sphere, while the public sphere is guarded as a neutral religion-free zone. The first strategy identified above, namely religious tolerance, might be felt to defend this distinction (which has not traditionally been supported in practice in the UK). The shift from tolerance towards non-discrimination in key areas such as employment, and claims for the "accommodation of religious differences" in the public is more problematic from the standpoint of religious tolerance. Moreover, contemporary societies are increasingly characterised by diversity in the types of religious belief of their citizens. This diversity can be called factual multiculturalism, in the sense that a great variety of different cultures and religions co-exist in Western liberal democracies. Individuals claim that their status as political right bearers is no longer a sufficient guarantee of freedom and equality, and now want their personal identity to be more substantially recognised by the State. This new politics raises an urgent point of principle: how should a liberal democratic state respond to claims by its citizens that their religion should move from its designated place in the private realm towards positive accommodation in the public sphere? This demand for the "accommodation of difference" can be

[1] *Copsey v WBB Devon Clays Ltd*, 2005] EWCA Civ 932, [2005] I.C.R. 1789; petition refused [2006] I.C.R. 205, HL. See the comment on the limits of the Human Rights Act as a way of securing civil liberties in the workplace. Hugh Collins, "The Protection of Civil Liberties in the Workplace" (2006) 69 M.L.R. 619.

labelled "normative multiculturalism". Identity politics is an observable social phenomenon: there has been a significant change in the form and content of the political claims made by minority groups in recent times. Many no longer ask for the "same" rights as the majority. Some of the most compelling demands of minorities now take the form of calls for the accommodation of "difference" in the public sphere and this is discussed in Chapter 3.[2] This social change is especially problematic for liberal multiculturalism. Claims for accommodation vary greatly: ranging from claims based on race, culture and religion through to gender and sexual orientation and disability. Legal regulation—at the EU and domestic level—covers all of these various grounds.[3] A further issue raised by multiculturalism in the context of religion is that new religious minorities are increasingly asking for protection against offence to their religious sentiments (with the extension of the law of blasphemy beyond Christians) or against hate speech. This has been especially true of Muslims as a religious minority within Europe and Britain. The "Salman Rushdie" incident was one such example and, more recently, the Danish cartoons controversy also illustrates this phenomenon. As this chapter illustrates, existing concepts of religious freedom, and state policy, have found it difficult to respond to these rapid social changes.

Traditional cultural and religious groups also raise a distinct set of problems for discrimination law for a number of reasons. Traditional norms and attitudes towards women and young girls, or gays and lesbians, which are especially prevalent in religious groups, can sometimes conflict with the principles that underlie discrimination law. The fact that all these grounds—race, religion, gender and sexual orientation—are all protected within the same normative structure of discrimination law raises the spectre of a "conflict of rights", e.g. where a religious groups argues that its particular practice require discrimination against women.[4] The proliferation of protected grounds within discrimination law also raises the problem of intersectionality, i.e. overlapping claims different grounds such as race and gender; religion and sexual orientation. This was discussed in Chapter 9. Here it is worth observing that the potential for a "conflict of rights" will raise special difficulties in any analysis of religious discrimination: e.g. in delineating the scope, nature and extent of the public accommodation of religious difference that is possible within liberal democracies.

[2] For a discussion of some of these issues see Tariq Modood, *Multicultutral Politics: Racism, Ethnicity and Muslims in Britain* (Minnesota: University of Minnesota Press, 2005).

[3] For a discussion of some of these issues see W. Kymlicka, "Introduction", *Rights of Minority Cultures*, W. Kymlicka (ed.) (Oxford: Oxford University Press, 1995) at p. 7. See also M. Malik, *Faith and the State of Jurisprudence*, Peter Oliver et al (eds) *Faith and Law: Essays in Legal Theory*, (Oxford: Hart Publishing, 2000) at pp.129–133.

[4] See Susan Moller Okin, "'Mistresses of Their Own Destiny': Group Rights, Gender, and Realistic Rights of Exit" Ethics 112 (January 2002): 205–230 and Susan Moller Okin, "Feminism and Multiculturalism" (July 1998) Ethics 108, 661–684.

II. Distinguishing "Religious Freedom"

The historical transformation in the claims of religious minorities—from (1) tolerance, through to (2) non-discrimination, and now including (3) accommodating difference—is also true of groups such as racial minorities. However, unlike other grounds of discrimination, there is a long standing precedent treating "religious freedom" as a special category for human rights based protection. Recognising "religion" as not only a ground for non-discrimination, but also a special delineated "freedom" via a specific human right, gives it a distinctive status by contrast with the grounds of discrimination. It may be that this is a historical anomoly.[5] Nevertheless, the special status of religion within a scheme of protecting individual freedom raises important issues for when analysing prohibited religion as a ground within discrimination law. In understanding religious discrimination it is, therefore, necessary to make a preliminary but critical distinction between "religious freedom" and "non-discrimination relating to religion". This distinction is becoming increasingly important for a number of reasons. International and regional human/constitutional rights protection for freedom of religion, such as Art.18 of the International Covenant of Civil and Political Rights, now co-exist with the right to non-discrimination on the ground of religion within discrimination. Futhermore, the Canadian Charter, s.2, protects freedom of religion, whilst s.15 guarantees equality on the ground of religion. The ECHR contains a provision for freedom of religion (Art.9), whilst at the same time containing a non-discrimination provision that covers religion in Art.14. The translation of these ECHR rights into EU and domestic discrimination law creates a similar dual system for dealing with religious discrimination. Article 9 of the ECHR also provides one of the sources for "fundamental rights" within the EU legal system and, at the same time, EU law has also now adopted a statutory norm to protect against religious discrmination in employment and training (via the Employment Equality Directive). In domestic discrimination law, the HRA ensures that Art.9 and Art.14 ECHR provide protection of religious freedom (particularly in the context of public authorities) whilst at the time there is now prohibition of religious discrimination in employment and training and also the provision of goods and services in the Employment Equality (Religion and Belief) Regulations 2003 and the Equality Act 2006. The recent case of *Copsey v WWB Devon Clays*[6] illustrates the way in which there will be an increasing overlap between these different prohibitions on religious discrimination. The discussion of "religion" in discrimination law often inflates "religious freedom" and "religious equality". It is, therefore, important to set out, in further detail,

[5] For a discussion of the special justifications of the place of religion to individual freedom and autonomy see Timothy Macklem, "Reason and Religion" in Peter Oliver, et al (eds) *Faith in Law: Essays in Legal Theory* (Hart Publishing: Oxford, 2000).

[6] [2005] I.R.L.R. 811.

some of the instructions between these different strategies for addressing how the law should safeguard religion and belief.

III. Religious Minorities in Britain

Chapter 3 discussed the ways in which liberal values such as freedom and autonomy can provide a justification for discrimination law. Values such as these are sometimes also key to provide that are the foundations of human rights and constitutional guarantees of individual freedom. It is therefore important to distinguish between religion as "freedom" in international and human rights law and religion as a ground of prohibited discrimination law. The distinction between "religious tolerance" and non-discrimination as strategies, discussed above, is important because it keeps distinct the myriad of forms that claims for "religious freedom" and "non-discrimination" can take. An example will serve to illustrate this point.[7] Imagine a political community which has a Sikh minority and introduces a number of legal rules:

- Rule 1: A general rule that it is a criminal offence to profess to be a Sikh;
- Rule 2: A general rule that full citizenship and a work permit is dependent on taking a public oath that requires an individual to swear loyalty to the Christian faith;
- Rule 3: A general rule that no Sikhs should be employed in the construction industry;
- Rule 4: A requirement that all employees in the construction industry must wear safety helmets.

All of these rules might be presented as examples of "discrimination against Sikhs on the ground of their religion". However, it is worth noting certain distinctions between them. Rule 1 is clearly an interferance with the individual right to religious freedom, i.e. the individual right to believe and manifest religion. Rule 2 also operates in this way by introducing a penalty and exclusionary condition for full and equal citizenship. Rule 2 would ensure exclusion of all Sikhs from a whole range of public goods and all employment. The restrictions in Rule 1 and Rule 2 could thus be said to constitute classic exampls of restrictions on religious liberty/freedom as articulated in Art.9 of the ECHR, which provides for the "right to freedom of religion, including the right to manifest this religion in practice and observance". Similarly, Article 27 IPPR which states that members of a minority group "[. . .] shall not be denied the right [. . .] to profess and practice their own religion." Rule 3 and Rule 4 are

[7] The following discussion is developed from the analysis of these issues in Brian Barry, *Culture and Equality* (Polity Press: London, 2001), especially ch.2.

different because they are examples of discrimination in accessing a specific good or opportunity such as employment in a specific context. Rule 3 is an example of denying opportunities to a specific religious group and would fall within definition of direct religious discrimination in employment. Rule 4 is an example of a netural rule which does not specifically mention religion: however Sikhs (whose beliefs require them to wear turbans) cannot comply with this netural rule because of their "religious difference". The argument that Sikhs should be granted an exemption from the application of this neutral rule because of their inability to comply with its requirement can be categorised as a "rule exemption" claim. This may also be an example of indirect religious discrimination.

These distinctions also illustrate the different role of choice in each of these fact situations. In Rule 1 and Rule 2 there is clear interferance with the right to believe and manifest religion in all aspects of the life of the individual. It could also be argued that Rule 3, by operating as a wide ranging ban on accessing an important good such as employment, is also an interferance with freedom (this is discussed below in the context of the ECHR contracting out cases).[8] However, Rule 4 operates in a different way. There is no general requirement to work in the construction industry: it is an example of a restriction that is faced by, and arguably chosen by, Sikhs because of their religious beliefs. There are clearly reasons to be concerned where an individual faces a significant penalty or impediment in accessing a key good because of their religious belief. This may be direct discrimination (as in Rule 3) or indirect discrimination (as in Rule 4). This is exactly the sphere in which discrimination law can make a distinct contribution in terms of supplementing an individual right to religious freedom. However, these "non-discrimination" arguments need to be kept distinct from the well established historical principle of religious tolerance which has been translated into individual rights to freedom of religion found in constitutional and human rights documents. It would, on this analysis, be possible to argue that a provision such as Rule 4 is indirect religious discrimination against Sikhs and, at the same time that Rule 4 is not an interference with their right to freedom of religion.

ECHR jurisprudence partially acknowledges, and facilitates, the distinction between "religious freedom" and "non-discrimination". We discuss the specific issues relating to the Art.9 right to freedom of religion below. In the context of distinguishing religion as "freedom" and religion as in terms of "non-discrimination" it is worth noting that the European Court of Human Rights places the concepts of choice and voluntariness at the centre of its

[8] See *Copsey v WBB Devon Clays Ltd* [2005] EWCA Civ 932, [2005] I.C.R. 1789; petition refused [2006] I.C.R. 205, HL. Lord Jusitce Mummery questioned ECHR jurisprudence that assumes that there can "voluntary contracting out" of the Art.9 right to religious freedom, and no interference with this right, as long as the individual has a choice to leave the employment. Mummery L.J. questioned whether it is reasonable to expect an individual to seek alternative employment in these contexts. For analysis, see: Hugh Collins, "The Protection of Civil Liberties in the Workplace" (2006) 69 M.L.R. 619.

analysis of the scope and nature of the Art.9 right to religious freedom. This is exemplified in the principle that an individual can voluntarily contract out of the right to freedom of religion. The European Court of Human Rights has adopted and endorsed this approach in a number of their cases. In *Steadman v the United Kingdom*[9] for example, it was held that a woman who objected that Sunday working was an interference with her right to freedom of religion could have left her job if she found that her employment was interfering with her individual right to religion.[10] More recently, in *Kosteski v The Former Yugoslav Republic of Macdeonia*, the Court held that there was no right under Art.9 for time off work for religious holidays, and that the failure to grant time off for a religious holiday for a Muslim employee was not a breach of Art.9 of the ECHR.[11]

In these circumstances, the fact that there is a viable choice open to an individual, which if exercised permits him to manifest his religion, is seen to be of critical importance, i.e. the individual can manifest his religion by leaving his job. These cases illustrate the classic distinction between freedom and non-discrimination in the context of religion: there is no interference with freedom of religion where the individual is left with a viable and voluntary choice to put himself in a position where he can manifest his religion even if this requires some personal sacrifice. On this analysis, these fact situations individuals have, through the exercise of choice, put themselves in a situation which limits their ability to manifest their religion. Moreover, they have a choice to remove themselves from the restrictive context. There remain important questions about this principle of voluntariness and its impact on the scope of religious freedom. One obvious critique of voluntariness in this context relates to whether or not the choices concerned are truly voluntary, i.e. is it really viable to expect individuals to give up their job in order to manifest their religion? Does this impact on the scope of their individual right to freedom of religion? There is some acknolwedgement, within ECHR jurisprudence that there are limits to the concept of voluntariness and choice in these contexts. There may be situations where expecting an individual to change their position in order to manifest their religion may be unreasonable.[12]

[9] *Steadman v United Kingdom*, App. No. 29107/95, 89—A Eur. Comm'n H. R. Dec. & Rep. 104, 107–8 (1997).

[10] Another example of permissible "contracting out" of the right to religious freedom is the case of the Muslim school teacher who was found to have limited his right to religious freedom when he accepted an employment contract which included set working hours which prevented him from taking time off for Friday prayers, see *X v United Kingdom*, App. No.8160/78, 22 Eur. Comm'n H. R. Dec. & Rep. 27 (1981)

[11] Decision of April 13, 2006. Case No. 55170/00.

[12] *Darby v Sweden*, 187 European Court of Human Rights (Ser. A) (1990). See the discussion by Carolyn Evans, *Freedom of Religion Under the European Convention on Human Rights* (Oxford: Oxford University Press, 2001) at p.127.

There have also been reservations expressed in the Court of Appeal[13] and House of Lords[14] about whether the costs associated with "voluntariness" and "choice" are compatible with the guarantee of a right to religious freedom. Nevertheless, despite these doubts, it is clear that both ECHR jurisprudence and domestic law now recognises that the right to freedom of religion under Art.9(1) is not restricted in those cases which fall within the *Steadman* and *Ahmad v ILEA* analysis, i.e. where it can be said that the individual has either subjected himself to the restriction voluntarily or that they have a choice to alter their position in a way that permits the manifestation of their religious belief. This analysis of the right to freedom of religion suggests that the exercise of the right may sometimes involve significant costs for the individual. This approach has been affrimed by the House of Lords in the *Shabina Begum* case, in which a majority Lords Bingham, Hoffman, and Scott affirmed that where there is a "voluntariness" and "choice" (in that case to attend a school that permitted the jilbab/robe) then there may be no violation of the Art.9(1) right to religious freedom. This case is discussed in more detail below.

Clearly, the costs associated with finding an appopriate context within which to manifest religious belief will be higher for minorities, who will be faced with mainstream political, social and economic structures that do not match their religious needs. Carolyn Evans has suggested that ECHR jurisprudence is much better at securing religious freedom for majority religions and that it has consistently failed to respond to minority religious practices: a point which be important given the increasing claims for "accommodation" within the public sphere being made by minority religions (e.g. in the context of religious dress).[15] However, as religions become more diverse in Western European liberal democracies, even some "majority" religions feel that they are faced with a public sphere that does not allow them to fully manifest their beliefs.[16] The introduction of the principle of non-discrimination on the ground of religion in specific areas such as employment can address many of these issues. However, this is a distinct and separate source of protection for those who want to manifest their religion. As stated above, there are good reasons to keep "religion as freedom" and "non-discrimination"—distinct. In the case of religious freedom, the argument that the individual voluntarily entered into a situation which restricts his ability to manifest his religion, and retains the choice to leave this situation, may be relevant to the issue of whether there has

[13] See the comments of Mummery L.J. in *Copsey v WWB Devon Clays Ltd* [2005] EWCA Civ 932 I.C.R. 1789.

[14] See the difference in the reasoning of judges in *R. (on the Application of Shabina Begum) v Headteachers and Governors of Denbigh High School*.

[15] See Carolyn Evans, *Freedom of Religion under the European Convention on Human Rights* (Oxford: Oxford University Press, 2001). See also a specific example of this argument in the context of the ECHR headscarf cases, Carolyn Evans. "The 'Islamic Scarf' in the European Court of Human Rights". 7 (2006) Melbourne J. of International L. 52.

[16] *Steadman v United Kingdom*, App. No. 29107/95, 89—A Eur. Comm'n H. R. Dec. & Rep. 104, 107–8 (1997) illustrates the problem of working on Sundays. *R v Secretary of State for Education and Employment Ex p. Williamson* [2005] H.R.L.R. 14 illustrates the problem faced by some Christian groups in the context of the ban on corporal punishment in all schools.

been an interference. In the case of non-discrimination, voluntariness and choice will not compensate for the fact that the individual is faced with a situation which is direct discrimination. Moreover, whereas there may be good reasons either not to allow or to limit the role of indirect rule-exemption claims in the case of freedom of religion, it may be feasible to allow claims for indirect discrimination. In the context of non-discrimination, the claim for a rule exemption operates as a claim for religious equality/non-discrimination on the ground of religion in a distinct and limited area such as employment, rather than widely framed as a constitutional right that can bind public duties with a wide ranging duty to accommodate a myriad of religious differences. This means that arguments about the "public accommodation of religious difference" may need to be assessed depending on the form of the legal provision and the specific context in which the claim is made. There may, in some cases, be valid arguments that permit the accommodation of difference in the context of statutory discrimination law (religious equality) which limits the scope of the principle of non-discrimination. A useful illustration of the way in which statutory discrimination law may be better able to accommodate the most pressing needs of religious groups, as compared with the ECHR approach to religious freedom, is the EAT case, *James v MSC Cruises Ltd*,[17] which concerned a challenge to Saturday working by a member of the Seventh-day Adventist Church. The Saturday working was found to be potentially a form of indirect religious discrimination although the EAT also found that it was justified as a "proportionate means of achieving a legitimate aim". Unlike claims for religious freedom under Art.9 of the ECHR where it is assumed that there is no interference with the Art.9(1) right where there is freedom to leave the employment in this case the Employment Equality (Religion and Belief) Regulations 2003 and statutory discrimination law provides a greater potential for examining issues of direct and indirect religious discrimination in specified areas such as the workplace.

A. *History*

The context for understanding attitudes to religion needs to be related to the role of "religion" in European and British history. The British Reformation and the European "wars of religion"[18] have ensured that "religion" is commonly associated with violence and war throughout Western Europe. There are two trends that are significant for our analysis of contemporary religious discrimination. First, the attitudes of nation states towards different religions and

[17] *James v MSC Cruises Ltd*, Case No. 2203173/05, (Decision of April 12, 2006, Central London Industrial Tribunal, Chair: RA Hemmings), discussed at "Saturday-working requirement did not give rise to indirect religious discrimination" (Oct 2006) 157 Equal Opportunities Rev. 32.

[18] For a historical discussion of the reformation in Europe see Diarmaid MacCulloch, *Reformation: Europe's House Divided, 1490–1700*, (Penguin: London, 2003).

religious groups; and second, the emerging process of secularisation in European nation states which had consequences for all religions and religious groups.

The liberal solution, adopted in many jurisdictions (although not strictly in the UK) was to ensure that religion became a matter for the private sphere, with the State endorsing any particular religion. This ensured that differences in religion were relegated to the private sphere. For example, in France the liberal solution was to entrench a strict principle of *laïcité* which keeps separate the state (French Republic) from religion. The historical origin of the principle of *laïcité* is linked with the development of democratic and constitutional politics: French revolutionaries explicitly disestablished the church as part of their rejection of the regime of the monarch and his religious supporters in the Catholic Church.

In Britain, by contrast a gradual process of toleration towards nonconformist Protestants, Catholics, Jews and other minorities has ensured the expansion of the concept of religious freedom. The Church of England was established as the official "state" church through the First and Second Acts of Supremacy in 1534 and 1559. The English Toleration Act 1679 allowed the established Church to exist, but individuals were no longer punished for not being members of the official Church. The main beneficiaries of the change were non-conformist Christians who were willing to sign loyalty oaths and able to have their practices "certified". Non-conformist Christians could, therefore, set up their own churches and also become members of Parliament. This settlement still excluded Catholics and Jews from holding public office. The right to be an MP and hold public office was extended to Catholics and Jews in the nineteenth century. This historical development is relevant to contemporary discussions of religious discrimination for a number of reasons. The confrontation between Protestants and Catholics remains significant for an analysis of religion in the contemporary period. Intolerance towards Catholics, and their exclusion from public office, meant that anti-Catholic prejudice prevailed in Britain. Moreover, the Act of Union of 1801 which ensured the incorporation of Ireland into the political entity of the United Kingdom had far reaching consequences for the status of Catholics in Ireland.[19] The exclusion of Catholics from public life as required by law, and the subsequent confrontation between Catholics and Protestants, translated into structural inequality and discrimination against the Catholic minority in Northern Ireland. This meant that discrimination law in Northern Ireland took a different form from legislation in England, Scotland and Wales. For example, although religious discrimination has only recently been prohibited in employment and training in England and Wales, there has been legislation in Northern Ireland (via the FETO) for a longer period. Moreover, the political

[19] For a general discussion of the British and French approach to the relations between Church and State, see C. Evans, *Freedom of Religion under the European Convention on Human Rights* (Oxford: Oxford University Press, 2001) and Joel S. Fetzer and J. Christopher Soper, *Muslims and the State in Britain, France and Germany* (Cambridge: Cambridge University Press, 2005).

context of the association of Catholics with foreign powers such as France and Spain, and the subsequent focus on the Irish as a source of domestic terrorism, meant that there were complex reasons for the racialisation of British Catholics as a "fifth column" and an "internal security threat".

There had been Jews in Britain since the time of William the Conqueror in the late eleventh century.[20] They were subject to massacres, hostility, harassment and discrimination. One notable and extreme example was the York Massacre of 1190 when almost the entire Jewish population of the city of York was murdered. Other examples of stigmatisation include the obligation for young Jewish men to wear a yellow badge on their outer clothing (introduced in 1218 and extended to adults and children from the age of seven upwards). Jews were expelled from Britain in 1290 and subsequently re-admitted by Cromwell in 1656.[21] During the period that followed, there was increasing settlement by Jews within Britain, and also a gradual accommodation of Jews into British public institutions: e.g. Jews were granted Royal Protection in 1664; Jews were allowed to swear in Court on the Old Testament in 1967; and a court venue was changed from a Saturday to avoid Jews giving evidence on a Saturday in 1674. There was also the gradual establishment of Jewish synagogues in the seventeenth century and the Jewish Board of Deputies in 1760. However, Jews continued to be excluded from public office because they were unable to take a pledge of allegiance which required using the phrase "on the true faith of a Christian". This barrier was finally removed with the passage of the Jewish Relief Act 1958 that enabled Jews to be free of legal restrictions in relation to taking up public office. Despite these changes there remained widespread prejudice about Jews and discrimination against them: these included anti-Jewish disturbances in South Wales in 1902 and Tredegar in 1911. The migration of large number of Jews fleeing persecution in Eastern Europe provided a new context for the racialisation of British Jews, and the re-emergence prejudice against Jews in Britain.[22]

As the example of Jewish minorities illustrates, religious tolerance and secularisation emerged in Britain through a gradual and incremental process. Unlike the French developments which led to a strict separation of the political and religious, in Britain there was, and remains, an established Church which enjoyed an officially recognised relationship with the State. As we have seen, a gradual process of negoitation (e.g. with non-conformist Protestants, Catholics and Jews) ensured that other religions came to be included within this set-

[20] For a discussion of the history of Jews in Britain see T. Endelman, *The Jews of Britain, 1656 to 2000* (California: Univ of California Press, 2002).

[21] For dates of the key events (and also a detailed bibliography) in the history of Jews in Britain see "A Chronology of Jews in Britain" documented at the archives of The Jewish Historical Society of England at *http://www.jhse.org/* (accessed November 30, 2006).

[22] Colin Holmes, *Anti-Semitism in British Society 1876–1939* (New York: Holmes and Meier Publications, 1979); Tony Kushner, *The persistence of prejudice: Antisemtism in British society during the second world war* (Manchester: Manchester University Press, 1989); Louise London, *Whitehall and the Jews, 1933–1948: British immigration policy, Jewish refugees and the Holocaust* (Cambridge: Cambridge University Press, 2000).

tlement over a period of time without explicitly challenging the established authority of the Church of England. This process of gradualism, rather than an explicit shift towards religious tolerance and secularism, has had a number of ongoing consequences for understanding the relationship between the state and religion in Britain. For example, state education grew out of, and in conjunction with, religious schools without any calls for a complete exclusion of religion from education. Moreover, the distinctive British history of the relationship between Church and state explains the substantial differences between British and French approaches to the demands of religious minorities, e.g. in cases concerning the Muslim headscarf. The change in the political power of religion in contemporary societies also raises the issue of whether there is scope for the accommodation of religious claims by newly emerging religious minorities. Moreover, changes in the status of religion in the contemporary period also raise a question about whether small concessions to the most urgent needs of religious minorities can now be justified within a general framework of liberal secular democracy, as compared with earlier historical periods when religion had greater political power and could have been a viable alternative to such democracies.[23]

B. *Contemporary Issues*

Surveys in England, Wales and Scotland give a picture of the nature of religious belief, and the spread of religious communities. In the next section we set out summaries of the figures in each part of Britain. The political conflict between Protestants and Catholics means that Northern Ireland is a special and distinct case for discrimination law and policy, and this also is dealt with separately. The quantitaive focus on the statistics is then followed by a qualitative discussion about the social, economic and political issues relevant to religion as a category in discrimination law.

[23] See Seumas Milne, "The struggle is no longer against religion, but within it", *The Guardian*, December 16, 2004.

1. Religion in England, Wales and Scotland

Religious composition of ethnic groups, April 2001, England & Wales
***http://www.statistics.gov.uk/* (accessed on February 16, 2006)**

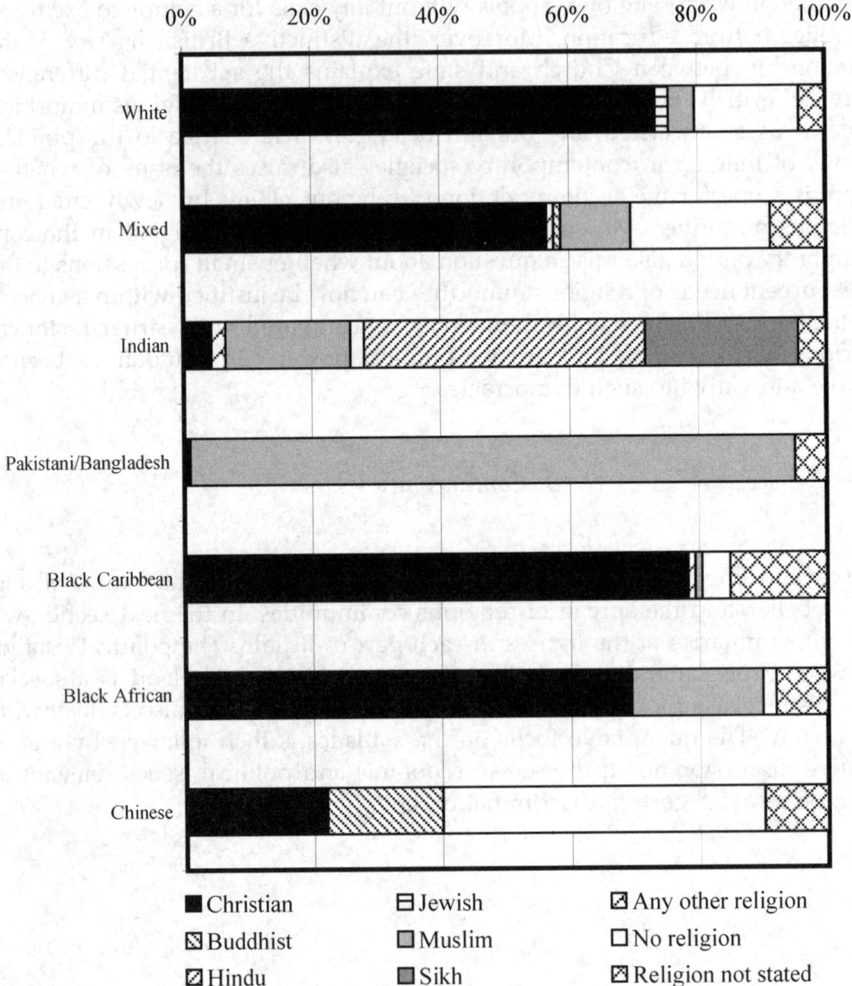

"The 2001 Census collected information about ethnicity and religious identity. Combining these results show that while the population of England and Wales is more culturally diverse than ever before, White Christians remain the largest single group by far. In England and Wales, 36 million people (nearly 7 out of 10) described their ethnicity as White and their religion as Christian.

Majorities of Black people and those from Mixed ethnic backgrounds also identified as Christian (71 and 52 per cent respectively). In total there were 810,000 Black Christians and 347,000 Christians from Mixed ethnic backgrounds.

Among other faiths the largest groups were Pakistani Muslims (658,000) and Indian Hindus (467,000) followed by Indian Sikhs (301,000), Bangladeshi Muslims (260,000) and White Jews (252,000).

The Indian group was religiously diverse: 45 per cent of Indians were Hindu, 29 per cent Sikh and a further 13 per cent Muslim. In contrast the Pakistani and Bangladeshi groups were more homogenous, Muslims accounting for 92 per cent of each ethnic group.

Some faith communities were concentrated in particular ethnic groups. For example, 91 per cent of Sikhs were Indian and 97 per cent of Jews described their ethnicity as White. Other faiths were more widely dispersed. Considerable proportions of Buddhists were found in the White, Chinese, Other Asian and Other ethnic groups.

Overall, 15 per cent of the English and Welsh population reported having no religion although variation by ethnicity was marked. Just over half of all Chinese people, and one quarter of people from Mixed ethnic backgrounds, stated they had no religion. Asian, Black African and White Irish people were least likely to have no religion. Fewer than 1 in 200 Pakistanis and Bangladeshis reported having no religion.

Fourteen per cent of people in the Other Black group chose not to answer the religion question, almost twice the average for England and Wales as a whole. Similar proportions of people in the Black Caribbean and Mixed ethnic groups also gave no answer.

Source: Census, April 2001, Office for National Statistics.

Notes: The Census question about religion was voluntary.

Published on January 8, 2004.

Population of Wales: by ethnic group, April 2001

Wales

	Numbers	Percentages
White British	2,786,605	95.99
White Irish	17,689	0.61
Other White	37,211	1.28
White	**2,841,505**	**97.88**
Mixed	**17,661**	**0.61**
Indian	8,261	0.28
Pakistani	8,287	0.29
Bangladeshi	5,436	0.19
Other Asian	3,464	0.12
Asian or Asian British	**25,448**	**0.88**
Black Caribbean	2,597	0.09
Black African	3,727	0.13
Other Black	745	0.03
Black or Black British	**7,069**	**0.24**
Chinese	**6,267**	**0.22**
Other	**5,135**	**0.18**
All non-white	**61,580**	**2.12**
All population	**2,903,085**	**100.00**

The 2001 Census collected information about ethnicity and, for the first time, religious identity. Religious and ethnic minorities in Wales formed a small proportion of the population, although Cardiff was considerably more diverse.

Ethnicity

Most of the population of Wales described their ethnicity as White, with 96 per cent White British, 0.6 per cent White Irish and 1.3 per cent from another White background. The remaining 2.1 per cent of the population were from ethnic backgrounds other than White, and together numbered 62,000 people.

More than 25,000 people were of Asian descent, the majority being either Indians or Pakistanis (8,000 each). Nearly 18,000 people were of Mixed ethnic origin, 7,000 described their ethnicity as Black, and 6,000 as Chinese. A further 5,000 were from other ethnic backgrounds.

People from ethnic backgrounds other than White were concentrated in the three biggest cities in Wales. In Cardiff they made up 8 per cent of the population, in Newport 5 per cent and in Swansea 2 per cent. By far the highest concentrations were in Cardiff. Around half of the Black and Asian groups and a third of the Mixed and Chinese groups lived in the capital.

The White group were older than other ethnic groups. The White Irish were oldest of all. Among White Irish people 32 per cent were above working age, compared with only 5 per cent of the Mixed group and 3 per cent of Bangladeshis. The Mixed group were youngest, with nearly half (47 per cent) under the age of 16.

Religion

Nearly three quarters of the Welsh population described their religion as Christian (72 per cent). The White group contained the highest proportion of Christians (73 per cent), and majorities of Black Caribbeans and people from Mixed ethnic backgrounds also identified as Christians (70 and 51 per cent respectively).

After Christianity, Islam was the next most common faith. Cardiff had the largest Muslim population (4 per cent of the local population) but in the country overall Muslims accounted for less than 1 per cent of the population (22,000 people). Most Muslims were from Asian backgrounds, including 7,000 Pakistani Muslims and 5,000 Bangladeshi Muslims, although nearly 3,000 White people also described themselves as Muslim.

Among other faiths the next largest groups were Indian Hindus (over 4,000) and White Buddhists (3,000), followed by White Jews and Indian Sikhs (both about 2,000).

Age structures of the different religious groups reflected their ethnic composition and the secular trend among the White population. Between 5 and 6 per cent of Muslims, Hindus and Sikhs were pensioners, compared with 24 per cent of Christians and 30 per cent of Jews.

Across Wales 19 per cent reported they had no religion and a further 8 per cent did not record an answer.

Source: Censuses, April 1991 and April 2001, Office for National Statistics.

Notes: Census Religion Question—'What is your religion?' Answers categories were None, Christian, Buddhist, Hindu, Jewish, Muslim, Sikh, or, any other religion.

Census Ethnic Group Question—In both 1991 and 2001 respondents were asked to which ethnic group they considered themselves to belong. The question asked in 2001 was more extensive than that asked in 1991, so that people could tick 'Mixed' for the first time. This change in answer categories may account for a part of the observed increase in the minority ethnic population over the period.

White British includes those who indicated their ethnicity was White English, White Scottish or White Welsh.

Working age—Males aged 16 to 64, females aged 16 to 59."

Published on January 8, 2004.

ANALYSIS OF RELIGION IN SCOTLAND IN THE 2001 CENSUS: Summary Report

"1. DEMOGRAPHICS

Scottish Population

Table 1.1: Current Religion in Scotland—All People

	Number (000s)	Percentage (%)
Church of Scotland	2,146.3	42.40
Roman Catholic	803.7	15.88
Other Christian	344.6	6.81
Buddhist	6.8	0.13
Hindu	5.6	0.11
Jewish	6.4	0.13
Muslim	42.6	0.84
Sikh	6.6	0.13
Another Religion	27.0	0.53
All Religions	3,389.5	66.96
No religion	1,394.5	27.55
Not Answered	278.1	5.49
All no religion / Not answered	1,672.5	33.04
Base	5,062.0	100.00

Just over two-thirds (67%) of the Scottish population reported currently having a religion. More than six out of ten people said that their religion was Christian (65%): 42% Church of Scotland, 16% Roman Catholics and 7% Other Christian.

The Other Christian group includes a wide range of groups which can be very different from each other in terms of their approaches to key issues. Examples of the write-in answers include the Church of England, Evangelical, Greek Orthodox, Jehovah's Witness, Methodist, Spiritualist and many others.

After Christianity, Islam was the most common faith with 42.6 thousand people in Scotland describing their religion as Muslim. This is followed by people from Other religions (27 thousand), Buddhists (6.8 thousand), Sikhs (6.6 thousand), Jews (6.4 thousand) and Hindus (5.6 thousand). These groups each accounted for less than 1% of the Scottish population. Even with these groups added together they still account for less than 2% of the overall population.

The profile of the non-Christian religious population is shown in Chart 1.1: **Chart 1.1: Current Religion of Non-Christian Religious Population**

Percentages

Just under half (45%) of the non-Christian religious population is made up of Muslims. The next largest non-Christian religious groups are Buddhists, Sikhs and Jews with 7% in each group. Those from other religion groups make up a significant proportion of the non-Christian group with 28% responding that they belong to a religion group out with those listed on the Census form. Further information on the write-in answers for those responding 'Another Religion' can be found in Annex A.2.

The Census religion questions (first question asked about current religion and the second asked about religion of upbringing) were both voluntary. Nevertheless, over 94% of people choose to answer the question on current religion. Around 28% of people in Scotland stated that they had no current religion."

In the case of the figures on religion in Scotland it is worth pointing out that like Northern Ireland there is a distinction within the term "Christian". In Scotland, the history of tensions between the Catholics and non-Catholics remains significant in the contemporary period with a recognition that these historical tensions can give rise to a more general "sectarianism" that can be a cause of discrimination. A recent study of sectarianism in Scotland concludes that there has been significant progress in this area:

Bruce, S, Glendinning, A., Paterson, I & Rosie, M "Sectarianism in Scotland", Edinburgh, cited in Louise McAspurren, *Religious Discrimination & Sectarianism in Scotland: a Brief Review of Evidence* (2002–2004), available at *www.scotland.gov.uk* (accessed February 14, 2006)

"Late Twentieth Century- Present Day.

3.7 When looking at discrimination in Scotland today, the authors note that older Catholic men are more likely to say discrimination exists against Catholics. Half of Catholics living in Scotland believe their religion makes a difference to how they are treated, and a third of other respondents share this view. However, only 1% report any experience of discrimination against them personally due to their religion. The authors suggest this shows the power of the myth of sectarianism. In reality they suggest that very few people experience any kind of discrimination because of their religion. From the 1980s onwards, it is suggested that Catholics no longer found discrimination on entering the workplace. Today, Catholics receive the same form of state protection in welfare, and there is no evidence to suggest that religious identity equals victimisation.

3.8 Furthermore, it is argued that the Catholic Church is very well respected- more so than some conservative Protestant groups. In looking at chaplaincy it is claimed that in the majority of cases where 2 chaplains work side by side, one is from the Church of Scotland and one is Catholic. This is said to be a large presence for a population that equals 16% of the Scottish population.

3.9 When looking at whether Catholics have a 'distinctive' identity, the following is claimed:

- Intermarriage is increasing with almost 50% of married Catholics marrying non-Catholics.
- Catholics living in Scotland are more likely to say they are Scottish not British, as

Protestants are more likely to say they are equally Scottish and British. There is no indication that Catholics in Scotland identify themselves primarily as Irish.

- 20% of those raised as Catholics now have 'no religion'.
- An increasing number of those identifying with Catholicism, feel the Church should comment on public issues but not private matters. This is possibly a move to secularism.

3.10 Other signs of tolerance in society include the backlash against those figures that are 'caught' airing sectarian attitudes and the decreasing membership of the Orange Lodge (estimated to be 50,000) in Scotland, compared to other countries.

Football and Violence in Scotland

3.11 There is a perception that the majority of sectarian attitudes and behaviour is linked to football and associated street violence. Whilst the authors recognise some individual cases, in particular the murder of Mark Scott by Jason Campbell and Campbell's connections to the UVF and planned bombing attacks on Glasgow pubs, they suggest that this is the extreme and not the norm. [...]

3.15 One final point that the authors raise is the question over what is allowed in a 'good society'. In other words, what does it mean to be sectarian? They caution that it should not be prejudiced to accept Irish Catholicism in various forms, whilst also choosing to disagree with some aspects of that tradition in favour of a Scottish Protestant background. It is suggested that it is more a question of tolerance whilst keeping one's own identity."

The final point made by Steve Bruce et al raises a wider theme in the context of religion and discrimination law. Can any religious tradition that has a history of intolerance towards other religions, women, or gays and lesbians, be the basis for a viable and recognised personal identity in contemporary legal systems? The issue of national identity and religious minorities is also important. Wales and Scotland have distinct and well established national identities that draw on linguistic and cultural differences. There has also been devolution of power to Wales and Scotland which enables the further development of distinct national political identities. It is worth emphasising that there may also be some intersection between race and religion within the category "Welsh" and "Scot".

Chapters 9 and 12 emphasise the importance of deconstructing concepts such as race and ethnicity to ensure that they do not merely reflect the viewpoint of those with greater social power. In this context, the overlap between claims to national identity and devolution, and the ongoing problems of sectarianism, are an example of the overlap between different grounds of discrimination. It is worth reiterating the importance of a method which is able to respond to intersectional discrimination, e.g. in this case, discrimination against a person because he is Scottish (national origin) but at the same time also Catholic. Processes of devolution of power, and the increasing recognition of national minorities, need to be sensitive to the fact that an overarching homogenous category such as "national minority" will often be composed of other social groups (e.g. smaller minorities). There is increasing recognition of the importance of linking issues of devolution to issues of intersectional discrimination, and recent quantitative research and academic literature has given priority to this overlap of protected grounds in discrimination law.[24]

A significant difference between the established Church of England and the disestablished Church in Wales, is that in England formally the sovereign is both the Head of State and the Supreme Governor of the Church of England. Moreover, there is a close relationship between Church and State in a number of other areas: for example, state processions, the appointment of religious officials and the requirement for parliamentary approval for key matters of governance in the Church of England.[25]

One alternative to religious establishment is strict constitutional neutrality and a strict division between religion and state. A versions of this approach can be found in France (the *laicite* principle). Furthermore, US constitutional law prohibits the use of religion as a classification for state action, i.e as the basis for conferring either a benefit or a burden (set out in the Free Exercise Clause of the First Amendment to the US Constitution. However, what appears to be a simple appeal to neutrality towards all religions masks a more complex contemporary political choice. In Britain there is acceptance that in some cases neutrality and equality will require taking some positive action thereby allowing a limited accommodation for religious differences in the public sphere, such as making allowance for Sikh turbans and Muslim headscarves. However, the stricter French *laicite* approach (discussed below) does not at first sight permit such exceptions to strict neutrality in the public sphere. At one level, a "*strict laïcité*" approach of neutrality requires treating everyone in exactly the same way through the universal application of a general rule in the public sphere. However, within discrimination law in some circumstances there may be good reasons why strict neutrality must give way and take account of relevant differences. This need to respond to "difference" in limited circumstances may justify a "soft *laïcité*" approach which corresponds to definitions of "substantive equality". As the discussion of the French headscarf ban later in this chapter illustrates, even within one political tradition such as French republicanism, there are often choices between strict and softer versions of *laicite* and different visions of political and social equality. In this context, a reductionist appeal to "*laicite*" or "neutrality" may be less useful than more refined concepts which separate out "strict" from a

[24] See for example the ESRC research project on "Devolution and Constitutional Change" which includes projects on the intersection between Scottish national identity and other categories such as gender, ethnicity and religion, *see www.devolution.ac.uk* (accessed on August 20, 2006). For qualitative academic literature see for example Catherine Bromley (ed.), John Curtice (ed.), David McCrone (ed.), Alison Park (ed.) *Has Devolution Delivered?* (Edinburgh: Edinburgh University Press, 2006) and Asifa M. Hussain and William L. Miller, *Multicultural Nationalism* (Oxford: Oxford University Press, 2006).

[25] See Rex Ahdar and Ian Leigh, *Religious Freedom in the Liberal State* (Oxford: Oxford University Press, 2005) at Ch.3.

"softer" version of laicite or neutrality.[26] As a number of commentators have noted, the strict laicite principle may have an unequal effect between established religions and newer religious minorities. The optimal state response to religion may, therefore, need to be reformulated in the light of increasing religious diversity in Europe and other liberal democracies.[27]

A more complex approach towards the relationship between liberal democratic politics and religion needs to open up a series of distinctions. An important preliminary question when choosing between different versions of liberal secularism in the contemporary context relates to the relationship between religious and political authories. Does the weakening of religious power justify a more permissive approach to the accommodation of religion, and religious minorities who are especially vulnerable?[28] Should they overlap, compete with or complement each other? Does one act as a check on the other? Does pluralism require the accommodation and simultaneous co-existence of both religious and political authority or does it require the state to act as the source of power (and arbiter) of whether, and on what terms, religion will be accommodated within the political or public sphere?

In the two extracts that follow, the first by Bhiku Parekh and the second by Anne Phillips, the relationship between politics and religion is discussed. Each writer develops alternative approaches to this relationship in liberal democracies. Each also has an alternative vision for how there can be a viable separation of religion from political power and public life. Bhiku Parekh argues in favour of the accommodation of religion into the political and public life of the state because of the *substantive* benefits of religion. Anne Phillips, by contrast, re-affirms the importance of maintaining limits on the place of religion in the political and public sphere. Yet, at the same time, Phillips develops a secular justification for policies which allow a limited accommodation of religion. However, Phillips justifies limited accommodation not because of the substantive value or truth of religion: rather, she argues that accommodation remains firmly rooted in liberal secular principles. Phillips' approach seeks to retain secularism as the pre-condition for determining the role of religion in politics, but it avoids a "militant secularism" in favour of an approach that

[26] Joel S. Fetzer and J. Christopher Soper, *Muslims and the State in Britain, France and Germany* (Cambridge: Cambridge University Press, 2005).

[27] Talal Asad gives as one example of the exception to the principle of a strict laicite the following: "Alsace-Moselle is the one region in which the state pays the salaries of priests, pastors, and rabbis, and owns all church property. There are historical reasons for this exception and the Stasi report suggests this exceptional arrangement be retained on the ground that the population of that area is especially attached to them—that is, because *they are part of its regional identity*. Retaining these arrangements does not, so the report insists, conflict with the principle of secular neutrality." See Talal Asad, "Reflections on Laicite and the Public Sphere" Keynote Address at the Beirut Conference on the Public Sphere, October 22–24, 2004, *http://www.ssrc.org/publications/items/v5n3/index.html* (accessed October 20, 2006). See also Talal Asad, "Trying to Understand French Secularism" in Hent de Vries (ed.), *Political Theologies* (New York: Fordham University Press, 2006).

[28] See Seumas Milne, "The struggle is no longer against religion, but within it", *The Guardian*, December 16, 2004.

seeks to "soften" secularism through limited public accommodation of some religious difference. The contrast between Parekh and Phillips also raises a question about the relationship between religion and secular liberal political power. Both writers assume that it is possible to sharply demarcate religion from liberal democratic politics, but a contrary view would be that such an assumption underestimates the relationship between these two categories. Even if it is assumed that secular liberal democracies can separate questions about religion from questions about politics[29], there is also a further question about whether, and to what extent, religious belief can make a contribution in justifying and providing a moral context for, a liberal political order.[30]

"Religion and Public Life"
Bhikhu Parekh
In Church, State and Religious Minorities,
Tariq Modood (ed.)
(London: Policy Studies Institute, 1997)

"There are then, four different interpretations of the concept of equal treatment of all religions:

(i) The state should not persecute or suppress *any* religion, but may privilege one that happens to be an integral part of its history and identity.
(ii) It should protect *all* religions equally.
(iii) It should not institutionalise or protect *any* religion.
(iv) It should protect a religion under threat in the same way that it grants extra protection to individuals under threat or in special need.

The question is therefore raised as to which of these four is the 'correct' or rather, the most reasonable interpretation of the principle of religious equality. The question is not easy to answer. If the principle is defined in terms of equal formal rights, only the second and the third interpretations qualify, and do so equally. If it is defined in terms of equal outcome or

[29] Talal Asad has noted:

"Yet the insistence that religion has an autonomous essence—not to be confused with the essence of science, or of politics, or of common sense—invites us to define religion (like any essence) as a transhistorical and transcultural phenomenon. It may be a happy accident that this effort of defining religion converges with the liberal demand in our time that it be kept quite separate from politics, law and science—spaces in which varieties of power and reason articulate our distinctively modern life. This definition is at once part of a strategy (for secular liberals) of the confinement, and (for liberal Christians) of the defense of religion.",

See Talal Asad, *Geneologies of Religion* (Baltimore, US: The John Hopkins University Press, 1993). Clifford Geertz has made a similar point in noting that a sharp dichotomy between a religious and secular perspectives under-estimates the important relationships and overlap between the two, see Clifford Geertz, *The Interpretation of Cultures* (London: Fontana Press, 1993) at Chapter 4.

[30] See Raymond Plant, *Politics, Theology and History* (Cambridge: Cambridge University Press, 1996), Pt II.

equally effective protection of all religions, then the second and the fourth but not the third would qualify. In either case the first would be grossly discriminatory and would have to be rejected. [. . .]

Religion also plays a valuable counterweight to the state, and nurtures sensibilities that give political life spiritual depth. Just as we need opposition parties to check the government of the day, we need powerful non-state institutions to check the statist manner of thinking, including the glorification of the state. If religion is prone to the vice of fundamentalism, the state is prone to the equally undesirable vice evil of nationalism. Again, religion is a source of important moral and social values and has inspired many empancipatory movements such as those against slavery and racism. What is more, since the modern state is too abstract, distant and bureaucratic to hold society together and to deal with such problems as the disintegration of the family, the rise in crime, and selfish disregard of others' interests, the state needs moral partners, of which religion is obviously one. Religion reaches areas of life the state cannot, and can complement its efforts.

For these and other reasons we need to consider the currently dominant secularist view of political life. Secularism has its virtues, but also its limitations. It keeps religious passions at bay, avoids social authoritarianism, discourages moral absolutism, etc. but it also nurtures moral positivism and cynical politics, undermines the wholeness of peoples lives, fails to mobilise their moral and spiritual energies, and homogenises public discourse. While secularism must remain an important voice in political life, it cannot be allowed to be the only one. Religion has much to say of great relevance about the good life, personal responsibility, family values, social justice, global redistribution of resources, the environment and other issues that dominate contemporary public agenda. We must therefore find new ways of giving it a public presence and role. In so doing, religion will also be subject to public scrutiny and the discipline of political responsibility and power. The established church is one way of doing this. But it clearly has its problems, including subjecting religion to the manipulation and pressures of the state. What alternative structure to put in its place and how to ensure a creative and mutually beneficial interplay between religion and politics is one of the important questions of our times. We cannot even begin to challenge it unless we answer the untenable and long-held beliefs that only a secular state can be liberal and democratic and that political discourse is manageable only when it is conceptually monolingual and homogenous. [. . .]

The discussion is further complicated by the fact that religious equality is an ambiguous concept. It could mean either equal respect for religions taken as collective wholes, or equal respect for the religious beliefs and practices of all individuals; that is, it could mean either equality of religions or equality *to* religion. In the first sense of the term, all but the first of the four interpretations mentioned above are valid; in the second sense, the first interpretation is not only valid but might even have an edge over the others. Once the religious beliefs of all individuals are equally respected, which is so under the first interpretation, no apparent injustice is done to minorities if the religion of the overwhelming majority of the citizens is given some precedence over others, especially when it has long enjoyed that precedence, it is built into the structure of the state and when doing so has no adverse effects on the rights of religious minorities."

"In Defence of Secularism"
Anne Phillips
In Church, State and Religious Minorities,
Tariq Modood (ed.)
(London: Policy Studies Institute, 1997)

"[...] religions almost invariably build into their moral prescriptions part of what have been the customs and conventions of the societies from which they arise; they then weigh these customs with all the power of religious prescriptions. [...]

Religion is better regarded as a matter of private choice and practice, and while this is in my view entirely compatible with the public funding of religious schools, it is not compatible with the state defining itself through one or more religions. [...] secularism also presents itself as the solution after all other voices have spoke, for in arguing for a separation between church and state, it promises to protect the beliefs and the practices of each from the pressures to go along with what any others believe. [...] Yet the original point about secularism remains: that it is the only approach that can even approximate equality of treatment between those who hold different beliefs. In a secular society that nonetheless contains a variety of religions, the interests of democratic equality cannot be well served by practices that privilege one church over the others; nor can they be well served by practices that privilege religious values over secular ones; nor—and this is the difficult one—can they be well served by practices that privilege secular values over religious beliefs. The difficulty remains that any way of formulating this puts it in the framework of a secular solution, and some will regard this as diminishing the significance of religion. But the secular separation of church from state is still the closest we can get to parity of treatment between those who are religious and those who are not, and between the followers of different religions. Equality is one of the only crucial principles of a modern democracy, and for this reason (even excluding all the others), the secular solution is the only one I could defend. [...] It is a serious misreading of secularism to treat it as evacuating the terrain of morality, or to treat it as excluding religious considerations from public debate. What secularism means, in this present context, is removing from our political institutions the anachronistic privileging of what is only one out of many sets of values. As such, it is a necessary part of a project for democratic equality, particularly important in a multicultural society, hardly even arising in a (mythical) monocultural state."

The contrast between Parekh and Phillips reveals the variety of options available in thinking about the place of religion in the public sphere. Significantly, neither Parekh nor Phillips advocates a strict separation of religion and state along the lines of the French *laicite* model. Parekh's argument about the substantive contribution of religion in the public sphere may be difficult to reconcile with ideas of liberal democracy, which focuses on individual autonomy and choice rather than groups (see further Chapter 3). Moreover, rather than providing a justification for the substantive inclusion of religion in public life, the increasing diversity of religion might be thought to provide a strong argument for the opposite proposition, i.e. that the existence of a range of diverse (and sometimes conflicting) religions makes it even more important to maintain a separation of political (public) space and religion (private) belief. Within this contemporary context, it might be thought that there is a need for a form of secularism which recognises that religion has, and continues to have, a limited role in the public sphere. From this perspective, Phillips' affirmation of secularism which reconciles the idea with equal citizenship becomes especially useful. Moreover, Phillips accepts that secularism does not exclude religion from the public sphere altogether.[31] Phillips endorses secularism, but in a version that permits some accommodation of difference. Phillips states:

> In a secular society that nonetheless contains a variety of religions, the interests of democratic equality cannot be well served by practices that privilege one church over the others; nor can they be well served by practices that privilege religious values over secular ones; nor—and this is the difficult one—can they be well served by practices that privilege secular values over religious beliefs [emphasis added].

Phillips' approach affirms that equality between all citizens in contemporary liberal democracies, between those with different religious viewpoints and also those with no religious viewpoint, can only be maintained by adopting the principle of secularism:

"[...] secularism also presents itself as the solution when all the other voices have spoken, for in arguing for a separation between church and state, it promises to protect the beliefs and the practices of each from the pressures to go along with what any others believe".[32] Yet, at the same time, and as the final sentence of the passage above suggests, it is important that this does not become "an arrogance of secular thinking when it becomes a majoritarian norm."[33]

It is significant that the Court of Appeal in the recent *Shabina Begum* case, recognised that there is a long standing British tradition of including religion as part of the education syllabus. In the contemporary period, this principle has been extended to include non-Christian religions. Lord Justice Brooke found that unlike Turkey, the UK does not enforce a strict verison of secularism. There are statutory duties on schools to provide religious education (e.g. s.80 of the Education Act 2002). Brooke L.J. states:

"The position of the School is already distinctive in the sense that despite its policy of inclusiveness it permits girls to wear a headscarf which is likely to identify them as Muslim. The central issue is therefore the more subtle one of whether, given that Muslim girls can already be identified in this way, it is necessary in a democratic society to place a particular restriction on those Muslim girls at this school who sincerely believe that when they arrive at the

[31] See also Maleiha Malik, "Faith and the State of Jurisprudence", in Peter Oliver, et al (eds), *Faith in Law: Essays in Legal Theory* (Oxford: Hart Publishing, 2000).

[32] Anne Phillips, "In Defence of Secularism" in Tariq Modood (ed.), "Religion and Public Life" in *Church, State and Religious Minorities*, (London: Policy Studies Institute, 1997) at p.27.

[33] *ibid.*

age of puberty they should cover themselves more comprehensively than is permitted by the school uniform policy."[34]

It might be argued that what is perhaps needed, is a version of secularism that can adapt to the changing relationship between politics and religion. Yet, at the same time, there may need to be a more explicit dissenting judgment in the recognition that secularism should not be used as a way of oppressing religious minorities. Strict versions of secularism may introduce the risk of the authoritarianism against vulnerable religious minorities. Judge Tulkens' dissent in the ECHR headscarf case, *Leyla Sahin v Turkey* recognises this risk. She concludes:

"In the present case, relying exclusively on the reasons cited by the national authorities and courts, the majority put forward, in general and abstract terms, two main arguments: secularism and equality. While I fully and totally subscribe to each of these principles, I disagree with the manner in which they are applied here and to the way they were interpreted in relation to the practice of the wearing the headscarf. *In a democratic society, I believe it is necessary to seek to harmonise the principles of secularism, equality and liberty, not to weigh one against the other.*"[35]

IV. Defining Religion and Belief

The regulation of religion within discrimination law raises a set of distinct issues not raised in relation to other categories such as race or gender. One aspect is that "religion" maps upon a different set of historical conditions to those relevant to the other prohibited groups. There is an ongoing controversy about the appropriate definition of religion within disciplines such as theology or religious studies. This section does not seek to address these controversies although it is argued below that it is advantageous, when seeking to understand the category "religion" within discrimination, law to use a method similar to that employed in relation to race in Chapter 12, i.e. rather than searching for an essential and ahistorical definition of religion we should instead use a "social construction" method which seeks to analyse religion as part of the social and political context within which discrimination law has to operate. Nevertheless, it is worth making some brief observations about the wider and distinct issues raised by the attempts to define religion. One aspect of these wider issues is the relationship between religion and politics in liberal democracies (discussed above). In earlier sections, we noted the historical

[34] *R (On the Application of Shabina Begum) v Headteachers and Governors of Denbigh High School.* [2005] H.R.L.R. 16 at para.74.

[35] *Leyla Sahin v Turkey*, European Court of Human Rights, Decision of November 10, 2005, Application No.44774/98, *per* Judge Tulkens, para.4 (emphasis added).

processes that have led European liberal democracies to demarcate a distinct space for religion, and separate this space from politics and the public sphere. The discussion of the headscarf case in France later in this chapter illustrates that these differences have real consequences for law and policy. Despite variations in religion-state relations throughout Europe, the approach in most liberal democratices assumes that it is possible to develop a sharp distinction between religion and the spheres within which secular political power is exercised. However, once we move away from an essentialist view of religion, such a sharp dichotomy becomes less easy to sustain. Talal Asad has noted:

"Yet the insistence that religion has an autonomous essence—not to be confused with the essence of science, or of politics, or of common sense—invites us to define religion (like any essence) as a transhistorical and transcultural phenomenon. It may be a happy accident that this effort of defining religion converges with the liberal demand in our time that it be kept quite separate from politics, law and science—spaces in which varieties of power and reason articulate our distinctively modern life. This definition is at once part of a strategy (for secular liberals) of the confinement, and (for liberal Christians) of the defense of religion."[36]

Clifford Geertz has made a similar point in noting that a sharp dichotomy between religious and secular perspectives under-estimates the important relationships and overlap between these two spheres.[37] This more complex view of the place of religion within the "public sphere", as well as a method that allows a socially constructionist approach to the definition of religion, opens the way for an analysis of religion that responds to contemporary social and political problems. The danger of using a more inflexible "essentialist" definition of religion is that it may render the idea either wholly irrelevant to the public sphere or construe religion as a set of immutable beliefs and practices that threatens to engulf the whole of the public sphere.

As with race, problems associated with the definition of religion for legal purposes can also be alleviated by using the constructionist approach. First, it is noteworthy that "religion and belief" will potentially cover a myriad of religious viewpoints and practices. This problem of definition, and the appropriate legal rules to address these problems, are discussed below. Here it is worth noticing that whilst there may be a problem of defining religion and belief in an abstract analysis, and that an essentialist approach may well fail to capture the diversity that is present in any social group (underlying a religion), it may be possible to address some of the difficulties by taking a more practical

36 Talal Asad, *Genealogies of Religion* (Baltimore, US: The John Hopkins University Press, 1993) at p.28.

37 Clifford Geertz, *The Interpretation of Cultures* (London: Fontana Press, 1993) at Ch.4. Note, however, the importance of separating religious and non-religious arguments in a constitutional democracy: Nicholas Bamforth and David A.J. Richards, *Patriarchal Religion, Sexuality and Gender: A Critique of New Natural Law*, (Cambridge: Cambridge UP, 2008), Ch.2.

and functionalist approach. Religion and belief become important, within this more functional analysis, not because of some essentialist commitment to their underlying values, but because they can operate in practical contexts as a source of injustice. Moreover, religion is also important, like other criteria such as race, gender or sexual orientation, because it provides a context for the well-being of individuals.[38] As with race, the main concern is not with the essential meaning of the term but rather with the way in which it is deployed in particular contexts. Therefore, as with the functionalist approach to race, the category religion can also be a marker for identifying individual needs and addressing injustice.[39] These injustices can arise where a particular religion or belief, and its manifestation, is a source of prejudice and discrimination. Injustice can also arise when religion becomes a barrier to enabling an individual to access key goods such as employment, education and public services. This is exacerbated in the case of minority religions which face a pre-existing public sphere which is not conducive to their particular beliefs, e.g. attending work or schools during minority religious festivals such as Diwali for Hindus or Eid for Muslims. A functional approach is also less concerned with arbitrary distinctions and bright-line drawing between religion, race and culture. Instead, it is more concerned with: identifying the needs of certain individuals and groups as they manifest themselves in practice; and then developing an appropriate response (informed by both principle and pragmatism) by the state, public and private bodies. The present system of legal regulation, which creates a hierarchy of protection and rights depending on whether a group falls within the category race or religion does not encourage this type of functionalist analysis. A move towards rationalising discrimination law in the form of a single statute covering all prohibited grounds of discrimination may, by contrast, help to ensure that arbitrary distinctions between race, religion and culture do not become the basis for providing differential rights, goods and services to individuals.

A strict distinction between race, religion and culture also under-estimates the extent to which certain ideas can operate simultaneously within different categories such as race, culture and religion and yet, at the same time, still racialise individuals and groups in a similar way. In Chapter 12 we noted how there can be a transfer of "race" ideas from previously racialised groups to new racialised groups. One important historical precedent for current processes of racialisation of minorities is the treatment of Jews as one of the earliest racial and religious minorities in Britian (see futher Chapter 12), we also examined the way in which Jews and Muslims have been racialised because of their religious culture. Here it is worth observing that some aspects

[38] See Timothy Macklem, "Reason and Religion", in Peter Oliver, et al (eds), *Faith in Law: Essays in Legal Theory* (Oxford: Hart Publishing, 2000).

[39] Tariq Modood, for example, makes the point that although there is diversity within social groups such as Christian or Muslim, this does not make it impossible or meaningless to identify the group: "Muslims and the Politics of Difference", The Political Quarterly 100 (2003).

of discrimination against groups such as Jews or Muslims may also be understood as a form of "religious discrimination" law.

At a legal level, one especially important source of overlap between religion and race occurs because of *Mandla v Dowell Lee* which defines ethnic religious minorities (e.g. Sikhs and Jews) but not non-ethnic minorities as a race. One consequence of this division is that despite the "religious needs" of Sikhs and Jews they may forced to construct their arguments in terms of racial criteria which may distort the "religious" dimension of their claim. Conversely, other groups will be forced to bring their argument within the criterion of "religion" despite the fact that the nature of the discrimination that has caused them harm either or also fits better into an analysis of race. For these reasons it would be preferable if there were not serious political and legal consequences that follow from the distinction between race and religion within discrimination law. However, as we saw in Chapter 2, race is prohibited as a ground of discrimination in a much wider range of situations than religion. Race discrimination is prohibited in the areas of employment and training, and also in the delivery of public and private goods and services. In addition there is a positive equality duty in relation to racial discrimination. In contrast, as we will see below, religious discrimination is mainly concerned with employment and training. A method which treats religion as a social rather than an essential category can also justify a shift of focus away from religious belief and on to religious needs in their wider social and political context. An essentialist approach fails to recognise the diversity that can exist within a social group. Nevertheless, there is a need to take seriously the way in which religion can operate as a source of discrimination and disadvantage. Therefore, an approach that can give some place to religion within the analysis, without treating it as an immutable characteristic, is of the greatest use in the context of discrimination law.[40] This strategy encourages a more comprehensive approach to tackling religious discrimination: one which uses law where necessary but which is also supplemented by the use of other strategies such as education and dissemination of information to challenge stereotypes about religions generally (but especially minority religions) that can manifest themselves as discrimination in the distribution of important goods and services.

This issue has taken on a particular salience in recent times for British and European Muslim minorities because of the domestic and international context of the "war on terror" which has led to a conflation of Islam, violence and terrorism. This raises the risk of the formation of sterotypes about minorities specifically around the category "Muslim" which can in turn filter down to manifest themselves as prejudice, violence or discrimination against those who are identifiable as Muslims. The most recent survey of social attitude

[40] Tariq Modood, for example, makes the point that although there is diversity within a social group, such as Christian, Belgian or Muslim, this does not make it either impossible or meaingless to identify the social group, see Tariq Modood, "Muslims and the Politics of Difference" (2003) 74 Political Quarterly 1 100–115.

confirms that there is increasing stereotyping of Muslims; fear is an increasing emotional reaction to the term "Muslim"; nearly a third of those surveyed felt that Muslims pose a physical or cultural threat; and there are assumptions that it is not possible to be Muslim and British.[41] The political context which renders Muslims vulnerable to this type of discrimination is also exacerbated by the socio-economic data which suggests that as a group Muslims are more likely to be concentrated in the lowest socio-economic groups in terms of income, housing, education and child poverty. The summary of recent findings on the social-economic status of ethnic minorities by Lucinda Platt set out in Chapter 12 confirmed that Pakistanis and Bangladeshis (which can be used as an approximate proxy for Muslim in the absence of statistics based on religion) are more likely to be disadvantaged in these spheres.[42]

It is because of the special risk of discrimination against Muslims, and particularly the risk that anti-terrorist legislation will exacerbate this risk, that the Government extended the existing provisions on racially aggravated offences in the Crime and Disorder Act 1998 to cover religously aggravated offences in the Anti-Terrorism Act 2002. Following the terrorist bombings in London in July 2005, there was the prospect of a specific risk of harm to Muslim more generally. As the monitoring work of the European Union Monitoring Centre in Vienna makes clear despite an initial spike in the figures of religious aggravated crime the rates of such "hate crimes" fell back to pre-July 2005 levels.[43] The EUMC report credits appropriate political leadership by the State, minority communities and a sensitive police and media response for this result. In addition, the EUMC report highlights the way in which extra-legal interventions in the public sphere in the form of representations of minorities, as well as targeted social exclusion programmes, can be a useful tool in preventing the formation of prejudice and stereotype before it becomes entrenched and manifests itself as harmful conduct. The place of interventions to prevent the formation of prejudice is also related to a more difficult question in the context of religion: should, and to what extent, should free speech be regulated, and if so to what extent? This raises a specific problem about the extent to which religious belief should be open to scrutiny in a secular society on the one hand, and to what extent free speech should be regulated to prevent the formation of prejudice and the harm of "hate speech". A further related aspect which is distinctive to religion is the place of the regulation of blasphemy, discussed in Chapter 8 on harassment, hate crimes and hate speech.

[41] See Dominic Abrams and Diane M. Houston, Equality, Diversity and Prejudice in Britain: Results from the 2005 National Survey, Report for the Cabinet Office Equalities Review, Centre for the Study of Group Processes, University of Kent (published October 2006).

[42] "Child Poverty in the UK, second report of session 2003–04, Vol.2, Written Evidence, House of Commons Papers 2003–04, 85-II. This report can be obtained via the official web site of the House of Commons, at *http://www.parliament.the-stationery-office.co.uk/pa/cm200304/cmselect/cmworpen/85/85we54.htm* (accessed November 10, 2005).

[43] "The impact of 7 July 2005 London bomb attacks on Muslim communities in the EU", 2005, (Vienna: European Monitoring Centre on Racism and Xenophobia, 2005.

A key issue for analysis in any discussion of religious discrimination is "how should religion and belief be defined?", whether for the purpose of legal regulation or policy formation.

There are distinct reasons that secular liberal democracies need to regulate religion through discrimination law. Legal regulation is not because of the essential truth claims of religious beliefs. Rather, it is because in some cases religion is a marker for social, economic and political inequalities or denials of dignity that undermine some of the central goals of secular liberal politics. As Anne Phillips suggests in the extract presented earlier, there is a powerful secular justification for the protection of religion in distinct and limited contexts. Once this policy is accepted it then becomes possible to set out the range of options about how religion should be defined for the purposes of discrimination law and policy.

A. *Options for Defining "Religion" and Belief*

One set of option for defining religion for law and policy was summarised by Bob Hepple and Tufyal Choudhry in the extract below:

Bob Hepple Q.C. and Tufyal Choudhury
Tackling Religious Discrimination: Practical Implications for Policy Makers and Legislators
Home Office Research Studies, 221 (London: Home Office, 2001)

pp.25–33: "The first option is to attempt a definition within the legislation or through a statutory code of practice. A starting point may be the classical sociological definition of religion set out by Durkheim:

> "A unified system of beliefs and practices relative to sacred things, that is to say, things set apart and forbidden—beliefs and practices which unite into one single moral community called a Church, all those who adhere to them."

Alternatively one could take the Oxford English Dictionary definition of religion as "action or conduct indicating a belief in, reverence for, and desire to please, a divine ruling power; the exercise or practice of rites or observances implying this . . . a particular system of faith and worship." [. . .]

Another broader formulation is that adopted by Ontario Human Rights Commission. The Ontario Human Rights Code prohibits discrimination on the grounds of "creed". Creed is not a defined term in the Code. The Commission's guidance states that:

> "Creed is interpreted to mean 'religious creed' or 'religion'. It is defined as a professed system and confession of faith, including both beliefs and observances or worship. A belief in a God or gods, or a single Supreme Being or deity is not a pre-requisite.

> Religion is broadly accepted by the Commission to include, for example, non-deistic bodies of faith, such as the spiritual faiths, practices of aboriginal cultures, as well as bona fide newer religions (assessed on a case by case basis). The existence of religious beliefs and practices are both necessary and sufficient to the meaning of creed, if the beliefs and practices are sincerely held and/or observed. 'Creed' is defined subjectively. The Code protects personal religious beliefs, practices or observances, even if they are not essential elements of the creed, provided they are sincerely held. 'Creed' is defined subjectively. The Code protects personal religious beliefs, practices or observances, even if they are not essential elements of the creed, provided they are sincerely held."

The advantage of utilising a statutory code of practice, to which courts must have regard, is that it provides guidance to users of the legislation on where to draw the line while leaving flexibility to deal sensitively with individual cases. However any definition will inevitably exclude some groups and would require further interpretation.

A **second option** is to have a list of recognised religions with a process and criteria for such recognition. The list system is operated to an extent in Germany, where certain religions are given the status of legal person in public law, through procedures in force under Article 140 of the Constitution. The status of legal person gives rise to certain rights, in particular the right to levy church taxes through the services of the State and the right to tax advantages and tax exemptions. A "cult" is granted the status of a legal person in public law when, in light of its statutes and its membership, it gives every indication of durability. Recognition requires a "measure of internal organsation, adequate financing, and a certain period of existence; in practice, existence for thirty or forty years is required before a religious community can be considered to have shown sufficient durability. Jehovah's Witnesses and the Church of Scientology and the Muslim community are among those who have so far not received recognition as legal persons in public law in Germany.

The creation of lists of accepted religions raises the issue of the recognition of new religious movements. Those who favour an official list system claim a number of advantages. It provides a system of executive supervision to prevent protection being given to fleeting beliefs, or ones which are believed to present a threat to other human rights and values. It also allows for a high degree of certainty as regards the scope of legislation for various purposes. If utilised in the case of anti-discrimination legislation, it would reduce the need for litigation to decide whether a religious group came within the scope of the Act. There is already some experience of official listing of religions in the UK. The prison chaplaincy service carries out an Annual Religious Census on which Scientologists, Black Muslims and Rastafarians are recorded as "non-permitted Muslims"

The main disadvantages of a list system are that it would require an administrative or judicial procedure in order to determine the status of a particular religion. The German system does not exist in the context of an anti-discrimination law, but serves the purpose of conferring a status for purposes such as the right to levy taxes or enjoy priveleges. Certainty may be outweighed by rigidity, and the possibly unfair exclusion of new and unpopular beliefs. A law against religious discrimination is primarily concerned with conferring protection on individuals in respect of their own sincerely held beliefs, rather than protecting or legitimating any particular religion.

The **third option** is to leave the definition of religion for the courts to develop. Article 14 of the ECHR prohibits discrimination on the grounds of religion without providing a definition of religion. Most anti-discrimination legislation in Australia, Canada and the United States which prohibits discrimination on the grounds of religion adopts this approach. The definition has been left to the courts, in some cases with guidance provided by the enforcement commission.

The meaning of "religion" may depend on the purposes of the statute or other legal instruments in which the word is used. Outside the area of discrimination law the legal system does have experience in attempting to define religion and in establishing principles by which to recognise religions. This shows that no single or universal definition of religion is possible."

Hepple and Choudhury go on and identify the areas of UK law in which definitions of religion can be found. These include inter alia: cases involving charitable trusts set up for the advancement of religion; tax; conscientious objection; and most significantly the experience of courts and industrial tribunals in defining "religious belief" and "conscience" in the context of exemptions from closed shop arrangments.

Legal systems have tended to have a preference for the third approach: which leaves the definition of religion for judicial development by the courts. This is also the preferred approach of the ECHR and the Employment Equality Directive. Neither the Employment Equality Directive nor the Employment Equality (Religion and Belief) Regs 2003 specify or define religion and belief in a statutory definition (option 1 and option 2 laid down by Hepple and Choudhury above). They leave the development of a definition to the courts. The decision of the ECJ in *Chacon Navas v Eurest*[44] on the meaning of disability (under the Employment Equality Directive) confirmed that "disability" would have a harmonised EU wide meaning. This suggests that other categories under EU discrimination law, such as race and religion, should also be subject to an autonomous and uniform interpretation. In domestic discrimination law, the Religion and Belief Regs (2003) do, however, indirectly introduce a partial list. The DTI Explanatory notes and the ACAS Code of Practice, which are used to interpret the Regulations, set out a list of religions which are widely recognised: Christianity; Islam; Judaism; Bhuddism; Sikhism; Rastafarianism; Baha'is; Zorastrianism and Jainism.[45] It is also worth noting that the wider definition of religion in the Directive has been transposed into the Northern Ireland directly into the FETO definitions of religious discrimination. The FETO structure introduced the prohibition of discrimination on the grounds of religion and political opinion. The FETO provisions are discussed below.

Before concluding the analysis of how to define religion and belief, it is worth connecting this issue with the previous discussion of the wider social and political context within which religious discrimination operates in liberal democracies. As suggested earlier, rather than being concerned with the objective truth claims of a religion, or defining its essence, discrimination law should be more concerned with justifications that draw on the value of religious belief to individual citizens as an important source of their self-respect; the possibility that certain religions and religious groups will have a lower status, something which has ramifications for the political, social and economic position of their members; and the secular argument for the recognition of religious difference. Once the paradigm is set in these terms, it becomes

[44] *Chacon Navas v Eurest Colectiviades SA* C—13/05, (decision of ECJ of July 11, 2006).

[45] ACAS, "*Religion or Belief and the Workplace*", November 2005 (available at www.acas.org.uk, accessed on August 20, 2006).

easier to adopt a more flexible definition of terms such as "religion" and "belief". For example, the Ontario Human Rights Code defines "creed" subjectively and according to the sincere beliefs of the individuals. Furthermore, Hepple and Choudhury's option (see extract above) which permits the courts to develop a definition of religion and belief depending on the statutory purpose of the legislation would also fit with this flexible approach. As Hepple and Choudhury observe, this would accord with the discrimination law paradigm because:

"The main purpose of discrimination law is to protect the individual from arbitrary treatment based on stereotypes or unjustified practices. The courts will not be concerned with the legitimacy of a particular creed, but rather with whether or not there has been discrimination because an individual is believed, rightly or wrongly, to subscribe to those beliefs."

While a focus on the subjective perspective of the individual, and the underlying objectives of discrimination law, may offer one appropriate method for analysis in cases involving definitions of religion and belief, it does however, raise the spectre of a myriad of different, and new, claims about "religion". As Hepple and Choudhury note:

Bob Hepple QC and Tufyal Choudhury
Tackling Religious Discrimination: Practical Implications for Policy Makers and Legislators
Home Office Research Studies, 221 (London: Home Office, 2001)

pp.31–33: "No one argues that there should be an official list of recognised beliefs. But is some definition necessary? The House of Lords Select Committee looking at Article 13 draft employment directive expressed concern that belief "would appear to encompass a wide range of political or ideological views" The issues and options raised by the definition of "belief" are similar to those surrounding the definition of religion.

Again, the first option would be to provide a definition in the legislation or a statutory code of practice. The second option would be to leave this to the courts.

The ECHR may be of some assistance here. The broad approach of the Convention organs to the interpretation of Article 9 has enabled them to accept, in principle, that its protection extends to Druidism, pacifism, veganism, the Divine Light Zentrum and the Church of Scientology. The European Court of Human Rights has said that Article 9 is a "precious asset for atheists, agnostics, sceptics and the unconcerned." This does not, however, mean that every individual opinion or preference constitutes a religion or belief. To come within the protection of this article the views must attain a certain level of cogency, seriousness, cohesion and importance. In McFeely v UK the Commission said that "belief" in Article 9 "means more than just 'mere opinions or deeply held feelings'; there must be a holding of spiritual or philosophical convictions which have an identifiable formal content." The courts may in future be guided, when interpreting Article 13 employment directive, by the EU Charter of Fundamental Rights, Article 1 of which says that "the dignity of the person must be respected and protected". Those beliefs which are essential to the dignity and integrity of the individual are likely to be protected as an aspect of freedom of belief. On the other hand, the courts may be unwilling to allow political or ideological views (e.g against the criminalisation of drugs or against genetically modified foods) to qualify as "beliefs".

The UN Human Rights Committee has also recognised that the definition of "religion or belief" should be subjected to certain limits. In the case of M. A. B.; W. A. T. and A. Y. T v Canada [...] The Committee said that the expression "religion or belief" does not encompass a belief which consists primarily or exclusively of the worship of and distribution of a narcotic drug."

One specific form of belief is, of course, political opinion. The sectarian conflict in Northern Ireland made the connection between religion and political opinion especially salient in the domestic context. The legal and policy response to this distinct problem is considered later in this chapter. Here it is worth observing that the protection of "belief" has also caused difficulty in other contexts. In a recent case, the Court of Appeal held that a far right British political party, the British National Party, could not claim to be protected by the RRA.[46] This left open the issue of whether this type of political belief can fall within the definition of religion or "belief" in the Religion and Belief Regulations 2003. This issue has also now been clarified in *Baggs v Dr FDA Fudge*.[47] In *Baggs* an Industrial Tribunal found that the British National Party was a political party, the views of which were not protected as a "philosophical belief" under Reg.2 of the Religion and Belief Regs 2003. The IT found that "belief" in this context needs to be similar to religious belief and for this reason the BNP fell outside the definition.[48]

B. *Legal Regulation of Religion and Belief*

Freedom of Religion is a well established individual right which is protected in a range of international and human rights instruments. At the international level, for example, Art.18 of the International Covenant on Civil and Political Rights states:

Article 18 of the ICCPR

"1. Everyone shall have the right to freedom of thought, conscience and religion. This right shall include freedom to have or to adopt a religion or belief of his choice, and

[46] *Redfearn v Serco Ltd (t/a West Yorkshire Transport Service)* [2006] EWCA Civ 659, [2006] I.R.L.R. 623.

[47] *Baggs v Dr FDA Fudge* (Chair, AC Tickle), March 24, 2005, case No.1400114/05, reported (Oct 2005) 157 Equal Opportunities Review 31–32.

[48] ibid.

freedom, either individually or in community with others and in public or private, to manifest his religion or belief in worship, observance, practice and teaching.

2. No one shall be subject to coercion which would impair his freedom to have or to adopt a religion or belief of his choice.

3. Freedom to manifest one's religion or beliefs may be subject only to such limitations as are prescribed by law and are necessary to protect public safety, order, health, or morals or the fundamental rights and freedoms of others.

4. The States Parties to the present Covenant undertake to have respect for the liberty of parents and, when applicable, legal guardians to ensure the religious and moral education of their children in conformity with their own convictions."

Article 9 ECHR replicates this structure by having two specific components to this fundamental freedom.

Article 9 of the ECHR

"1. Everyone has the right to freedom of thought, conscience and religion; this right includes freedom to change his religion or belief, and freedom, either alone or in community with others and in public or private, to manifest his religion or belief, in worship, teaching, practice and observance.

2. Freedom to manifest one's religion or beliefs shall be subject only to such limitations as are prescribed by law and are necessary in a democratic society in the interests of public safety, for the protection of public order, health or morals, or the protection of the rights and freedoms of others."

Article 14 of the ECHR introduces a norm of non-discrimination on the grounds of discrimination in the enjoyment of any of the ECHR rights:

Article 14 of the ECHR

"The enjoyment of the rights and freedoms set forth in this Convention shall be secured without discrimination on any ground such as sex, race, colour, language, religion, political or other opinion, national or social origin, association with a national minority, property, birth or other status."

There are a number of aspects of the ECHR provisions that are specially relevant in the context of religious discrimination. The Human Rights Act 1998 purports to give special status by including the following provision in s.13(1): "If a court's determination of any question arising under this Act might affect the exercise by a religious organisation (itself or its members collectively) of the Convention right to freedom of thought, conscience and religion, it must have particular regard to the importance of that right."[49] The general non-discrimination provision of Art.14 of the ECHR also applies to religion. In addition, provisions on freedom of expression (Art.10) will also be relevant to wider issues relating to religious freedom.

There are a number of specific points to make on the scope of Art.9 as a legal provision which protects religious freedom. The analysis of whether there has been an interference with Art.9 freedom of religion will turn on whether the state itself has interfered with the right of the individual; and whether the state has failed to secure and protect the individual from interference by private parties in a way that constitutes a breach of its obligation under Art.1 ECHR to safeguard Convention rights.

The analysis of the individual right in Art.9 requires further discussion. First, Art.9(1) contains the provision that protects "the right to freedom of thought, conscience and religion". Crucially, the first part of the text of Art.9 does not contain a reference to "belief". It gives special status to the internal aspect of this right which is associated with "thought and conscience". Although the first part of Art.9 does not contain a reference to belief it seems probable that belief would be included within the term "right to freedom of thought and conscience".[50] This internal aspect, sometimes known as *forum internum*, of the right to religious freedom in Art.9(1) is unqualified and restriction cannot be justified under Art.9(2). Article 9 therefore relies on a dichotomy between belief and action. Belief is given unconditional protection. This is in comparison to the right to manifest religion and belief, the restriction of which can be justified under Art.9(2). A number of commentators have noted the way in which this dichotomy underestimates the relationship between belief and action and, in particular, the way in which restrictions on action can have an important impact on the inner dimension of religion and belief. The belief-action dichotomy can be traced back to the classic exposition of religious toleration in John Locke's "A Letter Concerning Tolerance" where he argued that there could be no regulation of inner conscience on matters of religion. Moens has noted that the distinction between a wide range of latitude for belief, but a more restrictive approach to action, depends on some consensus about the social values that underlie religion. In increasingly plural societies, Moens argues, it will be difficult to apply the doctrine because it provides no substantive guide to what types of manifestation of belief fall within the permissible range.[51] More recently, Lord Nicholls, in *Williamson* stated that there was an important relationship between them:

[49] Although the Court of Appeal's treatment of an analogous attempt to give priority to Art.10 suggests that s.13 might not succeed in granting Art.9 any special status: see *Douglas and Zeta Jone v Hello Ltd* [2001] Q.B. 897.

[50] See the discussion by Carolyn Evans, *Freedom of Religion Under the European Convention on Human Rights* (Oxford: Oxford University Press, 2001) at pp.52–53.

[51] See Gabriel Moens, "The Action-Belief Dichtomy and Freedom of Religion" (1989–1990) 12 Sydney L. R. 195.

"It is against this background that Art.9 of the European Convention on Human Rights safeguards freedom of religion. This freedom is not confined to freedom to hold a religious belief. It includes the right to express and practise one's beliefs. Without this, freedom of religion would be emasculated. Invariably religious faiths call for more than belief. To a greater or lesser extent adherents are required or encouraged to act in certain ways, most obviously and directly in forms of communal or personal worship, supplication and meditation. But under Art.9 there is a difference between freedom to hold a belief and freedom to express or "manifest" a belief. The former right, freedom of belief, is absolute. The latter right, freedom to manifest belief, is qualified."[52]

The second part of Art.9 deals with the freedom to act upon these inner beliefs. This freedom is guaranteed by Art.9 as a manifestation of religion or belief. This aspect is more limited than the translation of the inner freedom of belief into all the external manifestations that follow from that belief. Therefore, a number of further questions arise for consideration. The discussion that follows focuses on three particular aspects. First, we examine what constitutes the manifestation of religion or belief. Second, we examine case law concerning situations in which individuals are deemed to have "contracted out" of Art.9. Third, we explore the extent to which Art.11, dealing with discrimination, can protect the religious claimant. In sections V and VI below, we consider two further questions, relating to the extent to which Art.9 goes beyond a negative freedom that protects individuals from state interference with religious freedom to a positive obligation to accommodate the specific needs of individuals in relation to religion or belief, and the qualification in Art.9(2) that permits the state to justify an interference with religious freedom under Art.9(1).

Beginning with the first point, courts needs to determine whether the conduct of the individual falls within the category "manifesting religious belief". Here there is a choice between an objective and a subjective test. The European Court of Human Rights approach is mixed. However, in a number of cases it has developed a more objective test which has focused on "necessity" as a marker for determining whether the conduct falls within the protection of Art.9. The necessity test was developed in the *Arrowsmith* case.[53] Generally, Art.9 is seen as protecting personal beliefs and religious creeds, falling within an area which is sometimes called the "forum internum". It also protects acts which are intimately linked to relevant beliefs and creeds, such as acts of worship or devotion which are also aspects of the practice of a religion or belief (in a generally recognised form)."[54] Both the "necessity" test and the "intimately linked" test seek to establish an objective causal analysis between

[52] *R v Secretary of State for Education and Employment Ex p. Williamson* [2005] H.R.L.R. 14 at para.16.
[53] *Arrowsmith v the United Kingdom*, App. No.7050/755, 8 Eur. Comm'n H. R. Dec. & rep. 123, 127 (1977).
[54] See *C v the United Kingdom*, Appl. 10678/83 D&R 37 (1984) at p.147.

the belief and the conduct/act that the individual is claiming should be protected. Article 9 also sets out certain examples of the manifestation of religious belief as "worship, teaching, practice and observance". The test for manifestation of religion and belief will be a critical stage of the analysis in order to determine the precise nature and scope of religious freedom under Art.9. Not every act that is motivated by, or inspired by, religion will necessarily fall within the ambit of Art.9 of the ECHR[55]. In *Arrowsmith*, the UK argued that the reference in Art.9 to the types of act that are protected was an exclusive list which provided an analogy for the types of manifestation of belief that fall within the scope of Art.9.[56] Although the Commission did not determine this issue in an explicit way the development of opinion and case law under Art.9 suggests that the range of conduct that falls within "practice" under Art.9 will be interpreted in a strict way. There has, for example, been a significant reluctance to create new rights under Art.9 case law.[57] The right to manifest religion under Art.9 has been found to include both an active and a passive component, i.e. it includes the right not to manifest a religion and belief. For example, it has been held that Art.9 includes the right not to have to swear an oath on the Gospels.[58] There is also an emerging hierachy in relation to types of manifestation of religion: worship is given the highest status; and the term observance has extended the range of protection and provided an more expansive reading of "worship". The term teaching has been problematic and requires a balancing between "improper proselytism" on the one hand and a limited right to proselytize as part of a manifestation of teaching religion and belief within Art.9.[59]

R. v Secretary of State for Education and Employment Ex p. Williamson House of Lords [2005] H.R.L.R. 14

These issues have been considered at length by domestic courts in the *Williamson* case. In *Williamson* the claimants were a group of head teachers, teachers and parents of children at four independent schools. The main claim was that the ban on corporal punishment in schools that had been extended to pupils attending all types of schools was incompatible with their Art.9, ECHR

[55] See *Arrowsmith v the United Kingdom*, App. No.7050/755, 8 Eur. Comm'n H. R. Dec. & rep. 123, 127 (1977) and also *Kalaç v Turkey*—20704/92 [1997] ECHR 37 (July 1, 1997).

[56] *ibid.*

[57] See the discussion by Carolyn Evans, *Freedom of Religion Under the European Convention on Human Rights* (Oxford: Oxford University Press, 2001) at pp.106.

[58] *ibid.*, at pp.107–109. On "teaching" see two cases: *Kokkinakis v Greece*, 260-A European Court of Human Rights (ser. A) (1993) and *Larissis v Greece*, 65 European Court of Human Rights (ser. A) at 17 (1993) cited and discussed in Evans.

[59] See the discussion by Carolyn Evans, *Freedom of Religion Under the European Convention on Human Rights* (Oxford: Oxford University Press, 2001) at pp.106.

right to freedom of religion. The claims were dismissed in the High Court and the Court of Appeal. The House of Lords also dismissed the claim.

PER LORD NICHOLLS:

[23]: "It is necessary first to clarify the court's role in identifying a religious belief calling for protection under Art.9. When the genuineness of a claimant's professed belief is an issue in the proceedings the court will inquire into and decide this issue as a question of fact. This is a limited inquiry. The court is concerned to ensure an assertion of religious belief is made in good faith: "neither fictitious, nor capricious, and that it is not an artifice", to adopt the felicitous phrase of Iacobucci J. in the decision of the Supreme Court of Canada in Syndicat Northcrest v Amselem (2004) 241 D.L.R. (4th) 1 at 27, para.[52]. But, emphatically, it is not for the court to embark on an inquiry into the asserted belief and judge its "validity" by some objective standard such as the source material upon which the claimant founds his belief or the orthodox teaching of the religion in question or the extent to which the claimant's belief conforms to or differs from the views of others professing the same religion. Freedom of religion protects the subjective belief of an individual. As Iaccobucci J. also noted, at p.28, para.[54], religious belief is intensely personal and can easily vary from one individual to another. Each individual is at liberty to hold his own religious beliefs, however irrational or inconsistent they may seem to some, however surprising. The European Court of Human Rights has rightly noted that "in principle, the right to freedom of religion as understood in the Convention rules out any appreciation by the state of the legitimacy of religious beliefs or of the manner in which these are expressed": *Metropolitan Church of Bessarabia v Moldova* (2002) 35 E.H.R.R. 306 at 335, para.[117]. The relevance of objective factors such as source material is, at most, that they may throw light on whether the professed belief is genuinely held.

[24]: Everyone, therefore, is entitled to hold whatever beliefs he wishes. But when questions of "manifestation" arise, as they usually do in this type of case, a belief must satisfy some modest, objective minimum requirements. These threshold requirements are implicit in Art.9 of the European Convention and comparable guarantees in other human rights instruments. The belief must be consistent with basic standards of human dignity or integrity. Manifestation of a religious belief, for instance, which involved subjecting others to torture or inhuman punishment would not qualify for protection. The belief must relate to matters more than merely trivial. It must possess an adequate degree of seriousness and importance. As has been said, it must be a belief on a fundamental problem. With religious belief this requisite is readily satisfied. The belief must also be coherent in the sense of being intelligible and capable of being understood. But, again, too much should not be demanded in this regard. Typically, religion involves belief in the supernatural. It is not always susceptible to lucid exposition or, still less, rational justification. The language used is often the language of allegory, symbol and metaphor. Depending on the subject matter, individuals cannot always be expected to express themselves with cogency or precision. Nor are an individual's beliefs fixed and static. The beliefs of every individual are prone to change over his lifetime. Overall, these threshold requirements should not be set at a level which would deprive minority beliefs of the protection they are intended to have under the Convention: see Arden L.J. [2003] Q.B. 1300 at 1371, para.[258].

[25]: This leaves on one side the difficult question of the criteria to be applied in deciding whether a belief is to be characterised as religious. This question will seldom, if ever, arise under the European Convention. It does not arise in the present case. In the present case it does not matter whether the claimants' beliefs regarding the corporal punishment of children are categorised as religious. Article 9 embraces freedom of thought, conscience and religion. The atheist, the agnostic, and the sceptic are as much entitled to freedom to hold and manifest their beliefs as the theist. These beliefs are placed on an equal footing for the purpose of this guaranteed freedom. Thus, if its manifestation is to attract protection under Art.9 a non-religious belief, as much as a religious belief, must satisfy the

modest threshold requirements implicit in this article. In particular, for its manifestation to be protected by Art.9 a non-religious belief must relate to an aspect of human life or behaviour of comparable importance to that normally found with religious beliefs. Article 9 is apt, therefore, to include a belief such as pacifism: *Arrowsmith v United Kingdom* (1978) 3 E.H.R.R. 218. The position is much the same with regard to the respect guaranteed to a parent's "religious and philosophical convictions" under Art.2 of the First Protocol: see *Campbell and Cosans v United Kingdom* 4 E.H.R.R. 293.
[26]: I turn to apply this approach in the present case. Here, different claimants express their beliefs with different emphases. This is to be expected. The underlying rationale is expressed in different terms. In practice the circumstances in which corporal punishment is administered differ. These individual variations do not mean each individual cannot hold what is, to him or her, a coherent belief on a matter of importance."

One point Lords Nicholls considered, which is set out in the passage above, was the issue of when a religious belief engages the protection of Art.9 of the ECHR. There is substantial case law on this issue where the Eur.Ct.H.R. sets out its test for when Art.9 is "engaged", before any further analysis of whether there has been an interferance or whether there is justification under Art.9(2). As Lord Nicholls notes in *Williamson*, there is a need to examine the nature of the religious belief that is being claimed as protected under Art.9. It is precisely at this point that a space opens up about the impact of different legal rules on the nature and extent of religious tolerance in liberal democracies. Provisions such as Art.9 guarantee not only the right to hold a belief (which cannot be limited under Art.9(2)) but also the right to manifest that belief (which can be justified under Art.9(2)). It is accepted that Art.9 of the ECHR does not cover all practices that are motivated by religion or belief (more widely defined). As discussed above in *Arrowsmith*[60], the Commission clearly established that in Art.9 cases a strictly subjective view of whether or not the act or practice was motivated by religion or belief was not practical: the term "practice" did not cover each act that was motivated or influenced by a religion or belief. The resulting analysis has come to be described by some commentators as a "necessity" test which requires the applicant to show that the manifestion or practice was required by their religion or belief.[61] Subsequent appliction of the *Arrowsmith* test suggests that it may not cover behaviour that is encouraged or permitted but not required by a religion.[62] For example, the Commission upheld the criminal conviction of a 21-year-old man who underwent an Islamic marriage to a 14-year-old woman without her parents' consent because Islam permitted rather than required marriage at an earlier age than British law.[63] In *X v United Kingdom* the Commission held that the there was no engagement of an Art.9 right where an applicant was refused

[60] *Arrowsmith v United Kingdom* App. No.7050/75, 8 Eur. Comm'n H. R. Dec. & Rep. 123 (1977).
[61] C. Evans, *Freedom of Religion under the European Convention on Human Rights* (Oxford: Oxford University Press, 2001) at p.115.
[62] *ibid.*, at p.116.
[63] *X v United Kingdom*, App. No.5442/72, 1 Eur. Comm H. R. Dec & rep. 89 (1981), cited in C. Evans, *Freedom of Religion under the European Convention on Human Rights* (Oxford: Oxford University Press, at p.116.2001) at p.116.

permission to attend a mosque for Friday prayers because the applicant had not shown that it was a requirement of the religion to attend Friday prayers.[64] Subsequent application of the *Arrowsmith* test, therefore, reveals a mixed picture in terms of the precise nature of the "objective" inquiry into whether or not the applicant's manifestation of religious belief engages Art.9.[65] Nevertheless, what does seem clear is that the test under Art.9 ECHR will not simply treat as sufficient the sincere and subjective claims of applicants that they were acting out of a religious belief. Yet it is precisely this more "subjective" approach that underlies Lord Nicholl's analysis in the *Williamson* case. As we noted earlier, difficulties are raised when discrimination law in secular liberal democracies requires a more subjective analysis of religious belief rather than an approach that focuses on the truth of religious claims. How could we filter out those ranges of subjective beliefs that can be accommodated within the legal system? What happens where subjective beliefs conflict with other aims of discrimination and the legal system? In *Williamson*, Lord Nicholls acknowledges the need for some "objective" filter to determine whether or not a practice should trigger Art.9 protection. He sets out the way in which this criterion provides "threshold" requirements: such as the fact that the belief relied on must relate to "matters more than merely trivial", "it must possess an adquate degree of seriousness and importance" and "it must be a belief on a fundamental problem".[66] In addition, and crucially, Lord Nicholls makes it clear that the belief must be consistent with basic standards of human dignity or integrity.

In *Williamson*, Lord Walker had reservations about the practicality of the judical process as a forum for investigating the "seriousness, cogency and coherence of theological beliefs" because it risked taking "the Court beyond its legitimate role."[67] Although this scepticism is important, it is also worth noticing that Lord Nicholls's approach at this stage. Lord Nicholls states:

"With religious belief this requisite is easily satisfied. The belief must also be coherent in the sense of being intelligible and capable of being understood. But, again, too much should not be demanded in this regard."[68]

This is a very low threshold criteria and seems to go some way towards answering the concerns of Lord Walker. As stated, Art.9 does not have a narrow definition of religion and in fact includes a wide range of belief. In these circumstances it will invariably be the case that courts will need to determine what practices fall within Art.9 protection and may also need to

64 *X v the United Kingdom*, App. No.8160/78, 22 Eur Comm H. R. Dec & Rep 27 (1981).

65 C. Evans, *Freedom of Religion under the European Convention on Human Rights* (Oxford: Oxford University Press, 2001) at p.116–120.

66 [2005] H.R.L.R. 14, at para.23.

67 [2005] H.R.L.R. 14, at para.58.

68 [2005] H.R.L.R. 14, at para.23.

distinguish between the core and peripheral practices of religions.[69] Lord Nicholls' solution is to have a low threshold test which performs these functions before moving on to apply an analysis that takes up the perspective of the individual claiming the right to religious freedom. After having passed this initial stage, the analysis that Lord Nicholls takes up the point of view of the applicant. Despite citing *Arrowsmith*, he does not explicitly adopt the "objective necessity" test as a guide to whether or not a practice is a manifestation of belief that engages Art.9. Instead, Lord Nicholls adopts an analysis that relies on *X v UK*,[70] which used the phrase "intimately linked",[71] as a guide to when the applicant's practice was a manifestation of religious belief under Art.9. Lord Nicholls states that:

"If, as here, the belief takes the form of a perceived obligation to act in a specific way, then, in principle, doing that act pursuant to that belief is itself a manifestation of that belief in practice".[72]

He goes on to apply this test for "perceived obligation" to the applicants in the case and finds that: "[...] the act of administering corporal punishment on a child is, *for that person*, an expression of his conviction in practice [...] It follows that when parents administer corporal punishment to their children in accordance with these beliefs they are manifesting these beliefs."[73]

There is clearly some need to develop a way of translating issues of religion into legal analysis because, as Brennan J. has ruled, "Religious conviction is not a solvent of legal obligation."[74] How can courts develop a legal rule that defines the scope of religion and religious tolerance in a coherent and intelligible way? As we have seen the *Arrowsmith* test suggests an objective necessity test. Lord Nicholls in *Williamson*, however, analyses the issue with more attention to the subjective beliefs of the applicant. There is a clear difference between an "objective necessity" test and a more "subjective test" that focuses on showing an "intimate link" between the religious belief and practice. The shift in analysis to pay greater attention to the belief of the applicant, followed by Lords Nicholls, is significant for a number of reasons. The choice of legal test for when a practice will be sufficient to trigger protection under the right to freedom of religion is of critical importance to the scope of religious tolerance. Underlying the whole approach of the ECHR to religious tolerance is an assumption that there is a viable dichotomy between religious belief and religious practice. The fact that religious belief has

69 For a discussion of the wider issues relating to the need for liberal democracies to distinguish between (a) culture and religion; and (b) central and subsidiary religious practices see Seyla Benhabib, *The Claims of Culture: Equality and Diversity in the Global Era* (Princeton, NJ: Princeton University Press, 2002) at pp.11–15.

70 *X v UK* App. No.10295/82, (1984) 6 E.H.R.R. 558.

71 [2005] H.R.L.R. 14, at para.33.

72 *ibid.*, at para.32.

73 *ibid.*, at paras 34–35, emphasis added.

74 Brennan J., quoted approvingly by Lord Walker in *Williamson* [2005] H.R.L.R. 14, at para.58.

unconditional protection under Art.9 whereas restriction of religious practice/manifestations can be jusitified via Art.9(2) is one consequence of this approach. This dichotomy assumes that a restrictive approach at the level of manifestation of a religious belief will not have any significant impact on the internal structure of religious belief. However, it is questionable whether this strict separation of internal belief and external practice is viable. It suggests that a person may hold a belief passionately but that they cannot always act on that belief by manifesting it in the public sphere. Obviously, this mirrors the liberal separation between the private and the public sphere. The sincere believer, however, may experience the world rather differently from the sincere liberal. There is, therefore, a risk that restriction of the manifestation of religious belief will have a significant impact on internal belief as experienced by the adherent of a religion. This is not to say that all manifestation of a sincerely held religious belief should fall within the scope of the legal protection of religion. If a more restrictive approach is followed, this might take the form of a stricter defintion of what constitutes religion or belief, or a stricter version of the type of threshold test set out by Lord Nicholls in *Williamson*.

Another difficulty with a restrictive legal test of manifestation, especially one that uses an objective or necessity test, is that it may be difficult to apply in cases where there are minority religions with which the mainstream legal and political institutions are not familiar. This is illustrated in some of the relevant cases where expert evidence is used to establish what is in fact a "necessary" manifestation of a religion. Use of expert evidence in these types of cases introduces a number of difficulties. In relation to a majority religion it may be reasonably unproblematic for a court to consider this evidence and determine what is a "necessary" manifestation of belief. In these cases it will be easier for a court to pick out those practices that it recognises as being familiar as also being necessary and reasonable. However, in other cases such an analysis will be more difficult. For example, in the case of minority and unusual religions, and those that lack a hierachical structure and a clear set of rules, it will be difficult to be led by expert evidence. One consequence may be that unusual and "minority" religions or beliefs will find it harder to establish that a practice is a necessary manifestation of their faith. Moreover, this approach may result in a conflict within religious groups if a court is faced with questions about whether or not a particular practice is "necessary" to a religious belief. These will be cases where someone who is a member of a religious group accepts some but not all of the rules or practices of that particular religion.

These problems with an objective/necessity test suggest that other legal solutions may be more appropriate. Lord Nicholls himself provides some way out of the objective test with his very low threshold approach and his focus on the subjective views of the applicants. There may also be the seeds of an alternative analysis in some ECHR decisions.[75] The approach of the US

[75] *Valsammis v Greece*, 2 European Court of Human Rights (ser. A.) (1968).

Supreme Court in the *Thomas v Review Board*[76] which provides a marked contrast to the *Arrowsmith* objective necessity test is significant. In *Thomas*, the claimant was a Jehovah's Witness who was tranferred from his work in a steel factory to a factory that was involved in the production of military tanks. He argued that this was in conflict with his religious beliefs and he asked for his employment to be terminated. The Indiana Supreme Court dismised his claim citing the reason that the applicant's decision was based on a "personal philosophical choice" rather than religious belief and dismissed his claim. On appeal, the majority in the US Supreme Court held that the guarantee of free exercise (the right to freedom of religion) was not limited to beliefs which are shared by all the members of a religious sect. The fact that other Jehovah's Witness followers felt able to work in the production of tanks, and the fact that the claimant himself was struggling with whether or not his faith permitted such work, did not negate this particular individual's claim. The US Supreme Court recognised that there were often differences within religious groups and, echoing Lord Walker's comments in *Williamson*, that the judicial process is not well suited to resolve such issues.[77] This approach, rather like that of Lord Nicholls in *Williamson*, focused on the nature of religious tolerance as an individual right. From this perspective, the key issue is the perspective of the individual who was seeking to rely on the right to freedom of religion. In the context of increasing diversity of religious belief in liberal democracies, it will be difficult to expect the judicial process to investigate and authoritatively define what is "necessary" for a particular religious group. A more subjective test, which treats the right to religious freedom as important because of the place that religious belief has *for that individual*, may be more appropriate.[78] Once we recognise that such an impact is likely, then a concern with protecting internal religious beliefs may at the same time require a more generous interpretation of the types of practice that constitute the manifestation of belief. The fact that it is possible to justify restrictions on these manifestations through provisions such as Art.9(2) ECHR suggest that this latitude should not be too problematic. Moreover, the US example in *Thomas* suggests that a more subjective test for manifestation of religious belief can achieve an appropriate balance between the maximum tolerance for individual religious belief and practice, and the need for some control over the types of practice that fall within the protection of an individual right to religion. Finally, the "secular" justifications for accommodating religious belief in a secular liberal democracy, e.g. arguments of Anne Phillips (considered above), support a more subjective test. On this analysis, the concern is not with defining religion or belief in an essential or "true" or "objective" sense; but rather with taking beliefs seriously because of their value for individual citizens.

[76] *Thomas v Review Board of the Indiana Employment Security Division*, 450 U.S. 707.

[77] *ibid.*, at pp.713–716.

[78] For a discussion of the need to take into account the subjective beliefs of the individuals see M. Malik, "Faith and the State of Jurisprudence" in S. Douglas-Scott, P. Oliver and V. Tadros, *Faith in Law* (Oxford: Hart Publications, 2000).

C. "Voluntary Contracting Out of Rights"

Where the individual has voluntarily accepted the practical context which is the cause of their inability to manifest their religion or belief, the ECHR has developed the doctrine of "voluntary contracting out" and found that such "voluntary" conduct cannot give rise to a breach of the Art.9, right to individual freedom of religion. For example, in *Ahmad v UK*[79] a Muslim man was taken to have accepted a limit on his right to manifest religion by accepting an employment contract that made it impossible to attend a mosque on Fridays; in *Steadman v UK*[80] a Christian woman who felt she could not work on Sundays was found not to have a claim under Art.9 because she was free to leave her employment if she found she could not work on Sundays for religious reasons. In *Karaduman v Turkey*, a Muslim student who entered into a secular university was taken to have agreed to abide by the rules of the institutions and therefore could not claim an interference with her Art.9 rights because she was required to take off the scarf for the purposes of an identity photograph.[81] The reasoning that informs the analysis in these cases is that the individual has had a choice in putting themselves in the social contexts in issue; and that they are free to change this social situtation thereby safeguarding their right to relgion and belief. This approach treats religion as "freedom". In these cases, it is possible to change the individual's position to preserve religious freedom, although the change in position entails a social cost and penalty for the individual. Where the ability of the individual to change their position to freely practice their religion becomes unreasonably high there may be an interference with religious freedom. In *Darby v Sweden*, the Commission rejected the argument that the choice of moving countries to Sweden that was available to the applicants, and which they did not exercise, meant that they had voluntarily accepted payment of a Church tax that breached their Art.9 rights.[82] However, Mummery L. J. in the *Copsey* case commented that "costs" on the individual such as a change in employment may not be compatible with the importance of the right to freedom of religion.[83]

Arguably, this approach forces individuals to make a choice between a deeply held religion or belief and their public social role. One social and economic role is that of "employment" which was the issue raised in *Ahmad v*

[79] *Ahmad v United Kingdom* App. No. 8160/78, 22 Eur. Comm'n H. R. Dec & rep. 27 (1981).

[80] *Steadman v United Kingdom* App. No. 2910/95, 89 A Eur. Comm'n H. R. Dec. & Rep. 104 (1997).

[81] *Karaduman v Turkey*, App. No. 16278/90, 74 Eur. Comm'n H. R. Dec. & Rep. 93 (1993).

[82] *Darby v Sweden*, 187 European Court of Human Rights (ser A) (1990). Discussed at See the discussion by Carolyn Evans, *Freedom of Religion Under the European Convention on Human Rights* (Oxford: Oxford University Press, 2001) at p.127.

[83] *Copsey v WBB Devon Clays Ltd* [2005] I. C. R. 1789 (C.A.) at para.34. *Copsey v WBB Devon Clays Ltd* [2005] EWCA Civ 932, [2005] I.C.R. 1789; petition refused [2006] I.C.R. 205, HL. See the comment on the limits of the Human Rights Act as a way of securing civil liberties in the workplace; Hugh Collins, "The Protection of Civil Liberties in the Workplace" (2006) 69 M.L.R. 619.

UK and *Stedman v UK*. Focusing the analysis on the terms of the contract of employment to which the individual has agreed may obscure the wider context within which the individual has agreed to this choice. In the employment context, the potential for a conflict between religion and belief on the one hand, and the social and economic needs of individuals in employment, has now been substantially reduced by the introduction of the Employment Equality (Religion and Belief) Regs 2003 that prohibit religious discrimination in employment and training.

The scope for protection of religion and belief in specific contexts specified by legislation, such as employment, may in some cases be wider than under Art.9, ECHR. This point was recognised *Copsey v WBB Devon Clays Ltd*[84] where the Court of Appeal confirmed the *Steadman* analysis that an individual who had agreed to work on Sunday could not subsequently claim that this interfered with her Art.9, right to freedom of religion. However, this affirmation of the approach of the European Commission on Human Rights to the "voluntary contracting out of rights" principle was criticised by Mummery L.J.:

Copsey v WBB Devon Clays Ltd [2005] I.C.R. 1789 (CA) para.[34]

"The rulings are difficult to square with the supposed fundamental character of the rights. It hardly seems compatible with the fundamental character of article 9 that a person can be told that his right has not been interfered with because he is free to move on, for example, to another employer, who will not interfere with his fundamental right, or even to a condition of unemployment in order to manifest the fundamental right."

Mummery L.J. goes on to state that the "free to resign" argument found no favour with the Court of Appeal in the *Denbigh* case, discussed below, which concerned the right of a Muslim school teacher to wear a robe which contravened her school uniform. However, despite these reservations, Mummery L.J. concludes:

"In the absence of the Commission rulings, I would have regarded this as a case of material interference with Mr Copsey's Article 9 rights. The rights would be engaged and interference with them would require justification under Article 9(2). Under the 1998 Human Rights Act, however, this court must take the Commission rulings into account, so far as they are relevant in determing a question which has arisen in connection with a Convention right: section 2(1)(c). They are relevant. It is not a case of an isolated ruling. So far as the Commission is concerned it seems to be well established that the qualified Article 9 right of a citizen in an employment relationship to manifest his belief is not engaged when the employer requires an employee to work hours which interfere with the manifestation of his religion or dismisses him for not working or agreeing to work those hours because he wishes to practice religious observances during normal working hours. As Lord Nicholls of Birkenhead said in *Williamson*, at para 38:

[84] [2005] I. C. R. 1789 (CA).

"What constitutes inteference depends on all the circumstances of the case including the extent to which in the circumstances an individual can reasonably expect to be at liberty to manifest his beliefs in practice."

Applying that approach to the specific situation of Mr Copsey in the light of the Commission rulings, there was no material or significant interference with his article 9 right and the decision of the employment tribunal that article 9 was not engaged was correct in law."[85]

In *Copsey*, the Employment Equality (Religion and Belief) Regs 2003 did not give the individual an actionable claim because they were not in force when the relevant breach (dismissal) had occurred. On the wider issue of the extent to which individuals should have the right to manifest their beliefs in the workplace Mummery L.J. made the following observations:

"**[39]** I am convinced that it is not the function of this court to question the non-interference approach taken in the Commission rulings. Rix L.J., the House of Lords or the Strasbourg court may take a different view of the Commission's rulings if the matter arises for their consideration. My own view, for what it is worth, is that in some sections of the community this is a controversial question which will not go away and that its resolution requires a political solution following full consultation between government, leaders of employers and trade unions, and religious leaders. Courts do not have access to the same range of expertise or to the same consultative procedures as legislation. Neither judges nor lawyers have relevant knowledge or experience. The adversarial trial processes in the courts and tribunals are not suited to deciding questions of this kind."[86]

This last comment raises the question of the best institutional framework—judicial, legislative or non-legal—for resolving issues relating to the accommodation of difference (see Chapters 6 and 7). One particular problem is that minorities will find it more difficult to exercise political power to influence legislative processes. This is significant because religious minorities are much more likely to face conflicts between their religious needs and the predominant social, economic and public roles that they find themselves in. For example, minority religions will not easily be able to fit within the existing structures of the working week and holidays, e.g. the needs of Jews for time off on a Friday afternoon or for religious holidays will conflict with the established working practices. However, as *Steadman* and *Copsey*, illustrate, the increasing weakening of religion as an influence on social, economic and political structures in the public sphere means that religious discrimination will increasingly impact on both majority and minority religions. The subject of *Williamson*, the House of Lords case on Art.9 corporal punishment and Christian belief, may be seen in this light as unforming, also confirms that religious freedom and religious equality are increasingly important for safeguarding the rights of established majority religions such as Christianity.

[85] *Copsey v WBB Devon Clays Ltd* [2005] I. C. R. 1789 (C.A.) at para.34–37.

[86] *ibid.*, at para.39. See Hugh Collins' critique of this decision: Hugh Collins, "The Protection of Civil Liberties in the Workplace" (2006) 69 M.L.R. 619.

D. *Religious Discrimination and the ECHR*

The right to non-discrimination in the exercise of ECHR rights under Art.14 will be reasonably unproblematic in cases where there is a rule or practice that clearly differentiates on the basis of religion. In *Hoffmann v Austria*,[87] the European Court of Human Rights recognised direct discrimination on the ground of religion (the case involved access to children for a mother who was a Jehovah's Witness). In *Hoffmann* there was found to be religious discrimination in the enjoymnent of Art.8 rights to privacy and family life, although the European Court of Human Rights found that the infringement was justified. The application of Art.14 will be more complex in those cases where the rule or practice that is being challenged is in fact framed in neutral terms, but has a disproportionate impact on a religious minority who cannot comply with it because of its specific religious difference. Obviously, religious minorities are more likely to find that majoritarian rules and practices operate to disadvantage them in this way.

In the previous section II, we identified different claims that can be made in the context of religion. It was argued, that it is important to maintain a distinction between "religion as freedom" and "non-discrimination on the grounds of religion and belief". It was also argued that rule exemption claims that involve the accommodation of difference of a religious group, and therefore create an exception to a universal rule, will be easier to justify if the claim arises within the context of non-discrimination rather than within the context of freedom of religion. Rule exemption cases raise issues of, and have implications for, the distribution of key resources such as employment or private and public goods in ways that do not exclude certain individuals.

Clearly, rule exemption claims will arise in the context of statutory discrimination law. As we see below, both EU and domestic discrimination law have responded to these claims by creating a distinct and detailed regime which permits a claim for indirect religious discrimination. Moreover, it has introduced both tests of necessity and proportionality have been introduced in the context of indirect religious discrimination; as well as general and specific "Genuine Occupational Requirements" to create an appropriate balance between the needs of religious minorities and the needs of other interested parties in spheres of private and public life, e.g. in employment and training.

Rule exemption claims have also arisen in the context of human rights instruments such as the European Convention on Human Rights. We now go on to examine the way in which different jurisdictions have responded to claims for "accommodation of difference" by religious groups.

[87] *Hoffmann v Austria* (1993) 17 E.H.R.R. 293.

V. Accommodating Religious Difference: negative and positive obligations

The ECHR solution to rule exemption claims by religious groups has been complex. In most cases the result has been to deny the claim of the religious groups seeking accommodation via an exemption from a neutral rule.[88] In the case of the British school teacher seeking time off on a Friday to attend the mosque, the Commission decided that there was no breach of his Art.9 rights because, inter alia, he had voluntarily accepted the employment contract that required him to be present at work on Fridays.[89] The Commission also noted that he had not passed the "necessity" test because he had not shown that it was a "requirement" to attend Friday prayers in a mosque. One exception to this general trend is *Thlimmenos v Greece*[90] where the European Court of Human Rights upheld the complaint of a Jehovah's Witness. In that case the complainant had been convicted whilst in the army for refusing to wear a military uniform on the ground that it was in conflict with his religious beliefs. Subsequently he was refused admission to the Institute of Chartered Accounts (the Greek professional accountants' body) according to its rules because of his previous conviction. The Institute did not distinguish between convictions based on religious belief and other types of criminal conviction. In *Thlimmenos*, the European Court of Human Rights held that there had been a violation of the right to non-discrimination in Art.14 taken in conjunction with the right to freedom of religion in Art.9. In the course of its judgment the Court stated that the right not to be discriminated against is also violated where a State without an objective and reasonable justification fails to treat differently persons whose situations are significantly different. Clearly, where there is a specific and clear difference in treatment between persons on the ground of religion there are good reasons for a high level of scrutiny of the relevant rules more recently.

Moreover, there will also be rules that are neutral but which have a dispropotionate impact on religious minorities. It is precisely in these cases that religious minorities will make a claim that indirect discrimination has occurred: and they will claim that principles of equality and non-discrimination requires that they be granted an exemption from the rule, thereby "accommodating" their religious difference. *Thlimmenos* is therefore an important extension of the principle of non-discrimination under Art.14 by including indirect discrimination. However, it is also worth noting that there were certain specific reasons for the decision in *Thlimmenos* which included the fact that the claimant was being penalised twice for his religious beliefs: once by being convicted in the army and second by being refused admission to the Institute and his chosen profession because of the same conviction. Given that

88 C. Evans, *Freedom of Religion under the European Convention on Human Rights* (Oxford: Oxford University Press, 2001) at Ch.6 and Ch.8.

89 *X v United Kingdom*, App. No.8160/78, 22 Eur. Comm H. R. Dec. & Rep. 27 (1981).

90 *Thlimmenos v Greece*—App. 34369/97 [2000] ECHR 162 (April 6, 2000).

experience from Canada suggests that accommodation of differences will raise significant and controversial questions relating to the allocation of resources between majorities and minorities, it may be that the Court of Human Rights will respond with caution to arguments for the extension of indirect discrimination under Art.14 in religious discrimination cases.

VI. "The Headscarf Cases"

A. *ECHR—The* Leyla Sahin *Case*

One testing ground for the ECHR approach to rule exemption claims (i.e. indirect discrimination and the accommodation of difference) is the response of the European Court of Human Rights to the "headscarf issue". Claims for the accommodation of the "headscarf" are perhaps the least troublesome form of rule exemption claims. There are, of course, public policy arguments about the meaning or symbolism of the headscarf (as a form of extremism or gender inequality) that we consider below. However, the malign effects of the grant of a rule exemption in this case might be said to be modest in the sense that the predominant impact of a "no headscarf rule" is on the individual. At the same time, an exemption from the rule has no explicit or overwhelming social or economic costs for the majority who are not being obliged to adopt a "headscarf". To this extent, the accommodation of the "headscarf", might be felt to be less serious than rule exemption claims that require the allocation of extra funds. Nevertheless, the approach of the European Court of Human Rights in the "headscarf" cases is clear and emphatic: there is no positive duty on states to accommodate such religious differences as part of their obligations under Art.9 and Art.14 of the ECHR.

In a series of "headscarf" cases the European Court of Human Rights has upheld the rights of States to restrict the ability of individual women to wear headscarves as part of their religious obligations.[91] There is also discussion of

[91] For a detailed discussion of the legal regulation (and legal cases) on headscarves see Dominic McGoldrick, *Human Rights and Relgion: The Islamic Headscarf Debate in Europe* (Hart Publications: Oxford, 2006); *R v Headteacher and Governors of Denbigh High School (Ex p. Shabina Begum)* [2006] UKHL 15 (*Shabina Begum*). *Ludin* BverfG, 2 BvR 1436/02 (September 24, 2004; decision of the German Federal Constitutional Court). For a detailed discussion of the *Ludin* case (both the decisions of the Federal Administrative Court and the Federal Constitutional Court) see Matthias Mahlmann, "Religious Tolerance, Pluralist Society and the Neutrality of the State: The Federal Constitutional Court's decision in the Headscarf Case" [2003] German Law Journal 11(4) pp.1099. *Karduman v Turkey* (1993), 74 Dec O& Rep Eur Comm H. R. 93; *Dahlab v Switzerland*, Application No.42393/98, ECHR 2001—V; *Leyla Sahin v Turkey* (European Court of Human Rights, Decision of November 10, 2005, App. No. 44774/98).

legislative intervention to prevent the wearing of headscards and in some cases the full facial veil in public.[92] Such cases have related to Turkey which has a constitutional commitment to strict secularism e.g. (*Karaduman*[93] and *Sahin*[94]). However, the European Court of Human Rights has also confirmed this general approach in *Dahlab*,[95] involving the wearing of a "headscarf" in Switzerland. The decisions in these cases recognise that the State can justify a ban on headscarves on public policy grounds as part of the justification defence, and that a margin of appreciation granted to the state, in Art.9(2). Most recently, *Leyla Sahin v Turkey* confirms the general approach of the European Court of Human Rights to granting states a significant margin of appreciation in the accommodation of religious difference generally, and more specifically on the headscarf issue. *Leyla Sahin* was one of a series of cases challenging the prohibition on the wearing of headscarves in Turkey in the public sphere. Leyla Sahin was a Turkish national who was a student at a medical school, who had been banned from attending lectures because she wore a headscarf. The Turkish government argued that the ban on headscarves was necessary to fight extremism and to preserve public order. The European Court of Human Rights deemed the ban to be permissible in terms of Art.9(2). The European Court of Human Rights summarised the rules that govern Art.9(2):

92 From September 2004, the school regulations of the Provincale Handelsschool Hasselt in Belgium stipulated a ban on wearing any sort of head cover in the classroom. Six Muslim girls, together with their families, constested this regulation. Initial reconciliation efforts by the Centre for equal opportunities and opposition to racism (CEOOR) did not result in an acceptable solution for the school and the families. In order to settle the situation, the girls started the proceedings against the regulation. On October 6, 2004 the court decided that "freedom of religion", as protected by the Belgian constitution, has its limtis and dismissed the application of the six girls. There has been no decision of a higher appellate court in Belgium on this issue to date. See "Racism and Xenophobia in EU Member States: trends, developments and good practice", Annual Report 2005—Pt 2, at pp.73–74, (EUMC: Vienna, 2005) (available at *http://eumc.eu.int*, accessed on October 18, 2006). In Netherlands the Equal Treatment Commission has issued recommendations concerning religious clothing such as the headscarf and the niqab (full facial veils) in schools. Following the Equal Treatment Act, schools are allowed to prohibit veils if they can provide objective justification for why the veil poses a problem. Objective justifications include, inter alia, the inhibition of communication between teachers and pupils; difficulties in the identification of students which may lead to problems in the identification of unauthorised people in schools. See "Racism and Xenophobia in EU Member States: trends, developments and good practice", Annual Report 2005—Pt 2, at pp. 73–74, (EUMC: Vienna, 2005) (available at *http://eumc.eu.int*, accessed on October 18, 2006). There is a current proposal in the Netherlands to ban the full facial veil in public, see "Netherlands moves toward total ban on Muslim veils" by Dan Bell, The Guardian, Saturday November 11, 2006.

93 *Karaduman v Turkey* (1993) 74 Dec O& Rep Eur Comm H. R. 93.

94 *Leyla Sahin v Turkey* (European Court of Human Rights, Decision of November 10, 2005). Case 4474/98.

95 *Dahlab v Switzerland* (European Court of Human Rights, Decision of February 15, 2001). Case 42393/8.

Leyla Sahin v Turket, Case 4474/98, Eur.Ct.H.R. decision of November 2005.

Legitimate aim

[99]: "Having regard to the circumstances of the case and the terms of the domestic courts' decisions, the Court is able to accept that the impugned interference primarily pursued the legitimate aims of protecting the rights and freedoms of others and of protecting public order, a point which is not in issue between the parties.

4. "Necessary in a democratic society"

(b) The Court's assessment

(i) General principles

[107]: The Court has frequently emphasised the State's role as the neutral and impartial organiser of the exercise of various religions, faiths and beliefs, and stated that this role is conducive to public order, religious harmony and tolerance in a democratic society. It also considers that the State's duty of neutrality and impartiality is incompatible with any power on the State's part to assess the legitimacy of religious beliefs or the ways in which those beliefs are expressed . . . and that it requires the State to ensure mutual tolerance between opposing groups . . . Accordingly, the role of the authorities in such circumstances is not to remove the cause of tension by eliminating pluralism, but to ensure that the competing groups tolerate each other (*Serif v Greece*, no. 38178/97, § 53, ECHR 1999-IX).

[108]: Pluralism, tolerance and broadmindedness are hallmarks of a "democratic society". Although individual interests must on occasion be subordinated to those of a group, democracy does not simply mean that the views of a majority must always prevail: a balance must be achieved which ensures the fair and proper treatment of people from minorities and avoids any abuse of a dominant position . . . Pluralism and democracy must also be based on dialogue and a spirit of compromise necessarily entailing various concessions on the part of individuals or groups of individuals which are justified in order to maintain and promote the ideals and values of a democratic society . . . Where these "rights and freedoms" are themselves among those guaranteed by the Convention or its Protocols, it must be accepted that the need to protect them may lead States to restrict other rights or freedoms likewise set forth in the Convention. It is precisely this constant search for a balance between the fundamental rights of each individual which constitutes the foundation of a "democratic society" . . .

[109]: Where questions concerning the relationship between State and religions are at stake, on which opinion in a democratic society may reasonably differ widely, the role of the national decision-making body must be given special importance . . . This will notably be the case when it comes to regulating the wearing of religious symbols in educational institutions, especially (as the comparative-law materials illustrate—see paragraphs 55–65 above) in view of the diversity of the approaches taken by national authorities on the issue. It is not possible to discern throughout Europe a uniform conception of the significance of religion in society . . . and the meaning or impact of the public expression of a religious belief will differ according to time and context (see, among other authorities, *Dahlab v. Switzerland* (dec.) no. 42393/98, ECHR 2001-V). Rules in this sphere will consequently vary from one country to another according to national traditions and the requirements imposed by the need to protect the rights and freedoms of others and to maintain public order . . . Accordingly, the choice of the extent and form such regulations should take must inevitably be left up to a point to the State concerned, as it will depend on the domestic context concerned . . .

[110]: This margin of appreciation goes hand in hand with a European supervision embracing both the law and the decisions applying it. The Court's task is to determine whether the measures taken at national level were justified in principle and proportionate . . . In delimiting the extent of the margin of appreciation in the present case the Court must have regard to what is at stake, namely the need to protect the rights and freedoms of others, to preserve public order and to secure civil peace and true religious pluralism, which is vital to the survival of a democratic society . . .

[111]: The Court also notes that in the decisions of *Karaduman v. Turkey* (no. 16278/90, Commission decision of 3 May 1993, DR 74, p. 93) and *Dahlab v. Switzerland* (no. 42393/98, ECHR 2001-V) the Convention institutions found that in a democratic society the State was entitled to place restrictions on the wearing of the Islamic headscarf if it was incompatible with the pursued aim of protecting the rights and freedoms of others, public order and public safety. In the *Karaduman* case, measures taken in universities to prevent certain fundamentalist religious movements from exerting pressure on students who did not practise their religion or who belonged to another religion were found to be justified under Article 9 § 2 of the Convention. Consequently, it is established that institutions of higher education may regulate the manifestation of the rites and symbols of a religion by imposing restrictions as to the place and manner of such manifestation with the aim of ensuring peaceful co-existence between students of various faiths and thus protecting public order and the beliefs of others . . .''

Applying this test to the facts of the case, the majority of the European Court of Human Rights found that the Turkish government had met the required standard in Art.9(2). It is particularly noteworthy that in the area of religion and its relationship to the state the Court felt that there was a particular need to exercise its supervision of freedom of religion under Art.9(1) in a way that recognised the diversity of possible ''church-state'' models in European Convention states. In light of the diversity in the practices of Convention states (see further below) the reluctance of the European Court of Human Rights to harmonise rules in a sensitive area like ''religion'' is understandable. However, what is less clear is whether there was sufficient scrutiny of whether the facts *Leyla Sahin* fall within the margin of appreciation as defined by the European Court of Human Rights. In particular, Judge Tulken's dissent, which criticises the majority for accepting without further scrutiny the assetions of the Turkish government that the wearing of the headscarf was a threat to public order, and the Turkish government's interpretation of the headscarf as a symbol of extremism.

Judge Tulkens questioned whether Leyla Sahin's wearing of a head scarf was a threat to public order. She calls for more detailed scrutiny of the reasons given by the Turkish state before it was granted a margin of appreciation in a case where interference with the fundamental right under Art.9(1) was already established. Although framed in a different conceptual structure, this alternative analysis is similar to the approach of the minority in the US case judgment *Smith v Employment Division*, in which the US Supreme Court argued that there needed to be clear evidence of harm before an interference with freedom of religion could be justified under the ''compelling interest'' test of the US Constitution's Free Exercise provisions.[96] One noteworthy aspect of the dissent of Tulkens J. argument is that there is a need to treat the Art.9 right as vested in the individual subject. Therefore, it does not follow that because there is a general assumption about the meaning of the headscarf as a symbol of religious extremism or gender inequality that this necessarily also applies to the individual. In this way, and like the German Constitutional Court in the German headscarf case *Ludin,* Tulkens J. constructs the headscarf as an "individual right" rather than as a symbol or idea. In her dissent Tulkens J. states:

[10]: "In fact, it is the threat posed by "extremist political movements" seeking to "impose on society as a whole their religious symbols and conception of a society founded on religious precepts" which, in the Court's view, serves to justify the regulations in issue, which constitute "a measure intended to [. . .] to preserve pluralism in the university" (see paragraph 115 of the judgment, *in fine*). The Court had already made this clear in its *Refah Partisi and Others v. Turkey* judgment of 13 February 2003, when it stated: "In a country like Turkey, where the great majority of the population belong to a particular religion, measures taken in universities to prevent certain fundamentalist religious movements from exerting pressure on students who do not practise that religion or on those who belong to another religion may be justified under Article 9 § 2 of the Convention" (§ 95).

While everyone agrees on the need to prevent radical Islamism, a serious objection may nevertheless be made to such reasoning. Merely wearing the headscarf cannot be associated with fundamentalism and it is vital to distinguish between those who wear the headscarf and "extremists" who seek to impose the headscarf as they do other religious symbols. Not all women who wear the headscarf are fundamentalists and there is nothing to suggest that the applicant held fundamentalist views. She is a young adult woman and a university student and might reasonably be expected to have a heightened capacity to resist pressure, it being noted in this connection that the judgment fails to provide any concrete example of the type of pressure concerned. The applicant's personal interest in exercising the right to freedom of religion and to manifest her religion by an external symbol cannot be wholly absorbed by the public interest in fighting extremism.

[11]: Turning to *equality*, the majority focus on the protection of women's rights and the principle of sexual equality (see paragraphs 115 and 116 of the judgment). By converse implication, wearing the headscarf is considered synonymous with the alienation of women. The ban on wearing the headscarf is therefore seen as promoting equality between men and women. However, what, in fact, is the connection between the ban and sexual equality? The judgment does not say. Indeed, what is the signification of wearing the headscarf? As the German Constitutional Court noted in its judgment of 24 September 2003, wearing the headscarf has no single meaning; it is a practise that is engaged in for a variety of reasons. It does not necessarily symbolise the submission of women to men and there are those who maintain that, in certain cases, it can even be a means of emancipating women. What is lacking in this debate is the opinion of women, both those who wear the headscarf and those who choose not to.

[12]: On this issue, the Grand Chamber refers in its judgment to the *Dahlab v. Switzerland* decision of 15 February 2001, citing what to my mind is the most questionable part of the reasoning in that decision, namely that wearing the headscarf represents a "powerful external symbol", which "appeared to be imposed on women by a religious precept that was hard to reconcile with the principle of gender equality" and that the

[96] *Employment Division v Smith* 494 U.S. 872 (1990), see the dissenting opinion of Brennan J., et al.

practice could not easily be "reconciled with the message of tolerance, respect for others and, above all, equality and non-discrimination that all teachers in a democratic society should convey to their pupils" (see paragraph 111 of the judgment).

It is not the Court's role to make an appraisal of this type—in this instance a unilateral and negative one—of a religion or religious practice, just as it is not its role to determine in a general and abstract way the signification of wearing the headscarf or to impose its viewpoint on the applicant. The applicant, a young adult university student, said—and there is nothing to suggest that she was not telling the truth—that she wore the headscarf of her own free will. In this connection, I fail to see how the principle of sexual equality can justify prohibiting a woman from following a practice which, in the absence of proof to the contrary, she must be taken to have freely adopted. Equality and non-discrimination are subjective rights which must remain under the control of those who are entitled to benefit from them. "Paternalism" of this sort runs counter to the case-law of the Court, which has developed a real right to personal autonomy on the basis of Article 8 (*Keenan v. the United Kingdom*, judgment 3 April 2001, § 92; *Pretty v. the United Kingdom*, judgment of 29 April 2002, §§ 65–67; *Christine Goodwin v. the United Kingdom*, judgment of 11 July 2002, § 90). Finally, if wearing the headscarf really was contrary to the principle of the equality of men and women in any event, the State would have a positive obligation to prohibit it in all places, whether public or private.

[13]: Since, to my mind, the ban on wearing the Islamic headscarf on the university premises was not based on reasons that were relevant and sufficient, it cannot be considered to be interference that was "necessary in a democratic society" within the meaning of Article 9§2 of the Convention. In these circumstances, there has been a violation of the applicant's right to freedom of religion, as guaranteed by the Convention."

Most significantly, Tulkens J. considered the challenge posed to liberal democracies by minority religious difference and concluded that:

"**[4]:** In the present case, relying exclusively on the reasons cited by the national authorities and courts, the majority put forward, in general and abstract terms, two main arguments: secularism and equality. While I fully and totally subscribe to each of these principles, I disagree with the manner in which they are applied here and to the way they were interpreted in relation to the practice of the wearing the headscarf. *In a democratic society, I believe it is necessary to seek to harmonise the principles of secularism, equality and liberty, not to weigh one against the other.*"[97]

Interestingly, the main focus for discussion in the *Leyla Sahin* case is religious discrimination: there is no discussion of the fact that the prohibition on headscarves has an almost exclusive impact on women who will be disproportionately excluded from access to public education. This aspect of the case—the intersection between gender and religion—is discussed in more detail in chapter 9, concerning multiple discrimination. The decision in *Leyla Sahin* became the key authority in the main case on headscarves that came before the British courts: the *Shabina Begum* case, which divided the Court of Appeal and the House of Lords, is considered below.

[97] *Leyla Sahin v Turkey*, European Court of Human Rights, Decision of November 10, 2005, Application No.44774/98, *per* Tulkens J. para.4 (emphasis added).

B. *The UK—The Shabina Begum case*[98]

In this case, a young Muslim woman wanted to wear a more extensive covering (a *jilbab*) than was permitted under the school uniform which allowed the wearing of a headscarf (a *hijab*). She challenged the decision of her school to refuse to allow her to attend if she was not willing to comply with their school uniform requirements. The school's uniform policy had been adopted after extensive consultation with parents. At first instance it was held that there was no interference with Art.9 ECHR right to freedom of religion. The Court of Appeal allowed the claimant's appeal. Brooke L.J. articulated the test that the school should set itself as a set of procedural questions which include the individual student's right to freedom of religion under Art.9. Brooke L.J. explicitly refrained from reaching a substantive conclusion on whether or not the applicant should be allowed to wear the jilbab. This decision was overturned in the House of Lords where it was held that the School had not breached any Art.9 ECHR right in reaching its decision on school uniform which prevented the applicant from wearing the jilbab. All the members of the House of Lords found that there was no Art.9 violation. Lord Bingham, Lord Hoffmann and Lord Scott found that there was no interference under Art.9(1) and that in any event there was sufficient justification for any interference under Art.9(2). Lord Nicholls and Baroness Hale found that there was an Art.9(1) interference but that this was justified under Art.9(2).

In this section the *Shabina Begum* case is discussed, with a comparison in the next section with the approach as adopted in France, Germany, the US and Canada. This comparison raises a key issue about the appropriate political and legal response to the needs of religious groups, but especially minority religions, within liberal democracies. These comparisons are of interest with other jurisdictions, because each takes a different political, constitutional and legal approach to the issue.

The UK solution to the adoption of the headscarf is permissive and differs from the French solution of prohibition,[99] or the German approach of treating this as an issue for the legislature.[100]

1. *Shabina Begum* in the Court of Appeal

Before moving on to focus on the House of Lords decision, it is worth noting the approach of the Court of Appeal which characterised the analysis required by the School in reaching its decision in procedural and administrative law terms. One reason for paying close attention to the Court of Appeal's use of a

98 [2005] H.R.L.R. 16 CA; [2006] UKHL15 (HL).

99 See the French ban on headscarves Law No.2004–228, of March 15, 2004.

100 Matthias Mahlmann, "Religious Tolerance, Pluralist Society and the Neutrality of the State: The Federal Constitutional Court's Decision in the *Headscarf* Cases" (2003) 4 German L.J. (Vol. No.11) 1099–1116.

"procedural" analysis is that it raises questions about whether the same standard of review should be available in all cases of the right to religious freedom. The Court of Appeal held that the school had failed to follow the proper decision-making procedure in order to determine whether there had been a possible infringement of an Art.9 right. The Court of Appeal held that the school should have asked itself, inter alia, the following questions:

(1) Had the claimant established that she had a relevant Convention right which qualified for protection under Art.9(1)?

(2) Subject to any justification that was established under Art.9(2), has that Convention right been violated?

(3) Was the interference with her Convention right prescribed by law in the Convention sense of that expression?

(4) Did the interference have a legitimate aim?

(5) What were the considerations that needed to be balanced against each other when determining whether the interference was necessary in a democratic society for the purpose of achieving that aim?

(6) Was the interference justified under Art.9(2)?

It is important to note that the Court of Appeal set these out as the procedural questions that the school should have considered, but failed to do so but did not, consider. Therefore, it found that the school had failed to consider properly the applicant's Art.9 right and found in her favour. However, the Court of Appeal (Brooke L.J.) explicitly stated that:

"**[81]** Nothing in this judgment should be taken as meaning that it would be impossible for the School to justify its stance if it were to reconsider its uniform policy in the light of this judgement and were to determine not to alter it in any significant respect."

[94] [. . .] What went wrong in this case was that the School failed to appreciate that by its action it was infringing the claimant's Art.9(1) right to manifest her religion. It should have gone on to consider whether a limitation of her right was justified under Art.9(2) in the light of the particular circumstances at the School. As it did not carry out this exercise it is not possible to conclude what the result would have been. The way matters progressed the claimant was excluded from the school without following the appropriate procedures and her Art.9(1) rights were violated in the process.

The sincerity of the claimant's belief in the correctness of the minority view was not in issue in these proceedings. She believed that her religion prohibited her from displaying as much of her body as would be visible if she was wearing the shalwar kameeze, particularly if she was not wearing the school jumper over it in hot weather. So far as the legitimacy of her belief is concerned, in *Hasan and Chaush v Bulgaria* (October 26, 2000: Application No.30985/96) the European Court of Human Rights said (at [78]):

"[The court] recalls that, but for very exceptional cases, the right to freedom of religion as guaranteed under the Convention excludes any discretion on the part of the State to determine whether religious beliefs or the means used to express such beliefs are legitimate."

It follows that her freedom to manifest her religion or belief in public was being limited, and as a matter of Convention law it would be for the School, as an emanation of the state, to justify the limitation on her freedom created by the School's uniform code and by the way in which it was enforced."[101]

As well as construing the analysis in procedural administrative law terms, Brooke L.J. found that there were distinctions between the political system in Britian and other countries (most notably Turkey) where the headscarf ban has been justified as legitimate and proportionate under Art.9(2). On the issue of the justification of the interference with the claimant's Art.9 right to wear her version of the "headscarf", the Court of Appeal distinguished the European Court of Human Rights case law on headscarves. Brooke L.J. found that the UK, unlike Turkey, is not a secular state. There are statutory duties to provide religious education in schools (e.g s.80 of the Education Act 2002). Brooke L.J. thus noted that: "The position of the School is already distinctive in the sense that despite its policy of inclusiveness it permits girls to wear a headscarf which is likely to identify them as Muslim. The central issue is therefore the more subtle one of whether, given that Muslim girls can already be identified in this way, it is necessary in a democratic society to place a particular restriction on those Muslim girls at this school who sincerely believe that when they arrive at the age of puberty they should cover themselves more comprehensively than is permitted by the school uniform policy."[102]

2. The Decision of the House of Lords

A majority of the House of Lords found that the School's decision to enforce its uniform code was not a breach of Art.9. Three of the Law Lords (Lord Bingham, Lord Hoffman and Lord Scott) found that there was no interference with the claimant's right to manifest her religion and belief (Art.9(1)). Moreover, even if there was an interference, they went to find that there was a justification under Art.9(2). Lord Nicholls and Baroness Hale preferred to base their decision on an analysis that accepted that there was an inteference with the right to religion (Art.9(1)), but that such interference was justified under Art.9(2).

As noted above, the European Court of Human Rights has deemed a voluntary or contractual agreement to limit the scope of religious freedom to place a situation outside Art.9(1). Therefore, where an individual either puts themselves into a situation that restricts their religious freedom in some way, or has a choice that would allow them to change their situation in a way that allows them to exercise their religious freedom, then it is assumed that there has been no interference. This issue caused tension and divided the judges in the House of Lords in *Shabina Begum*. The minority view is summarised by Lord Nicholls in the following terms:

[101] [2005] H.R.L.R. 16 at para.81.
[102] *ibid.*, at para.74.

[41] "I think this (i.e. the ability or choice to move to another school where the jilbab was permissible) may over-estimate the ease with which Shabina could move to another, more suitable school and under-estimate the disruption this would be likely to cause to her education. I would prefer that in this type of case the school is called upon to explain and justify its decision, as did the Denbigh High School in the present case."[103]

The majority position was summarised in the following passage by Lord Bingham who acknowledges the reservations expressed by courts in cases such as *Copsey* and *Williamson* (considered above):

[23] "The Strasbourg institutions have not been at all ready to find an inteference with the right to manifest religious belief in practices or observance where a person has voluntarily accepted an employment or role which does not accommodate that practice or observance and there are other means open to the person to practise or observe his or her religion without undue hardship or inconvenience.

[24] This line of authority has been criticised by the Court of Appeal as overly restrictive (*Copsey v WWB Devon Clays Ltd* [2005] EWCA Civ 932, [2005] ICR 1789, paras 31–39, 44–66), and in *Williamson*, above para 39, the House questioned whether alternative means of accommodating a manifestation of religious belief had, as suggested in the Jewish Liturgical case, above, para 80. to be "impossible" before a claim of interference under article 9 could succeed. But the authorities do in my opinion support the proposition with which I prefaced para 23 of this opinion. Even if it be accepted that the Strasbourg institutions have erred on the side of strictness in rejecting the complaints of interference, there remains a coherent and remarkably consistent body of authority which our domestic courts must take into account and which shows that interference is not easily established.

[25] [. . .] There is, however, no evidence to show that ther was any real difficulty in her attending one or other of these schools, as she has in fact done and could no doubt have done sooner had she chosen. On the facts here, and endeavouring to apply the Strasbourg jurisprudence in a reasonable way, I am of opinion that in this case (unlike *Williamson*, above, para 41), where a different conclusion was reached) there was no interference with the respondent's right to manifest her belief in practice or observance. I appreciate, however, that my nobile and learned friends Lord Nicholls and Lady Hale of Richmond incline to a different opinion. It follows that this is a debatable question, which gives the issue of justification under article 9(1) particular significance."

The Court of Appeal had adopted a procedural approach to the issue of whether the school had infringed the claimant's Art.9 right. In the House of Lords, Lord Bingham considered this issue in detail and set out in clear terms that it was the substantive result of the action of Denbigh School, rather than the procedure that the school adopted, that was relevant:

[29] "I am persuaded that the Court of Appeal's approach to this procedural question was mistaken, and for three reasons. First, the purpose of the Human Rights Act 1998 was not to enlarge the rights or remedies of those in the United Kingdom whose Convention rights have been violated but to enable thoes rights and remedies to be asserted and enforced by the domestic courts in this country and not only by recourse to Strasbourg. [. . .] But the focus at Strasbourg is not and has never been on whether a challenged decision or action is the product of a defective decision-making process, but on whether, in the case under consideration, the applicant's Convention rights have been violated. In

103 [2006] UKHL 15 at p.17, at para.41.

considering the exercise of discretion by a national authority the court may consider whether the applicant had a fair opportunity to put his case, and to challenge an adverse decision, [...] But the House has been referred to no case in which the Strasbourg Court has found a violation of Convention right on the strength of failure by a national authority to follow the sort of reasoning process laid down by the Court of Appeal. This pragmatic approach is fully reflected in the 1998 Act. The unlawfulness proscribed by section 6(1) is acting in a way which is incompatible with a Convention right, not relying on a defective process of reasoning, and action may be bought under section 7(1) only by a victim of an unlawful act.

[30] Secondly, it is clear that the court's approach to an issue of proportionality under the Convention must go beyond that traditionally adopted to judicial review in a domestic setting. [...]

[33] [...] I consider that the Court of Appeal's approach would introduce 'a new formalism' and be 'a recipe for judicialisation on an unprecedented scale.' The Court of Appeal's decision-making prescription would be admirable guidance to a lower court or legal tribunal, but cannot be required of a head teacher and governors, even with a solicitor to help them. If, in such a case, it appears that such a body has conseintiously paid attention to all human rights considerations, no doubt a challenger's task will be the harder. But what matters in any case is the practical outcome, not the quality of the decision-making process that led to it."

This point was also confirmed by Lord Hoffman, who stated:

[68] "[...] In domestic judicial review, the court is usually concerned with the whether the decision-maker reached his decision in the right way rather than whether he got what the court might think to be the right answer. But article 9 is concerned with substance, not which procedure. It confers no right to have a decision made in any particular way. What matters is the result: was the right to manifest a religious belief restricted in a certain way which is not justified under Art 9.2. The fact that the decision-maker is allowed an area of judgment in imposing requirements which may have the effect of restricting the right does not entitle a court to say that a justifiable and proportionate restriction should be struck down because the decision-maker did not approach the question in the structured way in which a judge might have done. Head teachers and governors cannot be expected to make such decisions with textbooks of human rights law at the elbows. The most that can be said is that the way in which the school approached the problem may help to persuade a judge that its answer fell within the area of judgement accorded to it by the law."

The House of Lords was unanimous in reaching a decision that the School's decision was justified. As already noted, for Lord Bingham and Lord Hoffmann, the question was whether or not the School acted in a way that was permissible under the ECHR rather than whether or not the School asked itself the right questions. It was clear on the authority of the ECHR case law, and in particular the recent *Leyla Sahin* case, that a ban on religious dress such as headscarves could be permissible under Art.9(2). For Lord Bingham, factors that were relevant to the Art.9(2) analysis included the following:

[32] "It is therefore necessary to consider the proportionality of the school's interference with the respondent's right to manifest her religious belief by wearing a jilbab to the school. In doing so we have the valuable guidance of the Grand Chamber of the Strasbourg court in Sahin, above, paras 104–111. The court there recognises the high importance of the rights protected by article 9; the need in some situations to restrict freedom to manifest religious belief; the value of religious harmony and tolerance between opposing or competing groups and of pluralism and broadmindedness; the need for compromise and balance; the role of the state in deciding what is necessary to protect the rights and freedoms of others; and the permissibility in some contexts of restricting the wearing of religious dress. [...]

[33] Each school has to decide what uniform, if any, will best serve its wider educational purposes. The school did not reject the respondent's request out of hand; it took advice, and was told that its existing policy conformed with the requirements of mainstream Muslim opinion."

The fact that the *Leyla Sahin* case involved Turkey, a country with a different political tradition to Britain (a point that influenced Lord Justice Brooke in the Court of Appeal), was irrelevant: Lord Hoffmann made this point explicitly when he stated:

[64] "In my opinion a domestic court should accept the decision of Parliament to allow individual schools to make their own decisions about uniforms. The decision does not have to be made at a national level and national differences between Turkey and the United Kingdom are irrelevant. In applying the principles of *Sahin v Turkey* the justification must be sought at the local level and it is there that an area of judgment, comparable to the margin of appreciation, must be allowed to the school. That is the way the judge approached the matter and I think that he was right."

As all their Lordships noted, in this case the School had taken immense care in devising a school uniform policy that responded to the needs of all its relevant constituents, e.g. students, parents and the local commuity. Lord Bingham concluded:

[34] "On the agreed facts, the school was in my opinion fully justified in acting as it did. It had taken immsense pains to devise a uniform policy which respected the Muslim beliefs but did so in a unthreatening and uncompetetive way. The rules laid down were as far from being mindless as unifrom rules could ever be. The school had enjoyed a period of harmony and success to which the uniform policy was thought to contribute. On further enquiry it still appeared that the rules were acceptable to mainstream Muslim opinion. It was feared that acceding to the respondent's request would or might have significant adverse repurcussions. It would in my opinion be irresponsible of any court, lacking the experience, background and detailed knowledge of the headteacher, staff and governors, to overrule their judgement on a matter as sensitive as this. The power of decision has been given to them for the compelling reason that they are best placed to exercise it, and I see no reason to disturb that decision."

3. *Shabina Begum* and Accommodating Difference

Shabina Begum illustrates the way in which the complex social and political challenges of multiculturalism and identity politics have made their way into domestic legal processes. There are numerous ways in which such claims can arise.[104] For example, in the British context the claims vary: the call for a change

[104] For a full discussion of these issues see Sebastian Poulter, *Ethnicity, Law and Human Rights: The English Experience* (Oxford: Clarendon Press, 1998).

to neutral dress codes to accommodate the wearing of turbans by Sikhs;[105] an exemption for Sikhs from the statutory obligation to wear protective head gear on building sites;[106] a claim by a Muslim school teacher for time off to attend a mosque on a Friday;[107] and a claim by a Christian employee for time off on a Sunday as a day of rest.[108] These cases suggest that what seems to be neutral rule applicable to all citizens, places some religious minorities at a particular disadvantage when they manifest a religious belief which is "different" to the public norm.[109] Of course this is most acute in the case of minority religions. However as *Williamson* illustrates, the issue is also relevant for Christian "majority" faiths faced with an increasingly secular public sphere.

One initial difficulty with the rule-exemption "accommodation of difference" approach is that there needs to be some understanding of which exemptions are to be treated as legitimate. This in turn requires a more detailed understanding of the specific needs of minorities and the way in which existing structures fail to accommodate these needs. The RRAmnd Act 2000 is an example of the statutory enactment of a rule-exemption approach in relation to race in the area of public services. In the context of religious discrimination, the problem is complex because of the massive diversity in the sorts of needs that can arise, especially when a wide definition is given to religion and belief. In Britain a Home Office study by Paul Weller, et al, entitled *Religious Discrimination in England and Wales*,[110] sought to identify some of the key demands of religious minorities in a wide range of areas. These included employment, which is now regulated via the Employment Equality (Religion and Belief Regulations) 2003. However, the study also identified specific needs for key religious minorities such as Sikhs, Hindus, Jews and Muslims in a number of other areas: education; criminal justice and immigration; housing and planning; health care and social services; public transport; statutory funding; and representations in the media. Some of these needs will be accommodated through an ovelap between race and religion which allows the RRAmnd Act 2000 process to reach into areas such as education, health care and social services and public transport.

A recurring theme is the question to what extent does religious freedom and non-discrimination require the accommodation of religious differences, as well as an obligation not to interfere with religion, belief and its manifestations. This is a controversial topic. Commentators are divided on the question of whether liberalism should or should not accommodate "difference". Some writers such as Will Kymlicka and Charles Taylor have argued that limited

105 *Mandla v Dowell Lee* [1983] 2 A.C. 548.

106 s.11 of the Employment Act 1989. For a discussion of these issues see Sebastian Poulter, *Ethnicity, Law and Human Rights: The English Experience* (Oxford: Clarendon Press, 1998) at ch.8.

107 *Ahmad v ILEA* [1978] Q.B. 36.

108 *Copsey v Wbb Devon Clays Ltd* [2005] I.C.R. 1789.

109 For a strong argument against accommodating these types of rule-exemption claims see B. Barry, *Culture and Equality* (Cambridge: Polity Press, 2001) at ch.2.

110 Paul Weller, Alice Feldman and Kingsley Purdman, *Religious Discrimination in England and Wales* (Home Office Research Study, Development and Statistics Directorate, February 2001).

recognition is required as part of the necessary "liberal" context within which individuals can exercise meaningful choice; and that the recognition of certain key aspects of culture and religion in the public sphere is essential to the well-being and autonomy of a person.[111] Brian Barry argues that in general there should be preference for universal rules, although he concedes that in some cases (such as *Mandla v Dowell Lee*) there can be an exception to the rule.[112] The British solution in *Shabina Begum* can usefully be compared with the experiences in other jurisdictions: the ECHR, France, Germany, USA and Canada.

Before moving on to that discussion it is worth observing that the issue of accommodation of difference or reasonable accommodation is a recurring theme in discrimination law. For example, the issue also comes up under other grounds of discrimination law. In the context of gender it comes up in the context of pregnancy, childcare and the "equality—difference" debate, and in the context of disability discrimination, as part of the discussion on whether a disability needs to be accommodated rather than eliminated. One central question in the context of religion is whether religious difference should be treated as analogous with those categories of discrimination law.[113] As stated above, an inteference with religion, belief and its manifesation will be a breach of Art.9. In the employment context this would be covered by the concept of direct discrimination. In terms of the impact of seemingly neutral rules on those who have a difference based on religion, the issue becomes more complex. As we saw, Art.9 permits a limited concept of indirect discrimination which was introduced in the *Thlimmenos* case. However, as we also see that the scope of religious freedom under the ECHR has been limited by doctrines which deem that the voluntary contracting out of rights is not an Art.9(1) infringement. Furthermore, at national level, *Copsey WBB Devon Clays* suggests that Art.9 provides very little protection for an employee who claims that her rights to religious freedom in the workplace are infringed, because of the jurisprudence of the European Court of Human Rights on "voluntary contracting out" of the right to freedom of religion.[114] These limits suggest that statutory discrimination law may be a more useful form of protection against religious discrimination than Art.9 in certain contexts.

The other main issue raised by the rule—exemption approach is that not all the needs of religious minorities can be comfortably accommodated within mainstream institutions and society. Where the manifestation of the religious

[111] See Will Kymlicka, "Introduction" in Will Kymlicka (ed.), *The Rights of Minority Cultures* (Oxford: Oxford University Press, 1995); Charles Taylor, *Multiculturalism and the Politics of Recognition* (Princeton, NJ: Princeton University Press, 1994)

[112] Brian Barry, *Culture & Equality: An Egalitarian Critique of Multiculturalism* (Polity Press: London, 2003, at p.62).

[113] For a discussion of these issues and the view that religious differences, unlike race, are more like handicaps that need to be accommodated see Michael McConnell, "Free Exercise and the Smith Decision" (1990) 57 U. Chi. L. Rev. 1109 at pp.1140–1141.

[114] *Copsey v WBB Devon Clays Ltd* [2005] EWCA Civ 932; [2005] I.C.R. 1789; petition refused; [2006] I.C.R. 205, HL. See the comment on the limits of the Human Rights Act as a way of securing civil liberties in the workplace; Hugh Collins, "The Protection of Civil Liberties in the Workplace" (2006) 69 M.L.R. 619.

practice causes substantial harm (such as physical assault on children in the corporal punishment claim in *Williamson*) these cases will be easier to resolve. However, there is very little guidance on how to use "harm" as a way of grading these different types of practice. It is also difficult to formulate an appropriate legal response in case where the manifestation of relgious belief does not cause an obvious harm but either causes harm in a more subtle way or conflicts with another important right or public policy aim such as gender equality.

It is worth noticing that it is not inevitable that the "headscarf" cases will give rise to a confict of rights between religious freedom and gender equality. Before an individual right is traded off in what seems to be conflict of rights there should be clear evidence of such a conflict. In *Shabina Begum*, neither the Court of Appeal nor the House of Lords constructed the wearing of a headscarf as a practice that was potentially a source of gender inequality. Baroness Hale, however, made the following explicit statement that confirmed that gender equality in this case focused upon the individual woman's right to choose: "If a woman freely chooses to adopt a way of life for herself, it is not for others, including other women who have chosen differently, to criticse or prevent her."[115] There was no evidence before the court that the young Muslim woman had adopted her preferred choice of dress for any reason other than sincere religious belief (although there was some suggestions that the adoption of more conservative dress might act as a form of pressure on other Muslim women who adopted the less conservative headscarf rather than the robe). Moreover, unlike the Eur. Ct. H.R. jurisprudence, the Court of Appeal and the House of Lords did not treat the headscarf (hijab) or the robe (jilbab) as a symbol or practice of gender inequality per se. In this way the British reluctance to extrapolate a necessary connection between wearing a headscarf and gender inequality is similar to the approach of the dissenting opinion of Tulkens J. in the *Leyla Sahin* case who noted:

"By converse implication, wearing the headscarf is considered synonymous with the alienation of women. The ban on wearing the headscarf is therefore seen as promoting equality between men and women. However, what in fact is the connection between the ban and sexual equality? The judgement does not say. Indeed, what is the significance of wearing the headscarf. As the German Constitutional Court noted in its judgement of 24 September 2003, wearing a headscarf has no single meaning: it is a practice that is engaged in for a variety of reasons. It does not necessarily symbolise the submission of women to men and there are those who maintain that, in certain cases, it can even be a means of emancipating women. What is lacking in this debate is the opinion of women, both those who wear the headscarf and those who choose not to."[116]

115 *Shabina Begum* [2006] UKHL 15 at para.96, p.39.
116 *Leyla Sahin v Turkey*, dissenting opinion of Tulkens J., para.11.

This approach will be preferable to those who believe that legal analysis in discrimination law should avoid constructing fact situations as a conflict between individual rights unless there is clear and unequivocal evidence that such a conflict does in fact exist,[117] and that the preferred approach should be to harmonise basic fundamental individual rights. As Tulkens J. noted in the *Leyla Sahin*:

"In the present case, relying exclusively on the reasons cited by the national authorities and courts, the majority put forward, in general and abstract terms, two main arguments: secularism and equality. While I fully and totally subscribe to each of these principles, I disagree with the manner in which they are applied here and to the way in which they were interpreted in relation to the practice of wearing the headscarf. In a democratic society, I believe that it is necessary to seek to harmonise the principles of secularism, equality and liberty, not to weigh one against the other."[118]

It might be argued that this approach to conflict of rights issues seeks to minimise the trade-off between rights. It also fits in with a "subjective" approach to religious belief, ensuring that the focus remains on the actual choices of the individual claiming the right, rather than assuming the reasons for the exercise of their choice from a wider set of attitudes or assumptions about religious practices such as wearing headscarves.

As noted, there had been widespread agreement in the school in *Shabina Begum* that some form of dress code was appropriate, perhaps reflecting the consensus underlying the British approach to this issue namely that mainstream Muslim dress can and should be accommodated. *Shabina Begum* also raised a different issue about how the legal and political system should treat those minority opinions within a religious minority that seek to manifest their religious practice in a way that is different (in this case more conservative on issues of the dress of women) from the majority view within that group.

4. *Shabina Begum* and "multiculturalism"

More generally, *Shabina Begum* case illustrates a common dilemma facing contemporary liberal democracies that are increasingly diverse in terms of the religious practices of their citizens. Multiculturalism and policies of "accommodating difference" challenges the classic liberal distinction between a "neutral" public sphere and a private sphere within which religious belief may be manifested. Of course this classic liberal approach allowed minorities to flourish through guaranteeing individual civil and political rights, e.g. free speech; free association and free exercise of religion. This provided an over-

[117] This is also the method preferred by the Canadian Supreme Court in a case which involved a conflict between religious freedoms and equality rights, see *Trinity Western University v British Columbia College of Teachers* [2001] 1 S. C. R. 772.

[118] *Leyla Sahin v Turkey*, dissenting opinion of Tulkens J., at para.4.

arching framework allowing them to pursue their way of life in the private sphere. The ECHR and Art.9 can be read as part of this classic liberal approach to religion. However, there has been a significant change in the form and content of the political claims made by minority groups in recent times. Many no longer ask for the "same" rights as the majority. Some of the most compelling demands of minorities now take the form of calls for the accommodation of "difference" in the public sphere. This social change is especially problematic for liberal multiculturalism.

Shabina Begum confirms the general approach of treating religious freedom as a fundamental individual right, which is construed broadly and from the point of view of the person seeking to rely on the right. It also provides an alternative way of constructing the "headscarf" issue. The British approach in *Williamson* and *Shabina Begum* confirms a focus on the subjective aspect of religious freedom: i.e, the fact that religious freedom is a right that needs to be understood from the perspective of the individual for whom that religious belief has point, value and significance. Moreover, although in some cases where there is a clear case of significant harm which makes it impossible to accommodate certain types of religious practices (corporal punishment in *Williamson;* or female genital mutilation which is criminalised in Britain), there are other cases where despite the fact that the religious practice may conflict with existing liberal norms it may be the subject of accommodation in the public sphere.

Finally, the *Shabina Begum* case also illustrates an acceptance of the need for pluralism in decision-making about the accommodation of religious and cultural differences. The House of Lords recognised that once the school had consulted widely to set its uniform rule, and given that ECHR jurisprudence permitted the restriction of a jilbab as compatible with Art.9 freedom of religion, the decision should not be overturned. Lord Bingham states early on in his judgment that:

"It is important to stress at the outset that this case concerns a particular pupil and a particular school in a particular place and particular time. It must be resolved on the facts which are now, for the purposes of this appeal, agreed. The House is not, and could not be invited to rule whether Islamic dress, or any feature of Islamic dress, should or should not be permitted in the schools of this country. That would be a most inappropriate question for the House in its judicial capacity, and it is not one which I shall seek to address."[119]

This approach, along with the general analysis that notes with approval the school's wide consultation with the local community, pupils and parents, confirms an approach of pluralism in relation to decision-making in the area of accommodating difference. Judicial power is one, but not the only source of authority, that can determine the appropriate response to these types of con-

119 *Shabina Begum* [2006] UKHL 15 at para.2.

flict. Lord Bingham's approach justifies deference to the school as the decision-maker which should determine the appropriate response to the accommodation of religious difference: "The power of decision has been given to them for the compelling reason that they are best placed to exercise it, and I see no reason to disturb that decision."[120] This recognition of the need for a balance of power between different institutions—the courts, the legislature and also schools.

Both the "external" regulatory features of law, and also the "internal" aspects, link law to social formations. Increasing diversity will make it more difficult for "regulatory" law to enforce or ensure compliance from citizens if the legal rule in issue is failing to reflect the social norms by which they organise their daily lives. This development has two aspects that are relevant for discrimination law: first, the increasing use of law as a locus around which social groups form their identity; and second, the use of law as part of the newly emerging politics of recognition.

Starting with the first issue, social groups will look to the ability of law's regulatory functions to safeguard their private identity and choices. However, the increasing use of legal challenges (e.g. through discrimination law) as a way of advancing the interests of diverse social groups puts a strain on the law. More specifically, the increasing calls for the accommodation private identity in politics and law challenges legal "centralism". It introduces the prospect of a fragmentation of principles of generality, universality and equality. Individuals and groups may also regard the law as an instrument of legal change. Disadvantaged and marginal groups who have been alienated or excluded may use law to advance their goals. The volume of individual litigation on the headscarf issue across Europe demonstrates that individuals, such as Muslim women, are increasingly using law in this way: i.e. making legal claims to wear the "headscarf" and to ask for the public accommodation of their private identity. This category raises a specific problem for liberal democracies. A core feature of modern western legal orders is their appeal to generality and equality before the law as a requirement of the rule of law. The fear of fragmentation is especially acute in the case of Muslim women and headscarves because it is also possible to understand the "headscarf issue", and the cultural and religious norms that underpin the practice of wearing headscarves, as an example of a parallel (informal) legal order.[121] The "headscarf issue" raises problems similar to those that arise when there is a

[120] *ibid.*, at para.34.

[121] A. Griffiths, "Legal Pluralism" in R. Banakar and M. Travers (eds), *An Introduction to Law and Social Theory* (Hart Publishing: Oxford, 2000). For a general discussion of the relationship between law and social spheres see Dennis J. Galligan, *Law in Modern Society* (Oxford: Oxford University Press, 2007) especially Chs 9 and 10. For a discussion of the way in which the religious cultural norms of Muslim societies can be understood as informal legal norms see L. Rosen, *The Anthropology of Justice: Law as Culture in Islamic Society* (Cambridge: Cambridge University Press, 1989).

parallel informal legal order, i.e. where State law intersects and co-exists with normative rules that are based on cultural or traditional norms.[122] Yet, at the same time as being problematic, the political mobilisations of these popular movements through law, and demands for public legal accommodation of their most pressing needs, is also "so closely associated with the self-image of modern societies, so fundamental to its legal structure, that neglect or reversion, while possible, would be difficult."[123]

The second point about the use of law as part of the "politics of recognition" is linked to the previous discussion. Law and legal institutions have always been viewed as instruments for change by social and political groups. However, they are also increasingly important as part of the politics of recognition. On this analysis, law and legal institutions are not merely a focus for this new form of politics because of the impact they have on individuals and groups. Rather, law and legal institutions are taking on a constitutive function which goes beyond regulating disputes and having an impact on individual litigants. The shared meanings and beliefs embedded in the law, and its institutions, are the bases for a common understanding which create and sustains a sense of community.[124] The law and legal institutions also play a role in constructing behaviour, giving it sense and meaning, and influencing the self-interpretation of the participants.[125] Moreover, proper understanding and compliance with law requires as one of its preconditions that the law "speaks" in a language which is accessible to the person whom it seeks to bind.[126] This complex social role assigns to law and its institutions an important public role: a bank of collective wisdom; a means of creating a cohesive community; and a public ritual.[127]

Once law is configured in this more complex way it becomes clear that it will be a primary focus for the "politics of recognition". At an obvious level, the inclusion of important sources of personal identity in discrimination law will become an important objective for popular movements. Moreover, where discrimination law either fails to recognise, or misrecognises and distorts, important features of an individual's personal identity, this will cause harm to their sense of personal autonomy and self-respect.[128] This is not to say that there should be a perfect correlation between discrimination law and personal

122 See the critique of state centrality and an analysis of legal pluralism in John Griffiths, "What is Legal Pluralism" (1986) Journal of Legal Pluralism 24 p.39.

123 Dennis J. Galligan, *Law in Modern Society* (Oxford: Oxford University Press, 2007) at p. 275.

124 Ronald Dworkin has explored the relationship between law and community in the common law tradition see R. Dworkin, *Law's Empire* (London: Fontana Press, 1986). More specifically Roger Cottrell has developed this vision of law's function as the creation of a "community" in Roger Cottrell, *Law's Community* (Oxford: Clarendon Press, 1995).

125 Gerald Postema, *Bentham and the Common Law Tradition* (Oxford: Clarendon Press, 1996) at 73.

126 See R. A. Duff, "Law, Language and Community: Some Preconditions of Criminal Liability" (1998) O.J.L.S. 18 p.189.

127 For a detailed discussion of these points see Maleiha Malik. "Faith and the State of Jurisprudence", in Peter Oliver, et al (eds), *Faith in Law: Essays in Legal Theory* (Oxford: Hart Publishing, 2000) at p.137.

128 *ibid*.

identity. Rather, a vision for discrimination law that sees it as a source of creating and sustaining common meaning in a community makes it important to ensure that individuals' personal perceptions are given some weight, and that they do not see important features of their personal identity as distorted or misrecognised in law. This approach is more likely to ensure that they can identify with the legal system. There is the potential of a greater coalescence between the experience of individuals in their daily and practical lives and normative legal institutions. This means that discrimination law is likely to "speak" to individuals in their own language, thereby ensuring meaningful identification and a higher degree of co-operation by citizens.[129]

For all these reasons, it might be argued that it is important that the legal characterisation of the headscarf issue does not distort or misrecognise the value of the headscarf to the individual women for whom it has significance. This is not to say that the wishes of these women, or their characterisation of their own practice, should have precedence or be authoritative. Rather, it means that their perspective is one additional aspect that legal analysis needs to keep in mind in order to ensure that, as well performing its regulatory functions, the law is able to generate a deeper form of identification from the women to whom it is addressed. This in turn also ensures ease of compliance which may promote the values of autonomy and dignity, which are frequently cited as the justification for discrimination law. The present analysis is therefore relevant to some points raised in Chapter 3.

VII. Accommodating Religious Difference: a comparative survey

A. *France*

France takes a very different view on the appropriate structure for the relationship beween religion and belief and the state/political processes. In Britain, an established Church of England ensures a close relationship between Church and state, but at the same time there is religious tolerance and accommodation of minority religious needs. The right to freedom of religion

[129] See R. A. Duff, "Law, Language and Community: Some Preconditions of Criminal Liability" (1998) O.J.L.S. 18 p.189, at p.206. In the context of criminal liability Duff writes: "[...] the identification and examination of the preconditions of criminal liability is an important task; that one of those preconditions concerns the accessibility of the language of the law to those whom it claims to bind, as a language which they could speak in the first person; and that it is a serious question whether, and how widely, that precondition is satisfied. There may still be a bridge that connects the language of the law to our extra-legal normative language: but for some citizens that bridge is so long, or so steep, that the law cannot reasonably demands that they cross it."

is, as we have seen, part of domestic law via the Human Rights Act 1998. France has a more explicit and entrenched source for religious freedom. Article 10 of the *Revolutionary Declaration des droits de l'homme et du citoyen* of 1789 states: "No one may be troubled on account of his or her opinions, even religious ones, provided that their manifestation does not disturb the public order established by law".[130] The modern articulation of this principle can be found in Art.1 of the 1958 Constitution of the French Republic which declares: "France is an indivisible *laique*, democratic, and social Republic. She ensures the equality of all citizens before the law without regard for [their] origin, race, or religion. She respects all beliefs."[131] The historical confrontation between religious and political authority, and the *laicite* doctrine of the separation of powers, has ensured that this tradition is applied in contemporary contexts. The most recent application of this doctrine is illustrated in the headscarves (*foulard*) controversy which culminated in the banning of religious symbols (which also covered Sikh turbans and other significant religious symbols) in French public schools. This legislative enatment followed the political controversy in which some headteachers in state schools sought to ban French Muslim schoolgirls from wearing headscarves citing the principle of laicite as their justification.[132] The response of the French government was to ask for a legal opinion from the Conseil d'Etat. The opinion (*avis*) of the Conseil d'Etat did not support the prohibiton of conspicuous religious symbols generally, or the headscarf in particular. The opinion states:

"In educational institutions, students wearing a symbol by which they intend to indicate their belonging to a [particular] religion is not in itself incompatible with the principle of *laicite* since [this display] constitutes one's exercise of the liberty of expression and the right to indicate one's religious beliefs; but this liberty does not permit students to display symbols of religious membership that, by their nature, by the conditions under which they are individually or collectively worn, or by their ostentatious or protesting character [...] disturb the order of normal functioning of public services."[133]

This legal opinion by the Conseil d'Etat left open the issue of the status of the headscarf in French state schools. In fact, the legal judgment of the Conseil d'Etat on the headscarf (as compared with the subsequent Stasi Commission report and the legislative restricitions that followed) are very similar to the

[130] Joel S. Fetzer and J. Christopher Soper, *Muslims and the State in Britain, France and Germany* (Cambridge: Cambridge University Press, 2005) at p.76.

[131] *ibid.*

[132] For a full discussion of this controversy see Francoise Gaspard and Farhad Khosrokhavar, *Le Foulard et la Republique* (Paris: Le Decouverte, 1995).

[133] Quoted in Joel S. Fetzer and J. Christopher Soper, *Muslims and the State in Britain, France and Germany* (Cambridge: Cambridge University Press, 2005) at p.78.

British approach to the issue as outlined earlier in this chapter. This approach recognises the need for a pluarlism in the allocation of power: balancing legislative and judicial power with the power of schools and local communities. At the same time, this approach also leaves some room to argue that, despite the fact that the right to wear a headscarf raises a freedom of religion issue, there can also be a justification for the interference with that freedom because of a concern with gender equality. This is also part of the reasoning in the report of the Stasi Commission[134] in 2003 that preceded, and was used as a justification for legislative restriction of the wearing of the headscarf. Despite the fact that the political context for reconsidering the role of religious symbols in public schools was the "headscarf", the legislation that followed was framed in a general way. Following the recommendations for prohibition of conspicuous religious symbols by the Stasi Commission, the French government introduced LAW No.2004–228 of March 2004 which states that in State primary and secondary schools, the wearing of signs or dress by which pupils overtly or conspicuously (*ostensiblement*) manifest a religious affiliation is prohibited. The emerging scholarship on the French *foulard* controversy confirms that there was a tension within France between those who wanted a strict *laicite* (including French feminists, the Republican left and teachers unions) and and those who preferred soft *laicite* (which included the multicultural left, many Christian and Jewish leaders, most French Muslims and many human rights advocates).[135] The strict *laicite* position included arguments that the headscarf was a "Trojan horse for other things": i.e. the acceptance of the headscarves would create a slippery slope and lead to demands to accommodate a vast and problematic set of religious differences.[136] The objection of French feminists to the *foulard* is stated in a number of ways that conceptualises it as a symbol of gender inequality and the oppression of women: the objection is stated as "more feminist than *laique* [...] to veil a kid that young struck me as obviously unacceptable, permitting the headscarf is to acquiece in a practice which is sexist and oppressive towards women".[137] By contrast, those who favored soft *laicite* also cite women's equality to justify their position: they claimed that excluding women who wear headscarves from mainstream public eduction would undermine their life choices and opportunities by segregating them in the public sphere. They argued that the assumption by French feminists about what the headscarf meant contradicted the choices of individual French Muslim schoolgirls:

[134] *Rapport au President de la République: Commission de réflection sur l'application du principe de laïcité dans la République*, Remis le 11 decembre 2003, (*http://www.ladocumentationfrancaise.fr*). The report has also been published in book form as *Laïcité et République, Commission présidée par Bernard Stasi* (Paris: La Documentation Française, 2004).

[135] Quoted in Joel S. Fetzer and J. Christopher Soper, *Muslims and the State in Britain, France and Germany* (Cambridge: Cambridge University Press, 2005) at pp.69–77.

[136] See the comments by Berguin quoted in Joel S. Fetzer and J. Christopher Soper, *Muslims and the State in Britain, France and Germany* (Cambridge: Cambridge University Press, 2005) at p.82.

[137] Quoted in Joel S. Fetzer and J. Christopher Soper, *Muslims and the State in Britain, France and Germany* (Cambridge: Cambridge University Press, 2005) at pp.82–83.

"What is funny is who is saying that [the *hijab* is a symbol of the oppression of women]. It's the non-Muslims."[138] This last point is also made by Talal Asad in the extract below when he questions why the Stasi Commission constructed the issue of the real choices of the French schoolgirls in an assymterical way. The Stasi Commission asked the question whether those girls who choose to wear the scarf are acting out of true desire rather than because of the constraints of their culture and religion. However, they never asked the question whether amongst those girls who choose not to wear the scarf some may in fact have a desire to do so, but are not fulfilling that desire because they are faced with a political and public sphere which is based on a strict principle of laicite. It is also noteworthy that the approach of the French feminists who objected to the headscarves took what we have in earlier discussion of race and religion constructed as an essentialist approach. They took the headscarf to be an unchanging and static cultural and religious symbol. This method diminishes the subject viewpoint and agency of the French schoolgirls themselves. It also under-estimates the extent to which the schoolgirls have the power to re-negotiate and re-signify the meaning that the headscarf has "for them", i.e. this would be a subjective interpretation of religious freedom, and one that is favoured in *Williamson*. This point is also made by Seyla Benhabib:

"Ironically, they (the school girls) used the freedom given to them by French society and French political traditions, not the least of which is the availability of free and compulsory pubic education for all children in French soil, to transpose an aspect of their private identity into the public sphere. [. . .] They used the symbol of the home to gain entry into the public sphere by retaining the modesty required of them by Islam in covering their head; yet at the same time, they left the home to become public actors in a civil public space in which they defied the state. [. . .]"[139]

The two passages that are set out below open up a discussion of some of these issues. The first extract is by a French journalist, Naima Bouteldja, who places the debate about secularism and laicite within a more political context. The second extract, by Talal Asad restructures the issue by using methods from postmodern scholarship. This is an analysis similar to that of Iris Marion Young, and that reveals the specific ways in which a group can be oppressed by the application of a seemingly netural univeral rule.

[138] *ibid.*, at p.84.

[139] Seyla Benhabib, *The Rights of Others: Aliens, Residents and Citizens* (Cambridge: Cambridge University Press, 2004) at p.189.

The reality of l'affaire du foulard
Naima Bouteldja
The Guardian
Friday, February 25, 2005

"[...] The reality of French secularism is far removed from such lofty idealism. The public debate about, and subsequent banning of, "conspicuous religious symbols" in schools has focused exclusively on the Muslim hijab rather than Christian or Jewish items, and with every new affaire du foulard (headscarf affair), the hysteria has reached a disturbing level. The intensity of this debate cannot be explained in terms of secular ideas.

French secularism is a historical construct that blossomed with the victory of the republic over the Catholic church. Its three founding juridical principles are the separation of church and state; the freedom of thought; and the free exercise and organisation of worship. Contrary to received opinion, the practical implementation of French secularism has been achieved in a piecemeal fashion.

Secularism has never led to the cleansing of all religious expression from the public sphere—collective expressions of religious life are tolerated so long as they do not affect public order. Neither has it led to an absolute separation of church and state, nor even to a strictly neutral and egalitarian treatment of all religions by the state.

Several measures place the Catholic church in a privileged position in relation to other religions, particularly Islam. The maintenance of buildings of worship built before 1905 is the responsibility of local authorities, a practice that discriminates against Muslims, whose presence was barely felt at that time.

With 5 million Muslims now in France, Islam constitutes the second most important religion in the country, but all mosques must be privately built and maintained by France's most impoverished community. Moreover, licences for the construction of buildings of worship can only be issued by local councils, and these are often denied for mosques.

But inequalities between religions are most glaring in education. The 1880 education laws made state education secular, free and obligatory. But it is a very Catholic kind of secularism. The state school calendar remains based around Christian holidays and, under pressure from the Catholic church, a day has been reserved in the middle of the week for religious education. However, no planning is allowed in schools for religious minorities, not even for the supply of halal or kosher food in canteens. More significantly, a series of laws enable private faith schools to have access to state and local funding in certain conditions: 95% of schools that benefit are Catholic.

It is in this context, well understood by Chirac's government, that the ban on religious symbols was passed a year ago, with the backing of all major political parties, including sections of the communist left—and despite a 1989 ruling by the state council, France's highest legal institution, that the 1880 statutes on secularism did not apply to pupils, only to schools, curriculum and teaching staff.

By imposing secularity on pupils for the first time in the history of the republic, the French government has called into question the very foundations of the secular school system—the right of every child to a free education. But the hijab ban had little to do with reinforcing secularism. In reality, the debate on the headscarf has served as a magnificent political diversion masking France's deeper social and economic problems around the rise of unemployment and casualisation.

The ban has also helped to undermine the growth of a serious and growing social movement opposed to public sector retrenchment, with the radical teachers and students of French schools at its nerve centre.

As the French philosopher Pierre Tévanian has argued, what is most interesting about this debate around the "veil" is not what it has veiled (social issues), but what it has unveiled. "There exists in France a cultural racism, which targets the descendants of the colonised, and primarily picks upon their Muslim identity." This post-colonial anxiety helps us to understand the ubiquity of appeals to "reaffirm" the secular principles of the republic, even as it reinvents and distorts those very traditions.

But if the basic texts from the 1880s do not justify in any way a ban on religious symbols worn by pupils, what then has to be remembered? One possibility, argues Tévanian, is that the ban reaffirms "a symbolic order . . . which we can call colonial, where certain people were considered sub-human primarily due to their Muslim identity, dedicated to remaining docile and invisible servants or targets and scapegoats".

Reflections on Laïcité & the Public Sphere
Keynote address at the "Beirut Conference on Public Spheres"
October 22–24, 2004
http://www.ssrc.org/publications/items/v5n3/index.html

"The [Stasi] commission's concern with the desires of pupils is expressed in a distinction between those who didn't really want to wear the headscarf and those who did. It is not very clear exactly how these "genuine desires" were deciphered, although reference is made to pressure by traditional parents and communities. Referring to the verbal and physical abuse offered young women who go bareheaded in the ghettoes, the report describes the headscarf as "offering them the protection that ought to be guaranteed by the Republic." Does it follow from this that pupils should be subjected to a sartorial rule in public schools? This may seem an odd leap, but if the rule is put in the context of the project of cultivating and governing secular subjects—who are free, equal and tolerant only *as properly-formed Republican citizens*—this exercise of state authority makes good sense.

However, it is worth remarking that solicitude for the "real" desires of the pupils applied only to girls *who wore the headscarf*. No thought appears to have been given to determining the "real" desires of girls *who did not wear the headscarf*. Was it possible that some of them secretly wanted to wear a headscarf but were ashamed to do so because of what their French peers and people in the streets might think and say? Or could it be that they were hesitant for more complicated reasons? However, in their case surface appearance alone was sufficient for the commission: no-headscarf worn means no-desire to wear it. In this way "desire" is not discovered but semiotically constructed.

This asymmetry in the possible meanings of the headscarf as a sign again makes sense if the commission's concern is seen to be not simply a matter of scrupulousness in interpreting abstract evidence but of promoting a certain kind of behavior—hence the commission's employment of the binary "coerced" or "freely chosen" in defining desire. The point is that in ordinary life the wish to choose one thing rather than another is rooted in dominant conventions, in loyalties and habits one has acquired over time, as well as in the anxieties and pleasures experienced in interaction with lovers and friends, relatives, teachers and other authority figures. But when "desire" is the objective of *discipline*, there are only two options: it must either be encouraged ("natural") or discouraged ("fictitious"). And the commission was certainly engaged in a disciplining project.

[. . .] The question remains as to whether there is any place in *laïcité* for rights attached to religious groups. And the answer is that indeed there is, although such groups are usually thought of as particular exceptions. Perhaps the most striking are state subsidized Christian and Jewish schools ("private establishments under contract to the government") in which it is possible, among other things, to display crosses and kippas, and where religious texts are systematically taught, and where pupils still grow up to become good French citizens. (Indeed, because they are able to be more selective and are often better funded than public schools, religious schools tend to maintain higher educational standards.) [Asad then goes on to give examples of other exceptions to the strict application of the principle of laicite]

So France is not—and never has been—a society consisting simply of individual citizens with universal rights and duties who can exchange ideas and information in the public sphere and arrive at rational conclusions. French citizens *do* have particular rights by virtue of their belonging to religious groups—and the power to defend them in public space. Thus early in 1984, when the Mauroy government attempted to introduce limited state intervention in religious schools, massive demonstrations in Paris and Versailles (about a million in the former) led to the government's fall. Although demonstrations are not in the normal sense part of a *debate*, they surely inhabit the public sphere to the extent that they express and defend political positions in public space.

To these religious groupings—all inhabiting the public space between the state and private life—belong many citizens, clerical and lay, and their identities and interests are partly shaped by that belonging. And since they participate with unequal power in the formulation of public policy, the claim of political neutrality of the secular state towards individual religious groups becomes problematic.

Since the Stasi commission was aware of exceptions to the general rule of *laïcité*, it explained them by distinguishing between the founding principle of secularism (that the lay Republic respect all beliefs) and the numerous legal obligations that issue from this principle but that also sometimes appear to contradict it. The report points out that the legal regime overseeing the public sphere is not at all a monolithic whole: It is at once dispersed in numerous legal sources and diversified in the different forms it takes throughout mainland France and in its overseas territories. The scattered sources and diverse forms of French secularism mean that the Republic has constantly to deal with exceptions. I want to suggest that *that* very exercise of power to identify and deal with the exception is what subsumes the diversity within a unity, and confirms Republican sovereignty—in the sense of sovereignty Schmitt has made us aware of. The banning of the veil can therefore be seen as an exercise in sovereign power, an attempt to dominate the entirety of public space."

Asad's analysis provides a specific example of the way in which a focus on power, rather than the formal guarantee of universal rights under a principle of laicite, is able to reconstruct the "headscarf" claims: from a principle of the universal application of a general rule, into an example of the state exercise of sovereign power against a minority. Asad also brings into sharp focus the analytical controversies and difficulties of accommodating religion, even within settled models of secular politics such as the one existing in France.

Constructing the issue of the headscarf in terms of political power to grant an exception to a minority request for limited accommodation, rather than seeing it as an issue of a minority asking for a special exception to an otherwise universal rule, significantly alters the nature of the analysis. For those who favour such a shift in analysis the headscarf can be used as an example of Young's category of "cultural alienation", i.e. the "face of oppression" through which a social group can be socially excluded from access to public goods and the public sphere. Furthermore, Asad's analysis, if accepted, illustrates the way in which what seems to be a universal rule that applies fairly to all citizens can also be understood in a very different way, i.e. as a rule that enables those with greater social and political power to define the public sphere in order to privelege their viewpoint and disadvantage minorities. As we saw earlier, one of the key issues in the legal analysis of claims of religious minorities is the difficulty of accommodating their legal demands where these are framed as "rule-exemption" claims. Once the issue is cast as a demand for accommodation in the public space, or as an act of negotiating political power, then a question arises as to institutional context is appropriate for these claims. It could be argued that the appropriate context to re-negotiate these issues of power is the political sphere rather than judicial institutions. Of course, that raises a particular difficulty for minorities who find it difficult to mobilise and make demand through political processes in which they are not always adequately represented.[140] Some of these institutional issues are discussed later in the chapter.

B. *Germany*

The German approach to religious freedom represents a contrast to both the British approach of an established Church of England with toleration and accommodation of other religions and beliefs in the public sphere; and the French *laicite* tradition. The German constitutional arrangement ensures a separation of official religion and state but permits mutual co-operation between the state and certain officially recognised religions which are granted a status as "public corporations."[141] This legal recognition, through Art.140 of the Basic Law (*Grundgesetz*), permits the government to carry out functions such as collection of money on behalf of religious organisations. These funds can be used for religious, social welfare and educational work. Moreover, Art.4 of the Basic Law ensures that the principles of "freedom of faith and conscience as well as freedom of creed, whether religious or otherwise", are inviolable and goes on to establish a right to practice by guaranteeing "the undisturbed practice of religion." Article 140 prevents State interference with civil liberties based on the "exercise of freedom of religion." Article 140 also permits the grant of status as public corporation to minority (e.g. not Protestant or Catholic) religions: "Other religious communities shall be granted like rights upon application where their constitution and the number of members offer an assurance of their permanency." Within the German federal system each federal unit (a *Land*) determines this issue.[142]

140 For a discussion of this dilemma for minorities see Maleiha Malik, "Minorities and the Human Rights Act" in Campbell, Ewing and Tomkins (eds), *Sceptical Approaches to the Human Rights Act* (Oxford: Oxford University Press, 2001).

141 For a summary, quoted in Joel S. Fetzer and J. Christopher Soper, *Muslims and the State in Britain, France and Germany* (Cambridge: Cambridge University Press, 2005) at pp.105–111.

142 For a summary, quoted in Joel S. Fetzer and J. Christopher Soper, *Muslims and the State in Britain, France and Germany*, (Cambridge: Cambridge University Press, 2005) at pp.108.

The example of headscarves that we have been tracing through in this discussion has also caused controversy in Germany. The situation in Germany is that a general ban on wearing headscarves would be an infringement of freedom of religion. Moreover, German schools have been overwhelmingly permissive in allowing schoolgirls to wear the headscarf. There has, however, been controversy relating to the issue of whether a teacher in a public school can wear a headscarf (an issue considered in the *Ludin* case in the German constitutional court).[143] This controversy is factually analogous to *Dahlab* where the European Court of Human Rights found that a ban on a Swiss school teacher wearing a headscarf in a public school was permissible, and fell within the state's margin of appreciation under Art.9(2) of the ECHR.[144] In the German case, an Afghan born German Muslim woman called Fereshta Ludin who wore a headscarf was not hired as a teacher in a public school because of her headscarf. The decision was made by the relevant minister in her local area (*Land*). In 2002, the Federal Administrative Court confirmed the decision of the minister. In 2003, the Federal Constitutional Court allowed Ludin's appeal on the basis, inter alia, that a prohibition on wearing headscarves can only be introduced via a legislative act.[145] In the course of reaching its decision the Court commented on the appropriate way to construct the use of religious symbols by individuals. They found, inter alia: that the headscarf cannot be reduced to a sign of the suppression of women; and that it does not, in and of itself, constitute a violation of the principles of the German constitution. They also distinguished between the adoption of a religious symbol by a state and the adoption of the same symbol by an individual. In the latter case, the toleration by the state of the adoption of a religious symbol by an individual does not make that symbol a *state symbol*. This clearly distinguishes this analysis from the strict *laicite* approach. It also connects with an issue raised earlier about the change in the relationship between religion and politics in the contemporary period, i.e. whether or not the accommodation of religious minority difference in the contemporary period can be distinguished from earlier definitions of secularism when religion had greater political power and was a greater threat to the individual freedom of those who were not believers. Moreover, the analysis of the German Federal Constitutional Court seeks to focus on the individual rights from the point of view of the subject. As we saw in section V, the approach and decision in *Ludin* were supported by Judge

143 See discussion in Matthias Mahlmann, "*Religious Tolerance, Pluralist Society and the Neutrality of the State: The Federal Constitutional Court's Decision in the Headscarf Case*", (2003) 4 German Law Journal (Vol.11) pp.1099–1116.

144 *Dahlab v Switzerland* (European Court of Human Rights, Decision of February 15, 2001) Case 42393/98.

145 For a detailed discussion of the *Ludin* case (both the decisions of the Federal Administrative Court and the Federal Constitutional Court) see Matthias Mahlmann, "Religious Tolerance, Pluralist Society and the Neutrality of the State: The Federal Constitutional Court's decision in the Headscarf Case [2003] 11(4) German L.J. 1099.

Tulkens in her dissenting judgment at European Court of Human Rights level in *Leyla Sahin*.[146]

It might also be argued that *Ludin* reinforces Talal Asad's suggestion that the Stasi commission was unable to accommodate the full range of desires of French women. More broadly, some might suggest that modest accommodation in the public sphere can be understood as within the range of the flexible response advocated by Anne Phillips' model of secularism, which was discussed earlier.

C. *United States: The Free Exercise Clause and the "Compelling Interest" Test*

As stated earlier, the US constitutional protection for religion is guaranteed by the Free Exercise Clause of the First Amendment, which states: "Congress shall make no law respecting estabishment of religion, or prohibiting the free exercise thereof [...]". One aspect of this provision is the obvious prohibition on government regulation of religious belief: the government cannot compel and enforce a state religion; it cannot punish religious doctrines; and it cannot impose penalties on the basis of a religious point of view or status. In addition, as the second part of the Free Exercise Clause makes clear, the constitutional protection of religion extends not only to "belief" but also to "actions" which are founded upon that belief. As with Art.9, the Free Exercise Clause covers both the internal aspect of religion and belief and also its manifestation. Michael McConnell, a US commentator on the Free Exercise clause, has observed that the US doctrine of religious freedom developed through case law, and that it was mainly concerned with issues of religious establishment in the early period of US constitutional law.[147] During this period, the fundamental question of the degree of latitude given to religious practice remained implicit rather than explicit. The decision of the US Supreme Court in *Employment Division v Smith*[148] made the issue of interpretation of the Free Exercise Clause, and the latitude that this gave to religious practice, more explicit. Moreover, *Employment Division v Smith* also raised issues about how the legal system in liberal democracies should respond to rule-exemption claims by individuals and groups who argue that they cannot comply with a universal legal rule because of their particular religion or belief. The case therefore provides an interesting comparison to the responses of other jurisdictions to these calls for the accommodation of religious (and belief based) differences by the legal system and in the public sphere. Before the decision in *Employment Division v Smith*, there was precedent to support the view that the Free Exercise Clause required the accommodation of religious difference by

146 *Ibid.*
147 Michael W. McConnell, "Free Exercise and the Smith Decision" (1990) 57 Univ. of Chicago L. Rev. 1109
148 494 U.S. 872 (1990).

granting religious specific exemptions from otherwise applicable universal rules.[149] In *Employment Division v Smith*, the respondents were dismissed from their employment with a drug rehabilitation organisation because they ingested peyote (a recreational drug which was deemed to be a controlled substance under the relevant state criminal law of Oregon prohibiting the possession and use of drugs). They were both members of a Native American Church and they ingested the peyote for sacramental purposes. When the respondents applied to the Employment Division for unemployment compensation they were deemed to be ineligible because they had been dismissed for work-related conduct. The Oregon Supreme Court held that Oregon does prohibit the religious use of peyote. The US Supreme Court was required to consider whether that prohibition was permissible under the Free Exercise Clause.

The majority of the US Supreme Court found that there was no interference with the Free Exercise Clause and concluded:

SCALIA J:
"The Free Exercise Clause of the First Amendment, which has been made applicable to the States by incorporation into the Fourteenth Amendment, . . . provides that "Congress shall make no law respecting an establishment of religion, or *prohibiting the free exercise thereof*. . . ." U.S. Const., Amdt. 1 (emphasis added.) The free exercise of religion means, first and foremost, the right to believe and profess whatever religious doctrine one desires. Thus, the First Amendment obviously excludes all "governmental regulation of religious *beliefs* as such." . . . The government may not compel affirmation of religious belief, . . ., punish the expression of religious doctrines it believes to be false, . . ., impose special disabilities on the basis of religious views or religious status, . . . or lend its power to one or the other side in controversies over religious authority or dogma . . .

But the "exercise of religion" often involves not only belief and profession but the performance of (or abstention from) physical acts: assembling with others for a worship service, participating in sacramental use of bread and wine, proselytizing, abstaining from certain foods or certain modes of transportation. It would be true, we think (though no case of ours has involved the point), that a State would be "prohibiting the free exercise [of religion]" if it sought to ban such acts or abstentions only when they are engaged in for religious reasons, or only because of the religious belief that they display. It would doubtless be unconstitutional, for example, to ban the casting of "statues that are to be used for worship purposes," or to prohibit bowing down before a golden calf.

[. . .] We have never held that an individual's religious beliefs excuse him from compliance with an otherwise valid law prohibiting conduct that the State is free to regulate. On the contrary, the record of more than a century of our free exercise jurisprudence contradicts that proposition. As described succinctly by Justice Frankfurter in *Minersville School Dist. Bd. of Ed. v. Gobitis*, 310 U.S. 586, 594–595, 60 S.Ct. 1010, 1012–1013, 84 L.Ed. 1375 (1940): "Conscientious scruples have not, in the course of the long struggle for religious toleration, relieved the individual from obedience to a general law not aimed at the promotion or restriction of religious beliefs. The mere possession of religious convictions which contradict the relevant concerns of a political society does not relieve the

149 See for example *Wisconsin v Yoder* 406 U.S. 205 (1972) where the Supreme Court that a generally applicable rule relating to school attendance did not apply to Amish children because of their religious differences. They held that the application of the general rule in the context of the Amish, which did not meet the compelling interests test, was an unconstitutional breach of the Free Exercise Clause.

citizen from the discharge of political responsibilities (footnote omitted).'' We first had occasion to assert that principle in *Reynolds v. United States*, 98 U.S. 145, 25 L.Ed. 244 (1879), where we rejected the claim that criminal laws against polygamy could not be constitutionally applied to those whose religion commanded the practice [Mormons, at the time]. ''Laws,'' we said, ''are made for the government of actions, and while they cannot interfere with mere religious belief and opinions, they may with practices. . . . Can a man excuse his practices to the contrary because of his religious belief? To permit this would be to make the professed doctrines of religious belief superior to the law of the land, and in effect to permit every citizen to become a law unto himself.'' *Id.*, at 166–167. [. . .]

The only decisions in which we have held that the First Amendment bars application of a neutral, generally applicable law to religiously motivated action have involved not the Free Exercise Clause alone, but the Free Exercise Clause in conjunction with other constitutional protections, such as freedom of speech and of the press, . . . or the right of parents, acknowledged in *Pierce v. Society of Sisters*, 268 U.S. 510, 45 S.Ct. 571, 69 L.Ed. 1070 (1925), to direct the education of their children, see *Wisconsin v. Yoder*, 406 U.S. 205, 92 S.Ct. 1526, 32 L.Ed.2d 15 (1972) (invalidating compulsory school-attendance laws as applied to Amish parents who refused on religious grounds to send their children to school). Some of our cases prohibiting compelled expression, decided exclusively upon free speech grounds, have also involved freedom of religion, cf. *Wooley v. Maynard*, 430 U.S. 705, 97 S.Ct. 1428, 51 L.Ed.2d 752 (1977) (invalidating compelled display of a license plate slogan [''Live Free or Die''] that offended individual religious beliefs); *West Virginia Bd. of Education v. Barnette*, 319 U.S. 624, 63 S.Ct. 1178, 87 L.Ed. 1628 (1943) (invalidating compulsory flag salute statute challenged by religious objectors). . . .

The present case does not present such a hybrid situation, but a free exercise claim unconnected with any communicative activity or parental right. Respondents urge us to hold, quite simply, that when otherwise prohibitable conduct is accompanied by religious convictions, not only the convictions but the conduct itself must be free from governmental regulation. We have never held that, and decline to do so now. There being no contention that Oregon's drug law represents an attempt to regulate religious beliefs, the communication of religious beliefs, or the raising of one's children in those beliefs, the rule to which we have adhered ever since *Reynolds* plainly controls. ''Our cases do not at their farthest reach support the proposition that a stance of conscientious opposition relieves an objector from any colliding duty fixed by a democratic government.'' *Gillette v. United States, supra*, 401 U.S., at 461, 91 S.Ct., at 842.

B

[. . .] Nor is it possible to limit the impact of respondents' proposal by requiring a ''compelling state interest'' only when the conduct prohibited is ''central'' to the individual's religion. ... It is no more appropriate for judges to determine the ''centrality'' of religious beliefs before applying a ''compelling interest'' test in the free exercise field, than it would be for them to determine the ''importance'' of ideas before applying the ''compelling interest'' test in the free speech field. What principle of law or logic can be brought to bear to contradict a believer's assertion that a particular act is ''central'' to his personal faith? Judging the centrality of different religious practices is akin to the unacceptable ''business of evaluating the relative merits of differing religious claims.'' . . . As we reaffirmed only last Term, ''[i]t is not within the judicial ken to question the centrality of particular beliefs or practices to a faith, or the validity of particular litigants' interpretations of those creeds.'' . . . Repeatedly and in many different contexts, we have warned that courts must not presume to determine the place of a particular belief in a religion or the plausibility of a religious claim. [. . .]

If the ''compelling interest'' test is to be applied at all, then, it must be applied across the board, to all actions thought to be religiously commanded. Moreover, if ''compelling interest'' really means what it says (and watering it down here would subvert its rigor in the other fields where it is applied), many laws will not meet the test. Any society adopting such a system would be courting anarchy, but that danger increases in direct proportion to the society's diversity of religious beliefs, and its determination to coerce or suppress none of them. Precisely because "we are a cosmopolitan nation made up of people of almost every conceivable religious preference," ... and precisely because we value and protect that religious divergence, we cannot afford the luxury of deeming *presumptively invalid*, as applied to the religious objector, every regulation of conduct that does not protect an interest of the highest order. The rule respondents favor would open the prospect of constitutionally required religious exemptions from civic obligations of almost every conceivable kind–ranging from compulsory military service, ... to the payment of taxes, ... to health and safety regulation such as manslaughter and child neglect laws, ... compulsory vaccination laws, ... drug laws, ... and traffic laws ...; to social welfare legislation such as minimum wage laws, ... child labor laws, ... animal cruelty laws, ... environmental protection laws, ... and laws providing for equality of opportunity for the races ... The First Amendment's protection of religious liberty does not require this."

Justice Blackmun, with whom Justice Brennan and Justice Marshall joined, set out the dissenting opinion, which is extracted below:

"This Court over the years painstakingly has developed a consistent and exacting standard to test the constitutionality of a state statute that burdens the free exercise of religion. Such a statute may stand only if the law in general, and the State's refusal to allow a religious exemption in particular, are justified by a compelling interest that cannot be served by less restrictive means. [...]

This distorted view of our precedents leads the majority to conclude that strict scrutiny of a state law burdening the free exercise of religion is a 'luxury' that a well-ordered society cannot afford, ... and that the repression of minority religions is an 'unavoidable consequence of democratic government.' ... I do not believe the Founders thought their dearly bought freedom from religious persecution a 'luxury,' but an essential element of liberty–and they could not have thought religious intolerance 'unavoidable,' for they drafted the Religion Clauses precisely in order to avoid that intolerance. [...]

The State's interest in enforcing its prohibition, in order to be sufficiently compelling to outweigh a free exercise claim, cannot be merely abstract or symbolic. The State cannot plausibly assert that unbending application of a criminal prohibition is essential to fulfill any compelling interest, if it does not, in fact, attempt to enforce that prohibition. In this case, the State actually has not evinced any concrete interest in enforcing its drug laws against religious users of peyote. Oregon has never sought to prosecute respondents, and does not claim that it has made significant enforcement efforts against other religious users of peyote. The State's asserted interest thus amounts only to the symbolic preservation of an unenforced prohibition. But a government interest in 'symbolism, even symbolism for so worthy a cause as the abolition of unlawful drugs,' ... cannot suffice to abrogate the constitutional rights of individuals.

Similarly, this Court's prior decisions have not allowed a government to rely on mere speculation about potential harms, but have demanded evidentiary support for a refusal to allow a religious exception. ... In this case, the State's justification for refusing to recognize an exception to its criminal laws for religious peyote use is entirely speculative. The State proclaims an interest in protecting the health and safety of its citizens from the dangers of unlawful drugs. It offers, however, no evidence that the religious use of peyote has ever harmed anyone. The factual findings of other courts cast doubt on the State's assumption that religious use of peyote is harmful. [...]

Finally, the State argues that granting an exception for religious peyote use would erode its interest in the uniform, fair, and certain enforcement of its drug laws. The State fears that, if it grants an exemption for religious peyote use, a flood of other claims to religious exemptions will follow. It would then be placed in a dilemma, it says, between allowing a patchwork of exemptions that would hinder its law enforcement efforts, and risking a violation of the Establishment Clause by arbitrarily limiting its religious exemptions. This argument, however, could be made in almost any free exercise case. [...]

Allowing an exemption for religious peyote use would not necessarily oblige the State to grant a similar exemption to other religious groups. [...] That the State might grant an exemption for religious peyote use, but deny other religious claims arising in different circumstances, would not violate the Establishment Clause. Though the State must treat all religions equally, and not favor one over another, this obligation is fulfilled by the uniform application of the 'compelling interest' *test* to all free exercise claims, not by reaching uniform *results* as to all claims. A showing that religious peyote use does not unduly interfere with the State's interests is 'one that probably few other religious groups or sects could make,' *Yoder*, 406 U.S., at 236, 92 S.Ct., at 1543; [...]"

The decision of the US Supreme Court in *Smith* raises a number of the key issues that we have been discussing. One feature is the insistence of Scalia J. and Blackmun J. that it is not appropriate to enter into a detailed analysis of the nature of the religious belief of the individual. This "subjective approach", which fits in with the US constitution's preference for "neutrality" in relation to the content of ideas and beliefs, is similar to the approach of Lord Nicholls in *Williamson* where he argued that this stage of the test for "religion" would be an easy hurdle to pass. Another noteworthy aspect of *Smith* is the clear division between the majority and the minority views of how a constitutional provision on freedom of religion should respond to rule-exemptions claims that require the accommodation of difference. Scalia J. took a strict approach to this issue, citing reasons such as, inter alia, the possibility of "anarchy" if there is a presumption that uniform laws can be avoided by those who argue that they are acting under the protection of freedom of religion. Moreover, by citing the increasing diversity of religious views and beliefs in society, this line of argument suggests the need for a strict approach to rule exemption claims as pluralism and diversity increases. This assumption, that rule exemption and the accommodation of difference will become more problematic under conditions of diversity, echoes the arguments of Brian Barry.[150] The only exception that Scalia J. admits is the hybrid situation where the right to freedom of religion is being exercised along with another constitutional right such as, for example, freedom of speech or the right to parental control.

In marked contrast, the dissenting opinion takes a more permissive approach to rule exemption claims under the Free Exercise Clause generally, and the specific claim to be allowed to use a drug "peyote" in particular. Blackmun J. argued that once it is established that an individual is acting under a right to freedom of religion under the Free Exercise Clause, there needs to be detailed inquiry into the reasons for an interference with this right (the "compelling interest" test). In undertaking this inquiry, the court must, he argued, investigate whether there is in reality such a compelling interest and whether there is potential harm. In *Smith*, Blackmun J. found that that the law prohibiting peyote was of "symbolic" rather than actual importance. He also

[150] Brian Barry, *Culture and Equality* (Polity Press: London, 2001) especially ch.2.

found that, on the facts, the assumptions about the harm caused by the use of peyote were speculative rather than real. This more thoroughgoing inquiry required before the "compelling interest test" is satisfied under *Blackmun*'s analysis can be contrasted with the majority approach to Art.9(2) of the ECHR in cases such as *Leyla Sahin* where the European Court of Human Rights did not require evidence of the harm caused by the wearing of headscarves to gender equality or democratic politics in Turkey.

Finally, Blackmun J. challenged the assumption that the grant of rule-exemption claims will lead to a "floodgate" of challenges to universally applicable laws. He pointed out that granting an exemption to a rule relating to the use of "peyote" did not necessarily oblige the accommodation of all other religious claims. The resulting complexity of the circumstances under which rule-exemptions are granted or refused is, Blackmun J. argued, an inevitable outcome of the commitment in the Free Exercise Clause to not giving prioirty to one uniform view of religion or belief over another. This final point, about the inevitable complexity that would arise were Blackmun J.'s analysis to have prevailed is also addressed by Michael McConnell in his trenchant critique of the majority opinion in *Smith*.

Michael W. McConnell
"Free Exercise Revisionism and the *Smith* Decision" (1990) 57 U. Chicago L. Rev. 1108

p.1152: "According to the Smith opinion, the argument for free exercise exemptions [e.g rule-exemptions and the accommodation of religious difference] "contradicts both constitutional tradition and common sense. Unfortunately, the Court never presents that argument so that readers might be able to judge for themselves. The argument is this: the Free Exercise Clause, by its very terms and read in the light of its historic purposes, guarantees that believers of every faith, and not just the majority, are able to practice their religion without unnecessary interference from the government. The clause is not concerned with facial neutrality or general applicability. It singles out a particular category of human activities for particular protection, a protection that is most often needed by practioners of non-mainstream faiths who lack the ability to protect themselves in the political sphere, but may on occasion, be needed by any person of religious convictions caught in conflict with our secular political culture.

For this protection the *Smith* opinion sustitutes a bare requirement of formal neutrality. Religious exercise is no longer to be treated as a preferred freedom; so long as it is treated no worse than commercial or other secular activity, religion can ask for no more. The needs of minority religion are no longer to be entitled to equal consideration from the state. If practioners of minority religions cannot protect themselves, that is the 'consequence of democratic government', which they should recognize as 'unavoidable' [...] if it is necessary to confront the normative question directly, I would say that a full guarantee of religious freedom is preferable to a largely redundant equal protection clause for religion, and that a genuinely neutrality towards minority religion is preferable to a mere formal neutrality, which can be expected to reflect the moral or religious superstitions of the majority."

McConnell's analysis sets out a defence of "religions freedom" and distinguishes this from equal protection on the ground of religion. Moreover, he argues that an important aspect of the protection of religious freedom is a trenchant judicial defence of minority religions from majoritarian politics, i.e. the democratic political processes which will be inhospitable to the claims and viewpoint of minority religions. This issue of institutional balance is considered later in this chapter.

D. *Canada*—Multani, *Freedom of Religion and Accommodation of Difference*

Canadian case law contains a well established constitutional doctrine for the protection of religious freedom. Section 2(a) of the Canadian Charter of Rights and Freedoms states that religious freedom is one of the "fundamental freedoms":

"Everyone has the following fundamental freedoms:

(*a*) freedom of conscience and religion;
(*b*) freedom of thought, belief, opinion and expression, including freedom of the press and other media of communication;
(*c*) freedom of peaceful assembly; and
(*d*) freedom of association."

The Canadian Supreme Court has confirmed the importance given to freedom of religion in a number of cases and most recently in the *Multani* case.[151]

In *Multani*, the applicants (father and son) were both orthodox Sikhs who believed that the son was required to wear a religious symbol of a kirpan (a dagger made of metal) at all times. In 2001, despite a decision by the School Board that as a matter of "reasonable accommodation" the boy would be able to carry a kirpan to school, the governing body of the school refused permission and applied the rule of the school's code of conduct that prohibited the carrying of weapons. That decision was upheld by the Board of Commissioners. The applicants asked applied for a declaration that the decision of the School Commissioners was void. The question was whether the boy's right to freedom of religion under s.2(a) of the Charter had been unjustifiably infringed.

The Supreme Court decided in favour of the applicants and held that the decision of the School Commissioners was void. The majority of the Supreme Court (McLachlin C.J., and Bastarache, Binnie, Fish and Charron JJ.) reached

[151] *Multani v Commission Scolarie Marguerite-Burgeoys*, [2006] SCC6.

their decision on the basis that the appropriate test was constitutional review. A minority (Deschamps and Abella JJ.) reached their decision on a different basis, namely, that this was a decision made by an administrative body the appropriate standard of review was that set down by administrative law.

Multani raised a number of important questions: on the definition of religious belief; on the degree of accommodation of difference that is required or permissible under constitutional protections such as the Charter; and also on the relationship between standards of review in constitutonal law as compared with administrative law. More generally, the final decision in *Multani* provides a vivid contrast to the approach of other courts as to how far "rule exemption" claims and claims for reasonable accommodation can be permitted. The Candian Supreme Court acknowledged that the type of harm associated with carrying a weapon was capable of justifying an interference with freedom of religion (although, like Blakmun J. in *Smith*, they argued that there needs to be clear evidence of harm before the intereference can be justified, see paras 59 and 60).

Despite this, the Canadian Supreme Court found that there should be reasonable accommodation of the religious need of the Sikh boy. Moreover, the majority argued that the school should ensure that it created an atmosphere of pluralism in which its pupils understood the need for a Sikh student to carry the kirpan as a religious symbol. This point was emphasised in the majority opinion in *Multani* which stated:

"Religious tolerance is a very important value of Canadian society. If some students consider it unfair that Gurbaj Singh may wear his kirpan to school while they are not allowed to have knives in their possession, it is incumbent on the schools to discharge their obligation to instil in their students this value that is, [...], at the very foundation of our democracy."[152]

(i) *Defining "Religious Belief and Manifestation"*

On the issue of how to define religious belief, whether subjectively or objectively, the Court in *Multani* stated:

para.35: "The fact that different people practise the same religion in different ways does not affect the validity of the case of a person alleging that his or her freedom of religion is infringed. What an individual must do is show that he or she sincerely believes that a certain belief or practice is required by his or her religion. The religious belief must be asserted in good faith and must not be fictitious, capricious or an artifice. In assessing the sincerity of the belief, a court must take into account, inter alia, the credibility of the testimony of the person asserting the particular belief and the consistency of the belief with his or her other current religious practices."

[152] *Multani*, ibid. at para.76.

(ii) *"Internal Restrictions" on Freedom of Religion*

One argument presented to the court in *Multani* was that the case could be resolved by delineating the right to freedom of religion in a certain way. According to this analysis, defined in the appropriate way, it would be possible to argue that there were certain internal limits to the right to freedom of religion under s.2(a) of the Canadian Charter which would take into account the issues of public health and safety. This "internal limits" analysis is similar to the point made about "voluntariness" and "choice" in the ECHR jurisprudence. This approach allowed the court to find that there is no infringement in cases such as *Steadman* or *Ahmad v ILEA*. However, in *Multani*, the Canadian Supreme Court did not following this line of reasoning. They preferred to treat this as a case where the right had been infringed under s.1 of the Charter rather than one of construction of internal limits of the right to freedom of religion under s.2(a). The Canadian Supreme Court stated:

"According to this line of reasoning, the outcome of this appeal would be decided at the stage of determing whether freedom of religion has been infringed rather than at the stage of reconciling the rights of the parties under s. 1 of the *Canadian Charter*.

This Court has clearly recognized that freedom of religion can be limited when a person's freedom to act in accordance with his or her beliefs may cause harm to or interfere with the rights of others (see *R. v. Big M Drug Mart* [1985] 1 S. C. R. 295, at p. 337, and *Syndicat Northcrest v. Amselem* [2004] 2 S. C. R. 551, 2004 SCC 47, at para. 62). However, the Court has on numerous occasions stressed the advantages of reconciling rights by means of a s. 1 analysis. [. . .]

This Court has consistently refrained from formulating internal limits to the scope of freedom of religion in cases where the constitutionality of a legislative scheme was raised; it rather opted to balance competing rights under s. 1 of the *Charter*.

In my view, it appears sounder to leave to the state the burden of justifying the restrictions it has chosen. Any ambiguity or hesitation should be resolved in favour of individual rights. Not only is this consistent with the broad and liberal interpretation of rights favoured by the Court, but s. 1 is a much more flexible tool with which to balance competing rights than s. 2(a)."[153]

This approach is similar to that taken by Lord Nicholls and Baroness Hale in *Shabina Begum*. They were both reluctant to view the case as raising no infringement of freedom of religion under Art.9(1) but rather preferred that the State should have to make out a case for justification of the interference with the right. This focus on a broad interpretation of the initial right in order to give the maximum space for individual freedom of religion, and then placing the burden on the state to justify any intevention, is in marked contrast to the ECHR jurisprudence which, as we have discussed, restricts the right to freedom of religion at a much earlier stage in the analysis.

[153] *Multani, ibid.*, at paras 25–26.

(iii) *Critique of the Unified Approach—separate opinion of Abella and Dechamps JJ. Substantive v Procedural Review*

One issue which divided the Supreme Court in *Multani* was the appropriate relationship between administrative law and constitutional law, in the context of a case where there was an allegation of a violation of the Canadian Charter. In *Multani*, two of the judges (Deschamps and Abella JJ.) set out alternative reasons, and disagreed with the majority also the basis of the decision. Deschamps and Abella JJ. argued that in the case of decisions and orders (rather than laws and regulations) it was more appropriate to use administrative rather than constitutional law. Their argument against a unified approach is summarised in their separate opinions. This is similar to the test formulated by Brooke L.J. in *Shabina Begum* who seemed to favour a "procedural approach" in those cases that involved the decision of a public body, as compared with the House of Lords which confirmed that a unified "substantive" test applied to both the legislature and public bodies.

Deschamps and Abella JJ. suggested that a:

> "distinct 'administrative law' approach should be maintained between (1) reviewing the decisions and orders of administrative bodies; and (2) the validity or enforceability of a norm such as a law, regulation or a similar rule of general application."

Therefore, the decision by the School Commissioners in this case about the interpretation of the school's code of conduct fell into the first category. Deschamps and Abella JJ argued that:

> "The idea that norms of general application should be dealt with in the same way as decisions or orders of administrative bodies, as suggested by Lamer J. in *Slaight*, may be attractive from a theoretical standpoint. However, apart from the aesthetic appeal of this unified approach, we are not convinced that there is any advantage to adopting it. The question is not whether an administrative body can disregard constitutional values. The answer to that question is clear: it cannot do so absent an express indication that the legislature intended to allow it to do so. The question is rather how to assess an adminstrative body's alleged breach—in a decision—of its constitutional obligations: by means of an analytical approach under s. 1 of the Canadian Charter or under an administrative law standard of review? As the instant case shows, as as we stated previously, it is difficult to imagine a decision that would be considered reasonable or correct even though it conflicted with constitutional values. Give the demanding nature of the standard of judicial review to be met where an administrative body fails to consider constitutional values, the result can be no different [. . .].[154]

Deschamps and Abella JJ. illustrate this analysis through a comparison of two similar concepts in Canadian public law: the principle of reasonable accommodation used in administrative law; and the principle of minimal impairment used in constitutional justification analysis. They conclude:

[154] *Multani, ibid.*, at para.[109]. See also paras [103–104].

The process required by the duty of reasonable accommodation takes into account the specific details of the circumstances of the parties and allows for dialogue between them. This dialogue enables them to reconcile their positions and find common ground tailored to their own needs. The approach is different, however, in the case of minimal impairment when it is considered in the context of the broad impact of the result of the constitutional justification analysis. The justification of the infringement is based on societal interests, not on the needs of the individual parties. An administrative law analysis is microcosmic, whereas a constitutional law analysis is macrocosmic. The values involved may be different. We believe that there is an advantage to keeping these approaches separate. Furthermore, although the minimal impairment test under s. 1 of the Canadian Charter is similar to the undue hardship test in human rights law, the perspectives in the two cases are different, as is the evidence that can support the analysis. Assessing the scope of a law sometimes requries that social facts or the potential consequences of applying the law be taken into account, whereas determining whether there is undue hardship requires evidence of hardship in a particular case.

These separate streams—public versus individual—should be kept distinct. A lack of coherence in the analysis can only be detrimental to the exercise of human rights. Reasonable accommodation and undue hardship belong to the sphere of administrative law and human rights legislation, whereas the assessment of minimal impairment is part of a constitutional analysis with wider societal implications.[155]

This higher bifurcation of the analysis, and the development of variable standards of review and proportionalty, may enable the courts to develop a different response to rule exemption claims depending on variables such as the nature of the organisation, the importance of the claim for accommodation, the risk of the harm caused by accommodation and the possibility of a conflict of rights.

VIII. Consequences of "Accomodation of Difference"

A. *Conflicts of Rights*

One recurring aspect of the headscarves issue is the argument about the potential conflict between the right to wear a headscarf and gender equality. This raises a more fundamental point about how contemporary legal systems resolve conflict of rights issues (a point articulated in the sixth question of discrimination law that we raised in chapter 1, namely "what happens when protection from discrimination clashes with other rights or values?") Given the spread of discrimination law beyond the traditional grounds of race and gender to include grounds such as sexual orientation, religion and disability, it is increasingly likely that there will be a conflict of rights between claims to religious freedom on the one hand and claims to protection from discrimination related to another prohibited ground (e.g gender equality or

155 *Multani, ibid.*, at paras 131–134.

sexual orientation). A number of jurisdictions have already considered these types of confict[156]. The potential conflict in the EU Framework Directive between religion and sexual orientation in the sphere of non-discrimination in employment is acknowledged and resolved through a compromise which allows religious groups a limited exemption from the general requirement of non-discrimination on the grounds of sexual orientation.[157]

B. *Institutional factors*

To the extent that claimants can rely on indirect discrimination arguments, it will be easier for them to make rule-exception claims and challenge facially neutral rules that do not accommodate their particular practice. However, as discussed, the extension of Art.14 ECHR by the European Court of Human Rights in *Thlimmenos* to discrimination cases has so far been limited and the Court has shown deference to national authorities in the 'headscarf' cases. The Canadian Supreme Court has been more permissive. It has taken a robust approach in cases such as *Multani* where there is an interference with freedom of religion. It has allowed indirect discrimination claims in the context of s.15 of the Canadian Charter but these have been in limited conditions and there are very few successful claims: *Eldridge v British Columbia (Attorney General)*[158] is one of the rare cases where such a claim was allowed and it is perhaps explicable because there was a discreet claim by a particularly vulnerable group (medical patients with hearing impairments) who were claiming a key public good (medical facilities). One reason for the caution of constitutional courts in the context of claims for indirect discrimination becomes clear from the reasoning of the Canadian Supreme Court in *Eldridge*. The court noted that permitting indirect discrimination claims in that case had significant implications for the distribution of resources, which were decisions usually best left to legislatures.[159] This raises a more fundamental question about the use of constitutional human rights protections as a mechanism for "accommodating difference". Such a strategy will raise important questions about the redistribution of resources and power between majorities and minorities. There is therefore a strong argument that legislative and representative bodies are the best institutional forum for reaching decisions on these issues. However, the obvious problem is that minorities are not well represented in these institutions. This is the point that McConnell makes in his critique of *Smith*, discussed earlier where he argues that judicial protection is required precisely because majoritarian democratic politics poses a specific type of threat to

[156] See the decision of the Canadian Supreme Court in *Trinity Western University v British Columbia College of Teachers* [2001] 1 S.C.R. 772.
[157] Employment Equality Directive, Council Directive 2000/78/EC of November 27, 2000.
[158] *Eldridge v British Columbia (Attorney General)* (1997) 3 S.C.R. 624.
[159] *Eldridge v British Columbia (Attorney General)* (1997) 3 S.C.R. 624.

minority religious viewpoints. This analysis has particular relevance in the context of the individual civil and political right to freedom of religion. In the context of the allocation of social and economic goods to religious minorities or accommodating their religious needs, there is an argument in favour of a greater "dialogue" between minorities and majorities that ensures that decisions are consensual and carry the commitment of both sides. Agreeing on controversial decisions about allocation of economic and social power through negotiation in assemblies and representative bodies may ensure a greater degree of commitment by both majorities and minorities to these decisions. It has therefore been argued that the fact that citizens are more likely to identify with the decisions of representative institutions makes the latter a preferable forum when minority protection policies require social change, re-allocation of power or resources or multiculturalism.[160] There are examples where minorities have succeeded in using political processes to advance their most pressing claims for the accommodation of their distinct needs, which suggests that legislative processes can be sometimes hospitable to minority claims.[161] It is also worth noting that legislatures and political processes may be more appropriate institutions to deliver wide ranging social reform to address the needs of minorities than courts and litigation.[162]

IX. Statutory Provisions and Religious Discrimination

As stated earlier, apart from the legislation in Northern Ireland which was a response to the long-standing sectarian conflict between Catholics and Protestants, there was until recently no prohibition in the UK on religious discrimination analogous to that in the areas of race and gender until very recently. There was however, indirect protection for some religious groups. Ethnic religious minorities such as Sikhs and Jews who fell within the *Mandla* definition of race were protected by the whole ambit of race relations legislation. In addition, those characteristics of religious groups that overlapped with race or culture could be protected via the indirect discrimination provisions of race relations legislation. For example, if a requirement to have short hair was introduced in a workplace it could perhaps be shown to have a disproportionate impact on African-Carribean groups as a "racial group", because large numbers of the members of those groups are also Rastafarians. However, such indirect protection was dependent on an individual being able to show an overlap between their religion and race or culture. It raised diffi-

160 Maleiha Malik, "Minority Protection and the Human Rights Act" in Tom Campbell, et al (eds), *Sceptical Essays on Human Rights* (Oxford: Oxford University Press, 2001) at 292.

161 See for example the example of Sikhs discussed in Sebastian Poulter, *Ethnicity, Law and Human Rights: The English Experience* (Oxford: Oxford University Press, 1998) at ch.8.

162 G. N. Rosenberg, *The Hollow Hope: Can Courts Bring About Social Change?* (Chicago: University of Chicago Press, 1991), especially at pp.20–25.

culties for converts to a religion who would not be able to bring themselves within the category race by relying on their religious difference. Moreover, unlike the full protection of direct discrimination provisions the reliance on indirect discrimination could be justified by employers on a number of grounds including business necessity.

These anomalies have been partially remedied through the introduction of the Employment Equality (Religion and Belief) Regulations 2003 (R and B Regs) which transpose the Art.13 Employment Equality Directive (EED) into law. As discussed earlier, the EED provides the basis for equality of treatment in employment and training on a number of grounds which include religion and also sexual orientation, disability and age. As Chapter 2 discussed, religious discrimination in the provision of goods and services is also now prohibited under the Equality Act 2006. In the next section, we will examine the main provisions of the EED; the form and content of the Religion and Belief Regulations. The EED states in Art.1 that "the purpose of this Directive is to lay down a general framework for combating discrimination on the grounds of religion or belief. There are, however, also a number of specific provisions in the Directive that set out the exact nature of the protection afforded to religion and belief.

A. *Defining Religion and Belief*

It is worth observing that there is no definition of religion or belief in the EED. There are, therefore, a number of options open to those who seek to regulate religion and belief: a statutory definition; an open or closed list; or a wide set of criteria. The EED contains no definition of religion or belief. Instead, there has been a preference for leaving the definition of religion and belief to the national authorities, courts and circumstances. This solution introduces the prospect of some confusion. The idea of "religion and belief" is, in some respects, more like race and ethnicity and also overlaps with these protected characteristics. The form and significance of the term "religion and belief", and its relationship to issues of race and political opinion, will vary considerably across the different Member States of the EU. This introduces the possibility of a wide range of variation in the definition of the term "religion and belief" across the Member States, with the consequence that there will be variable protection in each jurisdiction of an individual right which the EU regards as part of the fundamental non-discrimination right guaranteed by Art.13. On the other hand the strategy of leaving the definition to each Member State has considerable advantages as indicated in the discussion below.

"EU Proposals to Combat Discrimination"
Ninth Report of the EU House of Lords Select Committee
Session (1999–2000)

[61]: "The lack of definitions of key concepts is one of the most striking features of the proposed Directives. The grounds of discrimination ("racial or ethnic origin", "disability", and so on) are not defined; nor are concepts such as "social advantages", or "positive action". Definitions are, however, provided for direct and indirect discrimination, and these will be considered in due course.

[62]: The Commission's approach was described by Mme Quintin. The draft Directives were "proposals which set objectives without going into too much detail as to how those objectives should be achieved". The lack of detail would leave Member States "a lot of margin for manoeuvre to adapt their legislation in response to their specific cultural diversity". This was the only realistic approach: "we have deliberately chosen not to define the various grounds of discrimination but to leave it for the definition of Member States, in particular in the case of disability, because we know all the differences and all the difficulties which have been encountered . . . when it has been discussed to come to a common definition". However, the inclusion of Article 13 in the EC Treaty means that any measures to which it gives rise will be justiciable by the European Court of Justice. The Committee suggested to Mme Quintin that any definitions supplied by Member States in their implementing legislation would necessarily be subjected to the scrutiny of the ECJ, with the result that Community definitions would ultimately be necessary. Mme Quintin did not answer this point, but simply repeated her statement that "we believe that it is better to leave this issue to be dealt with in each individual national context" (QQ 35, 37, 43, p.25).

[63]: Other witnesses advanced widely differing opinions on this question. The Government broadly agreed with the Commission: "In the interests of subsidiarity we feel that it should be left to Member States to work out their own definitions within guidelines provided by the text of the Directive" (however, the draft Directives contain no such guidelines). Bert Massie (DRC) accepted that the Commission's approach was at least realistic: "if you have no definition [of disability], you have the advantage that at least the EU countries could agree on it". Professor Hepple, addressing the question of "religion or belief", echoed this view: "I am not sure that given the great differences among the 15 Member States and the enlarged Union one could really begin to have a definition which would satisfy all Member States. It may therefore be better to leave this . . . to case law development". It is notable however that Professor Hepple envisaged definitions evolving in the courts: "Ultimately the European Court of Justice has to decide the question". When challenged on the problems faced by those with learning disabilities, he argued that "if you leave [the Directive] fairly open-textured you do give the opportunity for development of the concept to deal with [such] situations". In this respect Professor Hepple echoed those disability groups who were also willing to rely on judges. John Wall (RNIB) suggested that the Commission's approach would allow greater flexibility: "I think that if it is left to judicial interpretation . . . I have sufficient faith in the judges of [the ECJ] to believe that they would be able to define disability in a way which would be consonant with the ethos of the time. This is one of the great advantages of common law over statute law" (p.11, QQ 246, 328, 333, 332, 245)."

Despite the reluctance of Mme Quintin (representing the European Commission) to concede that the European Court of Justice would ultimately adjudicate on issues about the definition of religion and belief it seems reasonable to predict that this will be a key issue for litigation under provisions which fall within the jurisdiction of the ECJ. It is also worth noticing that following the interpretation of "disability" as a prohibited ground of discrimination under the EED as having an EU wide autonomous meaning in the *Chacon Navas* case,[163] the ECJ is likely to also assume supervision over the term "religion". The development of an EU wide definition of "religion or belief" will need to strike a subtle balance between harmonising, and leaving much needed discretion to national courts to respond to local issues. Given the previous argument concerning the dangers of essentialist definitions, and the advantages of an approach that seeks to interpret "religion or belief" as socially constructed categories, it follows that there are good arguments for the term to be interpreted at a national level where there is likely to be a deeper understanding of local issues relating to discrimination and prejudice. The ECJ will need to ensure that the purpose of Art.13 to secure fundamental rights to equality in employment and training across the EU is secured, without developing a definition which excludes all national discretion to local issues of religious and belief based discrimination. The example of Northern Ireland, where there are positive action measures for ensuring that Catholics are included in the police, illustrates the need for regional variation in discrimination law within the UK. The specific form, and need for distinct exceptions, will vary across depending on factors such as differences of history, politics and society in different EU member states.

In the R and B Regulations, the term "religion or belief" is defined in Reg.2 in the following terms: "In these Regulations, 'religion or belief' means any religion, religious belief, or similar philosophical belief." As discussed earlier the term "similar philosophical belief" will act as a limiting factor. Nonetheless, the Regulations leave the matter of whether a particular religion or belief falls within their scope to courts and tribunals. There is some guidance provided via the DTI in its guidance to the Religion and Belief Regulations. This guidance explictly follows the Art.9, ECHR approach: it leaves open the precise definition of religion and belief including an open list of those religions which are recognised in Britain: Christianity, Islam, Hinduism, Judaism, Buddhism, Sikhism, Rastafarianism, Baha'ism, Zorastrianism and Jainism.[164] One example of the complexity of defining the terms is *Baggs v Dr FDA Fudge*[165]. In *Baggs*, a Tribunal found that the British National Party was a political party that was not protected as a "philosophical belief" under Reg.2 of the Religion and Belief Regs. The IT found that "belief" in the context of Reg.2 Religion and Belief Regs needs to be similar to religious belief and for this reason the BNP fell outside the definition.[166] There have been two other recent cases on the meaning of "religion and belief" under the R and B Regs.

163 *Chacón Navas v Eurest Colectividades SA European Court of Justice* C-13/05.
164 ACAS, *"Religion or Belief and the Workplace"*, November 2005, available at www.acas.org.uk (accessed on August 20, 2005).
165 *Baggs v DR FDA Fudge* (Chair, AC Tickle), March 24, 2005, Case No:1400114/05, reported (October 2005) 157 Equal Opportunities Rev. 31–32.
166 *ibid.*

In *Harris v NJL Automotive Ltd and Matrix Consultancy UK Ltd*, the EAT has held that Rastafarians are a similar philosophical belief to religion.[167] In *McClintock v Department for Constitutional Affairs* the EAT has held that a general opinion which is not related to a religious or philosophical belief.[168]

B. *Concept of Discrimination*

The EED sets out three specific aspects of what constitutes unlawful discrimination. Article 2 states that "for the purposes of this Directive, the principle of equal treatment shall mean that there shall be no direct or indirect discrimination whatsoever" on the ground of religion or belief. In addition, the Directive specifies that harassment is a form of discrimination. Direct discrimination is defined as less favourable treatment: where one person is treated less favourably than another is, has been or would be treated in a comparable situation. In addition, indirect discrimination introduces the EU ideas of "legitimate aim" and "proportionality". Harassment on the ground of religion and belief is also deemed to be a form of discrimination, as is victimisation. At domestic level, these concepts are found in Regs 3 and 4 of the Religion and Belief Regulations. The scope of the EED extends to all types of employment and vocational training in both the public and private sector (see Art.3).

The transposition of these concepts of discrimination into the R and B Regulations has raised a number of important points.

1. Direct and Indirect Discrimination

In relation to direct religious discrimination, the term less favourable treatment is included "on grounds of religion and belief" (Reg.3(1)(a)). This wording is significant because it ensures that the concept of direct religious discrimination extends beyond the obvious case of discrimination against an individual because of their religion and belief, and it also potentially includes:[169]

(a) treatment based on the perception of the persons' religion, e.g. a mistaken belief about the religion of a person leading to less favourable treatment;

[167] (Jan 2008) 172 EOR 22. Decision of EAT of October 3, 2007.
[168] *ibid*., Decision of EAT of October 31, 2007.
[169] For a full discussion of these issues and for examples below see Lucy Vickers, "Freedom of Religion and the Workplace: The Draft Employment and Equality (Religion or Belief) Regulations 2003" (2003) 32 Industrial L.J. 23 at 24.

(b) treatment based on the person's association with people of a particular religion, e.g. less favourable treatment based on friendship or marriage to a person of a particular religion;

Treatment based on the discriminator's religious views is not included within the definition of direct discrimination (Reg.3(2)).

It is also worth observing that because religion has a communal aspect, there will be cases where those who are religious or employers in religious organisations will undertake less favourable treatment on the grounds of religion. The prohibition on religious discrimination applies to religious employers and organisations but there are exceptions which permit some forms of discrimination in order to preseve the distinct character of religious organisations. This is the "religious ethos" requirement discussed below.

Indirect religious discrimination is set out in Reg.3(1)(b). The definition mirrors the new definition of indirect discrimination introduced into the RRA (see Chapter 2). It includes the terms "provision, criterion or practice" to identify the practice; and the justifiability test "to be a proportionate means of achieving a legitimate aim". As discussed indirect religious discrimination concept that can be used to advance "accommodating differences" arguments. The extent to which the R and B Regs will protect the manifestation of religion and belief in the context of the workplace will depend upon the way Reg.3 is interpreted. Unlike Art.9 and other human rights instruments, the indirect discrimination provision in the R and B Regs is necessarily more limited in scope covers employment and training. This suggests that, there will be a distinct analysis that applies to issues of accommodation of religious practices in the workplace. The fact that employees have voluntarily chosen to put themselves into a contractual relationship cannot be in and of itself a sufficient reason to assume that they have contracted out all of their rights to manifest their religion in the workplace. Here the distinction between "freedom of religion" and "non-discrimination on the grounds of religion", which was developed earlier in the chapter, becomes especially relevant. It might be possible, in the context of religion as freedom to argue that in the "voluntary contracting out cases" (e.g. where there has been an agreement by a Christian employee to Sunday working) there is still freedom because the individual is free to leave the employment if it conflicts with his religious obligations. However, in the context of non-discrimination arguments it is precisely the function of a prohibition on religious discrimination in employment that the employee should not have to accept "contract out" of his or her religious obligation. Therefore, in these cases the courts will have to consider the nature of the interference with the manifestation of religious belief of the employee; and then apply the legitimacy and proporitionality test to determine whether the employer can justify the interference. In the context of the R and B Regs, these provisions need to be read as protective legislation which is compensating the employee in the workplace. As Mummery L. J.'s observations in *Copsey* suggest, the "free to resign" argument in the context of employment can seem harsh: it gives the employee only the stark alternative of leaving their job and going elsewhere.[170]

The ECHR in cases such as *Ahmad v ILEA* and *Steadman* is quite clear: an employer has the right to keep his workplace free of manifestations of religion. In human rights claims, arguments for accommodation raise the spectre of rule-exemption claims from wider universally applicable laws, something which poses the danger of fragmentation of the rule of law which has been referred to in the US Supreme Court case of *Employment Division v Smith*. In statutory discrimination law, there is no such risk because the scope of the protection from religious discrimination is limited to a specific sphere, e.g. employment. The claim for accommodation is not in the form of a wide ranging rule-exemption. Rather it is a claim by employees against their employers as part of the allocation of power, rights and responsibilities in the workplace. This distinction is important because it suggests that courts may be able to develop a different and in some cases a more generous view of the type of accommodation that is possible under indirect religious discrimination provisions of the R and B Regs, as compared with provisions such as Art.9.

Before the introduction of the Religion and Belief Regulations (2003) there were a number of cases which argued for accommodation of religious beliefs within the indirect race discrimination provisions of the RRA. On the whole, these cases have not provided for the substantial "accomodation of religious difference" in the workplace. Such accommodation will be especially important for minority religions which are faced with public structures (such as holidays or weekend timing) which are not conducive to the practice of their faith. However, as the *Copsey* case itself illustrates, (the case concerned a Christian employee asking for time off on a Saturday), this is also increasingly an issue for majority religions such as Christianity as the public sphere increasingly moves away from reflecting any religious point of view. The key areas in which religious practice will raise questions of "accommodation" will be, inter alia: time off for religious festivals and holidays; time off for attendance for religious worship during working hours; and dress and appearance. Practical examples of this need for accommodation of religious difference could include, inter alia: weekend working arrangements permitting attendance at church for Christians;[171] leaving work at sunset on Fridays for Jews;[172] lunch time attendance at mosque on Fridays for Muslims;[173] the adoption of

[170] *Copsey v WBB Devon Clays Ltd* [2005] E. C. R. 1789.

[171] *Copsey v WBB Devon Clays Ltd* [2005] E.C.R. 1789 and *James v MSC Cruises Ltd* Case No.2203173/05, 12 April 2006, Central London Industrial Tribunal, Chair: RA Hemmings, (October 2006) 157 EOR 32.

[172] *Fluss v Grant Thornton Chartered Accountants*, COIT Case 30561/86, dated March 26, 1986 (cited in (December 1991) 439 Industrial Relations Legal Information Bulletin 2–9 and *London Borough of Tower Hamlets v Rabin*, EAT 260/88, dated June 6, 1989 (cited in (December 1991) 439 Industrial Relations Legal Information Bulletin 2–9).

[173] *Ahmad v Inner London Education Authority* [1977] I.C.R. 490.

beards and turbans by Sikhs[174] and wearing skirts by Asian (Sikh and Muslim) women;[175] and handling of meat based products for Hindus. Of these cases it is worth mentioning *Panesar v Nestle*,[176] in which there is a detailed discussion of the "business necessity" requirement under the indirect race discrimination provisions of the RRA. In *Panesar* the EAT upheld the IT decision that the prohibition of beards was justified in relation to a job at a chocolate factory for health and safety reasons, this was irrespective of the fact that other factories did not have such a protective rule.

A recent case under the new R and B Regs is *James v MSC Cruises Ltd*, which suggests that employers have scope to persuade Employment Tribunals that there is a "compelling business case" for a weekend working policy, which meets the requirements fo "legitimate aim" and "proportionality". In *James v MSC Cruises Ltd*[176a] the employee was a practising member of the Seventh-day Adventist Church who was offered a post that involved working from 9am to 1pm on a Saturday. The employee, Mrs James, argued that she could not work on Saturdays because of her faith which required her to observe the Sabbath strictly after sunset on a Friday (her faith provided an exception for essential services such as medicine). The tribunal accepted the employer's evidence that Saturday working was essential in the tourism industry, and that this required dedicated staff with a depth of experience. The employee countered this by arguing that a solution could have been reached after consultation with employees; and the emphasis/weight given to Saturday working was only a small part of the work. The tribunal accepted the employers reliance on the tourism standard, which in this case meant that the requirement of Saturday working would exclude practicing Seventh Day Adventists from the tourism industry. As suggested earlier, given that the R and B Regs limit the scope of "religious equality" and "non-discrimination on the grounds of religion" to employment and training, there is some scope for courts to develop a more flexible standard for the accommodation of religion difference in employment, than is available under the Art.9 of the ECHR. Moreover, it could be argued that the EU law test for indirect discrimination sets a higher threshold than the test under the RRA in cases such as *Panesar*. If this is correct, then the R and B Regs might, therefore, offer greater protection for employees from practices that are indirect religious discrimination.

[174] *Panesar v Nestle Company Ltd* [1980] I.R.L.R. 60.

[175] *Kingston v Richmond AHA v Kaur* [1981] I.R.L.R. 337 and *Malik v Bertram Personnel Group* (1991) 7 EOR 5.

[176] *Panesar v Nestle Company Ltd* [1980] I.R.L.R. 60.

[176a] Case No.2203173/05 (Decision of April 12, 2006, Central London Industrial Tribunal), discussed at "Saturday-working requirement did not give rise to indirect discrimination" (October 2006) 157 Equal Opportunities Rev.32.

2. Harassment and Victimisation

Harassment on the grounds of "religion and belief" is defined in Regulation 5 as:

"5.—(1) For the purposes of these Regulations, a person ("A") subjects another person ("B") to harassment where, on grounds of religion or belief, A engages in unwanted conduct which has the purpose or effect of—

(a) violating B's dignity; or

(b) creating an intimidating, hostile, degrading, humiliating or offensive environment for B.

(2) Conduct shall be regarded as having the effect specified in paragraph (1)(a) or (b) only if, having regard to all the circumstances, including in particular the perception of B, it should reasonably be considered as having that effect."

Victimisation is deemed to be discrimination under Reg.4. These provisions have been considered in chapter 8. Here it is worth observing that there may be special issues relating to "religion" that are relevant in the case of harassment. S.5(2) defines the relevant circumstances for the test of whether conduct constitutes harassment "including in particular the perception of B [i.e the victim of harassment]". This may suggest that an overly sensitive person's perspective is given undue weight in deciding whether conduct is harassment. However, it is worth noticing that the statutory provision requires attention to be paid to all the circumstances and introduces a test of reasonableness. Read in this context, the perception of the victim is clearly a relevant factor, but it need not be given determinative weight if it is deemed to be an overaction to the conduct using the test of reasonableness as developed by the courts. A second problem may emerge out of the conflict of rights point. The potential for conflict between traditional religions and beliefs and the protection given to groups such as women and gays and lesbians is a real possibility. Courts will need to deal with such cases with care, and to draw clear distinctions between the right of individuals to hold their religious or other beliefs generally on the one hand; and speech or conduct based on these beliefs that becomes unacceptable within the context of the workplace where women, gays and lesbians have a right to be protected against harassment.[177] One commentator, Ian Leigh, has suggested that:

[177] See one example of the types of facts situations that could arise from a case that arose before the introduction of the Religion and Belief Regs 2003 arose in *Berrisford v Woodard Schools (Midland Division) Ltd* [1991] I.R.L.R. 247 where a member of staff was dismissed by a Church of England school because she became pregnant without being married, and the employer argued that this conveyed an unacceptable moral message to pupils. The claim under the SDA was dismissed because it was held that a male school teacher would have treated a male member of staff in the same way.

"Attempts, whether by a public authority or a private employer, to deal with what it perceives to be 'homophobia' can too easily be perceived by the persons affected as oppressive discrimination against their religious beliefs."[178]

In relation to the Art.13 EED (in draft form) Leigh concluded:

"The proposed directive demonstrates how religious liberty can be at risk from privileging of a particular conception of equality and non-discrimination, especially where private action and belief are subordinated. It embodies a refusal to accept that private individuals are entitled to act on or form private moral judgments about homosexual conduct which depart from the 'correct' non-judgmental official position. [...] Despite amendments which were more sympathetic to the concerns of religious groups, the directive places a low value on 'associational' religious liberty as compared with religious rights. [...]".[179]

In the context of harassment, it is clear that individuals have the right to hold religious views until they are manifested in a way that constitutes the harm of harassment. Courts will have to determine the boundaries between free speech and harassment. However, once again, in the context of statutory discrimination law it may be possible to argue that the fact that protection from discrimination is limited to employment enables a more substantial protection against discrimination harassment without the risk that there will be a wide reaching interference with the right to religion and belief. The individual has a wide range of other contexts in which to express his or her views based on religion and belief. However, in the very specific context of employment there are special reasons, including the fact that individuals are working in close proximity, that suggest that this right should be limited.

This issue is bound to raise some difficult questions in many areas. In relation to minority traditional religions with distinct views about the role of women, there is also a risk that comments which an individual takes to be the expression of their "religion or belief" worldview are taken by others to be sexist or even to constitute sexual harassment. In relation to all religions there is a danger of a conflict between traditional religious beliefs and attitudes towards gays and lesbians.

[178] Ian Leigh, "Clashing Rights, Exemptions, And Opt-Outs: Religious Liberty and Homophobia" in Richard O'Dair and Andrew Lewis, *Law and Religion*, (2001) 4 Current Legal Issues 247 (Oxford: Oxford University Press, 2001) at p.248.

[179] *ibid.*, at p.272.

C. *Exceptions and the Genuine Occupational Qualifications*

(i) *General Exceptions for National Interests*

The EED contains important exceptions to the requirement of non-discrimination on the grounds of religion and belief. There is a general exception in Art.2(5) which provides that the Directive does not apply in relation to:

"measures laid down by law which, in a democratic society, are necessary for public security, for maintenance of public order and the prevention of criminal offences, for health protection and for the protection of the rights and freedoms of others."

This is introduced into the domestic law through the R and B Regs, 24–26 which creates an exception for national security. In addition, Reg.26 introduces a measure which ensures that any indirect discrimination against Sikhs which is based on the requirement that they wear safety helmets on construction sites cannot be justified. This provision ensures compliance with the special exemption provided to Sikhs from the requirement to wear safety helmets as part of the health and safety measures by s.11 of the Employment Act 1989, providing an interesting example of a rule exemption claim granted by Sikhs.

Reg 25 of the R and B Regs is an exemption for postive action measures. As with positive action measures in the area of gender discrimination, these are a permissible exception from the principle of equal treatment under Art.7 of the EED which provides that:

"with a view to ensuring full equality in practice, the principle of equal treatment shall not prevent any Member State from maintaining or adopting specific measures to prevent or compensate for disadvantages linked ot the grounds of religion or belief."

(ii) *Other sets of exceptions contained in Article 4 of the EED*

These exceptions are similar to the Genuine Occupations Requirements exceptions discussed in earlier chapters. Article 4 permits certain exceptions which relate to occupations requirements. It permits a difference of treatment which is based on a characteristic related to religion or belief where by reason of the nature of the particular occupational activities concerned or of the context in which they are carried out, such a characteristic constitutes a genuine and determing occupational requirement, provided that the objective is legitimate and the requirement is proportionate. Article 4 is transposed into domestic law in R and B Regs, Reg.7, which states::

"7.—(2) This paragraph applies where, having regard to the nature of the employment or the context in which it is carried out—(a) being of a particular religion or belief is a genuine and determining occupational requirement; (b) it is proportionate to apply that requirement in the particular case; and (c) either—

(i) the person to whom that requirement is applied does not meet it, or

(ii) the employer is not satisfied, and in all the circumstances it is reasonable for him not to be satisfied, that that person meets it,

and this paragraph applies whether or not the employer has an ethos based on religion or belief."

This provision is similar to GOR provisions for the other prohibited grounds, and a similar analysis relating to what is genuine and proportionate would appear to apply in this context. A key issue in interpreting this provision will be the extent to which a court will enter into a scrutiny of the claims of employers about their specific job function; whether there is a relationship between the job function and the religion and belief related criterion that the employer argues is an essential requirement; and the ability of the candidate to meet this criterion. The issue of how the job function is defined will be a key stage in this analysis. For example, if the issue relates to employment as a teacher in a school which is specifically for Christian children there are two ways of specifying the job function. First, it can be specified as a requirement for a Christian teacher. Second, it can be specified as a requirement for a teacher with a sufficient knowledge of Christianity to be able to perform the job as a teacher. Given that the GORs are an exception to the general principle of non-discrimination it is suggested that the second more restrictive interpretation should be preferred. It is also noteworthy that Reg.7(2)(ii) ensures that where there is doubt or controversy about whether a person meets the criteria, the issue is left to the employer subject to the requirement of context and reasonableness. This means that in the controversial area of determining a person's religious beliefs—or whether they meet the right criteria or denomination—the issue is resolved in favour of the employer.[180]

D. *Article 4(2)—Religious Ethos Exception and Protection the Group/Associational Aspects of Religion*

Article 4(2)(a) of the EED makes provision for the "religious ethos" of certain churches and similar organisations. This has been transposed into domestic discrimination law in Reg.7(3) of the Employment Equality (Religion and Belief) Regulations 2003

[180] Lucy Vickers, "The Employment Equality (Religion or Belief) Regulations 2003 (2003) 32(2) Industrial L.J. 191.

"This paragraph applies where an employer has an ethos based on religion or belief and, having regard to that ethos and to the nature of the employment or the context in which it is carried out—(a) being of a particular religion or belief is a genuine occupational requirement for the job; (b) it is proportionate to apply that requirement in the particular case; and (c) either—

(i) the person to whom that requirement is applied does not meet it, or

(ii) the employer is not satisfied, and in all the circumstances it is reasonable for him not to be satisfied, that that person meets it."

Article 4 and Reg 7(3) therefore provide a potentially wide exception to the general principle of non-discrimination on the ground of religion and belief in employment. There were some fears that this would allow a sweeping power to preseve the "religious ethos" of organisations by (a) employing only those of a certain faith; or (b) imposing strict criteria in terms of behaviour on employees.

This provision was introduced as a safeguard for the collective and associational aspects of religion: i.e the need for churches and other institutions to maintain their distinctive characteristics which may in some aspects entail discrimination on the ground of religion.

In the transposition of Art.4 into domestic discrimination law there are a number of ways in which this exception is limited. First, it has been made clear that Reg.7(3) will only apply to "organised religion". Only those institutions that meet the criterion of organised religion will be able to rely on this exception. Second, Reg.7(3) makes clear that the institution cannot allocate all the jobs as being for those of a certain religion and belief to maintain the ethos of that organisation. Reg.7(3)(a) still specifies that there is a need for religion or belief to be a requirement of the job for which the GOR is being sought.

X. Fair Employment and Treatment (Northern Ireland) Order 1998 (FETO)

The R and B Regs do not regulate religious discrimination in Northern Ireland where there has been legislation to prohibit religious discrimination on the ground of "relgion and belief" since the Employment Acts of 1976 and 1989. Therefore, the impact of the EED in Northern Ireland depends on its interface with the existing FETO regime. The need for legislation to prohibit religious discrimination in Northern Ireland at a time when there was no substantial regulation in the rest of the United Kingdom can be explained by the particular political situation in the area. There are two main religious groups in Northern Ireland: a majority of Protestants; and a significant Catholic minority, which had until the peace process of the late 1990s and early 2000s been engaged in sectarian conflict.

Census, April 2001, Northern Ireland Statistics and Research Agency

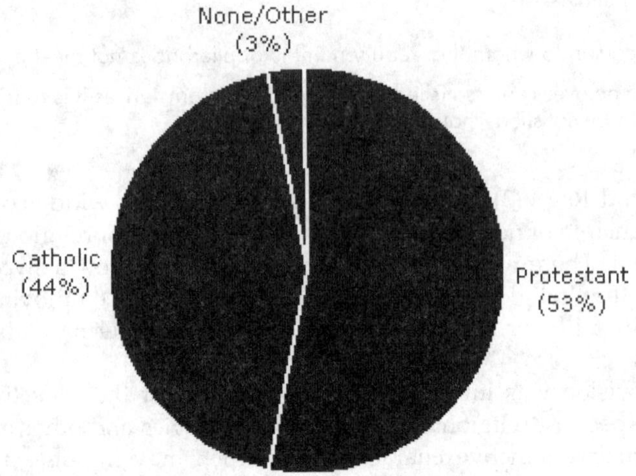

Community background (religion or religion brought up in), April 2001, Northern Ireland

"People from a Protestant community background make up the largest group in Northern Ireland. In 2001, 53 per cent of the population was from a Protestant community background. People from a Catholic community background made up the second largest group (44 per cent).

The relationship between these two groups has been marked by centuries of political sectarian conflict with the result of significant inequalities. Religious differences map onto political difference in complex ways: broadly speaking they correlate to the Protestant majority favouring political union with the United Kingdom; whereas the long standing demand of the Catholic minority has been for autonomy either in the form of a united Ireland or through a break with affiliation with the Union (and control by the Westminster Parliament). The profile of each community varies and some of these differences are set out below. Most significantly, the rates of unemployment of Catholics remain significantly higher than those for Protestants.

There were similar proportions of men and women in each of the communities. Forty-nine per cent of people from a Protestant background were men and 51 per cent were women. Among Catholics, 48 per cent were men and 52 per cent were women. In contrast, those with no religious community background were more likely to be men (55 per cent).

Northern Ireland data on religion are different to those for Great Britain because a very different Census question was asked in Northern Ireland. The religious categories were all divisions of the Christian category together with an "other religion" option. The distinction between Catholics and Protestants was not available for the rest of Great Britain.

People from a Protestant community background have an older age structure than those from a Catholic community background. In 2001, 17 per cent of Protestants were aged 65 years or over compared with 10 per cent of Catholics. Conversely, over a quarter (27 per cent) of people from a Catholic community background were under 16 years of age, compared with a fifth (20 per cent) of those from a Protestant background.

Northern Ireland is divided into five European Union geographic areas (NUTS), but only one of these areas, Belfast, was inhabited by roughly equal proportions of people from Catholic and Protestant community backgrounds in 2001 (47 per cent and 49 per cent respectively).

Outer Belfast and East of Northern Ireland were the areas with the highest proportions of people from a Protestant background (74 per cent and 62 per cent respectively). The highest proportions of people from a Catholic background were found in the West and South of Northern Ireland (65 per cent) and in the North of Northern Ireland (57 per cent).

The spatial concentration of the different religions can be seen at a smaller geographical level. People from Catholic and Protestant community backgrounds were represented in roughly equal numbers in only two of the 26 local government districts in Northern Ireland in 2001—Armagh and Belfast.

Protestants formed the majority population in 13 local government districts and in six of these districts they made up more than three quarters of the population. The highest concentrations of Protestants were found in Carrickfergus (85 per cent), Ards (83 per cent) and North Down (80 per cent).

Catholics formed the majority population in 11 local government districts. However, they accounted for more than three quarters of the local population in only two: Newry and Mourne (where 81 per cent were from the Catholic community) and Derry (where 75 per cent were Catholics).

Notes: The term community background refers to a person's current religion or if no current religion is stated, the religion that that person was brought up in. Protestant includes "Other Christian" and "Christian related", and those brought up as Protestants. Catholic includes those respondents who gave their religion as Catholic or Roman Catholic, and those brought up as Catholics.

NUTS stands for European Union Nomenclature of Units for Territorial Statistics. NUTS is a hierarchical classification of areas that provide a breakdown of the European Union's economic territory so that regional statistics that are comparable across the Union can be produced.

Published on October 11, 2004"

Northern Ireland Labour Market
Unemployment rate higher for Catholics than Protestants

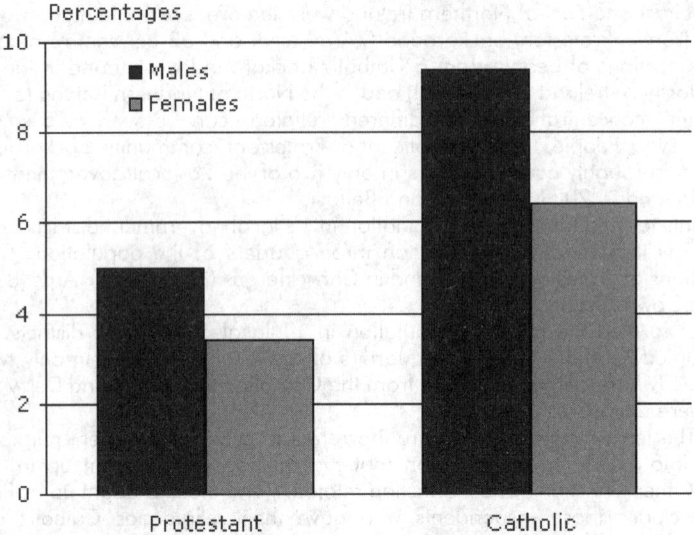

Unemployment rate: by religion and sex, 2002/03, Northern Ireland

"In Northern Ireland, unemployment rates among Catholics were higher than those among Protestants for both men and women in 2002/03.

The unemployment rate for Catholic men was 9 per cent compared with 5 per cent for Protestant men. Among women, the unemployment rates were 6 per cent for Catholics compared with 3 per cent for Protestants.

This difference is evident for both men and women, and among all age groups, except for men aged under 25. Within this group, unemployment rates for the two communities were very similar.

A higher proportion of Catholic than Protestant working age men and women were economically inactive, that is not available for work and/or not actively seeking work. Reasons for economic inactivity include being a student, being disabled or looking after the family and home.

Overall in 2002/03, 24 per cent of Catholic men were economically inactive compared with 18 per cent of Protestant men. This pattern was the same across most age groups.

Economic inactivity rates were higher for women than men, and there was a greater difference between the two religions among women than among men: 42 per cent of Catholic women were inactive compared with 31 per cent of Protestant women. This pattern occurred across all age groups.

Among men a higher proportion of Catholics than Protestants worked in the construction industry, 25 per cent compared with 15 per cent. There was little variation between Catholic and Protestant women in the industries in which they worked.

For most age groups there was little difference between Catholics and Protestants in educational achievement in 2002/03. However, Catholics aged 50 and over were more likely than Protestants of the same age to have no qualifications (49 per cent compared with 40 per cent).

In 2002/03, around one in ten of both Protestants and Catholics held a degree. Among both groups a quarter had GCE "A" levels as their highest qualification while a quarter had no qualifications.

Source: Labour Force Survey, Office for National Statistics

Notes: The period 2002/03 refers to the year beginning 1st March 2002 and ending 28th February 2003.

Respondents to the Labour Force Survey were asked: "What is your religious denomination?"

Unemployment rates are expressed as a percentage of the economically active population.

Analysis excludes those with No Religion and those belonging to Other religions.

Qualification questions are asked to people in employment aged 16 and over, and to all other people of working age (males 16–64 and females 16–59).

Published on October 11, 2004"

Discrimination law has played an important role in the attempts to resolve the sectarian conflict and divide in Northern Ireland. The introduction of the FETO 98 was an attempt to consolidate the policies of non-discrimination, and affirmative action and were part of an attempt to achieve greater political, social and economic equality between Protestants and Catholics. One noteworthy and significant feature of the Fair Employment Act 1989 and the FETO regime relates to the postive action duties and provisions that it introduced. There was political concern over the level of sectarian violence. A consensus began to emerge in the 1980s that addressing economic and social inequality could make a significant contribution to reducing it. This focus on equal opportunity issues in Northern Ireland was spurred by initiatives in the US where there was political interest in the issue because of historical links with US Irish Catholic communities. The emergence of the MacBride campaign put pressure on US companies who invested in Northern Ireland to ensure that there was compliance with principles relating to fair employment for Catholics (known as the "MacBride Principles").[181] As Christopher McCrudden notes:

"This American campaign began to fill, however partially and inadequately, the political vacuum caused by the failure of Northern Ireland's political institutions to address the issue adequately."[182]

The Standing Advisory Commission on Human Rights (SACHR) and the Policy Studies Institute, conducted research on and evaluations of the situation and existing discrimination law in Northern Ireland. The SACHR made a number of recommendations for reform of the Fair Employment Act 1976. Not all of the proposed reforms were adopted. However, significantly, the subsequent Fair Employment Act 1989 introduced a regime of affirmative action and postive action measures including compulsory monitoring, which is now also included in FETO, Arts 52–54. The details of the postitive action measures

[181] Christopher McCrudden, "The Northern Ireland Fair Employment White Paper: A Critical Assessment" (1988) 17 Industrial L.J. 162.

[182] *ibid.*, at 163.

in the context of Northern Ireland are discussed in chapter 7. Here, we set out a brief summary of the discrimination law structure in Northern Ireland.

The new Employment Equality Directive has been implemented in Northern Ireland through the FETO structure. The Fair Employment and Treatment Order (Amendment) Regulations (Northern Ireland) Regs 2003 have ensured that the provisions of the EED now apply to the FETO regime, e.g. discrimination on the ground of "religion or belief" is now prohibited. Moreover, this implementation of the EED has been comprehensive: the prohibition of discrimination in areas of employment and training covered by the EED—e.g. dismissal, harassment in employment, vocational training—extends not only to the protected grounds of "religion or belief" set out in the EED, but also to the explicit FETO protected ground of "political opinion." For example, the definition of direct discrimination in FETO is now amended via the FETO (Amendment) Regulations 2003, Reg.4 (2A). This provision states that direct discrimination occurs where, in the relevant context, a person discriminates against another person on the ground of "religious belief or political opinion" if he treats that other less favourably than he treats or would treat other persons. The prohibition of direct and indirect discrimination and harassment on these comprehensive grounds in "employment and training", as now required by the EED, gives substantive protection to all religious groups in Northern Ireland (and in particular Catholics). Employment discrimination cases are dealt with by specialist tribunals called the Fair Employment Tribunal. There is a three month time limit from the date of the act complained of. There are a range of remedies: declaration of rights; compensation; or a recommendation that the respondents take action to reduce or alleviate the discrimination. Moreover, the scope of FETO also extends beyond employment and covers the provision of education, goods and services. These cases are dealt with by the County Courts. Appeals in all cases can be made to the Court of Appeal.

One significant feature of the EED is that Art.15 makes a special provision for Northern Ireland. It permits differences in treatment, i.e. discrimination on the ground of religion and belief, in the recruitment of police officers and teachers where these are expressly authorised by national legislation. In the context of police officers, the difference in treatment is permissible where it is "to tackle the underrepresentation of one of the major religious communities in the police service in Northern Ireland". In teaching, the difference in treatment is permissible if it is "In order to maintain a balance of opportunity in employment for teachers in Northern Ireland while furthering the reconciliation of historical divisions between the major religious communities"

The prohibitions on discrimination in employment and the provision of goods and services are supplemented by stipulations concerning non-discrimination in the public sector under the Northern Ireland Act 1998. First, s.75 and Sch.9 of the Northern Ireland Act 1998 place a statutory obligation on public authorities to carry out their functions relating to Northern Ireland with due regard to the need to promote equality of opportunity. That is defined as equality between persons of different: religious belief and political opinion; racial group; age, marital status or sexual orientation; between men and women generally; between persons with a disability and persons without; and between persons with dependants and persons without. In addition, the provisions mean that, public authorities must have regard to the desirability of promoting good relations between persons of different religious belief, political opinion, or racial group. This wide-ranging public duty is discussed in more detail in chapter 7 on positive action. Here, it is worth observing that the public duty was introduced into Northern Ireland before its equivalents were introduced in the rest of the United Kingdom. Moreover, the NIA 98 merged the discreet equalities commissions in Northern Ireland, e.g. the Fair Employment Commission, and EOC and CRE for Northern Ireland, into a single body called the Equality Commission. Again, this change precedes and mirrors the recent creation of the Commission on Equality and Human Rights via the Equalities Act 2006.

XI. Conclusion

The inclusion of "religion and belief" as a prohibited ground of discrimination in EU and domestic law in relation to employment and training sits, not always easily, alongside the European Convention Art.9 right to "religious freedom" and Art.14's guarantee of non-discrimination in the enjoyment of the Art.9 right. As we have seen, these two dimensions to the legal protection of religion and belief interact and diverge in a variety of ways. At a deeper social level, there would also seem to be a complex set of overlapping reasons (relating to race, culture and poverty as well as religion and belief) that case the social exclusion of particular religious groups. Moreover, increasing religious and cultural diversity means that there are a wider range of religions and beliefs that will need to be protected from discrimination. In addition, the secularisation of modern liberal democracies means that there is a risk (actual or perceived) of discrimination for those who are from "majority" religions such as Christianity as well as from minority religions. "Religion and belief" also raises a particular problem for discrimination law because of the risk of conflict with other prohibited grounds of discrimination, most obviously sex and sexual orientation, or other important rights (such as freedom of expression). For all these reasons, the use of the European Convention on Human Rights, EU law and domestic law to regulate discrimination based on "religion and belief" is likely to remain one of the most controversial areas of discrimination law in the future.

14

DISABILITY DISCRIMINATION

I. Introduction

Disability discrimination law has often been treated as a separate, isolated and *sui generis* part of discrimination law, and is prone to being regarded by law teachers and practitioners as a specialised add-on to the mainstream of the subject. This may be due to a combination of factors, including the comparatively recent introduction of disability discrimination legislation, the under-development of international human rights norms that relate to disability issues, and the very distinct issues that arise in the disability context when compared to other prohibited grounds of discrimination. It is important to recognise the unique nature of disability discrimination law and of the wider demands of the disability rights movement in general. Specific conceptual and legislative frameworks have been developed to deal with the variety of barriers that disadvantage disabled persons: these frameworks often differ from the approaches that are adopted across the other prohibited grounds of discrimination, often because disabled persons suffer very distinct types of disadvantage. However, precisely because they are seen as different from other anti-discrimination norms, disability discrimination law and disability rights in general can often be marginalised and side-lined.

This isolation and neglect of disability as a prohibited ground of discrimination needs to be firmly resisted. The disability rights movement challenges some of the deepest and most ingrained forms of social prejudice, and the ways in which disability anti-discrimination legislation attempts to break down these patterns of disadvantage and exclusion constitute some of the most radical, ground-breaking and far-reaching applications of discrimination law. Students and practitioners in other areas of discrimination law can learn much from the evolution of disability discrimination law. A greater focus on disability could also help to sharpen and clarify many of the conceptual debates that surround discrimination law. (see Ch.1, above).

It is also important that the broad conception of discrimination law adopted throughout this book (see Ch.1) is also applied in the context of disability. The employment provisions of the Disability Discrimination Act 1995 usually form the core of any analysis or teaching of disability rights legislation. While important, this employment-centred focus runs the risk of neglecting the full range of human rights norms and legislative provisions that affect the lives of disabled persons, in particular by impacting upon their ability to access basic goods and services, as well as their opportunity to participate equally in social activity. A narrow focus on employment rights may therefore risk neglecting many of the legal tools used to address the problems faced by disabled persons and groups. An integrated account of disability discrimination law has also to include a social and historical analysis of the evolution of the disability rights movement, as well as the theoretical frameworks that have emerged from this process. Only by adopting this broad conceptual analysis can a full and comprehensive analysis of disability rights law be attempted.

II. Conceptions of Disability

The treatment of disabled persons has often been shaped by prevailing social conceptions of what constitutes a disability and the appropriate social role to be played by disabled persons. Oliver has argued that, with the development of modernity, disabled persons came to be viewed as economic non-participants in the new capitalist economies and as objects of pity and charity, rather than as individuals capable of active participation in society. Social policies of exclusion and segregation were justified by the "pervasive belief that people with disabilities were incapable of coping with social and other major life activities".[1] This belief was reinforced by what disability rights activists have characterised as the "medical model" of disability: an individual with a disability was perceived as having an ailment or medical problem that required a cure, and failing that, the individual had to be provided with alleviating treatment or care. The individual's disability was thus deemed to constitute a barrier to normal social participation and a deviation from the norm. Disabled persons were seen as requiring special protection and welfare, and perceived as largely incapable of participating in normal social processes.[2]

As a consequence, many of the measures taken to promote the well-being of disabled persons took the form of special welfare programmes, the provision of segregated educational and social environments, or the introduction of quota mechanisms that aimed to set aside employment posts for disabled persons who were deemed otherwise incapable of full participation.[3] The

[1] See Theresa Degener and Gerard Quinn, "A Survey of International Comparative and Regional Disability Law Reform", in *From Principles to Practice: An International Disability Law and Policy Symposium* (Washington D.C.: Hodges, 2000), p.3.

[2] See Jonathan C. Drimmer, "Cripples, Overcomers, and Civil Rights: Tracing the Evolution of Federal Legislation and Social Policy for People with Disabilities" (1993) 40 UCLA L. Rev. 1341. For an interesting comparison between the depiction of disabled persons underlying the "medical model" and similar stereotypes underlying assumptions about the "passive" nature of women, see Harlan Hahn, "Feminist Perspectives, Disability, Sexuality and Law: New Issues and Agendas" (1994) 4 S. Cal. Rev. L. & Women's Stud. 97.

philosophy underlying this has subsequently been described as "custodialism". For example, in the UK, the Disabled Persons (Employment) Act 1944 required employers with a substantial number of employees to employ a set quota of people registered as disabled. Similar schemes were established across much of Europe in the wake of the two world wars. These quota mechanisms were in the main not enforced or implemented. This was often partially due to a failure to treat the employment of disabled persons as a serious social objective. It was also reinforced by unwillingness on the part of disabled persons to participate in such schemes, which often only ensured that poorly paid posts of low social standing were set aside for the disabled. This in turn tended to reinforce the perception that disabled persons were not interested or capable of workplace participation, even in the limited form offered by the quota mechanisms.

The "medical model" was so entrenched that none of the major international human rights documents drawn up in the wake of the Second World War mentioned disability as a specific human characteristic that should be treated as a "suspect" ground for differentiating between persons. This was in spite of the Nazi sterilisation and extermination policies which were directed against certain categories of disabled persons, in particular those with mental disabilities. However, from the 1960s on, rights awareness grew among disabled groups, which was manifested in demands for self-determination within institutions and charities and an end to segregation and exclusion within wider society. Inspired by the US civil rights movement, many disabled rights activists called for greater integration for disabled persons into the social mainstream, through their absorption into mainstream employment, occupations and educational institutions. This approach has been labelled as "integrationalist": it also emphasised the extension of civil rights protection to disabled persons to enable them to challenge segregation and exclusion.[4]

Others went further and called for a fundamental reassessment of social norms. The "medical model" of disability came under increasing challenge from an alternative conceptual framework, the "social model". This theoretical approach views disability as a condition that does not stem from the individual's physical and mental capacities, but from the social environment in which an individual is situated, and the barriers to full participation erected by institutional and cultural norms that place disabled persons at a disadvantage.[5] Anita Silvers has described the social model of disability as attributing the disadvantages faced by disabled peoples to the existence of hostile environments that are "artificial and remediable": she provides as an example the perspective of a wheelchair-user, whose "disability" is experienced not by any inherent limitation but by lack of access to workplaces,

[1] See Degener and Quinn, n.1 above, p.11.
[4] See Jacobus tenBroek and Floyd Matson, "The Disabled and the Law of Welfare" (1966) 54 Cal. L.R. 809.
[5] See Colin Barnes, *Disabled People in Britain and Discrimination: A Case for Anti-Discrimination Legislation* (London: Hurst, 1991), p.1.

educational programs, medical services, and other areas that are otherwise open to the general public.[6] The social model therefore calls for the reconfiguration of existing social practices to eliminate exclusionary barriers that disadvantage disabled persons.[7] It recognises that simply insisting on similar treatment as non-disabled people would ensure that exclusionary social norms are left untouched and unchallenged: social change and transformation is needed to accommodate disabled persons.

The flourishing of the disability rights movement, and the ensuing political pressure exerted upon governments to remove barriers to participation by disabled persons in employment and other areas of social activity, resulted in the introduction of disability discrimination legislation in many jurisdictions. Notable examples included the Americans with Disabilities Act 1990 (henceforth referred to as the "ADA"),[8] the Australian Disability Discrimination Act 1992 and the UK Disability Discrimination Act 1996 (henceforth referred to as the "DDA"). With the inclusion of Art.13 in the EC Treaty in 1998, and the introduction of the Employment Equality Directive in 2000, disability discrimination in employment is now subject to the control of EU legal norms as set out in the Directive. Welfare, housing and educational policies that impact upon disabled persons have also often been subject to comprehensive reform, and human rights instruments, as discussed in the next section, have begun to be interpreted in such a manner as to extend a degree of protection to disability rights.

However, conceptual uncertainties remain embedded in disability discrimination legislation and in social policies that address disability issues. The "medical model" remains very influential in how definitions of disability are framed and how legislation is interpreted. For example, as discussed below, the protection offered by disability discrimination legislation is often only available to individuals who are deemed to have particular medical conditions that harm their ability to carry out "normal" day to day activities. Disabled persons are therefore usually required to classify themselves as afflicted by a medical condition and unable to operate within society in an ordinary manner, and at the same time have to argue that a failure to treat them equally and accommodate them within a workplace constitutes unfair discrimination. This "double bind" requires disabled persons to argue that they suffer from a medical condition but not to such a degree as to render them unemployable: it

[6] Anita Silvers, "Formal Justice in Disability, Difference, Discrimination: Perspectives on Justice", in A. Silvers *et al.* (eds) *Disability, Difference, Discrimination: Perspectives on Justice in Bioethics and Public Policy* (Lanham, MD: Roman & Littfield: 1998) 73–75.

[7] See Colin Barnes, "A Working Social Model? Disability, Work and Disability Politics in the Twenty-First Society" (2000) 20 Critical Social Policy 221. See also C. Barnes, G. Mercer, T. Shakespeare, *Exploring Disability: A Sociological Introduction* (Malden, MA: Polity Press, 1999); B. Hughes and K. Paterson, "The Social Model of Disability and the Disappearing Body: Towards a Sociology of Impairment" (1997) 12 Disability & Society 325–340; M. Priestley, "Constructions and Creations: Idealism, Materialism and Disability Theory" (1998) 13 Disability & Society 75.

[8] 42 U.S.C. 12101.

can substantially blunt the impact of disability discrimination legislation by making it difficult to win cases.[9]

Even where attempts are made to frame legislation and social initiatives in line with the "social model" approach to disability, conceptual problems arise. Criticisms have been made that the "social model" analysis places too much emphasis upon externally-imposed barriers and can overlook or neglect the reality of the functional limitations that may affect individuals. This can in turn lead to tensions between "integration" approaches, that emphasise the accommodation of disabled persons within existing social norms and in the workplace, and "post-integrationist" approaches, that call for the transformation of existing social norms in line with the "social model" analysis, while also emphasising that special treatment is necessary for those unable to integrate within existing workplaces and other social environments. Mark Weber has identified some of these tensions in his survey of the development of theoretical approaches to disability:

Mark C. Weber, "Disability and the Law of Welfare: A Post-integrationist Examination" (2000) University of Illinois Law Review 889

[899-900] "So far, there have been three major intellectual approaches to disability, and each has had its impact on the meaning of equality for people with disabilities ... the first two approaches are custodialism and integrationism. More recently, something that can be called post-integrationism has emerged. Each 'ism' has influenced what courts and commentators talk about as 'disability law'.

A. Custodialism

Custodialism is the idea that persons with disabilities are to be sheltered—that they should be kept separate from the population at large and given charity to compensate for their inability to survive in the world on their own ... Yet with support came compelled separation from others, often in almshouses or institutions ... The institutions kept people with disabilities out of sight and out of the public mind. When they were in public, they were frequently viewed not as individuals equal to others but as mere manifestations of their disabilities [...] The separation, however, more often protected those without disabilities from having to deal with the existence of anyone with a disability. Laws and the legal system created some of the most disturbing examples of compelled separation. Until 1973, Chicago had an ordinance prohibiting persons who were "deformed" and "unsightly" from exposing themselves to public view ...

[9] For an argument that the US ADA has been severely undermined by the attachment of the US courts to the "medical model", see Michael Stein, "Disability, Employment Policy, and the Supreme Court" (2002) 55 Stanford L. Rev. 607.

B. Integrationism

[901–912] "Proponents of integrationism believe that through the attitudinal and environmental changes compelled by antidiscrimination laws, together with the voluntary or compulsory application of technology, people with disabilities will be able to take their rightful places in the world. The ADA is a classic integrationist statute. It creates legally enforceable rights against segregation ... integrationist thinkers recognized that equal treatment for persons with disabilities is not the same as identical treatment. It is not equal or fair to give each law school candidate the same printed LSAT, whether the candidate is blind or not. Some form of adaptation is needed. Nevertheless, integrationist scholars hoped that once basic adaptations had been made, society would not be required to afford fundamentally different treatment to individuals with disabilities...

This absence of requirements for fundamentally different treatment marks the limits of the integrationist theory. For example, the obligations to afford special treatment embodied in the ADA's integrationist plan all have modest stopping points. Under the Act, an employer must provide employees with disabilities with reasonable accommodations ... The obligation ceases, however, when it imposes undue hardship ... These limits on social duties to accommodate the needs of persons with disabilities demonstrate that the ADA uses the person without disabilities as the norm and measures what it requires by the effort needed to depart from that norm...

Moreover, the rights are limited in their very design ... The role of the law is thus marginal—only when an accommodated person with a disability is able to do the job better than others, when the person with a disability overcompensates in some way, or when the disability was merely a perceived one in the first place, will the Act call for a result different from what would have occurred before the Act ... integrationism's emphasis on legally enforceable rights leaves behind those who are reluctant to assert rights, because of ignorance, irrational fear, or well-founded reluctance to disrupt existing relationships with those who have power over them ... Any benefits thus will go to the best off among those with disabilities...

The identification of the weaknesses of integrationist theory and the limits of the ADA do not negate the importance of either the theory or the legislation in advancing equality and making the world of today a better one than that of yesterday. Identifying the problems of integrationism is merely the first step in developing new theories to continue the effort of securing justice for persons with disabilities."

C. Post-Integrationist Theory

[912–921] "Post-integrationist ideas are still in the process of creation. Even at this time, however, it is safe to say that the ideas criticize integrationism, believing its reach to be limited. The ideas move beyond recognition of the limits of integrationism to include challenges to some of integrationism's underpinnings. They also explore new ideas about what equality means and how it should be applied in the disability context. Finally, they draw insights from feminist thinking to fashion new ideas about equality for persons with disabilities.

Post-integrationist ideas about disability are critical of what Sara Watson describes as "the image that all people with disabilities [are] easily employable and would happily remain employed at the same jobs forever, that disability [is] desirable, and that people with disabilities [are] a tight-knit minority with similar views." That image was crucial to combat the handicapping message of the segregationist era that disability was tragic, that it meant the end of employability, and that people with disabilities were simply the manifestations of diverse medical syndromes. Now, however, it is equally important to recognize that disability is far more complex and cannot be addressed simply by an integrationist message, just as barriers to employment cannot be addressed simply by reasonable accommodation.

The exploration of post-integrationist theory leads to several conclusions about disability and how society should respond to it: (1) in the world of today and in any foreseeable world of tomorrow, disability carries costs that will inevitably be borne by someone; (2) integrationist measures, such as the ADA, have limits in what they can accomplish for persons with disabilities because the measures use persons without disabilities as a social norm for the integration they promote; (3) welfare programs based on identification of disability will continue to be important simply for the survival of many persons with disabilities; (4) key premises of integrationism—the desirability of blending into the non-disabled population and making social and economic limits isomorphic with bodily ones—are questionable; (5) ideas of equal environmental adaptations, justice as fairness, balancing of social relations, and antisubordination call for significant redistribution of power and material resources in favor of persons with disabilities; and (6) just as some feminist thinkers have developed theories that call for rearranging differential social burdens in an effort to achieve real progress in women's equality, disability theory needs to embrace the notion that disability is a relevant difference for social policy..."

In line with elements of some post-integrationist thinking, certain disability rights activists have advocated a shift to a "minority rights" approach, calling for disabled groups to be classified and defined as a disadvantaged minority, and for group-centred action to eliminate the subordination and disadvantage that they face.[10] This approach draws a direct analogy between race discrimination and disability discrimination and calls for the same group-centred remedial action to be taken in both cases.[11] It has the advantage of emphasising the history of disadvantage faced by disabled persons and the need for strong rights-based protection and institutional support for disabled groups. It also can be strategically useful, as it makes a strong case for the "carry-over" of the approaches adopted for race discrimination to the disability context. The Americans with Disabilities Act 1990 (ADA) explicitly adopts the "minority rights" analysis first used in the in the Civil Rights Act 1960, stating that:

"[i]ndividuals with disabilities are a discrete and insular minority who have been faced with restrictions and limitations, subjected to a history of purposeful unequal treatment and relegated to a position of political powerlessness in our society..."[12]

However, in its turn, this approach has been criticised for encouraging an excessive emphasis upon defining who falls within the definition of "disabled", which as already discussed, can substantially limit the reach and effectiveness of disability discrimination legislation.[13] It also could reinforce

[10] See Harlam Hahn, "Towards a Politics of Disability: Definitions, Disciplines and Policies" (1985) 22(4) The Social Sciences Journal 87.

[11] *ibid.*

[12] ADA 1990, s.2(a)(7). For the background to the ADA, see generally Timothy M. Cook, "The Americans with Disabilities Act: The Move to Integration" (1991) 64 Temp. L. Rev. 393; Robert L. Burgdorf Jr., "The Americans with Disabilities Act: Analysis and Implications of a Second-Generation Civil Rights Statute" (1991) 26 Harv. C.R.-C.L. L. Rev. 413.

[13] See Michael Lynk, "A Dream Deferred" (1999) 15 International Journal of Comparative Labour Law and Industrial Relations 329–338.

perceptions of the separateness of disabled groups from the mainstream of society, lead to questions of conflict of resources between disabled and other groups, and generate tensions between different disabled groups themselves as to who should come within the umbrella of "disability".[14] Disabled persons often do not see themselves as part of a distinct social group and there is no real shared historical or social experience beyond a degree of shared disadvantage, which can vary considerably from group to group. Degener has cautioned that there is a need to avoid "essentialism", i.e. the perception that disabled groups are defined and separate by reason of their disability, which is deemed to be the key constituent factor in generating their self-identity.[15] For her, such essentialist accounts run the risk of trapping disabled persons in similar stereotypes as those that have contributed to their social exclusion. Bickenbach, et al. have commented that:

"disability is not a human attribute that demarks one portion of humanity from another; it is an infinitely various but universal feature of the human condition. No human has a complete repertoire of abilities ... disability policy is therefore not policy for some minority group; it is policy for all".[16]

An alternative post-integrationist approach advocated by Birkenbach and others has been described as the "universal design" model, which aims to restructure all aspects of human activity to ensure that every person can participate on an equal basis.[17] Zola has advocated a similar "universalist" approach, arguing for greater social respect for differences in capacity to be combined with a wider definition of what is deemed to constitute "normality".[18] These "universal" approaches share the insistence of the "minority rights" and "integrationist" approaches upon securing legally enforceable

[14] See also Jerome E. Birkenbach, "Minority Rights or Universal Participation: The Politics of Disablement", in M. Jones and L.A. Baser Marks (eds) *Disability, Divers-ability & Legal Change Series: International Studies in Human Rights*, vol. 56 (London: Martinus Nijhoff, 1999) 101–116; T. Shakespeare, "What is a Disabled Person?" in the same volume, 25–34. For a critique that the social model in general can be too deterministic, in automatically equating disability to disadvantage, see R. Pinder, "Bringing Back the Body Without the Blame?—The Experience of Ill and Disabled People at Work" (1995) 17(5) Sociology of Health and Illness 605.

[15] See Theresia Degener, "Disabled Persons and Human Rights: The Legal Framework", in Theresia Degener & Yolan Koster-Dreese (eds) *Human Rights and Disabled Persons* (Dordrecht: Kluwer Academic, 1995) 9.

[16] See J. E. Bickenbach, S. Charrerji, E. M. Badley, T.B. Ustun, "Models of Disablement, Universalism and the International Classification of Impairments, Disabilities and Handicaps" (1999) 48 Social Science & Medicine, 1173–1187, 1182. See also the point made by Peter Alldridge about attempts to construct group identity upon possession of disabilities: "I am sceptical when people use expressions like 'celebration of identity' in the context of disability. Let us by all means explore the analogies with race, gender, sexuality and so on, but still be aware that, as Tom Shakespeare wrote: '... the analogy between disability and gender/race/sexuality can be misleading. Disability may be more like poverty: not an identity to be celebrated.'" See P. Alldridge, "Locating Disability Law" (2006) 60 Current Legal Problems 445.

[17] Bickenbach, et al., *ibid.*, 1183.

[18] Irving K. Zola, "Towards the necessary universalising of a disability policy" (1989) 67 (Supp. 2, Pt. 2) Millbank Quarterly 401.

rights for disabled persons. However, they also retain the social model's insistence on the necessity of transforming social structures to allow universal access, seeing this as an aspiration that is relevant to all social groups, and not just those that come within narrow definitions of "disability".[19] Stein suggests that effective disability discrimination legislation modelled upon this approach can reduce the sense that disabled persons are "other", thereby achieving "belief change" and opening up the mainstream of social activity to disabled persons.[20] Alldridge illustrates how the universalist approach might clarify key issues:

"behind a Rawlsian veil of ignorance, we would agree that taps in public lavatories should be operated by levers not spindles, and that access to trains should be step-free."[21]

However, all post-integrationist perspectives must also engage with the reality that many disabled persons will not be able to integrate within the social mainstream, or even be able to access fully transformed social structures modelled in terms of "universal design". Stein acknowledges that the needs of disabled persons who will remain unable to integrate within even greatly expanded social norms have to be taken into account as an important element in disability law and policy.[22] Fredman makes a similar point, while emphasising that most disability-centred disadvantage stems from a failure to transform existing structures.[23]

This highlights that any coherent approach to disability has to a) aim to ensure the removal of barriers to the equal participation of disabled persons in employment, occupation and social activities in general; b) emphasise the transformation of existing social practices and norms to ensure that they are open to and can accommodate all who wish to participate; and c) provide support for those disabled persons who require special assistance to access social structures and also for those who may not be able to benefit from enhanced accessibility. Different "post-integrationist" approaches to disability will stress different elements: they may also adopt different priorities and set different targets. However, they all share these common concerns and may all be "useful" at different times and in different contexts.[24]

As a result, disability discrimination legislation has to be examined in

[19] Jerome E. Bickenbach, *et al.*, "Models of Disablement, Universalism and the International Classification of Impairments, Disabilities and Handicaps", cited above.

[20] Mark Stein, "Same Struggle, Different Difference: ADA Accommodations as Anti-discrimination" (2004) 153 University of Pennsylvania L. Rev. 579.

[21] See Peter Alldridge, "Locating Disability Law" (2006) 59 Current Legal Problems 445.

[22] Stein, "Same Struggle, Different Difference", cited above.

[23] Sandra Fredman,, "Disability Equality: A Challenge to the Existing Anti-Discrimination Paradigm?, in Caroline Gooding and Anna Lawson (eds), *Disability Rights in Europe* (Oxford: Hart, 2004) 199–218, 211–214

[24] For an excellent discussion of this, see Deborah Mabbett, "Some Are More Equal Than Others: Definitions of Disability in Social Policy and Discrimination Law in Europe" (2005) 34(2) J. of Social Policy 215–233.

conjunction with human rights standards, welfare legislation and other forms of social legislation. Equality for disabled persons cannot be analysed in isolation from social provision and other guarantees of basic entitlements. This chapter will primarily focus upon anti-discrimination measures. However, the importance of legislation and human rights provisions for those who may not be able to access employment or goods and services, even with the benefit of reasonable accommodation requirements, should not be forgotten. In general, Alldridge suggests that "disability law" covers:

"any interface of law and disability, and consequently [is] a far wider area of legal study than simply discrimination law ... On this broader account of disability law, there are many areas of law that impact upon disability ... A fuller account of specific areas of legal study that should be included would include parts of land law, mental health law, charity law, local government law, employment law, social security law, discrimination law and environmental law."[25]

Also, as discussed below, the concept of reasonable accommodation and other core elements of disability discrimination law have generated considerable debate as to whether these provisions are best classified as anti-discrimination measures, or as forms of special provision, positive action or redistributive measures designed to "favour" disabled persons. The reality is that attempting to distinguish between anti-discrimination and positive action in the disability context is a largely futile exercise. Disability discrimination legislation cannot confine its scope to removing obstacles that disabled persons face in attempting to access employment and other social goods. It also has to be concerned with ensuring that social practices and the surrounding physical environment are sufficiently capable of accommodating the special and particular needs of disabled groups: integration without transformation of social norms will never be sufficient for many disabled persons. No real distinction can be made between prohibiting discrimination and requiring accommodation to be made for disabled persons. This has considerable significance for how disability discrimination legislation is framed and implemented in practice, and will be discussed in greater detail below.

III. Disability and International Human Rights Law

Prior to the UN Convention on the Rights of Persons With Disabilities, which was adopted by the UN General Assembly on October 13, 2006, none of the

[25] See Peter Alldridge, "Locating Disability Law" (2006) Current Legal Problems 445.

major existing international human rights instruments included disability as one of the suspect forms of classification that are explicitly listed in their non-discrimination and equality clauses,[26] and there was also no specialist UN convention on disability rights, in contrast to race and gender. This gap reflected the predominance of the medical model of disability at the time of the drafting of the major UN and regional instruments from 1948 to the early 1980s. The exclusion of the disabled from society was seen as an unfortunate but inevitable consequence of their disabilities, and not as the product of discrimination *per se*.

However, there is a growing body of international human rights documents and resolutions that addresses the rights of people with disabilities, which the Convention now caps with a comprehensive statement of the rights of persons with disabilities. The UN General Assembly has adopted declarations which recognise that disabled persons have basic rights under the provisions of existing international human rights law.[27] These have been supplemented by non-binding resolutions that attempt to set standards for how disabled persons should be treated,[28] culminating in the 1982 World Program on Action Concerning Disabled Persons, which provides that:

"the general system of society, such as the physical, cultural environment, housing and transportation, social and health services, educational and work

[26] Note however that the UN Committee for Economic, Social and Cultural Rights, in their General Comment 5 on the International Covenant on Economic, Social and Cultural Rights, UN Doc. E/1995/22 at 19(1995), have indicated that both the UN Covenants should be interpreted as treating discrimination on grounds of disability as coming within the "other status" grounds of the anti-discrimination and equality clauses. Paragraph 15 of the General Comment defines disability-based discrimination under the ICESCR as including:

> "any distinction, exclusion, restriction or preference, or denial of reasonable accommodation based on disability which has the effect of nullifying or impairing the recognition, enjoyment or exercise of economic, social or cultural rights."

Paragraph 16 of the General Comment suggests the adoption of anti-discrimination legislation:

> "in order to remedy past and present discrimination, and to deter future discrimination, comprehensive anti-discrimination legislation in relation to disability would seem to be indispensable in virtually all states parties."

[27] The UN Declaration on the Rights of Mentally Retarded Persons Gen. Ass. Resolution 2856 (XXVI) of December 20, 1971 was the first international human rights instrument to be primarily concerned with disability rights. The purpose of the Declaration is "... to promote the integration of people with disabilities as far as possible, in normal life": however, the thrust of the Declaration largely adopts a "medical model" of mental disability, concentrating as it does upon ensuring certain basic standards of treatment for mentally disabled persons: see *http://www1.umn.edu/humanrts/instree/t1drmrp.htm*. Its title, unimaginable now, demonstrates how far the disability rights agenda has advanced in three decades. In 1975, the UN Declaration of Rights of Disabled Persons Gen. Ass. Resolution 3447 of December 9, 1975, explicitly affirmed, for the first time in international law, the right of people with disabilities to the basic civil and political rights: see *http://www.unhchr.ch/html/menu3/b/72.htm*.

[28] These resolutions were designed to provide impetus for the UN Decade of the Disabled Person from 1983–1993.

opportunities, cultural and social life, including sports and recreational activities are made accessible to all."[29]

Most importantly, the UN General Assembly in 1993 also adopted the Standard Rules on Equalisation of Opportunities for People with Disabilities.[30] The Standard Rules recognise participation by people with disabilities as an internationally recognised human right and suggest that governments:

"ensure that organisations of persons with disabilities are involved in the development of national legislation concerning the rights of persons with disabilities ... Any discriminatory provisions against persons with disabilities must be eliminated. National legislation should provide for appropriate sanctions in case of violations of the principles of non-discrimination."

Rule 14(2)) provides for countries to engage in a national planning process to bring legislation, policies, and programmes into conformity with international human rights standards:

"The principle of equal rights implies that the needs of each and every individual are of equal importance, that those needs must be made the basis for the planning of society and that all resources must be employed in such a way as to ensure that every individual has equal opportunity for participation."

The Rules are important in that they establish an international framework of standards for disability rights, and emphasise an integration and rights approach to disability, as distinct from the historically embedded medical model. By placing disability on the international human rights agenda, they have had some impact in encouraging the adoption of disability rights legislation in various jurisdictions.[31] The Rules also explicitly adopt the language of the "social model" and the "universalist" approach to disability, with their emphasis on "every individual" having "equal opportunity for participation". This approach has been strongly endorsed by the 2003 Report of the UN Ad

[29] UN Doc. A/37/51, Gen. Ass. (XXXVII) Supplement No.51: see *http://www.un.org/esa/socdev/enable/diswpa00.htm*. In 1991, the General Assembly of the UN also adopted the Principles for Protection of Persons with Mental Illness and the Improvement of Mental Health Care Gen. Ass. Resolution 46/119 of December 17, 1991 (see *http://www.un.org/esa/socdev/enable/diswpa00.htm*). These set standards to evaluate national mental health systems, and provide for a reporting framework.

[30] See the Annex to UN General Assembly Resolution No. 48/96, 20/12/1993, *http://www.un.org/esa/socdev/enable/dissre00.htm*. The UN also established a monitoring mechanism to monitor implementation of the Standards and appointed a Special Rapporteur for Disability Rights. Three of the four reports by the Special Rapporteur are available through the UN Enable website: 1997 report, A52/56, annex at: *http://www.un.org/esa/socdev/enable/dismsre0.htm*; 2000 report, E/CN.5/2000/3, annex at: *http://www.un.org/esa/socdev/enable/disecn003e1.htm*; and 2002 report, E/CN.5/2002/4, annex at: *http://www.un.org/esa/socdev/enable/disecn520024e0.htm*.

[31] See G. Quinn, T. Degener, et al., *Human Rights and Disability: The Current Use and Future Potential of United Nations Human Rights Instruments in the Context of Disability* (Geneva, UN High Commissioner for Human Rights, 2002).

Hoc Committee on the Rights of Persons with Disabilities, which stresses the concept of the "new universe of disability" and argues that "the data suggests that disability is a normal aspect of life; all kinds of disabilities can happen to all types of people at all stages in their normal lifecycles."[32]

However, the Rules do not constitute binding legal obligations. They also lack precision and specificity, as do other declaratory instruments that attempt to achieve similar results.[33] Therefore, there have been recent moves to establish legally binding standards in international law. At the regional level, the Inter-American Convention on the Elimination of All Forms of Discrimination Against Persons with Disabilities, adopted by the Organisation of American States in 1999, was the first binding treaty on disability rights to have been opened for signing. The UN also appointed an Ad Hoc Committee of the General Assembly to draft a proposed convention on the rights of people with disabilities: the long-drawn process of drafting this convention finally concluded in August 2006 with agreement on a final text for the new UN Convention on the Rights of Persons with Disabilities.

This Convention is intended to parallel the provisions of the Convention for the Elimination of Racial Discrimination and the Convention on the Elimination of Discrimination Against Women.[34] Framing the positive obligations of states proved a difficult and complex process: however, the final text represents a crucial moment, in that disability rights have achieved perhaps for the first time full recognition in international human rights law.[35] The Convention's provisions require ratifying states to change laws or customs that

[32] See Report of the Secretary General, *Issues and Emerging Trends related to Advancement of Persons with Disabilities* (A/AC.265/2003/1), paras 9–10.

[33] In January 2003, the Parliamentary Assembly of the Council of Europe adopted a recommendation entitled "Towards Full Social Inclusion of Persons with Disabilities". see Recommendation No.1592, Doc. 9632, January 29, 2003. The Recommendation adopts a social rights model, as it provides that:

> "The Assembly notes with satisfaction that in certain member states policies concerning people with disabilities have been gradually evolving over the last decade from an institutional approach, considering people with disabilities as 'patients', to a more holistic approach viewing them as 'citizens', who have a right to individual support and self-determination." The Recommendation goes on to state that:
>
> > "The right to receive support and assistance, although essential to improving the quality of life of people with disabilities, is not enough. Guaranteeing access to equal political, social, economic and cultural rights should be a common political objective for the next decade. Equal status, inclusion, full citizenship, and the right to choose should be further promoted and implemented."

See also ILO Vocational Rehabilitation and Employment (Disabled Persons) Convention, 1983 (No.159) (*http://www.ilo.org/public/english/employment/skills/recomm/instr/c_159.htm*), and paras 55–56 of the ILO General Survey, *Equality in Employment and Occupation: Introduction*, 1996 (see *http://www.ilo.org/ilolex/english/surlist.htm*). UNESCO and WHO declarations attempt to establish minimum standards of treatment for disabled persons. See J. Cooper, "Improving the Civil Rights of People With Disabilities Through International Law", in Jeremy Cooper, *Law, Rights and Disability* (London: Kingsley, 2000).

[34] For the final text of the Convention and information about the drafting process, see *http://www.un.org/disabilities/convention/*.

[35] See Anna Lawson, "The Human Rights of Persons With Disabilities: Extending Freedom to All", a lecture delivered at the London School of Economics on March 9, 2006 and available at *http://www.lse.ac.uk/Depts/human-rights/Lectures/HR_disability.htm*.

discriminate against or exclude disabled persons, to provide legal protection against discrimination or harassment, to recognise the equal right of persons with disabilities to life, education, autonomy and self-determination in their daily lives, and to provide the required support and assistance for disabled persons to live an independent life. In recognising that respecting the human rights of persons with disabilities requires states to implement positive obligations in a systematic and far-reaching manner, the Convention is a major break-though for the rights of disabled persons: indeed, Michael Stein has suggested that it may open the door to a fresh conceptualisation of human rights in general.[36]

IV. Disability Rights and the European Convention on Human Rights

The need for clear and specific standards in international human rights law is demonstrated by the uncertain and limited protection that exists for disabled persons against abuse and discrimination under the ECHR. As with the UN instruments, Art.14 of the ECHR does not explicitly prohibit unjustified discrimination on the ground of disability. Nevertheless, disability discrimination would appear to be covered by the "other status" limb of Art.14, as it can clearly be deemed to constitute a "personal status". Therefore, the protection offered against discrimination by Art.14 ECHR should be capable of being extended to the ground of disability.

However, the European Court of Human Rights has not as yet treated Art.14 as actively engaged in a disability rights case. As with other grounds of discrimination, this is partially due to the lack of concrete cases that have been brought before the Court. In the disability context, this dearth of cases is perhaps attributable to the real difficulties that many disabled persons face in accessing legal remedies throughout Europe. The cases related to disability that the Court has decided have arisen not under Art.14 but under other provisions of the Convention, in particular the Art.3 guarantee of freedom from inhuman and degrading treatment and the Art.8 right to personal privacy, home life and family life. These decisions have generated mixed results.

The Court has recognised that the failure to make special accommodation for a disabled person may give rise to an Art.3 breach, even where similar treatment of non-disabled persons would not. In *Herzcegfalvy v Austria*,[37] the European Court of Human Rights observed that "[t]he position of inferiority and powerlessness which is typical of patients confined in psychiatric hospitals calls for increased vigilance in reviewing whether the Convention has

[36] See M. Stein, "Disability Human Rights" (2007) 95 California L. Rev. 75–122.

[37] No.10533/83, 24/09/1993; (1992) 15 E.H.R.R. 437. See also *R (Wilkinson) v Broadmoor Special Hospital Authority* [2001] EWCA Civ 1545, [2002] 1 W.L.R. 419.

been complied with". In *Price v the United Kingdom,*[38] Ms Price, a woman with a physical disability who used a wheelchair and was described by the European Court of Human Rights as "four-limb deficient", was imprisoned on contempt charges for seven days in a cell without any modifications to accommodate a disabled person. She was forced to sleep in her wheelchair, with emergency buttons and light switches out of her reach and an inaccessible toilet: when finally given access to a toilet, she was left there for hours and undressed in front of male guards. The European Court of Human Rights found that this treatment constituted degrading treatment in violation of Art.3, even in the absence of intent to degrade, due to the nature of the treatment to which Ms Price was subject to in custody, and, in particular, the failure to make accommodation to prevent her suffering this treatment.

In a separate concurring opinion, Greve J. commented that:

> "In this [case] the applicant is different from other people to the extent that treating her like others is not only discrimination but brings about a violation of Article 3 . . . It is obvious that restraining any non-disabled person to *the applicant's level of ability to move and assist herself*, for even a limited period of time, would amount to inhuman and degrading treatment—possibly torture. In a civilised country like the United Kingdom, society considers it not only appropriate but *a basic humane concern* to try to improve and compensate for the disabilities faced by a person in the applicant's situation . . . The applicant's disabilities are not hidden or easily overlooked. It requires no special qualification, *only a minimum of ordinary human empathy*, to appreciate her situation and to understand that to avoid unnecessary hardship—that is, hardship not implicit in the imprisonment of an able-bodied person—she has to be treated differently from other people because her situation is significantly different."[38a]

Respect for the dignity of disabled persons may therefore require a departure from standard norms of treatment. Thus, in *Keenan v United Kingdom,*[39] the Court commented that:

> "**[112]** . . . While it is true that the severity of suffering, physical or mental, attributable to a particular measure has been a significant consideration in many of the cases decided by the Court under Article 3, there are circumstances where proof of the actual effect on the person may not be a major factor. For example . . . treatment of a mentally ill person may be incompatible with the standards imposed by Article 3 in the protection of fundamental human dignity, even though that person may not be able, or capable of, pointing to any specific ill-effects."

However, these decisions all concern a failure to accommodate basic needs while disabled persons are in confinement or in some way subject to the coercive power of the state. The Strasbourg court has not as yet recognised a right to have the basic needs of a disabled person accommodated *in general*, i.e. outside of the scope of immediate state control. It should also be noted that the

[38] No.33394/96, 10/07/2001; (2002) 34 E.H.R.R. 1285.
[38a] At p.1296 (emphasis added)).
[39] (2001) 33 E.H.R.R. 913.

threshold of denial of dignity required to "trigger" Art.3 is a high one. The protection the Convention extends under Art.3 is limited to treatment or a lack of treatment of a particularly degrading nature.

The Court has been prepared to accept that special provision for disabled persons may be required to vindicate their right to private life, home life and family life as recognised by Art.8 of the ECHR. This recognition that positive obligations exist to provide resources in certain circumstances to disabled persons is potentially very important. Article 8 has a greater scope than Art.3, and should guarantee to disabled persons the entitlement to enjoy the essential facilities that are required to enjoy a meaningful home, private and family life, thereby applying to much wider range of circumstances than Art.3. However, several disability cases that have attempted to use this Art.8 route have floundered, as the Court has been thus far unwilling to extend the scope of protection offered by Art.8 to include access to general social amenities. The Court has also refused to find that access to social amenities even came within the general ambit of Art.8, so as to trigger the application of Art.8.

In *Botta v Italy*,[40] the disabled applicant was unable to gain access to the beach and the sea at a private bathing establishment due to its failure to provide the disabled facilities required by Italian law. The applicant claimed that the failure by the Italian State to take measures to remedy the omission by the private resort breached his right to a private life and the development of his personality under Art.8, as well as constituting discrimination contrary to Art.14. However, the Court held that the right asserted, namely the right to gain access to the beach and the sea at a place distant from his normal place of residence during holidays, did not fall within the scope of Art.8, or even within its general ambit so as to engage Art.14.

Similarly, in *Zehnalová and Zehnal v Czech Republic*,[41] the applicants alleged an infringement of their Art.8 and Art.14 rights on the basis that many public buildings were not equipped with access facilities for the disabled in violation of Czech law. The European Court of Human Rights again held that the entitlement claimed did not come within the scope of Art.8 or of its general ambit, so neither article was engaged. The Court observed that:

> "The Court is of the opinion that Article 8 of the Convention cannot apply as a general rule and whenever the everyday life of the female applicant is concerned, but only in exceptional cases where a lack of access to public buildings and those open to the public would prevent the female applicant from leading her life so that her right to personal development and her right to make and maintain relations with other human beings and the outside world are in question (see the *Pretty v United Kingdom* judgment, No. 2346/02, §61, 29 April 2002). In a case like that, a positive obligation for the state could be established to ensure access to the buildings mentioned. Now, in the case in point, the rights invoked are too wide and indeterminate, as the applicants have failed to be specific about the alleged obstacles and to give convincing proof of an attack on their private lives. According to the Court, the female applicant has not managed to demonstrate the special

[40] (1998) 26 E.H.R.R. 241.
[41] No.3826/97, E.C.H.R. 2002-V, 14/05/2002.

link between the inaccessibility of the institutions mentioned and the particular needs concerned with her private life."

In *Marzari v Italy*,[42] the applicant suffered from a rare disease that, at times, constrained him to use a wheelchair. He complained that his Art.8 rights had been infringed, in that he had been evicted and that the alternative accommodation offered to him was not suitable, having regard to his special needs. The court observed:

"The Court must first examine whether the applicant's rights under Article 8 were violated on account of the decision of the authorities to evict him despite his medical condition. It further has to examine whether the applicant's rights were violated on account of the authorities' alleged failure to provide him with adequate accommodation. The Court considers that, although Article 8 does not guarantee the right to have one's housing problem solved by the authorities, a refusal of the authorities to provide assistance in this respect to an individual suffering from a severe disease might in certain circumstances raise an issue under Article 8 of the Convention because of the impact of such refusal on the private life of the individual. The Court recalls in this respect that, while the essential object of Article 8 is to protect the individual against arbitrary interference by public authorities, this provision does not merely compel the state to abstain from such interference: in addition, to this negative undertaking, there may be positive obligations inherent in effective respect for private life. A State has obligations of this type where there is a direct and immediate link between the measures sought by the applicant and the latter's private life."[42a]

However, the court went on to hold that it was not for it to review the decisions taken by the local authorities as to the adequacy of the accommodation offered to the applicant, observing that they had offered to carry out further works to make the accommodation suitable. In these circumstances the court held that the local authorities could be considered to have "discharged their positive obligations in respect of the applicant's right to respect for private life".

In all three cases, the court was willing to assume that Art.8 could be engaged, or that a disability issue could fall within its ambit so as to trigger an Art.14 claim. In addition, two important principles have been established in these cases. Firstly, the court appeared willing to accept that the concept of private life in Art.8 was sufficiently wide as to include the right to establish and develop relationships with others, as long as this could be linked to the manifestation of a "private life". Secondly, the court was prepared to accept that Art.8 could impose positive obligations upon member states to ensure that disabled persons were not denied the possibility of developing these relationships with other people.

However, while leaving the possibility of a successful claim open, in all three decisions the court was extremely cautious in determining the scope and even the "ambit" of Art.8. The sphere of protection conferred by this right as it

[42] (1999) 28 E.H.R.R. CD175.
[42a] At p.179)

emerges from these cases appears very limited: in particular, in *Botta* and *Zehnalová*, the court seems to presume that private life is not manifested through participation in certain public spheres and facilities. An interesting contrast exists with the court's decision in *Sidabras v Lithuania*, where a ban on the employment of former members of the KGB in particular professions was held to violate Art.14: the court was willing to find that the scope of these restrictions as to what the claimants could do in the public sphere of employment was so extensive as to impact upon their family and private lives, and therefore to come within the ambit of Art.8 and so trigger Art.14. The extent of the exclusion from core social amenities involved in *Zehnalová* in particular could be said to be of a similar order as that at issue in *Siadabras*, as could the actual effects of this exclusion upon the private lives in question.

Therefore, *Sidabras* appears to be out of step with *Botta* and *Zehnalová*. However, the latter decision may herald a new readiness by the court to utilise Art.14, and a greater confidence in its competence in discrimination issues:[43] by introducing an "effects" test in deciding whether external restrictions impact upon private and family life, it may open the door to successful disability rights cases. *Botta, Zehnalová* and *Marzari* (where the interference with private life was more direct and immediate) may have opened a door which could be utilised by creative judicial interpretation to lead on to a more developed jurisprudence. However, until this materialises, the ECHR as with other human rights instruments offers limited pickings for activists pushing for greater acknowledgement of disability rights. The absence of a comprehensive guarantee of equality in the ECHR remains a particular problem in this area. Until the UK signs and ratifies Protocol 12 to the Convention, disability cases will have to be squeezed through the routes of Arts 3, 8 and other existing Convention rights, which will inevitably limit what can be achieved using the ECHR.

However, the potential of Arts 3 and 8 as tools to push for greater rights for disabled people can be seen in the domestic decisions of *R (Bernard) v London Borough of Enfield*[44] and *A v East Sussex CC*.[45] In *Bernard*, the claimants were husband and wife, who had six children. The wife was severely disabled and confined to a wheelchair. The defendant local authority had provided the family with a small house but had breached (as the authority accepted) s.21(1)(a) of the National Assistance Act in failing to provide the family with accommodation suited to her disability. The consequences for the family and for the mother in particular, were severe. The claimants sought damages for breaches of Arts 3 and 8 of the Convention. With some hesitation, Sullivan J. concluded that the degree of severity of the claimants' predicament did not breach the Article 3 threshold. He held, however, that there was a clear breach of Art.8:

[43] Virginia Mantouvalou, "Work and Private Life: *Sidabras and Dziautas v Lithuania*" (2005) 30(4) E.L.R. 573, 581–82.

[44] [2002] EWHC Admin 2282.

[45] [2003] EWCA Admin 167.

"I accept the defendant's submission that not every breach of duty under section 21 of the 1948 Act will result in a breach of Article 8. Respect for private and family life does not require the State to provide every one of its citizens with a house: see the decision of Jackson J. in *Morris v LB Newham* [2002] EWHC Admin 262 at [59]–[62]. However, those entitled to care under Section 21 are a particularly vulnerable group. Positive measures have to be taken (by way of community care facilities) to enable them to enjoy, so far as possible, a normal private and family life...

Following the assessments in September 2000 the defendant was under an obligation not merely to refrain from unwarranted interference in the claimants' family life, but also to take positive steps, including the provision of suitably adapted accommodation, to enable the claimants and their children to lead as normal a family life as possible, bearing in mind the second claimant's severe disabilities. Suitably adapted accommodation would not merely have facilitated the normal incidents of family life ... It would also have secured her physical and psychological integrity. She would no longer have been housebound, confined to a shower chair for most of the day, lacking privacy in the most undignified of circumstances, but would have been able to operate as part of her family and as a person in her own right, rather than being a burden, wholly dependent upon the rest of her family. In short, it would have restored her dignity as a human being.

The Council's failure to act on the September 2000 assessments showed a singular lack of respect for the claimant's private and family life. It condemned the claimants to living conditions which made it virtually impossible for them to have any meaningful private or family life for the purposes of Article 8. Accordingly, I have no doubt that the defendant was not merely in breach of its statutory duty under the 1948 Act. Its failure to act on the September 2000 assessments over a period of 20 months was also incompatible with the claimants' rights under Article 8 of the Convention."

Sullivan J. awarded a considerable sum of damages to the claimants.[46] The Court of Appeal in *Anufiraja v Southwark*[47] adopted a more cautious approach to Art.8. It considered that the European Court of Human Rights' approach in *Botta* and *Marzari* had established that there were some circumstances in which a public authority was required to devote resources to make it possible for individuals to enjoy the right to privacy, family life and home life under Art.8. The court went on to approve Sullivan J.'s decision in *Bernard*, but however indicated that Art.8 claims would have to fall within or close to the definition of inhuman and degrading treatment:

"...our conclusion is that Sullivan J was correct to accept that Article 8 is capable of imposing on a State a positive obligation to provide support. We find it hard to conceive, however, of a situation in which the predicament of an individual will be such that Article 8 requires him to be provided with welfare support, where his predicament is not sufficiently severe to engage Article 3. Article 8 may more readily be engaged where a family unit is involved ... Family life was seriously inhibited by the hideous conditions prevailing in the claimants' home in *Bernard* and we consider that it was open to Sullivan J to find that Article 8 was infringed on the facts of that case."[48]

[46] Sullivan J. assessed damages at £10,000, £8000 to the mother and £2000 to the father, with the Court of Appeal confirming in *Anufiraja v Southwark* that this case was right at the maximum level of damages that could properly be awarded for a breach of Art.8 on the facts of such a case.

[47] [2003] EWCA Civ 1406.

[48] *ibid.*, para.43.

In *East Sussex*, two disabled persons were living in appalling conditions as a result of health and safety restrictions imposed by East Sussex County Council on manual lifting activities by carers. Munby J. in his judgment considered that these conditions were approximating the Art.3 floor of "degrading treatment", and indicated that the council had to factor in due consideration for the human dignity of the claimants in deciding how to exercise its powers to provide special support for severely disabled persons.

Therefore, a remedy under the HRA may exist where the treatment of disabled persons or a failure to make reasonable accommodation results in a high level of degrading treatment.[49] The HRA could also have an impact in discrimination cases under Art.14, although this remains untested at present. The HRA has had a considerable impact in the context of the treatment of individuals with mental health difficulties, requiring greater legal certainty and protection for their procedural rights.[50]

The HRA could also have a significant impact on the care and medical treatment received by disabled persons. In *R (Burke) v GMC*,[51] the claimant, Oliver Burke, suffered from cerebellar ataxia, and as his condition worsened, it was inevitable that he would need to receive food and water by artificial means. He contended that the relevant guidance issued by the General Medical Council (GMC) was incompatible with his rights under Arts 2, 3, 6, 8 and 14 of the ECHR, as it provided for the denial or withdrawal of the provision of artificial nutrition in certain circumstances. He sought judicial review of the guidance and clarification as to the circumstances in which artificial nutrition could be lawfully withdrawn from a patient in his position.[52] In the High Court, Munby J. emphasised the centrality of human dignity to the Convention scheme of rights. He considered that the GMC guidance did not adequately reflect the vision of human rights expressed in Arts 2,3 and 8 of the Convention, by downplaying the overwhelming importance of giving effect to the will of the individual in treatment decisions. The Court of Appeal disagreed with Munby J.'s analysis of the sufficiency of the existing guidelines, but this case does demonstrate the possibilities that the introduction for the HRA has opened up for challenging the paternalism and denials of agency that all too frequently afflict disabled persons. However, the decision of the House of Lords in *YL v Birmingham CC*[53] that restricted the scope of applicability of the HRA by adopting a narrow interpretation of what constitutes a "public function" for the purposes of s.6 of the HRA means that the Act's

49 See the excellent analysis in Anna Lawson, "Disability, Degradation and Dignity: the Role of Article 3 of the European Convention On Human Rights" (2006) 56(4) N.I.L.Q. 462.

50 See e.g. *R (KB) v Mental Health Review Tribunal* [2003] EWHC 193 (Admin).

51 [2005] EWCA Civ 1003.

52 The Disability Rights Commission was joined in the proceedings as an interested party, as they had previously been in *R (A, B, X and Y) v East Sussex CC and the Disability Rights Commission (No.2)* [2003] EWHC 167 (Admin), where Munby J. commented on the importance of the role of the Commission at paras 178–185.

53 [2007] UKHL 27.

potential impact upon poor treatment of disabled persons by private providers of service delivery may be severely limited.

In *Pretty v the United Kingdom*,[54] Mrs Pretty, who was in the final stages of motor neurone disease, claimed that criminal legislation that made it a crime to assist someone to commit suicide, but not to commit or attempt suicide oneself, discriminated against those who, like her, could not take their own lives without assistance because of a physical disability. She therefore claimed that this legislative prohibition on euthanasia violated *inter alia* Art.8 and 14, as it prevented the disabled, but not the able-bodied, to exercise their right to commit suicide. The European Court of Human Rights agreed with the Law Lords in rejecting Ms Pretty's claim, holding that the Convention did not create a right to commit suicide, and that the issue did not come within the ambit of any of the Convention rights.[55] *Pretty* is a difficult case from the perspective of disability rights. Permitting euthanasia could symbolically indicate that a certain level of disability is incompatible with a dignified life, and there are concerns that disabled persons will be very vulnerable to pressure to agree to their own deaths. However, Mrs Pretty's case could also be seen as an assertion of individual dignity and a challenge to paternalist laws that deny agency to those whose disabilities exclude them from options available to others.

Disability rights have been addressed increasingly within other jurisdictions through constitutional rights provisions. However, the experience has again yielded mixed results. In the United States, Oliver Wendell Holmes famously justified state-imposed sterilisation requirements in *Buck v Bell* on the ground that "[t]hree generations of imbeciles are enough",[56] and constitutional rights have rarely proved an effective avenue for the upholding of disability rights. The US Supreme Court in *City of Cleburne v Cleburne Living Centre, Inc*[57] ruled that a lower federal court of appeal had erred in deciding that the use of the fact that a group of persons suffered from "mental retardation" in denying a planning application (which was intended to provide housing for this group) could be considered a quasi-suspect form of classification, which would be subject to a more exacting standard of judicial review. The Supreme Court decided that the standard level of rational review was sufficient where distinctions were made on the basis of mental disability, while nevertheless striking down the zoning ordinance challenged in this case on the ground that it was the product of irrational prejudice. While the decision on its facts was positive, the judgment established that distinctions made on the ground of disability did not constitute a suspect category in US constitutional law.

However, the Canadian experience has arguably been more positive, and deserves some close analysis. The original text of the equality clause of the

[54] No.2346/02, 29/04/2002; (2002) 35 E.H.R.R. 1.
[55] See also the similar decision of the Canadian Supreme Court in *Rodriguez v British Columbia (A.G.)* [1997] 3 S.C.R. 519.
[56] 274 U.S. 200, 207 (1927).
[57] 473 U.S. 432 (1985).

Canadian Charter of Fundamental Rights and Freedoms (s.15) included no equality rights guarantee for persons with disabilities. The subsequent decision to include protection for persons with disabilities in the final version of s.15 was taken only after considerable debate. Again, it has yielded mixed results. In *Eaton v Brant (County) Board of Education*,[58] the Ontario Court of Appeal held that s.15 gives children with disabilities the right to be educated in an integrated setting with students without disabilities. Compulsory placement in segregated disability programs was only permissible if the school board could show that the child's needs could not be met in the regular school setting or other less restrictive environment, even after reasonable accommodation had been made. However, the Canadian Supreme Court rejected the argument that s.15 should be read as establishing a presumption in favour of integration, a decision that has generated some controversy. Nevertheless, the Court did recognise the importance of reasonable accommodation and the need to make special provision to enable disabled persons to enjoy full equality in Canadian society, explicitly adopting a "social model" analysis of disability. Sopinka J. remarked that:

> "The principles that not every distinction on a prohibited ground will constitute discrimination and that, in general, distinctions based on presumed rather than actual characteristics are the hallmarks of discrimination have particular significance when applied to physical and mental disability. Avoidance of discrimination on this ground will frequently require distinctions to be made taking into account the actual personal characteristics of disabled persons...
>
> The principal object of certain of the prohibited grounds is the elimination of discrimination by the attribution of untrue characteristics based on stereotypical attitudes relating to immutable conditions such as race or sex. In the case of disability, this is one of the objectives. The other equally important objective seeks to take into account the true characteristics of this group which act as headwinds to the enjoyment of society's benefits and to accommodate them. Exclusion from the mainstream of society results from the construction of a society based solely on "mainstream" attributes to which disabled persons will never be able to gain access. Whether it is the impossibility of success at a written test for a blind person, or the need for ramp access to a library, the discrimination does not lie in the attribution of untrue characteristics to the disabled individual. The blind person cannot see and the person in a wheelchair needs a ramp. Rather, it is the failure to make reasonable accommodation, to fine-tune society so that its structures and assumptions do not result in the relegation and banishment of disabled persons from participation, which results in discrimination against them. It is recognition of the actual characteristics, and reasonable accommodation of these characteristics which is the central purpose of s.15(1) in relation to disability."[58a]

This was an important recognition of the basic approach of the social model of disability, even if the decision did reject any assumption in favour of integration. In *Eldridge v British Columbia (Attorney General)*,[59] the Supreme Court

[58] [1997] 1 S.C.R. 241.
[58a] At paras [66]–[67])
[59] [1997] 3 S.C.R. 624.

further indicated its willingness to adopt a social model analysis in finding that deaf persons were entitled to publicly-funded sign-language interpretation to access medical services. The court stressed that disabled persons have been subject to historical patterns of exclusion, stereotyping, segregation and "paternalistic attitudes of pity and charity", and that "their entrance into the social mainstream has been conditional upon their emulation of able-bodied norms ..." The court emphasised that "the appellants ... ask only for equal access to services that are available to all", but accepted that reasonable accommodation of the needs of disabled persons could be required to vindicate this basic right to equal access and participation[59a].

In *Granovsky v Minister for Employment and Immigration*,[60] a social model analysis was applied again by the Supreme Court in finding that it was open to the federal government to relax a pension contribution requirement for permanently disabled persons, but not for temporarily disabled persons. The court considered that the proper focus of the s.15(1) analysis in disability claims should not be on the medical nature of the specific disability, but on the response of the state to the needs of the person with that disability. Also, in considering whether a difference of treatment on the ground of disability was justified, the court felt that it should consider whether the measure in question, in purpose or effect, perpetuated the view that persons with disabilities were less capable or less worthy of recognition as human beings or as members of Canadian society. Applying this approach, the court found that the differential treatment afforded by the contribution relaxation operated to ameliorate the position of those with severe and permanent disabilities: the failure to grant a similar waiver to those with temporary disabilities did not involve an attack on their dignity. Perhaps of more interest than the actual decision was the approach to disability issues outlined by Binnie J., which is worth quoting in detail:

Granovsky v Minister for Employment and Immigration [2000] 1 S.C.R. 703, S.C.C. 28, Binnie J.

"**28.** Unlike gender or ethnic origin, which generally stamp each member of the class with a singular characteristic, disabilities vary in type, intensity and duration across the full range of personal physical or mental characteristics ... The concept of disability must therefore accommodate a multiplicity of impairments, both physical and mental, overlaid on a range of functional limitations, real or perceived, interwoven with recognition that in many important aspects of life the so-called "disabled" individual may not be impaired or limited in any way at all ... The bedrock of the appellant's argument is that many of the difficulties confronting persons with disabilities in everyday life do not flow ineluctably from the individual's condition at all but are located in the problematic response of society to

[59a] At para.92).
[60] [2000] 1 S.C.R. 703, S.C.C. 28.

that condition. A proper analysis necessitates unbundling the impairment from the reaction of society *to* the impairment, and a recognition that much discrimination is socially constructed. Exclusion and marginalization are generally not created by the individual with disabilities but are created by the economic and social environment and, unfortunately, by the state itself. Problematic responses include, in the case of government action, legislation which discriminates *in its effect* against persons with disabilities, and thoughtless administrative oversight . . .

34. It is therefore useful to keep distinct the component of disability that may be said to be located in an individual, namely the aspects of physical or mental impairment, and functional limitation, and on the other hand the other component, namely, the socially constructed handicap that is not located in the individual at all but in the society in which the individual is obliged to go about his or her everyday tasks. This manner of differentiating among the different aspects of disabilities is elaborated upon in the medical context by the World Health Organization in the *International Classification of Impairments, Disabilities, and Handicaps: A Manual of Classification Relating to the Consequences of Disease* (1980); restated in: *United Nations Decade of Disabled Persons, 1983–1992: World Programme of Action concerning Disabled Persons* (1983), at pp. 2–3, and in the human rights area by Professor J. E. Bickenbach, *Physical Disability and Social Policy* (1993), and Professor M. Minow, "When Difference Has Its Home; Group Homes for the Mentally Retarded, Equal Protection and Legal Treatment of Difference" (1987), 22 *Harv. C.R.-C.L. L. Rev.* 111, at p. 124. (While the WHO, in the *medical* context, uses the word "disability" to refer to functional limitation (the second aspect), I prefer to use the expression "functional limitation" to emphasize that in *legal* terms it is all three aspects considered together that constitute the disability) . . .

37. . . . the third aspect (the socially constructed handicap) may wrongly attribute exaggerated or unjustified consequences to whatever functional limitations in fact exist. A government inclination to write people off because of their impairment justifies scrutiny even if the impairment has resulted in very real functional limitations.

38. Equally problematically, there are instances where society passes directly from the first aspect (physical or mental impairment) to the third aspect (imposition of a disadvantage or handicap) without going through the intermediate consideration of evaluating the true functional limitations, if any. An individual with a serious facial disfigurement, for example, or a person who is diagnosed with leprosy, may not have, and may never have, any relevant functional limitations, but may nevertheless suffer discrimination on account of the condition.

39. In summary, while the notions of impairment and functional limitation (real or perceived) are important considerations in the disability analysis, the primary focus is on the inappropriate legislative or administrative response (or lack thereof) of the state. Section 15(1) is ultimately concerned with human rights and discriminatory treatment, not with biomedical conditions."[61]

[61] Binnie J. in his judgment also cited D. Pothier, "Miles to Go: Some Personal Reflections on the Social Construction of Disability" (1992) 14 Dalhousie L.J. 526.

A similar readiness to scrutinise social norms for unjustified limitations imposed upon disabled persons has been present in the court's case-law.[62] While not without its defects, the court's disability case law has been marked by a willingness to at least engage with the social model.[63]

The Canadian jurisprudence could to a degree serve as a template for how the social model approach can be incorporated in the interpretation and application of human rights instruments, including the ECHR. Problems may always exist as to what can be achieved for disabled persons through rights activism. In particular, the reluctance of courts in engage in forms of resource allocation, and to intervene in areas of social policy which are debated and outside their natural sphere of competency, may inevitably blunt what can be achieved through rights-based litigation.[64] However, the Canadian cases do illustrate the partial gains that can be gained through the use of rights instruments in the context of disability.

It should also be noted that the European Committee of Social Rights in its comments on national reports on compliance with the European Social Charter, and in its new and developing case law stemming from the revised Social Charter's collective complaints procedure (which the UK has not as yet signed or ratified) has begun to emphasise the obligations of states towards disabled persons. For example, in its decision in the matter of *International Association Autism-Europe v France*, the committee came to the conclusion that France had failed to give adequate effect to the rights to education and non-discrimination in the charter by failing to provide adequate educational facilities for autistic children.[65] The impact of the committee's determinations is often limited: but this developing jurisprudence does show how human rights concepts are gradually being extended to protect the entitlements of

[62] See e.g. in *R. v Pearson* (1994) 36 C.P. (4th) 343, the British Columbia Court of Appeal affirmed the lower court's extension of a hearsay admissibility rule to an alleged sexual assault victim whose disability precluded him from giving a full, articulate account of the assault. In *British Columbia (Superintendent of Motor Vehicles) v British Columbia (Council of Human Rights)* [1999] 3 S.C.R. 868 (known as "*Grismer Estate*"), the appellant's eyesight was impaired by a stroke, and was assumed by the Superintendent of Motor Vehicles, without any individual testing, to be sufficiently visually impaired to disqualify him from holding a driver's licence. The Court held that the appellant was entitled to an individual test to determine whether the impairment did in fact exist to the degree alleged. In the gender discrimination case of *British Columbia (Public Service Employee Relations Commission) v BCGSEU* [1999] 3 S.C.R. 3, a woman fire-fighter failed a series of strenuous physical endurance tests, but succeeded in arguing that the physical standards that had been set were not related to the demands of fire-fighting but just reflected the physical performance of male fire-fighters. The problem did not lie with the individual, but with the substitution of a male norm in place of a fair, job-related performance analysis. A similar approach could be applied readily in the disability context, and is consistent with the approach taken in *Granovsky*, *Eldridge* and *Grismer Estate*.

[63] For a useful discussion, see M. David Lepofsky, "The Charter's Guarantee of Equality to People with Disabilities—How Well is it Working?" [1998] 16 Windsor Yearbook of Access to Justice 155.

[64] The decision in *Eaton*, discussed above, reflects this reluctance to intervene in areas of controversy and complex policy assessment.

[65] Complaint No.13/2002, Decision on the Merits November 4, 2003, European Committee of Social Rights.

disabled persons. The new UN Convention should help this process: while the formal position in the dualist UK legal system remains that the Convention can only be taken into account by the courts to assist in interpreting ambiguous legislation,[66] the growing salience of human rights standards in UK law means that it may prove a valuable resource in steering judicial interpretation of the Disability Discrimination Act (see below) and social welfare instruments that make provision for support for persons with disabilities.

V. Disability Discrimination Legislation

The main legal vehicle for addressing disability rights claims has been the introduction of various forms of legislation which attempt to improve the position of disabled persons. The initial steps taken to address the needs of the disabled were adopted as part of welfare measures to cope with and contain the needs of the "poor" in general, with whom the disabled were classed. Following the First World War with its huge toll of injury and wounded, the European states began to introduce measures to provide employment, rather than just welfare relief, for disabled persons. Waddington has described the initial forms of disability-related legislation introduced in the 1920s as adopting a combination of three separate approaches:

a) attempts to help disabled persons find work via the creation of specialist employment agencies and other measures;

b) the establishment of compulsory quotas for employers, requiring them to employ a certain proportion of disabled workers; and

c) the creation of separate "sheltered" labour markets, through the establishment of workshops and other forms of special employment for particular categories of disabled persons.[67]

All three approaches remained commonplace until recently, and elements of all three still persist in current legislation and policy. However, all three were based upon the medical model approach: the disabled person was presumed to be largely incapable of coping with normal social expectations, and special provision took the form of the creation of reserved areas of activity separate from the mainstream of society. This often served to ghettoise disabled workers within limited and narrow forms of activity, and ensured that mainstream social structures faced no demand to change to accommodate the needs of the segregated disabled communities. Some of these strategies yiel-

66 See *R v Secretary of State for Home Department, Ex p. Brind* [1991] 1 A.C. 696.

67 Lisa Waddington, "Changing Attitudes to the Rights of People with Disabilities in Europe", in J. Cooper *Law, Rights and Disability* (London: Kingsley, 2000) 33–57.

ded useful results for some disabled persons: sheltered employment played some role in giving dignity and employment to particular groups, and remains important today for a small proportion of disabled persons. However, in the main, these approaches proved limited and ineffective in securing meaningful employment for disabled persons.

For example, in the UK, the Disabled Persons (Employment) Act 1944 required private employers with 20 or more employees (public sector employers were not bound by the legislation, but agreed at the time to adopt a similar policy) to ensure that at least three per cent of their workforce was made up of disabled persons. The hiring of new employees was prohibited if it would bring the employer under quota, and the legislation also provided for criminal sanctions. The legislation did play a role in re-integrating some wounded combat veterans back into the workforce in the wake of World War II. However, in the main, and in common with similar quota-based legislation in other European countries, the Act was not a success. Block exemptions could be granted by the relevant Secretary of State: the legislation was also largely not enforced. In addition, there was no requirement to hold open particular categories of posts for disabled persons, or to adopt an equal treatment policy for disabled employees. Therefore, those employed under quota arrangements often filled low-profile and low-earning roles. This in turn discredited the quota scheme: many disabled persons chose not to register as officially disabled for the purposes of the legislation, with the Employment Service estimating in the early 1990s that only one-third of those eligible had signed on.[68] In 1993, only 18.9% of employers achieved the quota requirement.[69] The quota scheme also served to segregate disabled workers, and to reinforce the perception that disabled persons were only useful for low-level forms of employment. When the Disability Discrimination Act was introduced in 1996, the relevant provisions of the 1944 Act was repealed.

With the growing demands from disabled persons for greater meaningful equality, and the gradual shift towards forms of social model analysis, there has been a significant shift in how disability rights issues are addressed. The emphasis has now shifted in favour of the introduction of legislation prohibiting discrimination on the grounds of disability, with disability discrimination being conceptualised as a form of social exclusion comparable to other forms of discrimination. This has either been introduced as part of combined equality legislation, as in the Irish Employment Equality Act 1996 and Equal Status Act 2000, or else has taken the form of separate and specialised disability discrimination legislation, such as the Americans with Disabilities Act 1986. Disability discrimination legislation attempts both to

68 *ibid.*

69 *ibid.* See also L. Waddington and M. Diller, "Tensions and Coherence in Disability Policy: The Uneasy Relationship Between Social Welfare and Civil Rights Models of Disability in American, European and International Employment Law" in M Breslin and S Yee (eds), *Disability Rights Law and Policy: International and National Perspectives* (Ardsley, New York: Transnational Publishers Inc, 2002).

prohibit unjustified discrimination against disabled persons, but also to require reasonable accommodation of their needs: simply prohibiting discrimination would not achieve the positive transformation of social practices that the social model aims to achieve.

VI. Disability and the European Union

The EU has only recently acquired competence in respect of disability issues through Article 13 of the EC Treaty.[70] The Employment Equality Directive, introduced in 2000, prohibits unjustified discrimination on the ground of disability in employment, vocational guidance and training, and membership of professional, workers' and employers' bodies.[71] Importantly in the disability context, it does not apply to social security or social protection schemes (see below), or to other forms of social advantage.[72]

The key provisions of the Directive in the disability context are as follows (the non-binding recitals are included, as they have considerable persuasive force):

COUNCIL DIRECTIVE 2000/78/EC of November 27, 2000, establishing a general framework for equal treatment in employment and occupation

"Recitals

(16) The provision of measures to accommodate the needs of disabled people at the workplace plays an important role in combating discrimination on grounds of disability.

(17) This Directive does not require the recruitment, promotion, maintenance in employment or training of an individual who is not competent, capable and available to perform the essential functions of the post concerned or to undergo the relevant training, without prejudice to the obligation to provide reasonable accommodation for people with disabilities.

[70] For the development of disability policy at EU level, see Deborah Mabbett, "The Development of Rights-Based Social Policy in the European Union: The Example of Disability Rights" [2005] Journal of Common Market Studies 97; Anna Lawson, "The EU Rights based Approach to Disability: Strategies for Shaping an Inclusive Society" (2005) 6 International J. of Discrimination and the Law 269.

[71] O.J. L. 303/19. Under Art.18 of the Framework Directive, States may, if necessary, have an additional period of three years from December 2, 2003 (a total of six years) for implementation of the provisions on disability discrimination. The UK has not availed of this provision.

[72] Article 3(3) and Recital 13 clarifies that the scope of the Directive does not include state social security and social protection schemes whose benefits are not treated as income within the meaning given to that term within EC law, nor to "any kind of payment by the State aimed at providing access of employment or maintaining employment".

(18) This Directive does not require, in particular, the armed forces and the police, prison or emergency services to recruit or maintain in employment persons who do not have the required capacity to carry out the range of functions that they may be called upon to perform with regard to the legitimate objective of preserving the operational capacity of those services.

(20) Appropriate measures should be provided, i.e. effective and practical measures to adapt the workplace to the disability, for example adapting premises and equipment, patterns of working time, the distribution of tasks or the provision of training or integration resources.

(21) To determine whether the measures in question give rise to a disproportionate burden, account should be taken in particular of the financial and other costs entailed, the scale and financial resources of the organisation or undertaking and the possibility of obtaining public funding or any other assistance [. . .]

(26) The prohibition of discrimination should be without prejudice to the maintenance or adoption of measures intended to prevent or compensate for disadvantages suffered by a group of persons of a particular religion or belief, disability, age or sexual orientation, and such measures may permit organisations of persons of a particular religion or belief, disability, age or sexual orientation where their main object is the promotion of the special needs of those persons.

(27) In its Recommendation 86/379/EEC of 24 July 1986 on the employment of disabled people in the Community (1), the Council established a guideline framework setting out examples of positive action to promote the employment and training of disabled people, and in its Resolution of 17 June 1999 on equal employment opportunities for people with disabilities (2), affirmed the importance of giving specific attention *inter alia* to recruitment, retention, training and lifelong learning with regard to disabled persons. [. . .]''

Article 1

''Purpose

The purpose of this Directive is to lay down a general framework for combating discrimination on the grounds of religion or belief, disability, age or sexual orientation as regards employment and occupation, with a view to putting into effect in the Member States the principle of equal treatment.''

Article 2

''Concept of Discrimination

1. For the purposes of this Directive, the ''principle of equal treatment'' shall mean that there shall be no direct or indirect discrimination whatsoever on any of the grounds referred to in Article 1.

2. For the purposes of paragraph 1:

(a) direct discrimination shall be taken to occur where one person is treated less favourably than another is, has been or would be treated in a comparable situation, on any of the grounds referred to in Article 1;

(b) indirect discrimination shall be taken to occur where an apparently neutral provision, criterion or practice would put persons having a particular religion or belief, a particular disability, a particular age, or a particular sexual orientation at a particular disadvantage compared with other persons unless:

   (i) that provision, criterion or practice is objectively justified by a legitimate aim and the means of achieving that aim are appropriate and necessary, or
   (ii) as regards persons with a particular disability, the employer or any person or organisation to whom this Directive applies, is obliged, under national legislation, to take appropriate measures in line with the principles contained in Article 5 in order to eliminate disadvantages entailed by such provision, criterion or practice...

[...]"

5. This Directive shall be without prejudice to measures laid down by national law which, in a democratic society, are necessary for public security, for the maintenance of public order and the prevention of criminal offences, for the protection of health and for the protection of the rights and freedoms of others.

[...]

Article 5

"Reasonable accommodation for disabled persons

In order to guarantee compliance with the principle of equal treatment in relation to persons with disabilities, reasonable accommodation shall be provided. This means that employers shall take appropriate measures, where needed in a particular case, to enable a person with a disability to have access to, participate in, or advance in employment, or to undergo training, unless such measures would impose a disproportionate burden on the employer. This burden shall not be disproportionate when it is sufficiently remedied by measures existing within the framework of the disability policy of the Member State concerned.

[...]"

Article 7

"Positive action

1. With a view to ensuring full equality in practice, the principle of equal treatment shall not prevent any Member State from maintaining or adopting specific measures to prevent or compensate for disadvantages linked to any of the grounds referred to in Article 1.

2. With regard to disabled persons, the principle of equal treatment shall be without prejudice to the right of Member States to maintain or adopt provisions on the protection of health and safety at work or to measures aimed at creating or maintaining provisions or facilities for safeguarding or promoting their integration into the working environment."

These provisions are framed in very general terms. The Directive does not define what is to constitute a "disability", or who might be protected or benefit from the prohibition of disability discrimination. This could permit multiple different definitions of disability to be adopted across the EU. This could also ensure that a range of different "trigger" points will exist in different member states as to what forms of discrimination might be deemed to be illegal: different national courts may adopt very different approaches as to what constitutes a "disability" in a particular case, whether discrimination has occurred on the basis of that disability and whether justification can be shown. The recitals and text also give very little guidance on what might constitute "reasonable accommodation".

The European Court of Justice has clarified in the *Navas* decision that the Directive does not require member states to include discrimination based upon an employee's "illness" within the scope of their national disability discrimination laws. The Court emphasised that the concept of "disability" contained in the Directive was intended to encompass "physical, mental or psychological impairments", which hinder "the participation of the person concerned in professional life" over a "long period of time". This was distinguished from "sickness", which the Court viewed as a separate concept and one not covered by the Directive:

Case C-13/05, *Sonia Chacón Navas v Eurest Colectividades SA* [2006] ECR I-6467

"Concept of 'disability'

39. The concept of 'disability' is not defined by Directive 2000/78 itself. Nor does the directive refer to the laws of the Member States for the definition of that concept.

40. It follows from the need for uniform application of Community law and the principle of equality that the terms of a provision of Community law which makes no express reference to the law of the Member States for the purpose of determining its meaning and scope must normally be given an autonomous and uniform interpretation throughout the Community, having regard to the context of the provision and the objective pursued by the legislation in question (see, inter alia, Case 327/82 *Ekro* [1984] ECR 107, paragraph 11, and Case C-323/03 *Commission* v *Spain* [2006] ECR I-0000, paragraph 32).

41. As is apparent from Article 1, the purpose of Directive 2000/78 is to lay down a general framework for combating discrimination based on any of the grounds referred to in that article, which include disability, as regards employment and occupation.

42. In the light of that objective, the concept of 'disability' for the purpose of Directive 2000/78 must, in accordance with the rule set out in paragraph 40 of this judgment, be given an autonomous and uniform interpretation.

43. Directive 2000/78 aims to combat certain types of discrimination as regards employment and occupation. In that context, the concept of 'disability' must be understood as referring to a limitation which results in particular from physical, mental or psychological impairments and which hinders the participation of the person concerned in professional life.

44. However, by using the concept of 'disability' in Article 1 of that directive, the legislature deliberately chose a term which differs from 'sickness'. The two concepts cannot therefore simply be treated as being the same.

45. Recital 16 in the preamble to Directive 2000/78 states that the 'provision of measures to accommodate the needs of disabled people at the workplace plays an important role in combating discrimination on grounds of disability'. The importance which the Community legislature attaches to measures for adapting the workplace to the disability demonstrates that it envisaged situations in which participation in professional life is hindered over a long period of time. In order for the limitation to fall within the concept of 'disability', it must therefore be probable that it will last for a long time.

46. There is nothing in Directive 2000/78 to suggest that workers are protected by the prohibition of discrimination on grounds of disability as soon as they develop any type of sickness.

47. It follows from the above considerations that a person who has been dismissed by his employer solely on account of sickness does not fall within the general framework laid down for combating discrimination on grounds of disability by Directive 2000/78."

The ECJ therefore appears to conceptualise "disability" as an impairment that hinders participation in working life for a substantial period of time. Beyond this basic conceptual framework, it remains to be seen what conditions the Directive will be deemed to include within its scope.

Direct forms of disability discrimination in employment are prohibited,[73] as is harassment on the ground of disability,[74] instructions to discriminate[75] and victimisation.[76] In addition, Art.5 of the Directive requires that provision is made by employers for "reasonable accommodation" to enable access to employment and training. The somewhat awkward formulation of Art.2(b)(ii) permits member states to either prohibit indirect discrimination, or to rely upon the reasonable accommodation requirement to achieve the removal of obstacles and barriers to equal participation that the prohibition on indirect discrimination is designed to achieve across the other prohibited grounds of discrimination.

73 Art.2.
74 Art.2(3).
75 Art.2(4).
76 Art.11.

Member states were given this option due to the concerns of a few states (including the UK) that in the context of disability the standard prohibition on indirect discrimination would generate considerable legal uncertainty. A multiplicity of standard employment practices and requirements could be deemed to have an adverse impact on particular disabled persons: employers could therefore have to place extensive reliance upon the objective justification test to escape the possibility of a finding of indirect discrimination against many of these practices. As a result, some governments saw the reasonable accommodation requirement as offering a more precise and certain legal standard. However, as discussed below, permitting reliance solely upon the reasonable accommodation requirement does have disadvantages. In particular, the reasonable accommodation requirement is only triggered by a request for accommodation, whereas a requirement to refrain from indirect discrimination could require action even in the absence of a specific request for accommodation. The Directive could be critiqued as excessively cautious and permissive for permitting this opt-out.

As with the other prohibited grounds of discrimination, the Directive also imposes the burden of proof upon respondents to prove that there has been no discriminatory treatment once a person alleging discrimination establishes facts "from which it may be presumed that there has been direct or indirect discrimination".[77] Judicial and/or administrative procedures must be available to permit complainants to bring a legal action,[78] and member states will have to establish an effective system of remedies, as well as taking steps to bring existing legislation and collective agreements into conformity with the Directive's requirements. The Directive also clarifies that it is laying down minimum requirements, does not permit any reduction in existing protection for equal treatment (non-regression), and does not invalidate any national provisions which offer a higher level of protection for equality.[79]

The exceptions to the scope of the Directive are of particular relevance to disability. Article 3(4) permits member states to exempt their armed forces from the Directive's provisions, while Art.3(3) states that social security schemes and other forms of state welfare provision are not within its scope. Article 7(2) exempts measures which are aimed at safeguarding or promoting the integration of disabled persons into the working environment. This ensures that most forms of quota schemes, set-aside places and other forms of positive action that are designed to assist persons with disabilities to integrate into the workforce will not subject to the Directive's requirements. This means that these measures will usually not have to satisfy the proportionality test that positive action measures must satisfy across the other equality grounds.

Domestic disability discrimination law must now comply with the requirements of the Directive (and its interpretation by the ECJ). As discussed

[77] Art.10.
[78] Art.9.
[79] Art.8: see also Recital 28.

below, the Directive's provisions have not had a major impact upon the UK. The DDA 1995 had already prohibited disability discrimination in employment and occupation, as well as in the provision of goods and services and other areas where the Directive does not at present apply. However, to ensure compliance with the Directive, the Disability Regulations 2003 and Northern Ireland Regulations 2004 make some alterations in the DDA 1995. In particular, explicit provisions prohibit harassment on the grounds of disability, and the justification defence for a failure to make reasonable accommodation is removed, as is the justification defence for direct discrimination on the basis of the victim's disabled status and the exception for small employers originally contained in the 1995 Act.

However, concern exists that the Regulations do not adequately transpose the Directive. In particular, the DDA 1995 offers protection only to people who come within the statutory definition of "disabled" persons, rather than prohibiting discrimination and harassment "on grounds of disability", as the Directive requires. This means that under domestic legislation, individuals who are *perceived* as disabled or *associated* with a disabled person are not protected against any discrimination that stems from this association or false perception. This could substantially affect those who care for disabled persons, or who exhibit behaviour that is misinterpreted as the product of a disability: such individuals are denied protection under domestic legislation as it currently stands.

This gap in protection is perhaps due to a fear on the part of the UK government that prohibiting discrimination on the ground of association with a person with a disability will in practice mutate into a wider prohibition of discrimination on the ground of a person's status as a carer. Such a prohibition would appear in any case to be justified, but it may generate anxiety in the corporate sector about "rising costs". However, the UK government's failure to act to prohibit discrimination on the grounds of disability linked to association or perception does appear to be very questionable, and a strong case can be made that it was incompatible with the Directive.

This issue is currently the subject of a reference to the European Court of Justice in the case of *Coleman v Attridge Law*,[80] where the claimant who is not herself disabled is arguing that her employers discriminated against her because of her son's disability and her status as his principal carer. At present, she would not recover under domestic law, but the employment tribunal considered that a very serious case existed that the failure of the domestic legislation to cover discrimination on the ground of association with a disabled person is not in compliance with the Directive and therefore took the unusual step of referring this matter directly to the ECJ. The Disability Rights Commission (DRC) has also argued that both association with a disabled

[80] ET 2303745/05.

person and perceived disabled status should be covered by domestic legislation, and that this best reflects the wording and intentions of the Directive.[81] The ECJ decision on the association issue is awaited, and a finding that domestic legislation is not compatible with the Directive will probably trigger the extension of the legislation to include both association with a disabled person and discrimination on the ground of perceived disability.

VII. The Disability Discrimination Act

The Directive now constitutes the dominant legal standard when it comes to disability discrimination, to which domestic law must comply. However, as noted above, the bulk of its provisions have been part of domestic law since 1995. The Disability Discrimination Act 1995 (DDA) was the result of intense campaigning by disability rights activists and other groups, who were determined to secure a UK equivalent of the US ADA. Several private members bills were introduced in the early 1990s which focussed attention on this issue. Despite the initial reluctance of the then Conservative government to legislate, the DDA was eventually introduced as a government Bill and became law in 1995.

The reluctant and cautious approach of the government to adding further layers of regulation was however reflected in the contents of the DDA. While far-reaching in many respects, its original 1995 form fell short in its scope of the RRA 76 or the SDA 75. In particular, its definition of disability was problematic, its provisions were often unwieldy and lacked clarity, and it did not apply to education and other areas covered by the race and sex discrimination legislation. It also failed to provide for the establishment of a Disability Rights Commission (DRC) to play a similar promotion and enforcement role to the Commission for Racial Equality (CRE) and Equal Opportunities Commission (EOC).[82]

Nevertheless, the DDA's introduction was a major breakthrough in the struggle for disability rights. Caroline Gooding has described the DDA as "not the fully comprehensive civil rights legislation that disabled people campaigned for, but it does represent a significant milestone".[83] A series of subsequent legislative provisions have also improved the DDA and remedied some of the gaps in the original legislation. It now constitutes a reasonably comprehensive legislative code, but retains defects that stem from the lack of ambition that accompanied its origin.

[81] DRC, *Definition of Disability Within Anti-discrimination Legislation: Recommendation to the Government*, July 2006, Pt 8, available at *http://www.drc.org.uk/docs/Definition%20of%20disability%20recommendation%20to%20govt.doc.*

[82] Caroline Gooding, "The Disability Discrimination Act 1995: An Overview", in J. Cooper, *Law, Rights and Disability* (London: Kingsley, 2000) 139–163, 139.

[83] *ibid.*

The legislation is also marked by its reliance upon accompanying official guidance to flesh out some of its contents, in particular its definition of disability. Under s.3 of the DDA, guidance can be issued by Secretary of State as to aspects of the legislation, which is not legally binding: however, courts and tribunals are obliged to take account of the guidance when relevant. The Disability Rights Commission is also given similar powers as those enjoyed by the other equality commissions to issue codes of practice with the approval of the Secretary of State, which again are not legally binding but can be taken into account by courts and tribunals.[84] Both the guidance and codes of practice play important roles in the application of the DDA, in particular in clarifying the often opaque issues relating to the definition of disability that arise under the Act.

VIII. Definition of Disability

Most forms of anti-discrimination legislation, by protecting individuals against certain forms of illegitimate treatment based upon possession of a particular characteristic, also protect the particular social groups who tend to be treated negatively as a result of their sharing of the characteristics in question. Women as a group benefit from the prohibition on treating individuals differently on the ground of their gender, for example. The focus is on prohibiting the illegitimate use of the "suspect" characteristic: the protection of disadvantaged social groups is a side-product, if an important one. The DDA is different: only those who come within the statutory definition of disability are protected. This has the advantage of clearly establishing the existence and contours of the disadvantaged group to be protected. It also ensures that positive action in favour of disabled persons does not trigger the same legal complexities as arise across the other grounds, as discussed below: non-disabled individuals cannot challenge differences of treatment based on disabled status as they do not come within the definition, which makes it simpler to design and implement positive action schemes directed towards the disadvantaged groups. However, it has the disadvantage of ensuring that coming within the definition of disability is a precondition that must be satisfied before an individual can bring an action, which, as discussed below, can be a serious stumbling block.

This requirement to come within the definition of being "disabled" means that how "disability" is defined becomes a matter of considerable importance. Framing such a definition is a very complex issue. What personal characteristics will affect an individual's ability to operate within society will vary with

[84] The codes that have been issued by the DRC include the *Code of Practice for Providers of Post-16 Education and Related Services, the Code of Practice for Schools,* the *Code of Practice: Rights of Access—Goods, Facilities, Services and Premises* (revised 2000) and the *Code of Practice—Employment and Occupation* (revised 2004) (hereafter referred to as the *Employment Code of Practice*).

social structures, popular perception, class and income, and technological change.[85] Prior to the mass availability of spectacles, for example, short-sightedness could be a considerable impairment, especially for the working class and agricultural workers: now, short-sightedness that is corrected via spectacles will not constitute a disability under the DDA. Therefore, definitions of disability will inevitably have to be contextual in nature and be capable of being applied in a flexible way to reflect changing technology, work expectations and patterns of social interaction.

In addition, different persons may move in different ways in and out of the scope of a definition of disability. Individuals may be perceived as having a variety of disabilities over the course of their lives. As noted above, the UN Ad Hoc Committee on the Rights of Persons with Disabilities has suggested that "the data suggests that disability is a normal aspect of life; all kinds of disabilities can happen to all types of people at all stages in their normal life-cycles."[86] However, individuals may also be very reluctant to be shoehorned into a disability identity, and may resist being classified as disabled, or may not self-define themselves as disabled until subject to what they perceive as unfair behaviour. Therefore, there are often no fixed groups with a distinct "disabled" identity, again making the task of definition difficult.

The theoretical approaches to disability discussed above will also be of considerable significance in defining "disability". A possible form of classification is to define an individual as "disabled" if she or he suffers from a medically classified condition with distinct physical or mental manifestations, which impact in particular ways upon an individual's ability to function in current social frameworks. This type of definition is common in national disability discrimination legislation, has been adopted in the DDA, and can be seen as rooted in the approach to disability encapsulated by the "medical model": the disability is seen as the product of the individual's particular condition, rather than as the product of external social barriers.

Such a "medical model" definition runs the risk of excluding many individuals and groups from the scope of its coverage. It can leave untouched social barriers that are based on perception, or links to disabled persons, rather than directly stemming from the existence of a medical condition, as such an approach will usually require that the claimant must suffer from a distinct medical condition before a claim can be brought. Individuals may face considerable disadvantages due to prejudicial assumptions, but their condition may not be manifested in a manner that falls within the scope of a distinct medical condition, and therefore will not be able to class themselves as disabled. Due to the necessity to show that an individual has the required medical condition to qualify as "disabled", a medical-centred definition tends to ensure that a considerable emphasis is placed in litigation upon establishing

[85] See C. Gooding, *Disabling Laws, Enabling Acts* (London: Pluto, 1996), p.15.

[86] See Report of the Secretary General, *Issues and Emerging Trends Related to Advancement of Persons with Disabilities* (A/AC.265/2003/1), paras 9–10.

the exact nature and scope of the medical condition that affects a particular individual. Experience in the US and the UK has confirmed this (see below). In addition, as discussed above, a claimant may be forced into the invidious position of having to show first that he or she is sufficiently disabled to qualify for protection under the legislation, and then having to show that they are not sufficiently disabled as to be unable to perform the essential requirements of the post in question. This "double bind" has been a recurring problem in US case law and has been an issue in the UK.

In contrast, definitions based upon the "social model" can be formulated. An individual can be deemed to suffer from a disability if she or he suffers from the existence of social barriers, which are based upon or linked to particular types of physical or mental characteristic. The great advantage of this type of definition is that the focus shifts to the nature and origin of the obstacles faced by the claimant, not the precise medical contours of their condition. However, its potential disadvantage is that the class of potential claimants may be much wider than under a "medical" definition: this could result in a lack of legal certainty, generate resistance from employers and service providers who will face wider exposure to potential litigation and may produce a potential "dilution" of protection by courts and tribunals in response to these concerns.

However, no matter which approach is adopted, framing a workable definition involves a balancing act. On the one hand, a definition has to ensure that persons who are subject to substantial impairments due to their physical and mental characteristics are shielded from unjustified discrimination on that basis. On the other hand, a definition also has to limit the scope of the protection offered when it comes to those who may suffer detriment as a consequence of transient illness, personality traits and other characteristics which, if covered by the legislation, would stretch its potential impact beyond the limits of coherence, sustainability and practicality. Achieving this balance is difficult: the boundary between protected and unprotected individuals and groups may be almost impossible to delineate with precision.

The definition adopted in the DDA was based upon that originally used in the ADA, which in turn drew upon the definition in the US Rehabilitation Act which was designed to assist in the reintegration of World War II wounded veterans into civilian life. Unsurprisingly, given this historical provenance, the definition draws on the medical model in defining disability in terms of being affected by medically recognised conditions and sets tight restrictions as to who can come within the protected class.

Part 1 of the DDA (ss.1–3) and Schs 1 and 2 provide definitions of "disability" and "disabled persons", which are worth reproducing in full:

Disability Discrimination Act 1995

"Section 1—Meaning of "disability" and "disabled person"

(1) Subject to the provisions of Schedule 1, a person has a disability for the purposes of this Act if he has a physical or mental impairment which has a substantial and long-term adverse effect on his ability to carry out normal day-to-day activities.

(2) In this Act "disabled person" means a person who has a disability."

These very general provisions are supplemented by added detail in Sch.1 of the Act, additional regulations that clarify aspects of the legislation,[87] and (recently revised and updated) statutory Guidance on matters to be taken into account by courts and tribunals in determining questions relating to the definition of disability issued under s.3.[88] The EAT has emphasised the need for tribunals in adjudicating disability discrimination claims to take the Guidance into account.[89] The Disability Rights Commission's Code of Practice on Employment also offers guidance upon how the definition should be interpreted and applied:

Disability Rights Commission Employment Code of Practice 2004

2.2 "The concept of discrimination in the Act reflects an understanding that functional limitations arising from disabled people's impairments do not inevitably restrict their ability to participate fully in society. Rather than the limitations of an impairment, it is often environmental factors (such as the structure of a building, or an employer's working practices) which unnecessarily lead to these social restrictions. This principle underpins the duty to make reasonable adjustments described in Chapter 5. Understanding this will assist employers and others to avoid discrimination. It is as important to consider which aspects of employment and occupation create difficulties for a disabled person as it is to understand the particular nature of an individual's disability."

Individuals have in general to come within the definition of being "disabled" to bring a claim under the Act, so this definition acts as a gatekeeper to regulate who can benefit from its provisions. It must be satisfied regardless of whether a person is deemed to be "disabled" for the purposes of other legislation, or satisfies eligibility conditions for disability-related benefits or concessions. Therefore, complainants must first of all prove that they are disabled within the precise terms of the DDA.

87 *Disability Discrimination (Meaning of Disability) Regulations* 1996, SI 1996/1455; see also *Disability Discrimination (Meaning of Disability) Regulations (Northern Ireland)* 1996, S.R. 1996/421.

88 *Guidance on Matters to be taken into Account in Determining Questions Related to the Definition of Disability* (London: HMSO, 2005); separate guidance has been issued in Northern Ireland, to similar effect.

89 See *Goodwin v The Patent Office* [1999] I.C.R. 302; [1999] I.R.L.R. 4.

Therefore, how the definition is interpreted and applied is a crucial element of the DDA. Within the contours of this definition, four criteria need to be satisfied to establish the existence of a disability: there must be a) a physical or mental impairment, b) which must affect the ability to carry-out normal day-to-day activities, c) in a long-term and d) substantial manner. Satisfying all four elements can be difficult, especially as employment tribunals have often adopted a narrow and rigid approach to interpreting and applying these provisions, which has often required subsequent intervention by the Employment Appeals Tribunal or the Court of Appeal to remedy these constrained interpretations.[90]

A. *Impairment*

The first leg of the definition is the requirement that a claimant suffer from an "impairment" that is medically recognised or which fits into the general typology of medically-recognised aliments. Under the DDA, an impairment affects a person's ability to carry out normal day-to-day activities only if it affects their mobility, manual dexterity, physical co-ordination, continence, ability to lift, carry or otherwise move everyday objects, speech, hearing or eyesight, memory or ability to concentrate, learn or understand, or their perception of the risk of physical danger.[91] The Guidance provides more detail:

DDA Guidance on the Definition of Disability 2006

"**A3**. The definition requires that the effects which a person may experience must arise from a physical or mental impairment. The term mental or physical impairment should be given its ordinary meaning. In many cases, there will be no dispute whether a person has an impairment. Any disagreement is more likely to be about whether the effects of the impairment are sufficient to fall within the definition. Even so, it may sometimes be necessary to decide whether a person has an impairment so as to be able to deal with the issues about its effects.

A4. Whether a person is disabled for the purposes of the Act is generally determined by reference to the **effect** that an impairment has on that person's ability to carry out normal day-to-day activities. It is not possible to provide an exhaustive list of conditions that qualify as impairments for the purposes of the Act. Any attempt to do so would inevitably become out of date as medical knowledge advanced.

A5. It is important to remember that not all impairments are readily identifiable. While

[90] See the *cri de coeur* by Juliette Nash in Discrimination Law Association, *Briefings 377–390*, Vol.26, October 2005, 390: "after thirty years of European influence upon English courts, it is clear that expecting the EAT to give anything resembling a purposive interpretation to legislation is most unwise".

[91] DDA Sch.1 para.4(1).

some impairments, particularly visible ones, are easy to identify, there are many which are not so immediately obvious.

A6. A disability can arise from a wide range of impairments which can be:

- sensory impairments, such as those affecting sight or hearing;
- impairments with fluctuating or recurring effects such as rheumatoid arthritis, myalgic encephalitis (ME)/chronic fatigue syndrome (CFS), fibromyalgia, depression and epilepsy;
- progressive, such as motor neurone disease, muscular dystrophy, forms of dementia and lupus (SLE);
- organ specific, including respiratory conditions, such as asthma, and cardiovascular diseases, including thrombosis, stroke and heart disease;
- developmental, such as autistic spectrum disorders (ASD), dyslexia and dyspraxia;
- learning difficulties;
- mental health conditions and mental illnesses, such as depression, schizophrenia, eating disorders, bipolar affective disorders, obsessive compulsive disorders, as well as personality disorders and some self-harming behaviour; produced by injury to the body or brain.

A7. It may not always be possible, nor is it necessary, to categorise a condition as either a physical or a mental impairment. The underlying cause of the impairment may be hard to establish. There may be adverse effects which are both physical and mental in nature. Furthermore, effects of a mainly physical nature may stem from an underlying mental impairment, and vice versa.

A8. It is not necessary to consider how an impairment is caused, even if the cause is a consequence of a condition which is excluded. For example, liver disease as a result of alcohol dependency would count as an impairment, although alcoholism itself is expressly excluded from the scope of the definition of disability in the Act. What it is important to consider is the effect of an impairment not its cause—provided that it is not an excluded condition."

The definition requires the existence of an actual impairment: a wrongful perception that a person is disabled is not included, nor is association with an impaired person.[92] As discussed above, both these omissions may be incompatible with the Employment Equality Directive and the absence of protection on the grounds of association is currently the subject of a reference to the European Court of Justice in *Coleman v Attridge Law*.

In the Employment Appeals Tribunal decision in *Goodwin v Post Office*,[93] Morison J. set out the basic parameters of the definition of impairment, as set out in the legislation and the accompanying Guidance:

[92] In *Howden v Capital Copiers (Edinburgh) Ltd* (1997) IT, Case S/40005, 33 D.C.L.D. 1, severe pain in the abdomen was deemed to be an impairment even though exact cause not identified.

[93] [1999] I.C.R. 302, [1999] I.R.L.R. 4, EAT.

Goodwin v Patent Office [1999] I.C.R. 302

"*The impairment condition*

308 MORISON J.

[32] The applicant must have either a physical or mental impairment. Mental impairment includes an impairment which results from or consists of a mental illness provided that the mental illness is 'a clinically well-recognised illness'—see paragraph 1 of Schedule 1, but mental illness does not have the special meaning attributed to it in other legislation. Not all mental impairments will inevitably satisfy the impairment test, and some impairments [e.g. due to alcoholism or tobacco or kleptomania] are excluded: see paragraph 8 of the Guidance. On the other hand, persons whose names appear on the Disabled Persons Register both on 12 January 1995 and 2 December 1995 are to be treated as having a disability without further inquiry, until 2 December 1998. Thereafter, they are to be treated as a person who had a disability in the past, and tribunals will note in that connection the provisions of schedule 2 headed 'past disabilities'.

[33] As the Guidance makes clear, a sensory impairment such as blindness (complete or partial) or loss of hearing (complete or partial) fall within the definition of a physical or mental impairment. If there is doubt as to whether the impairment condition is fulfilled in an alleged mental illness case it would be advisable to ascertain whether the illness described or referred to in the medical evidence is mentioned in the WHO's International Classification of Diseases. That Classification would very likely determine the issue one way or the other: see paragraph 14 of the Guidance."

In the combined cases of *Rugamer v Sony Music; McNicol v Balfour Beatty Rail Maintenance*,[94] the demanding nature of the requirement to show that a concrete impairment is recognised by medical opinion was demonstrated. One of the complainants suffered from a psychological "overlay", whereby a previous accident was alleged to have produced a psychological effect whereby he experienced continuing injury to his neck and spine for which no physical cause could be detected. The industrial tribunal held that no physical or mental impairment existed, within the definition of the DDA, and the EAT upheld this decision. However, the decision can be criticised as contrary to the Guidance (para.A8), which states that it is not necessary to consider how an impairment was caused: the lack of a specific physical or mental "originating" impairment in this case was fatal, even though the existence of a continuing injury should perhaps have constituted a sufficient "impairment" in itself.

In contrast, in *College of Ripon & York St John v Hobbs*,[95] the EAT was willing to accept that a physical impairment existed either by proof of its cause or by the existence of symptoms. Lindsay J. (then President of the EAT) stated:

"[t]here is no statutory definition of 'impairment' and nothing in the Act or Guidance which requires that the task of ascertaining whether there is a physical impairment involves any rigid distinctions between an ongoing fault, short-coming or defect of or in the body on the

[94] [2001] I.R.L.R. 644, [2001] I.C.R. 381, EAT.

[95] [2002] I.R.L.R. 185, EAT: see M. Connolly, *Townshend-Smith on Discrimination Law: Text, Cases and Materials* (2nd ed.) (London: Cavendish, 2004), p.473.

one hand, and evidence of the manifestation of the effects thereof on the other. The Act contemplates that an impairment can be something that results from an illness as opposed to itself being an illness. It can thus be cause or effect. In the present case, therefore, it was appropriate, and not simplistic, for the tribunal to ask itself whether there was evidence before it on which it could hold, directly or by inference, that there was something wrong with the applicant physically, something wrong with her body."[96]

The Court of Appeal approved the approach of Lindsay J. in determining the appeal from the EAT decision in *McNicol v Balfour Beatty Rail Maintenance Ltd*.[97] This clarification was useful, as it is simpler and more straightforward to assess the effects of an impairment rather than its cause. In any case, if a claimant is suffering from an impairment that comes within the DDA, it should make no difference what the source or origin of this impairment is: the legislation makes no distinction, and all that should matter is the actual impact upon the claimant.

Mental Impairment

The DDA covers mental as well as physical impairments. Although "mental impairment" is not defined by the DDA, Sch.1(1) of the Act did originally state that if the mental impairment emanates from mental illness, disability will only be established if it is "from, or consisting of, a mental illness that is clinically well recognised". In *Morgan v Staffordshire University*,[98] the EAT evidenced considerable reluctance to recognise types of mental states as coming within the definition in the DDA that did not result from or consist of a medically recognised "mental illness". Medical evidence of "stress", "anxiety" and "depression" was not sufficient to establish the existence of a disability: inclusion in the World Health Organisation's International Classification of Diseases or a similar publication, or recognition by a respected body of medical opinion, or similar proof was considered to be necessary.

This requirement was a classic example of the persistence of a "medical model" approach, with its requirement that a mental impairment be positively classified as a medical aliment. It was widely criticised and tended to generate complex litigation and extensive reliance upon medical expert evidence. Section 18 of the DDA 2005 has now removed this requirement. Nevertheless, claimants will still have to demonstrate that a mental impairment comes within the full DDA definition in terms of having a long-term substantial impact upon day-to-day activities, which may be far from straightforward (see below).

96 Note that in *Dunham v Ashford Windows* [2005], I.C.R. 1584; [2005] I.R.L.R. 608, the EAT made it clear that evidence from a psychologist, as distinct from a medical practitioner, could be sufficient.
97 [2002] I.R.L.R. 711, CA.
98 [2002] I.C.R. 475; [2002] I.R.L.R. 190, EAT.

However, the EAT in *Dunham v Ashford Windows*[99] overturned a decision of the Employment Tribunal that had rejected a claim on the basis that the evidence from a consultant psychologist (1) did not prove that the applicant suffered from an identified or specific condition and (2) was not from a doctor. The EAT considered that the evidence established that the applicant suffered from "generalised borderline moderate learning difficulties", which was a specific medical condition, albeit general in effect. It also held that the psychologist's evidence was sufficiently expert and from a qualified, experienced and unchallenged source, and that evidence from a doctor was not essential. The *Morgan* decision was analysed as opening up three paths for establishing the existence of a mental impairment:

(i) proof of a mental illness specifically mentioned as such in the World Health Organisation's International Classification of Diseases;

(ii) proof of a mental illness specifically mentioned as such in a publication similar to the WHO list; and

(iii) proof by other means of a medical illness recognised by a respected body of medical opinion.

The EAT confirmed however in *Dunham* that a fourth "path" existed: if, as a matter of sound expert opinion, there may exist a state which is recognisable as a mental impairment but which neither results from nor consists of a mental illness, then such state could be accepted as a mental impairment within the DDA.[100] This decision can be seen as confirmation of a slightly less restrictive approach to recognising the existence of mental impairment.

B. *Impact Upon Day-to-Day Activities*

The next leg of the definition is the requirement that the impairment have an adverse impact upon a person's day-to-day activities, as distinct from suffering from an impairment that may prevent them from engaging in a particular employment or occupation or pastime. Once again, this reflects the "medical model" approach. A claimant under the Act must show that they are hampered by an impairment in their daily existence: thereby, they must fit the picture of a "disabled" person being more or less permanently afflicted by their aliment, rather than being impacted in a particular facet of their lives by a social practice or external physical obstacle, which the "social model" would consider to be a more appropriate test.

99 [2005] UKEAT 0915_04_1306.
100 See also *John Grooms Housing Association v Burdett* [2004] UKEAT/0937/03/TM.

Schedule 1 of the DDA and the accompanying statutory Guidance offer useful clarification of the vague wording used in the definition in s.1.

DDA Schedule 1 para.4(1)

"Normal day-to-day activities

4(1) An impairment is to be taken to affect the ability of the person concerned to carry out normal day-to-day activities only if it affects one of the following—

(a) mobility;

(b) manual dexterity;

(c) physical co-ordination;

(d) continence;

(e) ability to lift, carry or otherwise move everyday objects;

(f) speech, hearing or eyesight;

(g) memory or ability to concentrate, learn or understand; or

(h) perception of the risk of physical danger.

In the accompanying Guidance, this list is referred to as the "list of capacities".

DDA Guidance on the Definition of Disability 2006

D2. "The list of capacities should be looked at in a broad sense, and applied equally to both physical and mental impairments. For example, it is often assumed that for people with a mental impairment the relevant capacity will be "memory or ability to concentrate, learn or understand". The capacities of mobility and physical co-ordination, for example, are often seen as relevant only where there is a physical impairment. However, in many instances this will not be the case. A person with a mental impairment may also have difficulties carrying out activities that involve mobility or other "physical" skills, and people with a physical impairment may also have effects that involve mental processes such as the ability to concentrate (for example, as a result of pain or fatigue).

D3. An impairment will only be treated as affecting a normal day-to-day activity if it involves at least one of the capacities set out at D1 above. The substantial effect is determined by looking at the effect on the particular day-to-day activity, not the relevant capacity. So, for example, an inability to go shopping because of restricted mobility is in itself a substantial effect on a normal day-to-day activity: it is not necessary to show that all or any other aspects of the capacity of mobility are substantially affected.

Meaning of "normal day-to-day activities"

D4. It should be noted that the list of capacities ... is not a list of day-to-day activities. It is not possible to provide an exhaustive list of day-to-day activities, although guidance on this matter is given here. In general, day-to-day activities are things people do on a regular or daily basis, and examples include shopping, reading and writing, having a conversation or using the telephone, watching television, getting washed and dressed, preparing and eating food, carrying out household tasks, walking and travelling by various forms of transport, and taking part in social activities.

D5. The term "normal day-to-day activities" is not intended to include activities which are normal only for a particular person, or a small group of people. In deciding whether an activity is a normal day-to-day activity, account should be taken of how far it is normal for a large number of people, and carried out by people on a daily or frequent and fairly regular basis. In this context, "normal" should be given its ordinary, everyday meaning.

D6. A normal day-to-day activity is not necessarily one that is carried out by a majority of people. For example, it is possible that some activities might be carried out only, or more predominantly, by people of a particular gender, such as applying make-up or using hair curling equipment, and cannot therefore be said to be normal for **most** people. They would nevertheless be considered to be normal day-to-day activities.

Work-related and other specialised activities

D7. Normal day-to-day activities do not include work of any particular form because no particular form of work is "normal" for most people. In any individual case, the activities carried out might be highly specialised. For example, carrying out delicate work with specialised tools may be a normal working activity for a watch repairer, whereas it would not be normal for a person who is employed as a semi-skilled worker. The Act only covers effects which go beyond the normal differences in skill or ability.

D8. The same is true of other specialised activities such as playing a musical instrument to a high standard of achievement; taking part in a particular game or hobby where very specific skills or level of ability are required; or playing a particular sport to a high level of ability, such as would be required for a professional footballer or athlete.

D9. However, many types of work or specialised hobby, sport or pastime may still involve normal day-to-day activities. For example; sitting down, standing up, walking, running, verbal interaction, writing, making a cup of tea, using everyday objects such as a keyboard, and lifting, moving or carrying everyday objects such as chairs.

D10. The effects experienced by a person as a result of environmental conditions, either in the workplace or in another location where a specialised activity is being carried out, should not be discounted simply because there may be a work-related or other specialised activity involved. It is important to consider whether there may also be an adverse effect on the ability to carry out a normal day-to-day activity.

Indirect effects

D11. An impairment may not directly **prevent** someone from carrying out one or more normal day-to-day activities, but it may still have a substantial adverse long-term effect on how he or she carries out those activities. For example:

- pain or fatigue: where an impairment causes pain or fatigue in performing normal day-to-day activities the person may have the capacity to do something but suffer pain in doing so; or the impairment might make the activity more than usually fatiguing so that the person might not be able to repeat the task over a sustained period of time.

- medical advice: where a person has been advised by a medical practitioner or other health professional, as part of a treatment plan, to change, limit or refrain from a normal day-to-day activity on account of an impairment or only do it in a certain way or under certain conditions."

Importantly, para.D11 in this Guidance indicates that indirect effects of disability, such as pain or fatigue, can be classified as impairments. The Guidance also gives non-exhaustive examples of when impairments on mobility, manual dexterity, physical co-ordination, memory, the perception of physical danger, speech and hearing can give rise to interference with "day-to-day activities".

As emphasised by Wall J. in *Bruce v Chamberlain*, the claimant needs to be disadvantaged in their daily life by an impairment: it is not sufficient that they lost some life or career opportunities as a consequence of an impairment of some sort.[101]

This insistence on the impairment affecting the claimant in their quotidian life activities is reflected in how the Guidance makes clear that an individual's work is excluded from the definition of "day-to-day activities"[102]: this apparently nonsensical provision is the product of the desire not to have an individual defined as disabled just because they were unable to engage in a particular occupation or employment.[103] However, where work is the cause of an impairment which has an impact upon other day-to-day activities, or when the impairment manifests itself in the course of work as well as at other times, there is no bar upon the tribunal considering evidence of how the complainant was affected while working in determining the extent to which other activities are impaired.

Thus, in *Cruickshank v Vaw Motorcast Ltd*,[104] Altman J. held that "the Act is not restricted to the period when people who are only doing day-to-day activities; those activities are rather a 'barometer' or test of the degree of severity of the impairment".[105] Similarly, in *Law Hospital NHS Trust v Rush*,[106] the Court of Session overturned a decision by the ET which the EAT had confirmed, and which had disregarded Ms Rush's activities in work when considering the impact of her disability on her day-to-day activities. The Court of Session held that evidence of the nature of an applicant's work duties and the way they are performed, especially where they include or relate to day-to-day activities, could be relevant.

The requirement to show an impact upon day-to-day activities carries with it the risk of an excessively incremental approach being adopted, where the impact of the impairment is assessed in terms of the extent to which it affects different specific activities, rather than its overall impact upon daily life. There

101 [2004] EWCA Civ 1047.
102 See para. C3 of the *Guidance on the Definition of Disability*.
103 See "Interpreting the DDA—Part 1: The Meaning of Disability" (1998) 79 Equal Opportunities Rev. 13, 15.
104 [2002] I.R.L.R. 24; [2002] I.C.R. 729, EAT.
105 *ibid.*, at p.28.
106 [2001] I.R.L.R. 611.

is also an anger of underinclusivity, where an excessively narrow approach is taken to defining what constitutes "day-to-day activity". In *Goodwin*, Morison J. set out the approach to be adopted in determining whether a sufficient impact on daily life has taken place:

Goodwin v Patent Office [1999] I.C.R. 302

"The adverse effect condition

MORISON J.

[34] In many ways this may be the most difficult of the four conditions to judge. There are a number of general comments to be made. What the Act is concerned with is an impairment on the person's ability to carry out activities. The fact that a person can carry out such activities does not mean that his ability to carry them out has not been impaired. Thus, for example, a person may be able to cook but only with the greatest difficulty. In order to constitute an adverse effect, it is not the doing of the acts which is the focus of attention but rather the ability to do [or not do] the acts. Experience shows that disabled persons often adjust their lives and circumstances to enable them to cope for themselves. Thus, a person whose capacity to communicate through normal speech was obviously impaired might well choose, more or less voluntarily, to live on their own. If one asked such a person whether they managed to carry on their daily lives without undue problems, the answer might well be 'yes'; yet their ability to lead a 'normal' life had obviously been impaired. Such a person would be unable to communicate through speech and the ability to communicate through speech is obviously a capacity which is needed for carrying out normal day to day activities, whether at work or at home. If asked whether they could use the telephone, or ask for directions or which bus to take, the answer would be 'no'. Those might be regarded as day to day activities contemplated by the legislation and that person's ability to carry them out would clearly be regarded as adversely affected.

[35] Furthermore, disabled persons are likely, habitually, to 'play down' the effect that their disabilities have on their daily lives. If asked whether they are able to cope at home, the answer may well be 'yes', even though, on analysis, many of the ordinary day-to-day tasks were done with great difficulty due to the person's impaired ability to carry them out ... The focus of attention required by the Act is on the things that the applicant either cannot do or can only do with difficulty, rather than on the things that the person can do. The Act is looking to see whether the capacities listed in paragraph 4(1) have been affected. These capacities are those which will be required, to a greater or lesser extent, to carry out normal day-to-day activities, whether at home or at work.

[36] What is a day-to-day activity is best left unspecified: easily recognised, but defined with difficulty. What can be said is that the inquiry is not focused on a particular or special set of circumstances. Thus, it is not directed to the person's own particular circumstances either at work or home. The fact that a person cannot demonstrate a particular skill, such as playing the piano, is not an issue before the Tribunal, even if it is considering a claim by a musician. Equally, the fact that a person had arranged their home to accommodate their disability would make inquiries as to how they managed at their particular home not determinative of the issue.

[37] It will be borne in mind that the effect of a disability on a person's ability to conduct his daily life might have a cumulative effect, in the sense that more than one of the capacities had been impaired. It is not necessary for the tribunal to go further, if satisfied that one 'capacity' has been impaired, which is sufficient for the adverse effect condition to be fulfilled. Tribunals will bear in mind the provisions of paragraph 8 of Schedule 1 when considering what are described as progressive conditions.

[38] During argument an example was given of a person whose hearing was exceptionally acute. One might say that this was not likely to be regarded as a handicap to the person's ability to carry out his normal day to day activities. Certainly one might say that there was no adverse effect upon his hearing; quite the contrary. However, such a condition could well adversely affect other capacities: for example, such a person might find it impossible or difficult to cope with conversation in a group of people or to go to a busy shop or to concentrate. The condition from which he was suffering would not have a direct adverse effect on the particular capacity, but might well have an adverse effect on a different capacity."

Goodwin was a paranoid schizophrenic, who was dismissed by his employer following complaints from co-workers about his odd behaviour. The industrial tribunal decided that his day-to-day activities were not substantially affected as he could care for himself at home without assistance, get to work and carry out his normal work without assistance. However, the EAT concluded that the evidence should have lead the tribunal to the conclusion that Goodwin was unable to carry-on a normal conversation with his colleagues and this was sufficient to establish that a disability existed for the purposes of the DDA.

In *Vicary v British Telecommunications*,[107] the complainant suffered from an impairment that affected her right arm and hand, and as a result suffered pain when undertaking repetitive work, such as typing, or more physical work on a once-off basis. The EAT decided that in assessing whether "day-to-day activities" were affected, a tribunal should examine what the complainant could *not* do, rather than what he or she could do. Therefore, she was held to be disabled for the purposes of the DDA, even though she was not adversely affected in the mainstream of the activities involved in the performance of her job. It was sufficient that she could not perform certain day-to-day activities that were required to be carried out with reasonable regularity.

This purposive and broad approach adopted in *Goodwin* and *Vicary* has been subsequently applied by the EAT in a series of decisions that have attempted to steer clear of excessively narrow or incremental applications of the "day-to-day" test. For example, in *Ekpe v Commissioner of Police of the Metropolis*,[108] Mrs Ekpe was required to undertake a job involving extensive use of keyboards, and argued that she could not do this job, due to the wasting of the muscles of her right hand. The employment tribunal held that she was not disabled, as this impairment did not have a substantial adverse effect on day-to-day activities: while she could not carry heavy shopping, undertake certain domestic cleaning and cooking tasks, apply rollers to her hair or sometimes apply make-up with her dominant right hand, the tribunal considered that the latter two activities were not "day-to-day activities" for the population at large, and that as she only restricted in certain aspects of shopping and

[107] [1999] I.R.L.R. 680, EAT.

[108] [2001] I.R.L.R. 605; [2001] I.C.R. 1084, EAT. The EAT also clarified in this case that a normal "day-to-day activity" did not have to be performed by both sexes.

household tasks, the former two impediments did not sufficiently affect each particular activity in general. On appeal, the EAT reversed the decision, finding that the employment tribunal had erred by focussing on each activity, rather than making an overall assessment of the impact of the impairment upon her daily life.

Similarly, in *Leonard v South Derbyshire Chamber of Commerce*,[109] it was emphasised that satisfying the test was not a question of balancing abilities against the impairments suffered by the claimant. The EAT held that the industrial tribunal in this case had erred in contrasting the claimant's ability to eat, drink and catch a ball with their inability to negotiate pavement edges in reaching the conclusion that normal day-to-day activities were not affected. The tribunal should have just focussed upon the impact of the impairment upon the claimant's day-to-day activities.

C. *Long-term Effect*

The "adverse effect" must also be long-term, that is, to have lasted for at least 12 months, or the period that it can reasonably be expected to last is at least 12 months or the rest of the person's life (whichever is the shorter).[110] Once again, the preference for the "medical" approach is apparent: the claimant's ailment must "afflict" them for a prolonged period, which suits the medical model's underlying assumption of the "invalid" status of a disabled person. Given this approach, the issue of recurrence is particularly important in the content of this leg of the test: how often does an impairment have to recur to constitute a disability that has a long-term impact?

Schedule 1 para.2 DDA

"Long-term effects

2(1) The effect of an impairment is a long-term effect if—

(a) it has lasted at least 12 months;

(b) the period for which it lasts is likely to be at least 12 months; or

(c) it is likely to last for the rest of the life of the person affected.

(2) Where an impairment ceases to have a substantial adverse effect on a person's ability to carry out normal day-to-day activities, it is to be treated as continuing to have that effect if that effect is likely to recur.

109 [2001] I.R.L.R. 19.
110 DDA Sch.1 para.2.

DDA Guidance on the Definition of Disability 2006

Meaning of "long-term effects"

C1. **The Act states** that, for the purpose of deciding whether a person is disabled, a long-term effect of an impairment is one:

- which has lasted at least 12 months; or
- where the total period for which it lasts, from the time of the first onset, is likely to be at least 12 months; or
- which is likely to last for the rest of the life of the person affected (**Sch1, Para 2**).

For the purpose of deciding whether a person has had a disability in the past, a long-term effect of an impairment is one which has lasted at least 12 months (**Sch2, Para 5**).

Meaning of "likely"

C2. It is likely that an event will happen if it is more probable than not that it will happen.

C3. In assessing the likelihood of an effect lasting for 12 months, account should be taken of the total period for which the effect exists. This includes any time before the point at which the alleged incident of discriminatory behaviour which is being considered by the adjudicating body occurred. Account should also be taken of both the typical length of such an effect on an individual, and any relevant factors specific to this individual (for example, general state of health or age).

Recurring or fluctuating effects

C4. **The Act states** that, if an impairment has had a substantial adverse effect on a person's ability to carry out normal day-to-day activities but that effect ceases, the substantial effect is treated as continuing if it is likely to recur. In other words, it is more likely than not that the effect will recur. (In deciding whether a person has had a disability in the past, the question is whether a substantial adverse effect has in fact recurred.) Conditions with effects which recur only sporadically or for short periods can still qualify as impairments for the purposes of the Act, in respect of the meaning of "long-term" (**Sch1, Para 2(2); Sch2, Para 5**).

C5. For example, a person with rheumatoid arthritis may experience substantial adverse effects for a few weeks after the first occurrence and then have a period of remission . . . If the substantial adverse effects are likely to recur, they are to be treated as if they were continuing. If the effects are likely to recur beyond 12 months after the first occurrence, they are to be treated as long-term. Other impairments with effects which can recur, or where effects can be sporadic, include Menières disease and epilepsy as well as mental health conditions such as schizophrenia, bipolar affective disorder, and certain types of depression, though this is not an exhaustive list. It should be noted that some impairments with recurring or fluctuating effects may be less obvious in their impact on the individual concerned than is the case with other impairments where the effects are more constant.

C6. It is not necessary for the effect to be the same throughout the period which is being considered in relation to determining whether the "long-term" element of the definition is met. A person may still satisfy the long-term element of the definition even if the effect is not the same throughout the period. It may change: for example activities which are initially very difficult may become possible to a much greater extent. The effect might even disappear temporarily. Or other effects on the ability to carry out normal day-to-day activities may develop and the initial effect may disappear altogether.

C7. Regulations specifically exclude seasonal allergic rhinitis (e.g. hayfever) except where it aggravates the effects of an existing condition.

Likelihood of recurrence

C8. Likelihood of recurrence should be considered taking all the circumstances of the case into account. This should include what the person could reasonably be expected to do to prevent the recurrence. For example, the person might reasonably be expected to take action which prevents the impairment from having such effects (e.g. avoiding substances to which he or she is allergic). This may be unreasonably difficult with some substances. In addition, it is possible that the way in which a person can control or cope with the effects of an impairment may not always be successful: for example, because a routine is not followed or the person is in an unfamiliar environment. If there is an increased likelihood that the control will break down, it will be more likely that there will be a recurrence. That possibility should be taken into account when assessing the likelihood of a recurrence...

C9. If medical or other treatment is likely to permanently cure a condition and therefore remove the impairment, so that recurrence of its effects would then be unlikely even if there were no further treatment, this should be taken into consideration when looking at the likelihood of recurrence of those effects. However, if the treatment simply delays or prevents a recurrence, and a recurrence would be likely if the treatment stopped, as is the case with most medication, then the treatment is to be ignored and the effect is to be regarded as likely to recur."

The DDA does therefore recognise that impairments that are likely to recur can be deemed to have a long-term impact. In *University of Surrey v Mowat-Brown*,[111] a claimant diagnosed with multiple sclerosis had suffered from very few symptoms of this disability during the three or four years post-diagnosis: the tribunal accepted that the medical evidence established that the condition was quiescent and therefore no disability existed at that time.

There appears to be a degree of uncertainty as to the point in time at which a tribunal should assess what impact an individual's impairment has had or is having upon him or her. This is important, as it could have a substantial practical impact for claimants struggling to establish that they have suffered a long-term impact. Paragraph B8 of the Guidance suggests that tribunals should take account of the entire period where the impairment was having an effect, including time after the alleged discriminatory act. However, the DDA itself could be read as envisaging that the tribunal should consider just the circumstances leading up to and in place at the time of the alleged discriminatory act.

In *Greenwood v British Airways*,[112] the EAT applied the Guidance and concluded that the tribunal should consider the adverse effects of the complainant's condition up to and including the date of the hearing, and was not confined to assessing the "long-term" impact of the condition at the time of

[111] [2002] I.R.L.R. 235.
[112] [1999] I.C.R. 969; [1999] I.R.L.R. 600.

the alleged discriminatory act. In contrast, in *Cruickshank v Vaw Motorcast Ltd*,[113] the EAT considered that the scheme of the Act required that claims against the employer had to involve an examination of the employer's conduct at the time of the alleged discriminatory act, and therefore the impact of the impairment up to that time, and not subsequent developments. This approach, while consistent with the DDA's general structure, could permit the employer to discriminate against an individual on the basis of characteristics which at the time of the acts in question did not constitute a "disability" under the terms of the DDA, but which subsequently did have sufficient long-term impact so as to constitute a "disability". This again illustrates the problems that stem from a "medical" focus upon the condition in questions and its effect, rather than on the reaction of others, which the "social model" would place front and centre in its preferred approach.[114]

D. *"Substantial" Impact*

The final stage of the test is the requirement to show that an impact has been "substantial". This stage of the test is again intended to filter out "limited" impairments that have only a minor impact upon an individual's life and to ensure that claimants under the DDA are clearly within the protected class of disabled persons deemed to be deserving of protection. Again, this reflects the medical model's preference for seeing disability as afflicting a distinct group of individuals defined by their impairments, which are to be substantial and of long duration. The target of the Act is to protect these individuals, not so much to eliminate prejudicial barriers erected on the basis of perceived disability, which might exist even where an impairment is transient or only has minor effects. Therefore, the "substantial" requirement constitutes yet another hurdle for applicants to overcome.

Whether an impairment has had a "substantial" adverse impact is in general a question of fact, with the Guidance providing some examples, as well as emphasising that "substantial" means "more than minor or trivial".[115]

113 [2002] I.C.R. 729, [2002] I.R.L.R. 24.

114 For more discussion of this, see M. Connolly, *Townshend-Smith on Discrimination Law: Text, Cases and Materials* (2nd ed.) (London: Cavendish, 2004), pp.480–483.

115 *Guidance* Part 11, para.A1.

Guidance on the Definition of Disability 2006

"Meaning of "substantial adverse effect"

B1. The requirement that an adverse effect on normal day-to-day activities should be a substantial one reflects the general understanding of disability as a limitation going beyond the normal differences in ability which may exist among people. A substantial effect is one that is greater than the effect which would be produced by the sort of physical or mental conditions experienced by many people which have only "minor" or "trivial" effects. This section looks in more detail at what "substantial" means. It should be read in conjunction with Section D which considers what is meant by "normal day-to-day activities".

The time taken to carry out an activity

B2. The time taken by a person with an impairment to carry out a normal day-to-day activity should be considered when assessing whether the effect of that impairment is substantial. It should be compared with the time it might take a person who did not have the impairment to complete an activity.

The way in which an activity is carried out

B3. Another factor to be considered when assessing whether the effect of an impairment is substantial is the way in which a person with that impairment carries out a normal day-to-day activity. The comparison should be with the way that the person might be expected to carry out the activity if he or she did not have the impairment.

A person who has obsessive compulsive disorder follows a complicated ritual of hand washing. When preparing a simple meal, he washes his hands carefully after handling each ingredient and each utensil. A person without the disorder might wash his or her hands at appropriate points in preparing the meal, for example after handling raw meat, but would not normally do this after every stage in the process of preparation.

Cumulative effects of an impairment

B4. An impairment might not have a substantial adverse effect on a person's ability to undertake a particular day-to-day activity in isolation, but its effects on more than one activity, taken together, could result in an overall substantial adverse effect.

B5. For example, a person whose impairment causes breathing difficulties may, as a result, experience minor effects on the ability to carry out a number of activities such as getting washed and dressed, preparing a meal, or travelling on public transport. But taken together, the cumulative result would amount to a substantial adverse effect on his or her ability to carry out these normal day-to-day activities.

B6. A person may have more than one impairment, any one of which alone would not have a substantial effect. In such a case, account should be taken of whether the impairments together have a substantial effect overall on the person's ability to carry out normal day-to-day activities. For example, a minor impairment which affects physical co-ordination and an irreversible but minor injury to a leg which affects mobility, when taken together, might have a substantial effect on the person's ability to carry out certain normal day-to-day activities.

Effects of behaviour

B7. Account should be taken of how far a person can **reasonably** be expected to modify his or her behaviour to prevent or reduce the effects of an impairment on normal day-to-day activities. If a person can reasonably be expected to behave in such a way that the impairment ceases to have a substantial adverse effect on his or her ability to carry out normal day-to-day activities the person would no longer meet the definition of disability. For example, when considering modification of behaviour, it would be reasonable to expect a person who has back pain to avoid extreme activities such as parachuting. It would not be reasonable to expect him or her to give up, or modify, more normal activities that might exacerbate the symptoms; such as moderate gardening, shopping, or using public transport.

B8. Account should also be taken of where a person avoids doing things which, for example, cause pain, fatigue or substantial social embarrassment; because of a loss of energy and motivation. It would **not** be reasonable to conclude that a person who employed an avoidance strategy was not a disabled person. In determining a question as to whether a person meets the definition of disability it is important to consider the things that a person cannot do, or can only do with difficulty, rather than focussing on those things that a person can do.

B9. In some cases, people have coping strategies which cease to work in certain circumstances (for example, where someone who has dyslexia is placed under stress). If it is possible that a person's ability to manage the effects of an impairment will break down so that effects will sometimes still occur, this possibility must be taken into account when assessing the effects of the impairment...

Effects of environment

B10. Environmental conditions may exacerbate the effect of an impairment. Factors such as temperature, humidity, lighting, the time of day or night, how tired the person is, or how much stress he or she is under, may have an impact on the effects. When assessing whether adverse effects are substantial, the extent to which such environmental factors are likely to exacerbate the effects should, therefore, also be considered...

Effects of treatment

B11. The Act provides that, where an impairment is subject to treatment or correction, the impairment is to be treated as having the effect that it would have without the measures in question (Sch1, Para 6(1)). The Act states that the treatment or correction measures which are to be disregarded for these purposes include, in particular, medical treatment and the use of a prosthesis or other aid (Sch1, Para 6(2)).

B12. This provision applies even if the measures result in the effects being completely under control or not at all apparent. Where treatment is continuing it may be having the effect of masking or ameliorating a disability so that it does not have a substantial adverse effect. If the final outcome of such treatment cannot be determined or if it is known that removal of the medical treatment would result in either a relapse or a worsened condition, it would be reasonable to disregard the medical treatment in accordance with paragraph 6 of Schedule 1.

B13. For example, if a person with a hearing impairment wears a hearing aid the question as to whether his or her impairment has a substantial adverse effect is to be decided by reference to what the hearing level would be without the hearing aid. Similarly, in the case of someone with diabetes which is being controlled by medication or diet, or the case of a person with depression which is being treated by counselling, whether or not the effect is substantial should be decided by reference to what the effects of the condition would be if he or she were not taking that medication or following the required diet, or were not receiving counseling (the so-called "deduced effects").

B14. The Act states that this provision does not apply to sight impairments to the extent that they are capable of correction by spectacles or contact lenses. In other words, the only effects on the ability to carry out normal day-to-day activities which are to be considered are those which remain when spectacles or contact lenses are used (or would remain if they were used). This does not include the use of devices to correct sight which are not spectacles or contact lenses (Sch1, Para 6(3)).

B15. Account should be taken of where the effect of the continuing medical treatment is to create a permanent improvement rather than a temporary improvement. For example, a person who develops pneumonia may be admitted to hospital for treatment including a course of antibiotics. This cures the impairment and no effects remain."

Again, Morison J. in *Goodwin* set out the general approach to be adopted in determining whether an impairment has a "substantial" effect:

Goodwin v Patent Office [1999] I.C.R. 302

MORISON J:

[40] "On the assumption that the impairment and adverse effect conditions have been fulfilled, the tribunal must consider whether the adverse effect is substantial. This is a word which is potentially ambiguous. 'Substantial' might mean 'very large' or it might mean 'more than minor or trivial'. Reference to the Guide shows that the word has been used in the latter sense: see paragraph A1.

[41] The tribunal may, where the applicant still claims to be suffering from the same degree of impairment as at the time of the events complained of, take into account how the applicant appears to the tribunal to 'manage', although tribunals will be slow to regard a person's capabilities in the relatively strange adversarial environment as an entirely reliable guide to the level of ability to perform normal day-to-day activities.

[42] The tribunal will wish to examine how the applicant's abilities had actually been affected at the material time, whilst on medication, and then to address their minds to the difficult question as to the effects which they think there would have been but for the medication: the deduced effects. The question is then whether the actual and deduced effects on the applicant's abilities to carry out normal day to day activities are clearly more than trivial.

[43] In many cases, the tribunal will be able to reach a conclusion on these matters without reference to the statutory Guidance [which is there to illuminate what is not reasonably clear] see part II, paragraph A1 et seq [. . .]

[44] Although Parliament has linked the effect of medication to the 'substantial condition', as we have already said splitting the statutory words into conditions should not divert attention from the definition as a whole, and in determining whether the adverse effect condition is fulfilled the tribunal will take into account deduced effects."

This approach was applied and clarified in *Vicary v British Telecommunications*,[116] where the complainant suffered from an impairment that affected her right arm and hand, and as a result suffered pain when undertaking repetitive

[116] [1999] I.R.L.R. 680, EAT.

work, such as typing, or more physical work on a once-off basis. The EAT was of the view that "substantial" meant more than "trivial", it was for the tribunal and not expert medical witnesses to assess whether an impact was "substantial", and that as with looking at day-to-day activities, the tribunal was to examine what the complainant could not do, rather than what he or she could do. The tribunal was to determine this issue on the facts before it, and recourse to the Guidance should only occur in "marginal cases".

This was an important finding: if the EAT had adopted an approach that required tribunals to adhere closely to the wording of the Guidance, there would be a real risk that the Guidance could become a restrictive template, narrowing the definition of "substantial impact" to cases closely analogous to those set out in its text. Another important clarification was established in *M v SW School*,[117] where it was held that satisfying the test of being "substantial" did not require the claimant to show that the impairment was "significant", if the other elements of the DDA test were satisfied.

However, real problems can still arise in how the requirement to show "substantial" effect is applied, in particular in the case of mental disabilities. Firstly, there can be difficulties in establishing that some forms of mental impairment have a substantial and long-term adverse effect because the adverse effect may only be substantial for relatively short periods of time, unlike the case with many physical impairments which will rarely fluctuate over time. Mental impairments with substantial but time-limited impact will only come within the definition if it can be established that the impairment is "recurrent". The Guidance states that a substantial effect will be treated as continuing if it is more likely than not that it will recur. However, it will often be difficult to establish this clearly to the required standard of the balance of probabilities.

This means that a wide discretion will often be left to the tribunals in establishing that a "substantial" effect exists, especially in cases of mild mental illnesses, such as epilepsy, involuntary muscular movements and Tourette's Syndrome. Much will depend upon the facts of a particular case.[118] The problem is compounded by the fact that recent EAT decisions such as *Cruickshank v Vaw Motorcast Ltd* (as discussed above) have held that the correct point in time for assessing the impact of the impairment is the time of the discriminatory act, and that evidence to the effect that an impairment has in fact recurred since that date should not be taken into account. A further difficulty stems from the list of "normal day to day activities" contained in para.4 of Sch.1 of the DDA (set out above), inference with which is cited as an example of impairment. This list does not adequately cover areas of day-to-day activity where the range of effects that may accompany mental impairment are most

[117] [2004] EWHC 2586 (Admin).

[118] For example, in *Gittens v Oxford Radcliffe NHS Trust* EAT 193/99 (May 4, 2000), the EAT accepted that a nurse with bulimia had a clinically recognised medical condition but was not disabled for the purposes for the DDA, as the condition did not have a substantial effect on day-to-day activities.

pronounced. Therefore, courts and tribunals lack statutory guidance in this key area.

An amendment was introduced in the House of Lords during the passage of the Disability Discrimination Bill 2005 to make it easier for depression sufferers to establish that they suffered from a substantial and long-term disability: this provided that if a complainant had suffered from depression in the previous five years which would have had an effect on normal day-to-day activities for six months during that period, then it should be treated as likely to recur. However, the amendment did not make it into the statute book: sufferers from depression, as with others with mental disabilities, remain dependent upon the vagaries of tribunal fact-finding.

E. *Medical Treatment*

Schedule 1 para.6 of the DDA specifies that if an impairment would have had a substantial adverse affect but for corrective measures, then it is to be treated for the purposes of the DDA as if it did have that substantial impact.[119] In such cases, Morison J. in *Goodwin* suggested that tribunals should consider how a complainant's abilities had been affected at the material time, and then "deduce" the effect of medical treatment and decide would the impact of the impairment in the absence of such treatment be "more than trivial". The use of hearing aids, insulin, inhalers, anti-epilepsy medication and even counselling for mental illnesses such as depression[120] could all be examples of medical treatment whose impact should be "deduced" in determining the extent of the impact of the underlying condition. This provision is an interesting concession to "social model" thinking: it recognises that discrimination against a disabled person may exist even where medical treatment makes them more or less capable of functioning "normally".

F. *Progressive Conditions, "Severe Disfigurement" and Genetic Disorders*

Another example of a departure from a strict "medical model" approach in the DDA is its provision that a number of special conditions will automatically constitute a "disability" in certain circumstances, including progressive or asymptomatic conditions, controlled or corrected conditions, and severe dis-

[119] See *Guidance on the Definition of Disability*, B11–B15. This provision does not apply to correction of sight defects by means of spectacles or contact lenses: see Sch.1 para.6(3).

[120] See *Kapadia v Lambeth BC* [2000] I.R.L.R. 14, EAT; confirmed by the Court of Appeal [2000] I.R.L.R. 699. The EAT here rejected the argument that counselling was aimed at reducing the impact of symptoms rather than "curing" the condition, and therefore did not constitute medical treatment. See also *Abadeh v British Telecommunications Plc* [2001] I.R.L.R. 23.

figurement. Schedule I para.3 provides that a "severe disfigurement" is to be treated automatically as having a substantial adverse impact upon day-to-day activities.[121] A wide range of conditions can be covered by this term, including the possession of a club foot.[122] The inclusion of these provisions represents a nod towards the social model of disability: these conditions may not generate an actual impairment to the claimant's performance of day-to-day activities, but are often the source of external prejudice that serves to disadvantage unfairly a person suffering from these conditions.

Schedule 1 para.8 makes more limited provision for another specific situation where an impairment will be deemed automatically to have "substantial" impact:

Schedule 1, para.8

"Progressive conditions

8(1) Where—

(a) a person has a progressive condition (such as cancer, multiple sclerosis or muscular dystrophy or infection by the human immunodeficiency virus HIV infection),

(b) as a result of that condition, he has an impairment which has (or had) an effect on his ability to carry out normal day-to-day activities, but

(c) that effect is not (or was not) a substantial adverse effect, he shall be taken to have an impairment which has such a substantial adverse effect if the condition is likely to result in his having such an impairment."

This provision means that a person with a progressive condition that is likely to result in a *future* substantial impairment to the sufferer will only be treated as "disabled" for the purposes of the Act from the moment that any impairment arising from the condition has some effect on normal day-to-day activities.[123] In *Kirton v Tetrosyl*, the Court of Appeal gave this relatively narrow provision a purposive definition, finding that interference in day-to-day activities caused by remedial surgery for cancer should for the purposes of the

[121] The Guidance gives as examples of severe disfigurements "scars, birthmarks, limb or postural disfigurement or diseases of the skin", as well as providing that assessing severity will depend mainly upon the degree of disfigurement, but may also involve taking account of where the feature in question is: see B20–B21. The Regulations provide in Sch.1, para.5, that tattoos and piercings shall not be classed as severe disfigurements.

[122] *Tarling v Wisdom Toothbrushes Ltd t/a Wisdom* (1997) IDS Brief 15.

[123] See *Guidance on the Definition of Disability*, B17. In *Mowat-Brown v University of Surrey* [2002] I.R.L.R. 235, the EAT confirmed that it was for the complainant to demonstrate that the progressive condition was likely to have a substantial adverse impact upon her or his individual ability to carry out day-to-day activities: it was not enough that the condition itself was likely in general to produce substantial adverse impact upon sufferers, although medical evidence of the claimant's likely prognosis could of course be adduced as evidence.

DDA be regarded as a consequence of the cancer itself and so constituted an "impairment".[124] However, as made clear in Scott Baker L.J.'s judgment in this case, progressive conditions which have as yet *not* manifested any impairing effects will not constitute a disability for the purposes of the DDA.

This meant that until the 2005 Act, HIV positive status did *not* constitute a disability in the absence of any AIDS-related symptoms, and discrimination on the basis of other asymptomatic condition was possible, in the absence of any impact upon day-to-day activities.[125] Now Sch.1, para.6A, introduced by the 2005 Act, provides that persons with HIV, cancer and multiple sclerosis are deemed to be disabled, with the power retained for the Secretary of State to exempt certain forms of cancer from this provision via regulations.

While these provisions correct some of the more glaring gaps left in the DDA, it has left the basic structure of Sch.1, para.8 unchanged: only those asymptomatic conditions now expressly defined as disabilities for the purposes of the DDA in Sch.1(6A) are covered by the legislation. This means that, in particular, persons with latent genetic disorders are left without protection under the Act. This permits "genetic discrimination" by insurers, employers and other bodies that might choose to discriminate against a person on the basis of a real or perceived future risk of illness generated by genetic or family history factors.

This has resulted in calls for legislation prohibiting discrimination on the grounds of latent genetic disorders to be introduced. Defining what would constitute discrimination on the grounds of genetic make-up is potentially complex, as a case could be made out for a genetic "link" to virtually any characteristic, including intelligence, concentration or skill. However, the absence of protection for discrimination based on the potential that latent genetic disorders will emerge is a real problem, the importance of which may expand dramatically as knowledge of the impact of genetic factors upon health increases. Interesting issues exist as to whether this form of discrimination should be treated as a subset of disability discrimination, or as a ground in its own right.[126]

Schedule 2 of the DDA explicitly extends the protection of the legislation to fluctuating and recurring conditions, which are deemed to be continuing disabilities.[127] In addition, Sch.1, para.7 classifies automatically any person that was registered as disabled under the old quota legislation both in January 1995 (when the Bill was introduced) and in December 1996 (when the employment

124 [2003] EWCA Civ 619.

125 See the contrasting US case of *Bragdon v Abbott* 524 U.S. 624 (1998), where the US Supreme Court held that Abbott, an HIV positive dental patient, was disabled within the terms of the statute and therefore protected from disability discrimination.

126 Michael Stein and Anita Silvers, "An Equality Paradigm for Genetic Discrimination" (2002) 55 Vanderbilt L. Rev. 1341. For an argument that discrimination on the basis of genetic characteristics might be justifiable, see D. Hellman, "What Makes Genetic Discrimination Exceptional?" (2003) 29 American Journal of Law and Medicine 77.

127 See *Swift v The Chief Constable of the Wiltshire Constabulary*, EAT [2004] I.C.R. 909, EAT; [2004] I.R.L.R. 540.

provisions of the Act came into force) as disabled for the purposes of the new Act, for an initial period of three years.

G. *Past Disabilities*

Section 2 of the DDA provides that the provisions of the DDA shall apply to persons who had a disability as they apply to those who currently have a disability: in other words, the Act applies equally to past disabilities as it does to present disabilities, and can prohibit the targeting of individuals who have had a disability in the past for discriminatory treatment. The value of this section is best illustrated by the decision in *Greenwood v British Airways*,[128] where the complainant was held to have been subject to discrimination contrary to the DDA inter alia on the basis that his dismissal had been partially based upon his sickness record, which was the result of a bout of depression from which he appeared no longer to suffer from at the time of dismissal. This demonstrates how the DDA can protect against discrimination arising from the *consequences* of disability as well as discrimination arising directly from the existence of a disability. This is another nod towards the social model conception of disability, as it recognises that social practices may that disadvantage persons associated with disabilities may persist even after the medically diagnosed impairment has dissipated.

H. *Excluded Conditions*

Substance addictions and conditions with strong anti-social manifestations are excluded from the scope of protection of the DDA. These include smoking addiction, drug addiction, kleptomania, exhibitionism, voyeurism, and arsonist tendencies.[129] Tattoos and piercings are also excluded, as is hay fever. It is not altogether clear why hay fever should be classified with these other conditions as an excluded ailment. The logic underlying its exclusion is that it is too common an ailment to qualify as a special impairment worthy of qualifying for protection under the DDA. However, this means that irrational or unjustified mistreatment based upon a claimant's suffering caused by hay fever remains outside the legislation: again, the demand that an impairment be sufficiently serious to satisfy the medical model concept of a disability results in the limitation of the scope of the disability discrimination legislation.

128 [1999] I.C.R. 969; [1999] I.R.L.R. 600, EAT.
129 Disability Discrimination (Meaning of Disability) Regulations 1996, SI 1996/1455.

I. *Applying the Definition*

Determining whether an individual satisfies the definition of disability can be a difficult and complex process. Morison J. in *Goodwin v The Patent Office* suggested that tribunals should play an active role in examining the evidence to determine if the definition was satisfied:

"**[21]** The role of the Industrial Tribunal contains an inquisitorial element, as Rule 9 of their Rules of Procedure indicates ... There is a risk of a genuine 'Catch Twenty Two' situation. Some disabled persons may be unable or unwilling to accept that they suffer from any disability; indeed, it may be symptomatic of their condition that they deny it. Without the direct assistance of the tribunal at the hearing, there may be some cases where the claim has been drafted with outside assistance but which the applicant, for some reason related to his disability, is unwilling to support. Whilst we are sure that tribunals would be alert to such cases, some might feel constrained not to intervene perhaps as much as they would wish ...

[22] The tribunal should bear in mind that with social legislation of this kind, a purposive approach to construction should be adopted. The language should be construed in a way which gives effect to the stated or presumed intention of Parliament, but with due regard to the ordinary and natural meaning of the words in question ..."

However, the Court of Appeal in *McNicol v Balfour Beatty Rail Maintenance*[130] indicated that a more restrained approach was preferable: Mummery L.J. suggested that the legislation and the accompanying Guidance should be given their "ordinary" meaning and that tribunals should steer clear of "ambitious" attempts to substitute alternative wording for the statutory test. The EAT in *Rugamer v Sony Music; McNicol v Balfour Beatty Rail Maintenance*[131] similarly interpreted Morison J.'s comments as merely indicating that a tribunal should conduct hearings in a fair and balanced manner to ensure due consideration of the key issues, and suggested that a tribunal should steer clear from conducting a "free standing inquiry of its own". This reluctance to assume a more interventionist role can be problematic, especially when claimants are unrepresented or lack the ability, know-how and means to bring expert medical advice to the proceedings on their behalf.[132] In Canada, the tribunals play a much more active role in ascertaining whether a claimant does come within the definition of disability: the absence of such an approach in the UK, notwithstanding Morison J.'s comments in *Goodwin*, can in practice constitute a real problem for certain claimants.

130 [2002] EWCA Civ 1074; [2002] I.R.L.R. 711.

131 [2001] I.R.L.R. 644; I.C.R. 381, EAT.

132 It also sits uneasily with the overriding objectives of the employment tribunals, as defined in Reg.10 of the Employment Tribunals (Constitution and Rules of Procedure) Regulations 2001, of ensuring that the parties are on an equal footing and dealing with the case expeditiously and fairly.

This is one of several factors that make satisfying the definition of disability a major stumbling block to claimants. Most of the disability cases appealed to the EAT have arisen from issues relating to the definition, and as the discussion above shows, the law in this area is riddled with uncertainty, problems of definition and a general lack of clarity.[133] Sixteen per cent of employment claims under the DDA are rejected as a result of the failure of the claimant to show they are sufficiently "impaired" for the purposes of the Act: it is the most common reason for the failure of disability discrimination claims. This deters claimants,[134] and can ensure that many questionable practices are not subject to close analysis by courts and tribunals on account of a lack of clearly disabled litigants bringing cases.[135] In addition, the requirement for the individual to establish that she or he comes within this definition can expose applicants to demeaning cross-examination and significant costs in establishing the validity of their claim.[136]

These problems are not unique to the UK. In the USA, the ADA defines disability as "a physical or mental impairment that substantially limits one or more of their major life activities", and includes within its scope situations where a person is regarded as having such an impairment.[137] The argument has been made that this is a better and clearer definition than that used in the DDA, as it refers to "one or more major life activity" rather than the broader and less clear "day-to-day activities" term used in the DDA, and also explicitly covers those assumed to have such disabilities.[138] However, it still imposes a requirement on the claimant to show that they have or are perceived to have some sort of substantial impairment. This has repeatedly constituted a

[133] C. Gooding, "The Disability Discrimination Act 1995: An Overview", in J. Cooper, *Law, Rights and Disability* (London: Kingsley, 2000) 139–163.

[134] See Brian Doyle, "Reform of the Disability Discrimination Act", Working Paper 4 for the Independent Review of the Enforcement of UK Anti-Discrimination Legislation, University of Cambridge 1999: "[D]efendants in disability discrimination litigation have every strategic reason and encouragement to challenge the status of the claimant as a disabled person. This not only adds to the potential length and cost of litigation, but has a considerable psychological effect upon the willingness of a disabled person to mount or to continue litigation under the 1995 Act."

[135] See S. Leverton, *Monitoring the Disability Discrimination Act 1995 (Phase 2)* (London: Department of Work and Pensions, 2002).

[136] Increasingly it is the practice for tribunals to hear medical evidence as to whether an impairment objectively exists, although whether the impairment is substantial remains a question of fact for the tribunal alone to determine. See e.g. *Abedeh v British Telecommunications Plc* [2001] 156 I.C.R.

[137] 42 U.S.C.S. 12101(2).

[138] B. Doyle, "Employment Rights, Equal Opportunities and Disabled Persons: The Ingredients of Reform" [1993] I.L.J. 89; see also the US Supreme Court decision in *School Board of Nassau County, Florida v Arline* 480 U.S. 273 (1987): an impairment may not limit how a person performs a job, but may substantially limit that person's ability to work as a result of the negative perceptions of others.

serious obstacle to successful claims in the US case law.[139] For example, in *Sutton v United Air Lines*,[140] two very short-sighted pilots who were barred from long-haul routes were held not to have been treated as "impaired" by United Airlines, as they were permitted to fly short-haul routes and therefore were not subject to an impediment to their normal working activity.[141]

The requirement in both the US and UK legislation to show that a claimant comes within the class of disabled persons constitutes a substantial burden, and ensures that the focus is on what the applicant *cannot* do, rather than on what they *can* but are not being allowed to do.[142] Proving that the claimant is disabled can generate considerable evidential issues and complex legal questions, as the discussion above highlights.[143] The current definition can also create anomalies between individuals and groups suffering from different disabilities, or even between persons suffering from the same disability where the exact nature of the impairment in question varies.

This is the legacy of the "medical model" approach: claimants must show that they are within the "sick" class of clearly disabled persons and suffer from impairments not normally experienced by other persons before they can mount any challenge to even quite clearly problematic restrictions and barriers. This can reduce disability discrimination claims to complex and legalistic technical exercise of proof and definition.[144] Claimants who could benefit greatly from a small amount of flexibility or adjustment on the part of an employer can be denied a remedy under the DDA simply because their impairment cannot be shown to satisfy the myriad of conditions required under the DDA for it to qualify as a "disability".

The Disability Rights Commission has highlighted a number of cases as illustrating this point.[145] In *Gittins v Oxford Radcliffe NHS Trust*,[146] a nurse who

[139] See Robert C. Burgdorf, "Substantially Limited Protection from Disability Discrimination: The Special Treatment Model and Misconstructions of the Definition of Disability" (1997) 42 Villanova L. Rev. 409–536; Chai R.Feldblum, "Definition of Disability under Federal Anti-Discrimination Law: What Happened? Why? And What?" (2000) 21(1) Berkeley Journal of Employment and Labor Law 91–165; Cheryl Anderson, "'Deserving Disabilities': Why the Definition of Disability Under the Americans with Disabilities Act Should Be Revised to Eliminate the Substantial Limitation Requirement" (2000) 65 Missouri Law Review 83–150; Lisa Eichhorn, "Applying the ADA to Mitigating Measure Cases: A Choice of Statutory Evils" (2000) 31 Arizona State L.J. 1071–1120; Paula Berg, "Ill/Legal: Interrogating the Meaning and Function of the Category of Disability in Antidiscrimination Law" (1999) 18 Yale L. & Policy Rev. 1–51.

[140] 527 U.S. 471 (1999).

[141] See also *Albertson's, Inc v Kirkingburg* 527 U.S. 555 (1999); *Murphy v United Parcel Service* 527 U.S. 516 (1999)

[142] *Abedeh v British Telecommunications Plc* [2001] 156 I.C.R.

[143] See K. Wells, "The Impact of the Framework Equality Directive on UK Disability Discrimination Law" [2003] 32(4) I.L.J. 253–273, 256–257.

[144] See Jerome K. Bickenbach, "Minority Rights or Universal Participation: The Politics of Disablement" in M. Jones and L.A. Baser Marks (eds) *Disability, Divers-ability & Legal Change* (London: Martinus Nijhoff, 1999) Series: International Studies in Human Rights, Vol.56 101–116.

[145] See Disability Rights Commission, *Definition of Disability: Consultation Document* (London: DRC, 2006) paras 18–32.

[146] EAT/193/99.

was denied employment on the basis that she suffered from bulimia: however, the hospital trust did not seek to defend their decision against the charge of discrimination on the grounds of justification, which might have been hard to do, but rather successfully argued that since Mrs Gittins' condition did not impair her sufficiently for the requirements of the DDA definition of disability, she was not legally entitled to challenge their decision. In *Compton v Bolton Metropolitan BC*,[147] a man who had attempted suicide due to clinical depression, and had a job offer withdrawn as a result, was held not to be disabled because he could not establish that the substantial effects of his depression were likely to last 12 months or more. Even though the job withdrawal was directly linked to the existence of the mental impairment in question, no assessment of the legitimacy of this act could be undertaken by the tribunal in the absence of strong medical evidence of "long-term" impact.[148]

The lingering attachment to the "medical model", as discussed extensively above, has also ensured that problems exist with progressive conditions, some mental impairments and other conditions that do not come within the definition of an impairment. The 2005 Act has remedied some of the more obvious gaps, but others remain. In addition, the reluctance on the part of the UK to extend protection to those who are discriminated against on the grounds of association with a disabled person, or the perception of being disabled, can be attributed to the idea that protection under the legislation should be confined to those who are "ill" or medically classifiable as disabled. The current approach to defining disability limits the extent of protection available, distorts the central issues and generates immense complexity, costs and uncertainty, especially for those suffering from mental impairments (as discussed above).[149] Arguably, what should be the focus of disability discrimination legislation is not what impairment is at issue, but rather the reaction to a real or perceived impairment. By obscuring this question, the DDA's current approach is unsatisfactory.

Can an alternative approach be adopted? The Parliamentary Scrutiny Committee that examined the provisions of the draft Disability Discrimination Bill in 2004, has called for a review of the DDA definition to ensure that the focus is shifted from the functional limitations from which the claimant suffers to whether the external obstacles faced by the claimant arise from the existence of a real or perceived impairment on their part.[150] In other words, there have been demands for a new definition that better reflects "social model" analysis. Stein suggests that an alternative formulation is possible, that prohibits discrimination "on the basis of" a disability, a formula used in other dis-

147 Case No.2400819/00.

148 See also *Quinlan v B&Q Plc*, EAT 1386/97.

149 Jerome E. Bickenbach, *Physical Disability and Social Policy* (Toronto: University of Toronto Press, 1992); Barbara M. Altman, "Disability Definitions, Models, Classification Schemes and Applications", in Gary L. Albrecht, Katherine D. Seelman, Michael Burg (eds) *Handbook of Disability Studies* (Thousand Oaks: Sage Publications, 2001) pp.97–122.

150 See Disability Rights Commission, *Definition of Disability: Consultation Document* (London: DRC, 2006) paras 13–17.

crimination legislation.[151] Wells has similarly suggested that legislative definitions of "disability" should not describe the *group* protected under the law: they should rather define the *acts* that are prohibited by the use of a formula prohibiting unjustified discrimination which is "disability-based", or some similar form of words.[152]

Some countries have adopted legislative provisions that prohibit discrimination simply on the grounds of an "impairment", without further definition: Finland is an example. The Swedish legislation uses the term "functional limitation", to avoid language that implies lack of capacity. These forms of wording have the advantage of eliminating the need for claimants to show that an impairment is substantial, of long duration or that it affects day-to-day activities. Such a definition would be simpler to satisfy: any claimant with any level of "impairment" could receive protection from unjustified discrimination and reasonable accommodation. However, the absence of a definition might lead courts to impose a more restricted interpretation of what constitutes an "impairment" to prevent its wide scope from being potentially abused: some have argued that this concern has resulted in the narrow interpretation given to impairment by the US courts.[153]

It could therefore be better to give some indication of what constitutes an "impairment", to ensure some clarity and certainty. Degener suggests that

"[i]n order to avoid the medical/individual model of disability ... a definition should be ... related to impairment, chronic illness or malfunctions; should not be based on a certain severity of disability; [and] should cover past, present, future and imputed impairments or chronic diseases and associates."[154]

She suggests that the Irish definition of disability in s.2(1) of the Employment Equality Act 1998 could serve as a model:

[151] See Michael Stein, "The Definition of Disability in the Americans with Disabilities Act: Its Successes and Shortcomings", Proceedings of the 2005 Annual Meeting, Association of American Law Schools Joint Sections on Employment Discrimination Law, Labor Relations and Employment Law and Law, Medicine and Health, (2005) 9 Emp. Rts. & Emp. Pol'y J. 473.

[152] Katie Wells, "The Impact of the Framework Equality Directive on UK Disability Discrimination Law" (2003) 32(4) I.L.J. 253–273, 260–263.

[153] DRC, *Definition of Disability: Consultation Document*, paras 83–84.

[154] Theresia Dagener, "Definition of Disability", paper prepared for EU Network of Experts on Disability Discrimination, August 2004, p.11; see also Katie Wells, "The Impact of the Framework Equality Directive on UK Disability Discrimination Law" (2003) 32(4) I.L.J. 253–273, 260–263.

Section 2(1) Irish Employment Equality Act 1998

"disability means—

(a) the total or partial absence of a person's bodily or mental functions, including the absence of a part of a person's body

(b) the presence, in the body of organisms causing, or likely to cause, chronic disease or illness,

(c) the malfunction, malformation or disfigurement of a part of a person's body

(d) a condition or malfunction which results in a person learning differently from a person without the condition or malfunction, or

(e) a condition, illness or disease which affects a person's thought processes, perception of reality, emotions or judgement or which results in disturbed behaviour,

and shall be taken to include a disability which exists at present, or which previously existed but no longer exists, or which may exist in the future or which is imputed to a person."

Similarly, the Australian Disability Discrimination Act 1992 only requires the claimant to show the existence of an impairment to qualify as "disabled". In both countries, as in Finland and Sweden with their even more minimal definitions, the issue of whether claimants come within the definition of being "disabled" has not generated substantial litigation.[155] The advantage of this approach is that the claimant only has to show that he or she has been subject to disadvantage on the grounds that they possess or possessed a real or perceived "impairment", or are associated with an impaired person. Once this was done, the focus would be on the act of alleged discrimination and the need or otherwise for reasonable adjustment, rather than the particular characteristics of the individual.

This would correspond with other discrimination laws, which adopt a similar "on the grounds of" approach. It would also sit better with the wording of the Employment Equality Directive than does the current legislation.[156] Wells suggests that the restrictive approach of tribunals to the definition of disability under the DDA may be incompatible with the purposive approach that should be given to the Directive's provisions on disability discrimination: it may also ensure that a regular stream of cases go to the European Court of Justice challenging such restrictive definitions as contrary to the provisions of EU law.[157] The DRC has suggested that such a "social model" orientated approach could lead to a shift away from the DDA being perceived as about protecting "disabled people" to a new emphasis on the legislation

[155] See Wells, *op cit.*, 262.

[156] Richard Whittle, "The Framework Directive for Equal Treatment in Employment and Occupation: An Analysis from the Disability Rights Perspective" (2002) Employment L. Rev. 303, 323.

[157] See Wells, *op cit.*, 262.

being about preventing "disability discrimination". This could encourage "a more systemic approach to change and to the removal of barriers."[158]

As noted above, concerns exist that such a "social model" approach might diminish the credibility of disability rights, if the widened and more easily satisfied definition of impairment is abused by litigants. Courts might also react to a broader definition by closer scrutiny of whether such a disadvantage existed. There could be a loss of focus on "core" groups with particular needs. However, the DRC has suggested that a shift to the "social model definition" would still require claimants to establish that the legal "trigger" of "impairment" applied, and care would need to be taken to ensure that this trigger was appropriately worded to deter trivial claims.[159] Confining protection to those with "impairments" would also permit the current asymmetrical approach to disability discrimination to continue: only those within these group could be subject to unlawful discrimination on the grounds of their disability, so non-disabled people could not claim that positive action in favour of disabled persons was unlawful.

Hendricks has suggested abandoning the term or concept of "impairment" altogether, arguing that any attempt to define a closed class of those protected by the legislation, no matter how broad the definition and how easy to satisfy the entry criteria, will result in the difficulties of complexity and distortion that currently arise with the US, UK and many European definitions.[160] He advocates prohibiting unjustified discrimination on the basis of "capabilities", which would not require the claimant to have to shown that he or she is in some way deficient or impaired. This would have the advantage of eliminating the need to demonstrate the existence of an impairment with all the consequent difficulties of showing both that a functional limitation exists and that the claimant is still capable of performing the job in question. The potential disadvantage is that this approach could leave positive action in favour of disabled person vulnerable to potential challenge, on the basis that it was discrimination based upon "capability". As Hendricks himself notes, this approach would require a clear commitment by the legislature, courts and tribunals to an asymmetric approach to disability discrimination, which was centred on eliminating disadvantage and not on securing formal equality.

The Disability Rights Commission has made a formal recommendation to the government that the DDA definition of disability be altered to give protection from discrimination to everyone who has (or has had or is perceived to have) an impairment, and to remove any requirement that the effects of that

[158] The DRC also point out that it would correspond better with the provisions of the Special Educational Needs and Disability Act 2001, which provides entitlements to additional educational support not on the basis of the severity of impact of a child's impairment in the abstract, but on the basis of the degree of mismatch between the school and the particular child. See Disability Rights Commission, *Definition of Disability: Consultation Document*, paras 37–40.

[159] *ibid.*, para.67.

[160] Aart C. Hendriks, "Different Definition—Same Problems—One Way Out?", in: Mary Lou Breslin, Silvia Yee (eds), *Disability Rights Law and Policy: International and National Perspectives* (Ardsley: 2002) pp.195–240.

impairment have to be substantial or long-term. The DRC argue that this will have the advantage of simplifying the law and placing the emphasis on assessing the fairness of responses to disability, rather than on technical and complex debates about the definition of disability.[161]

What is clear is that there is a real need for serious consideration to be given to reviewing the current definition of disability, and for making the transition from a "medical model" approach to one based upon some sort of "social model" approach. Until this is done, the key element of disability cases will all too often remain the question of whether a person is sufficiently disabled to claim under a DDA, with all the complexity that this generates for courts, tribunals, litigants, employers, service-providers and policy-makers.

IX. The Scope of the Disability Discrimination Act

The disabled person who manages to establish that he or she comes within the existing DDA definition of disability can attempt to make out their actual discrimination claim, only if their complaint comes within the scope of the Act. When initially introduced in 1995, the DDA's scope, as with other aspects of the legislation, fell short of the race and sex discrimination legislation in several important respects. It did not apply to small employers, education, the performance of public functions, many elements of transport and other areas covered by the race and sex discrimination legislation. However, the requirements of the Employment Equality Directive 2000 and demands for greater protection by disability rights groups have resulted in a gradual extension of the scope of the Act.

Protection against disability discrimination in educational institutions was introduced in the Special Educational Needs and Disability Act in 2001. The Disability Discrimination (Employment) Regulations 2003 were passed to ensure conformity with the disability provisions of the Employment Equality. The DDA 2005 has extended the definition of disabled status to include HIV status, certain forms of cancer and previously excluded forms of mental illness, as discussed above. It also now extends protection against discrimination on ground of disability to the performance by public authorities of their public functions and widens the scope of coverage of the legislation to include clubs and local government representatives. These reforms have now given the DDA a similar scope of application to that of the race and sex discrimination legislation. However, this incremental process has also ensured that different legal standards apply in different areas. Considerable differences, for example, exist between the tests for reasonable accommodation to be applied in the contexts of employment, the provision of goods and services and the perfor-

[161] DRC, *Definition of Disability within Anti-discrimination Law—Recommendation to Government*, July 2006.

mance of public functions. Once again, complexity haunts the application of the DDA.

A. *Employment*

The DDA initially had a considerably narrower scope than the sex and race discrimination statutes in its application to employment, due to a number of prominent gaps being left in its coverage. It originally applied only to employers with 15 or more employees at the time of the alleged discriminatory act.[162] Regulation 7 of the Disability Discrimination Act (Amendment) Regulations 2003 now removes this lower limit in line with the requirements of the Employment Equality Directive,[163] as well as removing other blanket exemptions from the scope of the original legislation, such as employment on ships, planes, fire-fighters, prison officers and specialised police forces.[164]

The 2003 Regulations also plugged other gaps in the DDA. Part II of the DDA (its employment provisions) was extended to the police, barristers, advocates and their pupils,[165] partnerships,[166] qualification bodies and practical work experience.[167] The Regulations also now prohibit instructions to discriminate, pressure to discriminate, and discrimination after the employment relationship has come to an end.[168] This latter change confirmed and made explicit the interpretation of the original text of the Act by the Law Lords in *Jones v 3M Healthcare*, to the effect that the phrase "a disabled person whom he employs" in s.4(2) of the DDA extended to discrimination after the employment relationship has expired, provided that there was a substantive connection between the discriminatory conduct and the employment relationship.[169] Therefore, the *Jones* decision and now the provisions of the Regulations make it clear that victimisation after the employment relationship is terminated is covered, reversing previous case law.[170]

The scope of the DDA's provisions in respect of employment is now essentially similar to that of the SDA 75 and RRA 76. It applies across the activities encompassed by the extended definition of "employment" common to all three acts, as well as to discrimination by trade organisations, victimisation and discriminatory advertising. Section 4 of the original text of the DDA had utilised virtually equivalent wording to that contained in the SDA 75 and

162 s.7 of the DDA 1995.
163 Reg.7, repealing DDA s.7.
164 Regs 24–27.
165 Reg.8, inserting new ss.7A–7D.
166 Reg.6, inserting new ss.6A–6C.
167 Reg.13, inserting new ss.14A–14D.
168 Reg.15, inserting new s.16A.
169 See the collective appeals of *Relaxion Group Plc v Rhys-Harper, D'Souza v Lambeth LBC, Jones v 3M Healthcare Ltd* [2003] UKHL 33.
170 See *Post Office v Adekeye* [1997] I.C.R. 110, [1997] I.R.L.R. 105, CA.

RRA 76 to make discrimination in employment unlawful, including prohibiting subjecting an employee "to any other detriment" on the grounds of their disability: this meant that the SDA 75 and RRA 76 case law on harassment could be carried over to the disability context, with the result that harassment on the ground of disability could constitute unlawful discrimination. The Regulations have now introduced a new s.3B that explicitly prohibits harassment in employment that is related to the victim's disability. However, the requirement that the harassment relate to the *victim's* disability means that harassment on the ground of a family member's disability, or the mistaken belief that the victim has a disability, could remain lawful.

As made clear by s.55(3) of the Act, protection against disability discrimination extends to non-disabled persons who suffer victimisation as a consequence of a claim being brought under the DDA: this is the one element of the Act that extends protection to the non-disabled. In general, as discussed extensively above, the DDA does not prohibit discrimination on the ground of another's disability, thereby excluding those who might have carer responsibilities for disabled persons from the protection of the Act. Discrimination on the ground of perceived disability also falls outside the DDA's scope. These limitations may be incompatible with the provisions of the Employment Equality Directive: see above.

Occupational Pension Schemes and Insurance Services

Section 4G of the DDA requires trustees and managers of occupational pension schemes not to discriminate against a disabled person: any decisions relating to such schemes must therefore be made according to health, life expectancy and other factors, not according to the disabled status of the individual. Pension schemes and insurance services are now subject to the reasonable adjustment duty.[171]

B. *Goods and Services*

The DDA also applies to the provision of goods and services. Section 19 in Pt III of the DDA prohibits discrimination by a provider of services: this is defined as a person who is "concerned with the provision in the United Kingdom of services to the public or to a section of the public; and it is irrelevant whether a service is provided on payment or without payment",[172] a formulation that is very similar to the goods and services provisions of the RRA 76 and SDA 75.

Section 19(3) of the Act lists examples of services to which the sections

171 See s.4H of the DDA.
172 DDA, s.19(2).

apply, including access to and use of any place which members of the public are permitted to enter; access to and use of means of communication; access to and use of information services; accommodation in a hotel, boarding house or other similar establishment; facilities by way of banking, or insurance or for grants, loans, credit or finance; facilities for entertainment, recreation or refreshment; facilities provided by employment agencies; and the services of any profession or trade, or any local or other public authority. Discrimination by private clubs with a membership of twenty-five or more persons has also been prohibited by the 2005 Act.

Services cases, as with race and sex discrimination, are for the most part heard in the county courts, or in the sheriff courts. Due to the considerable importance of equality in services for disabled individuals, there has to be a notably greater emphasis upon service provision cases in the disability context than in other areas of discrimination law.

This is apparent both in the promotional and enforcement work of the Disability Rights Commission and in the cases that are actually brought by litigants.

A range of legislation, regulations and codes of practice have made specific provision for access requirements in the physical environment, fixing standards for public lavatories, ramps, lifts and other access tools in the public sphere.[173]

C. *Transport*

The provision of transport services is still only partially covered by the DDA, whose scope however has been considerably extended by the 2005 Act. Any services which involved "the use of a means of transport" or the provision of a vehicle were originally excluded from the DDA's scope.[174] However, transport infrastructure (such as roads, train stations and airports) was not covered by this exemption, and therefore is subject to the requirements of the DDA.[175] In *Ryanair v Ross*,[176] the provision of access to aeroplanes and the provision of services in an airport were held to be covered by the DDA and both airlines and airport authorities could be liable, whereas transport within an aeroplane would fall within the scope of the exemption. The Code of Practice similarly stated that transport in a ferry is not covered by the DDA, while service in the catering facilities of the ferry terminal would be,[177] as could assistance in a train station or the provision of booking facilities.

173 The Communications Act 2003 establishes minimum standards for proportions of programmes which should be produced with sub-titles, audio-description and sign-language interpretation.

174 s.19(5) of the DDA.

175 See the *Code of Practice on Rights of Access*, para.2.36.

176 [2004] EWCA Civ 1751.

177 See *Code of Practice on Rights of Access*, para.2.36.

Now, the 2005 Act has removed the sweeping exemption for transport providers, and replaced it with a more precise exemption exempting the provision or use of a vehicle, which is however subject to a power to remove or restrict this exemption by regulation. By Dec 2006, taxis, private hire vehicles, buses, trains and breakdown vehicles were subject to most of the DDA's key requirements, including the reasonable adjustment duty, although there is no obligation to alter the physical features of vehicles subject to the Act, except in limited circumstances.[178] However, Pt V of the DDA permits regulations to be introduced to set minimum access standards and disability-friendly operational requirements for buses, trams and trains.[179] These provisions permit the relevant Minister to ensure that transport systems are modernised, and that suitable provision is made for disabled persons. Aircraft and sea-going vessels are still exempted from the DDA's requirements. A voluntary code of practice exists for the aviation industry,[180] but the DRC has argued that this code is not working for disabled persons, citing the fact that a third of calls to its helpline concern access to flights: it has called for the government to extend the DDA to apply to aircraft.[181] EU regulations adopted in June 2006 impose certain accessibility and assistance requirements upon airlines in respect of air passengers with reduced mobility (a narrower category than the DDA definition of disability).[182]

D. *Education*

The provision of education services was originally excluded from the scope of the DDA: Pt IV of the Act only required schools and institutes of further and higher education to publish their policies on educating disabled persons.[183]

[178] See the Disability Discrimination (Transport Vehicles) Regulations 2005. The DRC has now published a new Code of Practice relating to the transport provisions of the DDA: see DRC, *Supplement to Part 3 Code of Practice; Provision and Use of Transport Vehicles* (London: DRC, 2006).

[179] Regulations governing access standards have applied to certain types of buses and coaches since the end of 2000: see SI 2000/1970, amended by SI 2000/3318. Access standards for rail vehicles entering into use from January 1, 1999 have been introduced: see SI 1998/2456. Since April 2001, s.37 of the DDA makes it illegal for licensed taxis to refuse to carry or impose an extra charge on a disabled person accompanied by a guide dog or human guide: see also SI 2000/2989. See also the provisions of SI 2000/3215, SI 2000/2990.

[180] See Department for Transport, *Access to Air Travel for Disabled People—Code of Practice* (London: DoT, 2005).

[181] See DRC, "DRC says voluntary airline code not working", press release, July 4, 2006, available at *http://www.drc-gb.org/newsroom/news_releases/2006/airline_code_2006.aspx* (last accessed August 20, 2006).

[182] PE-CONS 3681/05, 8510/06 ADD1. Under the regulation, a reservation or boarding can only be refused for justified safety requirements or if, due to the size of the aircraft or its doors, the embarkation or carriage of a disabled person or person with reduced mobility is physically impossible. In the event of refusal to accept a reservation or a refuse to baord, the person concerned should be offered an acceptable alternative, including a right to reimbursement or re-routing.

[183] See original Pt IV DDA 1995 ss.29 and 30.

These provisions have now been replaced by the extensive obligations and provisions protecting individual educational rights introduced by the Special Educational Needs and Disability Act ("SENDA") 2001, which amended Pt IV of the DDA. New sections 28A–28Q of the DDA now prohibit less favourable treatment of disabled school pupils, and require schools to take reasonable steps to make sure that disabled pupils are not placed at a "substantial disadvantage" when compared to non-disabled pupils. This duty is the equivalent of a reasonable accommodation anticipatory duty: see below. It is open to schools to justify their actions but their justification must again be material and substantial. Sections 28R to 28V make similar provisions for students over 16.

A special enforcement procedure was established by SENDA for parents of school pupils to challenge failures to implement the SENDA requirements, involving Special Educational Needs and Disability Tribunals in England and Wales, and the sheriff court in Scotland. Codes of Practice relating to both schools and post-16 providers have been published by the DRC. The Code for schools gives the following examples of less favourable treatment and justification:

> "1. A disabled boy is admitted to a secondary school. The school wants him to have all his lessons in a separate room in case other children are frightened by his muscle spasms and involuntary noises. This may be deemed less favourable treatment for a reason related to his disability and may be against the law.
>
> 2. A pupil with cerebral palsy who uses a wheelchair is on a trip with her school to an outdoor centre. The teachers arrange for the schoolchildren to go on a 12-mile hike over difficult terrain, but having carried out a risk assessment, they decide that the disabled pupil can't go on the hike for health and safety reasons. In this case, the school may be able to justify the less favourable treatment."[184]

The Code also provides the following examples of failure to take reasonable steps to prevent students being subject to substantial disadvantage:

- "A secondary school does not make special arrangements for disabled pupils who are taking public exams
- A deaf pupil who lip-reads is at a disadvantage because teachers continue speaking while facing away from him to write on a whiteboard
- A pupil with severe dyslexia is told she cannot have her teacher's lesson notes, and that she should be taking notes during lessons 'like everyone else'."[185]

Schools are not obliged to provide "auxiliary aids or services" under the DDA, as other service providers are required to do under Pt III of the Act. This is because the Special Educational Needs (SEN) framework is supposed to regulate the provision of such aid. Schools are also not obliged to make reasonable adjustments to buildings and the physical environment, or to remove or alter physical features. However, some physical alterations can be required by

[184] Disability Rights Commission, Code of Practice for Schools.
[185] *ibid.*

the longer-term planning duties imposed upon local authorities and schools by s.28D. These duties require the preparation of schemes addressing how the issues of improved access to the curriculum, physical improvements to increase access to education and improved information in a range of formats for disabled pupils are to be addressed. No mechanism is provided for enforcing these duties, which are to be monitored by the school inspectorates.

From September 2003, providers of education to over-16 year olds, unlike schools, have been required to provide "auxiliary aids and services". These may include the provision of information in alternative formats, such as sign language interpreters and Braille. From September 2005, such post-16 education providers have been obliged to make reasonable adjustments to remove barriers to physical access: no defence of reasonable justification exists in this area. Vocational education is treated as an adjunct of employment for the provisions of the Employment Equality Directive, and is subject to the employment provisions of the Directive and the DDA.[186]

E. *Housing*

The sale, rental and management of premises are covered by separate and more restricted provisions of the DDA than other forms of service provision. Sections 22–24 of the DDA originally prohibited less favourable treatment in housing, but did not require reasonable adjustments of any form. This meant that landlords could refuse to adapt or grant permission for the alteration of their flats or houses, and even refuse permission for tenants to have guide-dogs. The 2005 Act now imposes a duty upon landlords and leaseholders to make reasonable adjustments to their rental policies, practices and procedures, and to provide auxiliary aids and services, as well as being required to make reasonable accommodation to ensure that disabled people can rent and enjoy premises and related facilities.[187] Section 24(3) of the DDA makes special provision for the use of a justification defence in this context (see below). A small dwellings exception similar to that in the SDA 75 exists: the 2005 Act permits this to be modified or removed by statutory instrument. In *Manchester CC v Romano & Samari*,[188] the Court of Appeal held that evicting a person on the grounds of behaviour caused by mental health problems could constitute less favourable treatment for a disability-related reason under Pt 3 of the DDA: where this is the case, the treatment in question will need to be justified, for example, on health and safety grounds.

[186] See the Disability Discrimination Act 1995 (Amendment) (Further and Higher Education) Regulations 2006.

[187] Some ambiguity remains about whether this duty extends to common areas of rented buildings: for the pre-2005 Act absence of coverage of common parts: see *Richmond Court (Swansea) Ltd v Williams* [2006] EWCA Civ 1719.

[188] [2004] EWCA Civ 834.

F. *Public Functions*

The DDA originally contained no express provision extending protection against less favourable treatment to the performance by public authorities of their public functions. By analogy with the similar lack of such provisions in the SDA, which was interpreted by the House of Lords in *Amin v Entry Clearance Officer Bombay*[189] as thereby not extending to the performance of public functions, this meant that the decisions of public authorities in many core areas of public sector activity were exempt from any possibility of challenge on disability discrimination grounds. This omission has however been rectified in the 2005 Act.[190] This legislation also imposes a positive duty to eliminate unlawful discrimination and to promote equality of opportunity upon bodies performing public functions (see below).

G. *Territorial Application*

Unlike the other anti-discrimination legislation, the 1995 Act applies directly in Northern Ireland.[191] However, the 2005 Act does not: however, many of its main provisions, such as the prohibition on discrimination by public authorities and the introduction of a positive duty to promote equality were already put into place by the Northern Ireland Act 1998.

X. Direct Discrimination and "less favourable treatment"

Within its scope, the DDA prohibits direct discrimination on the grounds of a person's disability in *employment* only, but also prohibits "less favourable treatment" on the grounds of a person's disability in employment, access to goods and services and the performance of public functions, unless it can be

189 [1983] 2 A.C. 518 (HL). Despite a strong dissent from Lord Scarman, the majority in *Amin* recognised a distinction between the provision by public authorities of goods and services analogous to those provided by private bodies, and the performance of public functions. As the legislation did not specifically apply to this latter type of activity, the Law Lords held that public authorities were not bound by anti-discrimination legislation when performing public functions. See C. O'Cinneide, "The Race Relations (Amendment) Act 2000" [2001] P.L. 221.

190 s.2 of the 2005 Act. However, a blanket exception for acts done in the name of national security remains. See s.59 DDA. For an example of how this could impact upon decisions by public bodies, see the Australian case of *Waters v Public Transport Corporation* (1992) 173 C.L.R. 349, where the Victorian government was to introduce a new public transport ticketing system whereby plastic coatings on tickets were to be scratched off by the passenger for each section travelled. This was held to indirectly discriminate against persons with physical, intellectual and psychiatric disabilities.

191 s.70(6) of the DDA 1995.

justified. This justification exception, coupled with the absence of a ban on indirect discrimination and the distinction made in the employment context between direct discrimination and "less favourable treatment", means that the DDA varies considerably from the SDA and RRA.

A. *Employment*

Section 5(1) of the DDA originally prohibited less favourable treatment of a disabled person in employment for a reason related to that person's disability, if this treatment could not be justified. This provision has now been altered in certain important respects by the 2003 Regulations, but an analysis of the original provisions of the DDA is essential for understanding the case law since the Act came into force in 1996.

Previous Section 5(1) of the DDA

"(1) For the purposes of this Part, an employer discriminates against the disabled person if—

(a) for a reason which relates to the disabled person's disability, he treats him less favourably than he treats or would treat others for whom that reason does not or would not apply; and

(b) he cannot show that the treatment in question is justified.

(2) For the purposes of this Part an employer also discriminates against a disabled person if—

(a) he fails to comply with a section 6 duty imposed on him in relation to the disabled person; and

(b) he cannot show that his failure to comply with that duty is justified.

(3) Subject to sub-section (5), for the purposes of sub-section (1) treatment is justified if, but only if, the reason for it is both material to the circumstances of the particular case and substantial.

(4) For the purposes of sub-section (2), failure to comply with a section 6 duty is justified if, but only if, the reason for the failure is both material to the circumstances of the particular case and substantial.

(5) If, in a case falling within sub-section (1), the employer is under a section 6 duty in relation to the disabled person but fails without justification to comply with that duty, his treatment of that person cannot be justified under sub-section (3) unless it would have been justified even if he had complied with the section 6 duty."

This prohibition differed considerably in several respects from the discrimination provisions contained in other anti-discrimination legislation. It prohibits less favourable treatment of a *disabled person*, not less favourable treatment on the grounds of disability. This means that non-disabled persons cannot be victims and therefore cannot bring cases under the legislation, as discussed above. The DDA therefore adopts an asymmetrical model: its provisions are designed to combat disadvantage faced by the disabled, not to minimise the use of distinctions based upon disabled status.

As a result, positive action in favour of disabled persons, including preferential treatment measures such as quotas, set-aside places and special training, is entirely permissible under the DDA.[192] However, some ambiguity exists: positive action which could be interpreted as treating other disabled persons less favourably could still be vulnerable to challenge. If this is the case, this could prove problematic and limiting in some instances. A case perhaps exists for the insertion into the DDA of a broader positive action provision similar to that contained in Art.7(1) of the Directive, which would permit positive action directed towards particular and specific disabled groups, and Art.7(2), which would permit the introduction of special measures to promote the integration of particular persons into the workforce. This would ensure greater flexibility in the design of positive action measures, and reduce any lingering uncertainty as to when measures can be targeted at particular disabled groups rather than at the disabled in general.[193]

Another very significant difference between the original text of the DDA and the approach taken in other anti-discrimination legislation is that less favourable treatment of a disabled person that was related to her or his disability, even when it took the form of direct discrimination against the disabled, could be justified. This provision was inserted to permit employers to justify discriminatory treatment of disabled individuals on the grounds of impracticability, the nature of the occupation in question, cost or other factors. Any such justification was required by s.5(3) to be "both material to the circumstances of the particular case and substantial". (See below for an analysis of this test.)

The position has now been significantly altered by the 2003 Regulations. Original s.5 has been replaced by a new s.3A.[194]

[192] Note that a failure to provide preferential treatment for a disabled person would not constitute "less favourable treatment", unless it constituted a reasonable adjustment: see *Burns v South Yorkshire Pensions Authority*, EAT, April 26, 2005, UKEAT/0004/05/MAA, where a failure by an employer's operating manager to provide extra assistance to a disabled applicant when he called to the employer's office was held not to constitute "less favourable treatment".

[193] s.10(2) protects organisations that provide "supported employment" for particular groups of disabled persons, such as workshops for the blind or for those with particular mental impairments. Section 10(3) defines "supported employment" by reference to where facilities are provided or payments made under s.15 of the Disabled Persons (Employment) Act 1944.

[194] See reg.4.

Section 3A of the DDA

"3A Meaning of "discrimination"

(1) For the purposes of this Part, a person discriminates against a disabled person if—

(a) for a reason which relates to the disabled person's disability, he treats him less favourably than he treats or would treat others to whom that reason does not or would not apply, and

(b) he cannot show that the treatment in question is justified.

(2) For the purposes of this Part, a person also discriminates against a disabled person if he fails to comply with a duty to make reasonable adjustments imposed on him in relation to the disabled person.

(3) Treatment is justified for the purposes of subsection (1)(b) if, but only if, the reason for it is both material to the circumstances of the particular case and substantial.

(4) But treatment of a disabled person cannot be justified under subsection (3) if it amounts to direct discrimination falling within subsection (5).

(5) A person directly discriminates against a disabled person if, on the ground of the disabled person's disability, he treats the disabled person less favourably than he treats or would treat a person not having that particular disability whose relevant circumstances, including his abilities, are the same as, or not materially different from, those of the disabled person.

(6) If, in a case falling within subsection (1), a person is under a duty to make reasonable adjustments in relation to a disabled person but fails to comply with that duty, his treatment of that person cannot be justified under subsection (3) unless it would have been justified even if he had complied with that duty."

This new section retains the prohibition on less favourable treatment and the justification defence established by the original text of the DDA. However, in line with the requirements of Art.2 of the Directive, s.3A(5) now provides that direct discrimination *on the ground of a disabled person's disability* cannot be justified. This means that direct discrimination in the employment and occupation context against a person with a disability on the grounds of that disability, such as the denial of a post to a blind person solely due to her or his blindness, is unlawful and cannot be justified.[195]

The crucial distinction is that the prohibition on direct discrimination only extends to action taken directly on the ground of a person's disability, where the disabled person is treated less well than another person who is not so disabled and whose inherent *abilities* are the same as or not materially different from the disabled person. This should be distinguished from less favourable treatment that is *related to* a person's disability, but which is based upon the *consequences or impact upon an individual's abilities* of the disability in question.[196] This form of less favourable treatment remains subject to the original

[195] See *Tudor v Spen Corner Veterinary Centre Ltd*, ET Case No.2404211/05.

[196] "Unconscious discrimination" against a person with a disability is covered by the prohibition on "less favourable treatment": see *Williams v YKK (UK) Ltd* [2003] All E.R. (D) 141, EAT.

requirements of the DDA. It therefore can be justified if it is material to the circumstances of the individual case and substantial.

Unlike other anti-discrimination measures, the DDA does not prohibit indirect discrimination. The White Paper which preceded the introduction of the DDA in 1995 stated that a "general prohibition on indirect discrimination ... could have unforeseen consequences which were mainly unfairly burdensome for business".[197] This caution can be criticised: why should disability discrimination legislation alone among anti-discrimination legislation not ban unjustified indirect discrimination?

However, the scope of the DDA's prohibition on less favourable treatment on grounds related to a person's disability may be sufficiently wide to cover certain types of indirect discrimination. Practices that are applied in a neutral manner to everyone, but which negatively impact upon a disabled person for a reason that is linked to her or his disability, will come within the scope of the DDA, and require justification. During the passage of the DDA through Parliament in 1995, the sponsoring Minister accepted this, noting that:

> "The Bill is drafted in such a way that indirect as well as direct discrimination can be dealt with ... A situation where dogs were not admitted to a café, with the effect that blind people would be unable to enter it, would be a *prima facie* case of indirect discrimination against blind people and would be unlawful."[198]

However, the extent to which the "related to" test does overlap with the indirect discrimination approach adopted in other legislation remains uncertain, due to a lack of clarity as to the full extent of its reach. A purposive or wide-ranging interpretation of this test could cover a considerable amount of ground, potentially including within its scope means-test related charges,[199] educational qualification requirements and other "neutral" requirements that often disadvantage disabled persons. Alternatively, a narrower interpretation of "related to" that looks for a distinct, strong and well-defined causal link between the disability in question and the disadvantage suffered may substantially narrow the scope of the test. This could reduce its ability to fulfil the role that the indirect discrimination test plays in other anti-discrimination contexts. It remains to be seen which approach will predominate.

It should also be noted that the requirement to make reasonable accommodation for disabled persons imposed by s.6 of the DDA (see below) also plays a substantial role in filling the gap left by the exclusion of any prohibition on indirect discrimination. Often complying with the reasonable

197 *Ending Discrimination Against Disabled People*, Cmnd. 2729 (London: HMSO, 1995) para.4.5. Similar concerns about the potential unforeseen impact of a ban on indirect discrimination were also expressed in the preceding Green Paper, *A Consultation on Government Measures to Tackle Discrimination Against Disabled Persons* (London: Disability Unit, Department of Social Security, 1994) para.4.11.

198 253 HC Reports (6th Series) Col.150, January 24, 1995.

199 See the arguments made by counsel for the complainant in *R v Powys CC, Ex p. Hambridge (No.2)* [2000] 2 F.C.R. 69, which however were rejected in this instance by the court.

accommodation requirement will require the removal of obstacles and the alteration of practices generally applied by an employer in order to accommodate a disabled individual.

As discussed above, Art.2 of the Directive provides that indirect discrimination on the ground of disability should be prohibited, but permits Member States to use reasonable accommodation requirements as a substitute legal mechanism for the conventional route of a ban on unjustified indirect discrimination.[200] The UK has taken advantage of this provision in implementing the Directive, and did not introduce a ban on indirect discrimination in the 2003 Regulations on the basis that the DDA's prohibition on "less favourable treatment" and its reasonable accommodation provisions taken together constituted a perfectly adequate functional substitute.

However, as the reasonable accommodation requirement is only triggered when an employer knew or should have known of an individual employee's difficulties, and imposes no requirement to remove practices that have an indirectly discriminatory impact upon disabled persons but just to accommodate individuals as an exception to these practices, it is very questionable whether the approach of using reasonable accommodation as a substitute for a ban on indirect discrimination is entirely satisfactory (see below).[201] Combined with the uncertain scope of the "related to" test, a case exists for a ban on indirect disability discrimination to be introduced.

B. *Goods and Services*

A similar prohibition on less favourable treatment on grounds related to a person's disability is imposed upon goods and service providers by s.19 of the DDA. However, the prohibition on direct discrimination introduced in the employment and occupation context by the 2003 Regulations does not apply, as service provision is not subject to the Employment Equality Directive.

Section 19 of the DDA

"Discrimination in relation to goods, facilities and services

(1) It is unlawful for a provider of services to discriminate against a disabled person—

[200] See Art.2(2)(b)(ii).

[201] See the discussion in Whittle, "The Framework Directive for Equal Treatment in Employment and Occupation: An Analysis from the Disability Rights Perspective" (2002) Employment L. Rev. 303.

(a) in refusing to provide, or deliberately not providing, to the disabled person any service which he provides, or is prepared to provide, to members of the public;

(b) in failing to comply with any duty imposed on him by section 21 in circumstances in which the effect of that failure is to make it impossible or unreasonably difficult for the disabled person to make use of any such service;

(c) in the standard of service which he provides to the disabled person or the manner in which he provides it to him; or

(d) in the terms on which he provides a service to the disabled person.

(2) For the purposes of this section and sections 20 and 21 to 21ZA

(a) the provision of services includes the provision of any goods or facilities;

(b) a person is 'a provider of services' if he is concerned with the provision, in the United Kingdom, of services to the public or to a section of the public; and

(c) it is irrelevant whether a service is provided on payment or without payment.

(3) The following are examples of services to which this section and sections 20 and 21 apply—

(a) access to and use of any place which members of the public are permitted to enter;

(b) access to and use of means of communication;

(c) access to and use of information services;

(d) accommodation in a hotel, boarding house or other similar establishment;

(e) facilities by way of banking or insurance or for grants, loans, credit or finance;

(f) facilities for entertainment, recreation or refreshment;

(g) facilities provided by employment agencies or under section 2 of the Employment and Training Act 1973;

(h) the services of any profession or trade, or any local or other public authority."

Section 20 of the DDA

"20 Meaning of 'discrimination'

(1) For the purposes of section 19, a provider of services discriminates against a disabled person if—

(a) for a reason which relates to the disabled person's disability, he treats him less favourably than he treats or would treat others to whom that reason does not or would not apply; and

(b) he cannot show that the treatment in question is justified."[202]

[202] See the *Code of Practice (Revised): Rights of Access to Goods, Facilities and Premises*, paras 9.35–9.37 for practical examples of the application of each of these conditions.

All forms of less favourable treatment in service provision can be justified (for the operation of the justification defence in the context of goods and services, see below). Section 19 covers less favourable treatment in the manner, terms and standard of how services are delivered, as well as the refusal of treatment.[203]

XI. The Comparator Test in the Context of Disability

In determining whether a disabled person has been subject to direct discrimination on the ground of their disability contrary to s.3A(2) of the DDA, the standard comparator approach used in other discrimination contexts will be applied: the applicant must show that they have been treated less favourably on the grounds of their disability than a comparator (real or hypothetical) in similar circumstances.[204]

However, in contrast, in applying the prohibition in s.3A(1) on less favourable treatment on the ground of disability, the DDA provides for a radically different approach to determining when less favourable treatment has occurred. In particular, the requirement to show the existence of a comparator in similar circumstances but who did not suffer the less favourable treatment in question, which has constantly bedevilled much of discrimination law, is not applied in these "less favourable treatment" cases (or, as will be discussed later, in determining whether "reasonable accommodation" is required).

The leading case of *Clark v TGD Ltd t/a Novacold*[205] established that in determining when a disabled person has been subjected to less favourable treatment, the appropriate comparator is not a person in a materially similar situation as the complainant, but rather other persons to whom the reason for the treatment in question (i.e. the disability in question) would not apply. In other words, to determine whether less favourable treatment has taken place, it is possible to compare the employer's treatment of the disabled person with that of a person to whom the disability-related reason does not apply: this contrasts with direct discrimination, where it is required that a comparison to be made with a person without the disability in question but who is subject to the same relevant circumstances. In simple terms, there is no need for a dis-

[203] The Code of Practice notes that bad treatment is not necessarily the same as less favourable treatment, "although, where the service provider acts unfairly or inflexibly, a court might draw inferences that discrimination had occurred": see *Code of Practice (Revised): Rights of Access to Goods, Facilities and Premises*, para.3.5. It also notes that there is no obligation to stock special products for disabled persons to avoid providing a worse standard of service, although as a matter of good practice it might consider so doing: however, if a provider takes orders from other customers for special products, the same treatment should be accorded to disabled persons. See para.3.21.

[204] See the *Employment Code of Practice*, para.4.13–4.18.

[205] [1999] I.C.R. 951; [1999] I.R.L.R. 318.

abled person to find a comparator who is subject to the same or similar impairments as the disabled person but who is treated differently to show that he or she has suffered less favourable treatment: the disabled person need only compare their treatment to that accorded to non-disabled people, which greatly simplifies and clarifies the operation of the legislation.

In *Clark*, the complainant suffered a back injury at work in August 1996 and was diagnosed as having soft tissue damage around his spine. He was unable to work from September 1996 to January 1997, when he was dismissed. The defendants argued that any person unable to work that long would have been dismissed, and so the complainant had not been subject to any less favourable treatment. Mummery L.J. in the Court of Appeal, with whom Roch and Beldam L.JJ. agreed, rejected this argument. The Court held that where an employee was dismissed for sickness absence arising from his disability, in considering whether or not there had been less favourable treatment the comparison should have been made with the treatment of a person who is not absent from work, and who thus would not have been dismissed, instead of a person who is absent but does not have a disability.

Mummery L.J.'s very significant judgment is worth quoting at length:

Clark v TGD Ltd t/a Novacold [1999] I.C.R. 951

MUMMERY L.J.

"**[2]** Leading Counsel for the appellant described it as a 'revolutionary Act' aimed at the integration of disabled people into society and, in particular, into the country's workforce. It is certainly more ambitious in its aim and scope than the system of registered disabled persons and quotas in the Disabled Persons (Employment) Act 1944, now repealed. And it is without doubt an unusually complex piece of legislation which poses novel questions of interpretation. It is not surprising that different conclusions have been reached at different levels of decision.

[3] This state of affairs should not to be taken as a criticism of the Act or of its drafting or of the judicial disagreements about its interpretation. The whole subject presents unique challenges to legislators and to tribunals and courts, as well as to those responsible for the day to day operation of the Act in the workplace. Anyone who thinks that there is an easy way of achieving a sensible, workable and fair balance between the different interests of disabled persons, of employers and of able bodied workers, in harmony with the wider public interests in an economically efficient workforce, in access to employment, in equal treatment of workers and in standards of fairness at work, has probably not given much serious thought to the problem.

[59] In the historical context of discrimination legislation it is natural to do what the Industrial Tribunal and the Appeal Tribunal (though 'without great confidence') did, namely to interpret the expression 'that reason' so as to achieve a situation in which a comparison is made of the case of the disabled person with that of an able-bodied person and the comparison is such that the relevant circumstances in the one case are the same, or not materially different, in the other case. This might be reasonably considered to be the obvious way of determining whether a disabled person has been treated less favourably than a person who is not disabled.

[60] But, as already indicated, the 1995 Act adopts a significantly different approach to the protection of disabled persons against less favourable treatment in employment. The definition of discrimination in the 1995 Act does not contain an express provision requiring a comparison of the cases of different persons in the same, or not materially different, circumstances. The statutory focus is narrower: it is on the 'reason' for the treatment of the disabled employee and the comparison to be made is with the treatment of 'others to whom that reason does not or would not apply.' The 'others' with whom comparison is to be made are not specifically required to be in the same, or not materially different, circumstances: they only have to be persons 'to whom that reason does not or would not apply' . . .

[62] The result of this approach is that the reason would not apply to others even if their circumstances are different from those of the disabled person. The persons who are performing the main functions of their jobs are 'others' to whom the reason for dismissal of the disabled person (i.e. inability to perform those functions) would not apply.

[63] In the context of the special sense in which 'discrimination' is defined in section 5 of the 1995 Act it is more probable that Parliament meant 'that reason' to refer only to the facts constituting the reason for the treatment, and not to include within that reason the added requirement of a causal link with disability: that is more properly regarded as the cause of the reason for the treatment than as in itself a reason for the treatment. This interpretation avoids the difficulties which would be encountered in many cases in seeking to identify what the Appeal Tribunal referred to as 'the characteristics of the hypothetical comparator'. It would avoid the kind of problems which the English (and Scottish) courts and the tribunals encountered in their futile attempts to find and identify the characteristics of a hypothetical non-pregnant male comparator for a pregnant woman in sex discrimination cases before the decision of the European Court of Justice in *Webb v Emo Air Cargo (UK) Ltd*: see *Webb* (No 2) [1995] 1 WLR 1454 [. . .].

[89] In brief the legal position is that

(1) Less favourable treatment of a disabled person is only discriminatory under section 5(1) if it is unjustified.

[90]

(2) Treatment is less favourable if the reason for it does not or would not apply to others.

[91]

(3) In deciding whether that reason does not or would not apply to others, it is not appropriate to make a comparison of the cases in the same way as in the 1975 and the 1976 Acts. It is simply a case of identifying others to whom the reason for the treatment does not or would not apply. The test of less favourable treatment is based on the reason for the treatment of the disabled person and not on the fact of his disability. It does not turn on a like-for-like comparison of the treatment of the disabled person and of others in similar circumstances . . ."

Mummery L.J. also suggests that:

"**[30]** Contrary to what might be reasonably assumed, the exercise of interpretation is not facilitated by familiarity with the pre-existing legislation prohibiting discrimination in the field of employment (and elsewhere) on the ground of sex (Sex Discrimination Act 1975) and race (Race Relations Act 1976). Indeed, it may be positively misleading to approach the 1995 Act with assumptions and concepts familiar from experience of the workings of the 1975 Act and the 1976 Act."

The decision in *Clark* is important because it established that the test to determine whether less favourable treatment has occurred involves an analysis of the precise reason for the treatment suffered by the claimant. Evidence of how other persons lacking the claimant's particular disability have been treated may be relevant to determining whether a claimant's treatment was based upon their disability. However, a claimant is not required to point as a legal requirement to a comparator in a similar position who has not been subject to similar treatment.

This is a sensible approach. Identifying a comparator in a similar situation as the disabled claimant could be very difficult, and a requirement to unearth one would add layers of complexity to the test. The *Clark* test simply focuses instead on establishing whether the complainant has been subject to a disadvantage linked to their disability, with comparison with persons not having a similar condition used to establish whether less favourable treatment has actually occurred. The comparator requirement generates complex and messy difficulties of proof, and often operates to blunt the impact of discrimination law without having any real basis in firm principle. Its absence from the DDA case-law is not to be lamented.[206]

The approach set out in *Clark* was extended to goods and services cases in *White v Clitheroe Royal Grammar School*[207] and in *Glover v Lawford*.[208] In *Glover*, a café denied access to a disabled person with a guide dog on the basis that it operated a "no dogs in the eating area" policy. The District Judge held that there had been less favourable treatment, on the basis that "imposing a condition on entry which self-evidently was not applied to any person wishing to use the café without a guide dog ... must amount to less favourable treatment."[209] There was no requirement to show that a person in a similar position of being accompanied by a dog would have been treated differently: the treatment here stemmed directly from the claimant's disability.

In determining whether less favourable treatment stemmed from the fact of a claimant's disability, in *Cosgrove v Caesar and Howie*[210] the President of the EAT indicated that tribunals should ask the following questions:

[206] See Sandra Fredman, "Disability Equality: A Challenge the Existing Anti-Discrimination Paradigm?", in A. Lawson and C. Gooding, *Disability Rights in Europe* (Oxford: Hart, 2005) 199–218. Contrast the approach of the Australian High Court in *Purvis v New South Wales (Department of Education and Training))* [2003] H.C.A. 62, where the court held that the relevant comparator was a person who does not have the disability but who exhibits the same behaviour. This decision has limited the scope of protection by anti-discrimination legislation, in particular with regard to disabilities which cause aberrations in behaviour such as psychiatric illness, as it makes it difficult for a disabled person to show that they were subject to less favourable treatment on the ground of their disability when compared to others exhibiting the same behaviour.

[207] Preston County Court, Claim No.BB002640.

[208] Manchester Crown Court, Claim No.MA26303.

[209] In *McAuley Catholic High School v CC* [2003] EWHC 3045 (Admin), this approach was also extended to education cases under the new SENDA legislation.

[210] [2001] I.R.L.R. 653.

a) what was the "material reason" for the treatment?

b) was the material reason one related to the applicant's disability?

c) would the employer have dismissed another person to whom that reason did not apply?

Once again, it is worth emphasising that the third question is not a requirement for a comparator in the traditional anti-discrimination sense: it is just a requirement for some evidence that the treatment was linked to the claimant's disability.

Knowledge of the existence of the disability on the part of the employer is not required to make a finding that less favourable treatment existed: an objective standard will be applied, as made clear by Lindsay L.J. in *Heinz v Kendrick*:[211]

Heinz v Kendrik [2001] I.R.L.R. 144, Lindsay L.J.

"*(iv) The Employer's knowledge of the disability for the purposes of Section 5 (1) (b)*

[25]. ... without being, we hope, too far-fetched, one can imagine, for example, a postman or messenger who, at his engagement and for a while afterwards, successfully conceals the fact that he has an artificial leg and can walk only for short distances at a time. He may later be dismissed for a conduct or capability ground, namely that he had proved to be unacceptably slow in making his rounds, but still without his disability being spotted. His slowness could have been taken by the employer to have been by reason of idleness or absenteeism. If, however, the employee were then able to show that his slowness was by reason of his having an artificial leg then, as it seems to us, he would, in such a case, have been treated less favourably 'than others to whom that reason does not apply' (namely, as *Clark v Novacold* requires, less favourably than other employees who did their rounds at an acceptable pace). Moreover he would have been so treated for a reason—unacceptable slowness—which related to his disability. That, it seems to us, would be the case whether or not the employer ever knew before the dismissal that the reason for the slowness was that the employee was disabled. The employee would, as it seems to us, have been discriminated against within the Act even if the employer had assumed that the slowness was attributable only to laziness or absenteeism. As another example, one might imagine a secretary dismissed because he or she, despite repeated training, persisted in typing hopelessly misspelt letters, yet without the employer or, perhaps, even the employee knowing that the reason for the errors was not ignorance or carelessness but dyslexia.

[26]. ... there is no language in Section 5 (1) that requires that the relationship between the disability and the treatment should be adjudged subjectively, through the eyes of the employer, so that the applicable test should be the objective one of whether the

[211] [2001] I.R.L.R. 144, EAT.

relationship exists, not whether the employer knew of it. Indeed, unless the test is objective there will be difficulties with credible and honest yet ignorant or obtuse employers who fail to recognise or acknowledge the obvious . . ."[212]

In *Hall v Department of Work and Pensions*[213] an employee who suffered psychiatric problems had declined in her health declaration form to provide any information about disabilities or long term health conditions and had also refused permission for the employer to contact her doctor. Subsequently, she made an application for a disabled person's tax credit to HM Revenue & Customs via the employer's human resources department. Following her dismissal for misconduct, an employment tribunal held that the employer could be said to have had constructive knowledge of her disability and to have subjected her to less favourable treatment. The EAT upheld this decision, which illustrates the objective standard to be applied: constructive knowledge of a disability can be attributed to an employer, even if the employee has deliberatively refused to make the employer aware of the existence of his or her disability. (It is worth bearing in mind that many disabled persons will wish not to disclose the existence of their disability.)

Confusingly, in *Taylor v OCS Group*,[214] the Court of Appeal appeared to suggest that a disability-related reason had to be present in and affecting the mind of an alleged discriminator before unlawful discrimination could exist. This is controversial, and appears to go against the well-established position set out by the House of Lords in the sex discrimination cases of *Nagarajan v London Regional Transport*[215] and *R v Birmingham CC, Ex p. EOC*[216] that no conscious motivation is required on the part of the discriminator. However, the Court of Appeal in this case was also probably more correct in holding that an employer might have several reasons for dismissing an employee, and if one of these reasons was disability-related, then that would suffice for lawful discrimination to exist.

In establishing whether a difference in treatment was based upon a claimant's disability, a similar approach is taken to matters of proof as with race and sex discrimination. Therefore, the burden of proof will shift as required by the 2003 Regulations in the employment and occupation context: otherwise, the burden remains on the claimant, but inferences can arise in certain circumstances which an employer will have to rebut.[217]

A finding of less favourable treatment that is directly on account of that disability will constitute direct discrimination and therefore is now auto-

212 See also *London Borough of Hammersmith and Fulham v Farnsworth* [2002] I.R.L.R. 691, where an employer's knowledge of the existence of a disability was held to be irrelevant in determining whether less favourable treatment had occurred.

213 [2005] All E.R. (D) 128.

214 [2006] EWCA Civ 702.

215 [2000] 1 A.C. 501.

216 [1989] A.C. 1155.

217 *Roberts v Warrington BC* Appeal No.EAT/497/98, clarified in *Igen Ltd v Wong* [2005] I.R.L.R. 258, EWCA.

matically prohibited if it occurred in the employment and occupation sphere: otherwise, the employer will have to demonstrate that the less favourable treatment was justified to avoid a finding of a breach of the DDA.

XII. Justification of "Less Favourable Treatment"

A. *Employment*

The Disability Discrimination (Employment) Regulations 1996 make special provisions in respect of performance-related pay, contributory benefit plans, uniform contribution requirements and other specific features of employer-employee relationships, providing that particular arrangements shall be deemed to be automatically justified. Otherwise, the test for determining whether less favourable treatment is justified is an objective one,[218] and requires an examination of the treatment meted out by the employer and its underlying rationale, irrespective of whether the employer was aware of the disability or not.[219] The relevant provisions of the Code of Practice may be important in providing guidance to tribunals as to what will constitute adequate justification, which will be a question of fact[220] This justification defence cannot be argued where an employer has failed to make reasonable adjustment under s.6: in the context of employment, a failure to discharge this duty will automatically render less favourable treatment unlawful (see below).[221]

As with any justification defence, its impact upon polices and practices of employers will depend on the difficulty with which this defence can be made out. Basic functional requirements for a particular post,[222] necessary safety issues,[223] and other types of occupational requirement will come under the justification umbrella. In *Royal Liverpool Children's NHS Trust v Dunsby*,[224] excessive absences from work related to disability were held in the circumstances to give rise to a possibility of a successful justification defence. However, the width of this justification defence is considerably broader than for conventional genuine occupational requirement tests as used in the SDA 75 and RRA 76, which impose a strict objective justification requirement.

Under the DDA, if a justification is "material"—i.e. related and relevant to

218 See *Baynton v Saurus General Engineers* [1999] I.R.L.R. 604.

219 See *Callaghan v Glasgow CC* [2001] I.R.L.R. 724, EAT.

220 See Mummery L.J. in *Clark*: "The question whether treatment has been shown to be justified is a question of fact to be determined on a proper self direction on the relevant law. Such a self direction includes taking into account those parts of the Code of Practice which a reasonable tribunal would regard as relevant to the determination of that question."

221 See s.5(3): see also *Archibald v Fife CC* [2004] UKHL, Lord Hope of Craighead, para.10.

222 See *Fozard v Greater Manchester Police Authority*, unreported, Case 2401143/97.

223 *Smith v Carpets International UK Plc*, unreported, IT, Case 1800507/97.

224 [2006] I.R.L.R. 351.

the specific circumstances of that particular individual employer and employee—and "substantial", i.e. resting upon a suitably firm and legitimate basis, then this defence will be made out: both legs of the test must be satisfied. The DRC Employment Code of Practice[225] stresses that "material" means that there must be a reasonably strong connection between the reason given for the treatment and the circumstances of the particular case; "substantial" means that the reason must carry real weight and be of substance. The Code of Practice provides a series of examples to explain the scope of the defence.

However, in applying this justification test, the courts have permitted considerable leeway to defendants, by accepting that a "reasonableness" standard could apply in determining when a justification was material and substantial. In *Heinz*, Lindsay J. interpreted the DDA as requiring the employer to show "reasonable" justification, rather than imposing a more onerous standard.[226] This narrow approach was confirmed as correct by the Court of Appeal in *Jones v Post Office*, a decision which has limited the reach and impact of the DDA.[227]

This case concerned the dismissal of a Post Office driver who had developed first diabetes and then heart disease. He was restricted to two hours driving time in any twenty-four period after his diabetes required insulin treatment. He claimed disability discrimination, and the Post Office responded by claiming justification on the basis that its medical advice indicated that Mr Jones was at risk of hypoglycaemic attack and hence a health and safety risk existed. Jones challenged the accuracy of this advice. The EAT overturned the tribunal's initial determination in his favour, finding that the tribunal had wrongfully assumed the role of deciding for itself on the evidence before it whether it was reasonable to limit the complainant's driving. On appeal, the Court of Appeal interpreted s.5(3) DDA to the effect that (a) that materiality and substantiality were all that justification required, and (b) that what was material and what was substantial was for the employer to decide, the tribunal's only power being to decide whether the decision fell within the range of reasonable responses to the known facts.

Jones is a key judgment, and it deserves close assessment:

Jones v Post Office [2001] EWCA Civ 558

PILL L.J.:

[11] "This appeal turns on the construction of section 5(3). Miss Tether submits that, when the "reason" relied on by the employer for the purposes of the subsection is a belief about the effects of a disability, the subsection requires an employment tribunal to

225 See the *Employment Code of Practice*, paras 6.3–6.4.
226 [2001] I.R.L.R. 144, EAT.
227 [2001] EWCA Civ 558; [2001] I.R.L.R. 384.

determine objectively whether that belief is correct. If the employer wrongly believes that the disability constitutes a safety risk, the reason is not "material" for the purposes of the subsection. The employment tribunal can also decide whether the reason is "substantial". The tribunal must be entitled to test the reason and determine whether the employer's belief is well founded because the section would offer little protection if the employer's belief, right or wrong, is to be accepted. The tribunal should consider the medical evidence afresh, make its own risk assessment and decide whether, in the light of its conclusion on the evidence, the less favourable treatment is justified [...]

[24] I have to say that I have found little assistance, upon the construction of section 5(3), in other cases or in the wording of other statutes ... The 1995 Act is plainly intended to create rights for the disabled and to protect their position as employees but those intentions must be considered in the context of the employer's duties to employees generally and to the general public. I cannot accept, in a case such as the present, involving an assessment of risk, that Parliament intended in the wording adopted to confer on employment tribunals a general power and duty to decide whether the employer's assessment of risk is correct. The issue is a different one from whether a person has a disability, within the meaning of section 1 of the Act, which is to be determined by the employment tribunal (*Goodwin v Patent* Office [1999] IRLR 4).

[25] Upon a consideration of the wording of section 5(3) in context, I conclude that the employment tribunal are confined to considering whether the reason given for the less favourable treatment can properly be described as both material to the circumstances of the particular case and substantial. The less favourable treatment in the present case is the limit upon the hours of driving. The reason given for it is the risk arising from longer periods of driving. The respondent obtained what are admitted to be suitably qualified and expert medical opinions. Upon the basis of those opinions, the respondent decided that the risk was such as to require the less favourable treatment. In order to rely on section 5(3) it is not enough for the employer to assert that his conduct was reasonable in a general way; he has to establish that the reason given satisfies the statutory criteria ... Where a properly conducted risk assessment provides a reason which is on its face both material and substantial, and is not irrational, the tribunal cannot substitute its own appraisal. The employment tribunal must consider whether the reason meets the statutory criteria; it does not have the more general power to make its own appraisal of the medical evidence and conclude that the evidence from admittedly competent medical witnesses was incorrect or make its own risk assessment.

[26] The present problem will typically arise when a risk assessment is involved. I am not doubting that the employment tribunal is permitted to investigate facts, for example as to the time-keeping record of the disabled person or as to his rate of productivity, matters which would arise upon some of the illustrations given in the Code of Practice. Consideration of the statutory criteria may also involve an assessment of the employer's decision to the extent of considering whether there was evidence on the basis of which a decision could properly be taken. Thus if no risk assessment was made or a decision was taken otherwise than on the basis of appropriate medical evidence, or was an irrational decision as being beyond the range of responses open to a reasonable decision maker (a test approved by Sir Thomas Bingham MR in a different context in *R v Ministry of Defence ex p Smith* [1996] 1 All ER 257 at 263), the employment tribunal could hold the reason insufficient and the treatment unjustified.

[27] The tribunal cannot, however, in my judgment, conclude that the reason is not material or substantial because the suitably qualified and competently expressed medical opinion, on the basis of which the employer's decision was made, was thought by them to be inferior to a different medical opinion expressed to them. Moreover, a reason may be material and substantial within the meaning of the section even if the employment tribunal would have come to a different decision as to the extent of the risk...

[33] The limited function of the employment tribunal may in some circumstances place them in a situation which is less than straightforward procedurally. However, it is not one with which they are unfamiliar. It is different but not very different from the task employment tribunals have to perform in cases of unfair dismissal...

ARDEN L.J.:

[36] Section 5(3) uses the words "material" and "substantial". In my judgment, those words cover different subject matter. "Material" denotes the quality of the connection which must exist between, on the one hand, the employer's reason for discriminating against the employee and, on the other hand, the circumstances of the particular case. The circumstances of the particular case may include those of both the employer and employee (*Baynton v Saurus Ltd* [2001] ICR 375). Under section 5(3), this connection must be "material".

[37] Mr Griffith-Jones submits that "material" means "relevant". As to this, it is often said that there are degrees of relevance. In this context, I would add to Mr Griffith-Jones submission the rider that it is not sufficient that the connection is an extenuated one. The use of the word "material" rather than "relevant" or "applicable" indicates to me that there must be a reasonably strong connection between the employer's reason and the circumstances of the individual case. The strength of this connection involves largely a factual enquiry. It ought not to involve an enquiry into medical evidence since such an enquiry is relevant, if at all, only to the second limb of section 5(3).

[38] An example may help throw light on the function of the word "material" in section 5(3). Suppose that it is shown that diabetes (of either type) leads to diminished night-time vision and the employer of an employee with diabetes prohibits that employee from doing night-time shifts for the reason that he has diabetes. In this example there would be a material connection between the employer's reason and the circumstances of the particular case. Miss Tether sought to argue that materiality also involved correctness. However, in my judgment, if the employer in the example last given believed that diabetes diminished night-time vision but was entirely wrong in that belief, the requirement for materiality in the example which I have given would still be met. However, there would be difficulty in the employer meeting the second requirement of substantiality, to which I now turn.

[39] The second requirement in section 5(3) is that the reason should be "substantial". This means, in my judgment, that the reason which the employer adopted as his ground for discrimination must carry real weight and thus be of substance. However the word "substantial" does not mean that the employer must necessarily have reached the best conclusion that could be reached in the light of all known medical science. Employers are not obliged to search for the Holy Grail. It is sufficient if their conclusion is one which on a critical examination is found to have substance. Thus a reason which on analysis is meretricious would not be a "substantial" reason. It would fail to meet the test in section 5(3)...

[43] The fact that the true construction of a particular statutory provision indicates that the protection given to an employee in one respect is not the maximum protection that could have been conferred or as great as the protection conferred in other areas of statute law, is not of itself a reason for rejecting that construction. The right level is a matter for Parliament. It may be that in the case of disability discrimination Parliament had in mind that an employer has to balance the interests of the employee with a disability with those of fellow employees and indeed also of members of the public. Accordingly I reject Miss Tether's submission that it would be surprising if the criteria for review under section 5(3) of the Disabilities Discrimination Act 1995 were less rigorous than, for instance, under the Race Relations Act 1976 or the Sex Discrimination Act 1975."

Jones established that an employer's decision must be irrational in the sense of being beyond the range of reasonable responses. Jackie Davies has argued that:

"a low threshold for justification offers a clear advantage to employers and threatens the integrity of the Act ... [the] introduction of the concept of a 'range of reasonable responses' into the defence of justification further upsets the delicate equilibrium between employer rights to economic autonomy and disabled persons' rights to equality of treatment."[228]

She argues that the *Jones* approach fails to recognise that the DDA intended to *change* practice, not to permit employers to maintain existing practices that are not clearly unreasonable. She describes the carry-over of the "reasonableness" test from the unfair dismissal context as a "cuckoo in the nest" in discrimination law.[229] The DRC has a similar view, criticising the *Jones* test as permitting employers "too much latitude".[230]

Davies also criticises the *Jones* test as ensuring that tribunals will inevitably have to adopt a permissive approach to medical evidence, if it is brought forward by an employer to show their treatment was rational. The "reasonableness" standard recognised in *Jones* in effect permits reasonable reliance by an employer on an independent risk assessment, whether thought by the tribunal to be correct or not. This seems to be confirmed by the case law. In *Bonner v First Manchester*,[231] reliance by an employer upon a medical assessment to form the basis for a blanket policy, but which was not based upon an assessment of the disabled individual in question, was held to be reasonable. Medical evidence may not always be material to the specific individual's situation, even if it is substantial in nature: it could be argued that the medical assessment in *Bonner* was not "material", but the application of the permissive *Jones* standard resulted in an absence of close scrutiny of the employer's justification.

Note as well that in *Jones*, Pill L.J. considered that the correctness of the Post Office's opinion and the steps it had taken to verify its opinion, including the use of medical expertise, should be considered under the "material" leg of the test, while Arden L.J. saw it as coming under the "substantial" leg of the test. This distinction is potentially important. If Pill L.J.'s approach is followed, a mistake by an employer as to the impact of a disability in the particular circumstances at issue, if based upon an unreasonable or irrational failure to examine and assess the nature and extent of the disability, would mean that the treatment in question was not based upon a reason truly material to the particular circumstances of the case. It therefore could not be deemed to be justified, even under the loose test set out in *Jones*.[232]

228 See J. Davies, "A Cuckoo in the Nest? A 'Range of Reasonable Responses', Justification and the Disability Discrimination Act 1995" (2003) 32(3) I.L.J. 164, 166.

229 *ibid.*, p.178.

230 See DRC, *Legislative Review: First Review of the Disability Discrimination Act 1995-Consultation Document*, 38–9.

231 Case 2402931/01.

232 See *Holmes v Whittingham and Porter*, unreported, IT, Case 1802799/97: specialist medical advice should have been taken before dismissal, and reliance upon a general practitioner's opinion was not sufficient.

This approach would therefore require proper investigation of the impact of a disability as an initial precondition before the employer could claim the benefit of the permissive "range of reasonable responses" test.[233] However, under Arden L.J.'s approach, such a failure to investigate adequately could be justifiable, as it might be deemed to be a substantial or well-founded reason, even if lacking a real basis. This approach if widely adopted might further contribute to the weakening of the justification test already loosened by *Jones*, by opening a possible route for "normal" unexamined prejudices and assumptions to be classed as "substantial".[234]

Pill L.J.'s approach also has problems of its own: how are tribunals supposed to identify and define proper investigations? Also, as Davies points out, proper investigations are no guarantee of objective decisions: they produce information to be interpreted by the employer, who still has the freedom to apply subjective prejudices.[235] Will "normal" investigation practices will be deemed okay? Will tribunals lack the expertise to assess the adequacy of investigations?[236]

Subsequent cases have partially clarified some of these issues. In *Paul v National Probation Service*,[236a] the EAT emphasised that even if an employment tribunal felt that less favourable treatment was justified under the *Jones* test, it should give due consideration to whether the duty to make reasonable adjustment came into play. Therefore, even where an employer has a reasonable justification for treating a disabled person less favourably, there may be a violation of the duty to make reasonable accommodation (see below). It also stressed that employment tribunals had to be careful in identifying the precise nature of the less favourable treatment that was sought to be justified, and that the *Jones* standard did not preclude tribunals from assessing medical evidence that was plainly contentious.

Similarly, in *Quinn v Schwarzkopf*,[237] the EAT held that "an employer cannot justify disability discrimination where, in fact, it did not apply its mind during the currency of the employment to what should be done because it was ignorant of the disability". In other words, if an employer claims not to have known of the disability, the justification defence is not available. However, in *Callaghan v Glasgow CC*,[238] the EAT modified this decision, saying that:

> "insofar as this tribunal may have suggested in *Quinn v Schwarzkopf* that justification can never occur if the employer was ignorant of the fact of disability at the relevant time, that goes too far . . . Obviously the fact that the employer did not know that a disability exists may affect the justification issue but does not preclude it."

[233] See Davies, p.170.
[234] *ibid.*, p.178.
[235] *ibid.*, p.171.
[236] As Davies notes, the EAT accepted an apparently inadequate risk assessment as constituting sufficient justification in *Marshall v Surrey Police* [2002] I.R.L.R. 843: *ibid.*, p.182.
[236a] [2004] I.R.L.R. 190
[237] [2001] I.R.L.R. 67.
[238] [2001] I.R.L.R. 724.

In *Williams v J Walter Thompson Group Ltd*,[239] the Court of Appeal upheld an employment tribunal decision that a failure to provide previously promised special training and technical support, combined with a failure to transfer the applicant to work that she could without the extra training and support, could not be justified. The employer had employed the applicant in the full knowledge of her disability and of the need for this extra training and support: in these special circumstances, the failure to carry out a serious assessment of the cost of this training and support mean that the employer could not make out a justification defence.

Despite this decision, which was very much rooted in the particular circumstances at issue, the leeway given to employers in justifying less favourable treatment by the *Jones* decision remains a problem. It has substantially diluted the impact and application of the DDA prohibition on "less favourable treatment". Unless discrimination on the ground of a person's disability is direct, an employer will avoid liability for less favourable treatment unless their actions are clearly unreasonable. This constitutes a weaker level of protection than that applying in other areas of discrimination law. However, the Discrimination Law Review has proposed that the current justification defence be replaced with one that requires less favourable treatment to be a proportionate means of achieving a legitimate aim. If implemented, this could remedy many of the problems caused by *Jones*.[240]

B. *Goods and Services*

Less favourable treatment on the ground of disability that cannot be justified is prohibited in the provision of goods and services as well. In determining whether less favourable treatment has occurred, the *Clark v Novacold* approach to comparators is also applied in the context of goods and services, but there is no automatic prohibition on direct discrimination: see above. Section 20 of the DDA also provides for a similar justification defence in the context of the provision of services: however, there are some significant differences from how this test is applied in the employment context.

[239] [2005] I.R.L.R. 376 EWCA.

[240] See *A Framework for Fairness* (The Discrimination Law Review) (London: HMSO, 1997), paras 1.50–1.53.

Section 20 of the DDA

"*Meaning of "discrimination"*

(1) For the purposes of section 19, a provider of services discriminates against a disabled person if—

(a) for a reason which relates to the disabled person's disability, he treats him less favourably than he treats or would treat others to whom that reason does not or would not apply; and

(b) he cannot show that the treatment in question is justified.[241]

[...]

(3) For the purposes of this section, treatment is justified only if—

(a) in the opinion of the provider of services, one or more of the conditions mentioned in subsection (4) are satisfied; and

(b) it is reasonable, in all the circumstances of the case, for him to hold that opinion.

(4) The conditions are that—

(a) in any case, the treatment is necessary in order not to endanger the health or safety of any person (which may include that of the disabled person);

(b) in any case, the disabled person is incapable of entering into an enforceable agreement, or of giving an informed consent, and for that reason the treatment is reasonable in that case;

(c) in a case falling within section 19(1)(a), the treatment is necessary because the provider of services would otherwise be unable to provide the service to members of the public;

(d) in a case falling within section 19(1)(c) or (d), the treatment is necessary in order for the provider of services to be able to provide the service to the disabled person or to other members of the public;

(e) in a case falling within section 19(1)(d), the difference in the terms on which the service is provided to the disabled person and those on which it is provided to other members of the public reflects the greater cost to the provider of services in providing the service to the disabled person.

(5) Any increase in the cost of providing a service to a disabled person which results from compliance by a provider of services with a section 21 duty shall be disregarded for the purposes of subsection (4)(e)."

In addition, specific provisions are introduced by the Disability Discrimination (Services and Premises) Regulations 1996, which provide inter alia that where a provider of insurance services has treated a disabled person less favourably, that treatment will be justifiable if based upon information which is relevant to

[241] See the *Code of Practice(Revised): Rights of Access to Goods, Facilities and Premises*, paras 9.35–9.37 for practical examples of the application of each of these conditions.

the assessment of the risk to be insured, and if it is reasonable having regard to the information relied upon and any other relevant factors.

This justification test that is applied in the goods and services context is two-fold in nature: a) the service provider must have a genuine belief that one of the specified conditions exists, and b) it must be reasonable for the service provider to hold that belief. The important differences between this defence and that provided for in the employment context are the emphasis on the opinion of the service provider, and the requirement that they must be satisfied that one or more of the necessary conditions apply.

The reason for the difference between this approach and that adopted for employment was the perception that service providers were in a different position to employers and had to make more rapid and once-off decisions: hence the emphasis on the validity of the opinion held by the service provider, rather than on the objectively acceptable nature of the actual act of less favourable treatment, as it was felt that the service provider could not be expected to initiate the medical assessments and other methods for determining the impact of a disability that might be available to an employer. The list of conditions in turn was designed to ensure that the opinion of the service provider had to be based upon acceptable criteria, as was the requirement that the belief had to be reasonable in all the circumstances of the particular case.

However, a concern does exist that the emphasis upon the belief of the service provider may mean that deference may be given to opinions that are based upon subjective and even prejudicial assumptions. The Disability Rights Commission has argued that this "reasonable opinion" provision can allow scope for prejudice to be deemed to be justifiable.[242] It could be argued that the requirement for an opinion to be reasonably held and the rule that the service provider's actual opinion at the relevant time will be scrutinised, as opposed to any *ex post facto* rationalisations, may mitigate the risk of excessive leeway being given to prejudice and subjectivity. It should also be remembered that reasonable adjustment requirements may also apply, which a service provider may fall foul of even if they are not held to have engaged in less favourable treatment (see below).

However, concern still remains about the "reasonable opinion" test, illustrated by the case of *Rose v Bouchet*.[243] A landlord refused to let a flat to Mr Rose, who was visually impaired, for a week during the Edinburgh Festival on the grounds that the lack of handrail on the outside steps of the flat would make it too dangerous for a blind person. In the Sheriff's Court, the landlord accepted that he had subjected Mr Rose to less favourable treatment for a reason relating to his disability, but argued that he was justified on health and safety grounds. The sheriff dismissed the claim on grounds that the landlord's treatment of Mr Rose was justified because in Mr Bouchet's opinion that refusal was necessary in order not to endanger Mr Rose, and that the opinion

[242] Disability Rights Commission, *Disability Equality: Making it Happen* (London: DRC, 2003).
[243] [1999] I.R.L.R. 463; 199 S.L.T.

was reasonably held, in all the circumstances of the case. The Sheriff Principal dismissed the subsequent appeal, considering that while the requirement of a "reasonable opinion" meant that an objective assessment of all the relevant circumstances was required, there was no duty in the present case on the service provider to obtain more information before settling his opinion. Whether further inquiry was necessary depended upon the facts and circumstances of the particular case, and the complainant's conduct in ending the conversation with the landlord in an angry manner meant that the landlord could not be criticised for refusing to make additional investigations.

This decision shows that considerable leeway can exist for subjective and *ad hoc* decision-making to be upheld under the DDA, and also opens the door for the complainant's conduct to be a significant factor in lessening the obligations upon the landlord. Subsequently, the revised Code of Practice issued by the DRC specified that the reference to "all the circumstances of the case" in s.20(3)(b) included whether advice and the opinion of the disabled person had been sought.

In *White v Clitheroe Royal Grammar School*,[244] a more rigorous approach was adopted to the application of the s.20 justification test: the District Judge held that the belief that a boy's exclusion from a school trip was justified had not been based upon a reasonably held opinion that it was necessary in order not to endanger his health or safety, as there was no involvement of the boy or his parents in the decision making process, the perceived problem was never put to the boy or his parents for an explanation and there was no serious attempt to initiate a risk assessment, even taking into account the nature of the holiday and the medical realities.

In *Glover v Lawford*,[245] the District Judge rejected the justification defence put forward by the café owner for refusing to let Mr Glover in with his guide dog, finding that that the "no dogs" policy was primarily driven by financial rather than health and safety considerations, which were in any case marginal in nature: an argument that the space available in the café did not permit the entry of dogs was also rejected, on the basis that the defendant made no attempt to assess objectively the truth of this claim.

A similar justification defence is available in housing cases.[246] This was considered by the Queens Bench Division in *North Devon Homes Ltd v Brazier*,[247] which concerned an order for possession which had been granted in respect of a tenant with a psychiatric disorder: Ms Brazier had admitted to persistent anti-social behaviour, including shouting at neighbouring tenants, keeping them awake and using foul language. The District Judge found that the eviction was not necessary in order to protect the health and safety of any person, as, although her neighbours were subject to a great deal of discomfort, "they are not such as to endanger the health or safety of any person". This

[244] Preston County Court, Claim No.BB002640.
[245] MA26303.
[246] See s.24 of the DDA.
[247] [2003] EWCA 574, QB.

aspect of the decision was upheld by the Queens Bench, which also held that the DDA could control this matter, and superseded the provisions of the relevant piece of housing legislation, s.7 of the Housing Act 1988.

These cases show a real willingness on the part of the courts to assess the reasonableness of a service provider's opinion, and to require a degree of assessment as to whether the required conditions exist. Concerns remain, however, about the potential for subjective elements to creep into this justification defence. The DRC has recommended that the wording of the justification provision be amended to provide an objective test for justifying potential discrimination in goods and services matters.[248] The Discrimination Law Review has proposed that a single objective justification test be used throughout the legislation, to the effect that the treatment must be a proportionate means of achieving a legitimate aim. This would eliminate many of the problems that exist with the current tests.

XIII. Reasonable Adjustment

A. *Introduction*

The DDA imposes a requirement to make reasonable adjustments on both employers and service providers. This key duty to remove barriers to the equal participation of disabled persons where reasonable to do so is a central element of the legislation, and distinguishes the DDA from other forms of anti-discrimination legislation. The neglect of steps to accommodate disability as a human difference is a major source of disability discrimination: formal guarantees of equal treatment without the provision of special support and access mechanisms for disabled persons will not be sufficient to achieve genuine equality of opportunity.[249] Reasonable accommodation duties are designed to require employers and service providers to take such special measures. They represent a manifestation of the "social model" approach: the concept underlying these duties is that external barriers to the participation of disabled persons in the workplace and in accessing goods and services should be removed where practicable and possible.

"Reasonable accommodation" was first used in the US in the disability rights context in regulations issued in 1977 by the Office of Federal Contract Compliance Programs (OFCCP) of the US Department of Labor to implement s.503 of the Rehabilitation Act. The OFCCP regulations required federal contractors having contracts or subcontracts of $2500 or more to "make a rea-

[248] Disability Rights Commission, *Disability Equality: Making it Happen* (London: DRC, 2003).
[249] Samuel R. Bagenstos, "Subordination, Stigma, and 'Disability' (2000) 86 Virginia L. Rev. 397–534.

sonable accommodation to the physical and mental limitations of an employee or applicant unless the contractor can demonstrate that such an accommodation would impose an undue hardship on the conduct of the contractor's business." Title I of the Americans with Disabilities Act (ADA) took this a step forward, with the Act including in its definition of discriminatory employment practices the following:

2112(b)(5)(A) of the Americans with Disabilities Act (ADA)

"(A) not making reasonable accommodations to the known physical or mental limitations of an otherwise qualified individual with a disability who is an applicant or employee, unless such covered entity can demonstrate that the accommodation would impose an undue hardship on the operation of the business of such covered entity; or

(B) denying employment opportunities to a job applicant or employee who is an otherwise qualified individual with a disability, if such denial is based on the need of such covered entity to make reasonable accommodation to the physical or mental impairments of the employee or applicant."

A similar duty was inserted in the DDA and is now required in the Employment Equality Directive (see below). However, notwithstanding its crucial importance and centrality to disability discrimination legislation, the nature of the reasonable accommodation duty has generated a considerable degree of academic controversy.

B. *The Nature of "Reasonable Accommodation": Positive Action or Anti-discrimination Requirement?*

Much of this debate arises out of the US case law and concerns the weight to be given to the accommodation duty and whether it should be defined as an integral anti-discrimination requirement or a positive action provision of less compelling heft. In *School Board of Nassau County v Arline*,[250] the US Supreme Court declared that "[e]mployers have an affirmative obligation to make a reasonable accommodation for a handicapped employee". In *US Airways, Inc v Barnett*,[251] the Supreme Court considered that reasonable accommodation is part of the broader obligation not to discriminate on the basis of disability. Nevertheless, academic writers have argued that a belief persists in the approach of the US courts that people with disabilities require special accommodation due to their functional limitations, which are the result of

[250] 480 US 273 (1987).
[251] 122 S. Ct. 1516 (2002).

biology rather than social practices. Therefore, accommodating disabled persons means providing them with special treatment not normally available to others, the availability of which should be balanced against other, potentially competing, social needs.

In other words, reasonable accommodation is seen as a form of positive action that is a supplemental "add-on" to the legislative prohibition on disability discrimination, which a disabled person should be required to show was necessary in the circumstances. It is not seen as a right to which a disabled person is entitled to unless pressing countervailing considerations apply. So, for example, in *Cleveland v Policy Management Systems Corp*,[251a] the Supreme Court considered that a disabled claimant had to show that a form of reasonable accommodation was available that could overcome her disability: overcoming this burden can place a heavy burden on the claimant.

So what is the nature of the reasonable accommodation duty? Brian Doyle argues that this duty to make a reasonable adjustment "is an example of legally mandated positive action rather than a requirement of reverse or positive discrimination", while emphasising that it is of paramount importance.[252] Karlan and Rutherglen have described the reasonable accommodation requirement in the ADA as a form of affirmative action, albeit an unusual and distinct form that substitutes accommodation for an individual for the blunt-edged group-centred approaches used in other discrimination contexts.[253] Tucker also argues that reasonable accommodation duties are one form of affirmative action, requiring employers and service providers to spend money and/or reorganise their policies to treat a person with a disability differently.[254]

In contrast, others have argued that accommodation duties are a method of remedying discrimination and securing equality of opportunity. Christine Joll has argued that an economic analysis of accommodation mandates, e.g. "reasonable accommodation", and discrimination law, reveals that the two forms of legal intervention are similar rather than distinct.[255] Mark Stein has made similar arguments.[256] Hendriks and Waddington have suggested that it is appropriate to perceive a failure to make "reasonable accommodation" as a form of discrimination *sui generis*, which consists of a failure to make an adaptation to ensure equal opportunities, but which does not involve differentiation on a forbidden or seemingly neutral ground, which is the traditional

[251a] (1999) 526 U.S. 795

[252] Brian Doyle, "Enabling Legislation or Dissembling Law? The Disability Discrimination Act 1995" (1997) 60 M.L.R. 64, 74.

[253] Pamela S. Karlan and George Rutherglen, "Disabilities, Discrimination & 'Reasonable Accommodation' (1996) 46(1) Duke L. J. 1.

[254] Bonnie P. Tucker, "The ADA's Revolving Door: Inherent Flaws in the Civil Rights Paradigm" (2001) 62 Ohio State L. J. 335.

[255] Christine Jolls, "Antidiscrimination and Accommodation" (2001) 115 Harvard L. Rev. 642.

[256] Mark Stein, "Same Struggle, Different Difference: ADA Accommodations as Antidiscrimination" [2004] 153 Univ. of Pennsylvania L. Rev.

definition of discrimination.[257] In other words, reasonable accommodation should be seen as a remedy for a particular form of discrimination, the denial of access to equality of opportunity, which is particularly common and potent in the context of disability.

This debate is important, both from a conceptual perspective (which approach best captures the nature of the reasonable accommodation requirement?) and also because the perception that reasonable accommodation involves affirmative action has exposed the ADA to political attack in the US and has weakened its impact. However, Lisa Waddington has argued that this is less likely to be a problem in the EU, as the Directive can be clearly interpreted as recognising reasonable accommodation as a remedy for discrimination, rather than as a form of positive action.[258]

Lisa Waddington, *Implementing and Interpreting the Reasonable Accommodation Provision of the Framework Employment Directive: Learning from Experience and Achieving Best Practice* (Brussels: E.U. Network of Experts on Disability Discrimination, 2004)

[31–34] "In spite of . . . the plea for a revised approach to positive action with regard to reasonable accommodation put forward by authors such as Karlan and Rutherglen, it seems inappropriate to view the reasonable accommodation requirement found in the Framework Employment Directive in this light. Even though the Directive does not explicitly define a failure to make a reasonable accommodation as a form of discrimination, or enunciate on the relationship between 'reasonable accommodation' and positive action, it seems implicit in its wording that the two kinds of instruments are regarded as distinct. This can be surmised from the fact that 'reasonable accommodation' is a requirement under the Directive whilst Member States are given the freedom (but not the obligation) to allow for, and adopt, positive action measures in favour of people with disabilities under Article 7 of the Directive. This distinction arguably strengthens the argument that the obligation to make a 'reasonable accommodation' should be fitted into the non-discrimination framework.

This argument is reinforced by a theoretical analysis of the concept of and motivation behind reasonable accommodation norms. It is recalled that the reasonable accommodation requirement is designed to secure the removal of barriers which would other-

[257] See Lisa Waddington and Aart Hendriks, "The Expanding Concept of Employment Discrimination in Europe: From Direct and Indirect Discrimination to 'reasonable accommodation' Discrimination" (2002) 18(4) The International J. of Comparative Labour Law and Industrial Relations, 403. See also Samuel R. Bagenstos, "Rational Discrimination," Accommodation, and the Politics of (Disability) Civil Rights' (2003) 89 Virginia L. Rev. 825; Sharon Rabin-Margalioth, "Anti-Discrimination, Accommodation, and Universal Mandates—Aren't They All the Same?" (2003) 24 Berkeley J. of Employment & Labor Law 111.

[258] See also Robert L. Burgdorf Jr., "'Substantially Limited'" Protection From Disability Discrimination: The Special Treatment Model and Misconstructions of the Definition of Disability" (1997) 42 Villanova L. Rev. 409, 529–32. For a similar conceptual view in the US context, *see* Harlan Hahn, "Accommodation and the ADA: Unreasonable Bias or Biased Reasoning?" (2000) 21 Berkeley J. of Employment and Labor Law 166, 189–90.

wise prevent disabled individuals from benefiting from employment opportunities. Such barriers arise because, on occasions, the interaction between the physical or social environment and an individual's impairment result in the inability to perform a particular function or job in the conventional manner. Ignoring (by failing to accommodate) the impairment would result in denying a person equal employment opportunities.

The reasonable accommodation requirement therefore recognises that where people's impairments result in them being differently situated regarding employment opportunities, identical treatment may be a source of discrimination, and different treatment may be required to eliminate it. Recognition of this need for real, not merely formal, equality is the basis of the obligation to make individualised adjustments to permit particular disabled individuals to participate in particular employment related activities. In this situation inaction, as opposed to action, can amount to discrimination, and this is expressly recognised in the reasonable accommodation requirement which prohibits an employer from denying an individual with a disability an employment opportunity by failing to take account of the impairment when taking account of it—in terms of changing the job or physical environment of the workplace—would enable the individual to do the work.

Burgdorf has argued in the US context that the failure by some to recognize reasonable accommodation . . . stems from a lack of in-depth understanding of the dynamics by which employers disadvantage some applicants and workers because of their disabilities. One basic oversight is an unawareness of the extent to which employers accommodate to the needs of employees without disabilities. Burgdorf argues that what is often ignored is that, in almost all circumstances, employers, businesses, and government agencies put a great deal of money and energy into 'accommodating' the users of their services, facilities, and programmes without denominating their actions as such. . . .

Burgdorf's point is not that employers should somehow anticipate the actual physical or mental limitations of all future employees and have the work environment ready to meet their specific needs. It is, rather, that employers routinely devote considerable energy and money providing accommodations for employees based upon assumptions that workers will have standard physical and mental characteristics. He concludes that reasonable accommodation for workers with disabilities, then, is simply the same type of accommodation that is provided generally, but is tailored to the actual needs of the particular worker for whose benefit it is made . . .

. . . For employers to ignore the existence of disabled people in planning and structuring their jobs, and in designing and erecting their facilities, goes well beyond inadvertence and simple negligence and amounts to reckless indifference or a form of intentionality—a looking away and denying the existence of disabled people in the face of abundant evidence to the contrary."

Therefore, a strong case exists that reasonable accommodation is best conceived as an anti-discrimination measure within the framework of EU law. However, even if this is the case, there may be circumstances where giving effect to this anti-discrimination requirement may involve the provision of special treatment to disabled persons, as illustrated by the US Supreme Court decision in *US Airways, Inc v Barnett*[259] and the House of Lords decision in *Archibald v Fife* (see below). Hard distinctions in this area are difficult to draw. Nevertheless, it should be borne in mind that reasonable accommodation requirements are essential to address the exclusion of disabled persons: they cannot be an optional extra, as the prohibition on unjustified "less favourable treatment" is insufficient on its own to remove the barriers faced by disabled

[259] 122 S. Ct. 1516 (2002).

persons. A refusal to transform existing practices to accommodate disabled persons may have even greater exclusionary impact than a denial of access to existing arrangements, which may be unsuitable and inaccessible in any case. The right of access to a building may mean nothing if the building is inaccessible in practice. As Hendricks and Waddington have argued, reasonable accommodation is an essential remedy for discrimination and exclusion.[260]

Waddington also argues that reasonable accommodation requirements will often be justified as economically efficient, as they can remove obstacles to maximising the productivity of disabled employees and encourage the economic integration of disabled persons across the workforce in general.[261] However, she also suggests that not all accommodations can be justified by considerations of efficiency, as some necessary accommodations are "simply economically inefficient". For her, the core justification for the duty of "reasonable accommodation" does not lie in appeals to economic efficiency, but rather in the claim to equality of opportunity for people with disabilities.

C. *The Concept of "Reasonableness"*

If this is the case, to what extent should this equality duty be applied? How far should employers and service providers be required to modify practices and to remove physical obstacles in order to facilitate disabled persons? Waddington cites Kelman's argument that the reasonable accommodation norm establishes a distributive claim on real social resources that compete with all other social resource claimants, and that all such claims cannot be met.[262] Therefore, a claimant's claim to have his or her "right" to accommodation vindicated can be countered by claims that their demands are "unreasonable", in the sense that the resources that would have to be devoted to meeting these needs could be spent in a better fashion. "Reasonable accommodation" claims involve a balancing of demands, the outcome of which will depend on what allocation of costs to meet the needs of the claimant will be deemed to be

260 See Lisa Waddington and Aart Hendriks, "The Expanding Concept of Employment Discrimination in Europe: From Direct and Indirect Discrimination to 'reasonable accommodation' Discrimination" (2002) 18(4) The International J. of Comparative Labour Law and Industrial Relations 403.

261 See L. Waddington, *Implementing and Interpreting the Reasonable Accommodation Provision of the Framework Employment Directive: Learning from Experience and Achieving Best Practice* (Brussels: E.U. Network of Experts on Disability Discrimination, 2004), 64. See also J.H. Verkerke, "Is the ADA Efficient?" [2003] 50 UCLA L. Rev. 903, who argues that "the duty of reasonable accommodation may promote labor market efficiency by combating employee churning and scarring . . .".

262 L. Waddington, *Implementing and Interpreting the Reasonable Accommodation Provision of the Framework Employment Directive: Learning from Experience and Achieving Best Practice* (Brussels: EU Network of Experts on Disability Discrimination, 2004), 63; Mark Kelman, "Market Discrimination and Groups", Stanford Public Law and Legal Theory Working Paper Series, Working Paper No.8, February, 2000.

"reasonable". Therefore, defining what will constitute "reasonableness" in this context is crucial.

Defining what is "reasonable" in any given circumstance can be very difficult, and the term is notoriously unstable and open to differential interpretations. The US courts in applying the ADA have utilised the concept of "undue hardship", to be determined on the facts of each case. However, the majority opinion in *Barnett* reasoned that the ADA does not "demand action beyond the realm of the reasonable." Paragraph 21 of the Preamble to the Directive attempts to flesh out what "reasonableness" requires:

> "To determine whether the measures in question give rise to a disproportionate burden, account should be taken in particular of the financial and other costs entailed, the scale and financial resources of the organisation or undertaking and the possibility of obtaining public funding or any other assistance."

Waddington therefore argues that if an accommodation is theoretically possible, the Directive only permits a restraint of the duty to accommodate if the making of the accommodation would impose a "disproportionate burden on the employer". However, Katie Wells is concerned that the Directive frames the duty to accommodate as requiring the balancing of two elements: the effectiveness of the accommodation in enabling the disabled person to access employment is weighed against the financial cost of the accommodation for the employer. She regards it as unfortunate: "this polar opposition of individual gain versus employer cost is not conducive to tackling attitudinal and systemic forms of disability discrimination, and it may reinforce the perception that the principal result of accommodation of disabled people is expense and not benefit."[263] The Directive's language may insufficiently reflect the overall social benefit of an effective and rigorous application of the accommodation requirement. It does represent an attempt to put some flesh on an uncertain concept. Ultimately, however, what reasonableness requires will be established by case-law and the approach of courts and tribunals.

XIV. Reasonable Adjustment in Employment

Turning to the specific provisions of the DDA, a distinction is made in the legislation between the standard of accommodation required in employment and in access to goods and services, a distinction which was been reinforced by the introduction of the regulations giving effect to the Employment Equality Directive. Concentrating upon employment first, the DDA now requires reasonable accommodation in the following terms:

[263] K. Wells, "The Impact of the Framework Employment Directive on UK Disability Discrimination Law" (2003) 32(4) I.L. J. 253, 264.

Section 4A DDA—Employers: Duty to Make Adjustments

"(1) Where—

(a) a provision, criterion or practice applied by or on behalf of an employer, or

(b) any physical feature of premises occupied by the employer, places the disabled person concerned at a substantial disadvantage in comparison with persons who are not disabled, it is the duty of the employer to take such steps as it is reasonable, in all the circumstances of the case, for him to have to take in order to prevent the provision, criterion or practice, or feature, having that effect.

(2) In subsection (1), "the disabled person concerned" means—

(a) in the case of a provision, criterion or practice for determining to whom employment should be offered, any disabled person who is, or has notified the employer that he may be, an applicant for that employment;

(b) in any other case, a disabled person who is—

(i) an applicant for the employment concerned, or
(ii) an employee of the employer concerned.

(3) Nothing in this section imposes any duty on an employer in relation to a disabled person if the employer does not know, and could not reasonably be expected to know—

(a) in the case of an applicant or potential applicant, that the disabled person concerned is, or may be, an applicant for the employment; or

(b) in any case, that that person has a disability and is likely to be affected in the way mentioned in subsection (1)."

This new s.4A, inserted by the DDA 2004, replaced the original s.6 of the DDA, which imposed a similar requirement to make reasonable accommodation but referred to "arrangements" rather than provisions, criteria or practices and provided for a justification defence to a failure to make reasonable accommodation. Similar provisions now also exist for contract workers, office holders, partnerships, barristers and advocates, trade unions and professional bodies, qualifications bodies, practical work experience and occupational pension schemes. The 1996 Regulations define what constitute physical features that can be required to be altered:

Disability Discrimination (Employment) Regulations 1996

"Physical features

9. For the purposes of section 6(1) of the Act the following are to be treated as physical features (whether permanent or temporary)—

(a) any feature arising from the design or construction of a building on the premises;

(b) any feature on the premises of any approach to, exit from or access to such a building;

(c) any fixtures, fittings, furnishings, furniture, equipment or materials in or on the premises;

(d) any other physical element or quality of any land comprised in the premises."

A complainant can allege a failure to make reasonable accommodation in addition to or in place of an allegation of less favourable treatment[264]: often, it may be unclear which claim might best suit the particular circumstances of a case, or whether both may be applicable. New s.3A(3), inserted into the DDA by the 2003 Regulations, clarifies that a person also discriminates against a disabled person if he fails to comply with a duty to make reasonable adjustments imposed on him in relation to the disabled person. In *Heinz v Kentrick*, the EAT emphasised that a breach of the reasonable accommodation duty could arise even if no "less favourable treatment" had taken place, and vice versa.[265]

A. *When is the Duty Triggered?*

The duty is triggered in the employment context when a practice, policy or procedure puts a disabled person at a "substantial disadvantage". In contrast, Pt III of the DDA covering access to goods and services provides for reasonable accommodation only where it was "impossible or unreasonably difficult" for disabled persons to use a service (see below),[266] but the 2003 Regulations have modified this so that in the case of employment-related services, such as the provisional of vocational training, the "substantial disadvantage" standard now applies.[267]

In *Morse v Wiltshire CC*,[268] the dismissal of an employee was held to constitute a type of "substantial disadvantage". Physical obstacles in the workplace, work practices, occupational requirements and safety restrictions are examples of the type of factor that may cause a disabled person "substantial disadvantage", and thereby trigger the duty.[269] Originally, s.6 of the DDA had used the term "arrangement" in place of the new wording now in s.4A that

264 See Mummery L.J. in *Clark v Novacold* [1999] I.C.R. 951; [1999] I.R.L.R. 318: "A claim for a breach of a [reasonable accommodation] duty is not dependant on successfully establishing a claim [for less favourable treatment]. They are different causes of action, even though ... they may overlap."

265 [2001] I.R.L.R. 144, para.29.

266 See s.21(1).

267 SI 2003/1673, inserting new s.21A(6).

268 [1998] I.R.L.R. 352, EAT.

269 See the *Employment Code of Practice*, para.5.8.

refers to "provision, criterion or practice": the House of Lords in *Archibald v Fife CC*[270] gave a wide interpretation to the term "arrangement", considering it capable of covering an employer's arrangements for dividing up work, deciding who undertakes what job, determining pay scales, job descriptions or fixing employment terms, conditions and arrangements.[271]

In considering whether a disabled person has been placed at a "substantial disadvantage", the same approach is adopted as that established in *Clark v Novacold* as applying in determining whether discrimination amounting to "less favourable treatment" has occurred: there is no requirement for a disabled person to show that another person in the same circumstances would not have been disadvantaged by the failure to make accommodation in question.[272]

The Law Lords took the view in *Archibald* that the effect of the arrangements in question upon the disabled person could be compared with their effect upon the non-disabled persons subject to the same arrangements but who had not been subject to any disadvantage. This would clarify if a "substantial disadvantage" had occurred.[273] This approach was adopted by the Court of Appeal in *Smith v Churchills Stairlifts Plc*.[274] In this case, a disabled applicant for a sales job was dismissed from a training course for which he had initially been selected as he was unable to carry a radiator cabinet that the firm wished their salesmen to display as a sample to potential customers. At first instance, an employment tribunal had held that the disabled person had not been placed at a "substantial disadvantage", as his inability to carry the cabinet would have been shared by the majority of the general population and therefore he could not be said to have suffered any particular disadvantage that the majority of the population would not also suffer. However, the Court of Appeal held that the disabled applicant had been placed at a disadvantage by this arrangement, as a comparison should not have been with the general population at large, but rather with the effect of this requirement upon the nine other applicants who were accepted for the training course, unlike the applicant who had obviously therefore suffered a substantial disadvantage.

The duty is triggered in this way in respect of a particular individual: there is no general obligation to make a workplace accessible or to provide a service to disabled persons. The duty is therefore personal in nature, and only arises when the employer has sufficient knowledge of the needs of the "triggering"

[270] [2004] UKHL 32.

[271] The Court of Session in this case had adopted a narrower approach, which the Law Lords rejected.

[272] See the *Employment Code of Practice*, para.5.4:

> "It does not matter if a disabled person cannot point to an actual non-disabled person compared with whom he is at a substantial disadvantage. The fact that a non-disabled person, or even another disabled person, would not be substantially disadvantaged by the provision, criterion or practice or by the physical feature in question is irrelevant. The duty is owed specifically to the individual disabled person."

[273] "Substantial" is described by the Employment Code of Practice as meaning something "not minor or trivial": see para.5.11.

[274] [2005] EWCA Civ 1220.

individual. No anticipatory obligation arises, except that in the case of common disabilities which can be readily accommodated with clear and relatively straightforward adjustments, a failure to anticipate may constitute a failure to make reasonable adjustment, especially in the context of the delivery of goods and services.[275] An employer will usually be expected to have sufficient knowledge of the needs of his current employees, and knowledge held by an employee may in normal circumstances be imputed to the employee: however, in general, the employer or service provider will have to be made aware of the disability for the duty to be triggered, which may place disabled persons in a dilemma as to whether to disclose their disability or not.[276]

In *Ridout v TC Group*,[277] the complainant, who suffered from a particularly rare form of epilepsy, was interviewed for a post in a room with bright fluorescent lighting. On entering the room, she mentioned that she might be disadvantaged by the lighting, which the employers took as explaining why she was carrying sunglasses around her neck: she completed the interview without putting on the sunglasses. Her CV had referred to the fact she had epilepsy and that it was controlled by the drug Epilim. The EAT held that the employers had not acted in breach of the reasonable adjustment duty in holding the interview in that room, finding that the employment tribunal was justified in concluding that no reasonable employer could be expected to know that the arrangements made for the interview would disadvantage the complainant without her telling them. The EAT emphasised that the duty to make reasonable adjustment required the tribunal to measure the extent of the duty against the actual or assumed knowledge of the employer, both as to the existence of the disability and its capacity to cause a disadvantage. Tribunals should not impose upon disabled persons a requirement to explain their impairments in detail, but nor should they expect employers in normal circumstances to investigate the impact of a disability in great detail.

B. *Nature of the Duty*

If the duty is triggered, the question of what adjustments are reasonable in the circumstances is an objective one, and tribunals may substitute their own view of what is reasonable for that of the employer or service provider: which contrasts with the approach to the justification defence taken in *Jones v Post Office*.[278] The requirement of "reasonableness", nevertheless, means that employers may still maintain reasonable occupational requirements, cannot be expected to run up disproportionate costs and energy, and may not be obliged

[275] See e.g. *Williams v Channel 5 Engineering Services Ltd*, unreported, Case 2302136/97 (IT).
[276] See the *Employment Code of Practice*, paras 5.14–5.16.
[277] [1998] I.R.L.R. 628.
[278] See *Morse v Wiltshire CC* [1998] I.R.L.R. 352, EAT.

to maintain an individual's pay levels as a part of an accommodation.[279] The test focuses upon the reasonableness of the steps necessary to accommodate the disabled person in light of the circumstances of the employer or service provider, not on whether particular forms of adjustment are capable of being introduced, although of course the practicability and ease of making particular adjustments will be relevant to determining whether the employer or service provider acted reasonably.[280]

The DDA (s.18B(2)) includes some examples of steps an employer may need to take in order to comply with a duty to make reasonable adjustments: these include making physical adjustments to premises; allocating some duties to another employee; transferring the person to fill an existing vacancy; being flexible with regard to working hours or place of work; allowing absence from work for rehabilitation, treatment and assessment; giving or arranging special training; acquiring or modifying equipment; modifying instructions or reference manuals; modifying procedures for testing or assessment; providing a reader or interpreter; and providing supervision or other support. The DRC Employment Code of Practice on employment mentions other steps an employer might have to take, including modifying disciplinary or grievance procedures and modifying performance related pay arrangements.[281]

However, what is reasonable will be a question of fact to be determined in individual cases, with the detailed guidance provided by the Code of Practice being usually very influential. In *Kenny v Hampshire Constabulary*,[282] the complainant suffered from cerebral palsy and needed assistance while urinating: having been initially offered a post, a delay in processing an application for a support worker under the disabled Access to Work scheme meant that the job offer made to him was subsequently withdrawn, on the basis that there was an urgent need to fill the post. The EAT held that there had not been a failure to make reasonable accommodation, as the employer's duty was confined to "job-related" matters: not every failure to make necessary arrangements would fall under the employer's responsibility.

In *British Gas Services Ltd v McCaull*,[283] the EAT emphasised that a failure to consider or to be aware of what was required under the duty to make reasonable adjustments, or a subsequent attempt to argue that particular adjustments were not reasonable when no consideration had been initially given to the claim, did not in itself constitute an automatic breach of the duty:

279 *British Gas Services v McCaull* [2001] I.R.L.R. 60.

280 The use of written questions to assess the competencies of a deaf candidate was held to be a reasonable adjustment in *Hughes v Hillingdon LBC*, ET 6001328/98, July 27, 1999: the ease of this procedure meant that no unreasonable adjustment of practice was required of the employer.

281 *Employment Code of Practice*, paras 5.18–5.20.

282 [1999] I.R.L.R. 76.

283 [2001] I.R.L.R. 60, EAT.

the objective test of reasonableness is applied to what the employer did or did not do, not what he or she had failed to do.[284]

Section 18B(1) of the DDA also sets out a list of factors which should be considered in determining whether in the particular circumstances it is reasonable for the employer[285] to have to make a particular adjustment. The factors it lists include the following:

- the effectiveness of the particular adjustment in question in preventing the particular disadvantage;
- its practicability;
- any financial and other costs which would be incurred and extent of any disruption caused;
- the employer's financial or other resources;
- the availability to the employer of financial or other assistance (such as government grants under the *Access to Work* scheme, which aims to assist the integration of disabled persons into the labour force);
- the nature of the employer's activities and the size of its undertaking.

Increased risk to the health and safety of any person can also a relevant factor.[286]

The EAT in *Morse v Wiltshire CC*[287] set out a series of guidelines as to how tribunals should handle reasonable accommodation claims. In *Stevens v JPM International Ltd*,[288] the EAT emphasised the importance of adhering to the *Morse* guidelines in normal circumstances: in this case, the Tribunal had departed from these guidelines and had prematurely written-off the possibility of making reasonable adjustment. The Tribunal should have considered whether the employer had made unjustified assumptions about the complainant's lack of capacity to fulfil the demands of the job, whether the job requirements could be adjusted to accommodate her abilities, and whether there was proper medical evidence available to the Tribunal which would indicate that the complainant was not going to be capable of doing the post in the foreseeable future.

Often, in cases like *Stevens*, the issue before the tribunal is how far the duty requires the employer to modify existing arrangements. In *Cosgrove v Caesar &*

[284] See also *Tarbuck v Sainsbury's Supermarkets Ltd* UKEAT/0136/06/LA, June 8, 2006, where the EAT upheld the *McCaull* decision. However, for a contrary opinion to the effect that a failure to consider the possibility of reasonable accommodation could constitute an automatic breach of the duty, see *Mid-Staffordshire General Hospital NHS Trust* [2003] I.R.L.R. 566, EAT. The Court of Appeal in *Hay v Surrey CC* [2007] EWCA Civ 93 declined an invitation to clarify the position.

[285] Or, alternatively, the person responsible for the employment situation.

[286] See the Management of Health and Safety at Work Regulations 1999.

[287] [1998] I.R.L.R. 352, EAT.

[288] EAT No.EAT/910/98.

Howie,[289] the EAT decided that an employer has a duty to consider whether reasonable adjustments could be made, even if there is no guarantee they would have worked, and even if the complainant or her supporting medical expert had not suggested a practical accommodation that could be made. However, in *British Gas Services Ltd v McCaull*, the EAT confirmed that after an objective assessment, if no steps could be taken, then no breach existed.

In *London Borough of Hillingdon v Morgan*,[290] the complainant suffered from ME and found returning to work after sick leave stressful. The employer attempted to accommodate her through their redeployment programme, but refused to accommodate her request to work from home. The EAT, in upholding the initial decision in favour of the complainant, emphasised that the council was under a duty not just to treat her as they would have treated any other person under the redeployment scheme, but to go further and provide the necessary specific reasonable adjustments to retain her in employment. In such redeployment cases, as the employer will often be the only person in a position to be aware of what posts or alternative work methods might be available, the onus rests upon them to show that no reasonable alternative postings were available.[291] In *Igen Ltd v Wong*,[292] the Court of Appeal confirmed that the initial onus was on the claimant to make out a case that they had been subject to substantial disadvantage and that there were adjustments that could have been made: however, once this onus has been satisfied, the burden then shifts to the defendant to show no reasonable adjustments were possible.

In *Paul v National Probation Service*,[293] the EAT emphasised that even where occupational health reports had identified problems with employing a disabled person, employers were under a duty to give due consideration to making reasonable adjustments.[294] It also considered that offering the complainant an alternative lower-paid post did not constitute reasonable accommodation.[295] However, in *Mulligan v Inland Revenue*,[296] where the claimant was not meeting output targets, the EAT considered that the reasonable accommodation duty did not require a lowering of performance standards.

289 [2001] I.R.L.R. 653.
290 EAT/1493/98.
291 *Conoco Ltd v Booth*, January 30, 2001 EAT, unreported.
292 [2005] I.R.L.R. 258, EWCA.
293 [2004] I.R.L.R. 190.
294 In *Johnston v Oglesby Building Services Ltd* (Case No. ET/2603296/01), the Employment Tribunal made it clear what conduct was expected from employers:

> ". . . knowing that the applicant suffered a knee problem which made him limp and which made it difficult for him to perform aspects of his job the respondent really ought to have ascertained the proper medical position and then addressed its mind to what was required in order to assist the applicant to remain in employment if possible with appropriate adjustments being made. The brute truth of the matter is that the respondent did nothing in the area of adjustment. It simply saw the continuing absence of the applicant as a problem and, consequently, decided to dismiss him."

See para.23.
295 *ibid.*, para.32.
296 Dec 2, 1999, EAT, EAT/691/99.

Particular issues have recently arisen in relation to the application of the reasonable adjustment requirement in the context of sickness absence, sick pay and sick leave. This is obviously an important issue for disabled persons, who may require time-off for medical reasons and thus may be exposed to tough employer practices and controls on sick leave, absence and pay. Employment tribunals have held that disability-related absences should normally be disregarded or accommodated by employers, as part of reasonable accommodation.[297] This basic approach was confirmed by the EAT in *Pousson v BT*, where the application of a "poor performance attendance procedure" (PPAP) to a disabled worker suffering from diabetes resulted in a worsening of his medical condition and the eventual termination of his employment: the EAT agreed with the original employment tribunal decision that the PPAP should not have been applied in this case as part of reasonable accommodation of the employee's disabled status.[298] However, in *O'Hanlon v Commissioners for Revenue*,[299] the EAT held that a failure to award sick pay to a disabled employee absent from work would not in normal circumstances constitute a failure to make reasonable adjustment by itself.

C. *Reasonable Accommodation and Special Provision—The* Archibald *Decision*

The extent to which the duty to accommodate can require special provision for the claimant was at issue in the House of Lords decision in *Archibald v Fife*.[300] Mrs Archibald was a cleaning and hygiene worker for Fife Council who developed back problems that made it impossible for her to continue manual work. She applied for a transfer to an administrative post, which was however classified as being at a slightly higher grade than her previous post, as where all office posts that did not involve manual work. Fife Council required all applicants for such posts to undergo a competitive interview process: Mrs Archibald did not succeed at this stage, and lost her job as she was unable to be alternatively employed. She appealed unsuccessfully within the council and then complained to an employment tribunal.

The essence of her complaint was that she should not have been required to go though the competitive interviews for the administrative post if she could show that she was qualified and suitable for the job in question, as a transfer to this post was a reasonable accommodation in respect of her disability which the council was under a legal duty to provide. In contrast, the council's policy was that competitive interviews were required if applying for a job at a higher grade: if the claimant was exempted from the requirement, this would con-

[297] See *Cox v Post Office*, ET No.1301162/97; *Kerrigan v Rover Group Ltd*, ET No.14014006/97.
[298] The Code of Practice on Employment gives examples of reasonable adjustments to sickness policy and procedures that employers may have to take: see para.5.20.
[299] [2006] I.R.L.R. 840, EAT.
[300] [2004] UKHL 32; [2004] I.R.L.R. 651.

stitute preferential treatment which was not required under the accommodation duty.

The tribunal held that, as there was nothing apart from transferring her to this post that the council could have done, and the duty did not require normal eligibility rules to be suspended, the council was not in breach of its reasonable accommodation duty. The EAT dismissed Mrs Archibald's appeal, on the basis that there was nothing in the arrangements for the job interviews which placed her at a substantial disadvantage on the grounds of her disability, because the interview policy applied to everyone: therefore, the obligation to make an adjustment had not been triggered.

The EAT also held that, even if it had been triggered, the duty did not require employers to waive standard recruitment and promotion procedures for particular posts if necessary to accommodate a disabled individual, citing the provisions of the then s.6(7) of the DDA, which provided that nothing in the legislation should be interpreted as requiring a person to treat a disabled person more favourably than he treats or would treat others. (This provision is now contained in s.18D of the amended DDA.) However, the EAT appeared to overlook that para.2 of this subsection expressly excluded the duty to make reasonable adjustments under s.6 from the scope of this provision precluding more favourable treatment. Nevertheless, the Court of Session also dismissed her appeal, on the ground that the obligation to make an adjustment had not been triggered: Mrs Archibald had not been disadvantaged on the grounds of her disability either in being dismissed for not being able to perform her job, or in not being transferred to the new post.[301]

However, the House of Lords on appeal confirmed that the duty required employers to make reasonable adjustments for disabled people if they become unable to carry out their job due to their disability. This meant that the duty was triggered in this case. The Law Lords went on to hold that the duty to make reasonable accommodation may indeed require employers to waive standard procedures as part of making reasonable adjustments for a disabled person, and requires consideration of whether it is reasonable to transfer the disabled person to another vacant post, even if that post is at a higher grade. Therefore, Fife County Council was required by the duty to make provision for Mrs Archibald, without demanding that she go through the interview process.

Archibald v Fife CC [2004] UKHL 32

LORD HOPE:

[15] "The duty . . . is not simply a duty to make adjustments. The making of adjustments is not an end in itself. The end is reached when the disabled person is no longer at a

[301] [2004] I.R.L.R. 197.

substantial disadvantage, in comparison with persons who are not disabled, by reason of any arrangements made by or on behalf of the employer or any physical features of premises which the employer occupies . . .

[19] . . . The performance of this duty may require the employer, when making adjustments, to treat a disabled person who is in this position more favourably to remove the disadvantage which is attributable to the disability . . ."

LADY HALE:

[47] "According to its long title, the purpose of the 1995 Act is 'to make it unlawful to discriminate against disabled persons in connection with employment, the provision of goods, facilities and services or the disposal or management of premises . . .' But this legislation is different from the Sex Discrimination Act 1975 and the Race Relations Act 1976. In the latter two, men and women or black and white, as the case may be, are opposite sides of the same coin. Each is to be treated in the same way. Treating men more favourably than women discriminates against women. Treating women more favourably than men discriminates against men. Pregnancy apart, the differences between the genders are generally regarded as irrelevant. The 1995 Act, however, does not regard the differences between disabled people and others as irrelevant. It does not expect each to be treated in the same way. It expects reasonable adjustments to be made to cater for the special needs of disabled people. It necessarily entails an element of more favourable treatment. The question for us is when that obligation arises and how far it goes . . .

[57] It is common ground that the Act entails a measure of positive discrimination, in the sense that employers are required to take steps to help disabled people which they are not required to take for others. It is also common ground that employers are only required to take those steps which in all the circumstances it is reasonable for them to have to take. Once triggered, the scope of the duty is determined by what is reasonable, considered in the light of the factors set out in [the legislation]. The debate is about what triggers the duty. The council argue that its purpose is to enable the disabled person to overcome the obstacles which her disability puts in the way of her doing the job for which she has applied or is already employed. The examples of steps which the employer may have to take . . . are with [one] exception . . . all adjustments which might be made to the particular job—adapting the premises, reallocating duties, altering the hours, modifying equipment, or providing training, interpretation or supervision. Once those obstacles have been cleared out of the way, there is a 'level playing field' and the disabled person is free to compete on her merits with anyone else. There is no positive discrimination other than redressing the impact of the disability on her ability to do a job which she is otherwise well fitted to do. This duty cannot arise when the disability means that she cannot do the job at all and there is no adjustment to the arrangements for that job which can make any difference.

[58] The Disability Rights Commission, which has taken up the case on behalf of Mrs Archibald, argue that in such a case the duty is indeed triggered. The control mechanism lies in the fact that the employer is only required to take such steps as it is reasonable for them to have to take. They are not expected to do the impossible. But among the possible steps is (c)—transfer to fill an existing vacancy, which must include an existing vacancy for a different job. Inability to do the present job cannot mean that there is no duty at all. The Act was clearly intended to apply to existing employees who became disabled as well as to would-be employees who were already disabled. This is reflected in paragraph 4.20 of the Code of Practice, issued by the Secretary of State and laid before Parliament under sections 53 and 54 of the Act, which says this under the heading 'transferring the person to fill an existing vacancy':

> 'If an employee becomes disabled, or has a disability which worsens so she cannot work in the same place or under the same arrangements and there is no reasonable adjustment which would enable the employee to continue doing the current job, then

she might have to be considered for any suitable alternative posts which are available. (Such a case might also involve reasonable retraining.)' . . .

[65] The duty is to take such steps as it is reasonable in all the circumstances of the case for the employer to have to take. Could this ever include transferring her to fill an existing vacancy at a slightly higher grade without competitive interview? It is noteworthy that the council did do a great deal to help Mrs Archibald. They arranged retraining for her. They kept her on the books for a great deal longer than they normally would have done while she retrained and then looked for alternative posts. They automatically short-listed her for the posts for which she applied. They went rather beyond their normal policies in cases of redundancy or ill-health. They were behaving as if they did have a duty towards her . . . even if they did not think that they did. They would have been prepared to transfer her without competitive interview to another job at the same or a lower grade, even though there might be others better qualified to do it. But as she was at the bottom of the manual grade and all office jobs were nominally at a higher grade, there was no equal or lower grade job to which she could be transferred.

[66] Section 6(3)(c) merely refers to 'an existing vacancy'. It does not qualify this by any words such as 'at the same or a lower grade'. It does refer to 'transferring' rather than 'promoting' her, but as a matter of language a transfer can be upwards as well as sideways or downwards. Furthermore, transferring her 'to fill' an existing vacancy is clearly more than merely allowing her to apply, short-listing or considering her for an existing vacancy. If that were all it meant, it would add nothing to the existing non-discrimination requirements: the employer is already required by section 4(2)(b) not to discriminate against a disabled employee in the opportunities afforded for promotion, transfer, training or any other benefit.

[67] On the face of it, therefore, transferring Mrs Archibald to a sedentary position which she was qualified to fill was among the steps which it might have been reasonable in all the circumstances for the council to have to take once she could no longer walk and sweep. Is there any reason to hold to the contrary?

[68] The Employment Tribunal thought that there was. They relied upon that part of section 6(7) which provides that 'nothing in this Part is to be taken to require an employer to treat a disabled person more favourably than he treats or would treat others'. But this is prefaced by the words, 'Subject to the provisions of this section, . . .': so that, to the extent that the duty to make reasonable adjustments requires it, the employer is not only permitted but obliged to treat a disabled person more favourably than others . . ."

The crucial importance of *Archibald* lies in its emphasis upon the strength and extent of the reasonable accommodation duty. It confirms that conforming with the duty can require employers to make adjustments to their usual policies, and even depart from the policies and make special provision for disabled persons were necessary. The House of Lords also clarified that the question of whether less favourable treatment could be justified cannot be resolved until a determination has been made as to whether reasonable adjustments could have been made: in other words, less favourable treatment cannot be justified if reasonable accommodation could have been made. The judgment also confirmed that the duty to make reasonable accommodation also covered the situation where a person becomes incapable, through disability, of carrying out his or her job.

D. *The (Now Semi Defunct) Justification Defence*

The original text of the DDA had permitted a failure to make reasonable accommodation to be justified, if the employer could show that the reason for the failure was both material to the circumstances of the particular case and substantial, just as "less favourable treatment" can be justified. In *Morse v Wiltshire CC*,[302] the EAT set out the appropriate approach to be adopted by tribunals in determining employment-related cases of reasonable adjustment, and in considering when a failure to make accommodation would be justified. The *Morse* decision is notable for its very different approach from that subsequently adopted in *Jones v Post Office* in applying the justification test where less favourable treatment had taken place. In *Morse*, Bell J. established that a tribunal must apply an objective test to the materiality and substantiality issues, and reach its own decision on whether the correct balance has been struck. He rejected the suggestion that the "reasonable range of responses" test used in *Jones* should be applied in the context of the justification defence to reasonable accommodation, and the notion that the tribunal could not substitute its views for that of the employer.

This approach appeared to conflict with that of the Court of Appeal in *Jones*. However, the Court of Appeal confirmed in *Collins v Royal National Theatre Board*[303] that the tests for reasonableness and for justification were both objective in nature, and rejected the argument that the *Jones* test should be applied in the context of the reasonable accommodation requirement.[304] This different approach was justified as required by the language of the DDA, in particular the reference in the then s.6(1) of the DDA to "it is the duty of the employer to take such steps as it is reasonable, in all the circumstances of the case, for him to have to take", and the nature of the reasonable accommodation duty. In *Smith v Churchill Stairlifts*,[305] the Court of Appeal took a similar approach. It concluded that an employer's reason for refusing to make an adjustment, if genuinely held and material and substantial, could be sufficient justification for less favourable treatment of a disabled person, but would not constitute sufficient justification for a failure to make reasonable accommodation if the employer had failed to give real consideration to the possibility of altering the problematic arrangements. In other words, the justification tests were different for less favourable treatment and a failure to make reasonable accommodation, the latter requiring an objective assessment of the employer's failure.

The ability of an employer to justify a failure to make reasonable accommodation has since been removed. In 1999, the Disability Task Force reported

[302] [1998] I.R.L.R. 352, EAT.
[303] [2004] EWCA Civ 144.
[304] This was confirmed by the Court of Appeal in *Law v Pace Micro Technology Ltd* [2004] EWCA Civ 923, CA.
[305] [2005] EWCA Civ 1220.

that, while the defence of justification of less favourable treatment should be retained, the defence of justification of unreasonable failure to make adjustments appeared to cover many of the same issues as would already have been decided in asking whether accommodation was reasonable. In addition, it was difficult to see from both a practical and a conceptual viewpoint how an employer could (or should) be able to justify a failure to make reasonable accommodation: the "reasonableness" requirement that needed to be satisfied before the duty applied appeared to give the employer sufficient leeway, and the additional justification element merely added another level of unnecessary complexity.[306] The Task Force therefore recommended that the justification defence to a breach of s.6 should be removed.

The Employment Equality Directive subsequently contained no provision for a justification defence to a failure to make reasonable accommodation. Therefore, the justification defence of a failure to make reasonable accommodation in the employment and occupation context has been removed from the DDA with effect from October 1, 2004, by the 2003 Regulations. However, this justification defence still exists for service providers, despite the problems that it presents. Nevertheless, *Morse, Collins* and *Smith* remain good precedent in confirming that this test when still applied in the context of goods and services provisions is objective in nature, unlike the justification defence for less favourable treatment.

E. *Reasonable Adjustment in Service Provision*

A different accommodation duty applies in the context of goods and services provision. Section 21 of the DDA requires three types of adjustment to be made by service providers where required: reasonable steps to change practices, policies and procedures which make it impossible or unreasonably difficult for disabled persons to use a service;[307] changes to physical features of premises where they make it impossible or unreasonably difficult to use a service (these changes in turn fall into four categories: removing, altering, or providing a reasonable means of a avoiding the feature; or providing the service by a reasonable alternative method);[308] and providing an auxiliary aid or service (such as information on tape, or the provision of a sign language interpreter) where this would enable or facilitate disabled persons in using a service.[309] Physical access barriers, eligibility requirements and health and

[306] In *Williams v J Walter Thompson Group Ltd* [2005] EWCA Civ 133, Mummery L.J. commented at para.12 that "in practice ... if there was a breach of the s.6 duty [i.e. if the employer had not made reasonable accommodation], it was extremely difficult, if not impossible, to conceive of circumstances in which the defence of justification ... would be available to an employer."

[307] s.21(1).

[308] s.21(2).

[309] s.21(4).

safety restrictions are all examples of factors that might make access to services "impossible or unreasonably difficult". Section 19(1)(b) provides that it is unlawful for a service provider to fail to comply with these requirements, and s.20(2) states that an unjustifiable failure to comply with the s.21 duty amounts to unlawful discrimination.

Due to the potentially wide-ranging nature of these provisions, they have been brought into force gradually and in a staggered manner. The obligations relating to practices, policies and procedures, auxiliary aids and services, as well as provision of a reasonable alternative method of service, came into force in October 1999, with the remaining duties relating to physical features coming into force in October 2004. Since December 2006, similar duties apply to premises occupied by private clubs and to public authorities carrying out public functions.

These duties are all circumscribed by s.21(6), which states that nothing in the section requires a service provider to take any steps which would fundamentally alter the nature of the service in question or the nature of his trade, profession or business. The Code of Practice gives some examples of when this would apply—such as nightclubs, which do not have to adjust their lighting to accommodate customers who are partially sighted if this would fundamentally change the atmosphere or ambience of the club.[310] As service provision is not covered by the Employment Equality Directive, a failure to make an adjustment is still subject to a justification defence, similar to that which used to apply to employment-related adjustments: the restrictive scope given to this defence in *Collins v National Theatre* would presumably also apply here (see above).

These limitations on the adjustment duties are to a degree counterbalanced by the specific wording of s.21, which refers specifically to the duties being owed to "disabled persons", unlike the employment duty, which is owed only to distinct individuals (see above). This means that the service provision duties are anticipatory in nature, as they are owed to "disabled people" in general. This means that service providers need to ensure that they have considered and taken steps to ensure the accessibility of their services.[311] This is very important, as it prevents service providers from arguing that an adjustment was not required as they had not been informed in advance of the needs of the disabled person in question. Unlike the employment duty, these anticipatory duties require the transformation of existing practices and physical features without an initial "trigger" request: the existence of a potential problem or need is enough to trigger the duties, and therefore they are key elements in changing social practices.

However, what the duties require, and when the different time-limits kick in, can be unclear, due to the use of different and potentially overlapping triggers for each duty and the inherent uncertainty of the requirement that

[310] *Code of Practice (Revised): Rights of Access to Goods, Facilities and Premises*, para.4.28.
[311] See the *Code of Practice (Revised): Rights of Access to Goods, Facilities and Premises*, Chs 4 and 5.

adjustment is necessary when it is "impossible or unreasonably difficult" for a disabled person to access a service. A failure to improve the accessibility of services, to change polices and practices or to provide auxiliary aids will not in itself breach the legislation: the failure must mean that it is "impossible or unreasonably difficult" for the disabled person to use the service.[312]

This trigger requirement can be potentially difficult to meet: a service could be reasonably difficult to use but a disabled person may nevertheless have no remedy. It would appear to be more difficult to satisfy than the "substantial disadvantage" test used in the employment context, and in the education duty provisions in SENDA. In addition, while anticipatory in nature, the "unreasonable difficulty" must both affect disabled persons in general, and the individual complainant specifically, before an action can be brought. A two-stage test is involved: does the particular feature at issue make access impossible or unreasonably difficult for disabled people in general, and if it does, does it make access impossible or unreasonably difficult for the individual claimant?

This test, and in particular the "trigger requirement" that a service must be "impossible or unreasonably difficult" to access before a breach of the DDA will exist, has been the subject of criticism and was the subject of a recommendation for change made by the Disability Task Force in 1999. These concerns are reflected in the case law. In *Baggley v Kingston-upon-Hull Council*,[313] a wheelchair user was required to sit at the back of a concert hall for health and safety reasons, and as the rest of the audience was standing, was unable to see the performer. It was held that the inability to see the performance (by Mel C, aka "Sporty Spice") did not make it "impossible or unreasonably difficult to make use of the service". In *Appleby and Department for Work and Pensions*,[314] a person with a hearing impairment, who needed to supplement his use of hearing aids with visual clues, had tremendous difficulties in obtaining a National Insurance number at a benefits office, due to the failure to inform the complainant of the existence of an induction loop system, and the non-functioning of tannoy and display screen systems. It was held that the complainant's practice of asking a member of the public to notify the complainant of when it was his turn meant that it was not "unreasonably difficult" for Mr Appleby to use the service. However, the failure to inform the complainant of the existence of the induction loop system was held to be tantamount to a failure to have such a system in the first place, and a breach of the DDA duty was established. In both cases, a very high standard was set as to what would constitute unreasonable difficulty. The recent Discrimination Law Review has suggested having a single standard threshold whereby the duty to make reasonable accommodation is triggered, and has suggested the adoption of the employment "substantial disadvantage" threshold. If this becomes law, it will

312 See DDA s.19 (1)(b).

313 Kingston upon Hull, County Court, Claim Number KH101929.

314 Lambeth County Court, Claim No.LB001649, DJ Worthington.

mean that the problem of the excessively high standards that are currently required in the goods and services context will be lessened.[315]

As with the employment duty, a degree of uncertainty inevitably exists as to what will be deemed to constitute a "reasonable" adjustment. This uncertainty is exacerbated by the relative rarity of goods and services cases, very few of which are taken to the county courts. The Code of Practice indicates that the same basic factors that are taken into account in assessing what is "reasonable" in the context of the employment duty will be taken into account in the context of service provision, such as effectiveness, practicability, cost, disruption, resources, amount already spent on adjustments, and the availability of other sources of assistance.[316] The relationship between the trigger requirement that a disabled person be not subject to "unreasonable difficulty" and the requirement that adjustment need to be "reasonable" is uncertain: is it reasonable for a service provider to make only the necessary adjustments to make it "reasonably difficult" for a disabled person to use the service? To what extent will adjustments be necessary if most disabled people can access the service, but certain specific individuals face considerable difficulty?

There are specific provisions in the DDA for regulations to be made to prescribe, amongst other things, circumstances in which it is reasonable or not for a provider of services to have to take steps of a prescribed description.[317] This could allow the government to prescribe accessibility standards, which would provide a degree of clarity and certainty where these regulations apply. Regulations have been introduced to specify accessibility standards in new construction and other forms of building work,[318] but no other systemic regulations under these provisions have been introduced.

The Court of Appeal has however recently given guidance both as to what will constitute "reasonable accommodation" and what will constitute "unreasonable difficulty" in accessing a service, in *Roads v Central Trains*.[319] In particular, it has addressed the question of what constitutes "unreasonable difficulty" and the relationship between this trigger requirement and the need for adjustments to be "reasonable". In this case, the claimant (a wheelchair user) wished to change platforms at Thetford to catch a return train service to Norwich. However, changing platforms at Thetford Station was only possible by an inaccessible footbridge: the only other access route to the other platform was a distance of eight hundred metres via a busy road with no footpath. The claimant was offered free rail travel on to Ely, where there was an elevator which would have enabled him to change platforms there, and back to Thetford, which would have allowed him to access the desired train service, but would have added an extra hour on to his journey. The claimant wished a taxi to be provided instead, but at the relevant time, there was no taxi in

315 *A Framework for Fairness* (London: HMSO, 2007), paras 1.54–1.59.
316 See the *Code of Practice (Revised): Rights of Access to Goods, Facilities and Premises*, Ch.6.
317 DDA s.(21)(5)(a) and (b).
318 See Pt M of the Building Regulations, particularly SI 2000/2531 and SI 2003/2692.
319 [2004] EWCA Civ 1541.

Thetford with the necessary adaptations to carry him. Obtaining a suitably-adapted taxi from Norwich would have cost forty-five pounds, and the defendant did not wish to incur this cost, arguing that its obligations to Mr Roads would be discharged by conveying him to Ely and allowing him to change platforms there. The plaintiff alleged a failure on the part of Central Trains to make reasonable accommodation in line with s.21 of the DDA to enable him to access the train service without unreasonable difficulty.

At first instance in the Norwich County Court, Judge O'Brien concluded that it was not reasonable in the circumstances of the case for Central Trains to provide a taxi. Mr Roads appealed, as did Central Trains, who contended that the appropriate test under s.21 DDA should have been to ask whether it was unreasonably difficult for disabled persons generally, and not just Mr Roads, to use the alternative route unaided. The Court of Appeal concluded that Central Trains was a service provider for the purpose of Pt III of the DDA, and that the separation of platforms at Thetford station amounted to a physical feature which made it impossible or unreasonably difficult for him to make use of the service Central Trains was providing. As a result, the train company was under a duty to Mr Roads to provide reasonable adjustments to enable him to make use of their service, and the court held that it was unreasonable in the circumstances and consequently discriminatory not to supply the taxi. In response to the cross-appeal, which it dismissed, the court also clarified that the appropriate test under s.21 was to assess what constituted reasonable accommodation for persons with a similar kind of disability as the individual at issue, and not what constituted reasonable accommodation for disabled persons generally as a class. The fact that a particular group of disabled persons can access a service does not mean that the service will be treated as accessible to all. In *Roads*, the fact that some wheelchair users could have used the access route at the station did not mean that it was classified as accessible to all wheelchair users.

Sedley L.J.'s judgment is also notable for its analysis of situations where, as in this case, there are number of possible adjustments that could be put in place to enable a disabled person to use an otherwise inaccessible service. Where there is only one practicable solution, it may have to be deemed reasonable even if it is demeaning or onerous for disabled people. But where there are different possible adjustments, Sedley L.J. stated that:

"...the policy of the DDA is not a minimalist policy of simply ensuring that some access is available to the disabled: it is, so far as reasonably practicable, to approximate the access enjoyed by disabled persons to that enjoyed by the rest of the public."[320]

This sets a high threshold for service providers, and means that the mere fact that a service is accessible in some way may often not be enough. The service

[320] para.13, see below.

provider may be required to show that the adjustments they have provided make the service as accessible as possible to disabled people as it is to non-disabled people. In *Roads*, the provision of a taxi would have enabled the service to be provided in a way that was a close as possible to the service provided to non-wheel chair users, who would not be expected to make a 60 mile detour.[321]

Roads v Central Trains [2004] EWCA Civ 1541

per SEDLEY L.J.

[11]. "[...] Manifestly no single feature of premises will obstruct access for all disabled persons or—in most cases—for disabled persons generally. In the present case, for instance, the footbridge is not likely to present an insuperable problem for blind people. The phrase "disabled persons" in section 21(2) must therefore be directing attention to features which impede persons with one or more kinds of disability: here, those whose disability makes them dependent on a wheelchair. The reason why it is expressed in this way and not by reference to the individual claimant is that section 21 sets out a duty resting on service providers. They cannot be expected to anticipate the needs of every individual who may use their service, but what they are required to think about and provide for are features which may impede persons with particular kinds of disability—impaired vision, impaired mobility and so on. Thus the practical way of applying section 21 in discrimination proceedings will usually be to focus the question and the answer on people with the same kind of disability as the claimant.

[12] The personal right created by section 19 of the DDA operates by fastening a cause of action on to the section 21 duty if the effect of a breach of the duty is "to make it impossible or unreasonably difficult for the disabled person to make use" of the service in question. Thus there is a double test, albeit both limbs use the same phraseology: first (in paraphrase), does the particular feature impede people with one or more kinds of disability; secondly, if it does, has it impeded the claimant?

[13] There is a further question of the meaning and effect of section 21(2). What paragraph (d) requires the service provider to do is "provide a reasonable alternative method" of—in this case—access to the eastbound line. Central Trains' fundamental position was that the station at Ely afforded this, and that this was enough to satisfy the Act. But, as Mr Coppel fairly and rightly accepted, what is reasonable in this special field of law is not always straightforward. Where there is only one practicable solution, it may have to be treated as reasonable even if it is demeaning or onerous for disabled people to use it. If on the other hand there is a range of solutions, the fact that one of them, if it stood alone, would satisfy section 21(2)(d) may not be enough to afford a defence. This is because the policy of the Act, as I would accept, is what it was held to be by Mynors Ch (albeit by way of restricting the duty) in *In re Holy Cross, Pershore* [2002] Fam 1, §105: "to provide access to a service as close as it is reasonably possible to get to the standard normally offered to the public at large". While, therefore, the Act does not require the court to make nice choices between comparably reasonable solutions, it makes comparison inescapable

[321] Note that Central Trains had conceded that the cost of the taxi from Norwich was not a relevant factor in assessing whether providing this service was reasonable. The reasons for this concession are not clear, and Sedley L.J. indicated that this cost could have been a significant factor for assessing the reasonableness of this form of accommodation: see para.10.

where a proffered solution is said not to be reasonable precisely because a better one, in terms of practicality or of the legislative policy, is available. That was this case...

[32] [...] Mr Lissack goes on to attack the judgment at two specific points. One is the judge's taking into account against the claimant the small scale of the problem. The other is his failure to consider what able-bodied passengers would make of the inconvenience of having to travel to Ely and back in order to change platforms. The fact that this was likely to be only an occasional problem made it more reasonable, not less (in Mr Lissack's submission), for Central Trains to solve it when it occurred by summoning an adapted taxi; and if the alternative of going round via Ely was an inconvenience that no able-bodied passenger would be expected to put up with, why (Mr Lissack asks) should Mr Roads? It is only, he submits, if the judge, despite the concession, took the cost of the Norwich taxi into account that he can have arrived at his conclusion that the measure sought by the claimant was unreasonable.

[33] For Central Trains, Mr Philip Coppel submits that the scale of the problem lies squarely within the issues posed by section 21(2)(d), which directs attention to "all the circumstances of the case". These necessarily include, he submits, both the relative rather than absolute nature of the difficulty (and therefore the fact that other wheelchair users coped) and the infrequency of Mr Roads' encounters with the problem. The awkwardness of the round trip through Ely had been expressly considered in the judgment: "it adds a good hour whichever way one looks at it".

[34] These competing submissions are not all mutually exclusive. The relative infrequency of the problem is no doubt relevant, but it may point towards the reasonableness, rather than the unreasonableness, of making special provision to meet it. I agree with Mr Lissack, however, that the relevance of the fact that some wheelchair users cope with the Station Lane route is logically spent with the finding that access is nevertheless unreasonably difficult for disabled people generally and for Mr Roads personally. It cannot be brought in a second time to reduce the standard of provision which it is reasonable to have to make to alleviate the difficulty."

Roads strengthens the reasonable accommodation duty imposed on service providers by s.21, especially in its emphasis upon the need to make accommodation for disabled persons so that they come as close as possible to accessing services to the same degree as non-disabled persons. It remains to be seen how the objective "reasonableness" requirement will be interpreted and applied in other goods and services cases. As discussed above, it should also be remembered that a defence of justification for a failure to make reasonable accommodation is still available, by virtue of s.19. This suffers from the same problems of coherence and redundancy as did the similar defence that existed for a failure to make reasonable accommodation in employment and occupation: however, as the area of goods and services lies outside the scope of the Employment Equality Directive, the UK government has not yet considered it necessary to remove this defence, as was done with the employment and occupation justification defence. However, objective justification will have to be shown, as held in *Collins v Royal National Theatre Board* and *Smith v Churchill Stairlifts* (see above), which imposes a stiffer standard of justification than does the *Jones* test used in the context of less favourable treatment.

XV. Trends and New Directions

The DDA is far from flawless. The definition of disability used in the legislation generates complexities and difficulties, as do the reasonable accommodation duties imposed upon service providers. There are significant areas of omission, although the 2005 Act and the implementation of the Directive have remedied some of the more important gaps. The test set out in *Jones* dilutes the justification requirement in the context of less favourable treatment, and the lingering legacy of the "medical model" continues to be a problematic factor both in how the legislation is framed in places and also occasionally in how it is interpreted. However, in the main, the DDA as it currently stands is a very important legislative instrument, which has made a gradual but significant contribution to breaking down some of the barriers to full and equal participation by persons with disabilities in society.

By 2005, 8,908 cases had commenced in England, Scotland and Wales under the employment provisions in Pt II of the DDA, of which 1,757 had reached a hearing. By contrast, only 53 County Court or Sheriff Court cases had at that stage commenced under the goods, facilities and services provisions in Pt III, just 9 of which proceeded to trial.[322] This indicates that much of the case law being generated under the Act stems from the area of employment and occupation, but it should be borne in mind that the accommodation requirements imposed on service providers are also gradually creating a new environment of enhanced accessibility. The provisions of the DDA have also acted as a springboard for the DRC to launch formal investigations into the accessibility of websites, the qualifications of health carers and the treatment of disabled persons within the health system: the DRC's legal strategy of supporting significant or ground-breaking cases under the DDA has also generated high-profile victories, such as that in *Ryanair v Ross*.[323]

The DDA also breaks new ground in anti-discrimination legislation in general in its rejection of a "symmetrical" approach and the imposition of positive accommodation duties upon employers and service providers. Sandra Fredman has argued that disability discrimination legislation represents in certain ways a significant advance on existing anti-discrimination legislation:

[322] See the DRC website, *http://www.drc-gb.org/thelaw* for these figures.

[323] See *www.drc.org.uk* for information on the work of the commission, which now has been replaced by the Equality and Human Rights Commission, which contains a specialist Disability Sub-Committee within its institutional structure.

Sandra Fredman, "Disability Equality: A Challenge to the Existing Anti-Discrimination Paradigm?, in Caroline Gooding and Anna Lawson (eds), *Disability Rights in Europe* (Oxford: Hart, 2004) pp.199–218

[211–214] "... Firstly, it is expressly asymmetrical. Gender and race legislation deliberately do not target the disadvantaged group, but instead view any gender or race based criterion as unlawful. This means that it is unlawful to use such criteria even if the aim is benefit the disadvantaged group ... By contrast, the DDA aims expressly to benefit people with disabilities. It thus aims, not at neutrality, but at redressing the disadvantage experienced by a specific group.

Secondly, the conformist tendencies of the direct discrimination concept in the race and gender legislation have been mitigated ... from very early on, tribunals and courts found it difficult to find an appropriate able-bodied norm to function as the comparator in a direct discrimination claim ... In the seminal Court of Appeal case of *Clark v Novacold*, Mummery LJ noted the "futile attempts of the ... courts to find and identify the characteristics of a hypothetical non-pregnant male comparator for a pregnant woman in sex discrimination cases". He therefore deliberately distanced himself from the difficulties experienced under the race and sex discrimination legislation in identifying the characteristics of a hypothetical comparator. Instead, he held that the question was how a non-disabled person would be treated. The result is to minimise the role of the comparator, with the effect that it becomes unlawful simply to subject a person to detriment on grounds of their disability...

Thirdly, and most importantly, recognition that equality requires more than sameness results, in the form of the duty to make reasonable adjustments, in an explicit requirement that the norm be changed. This duty, modelled on the duty to make reasonable accommodations in the ADA, is in many senses a precursor to the positive duty to promote equality, or the fourth generation equality rights, allied to substantive equality."

Fredman's argument leads on to an analysis of the inevitable limits of the DDA, which are similar to those that affect other types of anti-discrimination legislation: it remains too individualistic in its focus to give true effect to the "universalist" or "substantive equality" approaches, which see disability rights as potentially a matter for all and stress the need for positive steps to remove disadvantages to permit "universal access" to social goods. She continues to argue that:

"However ... the DDA ... is severely constrained by the continuing adherence to individualism. Thus the DDA does not to include an indirect discrimination, disability being considered to be too individual a matter. This contrasts with legislation elsewhere. The ADA, for instance, has always had an indirect discrimination provision and the EU employment directive has had little difficulty incorporating one. The Canadian Supreme Court has recently characterised disparate impact discrimination as the major form of disability discrimination...

This individualism is reinforced by the duty to make reasonable adjustment, which, in the context of employment at least, is specifically formulated as an individual duty.

In this respect, it is far more limited than the positive duty found in fourth generation equality statutes. This too contrasts with legislation from other jurisdictions, where the group dimension of duty of accommodation is stressed. Some have already generalised the duty of accommodation to embrace all grounds of discrimination. Thus, South African employment equity legislation places a duty on designated employers to take affirmative action, which includes making reasonable accommodation for blacks, women and disabled people...

As argued above, substantive equality moves beyond what was increasingly recognised as a sterile equality-difference debate. Instead, the concept of equality itself is reconfigured, so that the norm itself is refashioned to incorporate social diversity... In the case of disability, this means that the norm can the wide range of disabilities which can affect anyone during their normal lifecycle, whether as a subject or a carer. In other words, disability becomes a normal aspect of life. Substantive equality therefore encapsulate the universalist analysis, according to which the aim of substantive equality is not different or special treatment, but universal access to all activities.

Substantive equality, understood in this way, requires that social institutions be restructured to reflect the widened norm. This in turn requires a radical departure from the established structure of discrimination law... Substantive equality requires a positive duty to promote equality, resulting in proactive structural change."

Peter Alldridge has made a similar point, arguing that while it is important that the DDA ensures that opportunities are opened up for persons with disabilities to have access to employment, goods and services within existing social structures, there is also a need to transform these existing social norms so that they can provide genuine opportunities for self-realisation for persons with disabilites. He suggests that:

"disability discrimination claims challenge the assumption made in the other [equality] cases that a fairly limited formal notion of equality is sufficient. While it is relatively easy to work out what equality would mean in cases of discrimination on the basis of gender, sex sexuality, race or age, because people want the same thing as the comparator, the claimant in disability cases usually wants something different".[324]

The imposition of a positive duty upon public authorities to eliminate disability discrimination, to eliminate the unlawful harassment of disabled persons and to promote equality of opportunity for disabled persons in the 2005 Act is therefore a significant step, requiring as it does public authorities to take proactive action to identify and to remove barriers faced by disabled persons.[325] This duty has applied since December 2006, and has considerable potential for making a difference to how disabled persons are treated by public authorities. (For more on positive duties, see Chapters 6 and 7.) Alldridge also draws attention to the recent Cabinet Office Strategy Unit policy document, *Improving the Life Chances of Disabled People*, which defines disability as "disadvantage experienced by an individual resulting from barriers to independent living or educational, employment or other opportunities that

[324] See Peter Alldridge, "Locating Disability Law" (2006) 59 Current Legal Problems 445.

[325] See DDA s.49A. See also Colm O'Cinneide, "A New Generation of Equality Legislation? Positive Duties and Disability Rights", in A. Lawson and C. Gooding, *Disability Rights in Europe* (Oxford: Hart, 2005), pp.219–248.

impact on people with impairments and/or ill health''.[326] As he notes, this clearly embraces the social model of analysis, which in turn reflects the ''universalist'' and ''substantive equality'' approaches.

However, Alldridge also warns about assuming that a focus on securing equal opportunities for disabled persons will be enough. He argues that the disability rights movement has focused upon equality rights in recent decades, and has been understandably suspicious of ''welfarism'', given the legacy of the paternalist medical model.[327] The DDA and other ''equality'' instruments concentrate upon securing rights for those who can work or access social goods if discriminatory practices are removed.[328] However, many persons with disabilities will always require state support and the special allocation of resources that match their needs. Therefore, issues of social entitlement, positive obligations under human rights instruments, socio-economic and welfare rights, and the fairness and justice of state welfare provision remain salient and important issues for disabled persons. This should not be forgotten: issues of non-discrimination, resource allocation and the positive obligations of the state cannot easily be separated in the context of disability.

In 2006, Lord Ashley of Stoke introduced a private member's bill into the House of Lords, the Disabled Persons (Independent Living) Bill, which if its provisions were enacted, would set out principles which would underpin the delivery of independent living by local authorities, health services and their partner organisations, such as the enabling of freedom, choice, control, self-determination and participation of disabled persons, and the protection of their dignity.[329] The Bill would also place a duty upon public authorities to co-operate between themselves and key partners (such as Jobcentre Plus) to promote independent living and improve outcomes for disabled people, and supplements this with provisions on minimum levels of support, transferring support entitlements if necessary, and establishing a coherent system for charging for support. This type of legislative initiative is as integral to giving effect to ideals of equality or dignity for many disabled persons as is the DDA, and this dimension should not be forgotten.

326 Cabinet Office, *Improving the Life Chances of Disabled People* (London: Cabinet Office, 2005), para.3.1.

327 See also L. Waddington, ''Evolving Disability Policies: From Social Welfare to Human Rights: an international trend from a European perspective'' (2001) 19 Netherlands Quarterly of Human Rights 141.

328 See Ruth O'Brien, *Crippled Justice: The History of Modern Disability Policy in the Workplace* (Chicago: University of Chicago Press, 2001).

329 See Disability Rights Commission, *A Briefing on Lord Ashley's Disabled Persons (Independent Living) Bill* (London: DRC, June 8, 2006), available at *www.drc.org.uk*.

15

AGE DISCRIMINATION

I. Introduction

Council Directive 2000/78/EC (the "Employment Equality Directive") required the UK to introduce comprehensive legislation prohibiting age discrimination in employment and occupation by December 2006.[1] Age discrimination regulations, initially published in draft form in July 2005 in the *Coming of Age* consultation document, were finally approved by Parliament in March 2006 and mainly came into force on October 1, 2006, with specific regulations governing particular age-related issues in the context of pensions coming into force in December 2006. In place of a long-established and largely ineffective policy of relying upon non-binding codes of practice to encourage employers to avoid age discrimination, the regulations transformed age into another unlawful ground of discrimination, albeit one which is subject to some very important exceptions.

Age discrimination legislation inevitably gives rise to a series of complex and genuinely difficult issues, both conceptual and practical in nature.[2] Many of these difficulties stem from real uncertainty about why age discrimination

[1] Special provision was made for age in the implementation requirements imposed by the Directive. Its general provisions had to be implemented by member states by December 2, 2003, but Art.18 permitted a member state to wait a further three years (to December 2, 2006) before implementing the provisions concerning age discrimination, "in order to take account of particular conditions." The UK took advantage of this additional time period.

[2] By way of illustration, it took thirty-eight years for the US Supreme Court to confirm in *Smith v City of Jackson*(544 US 228 (2005) 351 F.3d 183) that the Age Discrimination in Employment Act (ADEA) 1967 permitted recovery for disparate impact discrimination. The Supreme Court based their decision upon the statutory language of the Act and its similarity to the equivalent provisions of the Civil Rights Act, an acknowledgement that the ADEA was broadly equivalent to other forms of discrimination legislation. For a taste of the extensive academic debate that lead up to this decision, see E. H. Pontz, "Note—What a Difference ADEA Makes: Why Disparate Impact Theory Should Not Apply to the Age Discrimination in Employment Act" (1995) 74 N.C. L. Rev. 267; M. Ziegler, "Note: Disparate Impact Analysis and the Age Discrimination in Employment Act" (1984) 68 Minn. L. Rev. 1038; S. J. Kaminshine, "The Cost of Older Workers, Disparate Impact, and the Age Discrimination in Employment Act" (1990) 42 Fla. L. Rev. 229; P. H. Harris, "Note, Age Discrimination, Wages and Economics: What Judicial Standard?" (1990) 13 Harv. J.L. & Pub. Policy 715, 729–30; P. S. Krop, "Note, Age Discrimination and the Disparate Impact Doctrine" (1982) 34 Stan. L. Rev. 837.

should be prohibited, and how far this prohibition should be extended. Is age really comparable to other "suspect grounds" of discrimination? What exceptions to a general ban on age discrimination should be permitted? How does the prohibition of age discrimination tie into wider debates about globalisation, the ageing population of European countries and shifts in working practices?

Comparative experience from countries that have well-established prohibitions on age discrimination in place indicates that age discrimination cases will probably be relatively common, often hard-fought and may be difficult to resolve. In the Republic of Ireland, which has comprehensive anti-discrimination legislation extending across all the six major prohibited grounds of discrimination, 17 per cent of employment discrimination claims referred to the Equality Tribunals in the period 2000–2003 concerned age discrimination.[3] In the US in the 1990s, 170,000 age discrimination claims were filed with the Equal Employment Opportunities Commission (EEOC), and EEOC support for litigants under the Age Discrimination in Employment Act (ADEA) has produced several high-profile damages awards in recent years, including a 1999 settlement with a New York insurance and brokerage firm, which resulted in $28 million being paid out to 13 individuals following the firm's implementation of a policy that required employee-directors to retire at age 60 or 62.[4]

Age discrimination legislation is therefore a potential minefield for judges, lawyers, litigants and policy-makers. At first glance, it may appear to be a "backwater" ground of discrimination, which attracts less political controversy and dispute than other areas of discrimination law: however, its potential impact is considerable and should not be underestimated.

II. Why Ban Age Discrimination?

Successive UK governments have been reluctant to introduce age discrimination legislation: employers' organisations have expressed concerns about its potential cost and complexity. Many forms of age discrimination have been historically viewed as entirely acceptable and socially desirable, and are widely seen as part of the natural cycle of the workplace. Older people are usually seen as the prime beneficiaries of age discrimination legislation, and yet older workers (as distinct from retired persons, who will not benefit from

[3] This proportion has stayed fairly constant since 2003: see the Annual Reports of the ODEI/The Equality Tribunal, 2000–2003. Initial experience from the Netherlands and Belgium confirms this trend. see Age Concern, *Addressing Age Barriers* (London: Age Concern, 2004).

[4] See *www.eeoc.org* (last accessed August 5, 2006). The ADEA combines specific exemptions for particular professions and seniority systems with a general prohibition on "arbitrary discrimination", leaving it to the courts to determine when age discrimination outside the specified exceptions will be deemed not to be based on objective justification. It also only protects those over 40, a significant difference from the requirements of EU law.

employed-centred anti-discrimination legislation) would not appear to constitute a particularly disadvantaged or vulnerable social group when taken as a whole. Given this, it makes sense to delve a little deeper into the logic of why should the use of age-based criteria in employment and occupation should be controlled by discrimination law. Is age discrimination really capable of being equated to race, sex or other forms of serious discrimination?

Two major types of justification have been cited at EU and national level to justify the introduction of age discrimination legislation, and similar arguments have been made in the USA, Australia, Canada and elsewhere. These are a) the principled desire to eliminate irrational prejudice and stereotyping on the grounds of age, and b) the social utilitarian goal of removing obstacles to greater participation by particular age groups in the labour market.

The first justification is based upon the argument that age is often used unfairly as an arbitrary, irrational and stereotyping tool for making distinctions between individuals. Differences of treatment between different individuals or groups on the ground of age are often based on generalised assumptions or casual stereotypes, with age used as a "proxy" for other personal characteristics such as maturity, health or vulnerability. For example, younger persons are often assumed to lack maturity, judgment and any form of committed family responsibilities: older persons are often assumed to lack flexibility, motivation, reliable health, and the ability to absorb new ideas.[5] These assumptions are often the basis for the use of age as a shorthand in making recruitment, promotion, training or redundancy decisions, which can take the form of involuntary redundancy measures targeted at older workers, differential treatment in the provision of training, a refusal to recruit or promote workers of a certain age, and the framing of job requirements in age terms.[6]

The assumption that age is an accurate proxy for other characteristics is deeply embedded in modern societies: someone's age is often automatically assumed to indicate the possession of the other characteristics associated with being of a particular age. However, many of the most common assumptions about the performance in employment of particular age groups have come under sustained challenge in recent years. For example, using age as an automatic proxy for health, ability to absorb new information or competency has been critiqued as resting on very questionable assumptions,[7] while evi-

[5] See Sandra Fredman, "The Age of Equality", in Sandra Fredman and Sarah Spencer, *Age as an Equality Issue: Legal and Policy Perspectives* (Oxford: Hart, 2003) 21–70, especially 22–35. See also Australian Human Rights Commission, *Age Matters: A Report on Age Discrimination* (Canberra: Australian Human Rights and Equal Opportunity Commission, May 2000).

[6] See Ontario Human Rights Commission, *Discrimination and Age: Human Rights Issues Facing Older Persons in Ontario* (Toronto: Ontario Human Rights Commission, 2000).

[7] See J. Grimley-Evans, "Age Discrimination: Implications of the Ageing Process" in S. Fredman and S. Spencer, *Age as an Equality Issue: Legal and Policy Perspectives* (Hart: 2003, Oxford), 11–20. See also in the same book, T. Schuller, "Age Equality in Access to Education", 117–144.

dence suggests that, except in a limited range of jobs, work performance does not deteriorate to a substantial degree with age.[8] Even where such assumptions may have some broad statistical validity across a particular age group, they do not reflect the diversity of individuals within the relevant age groups,[9] or the individual qualities and abilities of the particular individuals concerned.[10]

Age-based stereotyping is therefore increasingly being called into question.[11] At both ends of the age spectrum, the automatic identification of a person's age with particular characteristics is increasingly challenged. However, these stereotypes appear to be deeply rooted and have considerable persistence. Age discrimination legislation can therefore be justified as a tool to deter the use of irrational yet socially-embedded age-based stereotyping, which could be eliminated and replaced by more accurate and rational methods of determining ability, competence, health and other factors, such as individual assessment.[12] A person's health, experience, maturity, ability to learn, experience, skill, willingness to work may often be ascertained by normal vetting procedures, individual assessments and good job specifications. A 50-year-old secretary, for example, could be assumed to have certain types of experience usually not open to a 20-year-old, but this alone should not justify an automatic selection of the older applicant without an assessment of the merits of the 20-year-old.

This "anti-stereotyping" argument can be extended and deepened: when individuals are subject to discrimination as a result of these age-based ste-

[8] See P. Meadows, *Retirement Ages in the UK: A Review of the Literature*, Employment Relations Research Series No.18 (London: DTI, 2003), 28–29.

[9] Assumptions of ill-health and inflexibility on the part of older workers, for example, are frequently erroneous or exaggerated in respect of the particular "cohort" or age group concerned, but crucially are also often completely inapplicable and irrelevant to many individuals within that cohort. See Grimley-Evans, above at n.7.

[10] The Irish case of *Byrne v FAS*, DEC-E2002–045 is a good example of a case involving discriminatory and unfair assumptions. A 48-year-old woman was refused a vocational training place, after having been told at interview that older students were less successful at technical drawing and had more problems reconciling work with family commitments. The Equality Officer found for the claimant, finding that no objective evidence to support these comments had been produced. See M. Reid, "Age Discrimination in Employment: Issues Arising in Practice", lecture delivered at Academy of European Law, Trier, October 2, 2004, available at *http://www.era.int/www/gen/f_19096_file_en.pdf* (last accessed September 17, 2005), p.7.

[11] See A. Taqi, "Older People: Work and Equal Opportunity" [2002] 55 International Social Security Rev. 120.

[12] George Rutherglen makes the point that justifications for the ADEA "have a surprising resemblance to the justification for recognizing claims for wrongful discharge": see G. Rutherglen, "From Race to Age: The Expanding Scope of Employment Discrimination Law" (1995) 24 J. Legal Studies 491, at 496. He suggests that the justification for age discrimination legislation lies principally in its role as ensuring fair treatment of individuals, and preventing abuse by employers. Christine Jolls makes a similar point, accepting the view that "the ADEA cannot be justified on traditional distributive or rights-based grounds." See C. Jolls, "Hands-Tying and the Age Discrimination in Employment Act", (1996) 74 Tex. L. Rev. 1813, at 1814.

reotypes, then their individual qualities are subsumed within the (often demeaning) stereotype.[13] Fredman has argued that age stereotyping can therefore be conceptualised as a denial of human dignity that can humiliate those individuals who face discrimination on the basis of their age alone, and therefore is ripe for regulation by discrimination law.[14]

A second, more pragmatic set of arguments has also been evoked to support the prohibition of age discrimination. Age stereotyping can produce negative social consequences, with particular age groups subject to formidable obstacles to their full participation in the labour market. As a consequence, these groups often suffer social exclusion and high levels of poverty, which in turn imposes substantial economic and social welfare costs upon society at large.[15] In particular, older workers following redundancy may experience considerable difficulties in acquiring jobs of a similar level of income and responsibility. This imposes large burdens on welfare services, as well as having a negative impact on the dignity and self-esteem of the individuals concerned. These problems are frequently acute in particular geographical areas, where the decline or dismantling of traditional industries in the 1980s resulted in a generation of middle-aged workers left without jobs, with a consequential crippling effect on many communities and families. Similarly, a reluctance to employ young school-leavers can result in high unemployment, demoralisation and a loss of incentive among disadvantaged youth, with knock-on effects of crime, poverty and social exclusion.

Discrimination is not the only reason that older and younger people may face access problems in entering or remaining within the workforce. Nevertheless, the exclusion of large numbers of able individuals from the workforce on age grounds appears to be a significant source of individual disadvantage and social exclusion. Age discrimination can also be viewed as economically wasteful, in that experienced and mature workers are excluded from employment, often for irrational reasons, with a consequent loss of their skills, valuable organisational history and the benefits of an age-diverse workforce.[16]

These concerns about the side-effects of age discrimination are amplified by wider economic and social trends. For most of the 1980s, the primary labour market concern for most EU states was youth employment. Although this remains a very significant problem in many states, it has recently been supplemented by concern at the greatly reduced rate of participation of older

[13] See Fredman, "The Age of Equality": see also Colm O'Cinneide, "Comparative European Perspectives on Age Discrimination" in Fredman and Spencer, *Age as an Equality Issue*, 195–218, especially 214–5.

[14] Fredman, *ibid*.

[15] See UK Employers' Forum on Age, *The Cost of Ageism* (London: EFA, 1998), quoted in Helen Meenan, "Age Discrimination in the UK" (2000) 4 International Journal of Discrimination and the Law 247–292.

[16] See Australian Human Rights and Equal Opportunity Commission, *Age Matters: A Report on Age Discrimination* (Canberra: HREOC, May 2000).

workers in the workforce.[17] Allied to declining birth rates across Europe and the changing demographic profile of the continent's population, this has resulted in a declining base of younger workers supporting an increasing number of inactive older workers, with consequential ever-growing pressure on state and private welfare systems.[18] The UK is not immune to this trend, albeit to a slightly lesser degree than some other European economies.[19] The Government research paper, *Winning the Generation Game*, found that in the period 1979 to 1999, the proportion of men between 50 and the state pension age who were not working had doubled, while a third of men and women in this age range (2.8 million people in total) were not working.[20]

Bob Hepple has summarised the issues thrown up by persistent patterns of age discrimination and the exclusion from the labour market of particular categories of workers.

Bob Hepple Q.C., "Age as Discrimination in Employment", in Sandra Fredman and Sarah Spencer, *Age as an Equality Issue* (Oxford: Hart, 2003), pp.71–96:

"Discrimination related to age seriously undermines [key] objectives of employment policy . . . there are principally two groups of older men detached from the labour market. The slightly smaller group is typified by middle-class men with access to pensions who have left work largely through choice. The majority is characterised by men who have been subjected to compulsory redundancy. Restructuring in the face of two major recessions involved a substantial fall-out of older craft and manual workers from declining manufacturing sectors. During the early 1980s and early 1990s downsizing was achieved by encouraging early retirement often funded by occupational pension schemes. Workers took such opportunities, sometimes reluctantly, and then found that they could not get another job. Older manual workers who used to move down to less strenuous jobs in the same or another organisation found themselves not working at all; they are also reluctant to take low-paid work where it exists because this would jeopardise their benefits or increase their tax liabilities. At the other end of the age scale, youth unemployment rates in the UK in the period 1995–2000 have remained significantly higher than overall unem-

[17] The decline of traditional industries, the obsolescence of certain types of skills generally possessed by particular age segments of the population, and corporate cost-cutting frequently aimed at more expensive older workers have all contributed to this trend, frequently encouraged by the existence of early retirement incentives in occupational benefit schemes. See Performance and Innovation Unit, *Winning the Generation Game* (Cabinet Office: London, 2000), Ch.4.

[18] Their cumulative effect ensured that by 1997 three out of five people in the active 55–60 age group across the EU had left the labour market. See European Industrial Relations Observatory (EIRO), *Industrial Relations and the Ageing Workforce: a Review of Measures to Combat Age Discrimination in Employment*, 2000, at *www.eiro.eurofound.ie/2000/10/study/TN0010201S.html*.

[19] See *End Ageism in Employment*, Manifesto of the Employers' Forum on Age, May 14, 2001, at *http://www.efa.org.uk/*.

[20] See *Winning the Generation Game*, Ch.3.1, p.13. Most of these did not appear to have left the labour market voluntarily, with the study estimating that no more than a third of the fall in employment rates arose from voluntary early retirement. See Ch.3.2, pp.19–25.

ployment rates, indicating structural problems relating to the integration of young persons into the labour market.

The statistics also indicate that the rise in female participation in the labour force has not benefited older women to the same extent as younger ones. Women aged 30 are nearly 50% more likely to be employed than 20 years ago, for women aged 50 the growth has been more modest and for those approaching pension age participation has remained stable. Moreover, women are less likely than men to return to a job after a period out of work because of lack of opportunities combined with greater family responsibilities than men.

The conclusion to be drawn is that loss of traditional job opportunities for men in former industrial sectors, the inadequacy of post-school training and work experience for young people, and the absence of opportunities for older women seeking 'family-friendly' working patterns is a substantial cause of detachment from the labour force. This lack of opportunity is in part due to the disappearance of traditional jobs and the lack of flexible working arrangements for older people.

Another substantial reason for detachment from the labour force is age discrimination. There is no shortage of surveys of age-discriminatory employment practices. Most of these relate to older people and are based on subjective accounts of the extent to which they believe that they have experienced age discrimination, or accounts by managers. Among the findings are: 55% of managers said that the used age as a criterion for recruitment, and 60% said that they focussed on older workers when restructuring; one in four people aged between 50 and 69 claimed to have experienced age discrimination at some point in their lives; 23 out of 25 older persons looking for a job gave up after 12 months because of the lack of opportunities; up to 41% of job adverts had age limits; the likelihood of receiving employer-based training peaks in a worker's 30s and 40s and then declines; and less than 10% of all training costs is spent on the older one-third of people of working age. Many young people believe they have been the victims of age discrimination, although managers frequently claim that it is the lack of training and experience of young persons which is the principal reason for not employing more of them.

There are many reasons for age discrimination against older people. First, there is widespread reluctance (especially among younger managers) to appoint older employees because of negative stereotypes of them as being hard to train, lacking creativity, over-cautious, unable to adapt to new technology and inflexible. In fact, chronological age is not a good predictor of performance. Variations in productivity within a given age group have been found to be wider than variations between one age group and another. Secondly, it often suits both management and trade unions to achieve downsizing by 'buying off' older workers with redundancy packages, while preserving the jobs of younger workers. This is partly due to the widely held belief that those who have had a 'fair innings' should make way for others, and partly because these packages favour older workers on the basis of age and seniority. Thirdly, managers have in the past tended to believe that it is in the interests of their organisations to formalise internal labour markets by using age and seniority-based remuneration and promotion systems; these systems are now being replaced by performance-based reviews which rely heavily on subjective judgments. While removing overt age discrimination, these reviews are open to prejudice and manipulation. Finally, there is the fact that age discrimination—unlike race, gender and disability discrimination—is not unlawful (and, indeed, is built into the institutions of the labour market and pension schemes). This encourages the perception that it is legitimate and fair."

There are therefore considerable potential economic and social benefits to be gained if successful attempts can be made to combat this trend, widen participation in the labour market and break down patterns of age-linked exclusion. At both European and national levels, a range of policy responses has been introduced with this goal in mind: the UK government has now combined together a variety of initiatives within an overarching strategy, outlined in the policy paper *Opportunity Age*.[21] This strategy recognises that combating age discrimination is a "crucial part of the jigsaw" in transforming employment opportunities for older people. These arguments suggest that a strong rationale exists for the use of age discrimination legislation as a useful tool in breaking down patterns of social and economic exclusion, a justification that Hugh Collins has suggested constitutes the basis for much of discrimination law in general.[22]

Therefore, two main sets of arguments exist for the introduction of anti-discrimination legislation: the utilitarian "economic exclusion" rationale and the "anti-stereotyping" rationale linked to conceptions of human dignity. Both have been cited as justifications for the introduction of age discrimination legislation by the UK government, and both also make an appearance in the recitals accompanying the Employment Equality Directive.[23] It should be noted that both arguments could also be used to support the extension of age discrimination legislation to goods and services, education, and other areas not currently covered. Age distinctions in access to health care, education and other services both ensure the exclusion of significant segments of the population from important forms of social support, generating alternative knock-on forms of social costs, and also are often based on age stereotyping and the denial of dignity to older persons in particular.[24]

Helen Meenan has discussed the growing number of international instruments that call for greater steps to ensure enhanced age equality, focusing in particular upon those concerned with older persons:

[21] The strategy places an emphasis on overarching principles of active independence, choice, and flexibility for older workers, the overhaul of public service delivery and provision to better reflect these principles, and encouraging much greater participation in labour market by older workers by achieving "culture change".

[22] H. Collins, "Discrimination, Equality and Social Inclusion" (2003) 66(1) MLR 16–43. An equivalent set of arguments could be made for a role for age discrimination legislation in helping to address persisting problems of youth unemployment.

[23] Recitals 8 and 25 refer to the EU Employment Guidelines, which place great emphasis on supporting older workers in order to increase their participation in the labour force. Protection against age discrimination is seen as "an essential part of meeting the aims set out in the Employment Guidelines and encouraging diversity in the workforce": see Recital 25. The recitals also refer to the importance of the fundamental rights of dignity and equality, and recognise that unjustified discrimination based upon stereotypes and prejudice violates these basic individual rights: see Recitals 4 to 6.

[24] See Fredman, "The Age of Equality", *ibid*.

Helen Meenan, "The Future of Ageing and the Role of Age Discrimination in the Global Debate" [2005] The Journal of International Aging, Law & Policy 1–41, 6–11:

"In the Political Declaration adopted by the Second World Assembly on Ageing, the representatives of Governments positively commit themselves to eliminating all forms of discrimination, including age discrimination. The recommendations for action speak of a society for all ages that encompass the goal of providing older persons with the opportunity to continue contributing to society. To work towards this goal it is necessary to remove whatever excludes or discriminates against older persons. Another recommendation calls for participants to ensure the full enjoyment of all human rights and fundamental freedoms by promoting the implementation of human rights conventions and other human rights instruments, particularly in combating all forms of discrimination. This recent emphasis on the human rights needs of older persons in the global agenda is welcome. There was no explicit reference to the rights of older persons in the UN's *International Covenant on Economic, Social and Cultural Rights, 1966* nor the *Universal Declaration of Human Rights, 1948*. This omission does not necessarily prevent older persons implicitly benefiting from the covenant and has been explained by the fact that at the time these instruments were adopted the problem of population ageing was not so obvious. The phenomenon of population ageing in and of itself has thus helped to improve awareness of the situation and human rights needs of older people...

The cause of discrimination in employment and occupation has been taken up since the 1950s by the International Labour Organisation The ILO rectified the omission of age from the definition of discrimination in its recommendation on discrimination in employment by adopting the Older Workers Recommendation, 198052 (OWR). This applies to older workers who are 'liable to encounter difficulties in employment and occupation because of advancement in age.' No definition of older workers is given, but Member countries are permitted to adopt a more precise definition when giving effect to the recommendation, 'with reference to specific age categories ... in a manner consistent with local laws' and local conditions. The OWR recommends that:

> 'Employment problems of older workers should be dealt with in the context of an over-all and well balanced strategy for full employment and, at the level of the undertaking, of an over-all and well balanced social policy, due attention being given to all population groups, thereby ensuring that employment problems are not shifted from one group to another.'

Despite its focus on older workers, the OWR recommends equality of opportunity and treatment for workers of all ages. It calls on the Members 'within the framework of a national policy to promote equality of opportunity and treatment for workers, whatever their age, and of laws and regulations and of practice on the subject, take measures for the prevention of discrimination in employment and occupation with regard to older workers.' This is important to ensure that workers do not suffer when older because of discrimination when they were younger. It also promotes an approach that recognises that age discrimination can affect younger workers."

Meenan's analysis is valuable in highlighting the growing salience of issues of age equality in international instruments, and the need for policies addressing age discrimination to be concerned with both younger and older persons.

III. The Sceptical Counter-case

However, do these arguments make out a sufficient case to treat age discrimination as equivalent to other forms of discrimination? Age discrimination is not generally based on bigotry, hatred or the fundamental denial of equal status or dignity as human beings: while age stereotyping is a problem, it cannot be said in normal circumstances to take the same virulent forms of other forms of prejudice.[25] Courts and commentators have frequently suggested older people as a group have in general neither suffered historical discrimination nor a lack of political power, and therefore do not constitute a disadvantaged group.[26] As a consequence, the argument has been made that the moral imperatives to eliminate discriminatory and stereotyping behaviour on the grounds of race and sex discrimination do not apply in the age context, or at least do not apply with anything like the same imperative moral force. Both the US Supreme Court and the House of Lords have held that the use of age distinctions by public authorities should be subject to the low-intensity "rational" standard of scrutiny when toe use of such distinctions has been challenged as contrary to equal protection rights under the US Constitution and Art.14 ECHR.[27]

The argument is also sometimes made that age discrimination legislation can cut across or conflict with other non-discrimination concerns.[28] There is some evidence that the principal beneficiaries of the American age discrimination legislation have been older, white males: therefore, the argument is made that age discrimination legislation will inevitably result in special protection for well-off older litigants in established posts, while blocking

[25] Note however that older persons can be subject to appalling and degrading treatment in care homes, in residential accommodation and in everyday life, based often on a denial of their basic human entitlements: see J. Watson, *Something for Everyone: The Impact of the Human Rights Act and the Need for a Human Rights Commission* (London: British Institute for Human Rights, 2001), 46–50.

[26] In *Massachusetts Board of Retirement v Murgia* (1976) 438 U.S. 285, the Supreme Court explained that "old age does not define a 'discrete and insular' group ... in need of 'extraordinary protection from the majoritarian political process.' Instead, it marks a stage that each of us will reach if we live out our normal span." George Rutherglen has similarly argued that the ADEA "cannot be justified in terms of opening opportunities to a historically disfavored group." See G. Rutherglen, "From Race to Age: The Expanding Scope of Employment Discrimination Law" (1995) 24 J. Legal Studies 491.

[27] See the US Supreme Court decision in *Murgia* above, and *R v Secretary of State for Work and Pensions, ex p. Reynolds* [2005] UKHL 27.

[28] Clare McGlynn has argued that evidence in the United States shows that there may be a tension between age discrimination legislation and race and gender discrimination laws, at least in terms of their effects. See C. McGlynn, "Age Discrimination and European Union Law", paper delivered to a workshop organised by the Swedish National Institute for Working Life, Brussels, 6–7 November 2000, p.11–12.

promotion and employment possibilities for younger workers.[29] Given the gender and ethnic composition of the older strata of the workforce, this could in turn block opportunities for ethnic minorities, women, disabled persons and other groups.

So is age discrimination thus fundamentally different from other forms of discrimination, or even in actual conflict with the mainstream of discrimination law concerns? It is true that age inequalities are not directly linked with historical narratives that deny equality of human status to particular groups. However, the suggestion that age discrimination legislation inevitably only benefits specific and relatively privileged social groups, and can even have an overall negative impact on disadvantaged groups, is very contestable. The US experience is a very unreliable guide, as the ADEA applies just to discrimination against those over forty years of age. In contrast, the Employment Equality Directive requires age discrimination legislation to protect all age groups in employment and occupation, which may break down an assortment of age barriers across the workforce, including those that impact upon younger workers.[30]

In fact, older or younger women, ethnic minorities and disabled persons may be the prime beneficiaries of age discrimination legislation, as they may be the most exposed to discriminatory treatment, the most vulnerable to its negative effects, and the least able to combat it. Much depends on how age discrimination legislation is framed and defined: but there is nothing *intrinsic* in age discrimination legislation that means that it inevitably cuts across other non-discrimination initiatives.

It can also be argued that age discrimination does disproportionately impact upon particular age groups, in particular those at either end of the age spectrum, for special forms of negative and demeaning treatment. The accumulated evidence of widespread age-linked social exclusion discussed above graphically demonstrates this. Also, discrimination on the ground of age denies individual equality of opportunity whenever it occurs: the fundamental argument remains that as a virulent form of stereotyping, it should be controlled by legislation.

Therefore, a strong argument can be made for treating age discrimination legislation as broadly equivalent in its goals and rationale to other forms of anti-discrimination protection. However, some critics have argued that the use of age-based criteria to differentiate between individuals is also an integral

29 See Rutherglen, "From Race to Age: The Expanding Scope of Employment Discrimination Law", *ibid.* at 495: "Most claims of employment discrimination are now claims of discriminatory discharge. Litigation under the ADEA, which concerns such claims almost exclusively, exemplifies this trend in its most extreme form."

30 Thus, for example, the US age discrimination legislation does not apply to firms employing fewer than 20 people or to people under 40, and it only includes direct discrimination. Its creation of a special and privileged protected class by its protection being confined to those forty and above has attracted criticism, as it involves the use of the type of arbitrary age limit the legislation was designed to discourage, and has created difficulties as to when discrimination against a member of this group can be inferred.

and inescapable element of how current employment practices are organised. As a consequence, there have been calls for a minimalist approach to age discrimination legislation, with its scope restricted to the specific instances where direct discrimination on the basis of age stereotyping has clearly occurred. For example, in the United States, Evan Pontz has argued that the ADEA should not be interpreted as permitting "disparate impact analysis" (otherwise known as indirect discrimination claims) to be applied in the context of age discrimination, due to fears about its potential interference with standard employment practice.[31]

Richard Posner has gone so far as to argue that the range of circumstances in which age discrimination is a necessary tool for effective decision-making in employment is so considerable as to justify the repeal or substantial dilution of the US age discrimination legislation. In particular, Posner has suggested that while age is not always a very accurate proxy for individual characteristics, it is economically an efficient way of ascertaining certain types of relevant information about individuals, such as willingness to work for longer hours or productive capacity, than many other methods.[32] In contrast, other forms of individual assessment of employees would be more expensive, inefficient and burdensome to both employers and workers in general. He therefore suggests that age discrimination legislation imposes unjustified and economically damaging burdens upon employers, and gives them insufficient scope to use age as a differentiating factor, despite its utility.[33]

Much of Posner's arguments could be accused of relying too heavily upon commonplace assumptions about the utility of the use of age-based criteria. For example, Posner tends to assume that productivity will usually decline with age, while evidence exists that, except in a very limited range of jobs, work performance does not in fact deteriorate with age, at least up to the age of 70, beyond which virtually no evidence about work performance exists.[34] Other forms of worker assessment, such as performance-based criteria, may often be much more economically efficient than the use of age. This may be true both for individual employers and for society at large when the "external" social costs of age discrimination are taken into account, which Posner's analysis neglects. His argument that the use of age-based criteria is inescapable and economically necessary is too general and sweeping to be sustainable.

31 E. Pontz, "What a Difference ADEA Makes: Why Disparate Impact Theory Should Not Apply to the Age Discrimination in Employment Act" (1995) 74 North Carolina L. Rev. 267.

32 See Posner, *Aging and Old Age* (University of Chicago Press: Chicago, 1997).

33 Posner also argues that the ADEA is unnecessary, by claiming that "employers have their own incentives, unrelated to law, to avoid firing competent employees of any age, even if replacements are available. The employer has invested in the employee, and if the employee is still productive the employer is continuing to earn a return on the investment." See Posner, *Aging and Old Age, ibid.*, 334.

34 See P. Meadows, *Retirement Ages in the UK: A Review of the Literature*, Employment Relations Research Series No.18 (London: DTI, 2003), p.18. In addition, gains in productivity and performance due to the experience of older workers, their interpersonal skills and relationships, and their embodiment of institutional memory, often offset any adverse effects related to aging. See Meadows, p. 18.

The US experience has shown that the use of alternative non-age based methods in employment decision-making is possible without the infliction of crippling economic costs.[35]

Other "sceptical" arguments suggest that age discrimination may be hard-wired into our economic and social systems, and any unfairness is counter-balanced by the benefits of age discrimination being enjoyed by different groups at different times. "Fair innings" or "life cycle" arguments make the argument that age is not an immutable characteristic, as a person's age changes over time and all humans pass through the ageing process. As a consequence, it can be legitimate to offer more opportunity in certain circumstances to those at earlier stages of the aging process, on the basis that those further along this aging process previously had their fair share of extra opportunities. In other words, victims of age discrimination may have benefited from beneficial treatment based upon their age at other points of their life-cycle, unlike the case with other forms of inequality: therefore, this trade-off could be seen as reducing the "sting" of age discrimination.

A sophisticated version of the "life-cycle" argument has been offered in a much-cited critique of the ADEA by Issacharoff and Harris. They have argued that the US legislation, and in particular its abolition of mandatory retirement in 1986, has thrown a spanner in a well-established employment "life-cycle", whereby younger workers are paid less and receive less status recognition than their actual productivity would warrant, in return for subsequent pay and status rewards at a later stage of their careers, when their productivity is less. They argue that this cycle is only sustainable on the basis that employers through mandatory retirement and other methods can limit the amount of time during which they have to pay these disproportionate rewards to older workers, and also "free up" posts for younger workers. However, for Issacharoff and Harris, the impact of the ADEA has principally been to enable a generation of embedded older workers with great financial resources to secure, via the threat of ADEA litigation, an economically unfair elongation of their high-earning stage of this cycle.[36] Their summary of their own argument deserves to be quoted:

[35] See L. Freedman, "Age Discrimination Law: Some Remarks on the American Experience", in S. Fredman and S. Spencer, *Age as an Equality Issue* (Oxford: Hart, 2003), pp.175–194.

[36] They describe its impact as "a significant one-time transfer of resources to the generation whose members are currently drawing to the close of their working careers" and cite the predominantly middle-class and well-paid status of most complainants to support their argument that the legislation is a classic case of interest group capture. *Ibid.*, at p.783.

Samuel Issacharoff and Erica W. Worth, "Is Age Discrimination Really Age Discrimination? The ADEA's Unnatural Solution" 72 N.Y.U.L. Rev. 780, pp.780–783:

"The elderly lack the critical features of disadvantaged group status that give some elementary coherence to an antidiscrimination model. Far from being discrete and insular, the elderly represent the normal unfolding of life's processes for all persons. As a group, older Americans do not suffer from poverty or face the disabling social stigmas characteristically borne by black Americans at the start of the civil rights era. Indeed, we shall look to extensive evidence that older Americans are a relatively privileged social group sharing none of the characteristics of groups to which society may owe an ongoing obligation of remediation.

This Article proceeds along several fronts. First, we look at the formal use of antidiscrimination law to address the problem of aging in employment. The ADEA draws its inspiration from the vivid image of hiring signs that limited applicants to those under forty-five, for example. This invocation of 'Elders Need Not Apply' allowed the incorporation of many of the statutory mechanisms of Title VII's prohibition on race and sex discrimination. Nonetheless, even the initial proponents of the ADEA acknowledged that the parallels to other antidiscrimination commands were imperfect—a point that apparently has been lost along the evolutionary trail of the ADEA. In order to draw out the unique features of age in the workforce, we conclude Part I by examining the economic structure of career employment. By reviewing the employment 'life-cycle,' we show both the unique disadvantages that older employees face and the distinction between these disadvantages and classic claims of discrimination in employment.

We next turn to the two central points of our argument. First, the ADEA statutory scheme misconstrues the antidiscrimination model. Antidiscrimination laws have proved most effective at breaking down formal barriers to entry in employment markets. When employers constrict the full range of employees they are willing to consider for hiring, this taste for discrimination imposes costs because employers predictably have to pay higher wages in order to satisfy their demand from a smaller supply of labor. Antidiscrimination laws that break down such inefficient preferences are remarkably successful in promoting rapid integration.

Unfortunately, the source of concern for older employees is overwhelmingly at the tail end of a lifetime of employment, not at the hiring stage. The antidiscrimination model not only does a poor job of explaining the late-career vulnerability of older employees but also understates the prevalence of such vulnerability. At heart, the antidiscrimination model works best when addressing aberrant behavior that departs from rational market commands. By contrast, the economic vulnerability of late-stage career employees is the norm rather than the exception and is made all the more complicated by the clear economic incentives that run counter to the interests of such employees.

This first point leads to the second and no doubt more controversial part of our thesis. The disjunction between the source of employment vulnerability of older employees and the antidiscrimination model underlying the ADEA has had consequences far beyond the theoretical. By unleashing a politically evocative and litigation-tested antidiscrimination law into the arena of the workplace, Congress created an invitation to special interest capture of unjustified wealth. To demonstrate this capture, we make three points. First, we show that the ADEA on its terms failed to alter significantly the difficulties of older employees seeking to enter the workforce. Second, we demonstrate that, particularly after the emergence of the American Association of Retired Persons (AARP) as a powerful lobbying presence, advocates of expansive ADEA remedies essentially abandoned the issue of job acquisition that had been at the heart of the initial passage of the Act. Third, we turn to the amendments of the ADEA in 1986 and 1990 to reveal how the Act became, paradoxically, the most far-reaching of the antidiscrimination statutes. Through a carefully orchestrated assault on mandatory retirement and targeted employee retirement incentive programs, the AARP-inspired amendments of the ADEA provoked a significant one-time transfer of resources to the generation whose members are currently drawing to the close of their working careers.

The final part of this Article returns to the problem of the actual incentives operating against older workers within individual firms. We propose a system of contract protections and an easing of mandatory retirement to grant some additional opportunity and dignity to older workers. At the same time, we part company with the wealth grabbing components of the recent ADEA amendments. Thus, we argue that employers should be relieved of the obligation to contribute to pension plans for employees beyond the age at which pensions and benefits vest. We will also argue that what are euphemistically termed 'negative salary increases' of employees beyond the expected retirement age should not serve as prima facie evidence of employment discrimination but, rather, should be expected as employee tenure advances.

Our goal in this paper is to find a middle ground between the loss of dignity and capture. With an increase in longevity and with the emergence of attachment to work as a central social institution, the portrayal of abrupt and mandatory removal from the workforce as an assault on the dignity of senior employees should come as no surprise. At the same time, the dramatic shift in wealth toward older Americans and the diminished job prospects of the young provoke grave concerns that a misguided antidiscrimination model has allowed a concerted and politically powerful group of Americans to engage in a textbook example of what economists would term 'rent seeking.'"

However, such "life-cycle" arguments attribute certain group characteristics to all individuals within particular age groups, irrespective of their actual circumstances or life history. Some older persons may have been able to maximise their life experiences: others have not been able to so do, often due to lack of political power or social capital, and deserve not to be judged on the ground of their age.[37] Jolls argues that age discrimination legislation can be seen as an effective tool for "tying the hands" of employers in general, preventing them from reneging upon their side of the "life-cycle" bargain.[38] Issacharoff and Harris' argument is also founded upon the "Lazear contract model", which relies on the premise that older workers are being paid more than their productivity would justify:[39] however, there is limited evidence to

[37] See Australian Human Rights and Equal Opportunity Commission, *Age Matters: A Report on Age Discrimination* (Canberra: Australian Human Rights and Equal Opportunity Commission, May 2000).

[38] See C. Jolls, "Hands-Tying and the Age Discrimination in Employment Act", (1996) 74 Tex. L. Rev. 1813; Issacharoff and Harris suggest unfair dismissal protection would cover this, but without the rigour of discrimination law standards, employees may find it difficult to challenge employer decisions based on "rational" cost-cutting requirements. See also S. J. Schwab, "Life-Cycle Justice: Accommodating Just Cause and Employment at Will" (1993) 92 Mich. L. Rev. 8; J. H. Verkerke, "An Empirical Perspective on Indefinite Term Employment Contracts: Resolving the Just Cause Debate" (1995) Wis. L. Rev. 837.

[39] E. P. Lazear, "Why is there mandatory retirement?" (1979) 87 (6) J. Political Economy 1261–1284. See also R. Hutchens, "Delayed Payment Contracts and a Firm's Propensity to Fire Older Workers" (1986) 4 J. Lab. Econ. 439; J. L. Medoff & K. G. Abraham, "Are Those Paid More Really More Productive? The Case of Experience" (1981) 16 J. Human Resources 186, both cited by Issacharoff and Harris.

support this, and some to contradict it.[40] The US experience with the ADEA and the abolition of mandatory retirement has not generated the negative consequences predicted by Issacharoff and Harris. As with other forms of anti-discrimination legislation, time-honoured assumptions tend to shrivel, once exposed to the rigour of justification demands. To lock the "life cycle" into place by diluting age discrimination legislation would be to protect unnecessary and often unfair employment practices, where better alternatives exist.

Sandra Fredman has extended this critique to the use of "life cycle" and "fair innings" arguments in health care and other areas apart from employment:

Sandra Fredman, "The Age of Equality", in S. Fredman and S. Spencer, *Age as an Equality Issue* (Oxford: Hart, 2003), pp.21–69, 46–50

"As with many social rights, the right to age equality is not unlimited . . . There are several ways in which the limits to equality have been framed. The first is the 'fair innings' argument. We have seen that discrimination against older people in the health service has been defended on the grounds that older people have had a 'fair innings' and therefore are less deserving of limited health and social care resources. Similarly, employers have argued that older workers have had a fair innings and should give way to younger workers. This was the argument which was used to justify the policy of early retirement in the recessionary period at the end of the twentieth century. It is still used to justify policies of mandatory retirement. Underlying these arguments is the view that it is wrong to consider a particular stage of life in isolation. The opportunities available to an individual throughout his or her life-span should be considered cumulatively, and once a person has had those opportunities, she or he should not expect any more. Indeed, it has distributive overtones: because older people have once arguably been treated to all the benefits of society, they should now let others have their share.

This argument, is, however, fundamentally unsound. In particular, the notion that older workers should give way to younger ones is based on flawed assumptions. It assumes that there is a fixed number of jobs which can simply be handed from one worker to another. But driving people out of the labour market at 50 does not create jobs for young unemployed people. Conversely, keeping older people in work does not 'use up' jobs which could be reallocated to younger people . . .

The fair innings argument is also flawed in its application to health resources. It might be argued that health care differs fundamentally from the labour market, since health care resources are finite. Therefore, the use of resources on older people inevitably 'uses up' resources that could otherwise be spent on younger people. However, as in the case of jobs, the use of health care resources is not a 'zero sum game'. Health care that facilitates

40 As Meadows has argued, few older workers remain in jobs that requiring physical strength or rapid processing of new information, where productivity performance does deteriorate with age, while data suggests that in Britain at least, there appears to be little if any difference between the productivity of older and younger workers in most jobs. Meadows, *ibid.*, pp.27–28. Meadows also notes that Lazear subsequently acknowledged that the restriction of mandatory retirement in the US had not had the effect that he had expected. See Meadows, p.17.

independence or improves health can actually pay for itself. As Sir John Grimley Evans demonstrates, the resources spent on interventions such as hip replacements for older people improve their quality of life dramatically, as well as decreasing the need for other resource input. In addition, a healthier older person might care for others. In fact, the fair innings argument only really applies to life threatening illness. Health care resources which are withheld from an older person with a chronic illness or disability will only reappear in the social services budget, or be financed from private family income (unless, that is, we are prepared, as society to countenance older people living in degradation and pain)..."

Therefore, the balance of argument indicates that it is possible to establish a broad equivalence between age and other grounds of prohibited discrimination, and to introduce comprehensive age discrimination legislation without fatal disruption to social and economic structures. The legislative trend across the common law world reflects this. Recent decades have seen age discrimination brought within the general scope of anti-discrimination legislation in many countries, including Canada, Australia and Ireland, with the Irish and Canadian legislation extending protection across the full scope of anti-discrimination legislation, including access to goods and services.

The Employment Equality Directive makes some special provision for the age ground, but in the main applies its general provisions across all the four ground of discrimination to which it applies, and it requires member states to take the same basic steps for each of the four grounds. In other words, the Directive appears to require a general equivalence approach for age as with the other grounds, and does not apparently define it as a lesser ground, deserving lower levels of protection. The European Court of Justice in its decision in *Mangold* confirmed that age discrimination should be treated as equivalent to other forms of discrimination within European law, and recognised that it was encompassed within the general principle of non-discrimination inherent in European law.[41]

However, Advocate General Mazák in the ECJ case of *Palacios de la Villa v Cortefiel Servicios SA* suggested that age discrimination was very different in nature and history from sex discrimination.[42] As a consequence, and given the lack of clear agreement on what forms of age discrimination were problematic and which were acceptable, he suggested that age discrimination should not be treated as belonging in the same category of seriousness as sex discrimination, but rather should be seen as a less serious form of unequal treatment. This is a controversial approach, which however was also adopted to some degree by Advocate Generals Jacobs and Sharpston in their separate opinions in *Lindorfer v Council of the European Union*.[43] Nevertheless, the ECJ did not adopt this line of reasoning in its decision in *Palacios de la Villa*, where it appeared to treat age discrimination as analogous to other forms of dis-

41 See *Mangold v Helm*, Case C-144/04, [2005] ECR 1-9981.
42 See Case C-411/05, Opinion of Mazák A.G. delivered on February 15, 2007.
43 Case C-227/04P, Opinion of Advocate General Jacobs, delivered on October 27, 2005, and Advocate General Sharpston, delivered on November 30, 2006.

crimination, albeit subject to special rules.[44] This shows how disputes about the conceptual basis of age discrimination and its relationship to other prohibited grounds of discrimination remain relevant and tremendously important. Sharp divisions exist as to how age discrimination is regarded, and it remains to be seen how these differences will have a practical impact upon the evolution of EU and UK age discrimination law.

IV. Justifying Age Discrimination

However, there may be a narrow but distinct range of situations where an arguable case for using age as a differentiating factor can be made out. Firstly, there may be limited circumstances where the use of age to differentiate between individuals may serve some useful social or economic objectives, while not involving harmful stereotyping. This can arise when the use of the age-linked criteria may yield accurate information about particular individuals, or meaningful statistical data about an "age cohort" in general, i.e. about a collective group of individuals having a similar age. An example of where this might arise is when an employer decides not to send an older worker on an intensive and expensive training course because the employee's age means that she or he is due for retirement in a year: this might mean in the circumstances that the employer would receive an inadequate return on the training.

There also may be some circumstances where no reasonable alternative to the use of age as a proxy for individual characteristics is available, and the use of age in these circumstances can provide objectively relevant information about the individuals in question.[45] An employer may have too many employees to make individual assessment a practical proposition, or concerns may arise about whether individual testing will satisfy health and safety concerns.[46] Age may also have to be used as a proxy for need in identifying appropriate recipients of particular forms of employment-related social insurance, special support or positive action. Making differentiations between different age groups may also be necessary to adjust to changing socio-economic conditions and to ensure what Robin Allen has described as "cross-generational equity".[47] Particular complexities arise in respect of the use of

[44] Case C-411/05, ECJ, October 16, 2007.

[45] This could arise when assessing the qualities of each relevant individual is not possible, or would be excessively costly or wasteful of resources in the circumstances.

[46] For example, an airline may want to argue that it cannot test all of its pilots annually beyond a particular age as there may be a risk that eyesight deterioration may not be picked up, and it is safer and more cost-effective to set a fixed retirement age at the point when statistical means indicate that significant sight deterioration begins.

[47] R. Allen, "Age Discrimination and Its Wider Context: Individual Rights and Social Solidarity", *Prepatory Symposium for the 2006 Global Conference on Aging*, London, September 5, 2005.

mandatory retirement ages by employers, which is commonplace and often seen as essential to ensure a turnover of employees.

Many of these exceptions involve direct discrimination on the grounds of age, or age-linked criteria. Nevertheless, they are reconcilable in the abstract with the general prohibition on age discrimination: they usually either involve scenarios where age and age-linked characteristics are not being used to stereotype, or are being used for the purpose of defining groups in need of positive action or special treatment, or are linked to achieving cross-generational equity and therefore can be seen as advancing overall age equality. However, these exceptions are also all capable of encompassing a broad range of age-based distinctions, and of being used as a cloak to camouflage the perpetuation of unnecessary and damaging age-based differentiation. The use of the objective justification test familiar from other discrimination contexts is useful in ensuring that these exceptions are only applied where their use is necessary and justified.

Therefore, age discrimination legislation has to delineate the circumstances in which differential treatment on the basis of age will be treated as objectively justified. This differs from race and sex discrimination legislation, where direct discrimination on the prohibited ground is only permissible when it constitutes a genuine occupational requirement, and generally only indirect discrimination can be shown to be objectively justified. In contrast, age discrimination legislation has to incorporate a justification defence to both direct and indirect discrimination. In addition, it may have to incorporate express exceptions to the general ban on age discrimination in the interest of clarity, certainty and operability, as well as making provision for the use of age as a genuine occupational requirement. There may also be circumstances in which age distinctions are essential for the purpose of taking positive action, which again the legislation has to make allowance for. This means that framing age discrimination legislation has to answer certain difficult questions. What scope for justification should be permitted? What express exceptions should be made? What standard of scrutiny will be applied by policymakers and the courts to assess the validity of alleged justifications?

In addressing these complex questions, age discrimination legislation has to be framed with suitable clarity. Otherwise, it has the potential to trigger uncertainty and confusion among employers, which can inhibit effective compliance, provoke resentment and generate long-drawn out and expensive litigation. Lack of clarity may also limit its impact to those best able to use the legal system.[48] The UK government, in its initial consultation on age discrimination, recognised the concerns about the possibility of "fuzzy law" that could "inhibit effective compliance and benefit neither worker nor employer".[49]

[48] See Joseph Rowntree Foundation, *Transitions After 50 Project, Age Discrimination Legislation: Choices for the UK, http://www.jrf.org.uk/knowledge/findings/socialpolicy/711.asp.*

[49] See *Towards Equality and Diversity*, DTI, December 2001.

To achieve this clarity, and to maintain a principled and coherent approach in determining when exceptions to the legislation are objectively justified, it is imperative that the design and structure of age discrimination is built around a firm and clear central set of guiding principles. If the same approach adopted in the context of the other prohibited grounds of discrimination when it comes to exceptions is applied in the context of age, the use of age and age-linked characteristics will generally be prohibited, unless clearly objectively justified.

However, as already mentioned, Mazák A.G. in the ECJ case of *Palacios de la Villa v Cortefiel Servicios SA* was of the opinion that the prohibition on age discrimination contained in the Employment Equality Directive should be given a narrow and restrictive interpretation, reflecting his view discussed above that age discrimination is legitimately regarded at present as different from and less serious than other types of discrimination.[50]

Jacobs and Sharpston A.GG. in their separate opinions in *Lindorfer v Council of the European Union*[51] adopt a similar view, arguing that the prohibition on age discrimination should be applied "less rigorously" than the prohibition on sex discrimination, and therefore that exceptions to the ban on age discrimination and the justification test that can permit age discrimination in certain circumstances should not "read down". In *Palacios*[52] the ECJ appeared not to adopt this view that the prohibition on age discrimination should be given a narrow interpretation, but did give states a relatively broad degree of leeway in justifying age restrictions linked to retirement ages. Once again, it bears reiterating that disputes about the nature of age discrimination inevitably will affect how any prohibition on age discrimination will be applied, and will also affect the scope of any exceptions to this prohibition and how justification defences are applied in practice.

V. Protection against Age Discrimination in Employment Law

Prior to the coming into force of the age regulations, some degree of protection against age discrimination was offered by unfair dismissal legislation and other aspects of employment law.[53] Contractual terms have been interpreted in some contexts so as to give some protection against dismissal on age grounds. In *Wall v British Compressed Air Society*, the Court of Appeal held that a 67-year-old, dismissed on the grounds of their age, could bring an unfair dismissal claim, as the retirement age set out in their contract was 70 and the Court

[50] See Case C-411/05, Opinion of Mazák A.G. delivered on February 15, 2007.

[51] Case C-227/04P, Opinion of Jacobs A.G., delivered on October 27, 2005, and Sharpston A. G., delivered on November 30, 2006.

[52] Case C-411/05, ECJ, October 16, 2007.

[53] See T. Buck and B. Fitzpatrick, "Age Discrimination in Employment: legal protection in the United States and in the United Kingdom" [1987] Anglo-American L. R. 192.

considered that this contractual term established an expectation that their "normal" retirement age would be 70.

However, this protection was very limited, with no remedy against the application of contractual terms permitting age-based discrimination, or the use of age-based criteria that fall short of obviously "unfair" standards of treatment.[54] For example, in *Taylor v Secretary of State for Scotland*, a prison officer who was required to retire at 55 attempted to challenge his dismissal on the grounds that his contract allowed his retention in employment until 60 at the employer's discretion, and that an equal opportunities policy circular issued in 1992 committed the Scottish Prison Service to avoiding age discrimination. However, the Court of Session held that the employee's contract had not been breached by the decision to trigger the early retirement provision, as the contract explicitly enabled the mandatory retirement age policy to be put into effect, notwithstanding the existence of the equal opportunities circular. In any case, prior to the introduction of the regulations, protection against unfair dismissal was no longer available when an individual reached the age of 65, or the "normal retirement age" for the employment in question.

Other forms of anti-discrimination legislation, in particular the prohibition on indirect sex discrimination, can offer some degree of limited protection against certain forms of age-based discrimination. In *Rutherford v Secretary of State for Trade and Industry*, an employment tribunal held initially that the age limit of 65 for bringing unfair dismissal claims constituted unjustified indirect sex discrimination against male workers, who were more likely to be affected by this limitation of employment rights as they were statistically more likely to work to that age. However, the Court of Appeal and the House of Lords held that the tribunal had taken the wrong approach in only considering those who were affected by the age limitation of 65, instead of considering the relative proportions of men and women of the entire working population that could be hypothetically affected by this provision at some point of their careers.[55]

VI. Age Discrimination and EU Law

Outside of this limited degree of protection, government policies for dealing with age discrimination have tended to rely solely upon voluntary measures, such as the unsuccessful Code of Practice. However, the Employment Equality Directive changed this situation, by requiring the UK to introduce comprehensive legislation prohibiting unjustified age discrimination in employment and occupation by December 2006. The Directive does not define "age", but unlike the ADEA, its scope is not limited to discrimination against those above

[54] [1999] Court of Session I.R.L.R. 36.
[55] [2006] UKHL 19.

a particular age. Therefore, both younger and older workers have rights to age equality.

Council Directive 2000/78/EC of November 27, 2000 establishing a general framework for equal treatment in employment and occupation

"Recitals

[...]
(6) The Community Charter of the Fundamental Social Rights of Workers recognises the importance of combating every form of discrimination, including the need to take appropriate action for the social and economic integration of elderly and disabled people [...]
(11) Discrimination based on religion or belief, disability, age or sexual orientation may undermine the achievement of the objectives of the EC Treaty, in particular the attainment of a high level of employment and social protection, raising the standard of living and the quality of life, economic and social cohesion and solidarity, and the free movement of persons [...]
(13) This Directive does not apply to social security and social protection schemes whose benefits are not treated as income within the meaning given to that term for the purpose of applying Article 141 of the EC Treaty, nor to any kind of payment by the State aimed at providing access to employment or maintaining employment.
(14) This Directive shall be without prejudice to national provisions laying down retirement ages [...]
(25) The prohibition of age discrimination is an essential part of meeting the aims set out in the Employment Guidelines and encouraging diversity in the workforce.
However, differences in treatment in connection with age may be justified under certain circumstances and therefore require specific provisions which may vary in accordance with the situation in Member States. It is therefore essential to distinguish between differences in treatment which are justified, in particular by legitimate employment policy, labour market and vocational training objectives, and discrimination which must be prohibited."

Article 6

"Justification of differences of treatment on grounds of age

1. Notwithstanding Article 2(2), Member States may provide that differences of treatment on grounds of age shall not constitute discrimination, if, within the context of national law, they are objectively and reasonably justified by a legitimate aim, including legitimate employment policy, labour market and vocational training objectives, and if the means of achieving that aim are appropriate and necessary. Such differences of treatment may include, among others:

(a) the setting of special conditions on access to employment and vocational training, employment and occupation, including dismissal and remuneration conditions, for young people, older workers and persons with caring responsibilities in order to promote their vocational integration or ensure their protection;

(b) the fixing of minimum conditions of age, professional experience or seniority in service for access to employment or to certain advantages linked to employment;

(c) the fixing of a maximum age for recruitment which is based on the training requirements of the post in question or the need for a reasonable period of employment before retirement.

2. Notwithstanding Article 2(2), Member States may provide that the fixing for occupational social security schemes of ages for admission or entitlement to retirement or invalidity benefits, including the fixing under those schemes of different ages for employees or groups or categories of employees, and the use, in the context of such schemes, of age criteria in actuarial calculations, does not constitute discrimination on the grounds of age, provided this does not result in discrimination on the grounds of sex.''

The recitals accompanying the Directive acknowledge the crucial importance of combating age discrimination in employment, and how it can harm both individual non-discrimination rights and important social objectives. It establishes a general framework for prohibiting discrimination in employment and occupation on any of four grounds of age, disability, religion or sexual orientation. Direct and indirect discrimination, harassment and victimisation on the ground of a person's age are prohibited, the burden of proof is shifted when a prima facie case is made out, and member states are required to legislate to ensure that victims of age discrimination can obtain effective and adequate remedies.

The Directive does not describe age discrimination as a subsidiary concern, nor an issue of lesser concern than the other prohibited grounds: however, as is inevitable with age discrimination legislation, the age provisions of the Directive depart from the standard format for the other prohibited grounds in permitting direct discrimination on the basis of age to be justified. Article 6 attempts to establish a framework for assessing the legitimacy and justification for the use of age distinctions, while also permitting member states to introduce some specific exemptions if they wish in certain narrowly-defined areas.[56] Age distinctions will be deemed justified in three circumstances:

a) when being of a particular age is a genuine and determining occupational requirement for a particular post (Art.4);

b) when a member state has provided that the use of an age distinction is objectively and reasonably justified ''within the context of national law'' as a proportionate and necessary measure to attain a legitimate aim. Art.6(1) also gives specific examples of the type of legitimate aim and

[56] See Recital 25.

differences of treatment that may be justified in this type of circumstance;

c) when a person is subject to what would otherwise constitute indirect discrimination on the grounds of age, but the application of the provision, practice or criterion in question is justified as objectively necessary and proportionate (Art.2(1)(b)).

In all three circumstances, objective justification in accordance with the proportionality test must be demonstrated, but *what* has to be demonstrated will vary in each case. For age to qualify as a genuine occupational requirement, it will have to be shown that is necessary to be of a particular age to perform a particular job. For direct age discrimination to be justified, the use of age as a "material factor" in decision-making will have to be shown to be proportionate and necessary. Finally, for indirect discrimination, the use of a neutral provision, practice or criterion that disadvantages persons of a particular age will have to be justified.[57]

The scope of the Directive (and thus the scope of the UK Employment Equality (Age) Regulations, as the UK has chosen only to implement the Directive and not to go further) extends only to employment and occupation. This means that access to goods and services, housing, education and "social advantages" in general are not covered by the Directive's prohibition on age discrimination.

Article 3(3) and Recital 13 also clarifies that the scope of the Directive does not include state social security and social protection schemes. Recital 14 also states that the Directive is "without prejudice to national provisions governing retirement ages": the meaning of this is unclear, but appears at least to confirm that state-imposed retirement ages related to pension provision are exempt from the reach of the Directive's age provisions. Taken together, these exceptions mean that the use of age distinctions in state social security and pension schemes are exempt and will not have to be objectively justified.[58]

57 The Dutch government, in implementing the age provisions of the Directive in legislation, has taken the view that as both direct and indirect age discrimination may be "objectively justified", and the same test applies to determining the existence of age as a genuine occupational requirement, any distinction between these three circumstances is redundant and unnecessary. See *Wet van 17 december 2003, houdende gelijke behandeling op grond van leeftijd bij de arbeid, beroep en beroepsonderwijs (Wet Gelijke Behandeling op grond van Leeftijd bij de Arbeid Staatsblad)* 2004, 30. This approach is somewhat questionable: Therefore, there exist good reasons for keeping the three circumstances where justification can be shown distinct and separate, as does the text of the Directive. See for a full and detailed commentary on this issue by Marianne Gijzen, M. Gijzen, Dutch Baseline Report for the European Network of Legal Experts in the Non-discrimination Field, *Transposition of the Racial Equality Directive (Directive 2000/43) and the Framework Employment Directive (Directive 2000/78) into Dutch Law* (Brussels: Migration Policy Group, December 2004).

58 Most comparative age discrimination legislation shies clear of legislating in respect of state welfare or pension entitlements, with the Irish legislation and the EU Directive both exempting social security schemes from their scope, and Australian legislation similarly exempting superannuation payments.

State financial inducements to employers to hire older or younger workers, direct inducements to particular age categories of worker to re-enter the workforce, variances on age grounds in unemployment benefit and jobseekers' allowance, and other state payments that give rise to issues of age inequality all appear thus to be exempt, including state national insurance provisions. What is not clear is the Directive's impact upon state rules that permit employers to set their own retirement ages. However, in the absence of any exemption in the main text of the Directive for employer-imposed retirement ages, it has been argued that Recitals 13 and 14 can be interpreted as referring only to retirement ages imposed as part of state social security schemes (exempt under Art.3(3)).[59]

However, Mazák A.G. in the ECJ case of *Palacios de la Villa v Cortefiel Servicios SA* was of the opinion that retirement ages established in collective agreements fell outside of the scope of the Directive by virtue of Recital 14, as they could be classified as "national provisions governing retirement ages".[60] He based this conclusion on his argument, discussed above, that the nature and history of age discrimination made it different from sex discrimination, and that the age provisions of the Directive should be given a cautious and narrow interpretation as a result. This is a controversial approach, which however was not adopted by the ECJ in its decision in *Palacios* where national collective agreements were considered to come within the scope of the Directive.[61]

The wide exception for state pension and benefit schemes set out in Recitals 13 and 14 does not appear to apply to any benefits, including occupational security and pension schemes, which may be provided by employers (including public bodies) to supplement national social security provision. Nevertheless, under Art.6(2) member states are permitted to introduce a special exemption from the age provisions of the Directive to allow occupational security schemes to fix ages for admission or entitlement to retirement or invalidity benefits (including fixing different ages for employees or groups of employees), or to use age criteria in actuarial calculations in such schemes, provided that this does not result in sex discrimination. This was done to allow occupational insurers and pension-providers to continue to use age-based criteria in offering entry terms, regulating costs across different age groups, assessing premiums and imposing a minimum age for eligibility for early retirement.[62] Article 3(4) also specifically permits member states to exempt their armed forces from the age provisions of the Directive.

59 See Ch.4 "Retirement Ages" in *Equality and Diversity: Age Matters* (London: DTI, 2003).
60 See Case C-411/05, Opinion of Mazák A.G. delivered on February 15, 2007.
61 Case C-411/05, ECJ, October 16, 2007.
62 See s.623 of the US Age Discrimination Act 1967.

VII. Age Discrimination in Domestic Law

Introducing age discrimination legislation in conformity with the Directive can be done in a number of different ways. The most common method since 2000 in the EU has been for states to introduce into national law a prohibition on direct and indirect discrimination on the grounds of age, subject to a general objective justification defence to cover the circumstances where age discrimination can be objectively justified. This has been described as the "open approach" to age discrimination legislation.[63] Such general exemption clauses usually protect age-based distinctions that are "necessary" and "justified", with no clear outline of what constitute "justified" objectives, or of the standard to be applied in proportionality analysis.[64] Such general exemptions in the US, Canada and Australia have often resulted in policy-making in this area deposited in the laps of the judiciary, which can generate uncertainty, ad hoc development and a lack of clear principles.[65] Nevertheless, many EU states have simply chosen to transplant the general wording of Art.6, with minor alterations.[66]

An alternative "closed" approach is possible: national legislation can specify the circumstances in which the use of age-based criteria will be automatically deemed to be objectively justified. "Closed" approaches provide employers with a degree of certainty that if they come within the scope of an exception, then they will be immune from suit. However, defining the limits and nature of an exception can generate its own difficulties, and anticipating each and every situation where the use of age-based criteria may be justified is very

[63] It also provides that an employer does not violate the ADEA by observing the terms of a bona fide seniority system or the terms of a qualified benefit plan, so long as neither was intended to evade the purposes of the ADEA. Employers may also defend an age discrimination claim on the rationale that the differentiation complained of was based not on age, but rather on a reasonable factor other than age.

[64] For example, the Belgian legislation prohibits discrimination that is not "objectively and reasonably justified"; the Finnish age discrimination legislation permits the use of age distinctions for a "justified purpose": see s. 7(1) (3) of the Non-Discrimination Act [*yhdenvertaisuuslaki* (21/2004)].

[65] For example, the ADEA provides for several general statutory defences, which either permit age discrimination in employment under certain conditions, or allow the employer to prove that the employment decision was based on factors other than age. These include a bona fide occupational qualification (BFOQ) defence, when such a requirement is "reasonably necessary to the normal operation of the particular business." This defence leaves it to the courts to determine when age discrimination outside the specified exceptions will be deemed not to be based on objective justification. See Z. Hornstein (ed.) *Outlawing Age Discrimination: Foreign Lessons, UK Choices*, Transitions after 50 Series, The Joseph Rowntree Foundation, July 2001, see *http://www.jrf.org.uk/knowledge/findings/socialpolicy/711.asp*.

[66] For example, the Cypriot Law on Equality of Treatment in Occupation and Employment (N.58 (1)/2004) reproduces almost verbatim the wording of the Directive. See N. Trimikliniotis, *Report on Measures to Combat Discrimination in the 13 Candidate Countries (vt/2002/47): Country Report Cyprus*: European Network of Legal Experts in the Non-discrimination Field (Brussels: Migration Policy Group, November 2004).

difficult. Often, exceptions introduced as part of this approach tend to be framed in very wide terms, which can dilute the impact of the legislation.[67]

"Half open approaches" combine elements of both approaches, usually introducing a general objective justification test but also expressly setting out particular exceptions when age discrimination is deemed to be automatically justified.[68] The UK has adopted this approach in transposing the Directive, on the basis that it combines the greater legal certainty generated by the "closed" approach (with specific exceptions where employers know their use of age distinctions cannot be challenged), with the flexibility and usefulness of a catch-all justification provision offered by the "general" approach. There is of course no obligation for member states to make full use of the possibilities to justify age discrimination that the Directive permits. However, in the Employment Equality (Age) Regulations, the UK has largely adopted a permissive approach that makes considerable use of the differences of treatment on age grounds permitted by the Directive.[69]

A. *The Employment Equality (Age) Regulations 2006*

The Employment Equality (Age) Regulations 2006 now implement the age provisions of the Directive, prohibiting direct and indirect age discrimination, harassment and victimisation in employment and occupation.

[67] The Irish legislation adopts this approach: see Colm O'Cinneide, "Comparative European Perspectives on Age Discrimination Legislation", in S. Fredman and S. Spencer, *Age as an Equality Issue* (Oxford: Hart Publishing, 2003), 195–218; Helen Meenan, "Age Discrimination: Law-Making Possibilities Explored" (2000) International J. Discrimination and the Law 247–292.

[68] For example, the Dutch Age Discrimination Act contains a general "objective justification" test (as previously discussed), but also provides that the dismissal of employees on age grounds who have reached the statutory retirement age of 65 is considered to be objectively justified, as is the use of age distinctions as part of government programmes to promote the participation of particular age groups in the labour market: see Art.7 of the Age Discrimination Act. Ireland has adopted a similar approach, permitting the use of reasonable and rational age distinctions to achieve certain legitimate objectives explicitly set out in the legislation, and also exempting certain specific occupations and practices.

[69] In para.4.1.10 of *Coming of Age*, the UK government states that "we will follow the approach set out in the Directive because we believe that it strikes the right balance between outlawing age discrimination where it is unjustified and on the other hand allowing those with duties under the Age Regulations to demonstrate that a certain practice is justified."

Employment Equality (Age) Regulations 2006

Discrimination on Grounds of Age

"3.—(1) For the purposes of these Regulations, a person ("A") discriminates against another person ("B") if—

(a) on grounds of B's age, A treats B less favourably than he treats or would treat other persons, or

(b) A applies to B a provision, criterion or practice which he applies or would apply equally to persons not of the same age group as B, but—

(i) which puts or would put persons of the same age group as B at a particular disadvantage when compared with other persons, and

(ii) which puts B at that disadvantage,

and A cannot show the treatment or, as the case may be, provision, criterion or practice to be a proportionate means of achieving a legitimate aim.

(2) A comparison of B's case with that of another person under paragraph (1) must be such that the relevant circumstances in the one case are the same, or not materially different, in the other.

(3) In this regulation—

(a) "age group" means a group of persons defined by reference to age, whether by reference to a particular age or a range of ages; and

(b) the reference in paragraph (1)(a) to B's age includes B's apparent age."

Harassment on the ground of a person's age and victimisation are also prohibited in subsequent regulations.

The scope of the Regulations is similar to the scope and provisions of other anti-discrimination legislation in the field of employment and occupation. However, the Regulations differ in some very important respects from other forms of anti-discrimination legislation, and it makes sense therefore to focus on these differences for now.

One important difference that immediately leaps out is that the prohibition on age discrimination is confined to employment and occupation, and does not extend to discrimination in the fields of goods and services, education, etc. Jonathan Swift has placed great emphasis on this decision to confine the scope of age discrimination legislation to the employment context, suggesting that it indicates how different age discrimination is from other forms of inequalities.[70] However, it should be noted that many jurisdictions (such as Canada and Ireland) extend their prohibition on age discrimination across the full ambit of social activities covered by other forms of discrimination law.[71] There is also

[70] Jonathan Swift, "Justifying Age Discrimination" [2006] 35 I.L.J. 232.

[71] See Colm O'Cinneide, "Comparative European Perspectives on Age Discrimination Legislation", in S. Fredman and S. Spencer, *Age as an Equality Issue* (Oxford: Hart Publishing, 2003), pp.195–218.

considerable pressure on the UK government to do likewise from Age Concern, Help the Aged and other activist groups, which may ensure that an extension of age discrimination to goods and services will be given serious consideration as part of the Discrimination Law Review.

However, focusing for now on the current scope of the Age Regulations, the most obvious difference between age and the other prohibited grounds of discrimination is that there is considerably more scope for justifying the use of age-based criteria than is the case for most of the other prohibited grounds (a comparison could be made with disability discrimination, but this is potentially very misleading: see below). The Directive permits direct discrimination on the grounds of age (uniquely) to be objectively justified.

The Regulations therefore make provision in Reg.3 for a general objective justification defence for both direct and indirect age discrimination. Secondly, the Regulations also make provision for a series of specific exceptions from the scope of the prohibition on age discrimination: the use of certain age-based or age-linked criteria, in particular in imposing mandatory retirement ages, fixing age limits in minimum wage and New Deal programmes, using seniority-based benefit schemes and fixing access requirements for occupational benefits, are exempted from any requirement to show that they are objectively justified.

The government has justified the insertion of these specific exemptions on the grounds that they constitute circumstances where the use of age criteria is clearly objectively justified. They can be challenged for being incompatible with the requirements of the Directive, and the TUC, Age Concern and other organisations have been very critical of the scope of some of these exceptions: the older persons' organisation, Heyday, has already launched a judicial review of the retirement age exception which has been referred to the ECJ, discussed further below.

B. *"Less Favourable Treatment"—When Age Discrimination Strikes*

The Age Regulations in line with Article 2(2)(a) of the Directive define direct age discrimination as occurring where someone treats one person less favourably on the ground of his or her age than he or she treats or would treat other persons in a comparable situation, and there is no objective justification for doing so.[72] As with the Disability Discrimination Act 1996, discrimination on "the ground of" a person's age is only prohibited when it affects that particular person, unlike the case in the areas of race, gender, religion or belief and sexual orientation discrimination, where discrimination on the grounds of

[72] The Regulations also state that direct discrimination on grounds of age can also include discrimination based on the perception of someone's age, whether the perception is right or wrong.

association with a person is also prohibited when based on a "suspect" characteristic. As with the similar gap in the disability discrimination legislation, the reference to the European Court of Justice in the case of *Corrigan v Attridge Law*, may result in a finding that the Regulations require amendment to remedy this defect.[73]

Problems often arise as to when inferences should be drawn that "less favourable treatment" has occurred on the ground of age. Determining when "less favourable treatment" has occurred in the age context will involve applying the usual comparator approach familiar from other non-discrimination contexts. However, the fluid and changing ways in which a person's age and the differences in position and expectations that often exist even between persons of very similar ages may make the application of the comparator test difficult in this context.

For example, if a 60-year-old worker's contract is not renewed and she alleges that this treatment was based on her age, citing the fact that a 57-year-old co-worker on the same grade had his contract renewed at the same time, should an inference arise? What happens if the employer cites the continuing employment of the 57-year-old as an example of their willingness to continue to employ older workers? Does the three-year difference constitute a significant age distinction at that stage of that particular career, or is the age difference of no real significance? The same problems could obviously arise in respect of indirect discrimination claims.

Courts and tribunals may often be able to identify with ease the appropriate actual or hypothetical comparators from the specific circumstances of a particular case. However, where an obvious comparator does not exist, then difficulties may arise and creative solutions might be required.[74] Otherwise, there is a danger that age discrimination litigation will often degenerate into a debate about comparators that could prove even more intractable than similar debates in other non-discrimination cases, as has tended to occur in the US.[75]

Complexities can also arise in deciding whether "less favourable" treatment has taken place when differentiating criteria are used which are not linked directly to an individual's age, but instead refer to characteristics that are in reality closely linked to age. "Seniority", "maturity" and "experience" are all

[73] Case C-303/06: see the discussion of this case in Chapter 14 on Disability Rights.

[74] See the discussion of the use of hypothetical comparators in the Irish age equality case-law in M. Reid, "Age Discrimination in Employment: Issues Arising in Practice", lecture delivered at Academy of European Law, Trier, March 2003, available at *http://www.era.int/web/en/resources/5_2341_604_file_en.580.pdf* (last accessed July 17, 2007).

[75] Questions of when the existence of direct discrimination can be inferred from particular facts have proved difficult and complex in ADEA litigation, where case-law requires a plaintiff to establish a "nexus" that directly links the age of the complainant to the complained of conduct : see *Laugesen v Anaconda Co*, 510 F.2d 307, 313 n.4 (6th Cir. 1975); *Kelly v American Standard, Inc*, 640 F.2d 974, 980 (9th Cir. 1981) *Lovelace v Sherwin-Williams Co*, 681 F.2d 230, 238–41). In *O'Connor v Consolidated Coin Caterers Corp*, 116 S. Ct. 1307, 517 U.S. 308 (1996), the US Supreme Court had to clarify that if the claimant was replaced by a person who was also within the age group protected by the US legislation (40 years and older), this could still give rise to an inference of age discrimination, but no automatic presumption would arise.

examples of this type of *age-linked characteristic*, as they are often only capable of being acquired by those who have spent a number of years in an activity. If an employer selects employees for redundancy on the basis of "experience", this may come close to making age the determining factor.

Bob Hepple has suggested that that courts and tribunals will simply apply the usual "but for" test utilised by the UK courts,[76] and ask whether a claimant's age was a substantial factor in the decision to subject the claimant to less favourable treatment, or played a role in the making of that decision.[77] The US Supreme Court adopts a similar approach in its case law on the US age discrimination legislation,[78] as does the Dutch Equal Treatment Commission in its age discrimination case law.[79] Hepple suggests that this test would mean that the use of age-linked factors which are "analytically separate" from age, such as seniority, experience, qualifications and pay levels would not be deemed to constitute direct age discrimination (even if they may give rise to issues of *indirect* age discrimination). However, factors that are essentially "age proxies", that is, which are directly linked and act as a proxy for a person's age, will be deemed to constitute direct discrimination, as age will actually be a "material factor" in the decision-making process.[80]

It may be important to keep *age-based* (i.e. where the treatment would not have occurred "but for" a person's age) and *age-linked* (such as seniority) factors distinct. The former may involve direct discrimination claims; the latter indirect discrimination. While both types of discrimination can be justified under the Regulations, how the test may be applied may vary: it may be likely, for example, that indirect discrimination based on *age-linked* factors will be easier to justify than direct discrimination on the ground of age.

C. *Indirect Discrimination*

According to Art.2.1.2(b) of the Directive, indirect age discrimination will exist where a) an apparently neutral provision, criterion or practice b) puts persons of a "particular age" at a c) "particular disadvantage" compared to others unless that provision, criterion or practice can be d) objectively justified. The UK regulations implement this by defining indirect age discrimination as

[76] See e.g. *James v Eastleigh BC* [1990] 2 A.C. 751.

[77] See Bob Hepple, "Age Discrimination in Employment: Implementing the Framework Directive 2000/78/EC", in Fredman and Spencer, cited above, at 82.

[78] See *Hazen Paper v Biggins* 507 U.S. 604 (1993)

[79] See I.P. Asscher-Vonk, "Towards One Concept of Objective Justification" in: T. Loenen and P.R. Rodrigues, *Non-Discrimination Law—Comparative Perspectives* (The Hague: Kluwer Law International, 1999) pp.39–51, at p.43; see also M. Gijzen, Dutch Baseline Report for the European Network of Legal Experts in the Non-discrimination Field, *Transposition of the Racial Equality Directive (Directive 2000/43) and the Framework Employment Directive (Directive 2000/78) into Dutch Law* (Brussels: Migration Policy Group, December 2004).

[80] Hepple, "Age Discrimination in Employment: Implementing the Framework Directive 2000/78/EC", at 82.

occurring where an apparently neutral provision, criterion or practice puts or would put persons of a certain *age group* at a particular disadvantage compared with other persons, when a person of that certain age group suffers that disadvantage and there is no objective justification for the provision, criterion or practice.

The same general approach that currently is adopted by national courts and the ECJ in indirect discrimination claims across the other equality grounds will presumably be applied in determining what constitutes a "provision, criterion or practice", when indirect discrimination can be inferred, and how the justification defence be applied in the age context.[81]

Many different types of criteria used in employment-linked decisions may have some sort of disparate impact upon one or more age groups. Experience, "know-how", educational qualifications, decision-making capabilities, and emotional maturity are all neutral criteria that might put persons of a particular age at a disadvantage.[82] However, commonsense application of the objective justification test should be capable of distinguishing stereotyping use of age-linked criteria from legitimate use in making rational economic decisions.[83]

VIII. The Objective Justification Test for Age Discrimination

The issue of when age discrimination will be objectively justified remains the key issue in the age context. The wording of the objective justification defence used in Reg.3 for both direct and indirect discrimination has been criticised by Age Concern and others as introducing a weak and uncertain test of objective justification. However, the government's explanatory notes that accompanied the text of the draft Regulations stated that the "legitimate aim" test used in the Regulations was intended to correspond with the well-established "real need" test in EC sex equality law,[84] and the "proportionate means" stage of the same test corresponded with the "appropriate and necessary means" test set out in Art.2.2(b)(i).[85]

Therefore, the objective justification test in the Regulations should be interpreted in line with how the test is applied across the other areas of discrimination law: this means that employers attempting to rely on the defence will have to show a) the existence of a legitimate aim, and that b) proportionate means where used to achieve this aim.

[81] See e.g. *Bilka Kaufhaus* C-170/84 [1986] E.C.R. 1607.

[82] For an example of this potential complexity, refusing to call "overqualified" applicants for interview may indirectly discriminate against older workers: see the Irish case of *Noonan v Accountancy Connections*, DEC-E2004-042.

[83] Fredman, 58–59.

[84] para.4.1.16.

[85] para.4.1.19.

A. *Legitimate Aims*

Any employer attempting to satisfy the "objective justification" test will therefore have to first show the existence of a legitimate aim. Neither the Directive nor the Regulations fix what aims will be deemed legitimate.[86] Article 6(1) of the Directive lists certain examples of potential legitimate aims, namely "legitimate employment policy, labour market and vocational training objectives". These examples are not exhaustive. Both UK consultation papers suggest that there are a wide variety of other potential legitimate aims, as long as they correspond to a real need on the part of the employer, including economic needs.[87]

Criticism by Eurolink and other age equality NGOs of the text of the Directive centred on the very broad and vague wording of the examples of legitimate objectives listed in Art.6(1), such as "legitimate employment policy", labour and training objectives. Their concern was that including such open-ended and broad examples in the text might encourage a loose approach to the objective justification test on the part of governments and national courts.[88] The draft Regulations contained a similar and even perhaps more expansive list, which however did not appear in the final text.

It could be argued that giving employers a wide ambit in defining their aims makes sense, given the amount of age-linked factors that exist and the frequency with which their use may be entirely legitimate: looking for experience, for example, should clearly be a legitimate aim in most circumstances. However, applying the standard approach in assessing the legitimacy of an aim in sex discrimination and human rights cases, the aim cited to justify the use of an age distinction cannot be discriminatory in itself.[89] Jonathan Swift has expressed strong concern that if this rule is applied, then employers will not be

[86] In *Age Matters*, the UK government canvassed opinion on whether it should list and definitely define what would constitute a legitimate aim. However, in *Coming of Age*, it was concluded that an exhaustive list of legitimate aims for direct discrimination would be too restrictive and prescriptive for employers. See *Coming of Age*, para.4.1.5, cited above.

[87] See *Coming of Age*, para.4.1.16: it is also noted there that discrimination will not be justified merely because it may be more expensive not to discriminate, as per the standard approach in discrimination law. Other examples set out in both papers of what may constitute a legitimate aim including health, welfare and safety concerns, including the protection of younger workers; the facilitation of employment planning; the particular training requirements of the post in question, such as the lengthy specialist and expensive training that air traffic controllers must undergo; the encouraging and rewarding of loyalty; and the need for a reasonable period of employment before retirement." See *Age Matters*, para.3.15; *Coming of Age*, para.4.1.17.

[88] See Eurolink evidence to the UK House of Lords Select Committee on the European Union, "EU Proposals to Combat Discrimination", HL Paper 68, May 16, 2000. See also Helen Meenan, "Age Equality after the Employment Directive" (2003) 10 *Maastricht J. European and Comparative Law* 9–38; S. González Ortega, "La Discriminación por Razón de la Edad" (2001) 59 Temas Laborales, pp.93–124.

[89] See para.4.1.18, *Coming of Age*. An example of a discriminatory aim would be an attempt to discourage older people from entering a restaurant or pub: an employer would struggle to justify refusing to hire fully qualified older staff on the basis that they might make a venue more welcoming to older persons, for example.

able to argue that it is legitimate for them to attract a youthful audience or assert the legitimacy of similar aims.[90] However, again, it is important to maintain the distinction between age-based and age-linked factors. When an employer is trying to sell goods to younger people, then the aim in question is to sell goods to an audience that will buy them: if this audience happens to be predominantly young people, then that aim is still nevertheless legitimate, as the aim in question is in itself no way discriminatory. There is nothing in the legitimate aims stage of the age objective justification test which has proved problematic in other jurisdictions.

B. *Proportionate Means*

In addition to showing the existence of a legitimate aim for their use of an age-based distinction, employers will have to satisfy the test of proportionality by showing the use of age was "appropriate and necessary". Age limits that are not linked to a clear justification may be very vulnerable, as will age limits which could be replaced with less restrictive methods of achieving the legitimate aim in question, such as the use of "robust job specifications based on clear, objective job descriptions", as suggested in the initial consultation outline on the Directive.[91]

Some criticism has been directed at the list of examples of justified uses of age distinctions set out in Art.6 of the Directive, and in particular the suggestion that minimum age requirements can be justified to ensure minimum conditions of seniority, return on training and required experience. The fear has been expressed by Age Concern and others that the possibly permissive nature of these examples could mislead employers about how easy it is to make objective justifications, and give the false impression of a "presumption" that the practices cited will be lawful. However, the practices contained in the list are examples, not exemptions. Employers will, if challenged, still have to show that in their circumstances the practice pursues a legitimate aim, and is an appropriate and necessary (or proportionate) means of achieving that aim (the test of objective justification).

As will probably be the case with the genuine occupational requirement (GOR) defence that the Regulations also permit, the use of age as a "proxy" for other characteristics should only be usually permitted where individual assessment is impracticable. A person's health maturity, ability to learn, experience, skill, willingness to work may often be ascertained by vetting procedures, individual assessments and good job specifications. In a Dutch case, a number of referees successfully challenged the age limits of 47 and 49

[90] This aim could be cited if an employer was for example arguing that her sales staff had to give an impression of vibrancy and general "hipness".

[91] See the DfEE (now Dept. of Works and Pensions) Initial Consultation Outline—AAG/04.

used by the Royal Dutch Football Association (KNVB) on the basis that an individual assessment of each referee's capability was entirely possible, and it was a breach of the proportionality principle to set a fixed age limit.[92] Even where age can be statistically linked to trends, as with increased ill health, the individual deviations from the statistical trend are so great that the use of age can constitute a very inadequate proxy for any given individual.[93]

Age limits may be necessary in particular industries to ensure a "turnover" of workers and to encourage recruits into a profession: the Dutch Supreme Court has upheld the imposition of a compulsory retirement age upon airline pilots for this reason.[94] However, the use of age limits that are intended to simply shift the age profile of the company or which unreasonably narrow the age spread of new recruitees may face great difficulties in showing objective justification. Sargeant has suggested that this might conflict with some of the government's use of "age diversity" rhetoric.[95]

C. *Which Standard of Justification will be Required?*

Much depends upon how the objective justification test will be applied, which in turn may depend on what view is taken of the importance of age discrimination as a problem.

This general objective justification test could be applied by adopting the standard proportionality requirement developed and applied in EC and UK indirect sex discrimination case law, whereby an employer would have to show the existence of a clear legitimate aim and that the use of age distinctions was reasonably necessary and clearly proportionate to achieve this aim. Alternatively, a looser "rational" standard could be applied, similar to the

[92] See Amsterdam Court of Appeal [Hof Amsterdam] 13–01–2000, JAR 2000, 42.

[93] The Canadian courts applied this approach in *O'Brien v Ontario Hydro* (1981) 2 CHRR D/504, where a 40-year-old man was refused an apprenticeship: the Board of Inquiry ruled that the employer's argument that age had relevancy when determining whether a person would adjust to particular job conditions was unjustified age discrimination.

[94] Dutch Supreme Court, October 8, 2004—Nr. C03/077HR—*16 pilots v Martinair Holland NV and the Vereniging van Nederlandse Verkeersvliegers*: this case concerned a challenge to a policy of compulsory retirement at the age of 56 of pilots employed with Martinair on the grounds of a breach of Art.1 of the Constitution and Art.26 of the International Covenant on Civil and Political Rights (ICCPR). (The case predated the coming into force of the Directive and the Dutch implementing legislation.) The rationale for retirement of pilots at 56 was to guarantee "circulation", based upon the idea that any pilot's career (starting with a very costly education and ending with early retirement) is structured in terms of the expectation that it will be possible for all pilots to reach the highest seniority level before retirement. Both the cantonal court and the district court ruled that this rationale formed an "objective justification". The Supreme Court affirmed this and rejected the applicants' claim. See also Dutch Supreme Court, October 8, 2004, Nr. C03/133HR, *Applicant v Koninklijke Luchtvaartmaatschappij NV (Royal Dutch Airlines) and the Association of Dutch Traffic Pilots*.

[95] Malcolm Sargeant, "The Employment Equality (Age) Regulations 2006: A Legitimisation of Age Discrimination in Employment" (2006) 35 ILJ pp.209–227.

unfair dismissal standard controversially adopted in the context of the justification defence for "less favourable treatment" under the DDA 1995.[96]

It is in applying this test that the question of how "serious" is age discrimination arises again: how much leeway should be given to employers to use age distinctions and to argue that these distinctions are in fact objectively justified? Jonathan Swift has suggested that there is a lack of clarity as to how this test will be applied in practice, which stems from a fundamental lack of social consensus about how seriously age discrimination should be treated. Given the lack of this consensus, he suggests that the looser standard used in the disability discrimination context might be more appropriate.

Jonathan Swift, "Justifying Age Discrimination" [2006] ILJ 302

"As already indicated, the one matter that sets the Regulations apart from anti-discrimination legislation to date is the possibility that acts which would otherwise amount to direct discrimination are capable of being justified, and as such, lawful. This is expressly provided for by Regulation 3 which (formulated positively) provides for direct discrimination to be lawful if the alleged discriminator can show the treatment identified as 'less favourable treatment' to be a 'proportionate means of achieving a legitimate aim' . . .

Although the availability of justification (in whatever form) is conveniently referred to as a 'defence', more properly, these provisions . . . are the ones that that are integral to what is meant by equality in this area, since they identify the forms of age discrimination that are legitimate (and therefore lawful) and those which are not. What equality should mean in this area is a thorny problem. In deciding what the scope of the justification defence should be, courts and tribunals will need to have regard to the conceptual difficulties that underlay any attempt at age discrimination legislation, and the fact that as a result of these difficulties there is no clear consensus on what the content of equality here should be.

Conceptually, age discrimination legislation is different from other antidiscrimination schemes. Unlike discrimination law to date, age discrimination legislation does not seek to address the difficulties faced by a discrete group identified by a fixed quality. We are all people 'of age', and in the course of a life it is likely that everyone will encounter the benefits and the detriments of age when decisions are taken that concern their interests. Outside the employment field Parliament's general expectation appears to be that people should have the fortitude to withstand these consequences, or at the least that it is not necessary for the law to intervene to define what is permissible and what is not. Within the employment field this is no longer the position, but the fact here that some forms of age discrimination will be lawful because they will be justified means that unlike in other areas the issue is not simply to demonstrate that age has been removed from any decision-making process. The consequence of Regulation 3, and for that matter Regulation 32, is that age can be a relevant consideration. What is not clear is the extent to which it is permissible to take it into account.

This leads directly to the issue of consensus (or rather the present lack of any relevant

[96] See *Jones v Post Office* [2001] EWCA Civ 558; [2001] I.R.L.R. 384, and the critique of this standard by J. Davies, "A Cuckoo in the Nest? A 'Range of Reasonable Responses', Justification and the Disability Discrimination Act 1995" (2003) 32(3) I.L.J. 164. See however the different approach applied to the justification defence to reasonable accommodation in *Collins v Royal National Theatre Board* [2004] EWCA Civ 144.

consensus). In relation to sex and race discrimination it is not just 30 years of practical experience that has formed the consensus in these areas. Although in those areas we may still argue as to the practical application of the principle of equality in specific circumstances, there is general acceptance of the substantive requirement of that principle: neither a person's sex nor their race should form the basis on which they are treated in a specific way. Even 30 years ago this was the premise that underpinned the legislation, and that premise was well-understood. The same cannot be said for age discrimination legislation. Although all would no doubt agree that neither the old or the young should be patronised or prejudged simply because they are old or young, the legislation as drafted is not about simply protecting the old or the young, it is about less favourable treatment on grounds of age. As such there is a conflict at the heart of the legislation not only because in the labour market conflicts of interest exist between the old and the young, but also because the characteristics of age are ones that we all possess and all use when making day to day decisions. If truthful, it is unlikely that there are many people who could honestly say that they have never allowed age to influence decisions relating to others, not merely personal decisions but also practical and professional decisions. Many occupations are dominated by notions of 'seniority' and 'experience' both of which are closely synonymous with age. Decisions are made on this basis every day. Although it is tolerably clear that the Age Discrimination Regulations are not intended to outlaw these considerations for all purposes, the language of Regulation 3 does not permit too many other certainties. What use may be made of considerations of 'seniority' or 'experience' will depend on the approach taken to the irritatingly vague notion of whether the treatment in question is a 'proportionate means of achieving a legitimate aim'. Yet the reason why this phrase is irritatingly vague is because as yet there is no consensus, or even leading view as to what equality requires for the purposes of age discrimination.

The existence of the justification defence requires us to distinguish between discrimination in the pejorative (and unlawful) sense, and discrimination in the sense of measured and appropriate choice. Both aspects of the defence as drafted—a 'legitimate aim' obtained by 'proportionate means'—will require Tribunals and other Courts to identify what our notion of equality is for these purposes. Of necessity this will start from case to case; ultimately a more principled approach might emerge."

Whether age discrimination legislation will have an impact will ultimately depend on how strictly the proportionality approach will be applied. While the Directive and Regulations give no indication that the looser "disability" standard should be adopted, neither instrument gives much guidance as to how the stricter standard might be applied in the age context. Much will depend therefore on how courts and tribunals apply the objective justification test.

Courts in various countries have often chosen not to apply a strict proportionality analysis in *human rights* cases challenging the use of age distinctions, often classifying age discrimination as a less problematic form of inequality than other forms of discrimination.[97] Courts and commentators have frequently suggested older people as a group have in general neither suffered historical discrimination nor a lack of political power, and therefore

[97] See *In the Matter of Article 26 of the Constitution and in the Matter of the Employment Equality Bill, 1996* [1997] 2 I.R. 321(SC); *Massachusetts Board of Retirement et al v Murgia* 427 U.S. 307 (SC).

do not constitute a disadvantaged group.[98] For example, the Canadian Supreme Court in applying the Canadian Charter's s.15 guarantee of equal treatment in *McKinney v University of Guelph*[99] applied a "rational" standard of analysis, in contrast to the "strict" standard required under race and sex discrimination cases, and concluded that the University of Guelph had a "reasonable basis" for their decision that mandatory retirement impaired the right to equality as little as possible given their legitimate objective of ensuring staff renewal.

Similarly, the House of Lords in *Reynolds* rejected an Art.14 ECHR challenge to the lower rates of jobseekers' allowance and income support paid to those under 25, on the basis that the age differentiation could be justified due to those under 25 having in general lower living costs than older persons, as many were still living with their parents.[100] While this generalisation did not necessarily apply to many of those unemployed and under 25, and relied upon a random age-limit, the Law Lords were willing to accept that the Secretary of State's justification was sufficient to overcome the lower justification threshold that exists for age. In his leading judgment, Lord Hoffmann drew a distinction between forms of discrimination that potentially infringed upon fundamental dignity and equal respect for the individual, which would require very strong justification to survive a HRA challenge, and less objectionable forms of discrimination, where the "general public interest" could be taken into account. He gave discrimination against older people as an example of a type of "borderline" form of discrimination, which might belong to either category.[101] However, he considered the use of age limits in paying less income support to younger workers as clearly justifiable in the public interest, and presumably therefore falling into the second category of discrimination.

There are good arguments for being cautious in applying a strict justification standard in human rights case-law, in particular given how often age is used as a differentiating tool in social welfare payments and other forms of social regulation, as where age limits on voting, purchasing alcohol and drawing down a state pension exist. However, it should not be presumed that a loose justification test will be adopted in applying the Age Regulations. The US, Dutch, Canadian and Irish courts have all applied a stricter standard than that advocated by Swift in applying age discrimination legislation.

For example, the US Supreme Court in *Western Airlines v Criswell* adopted a variant of the "necessity" proportionality test in interpreting the US age dis-

[98] In *Massachusetts Board of Retirement v Murgia* (1976) 438 U.S. 285, the Supreme Court explained that "old age does not define a 'discrete and insular' group ... in need of 'extraordinary protection from the majoritarian political process.' Instead, it marks a stage that each of us will reach if we live out our normal span." As previously noted, George Rutherglen has similarly argued that the ADEA "cannot be justified in terms of opening opportunities to a historically disfavored group." See G. Rutherglen, "From Race to Age: The Expanding Scope of Employment Discrimination Law" (1995) 24 J. Legal Studies 491.

[99] [1990] 3 S.C.R. 229. See also *Law v Canada* [1989] 1 S.C.R. 143.

[100] *R v Secretary of State for Work and Pensions, Ex p. Reynolds* [2005] UKHL 37.

[101] See para.17

crimination legislation.[102] Similarly, in applying the age discrimination provisions of the Ontario Human Rights Code, the Canadian Supreme Court in *Ontario Human Rights Commission v Etobicoke*[103] held that the employer had to show that the age requirement in question was reasonably necessary, although the Court recognised that the employer need not show that this standard was justified in respect of every employee affected where this was "impractical".[104]

Two questions have generally been asked by the Australian and Canadian courts in age cases: a) are the characteristics that are cited to justify the act of discrimination legitimate and justifiable grounds for distinguishing between two people, and b) is age an effective proxy for the relevant characteristics or a necessary differentiating tool for determining whether an individual possesses those characteristics?[105] Much will depend on whether the European Court of Justice interprets the Directive in a similar manner, and in particular whether it carries over its strict approach to the proportionality test over from the sex discrimination context.

In its first decision on the interpretation of the Framework Equality Directive and on age discrimination, *Mangold v Helm*,[106] the ECJ applied the proportionality test in a rigorous manner, which may vary from the approach suggested by Swift. The facts of *Mangold* deserve close consideration. German labour law provided that fixed-term contracts could only be concluded with employees if it was of less than two years duration, and could only be renewed three times within the two year time-limit: otherwise, objective justification was required. However, to encourage greater employment of older workers, legislation was introduced permitting employers to conclude fixed-term contracts with workers over the age of 58 without these restrictions, and with workers over the age of 52 until December 2006. This was challenged as constituting a lowering of protection for older workers contrary to the commitment of the German government to take effective measures to implement the age discrimination provisions of the Directive by December 2006, and not in the interim to take action which would conflict with the goals and purpose of the Directive.

The ECJ agreed that the less favourable treatment afforded to older workers

[102] No 83-1545. Stevens J. described the standard as one of reasonable necessity, not reasonableness, required that employers demonstrate that identification of unqualified persons on an age-neutral individualised basis was "impossible or highly impractical" before age restrictions could be justified.

[103] [1982] 1 S.C.R. 202. See also *Saskatchewan (Human Rights Commission) v Saskatoon (City)* [1989] 2 S.C.R. 1297.

[104] In *British Columbia (Public Service Employee Relations Commission) v BCGSEU*, the Supreme Court has tightened this standard again, prohibiting age-based distinctions and requiring individual assessment except where it is impossible or where it would cause undue hardship. [1999] 3 S.C.R. 3. See also *British Columbia (Superintendent of Motor Vehicles) v British Columbia (Council of Human Rights)* [1999] 3 S.C.R. 868 and *Greater Vancouver Regional District Employees' Union v Greater Vancouver Regional District* [2001] B.C.C.A. 435.

[105] See *Law v Canada (Minister of Employment and Immigration)* [1989] 1 S.C.R. 143, *Qantas v Christie* (1998) 152 A.L.R. 1295.

[106] Case C-144/04, *Mangold v Helm*, [2005] ECR 1-9981.

did constitute discriminatory treatment contrary to the German government's commitment not to take steps that conflicted with the Directive's requirements prior to its coming into force, and the general principle of equality recognised by EC law. The ECJ also rejected the German government's argument that the special measures were justified by the goal of ensuring greater employment of older workers.

Case C-144/04, *Mangold v Helm*, [2005] ECR I-9981

56. "In this regard, it is to be noted that, in accordance with Article 1, the purpose of Directive 2000/78 is to lay down a general framework for combating discrimination on any of the grounds referred to in that article, which include age, as regards employment and occupation.

57. Paragraph 14(3) of the TzBfG, however, by permitting employers to conclude without restriction fixed-term contracts of employment with workers over the age of 52, introduces a difference of treatment on the grounds directly of age.

58. Specifically with regard to differences of treatment on grounds of age, Article 6(1) of Directive 2000/78 provides that the Member States may provide that such differences of treatment "shall not constitute discrimination, if, within the context of national law, they are objectively and reasonably justified by a legitimate aim, including legitimate employment policy, labour market and vocational training objectives, and if the means of achieving that aim are appropriate and necessary". According to subparagraph (a) of the second paragraph of Article 6(1), those differences may include inter alia "the setting of special conditions on access to employment and vocational training, employment and occupation ... for young people, older workers and persons with caring responsibilities in order to promote their vocational integration or ensure their protection" and, under subparagraphs (b) and (c), the fixing of conditions of age in certain special circumstances.

59. As is clear from the documents sent to the Court by the national court, the purpose of that legislation is plainly to promote the vocational integration of unemployed older workers, in so far as they encounter considerable difficulties in finding work.

60. The legitimacy of such a public-interest objective cannot reasonably be thrown in doubt, as indeed the Commission itself has admitted.

61. An objective of that kind must as a rule, therefore, be regarded as justifying, "objectively and reasonably", as provided for by the first subparagraph of Article 6(1) of Directive 2000/78, a difference of treatment on grounds of age laid down by Member States.

62. It still remains to be established whether, according to the actual wording of that provision, the means used to achieve that legitimate objective are "appropriate and necessary".

63. In this respect the Member States unarguably enjoy broad discretion in their choice of the measures capable of attaining their objectives in the field of social and employment policy.

64. However, as the national court has pointed out, application of national legislation such as that at issue in the main proceedings leads to a situation in which all workers who have reached the age of 52, without distinction, whether or not they were unemployed before the contract was concluded and whatever the duration of any period of unemployment, may lawfully, until the age at which they may claim their entitlement to a retirement pension, be offered fixed-term contracts of employment which may be renewed an indefinite number of times. This significant body of workers, determined solely on the basis of age, is thus in danger, during a substantial part of its members' working life, of being excluded from the benefit of stable employment which, however, as the Framework Agreement makes clear, constitutes a major element in the protection of workers.

65. In so far as such legislation takes the age of the worker concerned as the only criterion for the application of a fixed-term contract of employment, when it has not been shown that fixing an age threshold, as such, regardless of any other consideration linked to the structure of the labour market in question or the personal situation of the person concerned, is objectively necessary to the attainment of the objective which is the vocational integration of unemployed older workers, it must be considered to go beyond what is appropriate and necessary in order to attain the objective pursued. Observance of the principle of proportionality requires every derogation from an individual right to reconcile, so far as is possible, the requirements of the principle of equal treatment with those of the aim pursued (see, to that effect, Case C-476/99 *Lommers* [2002] ECR I-2891, paragraph 39). Such national legislation cannot, therefore, be justified under Article 6(1) of Directive 2000/78."

The ECJ therefore was not satisfied that the German government had discharged its obligation to show sufficient objective justification for the use of age distinctions, despite the greater leeway given to national governments in areas of economic policy. This judgment indicates that the proportionality test may be applied with some rigour in age discrimination claims, although it remains to be seen how consistent the ECJ will prove. As noted above, Mazák A.G., in the ECJ case of *Palacios de la Villa v Cortefiel Servicios SA*, was of the opinion that the nature and history of age discrimination made it different from sex discrimination, and suggested that wide scope could be given to exceptions to the prohibition on age discrimination.[107] However, the ECJ in its judgment in *Palacios* did not give the exceptions to the Driective a wide scope, and subjected the rationale behind the maintenance of retirement ages in collective agreements to close scrutiny. The Court found that the retention of these retirement ages was proportionate as they were designed to ensure a degree of cross-generational equity. Nevertheless, the ECJ appeared to adopt a *Mangold*-style approach to the application of the proportionality test.[108]

In its consultations on the age regulations, the UK government appeared to assume that the proportionality test would be applied strictly. In the consultation on the draft age regulations, it was stated that "the test of objective justification will not be an easy one to satisfy. The principle remains that different treatment on grounds of age will be unlawful: treating people differently on grounds of age will be possible but only exceptionally and only for good reasons".[109] Concern still remains that UK courts and employment tribunals may veer between strict and looser applications of the test, and it may take time before a consistent standard is established. However, it is by no means certain that Swift's suggestion of a looser standard will be adopted, or that it is necessary and desirable: again, it is worth emphasising that the

[107] See Case C-411/05, Opinion of Mazák A.G. delivered on February 15, 2007.

[108] Case C-411/05, Judgment, October 16, 2007, ECJ.

[109] See para.4.1.13, *Coming of Age*.

tendency is for national courts to adopt a tougher line, and the ECJ appears so far to be doing likewise.

IX. Specific Exemptions

Aside from the general objective justification defence, the Regulations also set out a number of specific areas where the use of age-based requirements by employers is automatically deemed to be justified. To summarise, the key ones are:

- positive action;
- pay related to the national minimum wage;
- acts under statutory authority;
- retirement;
- pay and other employment benefits linked to seniority; and
- occupational pension schemes.

If an age-related criterion, provision or practice falls within the scope of one of these specific exceptions, then it will be deemed to be lawful: an employer will not have to demonstrate the existence of an objective justification.

The government's intention in establishing these specific exceptions was to provide greater certainty for employers by delineating areas where the use of age criteria would be automatically treated as justified and save employers the time and expense of showing the existence of objective justification. However, it should be remembered that these specific exceptions must comply with the provisions of the Directive and be themselves objectively justifiable as general exceptions.

A. *Positive Action and the Protection of Disadvantaged Groups*

Article 7 of the Directive allows states to maintain positive action measures to compensate or prevent disadvantage, meaning that the proportionate use of age distinctions to compensate for disadvantage will be deemed to be objectively justified, if such measures are "... introduced or adopted by a member state". Article 6(1)(a) also recognises that the promotion of vocational integration and the protection of vulnerable groups is a legitimate aim, which chimes with the overall ethos and orientation of the Directive.

The Regulations have however taken a narrow approach to positive action, which parallels the highly restrictive approach adopted for other prohibited grounds of discrimination.

Employment Equality (Age) Regulations—Exceptions for Positive Action

"**29.**—(1) Nothing in Part 2 or 3 shall render unlawful any act done in or in connection with—

(a) affording persons of a particular age or age group access to facilities for training which would help fit them for particular work; or

(b) encouraging persons of a particular age or age group to take advantage of opportunities for doing particular work;

where it reasonably appears to the person doing the act that it prevents or compensates for disadvantages linked to age suffered by persons of that age or age group doing that work or likely to take up that work."

Therefore, anything done in connection with giving persons of a particular age access to vocational training or encouraging persons of a particular age to use employment opportunities will be lawful, if reasonably expected to prevent or compensate for disadvantages suffered by such persons. Similar exceptions exist for trade organisations.

Satisfying the requirements necessary to come within this positive action exception will be easier for employers than jumping the hurdle of the objective justification test, as the legitimate aim of such measures is already approved by the regulation and in place of the requirement to show objective justification, it is only necessary to show that it reasonably appears that the measure pursues the aim of preventing or compensating for such disadvantages.[110] However, this exception will only apply to discrimination in two narrowly circumscribed situations: giving access to vocational training facilities and encouraging persons to take advantage of employment opportunities. This resembles the limited positive action provisions in the sex and race discrimination legislation, and any wider forms of positive action can only be justified through the general test of objective justification.[111]

As these exceptions are narrow in scope, being essentially confined to training and encouragement, their usefulness will be limited. The government

[110] *Coming of Age*, para.4.2.10.

[111] See *Coming of Age*, para.4.2.9. It is interesting that the UK government has introduced such a narrow provision, given that positive action on the grounds of age would appear to attract considerably less controversy and generate fewer issues of principle than positive action in respect of other equality grounds. This may reflect a preference to avoid reliance in general upon positive action provisions.

consultation on the draft regulations suggested that the positive action defence would be less significant than it could be for other prohibited grounds of discrimination, due to the existence of the general objective justification defence.[112] This is a valid point, but the scope of the defence may prove uncomfortably restrictive.

The position is more complex when employers implement practices which involve differentiation on the grounds of age and lie outside the scope of the positive action exception, but are designed to benefit older workers, especially those nearing retirement. This type of practice can include pre-retirement courses, extra payments, extra holidays and adjustments to work loads. Much will depend on the nature of the benefits in question, and whether they are designed proportionally: "preparing for retirement" should not be allowed to become a legitimate aim that could justify any preferential treatment for older workers. However, it would be also problematic if an excessive concentration upon achieving formal equality were to prevent employers introducing special provisions for older workers moving towards retirement.

While the Canadian courts have tended to treat these policies as justified,[113] the Dutch Equal Treatment Commission have taken the opposite view: in Case 2004/150 of November 15, 2004, the Commission held that an employer's policy of gradually reducing working hours and granting extra holiday time for employees of 57 years of age or older was not objectively justified.[114] This decision was based upon a strict application of the objective justification test, but it can be queried: should the provision for time-off for older workers to prepare for retirement be recognised as a legitimate positive act? Is the need to maintain age-neutral policies really so great as to require that such pre-retirement policies be jettisoned?

B. *The Use of Age Limits in Government Policy*

As discussed above, the use of age limits as tools of government policy is common: they are often used as a cut-off point to determine beneficiaries of particular policies, or to identify vulnerable groups who are to be excluded from a particular activity or subject to special requirements. The use of age limits in this way may deprive some individuals of benefits or support on the

112 *ibid.*, para.4.2.6

113 In the Canadian case of *Broadley v Steel Co of Canada Inc* (1991) 15 CHRR D/408 extended vacations for employers aged 61 or older were held to be justifiable discrimination on the basis that the transition to retired status was a major psychological and financial shift, and the extended vacations were a proportionate measure to alleviate the hardship that might be caused by an abrupt transition.

114 Similarly, in Case *2004–118* of 24 September 2004, the Commission found the granting of extra days of holidays to employees of 45 or older to employees who have more than 10 years of service with the employer, and the granting of reduced working hours to employees of 60 years and older, was unjustified.

grounds of age alone: however, given the reality of resource limitations, public programmes must be able to be targeted at specific elements of the population to achieve maximum impact, where there is no other reasonable method of targeting the appropriate group. Therefore the use of age distinctions in employment policy could be found to be objectively justified, unless the proportionality of the measure vis-à-vis the social harm it is designed to address cannot survive close scrutiny, as was the case in *Mangold*.[115]

For example, some government "New Deal" programmes have been restricted to the under-26s and over-50s, and upper age limits have been placed upon apprenticeships, student loans, or access to Jobcentre Plus and New Deal advice and training. The use of age limits in these circumstances could be replaced by more nuanced ways of identifying who might be the most appropriate beneficiaries of this special support: however, these alternative methods might be excessively time-consuming and resource intensive.

Similar arguments could apply when age limits are used to protect disadvantaged groups, as with the work restrictions imposed on younger persons by the Young Persons' Directive 94/33/EC: in the absence of any way of assessing each and every person's competency and maturity, age limits may be objectively necessary as they set a definite cut-off point that can be effectively enforced across an industry or across the country.

Regulation 27 exempts anything done under statutory authority, so any age limits provided for in legislation will remain in force and can only be challenged via a reference to the ECJ.[116] Another exception exists in Reg.31 for the age disadvantages faced by younger workers in several national minimum wage schemes, where they are often entitled to a much lower rate, or else completely excluded.[117] The exception allows employers to pay a lower minimum wage rate to those in young age bands (those aged 16–17 or those aged 18–21) than that paid to other workers, provided that no age differentiation is maintained within these bands.

The UK government has argued that this differential treatment can be justified as necessary to promote the interests of younger workers, who might otherwise face exclusion from the labour market due to their relative cost when compared to their lack of experience and training needs. Hepple suggests that the UK government has partially based its position on the advice of the UK Low Pay Commission, which would go some way towards showing

[115] Note that the use by the state of age distinctions in tax credits, employment benefits, employer incentives and other financial inducements to encourage worker integration will not be subject to the Directive, as they will be exempt as part of national social security schemes (Article 3(3)). See UK Department of Trade and Industry, *Equality and Diversity: Age Matters* (London: DTI, 2003), para.3.21.

[116] See also UK Department of Trade and Industry, *Equality and Diversity: Age Matters* (London: DTI, 2003), para.3.23.

[117] The government has argued that national minimum wage bands makes it easier to hire younger workers, and encourages younger people to stay in full-time education: see *Coming of Age*, para.5.2.1

justification.[118] In addition, challenges to similar age restrictions in Canada have been dismissed by the Canadian Supreme Court,[119] and by the House of Lords in the HRA decision of *Reynolds* (see above). However, the less favourable treatment of younger workers in this context remains controversial, based as it is on the assumptions discussed in *Reynolds* that younger workers have parental resources to fall back upon, and that employers need special incentives to hire younger workers, which remains contested. Some leeway has to be left for the use of age-based distinctions in public policy: but *Mangold* calls into question whether the use of such distinctions can be justified in the absence of compelling justification.

C. *Retirement Ages*

Great uncertainty surrounds the question of retirement ages and the extent to which the Directive's age discrimination provisions require existing national practices to be altered. This debate is ongoing across the globe, and is emerging as one of the crucial issues of law and policy in the UK. This section can only give a brief account of the key legal issues, and how they relate to the age discrimination rules.

It is important to distinguish between pensionable ages, state-imposed retirement ages, and contractual or employer-imposed retirement ages. *Pensionable age* is the age set by a member state at which individuals become entitled to a state pension (as distinct from the age at which individuals retire from work). Article 3(3) specifically excludes state social security systems from the scope of the Directive, and therefore age-based state pension rules are exempt from its scope. Article 6(2) also permits the use of age criteria for admission or entitlement to occupational social security systems including retirement benefits: thus, member states can choose to exempt the use of pensionable ages in occupational pension arrangements (see below).

However, the key issue for many member states concerns employer-set retirement ages, that is, whether employers are entitled to set retirement ages by contract, collective bargaining or unilaterally.[120] Any requirement now

[118] See Hepple, 95.

[119] See *Gosselin v Quebec* [2002] 4 S.C.R. 429.

[120] There is a distinction between unilateral mandatory retirement imposed by the employer, and contractual mandatory retirement, where a fixed retirement age is an explicit part of a voluntarily agreed employment contract. Contractual mandatory retirement is often part of a wider set of benefits and obligations involving mutual trade-offs freely negotiated between an employer and employee, and therefore not a suitable subject for legislative intervention. However, as such agreements can be "agreed" as a result of intense pressure being imposed upon an employee, the US has introduced legislation specifying conditions for the validity of such agreements. See the recent decision of *Jankovitz v Des Moines Indep. Cmty. Sch. Dist.*, Case No.04-3401 (8th Cir. Aug. 29, 2005), where the US Eighth Circuit Court of Appeals found an Iowa school district's early retirement incentive plan violated the Age Discrimination in Employment Act because it denied incentives to employees who were over the age of 65. The court found that the plan was discriminatory on its face and that the school district had failed to prove that the plan met the requirements of the ADEA's "safe harbour" provisions.

imposed by an employer that an employee must retire at a specified age amounts to less favourable treatment on grounds of age and will therefore be contrary to the Directive's provisions unless objectively justifiable under Art.6, or permitted by national legislation which in turn can satisfy the proportionality requirements, or which is exempt from the Directive's requirements.

Previously in the UK, employers could have been able to set retirement ages because legislation deprived employees over that age of protection from unfair dismissal.[121] As denying employment rights to those above a particular age would appear to be now contrary to the Directive, the UK has altered its approach. In the consultation paper *Age Matters*, the UK government considered two options: the introduction of a national default retirement age of 70, with the effect that employers would only have to provide objective justification for any retirement ages below the national default retirement age, or the abandonment of any attempt to retain a national default retirement age, with all employers having to individually provide objective justification for the introduction of any retirement age. After a mixed response to this proposal, *Coming of Age* opted for the "national default retirement age" model, but with the age set at sixty-five; this will have the effect of permitting employers to dismiss employees when they reach sixty-five without having to demonstrate objective justification.[122]

Employment Equality (Age) Regulations 2006—Exception for Retirement

"30(2) Nothing in Part 2 or 3 shall render unlawful the dismissal of a person to whom this regulation applies at or over the age of 65 where the reason for the dismissal is retirement."

To supplement this, the current upper age limit on unfair dismissal or redundancy claims will be removed, meaning that employees kept on after 65 will have full employment rights (see below): however, keeping employees on past the national default retirement age will not prejudice employers' rights to retire employees at or after the retirement age. Section 98 of the Employment

[121] Other countries, including France, provide that protection from unfair dismissal is lost when full pension rights accrue. See Art.L122-14-13 of the French Labour Code.

[122] This was originally announced by Patricia Hewitt, Secretary of State for Trade and Industry, to the UK Parliament, Age Discrimination: Treatment of Retirement Age", *Hansard*, HC Vol.428, 127 WS (December 14, 2004). Several other member states have chosen to introduce default retirement ages, and have provided in their national implementing legislation that reliance upon this default age will not have to be shown to be objectively justified. For example, Art.7(1)(b) of the Dutch Age Discrimination Act provides that the prohibition of age discrimination will not apply once an employee reaches the statutory retirement age of 65, or an older age if it has been laid down by a Act or governmental decree, or which has been mutually agreed by the parties involved.

Rights Act 1996 is amended to add another fair reason for dismissal, "retirement of the employee".

As compensation for the retention of mandatory retirement ages, employers will be subject to a duty to consider requests from employees to stay on beyond the fixed retirement age, who is obliged to give reasonable consideration to requests to work on, similar to their obligations in respect of part-time workers.[123] This however remains a mere duty to "consider", and employers do not have to give reasons. Employers are also required to inform employees of their right to request a continuation of their employment contract at least six months before its termination. A failure to follow this procedure, or a premature termination of a contract, can be remedied through unfair dismissal.[124]

If employers wish to impose a mandatory retirement age before the sixty-five-year limit, they will have to be able to show that this lower retirement age satisfies the general test of objective justification. The particular arguments in favour of the use of a mandatory age that are presented by a specific employer will have to measured against the proportionality standard, and the outcome will be a mater of case by case analysis.

The retention of the ability of employers to dismiss employees at 65 has generated considerable controversy. Heyday, an older persons organisation backed by Age Concern, have succeeded in obtaining a reference of the retirement age provisions of the Regulations to the ECJ (the *Heyday* case), arguing that the scope of the current exemption is disproportionate in that it fails to incorporate an objective justification test which employers should be required to satisfy before they can avail of mandatory retirement policies.[125] As some employees did not have a retirement age written into their contracts, the introduction of this new ability for all employers to dismiss at 65 could be contrary to EU law's standard "non-regression" requirements, if it is not exempt under Recitals 13 and 14 of the Directive (discussed above). In addition, the fact that an employer need not objectively justify their decision to dismiss, or even to give reasons for rejecting a request to stay on, is questionable.

The justification offered by government is that significant numbers of employers use a set retirement age as a necessary part of their workforce planning.[126] Also, the government has suggested that at present, if employers

[123] See Regs 47 and 48, as well as Schs 6 and 7, of the Employment Equality (Age) Regulations 2006.

[124] Given that the upper age limit for unfair dismissal claims will be removed, employees may be able to claim unfair dismissal if the employer did not comply with the duty-to-consider procedure, even where the retirement was above the national default retirement age.

[125] Two other references have already been made from Spain to the ECJ on the issue of mandatory retirement ages: *Palacios de la Villa and Cortefield Sericios SA* (case C-411/05) and *Garcia v Confederación Hidrográfica del Duero* (Case C-87/06), both of which involve compulsory retirement ages set under collective agreements.

[126] *Coming of Age* remarks that "whilst an increasing number of employers are able to organise their business around the best practice of having no set retirement age for all or particular groups of their workforce, some nevertheless still rely on it heavily." *Coming of Age*, para.6.1.14.

only had the option of individually justified retirement ages, this could risk the possibility that employers would reduce or remove work-related benefits they offer to employees to offset any increase in costs. The government has also announced that it will review whether it is still appropriate to have a default retirement age in 2011 (five years after the Age Regulations come into force). *Coming of Age* states that the decision to keep or abolish the default retirement age will focus mainly on two factors: whether, in the light of the evidence, the default retirement age remains appropriate and necessary to facilitate workforce planning and to avoid adverse effects on pensions and other employment benefits; and the influence of any other social policy objectives.[127] The government also has indicated that the six month notice time limit should help to encourage "planned retirement", and perhaps provide time for employees to persuade employers to reconsider. Presumably, there is also the hope that it may generate a culture change.

Nevertheless, the decision to retain a form of mandatory retirement remains controversial. Arguments do exist that as a practice, it may not be capable of being objectively justified in many contexts. It may be possible to justify certain exceptions in the context of specific forms of employment: however, it may be contestable whether it can be justified across the labour force as a whole.[128] It is worth noting that the retention of mandatory retirement is confined to employees: retirement ages for office-holders will have to be objectively justified.[129]

The use of mandatory retirement ages involves the creation of a bright-line categorical approach, involving the selection of an arbitrary chronological date (usually the 65th birthday). It fails to take account of the vastly different situations that older persons may find themselves in at that date.[130] The immediate transition from employment to leisure can result in damaging financial and psychological impact, and many employees experience their mandatory retirement as humiliating, degrading and denying them dignity. The ageing population, with increased health and life span and the need to increase the numbers of active income contributors, contributes an additional utilitarian dimension to the argument against mandatory retirement. These concerns are supplemented by considerations that arise from core principles: by denying access to the workplace, mandatory retirement can close off

[127] *Coming of Age*, para.6.4.5.

[128] Compulsory retirement is a major contributor to poverty in the elderly, especially in the case of women who may have taken years out for childcare and consequently lacked the opportunity to make an adequate level of national insurance or pension contributions.

[129] *Coming of Age*, para.6.1.13.

[130] See Ontario Human Rights Commission, *Discrimination and Age: Human Rights Issues Facing Older Persons in Ontario* (Ontario Human Rights Commission, 2000), p.4. Compulsory retirement is a major contributor to poverty in the elderly, especially in the case of women who may have taken years out for childcare and consequently lacked the opportunity to make an adequate level of national insurance or pension contributions.

opportunities for individual self-realisation and constitute a paternalist intrusion in personal life that violates the principle of human dignity.[131]

The argument has often been made that mandatory retirement is needed to promote job opportunities for younger workers. This contention often rests on questionable assumptions based around the "lump of labour" fallacy that there is a fixed number of posts, and that compelling the elderly to vacate theirs will automatically free new positions for the young. As with sex discrimination, evidence rarely supports this contention.[132] Such arguments also often make use of the "life cycle" arguments made by Issacharoff and Harris amongst others, already discussed above. Again, these arguments are less than convincing or compelling in the context of mandatory retirement, as many workers will not have benefited from the trade-off "life cycle" arguments suggest exists between lower pay/higher productivity at earlier stages of a career and higher pay/lower productivity later on. Also, older worker productivity remains reasonably constant after 65, so the alleged gains obtained via siphoning off older workers are again questionable (see above). The abolition of mandatory retirement in the US shows clearly that it is not a necessary part of employment policy and planning.

However, "life-cycle" concerns may have some validity in workplaces with very hierarchical and structured managerial systems, where some compulsory age restrictions may be necessary to ensure a turnover of older workers, whose ongoing employment may limit promotion opportunities and make restructuring difficult to achieve. The frequently cited example to illustrate this argument is academia, where there are a comparatively small and fixed number of academic posts and promotion opportunities. Without a degree of compulsory turnover, opportunities for younger staff may not open up and under-performing older colleagues may be impossible to remove.[133] The Dutch Supreme Court has upheld the imposition of a compulsory retirement age upon airline pilots for reasons of ensuring adequate promotion and guaranteed employment opportunities for younger pilots.[134]

Particular considerations may also exist for particular posts that justify the use of retirement ages. Health and safety requirements may require that cer-

[131] See L. Friedman, *Your Time Will Come: The Law of Age Discrimination and Mandatory Retirement* (Social Research Perspectives, No.10), (New York: Russell Sage Foundation, 1985).

[132] See P. Meadows, *Winning the Generation Game*, p.60. The latest version of the European Employment Strategy, agreed at the Lisbon summit in 2000, commits all EU Member States, including Britain to increasing the employment rate of older people. See also *Time for Action: Advancing Human Rights for Older Ontarians* (Toronto: Ontario Human Rights Commission, September 2000).

[133] Experience from the US has shown that those who choose to continue working after the normal retirement age tend to be those who are well educated with intrinsically interesting jobs and with a sizeable degree of authority and/or autonomy: senior academics fit this profile perfectly! See Meadows, 64–67.

[134] Dutch Supreme Court, 8 October 2004—Nr. C03/077HR—*16 pilots v Martinair Holland NV and the Vereniging van Nederlandse Verkeersvliegers*. See also Dutch Supreme Court, October 8, 2004, Nr. C03/133HR, *Applicant v Koninklijke Luchtvaartmaatschappij NV (Royal Dutch Airlines) and the Association of Dutch Traffic Pilots*.

tain employees retire before physical deterioration presents a risk, where individual assessment is not possible, or where it may not be sufficiently reliable. The need to guarantee a competent judiciary while avoiding individualised assessment which might rise real concerns about judicial independence would clearly justify fixing a set retirement age for judges.[135]

Arguments are also made that abolishing mandatory retirement could actually have negative implications for the dignity of older workers. Where there is no automatic retirement mechanism, competency tests may be required to assess continuing ability to deliver: their impact may be more intrusive and more demeaning for older workers, who may feel that the tests constitute a threat specifically directed at them.[136] Also, abolishing mandatory retirement could result in a reluctance to grant permanent contracts and an increasing contribution to the overall market trend of using fixed contracts. Reducing job security for older workers would be an unfortunate side effect of abolishing mandatory retirement.[137]

A related concern is that the state pension age can be viewed as reflecting a social consensus that there is a point beyond which people should no longer be obliged to work. Since 1989, when the earnings rule was abolished, people drawing state pensions have been able to work without penalty.[138] Thus, the existence of state pension age does not in itself justify mandatory retirement at that age.[139] However, trade unions have voiced concern that the abolition of mandatory retirement will mean that employers will be able to put greater pressure on people to continue working when they would really prefer to retire.

[135] See *Age Matters: A Report on Age Discrimination* (Canberra: Australian Human Rights and Equal Opportunity Commission, May 2000) p.42. The US practice of not imposing a retirement age on Supreme Court judges has not found favour in other countries.

[136] *Ibid*.

[137] Research into comparative experiences of age discrimination has concluded that forbidding mandatory retirement ages may make employers slightly less likely to hire older workers but that there is no evidence that this has been a major disincentive. See Z. Hornstein (ed.) *Outlawing Age Discrimination: Foreign Lessons, UK Choices*, Transitions after 50 Series, The Joseph Rowntree Foundation, July 2001, see *http://www.jrf.org.uk/knowledge/findings/socialpolicy/711.asp*. See also A. Taqi, "Older People: Work and Equal Opportunity" [2002] 55 International Social Security Rev. 120.

[138] Approximately eight per cent of men and more than a quarter of women continue working beyond state pension age, typically for a year or two for men, and up to age 65 for women: see Meadows, 64–67.

[139] Concerns have also been expressed about occupational defined benefit pension schemes, where the rate of return from additional years of service close to retirement is often disproportionately high in comparison with rates in earlier years: allowing members of such scheme discretion as to when to retire would therefore allow them to continue to obtain these higher rates and thereby obtain a "forced transfer" from employers and other scheme members. As Meadows argues, however, it is not retirement that is essential to control rates of return, but rather the ability to limit employees' ability to accrue these higher rates for a longer period. Retirement is the conventional means of doing this, but other approaches are possible, including the introduction of age, salary or length of service caps. Defined contribution schemes, which are becoming the norm, do not give rise to similar concerns, as benefits are related strictly to contributions rather than years of service. See Meadows, pp.64–67.

tpkeep1 >These concerns may be exaggerated. The US experience indicates that prohibiting mandatory retirement need not generate substantial negative effects, if only because the number of people who choose to postpone their retirement is likely to be limited, and those who stay beyond the normal retirement date for their employment will tend to do so for only a few years. Employers have become used to accommodate people leaving earlier than expected, due to increased workforce mobility and voluntary early retirement: the accommodating of a small number who choose to remain in employment longer may therefore not pose a considerable difficulty. Meadows suggests that "the effect on our national productive potential of any changes in mandatory retirement arrangements is likely to be very small".[140] However, the relevant evidence is less than certain (as with so many aspects of the mandatory retirement issue).[141]

Nevertheless, strong arguments do exist that as a practice, mandatory retirement may not be capable of being objectively justified in many contexts. It may be possible to justify certain exceptions in the context of specific forms of employment[142]: however, it is highly contestable whether it can be justified across the labour force as a whole. In more flexible labour markets and with the expansion in early retirement options, employers should arguably be able to achieve the same degree of certainty and planning by the use of effective human resource strategies and good performance management techniques rather than the blunt tool of a mandatory retirement age. It also seems to deviate from the core principle that age distinctions should be removed unless they are clearly objectively justified; it could be vulnerable to challenge under the Directive on this basis; and it appears to run contrary to the public policy challenges thrown up by the "greying" of the population, which seem to require greater encouragement of the older workers who choose to stay in employment after 65.

140 *ibid.*

141 Evidence about what happens in the workplace is drawn almost entirely from the United States. However, as with other aspects of age discrimination related issues, the US evidence has to be treated with some caution, since the provisions of the US legislation, many of the key features of the labour market, and the potential sources of income and welfare support available to people in retirement, vary considerably from those in Britain. In Australia, Canada and New Zealand, the abolition of mandatory retirement is generally too recent for any effects to have been measured. See Meadows, *ibid.*

142 See the Dutch Supreme Court decision in *Martinair Holland* referred to above.

Malcolm Sargeant, "The Employment Equality (Age) Regulations 2006: A Legitimisation of Age Discrimination in Employment" (2006) 35 I.L.J. 209–227

"The Government proposes to review the default retirement age after five years. Until then employers will be able to enforce retirement at the age of 65 years, and at other ages if this can be objectively justified. It is possible to view the employers' arguments in favour of the retirement age with scepticism, but it must be accepted that the abolition of a mandatory retirement age would cause problems for employers, especially small ones. The 'dignity' argument may also be accepted in a number of cases. These arguments, however, have to be balanced against the effect of mandatory retirement on employees who do not wish to retire. The effect of retirement upon individuals may also be significant when forced to leave the workforce. In this debate the Government has accepted, at least until 2011, the employers' view, but this must be at the expense of employees for whom the default retirement age represents another form of age discrimination at work.

Thus we are to have a default retirement age of 65 years. Retirement below the age of 65 years will need to be objectively justified and presumably this will be entirely possible and proper in some cases ... For retirement to be taken as the only reason for dismissal, it must take place on the 'intended date of retirement'. There is still the opportunity for the employee to claim that the real reason for dismissal was some other reason and that the planned retirement would not have taken place but for this other reason, or if the dismissal amounts to unlawful discrimination under the Regulations. This will not be easy and the 2005 Consultation states that there will be a heavy burden of proof on the employee ...

Thus the situation will be that where there is no consensual retirement, the employer may dismiss the employee and this dismissal will be a 'fair' dismissal provided it takes place on the retirement date and the employer has followed the statutory retirement procedure for consideration of any request from the employee not to retire. The Government's 2005 Consultation document stated that 'We want to encourage employers and employees to extend working life beyond the national default retirement age'. It is difficult to comprehend this measure achieving this objective, given the employers' enthusiasm for a default retirement age in response to the Government's 2003 consultation. The most likely outcome of any decision by the employer not to require the employee to retire at the intended retirement date is for the employer to agree a new date. In effect this will allow the employee to continue his or her contract for a fixed term. ...

Thus older workers, i.e. those over 65 or the normal retirement date, will continue to be discriminated against. This will be as a result of the Age Regulations which were, perhaps ostensibly, intended to stop age discrimination. Older workers will have no security, knowing that there employer can legitimately dismiss them at each new retirement date, provided a procedure of information and consideration is followed."

It remains to be seen whether the UK's mandatory retirement age survives challenge before the ECJ in the *Heyday* case. Mazák A.G. in the ECJ case of *Palacios de la Villa v Cortefiel Servicios SA* (which concerned the legitimacy of a collective agreement providing for compulsory retirement) was of the opinion that retirement ages established in collective agreements fell outside of the scope of the Directive by virtue of Recital 14, as they could be classified as "national provisions governing retirement ages".[143] If this approach had been followed by the ECJ, the UK government could have argued that legislative

[143] See Case C-411/05, Opinion of Mazák A.G. delivered on February 15, 2007.

provision for mandatory retirement could also qualify for exclusion as "national provisions governing retirement ages". However, as already discussed, the ECJ in its judgment in *Palacios*[144] considered that national rules governing retirement ages did come with the scope of the Directive. In this particular case, the ECJ considered that objective justification existed for the use of mandatory retirement ages in the collective agreements in question: the Court considered that the use of retirement ages was based upon a justifiable policy decision to ensure that job opportunities were available to younger workers as part of "cross-generational equity" planning. Therefore, it appears that the ECJ may be willing to grant states some leeway in maintaining retirement ages, but will nevertheless require that objective justification exists for such measures. *Heyday* will test whether the UK can show a similar objective justification.

D. *Employment and Redundancy Rights*

The denial or restriction of employment rights to workers above a particular age also raises serious questions under the Directive, as this will constitute direct age discrimination that again requires objective justification. The UK government has come to a similar conclusion, removing in the Regulations the previous statutory provisions that remove the right to protection from unfair dismissal upon reaching 65, or the normal retirement age for the post in question.[145] The Regulations also removes the lower age limit of 18 and the upper limit of 65 for entitlement to redundancy payments.[146]

Complex issues arose in the course of the implementation process about redundancy payments. Member states have historically provided for special benefits for older employees in redundancy decisions, as does the UK at present.[147] This constitutes age discrimination and will need justification. However, the UK government has decided to retain the current weighting of

[144] Case C-411/05, October 16, 2007, ECJ.

[145] UK DTI, *Equality and Diversity: Age Matters* (London: DTI, 2003) para.5.2–5.3

[146] Whereas in *Age Matters* para.XX, the suggestion was made that the upper age limit on redundancy payments should be retained if a default retirement age was introduced, the government decided to remove it in spite of the decision to have a default retirement age, on the basis that there are no legitimate aims supporting discrimination against older employees in the form of an upper age limit on redundancy payments. *Coming of Age* suggests that redundancy decisions should be made without regard to age, and the removal of the upper limit sends a clear signal that the default retirement age is an exception to the rule that older workers should receive the same treatment as younger workers. See *Coming of Age*, para.XX

[147] In the Netherlands, greater redundancy payments are also available for older workers. See M. Gijzen in the Dutch Baseline Report for the European Network of Legal Experts in the Non-discrimination Field, *Transposition of the Racial Equality Directive (Directive 2000/43) and the Framework Employment Directive (Directive 2000/78) into Dutch Law* (Brussels: Migration Policy Group, December 2004)

redundancy payments in favour of older workers, considering that it will be proportionate to retain higher payments for those nearing retirement.[148]

Length of service is also used to calculate redundancy payments, with minimum length of service requirements to qualify for eligibility: these elements could amount to indirect discrimination. However, the UK government has retained the use of length of service in computing these payments, on the basis that it is objectively justified as ensuring that compensation rewards past loyalty and commitment of the employee.[149] This raises the issue of seniority, and when its use will be justifiable as a method of distinguishing between employees.

E. *Experience and Seniority-Based Practices*

Distinctions based on experience, seniority (length of time of service), such as "last in first out" redundancy selection and pay scales which vary according to length of service, are common. However, they may be indirectly discriminatory, as they will often disadvantage younger workers, unless they can be objectively justified. Therefore, variations on the ground of seniority may have to be objectively justified by reference to the specific experience gained by actual work in the job in question, just as they may have to be in the context of sex discrimination.[150]

There are good reasons for maintaining the ability to make distinctions upon the grounds of seniority.[151] Rewarding loyalty and encouraging experienced employees to stay with an employer may be justifiable if they are required for good business reasons. Article 6(1)(b) specifically refers to the acceptability of justification of minimum conditions of professional experience or seniority in service for access to employment or employment-related advantages.

Other states have been content to assume that seniority distinctions are inherently justifiable, irrespective of the exact legitimate aim sought: others have introduced "seniority" exceptions into their new age discrimination legislation. For example, the Irish Equality Act 2004 now allows an employer to fix differential rates of severance payment based on seniority, and there are also specific exceptions for differences based on seniority in relation to remuneration or to conditions of employment. However, in the Irish case of *McGarr v Dept of Finance*,[152] the Equality Officer held that the express seniority exception in the Irish legislation must be strictly interpreted and could not be extended to permitting seniority requirements for promotion and for special

[148] UK DTI, *Equality and Diversity: Age Matters* (London: DTI, 2003) para.6.5.
[149] Reg.33 Employment Equality (Age) Regulations 2006.
[150] See *Cadman v HSE*, Case C-17/05, October 3, 2006.
[151] UK DTI, *Equality and Diversity: Age Matters* (London: DTI, 2003), para.9.3–9.5. Note that there was strong support among all social partners for the retention of seniority-based pay benefits.
[152] *McGarr v Dept of Finance*, DEC-E2003-036.

payments which were not objectively justified.[153] Similarly, in the Dutch Case 2004/141 of October 29, 2004, a pension regulation which remunerated on the basis of a length of service requirement was held to constitute unjustified *indirect* discrimination. These initial cases clearly demonstrate that seniority-based distinctions may be more vulnerable to challenge than is usually presumed, especially if they reflect an unquestioned assumption that longer service should be matched by greater rewards.

The use of seniority to encourage and reward loyalty was referred to in *Age Matters*, which proposed to "make specific provision for employers to be able to justify seniority conditions by reference to the aims ... [of] encouraging and rewarding loyalty."[154] The consultation revealed a considerable degree of consensus among respondents that loyalty-linked employee benefits were desirable and should be maintained.[155] To avoid the danger of employers having to justify each use of seniority criteria on a case-by-case basis, a general exemption for service rewards was built into the Regulations, along with two other more specific exceptions.

Employment Equality (Age) Regulations 2006—Exception for Provision of Certain Benefits Based on Length of Service

"32.—(1) Subject to paragraph (2), nothing in Part 2 or 3 shall render it unlawful for a person ("A"), in relation to the award of any benefit by him, to put a worker ("B") at a disadvantage when compared with another worker ("C"), if and to the extent that the disadvantage suffered by B is because B's length of service is less than that of C.

(2) Where B's length of service exceeds 5 years, it must reasonably appear to A that the way in which he uses the criterion of length of service, in relation to the award in respect of which B is put at a disadvantage, fulfils a business need of his undertaking (for example, by encouraging the loyalty or motivation, or rewarding the experience, of some or all of his workers).

(3) In calculating a worker's length of service for these purposes, A shall calculate—

(a) the length of time the worker has been working for him doing work which he reasonably considers to be at or above a particular level (assessed by reference to the demands made on the worker, for example, in terms of effort, skills and decision making); or

(b) the length of time the worker has been working for him in total;

and on each occasion on which he decides to use the criterion of length of service in relation to the award of a benefit to workers, it is for him to decide which of these definitions to use to calculate their lengths of service."

153 The Irish legislation has now been modified by the Equality Act 2004 to permit such seniority-based payments.

154 UK DTI, *Equality and Diversity: Age Matters* (London: DTI, 2003), para.9.5.

155 paras 5.1.5–5.1.6.

The use of length of service criterion for awarding or increasing benefits during the first five years of service is deemed to be clearly justified, and a complete and automatic exemption will apply: the employer need show nothing more. In contrast, making use of length of service requirements which are longer than five years may still be justified, but will not be automatically so: Reg.33 (3) sets out conditions to be fulfilled for this general exemption to apply:

a) awarding or increasing the benefit is meant to reflect the higher level of experience of the employee, or to reward loyalty, or to increase or maintain motivation of the employee; and

b) the employer has concluded that there will be a business benefit resulting from the achievement of these aims; and

c) the employer applies the length of service criterion similarly to staff in similar situations.

These conditions appear to be easier to satisfy than the full objective justification test. The employer does not have to show the existence of objective justification, but just to show that the use of the length of service criterion was done for a legitimate aim, applied consistently and was deemed necessary to achieve a "business benefit". However, these criteria still require the employer to justify the aim and effect of the benefit.

Both of these service exemptions are intended to distinguish between the use of legitimate "loyalty reward" schemes, which may often be appropriate and necessary means to achieve the legitimate aim of encouraging and rewarding loyalty, and the widespread use of seniority systems, which will often not be justifiable. However, some concern has been expressed that the general length of service exemption will legitimise the widespread use of length of service criteria, especially as the employer does not have to show that the use of the length of service condition is objectively justified.

Concern has also been expressed that the five year exemption of any length of service requirement may provide employers with too much leeway: five years is a considerable period of time in the contemporary workplace, and this time limit seems to be potentially disproportionate. It should be noted that length of service requirements may fall foul of the prohibition on indirect sex and race discrimination in certain circumstances.[156]

[156] See e.g. Case C-184/89, *Nimz v Freie und Hansestadt Hamburg* [1991] E.C.R. I-297.

F. *Occupational Pensions*

Article 3(3) of the Directive provides that it "does not apply to payments of any kind made by state schemes or similar, including state social security or social protection schemes". As previously discussed, this may exempt all state social security schemes from the scope of the Directive. On the other hand, employment-related occupational pensions and insurance are within the scope of the Directive. However, Article 6(2) of the Directive provides that:

> "Member States may provide that 'the fixing for occupational social security schemes of ages for admission or entitlement to retirement or invalidity benefits, including the fixing under those schemes of different ages for employees or groups or categories of employees, and the use, in the context of such schemes, of age criteria in actuarial calculations, does not constitute discrimination on the grounds of age, provided this does not result in discrimination on the grounds of sex.'

In other words, member states can choose to exempt the use by occupational schemes of age distinctions governing admission or entitlement to retirement or invalidity benefits and the use of age criteria in actuarial calculations under such schemes. This was done to allow occupational insurers and pension-providers to continue to use age-based criteria in offering entry terms, regulating costs across different age groups and in assessing premiums. Member states must actively invoke the exception. Most have done so.

The UK Regulations make it unlawful for trustees or managers of an occupational pension scheme, when carrying out their functions, to discriminate on grounds of age. However, certain age-related rules or practices in occupational pension schemes are exempted, and these are defined in a complex set of provisions in Sch. 2, Pts 2 and 3 of the Regulations. These excpetions include the setting a minimum level of pensionable pay for admission; having a normal pension age in a pension scheme (i.e. the age at which a person normally becomes entitled to receive retirement benefits) and the use of age criteria in actuarial calculations.[157]

The provisions in the Age Regulations are more restrictive than those set out in the original draft regulations. This unexpected tightening of the pension provisions was probably driven by concern that the width of the exceptions in the original draft regulations went further than was permitted by Art.6(2), especially those that related to the use of age distinctions in *paying out* benefits, as distinct from their use in fixing who is *entitled* to particular occupational benefits.[158] Any exceptions still in the Regulations that lie outside the scope of Art.6(2) will have to be shown to be objectively justified under Art.6.1.

These new provisions inserted at the last moment into the final text of the

[157] See *Coming of Age*, paras 7.1–7.

[158] The text of Art.6(2) referred to fixing conditions for "admission or entitlement", not to differentiation in how benefits are paid out after an entitlement has arisen.

Regulations caused a considerable degree of uncertainty and consternation in the pensions industry. There were differences of opinion between the government and some pension advisers as to the meaning of certain of these provisions, and in particular about whether employees who become entitled to a pension could in fact choose to work on while also collecting their pension.[159] As a consequence, the government delayed implementation of these provisions until December 1, 2006 (the absolute final deadline allowed under the Directive).

It should also be noted that the use of age distinctions in occupational schemes can still be challenged on the basis of sex discrimination, even if a member state has taken advantage of the exception. Given that the use of age-based criteria for admission and entitlement to benefits and of age-based actuarial criteria may give rise to serious issues of indirect gender discrimination, Art.6(2) provides at best a limited shelter from the scope of discrimination law.

X. Conclusion

Medical, social and economic trends have considerably altered or called into doubt many of the presumptions that could arguably once have justified wholescale age discrimination. Critical and ongoing scrutiny of age inequalities, affecting young and old, is on the increase. As with other forms of anti-discrimination legislation, time-honoured assumptions tend to shrivel, once exposed to the rigour of justification demands. To lock the "life cycle" into place by diluting age discrimination legislation may be to protect unnecessary and often unfair employment practices, where better alternatives exist. Swift is correct to say that there is no clear consensus as yet on the extent to which age discrimination is unacceptable: but the trend may point towards the reasonably rapid emergence of a broad consensus that the use of age-based criteria need to be largely abandoned, which was been the experience elsewhere, and which may quickly be reflected in EU and UK case law.

However, there may be a narrow but distinct range of situations where an arguable case for using age as a differentiating factor can be made out. Many of these exceptions involve direct discrimination the grounds of age, or age-linked criteria. Nevertheless, they are reconcilable in the abstract with the general prohibition on age discrimination: they usually either involve scenarios where age and age-linked characteristics are not being used to stereotype, or are being used for the purpose of defining groups in need of positive action or special treatment, or are linked to achieving cross-generational equity and therefore can be seen as advancing wider equality concerns.

However, these exceptions are also all capable of encompassing a broad

[159] See BBC News, "Age Rules on Pensions Postponed", September 8, 2006, available at *http://news.bbc.co.uk/1/hi/business/5326848.stm*.

range of age-based distinctions, and of being used as a cloak to camouflage the perpetuation of unnecessary and damaging age-based differentiation. The use of the objective justification test familiar from other discrimination contexts may be necessary to ensure that these exceptions are only applied where their use is necessary and justified. The justifications for prohibiting age discrimination may be different in certain respects from those that underpin other forms of discrimination law, but how age discrimination legislation may be applied and develop in practice may not be so different after all. The recent Discrimination Law Review has sought views on whether age discrimination in the provision of goods and services and other areas not currently covered by the 2006 Regulations should be subject to legislative control. Despite the potential complexities of achieving this, the Review's interest in ensuring that age discrimination legislation has a similar scope to other forms of discrimination legislation again illustrates how difficult it is to separate age out from other areas of discrimination law.

PART D

REMEDIES, ENFORCEMENT AND SOCIAL POLICY

16

INDIVIDUAL REMEDIES

I. Introduction

A recurring theme of this book has been the complexity of discrimination law. As we have seen, the legal regulation of equality and discrimination now includes vast types of legal forms including, inter alia: international, human rights and constitutional law; criminal law; civil law; and public law. The focus of this legal intervention is both the individual and collective action of a wide range of actors. Moreover, some of the state responses to inequality and discrimination also use non-legal responses (e.g. supply-side measures) to address the problem. It is therefore impossible to address all the enforcement and remedial issues that arise in the context of discrimination law. As a result, issues relating to remedies and enforcement are often treated as "technical" and summarily dealt with in final comments. In this chapter we take a different approach and treat an analysis of remedies as an essential part of the exploration of discrimination law. This approach to remedies is summarised by Peter Cane in his conclusion:

"The importance of remedies and sanctions to an understanding of historic legal responsibility must not be underestimated. This is obvious in the criminal context where the sentencing process is just as important a locus of responsibility judgments as the process of adjudicating guilt. More generally, the process of deciding what remedy or sanction ought to attach to any particular finding of legal liability provides important opportunities for the law, by establishing 'scales' or 'degrees' of responsibility, to modify and fine-tune responsibility judgments made in adjudicating upon liability. Because the sanctioning and remedial stage is much more highly formalised and developed in law than in morality, study of legal rules and principles governing remedies and sanctions can provide us with a depth of understanding about responsibility that could hardly be obtained by reflection on and observation of systems of responsibility that lack formalised and well developed remedial and sanctioning mechanisms and institutions."[1]

In this part of the book we focus on the remedies of the civil law, and in

[1] Peter Cane, *Responsibility in Law and Morality* (Hart Publications: Oxford, 2002) at p.44.

particular, the main EU and domestic discrimination law provisions. We address:

(1) individual and collective remedies;

(2) the work of the enforcement agencies; and

(3) the increasing use of non-legal and supply-side measures.

Before moving on to consider the legal issues relating to remedies in discrimination law, the first section sets out some of the theoretical issues that are relevant to attribution of individual responsibility for the harm of discrimination.

II. Individual Responsibility for Discrimination

Discussions of remedies raise more fundamental questions about the exact nature of the harm of discrimination which in turn justifies legal regulation in this area. Some of these issues are discussed in detail throughout the book and in particular in Part A of the book in the discussions on theory.

As stated earlier, domestic statutory discrimination law has created a private law statutory tort as the preferred legal form for the regulation of certain types of discrimination. In this way, the function of tort law to delineate interests that will enjoy legal protection has been applied to a new form of harm—"discrimination". Tort law has protected interests such as reputation through the law of defamation and psychological well-being through the intentional torts and the tort of negligence. Therefore, the protection of the interests of the individual in being free from the harm of discrimination can fall within this paradigm of tort law. In terms of remedies, the main aim of remedies in tort is to provide compensation for interference with this legally protected interest usually through financial damages, but also in some cases through injunctions. Therefore, the central aim of remedies in tort law which is to put the victim of the wrongdoing back in the position they would have been in had the wrong not occurred is achieved through giving financial compensation as a substitute for the harm that has been caused or the change in the position that has resulted from the tort.

There are, however, important distinctions between responsibility for harm and legal liability for harm. Responsibility is sometimes equated with liability but there are important distinctions between the two. A person may be responsible for harm caused but not be held to be liable in law, e.g. where a person disseminates ideas in the public sphere which are racist, misogynist or discriminatory but which are not liable to legal regulation. Equally, there may be cases where legal liability is imposed on an individual in circumstances where it is impossible (or difficult) to attribute moral responsibility, e.g. where public institutions are held liable for "institutional discrimination". In the following passage, Peter Cane sets out some of these issues which are relevant to discrimination law, and that relate to (a) the relationship between responsibility and legal liability; (b) the features of collective as well as individual responsibility; and (c) the link between responsibility and the imposition of sanctions using law.

Peter Cane: *Responsibility in Law and Morality* (Hart Publications: Oxford, 2002) pp.2–5; 40; 44

"Responsibility is an important criterion of legal liability, but not the sole criterion. Putting the point another way, liability is a trigger of legal penalties and remedies, whereas personal responsibility is one (but not the only) trigger of legal liability. [. . .] On the other hand, it is true that 'responsibility' is used much more commonly outside the law than in legal discourse to express ideas that underlie both it and 'liability'. Thus, we tend to speak of 'moral *responsibility*' and 'legal *liability*'. [. . .] Whereas law is necessarily a social phenomenon, a matter of convention and practice, morality is ultimately non-conventional and critical, providing ultimate standards for the ethical assessment of law and other social practices. Joel Feinberg puts the point well when he speaks, in relation to responsibility, of: 'a stubborn feeling [. . .] even after legal responsibility has been decided that there is still a problem ... left over: namely, is the defendant really responsible (as opposed to 'responsible in law') for the harm?"

[p. 40] According to the modern view of responsibility, individual responsibility is the only sort of responsibility there is. Adherents to the modern view need not deny that responsibility for an event can be shared by several individuals, but they would deny that groups can be responsible independently of the individuals who constitute them. Shared responsibility is a common legal phenomenon found in doctrines such as contributory negligence and contributions amongst wrongdoers. Group legal responsibility attaches to corporations. [. . .] In a physical and mental sense, we can reasonably say that human beings are 'natural' in a way that corporations are not. However, legal personality is not a matter of physical and mental attributes. [. . .] The legal personality of human beings is as much a social construct as the legal personality of corporations. [. . .] Neither in law or morality are there 'natural persons' or 'real responsibility'. Moral and legal personality and responsibility are all human artefacts.

[p. 43] One of the most important differences between law and morality is that law has much stronger and much more highly developed enforcement mechanisms and institutions than morality. Because morality lacks strong enforcement mechanisms and institutions, discussions of moral responsibility typically have little to say, in detail at least, about the relationship between responsibility and sanctions. Legal sanctions are of three basic types, punitive, reparative (or 'corrective') and preventive. Punitive sanctions focus on the person held responsible, whereas reparative and preventive sanctions also take account of the interests of those for whose benefit responsibility is imposed. Legal sanctions that benefit identified individuals are called 'remedies'. Punitive sanctions include imprisonment and fines. Reparative sanctions include orders to pay monetary compensation and restitution, and to take other types of action; and orders depriving instruments and decisions of legal effect. Preventive sanctions include detention, and orders prohibiting future conduct that would contravene some law or requiring action to avoid some legal contravention. [. . .]"

There are good reasons to focus on individual remedies as a focus for remedial provisions in discrimination law. If, as argued in Part A, discrimination law is a moral wrong, and a stigma for its victims, then allowing individuals to bring an action empowers them, makes them feel that they have control and vindication for a wrong, and it holds the perpetrator of discrimination responsible for his culpability. We have also seen, however, that along with the moral wrong of discrimination there are other features that cannot be easily accommodated within the paradigm of individual morality or responsibility. Structural discrimination, for example, cannot easily link the present wrong of discrimination to those who are often asked to bear the remedial costs, e.g. employers in indirect discrimination cases. This tension between discrimination as an individual and its collective structural aspect also raises complex issues in relation to remedies, In the next chapter we consider some of the ways in which the collective structural nature of discrimination is addressed, e.g. through the creation of enforcement agencies with powers of investigation; the use of contract compliance or the use of strategic public investment and supply side measures. In this chapter we consider individual remedies.

This division, however, needs to be put into context. Although individuals have a right to bring an action, the collective structural problems of discrimination will often mean that they lack the social, political and economic power to make this right to individual action into a reality. As we see in this chapter, this powerlessness is reflected in a number of ways: the pressure on employees to settle claims through arbitration even if it is not in their best interests; and the failure of employers to pay awards of damages. These problems are exacerbated by the forum and rules of procedure, evidence and costs in discrimination law cases: e.g. lack of legal aid for legal representation in cases which, despite the original intention to ensure that tribunals were a "user friendly forum", often raise complex issues of evidence and procedure.[2]

There has also been a tendency to rely on monetory compensation as the main remedy in discrimination law which ignores the structural nature of the problem. Monetary compensation cannot respond to the challenge to develop more proactive remedies that taget discrimination as a systematic practice which can cause harm to a whole social group rather than the one individual who is involved in bringing the claim. Reinstatement, for example, as discussed below, has become the "forgetten remedy". Domestic discrimination law has also not deployed the technique of mandatory injunction which would have a number of advantages in discrimination cases: e.g. allowing the judge to balance the needs of those in the social group and wider community other than the individual litigants; shifting the focus away from fault on to future consequences.[3] Some of the challenges could also be addressed through the introduction of US style class actions which would allow a whole group to

[2] See the discussion of these issues by Sandra Fredman, *Discrimination Law* (Oxford: Clarendon Press, 2002), Ch.6.
[3] *Ibid.*, p.171.

benefit from a decision. It has been argued that these would make it more difficult to bring cases. Even if class actions were thought to not be suitable, a more imaginative use of remedies and case management may be able to take into account the collective and "group" aspects of individual cases in discrimination law. In this chapter we consider individual remedies before moving on to a discussion of collective remedies in the next chapter.

III. Discrimination Remedies in International and EU Law

In this section we consider the remedies available in discrimination cases concerned with international legal provisions (including the European Convention on Human Rights) and, in so far as it is distinctive, EU law.

International law has distinct remedial and enforcement provisions which vary according to the international treaty that governs the relevant discrimination law provision. Moreover, the enforcement of international law obligations by individuals or organisations depends on whether the state which is a signatory to the treaty (State Party) and against which the right is being asserted has a "monist" or "dualist" approach to international law treaty provisions. "Monist" states have a system whereby a ratified international treaty automatically becomes integrated into domestic law. By contrast, in a "dualist" state's legal system, e.g. that of the United Kingdom, a ratified international treaty is binding on a State Party but it only becomes an enforceable part of domestic law once it is expressly incorporated into domestic law, e.g. in the case of the UK via an Act of Parliament.

Another marked difference between international treaty provisions and regional (e.g. EU) or domestic discrimination law relates to the remedies that are available. In the case of EU or domestic law the main remedies are damages or injunctions. In some contexts, such as public law, there are remedies such as declarations and in the Human Rights Act, there is the "declaration of incompatibility". This range of remedies is the main focus of this chapter. In the context of international discrimination law the range of available remedies is very different. The main focus of implementation of international law is (a) a periodic reporting process; and (b) adjudication before an international court or tribunal. Reporting systems are set up by the relevant international treaty which often sets up a committee structure to monitor the actions of a State Party. The relevant committee usually reviews the State Party's report in an open hearing and also refers to the documents/reports of non-government organisations (NGOs) which are set up to scrutinise state action in areas such as human rights and non-discrimination. The committee then produces its own report on the state's compliance with the treaty obligations: e.g. it highlights areas of compliance, breaches, trends and points of concern. These reports act as a basis for on-going negotiation (and also debate and dialogue) between the committees, member states and other interested parties (e.g. NGOs).[4] It is more unusual for an individual to have a right to adjudication where there has been an alleged breach of international discrimination law. However, in some cases states have the opportunity, and do, permit complaints by individuals which are then considered by relevant committees that sit in an adjudicative capacity. These committees do not have substantive enforcement powers but they do made recommendations to the relevant state about the complaint against them.

A. *ICCPR and other International Treaties*

As noted in earlier chapters, Art.26 of the ICCPR is the main relevant provision which establishes non-discrimination on the grounds of race, sex and religion (and other status) as a right in international law. Article 27 of the ICCPR deals with the "collective" aspect of the right of individuals to belong to a group. The ICCPR is legally binding on all State Parties with enforcement via reporting, under the supervision of the Human Rights Committee (established under the ICCPR). Art.40 of the ICCPR requires the relevant state to submit an initial report within one year of the Covenant coming into effect. Other reports are usually submitted at an interval of five years although reports can also be requested by the Human Rights Committee. The Human Rights Committee has a number of functions: inter alia, it provides guidance to states; and it considers representations of NGOs. It can also hear representations by individuals where the relevant State Party is a signatory to the Optional Protocol which allows an individual the right to petition where there is an alleged breach of right under the ICCPR. One example of this adjudicative remedy in international discrimination law is the *Lovelace v Canada*[5] case that was discussed at length in the chapter on intersectionality. In *Lovelace,* Canada had signed the Optional Protocol that allows its citizens a right to bring an individual complaint against the state before the Human Rights Committee (Lovelace's complaint was that Canada had breached Art.26 and Art.27 of the ICCPR). Other UN international treaties follow similar procedures, e.g. Art.9 of the International Convention on the Elimination of All Forms of Racial Discrimination (CERD) requires State Parties to submit first reports within one year of signing and then after every four years.[6] CEDAW (the International Convention on the Elimination of all forms of Discrimination

4 For an overview of these issues see Karon Monaghan, Max du Plessis Tajinder Malhi, *Race, Religion and Ethnicity Discrimination, A JUSTICE Report*, (Jonathan Cooper (ed.)), (London: Justice 2003).

5 See intersectionality, Chapter 9.

6 For an overview of these issues see Karon Monaghan, Max du Plessis Tajinder Malhi, *Race, Religion and Ethnicity Discrimination, A JUSTICE Report*, (Jonathan Cooper (ed.), (London: Justice 2003) at p.31.

Against Women) has analogous enforcement provisions as does the new Convention on the Rights of Persons with Disabilities (CRPD).

B. *Remedies for Breach of Convention Rights*

A number of the provisions of the ECHR provide a basis for equality and non-discrimination: most specifically Art.14 of the ECHR, but also other provisions such as Art.9, ECHR right to freedom of religion (Britain is not a signatory to the free standing right to non-discrimination in Protocol 12). ECHR rights are now enforced in UK law through the Human Rights Act, although the HRA does not remove the right to individual petition to the European Court of Human Rights.

C. *"Constitutional" Provisions on Remedies*

A number of provisions of the European Convention on Human Rights (ECHR) are relevant in the discrimination context. Most obviously significant is the Art.14 right to non-discrimination. However, since the UK has not signed Protocol 12 to the Convention, this must be raised by claimants in conjunction with another Convention right—for example, the Art.8 right to respect for private and family life, or the Art.9 right to freedom of religion—and the Court of Human Rights has been content in many cases to determine cases which appear, in common-sense terms, to involve "discrimination" using one of these other rights (these issues are discussed in detail in chapter 2).

Where the European Court of Human Rights finds against a signatory state on a petition brought by an individual "victim" (Art.34 of the Convention stipulates that the claimant must be a "victim"[7]), Arts 41 and 46(1) of the Convention come into play.

2. *European Convention*

Article 41. If the Court finds that there has been a violation of the Convention or the protocols thereto, and if the internal law of the High Contracting Party concerned allows only partial reparation to be made, the Court shall, if necessary, afford just satisfaction to the injured party.

Article 46(1). The High Contracting Parties undertake to abide by the final judgment of the Court in any case to which they are parties.

[7] For analysis, see Richard Clayton and Hugh Tomlinson, *The Law of Human Rights* (Oxford: Oxford University Press, 2000), paras 22.14 to 22.49.

(2). The final judgment of the Court shall be transmitted to the Committee of Ministers [of the Council of Europe], which shall supervise its execution.

The object of Art.41 is to return the claimant as far as possible to the situation in which they would have been but for the breach of their Convention rights.[8] The Court of Human Rights has in some cases awarded compensation as "just satisfaction"; however, it frequently deems the mere giving of a judgment in favour of the claimant to be sufficient.[9]

At national level, legislation must be interpreted, so far as this is possible, in a way which is compatible with Convention rights (under s.3(1) of the Human Rights Act 1998), an obligation which extends to both the cause of action and the available remedies contained in the legislation in issue. However, where legislation is incompatible with a Convention right and thus incapable of interpretation using s.3(1), s.4(2) stipulates that a court "may make a declaration of that incompatibility". As s.4(6) makes clear, however, such a declaration "(a) does not affect the validity, continuing operation or enforcement of the provision in respect of which it is given; and (b) is not binding on the parties to the proceedings in which it is made." While Parliament is likely to intervene to amend the legislation in issue for future cases, the claimant's only chance of a material remedy such as damages is via a successful petition to the Court of Human Rights.

HRA ss.6 to 8 establish a specific remedy against public authorities. HRA s.6(1) states that it is unlawful for a public authority to act in a way which is incompatible with a Convention right. HRA s.7 allows persons who count or would count as "victims" of the public authority's unlawful act to bring proceedings.[10]; HRA s.8 then stipulates that:

3. *Human Rights Act 1998*

s. 8(1) In relation to any act (or proposed act) of a public authority which the court finds is (or would be) unlawful, it may grant such relief or remedy, or make such order, within its powers as it considers just and appropriate.

(2) But damages may be awarded only by a court which has power to award damages, or to order the payment of compensation, in civil proceedings. [. . .]

(4) In determining—

(a) whether to award damages, or

(b) the amount of an award,

[8] *Pine Valley Developments v Ireland* (1993) 16 E.H.R.R. 379, para.[20]; *Papamichalopoulos v Greece* (1995) 21 E.H.R.R. 439, para.[38].

[9] Richard Clayton and Hugh Tomlinson, *The Law of Human Rights, ibid..*, paras 21.32 to 21.59.

[10] For critical analysis, see Joanna Miles, "Standing under the Human Rights Act 1998: theories of Rights Enforcement and the Nature of Public Law Adjudication" (2000) 59 C.L.J. 133 and "Standing in a Multi-layered Constitution", Ch.15 in Nicholas Bamforth and Peter Leyland (eds.), *Public Law in a Multi-layered Constitution* (Oxford: Hart, 2003). Note also the "collective enforcement" role of the Commission for Equality and Human Rights: Equality Act 2006, ss.9, 30 (see further Ch.17).

the court must take into account the principles applied by the European Court of Human Rights in relation to the award of compensation under Article 41 of the Convention....

Thus far, it has been assumed that s.8(1) allows a court to award such remedies as are conventionally available in a successful judicial review claim, as well as damages.[11] However, s.6(1) does not apply where "(a) as a result of one or more provisions of primary legislation, the authority could not have acted differently; or (b) in the case of one or more provisions of, or made under, primary legislation which cannot be read or given effect in a way which is compatible with the Convention rights, the authority was acting so as to give effect to or enforce those provisions" (HRA s.6(2)). In cases falling within s.6(2), the only option open to a court is to make a declaration of incompatibility concerning the legislation in issue.[12] National courts are obliged under Art. 13 of the Convention (not brought into domestic law by the Human Rights Act, but still applicable against the U.K. at Court of Human Rights level) to grant an "effective remedy" for violation of a Convention right. The Court has used Art. 13 to lay down minimum standards for the conduct of judicial review in national law.[13] For the moment it cannot be stated with confidence that the Human Rights Act declaration of incompatibility procedure is sufficiently "effective" for all purposes."[14]

D. *Other Remedial Mechanisms*

Other Council of Europe sources of discrimination law cannot be enforced in the same way as ECHR. The European Social Charter has not been incorporated into domestic law and is enforced through reporting mechanisms and a collective complaints mechanism, which however is optional and has not been adopted by the UK. Similarly, other sources such as the Framework Convention for the Protection of National Minorities (1995) and the European Charter for Regional or Minority Languages (1992) are also enforced through reporting, advice, opinions and recommendations. In the context of racism, the Council of Europe has developed special expertise by establishing the European Commission against Racism and Intolerance (ECRI) which comprises of independent experts from each member state who: receive reports from each

[11] For discussion of HRA damages, see Law Commission Report No. 266, *Damages under the Human Rights Act* (2000), pp.1–46; *Anufrijeva v. Southwark London Borough Council* [2003] EWCA Civ 1406; *R. (Greenfield) v Secretary of State for the Home Department* [2005] UKHL 14, [2005] 2 All E.R. 240; Duncan Fairgreave, "The Human Rights Act 1998, Damages and Tort Law" [2001] P.L. 695.

[12] See, e.g., *A. v. Secretary of State for the Home Department* [2004] UKHL 56, [2005] A.C. 68.

[13] *Smith and Grady v UK* (2000) 29 EHRR 493; *Hatton v UK* (2002) 34 E.H.R.R. 1 and (2003) 37 E.H.R.R. 28.

[14] Note the Court's doubts in its Chamber decision in *Miss Burden v UK*, Application no. 13378/05, December 12, 2006 (currently on appeal to the Grand Chamber).

member state; analyse the reports; and make suggestions on how to tackle problems.

As stated in earlier sections, European Union law operates as a special legal system which is supra-national but at the same time is distinct from international law. One consequence of this is that there is a well developed system of individual enforcement of rights in EU law, allowing individuals to enforce their EU rights and also in some cases to claim damages and other remedial relief in both domestic courts and the European Court of Justice. Significantly, the EU law doctrines of supremacy and direct effect mean that EU law can be enforced by domestic courts. Moreover, the principle in the *Francovich* case[15] means that an individual injured in certain circumstances by a Member State's breach of EU law can (in certain limited circumstances) claim damages.

In the area of EU discrimination law it is important to note that Art.141 does have direct effect, as established in the *Defrenne* case.[16] In relation to directives, such as the Equal Treatment Directive, the ECJ has established that these can only be enforced against Member States (and public bodies widely defined). In the *Marshall* case,[17] the Court held that ETD could be (vertically) directly effective to allow an applicant alleging discrimination to bring an action against a Member State. As stated above, the *Francovich* case principle allows individuals to also claim damages in some limited cases where non-implementation by the Member State has led to loss. Moreover, although the directives cannot be enforced against a private individual (i.e. they do not have horizontal direct effect) the increasing development of the doctrine of consistent interpretation[18] which requires domestic courts to interpret domestic law so that it complies with clear EU directives means that there is an "indirect" implementation of the norms of directives into the legal relationships and actions between private parties in domestic settings. The House of Lords has also affirmed that it will apply interpretative principles to ensure that domestic anti-discrimination legislation (e.g. the SDA) is interpreted in a way that is consistent with EU law.[19]

Moreover, as well as general remedies of enforcement and damages EU discrimination law also includes certain specific remedies which are set out and considered below. These remedies include both individual remedies in the form of "judicial and/or administrative procedures" including conciliation processes (such as ACAS). The remedial framework also includes the establishment of a collective enforcement body in the case of EU sex discrimination law (ETD, Art.8a) and EU race discrimination law (RED, Art.13) although there is no such requirement for the Equality Framework Directive in

[15] *Francovich & Bonifaci v Italy* (Cases C-6 & (/90) [1991] E.C.R. I–5357.

[16] *Defrenne v Belgium (Defrenne I)* Case 80/70, [1971] E.C.R. 445.

[17] *Marshall v Southampton and South West Hampshire AHA* (Teaching) Case C-152/84 [1986] 2 E.C.R. 723.

[18] See for example discussion in *Marleasing SA v Comerical Internacional de Alimentacion SA* Case C–106/89 [1990] E.C.R. I–4135.

[19] *Webb v EMO (Air Cargo) Ltd* [1995] 4 All E.R. 577.

relation to discrimination on the grounds of sexual orientation, religion, disability and age. In Britain, the new Commission for Equality and Human Rights is now the single body that deals with all these strands of discrimination. This is discussed in more detail in the following chapter.

EU law generally leaves the choice of specific remedies (e.g. criminal vs. civil sanctions) to individual member states, as long as the remedies are effective and the same as for the enforcement of national law rights through its main provisions on enforcement: the amended ETD, Arts 6, 8d; Race Equality Directive, Arts 7, 15; and the Framework Directive, Arts 9, 17.

Amended Equal Treatment Directive

"Article 6

1. Member States shall ensure that judicial and/or administrative procedures, including where they deem it appropriate conciliation procedures, for the enforcement of obligations under this Directive are available to all persons who consider themselves wronged by failure to apply the principle of equal treatment to them, even after the relationship in which the discrimination is alleged to have occurred has ended.

2. Member States shall introduce into their national legal systems such measures as are necessary to ensure real and effective compensation or reparation as the Member States so determine for the loss and damage sustained by a person injured as a result of discrimination contrary to Article 3, in a way which is dissuasive and proportionate to the damage suffered; such compensation or reparation may not be restricted by the fixing of a prior upper limit, except in cases where the employer can prove that the only damage suffered by an applicant as a result of discrimination within the meaning of this Directive is the refusal to take his/her job application into consideration.

3. Member States shall ensure that associations, organisations or other legal entities which have, in accordance with the criteria laid down by their national law, a legitimate interest in ensuring that the provisions of this Directive are complied with, may engage, either on behalf or in support of the complainants, with his or her approval, in any judicial and/or administrative procedure provided for the enforcement of obligations under this Directive.

Article 8a

1. Member States shall designate and make the necessary arrangements for a body or bodies for the promotion, analysis, monitoring and support of equal treatment of all persons without discrimination on the grounds of sex. These bodies may form part of agencies charged at national level with the defence of human rights or the safeguard of individuals' rights.

2. Member States shall ensure that the competences of these bodies include:

(a) without prejudice to the right of victims and of associations, organisations or other legal entities referred to in Article 6(3), providing independent assistance to victims of discrimination in pursuing their complaints about discrimination;

(b) conducting independent surveys concerning discrimination;

(c) publishing independent reports and making recommendations on any issue relating to such discrimination.

Article 8d

Member States shall lay down the rules on sanctions applicable to infringements of the national provisions adopted pursuant to this Directive, and shall take all measures necessary to ensure that they are applied.

The sanctions, which may comprise the payment of compensation to the victim, must be effective, proportionate and dissuasive. The Member States shall notify those provisions to the Commission by 5 October 2005 at the latest and shall notify it without delay of any subsequent amendment affecting them."

Race Directive

"Article 7 Defence of rights

1. Member States shall ensure that judicial and/or administrative procedures, including where they deem it appropriate conciliation procedures, for the enforcement of obligations under this Directive are available to all persons who consider themselves wronged by failure to apply the principle of equal treatment to them, even after the relationship in which the discrimination is alleged to have occurred has ended.

2. Member States shall ensure that associations, organisations or other legal entities, which have, in accordance with the criteria laid down by their national law, a legitimate interest in ensuring that the provisions of this Directive are complied with, may engage, either on behalf or in support of the complainant, with his or her approval, in any judicial and/or administrative procedure provided for the enforcement of obligations under this Directive. [...]

Article 13 Bodies for the promotion of equal treatment

1. Member States shall designate a body or bodies for the promotion of equal treatment of all persons without discrimination on the grounds of racial or ethnic origin. These bodies may form part of agencies charged at national level with the defence of human rights or the safeguard of individuals' rights.

2. Member States shall ensure that the competences of these bodies include:

— without prejudice to the right of victims and of associations, organisations or other legal entities referred to in Article 7(2), providing independent assistance to victims of discrimination in pursuing their complaints about discrimination,

— conducting independent surveys concerning discrimination,

— publishing independent reports and making recommendations on any issue relating to such discrimination.

Article 15 Sanctions

Member States shall lay down the rules on sanctions applicable to infringements of the national provisions adopted pursuant to this Directive and shall take all measures necessary to ensure that they are applied. The sanctions, which may comprise the payment of compensation to the victim, must be effective, proportionate and dissuasive."

Framework Directive

Article 9 [identical to Race Directive, Article 7]

Article 17 [identical to Race Directive, Article 15]

More generally, we need to consider the principles the ECJ will apply in this context. In a series of cases in the 1990s, the ECJ has negotiated the tension between two goals in relation to remedies in EU law: first, the principle that a national court should be free to apply all domestic rules which comply with the conditions of equivalence and practical possibility; and yet at the same time a second principle that national remedies must secure the effectiveness of EU rights. The fact that EU discrimination law contains requirements for a judicial remedy has meant that there has been strict scrutiny of national domestic remedies for a breach of EU discrimination law. For example, in the *Dekker* case,[20] where the applicant had sought damages for pregnancy discrimination, the ECJ found that although the national law could determine the remedy for a breach of the Equal Treatment Directive, the national remedy could not apply where it would in effect subject the claim to the burdensome requirement of fault or to a defence of justification. In *Dekker* the ECJ summed up its approach in the following terms:

"Article 6 of the Directive (ETD) recognizes the existence of rights vesting in the victims of discrimination which can be pleaded in legal proceedings. Although full implementation of the Directive does not require any specific form of sanction for unlawful discrimination it does entail that that sanction be such as to guarantee real and effective judicial protection (judgment in Case 14/83 *Von Colson* [1984] ECR 1891, paragraph 23). It must therefore have a real deterrent effect on the employer"[21]

During one phase of ECJ interpretation of the relationship between autonomy for national courts and ensuring the effective application of EU law there was an expectation that national courts should be proactive in ensuring that EU law was applied in an effective way in the domestic courts. The requirement in cases such as *Dekker* that the effectiveness of EU law should not be "impossible in practice" was increasingly interpreted as requiring that the right in EU law

[20] *Dekker v Stitchting voor Jonge Volwassenen (VJV) Plus* [1990] I—E.C.R. 3941.
[21] *Dekker v Stitchting voor Jong Volwassenen (VJV) Plus* [1990] I—ECR 3941, at para. 23.

would not be "excessively difficult" to exercise and make real.[22] Perhaps one of the most clear examples of this increasing willingness to interfere with national autonomy in the area of remedies was the ECJ decision in *Marshall (II)*.[23] In *Marshall (II)*, the House of Lords had asked the ECJ to give a preliminary ruling on the compatibility of maximum ceilings of compensation on employment tribunals: the issue was whether Art.6 of Directive 76/207 (ETD) could be relied upon to challenge national legislation that set a maximum limit on the amount of compensation that could be awarded by a tribunal in a sex discrimination case. The ECJ considered two of the rules in the national rules governing remedies: first, the substantive rule on the ceiling for damages; and second, the jurisdictional rule on the lack of power to award interest. In *Marshall (II)* the ECJ ruled that both of these rules would have to be disapplied and overridden to provide an effective remedy in EU law under the ETD.

Since the *Marshall (II)* case there has been a limited retrenchment from interference with national autonomy to determine remedies in EU law. In *Steenhorst Neerings*[24] the domestic national rule was a restriction on the retroactivity of a claim for benefit which clearly weakened the effectiveness of the provisions to eliminate discrimination in the areas of social security benefits for married women (Art.4(1) of Directive 79/7). The applicant in that case had been prevented (because of a national rule) from claiming benefits to which she would have been entitled had it not been for the failure of the State to implement the Directive correctly. The decision in *Steenhorst Neerings* suggests a more restrictive approach to the principle of adequacy of compensation in EU sex discrimination law cases was limited. This retrenchment has also been reinforced by the *Johnson (II)* case[25] where the ECJ held that restriction on a retroactive effect of a claim were compatible with EU law even where there were no issues of the State's administrative convenience of financial balance.

There is now an increasingly median position between an approach that restricts national autonomy to determine remedies and one that takes a more cautious approach. This more balanced approach requires that the principles of effectiveness and equivalence which have been developed by the ECJ must be applied by the national courts in an analysis that needs to determine whether or not the national rule relating to remedies that is at issue may end up undermining the practical exercise of the EU law right. Craig and de Burca have summarised this new balancing approach of the ECJ in the following terms:

[22] See Cases C-312/93, *Peterbroeck, Van Campenhout & Cie v Belgian State* [1995] E.C.R. I–4599, para.12, and C-430–431/93, *Van Schijndel & Van Veen v Stichtung Pensioenfonds voor Fysiotherapeuten* [1995] E.C.R. I-4705, para.17. For a full discussion of the development of ECJ case law see Paul Craig and Grainne de Burca, *EU Law: Text, Cases and Materials*, 3rd ed. (Oxford: Oxford, 2003) at pp.240–274.

[23] Case C–271/91, *Marshall v Southampton and South West AHA II* [1993] E.C.R. I-4367.

[24] Case C–338/91, *Steenhorst—Neerings v Bestuur van de Bedrijfsverenigning voor Detailhandel, Ambachten en Huisvrouwen* [1993] E.C.R. I–5475.

[25] Case C-410/92, *Johnson v Chief Adjudication Officer* [1994] E.C.R. I–5483.

"The 'balancing' approach to the relationship between the requirement of equivalence and effectiveness and the prima facie principles of national procedural autonomy thus introduces a kind of proportionality test for weighting the impact of a national rule on a particular Community right against the legitimate aim served by that rule, and consequently also introduces a considerable degree of uncertainty from case to case. Whether a national remedial rule will be lawful or not will depend not just on the intrinsic nature, aim and effects of that rule, but also on its application to a particular factual set of circumstances, when weighed against the aim and importance of the Community right in question."[26]

IV. The Forum for Litigation—Employment Tribunals and County Courts

Most cases of discrimination are dealt with in the employment tribunals or the country courts. However, in some exceptional cases there are special provisions where a body or an individual carrying out a statutory function has to deal with a complaint of discrimination. In these cases the statutory body or the individual is required to achieve a high standard of fairness in adjudicating the claim. For example, an Army Board exercising its statutory function of dealing with complaints of racial discrimination has to take into account a number of factors: the relevant provisions of the Race Relations Act; to consider whether there has been unlawful racial discrimination; and to give proper consideration to whether compensation or other redress should be granted. Moreover, and crucially, as the forum of last resort for dealing with the individual complaint the Army Board is required to ensure that it achieves the highest standards of fairness.[27] Similarly, where the Secretary of State for Health is hearing an appeal under the National Health Service Act which raises an issue of racial discrimination he must take into account the provisions of the RRA and exercise his appellant function in a fair way.[28]

As socio-legal critiques of private law actions for damages have revealed, the disparity of power between litigants and employers creates substantial barriers to access to justice for individuals. This disparity is especially pro-

[26] For a full discussion of the development of ECJ case law see Paul Craig and Grainne de Burca, *EU Law: Text, Cases and Materials*, 3rd ed. (Oxford: Oxford University Press, 2003) at p.252. Now see Paul Craig and Grainne de Burca EU: Law: Text, Cases and Materials, 4th ed. (Oxford: Oxford University Press, 2008).

[27] *R v Army Board of the Defence Council Ex p. Anderson* [1991] I.R.L.R. 425 DC, Michael Rubenstein, "Sex and Race Discrimination: Individual Remedies" in (2006) Discrimination Case Law Guide, Published by IRS on February 1, 2006.

[28] *R v Department of Health Ex p. Gandhi* [1991] I.R.L.R. 431 DC, Michael Rubenstein, "Sex and Race Discrimination: Individual Remedies" in (2006) Discrimination Case Law Guide, Published by IRS on February 1, 2006.

nounced in discrimination cases where the imbalance of power (e.g. between employees and employers) is compounded by the additional marginalisation of the employees who will be minorities (e.g. women, ethnic and religious minorities, gays and lesbians, the disabled and the old). In these circumstances the design of the forum for litigation and the availabilty of assistance for individual litigants become especially important. The main focus of this chapter is on individual remedies in the employment tribunal. Nevertheless, it is worth noting that claims for discrimination in the spheres of goods and services, education and housing are litigated in the County Court.

The current rules on the time limits for bringing a claim in the Employment Tribunals are set out below. It is worth noting that the imposition of time limits by tribunals by domestic discrimination law has been held to be compatible with EU discrimination law.

In relation to time limits although the ECJ has held that time limits are not incompatible with EU law there are limits to the way in which they are applied. The ECJ has confirmed that domestic time limits are compatible with EU law as long as there is (a) equivalence with other domestic law rights (i.e. not less favourable as for equivalent domestic law rights); and they are practically effective (i.e. they do not render the exercise of the EU rights impossible in practice).[29] In *Emmott*, the applicant sought a retrospective payment of a disability benefit for the period of time during which Council Directive 79/7 was unimplemented in Ireland, and during which time the applicant had been discrimination against on the grounds of sex. When the applicant applied for judicial review, the state representative department argued that her delay in initiating proceedings within the relevant time limit was a bar to the legal action. The ECJ held that although the national time limit was not such as to render her right to exercise her right impossible per se, in this case the fact that the Directive had not been implemented needed to be taken into account, and therefore the time limit could not be applied against the applicant (who was seeking to rely on the provisions of a directive) until that directive had been implemented.[30] *Emmott* was subsequently distinguished in *Steenhorst-Neerings,*[31] where the ECJ found that time-limits served an important function in ensuring that administrative decisions could not be subject to challenge indefinitely: in this way time limits could serve the functions of administrative efficiency and financial balancing. In *Johnson (II),*[32] a time limit that restricted the ability of an applicant to rely on EU law rights was upheld even where it did not impact on administrative efficiency and financial balancing. This line of cases has been interpreted as being a

[29] See for example the discussion in *Rewe-Zentralfinanz eG V Landwirtschaftskammer fur das Saarland* Case C-33/76 [1976] E.C.R. 1989.

[30] Case C-208/90, *Emmott v Minister for Social Welfare* [1991] E.C.R. I-4269.

[31] Case C-338/91, *Steenhorst—Neerings v Bestuur van de Bedrijfsvereniging voor Detailhandel, Ambachten en Huisvrouwen* [1993] E.C.R. I-5475.

[32] Case C-410/92, *Johnson v Chief Adjudication Officer* [1994] E.C.R. I-5483.

consistent with each other, and *Emmott* was treated as an exceptional case, in the *Denkavit Internationaal BV* case.[33] In *Denkavit*, it was suggested by Jacobs A.G. that *Emmott* could be explained as an exceptional case because the state itself was implicated in leading the applicant to make an error. Jacobs A.G. went on to affirm that legal certainty required that, as a general rule, the setting aside of time limits should be confined to wholly exceptional circumstances, as in *Emmott*. In this way the decision in *Emmott* was reconciled with the later more restrictive interpretations on the ability of the ECJ to interfere with national rules on time limits in cases such as *Steenhorst-Neering* and *Johnson (II)*.

In relation to domestic discrimination law, the general rule in employment discrimination cases (other than equal pay claims that are dealt with below) is set out in Section 111(2) of the Employment Rights Act 1996 (ERA) provides that:

"An employment tribunal shall not consider a complaint [of unfair dismissal] under this section unless it is presented to the tribunal—

(a) before the end of the period of three months beginning with the effective date of dismissal, or

(b) within such further period as the tribunal considers reasonable in a case where it is satisfied that it was not reasonably practicable for the complaint to be presented before the end of that period of three months."

There are a number of issues that have arisen in relation to time limits in Employment Tribunals and individual complaints of discrimination that need to be briefly considered. One issue relates to how a tribunal should exercise its discretion set out in ERA 1996, s.112(2)(b) about what is a "reasonably practicable" time period within which to present a claim. Judicial interpretation of this discretion suggests that a wide margin of discretion will be given to tribunals to determine what is reasonable in these circumstances. For example, in *London Borough of Southwark v Afolabi*[34], the Court of Appeal upheld the decision of a tribunal which allowed an employee to claim race discrimination nine years after the date of the appointment which was the discriminatory act. The tribunal had exercised its discretion on the basis that the claimant had only gained knowledge of the discriminatory act on seeing his personnel file nine years after he had failed to be appointed for the position for which he had applied (the act he was claiming was race discrimination). The tribunal allowed the time to run from the date on which the claimant saw the file and relied on the fact that he had no reason to inspect the personnel file before this

33 *Denkavit Internationaal BV v Kamer van Hopophandel en Fabrieken voor Middengelderland*, Case C-2/94 [1996] E.C.R. I-2827.

34 *London Borough of Southwark v Afolabi* [2003] I.C.R. 800.

date. In reaching their decision to uphold the exercise of discretion of the tribunal in this case, the Court of Appeal acknowledged that this was an exceptional case in which the lapse of nine years was a period of considerable magnitude. They found that the policy of the Act is made clear by the brevity of the limitation period; and that period of three months is in marked contrast to the limitation periods in ordinary litigation. Therefore, given that Parliament had envisaged that complaints for these types of cases would be determined within the shorter time period, it would only be in very exceptional cases that a tribunal could decide that there can be a fair trial despite a long period (such as nine years) passing after the original events. However, in this case the Court of Appeal found that there was no prejudice to the employers over and above that to the employee who was complaining of discretion and upheld the exercise of discretion of the tribunal.

It has been confirmed in *Royal Bank of Scotland Plc v Theobald* that where an applicant has official advice (e.g in this case from the Citizen's Advice Bureau) that he should wait before filing a complaint in an Employment Tribunal, and where he acts on this advice, then it may be found that it was not reasonably practicable for the claimant to have filed his application in time, and he may be allowed to proceed with his claim. In *Royal Bank of Scotland Plc*, on the facts, the EAT found that the applicant could have filed the complaint in time.[35] Moreover, the tribunal has some discretion about allowing claims on the basis of what is "just and equitable" in all the "circumstances of the case" as set out in ERA 1996, s.11. In *Virdi v Commissioner of Police of the Metropolis*, the EAT found that, on all the facts of the case, they would allow the claimant to proceed against one of the respondents although the complaint was filed one day late, but he could proceed against a second respondent against whom the complaint was filed three months late (without good reason for this delay).[36]

A number of recent cases have set out some of the principles that can act as a guide to what constitutes an "act" or "continuing acts" of discrimination for the purposes of determining the date of the three month time limit. It is clear that in relation to a claim for discrimination in relation to a contractual term, the three month time limit applies from the end date of the claimant's employment,[37] and that in a case of constructive dismissal the time limit runs from the date of the repudiatory act rather than the acceptance of the act.[38] In *Humpheries v Chevler Packaging Ltd*, the EAT held that the continuing failure to

[35] *Royal Bank of Scotland Plc v Theobald* EAT/0444/06 (1 report), discussed in Pennie Christie, "Points of Procedure Roundup" (2007) 865 IRS Employment Review.

[36] *Virdi v Commissioner of Police of the Metropolis* [2007] I.R.L.R. 24 EAT (2 reports), discussed in Pennie Christie, "Points of Procedure Roundup", (2007) 865 IRS Employment Review.

[37] See Aileen McColgan, *Discrimination Law: Text, Cases and Materials* (Hart Publications: Oxford, 2005) at p.327.

[38] Commissioner of Police for the *Metropolis v Harley* [2001] I.C.R. 927, Aileen McColgan, *Discrimination Law: Text, Cases and Materials* (Hart Publications: Oxford, 2005) at p.327.

make adjustments as required under the DDA 1995 constituted an ommission so as to extend the time limit for bringing a claim.[39]

In the context of a series of acts that were claimed to be race discrimination, the EAT has applied the Court of Appeal definition of a "continuing act" given in *Hendricks v Commissioner of Police of the Metropolis*. In that case, Mummery L.J. had said of the claimant:

"She is, in my view, entitled to pursue her claim ... on the basis that the burden is on her to prove, either by direct evidence or by inference from primary facts, that the numerous alleged incidents of discrimination are linked to one another and that they are evidence of a continuing discriminatory state of affairs covered by the concept of 'an act extending over a period".

Mummery L.J. concluded that the central question was whether there was an "act extending over a period of time", as distinct from a series of unconnected isolated acts for which time would begin to run from the date when each of the specified acts was committed[40] However, the idea of a "continuing act" comes to an end once the ongoing situation of discrimination has ended, so that after this end point the normal rules relating to time limits apply. In *Lyfar v Brighton and Sussex University Hospitals*, the Court of Appeal upheld the tribunal and EAT decisions that applied this approach to "continuing acts" of discrimination and held that that the majority of a race discrimination claim could not be allowed to proceed on the basis that it was time-barred.[41]

In *Pugh v The National Assembly for Wales* the EAT has also recently held that it is not necessary for there to be an explicit "policy" of discrimination for a series of acts, practices or rules to constitute a "continuing act of discrimination". The decision confirms that employment tribunals need not take too restrictive a view of what constitutes an "act extending over a period" although the claimant had to prove that there was such an act for the claim to proceed.[42]

The EAT has also recently considered how time limits should be construed where there have been procedural difficulties in the sending, receipt or filing of the application. It has held that the time for the presentation of a response (i.e. rule 4(1) of the Rules of Procedure which state that a claimant should file

39 *Humphries v Chevler Packaging Ltd* EAT/0224/06 (3 reports), discussed in Pennie Christie, "Points of Procedure Roundup", (2007) 865 IRS Employment Review.

40 *Hendricks v Commissioner of Police of the Metropolis* (CA) [2002] EWCA Civ 1686, [2002] IRLR 96, discussed in Pennie Christie, "Points of Procedure Roundup", (2007) 865 IRS Employment Review.

41 *Lyfar v Brighton and Sussex University Hospitals Trust* [2006] I.R.L.R. 345 (1 report), discussed in Pennie Christie, "Points of Procedure Roundup", (2007) 865 IRS Employment Review, published by IRS Feb 16, 2007.

42 *Pugh v The National Assembly for Wales* EAT/0251/06 (1 report), discussed in Pennie Christie, "Points of Procedure Roundup", (2007) 865 IRS Employment Review (*ibid*).

his response to the ET within 28 days of the copy of the claim being sent to him) runs from when the response is sent rather than when it is received.[43]

Also, where a respondent employer has failed to file a response within the time limit then Rule 9 of the Rules of Procedure apply, which state that where a respondent has not presented a response to a claim, or has had its response rejected, it shall not be entitled to take part in the proceedings except to:

(i) make an application for a review of a default judgment;

(ii) make an application for preliminary consideration of an application for review;

(iii) be called as a witness by another person; or

(iv) be sent a copy of a document or corrected entry.

The EAT has held that in these circumstances there are two procedural options open to the employer respondent: first, it can challenge the default judgment under rule 33; or second, it can apply for a review of a refusal to accept a response under rule 34.[44]

In relation to equal pay claims there are special time limits of six months. These have been challenged in *Preston v Wolverhampton Healthcare NHS Trust*.[45] In *Preston* the ECJ had been asked for a preliminary ruling to determine whether the six month time limit was compatible with the exercise of rights under Art.141 of the EU Treaty. The ECJ ruled that the six-months time limit did not make it more difficult or excessively difficult to exercise rights conferred by EU Art.141. The ECJ also ruled in that case that in relation to successive fixed term contracts the relevant time limit should run from the end of the "stable employment relationship". In *Preston*, the House of Lords affirmed this approach. It held that in relation to successive employment contracts the six months time limit runs from the end of the period of each contract of service, which led to the amendment of the Equal Pay Act.[46]

V. Proof of Discrimination—Burden of Proof

As with other civil cases, the burden of proof in discrimination law is on the complainant and the standard is on a "balance of probabilities". Unlike other

[43] *Bone v Fabcon Projects Ltd* [2006] I.R.L.R. 908, discussed in Pennie Christie, "Points of Procedure Roundup", (2007) 865 IRS Employment Review (*ibid*).

[44] *(1) D&H Travel Ltd and (2) Henderson v Foster* EAT/0226/0, discussed in Pennie Christie, "Points of Procedure Roundup", (2007) 865 IRS Employment Review (*ibid*).

[45] *Preston v Wolverhampton Healthcare NHS Trust* [2001] 2 A.C. 455.

[46] Equal Pay Act, ss.2(4). For a full discussion of time limits in equal pay cases see Aileen McColgan, *Discrimination Law: Text, Cases and Materials* (Hart Publications: Oxford, 2005) at pp.326–338.

civil cases, however, it is rare for there to be explicit and direct evidence of discrimination which raises particular problems for complainants. More specifically, the need to relate conduct to the requirement that it is "because of" race or sex or another prohibited ground. This, however, is something which is almost exclusively within the knowledge (and therefore) control of the discriminator. This paradigm once again reveals the way in which although discrimination law operates in a civil law paradigm, it often raises challenges of establishing inner mental states which are similar to those faced in the criminal law. In many cases, this can only be established through examining the discriminator's state of mind which will usually be impossible.

Therefore, in many cases the proof of discrimination has to be inferred from other primary facts. For these reasons, the EU discrimination law approach to burden of proof is that once the complainant has made out a prima facie case, it is then for the discriminator to establish the non-discriminatory reason for the decision. This approach was developed in number of ECJ decisions which established the rules on how direct and indirect discrimination should be proven in EU law.[47] *Enderby v Frenchay* AHA was a particularly important case in this context because it affirmed that (a) the existence of a prima facie case of discrimination places the burden of proving objective justification on the employer; and (b) affirmed that a prima facie case might be made out where "significant statistics disclose an appreciable difference in pay between two jobs of equal value, one of which is carried out almost exclusively by men and the other predominantly by women."[48] The Burden of Proof Directive[49] now explicitly sets out how this process will work in EU sex discrimination law. Identical rules are now contained in the Race Equality Directive and the Employment Equality Directive. The Burden of Proof Directive Art.4(1) states:

"Member States shall take such measures as are necessary, in accordance with their national judicial systems, to ensure that, when persons who consider themselves wronged because the principle of equal treatment has not been applied to them establish, before a court or other competent authority, facts from which it may be permitted that there has been direct or indirect discrimination, it shall be for the respondent to prove that there has been no breach of the principle of equal treatment."

47 See for example *Handels- OG Kontorfunktionaerenrdes Forbund I Danmark v Dansk-Arbejdsgiverforening* Case 109/88 [1989] E.C.R. 3199.

48 Case C-127/92 [1993] ECR I-5535, see Evelyn Ellis, *EU Anti-Discrimination Law* (Oxford: Oxford University Press, 2005) at pp.100–101.

49 Directive 97/80, extended to the UK and amended by Directive 98/52. For a full discussion of this issue in the context of EU anti-discrimination law see Evelyn Ellis, *EU Anti-Discrimination Law* (Oxford: Oxford University Press, 2005) at pp.101–103.

A. *Pre-existing Case Law—Burden of Proof in Areas where EU Discrimination Law does not Apply*

Before the introduction of the new statutory provisions on burden of proof (that introduced the EU standard into domestic discrimination law) there was a pre-existing case law. This pre-existing case still applies to those cases where there has not been statutory amendment to ensure compliance with the EU standard.

Two key cases established this older pre-existing standard for burden of proof. In *King v Great Britain China Centre* the Court of Appeal considered a claim under the RRA by a Chinese woman. The complainant's claim was upheld by the tribunal who found that the employer had failed to show that the unfavourable treatment that she had suffered was not because of her race. The EAT had overturned this decision because they stated that it incorrectly placed the burden of proof for discrimination on the employers. The Court of Appeal overturned the decision of the EAT and upheld the decision of the original tribunal. They stated that in cases of discrimination law, it was permissible to draw inferences from primary facts. They also held that that where it was shown that there was a less favourable treatment on racial grounds (i.e. a difference in treatment and a difference in race) it was permissible for the tribunal to require the employer to give an explanation for this discrimination. If no adequate explanation was provided, it was possible to infer discrimination from the primary facts. This did not reverse the evidential burden of proof. The main summary of the decision was given in the judgment of Neil L.J.:

King v Great Britain–China Centre Court of Appeal CA (Civ Div) [1992] I.C.R. 516

"From these several authorities it is possible, I think, to extract the following principles and guidance. (1) It is for the applicant who complains of racial discrimination to make out his or her case. thus if the applicant does not prove the case on the balance of probabilities he or she will fail. (2) It is important to bear in mind that it is unusual to find direct evidence of racial discrimination. Few employers will be prepared to admit such discrimination even to themselves. In some cases the discrimination will not be ill-intentioned but merely based on an assumption that 'he or she would not have fitted in.' (3) the outcome of the case will therefore usually depend on what inferences it is proper to draw from the primary facts found by the tribunal. these inferences can include, in appropriate cases, any inferences that it is just and equitable to draw in accordance with section 65(2)(b) of the Act of 1976 from an evasive or equivocal reply to a questionnaire. (4) though there will be some cases where, for example, the non-selection of the applicant for a post or for promotion is clearly not on racial grounds, a finding of discrimination and a finding of a difference in race will often point to the possibility of racial discrimination. In such circumstances the tribunal will look to the employer for an explanation. If no explanation is then put forward or if the tribunal considers the explanation to be inadequate or unsatisfactory it will be legitimate for the tribunal to infer that the discrimination was on racial grounds. this is not a matter of law but, as May L.J. put it in North West thames Regional Health Authority v. Noone [1988] I.C.R. 813, 822, 'almost common sense.' (5) It is unnecessary and unhelpful to introduce the concept of a shifting evidential burden of proof. At the conclusion of all the evidence the tribunal should make findings as to the primary facts and draw such inferences as they consider proper from those facts. They should then reach a conclusion on the balance of probabilities, bearing in mind both the difficulties which face a person who complains of unlawful discrimination and the fact that it is for the complainant to prove his or her case."

That passage was approved by the House of Lords in *Glasgow CC v Zafar*.[50] In *Zafar*, Lord Browne-Wilkinson stated that:

Glasgow CC v Zafar [1998] I.C.R. 120

"On racial grounds

The industrial tribunal, having wrongly drawn the inference of less favourable treatment, then held that, in the absence of any satisfactory non-racial explanation for such treatment, it was *bound* (author's emphasis) by authority to draw the inference that such less favourable treatment was on the grounds of the applicant's race. [...] If the tribunal meant to decide that, at this very last stage in the dealings between the parties, the attitude of the local authority on racial discrimination had changed and it had become racially prejudiced, the tribunal must surely have said so in the clearest terms. Instead it expressed itself as having "no choice but to draw [the] inference" of racial prejudice, i.e. it held it was bound in law to draw the inference of racial prejudice in the absence of any other satisfactory explanation given by the local authority of the differential treatment accorded to the applicant."[51]

In *Zafar* the House of Lords also clarified one crucial point. The King decision had confirmed that it was permissible and legitimate for tribunals to infer unlawful discrimination: from primary facts and in the absense of an adequate explanation by the employer using a test of a balance of probabilities. In *Zafar* the House of Lords made it clear that this permits the tribunals to draw such inferences. However, as the emphasis in the passage extracted above confirm, the House of Lords confirmed that tribunals are not *bound* to draw such inferences. This is an important point of difference between the preexisting case law on burden of proof which was developed before the EU standard was introduced. As the discussion of the Inge case below confirms, in relation to the statutory provisions that are under the new EU burden of proof standard there is now a requirement to draw such inferences and an explicit shift in the burden of proof to the employer."

Zafar also illustrates a particular difficuly in discrimination law cases that arise because of the weight that is given to the comparator. In the case Lord Browne Wilkinson stated:

[50] *Glasgow CC v Zafar* [1998] I.C.R. 120.
[51] *Ibid.*, 124–125.

"Less favourable treatment

The reasoning of the industrial tribunal on this issue is wholly defective. The Act of 1976 requires it to be shown that the complainant has been treated by the person against whom the discrimination is alleged less favourably than that person treats or would have treated another. In deciding that issue, the conduct of a hypothetical reasonable employer is irrelevant. The alleged discriminator may or may not be a reasonable employer. If he is not a reasonable employer he might well have treated another employee in just the same unsatisfactory way as he treated the complainant in which case he would not have treated the complainant 'less favourably' for the purposes of the Act of 1976. The fact that, for the purposes of the law of unfair dismissal, an employer has acted unreasonably casts no light whatsoever on the question whether he has treated the employee 'less favourably' for the purposes of the Act of 1976."[52]

As this passage confirms, the test for discrimination is whether the complainant is treated less favourably than the relevant comparator. The fact that the relevant comparator would also have been treated badly or unreasonably does not negate the fact that in this case there will be identical treatment and therefore no discrimination. This analysis confirms the criticisms of basing discrimination law on a procedural concept of equality as the treatment of "like with like", rather than a substantive concept of equality or autonomy which is more concerned with ensuring just and fair treatment. In the context of evidence and burden of proof, the *Zafar* approach means that an employer who can show that he would have treated all employees equally badly will not be found to be discriminatory.

In a subsequent case, the Court of Appeal has confirmed that it is important to distinguish between (a) general unreasonable treatment on the one hand; and (b) discriminatory treatment based on the fact that the employer's reasons for acting are linked to the prohibited grounds, e.g. that the complainant was black or a woman. This point was confirmed by the Court of Appeal in *Law Society v Bahl*, where they confirmed (the approach in *Zafar*) that proof that an employer acted equally unreasonably to other employees of any race or gender could be a reason negating an inference of discrimination. However, this was not the only method of disproving discrimination and its absence did not automatically render the treatment discriminatory.

In *Bahl*, the Court of Appeal approved the reasoning of Elias J. who had given the judgment in the EAT. Elias J. had stated:

"We do, however, respectfully accept that Sedley LJ was right to say that racial bias may be inferred if there is not explanation for the unreasoanble behaviour. But *it is not then the mere fact of unreasonable behaviour which entitles the tribunal to infer discrimination; it is not, to use the tribunal's language, unreasonable conduct 'without more', but rather the fact that there is no reason advanced for it.*"[53]

52 *ibid.*
53 *The Law Society v Bahl* [2003] I.R.L.R. 640, at p.96.

This distinction between unreasonable conduct and discriminatory conduct is crucial to ensure that discrimination is jusified as an independent wrong which justifies legal regulation. More specifically, this approach confirmed the need to ensure that there is a link between the employer's wrongful conduct and the prohibited grounds. Elias J. goes on to summarise this core aim in the following terms:

"The basic concepts inherent in the concept of unlawful discrimination are not difficult to state; the difficulties which tribunals regularly have is with their application. It is trite but true that the starting point of all tribunals is that they must remember that they are concerned with rooting out certain forms of discriminatory treatment. If they forget that fundamental fact, then they are likely to slip into error. The point was made by Lord Scott in the case of *MacDonald v Advocate General for Scotland* [2003] UKHL 34, when he said this:

> 'These two appeals demonstrate the importance, in my opinion, when dealing with complaints under the 1975 Act and the other discrimination Acts, of keeping in mind that they are intended to combat discrimination. They are discrimination statutes. Absent discrimination, objectionable conduct by employers must be countered by other means than complaints under these Acts.' "[54]

In the context of the changes to the pre-existing case law to take account of the new EU law standard this link is preserved by paras 11 and 12 of the amended *Barton* guidelines developed in *Igen* which shift the burden of proof to disprove this link on to the employer and state. To discharge that burden, it is necessary for the employer to prove, on the balance of probabilities, that the treatment was in no sense whatsoever on the grounds of sex, since "no discrimination whatsoever" is compatible with the Burden of Proof Directive; (12). This requires a tribunal to assess not merely whether the employer has proved an explanation for the facts from which such inferences can be drawn, but further that it is adequate to discharge the burden of proof on the balance of probabilities that sex was not a ground for the treatment in question. In these cases, the employer can still discharge the burden if he is able to show that his conduct is unreasonable conduct that is not related to the protected grounds of discrimination.

B. *EU Burden of Proof Directives and Changes in Domestic Law*

Changes in EU discrimination law on burden of proof also required changes in domestic discrimination law. The piecemeal nature of the changes has meant

[54] *Ibid.*, at para.94

that the amendments were carried out to each domestic statute to ensure compliance with EU law rather than harmonising all the legislation by introducing one standard of proof in all discrimination cases. This was achieved through amendments to the SDA, s.63(2)A now establishes the standard of proof as s.63A of the SDA (as inserted by reg.5 of the Sex Discrimination (Indirect Discrimination and Burden of Proof Regulations 2001):

"Where, on the hearing of the complaint, the complainant proves facts from which the tribunal could, apart from this section, conclude in the absence of an adequate explanation that the respondent—(a) has committed an act of discrimination against the complainant which is unlawful by virtue of Part 2 [...] the tribunal shall uphold the complaint unless the respondent proves that he did not commit, or, as the case may be, is not to be treated as having committed, that act."

The amendments to the burden of proof in sex discrimination cases only apply to employment discrimination (including pupil barristers and vocational training). Other areas such as goods and services, education and housing are not covered by the EU standard and they are still governed by the domestic case law on burden of proof.

The RRA has now also been amended to meet the EU law standard of proof (s.54A of the RRA 76, as inserted by reg.41 of the Race Relations Act 1976 (Amendment) Regulations 2003). However, the piecemeal nature of the amendments means that there are now two different standards of proof in race discrimination cases. Significantly, the changes to the RRA are not limited to employment cases because the Race Equality Directive covers not only employment but also other spheres (e.g goods and services, education). In relation to those protected grounds that are explicitly covered by EU race discrimination legislation (e.g race or ethnic national origin), the EU law standard has been introduced via an amendment to the RRA (RRA ss.54A and 57A). However, in relation to the other grounds referred to in the RRA but not EU race discrimination (e.g. colour or nationality) the burden of proof standard is governed by the domestic case law.

In those cases where the new burden of proof standard applies, (RRA ss.54A and 57A) states:

"Where, on the hearing of the complaint, the complainant proves facts from which the tribunal (or county court) could, apart from this section, conclude in the absence of an adequate explanation that the respondent—(a) has committed such an act of discrimination or harassment against the complainant [...] the tribunal (or county court) shall uphold the complaint unless the respondent proves that he did not commit or, as the case may be, is not to be treated as having committed, that act."

In those areas of law which are covered by the EU Employment Equality

Directive, the EU standard of proof also applies: i.e. the Employment Equality (Sexual Orientation) Regulations 2000, reg.29; Employment Equality (Religion and Belief) Regulation 2000, reg.29; DDA 17A(1C) of the Disability Discrimination Act 1995, as inserted by regs 3(1) and 9(2)(c) of the Disability Discrimination Act 1995 (Amendment) Regulations 2003 (SI 2003/1673). New standards for burden of proof have also been introduced into FETO (Arts 38A and 48A). As with the SDA, in non-employment related disability and FETO discrimination the domestic case law on burden of proof applies.

The way in which domestic courts will interpret the new EU law standard of proof in the areas in which it applies has been considered in *Barton v Investec*,[55] which was an action by a woman analyst who alleged discrimination under the EqPA and the SDA in the payment to her of a non-contractual bonus by her employer who was a financial services company. The facts in *Barton* were complex and raised difficult issues about the drawing inferences, from primary facts; and also from the employer's disregard for a statutory code of practice. In *Barton* the EAT affirmed that courts have always recognised that it is rare for complainant's in discrimination law cases to have evidence of overtly discriminatory words or actions. Therefore there is a need for an approach to proof that allows the use of affirmative evidence which consists of inferences drawn from primary facts. However, *Barton* also confirmed the tribunal's fact-finding role in these cases was emphasised in *Anya v University of Oxford*[56] where Sedley L.J. referred to the "ubiquitous need to make the findings of primary fact without which it is impossible to consider the drawing of relevant inferences". Barton also affirmed the decisions in *King v Great Britain—China Centre and Glasgow Council v Zafar* and stated that the new EU burden of proof (and consequent statutory amendments to the UK discrimination law set out above) had led to a new standard.

In *Barton*, the EAT summarised the approach to the new burden of proof in a set of "guidelines" which were subsequently amended by the Court of Appeal in the *Igen* case, and which are set out in the extract of the *Igen* case below. *Igen* also clarified one issue that had remained confused after the decision and the guidance in *Barton*. This was the process and stages through which the burden of proof shifts between the parties.

Igen was a case that joined a number of individual cases all of which raised an issue about the how to interpret the new burden of proof that had been introduced by the amendments to the SDA and RRA, and which was similar to the standard of proof under the DDA, the EE(SO), reg.29, and EE(RB), reg.29. More precisely, the issue was about when and how there is a shift in the burden of proof between a complainant and the respondent under the new burden of proofs standards introduced through these statutory provisions. The Equal Opportunities Commission, the Commission for Racial Equality

[55] *Barton v Investec Henderson Crosthwaite Securities Ltd*, EAT, 2003 March 6; April 3 [2003] I.C.R. 1205.

[56] [2001] I.C.R. 847, 855D-E, para.10

and the Disability Rights Commission intervened in the case because of the significant impact of the decision in a wide range of discrimination cases.The extract of the case below sets out the general arguments and includes the amended guidelines developed in *Barton*. However, before moving on to consider the general test and the amended *Barton* guidelines, it is necessary to summarise the three joint cases.

"Discrimination: Burden of proof finally reversed in direct discrimination claims"

820 (2005) IRS Employment Review Publisher IRS, on March 25, 2005

Igen Ltd and ors v Wong. The tribunal had directed itself correctly and there was no error of law. Inferences were drawn from the employer's unexplained unreasonable conduct, thereby satisfying the first stage of the burden of proof process. At the second stage, the tribunal found the appellants' explanations inadequate and had set out its reasons why.

Chamberlin Solicitors and ors v Emokpae. In Emokpae—a case in which the complainant was dismissed as a result of rumours of a relationship between herself and the officer manager—the tribunal and the EAT were incorrect to conclude that there was discrimination on the grounds of sex on the basis of an assertion that there would have been no rumours but for Ms Emokpae being a woman. The tribunal's finding that the reason for the dismissal was the rumours, not the complainant's sex, meant that her case failed at the first stage. Further, (obiter), it was not an error of law for a tribunal to fail to identify a hypothetical comparator where no actual comparator can be found. However, the failure to identify the characteristics of some sort of comparator might lead the tribunal not to focus correctly on the key issues.

Brunel University v Webster. The Court considered whether the use of the word "could" in s 54A of the RRA 1976 meant that the complainant did not have to prove that the respondent actually committed the act of discrimination complained of, as long as the complainant proved that there was an act of discrimination, which could have been committed by the respondent. The Court rejected this construction. It took the view that the respondent needs to provide an explanation for his conduct once he is shown to have acted in a certain way. He does not need to prove that he did not even carry out the act in the first place. It is for the complainant to prove the probability of the facts complained of, not just the possibility. The Court took the view that to construct the statute otherwise would result in a great injustice to the respondent. The claim therefore failed at the first stage of the two-stage process."

(1) Igen Ltd (Formerly Leeds Careers Guidance) v Wong; (2) Chamberlin v Emokpae; (3) Webster v Brunel University [2005] EWCA Civ 142, CA (Civil Div) Kennedy, Peter Gibson and Scott Baker L.JJ.

"16 Before us there has been no challenge to the broad outline of the Barton guidance, although suggestions have been put to us as to how it might be improved. Some criticisms have been made and suggestions put forward by the Employment Appeal Tribunal in other cases. We shall return to the wording of the guidance later. However it is important to stress at the outset that employment tribunals must obtain their main guidance from the statutory language itself. No error of law is committed by a tribunal failing to set out the Barton guidance or by failing to go through it paragraph by paragraph in its decision.

17 The statutory amendments [*to the burden of proof to ensure compliance with EU law—added by author*] clearly require the employment tribunal to go through a two-stage process if the complaint of the complainant is to be upheld. The first stage requires the complainant to prove facts from which the tribunal could, apart from the section, conclude in the absence of an adequate explanation that the respondent has committed, or is to be treated as having committed, the unlawful act of discrimination against the complainant. The second stage, which only comes into effect if the complainant has proved those facts, requires the respondent to prove that he did not commit or is not to be treated as having committed the unlawful act, if the complaint is not to be upheld.

18 There was some debate before us as to whether the statutory amendments merely codified the pre-existing law or whether it had made a substantive change to the law. [...] We think it clear, as Mr Allen submitted and as Miss Slade accepted, that the amendments did not codify, but altered, the pre-existing position established by the case law relating to direct discrimination. It is plain from the Burden of Proof Directive that member states were required to take measures to ensure that once the complainant established facts from which it might be presumed that there had been discrimination, the burden of proof shifted to the respondent to prove no breach of the principle of equal treatment. Looking at Neill LJ's guidelines in King v Great Britain-China Centre [1992] ICR 516 (set out in para 6 above), it is plain that paras (1), (4) and (5) need alteration. It is for the applicant complaining of discrimination only to make out his or her case to satisfy the first stage requirements. If the second stage is reached, and the respondent's explanation is inadequate, it will be not merely legitimate but also necessary for the employment tribunal to conclude that the complaint should be upheld. The statutory amendments shift the evidential burden of proof to the respondent if the complainant proves what he or she is required to prove at the first stage.

19 Although we have referred to the two stages in the employment tribunal's decision-making process, we do not thereby intend to suggest that employment tribunals should divide hearings into two parts to correspond to those stages. No doubt tribunals will generally wish to hear all the evidence, including the respondent's explanation, before deciding whether the requirements at the first stage are satisfied and, if so, whether the respondent has discharged the onus shifted to him.

20 One issue which arose before us was whether the words of the statutory amendment, quoting the absence of an adequate explanation, precluded consideration of the respondent's explanation at the first stage. The words 'in the absence of an adequate explanation', followed by 'could', indicate that the employment tribunal is required to make an assumption at the first stage which may be contrary to reality, the plain purpose being to shift the burden of proof at the second stage so that unless the respondent provides an adequate explanation, the complainant will succeed. It would be inconsistent with that assumption to take account of an adequate explanation by the respondent at the first stage. [...]

23 We accept Mr White's suggestion that in view of our conclusion it may be helpful for the Barton guidance to include a paragraph stating that the employment tribunal must assume no adequate explanation at the first stage.

24 We draw attention to another related point on the language of the statutory amendments, although there was no dispute before us on it. The language points to the complainant having to prove facts, and there is no mention of evidence from the respondent. However, it would be unreal if the employment tribunal could not take account of evidence from the respondent if such evidence assisted the employment tribunal to conclude that in the absence of an adequate explanation unlawful discrimination by the respondent on a proscribed ground would have been established. Paras (6) and (7) of the Barton guidance give examples of unsatisfactory conduct by the respondent, in response, for example, to the statutory questionnaire or in breach of a code of practice, being relevant to the drawing of inferences at the first stage, and it cannot matter whether the claimant or the respondent gave that evidence.

25 An important point of construction is raised by the decision of the appeal tribunal in Webster. We shall come to the particular circumstances of that appeal later, but the short point raised is whether the word 'could' in the statutory amendments imports that it is not necessary for the complainant to prove that the respondent in fact committed the act of discrimination complained of so long as the complainant proves that there was an act of less favourable treatment on a prohibited ground and that that act could have been committed by the respondent. As Burton J put it in para 34 of the judgment of the appeal tribunal: 'It will be for a tribunal to ask itself, having found the facts as to what occurred, whether the treatment, which it, on the balance of probabilities, has established, could have been by the respondent.' [...]

28 With all respect to the appeal tribunal, we cannot accept its construction. We have no hesitation in agreeing with Mr Vickery. The language of the statutory amendments seems to us plain. It is for the complainant to prove the facts from which, if the amendments had not been passed, the employment tribunal could conclude, in the absence of an adequate explanation, that the respondent committed an unlawful act of discrimination. It does not say that the facts to be proved are those from which the employment tribunal could conclude that the respondent 'could' have committedquot such act.

[...] On the contrary: the Directive requires the complainant to establish facts from which it may be presumed that there has been discrimination by the alleged discriminator. [...]

31 The scheme of the statutory amendments appears to us simple and to make good sense given that a complainant can be expected to know how he or she has been treated by the respondent whereas the respondent can be expected to explain why the complainant has been so treated. Of course there may be cases where the complainant will have difficulty in proving that it was the employer who committed the unlawful act. But that is a difficulty faced by many who feel aggrieved and would wish to obtain redress through the courts or the tribunals. The complainant may have no less difficulty in establishing others of the essential facts, but that does not mean that it is sufficient for the complainant to prove only the possibility rather than the probability of those other facts at the first stage.

32 The appeal tribunal has read too much into the word 'could' without appreciating that its use is linked to the assumption 'in the absence of an adequate explanation'. The very word 'explanation' seems to us a pointer to the legislative intention that the respondent should explain why he has done what he has been proved by the complainant to have done, rather than to the respondent having to prove the fact that it was not he who did it at all.

33 Finally, if there is any doubt at all as to the correct interpretation, it must surely be resolved by the consideration that, if the appeal tribunal is right, a very real injustice may be done to the respondent. Take any case where there is a possibility that the alleged discriminator, through an employee, has done the unlawful act but there is also a pos-

sibility that a person who has nothing to do with the respondent did it, and the respondent not only does not know any more than the complainant does but has no means of proving that it was not his employee who committed the act. What is the justice of imposing the burden of proof and hence liability on him rather than the complainant? We would add that it does not appear to us to be a sound basis for deciding whether the requirements of the first stage are satisfied by counting heads, in the example given by the appeal tribunal as set out in para 26 above. Once it is accepted that the mere possibility of an employee having uttered the word 'Paki' is sufficient to satisfy the first stage requirements, the burden of proof must shift, whether or not employees outnumber non-employees. [...]

51 [...] Whilst we would caution employment tribunals against too readily inferring unlawful discrimination on a prohibited ground merely from unreasonable conduct where there is no evidence of other discriminatory behaviour on such ground, we cannot say that the tribunal was wrong in law to draw that inference, and we repeat that there is no perversity challenge. At the second stage it did consider whether the appellants had discharged the onus on them by their explanations, but it found those explanations inadequate for the reasons which it gave. It did expressly refer to the conduct of Ms Wong and Mr Dawes. The fact that one finding favourable to Ms Parsons has been made does not preclude another finding unfavourable to her. No error of law has been disclosed. [...]

The revised Barton guidance [title added]

76 As this is the first time that the Barton guidance has been considered by this court, it may be helpful for us to set it out again in the form in which we approve it. In Webster Burton J (President) refers to criticisms made of its prolixity. Tempting though it is to rewrite the guidance in a shorter form, we think it better to resist that temptation in view of the fact that in practice the guidance appears to be offering practical help in a way which most employment tribunals and appeal tribunals find acceptable. What is set out in the annex to this judgment incorporates the amendments to which we have referred and other minor corrections. We have also omitted references to authorities. For example, the unreported case referred to in para (6) of the guidance may be difficult for employment tribunals to obtain. We repeat the warning that the guidance is only that and is not a substitute for the statutory language.

Annex

(1) Pursuant to section 63A of the 1975 Act, it is for the claimant who complains of sex discrimination to prove on the balance of probabilities facts from which the tribunal could conclude, in the absence of an adequate explanation, that the employer has committed an act of discrimination against the claimant which is unlawful by virtue of Part 2, or which, by virtue of section 41 or section 42 of the 1975 Act, is to be treated as having been committed against the claimant. These are referred to below as 'such facts'.

(2) If the claimant does not prove such facts he or she will fail.

(3) It is important to bear in mind in deciding whether the claimant has proved such facts that it is unusual to find direct evidence of sex discrimination. Few employers would be prepared to admit such discrimination, even to themselves. In some cases the discrimination will not be an intention but merely based on the assumption that 'the or she would not have fitted in'.

(4) In deciding whether the claimant has proved such facts, it is important to remember that the outcome at this stage of the analysis by the tribunal will therefore usually depend on what inferences it is proper to draw from the primary facts found by the tribunal.

(5) It is important to note the word 'could' in section 63A(2). At this stage the tribunal does not have to reach a definitive determination that such facts would lead it to the conclusion that there was an act of unlawful discrimination. At this stage a tribunal is

looking at the primary facts before it to see what inferences of secondary fact could be drawn from them.

(6) In considering what inferences or conclusions can be drawn from the primary facts, the tribunal must assume that there is no adequate explanation for those facts.

(7) These inferences can include, in appropriate cases, any inferences that it is just and equitable to draw in accordance with section 74(2)(b) of the 1975 Act from an evasive or equivocal reply to a questionnaire or any other questions that fall within section 74(2) of the 1975 Act.

(8) Likewise, the tribunal must decide whether any provision of any relevant code of practice is relevant and, if so, take it into account in determining such facts pursuant to section 56A(10) of the 1975 Act. This means that inferences may also be drawn from any failure to comply with any relevant code of practice.

(9) Where the claimant has proved facts from which conclusions could be drawn that the employer has treated the claimant less favourably on the ground of sex, then the burden of proof moves to the employer.

(10) It is then for the employer to prove that he did not commit, or as the case may be, is not to be treated as having committed, that act.

(11) To discharge that burden it is necessary for the employer to prove, on the balance of probabilities, that the treatment was in no sense whatsoever on the grounds of sex, since 'no discrimination whatsoever' is compatible with the Burden of Proof Directive.

(12) That requires a tribunal to assess not merely whether the employer has proved an explanation for the facts from which such inferences can be drawn, but further that it is adequate to discharge the burden of proof on the balance of probabilities that sex was not a ground for the treatment in question.

(13) Since the facts necessary to prove an explanation would normally be in the possession of the respondent, a tribunal would normally expect cogent evidence to discharge that burden of proof. In particular, the tribunal will need to examine carefully explanations for failure to deal with the questionnaire procedure and/or code of practice."

Igen is an important case for a number of reasons. As well as amending and affirming the *Barton* guidelines the Court of Appeal's decision confirms that there is a significant change to the burden of proof test in those cases that are covered by the new post EU Burden of Proof directive statutory provisions. The CA categorically states that the new burden of proof rules do not merely codify the existing law in *King* and *Zafar*, but in fact they substantively change the rules. Whereas under *King* and *Zafar* the tribunals were *permitted* to draw inferences from an absence of an adequate explanation by an employer, the new test is much stronger. Following *Igen*, where the context is appropriate, the tribunals are now *required* to draw inferences of discrimination in the absence of an adequate explanation by the employers. Moreover, the *Barton* guidelines are now amended. The CA has clarified that the amended *Barton* guidelines are relevant in burden of proof cases although they have also emphasised that they are merely a guide and not a substitude for statutory construction. This analysis treats the new (i.e. where the EU standard of proof applies) standard as requiring a shift in the burden of proof, once the inference of discrimination has been established by the complainant. This is also similar to the approach taken in *Dresdner Kleinwort Wasserstein Ltd v Adebayo*[57] which

[57] [2005] I.R.L.R. 514 EAT.

was a race discrimination case decided before the decision in *Igen*. *Dresdner* is also significant because it includes a detailed discussion by the EAT of the 'first stage' of the analysis. In *Dresdner*, the EAT confirmed that it will not be enough at this initial first stage for the complainant to show that there was an appopriate comparator. The complainant also has to show that the comparator was similarly situated (which is a statutory requirement in provisions such as RRA, s.3(4)). At this first stage, the complainant has to prove the primary facts (on a balance of probablities) from which inferences can be drawn that there has been race discrimination. The burden then shifts to the respondent to provide an explanation.

It is worth noting that in *Igen* the CA has emphasised that although they do not want to introduce a categoric and sharply divided test, they have confirmed that there are two stages to the analysis of the burden of proof under the new statutory rules. At the first stage, the complainant is required to prove the primary facts, e.g. in direct discrimination cases this will be evidence that there was less favourable treatment which is to be established on a balance of probabilities. Once these facts have been established, the burden shifts on to the respondent to provide an explanation for the less favourable treatment. This approach confirms a shift away from a more stringent test in *University of Huddersfield v Wolff*[58] which suggested that the claimant has to show a causal relationship at the first stage: i.e. that the less favourable treatement had been caused by the difference in sex or race.

Although *Igen* represents a shift away from a more restrictive approach to burden of proof in cases such as *Bahl* and *University of Huddersfield v Woolf*, there are still still conditions that have to be met before there can be an inference of discrimination. As the passages above confirm, there need to be some primary facts established at the first stage from which the inference is drawn, e.g. the failure to comply with statutory codes of practice or unequivocal or unsatisfactory replies to statutory questionannaire procedures. The burden of proof then shifts to the employer and it is for him to prove that the conduct was not because of discrimination. Here, the CA applies a stringent test for such proof that is set out in paras 12 and 13 of the amended *Barton* Guidelines. Paragraph 12 specifies that the tribunal has to establish whether the employer has proved, on a balance of probabilities, that the treatement was based on prohibited discrimination. Since the respondent will normally have the facts necessary to provide an explanation for the less favourable treatment, para.13 makes clear that the tribunal would require cogent evidence to discharge the burden of proof, and that they will carefully examine any failure to deal statutory codes of practice or the questionnaire procedure.

In recent cases, the EAT and the CA have confirmed that there needs to be a substantive enquiry at the "first stage" of the new burden of proof as set out in *Igen*. There must be primary facts from which an inference of discrimination can be made before there is any shift in the burden of proof. In *Network Rail*

58 [2004] I.C.R. 828.

Infrastructure Ltd v Griffiths-Henry,[59] which was a case involving a claim of discrimination by a black woman who was not selected for a post, the EAT observed that there was a need for careful analysis of the evidence before a tribunal could conclude that there was discrimination in the selection process. The EAT stressed that there was a difference between unreasonable conduct which renders a process or a dismissal unfair and discriminatory treatment. They also stated that it did not follow that there was unlawful discrimination everytime a black or woman candidate was treated unfairly. This approach to the threshold requirement at the first stage of the burden of proof as set out in *Igen* was confirmed in *Madarassay v Nomura International Plc.*[60] In *Madarassay,* the Court of Appeal confirmed, in a pregnancy discrimination case, that mere difference of treatment was not sufficient to establish a prima facie case of discrimination which shifted the burden of proof to the employer. These cases suggest that the tribunals will need to focus on the difference in treatment and also the reasons for the difference in the treatment (e.g. was it for prohibited reasons/grounds) at the prima facie stage of the burden of proof analysis.

C. *Comparators and the Burden of Proof*

Another issue in *Igen* related to the role of the comparator in the context of proof of discrimination. In this context the CA held:

"34 (per Peter Gibson L.J, We also heard argument on the need for there to be a comparator in the ingredient of less favourable treatment which the complainant must prove for there to be sexual or racial discrimination. However there was no real dispute before us on this point. That a comparison must be made is explicit in the language of the definition of discrimination. In section 1(1)(a) of the 1975 Act, substituted by regulation 3 of the Sex Discrimination (Indirect Discrimination and Burden of Proof) Regulations 2001, one finds 'the treats her less favourably than he treats or would treat a man'. In section 1(1)(a) of the 1976 Act one finds 'the treats that other less favourably than he treats or would treat other persons'. The comparison must be such that the relevant circumstances of the complainant must be the same as or not materially different from those of the comparator. It is trite law that the complainant need not point to an actual comparator. A hypothetical one with the relevant attributes may do. Our attention was drawn to what was said by Elias J, giving the judgment of the Employment Appeal Tribunal in Law Society v Bahl [2003] IRLR 640, paras 162–163. There it was held that it is not obligatory for employment tribunals formally to construct a hypothetical comparator, though it was pointed out that it might be prudent to do so and that the employment tribunal might more readily avoid errors in its reasoning if it did so. Similarly, when Bahl went to appeal, this court [2004] IRLR 799, para 156 said that it was not an error of law for an employment tribunal to fail to identify a hypothetical comparator where no actual comparator can be found. However, this court also said that not to identify the characteristics of the comparator might cause the employment tribunal not to focus correctly on what Lord Nicholls of Birkenhead in Shamoon v Chief Constable of the Royal Ulster Constabulary [2003] ICR

[59] [2006] I.R.L.R. 865 EAT.
[60] *Madarassy v Nomura International* Plc [2007] EWCA Civ 33, CA.

337, para 7 called 'the "less favourable treatment" issue' (viz whether the complainant received less favourable treatment than the appropriate comparator) and 'the "reason why" issue' (viz whether the less favourable treatment was on the relevant proscribed ground). The importance of a failure to identify a comparator or the characteristics of the comparator may vary from case to case, and may be thought to be of particular relevance to the appeal in Emokpae."[61]

In relation to the *Emokpae* appeal, the Court of Appeal held that where there was no actual comparator to be found it was not a total failure for a court not to be able to use a hypothetical comparator, although it was stated that the failure to identify the characteristics of a comparator could lead to a focus on the wrong issues. The flexible approach to the use of comparators generally, but especially during the analysis of burden of proof (and drawing inferences of discrimination) is particularly important in cases of multiple or intersectional discrimination. This issue was also raised in *The Law Society v Bahl*[62] case where the tribunal had held that "there was no basis in the evidence for comparing her treatment with that of a white female or a black male office holder". Although this statement is unclear, there is a more fundamental point about the appropriate choice of comparator in cases such as this where the complainant is Asian and a woman and therefore falls within two protected grounds (race and sex). As indicated in the earlier chapter on multiple discrimination, the single axis focus on discrimination law means that these types of cases are under-inclusive: the exisiting categories of discrimination on the grounds of race or sex will not fully accommodate the ways in which there can be discrimination against an individual who fall in both categories simultaneously. For example, if the enquiry is about gender, an employer may not have discriminated because he would have treated a white (man) as compared with an Asian (man) in the same way. Alternatively, if the enquiry is about race, the employer may be found not to to have discriminated because he would have treated a (white) woman as compared with an (Asian) woman in the same way. However, this analysis will miss out evidence about whether he would have treated (i) an Asian woman in the same way as compared with (ii) a white man; (iii) a white woman; and also (iv) an Asian man. The evidence that would be required to analyse whether discrimination had taken place using each of these different comparators will be different. This issue is explored in more detail in chapter 9. Here it is worth observing that one way to compensate for the defects of single axis discrimination law would be to have a more flexible approach the hypothetical compator (i.e. recognise that there is a need to use a compator of an Asian woman rather than just woman). Gaps in single axis discrimination law could also be minimised by having a wide ranging enquiry, which not only allows evidence in respect of each of the categories but also examines whether there is evidence of discrimination when both the categories are taken together.

[61] *Igen Ltd v Wong* [2005] WCCA, Civ 142.
[62] *The Law Society v Bahl* [2003] I.R.L.R. 640.

This was not the approach taken by the EAT or the CA in *The Law Society v Bahl*. Although Elias J. did endorse the generally more flexible approach to the need to identify a hypothetical comparator (developed in cases such as *Shamoon* discussed in chapter 4 on direct discrimination). This does assist in compensating for some of the problems of the single-axis approach to discrimination, However, Elias J. did not extend this flexible approach to distinguishing between the grounds of discrimination, at the stage of analysing the evidence and drawing inferences. After considering the tribunal approach, which did not distinguish between race and discrimination in the context of the choice of comparator, Elias J. stated that:

> "*Failing to distinguish racial and sexual discrimination.*
>
> 158. Plainly it is possible for a tribunal to infer that there may be discrimination both on grounds of race and sex after considering the evidence in respect of each. But if the evidence does not satisfy the tribunal that there is discrimination on grounds of race or on grounds of sex, considered independently, then it is not open to a tribunal to find either claim satisfied on the basis that there is nonetheless discrimination on grounds of race and sex when both are taken together. That would fail to give effect to the fact that the burden of proof is on the applicant. Nor can the tribunal properly conclude, if it is uncertain about whether it is race or sex, that it will find both. [...]
>
> 159. Mr de Mello submits that the tribunal was entitled to adopt this approach. It was not obliged to separate out the two strands of race and sex from the mix. The applicant had put her case before the tribunal on the basis that she was a black woman, and it was entitled to treat the two elements together. It was a unique case and the tribunal was justified in treating the evidence in the round without identifying those aspects which it considered justified the inference of race discrimination and those which justified a finding of sex discrimination.
>
> We do not accept that submission. In our view the tribunal did err in law in failing to distinguish between the elements of alleged race and sex discrimination. The result was that it failed to reach properly reasoned findings on the question whether Dr. Bahl had satisfied the tribunal—the burden being on her—that discrimination had occurred in respect of either ground. This would, in our view, be a sufficient basis for upholding these appeals even in the absence of any other error of law.[63]"

In *The Law Society v Bahl* the Court of Appeal endorsed this approach and reiterated the need to establish evidence of each head of discrimination (race and sex) in distinct and separate analysis. They held (per Peter Gibson L.J.):

[63] [2003] I.R.L.R. 640, paras cited above, In a recent case *Network Rail Infrastructure Ltd v Griffiths-Henry* [2006] I.R.L.R. 865, EAT, Elias J. has re-iterated the test in *Bahl* although he has refined the issue by stating that where the employer does not raise any distinction between the two grounds (e.g. race and sex), and where the distinction is not relevant to the analysis of discrimination or the burden of proof, the tribunal does not err in law if it does not explicitly the treat the two grounds separately.

Kamlesh Bahl v The Law Society et al [2004] EWCA Civ 1070.

Para. 135. "Mr. de Mello submits that the ET made no error of law in saying as it did in para. 7.4.19: 'We do not distinguish between the race or sex of the Applicant in reaching this conclusion. Our reason for that is simple. The claim was advanced on the basis that Kamlesh Bahl was treated in the way she was because she is a black woman. Kamlesh Bahl was the first office holder that the Law Society had ever had who was not both white and male. There was no basis in the evidence for comparing her treatment with that of a white female, or a black male, office holder. We can only draw inferences. We do not know what was in the minds of Robert Sayer and Jane Betts at any particular point. It is sufficient for our purposes to find, where appropriate, that in each case they would not have treated a white person or a man less favourably. If we need to refine our approach for the purposes of dealing with remedy the parties may address this issue at that stage.' He says that the ET was entitled to treat the two discriminatory elements together given its finding that it was a unique case.

136. This is a puzzling passage. It says that there was no basis in the evidence for comparing the treatment of Dr. Bahl with that of a white female, or a black male office holder, and yet the ET had to make a comparison on the evidence between her treatment and that of an appropriate comparator. It is not disputed that to find discrimination on the ground of race or sex the ET must find that subjectively racial or sexual considerations were in the mind of the discriminator, but here the ET says that it does not know what was in the minds of Mr. Sayer and Mrs. Betts at any particular point. It acknowledges that there may be a need to refine its approach at the remedy stage, but why should that need arise at so late a stage in the proceedings if the ET has properly found both sex and race discrimination?

137. What the ET has plainly omitted to do is to identify what evidence goes to support a finding of race discrimination and what evidence goes to support a finding of sex discrimination. It would be surprising if the evidence for each form of discrimination was the same. For example, so rare is it to find a woman guilty of sex discrimination against another woman that one might have expected the ET to spell out the evidence which led it to infer such discrimination by Mrs. Betts against Dr. Bahl. In our judgment, it was necessary for the ET to find the primary facts in relation to each type of discrimination against each alleged discriminator and then to explain why it was making the inference which it did in favour of Dr. Bahl on whom lay the burden of proving her case. It failed to do so, and thereby, as the EAT correctly found, erred in law."[64]

A more flexible approach to hypothetical comparators does alleviate some of the problems faced by complainants who have suffered from multiple or intersectional discrimination. The analysis of the facts and evidence in the EAT and CA confirms that one difficulty in *The Law Society v Bahl* was that there was no substantial evidence or primary facts from which to draw inferences that there was discrimination on the new category (e.g. Asian woman) even though there would have been no discrimination under the separate categories race or sex. If there was a stronger case, it could be argued that a more flexible approach that does not sharply distinguish between the analysis of race and sex may be justified. There is increasing evidence that tribunals are adopting a more flexible approach. There are now a number of decisions where tribunals

[64] *Kamlesh Bahl v The Law Society, Robert Sayer, Jane Betts* [2004] EWCA Civ 1070, CA EAT105601 DA.

have found that there has been discrimination on multiple (overlapping) ground even if there would not have been sufficient proof of discrimination on each ground by itself. For example, in a case the tribunal explicity recognised that there are distinct sterotype that relate to Asian women that do not operate in relation to (i) white women; (ii) white men; or (iii) Asian men, set out below.[65]

Mrs S Ali v (1) North East Centre for Diversity & Racial Equality (2) Jamiel Bux Case No: 2504529/03

"Mrs A, a finance officer, claimed that she had been treated less favourably on the grounds of her race and sex when she suffered humiliating treatment by Mr B. in front of her colleagues and her family. She received demands that she cook for Mr B., received unjustified complaints about her work, and was required to be involved in dubious financial arrangements.

The tribunal described as extraordinary, Mr B's insistence that Mrs A. attend at his house with her family for work-related issues and found it to be harassment on grounds of sex and race. The tribunal made the same finding in relation to an incident when Mrs A. sought advice from a male colleague regarding her banking duties and became so upset by Mr B's reaction that she needed to attend hospital and never returned to work at the centre.

The tribunal found that the treatment of Mrs A. amounted to harassment on the grounds of sex and race and was the result of a perception of Mrs A. as being *compliant because she was a Pakistani Muslim woman who had been brought up in Pakistan. Mr B. decided that he could manipulate her. The tribunal considered that Mr B. would not have made the same demands of a white female employee nor of Muslim female employees who had been brought up in Britain (emphasis added)*. He would not have acted in the same way towards the men employed."

A number of commentators have argued that there is a need to reconsider the structure of discrimination law to take into account the challenges posed by multiple and intersectional discrimination. Aileen McColgan specifically cites the importance of being able to prove discrimination in these cases. She argues that where a claimant falls in more than one ground, and most importantly where that ground is specifically associated with disadvantage, this may act as a trigger for "an easy shift in the burden to the employer to disprove discrimination"[66]

[65] EOC case summaries on race and sex cases—multiple discrimination, *http://www.eoc.org.uk/Default.aspx?page=15655*, Accessed May 2006. Document also with the authors.

[66] Aileen McColgan, "Reconfiguring Discrimination Law" (2007) 1 P. L. Spring, 74–94, at p.94.

D. *Other Rules of Evidence in Discrimination Cases*

In many civil law cases the discussion of terms of settlement using a discussion or letter that is entitled "without prejudice" is a useful tool of litigation. In discrimination law, however, the EAT has held that the overriding need to get to the truth means that the tribunal has a discretion to override the rule preventing private settlement offers and discussions from being admissible in evidence.[67] It is significant that in overruling the tribunal which had refused to allow the "without prejudice" information and discussion as evidence, the EAT held that the public interest in eradicating discrimination was more important than public interest in preserving the confidentiality of "without prejudice" discussions between the parties.

E. *Questionnaire Procedure; Statistical Evidence*

One consequence of the focus on informality and a lack of a right to legal representation in employment tribunals is the use of a less formal form of pleadings. In the context of discrimination cases, there are statutory provisions which set out a questionnaire procedure. The form used is set down in statutory instruments (passed under the primary legislation such as SDA, s.65) and covers all the relevant discrimination claims: e.g race, sex and disability; FETO; and now also sexual orientation and religion and belief.[68] The questions and answers can be used as evidence in the proceedings. In addition, where there is a failure to reply within a reasonable period without a reasonable excuse, or where the answer is evasive or equivocal this can be used as evidence. The tribunal can draw an inference from this conduct which it considers to be just and equitiable, including an inference that the party questioned committed an unlawful act (see RRA, s.65; SDA, s.76; DDA, s.56; FETO, Art.44; EE(SO), reg.33; EE(RB), reg.33.

The failure to answer the questionnaire or being obstructive about the procedure can also be the basis for an award of injury to feelings or aggravated damages.

[67] *Brunel University v Vaseghi* EAT/0307/06, discussed in Pennie Christie, "Points of Procedure Roundup", (2007) 865 IRS Employment Review, Published by IRS, Feb 16, 2007.

[68] See for example the Race Relations (Questions and Replies) Order 1977, (SI 1977, No.842, Sch.1); Sex Discrimination (Questions and Replies) Order 1975, (SI 1975, No.2048); Disability Discrimination (Questions and Replies) Order 1996 (SI 1996 No.2793).

VI. Procedure for Litigation

A. *Procedure in Employment Tribunals/County Courts*

Although the predominant focus of domestic discrimination law is on employment discrimination, it is also worth remembering that there are other forms of discrimination in areas such as education or housing that are also prohibited. Employment discrimination claims are dealt with in employment tribunals whereas other types of legal actions are enforced via County Courts. It is also worth recalling some of the main statutory provisions that set out the legal regime for the enforcement of British statutory discrimination law.

One important feature of employment tribunals is that they include adjudicators who are not only judges, but also individuals who represent employers and employees. This has the advantage of introducing specialist knowledge into the decision-making process. This feature was originally justified as a way of ensuring that employment tribunals were a specialist body for dispute resolution rather than a mirror of ordinary courts. However, in some cases the introduction of non-judicial decision-makers has led to allegations of bias. There are existing tests for bias in a tribunal of whether a tribunal is biased, but the issue has also been considered in the specific context of employment tribunals. The Court of Appeal has held that the mere complaint of bias against a tribunal chair does not give an automatic right to have him removed. [69] However, where there is a more direct connection between the tribunal chair and some aspect of the proceedings it may be easier to argue that a "fair minded and impartial observer" may feel that there is a bias. In one case, a GMB branch secretary who had been reprimanded for not following the GMB policy on equal pay claims bought an action against the GMB. One member of the tribunal was a senior member of the UNISON trade union which shared the same policy on equal pay as the GMB. Although there was no evidence of bias in favour of the GMB, the EAT held that this was a case in which a "fair minded and impartial observer" may feel that there was bias. Therefore, the EAT held that there should be a new hearing before a differently constituted tribunal.[70]

In relation to the tribunal proceedings, although there is an emphasis on informality there are certain set requirements that have to be met. These are set out in the Rules of Procedure and in a number of different sources: e.g. the Employment Tribunals (Constitution and Rules of Procedure) Regulations 2004 (SI 2004/1861). Schedule 1 of the Regulations contains the Employment Tribunals Rules of Procedure (the Rules of Procedure).

[69] *Ansar v Lloyds TSB Bank Plc* [2007] I.R.L.R. 211 CA, discussed in Pennie Christie, "Points of Procedure Roundup" (2007) 865 IRS Employment Review, Published by IRS, Feb 16, 2007.
[70] *Humphries v Chevler Packaging Ltd* EAT/0224/06, discussed in Pennie Christie, "Points of Procedure Roundup" (2007) 865 IRS Employment Review, Published by IRS, Feb 16, 2007.

The EAT has confirmed that it will take a broad brush approach to procedural formalities in employment tribunal. In one case, despite the fact that the rules state that the employment tribunal claim must be in writing and contain required information including the name and address, the EAT held that the procedural failure to include the address was not relevant. The EAT emphasized that the tribunal should ask itself whether or not the failure was relevant.[71] However, there are some important limits to this informality and "broad brush" approach. For example, the EAT has emphasized that it will not take a flexible approach to the nature of the pleadings and allow on-going amendment of a claim. In these circumstances, the tribunals have a general discretion to manage the proceedings. However, in a disability discrimination case where the claimant wanted to amend his claim on the first day of proceedings the EAT emphasised that the tribunal has the ultimate discretion and should take into account all the circumstances and balance the factors in favour of amendment against the hardship or refusing it. In that case, the EAT upheld the decision of the tribunal to refuse the amendment and approved of the factors that the tribunal cited in support of its refusal: the claimant had been legally represented throughout; the issues had been discussed at pre-trial hearing at which stage the complainant had not raised the new factors; the complainant had refused requests from the employers for particulars of the case in relation to reasonable adjustments; he had not included the new facts in a medical report served ten days before the hearing. Generally, the EAT emphasized that it was important for the parties to put forward their whole case at the directions hearing.[72]

The Court of Appeal has confirmed the decision of the EAT that a tribunal has no jurisdiction to set aside a notice of withdrawal. In these cases the complainant cannot restart the proceedings after the withdrawal of a claim and the withdrawn claim cannot be revived.[73] The tribunal also has powers to strike out claims where the manner of the proceeding's conduct by the claimant has been scandalous, unreasonable or vexatious but the EAT and the Court of Appeal have emphasised that this power should be exercised only in the most wholly extreme cases and as a sanction of last resort.[74] In cases where there is obstructive action by the claimants or the claims are not being actively pursued the use of adjournment or costs order are often a more appropriate

[71] *Hamling v Coxlease School Ltd* [2007] I.R.L.R. 8 EAT, discussed in Pennie Christie, "Points of Procedure Roundup", (2007) 865 IRS Employment Review, Published by IRS, Feb 16, 2007.

[72] *Martin v Microgen Wealth Management Systems Ltd* EAT/0505/06, discussed in Pennie Christie, "Points of Procedure Roundup" (2007) 865 IRS Employment Review, published by IRS, Feb 16, 2007.

[73] *Khan v Heywood and Middleton Primary Care Trust* [2006] EWCA 1087, discussed in Pennie Christie, "Points of Procedure Roundup", (2007) 865 IRS Employment Review, Published by IRS, Feb 16, 2007.

[74] *Blockbuster Entertainment Ltd v James* [2006] I.R.L.R. 630 CA, discussed in Pennie Christie, "Points of Procedure Roundup", (2007) 865 IRS Employment Review, Published by IRS, Feb 16, 2007.

response than the use of a striking out power.[75] The tribunal has discretion in relation to making costs orders which can be made throughout the proceedings, and the £10,000 limit on costs is per order and not per proceedings.[76]

B. *Domestic Discrimination Law—Individual Enforcement*

1. Problems with the present system of individual enforcement

There are a number of features of the paradigm of damages in tort that make it useful for discrimination law. The focus on damages recognises that in fact discrimination does cause a tangible harm to core interests of individual victims for which the individual discriminator should be held responsible. Moreover, the fact that the individual action for discrimination is a private law action can sometimes usefully open up a wider range of issues that need to be addressed. To this extent, the private law action performs a "public" function by highlighting what have come to be regarded as constitutional norms of equality and non-discrimination. However, the use of a private law action in tort also raises difficulties in the context of discrimination law. For example, where private parties to an action in discrimination law settle their claim for a sum of money, and in particular where they agree to keep the terms of the settlement confidential, some key issues of constitutional importance relating to equality and non-discrimination may remain masked and unresolved.[77] In this sense, there is what Hugh Collins has labelled "subversion by conciliation" in the context of settlement of cases for unfair dismissal: i.e. "The public good of affirming the importance of procedural fairness is subverted by the ease of and pressures of private settlements."[78] Moreover, the private law paradigm that seeks to translate the harm of discrimination into financial damages, and prefers individual litigation in employment tribunals where there is no legal aid available. This introduces a large number of further difficulties in developing principled and effective enforcement and remedial provisions in discrimination law.

In particular, all the difficulties that are associated with individuals accessing the civil law system to make claims for financial damages for the harm

[75] *Ridsdill v D Smith & Nephew Medical* EAT/0704/05, discussed in Pennie Christie, "Points of Procedure Roundup", (2007) 865 IRS Employment Review, Published by IRS, Feb 16, 2007.

[76] *Blockbuster Entertainment Ltd v James* [2006] I.R.L.R. 630 CA, discussed in Pennie Christie, "Points of Procedure Roundup", (2007) 865 IRS Employment Review, Published by IRS, Feb 16, 2007.

[77] Research in the context of race discrimination cases (which raise controversial issues about equality and non-discrimination) has confirmed that large numbers of cases are settled rather than upheld, raising the issue of whether private law actions are a useful forum for resolving the social issues concerning racial equality. For a discussion of race discrimination cases see Christopher McCrudden, David J. Smith and Colin Brown (with the assistance of Jim Knox), *Racial Justice at Work* (London: Policy Studies Institute, 1991) at p.153.

[78] Hugh Collins, *Justice in Dismissal: The Law of Termination of Employment* (Clarendon Press: Oxford, 1992) at p.138.

they have suffered are re-introduced into the system for remedies in discrimination law. A number of scholars of the tort system have now shown that the tort system of remedies is both unfair and inefficient. In particular, the socio-legal critique of the legal system which has highlighted the inequalities in access to justice which undermine the rule of law's claim to equality before the law have a particular relevance in the context of discrimination law. This is because discrimination law is concerned with the protection of the rights of those who are marginalised from power on a number of overlapping criteria, e.g. race, gender, disability, sexual orientation, religion, age as well as class.[79] This increased marginalisation of victims of discrimination in accessing individual justice means that, despite formal equality between the parties in a private law action, the inequalities of power between the parties have a significant impact on both their ability to access justice; and also their ability to handle and present their case in a competent and efficient way. The socio-legal critique emphasises the way in which structural inequality and unequal bargaining power between the parties creates uncertainties and risks can distort the legal issues at stake in individual litigation and the settlement of claims. The unavailability of legal aid compounds this inequality, although the availability of support for individual litigation by the enforcement agencies (now the Commission for Equality and Human Rights—CEHR) goes some way towards redressing the balance in favour of the victims of discrimination. This makes the issue of the past performance of the enforcement agencies (the CRE, EOC and the DRC), as well as the future performance of the CEHR in the area of support for individual complaints, particularly important. The difficulty of assigning a financial sum to "wrongs", which is another criticism of the tort system of remedies, is also compounded in the case of discrimination law where the intangible nature of the harms—e.g. unequal treatment, stigma, procedural unfairness—are difficult to translate into a monetary sum.[80] Some of these difficulties of translating the wrong of discrimination into a financial sum for an individual become clear in the discussion of the difficulties faced by individual courts who struggle to develop a tarriff for discrimination, and use concepts such as aggravated damages to give sense to the full range of harms that are caused by discrimination.

2. Individual Enforcement of Domestic Discrimination Law

Domestic anti-discrimination legislation is primarily enforced via employment tribunal (for employment discrimination) or county courts in England and Wales (other areas). The statutory provisions which confirm this legal arrangement are as follows: SDA, ss.63, 65 (employment), 66 (other areas); RRA, ss.54, 56 (employment), 57 (other areas); DDA, ss.17A (employment), 25

[79] Donald Harris, David Campbell, Roger Halson, *Remedies in Contract and Tort* (London: Butterworths, 2002) at p.430.

[80] Ibid., for a detailed discussion of these issues see Ch.24.

(other areas); EE(RB)R, regs 28, 30 (employment), 31 (other areas); EE(SO)R, Regs 28, 30 (employment), 31 (other areas). The primary focus of this chapter is on remedies in employment tribunals which is the distinct enforcement mechanism created by domestic discrimination law, and which is the most prominent forum for claims. County Courts are the forum for claims for discrimination in the areas of goods and services, education and housing. These claims proceed in the same way as claims in tort in the civil law, although it is made clear that damages for injury to feelings are available in these cases. (discussed below). In the next section we: (a) discuss the different types of remedies that are available in the Employment Tribunal (e.g. orders and damages); (b) discuss the procedure for bringing an action; (c) discuss how discrimination is proved; and (d) discuss the appropriateness of Employment Tribunals as the main forum for enforcement of discrimination law.

VII. Individual Remedies in Employment Tribunals

In the context of Employment tribunals, provisions such as SDA, s.65 and RRA, s. 56 make it clear that a three sets of remedies are available: (a) an order declaring the rights of the complainant and the respondent in relation to the act to which the complainant relates; (b) an order requiring the respondent to pay to the complainant compensation of an amount corresponding to any damages he could have been ordered by a county court to pay to the complainant; and (c) a recommendation that the respondent take within a specified period action appearing to the tribunal to be practicable for the purpose of obviating or reducing the adverse effect on the complainant of any act of discrimination to which the complainant relates (The DDA replaces the word "practical" with the formulation of "reasonable in all the circumstances of the case").

This is the general structure for individual remedies in the main statues the SDA and RRA. Significantly, the FETO provisions include the power to make an order or recommendation which the tribunal considers to be practicable "for the purpose of obviating or reducing the adverse effect on a person other than the complainant of any unlawful discrimination to which the complainant relates" (FETO, Art.39). This is significant because it enables a tribunal to make an order which alleviates the adverse effect of the discriminatory act on those who are affected by it other than the complainant, thereby acknowledging the individual action for discrimination has a wider effect and that individual discrimination law needs to be related to the wider and collective structural problems of discrimination. Unfortunately the SDA, RRA and DDA retain the individualistic focus on the complainant (rather than the collective impact of a discriminatory practice) which draws a sharp dichotomy between individual and collective remedies.

Although remedies available in the County Court are also an important form of redress for discrimination in non-employment contexts, the most significant individual remedy in discrimination law cases is the action for damages in the Employment Tribunals which is the predominant focus of this chapter. In the context of individual enforcement in Employment Tribunals other forms of redress such as orders, recommendations and reinstatement (s.1), reinstatement (s.2) and conciliation (s.3) are used less often. Nevertheless, they also provide distinct and important forms of addressing discrimination that were introduced as part of the distinct remedial framework within the tribunal system. Therefore, in the next section we discuss these alternative remedies before moving on to a discussion of individual damages for discrimination (s.4 below).

A. *Conciliation*

Domestic discrimination law provides a structure within which conciliation is available in unfair dismissal cases generally, and also in cases that involve claims of discrimination. The Employment Tribunals Act 1996 provides for this in cases where there is a claim of discriminatory dismissal.

In addition, s.27 of the Equality Act 2006 gives the CEHR the power to make arrangements for the provision of conciliation services (as defined in subs.27 (9)). Conciliation services can be provided in relation to disputes where proceedings have been or could be brought under specified sections of the equality enactments (listed in s.27(1)). These are civil proceedings in respect of:

- goods, facilities and services, premises, public functions and education under the SDA;
- goods, facilities and services, premises, public functions and education under the RRA;
- goods, facilities and services, premises, public functions and education under the DDA (except for proceedings about admissions and exclusions);
- goods, facilities and services, premises, public functions and education under the provisions for religion and belief in this Act;
- activities covered by the Sexual Orientation Regulations that can be made under Pt 3 of this Act, and;
- further and higher education under the Employment Equality (Sexual Orientation) Regulations and the Employment Equality (Religion or Belief) Regulations.

The main body that is involved in conciliation is the Arbitration and Conciliation Advisory Council which is a statutory body providing advice and conciliation officers who seek to resolve the dispute between the parties. It is sometimes argued in the context of the use of conciliation in the context of employment disputes, that this mode of dispute resolution acts against the interests of employees. However, research by Linda Dickens, et al suggests that wide ranging criticism that ACAS officers as not neutral is misplaced, because this criticism fails to recognise that they are limited by their statutory functions. Dickens also notes that confusion arises from judging the work of conciliation officers against a model which differs from that of ACAS itself. Dickens goes on to state that pressures on the system of remedies in employment cases are not replicated in the work of ACAS officers, and that these pressures bear unequally on the parties.[81] Hugh Collins, on the other hand, has argued that conciliation in unfair dismissal cases can in fact weaken the standards of procedural fairness. He argues, first, that procedural standards do not play a very significant role in the decision of whether or not to settle, even or the amount for which the claim will be settled. In these cases, the public good of affirming procedural fairness is being subverted by the ease of private settlements which will not always reflect the need to affirm procedural fairness. Collins also argues that the structural and statutory function of conciliation is defined in a way that encourages the settlement of cases in order to reduce the costs of administering justice. Therefore, the intrinsic statutory function of conciliation is not neutral: the requirement to give impartial advice is "tainted" by the statutory aim of conciliation to promote settlement. This, Collins argues, breaches the requirements of natural justice in resolution of individual disputes. As an alternative, Collins suggests a way of defining the role of conciliation which require conciliation officers to push employers to go through all the fair procedures and reach a correct decision on the correct information, rather than attempting to advise employees on whether or not to settle. This alternative focus, Collins argues, would provide an incentive for employers to meet the standards of procedural justice if they are to enjoy the benefit of cheaper out of court settlement of a dispute. Collins concludes that:

"instead of performing a role which would at once have been conducive to fairness towards the dismissed employee and at the same time beneficial to harmonious industrial relations, the conciliation officers routinely and subtly undermine the force of procedural requirements by encouraging employees to take quick settlements which reflect a mixture of the substantive merits of their cases and their employers' estimates of the likely cost of litigation."[82]

Conciliation in the context of race discrimination law claims raises additional difficulties. Evidence suggests that in "race" cases there are strong feelings

[81] L. Dickens, M. Jones, B. Weekes, *Dismissed: A Study of Unfair Dismissal and the Industrial Tribunal System* (Oxford: Blackwell, 1985) at p.170.

[82] Hugh Collins, *Justice in Dismissal: The Law of Termination of Employment* (Oxford: Clarendon Press, 1992) at p.138–139.

and a tendency to prefer the resolution of the merits of the case over settlement as compared with other types of unfair dismissal cases. There are also practical difficulties of ensuring conciliation in race cases: e.g. unfamiliar law; difficulties of establishing tariffs and the level of compensation; and problems of proof in race cases which arise from deep disagreement about facts combined with less access to "hard evidence" that can be the basis for advice about the merits of the case.[83] In addition, race discrimination cases raise a high degree of emotion which is not present in other unfair dismissal cases or even other types of discrimination cases e.g. sex discrimination. McCrudden et al. summarises this trend in the following terms:

"There seems to be something uniquely sensitive about racial discrimination. And the strong responses of employers do not seem to be based on a simple fear of losing ethnic minority trade. One COT, who had worked in areas with both high and low levels of minority residence, said: 'There's a real stigma about race cases, felt by all employers. Its as bad here, where there are few ethnic minorities, as it is in London, so it's not just a pragmatic concern about trading. I don't know why. There's less stigma about sex cases.' "[84]

In "race" cases, the parties seem to be more concerned about setting and keeping a standard rather than just settling their individual dispute. However, conciliation does not always provide them with the option of resolving issues of fault. In this context, the parties see conciliation as a lesser form of settlement than adjudication because it cannot set the public standard or provide a public acknowledgement of fault. One way of overcoming this problem would be to raise the status of conciliation and settlements so that higher settlements come to be seen as a proper compensation and a recognisable penalty for discriminatory conduct.[85]

Recent case law confirm the preference for a model of conciliation which puts a predominant focus on the ACAS conciliation officer having a role to "promote" settlement rather than ensuring that the settlement is just or fair. In *Clarke v Redcar and Cleveland BC* and *Wilson v Stockton-on-Tees BC*,[86] the EAT upheld the validity of conciliation agreements, drawn up with the assistance of ACAS following negotiations between the employer and trade unions, the effect of which was to preclude the employees from bringing equal pay claims. In this case, the facts suggested that the individual employees had benefited from a collective settlement made with the employers. In these circumstances,

[83] Christopher McCrudden, David J Smith, Colin Brown (with the assistance of Jim Knox), *Racial Justice at Work: Enforcement of the Race Relations Act 1976 in Employment* (Policy Studies Institute: London, 1991) at p.190.
[84] *Ibid.*, at p.191.
[85] *Ibid.*, at p.197.
[86] [2006] I.R.L.R. 324. For discussion of the case see "Conciliation Agreements: ACAS Conciliation-agreements Upheld" (2006) 852 IRS Employment Review, published by IRS on August 4, 2006.

it seemed to follow that individuals should be bound by the terms of the collective settlement and not resort to individual action that would undermine the settlement.

The cases also raised an important point about the role of conciliation and the ACAS officer in employment cases, which is a point that is emphasised by Collins in his critique of the way that conciliation is presently defined. The EAT accepted submissions on ACAS officers' remit, derived from *Moore v Duport Furniture Products Ltd*[87] and *Slack v Greenham (Plant Hire) Ltd*,[88] that the statutory duty requires an ACAS officer to "promote a settlement", rather than to give legal advice on the merits of a proposed compromise. The main duty and focus of the work of the ACAS officer is to promote settlement and not to be responsible for ensuring that the terms of the settlement are fair to the employee. The affirmation by the EAT also affirms the earlier decision in *McAllister v Old Moat Inn* (1993)[89] where the Fair Employment Tribunal found that an employment tribunal is not entitled to set aside an agreement between the parties on the grounds that the conciliation officer had given mistaken advice on issues of law or the settlement of the case. In *McAllister*, the case arose in the context of the Northern Ireland legislation on religious discrimination. The applicant argued that she had been mistakenly been advised to settle her case by a conciliation officer. She sought to retract the withdrawal of her case on the grounds that the advice that she had been given was misleading. The Fair Employment Tribunal (FET) declined to set aside the conciliation settlement and agreement. The conciliation officer had not acted in bad faith or adopted methods which were malicious or not designed to promote settlement (or were to disadvantage one party and benefit another). The FET found that an employment tribunal does not have the ability to assess the fairness of the conciliation officer's performance. Therefore, unless there is evidence of bad faith or malice the employment tribunal cannot set aside an agreement on the grounds of mistaken advice or the adequacy of the settlement. The FET concluded that "there is no duty on a conciliation officer endeavouring to promote a financial settlement to ensure that the settlement is fair."

This line of cases support Collins' analysis that conciliation favours settlement at the cost of upholding procedural fairness. This also suggests that the solution to this interpretation of the role of conciliation lies in changes to the statutory function of conciliation and the role of ACAS conciliation officers.

The recent annual report of ACAS confirms that there is an increasing

[87] [1982] I.R.L.R. 31, discussed in [2006] I.R.L.R. 324. For discussion of the case see "Conciliation Agreements: ACAS Conciliation-agreements Upheld" (2006) 852 IRS Employment Review, published by IRS on August 4, 2006.

[88] [1983] I.R.L.R. 271, [2006] I.R.L.R. 324. For discussion of the case see "Conciliation Agreements: ACAS Conciliation-agreements Upheld" (2006) 852 IRS Employment Review, published by IRS on August 4, 2006.

[89] *McAllister v Old Moat Inn* [1993] IT/164/92, reported and discussed at "No duty to ensure fair settlement" (1993) 17 Discrimination Case Law Digest, published by IRS, September 1, 1993.

demand for their services (both telephone advice and also conciliation officers) in discrimination law cases. The latest annual report from ACAS shows an increase in demand for its services, including equality help and advice. In 2005–06, the ACAS Equality Direct helpline received 5,061 calls, an increase of 7 per cent on the previous year. ACAS equality advisers also dealt with more cases than in the previous year, opening 135 cases compared with 99 in 2004–05—a 36 per cent rise. Equal pay claims have resulted in an increased workload for conciliation officers, with some 30,000 actual or potential claims arising in 2005–06. The number of independent experts appointed in equal value claims has also given rise to unprecedented numbers: 37 in 2005–06 compared with 12 the previous year.[90]

ACAS has recently undertaken a policy review of its work on equality and diversity issues. In their report *Back to basics*,[91] the fifth in a series of ACAS policy discussion papers, ACAS focuses on how employers and employees are dealing with the profound changes presented by the equality and diversity agenda. The policy paper highlights a number of aspects of equality and diversity work that emerge from ACAS work and experience in this field. These include, inter alia, that although awareness of equality and diversity has changed dramatically in the past ten years, there are still areas of work in which norms have not shifted and where there are common misconceptions about the law and negative attitudes towards equality and non-discrimination norms. Areas in which there is the greatest misunderstanding amongst employers and employees include: the definition of disability; rights of pregnant workers; the right to request flexible working; and the rights of migrant workers. The report also notes attitudinal barriers towards progress on equality such as lack of awareness, entrenched attitudes, embarassment, and an absence of clear lines of responsibility for equality and diversity issues. The paper recommends: demystification of the concepts of equality and diversity especially through the greater use of plain language; more support for employers to help change attitudes and behaviour of staff; more training for line managers including an understand of the benefits of workplace training and mediation around these issues; the greater use of procurement by public authorities to encourage good practice in equality and diversity; and better education of school leavers on rights and responsibilities on equality and diversity before they enter the workplace, e.g. through a campaign to be led by the Commission on Equality and Human Rights.

[90] See ACAS Annual Report (2005–2006) available at *www.acas.org* (accessed on March 13, 2006).

[91] Available at *Back to basics. Acas's experience of equality and diversity in the workplace*. A copy of the full report is available at *www.acas.org* (accessed on March 13, 2006)

B. *Orders, Recommendations*

Although there has always been a provision for an Employment Tribunal to make orders on the rights of the parties, and recommendations for action by the respondent, these are (unlike FETO) only limited to the purpose of dealing with the complaint by the original complainant and do not "reach" the structural problems in the employer's workplace practices and organisation. The proportion of cases that result in these types of remedies is much smaller than those that result in damages. Nevertheless, the availablity of these alternative forms of remedies remains significant not least because they are potentially important levers to ensure substantial change in workplace procedures and employer attitudes. It is also significant that in the context of race discrimination *"Racial Justice at Work"*, a major study published in 1991, confirmed that: "evidence presented in later chapters suggests that honour and self-respect are at stake more than monetary compensation. However, there is little scope, as matters now stand, for tribunal proceedings to influence the behaviour, policy or practices of employers."[92]

Although the remedies to make an order on the rights of the parties or a recommendation have not been used with frequency (and they are limited by requiring an atomistic focus on the complainant rather than wider behaviour, policy or practices) there is an emerging body of case law that provides a guide on how the courts could develop ways of influencing the policies and practices of employers without resorting to financial penalties. As well as the RRA, s.56 power, the Employment Tribunals also has a discretion under s.116 of the Employment Rights Act 1996 which, in unfair dismissal cases, confers a discretion on tribunals to make an order for reinstatement or re-engagement of a successful complainant.

In *Chief Constable of West Yorkshire Police v Vento (No.2)* the EAT confirmed that the statutory provisions on action recommendations give the employment tribunal an extremely wide discretion.[93] However, in a number of cases the courts have developed principles that guide the exercise of discretion on making orders, recommendations and using reinstatement as a remedy. For example, in *Ministry of Defence v Jeremiah* the EAT confirmed that tribunals did not have the power (under SDA, s.65) to make an order to discontinue a discriminatory practice. Moreover, their power was limited to one of the three options set out in that statutory provision: an order declaring the rights of the parties; recommendations; or an order requiring the payment of compensation.[94] In addition, where an ET is exercising its power to make a recommendation, this power (SDA, s.65(1)(c)) does not also include the power to

92 Christopher McCrudden, David J Smith, Colin Brown, with the assistance of Jim Knox, *Racial Justice at Work: Enforcement of the Race Relations Act 1976 in Employment* (Policy Studies Institute: London, 1991) at p.156.

93 *Chief Constable of West Yorkshire Police v Vento (No.2)* [2002] I.R.L.R. 177 EAT.

94 *Ministry of Defence v Jeremiah* [1978] I.R.L.R. 402 EAT.

make a recommendation on payment of remuneration. Monetary compensation is to be dealt with as a separate remedy under SDA 75, s. 65(1)(b) as confirmed by the Court of Appeal in *Irvine v Prestcold* where Fox L.J. concluded:

"When one comes to the language of para. (c) itself, I do not think that it is at all apt to cover recommendations as to payment of remuneration. The paragraph authorises the making of 'a recommendation that the respondent take within a specific period action appearing to the Tribunal to be practicable'. The paragraph is, therefore, concerned with the taking of some action 'within a specified period'. It is I think concerned with the taking of action without undue delay; an example is that given by the Appeals Tribunal, namely the provision of training facilities within a specified period. It seems to me that the words 'within' a specified period are inapt to cover a recommendation as to the payment of a particular remuneration during a period which might well extend over several years and even (if, for example, the position in question did not become vacant) over the whole of the employee's future period of employment by the employer. I am not saying that the taking of action may not extend over a substantial period but only that the payment of remuneration for employment does not, as a matter of the ordinary use of English fit the description 'take within a specified period action, etc'. Accordingly, I think that the Appeal Tribunal reached the correct conclusion as to the ambit of para. (c) in s.65(1)"[95]

Moreover, a tribunal was limited in relation to the terms of the recommendation that it makes under the relevant provisions of the SDA, s.65 and RRA 76 s.56. In *Noone v North West Thames Regional Health Authority (No.2)* (1988)[96] the Court of Appeal considered that the power to make recommendations under RRA s.56 to the effect that an employee who was an NHS doctor who had been discriminated against, should be appointed to the next vacancy for the post that became available. The Court of Appeal held that the ET could not make such a prescriptive recommendation, and noted that this would be equivalent to not requiring the usual advertising of the post and would require special permission to bypass the special statutory procedures for the appointment of NHS consultants. *Noone* can be partially explained because there are complex statutory guidelines in place for the appointment of NHS consultants which can be justified as a requirement of the public good. This leaves open the question of whether, in the absence of these special rules for promotion and appointment, a tribunal could not exercise its wide discretion (as confirmed by cases such as *Vento* above) to make a recommendation that the next available promotion or job should be made available for an applicant who has suffered from unlawful discrimination. Such a recommendation would have to respect the prohibitions on positive action in domestic discrimination law. Therefore, the tribunal cannot recommend the appointment of a complainant who has

[95] *Irvine v Prestcold Ltd* [1981] I.R.L.R. 281.
[96] *Noone v North West Thames Regional Health Authority (No.2)* [1988] I.R.L.R. 530 CA.
[1] *British Gas Plc v Sharma* [1991] I.R.L.R. 101 EAT.

suffered unlawful discrimination to a job for which he is not suitably qualified or where there are other applicants who have more superior qualifications because this would be tantamount to direct discrimination against those other applicants.[97]

One particular limit on these remedies is that the recommendation must be framed in a way that specifically obviates or reduces the impact of the discriminatory act. In *Leeds Rhinos Rugby Club v Sterling* (2001)[98] the EAT held that the tribunal had erred in law in making a recommendation under the RRA 76, s.56. In that case, Mr Sterling was employed by Leeds Rhinos Rugby Club to play rugby league football. He entered into the last of the contracts under which he was employed in November 1999 which stated that it would remain in force until November 30, 2000. In early 2000, Mr Sterling was excluded from the first team training squad for three which the tribunal held was unlawful race discrimination under the RRA. The tribunal also found that two other employees had victimised him by failing to investigate properly his complaint of discrimination. The tribunal awarded Mr Sterling compensation. In addition, they found that the applicant was likely to be considered a "trouble maker" because he had bought an action against his employer. This made it less likely that he could get suitable alternative contracts of employment at another club. Therefore, the tribunal made a recommendation, under s.56(1)(c) of the RRA, that the Club should offer him a contract by December 2000 on the same terms as that of his contract of November 1999. The tribunal justified the recommendation as necessary for the purpose of obviating or reducing the adverse effect on Mr Sterling of the act of discrimination and its consequences. The tribunal also took the view that taking on one extra player would not cause the Club any significant financial difficulty.

On appeal to the EAT, the Club argued that the tribunal had not exercised its discretion appropriately for a number of reasons: it had wrongly focused on the publicity generated by the case rather than the effect of the discriminatory act on the complainant; that it should consider practicality under RRA, s.56 from the perspective of both parties; and the renumeration advantage of the recommendation would be greater than an award of financial renumeration and this was therefore in breach of *Irving v Prestcold* (discussed above). The EAT agreed with the Club that the tribunal should not have focused on the issue of publicity and should have focused on the immediate consequences to which the discriminatory act related. It cannot be aimed at the effect of some other act or acts (such as unfavourable publicity generated by the litigation) or the act of a third party. Therefore, the recommendation went beyond the adverse effect of the discriminatory act. The EAT held that, in relation to practicality, although the focus was on the impact on the complainant, the tribunal should also consider the practicality of carrying out the recommendation from the point of view of the discriminator. It would, therefore, be

[98] *Leeds Rugby League Club v Sterling* EAT/267/01 (2003) 779 IRS Employment Review (Published by IRS July 3, 2003).

improper to make a recommendation compliance with which was completely impractical for a discriminator.

Cases such as *Noone*, *Leeds Rhinos Rugby Club v Sterling* and *Irving v Prestcold* reveal the limits of using recommendations that include a requirement to promote the victim of discrimination in a future job or the award of contracts that are a form of renumeration. The power to make recommendations by a tribunal will be significantly limited by the conditions that have been developed in these cases. However, one particular area in which recommendations have been made and where they have the potential to influence employer behaviour and practices is in the area of equal opportunities awareness and training. In this context, the employment tribunal faced with a discriminatory act (especially in cases where there has been personal misconduct such as abuse or harassment) can suggest that the discriminator should participate in forms of equal opportunities training to make him more aware of the way in which his or her personal conduct has contributed to the discrimination.

For example, in *Vearer v BPCC Magazines Colchester Ltd*[99] the tribunal upheld a complaint by six women who were casual workers that they had been discriminated against when only male casual workers were offered permenant posts. The tribunal made a recommendation under SDA, s.65(1) that "all members of the respondents' management should receive training in equal opportunities within the next six months." The tribunal also recommended that the respondents notify the applicants of all permenant vacancies in the establishment for a period of three years.

Equal Opportunities training has also been recommended in cases where inappropriate or offensive language has been used, or where there have been ineffective procedures for recruitment and interviewing, particularly where the discrimination is a result of lack of understanding rather than malice.[100] There is also the option of a focused recommendation that remedies the specific act which is the cause of the discrimination, such as the re-writing of a reference in a more favourable way to recommend more accurately the positive assessment of the complainant who has suffered discrimination by getting a unfavourable reference.[101]

99 *Vearer v BPCC Magazines Colchester Ltd* [1993] IT/49675/91, see (1993) 16 Discrimination Case Law Digest (Publisher IRS, June 1, 1993)

100 *Mahon v Black Country Small Business Service Ltd*, December 7, 2005; Case No.1301883/05 (inappropriate language); and *Mba v Marshall and Gaplin*, November 18, 2005; Case No.2700543/05 (inadequate procedures for recruitment and interviewing) reported at (2006) Discrimination Compensation Guide (Published by IRS, August 1, 2006).

101 In *Melloy v HM Prison Service*, October 7, 2005; Case No.1400772/04. The tribunal recommended that the respondent agree an amended form of reference with the claimant to reflect the "very positive appraisal" of the claimant's performance at Erlestoke Prison, in which it was "clearly anticipated [that] the claimant would succeed in achieving promotion". reported at (2006) Discrimination Compensation Guide (Published by IRS, August 1, 2006).

1 *X v (1) Coral Racing (2) Mr Y*, November 25, 2005; Case No.2301932/05, reported at (2006) Discrimination Compensation Guide (Published by IRS, August 1, 2006).

In one case, the tribunal awarded the claimant £9,000 compensation for injury to feelings and fixed a second date for a further remedies hearing. It said that if before that date the respondent provided evidence that Mr Y had been moved and that the two men had attended appropriate training courses, then the remedy hearing would be set aside.[102]

In some cases, employment tribunals have recommended that the discriminator make an apology. For example, in *Newton v West Herts Hospital NHS Trust*[103] the tribunal accepted the complainant's evidence that he would feel better and the injury to his feelings would be mitigated if the respondents were to provide an apology to him. A recommendation was made that the respondent provide the applicant with an apology for the treatment he endured during the course of his employment within 21 days of the promulgation of the tribunal decision. The apology was to be drafted and signed by somebody within the respondent organisation at an appropriately senior level.

If, as McCrudden, et al argue, an important part of the harm that is experienced by victims in race discrimination cases is about honour and self-respect, then these types of recommendations may have an important role to play as a remedy in some appropriate cases, rather than a sole reliance on financial compensation for hurt to feelings.[103a] There are obvious limits on the use of non-compensatory remedies that require specific and personal acts by discriminators. For example, it has been recognised that where the apology would not be sincere then it may not have a productive role to play as a remedy in a discrimination law action.[104]

Even where they have not formally used recommendations under their statutory remedial powers, tribunals have been flexible about allowing informal arbitration, conciliation and negotiations to continue between the parties in order to resolve the dispute by encouraging them to "find a mutually acceptable resolution to the claimant's employment problems."[105] For example in *Chief Constable of West Yorkshire Police v Vento*[106] the EAT found that the tribunal had not made an error when it made a recommendation that the Deputy Chief Constable should interview named police officers and dis-

[102] *X v (1) Coral Racing (2) Mr Y*, November 25, 2005; Case No.2301932/05, reported at (2006) Discrimination Compensation Guide (Published by IRS, August 1, 2006).

[103] *Newton v West Herts Hospital NHS Trust*, August 23, 2004; Case No.3300453/03, reported at (2006) Discrimination Compensation Guide (Published by IRS, August 1, 2006).

[103a] Christopher McCruden et al, *Racial Justice at Work*, ibid.

[104] For example, in *Riaz v City of London Police*, September 9, 2005; Case No.2201494/04 the tribunal commented:

> "We do not make a recommendation that Mr Farrell and Mr Moore make a written apology to the claimant. We doubt whether such a recommendation could be enforced against them. Further, in the light of their earlier refusal to apologise, it is doubtful whether such a forced apology would be seen as sincere."

Reported at (2006) Discrimination Compensation Guide (Published by IRS, August 1, 2006).

[105] *Noronha v (1) Sheila Blackburn (2) Bromley Hospitals NHS Trust (3) Carol Doyle (4) Deanna Kingsmill*, November 15, 2005; Case No.1100216/05. Reported at (2006) Discrimination Compensation Guide (Published by IRS, August 1, 2006).

[106] *Chief Constable of West Yorkshire Police v Vento (No.2)* [2002] I.R.L.R. 177 EAT.

cuss with them the relevant parts of the legal decisions relating to liability for sex discrimination.

C. *Reinstatement*

Although there is no specific remedy for reinstatement in the RRA, s.56 or SDA, s.65, there is a general discretion to make an order which has been described in the *Chief Constable v Vento (No.2)* case, as extremely wide. Therefore, under the appropriate circumstances an employment tribunal can make a recommendation for reinstatement. In relation to unfair dismissal generally, the employment tribunal has a wide ranging power under the Employments Rights Act 1996 s.114–116 to make an order for reinstatement or re-engagement of a successful complainant. The rationale for putting in place a tribunal system was that it could be a more informal and less adversarial system which had the option for conciliation and arbitration. This would have provided a more appropriate context in which the relationship between the employee and employers—the parties to the litigation—did not break down. In this context reinstatement would remain a viable remedy for both parties after their dispute had been resolved. However, as we see in the discussion below, the tribunal system has not achieved its ambition of being a forum which is informal and conciliatory rather than adversarial, therefore the sometimes adversarial context of litigation in discrimination law cases, reinstatement is often not a realistic remedy open to employment tribunals.

Moreover, and more generally in unfair dismissal cases, there are other reasons why, as Hugh Collins has argued, reinstatement and reengagement have become the "lost remedy".[107] Collins argues that reinstatement is undermined as a remedy because it operates within a general paradigm of private law litigation with a focus on the individual. He concludes that "the major reason for the absence of reinstatement orders is the predictable result of the distortion of this apparent policy of the legislation by the private interests of both employers and employees".[108] Collins argues that employers are resistant, in the last resort, to orders by employment tribunals about who should be employed by them. Collins paces this resistance within the broader paradigm and attitude that employment is a private matter which should not be subject to interference by outside parties. Employers, Collins argues, routinely ignore orders for reinstatement "hoping either that the claimant will not pursue his or her remedy for an additional award, a hope usually justified in fact, or being prepared to pay the additional sum in order to ensure a break of contract with the employee."[109] Williams and Lewis report one instance

[107] See L. Dickens, M. Hart, M. Jones and B. Weekes, "Reinstatement of Unfairly Dismissed Workers: The Lost Remedy" (1981) 10 I.L.J. 160.

[108] Hugh Collins, *Justice in Dismissal: The Law of Termination of Employment* (Oxford: Clarendon Press, 1992) at p.234.

[109] *ibid.*

"where a Tribunal told an employer in advance that the cost of not complying with the order would be £138 it was promptly accepted as a bargain."[110]

Employees are also resistant to reinstatement because of the individuated nature in which the remedy operates. They are concerned with their own personal interests rather than the wider interests of the workforce. Within this context, during litigation, a number of factors suggest that even where employees are keen on reinstatement at the start of the proceedings they are less keen during the course of litigation and towards the end of their case. These factors include, inter alia, the breakdown of the relationship; fear of victimisation; and belief that employer behaviour is so bad that the employee does not want to work with them again. These factors, which are relevant in all unfair dismissal cases, will be especially aggravated in discrimination law cases which are often perceived by both parties as raising more sensitive issues about identity and self-esteem. Collins suggests that a further significant reason may be that employees enter into litigation with a personal interest of maximising the compensation that they will be awarded. He therefore concludes that an important reason that reinstatement is not more readily used in employment tribunals cases is the structural nature of the remedy of reinstatement—with its focus on a private law and individuated paradigm for litigation. This means that financial compensation will remain the preferred remedy for not only employers, but also employees, even if tribunals adopt a more flexible approach towards reinstatement through a wider test of when it is "practicable" or "just".

There have been cases where employment tribunals have recommended reinstatement as the preferred remedy in discrimination cases. In *D'Souza v London Borough of Lambeth*,[111] for example, the original tribunal made an order for reinstatement which was not complied with by the employers. In a case where an order for reinstatement is made, but the unfairly dismissed employee is not reinstated albeit that it *was* practicable to comply with the order, the industrial tribunal must make an additional award and a compensatory award. In this type of case, the order for reinstatement is a two-stage process. The first order is "provisional" and all questions of compensation are deferred. If the order for reinstatement is not complied with, the employment tribunal can then make an additional compensatory award. The decision of the EAT in *De Souza* also confirms that employment tribunals should be wary about making an order for reinstatement where the employer is not present at the hearing, as the co-operation of the employer and their view on what is practical is a key issue in making a decision about whether reinstatement is a practicable remedy in the circumstances.

Reinstatement has also been ordered under the SDA. In *Winn v Northwedge*

110 Hugh Collins, *Justice in Dismissal: The Law of Termination of Employment* (Oxford: Clarendon Press, 1992) at p.235.

111 *D'Souza v London Borough of Lambeth* [1997] I.R.L.R. 677 EAT.

Ltd,[112] a tribunal recommended the reinstatement of a female bouncer who was dismissed because of her sex. The applicant was the only female among five bouncers employed by a nightclub. In February 1995, the company took a policy decision not to employ female bouncers and Ms Winn was offered bar work. She refused the offer and was dismissed. The company admitted sex discrimination. The tribunal awarded financial compensation including compensation for injury to feelings. It also considered it appropriate to recommend reinstatement, to take effect from two weeks of the hearing date.

In reaching a decision about the practicability of reinstatement as a remedy the tribunal took into account a number of factors. Although a replacement had been appointed for the applicant's post, the tribunal noted that there was no evidence that this was a permenant replacement and in any event there was no evidence that the replacement could not be offered other employment. Moreover, the tribunal also took into account the fact that the employer knew early on in the proceedings that the applicant would be seeking reinstatement. Significantly, they found that the relationship between the parties had not broken down. The tribunal stated that "Where an applicant has gone to a tribunal and the parties have given evidence, this is likely to sour relations between them and make the restoration of that relationship more difficult."[113] They went on to note that in this case there was evidence that there was an ongoing working relationship between the employer and employee and noted that "Firstly, perhaps unusually, the applicant herself wants to return to this job. Secondly, even after the application was threatened the respondents made it clear that they were willing to offer her bar work."[114]

D. *Individual Damages*

In most cases the remedy for discrimination is individual damages and the case is before either the employment tribunal or the county courts. It is worth noting that there are also special procedures for remedies for individual damages are now available in most, but not all, cases of discrimination. However, there remain some cases of unintentional indirect discrimination where damages will not be available which we will briefly examine before moving on to examine the principles that govern an award of damages in discrimination law. The same approach to compensation is taken under the SDA, the RRA, the DDA, the Employment Equality (Sexual Orientation) Regulations 2003, the Employment Equality (Religion or Belief) Regulations 2003, and the Employment Equality (Age) Regulations 2006. However, the rules on compensation for indirect discrimination on the grounds of colour

[112] *Winn v Northwedge Ltd* [1995] IT/16706/95 (1 report), reported at (1995) 25 Discrimination Case Law Digest (Published by IRS, September 1, 1995).
[113] *ibid.*
[114] *ibid.*

and nationality differ from those relating to indirect discrimination on other grounds.

1. Unintentional indirect discrimination

Claims under Pt III of the RRA and which relate to non-employment-related fields (e.g education, housing, goods and services) of discrimination, still require proof of intent in indirect discrimination cases before there can be an award of individul damages. RRA, s.57(3) states that for non-employment-related discrimination (under Pt III) there can be no award of damages for indirect discrimination (RRA 76, s.1(1)(b)) if the respondent proves that the requirement or condition was not applied with the intention of treating the claimant unfavourably on the racial grounds. In non-employment-related sex discrimination cases, the analogous provision is SDA s.66(3). The piecemeal nature of the reforms of the RRA mean that there is also no claim for damages for unintentional indirect discrimination where the grounds for discrimination are "nationality or colour", i.e. grounds which were explicitly included in the original RRA but which are not included in the Race Equality Directive.

A number of cases illustrate the way in which "intention" will be defined in the context of claims for damages in non-employment indirect discrimination cases. In an early case of *Orphanos v Queen Mary College*[115] in 1985, the House of Lords held that intention in RRA, s.57(3) requires a focus on the subjective intention of the discriminator. This view of intention under RRA, s.57(3) was also affirmed by the EAT in *J H Walker v Hussain*.[116] In *Hussain*, the EAT confirmed that intention in this context is concerned with the state of mind of respondent (i.e. it is subjective) in relation to the consequences of his act. Therefore, the analysis requires examining whether at the time the discriminatory act is done, the discriminator wanted to bring about the less favourable treatment on racial grounds or knew that such treatment would result from his acts. The EAT also affirmed that the motive of the discriminator is not relevant to the analysis, thereby confirming the case law that has moved away from an analysis of motive in a definition of direct discrimination.

In the context of non-employment-related sex discrimination, the EAT has also confirmed that the focus in these cases should be on the way in which the requirement or intention is applied by the discriminator rather than on a generalised enquiry about why the requirement or condition was introduced. In *London Underground v Edwards*,[117] the EAT confirmed that under SDA s.66(3), where the discriminator has applied a requirement or condition with knowledge of its likely unfavourable consequences for the woman complainant, this is sufficient to establish intentional indirect discrimination.

[115] [1985] I.R.L.R. 349, HL.
[116] [1996] I.R.L.R. 11 EAT.
[117] *London Underground Ltd v Edwards* [1995] I.R.L.R. 355 EAT.

2. Principles for awards of damages in discrimination law

This section sets out and summarises the main issues that are relevant to claims for pecuniary and non-pecuniary damages in discrimination cases. Discrimination is a statutory tort and, therefore, the main principles that govern an award of damages in discrimination cases are based on the tort law principle of compensation of putting the victim back in the position that they would have been in had the tort (the wrong of discrimination) never been committed.[118] Moreover, appellate courts are entitled to interfere with an award of damages made by a tribunal where the tribunal was acting under a wrong principle of law, where it had misunderstood the relevant facts or where the amount awarded for damages was such that made the award an erroneous estimate of the damage suffered.

Before moving on to consider the principles that guide courts in making awards for compensation in discrimination law cases, it is worth summarising the practical context. Previously, there was a maximum ceiling on awards of damages in discrimination cases. The limit in sex discrimination cases (SDA, s.65) was held to be incompatible with EU sex discrimination law (Equal Treatment Directive, Art.6) in *Marshall (No.2)*. In *Marshall*, ECJ stated: "It also follows from that interpretation that the fixing of an upper limit of the kind at issue in the main proceedings cannot, by definition, constitute proper implementation of Art.6 of the Directive, since it limits the amount of compensation a priori to a level which is not necessarily consistent with the requirement of ensuring real equality of opportunity through adequate reparation for the loss and damage sustained as a result of discriminatory dismissal."[119] Following *Marshall*, the upper limit on damages in sex discrimination cases was removed. The Race Relations (Remedies) Act 1994 removed the then £11,000 limit in the RRA.

Recent high profile sex and race discrimination cases have hit the media headlines and suggest large sums of money are awarded in discrimination cases. For example, high profile cases and also settlements involving sexual harassment claims against investment banks have led to awards in the range of half a million to one million pounds.[120] However, these high profile cases do not reflect the reality of awards in discrimination cases, as noted by Nicola Dandridge in her summary of recent trends in compensation in discrimination law cases:

118 *Ministry of Defence v Wheeler* [1998] I.R.L.R. 23, CA.

119 *Marshall v Southampton and Sout West Hampshire AHA (No.2)* Case C–271/91 [1993] E.C.R. I–4367 at para.30.

120 Merill Lynch Bank, for example, settled a case without admitting liability for £1 million. The case involved a woman lawyer at the bank who brought an action for sexual harassment, constructive dismissal and victimisation claiming that a senior lawyer at the firm made remarks about her breasts and sex life at the office Christmas party. See "Investment Banks Make Huge Discrimination Payouts" in July 13, 2004, Management Issues, (*www.management-issues.com*, accessed March 13, 2006). See also a recent claim for £5 million pounds for sexual orientation discrimination, Audrey Gillan, "I was sacked for being gay, banker tells tribunal", *The Guardian*, March 8, 2006.

Nicola Dandrige, "Discrimination Compensation Guide, 2006, Forward", (2006) Discrimination Compensation Guide 2006 Published by IRS on August 1, 2006

"[...] compensation awards increased significantly in 2005. In 2004, the highest award in a race case was £90,158, whereas in 2005 it had increased to £372,357. In sex discrimination claims, the highest award was £175,000 in 2004 and in 2005 that had increased to £217,111. These are, of course, the headline awards. Probably much more useful for practitioners are the average or median awards. But here, too, we see increases in 2005. The median race award in 2004 was £6,104, increasing to £8,270 in 2005. For sex discrimination claims the median in 2004 was £6,243 increasing in 2005 to £7,497. Interestingly, the disability median decreased, from £10,712 in 2004, to £8,373.

Compensation totalling more than £5 million was awarded by employment tribunals in discrimination cases in 2005—a 16% decrease on the previous year. The number of awards made also decreased. Our survey covers 355 awards of compensation for discrimination—13 fewer than in 2004, continuing a downward trend, although the number of awards in race discrimination cases increased. The overall average award has fallen to £14,228, although the median has increased to £7,567.

Key points

- The total amount awarded for compensation in 2005 decreased by 16% compared with the previous year.
- The number of awards made dropped once again by 13—a fall of 3.5%.
- The number of awards in disability and sex discrimination cases fell, whereas race discrimination awards increased in 2005, bringing the number back to the same level as in 2003.
- The overall average award (that is, across all jurisdictions) fell to £14,228—a decrease of 12.5%.
- The overall median, however, rose by 7% to £7,567.
- The average in disability and sex discrimination cases fell over the year, although the median award in sex cases went up.
- The average in race discrimination awards showed a huge 41% increase, with the median also increasing, by 35%.
- The increase in the average in race cases reflects the highest award for race discrimination, which was exceptionally large at more than £300,000.
- There were only four awards over £100,000 in 2005, compared with 11 such awards in the previous year.
- However, the large increase in the median level of awards generally shows that tribunals were making more awards at the higher levels, albeit not at the highest level.
- Cases involving more than one jurisdiction attracted awards at much higher levels than the previous year, with both the average and median more than doubling.
- For the first time, awards were made for sexual orientation and religious discrimination. However, the number of cases is still very low (seven and four respectively).

- The average award for injury to feelings overall has risen by 29% with a 43% increase in the median. Almost half of awards for injury to feelings fell within the lowest band identified in *Vento*, compared with two-thirds of awards the year before. Almost one-third fell within the middle band in 2005."

The case law of the EAT and the Court of Appeal confirms that they will apply the normal principles of assessing pecuniary loss in tort cases (e.g. principles of mitigation and percentage chance of completion or loss of job in relation to a loss of future wages claim) in their analysis of damages for pecuniary loss in discrimination cases. The different heads of damage in discrimination cases are considered below, and they include: financial loss; injury to feeling; personal injury including pyschiatric damage; and aggravated damages. If the claimant has succeeded in unfair dismissal and unlawful discrimination and the financial loss exceeds the maximum that can be awarded for unfair dismissal, the award should be made under the anti-discrimination legislation so that the claimant can be compensated in full.[121] A claimant is under a duty to mitigate loss and the burden is on the respondent to prove that there has been a breach of this duty. The normal principles of tort law will apply to determine whether or not the claimant has taken reasonable steps to mitigate loss.[122]

Before moving on to consider the details of claims for damages, we will examine one case in detail to illustrate the general approach taken by appellate counts. In *Vento v Chief Constable of West Yorkshire Police*, which is set out in detail below, the Court of Appeal confirmed a number of key issues which are highlighted in the passages extracted below. First, the Court of Appeal confirmed that it is a second appellate body that can review the decisions of both Employment Tribunals and the Employment Appeal Tribunal in relation to compensation and awards of damages. Second, they affirmed that in reviewing awards for future loss of earnings, tribunals are allowed to rely on statistical evidence, and an appellate court should not overturn the decision of a tribunal based on evidence unless that decision is "perverse". This part of the decision is extracted and discussed in the section on injury to feeling (see below). Third, the Court of Appeal set out the principles that should guide awards for hurt feelings in discrimination law cases. Previous case law provides a guide to making an assessment about injury to feelings. In addition, the Court of Appeal confirmed that an appellate court should not interfere with such awards by tribunals unless (a) the tribunal had acted under a mistake of law; (b) had misapprehended the facts; or (c) had made a wholly erroneous estimate of the loss suffered.

121 *D'Souza v London Borough of Lambeth* [1997] I.R.L.R. 677 EAT.

122 See the recent decision of the Court of Appeal that an employee can reclaim costs reasonably incurred in mitigating loss, e.g. by setting up a business, see *AON Training Ltd v Dore* [2005] I.R.L.R. 891, CA.

Vento v Chief Constable of West Yorkshire Police [2002] EWCA Civ 1871 Court of Appeal CA (Civ Div) Ward, Mummery and Jonathan Parker L.JJ. 2002 Oct 2; Dec 20

"The facts are summarised in the case reports. The applicant joined the respondent's police force as a probationary officer at the age of 28, when she was married with three children. Two years later her marriage began to break down, and at the same time incidents occurred at work where fellow police officers criticised her conduct, her personal life and her character in an unwarranted, aggressive and demoralising manner. She became clinically depressed but tried to continue. Further discrimination resulted in suicidal impulses, and she was subsequently dismissed from the force for alleged lack of honesty and performance. Her complaint of sex discrimination against the chief constable was upheld by an employment tribunal, and, on a remedies hearing, the tribunal concluded that the applicant would have completed her probation and qualified as a police officer and that she would have had a 75% chance of working in the force for the rest of her career. The applicant was awarded £165,829 for loss of future earnings, £65,000, including £15,000 aggravated damages, for non-pecuniary loss for injury to feelings and £9,000 for psychiatric damage. An appeal by the chief constable was allowed by the Employment Appeal Tribunal who remitted the calculation of loss of future earnings to a freshly constituted tribunal, on the ground that the employment tribunal had erred in law in proceeding on the basis that the applicant had a 75% chance of completing her police career, and substituted a sum of £30,000, to include aggravated damages of £5,000, for injury to feelings, on the ground that £65,000 was so excessive as to amount to an error of law. The Court of Appeal allowed Ms Vento's appeal against this decision because the EAT had wrongly interferred with the decision of the tribunal about the amount awarded for loss of future earnings. The Court of Appeal made a number of points of principle.

1. Jurisdiction of the Court of Appeal in compensation awards by tribunals

[para.25] The true position, on authority and in principle, is that the Court of Appeal exercises a second appellate jurisdiction in respect of decisions of the employment tribunal. It has been settled by decisions binding on this court that the question for the Court of Appeal is whether there is an error of law in the decision of, or in the proceedings before, the employment tribunal. [...]

[para.31] The appeal to this court involves a determination of the very same questions as were before the appeal tribunal, i e is there an error of law arising in the decision of, or in the proceedings before, the employment tribunal? And, if so, what should be done about it? As in the case of appeals from the ordinary courts, the focus of the appellate body, whether at the first, second or any remoter tier of appeal, is on the determination of the proceedings in the trial court or tribunal. Attention and respect will be paid by the Court of Appeal to the conclusions of the appeal tribunal in the exercise of its specialist appellate function. But we are unable to accept the contention that the intervening decision of the appeal tribunal has the effect of preventing this court (or any higher court) from taking the decision of the employment tribunal as the relevant point for deciding whether there is an error of law and, if there is, how the appeal court should exercise its powers to rectify the error.

2. Conclusion on future loss of earnings

[para.38] The decision of the employment tribunal on this point ought only to be overturned if it is shown to be a perverse conclusion, that is a decision which no reasonable tribunal, properly directing itself on the law and on the materials before it, could reasonably have reached. An appellate tribunal or court is not entitled to interfere with such a conclusion simply on the basis that it would itself have reached a different conclusion on the same materials.

[para.39] It has to be accepted that the figure of a 75% chance of a full career is certainly on the high side. We doubt whether we would have estimated Ms Vento's chances as high as that had we been sitting in the employment tribunal. It was, however, an option reasonably open to the employment tribunal. The decision on that point ought not to have been interfered with by the appeal tribunal. We would allow Ms Vento's appeal. [. . .]

[para.42] In our judgment, the employment tribunal was entitled to approach the statistics with circumspection. [. . .]

[para.44] In our judgment, the employment tribunal did not apply any wrong principle of law or reach a perverse decision in the difficult and imprecise exercise of assessing the relative future chances. There was material on which its evaluation could be justified. It explained its conclusion sufficiently to comply with its duty to give sufficient reasons for its decision. The parties were able to tell in broad terms why they had won or lost on that issue. It is difficult to see what further reasons or explanation could reasonably be expected of the tribunal on a point such as this. It referred to the statistics on which the police relied. It also referred to the factors casting doubt on the applicability of past statistics to the future prospects of this particular police officer."

Vento makes it clear that a wide margin of discretion will be given to tribunals to consider facts and to reach a conclusion on issues such as future pecuniary loss. Moreover, as subsequent case law confirms, the principles that are applied in discrimination cases are similar to, but do not necessarily have to replicate, the principles in cases of non-discriminatory dismissal. In *Abbey National Plc v Formoso*,[123] a case involving pregnancy discrimination the EAT made it clear that the principles applied in calculating the amount of pecuniary loss in cases of discriminatory dismissal not be identical to cases of unfair dismissal. The correct questions to ask were what were the chances that the employer would have dismissed the claimant had she not been pregnant, and had a fair procedure been followed, rather than what a "reasonable employer" would have done. Moreover, the case confirmed that the "reasonable employer" approach is appropriate when considering the fairness of a dismissal, but not when assessing the loss flowing from a discriminatory dismissal. The calculation of loss of wages requires taking into account the fact that they earned wages elsewhere. In *Ministry of Defence v Wheeler*[124] the Court of Appeal confirmed that the calculation of compensation for pregnancy dismissal required taking into account: the sum the complainant would have earned if she stayed in the job; deducting the amount which she did, or should, have if the loss was mitigated, discounted for the net loss by a percentage to reflect the chance that she might have left the job for some other reason. In *Ministry of Defence v Hunt*,[125] the EAT confirmed that where an employment tribunal has assessed a percentage chance of completing a certain number of years service, and has also found some failure to mitigate on the

[123] *Abbey National Plc v Formoso* [1999] I.R.L.R. 222.
[124] *Ministry of Defence v Wheeler* [1998] I.R.L.R. 23, CA.
[125] *Ministry of Defence v Hunt* [1996] I.R.L.R. 139 EAT.

part of the claimant, the tribunal should deduct the failure to mitigate figure before, rather than after, applying the percentage chance figure.

In relation to the calculation of future uncertainty in calculating pecuniary loss in *Ministry of Defence v Cannock*,[126] the EAT confirmed that although there is no separate head of damage for loss of career prospects, the financial consequences of being deprived of the opportunity of promotion can and should be compensated for under damages for loss of employment. The case also confirmed that an award for injury to feelings (discussed in more detail below) should include a sum for the injury to feelings sustained as a result of the loss of chosen career. In *Cannock*, Morison J. in the EAT overturned a large award in a pregnancy discrimination case against the Ministry of Defence and concluded:

"*Argument 1*

[. . .] It seems to us quite clear that the correct measure of damage is based on the principle that, as best as money can do it, the applicant must be put into the position she would have been in but for the unlawful conduct of the MoD in dismissing her by reason of her pregnancy.

We reject the MoD's submissions to the effect that a contractual measure of damage is appropriate [compensation only for notice period].

The Sex Discrimination Act (s 66(1)) treats unlawful acts of discrimination as statutory torts. There would be no sense in applying the contract test, and, indeed, Mr Pannick QC felt unable to contend that the contract test should be fully applied. He shrunk from the proposition that because all commissions can be terminated at will, the applicants were entitled to no loss of earnings. . . .

[. . .] In our guidance, we respectfully suggest that Industrial Tribunals need to keep a due sense of proportion when assessing compensation. Some of the applicants have received awards more appropriate for a person who has lost a career due to some kind of continuing disability. [Mrs. Cannock had been awarded £173,000.] All of these applicants who were entitled to any award of compensation for loss of earnings are assumed to have been ready, willing and able to resume their career in the services six months after their first child was born and therefore, ready, willing and able to undertake reasonably suitable alternative employment. To this extent, their compensation for loss of earnings is not likely to be different from the thousands of cases of unfair dismissal with which the Industrial Tribunals are having to deal each year, albeit that there is no cap on the award . . ."

More generally, in relation to the issue of mitigation in discrimination law damages awards, in *Ministry of Defence v Hunt* the EAT also affirmed that the burden of proof in cases where there is a claim of a failure of mitigation is on the person who asserts the claim. Moreover, the claim that there is a failure to mitigate must be backed up by evidence which needs to be established in the tribunal through examintion or cross examination during the proceedings.

In terms of pecuniary loss, the claimant can claim for any pecuniary loss that is attributable to an unlawful act of discrimination.[127] This includes financial

[126] *Ministry of Defence v Cannock* [1994] I.R.L.R. 509 EAT.
[127] *Coleman v Skyrail Oceanic Ltd* [1981] I.R.L.R. 398, CA.

loss as well as damages for all forms of personal injury including psychiatric damages as long as a "causal link" can be established between the discriminatory act and the damage claimed.[128] The nature of the causal link required to make a claim for damages in discrimination cases was discussed by the Court of Appeal in *Essa v Laing Ltd*.[129] *Essa* established that the complainant who was the victim of racial abuse was entitled to compensation for all loss that arose naturally and directly from the wrong (the discriminatory act).

In *Essa*, the complainant had suffered from pecuniary loss in the form of loss of wages and also a depressive illness following racial abuse. It was clear that the extent of his reaction to the abuse was severe and caused him serious psychiatric injury, and one of the questions related to what principles should determine the extent of damages that were recoverable following a discriminatory act. The employer argued that there was no liability for damages for all the consequences of the discriminatory act and, moreover, that it had not been established that psychiatric injury was reasonably forseeable. The Court of Appeal confirmed that the award for the depressive illness was recoverable, and that it was not necessary in discrimination cases for the claimant to show that the particular type of loss was reasonably forseeable. In *Essa*, the Court of Appeal used the normal principles of tort law to analyse the issue of remoteness in the context of discrimination law. The majority held that because discrimination is a statutory tort, all the loss that arises as a natural and direct result of the discriminatory act is recoverable. Moreover, there is no requirement of reasonable forseeability in addition to causation. In any event, the Court of Appeal found that psychiatric damage was reasonably forseeable in this case.[130] Mr Justice Pill applied the normal rules that establish remoteness of damage in tort cases, and he applied the standard applied in negligence cases.

In earlier cases, the principles for an award of damages in discrimination law cases were set out. In *Alexander v Home Office*,[131] the Court of Appeal confirmed that awards of damages for unlawful discrimination were not limited to pecuniary loss. The different heads of damages in these cases were summarised in the following terms: (i) compensation for the harm caused to the claimant by the wrongful act (i.e. discrimination); (ii) this included pecuniary loss (e.g. loss of wages), and could also include putting a financial sum on other non-pecuniary loss. In addition, in discrimination law cases it may be possible to make a claim for injury to feelings and aggravated damages. Aggravated damages are discussed in detail below. Here it is worth noting that RRA, s.57 and SDA, s.66 explicitly recognise that injury to feelings can in the appropriate circumstances, be included in an award of damages in discrimination law cases. In *Alexander*, the Court of Appeal confirmed that

128 *Sheriff v Klyne Tugs (Lowestoft) Ltd* [1999] I.R.L.R. 481, CA.
129 *Essa v Laing Ltd* [2004] I.R.L.R. 313, CA.
130 *Ibid.*
131 *Alexander v Home Office* [1988] I.C.R. 685, CA.

injury to feelings will often be an important component of the claim for damages in a race discrimination case. However, the Court of Appeal also confirmed that the mere fact that there was a case of racial discrimination does not of itself allow a tribunal to infer (without other facts or circumstances) that there is an injury to feelings.

3. Financial loss

The extract from *Vento* above confirms that courts and tribunals will apply normal principles for the calculation of pecuniary loss in discrimination law cases. Loss has to be established on the civil law standard of a balance of probabilities. It can include: loss of earnings, which includes loss of a pension; loss of other contractual or non-contractual benefits; as well as all other costs that have been suffered because of the discrimination. Moreover, as with other damages calculation, the loss should be calculated on a net basis (i.e. after deducting for tax and national insurance)[132] Pension loss raises special issues for calculation and has given rise to special guidance for tribunals.[133]

In calculating financial loss, and deciding issues such as the extent of the loss and whether there has been a break in the chain of causation, the courts will focus on whether the claimant took reasonable steps in the circumstances.[134] For example, in *Orthet Ltd v Vince-Cain*[135] the EAT held that the tribunal could award compensation for loss of earnings for four years for retraining at University where the employer was unable to prove that there was suitable work that the claimant should have taken up.

In applying the principle of putting the claimant back in the position that he would have been in had the discrimination (wrong) not occurred, it will often be necessary for the tribunal to evaluate the chances of certain events happening, e.g a future increase in pay or a promotion or a future dismissal.

There are normal principles of tort law that govern this analysis, e.g. the use and calculation of the multiplier using actuarial guides. In *Ministry of Defence v Wheeler*, the Court of Appeal took into account the chance that the claimant would have otherwise worked for the Ministry of Defence and the chance of finding alternative employment at the same rate and pay in the future.[136] Deductions will also be made from an award in discrimination cases by using similar principles to other tort cases, e.g. with a view to reducing the sum for

[132] *British Transport Commission v Gourley* [1956] A.C. 185 HL.

[133] See *Greenhoff v Barnsley Metropolitan BC* (May 31, 2006; appeal No.UKEAT/0093/06). The EAT recognised "the great difficulties for tribunals in ascertaining the value of the loss of pension rights", cited in discussion by Nicola Dandrige in (2006) *Discrimination Compensation Guide*, published by IRS on June 1, 2006, s.1. Dandrige also cites the following guide to pensions: "There are guidelines to assist tribunals in calculating pension loss. *Compensation for loss of pension rights* (third edition), which is written by tribunal chairs David Sneath and Colin Sara, the government actuary and a member of the Government Actuary's Department."

[134] *ICTS (UK) Ltd v Tchoula* [2000] I.R.L.R. 643.

[135] *Orthet Ltd v Vince-Cain* [2004] I.R.L.R. 857.

[136] *Ministry of Defence v Wheeler* [1998] I.R.L.R. 23, CA.

benefits received such as income support.[137] The same principles apply for deductions as for personal injury cases. Also, a claimant cannot recover damages in respect of loss that should be mitigated; and charitable payments resulting from the benevolence of third parties and from an insurance policy for which a claimant has paid or contributed to the premiums will not be deducted.[138]

4. Personal Injury and Non-pecuniary loss

As *Vento* confirms, the employment tribunal will calculate damages on the basis of tort law principles. This includes all personal injury which is caused by unlawful whether physical or psychiatric damage.[139] In most cases the pyschiatric damage element will be dealt with is a global assessment which includes the sum for injury to feelings. These issues are discussed in more detail in the section on injury to feelings. *Vento* also confirms that employment tribunals will often refer to the Judicial Studies Board's Guidelines for the Assessment of General Damages in Personal Injury Cases to help them to assess appropriate awards. These guidelines include different types of illness. They suggest that the following factors are relevant in the assessment of the value of a claim: the injured person's ability to cope with life and work; impact of injury on relationship with family and friends; the extent to which treatment is successful; whether medical treatment was sought; and whether (a) the harm was the result of sexual or physical abuse or a breach of trust; and (b) the nature of the abuse, its duration and the symptoms caused by it.[140]

Non-pecuniary loss includes claims for psychiatric damage, injury to feelings, aggravated damages and in some cases exemplary damages. Some cases have suggested that injury to feeling is so "fundamental" to sex discrimination that all that needs to be established is the statement that there was hurt feeling to trigger an award.[141] However, subsequent case law such as *Alexander v Home Office* has confirmed that an award for injury to feeling does not automatically follow whenever there is proof of unlawful discrimination. The non-pecuniary injury to feeling must arise from the knowledge of the claimant that he has suffered discrimination,[142] and injury to feelings unrelated to discrimination should be disregarded from an assessment of compensation.[143] Moreover, it

[137] *Chief Constable of West Yorkshire Police v Vento (No.2)* [2002] I.R.L.R. 177, CA.

[138] In *Atos Origin IT Services UK Ltd v Haddock* [2005] I.R.L.R. 20, the EAT held that payments from an accident or health insurance policy for which the premiums had been paid by the employer, without contribution from the employee, should be deducted in calculating an award of financial loss under the DDA 1995.

[139] *Sheriff v Klyne Tugs (Lowestoft) Ltd* [1999] I.R.L.R. 481.

[140] Nicola Dandrige in (2006) *Discrimination Compensation Guide*, published by IRS on June 1, 2006, s.1.

[141] *Murray v Powertech (Scotland) Ltd* [1992] I.R.L.R. 257, EAT.

[142] *Alexander v The Home Office* [1988] I.R.L.R. 190, CA.

[143] *Coleman v Skyrail Oceanic Ltd* [1981] I.R.L.R. 398, CA.

must be proved even though it will be reasonably easy to establish that acts of discrimination have injured the claimant's feelings.[144]

An award for injury to feelings should not be made automatically to be made whenever unlawful discrimination is proved or admitted. Injury must be proved, though it will often be easy to prove because no tribunal will take much persuasion that the anger, distress and affront caused by the act of discrimination has injured the claimant's feelings.

In *Vento*, the general approach and guidelines to the assessment of non-pecuniary loss was developed by the Court of Appeal. These are discussed in the following passage:

Vento v Chief Constable of West Yorkshire Police [2002] EWCA Civ 1871 Court of Appeal CA (Civ Div) Ward, Mummery and Jonathan Parker L.JJ. 2002 Oct 2; Dec 20

"The relevant facts in relation to calculation for injury to feelings include, inter alia: Two years later her marriage began to break down, and at the same time incidents occurred at work where fellow police officers criticised her conduct, her personal life and her character in an unwarranted, aggressive and demoralising manner. She became clinically depressed but tried to continue. Further discrimination resulted in suicidal impulses, and she was subsequently dismissed from the force for alleged lack of honesty and performance. The original award for non-pecuniary loss was £74,000 which was held to be excessive by the Court of Appeal. The CA summarised the relevant cases, set out a guide to assessment of non-pecuniary loss in discrimination cases and held that a sum in the total of £32,000, made up as to £18,000 for injury to feelings, £5,000 aggravated damages and £9,000 for psychiatric damage was reasonable.

3. Compensation for injury to feelings: the law

[46] This is the first time for many years that the Court of Appeal has had the opportunity to consider the appropriate level of compensation for injury to feelings in discrimination cases. Some decisions in the employment tribunal and in the appeal tribunal have resulted in awards of substantial sums for injury to feelings, sometimes supplemented by compensation for psychiatric damage and aggravated damages. Cases were cited to the court in which employment tribunals had, as in this case, awarded compensation for injury to feelings (plus aggravated damages) larger than the damages separately awarded for psychiatric injury, and totalling well in excess of £20,000. The court was shown the decision of an employment tribunal in a race discrimination case awarding the sum of £100,000 for injury to feelings, plus aggravated damages of £25,000: *Virdi v Comr of Police of the Metropolis (8 December 2000, London (Central) Employment Tribunal, Case No: 2202774/98)*. (This pales into insignificance in comparison with the reported award in 1994 by a Californian jury of $7.1m to a legal secretary for sexual harassment, and even with the subsequent halving of that sum on appeal.)

[47] Compensation of the magnitude of £125,000 for non-pecuniary damage creates concern as to whether some recent tribunal awards in discrimination cases are in line with

144 *Ministry of Defence v Cannock* [1994] I.R.L.R. 509, EAT.

general levels of compensation recovered in other cases of non-pecuniary loss, such as general damages for personal injuries, malicious prosecution and defamation. In the interests of justice (social and individual), and of predictability of outcome and consistency of treatment of like cases (an important ingredient of justice), this court should indicate to employment tribunals and practitioners general guidance on the proper level of award for injury to feelings and other forms of non-pecuniary damage. [...]

[50] It is self evident that the assessment of compensation for an injury or loss, which is neither physical nor financial, presents special problems for the judicial process, which aims to produce results objectively justified by evidence, reason and precedent. Subjective feelings of upset, frustration, worry, anxiety, mental distress, fear, grief, 0anguish, humiliation, unhappiness, stress, depression and so on and the degree of their intensity are incapable of objective proof or of measurement in monetary terms. Translating hurt feelings into hard currency is bound to be an artificial exercise. As Dickson J said in *Andrews v Grand & Toy Alberta Ltd* (1978) 83 DLR (3d) 452, 475–476, (cited by this court in *Heil v Rankin [2001] QB 272*, 292, para 16) there is no medium of exchange or market for non-pecuniary losses and their monetary evaluation:

> 'is a philosophical and policy exercise more than a legal or logical one. The award must be fair and reasonable, fairness being gauged by earlier decisions; but the award must also of necessity be arbitrary or conventional. No money can provide true restitution.'

[51] Although they are incapable of objective proof or measurement in monetary terms, hurt feelings are none the less real in human terms. The courts and tribunals have to do the best they can on the available material to make a sensible assessment, accepting that it is impossible to justify or explain a particular sum with the same kind of solid evidential foundation and persuasive practical reasoning available in the calculation of financial loss or compensation for bodily injury. In these circumstances an appellate body is not entitled to interfere with the assessment of the employment tribunal simply because it would have awarded more or less than the tribunal has done. It has to be established that the tribunal has acted on a wrong principle of law or has misapprehended the facts or made a wholly erroneous estimate of the loss suffered. Striking the right balance between awarding too much and too little is obviously not easy. [...]

[53] In *Prison Service v Johnson [1997] ICR 275* Smith J reviewed the authorities on compensation for non-pecuniary loss and made a valuable summary of the general principles gathered from them. We would gratefully adopt that summary. Employment tribunals should have it in mind when carrying out this challenging exercise. In her judgment on behalf of the appeal tribunal Smith J said, at p 283:

> '(i) Awards for injury to feelings are compensatory. They should be just to both parties. They should compensate fully without punishing the tortfeasor. Feelings of indignation at the tortfeasor's conduct should not be allowed to inflate the award. (ii) Awards should not be too low, as that would diminish respect for the policy of the anti-discrimination legislation. Society has condemned discrimination and awards must ensure that it is seen to be wrong. On the other hand, awards should be restrained, as excessive awards could, to use the phrase of Sir Thomas Bingham MR [in *John v MGN Ltd [1997] QB 586*, 611], be seen as the way to "untaxed riches". (iii) Awards should bear some broad general similarity to the range of awards in personal injury cases. We do not think that this should be done by reference to any particular type of personal injury award, rather to the whole range of such awards. (iv) In exercising that discretion in assessing a sum, tribunals should remind themselves of the value in everyday life of the sum they have in mind. This may be done by reference to purchasing power or by reference to earnings. (v) Finally, tribunals should bear in mind Sir Thomas Bingham's reference to the need for public respect for the level of awards made.'

[54] The appeal tribunal in that case was concerned with a serious case of race discrimination suffered by a black auxiliary prison officer, who was the victim of a campaign of racial harassment and humiliation over a period of 18 months, involving elements of pure malice and victimisation on the part of his persecutors. In August 1995 the employment tribunal awarded him £21,000 for injury to feelings and £7,500 for aggravated damages. That was the largest reported award at that time. The appeal by the Prison Service against those awards was dismissed on the ground that it could not be said that the employment tribunal had erred in law. The appeal tribunal concluded that, although the award of £21,000 for injury to feelings was on the high side, it was a serious case of discrimination and the level of the award was not obviously out of line with the general range of personal injury awards or with sums awarded for injury to reputation.

[55] The appeal tribunal also upheld the award of aggravated damages holding that such damages were available in discrimination cases having regard to the manner in which the acts of discrimination were committed and other aspects of the conduct of the discriminator. The appeal tribunal held that the award of £7,500 was not outside the bracket of reasonable awards. It was a very serious case, in which the treatment of the applicant had been appalling affecting both his work and home life, but not, apparently, inflicting any injury to health. The discrimination had been aggravated by the failure of the Prison Service to investigate his complaints.

[56] The general approach laid down in *Prison Service v Johnson* has been followed in three recent cases in the appeal tribunal, which provide useful illustrations of the range of awards of compensation to damages for feelings. [...]

[58] In *Tchoula v ICTS (UK) Ltd [2000] ICR 1191* the appeal tribunal (Judge Peter Clark presiding) allowed an appeal against an award of £27,000 in a race discrimination case brought by a security officer. The employment tribunal awarded £22,000 for injury to feelings and £5,000 for aggravated damages. The appeal tribunal considered that the total sum awarded was so excessive as to be in error of law. It was a relatively serious case, but fell within the lower category of awards. It was not a case of a campaign of discrimination. Having referred to the guidelines of the Judicial Studies Board, the appeal tribunal reduced the sum awarded to an overall sum of £10,000.

[59] The most recent reported case is the decision of the appeal tribunal (Mr Recorder Underhill QC presiding) in *Prison Service v Salmon [2001] IRLR 425*. That was a serious case of sex discrimination brought by a woman police officer complaining of humiliating and degrading conduct, which was so serious that she had suffered psychiatric harm for which she received an award of £11,250. In addition, the sum of £20,000 for injury to feelings, including £ 5,000 aggravated damages, was awarded. The appeal tribunal dismissed the appeal of the Prison Service against those awards, holding that they were not so excessive as to constitute an error of law by the employment tribunal. While accepting that employment tribunals must be aware of the danger of allowing double recovery for overlapping areas of loss, the appeal tribunal did not consider that in that case there had been any vitiating double counting.

[60] Being fully aware that awards in other cases only assist in a very general way, Mr Bean was brief in his citations of decisions in the personal injury field indicating that the awards by the employment tribunal and the appeal tribunal in this case were excessive. He cited decisions of this court and of the Criminal Injuries Compensation Board in which much lower sums have been awarded in recent years by way of general damages for post-traumatic stress disorder, for psychological harm involving serious personality change and damage and dysfunctional relationships, feelings of low self-esteem, eating disorders, panic attacks, personal and social unhappiness, anger and distress in serious cases of, for example, persistent sex and physical abuse of children by parents, step-parents and other carers. The level of awards ranged from about £15,000 at the lower end to £31,000 in cases where psychiatric damage had also been suffered. The cases cited were drawn from recent headnotes in *Kemp & Kemp The Quantum of Damages*. Mr Bean agreed that the

sums mentioned in the headnotes should be given their current value in accordance with the *Heil v Rankin [2001] QB 272* uplift.

[61] At the end of the day this court must first ask itself whether the award by the employment tribunal in this case was so excessive as to constitute an error of law. That was the conclusion of the appeal tribunal and it is clearly right. The totality of the award for non-pecuniary loss is seriously out of line with the majority of those made and approved on appeal in reported Employment Appeal Tribunal cases. It is also seriously out of line with the guidelines compiled for the Judicial Studies Board and with the cases reported in the personal injury field where general damages have been awarded for pain, suffering, disability and loss of amenity. The total award of £74,000 for non-pecuniary loss is, for example, in excess of the Judicial Studies Board guidelines for the award of general damages for moderate brain damage, involving epilepsy, for severe post-traumatic stress disorder having permanent effects and badly affecting all aspects of the life of the injured person, for loss of sight in one eye, with reduced vision in the remaining eye, and for total deafness and loss of speech. No reasonable person would think that that excess was a sensible result. The patent extravagance of the global sum is unjustifiable as an award of compensation. It is probably explicable by the understandable strength of feeling in the tribunal and as an expression of its condemnation of, and punishment for, the discriminatory treatment of Ms Vento.

[62] The next question is what is the appropriate amount to award under this head? For the reasons already stated we reject Mr Jeans's submission that this court is inhibited from reducing the sum below that substituted by the appeal tribunal. It is not a question of whether the appeal tribunal assessed a reasonable sum in the exercise of a discretion, with which this court ought not to interfere. The question for this court is what is the reasonable, fair and just sum to put in place of the award made in error of law by the employment tribunal. Neither side has contended that this matter should be remitted to the employment tribunal.

[63] In our judgment, taking account of the level of awards undisturbed on recent appeals to the appeal tribunal and of the Judicial Studies Board guidelines, the fair, reasonable and just award in this case for non-pecuniary loss is a total of £32,000, made up as to £18,000 for injury to feelings, £5,000 aggravated damages and £9,000 for psychiatric damage, which took the form of clinical depression and adjustment disorder lasting for three years (and against which there was no appeal). We also bear in mind that there was no finding by the employment tribunal that the injury to Ms Vento's feelings would continue after the psychiatric disorder had passed. During the period of psychiatric disorder there must have been a significant degree of overlap with the injury to her feelings.

[64] It should be understood that the reduction in the amount of compensation is made solely to bring the global award more into line with conventional wisdom on levels of compensation for non-pecuniary loss generally. The reduction does not mean that this court takes a less serious view than the employment tribunal did of the persistent unlawful discrimination suffered by Ms Vento at the hands of her colleagues in the police service, which is expected to set an example of abiding by the law, including the law governing all forms of discrimination."

The analysis in *Vento* confirms that there will often be an overlap between different categories of non-pecuniary loss and that these will be difficult to separate. Moreover, the case also affirms that aggravated damages can be claimed in the appropriate circumstances. Nevertheless there are existing principles on the calculation of non-pecuniary loss that can be applied in discrimination cases. *Vento* suggests that the top band should be between about £15,000 and £25,000. Awards of damages in this range should be for the most serious cases where there has been a series of events or a sustained campaign of harassment (*Tchoula* was noted as an excessive award because there was no such lengthy campaign). A middle band of between £5,000 and £15,000 was appropriate for less serious cases. The lower band of awards of about £500 and £5,000 were appropriate for less serious cases where the discrimination was a one off event or an isolated incident. Finally, awards lower than £500 should be avoided because they carry the risk of being so low as to not be a proper compensation for injury to feelings and these show a disregard for the goals of discrimination law[145] Yet, at the same time, awards should not be so high as to bring discrimination law into disrepute.[146]

Vento affirms principles articulated in other cases on injury to feelings.[147] In particular, these cases confirm that the awards for injury to feelings should be compensatory rather than a reflection of the indignation at the conduct of the tortfeasor, although aggravated damages are permitted in the appropriate circumstances. Awards should not be too low as that would diminish respect for the policy of the anti-discrimination legislation. Awards should bear some broad general similarity to the range of awards in personal injury cases. This should be done by reference to the whole range of such awards, rather than to any particular type of award. In exercising their discretion in assessing a sum, tribunals should remind themselves of the value in everyday life of the sum they have in mind. This may be done by reference to purchasing power or by reference to earnings. Tribunals should bear in mind the need for public respect for the level of awards made. *Vento* also confirms that although the calculation of non-pecuniary damages will often be difficult and lack the solid evidential basis of calculation of pecuniary loss, it is possible to use previous awards and guidelines from the Judicial Studies Board to formulate an approximate guide to what constitutes an appropriate award. The case also confirms that because there is more discretion involved in the calculation of non-pecuniary damages the appellate courts should be more cautious of overturning the decisions of tribunals.

Vento breaks down each of the different elements of non-pecuniary loss but it also takes a global approach to assessing the adequacy of compensation. Where there are a series of acts of discrimination, *ICTS v Tchoula* confirms that it is preferable to have a general award to represent the loss suffered by all the acts rather than making separate awards in respect of each of three acts of discrimination, since it would be unrealistic to seek to ascribe to each act of discrimination a proportion of the overall injury to feelings suffered.[148] However, where there is an overlap between different types of non-pecuniary

[145] See the discussion of *Vento* in Michael Rubenstein, "Sex and Race Discrimination: Individual Remedies" in (2006) *Discrimination Case Law Guide*, Published by IRS on February 1, 2006.

[146] *Alexander v The Home Office* [1988] I.R.L.R. 190, CA.

[147] *Armitage, Marsden* and *HM Prison Service v Johnson* [1997] I.R.L.R. 162 EAT (3 reports). See the discussion of *Vento* in Michael Rubenstein, "Sex and Race Discrimination: Individual Remedies" in (2006) *Discrimination Case Law Guide*, Published by IRS on February 1, 2006.

[148] *ICTS (UK) Ltd v Tchoula* [2000] I.R.L.R. 643, EAT.

loss such as injury to feelings and psychiatric damage, the tribunal needs to be aware of the risk of double compensation, i.e. the same suffering may be compensated under different heads of damage.[149] The EAT has considered the assessment of awards for psychiatric damage caused by unlawful discrimination in *HM Prison Service v Salmon*.[150] As in *Vento*, the EAT held that assessment of psychiatric injury is a matter of fact for the employment tribunal which can only be overturned on appeal if there is an error of law, a misunderstanding of facts or if it is a figure so high or low as to be perverse. In *Salmon*, the EAT noted that injury to feeling can cover minor instances such as upset and distress caused by one-off episodes of discrimination. In more serious cases, the injury to feelings may include prolonged feelings of humiliation, low self-esteem and depression. In the more serious cases it will often be impossible to separate out with certainty or precision when distress or humiliation become transformed into a recognisable psychiatric injury such as depression. It will also, therefore, be arbitrary whether the claim for non-pecuniary loss is framed as a claim for injury to feelings or as psychiatric damage supported by formal diagnosis or expert evidence. This analysis reinforces the more general argument that there is a need to treat awards under these two heads of injury to feelings and psychiatric damage as a global award.

Whereas in an award of future loss of earnings it is proper to take into account the fact that the claimant would be fairly dismissed within a relatively short period, in the case of injury to feelings this future contingency does not justify the reduction of an award for injury to feelings.[151] However, there are other issues that may reduce the amount awarded for non-pecuniary damages such as injury to feelings and psychiatric damage. For example, the nature of the job may be relevant to determine the issue of the injury to feeling (e.g. if it is a part-time rather than full time job and their whole career).[152] Also, the willingness of an employer to admit that the act was discriminatory may help to alleviate the hurt feelings and therefore reduce the hurt of further explanation of the nature of the treatment.[153] Concern at the "complete failure" of a respondent's equal opportunities policy does not properly form part of a compensatory award for injury to feelings[154]

5. Levels of awards for injury to feelings

Awards for injury to feeling have been made in a wide range of discrimination law cases, and especially in harassment cases.

[149] *HM Prison Service v Salmon* [2001] I.R.L.R. 425, EAT.
[150] *Ibid.*
[151] *O'Donoghue v Redcar & Cleveland BC* [2001] I.R.L.R. 615, CA.
[152] *Orlando v Didcot Power Station Sports & Social Club* [1996] I.R.L.R. 262, EAT.
[153] *Ibid.*
[154] *Corus Hotels v (1) Woodward (2) Rushton EAT/0536/05*, see Nicola Dandrige in (2006) *Discrimination Compensation Guide*, published by IRS on June 1, 2006, s.1.

In race discrimination cases, there have been both low and middle range awards for injury to feelings. The types of fact situations that give rise to such awards as well as the monetary amount awarded are summarised below.

In relation to one off comments and a transient injury, the awards have been low. For example, in a case involving racism against someone English by an Asian employer the relevant conduct included the following: calling the claimant an "English twat"; and saying that Asian people were buying up his country and taking women. The complainant said that he had never before experienced racism and this left him feeling intimidated. The tribunal awarded a sum of £750 to reflect the fact that this was a serious but one-off event.[155] A failure to promote a one-off act will also attract a modest sum for injury to feelings.[156] An Irish claimant who suffered a one off incident when offending words were used about the Irish[157] and were not subsequently removed (in breach of the code on equality and harassment) was awarded £3,000. The range for one-off comments or acts is at the lower end and tends to be between £750 and £3,000. Where a black applicant was told by her employer that she stuck out like a sore thumb,[158] a tribunal awarded her an award for injury to feelings of £1,500.

More serious cases of race discrimination have led to higher awards for injury to feeling in a range from £5,000 onwards. In cases where the conduct was not an isolated one-off event, and was real and significant, higher awards have been made.[159] In one case, a black African man was subjected to race discrimination and victimisation. There was a failure to investigate his complaint of racial discrimination and unfair dismissal. The complainant lost his job of five years. Moreover, on return to the job for a hearing he saw a picture of himself displayed in the workplace. The complainant received £6,000 for injury to feeling.[160]

Other relevant cases in this higher band for awards for race discrimination include the following:

- A claimant labelled a serious threat to colleagues which was not proven

[155] *Peter v Carmichael's Restaurant-Bar Ltd*, February 15, 2005; Case No.2511252/04. For other modest awards for one off events see *Lewis v (1) All Emergency Services (2) R Jones*, August 8, 2005; Case No.2301047/04 where the tribunal awarded £2,000 for injurty to feelings. Cited in Nicola Dandrige in (2006) *Discrimination Compensation Guide*, published by IRS on June 1, 2006, s.1.

[156] *Molero v Computershare Investor Services Plc*, October 26, 2005; Case No.1400719/05. Cited in Nicola Dandrige in (2006) *Discrimination Compensation Guide*, published by IRS on June 1, 2006, s.1.

[157] *Neylan v Royal Berkshire Fire Authority*, June 1, 2005; Case No.2701259/03. Cited in Nicola Dandrige in (2006) *Discrimination Compensation Guide*, published by IRS on June 1, 2006, s.1.

[158] *Bishop v Nails Inc*, June 3, 2005; Case No.3301860/04. Cited in Nicola Dandrige in (2006) *Discrimination Compensation Guide*, published by IRS on June 1, 2006, s.1.

[159] *Mahon v Black Country Small Business Service Ltd*, December 7, 2005; Case No.1301883/05. Cited in Nicola Dandrige in (2006) *Discrimination Compensation Guide*, published by IRS on June 1, 2006, s.1.

[160] *Oyewole v Aktrion Group Ltd*, May 4, 2005; Case No.3301858/04. Cited in Nicola Dandrige in (2006) *Discrimination Compensation Guide*, published by IRS on June 1, 2006, s.1.

was considered to be a serious allegation, and although a one-off act, this had serious consequences (£6,500 award for injury to feelings).[161]

- An employment tribunal found that Miss Gordon, who is black, was shunned for the four days she worked with the respondent. She was told that she was to be dismissed because she did not fit in. When she asked whether this was because she was black, her manager simply shrugged his shoulders. When she sought to challenge what had happened to her and asked for reasons for her dismissal in writing, they were not forthcoming. (£7,000 awarded for injury to feelings).[162]

In some cases, there have been incidents of racism that are ongoing and that have not been dealt with by the management through its equal opportunities policies. The creation of a racialised working atmosphere has been found to justify a high award for injury to feelings because of the continuing nature of the problem and the structural problems of the management refusing to deal with the racism. In one case, a complainant who was British African Carribean was subjected to offensive comments which were not just isolated incidents. The management did not deal with these complaints using its equal opportunities policy. An award of £12,000 was made for injury to feelings.[163] In *Obonyo v Wandsworth NHS Primary Trust*, the failure to follow its harassment policy which led to ongoing racial harassment of a complaiant, which the tribunal said created a racialised hostile working environment, led to the award of a sum of £18,000 which represented a sum for injury to feeling and also for psychiatric injury.[164]

Higher awards will also be justified where the conduct is serious and carried out over a longer time period. For example, where an employer's discriminatory conduct consisted of questioning the complainant's integrity and caused him concerns and fears about his safety, the tribunal made an award of £10,000.[165]

There are a number of recent cases that have attracted very high awards for injury to feelings in race discrimination cases which are worth examining and which confirm that length of service in employment and also the duration of the discriminatory conduct are relevant factors in deciding whether the cases fall within the higher bracket of awards for injury to feelings. In one case, there was a prolonged period of humiliating the complainant who was Jamaican

[161] *Abdillahi v Barts and London NHS Trust*, February 7, 2005; Case No.3203494/03 cited in Nicola Dandridge in *Discrimination Compensation Guide*, published by IRS on June 1, 2006, s.1.

[162] *Gordon v Telewest Communications Plc*, May 13, 2005; Case No.1302692/04. Cited in Nicola Dandrige in (2006) *Discrimination Compensation Guide*, published by IRS on June 1, 2006, s.1.

[163] *Richards v Ryder Plc*, May 13, 2005; Case No.1304622/04. Cited in Nicola Dandrige in (2006) *Discrimination Compensation Guide*, published by IRS on June 1, 2006, s.1.

[164] *Obonyo v Wandsworth NHS Primary Care Trust*, November 7, 2005; Case Nos 2306630/03 and 2302820/04. Cited in Nicola Dandrige in (2006) *Discrimination Compensation Guide*, published by IRS on June 1, 2006, s.1.

[165] *Melloy v HM Prison Service*, October 7, 2005; Case No.1400772/04. Cited in Nicola Dandrige in (2006) *Discrimination Compensation Guide*, published by IRS on June 1, 2006, s.1.

and who had worked for the company for 34 years. Rather than an honourable retirement, the tribunal found that the complainant had been the victim of racist insults and unfair redundancy dismissal (which the tribunal said was a devastating blow at the end of his career). In light of the length of service of the complainant and the continuing nature of the insults, the tribunal made an award of £15,000 for injury to feelings.[166]

(i) *Sex Discrimination Cases*

As with race discrimination cases, brief one-off transgressions and incidents of sex discrimination will fall within the lower band of the *Vento* scale for awards for injury to feelings. For example, in a case involving a complainant (a pregnant woman) who received two offensive emails led to an award of £4,000 for injury to feelings. The fact that the emails were from a senior colleague was treated as an aggravating feature.[167] Failure to agree to part-time work or flexible working arrangements for full time female workers, where these requests are treated in a peremptory way, have also led to awards for injury to feelings in the lower band. One case involved the refusal to allow part-time work (after the birth of a child) to a complainant who had worked full time. The treatment constituted indirect discrimination. The peremptory treatment of the claim, and resulting uncertainty, were cited as reasons which justified an award of £3,000 for injury to feelings.[168] Even in a case where the employer's failure to grant flexible working time to a full time mother is deemed to be indirect discrimination, which has been justified by the employer the tribunal has awarded £2,000 as compensation for injury to feelings to reflect the stress and uncertainty experienced by the complainant.[169]

Cases that fall within the middle band of compensation are those where the treatment is more serious or for a longer time period. Sexual harassment and pregnancy discrimination are two categories of cases that frequently give rise to awards of injury to feelings in the middle or higher range. Harassment cases raise particularly challenging questions for calculation of injury to feelings because of the nature of the harm and the facts that give rise to the discriminatory conduct. In *Snowball v Gardner Merchant Ltd*, the EAT held that compensation for sexual harassment must relate to the degree of the detriment suffered.[170] This requires an assessment of the injury to the victim's feelings: with reference to what an ordinary reasonable female employee would feel (to establish the standard objectively); and then also by reference to the actual

166 *(1) Laing v Copal Castings Ltd*, February 8, 2005; Case No.1303701/02. Cited in Nicola Dandrige in (2006) *Discrimination Compensation Guide*, published by IRS on June 1, 2006, s.1.

167 *Cole-Emodogo v Syracuse (UK) Ltd*, November 11, 2005; Case No.2301549/05. Cited in Nicola Dandrige in (2006) *Discrimination Compensation Guide*, published by IRS on June 1, 2006, s.1.

168 *Thompson v Stephen Davies Associates*, February 17, 2005; Case No.2401870/04. Cited in Nicola Dandrige in (2006) *Discrimination Compensation Guide*, published by IRS on June 1, 2006, s.1.

169 *Venkatasamy v Dhillon & Co Solicitors*, September 27, 2005; Case No.3203381/04. Cited in Nicola Dandrige in (2006) *Discrimination Compensation Guide*, published by IRS on June 1, 2006, s.1.

170 [1987] I.R.L.R. 719, EAT.

harm suffered by the claimant (established subjectively). The fact that there are not large number of previous complaints about the treatment may be caused by the claimant's fear of losing her job, and this factor is not therefore a conclusive guide to the degree of detriment the victim had suffered or the extent of injury to her feelings.[171]

In the context of a harassment case, the receipt of sexually explicit emails of a few a week over a twenty one month period has been held to be sex discrimination which attracted damages in the amount of £7,500 for injury to feelings.[172] In this case, the tribunal cited the following factors to justify treating this case as a middle rather than lower band case under the *Vento* scale: the age and religious background of the complainant; the nature of the emails; the length of time and regularity of exposure to emails; the effect on the working environment; and the failure of the senior partner to address what was a senior complaint. Moreover, a tribunal has held that comments that no employer should take on women of child bearing age that were made to an employee who had just returned from maternity leave went beyond free speech, and gave rise to an award for injury to feelings of £7,500.[173] A similar award of £7,500 was made for injury to feelings where a man's complaint of harassment was not dealt with after a lengthy period of harassment.[174] Aggravating features such a breach of trust by a senior manager can push up the awards in the middle/higher band. For example, in one case the sexual harassment of a younger woman by an older man who was a director of the company for a lengthy period, and where there was no recourse to grievance procedure, led to an award for injury to feelings of £8,000.[175]

A number of decisions in pregnancy discrimination cases suggest that conduct that is sex discrimination, that is carried out during the period of the complainant's pregnancy, can in the appropriate context give rise to awards for injurty to feelings. For example, one case where a complainant suffered sex discriminatory redundancy in the later stages of her pregnancy which caused her stress led to an award of damages in the middle band of the *Vento* scale of £6,000 for injury to feelings.[176] Indirect discrimination, which is not justified and arises from a failure to accommodate a complainant's childcare responsibilities, has led to an increase in the award of injury to feelings from £5,000 to £7,000 for injury to feelings (the tribunal cited the failure to follow statutory

[171] *Wileman v Minilec Engineering Ltd* [1988] I.R.L.R. 144, EAT.

[172] *Hawkins v McClure Naismith*, March 8, 2005; Case No.2203986/04. Cited in Nicola Dandrige in (2006) *Discrimination Compensation Guide*, published by IRS on June 1, 2006, s.1.

[173] *Flanagan v Philip A Roberts*, December 20, 2005; Case No.2201180/05. Cited in Nicola Dandrige in (2006) *Discrimination Compensation Guide*, published by IRS on June 1, 2006, s.1.

[174] *(1) Rance (2) Jennings v (1) NCH (2) Andrew Tasker*, March 23, 2005; Case Nos 3301043/04; 3301076/04; 3301960/04. Cited in Nicola Dandrige in (2006) *Discrimination Compensation Guide*, published by IRS on June 1, 2006, s.1.

[175] *Richardson v (1) The Restoration Packaging Company Ltd (2) Alan Wood*, April 21, 2005; case no.2500377/05. Cited in Nicola Dandrige in (2006) *Discrimination Compensation Guide*, published by IRS on June 1, 2006, s.1.

[176] *Pooni v Lloyds Pharmacy*, January 13, 2005; Case No.1303458/04. Cited in Nicola Dandrige in (2006) *Discrimination Compensation Guide*, published by IRS on June 1, 2006, s.1.

grievance procedure as a reason for the increase in the award).[177] There are a number of cases which confirm that a failure to follow procedures will justify a higher award for injury to feelings in these types of cases.[178] Cases in the higher band of the *Vento* scale are likely to be those where the sex discrimination is likely to be serious and consistent. For example, in one case of pregnancy discrimination and failure to consider flexible working arrangements there was "serious and persistent" discrimination during pregnancy which led to an award of £10,000 for injury to feelings.[179]

(ii) *Disability Discrimination*

In disability discrimination cases, with awards for injury to feelings in race and sex discrimination cases, one off and less serious incidents will lead to modest awards that fall at the lower end of the *Vento* scale. For example, where there was a failure to properly apply the employers policy which led to disciplinary action for absence, the tribunal found that the quick rectification of the error meant that the award was modest sum of £500.[180]

It is worth noticing, however, that, in disability discrimination cases, a one off event of discrimination can sometimes give rise to awards in the middle and top bands of the *Vento* scale where it has a serious impact on the claimant. For example, in the case of a claimant who suffered from a bipolar affective disorder which was fully known to the employer, there was a one off discriminatory act where the employer did not make an adjustment, but insisted instead on a "robust" return to work. Although, the tribunal recognised that in general a one off act would not lead to an award in the top end of the *Vento* scale, in this case the tribunal awarded £20,000 for injury to feelings. They cited the fact that the employer had full knowledge of the disability, and also the fact that the discriminatory act had led to a catastrophic damage to the claimant.[181]

Awards in the middle range of disability discrimination are in the region of £10,000 to £15,000. In a case where the employer refused to allow a disabled employee to return to work, which caused depression and loss of confidence

[177] *Giles v Geach and Jones t/a Cornelia Care Homes*, August 8, 2005; Case No.3100720/05. Cited in Nicola Dandrige in (2006) *Discrimination Compensation Guide*, published by IRS on June 1, 2006, s.1.

[178] *Farn v Lightning Freight Services*, October 26, 2005; Case No.2501256/05; *Newing v Toni & Guy (Andover) Ltd*, October 5, 2005; Case No.3100441/05; *Sutton v The Ranch Ltd*, December 1, 2005; Case No.100497/05. Cited in Nicola Dandrige in (2006) *Discrimination Compensation Guide*, published by IRS on June 1, 2006, s.1.

[179] *Rust v Dr Navin Shankar*, August 15, 2005; Case No.1200083/05. Cited in Nicola Dandrige in (2006) *Discrimination Compensation Guide*, published by IRS on June 1, 2006, s.1.

[180] *George v Bristol* CC, March 31, 2005; Case No.1402065/04.

[181] *Reverend Irvine v Gloucestershire Hospitals NHS Trust*, November 21, 2005; Case No.1401503/04.

the tribunal awarded £12,000 for injury to feelings which it said was in the middle range of the *Vento* scale.[182]

Moreover, as with sex discrimination cases, there is the possibility of awards of injury to feelings where there is indirect discrimination and a failure to accommodate. In one disability discrimination case, an employer's failure to make adjustments led to such an award, but the amount was reduced to reflect the lack of malice of the employer and the recalictrance of the claimant.[183] Where there is a serious and ongoing failure to take steps which are practicable over a longer period of time, there may be a much larger award for injury to feelings. For example, in a recent case, the tribunal has awarded £10,000 for injury to feelings where it found that adjustment was practical and would have allowed the claimant to continue work. It cited the following factors as relevant for the higher award: the steps were practical without much financial costs; the claiminant's disability caused him great difficulty in performing his duties but he continued despite the agonising pain; the attitude of the manager was obstructive therefore the claimant had a profound sense of injustice at the position that he found himself in and said he had never "been so low".[184] Where the failure to make an adjustment is accompanied by long service the award for injury to feelings has in one case been as high as £12,500.[185]

(iii) *Religious discrimination*

In the case of a Jewish employee who claimed indirect discrimination because of the employer's refusal to allow a Saturday holiday for Yom Kippur, the tribunal made an award for injury to feelings of £500, but said that this was on the lower scale because the claimant had acted irresponsibly in not booking his holiday in good time.[186] A higher award was made where the employer was told at the interview that the claimant was a practicing Christian who needed to attend Church on a Sunday. Despite this, the employer imposed a permenant rota for Sunday working on the claimant that made it impossible for her to attend the only church service that she could attend. It was found that there was constructive dismissal and indirect discrimination under the Employment Equality (Religion and Belief) Regulations 2003. An award of £4,000 was made. This high sum was justified because there had been an abuse of trust by the

[182] *Chalkley v TNT UK Ltd*, February 25, 2005; Case Nos 1200526/04 and 1201376/04. Cited in Nicola Dandrige in (2006) *Discrimination Compensation Guide*, published by IRS on June 1, 2006, s.1.

[183] *Hay v Surrey* CC, October 13, 2005; Case No.2304467/04. Cited in Nicola Dandrige in (2006) Discrimination Compensation Guide, published by IRS on June 1, 2006, s.1.

[184] *Godfrey v Royal Mail Group* Plc, July 18, 2005; Case No.3103936/04. Cited in Nicola Dandrige in (2006) *Discrimination Compensation Guide*, published by IRS on June 1, 2006, s.1.

[185] *Dicks v Smiths Aerospace Ltd*, April 20, 2005; Case No.1402034/04. Cited in Nicola Dandrige in (2006) *Discrimination Compensation Guide*, published by IRS on June 1, 2006, s.1.

[186] *Fugler v MacMillan, London Hairstudios Ltd*, July 20, 2005; Case No.2205090/04.

employer who had knowledge of the employee's religious needs at the interview but still imposed a Sunday rota.[187]

The Employment Equality (Religion and Belief) Regulations 2003 protect both religious belief and non-belief. A case which involved a non-Christian working in an organisation with a religious ethos confirms that direct discrimination against a non-Christian can also give rise to damages for injury to feelings. The claimant had a philosphical commitment to being a non-Christian which he discussed openly at his appointment and once he started the job. The evidence suggested that he did his job as a learning skills adviser with competence. Despite this, he was not provided with the level of support and respect that he would have received if he was a Christian which was direct religious discrimination. The tribunal awarded £5,000 for injury to feelings (no detailed reasons were provided for the decision).[188]

(iv) *Sexual Orientation Discrimination*

The statutory regulation of sexual orientation on the grounds of sexual orientation in employment and training was introduced by the Employment Equality (Sexual Orientation) Regulations 2003. Since then, there have been cases where there have been awards for injury to feelings for sexual orientation discrimination. In one case, a blank refusal to interview a gay man who was in a same sex partnership because the employer was looking for a "male—female couple" was held to be sexual orientation discrimination. The tribunal made an award for injury to feelings in the low band of £3,500 because there was no evidence of serious trauma this was nevertheless an example of "blatant" and "high handed" discrimination. The tribunal took into account the fact that the complainant had been gay for nearly twenty years and that this was the first time he had come across such a clear case of discrimination.[189] In another case, there was an incident of verbal abuse where the complainant heard his general manager refer to him in abusive homophobic terms. After this time the complainant felt that the manager's treatment towards him was coloured by homophobia. The complainant's resignation was treated as constructive unfair dismissal and direct discrimination and harassment on the grounds of sexual orientation under the Employment Equality (Sexual Orientation) Regulations 2003. The tribunal found that this was a one off comment but that it was "exceptionally offensive". Therefore, they awarded an amount of £4,000 for injury to feelings.[190] In a recent case, a significant sum of £39, 268 was awarded for sexual orientation dismissal, which included an

[187] *Williams-Drabble v Pathway Care Solutions Ltd*, January 11, 2005; Case No.2601718/04

[188] *Nicholson v The Aspire Trust*, July 19, 2005; Case No.2601009/04.

[189] *Hubble v Brian Brooks*, July 26, 2005; Case No.1600381/05.

[190] *Whitehead v Brighton Palace Pier*, May 5, 2005; Case No.3102595/04. Cited in Nicola Dandrige in (2006) *Discrimination Compensation Guide*, published by IRS on June 1, 2006, s.1.

award of £2,000 for injury to feelings suggesting a willingness by tribunals to make such awards in cases of sexual orientation discrimination.[191]

(v) *Intersectional Discrimination*

In Chapter 9 the theoretical and legal issues relating to multiple and intersectional discrimination were discussed. The increase in the number of prohibited grounds of discrimination means that this type of "multiple" or "intersectional" discrimination case is likely to increase. In the context of remedies and enforcement, there are examples of awards for injury to feelings which take into account combined discrimination claims.

One common form of overlap is experienced by minority women who can face discrimination on the grounds of both race and sex. In one recent case the respondent made offensive comments addressed to the Argentinian complainant about "escorts and prostitutes", and also her South American origins, and finally fired her using offensive language within six months of the start of her job. The tribunal found that there was injury to feelings on the grounds of race as well as sex. They calculated and compensated for each ground of discrimination separately. The unanimous agreement was for the award of a total sum of £11,000 for injury to feelings, with the majority considering that this divided into £4,000 for race and £7,000 for sex discrimination.[192] In a more serious case, an Asian woman who was hired as a finance officer was subjected to humiliating treatment by a senior manager who asked her to cook his food and impugned her honesty. The complainant suffered from a serious nervous breakdown. The tribunal held that this fell within the borderline between the middle and upper band of the *Vento* scale and awarded her £15,000 for injury to feelings (as well as £7,500 for aggravated damages and £10,000 for personal injury).[193]

In cases of a combination of race and disability discrimination, the awards have also fallen in the middle to high range of the *Vento* scale. For example, in a case involving an Asian woman, the tribunal found that the manager was inclined to treat the Asian staff less favourably. They also found that the manager had not taken reasonable steps to accommodate her need for sick leave, which constituted disability discrimination. The tribunal made a joint award of £10,000 for injury to feelings.[194]

191 *X v Y* [2006] ET/2201308/06, (Case No.2201308/06 of October 6, 2006), reported in (2007) 165 EOR, published by IRS on June 1, 2007.

192 *Yeomans v Dymore-Brown t/a Walkabout*, November 30, 2005. Cited in Nicola Dandrige in (2006) *Discrimination Compensation Guide*, published by IRS on June 1, 2006, s.1. no.2303136/05. Cited in Nicola Dandrige in (2006) Discrimination Compensation Guide, published by IRS on June 1, 2006, s.1.

193 *Ali v (1) North East Centre for Diversity and Racial Equality (2) Jamiel Bux*, January 12, 2005; Case No.2504529/03. Cited in Nicola Dandrige in (2006) Discrimination Compensation Guide, published by IRS on June 1, 2006, s.1.

194 *Kanadia v (1) Royal Bank of Scotland Group Plc* (2) Styles, January 21, 2005; Case Nos 3300003/03 and 3302534/03. Cited in Nicola Dandrige in (2006) *Discrimination Compensation Guide*, published by IRS on June 1, 2006, s.1.

In another case where there was an overlap between the claimant's race (Pakistani) and religion (Muslim). He claimed that he had been discriminated against on the grounds of both race and religion by the respondent company whose directors were Indian Hindus. The claimant cited a range of acts as evidence of discrimination: being asked to pray outside the office; a reduction in his lunch break; and derogatory comments about Pakistan's political leaders. The tribunal found that there was no satisfactory explanation for the complainant's dismissal, and that the respondent employer's did not make sufficient allowance for the claimant's religion. Moreover, the tribunal found that although this was a single event it had a serious impact on the claimant's confidence up till the time of the hearing. Therefore, the tribunal awarded £7,500 for injury to feelings.[195] In a recent case where there was both sex and sexual orientation discrimination, because the female complainant was replaced by a gay man which caused her to suffer anxiety and sleepless nights, the tribunal awarded £3,000 to cover both grounds of discrimination.[196]

6. Exemplary damages

Exemplary damages are designed to punish the wrongdoer rather than to compensate the claimant for loss suffered as a result of the wrong. There was previously some authority that exemplary damages could not be awarded in discrimination case.[197] However, the House of Lords decision in *Kuddus v Chief Constable of Leicestershire Constabulary*,[198] although not a discrimination case itself, has now opened up the possibility of exemplary damages being awarded in appropriate discrimination cases. Moreover, the EAT in *Virgo Fidelis Senior School v Boyle*,[199] has stated there is no reason in principle why exemplary damages should not be awarded in discrimination cases if the conditions in *Rookes v Barnard* are met, i.e. that there is oppressive, arbitrary or unconstitutional action by the servants of the government; or the respondent's conduct is calculated by him to make a profit for himself. Awards of exemplary damages in discrimination cases are likely to be very rare. It is more likely that tribunals will, and are (given the larger volume of awards), using aggravated damages as a way of compensating victims for especially serious acts of discrimination.

[195] *Shah v Harish Finance Ltd*, July 19, 2005; Case No.3302110/04. Cited in Nicola Dandrige in (2006) Discrimination Compensation Guide, published by IRS on June 1, 2006, s.1.

[196] *Hegarty v The Edge (Soho) Ltd*, 28 June 2005; case no.2200027/05. Cited in Nicola Dandrige in (2006) *Discrimination Compensation Guide*, published by IRS on June 1, 2006, s.1.

[197] *Deane v London Borough of Ealing* [1993] I.R.L.R. 209, EAT.

[198] *Kuddus v Chief Constable of Leicestershire Constabulary* [2001] (3 All E.R. 193).

[199] [2004] IRLR 268

7. Aggravated Damages

As the extracts from the *Vento* case above confirm, it is possible to claim aggravated damages in appropriate discrimination law cases where the defendant has behaved in an arbitrary or malicicious or insulting manner.[200] Claims for aggravated damages in tort are awarded in certain exceptional circumstances where the damages are general. They have typically been awarded in torts such as defamation, false imprisonment, malicious prosecution. Factors relating to the defendant's state of mind and conduct are relevant in the calculation, e.g. his motive and intent; his conduct; and high-handed, malicious or oppressive behaviour. Courts will also take into account the way in which the behaviour of the defendant may have caused an injury to the dignity of the complainant. Aggravated damages are compensatory in nature as they seek to make up for the extra harm that has been suffered by the complainant. However, the imprecision of the calculation of this type of damage, and the fact that in discrimination cases the conduct of the employee is often the main aggravating feature, makes it difficult to identify whether the court is making an award for aggravated damage (compensatory damages) or seeking to punish or deter the discriminator (exemplary damages).[201]

Early case also confirs that tribunals did make awards of aggravated damages. In *Scott v Commisioner of Inland Revenue*,[202] the Court of Appeal indicated that aggravated damages reflect the fact that the injury is inflicted by the conduct of proceedings in a high-handed, malicious or oppressive way. Therefore, aggravated damages should not be aggregated with or treated as part of the general award of injury to feelings. There needs to be causal connection between the conduct or motive that is being claimed, is the aggravating feature and the damage that is suffered by the claimant. Therefore, there needs to be some knowledge or suspicion of the conduct or motive is required to support the claim for aggravated damages.[203]

The type of conduct that is "high-handed, malicious or oppressive" includes the manner in which the defence of proceedings are conducted[204]. For example, a failure to fill in a quetionnaire which was required to conduct the proceedings could in the appropriate context be the basis of a claim for aggravated damages.[205] As the examples below illustrate, the tribunals will often take procedural defects such as a persistent failure to treat the claim properly or a lack of consultation as a basis for making an award for aggravated damages.

200 *Alexander v The Home Office* [1988] I.R.L.R. 190 CA. See also *(1) Armitage, (2) Marsden and (3) HM Prison Service v Johnson* [1997] I.R.L.R. 162, EAT. Cited in Nicola Dandrige, *Op. cit.*

201 Mark Lunney and Ken Oliphant, *Tort Law: Text and Materials*, 2nd ed. (Oxford: Oxford University Press, 2003), at Ch.15.

202 *Scott v Commissioners of Inland Revenue* [2004] I.R.L.R. 713, CA.

203 *Ministry of Defence v Meredith* [1995] I.R.L.R. 539, EAT.

204 *Zaiwalla & Co v Walia* [2002] I.R.L.R. 697, EAT.

205 *City of Bradford Metropolitan Council v Arora* [1989] I.R.L.R. 442, EA, Nicola Dandrige in (2006) *Discrimination Compensation Guide*, published by IRS on June 1, 2006, s.1.

Summarised below is a list of the types of conduct that have given rise to aggravated damages:

- Failure to investigate allegation of race discrimination and dismissal after the claimant alleged discriminatory conduct by a fellow employee (£1,000 aggravated damages).[206]
- Discriminatory appraisal that put a claimant's career in jeopardy combined with the respondent deliberately and falsely accusing the claimant of racism (£2,000 aggravated damages).[207]
- High-handed, dismissive manner and a lack of meaningful consultation (£3,000 aggravated damages).[208]
- Reasons for rejection could not be supported—maintained throughout the liability hearing.
- Genuine concerns dealt with in a high-handed manner and without proper investigation (£3,000 aggravated damages).[209]
- Misleading reference which was particularly bad and reprehensible conduct that led to loss of employment and a decline in the health of the claimant (£5,000 aggravated damages).[210]
- Delays that were not justified in conducting the case which led to the need to reconvene the hearing, and a high-handed manner.[211]
- In *British Telecommunications Plc v Reid*, aggravated damages were awarded where the complainant was forced to undergo an unjustified disciplinary investigation of his own conduct which exacerbated the injury to feelings arising from the unlawful discrimination. The CA also confirmed that although there is no principle that the employer cannot promote an employee who was facing disciplinary proceedings about an allegation of discrimination, it was possible that taken along with other factors this could be a material factor in demonstrating the high-handedness of the employer.[212]

Aggravated damages have also been awarded in cases involving disability

[206] *Oyewole v Aktrion Group Ltd*, May 4, 2005; Case No.3301858/, Nicola Dandrige in (2006) *Discrimination Compensation Guide*, published by IRS on June 1 2006, s.1.

[207] *Riaz v City of London Police*, September 9, 2005; Case No.2201494/, Nicola Dandrige in (2006) *Discrimination Compensation Guide*, published by IRS on June 1, 2006, s.1.

[208] *Laing v Copal Castings Ltd*, February 8, 2005; Case No.1303701/02, Nicola Dandrige in (2006) *Discrimination Compensation Guide*, published by IRS on June 1, 2006, s.1.

[209] *Gordon v Telewest Communications Plc*, May 13, 2005; Case No.1302692/04, Nicola Dandrige in (2006) *Discrimination Compensation Guide*, published by IRS on June 1, 2006, s.1.

[210] *Melloy v HM Prison Service*, October 7, 2005; Case No.1400772/04, Nicola Dandrige in (2006) *Discrimination Compensation Guide*, published by IRS on June 1, 2006, s.1.

[211] *Harkness v Topcoat Construction*, March 15, 2005; Case No.3201599/03, Nicola Dandrige in (2006) *Discrimination Compensation Guide*, published by IRS on June 1, 2006, s.1.

[212] *British Telecommuncations Plc v Reid* [2004] I.R.L.R. 327, CA.

discrimination. For example, in *Chalkley v TNT UK Ltd*[213] which was a case of disability discrimination the respondent had repeatedly ignored the claimant's request for medical examination, risk assessment, and had belittled the claimant's injury. The tribunal found that the respondent had ignored the code of practice which required a flexible approach. The tribunal took into account the respondent's offered reinstatement and apology although this was said to be "too little, too late". The tribunal awarded £3,000 for aggravated damages in addition to the award of £12,000 for injury to feelings. Failure to make reasonable adjustments under the DDA, which is caused by personal animosity, has led to an award of £5,000 for aggravated damages.[214]

Harassment cases often involve the type of fact situations that justify additional awards for aggravated damages. Often, the serious nature of the conduct and harm in these cases are addressed in the award of injury to feelings (discussed above). However, in some serious cases of harassment separate awards have been made for aggravated damages. In one case, the sexual harassment of a younger woman attracted an additional sum of £2,000 for aggravated damages because her vulnerability was taken into account.[215] In another case, the conduct of the hearing by the respondents disseminated untrue allegations about the complainant in the public.

The tribunal concluded that the content of the press reports was almost exclusively due to the way the respondents conducted their defence, which had an obvious and hurtful effect on the claimant. It made an award for aggravated damages of £7,500. It said it could easily have made a higher award but tempered the amount by taking into account the "youth and naivety" of some of the witnesses.[216]

8. Other procedural issues in individual damages claims

(i) *Awards against individual respondent*

In discrimination law cases where there is more than one respondent who can be held liable, the tribunal will use principles of apportionment to apportion liability between them. The main respondent will usually be the employer who will be liable on the basis of vicarious liability for the act of his employee. In addition, there may also be an award of damages against individuals who carry out the discriminatory act, although whether or not it is worth bringing an action in damages against the individual will depend on whether they are able to pay financial damages. In most cases, the tribunal will make a separate award against each respondent. However, the tribunal may if it is necessary to

213 *Chalkley v TNT UK Ltd*, February 25, 2005; Case Nos 1200526/04 and 1201376/04,

214 *Godfrey v Royal Mail Group Plc*, July 18, 2005; Case No.3103936/04, Nicola Dandrige in (2006) *Discrimination Compensation Guide*, published by IRS on June 1, 2006, s.1.

215 *Miss X v Mr Y and ITCW Ltd*, April 5, 2005; Case No.1600142/05. Cited in Nicola Dandrige in (2006) *Discrimination Compensation Guide*, published by IRS on June 1, 2006, s.1.

216 *Lodge Hotel (2) Mr N Crowe*, April 6, 2005; Case No.1501774/04. *Cited in* Nicola Dandrige in (2006) Discrimination Compensation Guide, published by IRS on June 1, 2006, s.1.

do so make a joint and several award of compensation against the joint respondents (A and B). In this way, the amount can be enforced by the complainant either (a) against one respondent only; or (b) part of the amount against respondent A and another part against respondent B.[217] In one recent case, the Court of Appeal upheld a joint and several award of £25,000 for injury to feelings against the director (the claimant's line manager) and majority shareholder (representing the company employing the claimant).[218]

(ii) *Taxation of awards and interest*

Tribunals will consider whether part or all of an award is likely to be taxable, and they should ensure that awards are calculated on a net basis after the reduction of tax. However, the EAT has held that awards for injury to feelings are not taxable.[219]

Interest is awarded on discrimination awards for: past financial loss; injury to feelings; Equal Pay Act awards for arrears of remuneration or damages under the Employment Tribunals (Interest on Awards in Discrimination Cases) Regulations 1996. In the case of injury to feelings, the EAT has held that interest should be calculated from the date of the discriminatory act.[220] The Employment Tribunals (Interest on Awards in Discrimination Cases) Regulations 1996 contain the guide on the award to interest in discrimination cases. These preserve the right of the employment tribunal to award interest for a different or a longer period than that specified in exceptional cases, and the determination of what is an exceptional case is a matter for the employment tribunal. Interest is not awarded on future loss. The Court of Appeal has held that where tax and national insurance contributions are to be deducted from an award, interest should be calculated on the net sum after deductions, rather than on the gross sum.[221]

(iii) *Problems with Individual Litigation and the Enforcement of Awards*

Discrimination cases can be litigated in either the Employment Tribunals (ET) or County Courts. In ET's the usual rules relating to legal aid (legal assistance) do not apply. In Scotland there is access to legal aid for employment discrimination cases, and there is also some limited legal aid assistance in England and Wales at the appellate level or via the Green Form scheme which allows limited access to preliminary advice in some cases. Moreover, the fact that ET's do not as a general rule award costs. Legal aid (legal assistance) is more widely avaible for discrimination law cases in the County Courts but the

217 *(1) Peter Way (2) Intro Cate Chemicals Ltd v Crouch* [2005] I.R.L.R. 603 EAT.
218 *Miles v Gilbank* [2006] EWCA Civ 543.
219 *Ministry of Defence v Cannock* [1994] I.R.L.R. 509, EAT.
220 *Derby Specialist Fabrication Ltd v Burton* [2001] I.R.L.R. 69, EAT.
221 *Bentwood Bros (Manchester) Ltd v Shepherd* [2003] I.R.L.R. 364, CA. Cited in Nicola Dandrige in (2006) *Discrimination Compensation Guide*, published by IRS on June 1, 2006, s.1.

usual rules of "means testing" and the general rule of an award of costs which requires the loser of the case to pay costs acts as a disincentive to litigation. Moreover, in those cases where there is an award of damages to the applicant, there is increasing concern that there is insufficient leverage to make employers pay the award of damages that has been awarded, as the following research the Citizen's Advice Bureau makes clear.

"Employers failing to pay tribunal awards"
2004 (135) Equal Opportunities Review

"Evidence from the network of Citizens Advice Bureaux (CAB) in England and Wales suggests that non-payment of employment tribunal awards is widespread and could be on the increase*.

Many awards are not paid simply because employment tribunals have no power to enforce them, says Citizens Advice.

As a result, where an employer fails to pay a tribunal award, the claimant must seek enforcement through the civil courts. Apart from being dauntingly legalistic, this process is both costly and time-consuming.

In the majority of cases of non-payment reported by the CAB, the tribunal award is relatively small. This reflects the fact that tribunal awards are calculated according to the claimant's pay and most of those seeking help with an employment problem from the CAB are low-paid.

Faced with the prospect of having to pay, but with no guarantee that they will then receive their award, many claimants feel they cannot take any further action.

The report also highlights the problem with enforcing Acas-conciliated settlements, as there is confusion as to which civil court is the correct forum for the attempted enforcement of such settlements. Again, attempted enforcement involves expenditure of time and money by the claimant, with no guarantee of success.

Citizens Advice recommends that the Department of Constitutional Affairs and the Department of Trade and Industry should undertake an urgent joint review of the enforcement of employment tribunal awards. The charity believes that provision for a mechanism to better enforce awards should be included in the Courts and Tribunals Bill being brought forward next year. It suggests that the state should pay the award to the claimant and then itself pursue the employer.

A spokesperson for the charity said: "All too often a favourable tribunal ruling proves to be a meaningless victory. There are just too many legal and financial obstacles to the enforcement of awards. The government must act to improve the system and make sure that successful claimants are not denied justice."

**Empty justice: the non-payment of employment tribunal awards, for details www.nacab.org.uk.*

These disincentives and risks to individual litigation of discrimination law cases make it especially important for the individual commissions (now the CEHR after September) to use their power to provide financial and practical assistance for individual litigants. Previously the CRE, EOC and DRC had the power to provide financial and practical assistance to individual litigants.

These powers have now been transferred to the CEHR. These issues are discussed in the next chapter which considers collective remedies.

VIII. Conclusion

This chapter has addressed the ninth question of discrimination law that we identified as "what legal remedies are available, and who may seek them?" in the context of individual remedies for discrimination. An effective system of remedies, enforcement and access to justice is a pre-condition to realising the goals of discrimination law. The present system of remedies, especially in the context of discrimination law, often fails to meet this criteria. The Discrimination Law Review (DLR) has proposed reform of the system of individual remedies in domestic discrimination law.[222] It identifies the 'protection of individuals from unlawful discrimination' as one of the two central goals of discrimination law.[223] In non-employment related cases, the DLR recommends promoting early dispute resolution through ADR; and improving accessibility, efficiency and effectiveness of procedures in discrimination law cases (DLR, para.7.2). In employment related cases, the DLR adopts the analysis of the DTI consultation paper *Resolving Disputes in the Workplace*.[224] This approach shows a strong preference for ADR: e.g. encouraging good practice in resolving disputes for those who do not resort to tribunals; a new telephone and internet advice service; and simplification and improvements in procedure and case management in tribunals (DLR, para.7.11). It is true that disputes should be resolved early where possible and that ADR has an important role in discrimination law. However, it is also true that voluntary ADR is not always a perfect or adequate substitute for a system of individual legal remedies. The DLR promotes ADR with little concern that individuals who are from disadvantaged social groups will often lack the power to negotiate fair settlements, and this may consequently result in the "subversion" of their rights 'through conciliation'[225] Discrimination cases are often complex; and litigants from disadvantaged social groups lack the personal skills and financial resources to manage litigation without legal representation or additional support from agencies or trade unions. The DLR contains no concrete proposals for improving legal aid and the quality of legal representation where individuals choose not to use ADR.

Although the DLR includes some suggestions for improving procedures

222 *Discrimination Law Review. A Framework for Fairness: Proposals for a Single Equality Act for Great Britain.* (Department of Communities and Local Government: London, 2007)

223 The DLR states that the two central goals for discrimination law that it identifies—to "protect individuals from discrimination" and "tackle disadvantage" — "reflect basic values of our society" (DLR, pp.60–62).

224 *Resolving Disputes in the Workplace.* (Department for Trade and Industry: London, 2007).

225 Hugh Collins, *Justice in Dismissal*, Oxford: Clarendon Press, 1992, at Ch.4.

and case management, it contains no systematic reforms for transforming or improving the nature of remedies in discrimination law. There are no clear proposals, for example, to increase and extend the use re-instatement, re-engagement and recommendations in appropriate cases, thereby ensuring that domestic discrimination law complies with the EU requirement that legal sanctions should be "effective, persuasive and dissuasive".[226] The failure to strengthen the system of individual remedies for discrimination makes it essential to strengthen collective forms of enforcement. It also makes it especially important to consider the question of "how far should we look outside the law for solutions?"—the tenth question of discrimination law that we identified—in the form of extra-legal measures and supply side measures. We consider these issues relating to collective enforcement and social policy in the next chapter.

[226] Hepple et al, *Report of the Independent Review of the Enforcement of UK Anti-Discrimination Law*, (Hart Publishing: Oxford, 2000) Recommendations 50–53.

17

COLLECTIVE REMEDIES AND EXTRA LEGAL STRATEGIES

I. Introduction

Earlier chapters have emphasised the structural form of discrimination against some social groups. One consequence of the persistent structural nature of discrimination is that the lack of social, political and economic power of individuals from these groups makes it difficult for them to access individual remedies under existing discrimination law structures. The adversarial and adjucative nature of individual remedies for discrimination is not suited to address the collective and structural aspects of inequality: this has been identified as the most persistent problem that faces discrimination law.[1] As the previous chapter confirms, there are a number of obstacles in the way of individual litigants: most specifically, the lack of legal aid in Employment Tribunals and the failure to pay awards by employers. Problems with collecting evidence and the complexity of procedures makes this process especially difficult for individual litigants who are not assisted by legal aid. In this chapter we consider some of the ways in which individual remedies can be supplemented. We start by discussing the role of the equality commissions in supporting individual litigants and in developing a strategic role which addresses structural discrimination.

A further consequence of structural discrimination is that individual remedies are not able to restructure the public and private sphere is a way that can compensate in the present for systematic patterns that are a result of past discrimination. These issues were considered in detail in the earlier chapters, especially in the discussion on indirect discrimination and positive action. One response to these structural problems has to be to introduce "fourth generation" equality laws which shift the focus away from an individual and adversarial system and towards addressing the collective nature of the problem of discrimination. "Fourth generation" equality laws include positive duties and mainstreaming which have been discussed in earlier chapters. In

[1] Richard H. Fallon, Jr., Paul C. Weiler, "Firefighters v. Stotts: Conflicting Models of Racial Justice" (1984) The Supreme Court Review, Vol.1984, pp.1–68.

Part II we continue this discussion by considering the EU and domestic law on public procurement, and the role of contract compliance and "best value" targets as techniques for using the financial power of the public sector to achieve the goals of discrimination law. These are forms of positive action measure that are also discussed in the earlier chapter, and they are discussed here as part of our analysis of the use of collective remedies. Part III sets out some of the ways in which the law itself is a limited response to the problems of discrimination and considers other non-legal strategies (e.g. supply-side investment measures that take into account some of the goals of discrimination law) as a lever to achieve change.

II. The Equality Commissions

The Commission for Racial Equality (CRE) and the Equal Opportunities Commission (EOC) were established in the mid-1970s, and the Disability Rights Commission (DRC) in 1999. Like the SDA 75 and RRA 76, they are another feature of British discrimination law which has been borrowed from the US: the original model on which the new Commissions were based was the Equal Employment Opportunity Commission, a public agency set up to perform a number of functions for the enforcement of discrimination law and policy.[2] This model has now been exported to the EU through the requirement to set up national bodies for the protection of equal treatment contained in Race Equality Directive, Art.13 which states "Members shall designate a body or bodies for the promotion of equal treatment of all persons without discrimination on the grounds of racial or ethnic origin. These agencies may form part of agencies charged at national level with the defence of human rights or the safeguard of individual rights." As well as requiring agency support at the national level, the EU has also set up an EU wide agency which is called the Fundamental Rights Agency (FRA—which continues the work of the European Union Monitoring Centre based in Vienna).[3] The FRA was established through a EU Council Regulation in 2007 which states, inter alia, that the function of the FRA is to support EU institutions and Member States "through assistance and expertise relating to fundamental rights in order to support them" in the field of fundamental rights (see Art.2); and these tasks include collecting information, setting standards and putting in place mechanisms for co-operation and dialogue between relevant stakeholders (Art.4).

[2] See Jeffrey Jowell, "The Administrative Enforcement of Laws Against Discrimination" (1965) P.L. 119.

[3] Council Regulation EC No.168/2007 of February 15, 2007 establishing a European Union Agency for Fundamental Rights, Official Journal of the European Union, O.J. L.53/1, 22.2.2007.

A. *Assistance to Individuals Provided by the Equality Commissions*

Since the establishment of the Commission for Racial Equality (CRE) and the Equal Opportunities Commission (EOC) in the mid-1970s, and the belated establishment of the Disability Rights Commission (DRC) in 1999, all three equality commissions have had the power to provide financial, legal and practical assistance to individual litigants.[4] These powers have now been transferred to the new Commission for Equality and Human Rights (CEHR) under s.28 of the Equality Act 2006. The Equality Commission for Northern Ireland (ECNI) has a similar power. This allows the commissions to select individual cases that they wish to support, whether due to their strategic importance, their facts or the contribution the cases may make to clarifying or strengthening discrimination law. The commissions in effect provide legal services for the individual litigant, absorbing the costs of the action themselves.

It was initially expected that the equality commissions would rely primarily upon their powers to launch formal investigations into the conduct of particular "named" employers and service providers.[5] Their power to support individual cases was seen as supplemental. However, the difficulties the commissions faced in using their investigation power meant that they turned increasingly from the early 1980s to supporting individual cases as their principal method of ensuring the enforcement of anti-discrimination legislation. This ability to support individual cases has allowed the commissions over the years to support many key discrimination cases. This strategy produced some notable results. In particular, the EOC's highly successful "strategic litigation" policy, which involved taking selected cases to the higher UK courts and ultimately to the European Court of Justice, and served to clarify and considerably widen the scope of UK and EU sex discrimination law as it applied to employment and occupation.[6] The CRE and DRC have adopted similar strategies, again with some success.

This policy of selecting particular individual cases for support has thus been quite successful. Also, it has been important that the commissions have provided support for some individual victims of discrimination. This has allowed some individuals to bring claims that would otherwise not have seen the light

[4] SDA 75 s.75 (see ss.53–61, 67–74 for other powers); RRA 76 s. 66 (see ss.43–52, 58–65 for other powers); Disability Rights Commission Act 1999, ss.7–8 (see ss.1–6, 9 for other powers).

[5] See the original White Paper, *Race Discrimination* (London: Department of Employment, 1975), Cmnd.6234, which anticipated that the primary method of enforcing the legislation would be through the CRE's investigative powers. See also A. Lester, "Discrimination: What Lawyers Can Learn From History" [1994] P.L. 224–237, 226–7; V. Sacks and J. Maxwell, "Unnatural Justice for Discriminators" (1984) 47 M.L.R. 334, 334–5.

[6] See C. Barnard, "A European Litigation Strategy: The Case of the Equal Opportunities Commission", in J. Shaw and G. More, *New Legal Dynamics of European Union* (Oxford: Clarendon Press, 1995). Barnard estimates that by the early 1990s, cases supported by the EOC represented about one third of all references heard by the European Court of Justice on matters relating to equal pay and equal treatment at the workplace.

of day. This is particularly so given the absence of legal aid or alternative sources of support for employment discrimination claims, which have constituted the bulk of the cases supported by the commissions.

However, the power to support individual cases is confined to cases brought under the anti-discrimination legislation. The CEHR cannot support individual cases brought under the HRA, even equality cases rooted in Art.14 ECHR, or cases based upon any other cause of action apart from anti-discrimination legislation.[7] The government's rationale for the distinction between HRA and anti-discrimination legislation cases is that legal aid is available for meritorious human rights claims, unlike for most discrimination cases. The CEHR may nevertheless be able to support cases that combine both discrimination and human rights claims, and some claims relating to disability that fall outside the scope of the disability discrimination legislation.[8] However, the difference between the CEHR's powers in respect of discrimination and human rights cases may nevertheless give rise to confusing and potentially unworkable distinctions. Also, the equality commissions cannot bring a case in their own name on behalf of victims of discrimination, unlike the Health and Safety Executive and other regulatory agencies.[9] However, the new commission can bring judicial proceedings under the HRA against public authorities without having to be a "victim" of a breach of the convention, as is normal.

The budget of the commissions has remained limited and the volume of discrimination cases remains high, support for individual cases inevitably involves selecting a tiny minority of "strategic" cases from a vast array of individual claims. In addition, strategic litigation can be an uncertain, often expensive and sometimes counter-productive business. Cases may often generate considerable costs, often stretching the budgets of the commissions to breaking point.[10] Therefore, the ability of the equality commissions to assist individual cases is ultimately limited.

Therefore in recent years, the commissions have tended to place more

[7] The Scottish Human Rights Commission is similarly barred from supporting individual human rights actions. The DRC had a reserved power under s.7(1)(b) of the Disability Rights Commission Act 1999 to assist individuals in cases based on the HRA, but this was never brought into effect by the necessary Ministerial order.

[8] s.28 of the Act provides for a ministerial power to establish via secondary legislation when the Commission can continue to support such cases even when the anti-discrimination element has fallen away. A similar ministerial power can also be triggered to permit the Commission to support a wider range of cases if they relate to disability issues, which may permit the CEHR to support litigation on issues of independent living and disability services provision. These provisions mark an improvement on the strongly criticised proposals contained in the Equality Bill when it first reached Parliament, which would have prevented the CEHR being able to continue to support any ongoing case where the anti-discrimination element had fallen away.

[9] The US, Belgian, Canadian, New Zealand and Australian equality bodies can all bring litigation in their own name: see C. O'Cinneide, "The Commission For Equality And Human Rights: A New Institution For New And Uncertain Times" 36(2) I.L.J. 141–162, 157.

[10] The legal budget of the Northern Irish Equality Commission became severely overstretched in 2000–1, requiring substantial cutbacks: see ECNI, *Annual Report 2002–03* (Belfast: ECNI, 2004), pp.20–21.

emphasis on alternative enforcement and promotion strategies. For example, the commissions have tried to influence the development of case-law through interventions before courts in ongoing litigation, and also try to make greater use of promotional strategies to try to influence public debate. The use of these strategies reflects a general shift in emphasis in discrimination policy towards addressing issues of structural equality via the use of mainstreaming policies and positive duties: there is less reliance upon individual litigation to bring about social change.[11]

Data from previous years confirms that enforcement bodies have not taken up a very large number of individual cases. The CRE in the calendar year 2005 only supported three fully funded individual cases, which marks a considerable reduction from previous periods.[12] The following extract summarises the most recent data on the work of the CRE, EOC and DRC in the area of individual enforcement:

"Equality Commissions Publish Annual Reports" (2006) 156 Equal Opportunities Review

"The Commission for Racial Equality, the Equal Opportunities Commission and the Disability Rights Commission have published their annual reports.

Applications for assistance to the Commission for Racial Equality (CRE) in 2005 were up by 85% on the previous year, according to the CRE's annual report 2005*. In 2005, the commission received 1,028 applications for assistance—with many more individuals being helped by the local racial equality organisations, funded by the CRE to the tune of more than £3.3 million.

Legal work continues to lie at the heart of the CRE's mission, says the commission's report, and in 2005, 503 applicants were given full advice and assistance, while 10 were offered advice and assistance limited to conciliation. Three applicants (one black African, one black Caribbean and one white) received full CRE representation. At the end of the reporting period, two of these were awaiting a hearing, and negotiations were under way for settling the third. The commission also intervened in three legal cases, and obtained leave to intervene in another.

Almost two-thirds of all applications for assistance were from men. The ethnic group that made most applications was black people, who sought assistance in 477 instances out of a total of 1,028 (see table).

Just over half (52%) of the applications for assistance received in 2005 were related to employment. By sector, most applications (53%) came from the public sector, with the largest number (158), as in 2004, coming from the courts, police, prison and probation services.

[11] See J. Clarke and S. Speeden, *Then and Now: Change for the Better?* (London: CRE, 2001).

[12] See CRE, *Annual Report* 2005 (London: CRE, 2006), available at *http://www.cre.gov.uk/downloads/ar05_main.pdf*. In contrast, between 1977 and 1984, the CRE supported approximately one-fifth of all race discrimination claims that were referred to it (150 in total). Of course, the case-load volume was much less in that time period: by the period 1994–1998, 1,750 cases on average were being referred to the CRE, who were obliged to reduce their level of support from the earlier peak period. See J. Clarke and S. Speeden, *Then and Now: Change for the Better*, 27–28.

Equal Opportunities Commission

According to the Equal Opportunities Commission's (EOC) annual report 2005–06†, there were almost 22,000 enquiries in that year, by phone, email or letter, to the EOC's main helpline, which is down by about 7% from the previous year. During the year, the commission also used its enforcement powers actively to support and achieve its key objectives.

It supported a small number of individual cases under s.75 of the Sex Discrimination Act (SDA), the successful conclusion of which, says the report, led to significant strategic change.

The report highlights "two extremely important cases relating to the rights of pregnant women"—*Alabaster v Woolwich Building Society* (Equal value update 2006) (which closed a loophole preventing women on maternity leave from bringing pay claims) and *Fletcher & others v NHS Pensions Agency, Student Grants Unit and Secretary of State for Health* (which secured new rights for health service trainees on maternity leave).

There were "three significant test cases on the priority issue of equal pay": *Cadman v Health and Safety Executive* (Equal value update 2006) (Court of Appeal/European Court of Justice); *Derbyshire v St Helens Borough Council* (House of Lords); and *Sharp v Caledonia* (Equal value update 2006) (Court of Appeal). The EOC also completed 16 assessments of organisations that were potentially in breach of the SDA and the Equal Pay Act. Based on these assessments, the commission negotiated formal agreements with major organisations to change their policies and practices.

The commission continued its strategic enforcement work with major employers where discrimination appears to be widespread. This included the continuation of its work on the commission's two (suspended) formal investigations into sexual harassment at the Royal Mail and the Ministry of Defence respectively.

A new investigation was started into the "transformation of work", exploring how working time can be better organised to meet the needs of both employees and employers, and the first Scotland-specific "general formal investigation" was launched looking at the pay and conditions of classroom assistants. The start of the EOC's investigation into the labour market position of Pakistani, Bangladeshi and black Caribbean women, "Moving on up?", "marked an important milestone in the commission's objective to better understand why some groups of ethnic minority women succeed better in employment than others".

Disability Rights Commission

The Disability Rights Commission's (DRC) annual report 2005–06** records that the commission directly supported or intervened in 55 new legal cases, placing a particular emphasis on strategically important cases at the precedent-setting higher levels of the tribunals and courts.

The DRC helpline dealt with just under 94,000 calls and enquiries. The largest proportions of these were from disabled people and their representatives, and around one-third were from employers and service providers.

During the year, the DRC commenced major programmes of external capacity building among appropriate external bodies at local level to promote disability rights, combined with widespread transfer of expertise on disability issues. At the same time, the commission wound down its provision of in-house advice and support for individuals."

As noted above, the commissions have continued to support some important employment and services discrimination cases.[13] The EOC and DRC in particular have supported several successful and high-profile cases that have both

[13] See *Cadman v Health and Safety Executive*, Case C-17/05, [2006] I.R.L.R. 969.

generated considerable publicity and clarified the scope of the Disability Discrimination Act.[14] However, there has been a shift away from supporting individual cases, and this has attracted criticism.[15] Concern has been expressed that the reduction of support for individual cases has eroded the already limited support available for claimants in this area. There is a real risk that discrimination in the employment context may increasingly be left unchallenged, due to a lack of support for individuals brave enough to attempt to bring a claim. However, there are inevitable limits on the effectiveness of individual litigation. Alternative strategies may at times be a more effective way of accelerating progress in certain circumstances.

The new CEHR will have to ensure continuing support for important and deserving individual cases, but also use their collective enforcement tools to try to bring about change when support for individual cases will not be sufficient. It is also worth noting that Art.8a of the amended Equal Treatment Directive and Art.13 of the Race Equality Directive both require member states to establish independent enforcement bodies which can provide "independent assistance to victims of discrimination in pursuing their complaints about discrimination". It is not completely clear what providing "independent assistance" requires, but it could be argued that a failure by the CEHR to provide a certain level of support to individual complainants, or the UK government to provide the new CEHR will the required resources to play this role, could result in the UK being in violation of its obligations under EU law.[16]

B. *Formal Investigations by the Equality Commissions*

Almost from the initial introduction of discrimination law in the UK, it was recognised that individuals would often lack the ability to challenge structural problems of inequality by bringing actions themselves, either because of lack of resources, or problems with proof, or due to fear of retaliation, or other factors. In addition, experience from the US has showed that it was necessary to establish a state-supported discrimination agencies charged with both enforcing the law and promoting equality. This resulted in the establishment of the Commission for Racial Equality and the Equal Opportunities Commission in the RRA 76 and the SDA 75 respectively as discussed above. Both commissions were given powers to support individual cases, as again dis-

[14] For an analysis of the DRC's enforcement and promotion strategy, see N. O'Brien, "The GB Disability Rights Commission and Strategic Law Enforcement: Transcending the Common Law Mind", in A. Lawson and C. Gooding, *Disability Rights in Europe* (Oxford: Hart, 2005), 249–263.

[15] See the reported remarks by Ken Livingstone to the effect that the CRE is now a "vast press department", Black Information Link, *www.blink.org*, 4/9/2006.

[16] Note that there is no equivalent provision as yet in the 2000 Framework Equality Directive, meaning that this obligation on member states to ensure that an independent body provides assistance to complainants only applies to the race and gender grounds thus far.

cussed above. However, both were also given extensive powers to both promote respect for equality via research, policy activism, media campaigns and other campaigning work, and also to enforce the existing law, through not just support for individual actions but also through the use of special investigative powers conferred upon the new commissions. The commissions were also given the power to draw up codes of practice with the final approval of the relevant Secretary of State, which while not legally binding could be drawn upon by courts and tribunals.

However, as noted above, the investigative powers were intended to be the main tool that the commissions would use to enforce discrimination law. These powers enabled the commissions to investigate private and public bodies, to call evidence and summon witnesses, and to issue notices requiring compliance with the anti-discrimination legislation in certain circumstances, which could then be enforced by means of a court order if required. The intention was for the equality commissions to use these wider powers to act in the public interest by investigating and scrutinising questionable practices.[17]

The equality commissions have retained these powers, and, when established in 1999, the Disability Rights Commission was given similar powers. However, the ability of the commissions to use these special investigative powers has been severely restricted by the narrow interpretation given to their scope by the UK courts. This has discouraged the commissions from using these powers, arguably leaving a gap in the enforcement structures in UK law.

Colm O'Cinneide, "The Commission For Equality And Human Rights: A New Institution For New And Uncertain Times' 36(2) I.L.J. pp. 141–162

147–149 "Since the establishment of the CRE and EOC in the late 1970s and the belated creation of the DRC in the late 1990s, the equality commissions have attempted to strike a balance in their work between the promotion of equality of opportunity and the enforcement of anti-discrimination legislation. Their promotional work has involved campaigning, media work, education, the preparation of codes of practice and the provision of guidance, advice and assistance to public and private bodies. Their enforcement work has principally involved supporting claims brought by individual complainants, particularly in cases involving discrimination in employment, along with some use of judicial review and their power to conduct formal investigations into alleged breaches of anti-discrimination law. Both the promotional and enforcement aspects of the work of the commissions are important and need to be combined in a common strategy: the 'carrot' of promotion becomes more attractive when the 'stick' of enforcement is a real threat. However, striking the right balance between promotion and enforcement has proved difficult.

The CRE and EOC were initially expected to act primarily as regulatory and enforcement agencies. In particular, it was expected that there would be considerable reli-

[17] For a full discussions see V. Sacks and J. Maxwell, "Unnatural Justice for Discriminators" (1984) 47 M.L.R. 334.

ance upon their powers to launch formal investigations into the conduct of particular 'named' employers and service providers. This power included the ability to require the production of evidence if approved by the relevant Secretary of State, and these investigations could result in a finding that a body had committed an unlawful act of discrimination, entitling the commission to issue a 'non-discrimination notice' which could be enforced through the courts. The CRE and EOC presumed that this power permitted it to conduct investigations both when an allegation of discriminatory treatment had been made and also where there had been no allegation of unlawful discrimination. Both types of investigation were therefore initially launched with great enthusiasm, in particular by the CRE. However, the use of these 'named investigation' powers was severely constrained by the decisions of the House of Lords in *R v CRE, ex parte Hillingdon Borough Council*[18] and *In re Prestige*.[19] In *Hillingdon*, the Law Lords held that the equality commissions had to have sufficient evidence 'to raise in the minds of reasonable men . . . a suspicion that there may have been acts by the person named of . . . discrimination of the kind which it is proposed to investigate'.[20] The subsequent *Prestige* decision made it clear that a named investigation could not be launched where no allegation of unlawful discrimination existed.

These decisions were decided against a background of considerable political and judicial disquiet about the use of the investigative power against private employers in particular,[21] and they considerably limited the scope and usefulness of the named investigation power.[22] The commissions subsequently tended to err on the side of extreme caution in deciding whether to launch formal investigations, especially where private employers were concerned. Subsequent attempts by the commissions to bring judicial review actions against public authorities where equality issues were at stake had more success: the courts were prepared to recognise that the commissions had standing to bring such actions, when the issue in question came within their general fields of responsibility.[23] However, the persisting fear of legal challenges, concern about political hostility and further judicial 'reading down' of their powers continued to cast a pall over the use by the commissions of their special statutory investigative powers."

Therefore, the *Prestige* and *Hillingdon* decisions led to a restriction on the ability of enforcement agencies to launch a formal investigation without first having sufficient threshold evidence.[24] It made it more difficult to launch formal investigations into structural discrimination.[25] This has acted as a serious barrier to attaining an optimal mix of remedial responses to the problems

[18] [1982] A.C. 779.

[19] [1984] I.C.R. 473. See V. Sacks and J. Maxwell, "Unnatural Justice for Discriminators" (1984) 47 M.L.R. 334, 334–5; see also G. Appleby and E. Ellis, "Formal Investigations: The Commission for Racial Equality and the Equal Opportunities Commission as Law Enforcement Agencies" [1984] P.L. 236.

[20] [1982] A.C. 779 at 791.

[21] See the report of the House of Commons Home Affairs Committee, *Commission for Racial Equality*, HC 46 (session 1981–2), November 1981. See also the comments of Lord Denning in *Science Research Council v Nassé* [1979] Q.B. 144, who used extraordinarily intemperate language in comparing the use by the CRE of its investigative powers to "the days of the inquisition".

[22] See E. Ellis and G. Appleby, "Blackening the *Prestige* Pot? Formal Investigations and the CRE" (1984) 100 L.Q.R. 349.

[23] See e.g. *R v Secretary of State for the Home Department, Ex p. Equal Opportunities Commission v Secretary of State for Employment* [1995] 1 A.C. 1, HL.

[24] E. Ellis and G. Appleby, "Blackening the *Prestige* Pot? Formal Investigations and the CRE" (1984) 100 L.Q.R. 349, 354.

[25] See CRE Annual Report for 1988 and V. Sacks, "The Equal Opportunities Commission: Ten Years on" (1986) 49 M.L.R. 560, 581–2.

of structural discrimination.[26] As Mary Coussey argues in the passage below, formal investigations before the *Prestige* decision did uncover structural problems that informed the response of the equality commissions to entrenched discriminatory practices.

Mary Coussey, "The Effectiveness of Strategic Enforcement of the Race Relations Act 1976" In B. Hepple and E. Szyszcak (eds.) *Discrimination: The Limits of Law* (Mansell: London, 1992)

"The strategic investigations carried out by the CRE before the *Prestige* decision in 1984 were chosen with reference to the broad labour market position. It was decided to carry out a rolling programme of general enquiries into the extent of inequality in a number of representative industries located in areas of significant ethnic minority population. In this way, it would be possible to build up a range of models, demonstrating in practical terms how discrimination operates. Over a dozen such enquiries were started. By selecting large companies in industrial sectors in which ethnic minorities were concentrated, it was anticipated that the findings of the investigations would be relevant to other employers in the same industry.

These enquiries combined a strategic and inspectorial approach. However, their aims were not fulfilled because many of the early strategic investigations had to be abandoned after the *Prestige* decision. But the experience gained was the basis for many of the recommendations in the Code of Practice, as these enquiries identified most of the potentially discriminatory practices and other barriers caused by disadvantage in the labour market."

Nevertheless, despite the great usefulness of the investigation power, the impact of *Prestige* and *Hillingdon* seems to have deterred the equality commissions from extensive use of these powers for the best part of two decades.[27] However, in recent years, the equality commissions have tentatively begun to make more use of their investigative abilities. The DRC, EOC and CRE can all conduct investigations (otherwise known as "general investigations" or "inquiries") into particular equality issues (such as pregnancy discrimination or discrimination in immigration and asylum processes) or areas of activity or "sectors" (such as policing, the insurance industry, etc.). While these inquiries may uncover evidence of discriminatory acts, they are not initially directed

[26] See C. McCrudden, "The Commission for Racial Equality: Formal Investigations in the Shadow of Judicial Review" in P. Craig and C. McCrudden, *Regulation and Public Law* (London: Weidenfield & Nicolson, 1987) 227–266: See also M. Munroe, "The *Prestige* Case: Putting the Lid on the Commission for Racial Equality" (1985) Anglo-American L.Rev. 187.

[27] The EOC has conducted very few formal "named" investigations, and none between 1993 and 2003. See V. Sacks, "The Equal Opportunities Commission—Ten Years On" (1986) 49 M.L.R. 560, 581–85. Almost half of the formal investigations ever conducted by the CRE predated the *Hillingdon* and *Prestige* decisions: see C. McCrudden, D. Smith and C. Brown, *Racial Justice at Work* (London: Policy Studies Institute, 1991), ch.3, s.4 of the Disability Rights Commission Act 1999 appears to confer a less-constrained named investigatory power upon the DRC: however, the DRC did not test the uncertain limits of this power.

"against" particular named bodies or towards the investigation of alleged specific discriminatory acts. Therefore, the use of these powers is not subject to the same procedural restraints as were imposed in *Prestige* and *Hillingdon* on "named" investigations.[28] This greater flexibility means that the commissions increasingly use this inquiry power, often in tandem with limited named investigations. For example, the EOC has in recent years carried out a formal named investigation into sexual harassment in the Post Office, and general inquiries into occupational segregation, pregnancy discrimination, working carers, and part-time and flexible work.[29]

C. *The Commission for Equality and Human Rights (CEHR): A New Beginning?*

The DRC, EOC and CRE are now to be merged within the new CEHR, which will have responsibility for promoting equality of opportunity and enforcing compliance with discrimination law across all the equality grounds. It will also have the ability to promote and enforce compliance with human rights standards, although as already discussed above in the context of supporting individual victims, its powers in respect of human rights will be more circumscribed. The establishment of the CEHR was controversial, with some groups questioning whether a single combined commission could cater for the needs of each of the different equality grounds. There was also concern that the new body would not adopt a strong position on enforcing anti-discrimination legislation.[30] However, there is nothing in the provisions of the Equality Act 2006 which establish the CEHR that requires the new Commission to take a "softly-softly" stance: in fact, as the following extract makes clear, the new Commission has somewhat greater powers than its predecessors.

Colm O'Cinneide, "The Commission For Equality And Human Rights: A New Institution For New And Uncertain Times" 36(2) Industrial L. J. pp.141–162

153–155 "[T]here is nothing in the Equality Act 2006 that necessarily commits the CEHR to adopting . . . [a] weak approach. In fact, the legislation strengthens the powers and freedom of action of the new body in comparison to its predecessor commissions: in some

[28] See C. O'Cinneide, *A Single Equality Body: Lessons from Abroad* (Manchester: EOC, 2002), pp.20–22.

[29] See the EOC website, *www.eoc.org.uk*.

[30] C. O'Cinneide, "The Commission For Equality And Human Rights: A New Institution For New And Uncertain Times" (2007) 36(2) I.L.J. pp.141–162, 141–146.

important areas, lessons from previous experience appear to have been taken on board. S. 3 of the Act places the Commission under a 'general duty' to use its powers and functions to work towards the development of a society where equality and rights principles have become rooted, which is defined as follows:

'(a) people's ability to achieve their potential is not limited by prejudice or discrimination,

(b) there is respect for and protection of each individual's human rights (including respect for the dignity and worth of each individual),

(c) each person has an equal opportunity to participate in society, and

(d) there is mutual respect between communities based on understanding and valuing of diversity and on shared respect for equality and human rights.'

These duties are an ambitious and fascinating attempt to give a legislative definition to the idea of a rights-based society. More pragmatically, the width of these statutory responsibilities also gives the Commission an expansive field of action,[31] ensuring that it will have standing to bring judicial review proceedings and to intervene across a wide range of issues such as asylum, social conditions and intersectional forms of discrimination.

A similar set of expansive duties and functions guide how the Commission is to use its powers that relate to equality and anti-discrimination in s. 7 and its human rights powers in s. 8. The Commission's remit extends across all the anti-discrimination grounds, and also includes the promotion of equality of opportunity and 'understanding of the importance of equality and diversity'. It also is extended in s. 10 to include the promotion of good relations and prevention of hostilities between different communities and 'groups' in British society. The CEHR is similarly given a wide-ranging remit to promote compliance with, and understanding of, human rights. This includes rights contained in international instruments which have not been formally incorporated into UK law, although the Commission is to pay 'particular regard' to the ECHR rights. The CEHR can also monitor and advise on the effectiveness of equality and human rights instruments, and is obliged to monitor and produce periodic reports on progress towards the social goals set out in s. 3 of the Act. However, the CEHR is precluded from taking 'human rights action' in relation to devolved matters in respect of which the Scottish Parliament has conferred competence on the newly established Scottish Human Rights Commission.

In addition to these wide-ranging functions, the Act confers the powers of the existing equality commissions on the CEHR, and extends them across the six equality grounds. These include the promotional, investigative, inquiry, case support and positive duty enforcement powers discussed above, but also the ability to give information and advice, issue codes of practice with ministerial approval, arrange for the provision of conciliation services in discrimination cases and bring actions to prevent discriminatory advertising and instructions to discriminate. The Act clarifies and enhances the scope of some of these powers. S. 30 places the ability of the CEHR to apply for judicial review and to intervene in court proceedings on firmer ground, by making explicit statutory provision for these powers. The Commission is given a new power to assess the compliance of public authorities with the general positive equality duties, and to issue a 'compliance notice' when it concludes following such an assessment that a public authority is not complying with the requirements of a general duty.[32] This is a potentially significant new power: it allows the CEHR to assess whether public authorities are taking adequate steps to promote

[31] *See Fairness for All: A New Commission for Equality and Human Rights*, paras 1.10–1.11.
[32] ss.31–32 of the Equality Act.

equality of opportunity, and not just whether they are complying with anti-discrimination law or with specific statutory duties.[33]

The CEHR is also given a potentially very useful power to enter into (and to enforce via legal action if necessary) binding agreements with employers and other bodies. This power was held by the DRC, but not by the other two commissions: it could be used to make employers and other bodies undertake to avoid certain discriminatory acts and to implement equal opportunity measures such as pay audits, in response for avoiding the bad publicity of an investigation. The Commission is also now able to seek an injunction to prevent someone committing an unlawful discriminatory act, another new power.

The Commission's general inquiry and formal investigation powers are also clarified, with s. 20(2) extending the scope for the use of 'named' investigations by proving that the Commission can investigate if it has a 'suspicion' that a body has committed an unlawful discriminatory act, a loosening of the 'reasonable suspicion' standard imposed by the Law Lords in *Hillingdon*. This may lower the evidential threshold of 'reasonable suspicion' to something closer to the irrationality standard in administrative law: i.e. a decision by the Commission to initiate a named investigation into the conduct of an employer or another particular body should only be reviewable by the courts if strongly disproportionate or irrational in nature, as distinct from being 'unreasonable'. This could help provide a remedy for the current Catch-22 situation, where the equality commissions are often unable to launch a named investigation precisely because it lacks the necessary evidence to demonstrate 'reasonable suspicion'. The CRE had to wait over ten years after it first became concerned about race discrimination in the army before it could launch a formal investigation, which only was able to go ahead when the *Hillingdon* threshold was satisfied by the evidence produced by an Army Board of Inquiry into racial discrimination in the Household Cavalry. The procedure for the conduct of these investigations is also streamlined and clarified by the 2006 Act."

There are restrictions on the scope of the new Commission's powers. In the field of human rights, the CEHR can carry out general inquiries into matters concerning compliance with human rights instruments, and also has the important power under s.30(3) of the Act to bring judicial review proceedings under the HRA against public authorities: it is not subject to the usual requirement to be a "victim" of a breach of the ECHR before such action can be taken. However, the CEHR cannot initiate "named investigations" into whether particular authorities are complying with the HRA, or, as discussed above, support individual human rights cases unless there is a discrimination dimension to them. Also, despite the greater flexibility given to the CEHR as to when it can launch named investigations, a good case exists that the effect of the *Prestige* decision should have been wholly reversed: the CEHR could have been permitted to launch named investigations even in the absence of allegations of breaches of discrimination law. The Irish Equality Authority can conduct "equality audits" into private and public sector employers with 50 employees or more and recommend improvements to their employment and pay polices, even in the absence of specific allegations of discrimination: the

[33] The existing commissions can at present only enforce the more detailed and narrower specific race and disability positive duties imposed on public authorities, which are essentially procedural in nature. See C. O'Cinneide, "A New Generation of Equality Legislation? Positive Duties and Disability Rights", in A. Lawson and C. Gooding, *Disability Rights in Europe* (Oxford: Hart, 2005), pp.219–248.

Equality Commission for Northern Ireland has similar powers in respect of the fair employment legislation.[34]

Therefore, the CEHR is limited to some degree by being largely cast in the mould of its predecessor commissions. It will be interesting to see how it chooses to use its powers, and in particular its investigative powers. It is confronted by some of the same dilemmas as those faced by its predecessor commissions. Should the CEHR be principally concerned with a relatively narrow agenda of enforcing respect for equality and human rights through the incremental support of individual claims for justice, or can and should it aim to play a wider and more strategic role? The latter option offers more potential for achieving wide social change, but might also leave the Commission open to the charge of sacrificing support for individual claims in favour of initiatives which might ultimately lack specific focus and real teeth.

What is clear is that litigation brought by individual victims can serve an important function to highlight structural problems, but these problems may only be fully addressed by the use of other remedial responses such as strategic investigation by the enforcement agencies, or positive action remedies. Individual remedies need to be supplemented by alternative remedies, and the CEHR needs to be to the forefront in making use of these other remedies.[35]

III. Contract Compliance, Public Procurement and "Best Value"

Chapter 7 on positive action sets out some of the ways in which discrimination law can move beyond an individual model towards remedial solutions that target the structural nature of discrimination. One feature of the positive action policies that have been given effect through law (e.g. the positive duties) is that they target the public sector. This strategy is effective because the public sector is a large employer and provider of key services: non-discrimination and ensuring equality in this context will therefore be an effective tool. Moreover, the social exclusion of many minorities makes them disproportionately dependent on public services which makes it especially important to eliminate discrimination and promote equality in this context. This strategy can also be justified because, after all, as citizens who contribute to public services, individuals from minority groups can legitimately claim that the state and public institutions should (a) not discriminate against them; and (b) accommodate their most urgent and pressing needs where this is

[34] See C. O'Cinneide, *Single Equality Bodies*, p. 62. The Northern Irish Commission has found that the absence of a requirement to have "reasonable suspicion" has meant that the conduct of such investigations has proved much less confrontational than named investigations that have to be based upon specific allegations. See Equality Commission for Northern Ireland, *Legislative Reform: Commission Powers/Judicial Process* (Belfast: ECNI, August 2003).

[35] For more on the composition of the CEHR, and the legislative provisions that protect its independence, see C. O'Cinneide, "The Commission For Equality And Human Rights: A New Institution For New And Uncertain Times" (2007) 36(2) I.L.J., pp. 141–162.

appropriate and possible. The focus on the public sector, however, means that the power of private employers and business is often marginalised from debates. The private sector is also becoming especially important as public sector reform delegates many services to private service providers. In this section we consider these issues in the context of mechanisms of "contract compliance" which allows the public sector to use its economic power to negotiate clauses in private contracts which can promote some of the central goals of discrimination law. The technique of contract compliance can achieve this by making the award of public contracts to private companies conditional on meeting certain criteria (e.g. non-discrimination and equality standards; labour or environmental standards).

Contract compliance mechanisms, whereby public authorities require contractors to introduce rigorous equal opportunity policies, could be very effective tools to require private contractors seeking public tenders to adopt positive action initiatives as discussed later.[36] However, the use of such incentives and requirements has not found favour with the UK government, outside of the Northern Irish context.[37] Pragmatic concerns about the excessive costs of business regulation have meant that no attempt has been made as yet to introduce private sector duties or general reasonable accommodation requirements in Britain. Indeed, the use of contract compliance policies by public authorities has been reined in and positively discouraged. Part 11 of the Local Government Act 1988 Act restricted or eliminated the ability of local authorities to use contract compliance measures outside of the race equality context.[38] Even the marginal loosening of these controls with the introduction of the "Best Value" contracting regime in 2000 has not deterred the "chilling effect" such controls have exercised upon the use of contract compliance by public authorities.[39] The positive duties may be able to open some additional chinks in these regulatory constraints on the use of contract compliance. However, an effective framework for the use of contract compliance can only be put into place if the existing statutory restrictions are removed or comprehensively reformed: tinkering at the edges can only go so far. It remains to be seen whether the Discrimination Law Review being conducted at present will make any recommendation on this point, or on the introduction of other forms of positive requirements upon private employers.

[36] See C. McCrudden, "Using Public Procurement to Achieve Social Outcomes" (2004) 28(4) Natural Resources Forum 257–267.

[37] Northern Ireland, as in may other areas of equality policy, is seen as an exceptional case.

[38] See P.E. Morris, "Legal Regulation of Contract Compliance: An Anglo-American Comparison", pp. 103–121; C. McCrudden, "Codes in a Cold Climate" (1988) M.L.R. 409. Despite the potentially greater scope for equality-based measures opened up by the *Helsinki Concordia Bus* decision (Case 513–99, [2002] ECR I–7213), and the recent legislative package clarifying the scope for social considerations available in public procurement (Directives 2004/17/EC and 2004/18/EC), EU legislation in this area has also consistently lacked real clarity as to when the introduction of such contract compliance requirements are compatible with EU law. See C. Tobler, "Encore: 'Women's Clauses' in Public Procurement under Community Law" [2000] 25(6) *European L. Rev.* 618–631; the *Hepple Report*, paras 3.71–3.73, pp.83–84.

[39] See the analysis in A. McColgan, *Discrimination Law* (2nd edn) 386–407.

A. *International, American and Canadian Approaches to Contract Compliance*

There are international standards to ensure fair wages and just labour standards in public services. The Fair Wage Resolution of 1946, and ILO Convention No.94 all support this principle. ILO Convention No. 94 of 1949 on Labour Clauses (Public Contracts), modelled on the 1946 Resolution, requires contracts to include clauses ensuring working conditions. It states and requires:

"... not less favourable than those established for work of the same character in the trade or industry concerned in the district where the work is carried on—(a) by collective agreement or other recognised machinery of negotiation between organisations of employers and workers ...".

The Convention was ratified by the UK in 1950, but the Thatcher government denounced it in 1982. Nonetheless, ILO Convention No.94 has been ratified by eight EU Member States, and similar policies are in effect in six others. The UK remains the only EU Member State without a formal policy requiring fair labour standards in public procurement. In its recent evidence to the House of Commons Select Committee on Fair Trade, the Trade Union Congress reiterated its call for the UK to ratify this international labour standard as part of a commitment to just labour standards.[40]

In the US, contract compliance has been available as a federal remedy against discrimination. There is regulation of racial or sex discrimination by recipients of federal funding through a number of specific statutes in areas such as education.[41] The main form of contract compliance in the US context, however, relates to employment discrimination. This power is derived from a presidential order rather than a statute. It was introduced through Executive Order 11,246 which prohibits discrimination and requires affirmative action on the basis of race, national origin, sex and religion.[42] The executive order is enforced by the US Office of Federal Contract Compliance Programs (OFCCP) in the Department of Labor which sets out the detailed terms of regulation. Significantly, the executive order has never been explicitly enacted by Congress which, as George Rutherven observes, "gives rise to persistent questions about its scope and validity."[43] The executive order is distinct from US statutory discrimination law in a number of respects: it requires affirmative action as well as prohibiting discrimination; it is enforced through administrative

[40] Written Evidence and Memorandum of the TUC to the International Development Committee of the House of Commons, (2006–7 session), Written Evidence, Vol.II, (2006–7), HC 356–II.

[41] George Rutherglen, *Major Issues in the Federal Law of Employment Discrimination*, 4th edn, (Washington DC, USA: Federal Judicial Center, 2004), at pp.167–168.

[42] Executive Order 11,246, 3 C. F. R. 339 (1964–1965), reprinted as amended in 42 U.S.C. section 200e (2000).

[43] Executive Order 11,246, 3 C. F. R. 339 (1964–1965), reprinted as amended in 42 U.S.C. section 200e (2000).

procedures rather than private litigation; it is interpreted and implemented through administrative regulations rather than judicial processes.[44]

Rutherven summarises the main features of Executive Order 11,246 by pointing out the following key features. It applies to all contractors with contracts in excess of $10,000, it imposes increased compliance and reporting requirements on contractors with contracts in excess of £50,000. It also imposes nondiscrimination and affirmative action obligations (which have been controversial). Employers with contracts in excess of $50,000 must prepare written affirmative action plans: containing a "work force analysis"; a determination whether any racial or ethnic minority group or women have been "underutilized" by the employer; and "goals and timetables" to remedy any underutilization by them". These requirements can also be expanded and detailed through regulations. Compliance is ensured through administratively imposed sanctions. Special provisions apply in relation to federal construction contracts in excess of $10,000. Significantly, given the current British concern with segregation, the OFCCP can set goals for employment of women and minority groups in most major geographical areas. Although administrative decisions are the main form of ensuring enforcement, there is the possibility to bring an action against contractors to enforce their obligations under the executive order. Private individual cannot sue, although they can in some circumstances take enforcement action.[45] Rutherven notes that most enforcement actions by the OFCCP result in negotiated settlements, which ensures flexibility in the way in which contract compliance operates, and explains why there have been very few challenges to the OFCCP decision-making process. Earlier legal challenges (in the early 1970s) to the OFCCP regulations were rejected on the grounds that they served a government interest in eliminating past discrimination.[46] Since then, however, the Supreme Court has raised the level of scrutiny of all racial classifications by government, and some of these issues are discussed in the context of affirmative action in the earlier chapter on positive action (Positive Action I). Rutherven also notes another interesting potential basis for challenging the OFCCP regulations. Rutherven notes that Executive Order 11,246 has been indirectly, rather than explicitly, confirmed by congressional authority. He concludes, however, that although a few lower

[44] This summary of Executive Order 11, 246 draws on George Rutherglen, *Major Issues in the Federal Law of Employment Discrimination*, 4th edn, (Washington DC, USA: Federal Judicial Center, 2004), at pp.165.

[45] See George Rutherglen, *Major Issues in the Federal Law of Employment Discrimination*, 4th edn, (Washington D.C., USA: Federal Judicial Center, 2004), citing *Legal Aid Society v Brennan*, 608 F. 2d 1319 (9th Cir. 1979).

[46] See for example, *Northeast Construction Co v Romney*, 485 F. 2d 752, 757–58 (D.C. Cir), cited in George Rutherglen, *Major Issues in the Federal Law of Employment Discrimination*, 4th edn, (Washington D.C., USA: Federal Judicial Center, 2004), citing *Legal Aid Society v Brennan*, 608 F. 2d 1319 (9th Cir. 1979).

courts have relied on this ambivalence in restricting the scope of the executive order, there is overall de facto validity for Executive Order 11,246 based on the length of time in which Congress has acquiesced in its operation.[47]

In Canada, the Employment Equity Act 1995 (and accompanying regulations) provide the basis for a federal structure of contract compliance.[48] This puts into place a system which requires employers and contractors bidding for contracts with the federal government to meet standards of employment equity which require "an action orientated approach that identifies under-representation or concentration of, and employment barriers to, certain groups of people, and provides a number of practical and creative remedies."[49] The Canadian Employment Equity Act 1995 contains a purpose clause which makes clear that it is using the economic power of the government to promote equality goals. The purpose clause states in s.2:

"Purpose of Act—The purpose of this Act is to achieve equality in the workplace so that no person shall be denied employment opportunities or benefits for reasons unrelated to ability and, in the fulfilment of that goal, to correct the conditions of disadvantage in employment experienced by women, aboriginal peoples, persons with disabilities and members of visible minorities by giving effect to the principle that employment equity means more than treating persons in the same way but also requires special measures and the accommodation of differences."

Like the equivalent US contract compliance regime, the Canadian Employment Equity Act has a focus on compliance through the use of administrative bodies and with an emphasis on negotiated settlements with employers. The Canadian Human Rights Commission has a role in enforcement which includes powers to direct employers to remedy any non-compliance (see Pt II of the Act). Employers can request that the Commission set up an Employment Equity Review Tribunal if it believes that the direction is unfounded or the Commission can request a Tribunal if it believes that direction has not been implemented (s.28). This Tribunal is an independent quasi-judicial body with the power to order, confirm, vary or rescind the Commission's direction, and to make any order it considers appropriate (s.30). Decisions of the Tribunal can be the subject of judicial review in federal courts (s.30); and, moreover, the decisions of Tribunals can be translated into orders of the Federal Court for the sake of enforcement (s.31).

In terms of the content of the duty on the employer, the Canadian contract

47 This regime contrasts to the specific mandate for federal level affirmative action in the areas of disability discrimination. Section 503 of the Rehabilitation Act of 1973, codified at 29 US Code s.793, has explicitly authorised the President to regulate discrimination and to encourage affirmative action by federal contractors on the basis of disability.

48 For a discussion see Aileen McColgan, Discrimination Law, 2nd edn, (Oxford: Hart Publications, 2005) at pp.386–387.

49 *Ibid.*

compliance regime puts into place a number of requirements on employers. First, the employer is required to take action to identify any potential patterns of inequality by, for example, conducting a workforce survey to ascertain the proportion and position of women, aboriginal, disabled and "visible minority" workers; undertaking a "workforce analysis" to determine the degree of under-representation, if any, of the groups within the workforce; and undertaking an "employment system's review" to determine what, if any, barriers "prohibit the full participation of designated group members within the employer's workforce." (ss.5 and 9). Second, the employer is required to develop a response to the problems identified. This requires developing an "employment equity" plan which should include positive policies and practices to accelerate the integration of designated group members in employers' workforces; elimination of employment barriers pinpointed during the employment systems review; a timetable for implementation; short term numerical goals; and longer term goals. Third, the employer is required to monitor the implementation of the plan, reviewing and revising it as necessary (e.g. ss.12 and 13). There is also a record and reporting system. Section 17, for example, requires "record keeping" and producing an employment equity report; and s.19 makes clear that these reports should be made available for public inspection.

The Canadian contract compliance regime is likely to cover a wide range of employers: it covers contractors with more than a hundred employees, and in relation to contracts worth at least $200,000. Although the Canadian system of contract compliance puts into place a detailed regime with significant powers of enforcement, there is also a mechanism to balance the needs of employers with the goals of discrimination law and equality. So, for example, there is a provision that the Commission may not give a direction and no Tribunal may make an order that would cause undue hardship on an employer, require an employer to hire or promote unqualified persons, or impose a quota on an employer, meaning a requirement to hire or promote a fixed and arbitrary number of persons during a given period (s.33). Another noteworthy feature of the Canadian contract compliance regime is that it creates a duty on employers to consult with employees in putting into place equity plans (s.15 of the Canadian Employment Equity Act 1995) in a way that is similar to the increasing requirements for social dialogue in EU public procurement law. The next section discusses the EU and British approach to contract compliance.

B. *EU and British approaches to contract compliance*

The emergence of the EU as a single economic market, and the confirmation that mainstreaming and contract compliance are legitimate ways of pursuing the EU goals of equality and non-discrimination, are of great significance for a number of reasons. The EU wields massive economic power with which it can force social change. The earlier chapter on positive action has emphasised the increasing importance of EU mainstreaming measures. EU employment strategy and structural funds are also important policy levers to deliver social reform and to achieve equality and non-discrimination goals. There is, therefore, widespread agreement that the use of economic power to pursue these social goals is legitimate. In the context of gender equality, for example, it has been stated that mainstreaming:

> "involves not restricting efforts to promote equality to implementation of specific measures to help women, but mobilising all general policies and measures specifically for the purpose of achieving equality by actively and openly taking into account at the planning stage their possible effects on the respective situation of men and women. This means systematically examining them: thus, development policies, the organisation of work, choices relating to transport or the fixing of school hours, etc, may have significant impact on the situation of women and men which must therefore be duly taken into consideration in order to further promote equality between women and men."[50]

The previous discussions on positive action have discussed some of the legislative framework for EU positive action and mainstreaming. In the next section we consider some of the non-legal supply-side policies (e.g. investment in education or transport) that can often achieve magnified benefits for women and minorities. In this section we consider the issue of the contract compliance and the use of the economic power of the state and public sector to motivate changes in the private sector.

The EU approach, as illustrated in the previous quote, readily accepts the principle that social and economic policy can legitimately be used to promote the goals of equality and non-discrimination. Britain, however, has had a more troubled history with the use of contract compliance to promote social policy generally, and equality goals in particular. The compliance policy of the Greater London Council in the 1980s, for example, which included duties to promote equality caused great controversy. The GLC based its policy on RRA 76 s.71 which imposed a duty on public authorities to promote equality and eliminate discrimination. This led to the introduction of s.17 of the Local Government Act which prohibited local and other public authorities from taking "non-commercial matters" into account in exercising their contractual functions. This provision covered equality issues which fell within the definition of "non-commercial" matters which included "terms and conditions of employment by contractors of their workers or the composition of, the arrangements for the promotion, transfer, training of or the other opportu-

50 "Incorporating equal opportunities for women and men into all Community policies and activities", Communication, COM (1996) 67, final, at 2.

nities afforded to, their workforces."[51] Section 18 of the LGA 1988 allowed local authorities to gather some data on ethnic monitoring but this was subject to conditions and limited to strict compliance with the requirements of the RRA 76, s.71. This restriction of the ability to rely on contract compliance had an impact on the ability of local authorities to make equality and non-discrimination issues a part of their contracting process with the private sector. The CRE concluded that

"If it had not been for the existence [RRA 76 s.71], the probability is that Government would have banned local authorities altogether from considering equal opportunities in their contracting processes [...] the SDA contains no similar provisions and Government did ban local authorities from considering equal opportunities between men and women in their contracting process."[52]

As Christopher McCrudden concluded, this restriction of local authority power to pursue equality goals was an accession to "requests from the CBI and the construction and civil engineering employers to introduce legislation restricting local authority powers to impose contract compliance policies on those with whom they contracted."[53] The restrictions on the ability of local government to address discrimination through contract compliance were accompanied by an economic policy which put previously public services into the private sector through "compulsory competitive tendering" (CCT). As Linda Dickens has noted, CCT had a

"disproportionately adverse effect on women and ethnic minorities, (in particular black women), who tend to be over-represented in those jobs which have been effected. [...] the major impact has been on women who have lost jobs, had hours reduced and work intensified, experienced pay reductions and loss of benefits."[54]

One consequence of this disproportionate impact on women was the increase in the use of equal pay legislation by unions. Commenting on this period in British industrial relations, and the history of contract compliance, Dickens concluded that there had been a possibility that the economic goal of subcontracting could have been used in a way that promoted equality through duties of contract compliance: instead a "contrary path" was taken in which the policies of contract compliance were curtailed by the LGA, s.18. Some of these issues are considered in the passage below.

[51] Aileen McColgan, *Discrimination Law*, 2nd edn, (Oxford: Hart Publications, 2005) at p.388.
[52] Quoted in Aileen McColgan, *Discrimination Law*, 2nd ed., (Oxford: Hart Publications, 2005) at p.388.
[53] Christopher McCrudden, "Codes in a Cold Climate", (1988) 51 M.L.R. 409, 429.
[54] Linda Dickens, "Gender, Race and Employment Equality in Britain: inadequate strategies and the role of industrial relations actors." (1997) 28 Industrial Relations L.J. 282.

"Best Value, Best Equality" (1998) Equal Opportunities Review (IRS, London, May 1, 1998)

"CCT and equal opportunities

Since the early 1980s, several services provided by local authorities have been subject to outside competition. The Local Government Planning and Land Act 1980 and then the Local Government Act 1988 applied compulsory competitive tendering to a range of local authority services, including building-cleaning, refuse collection, street-cleaning, catering, grounds maintenance and vehicle maintenance. The National Health Service (NHS) and Community Care Act (1990)), which gave local authorities primary responsibility for care in the community, extended competitive tendering and market testing to council social services departments, and in January 1991 sports and leisure management was added to the list of services covered.

In particular, the 1988 Local Government Act (LGA) regulated the way in which local authorities administered their tendering processes for all contracts for goods, works and services and had a far-reaching effect on local authority purchasing and contracting. It meant that a local council could only carry out certain defined activities in-house, through its own Direct Labour Organisation or Direct Service Organisation, if the work had first gone out to tender and been won in open competition. Specifically, Part II of the 1988 Act removed local authorities' ability to consider "non-commercial" matters when selecting contractors and awarding contracts. An increasing number of councils had been using equal opportunities criteria as part of the tendering process when selecting contractors. Part II prevented councils from taking equal opportunities into account when contracting out and virtually ended the use forward-thinking councils had made of the tendering process to promote equality.

Women's employment seriously damaged

Given the high numbers of women employed in the public sector, both of the statutory sex equality agencies became increasingly concerned about the impact CCT was having on women's employment. Research published by the British Equal Opportunities Commission (EOC) in 1995 (EOR 61) and by the EOC for Northern Ireland (EOCNI) a year later (EOR 66) confirmed what both organisations had suspected: that the CCT process had "hit women harder than men". Female council workers experienced reductions in hours, pay and employment and increased job insecurity, as predominately part-time workers were pushed outside the employment protection and national insurance (NI) systems.

Local authorities in Britain employ around 2.3 million people, in a wide range of occupations, including teachers, gardeners, cooks, computer analysts, refuse collectors, home-helps, town planners and nursery nurses. Around 70% of local council workers are women, many of whom work part time. Two out of five employees are female part-timers. Women are particularly prevalent in the jobs most affected by competitive tendering, such as building-cleaning, education catering and community care. A similar situation existed in Northern Ireland at the time of the research, when 41% of women worked in the public sector compared with 34% of men. Women made up just over half of all public sector workers (50.4%), and were particularly prevalent in the jobs most affected by competitive tendering, forming 80% of those employed in personal and protective services, such as domestic and catering services, and 79% of those working in personal and protective services in the education field. Women earned only 46% of male earnings in this group of jobs.

In Britain, the Centre for Public Services (CPS), on behalf of the EOC, analysed 71 contracts agreed by 39 local authorities for the contracting-out of five services—building-cleaning, education-catering, refuse collection, community care, and sports and leisure—and compared the employment position of women and men before and after the award of a contract. The EOCNI conducted its own general formal investigation, examining 20 contracts in the ancillary services of health and education, about 23% of the total awards up until November 1993. They included catering, domestic service, linen and grounds maintenance.

The research found:

- **Job losses.** In Britain, women's total employment fell by 22% during the first round of the CCT process, compared with 12% of job losses for men. Women accounted for 53% of "pre-contract" employment and for 96% of the net job losses. Since 91% of employment prior to the introduction of CCT was part time, part-time workers accounted for 95% of the total decline in employment. Similarly, in Northern Ireland, there was a higher rate of overall job loss for women (14%) than for men (6%). This leapt to a 37% female job loss compared to a 2% male gain in contracted-out services.
- **Pay reductions.** In Britain, in the female-dominated services, catering and cleaning, hours fell by 16% and 25% respectively. In contrast, in the male-dominated service of refuse collection, pay levels increased and contractual hours remained the same. There was also evidence that some local authority Direct Service Organisations and private contractors, particularly in cleaning and catering, deliberately attempted to keep the wages below the NI threshold to avoid paying employer NI contributions.

  A similar picture emerged in Northern Ireland, where women's average working hours were reduced by 11% compared to 5% for men, and a higher proportion of women (87%) than of men (67%) had their wages reduced after competitive tendering. There was a 3% increase in overall differential between women's and men's weekly pay after competitive tendering.
- **Part-timers.** Both investigations showed that female part-timers were the worse affected, with lower pay, fewer hours and worse terms and conditions of employment. Fewer hours and wage cuts meant that many female part-timers' weekly earnings dropped below the NI Lower Earnings Limit and so they no longer qualified for state benefits such as maternity pay, statutory sick pay, unemployment benefit and state pensions. This also led to an increasing number of female part-timers needing to have more than one job to make ends meet.
- **Temporary staff.** There was also a significant increase in the use of temporary and casual staff, particularly in female-dominated services. These employees had fewer rights and worse conditions than permanent staff.
- **Savings.** In Britain, the female-dominated services of catering and cleaning accounted for more than 90% of the savings generated by Direct Service Organisations.
- **Equal opportunities.** The Northern Ireland report confirmed that there was only minimal consideration of equal opportunities issues in the tendering process. Yet the British findings clearly showed that the adverse impact on women's terms and conditions could be reduced when care and attention was given to the tendering specification and service standards.

Calls for government action

As a result of these findings, the Equal Opportunities Commission called on:

- **government** to make equal opportunities a key measure in the selection of contractors and evaluation of bids, and to draw up guidelines for those who are tendering to provide public services, to help them comply with the sex equality legislation and treat men and women fairly;
- **local authorities** to make equal opportunities an integral part of the CCT process;
- **private contractors** to adopt basic equal opportunities practice, such as monitoring of the workforce; and
- **unions** to develop policies aimed at avoiding discriminatory impact when tendering.

In addition, the EOC also proposed that "the Local Government Act 1988 [should be] amended to allow terms and conditions to be a commercial matter. This would enable local authorities to ask potential contractors questions under the Sex Discrimination Act, as well as the Race Relations Act, as a means to assess their terms and conditions of service and their equal opportunities policies in relation to gender, race and disability."

As a result of its findings, the EOCNI called on the Government to suspend its policy of competitive tendering in health and education services in Northern Ireland, pending a full review of its policy, and recommended that the legislation be amended to allow for the full consideration of equal opportunities in the tendering process. In particular, the Commission called for the Government's own guidelines on Policy Appraisal and Fair Treatment to be used to monitor the gender implications of the tendering process.

Local authorities—England and Wales

Employees at December 1997

	Male	*Female*	*All*
Full time	506,433 (24.4%)	615,118 (29.6%)	1,121,551 (54.0%)
Part time	99,478 (4.8%)	856,530 (41.2%)	956,008 (46.0%)
Total	605,911 (29.17%)	1,471,648 (70.83%)	2,077,559 (100%)

Source: Local Government Management Board.

Local authorities—Scotland

Estimated employees at September 1997

	Male	*Female*	*All*
Full time	99,001 (34.1%)	89,557 (30.8%)	188,558 (64.9%)
Part time	8,757 (3.0%)	93,309 (32.1%)	102,066 (35.1%)
Total	107,758 (37.07%)	182,866 (62.93%)	290,066 (100%)

Source: Convention of Scottish Local Authorities.

The extract above confirms the basis of the criticism of CC by the EOC and EOCNI, and the reasons for their calls for greater mechanism to monitor and regulate the impact of tenders on women. In the Northern Ireland context the Fair Employment Treatment Order contains a limited form of contract compliance (Art.64). It prevents local authorities from entering into contracts with "unqualified" persons. The term "unqualified person" is declared by the Equality Commission, and includes those who have failed in relation to an "equalities obligation", e.g. to meet registration or monitoring requirements;

failed to submit a monitoring form; or failed to comply with an order of the Commission.[55] The Northern Ireland model of focusing on penalties as a deterrence can be characterised as *penalty* model for contract compliance; which can in turn be contrasted with the models of *incentive* model used in the US and Canada.

The clear evidence of the discriminatory impact of CCT, combined with the restrictions on the ability to compensate for these through contract compliance, is set out in detail in the passage above. This example illustrates the importance of supplementing discrimination law with social and economic policy, and it also shows that political leadership (or lack of leadership) is a key factor. This historical experience also illustrates the way in which the normative arguments in favour of equality and non-discrimination can conflict with private business able to use arguments about "light touch" regulation, e.g. the lobbying by stakeholders such as the CBI which led to the restrictions on contract compliance through the Local Government Act 1988. The call for "light touch regulation" as a response to increased regulation of discrimination is a recurring theme in the context of attempts to regulate the private sector. A further example, discussed below, is the recent failure of the Women and Work Commission Report—*Shaping a Fairer Future* (2006)—to recommend the introduction of mandatory pay audits to force private sector employers to comply with equal pay legislation, to mirror the equality reviews carried out in the public sector.[56]

C. *EU Public Procurement Law and Policy*

In relation to EU law and contract compliance, as the previous discussion indicated, there is increasing recognition that the EU can legitimately use its economic power to promote its social policy and goals through its structural funds and through implementing mainstreaming in decision-making. Yet, at the same time, there is an increasing pressure to ensure that the tendering process throughout the EU is open to competition. The policy was aimed at strengthening the single market: national bias in public procurement was perceived to be a significant obstacle to a single market, because it can cause distortion in patterns of trade between Member States. This two often conflicting goals within procurement policy were reflected in the political background to the introduction of the current EU legal regime on public procurement, when the Commission proposed an amended Procurement directive based on the principles of lowest price which would have precluded criteria relating to social policy, whereas the European Parliament opposed

[55] See Aileen McColgan, *Discrimination Law*, 2nd edn, (Oxford: Hart Publications, 2005) at p.389.
[56] "Commission Rejects Mandatory Equal Pay Reviews" (2006) 151 EOR (IRS: London, published April 1, 2006).

this approach.[57] The outcome was that the regime on procurement, with a number of directives that went back to the early 1970s, has now been extended and consolidated. In the context of awards by the public sector there are two main relevant provisions: the Public Sector Directive (Directive 2004/18/EC) and the Utilities Directive (Directive 2004/17). The Public Sector Directive applies to most awards by government or a public body: the Utilities Directive covers four large public sector bodies: water; energy; transport; and postal services.[58]

The central concern for discrimination law, in relation to EU law and policy on procurement, is whether it enables contact compliance which is conditional on meeting social policy goals of equality and non-discrimination. Although the EU directives are not explicit on this issue, like US and Canadian contract compliance regimes, they are sufficiently permissive to allow some forms of contract compliance regimes to be established in Member States. There are, however, some limiting conditions which may restrict the ability of member states, such as Britain, to introduce a wide ranging contract compliance regime. Although the preamble to the Public Sector Directive suggests that social policy can legitimately be a relevant factor, there is no explicit reference to this: in the text of the Directive, however the criteria of "lowest price" is not included which should allow a wider interpretation of the range of factors that can be legitimately placed as a condition on the grant of a tender.

In an early case decided in 2000, *Commission v France*,[59] the ECJ held that a public authority could make the award of a public contract to build a school conditional on meeting certain employment conditions designed to combat unemployment. This was subject to the conditions that the clause was consistent with all the fundamental principles of the EU and met the procedural conditions in EU public procurement directives. As we see below, the ECJ has built on this strategy on allowing contract compliance to pursue social goals but also, at the same time, has limited the way in which these conditions can be imposed on contractors.

This issue has now also been considered by the ECJ which considered these issues in the *Concordia Bus Finland Oy Ab v Helsingin kaupunki and HKL-Bussiliikenne (Helsinki Bus)* case.[60] The ECJ held that procurement conditions under the Directive did not need to be limited to a issues which were of a purely economic nature. This opens up the prospect of using contract compliance to

[57] See Aileen McColgan, *Discrimination Law*, 2nd edn, (Oxford: Hart Publications, 2005) at p.389.

[58] For a detailed discussion see Sue Arrowsmith, "The Past and Future Evolution of EC Procurement Law: From Framework to Common Code", (2006) 35(3) Public Contract L.J. 337. See also Niklass Brun and Brian Bercusson, "Labour Aspects of Public Procurement in the EU" in Ruth Neilsen and Steen Trumer (eds), *The New EU Public Procurement Directives*, (Copenhagen: DJOF Publications, 2005)

[59] Commission of the *European Communities v French Republic* Case C-225/98 [2003] E.C.H.R. I-07445.

[60] Case – 513/99, *Concordia Bus Finland v Helsinki* (2002) E.C.R. I-7213.

promote social policies, although there has been controversy about the extent of the potential to promote these objectives.[61] Although there is, therefore, some room within EU procurement law for using contract compliance to promote equality and non-discrimination, there are also some limits on the way in which Member States can pursue contract compliance. Judicial interpretation of the Directives has led to a number of limiting conditions which are summarised by Sue Arrowsmith as:

"First, the ECJ has interpreted the public sector rules as precluding Member States from excluding suppliers merely because those suppliers have failed to comply with social policies formulated by the procuring entity (such as fair recruitment policies) or because the procuring entity believes the supplier will be unable to comply with a contract condition of a social or environmental nature (for example, requiring use of certain disadvantaged workers on the contract). In the latter case, the procuring entity must allow the supplier to conclude the contract and then to take action only if the supplier does not actually comply (which may be impractical and costly). Such a restriction is not written into the public sector rule, but the ECJ concluded that the grounds for exclusion referred to in the public sector rules—namely technical capability, financial standing,, and criminal convictions—are generally exhaustive. [. . .] Secondly, the ECJ has ruled that award criteria must relate to the subject matter of the contract."

Sue Arrowsmith concludes that "There has been much debate over the merits of using procurement to implement 'collateral' policies and over the merits of exclusion and contact award criteria as mechanisms for doing so; but it suffices to say for the present purpose to point out that, by imposing sanctions on Member States in order to open up markets, the ECJ has deprived states of much of their previous freedoms to consider if and how to implement such policies in light of their own national circumstances."[62]

D. *Current Issues in British Contract Compliance—PFI and Best Value*

In the 1980s, policies to restrict public expenditure through reductions in the Public Sector Borrowing Requirement (PSBR) were accompanied by changes to funding and running of public services. During this period Compulsory Competitive Tendering (CCT), which sought to set standards in public services, was controversial and it was resented by local government and the trade unions. The present social, political and economic context for contract com-

[61] See Sue Arrowsmith, "The Past and Future Evolution of EC Procurement Law: From Framework to Common Code", (2006) 35(3) Public Contract L.J., 353.
[62] *Ibid.*, 353–354.

pliance differs from that of the 1980s when the Local Government Act 1988 was introduced. Yet, like previous mechanisms for increasing the role of the private sector, it seeks to realign the relationship between the private and public sector. In the present context, the contract compliance framework has drawn on the mechanism of Private Finance Initiative (PFI) which is a form of generating investment in public infrastructure projects such as hospitals, schools and prisons, as well as transport and local government. Previously the Government borrowed to invest in new public infrastructure. PFI is a long-term leasing arrangement under which private consortia borrow the cash to build and run new schools, hospitals and prisons for a length of time in exchange for an annual fee by the taxpayer. Despite differences, some experts on local government noted that there was also a continuity between CCT and the new PFI regime. Jane Sillett of the Local Government Information Unit, for example, noted that "PFI shares some of the same characteristics as CCT and market testing; it represents some loss of control and blurring of accountabilities; it can fragment service provision; and, in some cases, in-house workforces will be privatised and may suffer a deterioration in conditions."[63] PFI contracts were for a longer period than the requirements under CCT and a large number of them related to service sector jobs rather than just infrastructure creating a risk that cost efficiencies would be achieved at the expense of pay and conditions, especially of women and minorities. More specifically, there was a risk pay and conditions would be set by private contractors at private sector rates, leading to a two tier system for employment protection which would undermine single status agreements which had been achieved by public sector unions such as Unison. There was also the potential that increased flexibility requirements (e.g. changed job descriptions and casualisation) would impact disproportionately on women and minorities. The shift to the private sector, and the requirement for commercial confidentiality by contractors, would also make it more difficult to monitor and collate data in the area of equal opportunities.[64]

The present Government replaced the widely unpopular CCT regime with the concept of "Best Value and Inspection" in public services, which aims to ensure council services meet performance targets. This change from the CCT regime to a Best Value approach has opened up the potential for the greater use of contract compliance to pursue equality and non-discrimination goals. The transformation has taken place through a number of legal provisions. The best value standard and inspection regime was introduced by the Local Government Act 1999 (and relevant secondary legislation). There is still however a restriction on the ability of local authorities to take into account "non-commercial matters" (LGA s.17). LGA s.19 also states that the Secretary of State can deem a specified matter to "cease to be a commercial matter" for

63 Jane Sillett, "Local Government and the Private Finance Initiative", quoted in "Best Value, Best Equality" (1998) 79 EOR, published by IRS, May 1, 1998.
64 "Best Value, Best Equality" (1998) 79 EOR, published by IRS, May 1, 1998.

the purposes of "best value".[65] However, secondary legislation has been passed which deems issues relating to terms and conditions of employment contractors of their workers (including composition of the workforce, arrangements for promotion, transfer and training) to cease to be non-commercial matters (reg.3 Local Government Best Value Order 2001).[66] There is also an explicit recognition that despite the restrictions on local authorities to take into account non-commercial matters, they can undertake questionnaires and monitoring to ensure compliance with their public duty to promote equality in the RRA 76 s.71 (LGA s.18).

Best Value is administered by the Audit Commission which carries out regular best value inspections on council services and there is also an inspectorate for housing. (LGA 99 ss 10–15). Inspection reports give councils a start rating based on performance. There is a duty to publish the information (LGA 99 s.20). The Audit Commission has developed a system of ranking, publications and evaluation around the concept of Comprehensive Performance Assessments (CPA). This is being evolved into a regime of Comprehensive Area Assessment (CAA) in 2009 which aims to focus on a number of goals: increasing accountability; transparency and building local strategic partnerships between local organisations.[67]

E. *Impact of Best Value Scheme on Equal Opportunities*

Although the Best Value scheme was more welcome than CCT by those who work in the area of equal opportunities, there are concerns about using the scheme to achieve the goals of discrimination law. There are no explicit shifts towards the adoption of contract compliance as a mechanism for delivering equality objectives as there are in the US or Canada. The EOC, for example, asked for amendments to the LGA 99 to make this explicit commitment. They suggested that the Best Value criteria should explicitly incorporate guidance on equalities issues, possibly through a Code of Practice which could be the basis for a minimum standard to be followed by local authorities, and could therefore be subject to the inspection, monitoring and publication requirements contained in the LGA 99.[68] The CRE also called for the legislative framework to reflect racial equality aims more forcefully and concluded that:

[65] Local Government Act 1999 and Local Government Best Value (Exclusion of Non-commercial Considerations) Order 2001. See Aileen McColgan, *Discrimination Law*, 2nd edn, (Oxford: Hart Publications, 2005) p.400.

[66] The Local Government Best Value (Exclusion of Non-commercial Considerations) Order 2001, Statutory Instrument 2001, No.909.

[67] "The Evolution of Regulation": Comprehensive Area Assessment and the Changing Face of Public Service Improvement, Audit Commission, Public Service Consultation April 2007, (Audit Commission: London, 2007).

[68] "Best Value, Best Equality" (1998) 79 EOR, published by IRS, May 1, 1998.

"At stake is not just the way in which services themselves are delivered, but also the added value to be obtained through action to ensure that those providing services enjoy demonstrable equality of opportunity in employment".[69]

There have been other concerns expressed about the potentially discriminatory impact of the Best Value scheme, and the failure to use it positively to promote equality goals. When the new scheme was being introduced a range of public policy specialists (e.g. Centre for Public Studies and the Local Government Information Unit) expressed their concern about the discriminatory impact of Best Value schemes. The Centre for Public Services concluded that the lack of explicit reference to equal opportunities in Best Value was a significant lacuna which could lead to a detrimental impact or marginalisation of equality issues.[70] The Local Government Association and large public sector unions such as Unison, TGWU and GMB also shared this concern. Unison, in particular, set out a strong response to the Best Value initiatives which argued that local authorities should be legally obliged to evaluate antidiscrimination law indicators (as well as pay, conditions and health and safety).

The concerns of unions about the risks created by the Best Value scheme, and the potential for the creation of a "two tier workforce", led to ongoing negotiations with the Government which culminated in the publication of a Code of Practice in 2003. The code—Code of Practice on Workforce Matters in Local Authority Service Contracts—provided that service providers who sought to cut down costs by reducing levels of terms and conditions of their staff, fell outside the definition of "best value", and would not qualify to provide services. The Code also dealt with issues relating to the transfer of undertakings and pensions. The main key points of the Code relevant to this discussion are extracted below:

CODE OF PRACTICE ON WORKFORCE MATTERS IN PUBLIC SECTOR SERVICE CONTRACTS
Published by the Cabinet Office, March 2003.

"1. This document sets out an approach to workforce matters in public sector service contracts which involve a transfer of staff from the public sector organisation to the service provider, or in which staff originally transferred out from the public sector organisation as a result of an outsourcing are TUPE transferred to a new provider under a retender of a contract. This Code will form part of the service specification and conditions for all such

69 "Best Value, Best Equality" (1998) 79 EOR, published by IRS, May 1, 1998.
70 "Best Value, Best Equality" (1998) 79 EOR, published by IRS, May 1, 1998.

contracts, except those where the Best Value Code of Practice on Workforce Matters in Local Authority Service Contracts applies, or where other exemptions have been announced.[71]

2. The Code recognises that there is no conflict between good employment practice, value for money and quality of service. On the contrary, quality and good value will not be provided by organisations who do not manage workforce issues well. The intention of the public sector organisation is therefore to select only those providers who offer staff a package of terms and conditions which will secure high quality service delivery throughout the life of the contract. These must be sufficient to recruit and motivate high quality staff to work on the contract and designed to prevent the emergence of a "two-tier workforce", dividing transferees and new joiners working beside each other on the same contracts.

3. Service providers who intend to cut costs by driving down the terms and conditions for staff, whether for transferees or for new joiners taken on to work beside them, will not be selected to provide services for the public sector organisation. However, nothing in this Code should discourage public sector organisations or service providers from addressing productivity issues by working with their workforces in a positive manner to achieve continuous improvement in the services they deliver.

9. The service provider will consult representatives of a trade union where one is recognised, or other elected representatives of the employees where there is no recognised trade union, on the terms and conditions to be offered to such new recruits.

(References to "trade unions" throughout this code should be read to refer to other elected representatives of the employees where there is no recognised trade union.) The arrangements for consultation will involve a genuine dialogue. The precise nature of the arrangements for consultation is for agreement between the service provider and the recognised trade unions. The intention is that contractors and recognised trade unions should be able to agree on a particular package of terms and conditions, in keeping with the terms of this Code, to be offered to new joiners. [. . .]

Monitoring arrangements

11. Throughout the length of the contract, the service provider will provide the public sector organisation with information as requested which is necessary to allow the public sector organisation to monitor compliance with the conditions set out in this Code. This information will include the terms and conditions for transferred staff and the terms and conditions for employees recruited to work on the contract after the transfer.

12. Such requests for information will be restricted to that required for the purpose of monitoring compliance, will be designed to place the minimum burden on the service provider commensurate with this, and will respect commercial confidentiality. The service provider and the public sector organisation will also support a review of the impact of the Code, drawn up in consultation with representatives of the public sector organisations, contractors, trade unions and will provide information as requested for this purpose. Such requests will follow the same principles of proportionality and confidentiality.

Enforcement

[the code then sets out terms for enforcement which include: direct meetings between employees and trade unions with the service provider, and if these meetings fail and there

[71] Exemptions include: public corporations and trading funds, Independent Sector Treatment Centres, transfers where the Retention of Employment Model for NHS PFI contracts applies, higher and further education institutions and Academies.

is non-compliance then in the final instance "the public sector organisation will not be bound to consider that provider for future work" (para 13); and Alternative Dispute Resolution Mechanism set out in Annex A of Code (para 14); and publication by Government Departments of contact details for employees and trade unions to seek advice in cases where they consider that the public sector organisation has failed to meet its responsibilities (para 15).

Operation of the Code

17. Government departments will monitor the operation of the Code, following consultation with relevant employers and trade unions."

The code contains many of the features of the established contract compliance regimes such as the US or Canada, e.g. it has systems for setting standards and obligations; monitoring; and enforcement. However, a comparison also makes clear that this code is a much weaker form of contact compliance. The most striking difference is that the Code does not refer explicitly to equality or non-discrimination as a specific goal, or a specific requirement of good practice. This means that there is still in effect, a gap: there is no strong contract compliances measure in Britain like those that are available in US or Canadian discrimination law. There are also weaker forms of monitoring and enforcement. For example, unlike the Canadian system it is not subject to enforcement through an established commission. Nor are there any provisions of judicial or administrative interpretation of the Code as in the US or Canada: the British code leaves issues relating to the monitoring of the Code to the relevant Government departments following consultations with relevant employers and trade unions. As well as considering comprehensive reform through the introduction of legislation like that in the US or Canada, there are also more incremental changes that could improve the working of the existing regime of contract compliance. The Code of Practice could be modified to make a more explicit reference to equalities norms, which are incorporated as one of the specified outcomes of Best Value, and enforced and monitored by the Audit Commission: Secretary of State could more extensive use of powers to specify questions and evidence from contractors.

There is evidence that the standards that are already in place using Best Value are not delivering results in terms of equality and non-discrimination social policy goals. There is "Equality Standard for Local Government" which has been developed in consultation with the equality commissions as part of the Best Value Performance Indicator. This allows local authorities to assess their progress according to a number of criteria: commitment to a comprehensive equality policy; assessment and consultation; setting equality objectives and targets; information systems and monitoring against targets; and achieving and reviewing outcomes. Early results suggest that local authorities are not easily meeting these targets.[72]

[72] Aileen McColgan, *Discrimination Law*, 2nd edn, (Oxford: Hart Publications, 2005), p.404.

There are, therefore, ongoing concerns that the difficulties of moving public jobs into the private sector will continue to have a negative impact on equality:

"the government's modernisation programme conflicts with its equality policy statements. The inclusion of equality policies and public duty responsibilities in contract documents between the public and private sectors is unlikely to prove adequate protection given the historic difficulties of ensuring that equality policies are applied and implemented."[73]

The Discrimination Law Review has tentatively suggested that there should be some clarification of the law relating to public procurement. The Governance of Britain consultation paper states that the "Best Value" duty should be changed to "ensure that authorities inform, consult, involve and devolve to local authorities", which if implemented might open up more room for equality initiatives in this area.[74]

There is some evidence that large private sector suppliers of public services would welcome greater use of procurement as a policy lever to promote equality and diversity. Serco, the largest private sector supplier of public services, has stated this as a key objective and they have called for the incorporation of a "diversity dividend" so that:

"competition by private companies for the provision of public services would favour companies that invest in good diversity practices. This should include, for example: targets built into service performance, for instance, in relation to occupational segregation and encouraging women into non-traditional roles; plans agreed for the introduction of equality-proofed pay systems; rejecting tenders from employers that cannot demonstrate a track record and future commitment to diversity; and stimulating innovation in the private sector by rewarding progressive practices."[75]

There remain, however, some questions about whether private business as a whole would welcome further regulation in this area. The recent experience of resistance to the introduction of mandatory equal pay reviews for the private sector, which led to the failure to make them part of the recommendations of the Women and Women's Work Commission's Report *Shaping a Fairer Future*, suggests that there is still considerable resistance by private business and a lack of political will to making the private sector more accountable and responsive in the area of equality and non-discrimination.

[73] Karen Escott and Dextor Whitfield, *Promoting Equality in the Public Sector*, (EOC: Manchester, 2002), at p.22.

[74] "The Governance of Britain", Presented to Parliament by the Secretary of State for Justice and Lord Chancellor, July 2007, HC CM 7170, at p.50.

[75] "Promoting Diversity in Public Services" (2007) 161 EOR, published by IRS on February 1, 2007.

IV. Conclusion

This chapter has considered the collective aspect of the ninth question of discrimination law that we identified—"what legal remedies are available, and who may seek them"—with particular focus on the work of the new Commission for Equality and Human Rights (CEHR). In the context of the CEHR, it is surprising that the Discrimination Law Review has not raised any questions about the independence of the CEHR in the light of recent constitutional reform proposals to introduce greater scrutiny of public appointments and public power by Parliament[76] At present, the CEHR functions as a human rights and minority protection agency, but it is subject to political control over its appointments and budget.[77] The CEHR could easily be transformed into a more independent institutional structure by making it accountable to Parliament through the supervision of the Joint Committee on Human Rights. This would have the further advantage of providing a forum in which domestic discrimination law is analysed within the paradigm of existing international and European human rights obligations, e.g. ILO standards, equality provisions such as ECHR Art.14 and other human rights such as freedom of speech. The JCHR could also evaluate the operation of the Single Equality Act and provide an annual review of discrimination law. Rather than a "once in a lifetime" review, this would institutionalise discrimination law reform as an ongoing process.

The chapter has also discussed extra-legal measures, as well as supply-side investment measures. These issues address the tenth question of discrimination law—"how far should we look outside the law for solutions"? The discussion suggests that there is insufficient use of extra-legal measures such as contract compliance and public procurement to pursue the underlying goals of discrimination law, especially as compared with jurisdictions such as the US or Canada. The Discrimination Law Review (DLR) has proposed reform of these types of extra-legal measures in domestic discrimination law.[78]

The DLR suggests that the organisations like the CBI support greater use of public procurement as long as the guidelines are clear and there are the appropriate skills to deliver results (DLR, para.5.99). This represents a dramatic shift from the 1980s when the Local Government Act 1988, s.18 was introduced as a response to requests from the CBI and employers to restrict local authority powers to impose contract compliance policies. The DLR could have built on this emerging consensus by strengthening the legal framework; but instead, it fails to make any significant recommendations which would require or encourage public procurement to promote equality. Of course, the DLR's focus on greater clarity about the goals of public procurement through

76 *The Governance of Britain*, July 2007, HC Cmnd. 7170.
77 Equality Act 2006, Sch.1.
78 *Discrimination Law Review. A Framework for Fairness: Proposals for a Single Equality Act for Great Britain.* (Department of Communities and Local Government: London, 2007).

guidance notes, training and good practice, as suggested by the CBI, is necessary and important (DLR, paras 5.96–5.98). However, it is difficult to see why this requirement for clarity does not also extend to making crystal clear that public authorities can and should actively use public procurement to promote their equality duties (an idea which is rejected by the DLR, para.5.93). The DLR does not propose the introduction of a specific clause clarifying that the public sector duty entitles public bodies to use public procurement to promote their equality goals.[79] Nor does the DLR recommend the introduction of a statutory power which allows the Secretary of State to designate that specified public authorities are required to use public procurement to promote equality where there is large scale outsourcing of their functions. It is therefore difficult to avoid the conclusion that the DLR has failed to create an effective legal framework, or significant incentives, for a more extensive use of public sector procurement to promote equality.

[79] Equalities Review, Cabinet Office, February 2007, p.119).

INDEX